ECONOMIC MAN

In Two Volumes: VOLUME TWO

Economic Man

IN RELATION TO HIS NATURAL ENVIRONMENT

C. Reinold Noyes

VOLUME TWO

Columbia University Press
NEW YORK · MORNINGSIDE HEIGHTS
1948

PUBLISHED IN GREAT BRITAIN AND INDIA
BY GEOFFREY CUMBERLEGE
OXFORD UNIVERSITY PRESS, LONDON AND BOMBAY

MANUFACTURED IN THE UNITED STATES OF AMERICA

CONTENTS

Part III: Environment

Appendices

Part III

ENVIRONMENT

II

NATURAL RESISTANCES

A. THE ECONOMIC RELATION OF MAN TO HIS ENVIRONMENT

1. THE CLASSICAL SCHEME

FROM WHAT we have termed the "obdurately physical" viewpoint, which has been generally adopted in economics, the natural environment in which man lives his economic life has been treated as a congeries of material objects and forces which *co-operate* in the production of the means to the satisfaction of human wants. By an acknowledged convention this environment—or "nature"—has been given the name of its chief proprietary category, *land*,[1] and, as such, has been built into the structure of a logically symmetrical system as one of the three "agents" or "factors" of production.[2] The character of the terminology suggests the almost anthropomorphic view of nature which permeated the thinking of the earlier economists.[3] Since then, perhaps under the influence of nineteenth century developments in chemistry, product has come to be regarded as a sort of compound of the three constituents, "land, labor, and capital"—almost the result

[1] For our purposes this term must be rejected. And that not only because it is both non-descriptive and non-analytical, but chiefly because it is preferable to preserve it—like the term "capital"—for its more indispensable technical use in the proprietary or legal field. There, land as an object of property always comprises "everything which is attached to the earth whether by the course of nature . . . or by the hand of man." In that usage it includes the site, the natural resources (materials and powers) located therein or thereon or accessible thereto, and all the economic artifacts (products of effort) which are embraced by the legal term "improvements." For a more thorough statement of this conglomerate, see the author's *Institution of Property*, *313*, 395–396, 438.

[2] In an illuminating study of the techniques, or "approaches," to "so-called social science," Kroeber (*244*, 324–325) has given the name "logistic" to that "quasi-scientific" or "immature" approach which seems to have been the first stage of most sciences. Of this "approach," or stage, he considers economic theory "a classical example." It "seems to be scholastic in the sense that the science of Aquinas was scholastic." One of the inherent characteristics of this approach seems to be the necessity that its patterns conform to the requirements of an intellectual aesthetic—of which a chief one is symmetry.

[3] On a possible source of this fancy, see Veblen, *413*, 74–83.

of a reaction among these three reagents.[4] But, unlike the compounds of the chemical elements, these economic compounds do not have each its own invariable formula. Instead the proportions of the three constituents are conceived to be almost infinitely variable. One can procure the same result if one uses a "little more" "labor" and a "little less" "land," and vice versa; in the same way "doses" of "capital" can be substituted for those of "land" or "labor," and the reverse. The artful blending of these three elements or requisites constitutes the practice of economic life, and the marginal proportions, determined by the necessarily finite quantities of each which are available, settles the division of product among the three basic classes of a particular form of human society for which these abstract terms have been, in effect, but pseudonyms.[5]

From this orthodoxy there have developed two heresies, neither of which, however, does more than modify the scheme as the fundamental basis of economic analysis. One is a simplification; one is a "complification." The first arose because certain acute thinkers came to recognize that "capital" is not itself an original "factor," but is, instead, a product of the other two. Being product, it must itself be like all other product, a result rather than a primary cause. Thus, by some, the "factors" have come to be reduced to two only, "land" and "labor"—a still more picturesque and alliterative formulation.[6] On the other hand, those who were mathematically inclined found that it was impossible to define and therefore to treat the three original "factors"

[4] To Walras (*420*, 175), products result from the *association* of productive elements such as lands, men and capitals; or, more exactly, from that of the "service des facultés personnelles," the "*rente* ou le service des *terres* et le *profit* ou le service des *capitaux*." Probably *rente* and *profit* were thought of by him in their, purely French, physical sense of *use*, not in their financial sense. Nevertheless, it is clear that to him all three were *associated* by active forces similar to our notion of atomic valences in chemistry.

[5] As a first step in scientific analysis the notion of factors actually arose as a way of accounting for existing income distribution. This is quite evident, for instance, in Adam Smith. Of course, today "the classification of the factors of production is not a classification of men or groups of men, but of functions," as Mises puts it (*300*, 331). Nevertheless, the notion of function was derived from the type of income and not vice versa.

[6] I ignore the "fourth factor" enterprise, introduced by the French, since, except for the differential element, it is always treated as a kind of labor; also the fourth factor "natural materials" proposed by Cassel (*74*, 159) which we ourselves shall have to consider, but which has not been accepted; also the fourth factor "organization" proposed by Marshall (*291*, 138 ff.), who otherwise agreed that "in a sense," there are but two. In general, the Austrian acceptance of the two-factor notion was due to the fact that this school had adopted Böhm-Bawerk's realistic theory of capital, which made capital unsymmetrical (no longer physical) and hence not precisely a "factor" at all. That made physical "capital" "an intermediate product of nature and labour, nothing more" (*38*, 96). We are now engaged in making "land" unsymmetrical as well.

as homogeneous or even commensurable entities. Obviously, there are qualitative differences within each kind of "factor" which seemed to prevent their being used as such in purely quantitative treatment. But a mathematical principle saved the day. Since it can be assumed that, by the nature of the case, regardless of the number of homogeneous "factors" in use and the number of homogeneous products, there can be no more unknowns than there are equations (that is, every factor must enter into one or more products), it becomes possible to leave the analysis of "factors" out of consideration altogether by conveniently assigning to each member of a hypothetical myriad some sign for an unknown quantity.[7] Thus, in mathematical economics, the notion of "factor" has been relegated to an unlimited, undefined, and unclassified list of causative agents which may not even be specifically named, but are left to the imagination.[8] Nevertheless, the assumption remains that these causative agents can be grouped in at least the above two, or even the original three, general orders. It is the false system of energetics, based on these general orders, which, perhaps more than all else, has deformed or even defeated accurate economic analysis.

2. ENVIRONMENT IN TERMS OF ECONOMIC ENERGETICS

If we undertake *de novo* to survey the relationship of man, as an organism, to his natural environment, as host, in respect of what we call his economic life—that is, his making a living or, more broadly, the satisfying of his wants—these analytical formulations seem to lack realism. We then perceive that what we call nature—the environment—consists of a vast complexity of interlocking processes, distributed in space and over time, which proceed *regardless* of man. Man, placed perforce in this environment as it is, finds that certain of these processes, or stages in them, are potential means to the satisfaction of some of his wants—states that he wishes to get rid of—while others are potential causes of others of his wants—states that he wishes to prevent. Therefore, though nature proceeds regardless of man, man

[7] The reader is, of course, familiar with the formulae of general equilibrium theory. We may refer to Cassel's convenient presentation of it (*74*, 134–142).

[8] See especially Wicksteed (*441*, 365–367) who goes so far as to deny the utility of such analysis in terms of factors. Pareto (*317*, 377–379) ridicules the division into three or two factors, or the Marxian labor theory (one factor). To him every ingredient is a species by itself—for Rhine wine, Rhine land (not "land"); for a statue, a sculptor (not "labor"); for a locomotive, something with precisely the form of a locomotive (not any "capital mobilier"). To Walras the tripartite system was non-essential. Jevons did not reach the stage of analysis that would lead him to question or discard it.

cannot proceed regardless of nature.[9] Instead of acting as a co-operating "agent" or servant of man it would appear that nature, in this respect, plays rather the two roles that the horse's hide and his tail play to the horsefly.[10]

Moreover, if the combined formula of the economic process, which we have previously been following as the basis of our analysis, represents reality even incompletely, another difficulty appears. It is quite impossible to reconcile the view of nature as an actively beneficent agent with the view that man satisfies his wants almost wholly by means of his own efforts; nay even with the recognition that effort is required at all. At the beginning of Chapter 9 we recognized that the system of economic energetics we are developing involves the necessity that there must be an external resistance which is overcome by means of human activities.[11] Here we may formulate that proposi-

[9] Too much the "struggle for existence" has come to mean, to the modern economist and particularly to the reformer, a struggle *among men* (i.e., competition). But the real struggle, the struggle against nature, still exists, however much it has been concealed by the complexity of modern economic organization and by the fact that a portion of the community habitually underwrites most of the burden of this struggle and thus practically shields the rest from most of its effects. It is still true, as always, that, as to men themselves, they "are the best who conform most perfectly to the demands of Nature. . . . Nature eliminates those who do not satisfy her requirements, and from Nature's decree there is no appeal" (Brooks Adams, *2*, XXV).

[10] It has seemed to me that in the background of human thought in Western Europe during the last two centuries, there have lain certain assumptions as to the economic relations of man and nature, which have influenced without entirely convincing later economists. In the eighteenth century, roughly, the "bounty of nature" viewpoint prevailed. Locke, the Physiocrats, and even Smith were tainted with it. Then nature appeared as a caterer providing a single *menu* on the *table d'hôte* plan. The mental picture seems to have visualized mankind, seated at a festive board piled high with choice viands and weighed down with flowing bowls, while Dame Nature, in the background, is busying herself with preparing her new "plenties." To complete the picture in true eighteenth century style one might even add nymphs and dryads as serving maids.

When the vast technical progress of the nineteenth century had slightly turned men's heads, this picture was modified in two important respects; the *menu* became *à la carte*, and the allegorical figures were replaced by "iron slaves" and abstract forces represented in "modernistic" style. We had entered the "man's command over nature" period.

The first of these two viewpoints was, of course, confined to the leisure classes—those for whose exclusive benefit the late post-feudal economies seemed to themselves to be organized. The second has permeated most of those members of society whose economic activities take place above (or after) the level of extraction. And Veblen was its prophet.

[11] We may remind the reader of the analysis given at that point when we were engaged in distinguishing internal from the external resistances. Both present wants (PW) and future wants (FW) meet external resistances (N) in so far as they require bodily activities. But present wants meet no internal resistance. Thus the formula for them is PW *vs.* N. On the other hand, to future wants there is first opposed the internal resistance involved in effort. As resistance we may call this ER, one of the two aspects of

tion more exactly. The environment *gives* nothing to man. It only opposes resistance to the satisfying of his wants.[12] However much various material stages or kinetic phases in its wholly independent processes may afford potential means to the satisfaction of his wants to be got rid of, the fact remains that he must always "come and get it," with all that may involve. If, on the other hand, these stages threaten potential causes of his wants of prevention, nothing can save him from the necessity of finding his own ways of escaping. We do not regard all man's activities vis-à-vis nature as involving effort. That point has already been clarified. Nevertheless, from the physical viewpoint, there is no fundamental difference in kind between the activities of direct consumption, such as breathing the air, enjoying the view, or killing mosquitoes, on the one hand, and the activities of production, such as raising crops, painting pictures or building houses, on the other. All alike consist of human activities taking from the environment what will satisfy wants to be got rid of or of active intervention to avoid what will cause wants to be prevented. However, from the economic viewpoint, we have agreed to include the first kind of activities in one of the rubrics of leisure, either direct consumption or playing; while the second kind of activities, by reason of the fact that they involve the component which we have called effort—the necessity of overcoming some sort of internal as well as external resistance—is classified as working and retaining.[13]

volition, V. The other aspect of volition exerts the force of effort (EF) which then overcomes external resistance (N). Thus the formula for future wants is FW *vs.* ER ⟵ V ⟶ EF *vs.* N.

[12] Böhm-Bawerk, as a representative of the marginal utility school, has nothing but scorn for those who fall back on the notion of the "resistance of nature to man" (*38*, 139). But, in this connection, it is refreshing to read Commons on Ricardo and his followers (see *93*, 263–265).

[13] What is taken from the environment under the first category has been called in economics "free goods" or, in law, "common resources," or *res communes* and *res nullius*. Of this, more hereafter. The general confusion in economics between the proprietary situation and the condition of natural resistance requires to be cleared up. We are considering only the latter at this point. Natural phenomena which can be taken advantage of by means of activities which are not called effort—direct consumption—may be conventionally classed by themselves. They are not, however, "free" (i.e., strictly costless); they do require human activity; and it is only because of the different source of the energizing that this activity is not classed as effort and therefore not included as a cost of production. Moreover, it is this and no other criterion that determines the class. It is not the fact that such phenomena exist in superfluity (i.e., no scarcity) that causes us to exclude them from consideration in the process of production. That, as we shall see, is true of innumerable materials and powers that cannot be had without effort. The

In this light our analytical scheme presents itself as follows: As a system, the human organism and its environment are so constituted that human activities are necessary for the satisfaction of most wants.[14] And this because to these satisfactions nature offers resistances that can only be overcome by various forms of activity. Whether these activities constitute effort or not is determined by the preferred or unavoidable timing of the activity with relation to the occurrence of the want. If the timing places the activity before the want exists, the activity is effortful; if it places it (roughly) simultaneously with the want, it is effortless (consummatory reactions and play); but equally in both cases the activity is occasioned wholly by the necessity of overcoming the natural resistances. If, then, we wish to include natural resistances in our combined formula for a system of economic energetics, we must restate the first part of it as follows: future wants-efforts providing means against natural resistances. Or, in more explicit form: man, urged on by the expectation of his wants, exerting effort against the resistance of nature in order to provide for the satisfaction or prevention of his wants. The term resistance is perhaps as good as any other. But it must be understood to include both kinds—what may be called *passive* resistance, in the form of obstacles[15] to attaining means, and *active* resistance, in the form of externally imposed or threatened causes of wants. The latter type, the compulsion to avoidance, is as prevalent and important a cause of effort as is the former. In this formulation the efforts of man become the only agencies at work in the economic operations of production; they are *caused* by future wants; they are *directed* toward ultimate satisfactions (including preventions); they are *necessitated* wholly by the fact that nature invariably opposes resistance to the attainment or maintenance of these satisfactions.[16]

light of the sun is absent at night and the heat of the sun is greatly reduced in northern countries in winter; both must be replaced artificially. Rainfall is occasional; and other water is available only at cetain sites. Breathable air is almost, but not quite, universal. It is the fact that these phenomena, when and where they are available, may be taken by *effortless* activity that is the true ground of the distinction.

Marshall recognized the latter criterion; but in line with tradition he tried to combine it with the proprietary one. He says (*291, 55*), "Those goods are *free*, which are not appropriated and are afforded by nature without requiring the effort of man." And this statement is typical of the general position.

[14] Some few may, under favorable natural conditions or when of extreme intensity, be satisfied by inactivity (rest).

[15] Not used in the Paretan sense. On this see Chapter 12.

[16] Thus there is but one economic agent, with two functions, who acts in a medium and subject to its laws. That is, nature conditions man's economic activities; it does not

While this dynamic version seems far more precise and useful as a way of analyzing economic operations, it should be noted that, in two respects, it does not, in so simplified a form, cover the entire field. In the first place, it rests on the assumption, which needs to be explicitly stated, that there are available somewhere in the natural environment the physical objects and processes which make of that environment a possible habitat for man. But, since we are studying the observable fact of the economic life of mankind, it is not unreasonable merely to take it for granted that such life is possible. The formula, then, tacitly posits a habitable globe as an arena for the operations.[17] In the second place, this formulation may emphasize too exclusively the supply side —the aspect of "real costs." From the demand side—in the aspect of means—it is the observation of nature and the experiencing of the environment which generate many of man's wants, and which disclose gradually the means to new satisfactions that could not have been conceived *in vacuo*.[18] The formula, then, must recognize that the natu-

carry them on; it does not even co-operate. There is no "bounty"; there is only the "struggle for existence."

[17] In this sense nature is one of the "requisites" or "conditions" of production, in Mill's more advanced view (see *298*, I, 205–206).

[18] Those who are habituated to the old physical viewpoint may find these qualifications inadequate and inconsistent with our concept of usefulness. They will agree that, from the supply side, nature contributes no part of the "real costs" of production. That has always been agreed. They may even agree that it is nature which imposes the necessities of "real costs" by reason of her resistances. But, from the demand side, they may hold that it is nature, in the main, which contributes usefulness. This, however, is a matter of definition.

Some of the attributes of means, which we have defined as the relata of usefulness, exist in the state of nature. Some few natural materials and powers, containing such attributes, exist under conditions which make them usable in their natural state without production. Such use we regard as direct consumption. All the rest can only be made usable through production. Therefore such natural materials and powers in their natural state, though they contain such attributes, represent only potential usefulness. Production is necessary to make the usefulness actual.

Furthermore, most of the attributes of means, which we have defined as the relata of usefulness, do not exist in the state of nature. These attributes are entirely conferred by production.

Thus an iron sword was more useful than a bronze sword because it was harder (natural attribute). But its cutting edge is a produced, not a natural, attribute. And even its hardness only existed as a potential in its natural state (ore). Moreover, before the iron age that attribute did not represent even potential usefulness. Thus, for the most part, the worked-up material was merely a carrier of the usefulness contributed by production (effort).

Therefore, even from this semi-physical viewpoint, natural materials and powers represent almost wholly only potential usefulness. In their natural state they are purely latent, economically regarded, and only become economically active as conveyors or modifiers of usefulness when man's efforts have overcome a certain "critical" resistance to their release.

Furthermore, in Chapter 9, in the section on Product, we gave our reasons for finding

ral environment is also the source of much of man's purposive or wishful thinking; it is the material of phantasy, whether as an incitement to an attack on reality, or as a way of escape from it. But the hard fact remains that, if the realization of these imagined satisfactions requires alterations in the objective world, such alterations can only be procured at the cost of human effort. And perhaps it is serviceable to permit the formula to keep its simple form in order the better to emphasize that essential point.

At first sight this formulation may seem unsatisfactory in another regard as well. While it is true that, in respect of all the stages or phases of its processes, nature offers at least some resistance to man when he undertakes to use these processes for the satisfaction of his wants, it is also true that he has found it possible to avail himself of a great variety of, in this sense, secondary natural processes (or even materials) in order to overcome for him the resistances offered by that one with which he is primarily concerned. When this takes place it is no longer the gross resistance of the primary process that he must meet with his own physical effort but only its net resistance—that is, its gross resistance less the *assistance* of the secondary process. But, as Mill nicely pointed out, this secondary use of one natural process to overcome the resistance offered by another—the result of which is desired—consists in "putting things into fit places for being acted upon by their own internal forces, and by those residing in other natural objects." [19] Thus to bring the second process into play at all requires additional or different effort. First, it involves the mental effort necessary to arrive at an understanding of the processes of the natural environment and to discover and scheme out the ways in which these may be converted to man's ends—and these tasks require working-time of themselves; second, there is added the physical effort involved in overcoming the resistance these secondary processes themselves offer to being so converted—which also requires working-time; and, third, the mental activities required to apply the secondary process usually make that a

it analytically advantageous to regard usefulness—except of non-produced means—as something which appears *de novo* at the end of the production process. That most nearly represents the facts; and it detaches usefulness—a subjective attribution—from both nature and effort as effect.

[19] Mill, *298*, I, 47–48. Böhm-Bawerk says the same thing (*38*, 12). But he also says of man that (*ibid.*, VII), "to a large extent, he remakes the natural world to suit his purposes." Marshall's more cautious statement (*291*, 248) of "man's prerogative" seems preferable.

much greater component part of the total effort expended, though not necessarily adding to the working-time by itself. Thus, in the end, there must be considered along with the nullified or reduced resistance which remains to be overcome by physical effort in the primary process, the resistance which nature offers to our understanding, our learning how to adapt and our actual adaptation of the secondary one.

This playing of one process of nature off against another composes most of what we call technique.[20] To put it less picturesquely, technique—or, if you will, the progress of technique—consists in reducing the effort required to overcome the resistance which nature offers to the attainment by man of the satisfaction or prevention of his wants. This may take place either by way of a reduction of the absolute quantity of effort required to procure a given satisfaction, or by an increase in the quantity of usefulness per unit of resistance (improvement of product), or even by making available a wholly new and otherwise unobtainable means of satisfaction (synthetic product, etc.). To the extent that technique is generalized in an economy and can be passed from generation to generation by tradition, the effort occasioned by the resistance to its arrival at that stage—that is, the mental effort involved in coming to an understanding of, and in discovering how to adapt, natural processes for some new purpose—once performed, is for each stage in part eliminated. Nevertheless, as to each individual, there remains the frequently arduous mental effort of learning even this generalized technique.[21] And there remains also the difficulty that the more advanced the technique the greater, generally speaking, becomes the mental as opposed to the physical component in the effort required actually to apply it. Thus we must think of the reduction of effort in terms of working-time as consisting of a decrease in the expenditure of man's physical energy by reason of assistance, a simultaneous increase in that of his mental activities, changing the character of the effort, together with the inclusion of some periods of "deliberation" when nothing but mental activity is required. From the physical

[20] Actually we have little or no control over nature. We act as catalytic agents. And, independently of us as well, "we have nature playing one hand against the other, or trumping her own trick," as John Burroughs put it (*54*.)

But, as Böhm-Bawerk says (*38*, 21), "The condition of our success is, that we are able to control the materials on which the power that helps us depends, more easily than the materials which are to be transformed into the desired good." A partial statement, but good, so far as it goes.

[21] It was not so long ago that generalization was very limited. At that stage learning consisted in being initiated into the "mysteries of the craft."

standpoint it is true that the physical effort required to "handle" the secondary process plus the remaining physical effort required in the primary process may become very small compared to what they were at the no-technique (brute force) stage. But the collaborating mental component becomes correspondingly intense, though not necessarily prolonging the working-time. And, in any case, it must be recognized that it is never possible to eliminate effort altogether. Nature never becomes automatic in serving man.[22]

While the interrelation of multiplex processes in this way is of great interest to economic man, it constitutes the subject of technology, not that of economics. From the economic point of view—in the light of our proposed system of energetics—we are concerned solely with technique, whatever it is in each case and in each "state of the arts," as the determinant or expression of the ratio between the total resistance offered by nature and the human effort required to overcome it. The progress of technique from the brute-force stage consists in reducing the effort involved for given resistances, both by introducing assistance and in other ways. Since, then, the natural resistances are a prime and always to some extent an unavoidable factor, we will, as we proceed to analyze the characteristics of the natural environment as a habitat for man's economic activities, concern ourselves with the analysis of the nature and kinds of this resistance.

B. THE THREE ASPECTS OF THE ENVIRONMENT

1. IN RELATION TO WANTS TO BE GOT RID OF

Nature, as host to the organism man, appears in three general aspects which are quite different each from the other and can by no means be treated together. The first aspect is primarily spatial; it has been called the surface of the earth; but this can no longer be taken as correct unless we resort to the traditional legal definition and include therein the space extending in both vertical directions from the surface. All forms of economic activity, whether of production or consumption, must take place within this space. Or, conversely, each activity must have a locus, sometimes stationary and sometimes moving, usually on or just under the surface, though recently also above

[22] We are here considering only production, or effortful activities. But nature is not automatic even for direct consumption.

the surface.[1] In this aspect the environment serves as *site.* As such it represents the stage upon which economic life is played. It will at once be noted that most of the features which have been attributed to "land" as a "factor" have nothing whatever to do with this purely spatial aspect of the environment, and only rarely and in part have there been mentioned any of the conditions which its characteristics inevitably impose upon man's economic activities. In the purely spatial aspect the economically important features of site are its size, its elevation, etc. But one must consider also the interrelationships of sites as a whole, their arrangement (geography), and, therefore, from the point of view of the individual site, the *location* of each. It is evident that, in this spatial aspect, every site is unique and, by definition, completely immobile. However, since the globe itself, its waters, and its circumambient atmosphere are material, it follows that the environment, as site, cannot be treated only in its spatial aspect. Nevertheless, the material *composition* or *contour* of site as a locus for economic operations affects men quite differently from the other material aspect of the environment next to be mentioned. The germane considerations in this respect are whether the site is solid or fluid (or even gaseous—the air); if the former, what is its shape and composition; if the latter, whether the material is still or moving. It is equally evident that, in this material aspect, sites vary widely, but are nevertheless subject to rough classifications according to more or less close resemblances; it is also clear that the material of which they are composed is not necessarily completely immobile. What holds true of site regarded spatially is therefore only partly or not at all true of site regarded materially.

The second aspect of the natural environment is wholly material, in the sense of old-fashioned physics. For the purpose of satisfying his wants man requires certain substances which we have referred to as stages in natural processes. It is these substances that he must remove from their natural state and in which he embodies his efforts, except when his working takes the form of an act only. It is these substances in which he thus incorporates or makes available usefulness. In this aspect the environment serves as a source of raw material; it contains, as we say, natural resources. We shall use the term "natural

[1] Even so recently as 1874, Walras was able truthfully to say, "On ne fait point de l'industrie et du commerce entre ciel et terre; il faut se poser quelque part sur le sol" (*420*, 388).

materials" when we are referring to such materials as raw and *in situ* (i.e., not extracted).[2] That qualification points to the fact that all natural materials must exist somewhere—that is, they too, like economic operations, must have some locus in a site; they too must be on, in, or over some portion of the surface of the earth. But, when we classify these materials into kinds, we find that some are generally distributed among all sites, while others are concentrated in a few sites only. The greater number fall between these two extremes. Some materials are, when removed from the site, replenished there by natural process, continuously, periodically, or sporadically; some not at all. Some materials are extracted in the form in which they have long existed; some are snatched at a particular stage in a natural process. Some involve so little human activity in their extraction that they can be taken when and as present wants require them—then we elide the notion of production and call their taking direct consumption; some require long-sustained effort, a part of which may be applied at earlier stages in a natural process than the one at which the material is "ripe" for taking for human use. If we are to be literal we must include in the material aspect such elements of climate as rainfall or other flow of water, atmospheric ingredients, etc., which become a part of the physical resource itself.

In the conditioning to which our environment subjects us, this material aspect persists, however, even after the material resources *in situ* have been extracted and are in the further processes of production. There are characteristics of the various materials that we use which are "given," and which provide continued resistance, and therefore the occasion for human effort, while they are being moved or changed to the place or form in which they will finally serve as finished product, directly or indirectly, for the satisfaction of wants. If this is not the case; if the material exists, and is continuously replenished, everywhere, and therefore requires no transportation; and if it offers so little resistance that we do not need to class the activity as effort; then we have agreed to treat its abstraction and use as direct consumption. Since this exception is eliminated by our definition, the whole process

[2] But in view of the habitual glozing over of the true nature of these resources by the use of the term "land," derived from an earlier day, it is well to keep in mind, in considering the resistances, that we are including in this material aspect the atmosphere; superficial water and water supply from all sources; all the constituents of the earth's surface which are extracted by excavation or mining, or by biological processes; and all organic growths that are located on, or are moving about, the earth's surface, whether on land, in the air, or in water.

of production must be conceived to be conducted against natural resistance. Nature resists to the last, so to speak. But, at this later stage, the natural resistance which persists will be determined wholly by the characteristics of the material itself and by the *location* only of its source. It will no longer depend at all on the material conformation or composition of its original locus. Thus the material aspect in its totality includes the composition and contour of site, the material resources *in situ*, and then these latter again, after extraction, as the physical carrier or embodiment of all material product.

The third aspect of the environment, which it is not altogether easy to differentiate from the foregoing at their mutual border line, consists of the phases of natural processes themselves.[3] It may serve our purpose to call these *natural powers*.[4] They are usually included with the *materials* in the rubric "natural resources." But their behavior with reference to man's economic activities is sufficiently different in important respects to necessitate their separation in a class by themselves. Like both the foregoing, the generation of powers requires a site; [5] but in addition powers also require a material medium.[6] Natural processes must have a place to work in and also a medium to work upon. By the term "natural powers" we distinguish all those features of the environment that consist in movement or change of material elements which, once started, are automatic so far as man is concerned—flows of wind or water; biological processes; other chemical processes, including oxi-

[3] The verbal distinction which we have made between a stage and a phase of natural processes is intended to discriminate between what exists at some point in the process (stage) and what occurs between two points of the process (phase). The former can generally be regarded as objects or materials; the latter cannot. As to the powers residing in materials see note 19, above. Böhm-Bawerk remarks (*38*, *57*), "The function of materials of production is not simply to serve as a 'dead and plastic mass'; by means of the natural powers residing in them these materials take a share in the work of production which is, indeed, less prominent, but is, essentially, no less active." And Veblen, the technological economist (*412*, 5 and 6) regards as similar the part played by the "chemical properties of minerals" and the "motions of those mechanical appliances by whose use the minerals are handled." Not only does the apparatus reshape the minerals; "the materials reshape themselves by the help of the apparatus."

[4] This term of Mill's (*298*, I, 46) is not ideal, but it will do.

[5] As Carver puts it (*73*, *185*), nature's bounties "can only be utilized in connection with considerable areas of the earth's surface." But, showing the tenacity of the old idea of "factor," he proceeds to assert that there are plenty of bounties but the "ground space is limited" (*loc. cit.*) and concludes that "these productive forces are in reality parts of the land" (*ibid.*, 186).

[6] Some may be said to be *inherent* in the material under suitable conditions (combustion of coal, or a chemical reaction requiring the heat of an electric furnace); others are inherent in the location of the material (the flow or fall of water). But many have to be externally induced (the spark applied to the gasoline-air mixture, or yeast applied to dough).

dation and combustion; physical processes such as heat (including that of the sun), electrical activity, light, gravity, etc.; animal activities, etc.[7] For the most part these phases of natural processes do not serve directly as means to the satisfaction of man's wants. Their effectiveness for his purposes lies in moving him or his material product and in changing material from one form, which does not, to another which does fit his needs. For that reason it is particularly these which were referred to as secondary processes (or assistances) above. It follows that the ways in which they may be adapted to the satisfaction of man's wants, or, more particularly to the overcoming of resistances elsewhere, is not so readily (naïvely) perceived, nor so simply contrived as the taking of materials. Many of these processes are generalized at all sites. In fact, many of them are so mobile that they can be generated anywhere, once it is discovered how to generate them at all. Some few are restricted. Those which are restricted as to site are obviously immobile. Probably none is strictly unique.

Again, in this case, to the extent that natural powers themselves move or can be transmitted away from the site which is their source, or to the extent that they are generated through the medium of materials so moved, the factor of resistance may continue throughout the process of production and not merely occur at the stage of extraction. In this respect powers are analogous to materials. In fact, in this connection, it becomes difficult to divide materials from powers. Coal and oil are materials which are extracted as such from deposits found on certain sites. But the chief purpose for which they are extracted is to serve, at some other locus, for the generation of powers—heat, expansion, etc.—and, for the most part, at later stages of production or even in consumption. Similarly in the case of the hydro-electric system. There the power is generated by the fall of water (flow and gravity), is converted into electric current for purposes of transmission, and may be used at distant sites and in later processes of production or consumption.[8] But, in both cases, the resistance of nature occurs not only at the

[7] The generation of human power is treated as effort—one part of some kinds of working. The generation of natural power, animal or other, is treated as a natural resource. It is difficult for us to keep in mind how recent this "other" is, as an economic factor. Adam Smith says somewhere that neither windmills nor watermills were known in England at the beginning of the sixteenth century.

[8] The distinction between materials and powers is here purely conventional. In the case of water power, used on the spot, we think of it as being extracted in the process of using it and as an attribute or use of the site. In the case of steam power which is developed

point of extraction of the material or power resource. It continues during transportation or transmission and during conversion into heat, light or power; for these last phases only take place in suitable apparatus, by conjunction with other agencies, and, if they are to be useful, under human control. Even the process of final application itself offers resistance, and therefore requires human effort to overcome it. This characteristic is also found in certain materials which remain material until consumed. But there, we conventionally regard the resistances—such as that to digestion and assimilation—as consumption, not as effort.

2. IN RELATION TO WANTS TO BE PREVENTED

In the preceding pages we have examined the three aspects of the natural environment which are requisite for man's economic activity in the satisfaction of his wants. But these have only been viewed from the standpoint of those wants which consist of states he wishes to get rid of. The relation of nature to those of his wants which consist of states which he wishes to prevent is of a quite different character. Here nature herself may be the cause of the want. But, as to this class, another distinction should be made. In large part these wants of prevention are not threatened by external nature, but by "man's inhumanity to man." And these latter are the occasion of a considerable portion of his efforts.[9] But, in the first place, it is necessary to distinguish between the natural, or external, environment, on the one hand, and the human, or social, environment, on the other. The foregoing discussion has been confined to the natural environment only. In the second place, our analytical entity, a direct economy, to the study of which we are now exclusively devoting ourselves, precludes by definition all interhuman relations, including these. Therefore wants of prevention occasioned by human agency must be reserved for study in connection with the sociological or institutional part of the subject.

With regard to this class of wants the environment in the aspect of site has no special bearing. The agencies which threaten must

from a material resource—coal—that has been removed from its site, we think of it as the use of a product previously extracted and we regard the power as embodied in the material resource.

[9] "En outre, des parasites vivent dans ce milieu, en s'appropriant les biens produits par les autres individus" (Pareto, *316*, 71).

threaten *somewhere*—and that is all that need be said. It is only in the aspects of natural materials and powers that the environment gives rise to wants of prevention. The most conspicuous natural causes for such wants, and the only ones which have been embraced—if unsystematically—in economic analysis, are what have been called "the elements." This phrase constitutes a partial recognition of the fact that the same powers, or phases of natural processes, which we have already found assisting man at certain times and places, are also constantly threatening to intrude upon him at times or in ways in which they are not wanted. As a result, a large part of man's wants of prevention can only be satisfied by what has been called "protection" from "the elements." That this is a very insufficient concept will be seen from a few illustrations. The heat of the sun may be excessive or deficient; the light from the sun may be too bright; the air may be too mobile; the rain too wet. And these are strictly "the elements." Man may desire to take steps to prevent the effects they would have on him by means of artificial shelter and clothing, by artificial shade, by walls, by roofs. But, in addition, he will desire to protect himself against fire, lightning, flood, falling from high places; in fact from all the aforementioned natural powers when they are unmanaged—that is, when their effects are undesired. How little we do, in fact, perceive this hostile aspect of nature in the light of the "bounty" theory is evidenced very curiously by the phrase we use to describe the undesired activities of natural powers when these are on such a rampage that we cannot protect ourselves against them. Then we call them "acts of God."

Also, and hardly separable from the natural powers, there are innumerable undesired intrusions of natural materials, from the inorganic through the organic (including the animal) worlds. And here it is often impossible to separate the presence of the noxious material from its objectionable activity. For example dust, ordure, swill, bacteria, parasites, beasts of prey all constitute external causes of wants of prevention. Man desires to protect himself against these materials or powers of nature and thus to prevent the state which they might bring about within him.

The fact that "nature proceeds regardless of man" has the result, then, that man desires to take some of her materials and to get rid of others; that he desires the effect of some of the processes and to protect himself from the effect of others, or even to avoid them altogether. The notion of nature as a "factor" or "agent" of production is wholly incapable of grasping this dual role. But when we envisage the part played by nature as a varied system of resistances to the satisfaction of man's wants, we make due place for both roles. For, then, the occasion for effort in satisfying wants of the first class—states to be got rid of—is the fact that nature imposes resistance to the taking of her materials or the diversion of her processes. And the occasion for effort in satisfying wants of the second class—states to be prevented—is, so far as external nature is concerned, the fact that she imposes resistance to the elimination of her materials or the avoidance of, or opposition to, her processes.

It should be noted in passing that man, in using the materials and powers of his environment toward the end of satisfying his wants of the first class, also encounters these unwanted materials and processes and must eliminate, protect against or avoid them. But, in our scheme, this active interference by nature, in its indirect effects, may more conveniently be classed with the general resistance she sets up to the utilization by man of any of her materials and powers. It is neither necessary nor even possible to separate the difficulties of eliminating the slag from the ore, from those of eliminating water from the mine; the difficulties of irrigating a field, from those of preventing its erosion; the difficulties of applying some powers to productive results, from those of protecting the process from external interference by housing it.[10] It should also be noted that all productive processes, even those that are aimed at the prevention of wants or at the protection of other processes against these unwanted and interfering natural materials or powers, meet in their turn all the same resistances that are encountered when the processes are directed toward the satisfaction of wants to be got rid of. Thus protection is provided by securing the assistance of some natural materials and powers against others. For these reasons, in connection with all productive operations, as we have defined them, we shall treat the resistance set up by the natural environment as of one order, whether it be to the use of the toward or

[10] Jevons attempted to include both the direct and indirect forms of the active interference (or resistance) of nature with man's satisfactions under the one rubric "discommodity." In fact, he went so far as to include all natural obstacles (i.e., our resistance, including the passive form) in this category and to regard them as disutilities (see *224*, 127–129). But we cannot admit that the physical obstacles imposed by nature are psychological entities. It is the effort they necessitate that constitutes the "disutility." And the term "discommodity," if it is used at all, should be reserved for the direct forms of active resistance by nature, the *rejectanea*, as he calls them.

to the avoidance of the untoward. And this latter distinction will be reserved, or short-circuited, so that it applies only to the relation of nature directly to the human want and its satisfying (consumption). This seems to carry the analytical distinction as far as it is useful.

Since we have recognized that the need of human effort to satisfy human wants is occasioned only by the resistances of the environment, it is necessary to consider along with the foregoing three aspects of nature that of time. We may regard time as a datum, either objective or subjective, as we prefer. In either case we have to recognize that the "then" is not the "now," that the distinction between the future and the present is one which we are compelled to make by the conditioning of our own make-up or of our environment, and that the duration of an actual experience or the degree of futurity of an expected one enforces on us some sort of measurement of this magnitude, whatever its nature. It is clear that, whereas man's productive activities deal with the foregoing three aspects of nature by means of effort in the form of working over time they deal, and can only deal with this fourth aspect by itself through effort in the form of retaining. Whether or not time is to be conceived as one of the resistances is immaterial. It is part of our conditioning and beyond our control. With this acknowledgment of the fact at this point we shall defer, for the moment, consideration of the respects in which the environment imposes delay between working and ultimate satisfaction and therefore the extent to which retaining as a "real cost" lies beyond the purview of choice.

C. TYPES OF RESISTANCE

1. SPATIAL AND MATERIAL RESISTANCES UPON THE SITE

This cursory analysis of the chief aspects of his environment which condition man's economic life serves as a basis for a somewhat more thorough examination of the kinds of resistance offered to the satisfaction of his wants and, therefore, the ways in which are determined the various quantities of effort required to accomplish his several purposes.[1] Some few of these resistances are absolute. That is, they can-

[1] Our terms for these resistances will be purely figurative language, like all terms for the "properties of bodies" in nineteenth century physics—i.e., impenetrability, porosity, cohesion, affinity (chemical), adhesion, compressibility, elasticity, inertia, etc. All are merely names for classes of observed facts, not explanations of them; but they class these facts with sufficient precision so that they can be measured as magnitudes.

not be overcome by effort at all. Most, however, are not insuperable, although they vary widely in the quantity of effort required to overcome them. Even the absolute resistances may, in a sense, be evaded or got round.

The "ideal type" for an economy, in economic analysis, is too often one which is not projected in space. It is conceived as if it existed at a point. The essential condition of space is omitted.[2] Therefore, before we consider the resistances due to the aspect of site, spatial and material, we must set up for ourselves a mental diagram of the inherently necessary ground plan of economic operations—a system of production and consumption—an economy. And this because the natural resistances are only relative, economically speaking, to these operations. For this purpose it will be convenient to establish a plan which appears only in rudimentary form in a direct economy—necessarily limited in area and free from exchange—but which will represent as well the fundamental geographical arrangement we find in the more complex indirect economy. The essential ground plan of a direct economy consists of a site at which consumption takes place, of a set of tributary sites at which extraction of various materials or powers takes place, and of a set of loci, at these or other sites, at which the remaining members of the series of operations, constituting production of each of the various products, take place. Such an economy, then, presupposes an area which includes several not necessarily contiguous sites, to one of which is ultimately directed all movement.[3] It is not necessary for us to define any unit size of area as *a* site. Site, in the economic sense, is the locus at which a stationary or moving economic operation takes place. It is whatever area is actually utilized for the operation. But at least we must regard as separate sites areas which are not contiguous, though they may be used for one and the same process.[4]

[2] Marshall, at one point (*291*, 145), notes three of the conditions imposed by environment on site: the necessary locus for an operation, a means of access at least to ubiquitous material resources, and definite location with reference to other sites (distance).

But, as Enke has recently pointed out in a very interesting and original analysis of "Space and Value" (*138*), Marshall usually "ignores space in his apparatus." Enke also confirms our statement in the first sentence of this paragraph of the text. "The theory of value does not commonly include considerations of space" (*ibid.*, 627).

[3] With due allowance for the fact that all producers and all consumers are, in a direct economy, one and the same, Case II in Enke's article, quoted in the previous note (see *138*, 629), conforms to this ground plan of ours.

[4] That this ground plan of a direct economy is not imaginary may be confirmed by an observation of my own during the first World War. At one time I was quartered upon a French peasant whose farmhouse was built into a cave in the bluffs over the River Cher. His was a considerably self-sufficient economy. His landholdings consisted of a

With respect to the relation between this ground plan and that aspect of the natural environment which we have called site, both on its spatial and on its material side, there are two fundamental forms of resistance, both of which are absolute. The first is commonly stated in geometry in the form of an axiom, "Two solid bodies cannot occupy the same space at the same time." Or, we may say, to the extent that a particular lot of physical material—including man—is impenetrable, then, if it is already occupying certain space, it is necessary to move it before any other material can occupy that space. At the opposite pole we have another axiom. No particular lot of physical material—including man—can occupy two different positions in space at the same time. Again, if it is already in one position, it is necessary to move it before it can be located in the other. Thus two material objects may occupy the same space, and one object may occupy two different positions in space, only successively, not simultaneously. The natural resistance to the operations of an economy on a system of sites arises from these two hard and fast conditions. The first form of resistance may be called *pre-occupation* of space,[5] and the second, *economic distance* or *depth*. But the practical effect of both takes the form of resistance to motion; and, while the obstacle, pre-occupation, is essentially material and the obstacle, distance or depth, is essentially spatial, it will be realized that the resistance to any motion required to evade these obstacles depends as much upon the character of the material moved and the medium through which it is moved as it does upon the distance to be moved.

It may seem to the reader that the setting up of these self-evident truths, or axioms, of natural resistances in the aspect of site is supererogatory. Nevertheless, as has already been noted, the fact is that they have never been systematically embraced in economic analysis, and at times they have been ignored. There has been a tendency to relieve

---

large number of detached pieces of varying size, some at a distance of more than a mile from his house. Yet he claimed that this plan represented ideal integration, since each piece was of exactly the right character and size to supply some element in his whole requirements, and each was approximately as near his home as possible for its particular character.

Such a ground plan, but not in abstract form and only for an indirect economy, lies at the root of the analysis contained in von Thünen's *Der isolierte Staat* (399). Because it was not reduced to abstract form this implicit ground plan seems to have influenced economic analysis less than it should have.

[5] The general term in physics for this property of matter has been "impenetrability." That is the ultimate cause. But we do not want to use the term because impenetrability cannot be overcome by moving; pre-occupation can.

economic abstractions from the necessity of conforming to the conditioning of space, whereas economic categories which have a physical representation can exist only in space and are absolutely subject to its laws. This evasion will be found to be especially misleading when we come to consider the notion of "market" which, in an ill-defined form, occupies so considerable a position in economic analysis. It is also true of the so-called "law of rent" and of the "law of diminishing returns," whose only existence as "laws" is due to these underlying and inescapable conditions, to which they should be, but have not been, ascribed. And, generally speaking, it is well to recognize that the reasons we cannot all live on one building site, or enjoy the country while we are in the city, or produce all our wheat on one farm are not ultimately economic, but are rather conditions imposed on man by the physical facts of his environment.

Consider, first, any economic operation upon its necessary locus—a particular site. The material composition and conformation of the site may be suitable to this operation as it stands. If not, either or both must be changed; the site must be deforested, graded, drained, etc. All these processes consist in removing unsuitable material that preoccupies the space in order to replace it with other material, or leave it empty (replaced by air) as the case may be. The quantity of resistance to such removal depends on the nature of the material and the distance or depth over which it must be moved. Such resistances may be regarded as the measure of the *unsuitability* of the site and as the obstacles to its *adaptation* to any particular use. If the particular operation is to be an extractive one, then the site must be regarded as a means of access to the materials. It will often be impossible to get at the desired natural materials directly. This is not the case if the operation is cutting timber or removing other material from the surface. But, if it is desired to produce materials the deposits of which are under the surface, intervening material must be removed. And, even if the process is an agricultural one and the latent resources are extracted by a biological process, nevertheless it is usually necessary to move (break up and overturn) the top soil, though not to remove it, in order that the plant can get at the material resources.[6] Again, in extraction, the quantity of resistance depends first on the nature

[6] Throughout our discussion of the environment we are regarding all agriculture or horticulture or arboriculture as kinds of extraction by biological process—more literally as biological mining. Most of the materials the plant uses, including water, are drawn up from the soil. Only the powers, light and heat, and the material, air, come from

of the intervening material, if any, and the distance over or depth from which it must be moved, once and for all; and thereafter, continuously, periodically, or progressively, on the nature of the material extracted and the distance (or depth) it must be moved. All of these resistances may be conveniently included in our rubric, *economic depth*.[7]

We may assume, in general, that any economic operation upon a site is for the time being exclusive. It is usually not possible to conduct two such operations upon the same site at the same time. And, usually, a change of operations, successively, will require removal of the apparatus, or wrecking of inappropriate buildings, or changes in the conformation, left by its predecessor. That is, the resistance nature provides to the adaptation of site to one use is usually repeated or even enhanced when the site is converted to a new use.

These forms of natural resistance also affect an economic operation upon a site in another way. Considered from the standpoint of the persons performing the effort and the apparatus used by them, there are two extremes to be avoided. The concentration of such a process in point of space—both superficially and three-dimensionally—results in increasing interference by reason of the pre-occupation of space by other persons and apparatus. There ensues the kind of resistance we imply by the word *congestion*. On the other hand, the more diffuse is the application of effort over space by any single person or piece of apparatus, the greater the proportion of the effort which is consumed in moving its point of application from place to place. Thus, at the other extreme, an operation encounters an increasing resistance, in the form of economic distance (or depth), from what we may call *dissipation*. Thus for any economic operation on land as site, there is increasing resistance in one direction—dissipation of effort—due to the increasing time spent in mere horizontal or vertical movement of the agent; and there is increasing resistance in the opposite direction —the concentration of effort, or congestion—due to increasing interference among the agents. Both forms of resistance are due to the physical characteristics of space and matter and not to economic considerations. The former is one of the chief factors in setting the limit

---

above. The forces and some of the materials are replenished naturally as used up; some of the materials are not. But all, at some time or place, are apt to be or become deficient and are replenished artificially—that is, as product.

[7] This because we wish to reserve the term "distance" chiefly for that between sites.

to *extensive* use of site; the latter affects the limit of its *intensive* use. The second of these extremes is not so obvious or quickly reached in the case of a direct as it is in the case of an indirect economy, because it arises principally from a plurality of workers. Nevertheless, even a single worker and his apparatus need a minimum of "room." The opposite extreme is equally characteristic of both forms of economy, since workers are necessarily individual. While dissipation and congestion are relations between the economic operation and the site, they are not attributes of the site, and should therefore be treated as resistances due to manner of operation.

All the foregoing applies as well to the preparation for, and the actual extraction of, natural powers at a site. But, in that case, the form which the natural resistance takes arises chiefly from the difficulty of *canalizing* the powers; the effort is principally required to install and operate the apparatus which will accomplish this result.[8] This will be treated more fully as we proceed.

Consider, second, the complex of economic operations upon a set of sites which form the ground plan of an economy. Here there is necessarily involved the spatial resistance we have called *economic distance.* Since all forms of natural materials and powers are not available at every site, it follows that the economy must extract those missing ones which it finds desirable for satisfying its wants at whatever points they happen to be available. And it must then usually convey them

[8] It is worth while, at this point, to call attention to the difficulties into which the older and physical view gets us. These may be exemplified by a reference to J. M. Clark (*83*, 72). He says, "Not merely such things as air and water, but the underlying forces of nature may be regarded as free goods . . . we never utilize such things up to the point of increasing resistance. Indeed, that is the reason why they are free." They are free because they "have unlimited capacity"; it is only "the equipment [necessary] to harness these forces [that] has limited capacity."

In this brief statement, in connection with the discussion of the notion of capacity, all the essential distinctions are confused. The word "free" is used both in the proprietary sense ("limits set by patents and secret processes") and in the economic sense (absence of the necessity of effort to utilize). But, in the latter sense it is misused. True, there are forces which can be utilized *in situ* without effort (e.g., the heat of the sun in "a place in the sun"). This we have called direct consumption. But the very fact that other forces, or these at other times, require to be "harnessed," makes them non-free in this sense from the beginning. That contradicts the statement that they are never utilized up to the point of increasing resistance. On the contrary, they are always used against some resistance, and almost always up to the point of increasing resistance, as we shall point out in the next chapter. Of course, the initial resistance is not due to limited quantity (capacity); it is due, rather, to the resistance of these forces to being canalized (harnessed) for our purposes in any quantity at all. However, as we shall also see, the ultimate increasing resistance is due in some respects to the limited quantity available on any one site.

from where they are to the ultimate destination—the locus of consumption. Frequently they must pass through intermediate sites at which they are further produced. All this involves going and coming of persons as well as moving of materials. The natural resistance to such movement varies not only with respect to location (horizontal distance) but also with respect to conformation in general. Is the intervening surface level; is it clear; is it solid or liquid; is it still or moving? Finally, the resistance to moving of materials varies also with the nature of the materials, which factor we have not yet considered. But this we cannot include in the aspect, site.

For our further use, all these various ways in which the natural environment (in the aspect of site, spatial and material) resists man can be reduced to a generalization and a set of technical terms. Taking as the center (figuratively speaking) the site at which the consumption of an economy takes place, those other tributary sites necessary to its productive activities are more or less *accessible* according as the radial economic distance to the center is less or more. That is, *accessibility as site* is the reciprocal or converse of economic distance. Each individual site is more or less *suitable* for any particular use according as the changes in its composition or conformation that would be necessary in order to fit it to such use are less or more. That is, *suitability as site* is the reciprocal or converse of the resistance to its adaptation to any one use on account of pre-occupation or economic depth or distance on the site (distance of removal only). Finally, for extraction only, each individual resource of material or power, at each individual site where it exists at all, is more or less accessible upon the site according as the combination of (chiefly) vertical economic distance (depth) upon the site and recurring pre-occupation of this distance by intervening material is less or more. That is, *accessibility of resources upon the site* is the reciprocal or converse of the compound resistance set up by what we may call, after its commonest form, *economic depth.*[9] We may abbreviate this third phrase to *accessibility*

[9] In general, we use the term "economic distance" to signify horizontal inaccessibility, and "economic depth" to signify vertical inaccessibility. But it will be convenient to use economic distance to cover the resistance to motion between sites, which may include a vertical component; and economic depth to cover the resistance to motion upon a site, which may be partly horizontal (e.g., lateral "drifts" in mines).

Though we have used physical terms we must remember to keep these resistances dissociated from mere physical distance or depth. These two are purely analytical categories. What we are calling "economic distance" is the totality of natural resistances to movement, or "transportation" between sites. It is not proportionate to the mileage alone, but to all factors, other than the characteristics of what is to be transported, *as* (locus of, *sc.*) *resources.* And, in connection with it, we must remember that this is an attribute of the site, not of the resources. In this connection the site must be regarded as a means of access to resources. The function of applying effort to overcoming economic distance is generally called transportation and communication; that of applying effort to adapting site or to overcoming economic depth goes by many different names. All these attributes of site are relative to a particular use or material or power. And all are comparative for that. Resistance to the motion of the agent depends also upon the agent; that to the motion of material or power depends also on the nature of these.

2. RESISTANCES OF MATERIALS AND OF POWERS

When we come to consider the kinds of resistance which the natural environment, in its second or material aspect, opposes to man's efforts, we must exclude entirely the aspect of site. Therefore, considering first only the materials, these resistances must be limited to those which depend wholly upon the nature and characteristics of the desired substances themselves. From this standpoint the chief types are three; the first may be called the *economic refractoriness* of the material; the second results from its lack of *concentration;* the third may be called the *economic inertia* of the material. All the way along the process of production, from the "state of nature" to the finished product, materials of some kinds prove to be easy to "work up" (modify or shape), while others prove to be difficult. These varied resistances, embraced under the phrase "economic refractoriness," are data of external nature. At the same time few materials exist in their natural state in the condition of concentration in which they are desired for the finished product. They are mixed, or diluted, or encased, etc. According as the proportion of unwanted material, from which they must be separated at some stage in the process of production, is great or small, and according as this separation is difficult or easy, the materials in their native state may be said to oppose more or less resistance to use on

which fix the amount of effect necessary to be produced by effort in order to accomplish the result. Similarly, in "economic depth" we may conveniently include all forms of resistance not included in the characteristics of the material itself *in situ* (see below). Thus the operations of logging, of mining, of quarrying, of cropping land encounter innumerable and varied forms of resistance upon the site, in its adaptation and in extraction, before the literal processing of the material begins, which are due to the way the material exists or grows on the site, and not to its own character.

account of lack of concentration (dilution).[10] Again, during the whole process from extraction to consumption, materials oppose various resistances to being moved in the mass. These we have included under the term "economic inertia." Inertia is due to weight, bulk, fragility, liquidity (necessitating a container), injuriousness of all sorts (explosives, acids, poisons, etc.), and other analogous characteristics. Corresponding to accessibility and suitability in respect of site, we have then ductility, let us say (or, conversely, refractoriness), degree of concentration (or, conversely, dilution) and ease of transport (or, conversely, inertia) in respect of material.

In connection with the aspect of nature that we have called the natural powers, there is no specific form of resistance other than the difficulty of *canalization.* With this mere mention we will reserve discussion of that form of resistance and the methods by which it is met. But, in general, the extraction or use of these powers is also subject to many of the resistances considered above in reference to the aspects of site and material resources. However, it is chiefly by means of these powers—though in this respect they may also be viewed in their material form—that the environment adds to the total of resistances through *interference* with the operations of production. One of the chief occasions for man's effort, imposed on him from without, is the necessity of excluding interfering factors from his productive operations. In general we may call this exclusion, *protection.* It is difficult to classify; its needfulness depends partly upon the site, partly upon the character of the material, but is largely due to and directed against the natural powers. In the last case, it is difficult to distinguish from the resistance to canalization itself. By way of illustration we may note that outdoor work, production not housed, is almost exclusively confined to the extraction of material resources—agriculture, forestry, fisheries—or to the material alteration of, and construction upon, site. Almost all later stages of production require to be protected against interfering natural powers, at least in northern climates. Thus necessity for this form of protection depends somewhat on site but also on the step in the process. On the other hand, building stone, for instance, is not ordinarily housed at any stage of its production. Therefore, the need for protection depends partly on the material. With reference to the need for protection from other agencies than "the ele-

[10] But we stretch this matter of concentration *vs.* dilution to cover all quantitative relations between materials or powers that are wanted and the space in which they exist, in so far as these cause resistance.

ments" it must be noted that agriculture is one of the most vulnerable of all productive processes. Cultivation consists in the elimination of competitive plant life; fields must be fenced against animals; plants and trees must be sprayed against insects and fungi, and so on *ad infinitum.*

Finally, during the phases of production there occur—just as we have already noted there occur during consumption—multifarious kinds of *spoilage*, or destruction by "numerous gradual agents which we call collectively *time*," as Senior put it. Upon the nature of the material from which a product is made depends largely its physical durability—that is, its capacity to endure the activity of these agencies. And upon its physical durability then depends, to that extent, its economic durability. In so far as the net product is less than the gross by reason of spoilage or destruction during the process of production, and in so far as the product in use in consumption needs to be replaced more rapidly by reason of the action of these external agents called "time," then these agents must be regarded as hostile or interfering powers of the natural environment which go to increase the resistance to man—and therefore to increase the effort required—in the satisfying of his wants.

Taking into consideration all these types of resistance, offered by the environment in its several aspects, we may assume, as a first approximation, that an economy will seek so to organize its complex of sites that, for each required operation, the sum of economic distance and depth is at a minimum, with due consideration for the initial resistance to adaptation of site, and that the happy medium (or minimum resistance point) between dissipation and congestion is striven for. That is, where there is a choice, the economy will seek to apply its effort for each purpose at the site where, and in the way in which, the quantity of effort required to overcome these compound resistances is least per unit of product. And, measured in terms of these respective quantities of effort, as experienced or estimated, it will come to arrange the sites available for each purpose along a scale, representing their accessibility in both aspects. In general, also, it will seek to find and use, as the material necessary to satisfy each want, that one whose resistance on account of refractoriness, lack of concentration (dilution) and inertia is least in proportion to the usefulness which it has or which can be incorporated in it and, perhaps also, to its physical durability. For each purpose it will seek to select, from the natural powers it has learned to control, that one which opposes the least resistance to canalization in proportion to its effectiveness. Finally, there will be added to each of these forms of resistance, in calculating them, such known resistances as are imposed by the interfering natural powers, and which can be protected against or which necessitate an allowance for loss.

It should be noted that the foregoing applies only in part to that "central" point in the essential ground plan of an economy which represents the site at which most consumption takes place. At that point, the site may be so small that economic distance on the site (depth) is almost negligible; and some materials and powers may be available at the cost merely of activities which we do not regard as involving effort, or of effort so slight that their accessibility approaches close to the conceptual limit of no resistance. To this extent, then, the use of the environment at this point offers a resistance that is within our conventional limit, involves no production, and becomes, therefore, direct consumption.

3. THE RATIO OF EFFORT TO THE RESISTANCES—TECHNIQUE

Some of these natural resistances can be measured and compared in physical terms—technologically—and therefore in terms of the amount of force, static or dynamic, which natural powers or human physical energy are required to supply in order to overcome them. But the only way to measure and compare all of them is in economic terms. Such terms would appear to be the quantity of working-time they compel per unit of product. Economics is directly concerned only with the second form of comparison and measurement. Yet we have to recognize that this working-time is applied via a technique. If that varies, working-time will vary even for fixed resistances. If working-time varies, so does work incorporated; for working-time is measured in terms of standard units of work performed per hour. It is evident then that, among these three factors, resistance, effort, and technique, it is only possible to compare resistances in terms of effort, if technique remains the same; to compare quantities of effort in its own terms, if the resistances given by natural conditions are the same and the technique is uniform; and to compare techniques, if the quantities of effort are measured against a single set of natural resistances. Nevertheless, however complex this may sound when so formulated, it is exactly the procedure by which man determines the most favorable of several sets of natural conditions and the most economizing of several kinds of technique. He measures both in terms of the effort they economize for any given purpose, and he ascribes to each kind, entirely independently of the other kind, its own effect relative to others of its own kind. He does not conclude that, when one site offers less resistance than another, it is due to a greater effectiveness of effort; nor, when one technique reduces the ratio effort to resistance, that is due to an improvement in the quality or intensity of his effort.[11] Both greater accessibility and better technique are recognized as making the task *easier*. The fact that it may be difficult or impossible, in borderline cases, to assign changes in effort per unit of product to any definite one of these three factors does not make it any the less important to do so in so far as that is possible.

In order to convert these observations with regard to practical procedure into a useful scientific statement of the relations among these magnitudes, for our further analysis, we may recall our definition of the magnitude of effort. Since the component "retaining" does not appear to be so directly related to the natural resistances, and therefore to their interrelations with effort via technique, we will have to examine the part it plays separately and in the next subsection. Here we may remind ourselves that the component of effort, working, is quantitatively measured in terms of a standard quantity of work performed per unit of time. Thus we have reduced variations in efficiency to terms of quantity. The interrelations between working and resistances can then be stated as follows: The magnitude of natural resistance, in spite of the fact that it is wholly physical and largely mechanical, can be quantitatively conceived as the resistance offered to the production of a standard quantity of work at any particular task. This measure is wholly economic; but the two magnitudes are connected via the physico-economic entity, technique. Without that relation—that is, at the no-technique or brute-force stage—effort in physical terms would have to equal resistance in physical terms. Then, if the natural resistance were greater, the duration (quantity) of the working would have to be greater in order to accomplish the same results. But this assumes no technique; for any improvements of technique from this brute-force level change the ratio of effort to resist-

[11] It may be due in part to an increase in the mental component of effort, and thus to super-standard working as we have called it. As to that more hereafter.

ance and even the composition of the effort. We will give natural resistance the dimension N, since we have already used R for retaining. We will give technique, or the state of the *arts*, the dimension A, since we have been using T for time. It should be noted that, since we are using the dimension A as a multiplier, the stage of no-technique is unity, not zero, for A. Having fixed as a unit of resistance that quantity of it which requires the expenditure of a unit of work at any given task under no technique, so that 1 W = 1 N, we substitute a technique under which, for the same resistance, only ½ W is required. Then, while $1\ W \times A_1 = 1\ N$, $\frac{1}{2}\ W \times A_2 = 1\ N$. But, more often, we recognize that the absolute quantity—or extent—of physical resistance encountered is increased by the more advanced technique. It is necessary to conduct two processes in order to accomplish the same ultimate result. Nevertheless, in order to be an improvement, the quantity of work per unit of final product must thereby be decreased. We find then that $\frac{1}{2}\ W \times A_2 = 1\frac{1}{2}\ N$ per unit of final product. In other words, A_2 has made possible the overcoming of resistance at three times instead of only twice the previous rate. This formulation is useful as an analytical tool even if it appears that absolute units are impossible to come by and even if the whole system cannot be applied numerically, but only by comparisons of equalities and of more or less. Nevertheless, as we have seen, there is a definite unit of working in a direct economy. For, there, the working being necessarily assumed to be homogeneous, a unit of work of any kind will be the quantity that can be achieved under the least advantageous technique (or no technique) in one time unit of working. Progress in technique will then be construed as a reduction in time units of working required for the same quantity of final product under the same conditions of resistance, and will ignore the fact that the component of mental activity required may have been enlarged. Differences in the economizing of two techniques can thus be measured. But, only if the measure of resistance is based on no technique (i.e., brute force) can the absolute value of any technique be stated. And, to a small degree in close comparisons but to a great degree in terms of such absolute values of technique, the composition of the working would be so different that it would be difficult to determine its magnitude in the old units.[12] On the

[12] The reader may have noticed that we have now introduced another discrepancy between the magnitude of product as a compound of work and that of its objective or subjective size. This discrepancy must be admitted here. But we are not yet ready to

other hand, preference for certain natural conditions (sites, etc.) will be determined by differences in time units of working under the same technique and, for the same quantity of final product, under the different natural conditions available.

4. THE RELATION OF TIME TO THE RESISTANCES

We alluded above to another aspect of the environment which conditions man's economic life—namely, time or the passage of time. To complete our analytical scheme of the natural setting of economic activities we must now undertake briefly to show the influence of time on the natural resistances and therefore on man's efforts. We recognize, of course, that all processes require time. Thus the process, working, does so. But, for working, time does not constitute a separate resistance. Neither does it do so in the case of the ravages upon product which we "collectively call time" (Senior). These, too, can only take place with the passage of time. But we have treated all sources of such ravages as themselves a kind of natural resistance. They do not occur apart from time.

The only way in which the passage of time appears as itself a proximate factor in the relation is when there is imposed by the environment—not by man's choice—a delay or interval between the overcoming of some of the resistances already considered and the overcoming of others, or the ultimate satisfaction to which this overcoming was directed. Of course, time is not the cause of such delays. They are the results of the nature of things in several of its characteristics. Time, or an interval, is merely the form in which the delays appear. But it is convenient for us to view the delays in this proximate form, for, by doing so, we relate them to the only kind of effort that is involved in meeting them—the effort of retaining. It is true that we found such delay to be the criterion of working as well—that it is the facts of nature which preclude most means unless they are provided beforehand, and that it is this condition that differentiates consumption of product from direct consumption. However, we established a convention by which such brief delays—to the following consuming-day—would not be regarded as requiring retaining. And we can well maintain that convention here. Thus all we need to consider here is the influence of

---

deal with it comprehensively. That must be reserved to the end of Chapter 12, where all its circumstances are brought together under the headings of differentials and economic progress.

the environment in compelling retaining by imposing delays of more than a day during the production process or between that and consumption.

It is not necessary to review in this new light the several types of natural resistance we have just been examining. Suffice it to say that most of them, in themselves, and all of the techniques gradually devised to overcome them, impose delays, and therefore impose retaining as well as working. When we viewed the function of retaining from the standpoint of the occasions for it, in the previous chapter, we found many occasions that grouped themselves into the three types of technical necessity. All these are imposed by the conditions of the environment to a greater or less extent. Technique, which may be regarded as a way of getting around nature, must usually express itself via the technical options, and especially the second type which utilizes intermediate product. But, if technique resolves itself into a way of avoiding some of the resistances to working, or of securing assistance in overcoming them, it must be seen to be, at the same time, a way that incurs delay and therefore imposes the necessity of retaining. Or, rather, it is not so much that technique itself does this as that the ways and means it adopts involve inescapable delays that are imposed by the environment. Thus, from still a third viewpoint, progress in technique consists, in part, of a movement from the hand-to-mouth economy, through the day-to-day economy, to the long-range economy. By those very terms for the several stages there is connoted the increasing part played by the time interval—the delay. Such delay is not introduced chiefly because per se the satisfaction of wants is increased thereby. It is introduced because it cannot be helped. Delay is the "kick-back" which nature demands for allowing herself to be got round.

With all this in mind it becomes evident that it will be unprofitable, in much of our further analysis, to try to disentangle the two kinds of human effort that are involved in meeting or overcoming the various natural resistances. We will recognize that the resistance, if it should be regarded as such, which takes the form of delay and imposes retaining, is conjured up in most dealings with nature as an incident of working against the resistances that only working can overcome. When, therefore, we refer, in general, to efforts against natural resistances these efforts should be conceived to be an unanalyzed compound of various proportions of the two kinds of effort. Only when it is necessary for a specific purpose shall we take the compound apart and examine its composition or its components separately.

D. NATURAL ENVIRONMENT *vs.* EXTANT PRODUCT

One of the considerable sources of confusion in the classic formulation—land, labor, capital—has been due to disagreement as to where to draw the line between "land" and "capital." This is perhaps typical of the early stages of any science before there has arisen general agreement as to the relative importance of the various criteria that may be made the basis of classification. The dispute revolves around two questions; the one, whether man-made "improvements" in land are a part of the "land" or are, rather, "capital"; and the other, whether exhaustible materials are to be included in the former or in the latter class. These questions are not important in themselves; but solution of the questions indicates what type of system of energetics is being used. And that is of the most fundamental importance.[1]

[1] By way of a few examples we may cite the following: Marshall (*291*, 144) seems to accept the older view of both classes which assigns "those material things which owe their usefulness to human labour" to "capital" and "those which owe nothing to it" to land. This, as usual, he somewhat qualifies (for example, see *ibid.*, 147). His reason seems to be that the quantities of those things which are "given" by nature are fixed and therefore there is no "supply price" for them. But he adds the further reason that the latter class is permanent, although this is certainly not true of the exhaustible materials. Walras adopts almost the same distinction (*420*, 182 ff.). Lands are "*naturels et non artificiels ou produits.*" Also they are "*inconsommables*" and cannot even perish by accident. They are peculiar, therefore, in that one does not produce them or consume them. Therefore (*ibid.*, 184) land is separated from buildings, walls (including retaining), irrigation and drainage, which belong with seed, harvest, etc., under "*revenus.*"

Cassel (*74*, 257) takes the opposite position as to materials. He disregards the criterion of fixed quantities and only accepts that of permanence—the fact that some attributes are not used up, or are, in Ricardo's terminology, "indestructible." Therefore "materials" in so far as they are "exhaustible" are to him capital, and all the rest of the environment is land. "As natural materials are not durable goods," their prices "are simply prices of consumable articles that are found in nature." Which leads him to the erroneous conclusion that these materials are actually, in economic practice, valued *in situ* like other goods. We shall examine that error later. On this one of the two questions Wicksell is in accord with Cassel. He allows to land only the "natural resources which renew themselves continually." Its "actual ingredients . . . have rather the characteristics of capital" (*439*, I, 107).

Pareto may be cited as an example of those who take the opposite position as to improvements. He finds it impossible to separate the *capitaux mobiliers* from the *capitaux fonciers* in which they have been incorporated. He therefore throws them into the same class (land), the peculiar characteristic of which is that it is difficult to reproduce (see *317*, 435).

As taking the opposite position on both counts we may refer to Davenport. While he recognizes the old distinction between "natural" and "artificial" environment (*107*, 415), between "original environment" and what an "isolated individual" "has added to it" (*ibid.*, 415) and thus between "original" and "present" environment (*ibid.*, 161), he

These questions are clearly settled for us by our system of energetics. We are not viewing the natural environment in terms of a congeries of physical objects and forces; rather we regard it as a system of resistances opposed to man in his efforts to wring a living on and from it. The physical objects and forces—the sites, materials, and powers—are merely the points of reference to which we assign these varied and relative resistances. The results of successful past efforts to overcome the resistance imposed by a site to a certain use—its unsuitability—were necessarily to be defined as product at the time. If they remain in the present, they are extant product—that is, they are economically extant, as defined in the previous chapter, until they are consumed, used up, or lost. The fact that they may become physically indistinguishable has nothing to do with the question. They are distinguishable in economic analysis, and must be kept so. In effect, that means in this connection that, if they still serve to reduce the current resistance to the particular operation as compared with the original resistance of the raw land, they have survived and are extant. Therefore, all "improvements" that continue to economize current working, as compared with that required by the original state, are extant product. The work they involved in the past, as well as the retention they have involved since, have been and should continue to be added to (spread over) the current effort against the remaining current resistance as long as the site continues to be used for that purpose.[2]

The second question divides itself into two parts. Materials or powers *in situ*, while they offer potential resistance to extraction, are not yet product in so far as they have as yet had no effort incorporated in them. This compels us to discriminate. If the materials or powers, in

---

concludes for various reasons (*ibid.*, 162–172), not merely to throw the artificial in with the natural, but to treat the whole as capital. And this because capital is "all durable and objective sources of valuable private income" (*ibid.*, 161). Knight, for his own purposes, adopts the same course on the ground that "finding of new natural resources is equivalent to their creation" (*240*, 337)—that there is no "final distinction" between "pre-emption and production" (*ibid.*, 354, note 1). Finally Wicksteed (*441*, 365) deems the distinction "theoretically worthless" even if it can be drawn.

But all this is as if economic analysis needed to take no interest in the question how product comes into existence or how it comes to remain extant, but could take its appearance or existence for granted—as a datum merely to be accepted—like that of the natural environment. The real point is that product is what must be *done*, for it cannot *happen;* while nature is what *happens* and cannot be *done*.

[2] The longer the use the more thinly the original work is spread. But the original work measures the quantity of retaining, as effect; the retaining is done all along.

their natural state, are located upon the site wholly by reason of natural processes, they cannot be treated as product nor, therefore, as extant product. If, however, their being on that site or their arrival in the condition in which they are at present is due to the effort of man, then, to that extent, they are construed as product—even if unfinished—and therefore as extant product.[3] And here we customarily draw some arbitrary lines, for convenience, according as we construe the effort expended to have been incorporated in the materials or powers, or upon the site. We treat it as incorporated in the materials or powers if it has constantly to be repeated each time the operation of production is performed, or for each season, and as incorporated in the site, if not. In accordance with these several criteria buildings, plants, etc., are regarded as product and, to the extent that they are irremovable without demolition, as incorporated in the land. Again, bodies of ore "opened up" are not themselves product, as yet, though those "works" upon the site which, by the "opening up," have rendered it more suitable for their extraction, were product and are extant product incorporated in the site. Thus, too, clearing, or drainage, etc., of agricultural land is extant product incorporated in the site. But the materials and powers which exist naturally in it (fertility), until the soil begins to be prepared for a crop, are not yet product at all. As they stand they are nothing but potentials, useless and unusable until produced. On the other hand the seed, or the artificial fertilizer are both product, regarded as incorporated in the expected crop, the materials, not in the site.[4]

[3] Thus domestic animals are product to the extent that human effort is incorporated in them.

[4] Since there have grown up certain economic conventions which do not seem to conform to the agronomic facts, let us say that, in making use of the biological processes of growth in converting natural resources into desired products, no aspect of the environment is "inexhaustible" except site. All others are used up, sooner or later, by the process. The necessary supplies of some—heat, light, air, moisture—may be replenished by natural process. But in some form of culture or other, each one of these "climatic conditions" may instead have to be produced or avoided—eked out or tempered. The necessary supplies of others—constituents of the soil—must usually be replenished from below by ploughing or even brought from other sources. Even the "lay of the land" may be exhausted by erosion, or, if it is artificial (produced), by tilling itself (e.g., terraces). For all these reasons the resistance offered by nature to the continued use of a site for agricultural purposes must be conceived normally to increase with the passage of years.

E. THE LIMITATIONS UPON SITES, MATERIALS, AND POWERS

1. THE NOTION OF RELATIVE SCARCITY

In the previous examinations of the several economic entities, wants and their satisfactions, and the two forms of effort, working and retaining, our procedure has been, first, to arrive at a qualitative analysis, as definite as possible, and then to determine what limitation, if any, is set upon the quantity of the entity by its own characteristics. In that connection we considered several possibilities of limitation of the "extensity" of individual wants—due to various sorts of discontinuous and of continuous decline in intensity; but we found no apparent quantity limitation on the number of wants except an external one—the capacity to satisfy them. This latter, in turn, appeared to derive from the autonomous limitations of effort. That, in turn, as to working, was fixed at that point at which the force behind the product of working is equal to the sum of the internal resistance to the working required and the force behind not-working (leisure). And, as to retaining, the limitation was found to lie along the range at which the force behind any provision for the future is just greater than the sum of internal resistance offered by the retention involved and either the force behind the current provision that will have to be forgone or the internal resistance offered by longer working-hours, whichever is greater. Following the same procedure, we must now consider whether any self-set limitations appear in the matter of environment, in any of its aspects and either in the aggregate or in detail; and, if so, what they are.

From the usual physical viewpoint of economists the "factor" land—or the respective aspects which go to compose it, sites, materials, and powers—is regarded as consisting of a great variety of definite quantities of physical objects or phenomena. Among these definite quantities some are conceived to be "unlimited" while most are "limited," relatively at least to the quantity desired by human beings for the satisfaction of their wants. The latter are then defined as relatively "scarce." Since this relative scarcity connotes the fact that there is "not enough of them to go round," it is supposed to become necessary to subject the objects which exist only in "limited" quantities, in this sense, to appropriation or pre-emption—by which fact they become "economic goods." The men who "get there first," or those who seize and occupy them, may monopolize them, while the rest go without. Or, in an indirect and exchange economy, those who set the highest value upon their possession, and are at the same time able to give in exchange their equivalent to the next highest valuers, may monopolize them, while others not included in this elect class go without. Or, finally, these principles may not apply absolutely, but only relatively. The outcome may not be on an all or none basis. It may be that the quantity that each may possess is merely restricted by reason of the limited quantity available, so each is only partially satisfied by a more or less exigent quantity.[1]

It would be difficult to devise a scheme more utterly false to the facts. And this will be readily perceived if we survey these facts without prejudice or confirmed prepossessions. It must be immediately

[1] One could write a lengthy essay on the development of this scheme, running from, let us say, the early classical economists to its culmination in Cassel. One of its origins seems to have lain in the early distinction of "free" goods, which "bear no price" and are therefore not appropriated because they exist in "unlimited" quantities. Obviously, these must all be natural materials and powers. We may cite the summation of the classical school (Mill, *298*, I, 52) as representative. But this fallacy has persisted even to Marshall, as we have noted (see Section D, note 1, above). Another origin seems to have been the puzzling problem presented by "goods" which have great "value in use" with little or none "in exchange," and vice versa. This was closely allied to the first, but extended to product as well. A third origin must be suspected. That was the refutation of the labor-cost theory of value which, in the hands of Marx and his followers, had been twisted away from its original meaning into an exclusive explanation of all production and a peg on which to hang all dissatisfaction with society as organized. The full development arose when the various marginal utility schools began—partly by way of solving the problem of the above-mentioned discrepancy in value, and partly by way of exposing Marxism—to develop their theory of value. For then value came to be determined by the point on a usually negatively inclined curve of utility to which a *limited* supply stretched. The definition "limited" came then to be applied to those "goods" whose quantity (whether of stock or flow) did not reach to the full "extensity" of the curve; and the definition "unlimited" covered all those whose quantity reached to or beyond that point.

The feature we are concerned with here is not the general thesis but only its application to the environment in its raw state ("land"). All sites, and most materials and powers were conceived to be "limited" and therefore "relatively scarce." This scarcity then persisted through production. That was at least the chief, and sometimes the only acknowledged, cause of the fact that almost all products exist or flow in quantities less than that required for satiety for all persons (i.e., "the quantity demanded at the price of zero"—Walras). One may cite, by way of a few examples: in the Austrian group, Menger, *296*, 61 and note, Wieser, *442*, VIII and 70, Böhm-Bawerk, *38*, 135–137; in the Lausanne group, Walras, *420*, 23–26, 31, 166–169 (it should be noted, as Pareto does, in *316*, I, 34—and as we have done in Appendix IV—that Walras's limitation of quantity is the cause of, but not identical with, his *rareté*), Pareto, *317*, 315–316, and particularly Cassel, as the arch-apostle of "relative scarcity" (see *74*, in general, and *ibid*., 16 ff. and 90, in particular); in the English group, Wicksteed (*441*, 45–46); and, as a sample of its permeation of economic thinking, Davenport (*107*, 17 and 103). This list could be prolonged indefinitely. But even so much may be redundant.

admitted, of course, that since the aspect of site—regarded two-dimensionally—consists of the earth's surface, and since that of materials and powers consists of physical phenomena, the actual quantities of each, as a whole, and of each subordinate kind or variety, must necessarily be finite. However, that has no bearing on the question, since it is only rarely that economic operations have ever put to use any individual variety of site, material, or power in quantities even remotely approaching these finite limits.[2] Let us examine the data in some detail. Take first the land surface of the earth regarded in its primary and essential aspect as provision for living space—that is, as site for consumption activities, or leisure. If we divide the area of this surface by the number of human families in existence—since presumably mankind cannot live except in some form of biological grouping which provides for procreation and for nurture of the immature—we arrive at a figure of something over sixty acres per family.[3] We recognize at once that almost no human families are using such an area exclusively as a site for consumption, and that none need to do so. On the contrary, most human families prefer to live in such a way that their site for consumption is very small. And this necessarily follows from the fact that mankind in general is gregarious and social. What most human beings like in this regard approaches what we have called congestion. They can hardly be too close together to suit them. It is true that there are parts of this land surface of the earth which will only be used by those who are willing (or prefer) to live in igloos, and other parts by those who will, or like to, live in tents on the borders of desert oases. On the other hand, some like to live on the sea in ships—not on the land surface at all. At any rate, it is evident that there is plenty of "living room"; that the actual limit of the finite quantity of land cannot be accused of being even remotely effective as a limitation on man in this respect; that there are vast areas of quite habitable land which are unused for this purpose; and that crowding in this respect, is ultimately due entirely to human preferences and not in the least to physical limitations. These preferences do run up against our first axiom of space—what we have called the absolute resistance of pre-occupation

[2] Just as a matter of logic, none of these natural manifestations can be held to be "unlimited" if they necessarily exist only in finite quantities. And if the use of that distinction is justified by stating that the meaning is "unlimited in relation to human wants," then one is spitted upon the other horn of the dilemma, as we shall see. For so, at present, are all the others.

[3] Raymond Pearl (*322, 252*) estimates the density of world population in 1937 at 40.9 persons per square mile. Families would, I suppose, average about four persons.

—but not in the slightest degree because the quantity of land available is limited.

Take next the aspect of site as a locus of the operations of production other than extraction. The most casual observation shows that only a minute portion of the land surface is occupied by plants, railways, office buildings, etc., and that so little of the ocean surface is occupied by sea-ships or of the air by air-ships that one may sail or fly for a day and a night without sighting another. Obviously, the reason office buildings rise toward the sky, and the reason manufacturing plants are congregated in centers is in no respect due to lack of land—to a limitation in the total quantity—even after deducting that required as sites for consumption. Instead, it is due to preferences. And obviously railroads and ships might just as well be somewhere else. There is an abundance of room for them.

If then the finite limit is so far from being effective in respect of site as a locus for consumption and for production other than extraction, is it possible that, in this notion of limited quantity, economists were thinking solely of the environment as the site of natural recources—that is, as a source of those materials and powers that are generally wanted but are not generally available at all sites. In this respect we need to think of each particular material and of each particular power by itself; for, while it may be true that, for each material or power, some others can always be substituted, yet, if this substitution is compelled because the finite quantity of these others, which was in existence *in situ*, has been exhausted, the notion of limited quantities would to that extent be justified. In the first place, we must recognize that no natural limitation on the quantity of any material or power can logically be said to be effective so long as such material or power continues to be extracted. If we take account of each material and power only while it is extant, in our sense—that is, if we include only the quantity which is in the process between the beginning of extraction and final consumption or using-up—the limitation cannot be ascribed to the natural environment at all. It is wholly man-made. To increase the quantity, man is at liberty to use up less or to extract more. If, on the other hand, we are considering these quantities in terms of flow, not as static magnitudes extant, the same conclusion is reached. For, as long as there is any flow into production at all, the rate of such flow must necessarily be seen to depend on human choice—upon the effort expended—and not in the least upon any fixed limit of the quantity in its natural state. In other words, so long as a material or power continues to be extracted, it follows that there must be deposits remaining *in situ*, and the rate of extraction can then be increased if that is preferred. This rate is therefore again a matter of preference, not of limitation of quantities.

In the second place, if we take account of materials and powers also, or only, while they remain potentials in the sites at which they happen to exist (i.e., before extraction begins), we come then to disregard the rate of extraction and to consider only the number of sites, and the quantities at each site, at which each material or power exists. In this view the ultimate supply might be limited by nature even while the extant product or the current flow was only limited by man. From this restricted viewpoint we would need to examine the question whether, as a matter of fact, such limits to the ultimate supply, if they exist, are actually effective in limiting the current supply, or whether they serve merely as the source of fears for the welfare of our descendants and the basis of programs by the advocates of the "conservation of natural resources." If they do not limit the current supply—either as stock or as flow—they cannot be said to be the effective limits.

Considering, first, the number of sites at which the various desired natural materials or powers are available, the question resolves itself into this: Are there any such materials or powers of which every known deposit or source is being worked at the present time? It is clear that if, in every case, there are at least some known sources which are not being worked, the finite limit of the known quantity—much less the actual quantity—is not at present effective. I have made a somewhat thorough search to find such an instance and have been unable to do so. It is a matter of common knowledge that sources of all the common materials and powers still exist in a considerable degree of superfluity. It is estimated that the additional tillable acreage which can be made available in the four chief wheat exporting countries alone is almost three times that now in use there.[4] There are still vast areas of the earth's surface covered with native forest. There are innumerable geologically determined deposits of common minerals which are untouched.[5] As to the so-called rare minerals, one has only to consult a mineralogist to learn that, in every case, there are known to be sources

[4] Based on East's estimates (*129*, Chapter IV) and the figures of the International Institute of Agriculture for 1924. Actual acreage 482 (millions), potential, 1340 (millions).

[5] It is said that the largest and one of the best (in concentration) deposits of iron ore in the world lies under the harbor of Halifax, Nova Scotia.

which, for one reason or another, are still or now unworked. When the generalization made above is correctly understood it seems hardly likely that it will be contested. Therefore, it is not worth while to support it with an assemblage of the detailed evidence which is available to everyone.

Considering, second, the quantities of natural materials and powers that are in existence *in situ* in the various sites which are now being worked as sources, we arrive at the same conclusion. In every case these quantities must be regarded as finite. But I think no case can be found in which the finite quantity constitutes the actual limit of the quantity that is being, or will be, extracted. In every agricultural operation there is always some portion of the land which is not used for extraction of any kind—some "fertility" unused. On the site of every logging operation there is always some timber which is left uncut. In every mine there is always some part of the deposit which is "unpayable" and which is left unworked or, if worked, goes to the dump. In every oil district there are some wells that it is not worth while to pump.

2. THE SCALE OF INCREASING RESISTANCE

If we conclude from the foregoing that there do not exist now, and therefore have probably never existed, actual effective limitations of quantity to bar the increased use by man of any of the various kinds of sites, materials, and powers which the environment affords, what is the quantitative relation of nature to the economic scheme, if any? Our answer has already been suggested. It is the graduated system of indefinitely increasing resistance to each and every use or extraction.

Regarded as a locus for living—leisure in general—various sites become almost direct means for satisfying wants. Or, rather, they become the means of access to those materials and powers which are available everywhere and which can be directly consumed by effortless activities; and they conduce in various other ways—conformation, composition, etc.—to these and other satisfactions. There arises from the differences among various sites in these respects a preference by man for one over another. They become arranged, for each man, in an order of preference extending almost without limit from the most satisfactory down. These preferences are largely a matter of accustomedness. Nevertheless, they vary widely among individuals. To a large extent these series of preferences for sites of various economies, or groups, in any one indirect or compound economy conflict, or compete. On the other hand, there are few climates or lays of the land that are not preferred by somebody. If it happens that very many orders of preference coincide at their upper ends, the result is likely to be what we have called congestion, and the area occupied by each for the purpose of leisure is apt to be very narrow. The spatial axiom we have called pre-occupation comes into play to prevent too great an extreme in this respect. Nevertheless, it is surprising how far the tendency can go, not only from rivalry for the preferred sites, but because the comminution of these sites actually seems to serve the purpose of conducing to the satisfaction of gregariousness. Strictly speaking, in considering one direct economy only, this conflict or competition could not arise. Therefore, with this brief indication of the fact that it exists, we will leave its further examination until we are considering the compound or indirect economy.

Having once fixed the central site for all its final economic operations—the point upon which the flow of all product must ultimately converge—it is clear that the order of preference of any economy among the various sites at which each desired material or power is available for extraction will be objectively fixed by the order of increasing total resistance of these respective sites. This total resistance will be the sum of what we have called economic distance and economic depth; that is, it will be measured by the effort required per unit of product in going and coming to work and in transporting the product between the site and its destination, together with that required upon the site for extraction itself. And the latter will depend upon the complex of factors we have already discussed under the rubric economic depth, together with those included under that of initially rendering the site suitable for the operation of extraction. Thus, the order in which all available sites for each purpose will be arranged will be in the ratio of their respective accessibilities as site, suitabilities as site, and accessibilities as resources. And, in these ratios, each of the component factors will be weighted, so that the final form will state the quantity of effort required per unit of product delivered to destination from each of the potential sites, respectively. By experiments or calculations the optimum site for extraction for each purpose can thus be selected—that one in which the resistance is least.

However, supposing that some of these sites are available for two or more kinds of extraction—that the various series coincide at some points—it will not be safe for us to conclude, at this stage of our analysis, either that the combination of sites chosen for each purpose will be that in which the effort per unit of product is least or even that the combination for all purposes will be that in which total effort required is least. For, in the latter case, the quantity of each material or power to be extracted would need to be given. But we do not know as yet whether or not that is given without reference to the quantity of effort per unit of product, and, necessarily, these would vary for each product under each of the possible alternative combinations. The problem is further complicated by supposing—as is, in fact, the case—that many final products will be combinations of several materials, or the result of the action upon materials of certain natural powers, which are only available at certain sites and are not transmittable. For, then, materials must first be transported to the locus of power, or one material must be transported to the locus of another, or both to some third site, depending on the nature of the operation and the technique used. On the other hand, after the assemblage of natural materials and the use of natural powers which are only available at certain sites is completed, there still remains the problem whether or not the most satisfaction will be derived and the least effort occasioned by conducting further productive operations at or near the final destination. This will frequently not be the case. The operation may itself injure the neighborhood of the site for living. Or the degree of concentration of the material may be such that the reduction in effort by reason of not transporting the unwanted portions of the mixture will overbalance the increase of effort caused by conducting this "purifying" operation somewhere between the source and the destination. Thus the final solution—the selection of all the sites for production, at all stages and for all products—becomes an extremely complex affair. But, this enables us to have its principles clearly in mind and, in the next chapter, we will elaborate it so far as is necessary for the purposes of our analysis.

Further, we must conceive the natural materials themselves as being ranged in a long series in proportion to the resistance they offer to being used by man, on account of their own characteristics. This resistance, besides depending on the degree of concentration in which they occur in each particular deposit, depends also upon the refractoriness and the economic inertia of the pure material itself. Thus, for each purpose for which a variety of materials is suitable, there is an order of total resistance of this kind; and all products, once the optimum material is chosen, may be arranged in a series according as this type of resistance is greater or less. To a certain extent the same statements are also true of natural powers, though here, as noted before, the chief resistance is to their canalization.

Finally, all these graded series must be corrected by the inclusion of the necessary allowance for resistance, at each site or for each material or power, offered by interfering powers and materials of extraneous natural processes. This will be measured, in part, by the effort required to provide protection in order to overcome such resistances and, in part, by allowances for loss on account of such resistances as are not or cannot be overcome.

By means of this re-examination of the actual facts of the environment we have arrived at a formulation of the quantitative relation between the environment and man's economic activities which is quite different from the customary one. We have admitted that all the resources of nature—sites, materials and powers—exist in finite quantities only; but we have found that these finite limits are not, in practically any case, effective as limitations upon economic activities. Instead, the actual limitation seems to be due, in almost every case, to the fact that, as the quantity of each of man's uses of sites and his extraction of each material or power is expanded, he meets increasing resistance from the environment. At some point in this expansion of each kind the effort required to overcome this resistance will cease to be justified by the amount of product. At this point will be fixed the limit. In a sense, therefore, it is fixed by nature—or, rather, natural conditions are one of the three factors in fixing it. But it is not fixed by, or in terms of, quantities of land, materials or powers. Instead it is fixed by, and in terms of, degrees of (intensity of) resistance. When the conditions set by the environment for man's economic operations are thus realistically examined, it is found that the notion of "relative scarcity" is wholly inapplicable to them.

12

THE DETERMINANTS OF "REAL COSTS"

A. INTRODUCTORY

WE HAVE, in the previous chapters, separately analyzed each of the several chief elements in the formula which represents for us the system of economic energetics—future wants-efforts providing means against natural resistances-present wants-effortless behavior using provided means-satisfactions. We shall undertake, in this chapter, to combine our analysis of efforts with that of natural resistances—that is, to formulate the scheme of qualitative relations which exist between them and of quantitative effects which these relations have upon product ("real costs"). In Part IV we shall combine this scheme with the prior analysis of wants and their satisfactions, in order to formulate the scheme of quantitative relations, mediate and immediate, which "real costs" have with the want system—which relations may have a bearing upon behavior. But, before proceeding to undertake the combination of our separate studies of efforts and of resistances in order to develop an analysis of comparative "real costs," it may be helpful to look back again at the ground we have covered, to attempt to draw together the detached parts into a connected whole, and, however difficult that may prove, to reduce this necessarily great complexity to a sufficient degree of simplicity so that a not too inexact representation of the whole of our results may be kept in mind.

1. THE SETTING FOR THE DETERMINATION OF "REAL COSTS"

From the traditional viewpoint of economics, its elements are taken to be consumers, on the one hand, and, on the other, the "factors" of production—"land," "labor," and "capital." All of these consist of physical objects. That viewpoint is essentially a technical one, and, as we have already noted, has developed a sort of economic chemistry which observes the mixing of these "factors" in various proportions—

with resulting "transformations" or "transpositions" into product for the consumers. But, if we go behind these superficial or proximate physical phenomena in their technical aspect—this economic chemistry—and examine the same field in its purely economic aspect, the ultimate phenomena organize themselves into something more akin to an economic physics. That is, the data then appear as a vast complex of interrelated human activities and natural processes—happenings, not things. The second viewpoint is equally as objective and as little abstract as the first. In fact, modern physics is teaching us that all we actually observe is events and that the notion of a static object is an illusion, due to our inability to "perceive," by direct sensuous means, the process which is occurring. Moreover, examined in this way, the phenomena lend themselves to interpretation in terms of our economic (and therefore complete) rather than in those of a purely mechanical (and therefore partial) system of energetics. The physical viewpoint serves its purpose for technology; it is not literally false for economics; but it does not disclose the fundamental conditions of economic behavior.

The way human wants recur or occur, in experience or expectation, the way they organize themselves into an order of priority and into constellations, and their behavior as they are being satisfied, these are all data of human nature which we may take as "given"—as biological facts. We identify these wants according to their physiological source, or, where that is unknown, as some psychological entity, and not according to the objective means or kind of means required to satisfy each (the thing wanted). Thus we also discard the physical viewpoint in the analysis of wants and substitute for that a purely economic (or psycho-physiological) viewpoint. We view these wants as the primary and, in a direct economy, the sole, ultimate incentive to human activity—the *raison d'être* of economic life—and the derived future wants as the cause of the energizing which leads to effort. In such a direct economy, these future wants lead directly to efforts to overcome resistances and thus secure satisfactions. But, in an organized (indirect) economy, wants appear only as the ultimate—or even the merely potential and ineffective—pull which we call demand—effective or ineffective. For, there, the system of energetics has become at least indirect, and perhaps the circuit has even been broken. In a direct economy the system of wants also functions as the determinant of the kind of product wanted or preferred, as well as of the quantities of each kind wanted (or perhaps it is only one of the influences fixing these quantities); and, if we include the location and organization of the activity of consuming as the locus, or point of application, of the ultimate energizing force arising from the system of wants, this system is also the determinant of the place where, as well as of the time when, these various products are wanted.

We have continued to use the ordinary economic term effort—perhaps at some inconvenience—to cover those human activities which contain the component of effort to the extent that they are not carried on for their own sake, and for the reason that they are directed rather toward the satisfaction of future wants, including those of the following consuming-day. Needless to say we have also here completely discarded the physical viewpoint. We do not mean by working merely the application of physical energy to the moving of things; we mean every mental or physical activity which is aimed to conduce to production. Nor do we mean by retaining the keeping of an object physically intact; we mean the keeping of the usefulness—or any part of the usefulness—which has been embodied in it, unconsumed or unused for future use.[1] Product is the result of working, and may have either material or immaterial form. Extant product is the combined result of working and retaining, and has necessarily a material form. It owes the fact that it is product entirely to working and the fact that it is extant entirely to retaining. The one form of effort can by no possibility supply the deficiencies of the other.

From the completely physical or technical point of view of production nature creates everything, man nothing. If we let the notion of production become equivalent to that of creation, then production is exclusively the work of natural processes. If, however, we concede

[1] We have distinguished between those physical and mental activities which involve effort and those which do not. The element of effort then enters as a qualitative factor which is required when the activity will not be carried on for its own sake. It is therefore apparently equivalent to some sort of internal (psychical) resistance, which only in this case becomes obvious. On the other hand, in the case of activities carried on for their own sake no such resistance is evident.

Now all physical and mental activities require something in the nature of force or energy and this energy is only required because there is resistance. We may more conveniently treat the non-psychical aspect of this resistance as external. Included, therefore, in external resistance is that which requires physical energy to move the body or its parts, or to "deliberate" (think).

It is not necessary, however, to draw a line between this hypothetical internal and such external resistance. We may lump both together and treat them as the opposition which any activity has to overcome. In what we may call spontaneous activity the overcoming of resistance is not *felt* as effort; in working and retaining it is.

that production consists, not in creation, but in transformation and transportation of natural materials and powers in point of space, then man comes to play a part, at least in respect of his working. His retaining cannot be conceded to be *doing* anything physically. Nevertheless, since these reshapings, movements, and preservations of natural phenomena require power to effect, and since the great bulk of the power applied is, and has for long been, the natural powers (including those of animals), the part played by man is still a small one.[2] Even from that viewpoint working would have to be regarded not so much as power but as a sort of catalytic agent which makes natural materials and powers react in a way in which they would not react of themselves. As a result, the proximate productive agencies would appear to be solely workers and natural powers which operate on inert media, land and natural materials, through the instrumentality of further inert media (extant product) in the shape of machines, etc. Thus, in this partially physical view, the two-factor scheme is justifiable if the second one is limited so as to include only nature's powers. But if we disregard both the wholly physical and the partially physical aspects as purely technical, and adopt the economic viewpoint instead, then the part played by man becomes the whole of the process of production, his working effort becomes chiefly mental and only slightly "manual," and the only agencies (or functions) of production turn out to be working and retaining by human beings.

To regard the environment as an independent *economic* agent is anthropomorphism; to regard it as a driven but co-operating factor is to take the purely, or the partially, physical or technical viewpoint. Physically the environment is the stage on which economic life takes place, the substance on which much of man's effort is expended, the energy which may reinforce his physical energy, and the innumerable forms of active interference with his striving. But economically the environment is not even purely passive; it is actually resistant; for, as a locus upon which, and a medium through which, the efforts of man contrive to satisfy his wants, it consists of the opposing forces which condition his economic operations. From this purely economic viewpoint the productive province of an economy in its environmental setting resolves itself into a system in which all energy is generated as

[2] Böhm-Bawerk compares the "enormous mass of powers which the natural world exerts spontaneously year out and year in" and the "much more limited natural powers which reside in the human organism" (*38*, 78). But he admits that it is only "technically" true that "these two elements . . . do everything in the work of production."

a result of future wants and takes the form of the two varieties of human effort—working and retaining—necessitated in order to overcome, by man's own or by "natural" physical energy, the resistances opposed by the environment to the satisfaction of wants. These last—the resistances—prove to be the sole occasion for effort because they exist as obstacles interposed between wants and their satisfaction; and this, in part, because of the characteristics of the environment as the necessary arena for all human activities [3] and, in part, because of its characteristics as the necessary source of all materials and powers, other than man himself, which he wishes to use or to avoid.[4]

From neither the physical nor from the economic viewpoint is extant product an agency of production at all. In fact, it is a completely inert mass—even more so than is nature, since nature includes powers. Extant product represents embodied effort of the past aimed to conduce, directly or indirectly, to the satisfaction of future wants. To the extent that it consists of final product, the requisite expenditure of effort is in various degrees completed thereon and the usefulness more or less fully reached or remaining therein, against the time that man's activity or inactivity of consuming will use up the usefulness and "charge off" the effort. To the extent that it consists of intermediate product—that is, of objects which are not to be physically incorporated in final product—its bearing upon the satisfaction of wants is only indirect. But, then, it is an equally inert or inactive mass whether it be regarded from the semi-physical view suggested above—physical powers—or from the purely economic. It consists exclusively of apparatus through which human or natural powers may be used or avoided—purposefully canalized or protected against.[5] Though we have discriminated between consumption—the using-up of the usefulness of final product—and use in production—the using-up of intermediate product—the two processes are similar in all respects except

[3] To include land, in this aspect, as a factor or agent of production is a good deal like regarding, as the three reagents of a chemical reaction, the beaker, the acid, and the alkali.

[4] We might say, picturesquely, that, in this economic game of chess, the environment is the board and the rules for the moves, natural materials and powers are the "men," and human beings are the players.

[5] Extant intermediate product only *does* something physically when powers are applied to it. Therefore, the term "automatic machinery" is deceptive. Thus it becomes part of the process of canalizing of powers. And, since these—other than human—require effort to divert them, the economic aspect elides both the natural material and the natural powers and takes account only of the effort required to produce the ultimate result.

their immediate destination.[6] Again, intermediate extant product may be at all stages of completion or using-up and therefore represent various degrees of its full complement of effort. But it is customary to regard the effort which has been "charged off" on account of using-up in the operations of production as having been transferred into the final—or further intermediate—product for the production of which it has been used. And this effort which is applied to final product via the using-up of the intermediate product in which it has been embodied we classify as *indirect* effort. So far as its ultimate destination is concerned it may be classed as indirect effort from the time it is first applied. However, so far as it is regarded as a part of the "real cost" of final product it only enters that category as and when the intermediate product in which it is embodied is used in production of final product. In the meantime it is suspended or *retained*. Therefore, once the working on itself is finished, the only further effort required for intermediate product is the continued retaining of its unused portion until it is used up.

Analyzed in this way, the functioning of each element in the whole process is seen to be unique and entirely disparate with that of each of the others. Their quantitative relations become incapable of being stated in terms of limited or unlimited quantities of each. Instead, they must be stated in terms, first, of the quantity of each that is related to some quantity of another and then, as to the aggregate, only in terms of a scale of rising intensities as to each element and thus in terms of greater, less, or equal intensities between the elements. We have found that wants may be arranged (analytically) in an order of declining intensity (priority); and also that effort—at least working effort—tends to rise in intensity as it continues over time. And we will find

[6] Any use of the term "consumption" to describe the using-up of materials or powers in the process of production is confusing. What occurs up to the point of consumption of final product is transference. Water going through a turbine remains water though losing its energy of position; coal under a boiler becomes ashes when it loses its heat energy; similarly, gas in a burner is converted into another gas when it loses its energy. Yet the economic result may only be consumed at a distant point and even at a distant time.

Materials which become part of final product are not consumed in the process. They may be converted by a chemical process or reformed by a mechanical one; but the material subsists economically. By a naïve but useful convention, already noted, we discriminate from these the materials which are used up as intermediate product. But here again the process is one of transference—and often of delayed transference—not one of economic disappearance of the order of consumption. The distinction between intermediate and final product is not easy to apply—perhaps cannot be applied exactly at all. It is, however, useful analytically to divide the process of production into steps, even if their physical demarcation is not important.

that the natural resistances which must be met for the production of the several individual products, or even the same product under different natural conditions, also vary over a wide range. All this suggests the general outline of the synthesis toward which we are proceeding. Since there is literally nothing "free" in the environment—nothing which can be applied to the satisfaction of man's wants without some activity on his part— [7] the intensity of natural resistance will fix some quantity of effort as necessary in each case. Since, as the thus-imposed quantity of effort increases in the aggregate, its intensity also increases, therefore it will, at some point, equal the declining intensity of successively satisfied wants, and the process will stop. This turns out to be a rough definition of the term "capacity" which we have used hitherto in its incomplete form. It will serve to complete our analysis of the limitation of working because it defines the missing link—the determinant which makes possible the comparison of the intensity of a want with the intensity of work by relating any quantity of a product to its requisite quantity of work. By this route the extent of capacity is seen to depend inversely on the specific resistances of the environment and directly on the duration of working within its limit, which is, in turn, a resultant of the intensity of wants and the willingness of man to work. This also puts "economizing" in its proper place. The problem of "economizing" [8] turns out not to be the economizing of "scarce" "factors" by finding the optimum proportioning of limited quantities of mutually substitutable "factors" to produce that mixture which will satisfy the largest subjective quantity of wants. Rather it becomes, in general, the finding of the way of least natural resistance to the satisfying of each want, so that, in the course of economizing working with or without the usual concomitant of increasing retaining, the requirements of the sum of the two non-interchangeable forms of effort which that resistance compels is at a minimum. Behind this proximate objective the ultimate objective is that the process of satisfying wants may be carried as far as possible along the order of preference, before this minimum of effort per satisfaction ("real cost") rises to an intensity, in the course of the working-day, at which it is exceeds the intensity of the next want in order remaining unsatisfied and a limit is thus set to further effort.

[7] It is hardly necessary to keep repeating our conventional exclusion of direct consumption—activity not defined as effort.

[8] This is analyzed more fully at the end of this chapter under the title "maximization."

This, then, is the scheme into which our elements are fitted. It follows that, in our analysis of "real costs," we are measuring the quantities of two human functions which must be applied directly or indirectly to product in order, by means of the physical energy of man or of natural powers, to overcome the natural resistances which the environment places in the way of the satisfaction of man's wants.

2. ATTRIBUTION OF PRODUCT TO ITS ECONOMIC CAUSES

Since economic analysis has approached the subject of the quantitative relation between effort and product almost wholly from the standpoint of value theory, it is necessary for us, at the outset, to make clear a distinction which that prepossession is likely to obscure. Hitherto, we have chiefly regarded product in its two economic aspects—on the one hand, as the result of the process of production or contribution, in which aspect it represents quantities of work and perhaps retention; and, on the other hand, as a means for the satisfaction of wants, in which aspect it represents usefulness. But we have also used a third and non-economic aspect—that is, objective homogeneity (qualitative) and objective quantity (quantitative). At this point in our analysis this third aspect becomes essential, for it is actually the only nexus or common point through which the first two aspects can be related. In discussing the subjective measurement of means in Chapter 7, we noted that one relatum of the relation is the means, or its attributes, objectively regarded. It is only because we first determine by our senses, directly or indirectly, what is a single means, and then count it or find out how to measure quantities of it in terms of arbitrary units in such a way that its stated magnitude may be assumed to remain the same, that we attain any fixed point whatever to which to attach usefulness. But the objective determination of the kind and quantity of this common intermedium is equally essential in relation to the second aspect; for it is also only by means of the establishment of such a unit that we are able to assign, as its "real cost," what is merely a record of past effort expended on this particular objective magnitude. This conclusion is not so obvious in the case of product which is not embodied in material form. Nevertheless, it is true there as well. There is not and there cannot be any exact direct comparisons between efforts and satisfactions.[9] Such as there are may only be conducted indirectly in terms of natural, produced, or arbitrary units of objectively homogeneous kinds of product as the intermedium.

Thus we come back to the objective units of objectively classified means which we developed in Chapter 7. When the differences between two masses of product are objectively "unnoticeable"—not when they are merely subjectively indifferent—these constitute a single product. But mere naïve identification, as of the same form, is not sufficient for economic analysis. To this we must add co-occurrence or co-existence in point of space and time; and these, of course, are also objectively determinable. That is, complete identity of kind can only exist from some single given standpoint in space and time. The quantitative determination in terms of objective size or number has already been sufficiently discussed. There is, however, one complication implicit in this statement which requires notice here. The fact that such objects or acts are product at all, according to our definition, is not directly determinable from the objective viewpoint. That characteristic has only a subjective origin—that is, it is due to the attachment to the object or act of the relation of usefulness for some want at the time when, and only if, effort is being applied to its production. We shall see shortly that this point helps to clarify an otherwise confusing issue.

Taking as our starting point a single unit of *a* product, in this sense, we note that it is, by definition, a result of contribution—that is, it owes its economic existence as product to the fact that effort has been expended upon it to bring it to this state, locus and moment. From the standpoint of the effort expended upon it the product has, then, been *contributed*. The quantity of this contribution is not, however, the quantity of the product, objectively considered, but rather the amount of effect incorporated in it by the two forms of effort. In the case of working, one may say that one unit of effort has contributed one unit of effect to product.[10] Conversely,[11] from the standpoint of the product, the unit of effect is to be *attributed* to the effort which

[9] Thus we cannot have a direct balancing of Fisher's "desirable mental experiences" with "certain undesirable ones"—"efforts" (*142*, 326), because they do not occur simultaneously and therefore cannot be co-terminous.

[10] Since we are measuring effect (work) in terms of standard working, the units correspond.

[11] All relations are at least bipolar. What we can say about them depends always upon the pole they are viewed from—which we choose as the relate.

has produced it. But, again, the quantitative relation in this direction is not with the quantity of product, objectively considered. *Attribution* is, instead, an accounting for the effect incorporated in the product by attributing it to its causes, in terms of quantities of effort.[12] So, here, one says that the effect embodied in a unit of product is to be attributed to a unit of effort. Since the only effect of retaining is to keep product the same, the quantity of retention performed cannot be observed in the same way. The only way to attribute extant product to the retaining effort performed on it is to measure the work and the time elapsed since the work was performed. But this is also objective measurement and therefore permits attribution.

Attribution—or the assigning of product to its economic causes—is the basis for the assessment of "real costs." It is the determination of how much effort of the two kinds has been required to bring an objective unit of any particular product to its present stage in the process—that is, to produce the effect that has been produced upon it and to maintain that for the duration that it has been maintained.[13] In attribut-

[12] This abstract statement sounds excessively meticulous. Nevertheless, it is merely a statement, in abstract form, of what every producer does in any economy—direct or indirect—with reference to everything he produces. While the "imputation" of *value* from product to its causes hardly arises in a direct economy, attribution of product to its causes arises of necessity at once and alike for all production in any economy. In fact "imputation" is always dependent on prior attribution. If one does not first know to what attribute product one can hardly do any "imputing." Therefore we are making the essential distinction now and will build up here an analysis of attribution in actual practice in order that, when we come to "imputation" in considering an indirect economy later, this groundwork will have been laid. To imply, as some seem to have done, that attribution is impossible, is absurd. It is being done, and must be done, continually as to all product, however inexactly or even incorrectly.

[13] Here, in modified terminology, we are exactly following Marshall. He makes the essential distinction between the efforts which produce and the inducements which call forth these efforts. "The exertions of all the different kinds of labour that are directly or indirectly involved in making it; together with the abstinences or rather the waitings required for saving the capital used in making it: [for "waiting is an element of cost as truly as effort is"; *291*, 353] all these efforts and sacrifices together will be called the *real cost of production* of the commodity. The sums of money that have to be paid for these efforts and sacrifices will be called either its *money cost of production*, or, for shortness, its *expenses of production;* they are the prices which have to be paid in order to call forth an adequate supply of the efforts and waitings that are required for making it; or, in other words, they are its supply price" (*291*, 328).

These attributed "real costs" (causes) are Walras's "coefficients de fabrication des produits . . ." (*420*, XIII), which he defines (*ibid.*, 211) as "les quantités respectives de chacun des services producteurs (T), (P), (K) . . . qui entrent dans le confection d'une unite de chacun des produits (A), (B), (C), (D)." And, while he includes land, as he should not, and as Marshall does not, he too distinguishes between the "services" and the pay. Thus, as noted above (*ibid.*, 184), *rente* is the *service* of land, *fermage* its pay; *travail* is the *service* of labor, *salaires* its pay; *profit* is the *service* of capital, *interêt* its pay.

Pareto's term is "*coefficients de production*" or "*facteurs de la production*" (*317*, 304).

ing the entire effect to effort we must remind the reader that we are not using the term effort in the sense of expenditure of physical energy. True enough, the physical effects have been produced by the application of physical powers, non-human (natural powers) as well as, perhaps, human. But, from the economic viewpoint, these former are inert media; for their application to procure these effects is wholly due to human effort. Thus effort is the ultimate cause which *directs* powers, natural and human, to its ends. Nor are we measuring the effort in any respect in terms of the "pain" or "dissatisfaction" which it involves. Neither are we alluding to the sacrifice (the forgone alternative) involved. The "pain," etc., give to it its qualitative character as effort; but we have agreed that the only way we can deal quantitatively with effort is in terms of its performance—the effect it has produced.[14] Thus we can adopt an arbitrary standard unit for working effort expended on each specific kind of task. We can say that carrying so many brick up one story constitutes a standard quantity of work (effect)

But his qualitative distinction is even worse. For both consist of "quantités d'autres produits et de services de capitaux"—and everything goes under those heads. And to him "facteurs" are not kinds, and "*coefficients*" quantities of kinds. Instead both are quantities and the only kinds are, as we have noted, specific articles. Thus his use of the terms eliminates the distinction between kinds and quantities, and by the same road that Fisher uses when he treats "price" as that of a unit only and "value" as the price of any other quantity (see *142*, 13).

As stated above, Cassel's term is "technical coefficients" (*74*, 139 ff.).

[14] The amount of "real costs"—in the Marshallian sense in which we are using the term—which is required for the production of a unit of any product, does not hinge in any way, shape, or manner upon the "effortfulness" involved in these "real costs" (efforts). Neither does the quantity of satisfaction to be derived—though the latter is in part proportionate to these "real costs," in terms of their effect.

J. B. Clark's "pain suffered by society as a whole in the final period of daily labor" is one of the two factors in the limitation of working effort. But it cannot be the "ultimate unit of value," as he says it is, because it has no relation with any but the last or least important task performed (see *80*, 392).

This same defect is found in Jevons and his following, in that they overlook the fact that, while the critical ratio of "pleasure" to "pain," satisfaction to "dissatisfaction," influences the aggregate of effort put forth, it has no bearing whatever on the allocation of that aggregate among the various products that come within that limit. The problem that we are leading up to is that of the criterion which governs such allocation. Therefore, we ignore intramarginal differences in the constituent which makes effortful the behavior we are calling effort. It is possible, of course, that even in a direct economy, the nature of certain tasks, or the time they were performed, might make them more effortful than others. And conceivably, this may affect allocation. As Knight says (*240*, 75) of his example of a direct economy, "It will not be true that all things produced in equal times will be equated, for there are elements of 'irksomeness,' etc., which have to be taken account of." Therefore, time is merely a " 'first approximation.' " However, we must leave this complication and refinement out of consideration at this time. The problem is difficult enough without it.

for one hour's working. Then we can measure working effort expended on a whole load of brick in terms of this unit. That does not mean, however, that we have also rendered uniform the physical energy that may have been expended. A man has to carry himself as well as the brick; and, if one man weighs twice as much as another he has expended twice as much energy as the other on the non-payable load. Nor does it mean that such units of working effort are equal in point of "pain" or "dissatisfaction." In a direct economy, where the worker is regarded as homogeneous, we can relate different kinds of effect of working—different tasks—through their common denominator, one hour's working, thus adopting a standard unit of effect for each kind. When we come to deal with an indirect economy with heterogeneous workers whose standard effects at different tasks may vary in their ratios or may seem to be undeterminable, the problem becomes more difficult. But, even there, it may prove to be more soluble and more solved in actual practice than economists have been accustomed to concede. As a matter of fact, even there, approximately correct attribution is learned by observation and experience. It is studied by every producer all of the time. It must be, for it is one of the two essential bases for determining the allocation of effort.

Finally, it must be said that in no sense is this a "valuation" process.[15] We are making no assertions as to the "values" of product or, through "imputation," as to the "values" of the kinds and quantities of effort to which the effect produced on the product is due. All we are asserting is that this process of attribution is a necessary preliminary and basis for any "imputation," although it has not been recognized as such, or has only been tacitly assumed in "imputation" theory.[16] If

[15] We are not saying with J. B. Clark (*81*, 318) that "the psychological currency that ultimately measures all values is inherently bimetallic—that it is composed of two disutilities," "the sacrifices respectively involved in effort and abstinence." We are only saying, in a different terminology, that these are the "real costs" to which all product must be attributed.

[16] As an example of those who disregard this predicate—"real cost"—entirely, we may cite Davenport. Costs to him are taken from the point of view "of him who pays," not from that of "him who receives the pay"; they are "resistances" not "remunerations" (*107*, 446). They "cannot be reduced to any common denominator of pain"; nor do they "sum up or report the amount of labor . . . incorporated in the product, but only the sum of marginal sacrifices reduced to the common denominator of price." Or, again, "cost of production is, indeed, patently circuitous" because it "purports to explain the prices of products purely by an appeal to other prices—to the prices of the materials consumed, to the price wages of the labor applied, and to the price rents of the land and instruments employed."

If cost analysis does not first "sum up or report the amount of labor . . . incorporated," how can it be determined to what quantity of labor the value shall be imputed

production under any regime were unable to determine what quantities of "factors" were accountable for product, it would, of course, be unable to "impute" at all, since imputation is in terms of units of "factors" accountable. And if production actually depended on the application of the usual theory of substitution—marginal product—it would be going it almost blind. Precise determination and measurement of effect and its causes necessarily come first. But, even then, imputation of "value" to these causes does not follow directly. That is only the result of a synthesis which we are not yet prepared to make. However, when this synthesis is made it does not dissolve the "real costs." For one of the chief problems of economics in many economies is to study the relations between the two sets of independent variables, quantities of effort per unit of product (attribution) and, through that, values per unit of effort (imputation). To accomplish this purpose it is essential always to differentiate between the two. Moreover, if this analysis of the fundamental conditions, which face all economies alike, is to be made to apply to all economies no matter how they may be or might be organized, this distinction is necessary for another reason. In a slave economy the slave becomes an instrument, bought and maintained, like domestic animals or other extant product. His working effort may have no price. So, in a socialist economy, retaining effort may have no price; it may be compulsory. But, since we regard as effort all that is expended by human beings, excepting only non-human agencies, regardless of the form of the inducement (whether reward or compulsion), we must necessarily maintain our category of "real costs" even when the price, and therefore "imputation," has disappeared from the picture.[17]

Two complications arise in the primary problem of attribution. The first concerns the question as to the precise dividing line among all results of effort between what is and what is not product. Obviously, no effort will be intentionally devoted to processes which have no product. But the matter is not so simple as that. In many processes, extractive and other, the result of the application of effort is not a single objec-

---

and the "price wages" applied? If it does do this summing up, then it has determined the "real costs."

[17] For these reasons we must disagree with Knight (*240*, *75*) that the notion of "real costs" is merely "a mediating, instrumental idea," because "the use of effort to measure other things amounts to an evaluation of effort in terms of other things." On the other hand, we welcome his concession that "the concept of a quantitative outlay cost" means "something more than merely *any* sacrificed alternative."

tively homogeneous object or act, but several. Thus, in the concentrating of natural materials, we have both the material purified and the residue removed; after the slaughter of an animal we have its innumerable separate parts; in the adaptation of a site we may have the material removed from the site as well as the effect of this removal which remains on the site. For this reason it is necessary in each case to determine which of the several objectively homogeneous results constitute product and which do not, in order that all the "real costs" shall be assigned to product and none to what is not. We noted above that the objective definition of product is not sufficient for this purpose. Nor, evidently, is the fact that effort is expended on it. To be product requires also the subjectively assigned relation of usefulness at the time this effort is expended. And this provides the criterion for attribution. To what is determined to be residue (useless), no share of the "real costs" is assigned; but what is determined to be by-product or joint product must bear some share of the "real costs." So far as concerns the attribution of these conglomerates of several joint products to the effort which caused them—the "charging" of "real costs"—there is no basis for division. The conglomerate is a result of a mass of effort. So long as the conglomerate remains undivided, its costs are not only undivided but indivisible, except on some basis which, so far as attribution is concerned, is purely arbitrary.[18] The "real costs" of further processes, after separation, are, of course, assignable to each product separately. Thus the problem of what can be strictly called joint costs is insoluble upon the basis of attribution (economic causation) alone.

The second complication concerns the question of the precise divid-

[18] There are two equally logical bases upon which strictly joint "real costs" may be arbitrarily divided between the joint products. The first is to divide them equally over all the common units (say pounds) of all products when separated; the other is to divide them equally between the several batches of product regardless of quantities produced of each. On the first basis, the strictly joint costs of extracting and treating a ton of ore (say), which yields 1,000 lbs. of one metal and 100 lbs. of another, would be divided at an equal rate per lb. over 1,100 lbs. of product. On the second basis, the 1,000 lbs. of one metal would bear half and the 100 lbs. of the other the other half. There is another logical factor which may enter. Provided we can assume a definite and limited quantity wanted for each joint product, then it may occur that the quantities wanted do not bear the same ratio to each other that the quantities of each constituent in the raw material bear to each other. The "real costs" of whatever extra quantity of raw material must be produced in order to yield the required excess of one or the other should then logically be charged entirely to that one. The result will be two different "real costs" for the two portions of that product a surplus quantity of which is wanted. While these logical considerations influence the actual charging of joint "real costs," other considerations enter from the demand side which usually distort the picture.

ing line among all units of effort expended between those which can properly be "charged" to such product and those which cannot. And this, too, involves something beyond pure attribution. Nevertheless, this is a convenient point at which to introduce it. Presumably at the time the effort is expended it is estimated that all of it can properly be "charged" to the product envisaged as its result. And this will be done even if the result is smaller than expected (i.e., the product will have been produced at a higher "real cost"). Nevertheless, this record of the past which accompanies the product until it is used up and the "real cost" is "charged off," may have to be altered during that time for other reasons. These reasons have already been mentioned in previous chapters. If a portion of the product is physically destroyed, or damaged, or spoiled, and its usefulness is thus lost or diminished through the action of other agencies than those which are at work during its using-up, or through that of the same agencies but at a greater than normal rate, we say that the effort which has gone into such portion is to that extent wasted. In other words, attribution assigns to the net product not the whole effort expended on the gross product, but only its proportion of the whole effort. There is, however, an important exception to this rule based on a distinction between expected (insured) and unexpected disappearances of usefulness for these reasons. To the extent that the average of such more or less regular losses can be allowed for, they are included as a "real cost"; that is, the portion of total effort expended on product whose usefulness disappears in whole or in part is spread over the undestroyed, undamaged and unspoiled product. This "surcharge" is therefore included hereafter as one of the occasions for "real cost."

Our notion of disappearance also covered loss of usefulness due to a change in the order of priority of wants or in the unweighted terms of substitution among means. Here the problem of attribution is hardly affected. Even if the product, after it is produced, turns out at some stage of its life to have less usefulness than was expected, it is still conceived to bear its own "real costs." Such effort is to that extent wasted, to be sure; but since it is wasted as to the whole output, presumably, there is no net product, in the sense of the first case, to be separated from the gross, and therefore no question of attribution involved. Only in so far as losses due to obsolescence of this kind can be reasonably calculated in advance can the figure of waste effort be reduced by assigning it as a surcharge to other output. And then it can only be assigned to prior output and never to some other portion of current output.[19]

3. SCARCITY THEORY

Before proceeding to develop the analysis of comparative "real costs" upon the basis of the system of economic energetics that we have been following, it becomes necessary to attempt to clear the road of some interfering prepossessions which have arisen as a result of other formulations. In considering the subject of "real costs" in terms of the quantitative relation between the measurable efforts of men to secure the satisfaction of their wants and the resistance offered by the environment, which is the occasion of these efforts, we are adhering rather closely to the Ricardian tradition. But we are definitely taking issue with some of the favorite and not mutually incompatible viewpoints of recent times. These latter consist chiefly of two great pieces of economic synthesis—or possibly one, with variations—which, while they do not themselves represent analyses (or theories) of "real cost," because they rather elide than dispose of the subject, nevertheless have succeeded, more or less speciously, in glozing over the place in the whole scheme which they leave empty.

The first of these syntheses is best represented by Cassel's combination of the notion of scarcity, which has been an inherent assumption in most economic analysis from the beginning,[20] with the theory of general equilibrium (of prices and quantities) developed especially by the Lausanne school. Fundamentally this synthesis confines itself to the method of imputation of "value" to the "factors" of production, which are assumed to be limited with relation to demand because they are either absolutely or relatively scarce. That is, in this synthesis, quantities of all "factors" are taken as "given," and, usually, the necessary proportions in which they shall be combined to result in product ("technical co-efficients") are also taken as "given." A number of

19 It will be noted that in both these "surcharges," as contrasted with waste, we are following the distinction Knight has made between "risks" and "uncertainties." The effort corresponding to "risks" is a cost burden upon good product; that corresponding to "uncertainties" is waste. This particular "risk" category of costs is also used by Pareto under the title "assurance" (*317*, 300–301).

20 For instance, R. T. Bye (*56*, 647) goes so far as to weave it into his definition of economics, thus expressing the old and general prepossession. He says, "Economics is that branch of learning which deals with the social organization and process by which scarce means of production are directed toward the satisfaction of human wants."

specific technological and institutional conditions are necessary to make this synthesis valid even so far as it goes. Assuming these conditions, it is useful. When they do not exist, it is useless. It eliminates the distinction between "real" contribution—the converse of the quantity of effect upon product to be *attributed* to each cause—except as this is assumed to be "given" in the "technical coefficients," and, on the other hand, "distribution"—that is, the "value" which shall be *imputed* to, and the reward which shall presumably be paid for, each contributing factor. It undertakes to cover only ideal "distribution" to free-moving "factors" in a free-market economy. Therefore, for the most part, it is not false; it is merely inadequate.[21]

In one serious respect, however, this synthesis is false; for it depends on the notion of scarcity. Cassel makes this the keystone. He tells us that the scarcity of the relevant means of production is the only essential requisite for his definition of cost. That is an "idolum theatri," conceived in order to preserve an error retained by tradition from earlier economics. Absolute scarcity may be said to exist as to every-

[21] One might say that to Cassel—as to many others—"cost" is ideal *reward* to factors. Cassel says (74, 90), "In Marshall's opinion cost chiefly represents a personal exertion, a sacrifice which must have some compensation if it is to be made." I should say that Marshall, in the Ricardian tradition, recognizes the fact of "real costs," which is not a matter of opinion at all, and that he distinguishes these from the inducement. Cassel continues, "Here we take cost in a purely objective [*sic*] way, as the result of the price-fixing process" (i.e., as the imputed value of the effort, or ideal "compensation," not the cost at all). This confusion of the causes of production—"real costs"—with the results of production—"compensation"—precludes economic analysis in terms which will cover many institutional economic systems which have been proposed or tried out—e.g., German Nazi and Russian "Communist"—and even some which have existed in the past. There are other means of restricting demand besides price systems; there are other means of inducing effort besides "distribution" systems.

In an indirect economy, when the restriction of demand as it exists in a direct economy is removed, it is necessary that there be some system for limiting demand to whatever supply is made available. This is accomplished in a free-market economy by the means Cassel has so well analyzed—namely the automatic price system. But rationing is an alternative method in other types of economy. Again such a price system furnishes a useful guide to the best allocation of resources. But that is a matter of almost no interest in a rigid guild economy. Finally it furnishes an ideal basis for imputing value to factors and thus determining compensation. However, that question does not arise in a slave economy.

It may be noted that general equilibrium theory as a whole assumes, as a necessary basis, a somewhat ideal freedom on the part of the contributor in directing the allocation of his resources (or organizations of combined resources), which has been a goal striven for but never reached under our economic system in the past.

However, our fundamental objection to Cassel's synthesis is that it is typical of that constantly evinced desire to bring all possible phenomena under one unifying conception which has the failing that it necessarily views them in one aspect only or, worse still, tends to force heterogeneous phenomena into one mold. Also, it tends to bar further analysis.

thing of which the quantity is finite—that is, as to everything. But in almost all cases the actual quantity used is far within this limit. If we properly confine "factors" to the human functions of working and retaining, we recognize that there are absolute limits to the quantities of these functions than can be performed. That is, working-time cannot exceed twenty-four hours a day, and retaining cannot retain more than the entire output of product. But, as we have noted, the actual limitation upon the performance of both these functions is at a point well within these limits. If choice is free, the limit, in the case of working, is at the point where leisure is preferred to further production; [22] and, in the case of retaining, it is at the point where the least current want within the limit of working has greater force than the greatest future want remaining unprovided. In other words, the limitation for both is always a matter of preference.[23] As to the third "factor," environment, we may recall our discussion, in the previous chapter, of the subject of scarcity. There, again, everything exists in finite quantities. But these rarely, if ever, constitute the actual limits. Nothing, or practically nothing, in nature is absolutely scarce. But almost everything occurs over a wide range of accessibility. That, being converted into terms of the increasing effort required to overcome increasing resistance, means that, at some point, increase of quantity of any product is not worth the effort. In other words, the effective limitation via "real costs" is the same as before—the limitation on effort.[24] So, in respect of both the functions performed and the conditions under which they must be performed, there is but one limit and that is a matter of preference, not one of "relative scarcity."

It is customary to qualify the notion of scarcity, as to working, in some such way as the foregoing, so that, in reality, it becomes something other than scarcity; this is less frequently done as to retaining ("capital") and almost never as to environment ("land"—materials, powers, and sites). But even the verbal remnant—the use of the term —is unfortunate. In the analysis of a direct economy the whole no-

[22] We might say, somewhat picturesquely, that wants not requiring produced means (in fact requiring the non-production of means) conflict with and limit the satisfaction of those which do.

[23] On the scarcity theory cigars are "relatively scarce" for me because I prefer a pipe, and one cannot smoke both at the same time.

[24] There seems to be something wrong with an "analytical tool" which obliges one to say that the "relative scarcity" of copper is due to the "relative scarcity" of leisure. Why treat "scarcity" as the cause of limited quantities of product when the ultimate cause of the scarcity is the "real cost" of the product—i.e., the effort involved in producing it and, further back, the internal resistance opposed to the effort?

tion of scarcity is inappropriate; in that of an indirect economy even the term becomes absurd. Some say we do not live in an economy of scarcity, but rather in one of "abundance," nay often of superabundance. Both notions are equally beside the point, for both evade the direct connection between effort and satisfaction which is modified only by natural resistances, technique, and organization. We live in economies of worse or better techniques and with organizations which work more or less well. But there is this much in the notion of abundance. It is true that it is difficult to analyze, in terms of "relative scarcity," an economy which suffers from large-scale unemployment, which finds it necessary to plough under unsalable surplus crops, etc.[25] On the other hand, even with the best available technique and an ideal working of the organization, it is still true that almost the only limit upon an economy in the satisfaction of its wants is the ability or willingness of its members to incur "real costs" in the face of the necessity

[25] It may be well to attempt at this point to exorcise the notion of "relative scarcity" by attacking it in its stronghold, to which we have previously referred. It has been the criterion according to which "goods" (usually envisaging natural materials only) have been divided into non-economic ("free") goods and economic goods. According to Menger (*296*, 51 ff.), whose statements we may use as an example, the former are those "deren verfügbare Quantität grösser ist, als der Bedarf an denselben" (*ibid.*, 58) while the latter are those of which the disposable quantity is equal to, or less than, the requirements. Walras's (*420*, 23) distinction is the same, except that he confounds it with "appropriability" (i.e., a proprietary basis) which Menger expressly denies (*296*, 59). Menger argues (*296*, 61, note) that "costs of any sort are per se irrelevant to the question of whether a good is economic or non-economic" (quoted from Stigler, *386*, 236). If "goods" are economic because they are scarce and are scarce almost exclusively because there are costs of procuring them, that is obviously not true. He has taken the proximate for the ultimate cause.

One readily sees how Menger's incomplete analysis led him astray. His examples (*296*, 61, note) are that alluvial land and water power are economic and yet represent no work. Actually, there are plenty of unused sites of such materials and powers. There is no scarcity of them. Their economic quality (he means value) is due to the fact that some are more accessible, therefore involve less resistance, and therefore require less effort to use, than the surplus sites which remain unused (non-economic). On the other hand, he says (*ibid.*, 28) that, in the most primitive economy which confines itself to collection of "goods" of the lowest order from nature, man assumes no influence in production. These "goods" are conceived as "free" (non-economic) because his view of production is limited to transformation and does not include transportation. Yet their collection may involve effort and, if so, their quantity is limited by that fact.

The true distinction rests not on quantities available, which are almost without exception in excess of requirements, but upon comparative accessibility. There are materials and powers which are so readily accessible at practically all sites that the activity required to use them is not effortful (direct consumption). All others require activity which is effortful, and by that fact must be *produced* before they can be *consumed*. Wherever the line is drawn between effortless and effortful behavior you have determined the line between non-economic and economic "goods," because at that point the tendency toward restriction of quantity imposed by "real costs" begins to come into play.

imposed by the resistance of nature that they must do so if they are to secure satisfactions. The term scarcity leads to a superficial and a misleading analysis. It is misleading because it represents as if it were an involuntary limitation what is actually almost wholly a voluntary limitation of quantities. Only confusion can result from calling both limitations by the same name.

But we must not throw out the baby with the bath. If we discard "relative scarcity" as a mere blind for "real costs," we must retain "absolute scarcity," if we find that it exists. If at any time more of some final product is wanted and it is impossible to increase the quantity by a different allocation of effort and of the resources of the environment, then there may be said to exist as to that product the condition of "absolute scarcity." It appears, upon reflection, that the various causes and effects which have usually been attributed to such a condition can hardly be conceived to occur in a direct economy. Moreover, in order to analyze them in an indirect economy, where they do occur sporadically, we shall find necessary a number of categories and relations which we have not yet developed. Therefore, without discarding or even qualifying the notion of "absolute scarcity" at this point, we shall reserve examination of it until we can include it in its proper setting.[26]

4. THEORY OF OPPORTUNITY COST

In effect, the other synthesis referred to above, the scheme of "opportunity costs," is in part a way of stating that between two alternatives, the *preferred* alternative is chosen. Thus, essentially, it has brought into the foreground what we shall call the *motive of maximization.* Presumably that means the maximization of satisfaction of wants.

[26] Logically, to be absolutely scarce, the supply of a product must be strictly non-expansible. This might be because it is itself non-reproducible or because, in turn, some indispensable physical element or form of effort which goes into producing it is non-expansible. But since some other product may be a substitute for it, and, almost always, some other site, material, power, or form of effort can be substituted in the process of production, the application of the notion of "absolute scarcity" depends upon the limit of tolerance in substitution—that is, it depends upon what is defined as *a* product. Apart from those products which satisfy the want for rare objects, *qua* rare, and which are therefore defined by finicky criteria, we shall find this class to be of very limited importance. There are, however, several other limitations, inherent or arbitrary, on the re-allocation of resources that work to produce, in an indirect economy, variations from what we may call, tentatively, the ideal combination of quantities of the several products. And these we will need to study carefully when we reach that subject.

For a few incidental remarks on this subject, see Appendix VI, Section A.

We shall have to consider, in this and the next chapters, how that works in a direct economy, and whether its operation is as simple as this formulation makes it out to be. But when we come to consider indirect economies we shall find that the question will often arise—maximization of what? Therefore, we cannot accept even this feature of the scheme without reserve. However, our objections to this scheme, in connection with the subject of costs, are somewhat different. In the first place, this formulation, when it deals with the choice between product and no product, does not pose the true alternatives. It is true that we cannot go in two directions at the same time; nor can we do two different things at the same time (at least, we have already found that we do not do so). That is, we are compelled always to choose between two mutually exclusive alternatives. Now leisure today and eating tonight are not, in this sense, mutually exclusive alternatives. But leisure today and working today are such, because both would have to take place during the same hours. Since leisure today is a satisfaction, while working today is the opposite of one, there is no possibility that anyone would choose the latter for itself. The only reason for choosing the latter arises from an entirely different relation which is not envisaged at all in "opportunity costs." This relation is that nature imposes on us the necessity that we shall work today in order to eat tonight. That is, eating tonight has a "real cost"—working today—while leisure today has no "real cost." Thus the true comparison and choice —our true opportunities—are between the satisfaction of leisure today, on the one hand, and, on the other, the satisfaction of eating tonight less the "dissatisfaction" of working today ("real cost").[27] And ultimately the alternative to eating is not leisure, it is death. Thus "real costs" are not represented by the alternative forgone; they are a condition imposed by natural resistance to provision for certain satisfactions.

In the second place, when this formulation deals with the choice between two products, it cannot stand on its own feet. In this case it states that the cost of the preferred and elected alternative is the next best alternative which is rejected. Let us now represent (Fig. 29) a series of current provisions for wants *a* to *j* the force behind which declines according to the order of priority of the wants. The solid horizontal line from *r* represents what we regard as the "real cost" per provision (here, for simplicity's sake, the same for all). Under the interpretation

[27] The reader will recall the formula for this given in Chapter 10.

of opportunity costs, the cost of each provision, as it is elected, is the significance of the next in order; that of *d*, for instance, is provision *e*. Now it must be noted that this assumes that what we regard as "real costs" for *d* and *e* are equal; for, otherwise, these two are not, strictly speaking, alternatives—that is, they would then not represent allocations of the same amount of working effort. This proves that the terms of choice implicitly include the "coefficients of production" (i.e., our "real costs"). Thus, in reality, the idea of "opportunity costs" tacitly assumes that the choice between alternatives is based on the comparative usefulness of two products per unit of "real cost." That may be true; we shall examine the question in Part IV. Even if it is true, such a proposition can only be formulated at all if it is stated in this form: as between two products, *d* and *e*, having the same "real cost," r_1 and r_2 (below the solid cost line) *d* will be preferred. That introduces an entirely different relation as the "real cost." [28] No longer can *e* be called the cost of *d*.[29] This demonstrates that the notion of "opportunity costs" merely elides the crux of the question by means of its tacit assumptions. It assumes that the efforts which *produce* the product are given ("free"). And the true nature and bearing of comparative "real costs" of product remain unexplored. It is a grand synthesis which, like many another, lumps together a number of discrete elements and thus precludes, instead of aiding, further analysis.[30]

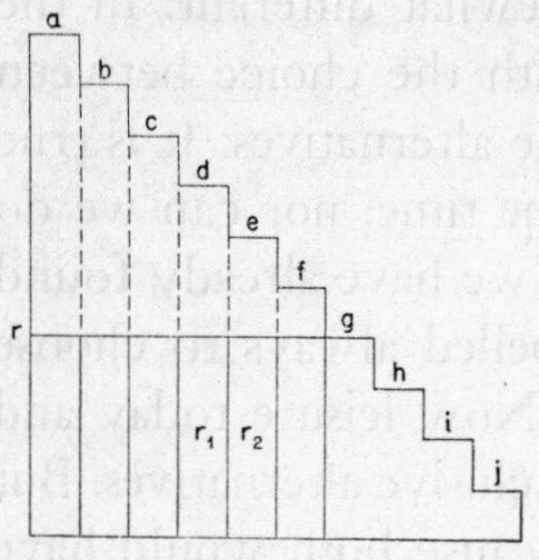

FIG. 29

[28] The formula for this relation was also given in Chapter 10.

[29] Under our "cost system" the cost of *a* to *f*, inclusive, is 6 *r*; under the "opportunity cost" system it is $b + c + d + e + f + g$. This shows that the difference is more than a dispute about words. It is a question of ignoring or not ignoring one of two sets of related facts.

[30] In his introduction to the reprint of Wicksteed's *Common Sense of Political Economy* (*441*, XVIII), Robbins states that "The conception of real costs as displaced alternatives is now accepted by the majority of theoretical economists." But it is worth recalling that Pareto (*317*, 218) considered that it is "inutile et ne fait qu'engendrer des équivoques." This "pseudo coût de production" (*ibid.*, 219) serves merely to call attention to the equal (in his view) marginal utility of all products consumed. And J. M. Clark finds it difficult to apply in practice (see *83*, 187). Even from the standpoint of clear thinking the conception is unfortunate. As Commons points out (*93*, 88) a choice is essentially three-dimensional—performance, avoidance, forbearance. Performance is what is done or given, avoidance is the alternative performance rejected or avoided; and forbearance is the limit placed on performance. We can analyze the process in such terms. To get *this*, which I prefer to *that*, I will do or give so much, but no more. What

B. "REAL COSTS" IN DIRECT EFFORT

Having determined what we mean by an objectively measured quantity of an objectively identified product and how we go about attributing such a quantity of product to the effort which has brought it to its present economic state—determining its "real costs"—let us consider what are the various features of the product and of the conditions under which it has been produced which fix the quantities of effort that have been required. Fundamentally, these features and conditions determine the amount of effect which it has been necessary to accomplish. This effect, in turn, has involved the overcoming of natural resistances of the various sorts analyzed in the previous chapter. And, through this intermediation, these resistances have fixed, subject to technique, the quantity of effort that has been required.

Allowing, at first, for no variations of technique and considering, at first, only direct effort, the "real cost" of a unit of product will depend upon a complicated set of variables. We may undertake to analyze them as follows:

I. Due to Characteristics of the Product Determined by Demand

A. Uniform for Each Product—Affecting Work Only

1. Optional Size of Unit. Where the unit is the "as-if separate" part of a continuum (lbs., gals., etc.), it is used for measurement only. Demand determines only the quantity wanted. This quantity is then stated in terms of the arbitrary units of measurement, varying inversely with their size. But then demand does not determine the size of the unit. Where a separated unit occurs in nature (an orange, a horse, etc.) its size may be ignored by demand. If not, then the various sizes which nature affords are not objectively indifferent and therefore constitute different products. Again, demand does not determine the size of a unit nor the range of sizes available. However, where the

---

I do or give is the cost. But we cannot analyze it in terms merely of avoidance—what I do not choose to do.

We said above that the two syntheses—scarcity and "opportunity cost"—were not mutually incompatible. The link is the "reserve price" of general equilibrium theory. This construes a restriction of supply as if it were an expansion of demand, and is conceived in terms of traders', not consumers', psychology. But, like "opportunity cost," it throws all possible choices into one class. Thus the limitation of efforts in general (capacity) is confused with their allocation in particular.

separated unit is wholly a result of production (a dress, a house, etc.) then its size—which, as a continuum, may be measured, in turn, in arbitrary as-if-separated units—is entirely determined by demand and is produced to fit this requirement. So, too, with units of services (a haircut, a theatrical performance). Therefore, if the product exists in separate units made to a size, this variable operates as to all such product, whether material or not, and as to all processes concerned in its production.

2. *Optional Elaborateness.*[1] The extent to which any product is elaborated is also determined by what is wanted (demand). This is true regardless of its size or how it is measured or whether it is material or not. Therefore this variable operates as to all product without qualification, and as to its entire process of production.

3. *Optional Material or Materials.* Where the material is not inherent in the nature of the product, the selection of the material or combination of materials of which a product is composed is made entirely in response to demand. Where the material is inherent, the definition of the product defines the material as well. In either case demand may be said to determine the material. Obviously, this variable operates only as to material product, but it concerns, or may concern, all processes of production.

In so far as those characteristics of the product itself that affect its "real cost" in work are concerned, all such characteristics can be included under one of the three foregoing rubrics.

B. Variable for Each Extant Product with Optional Life—Affecting Retention Only

4. *Optional Life.* The life of any product beyond the next consuming-day may be wholly determined (future provisions) or largely influenced (durables) by preferences (demand). This variable operates, of course, as to material product only. But, as to that, it concerns only the period of use after production and not the period of production. It is the result of:

a) Future provision, against contingencies of the first type;

b) Future provision, against contingencies of the second type;

c) Durables, in so far as the durability is a matter of choice in each case.

[1] By "elaborateness" we mean the degree to which the product is worked-up.

After the elaborateness and the material (if any) of a certain product have been defined by demand—under I A—and after the size of its unit has been determined either by demand, or by nature, or arbitrarily as an as-if-separated part of a continuum, the "real cost" per unit in respect of work only will depend upon the following variables, all of which measure quantities of the various kinds of natural resistances:

II. Due to Characteristics of the Product

A. Uniform for Each Product—Affecting Work Only

1. Size of Unit. Other things being equal, the aggregate of all the specific resistances enumerated below will vary with size of unit, optional or arbitrary. To the same degree the "real cost" in work will vary in the same proportion. This is always true of units fixed by demand. The building of a house meets greater resistance than the building of a shed, the making of a coat more than that of a glove, a wagon more than a go-cart; so, too, the journey of a messenger for six miles (or two hours) as against three miles (or one hour). Generally speaking, this variable also operates as to natural units when other things are actually equal (i.e., a grapefruit *vs.* an orange, etc.). It is quite obvious in the case of arbitrary units. Producing one gallon necessarily meets more resistance than producing one pint. This variable concerns all product, whether material or not, and all stages of the process of production.

2. Elaborateness. The degree of elaborateness prescribed in the specifications of the product wanted will determine, other things being equal, the amount of fabrication required. As to material product the resistance to fabrication arises chiefly from the refractoriness of the material, or the materials, and incidentally from the number of parts, perhaps of different materials, to be combined. As to non-material product it is proportionate to the "complexity" of the service. An elaborate "hair-do" requires more effort than a simple one. But, in general, a carved chair, an inlaid chest, an ornamented dress composed of different materials, are more elaborate than plain specimens. White flour is more elaborate (processed) per barrel than is whole wheat flour. Goods delivered to the home and "charged" are more elaborate than "cash and carry" goods. Again this variable concerns all product, material and non-material, and all parts of the process of production.

III. Due to Natural Conditions under Which Produced

A. Variable among Different Materials, but Uniform for Each Material—Affecting Work Only

1. Economic Refractoriness of Material. All materials present some resistance to extraction and fabrication, but this resistance varies greatly among them. For instance, working in clay or wood present less resistance than working in marble or iron. Other things being equal, the effort ("real cost") involved will be proportionate to the degree of this resistance. This variable concerns only material product, of course, but it may reach along the process of production as far as any change of form is taking place.

2. Economic Inertia of Material. The moving of any material, raw or in the form of product, presents different degrees of resistance according to its density (weight), low viscosity (necessity of a container), fragility, noxious qualities, etc. Moving stone, grain, glass, or acids, respectively, offers more resistance than moving wood, hides, boards, or water. Again this applies only to material product; but its effect necessarily reaches along the whole process from extraction to final arrival at the point of consumption.

B. Variable for Each Source as Well as Each Kind of Material—Affecting Work Only

3. Concentration of Material in Situ. The more dilute any material is *in situ* the greater is the resistance to its extraction per unit of resulting pure material.[2] Also, thereafter, the greater the proportion of unwanted residue which must be separated, the greater the resistance to purification. Of course, as between two different materials, the same degree of dilution does not offer the same degrees of resistance (the bark on lumber constitutes greater resistance to removal than the husk on corn). But between two lots of the same material there is also considerable variance; and, there, the degree of dilution is comparable, the residue being of the same or similar kind. This latter variation may occur, as we shall see, among "deposits" on a single site as well as between different sites. Therefore, our term source is intended to dis-

[2] We shall have more to say shortly with reference to the notion of concentration and dilution in connection with extraction performed by biological processes (i.e., agriculture, etc.). We shall also distinguish between the way these resistances affect materials and powers which are replenished by natural processes—which *replace themselves*—and those which are not.

tinguish all "deposits" when there are differences in this respect. To the extent that the purification process is not completed at the source, this variable may influence economic inertia by reason of the necessity of moving some of the unseparated residue along with the wanted material to the site of later processes. There is not much difference between the degree of concentration of some materials at their different sources (grain, for instance), while, with others, the difference may be marked (metals, for instance). This rubric includes the resistance incurred by all such processes as threshing, cleaning, and hulling grain, concentrating and smelting ores, etc. The variable affects only material product, but affects all material product more or less; and, while it applies chiefly to extraction, it may have a considerable influence all along the processes of production up to the point at which the material is sufficiently purified for fabrication.

4. Economic Distance as to Product. The greater the true economic distance between the site where extraction takes place and the site of consumption (center), and the greater the aberration from a bee line by reason of the location of the series (perhaps) of sites at which production processes subsequent to extraction take place, the greater, other things (chiefly inertia) being equal, will be the resistance on account of transporting the material, raw and as product.[3] This includes the converse of what we have called "accessibility of site" as a source of materials. Obviously, it affects material products only, but it influences all these from extraction all the way along to the point of consumption.

5. Economic Depth. In any extractive process some of the resistance on account of pre-occupation (material) and on account of economic depth proper (spatial) must be overcome concurrently even if no permanent adaptation of the site has been undertaken. Thus plowing meets the first (pre-occupation) and hoisting up natural grades (logging) or out of pit mines and quarries meets the second (economic depth). After adaptation, the concurrent resistance of depth may be increased and may apply both to product and workers (elevation in deep mines), or it may be decreased if horizontal (gravity) shafts can

[3] It should be noted that, for our analytical purposes, we are assigning to the extractive process, and therefore to raw material (or power) costs, all the "real costs" of transport of material product from source to center, except to the extent that intermediate processes are not conducted along an economic bee line (i.e., the shortest economic distance) from the site of the extraction to the consuming center. And this because the site of the extraction alone fixes this cost.

be used instead of vertical ones. This resistance, which as a whole we have called economic depth, is part of the converse of accessibility of site as resources. In its natural form it influences the "real costs" of extractive processes for material product only. In an artificial form we shall see that it concerns exclusively post-extractive processes.[4]

C. Variable for Each Site of Every Productive Process—Affecting Work Only

6. *Dissipation or Congestion of Process.* Variation from the optimum dispersion of any given quantity of any process on a site, toward either pole, increases the resistance to be met. If this variation is in the direction of dissipation (spreading out), it necessarily involves more time (work) in going to and fro on the site and in moving apparatus (if any) thereon (economic distance or depth on site). All such time is, in reality, unproductive time. If this variation is in the direction of congestion (concentration), the workers and the pieces of apparatus will get more and more in each other's way (pre-occupation of space). The way either extreme is avoided and some sort of happy medium is struck has become so much a matter of course that the resistances themselves are usually forgotten. Nevertheless, no optimum can avoid meeting some of both. Therefore, the sum of these two resistances, at whatever point between the poles is chosen in each instance, will vary. It will vary not only as between different processes, but as between different operations of the same process on different sites or under different conditions. This variable affects, therefore, every productive process from extraction through to delivery upon every product whether material or not.

7. *Economic Distance as to Workers.* Similar to the effect of dissipation upon a single site is the effect of economic distance between the site of any process and the consuming center, by reason, in both cases, of the unproductive time occupied by workers in moving to and fro. This is, again, a part of the converse of accessibility of site, but now in respect of the moving of workers not materials. Like the other, therefore, it applies to all processes from extraction up to final delivery; but, unlike the other, it also applies to all product, whether material or not.

[4] See below under reduplication of superficial area of site.

D. Variable among Kinds of Materials or Processes and among Sources or Site for Each—Affecting Work Only

8. Interferences. When protection against natural materials or powers which interfere with processes or damage product takes forms that are ephemeral or that become part of the product the work they represent is direct effort. Thus cultivating (as weeding), driving away pests, "preserving," packaging (one-use packages), for instance, represent effort expended to overcome the resistance of nature in these active forms (i.e., the diversion or avoidance of natural processes the result of which is not wanted). Such resistances vary with climate, etc., as well as with the nature of the process or product. But they are met with, in some degree, in the case of most processes and products, whether material or not.

9. Spoilage. To the extent that protection fails, whether provided in the foregoing or in "permanent" form—to be considered later—there is loss of, or damage to, product. The result is that such part of the resistance of natural powers or materials as has not been overcome has increased the "real cost" of the net good product.[5] In a sense this is the complement of the preceding resistance. But the two do not fit together neatly. Protection may be expensive and yet ineffective; or it may be inexpensive and yet very effective. Though the quantity of interfering process or material, and therefore the resistance in a strict sense, may be the same in both cases, yet in the first they occasion large "real costs" on both counts, and, in the second they occasion small "real costs" on both counts. Again, spoilage takes place, more or less, as to most processes and products, whether material or not. It is more difficult to conceive of it with services; but even these may be rendered less effective or ineffective by the interference of natural powers or materials.[6] For the most part we shall be considering, hereafter, spoilage of material product.

In addition to the foregoing, all of which affect "real cost" in work only, there are certain natural conditions—in a sense also resistances, though more difficult to conceive as such—which affect "real cost" in the form of retention. These are:

[5] That is, in so far as the loss can be "insured" by spreading the "real cost" of spoiled product over the rest of the concurrent product. Under "spoilage" we are, of course, not including the inevitable accompaniments of consumption or use, even if these are not the direct results of same (Senior's "time").

[6] On a hot day the seeds of knowledge may be sowed on stony soil.

E. Variable for Each Extant Product with Necessary Life—Affecting Retention Only

10. Necessary Life. In the case of several of the occasions for retaining enumerated in Chapter 10, natural conditions impose the necessity that the product shall have a life of more than one day and therefore the probability, though not the necessity, that its usefulness will continue for more than one day. This variable operates, of course, only as to material product.

a. Seasonal cycles, etc., make it necessary that some natural materials be retained either as raw material or as product, since they are available for future provision for occasions under the first type of technical necessity only at certain times. Strictly speaking, this particular variable, by itself, is determining only as to the interval between extraction and use (consumption), but this may vary over a wide range if more than one day's provision is made.

b. The physical durability of a durable product is the result of the characteristics of its material, and these in turn constitute a natural condition. Nevertheless, for different uses the durability of the material may be different. In this complex way, and subject to the kind of use and the continuance of usefulness, the fact that only durable products are capable of satisfying certain wants compels retaining. This variable affects the "real cost" of retention only in respect of the period during which the product is in use (consumption)—that is, the number of installments composing it. For it is not inherently necessary that a durable should require more than one day to produce.

c. In two respects what we have called long processes—and even large-batch technique—may be dictated by natural conditions. In this way the length of interval between the beginning of work on a product and the completion of its using-up (consumption), and thus the time during which retaining is required, may be in part a matter of necessity rather than of choice. The first respect is the time required for some natural process to be completed if it intervenes during the production process (i.e., after work has begun to be applied to the material through which or on which the process works). Examples are growth after tilling and seeding, "working" after pressing, curing after picking, cooling after smelting, etc. Usually this is justified only if large-batch technique is used. The second respect is due to the fact that time is required for moving from place to place. If the time needed to go to the source of a material and to return with it or its product exceeds one day, or if, to justify at all the expenditure of the working-time required for going and coming, it is necessary to bring back more than one day's provision at a time (large-batch technique), retaining is compelled. Since this situation exists only when the nearest "deposit" of some non-ubiquitous material is at a comparatively distant site (or is more accessible on all counts at that site), it is due to natural conditions in each particular environment. In so far as either of these conditions does not lead necessarily to the production of more than one day's provision at a time, it affects only the duration of retaining required in the process of production—that is, the interval between the beginning of work on the product and its completion ready for use (consumption). But if these conditions also necessitate large-batch technique—and this occurs with many of the products affected—then the imposition of this alternative technique, as the only way of adapting to the system of preferences, is due to the existing natural conditions, and these must also be held accountable for the quantity of retention required from the time of completion until the large batch is used up (consumed). This subsequent retention, after production is completed, is always additional to the retention during production, when due to natural processes, but it may be necessitated without any retention during production when large-batch technique is induced by distance of transportation. For, then, though the journey would not be made for a single day's provision, it may be made for a large batch, though the whole working time is less than one day.

This tabulation [7] of those of the natural resistances, as analyzed in the previous chapter, which require to be overcome by direct effort, enables us to clarify certain conclusions.[8] In the first place, as between

[7] The foregoing analysis is not intended to be exhaustive. It is, I think, sufficient, first, to illustrate what we mean by natural resistances and, second, to demonstrate that the occasion of *all* "real costs" is the various kinds of resistances from the environment.

[8] This may be the place to note more fully the radical differences between Pareto's "obstacles" and our "resistances." He, too, opposes wants to the obstacles in the way of their satisfaction (*317*, 150). But his obstacles are a curious hodge-podge derived from his notion of equilibrium. They consist, briefly, of the following (*ibid.*, 175), which he describes (at least for the most part) as "*sacrifices ou coûts*" (*ibid.*, 312):

I. a. Limitation of quantities of product—assumed to be fixed.
   b. Given coefficients of "*transformation matérielle.*"
   c. Necessity of "*transformation dans l'espace.*"
   d. Necessity of "*transformation dans le temps.*"
   e. Social organization.

II. Limitation on freedom of choice due to the wants (*ibid.*, 155) of other men (terms of trade due to competition).

We do not admit Ia. Ib, c, and d are the processes, not the resistances overcome. Ie

two units of different products, with given techniques, the comparative "real costs" in direct effort will be fixed by the sum of all these resistances actually incurred in their respective processes; for these resistances determine the amount of effect necessary to arrive at each of the units of finished product, and that effect, with any given technique, determines the amount of effort (work and retention) necessary to produce it.

In the second place, also with given technique, as between two different units of the same product, objectively defined, which are produced concurrently, the same difference in comparative "real costs" actually incurred may arise, but only in part. In this case the two variables listed under I A will be constants. Therefore, the same variables, listed under II A, where they refer to the resistances encountered, will also be constants. The variable I B will vary only according to destination (preference). Since the material is necessarily the same for two units of an objectively indifferent product there can be no difference between them in respect of the resistance listed as III A. But, if the two units come from different sources, or by way of different intermediate production points, or are produced under conditions different in respect of any of the other variables listed under III, the sum of these resistances may vary; if so, with any given technique the effect necessary and therefore the effort involved will also vary in the same proportion. This will almost inevitably be the case with the resistances included under III B and III C; and climatic conditions as well, perhaps, as special local conditions (wilderness, endemic pests, etc.), may cause variations in those under III D. The same may be true of those variables given under III E, in so far as "different natural conditions" include differences in the seasons or produce differences in durability of the same material, or involve differences in the length of the growing season, etc. And, certainly, if transportation requires more time than can be included in a single day's working, this time will vary between different sources or different series of successive production points. For the sake of brevity we may ascribe all these possible differences in the comparative "real costs" of different units of a single product, produced at the same time, to the differences in the conditions under which they are produced in the various *channels* through which they

(other than human interferences) and II are reasons why man may have to work further along the scale of increasing natural resistances, or use a worse technique, but they are not themselves resistances.

arrive. It is evident, then, that it is not possible to compute the comparative "real costs," in general, of two different products, but only those for some particular channel of each. Thus we might compare such products in terms of the lowest cost channel of each, or in terms of the highest cost channel of each actually operative, or even of the weighted average of all channels of each actually operative.[9]

In the third place, as between two different units of the same product, produced in a single channel but not at the same time, differences in comparative "real costs" actually incurred may arise; but again only as to a few of these variables. Wherever a natural process intervenes or affects production it is impossible completely to control the conditions requisite for it. Even in a chemical reaction it is impossible to exclude all interfering factors, even *in vitro*, so that the theoretical conversion is never fully realized. The result, as to all natural processes, is that for given effort and effect the output will vary as the conditions are more or less favorable. The chief variable which determines these differences comes under the general class of interferences, which may be construed as requiring more or less protection, or as resulting in more or less spoilage, at different times, though under conditions otherwise the same. But, to a great extent in the extraction of materials and powers which replace themselves,[10] and to a limited extent in later processes which utilize powers,[11] the degree to which they do replace themselves varies, particularly from season to season. These may be construed as changes in concentration.[12] Thus the only resistances which vary under these circumstances are those listed under III as 3, 8, and 9. Naming this class of variations after their commonest variety we may say that the comparative "real costs" of different units of a single product from a single channel are subject to these limited differences in the successive *seasons* during which they arrive. Again it becomes necessary in comparing the "real costs" of different products

[9] Since some of these variables may favor one channel and others another, etc., it is obvious that a comparison of any two channels is in terms of the net of an algebraic sum of all the differences, plus and minus, from some standard resistance of each kind.

[10] Or, more exactly, which are replenished by natural process. This primarily concerns agriculture and, through agriculture, animal husbandry.

[11] Such, for instance, as the use of flowing water for irrigation where the flow may change during a season or from season to season.

[12] While our previous illustrations of the resistance due to lack of concentration concerned themselves chiefly with purification, or the separation of unwanted residue, the concept can be stretched to include any quantitative relation between what is wanted and its spatial integument which causes a resistance either to man's working or to the natural processes he utilizes.

to specify not only the channel of each but, if they are subject to these variations, also the season of each. Because in these special cases the output varies from the planned quantity (or the quantity is only roughly planned at all), it has been customary to think of the "real costs" as fixed *in toto* and the output as uncontrolled and variable. To a limited extent it is necessary to preserve this point of view, for this is the one case where quantity wanted is not exactly governing as to quantity produced. But from the viewpoint of the formula of our system of energetics the actual variable is not the quantity produced but the resistances met per unit of product. Theoretically at least, if the variation in resistances was overcome by a corresponding variation of effort, the quantity of product would always be uniform.

C. "REAL COSTS" IN INDIRECT EFFORT

1. SPECIAL RESISTANCES TO INDIRECT EFFORT

It is impossible to examine those "real costs" of final product which take the form of indirect effort without reference to technique. Nevertheless, exposition will be made simpler if we reserve the discussion of technique until a later section, merely assuming it in this. By indirect effort, as already stated, we mean all effort the effect of which is applied to final product only through the medium of intermediate product; and we have defined intermediate product as all product which is not physically incorporated (the naïve criterion) in final product. Since intermediate product is not an end in itself, but is produced only for the purpose of being used up (or serving) directly or indirectly in the process of producing final product, and since only the latter can serve directly for the satisfaction of wants, it is more convenient to regard intermediate product as a stage in the process and to consider all effort which is contributed to it, directly or indirectly (through other intermediate product), as being contributed indirectly to the ultimate end, final product.[1]

[1] This is, of course, the Austrian innovation of the nineteenth century. To treat intermediate product as a *ding an sich*, a participant in, or factor of, production (the English view), to impute to it a share in the final product (quasi-rent) is to make a similar error to that which regarded as "capital" the "subsistence" of the workers. This subsistence is a flow, not a stock; and it constitutes a part of the results of production, not a part of its causes.

Intermediate product is also a part of the results of production, not of its causes. It is merely not the final result. But its causes are the same as those of all other product; it consists of embodied effort; and its only distinction is that the effort which has been ap-

Viewed from the standpoint of any one intermediate product by itself, in so far as it is the exclusive result of effort applied directly to it, the resistances which this effort is required to overcome in producing it are exactly the same as those already examined under final product (i.e., direct effort). But, viewed from the standpoint of the ultimate result—the final product in the production of which this intermediate product is used—there are three further kinds of resistance which the intermediate product is designed to overcome.

The first form of natural resistance which occasions indirect effort, and therefore requires intermediate product, consists in any degree of unsuitability of any site to any particular use that it is worth while to correct. In the previous chapter we analyzed this resistance into terms of pre-occupation (material), economic distance [2] and depth, and we indicated that the result of the effort is conventionally treated as intermediate product if it does not require to be repeated each time the operation of production is performed or concurrently with it. Moreover, the result, then, only ceases to be intermediate product when, as and if it is used up, or lost.[3]

The second form of natural resistance which occasions indirect effort is the interference of natural powers or materials with economic processes. If the necessary protection of product or process is not accomplished in ways which are ephemeral or by means which become part of the product itself it must take the form of intermediate product.[4] This is a wide category; it includes not only housing of process or product, but the prime purpose of containers for product, etc., etc.[5]

Another form of resistance which at times occasions indirect effort, and therefore intermediate product, is congestion. This has already been included among the resistances overcome by direct effort. But

plied to it is to be transferred to, or included in, final product immaterially (indirectly). If we define *a* final product, ontogenetically, as a continuing bit of substance (material), we exclude all that enters into it economically but does not enter it materially. Nevertheless, economically speaking, what is excluded enters into it on exactly the same basis as what is included. Economically, intermediate product becomes part of final product in the same way that raw material does. And it is only in attribution—in measuring "real costs"—that it becomes essential to distinguish the two.

[2] Only in respect of the distance to which material parts of the site must be removed, or from which they must be brought.

[3] The reader will recall that using-up is construed as the "charging off" of the "real cost" to the final product upon which it has naturally been expended; loss is disappearance due to other economic or to physical causes.

[4] "Housing for the internal operations of a machine shop cannot be supplied from moment to moment; nor can it be supplied economically from year to year"—Canning (57, 235).

[5] These latter also serve for overcoming inertia in moving.

to the extent that it can only be overcome by reduplicating the area of site,[6] it also calls for intermediate product and therefore indirect effort. However, since this intermediate product is actually inseparable from the above-mentioned permanent means of protection provided against interferences, it will be convenient to include it in that class.

The third form is the resistance to the canalization of natural powers. In practically all cases this requires intermediate product (indirect effort).[7] Also it is more exact as well as more convenient to regard all such means of canalization as intermediate, not final, product. For even when the effect of the natural power is itself consumed, rather than used in further production, it is this effect and not the apparatus through which it is brought to bear which constitutes the product actually consumed. Thus one consumes neither the telephone nor the radio, nor the power required to operate them, but the sound thus transmitted; one does not consume the electric light bulb, nor the electric current which makes it luminous, but the light; nor the coal, the furnace, the radiator, and the water it contains, but the heat. The natural power through its various transmutations remains natural power; the apparatus in which it is generated, or through which it is transmitted, or by which it is finally converted into the final desired effect, is intermediate product, the only need of which is due to the resistance of these powers to such canalization; and only the terminal effect is final product and then only if consumed as is.

And here it is necessary to pause for a moment to clarify a region in which the duplicity of the mixed physico-economic viewpoint and the fact of the evolution of machines from tools has left much confusion. From the physical viewpoint (mechanics) there are two forms of power; natural (including animal), and human; in this aspect both do "work" in the sense in which that term is used in mechanics. But even from this viewpoint both the machine and the tool are inert; they are merely the vehicles through which power is applied. The term

[6] Any building with more than one story enlarges the utilizable area above that of the site itself, regarded as a part of the earth's surface.

[7] Swimming downstream is a way of using a natural power without intermediate product—unless a bathing-suit is required by the "blue laws." But these cases are so few and far between and are so largely confined to direct consumption, not production, that the generalization is justified that the need for canalization offers a resistance which can only be overcome by intermediate product.

Flux (*143*, 89) remarks that "capital has been said to be the harness by which natural powers are guided so as to assist mankind in his efforts." This is a nice statement of the relation of canalization to intermediate product. But it is, of course, far too narrow a definition either of intermediate product or, for that matter, of "capital."

"automatic" when referring to machinery is thus deceptive. Its only automatic feature is that it is wholly, or almost wholly, a vehicle for the application of natural, not human, power, in this mechanical sense. On the other hand, from the economic viewpoint ("real costs") the only working performed in the machine process is the human working done indirectly in harnessing the natural power via this intermediate product and that done directly in operating this intermediate product (i.e., using it in production). In considering such working we do not differentiate between physical and mental exertion. It is all one from the standpoint of effort; and the mental is far more effective than the physical from the standpoint of result, even in the case of the operative alone. Moreover, this working is not the only effort required; retaining is required as well. From this economic viewpoint, then, natural power is not a cost; it works for nothing.[8] Nevertheless, its canalization occasions a cost because it presents a resistance to diversion to our purposes. This cost takes the form of indirect effort —the production of the intermediate product which canalizes the power—and of direct effort—the operation of this intermediate product in the process of producing final product.

There are two further types of intermediate product which differ from the foregoing in that they are not aimed to overcome, nor necessitated by, special forms of natural resistance to the production of final product. The first is merely one stage in some processes which ends up in the form of the third type above. This type includes all the natural materials which are utilized to generate natural powers—either as ultimate or merely proximate result. During the stages of the economic process in which they exist in the original material form, their production has involved no different kinds of natural resistance than any other material product. When they come to be used to generate natural powers, the resistance to this step takes the form of the third type above—the resistance to canalization. The proximate

[8] This has been said many times; but not always correctly and, so far as I know, never with its proper corollaries. As to the first, for instance, Ricardo said (*337*, 191) that natural agents and machinery "are serviceable to us, by increasing the abundance of productions, by making men richer, by adding to value in use; but as they perform their work gratuitously, as nothing is paid for the use of air, of heat, and of water, the assistance they afford us adds nothing to value in exchange." Obviously this is true only of "natural agents"; and it ignores the fact that "natural agents" without "machinery," in its broadest sense, are never serviceable to us except in direct consumption.

As to the second, Böhm-Bawerk, for example, says (*38*, 81), ". . . the cooperation of the free natural powers, which, technically, is also indispensable, is given without question and without cost." Itself is without cost, but its canalization is not.

as well as the ultimate result may be a canalized natural power, if the effect is used in consumption or in production. But the ultimate result may also be a new material (product of chemical reaction, coke, etc.) which is literally synthetic (not extracted as such), if the effect of the action of the power is to destroy the old and create a new material; and this new material may in turn constitute the substance of a product. The criterion of such transmutation may be whatever you please.

The last type of intermediate product, or occasion for indirect effort, differs from all the foregoing in that at no stage does it represent a means of overcoming a special resistance to the production of final product. This type may be called the *tool*, if we restrict the meaning of the term to such intermediate product as is designed to canalize human exertion, physical or mental, exclusively. There cannot be said to be a natural resistance to such canalization.[9] True, the production of the tool itself meets all the resistances offered to that of any other material product. But, as a way of applying indirect effort to the final product upon which it is used, it merely meets the same resistances which are met by direct working without the tool.[10] Presumably it does so in such a way that the sum of indirect and remaining direct effort is less than was direct effort alone. That is, the purpose of the canalization is to produce more effect with the same effort (change of technique) or to produce an effect impossible without the tool, which thereby effects an economizing in terms of equivalent quantities of usefulness. The tool has frequently been taken as the type of all intermediate product. However, not only has it become today the least important variety, but it is actually atypical, in spite of the fact that it was most probably the first, from which intermediate product for the canalizing of natural powers evolved.

While we are necessarily deferring the consideration of technique, one of its influences must be shown at this point in order to make clear to the reader the viewpoint as to intermediate product which we are adopting. Not only are we regarding it as only a stage in the process of producing final product but we also see it as a conglomerate artifact rather than in the aspect of the individual constituent products. And this for the reason that, except for the primitive tool, any par-

[9] There might be conceived to be human resistances to the use of a tool. But these would constitute merely reductions in the economizing of effort, not new or added natural resistances.

[10] Therefore, the best way in which it can be fitted into the general scheme can more conveniently be considered when we are treating of technique.

ticular technique always prescribes a congeries of intermediate products which must be used together (i.e., no one of which is dispensable). Thus while every part of this congeries is not necessarily limited to one objectively indifferent product, all parts are, in the usual sense, "perfectly complementary." [11] It should also be noted that the notion of a single technique also sets both minimum and maximum limits to the size of the units—or to the number of units, or to both—of the individual intermediate products of which this conglomerate is composed. For this reason, and for others which we shall give hereafter, the notion of a single technique envisages a limited range for the scale of operation to which it is adapted.

2. THE ATTRIBUTION OF FINAL PRODUCT TO INDIRECT EFFORT

By definition, indirect effort is not applied directly to the production of final product; nor, for that matter, is it necessarily applied directly to the production of all intermediate product with which it is concerned; it may be applied directly to the production of one intermediate product which is used in the production of some other intermediate product which comes later in the series.[12] Thus, the connection of indirect effort with final product may be through several steps or stages of intermediate product in succession. Now it is obvious that this single, or these successive, *uses* of intermediate product in the production of final product accomplish some definite result with reference to the latter or on the process of production of the latter; otherwise the indirect effort would not be made. It is also evident that there is another and somewhat independent connection between the two; that is, that the "real cost" in indirect effort must in some manner be absorbed in the "real cost" of final product, for the purpose of producing which it was solely incurred. Let us examine these two connections in the order stated.

We have already examined the chief purposes served by the use of intermediate product in the production of final or other intermediate

[11] While "perfect complementarity" is not an entirely adequate criterion for the study of demand for individual, objectively indifferent, intermediate products, its use here, within its limitations, is as far as we find it necessary to apply it at all in our analysis. We assume that the optimum among all possible substitutes for complementary parts will always be preferred.

[12] This is, of course, the general idea of "goods of a higher order"—the "higher" in the non-temporal series being the earlier in the temporal series—which Menger originated and which the Austrian school has made familiar.

product. The first is the adaptation of site. It is clear, in the first place, that the more or less permanent reduction of the natural resistance on account of the unsuitability of site will reduce direct effort per unit of product by a readily calculated amount. Nevertheless, the adaptation will not justify the total indirect effort it involves unless, during its effective life, it thereby reduces the total direct effort to be expended upon the process conducted on that site by a greater amount. The question must then arise as to what quantity of process upon the site will receive the benefit of this reduction in direct effort. The indirect effort, made once for all, is fixed in quantity, but its life in use is not fixed; moreover, the process located on the site extends more or less indefinitely into the future and involves more or less uncertain quantities of product. The ratio indirect effort expended to direct effort economized, both per unit of product, is therefore necessarily an estimate. It is also clear, in the second place, that the question whether this reduction of resistance per unit of product is worth while cannot be settled apart from the question of whether, in view of the estimated total effort, direct and indirect, per unit of product, remaining, this is the best available site to allocate to this process in view of the general scheme of allocation of sites to be described below.

The second purpose served by the use of intermediate product is the protection of final or other intermediate product or their processes. In the last analysis this, too, is always a way of economizing direct effort. In part, it operates to reduce direct effort per unit of product by reducing the natural interferences with the process; in part, it does so only as to the aggregate, by increasing the quantity of product—that is, by reducing the direct effort wasted on product that is spoiled. In this case the estimate must consider all the factors mentioned in the previous case as determining the ratio of indirect effort expended to direct effort economized, but also the fact that, here, the latter can only be very roughly approximated from past experience. In fact, today, the extra direct effort that would be incurred without protection has been to a large extent forgotten, and it is taken for granted in most processes that a minimum of protection is always justified.[13] Of course, in this case, the system of allocation of sites only enters the

[13] This is not true in all climates, nor of all processes in the least favorable climates. Actual extraction usually take place "out of doors," though even then some permanent protection, roofs or artificial shade, may be provided. So, too, the construction of protection itself and the post-extractive processes of production on many of its materials, are, in great part, unprotected.

picture in so far as the intermediate product intended for protection is more or less permanent and immovable (i.e., identified with the site). And, in this case, much of such intermediate product is not permanent, and still more is not immovable.

Whereas, when it consists of either one of these two kinds, the effect of the use of intermediate product does not appear positively in the final product itself, but only in the economizing of direct effort, that is usually not conceived to be true of the third kind. As we have already noted, the use of intermediate product whose purpose is to canalize natural powers seems, naïvely, to consist in the application of these powers to final, or other intermediate, product. That is again the physical rather than the economic viewpoint. For, economically speaking, it is equally true of this kind that the intermediate product upon which the indirect effort has been expended does nothing itself to final product. It is merely the channel through which the stream (power) flows. No more can one say that a machine produces product than that the channel of a river carries a boat downstream. On the other hand, natural power is not product at all. It exists or is generated by natural processes. Only the apparatus which transmits it, or in which it is generated, or by means of which it is applied, is product. Therefore, of the third kind, just as of the first two, the use consists only in accomplishing a reduction in the direct effort required. As in the first case, this reduction per unit of final product is rather readily estimable and the only difficult questions are the life of the intermediate product and the quantity of final product over which the indirect effort it involves must be spread. In this class we might as well include the type of intermediate product which exists first as a material, is then used to generate a power, and eventuates either in that power or in a new (synthetic) material.

From the physical viewpoint the type of intermediate product we have called the tool is somewhat similar to the last case. For, in this view, the tool is a medium through which man applies his own direct working effort, both physical and mental, to accomplish upon the final product the same effect he would accomplish without the tool, or one which he could not accomplish without it. But, again, from the economic standpoint this is but a way of economizing direct effort, by substituting for some of it a less quantity of indirect effort expended upon the tool. So, here too, for any given reduction in direct effort per unit of final product, the only question is the amount of indirect effort expended upon the tool, the life in use of that tool, and the quantity of final product upon which it will be used.

All this makes quite clear that the effect of the use of any intermediate product in economizing direct effort expended upon a unit of final product (or other intermediate)—that is, the first connection between the two—is rather readily and exactly calculated. But it also shows that the second connection, the deduction from this economizing per unit of final product that should be made in order that the entire "real cost" in indirect effort shall be correctly charged to the final product for the production of which it was expended, is far more difficult to calculate. And this for the reasons that the two factors which enter into it, the life in use of the intermediate product and the total quantity of final product to which its use will be applied, are somewhat independent of each other, and both are, within limits, matters of estimate of a somewhat uncertain future. Certain of the individual intermediate products among several of the various types enumerated are non-durables or one-use products (e.g., coal or paper containers). With these the life in use is easily ascertained. It is one use; and to that use must be charged the whole of the indirect effort expended. But the great bulk of intermediate product consists of durables of various durations of life in use. This raises difficulties. Furthermore, in most of these cases the life is not exactly correlated with the quantity of use;[14] in almost no case does the intermediate product gradually disappear as a physical entity; in many cases it does not greatly change in physical aspect during its life in use; and in many other cases such change as does take place is due, not to use, but to the gradual ravages of those natural processes we call, "collectively, time" (Senior). Furthermore, the quantity of final product in connection with which it will or can be used is also subject to many contingencies. The intermediate product (1) may be irreparably damaged or destroyed by accident (no longer usable); (2) if it is immovable (adaptation and certain protections), the process may move, due to changing conditions, and leave it unusable; (3) it may be superseded by an intermediate product so superior that it is no longer used; (4) the quantity of final product wanted, per period, may permanently decline or

[14] The life of a piece of grading or draining (adaptation of site) cannot be said to depend on how fast it is used up, for it is never used up. The life of a building may be shortened by non-use; and this even if repairs are made. A machine remains physically intact and continues to perform its function, perhaps with declining economizing, until it is discarded.

disappear; finally, (5) the quantity of final product wanted may fluctuate widely from period to period within a limited maximum. The first contingency leads to an allowance for "insurance" which may be calculated actuarily over a sufficient number of instances; the second, third and fourth are almost unpredictable, but lead nevertheless to some allowances for what is called, collectively, "obsolescence"; while the fifth tempts to that system of uniform charge per unit of final product which is usually advocated by economists, and which seems, on the face of it, the ideal system. But since movement of process (2), progress in technique (3), permanent changes in demand (4), and the ravages of time take place regardless of use, and since these constitute in the aggregate one of the chief determinants of life in use, the practical custom is to charge to the final product of each year (this may vary from year to year) a fraction of the indirect effort represented equal to the reciprocal of a conservatively estimated number of years in use. This method represents a compromise between the estimated influence of average expected use and the estimated influence of the factors which have their effect over time regardless of use.[15] To this is added, on the same basis, the allowance for "insurance" (1).

Since, in the last analysis, this charge for indirect effort depends not only on the quantity of indirect effort to be charged but also upon the quantity of final product over which it is to be distributed, one other element, not yet mentioned, enters as an influence in the case of durable intermediate product. For the particular conglomerate of intermediate product required for any one technique as to any one process there is a limit to the final product which can be produced in a given period of time. The maximum amount of final product per annum, against which these indirect costs can be charged on a per annum basis, is more or less rigidly fixed by technical considerations and thus establishes a minimum for the charge per unit. Usually the actual output is well within this maximum.[16]

[15] J. S. Bain (*15*) analyzes depreciation in two parts. One is a function of time and includes obsolescence and deterioration by the elements; the other is a function of output and depends on the rate of use. The separate influences are not necessarily "additive" or "cumulative." Actual depreciation may be the result of the strongest influence only, or of that plus some effect of the others. But there is a critical point in output beyond which further production will augment actual depreciation above that due to the time elements alone.

[16] Since this kind of "capacity" (of intermediate product) has wholly different causes and effects from the kind we have referred to previously (quantity of effort available),

The result of this customary method of "charging off" intermediate product, which is perhaps the wisest, is a convention according to which, in order so far as possible to make certain that all the indirect effort expended shall be charged to final product while the intermediate product is actually used, this charge is very considerably in excess of the physical wear and tear that use per unit of final product entails. The net economizing is thus made to appear less than it theoretically might be, but probably no less than it actually is. Moreover, this charge, since it is divided over more or less final product in different periods, may at times cause the net economizing entirely to disappear (or worse), while, at others, when output is at its maximum, it will be exaggerated. We may agree, at least, that this would be the wisest method for a well-managed direct economy which is, of course, vitally interested in avoiding any waste of effort. It would be desirous of avoiding, above all things, any self-deception that would lead it to apply indirect effort which *might not* result in net economizing. For, of course, it would consider all effort to be chargeable in full to the purpose for which it was intended, even though, after the water was over the dam, it might turn out to have been a dis-economizing.

3. DIFFERENTIATION IN THE ATTRIBUTION OF FINAL PRODUCT TO THE TWO KINDS OF INDIRECT EFFORT

Hitherto, we have been considering indirect effort as if it were a homogeneous function without reference to the fact that it is composed of two distinct components—working and retaining. We are now prepared to analyze the different ways in which the substitution of indirect for direct effort (the use of intermediate product) involves the two kinds of effort, and to what extent and how they are separately charged. In general we may say that the economizing of "real cost" in total effort by such substitution always involves the reduction of total work and the increase of total retention. There is one exception, noted hereafter.[17] Indirect working is not literally a substitute for direct working; its only effect is via the use of intermediate product, in the various ways cited, which presumably results in a sufficient reduction of direct working to offset the indirect and thereby result in economizing of

and since it can be best studied in its most advanced technological setting, we are reserving our examination of it for our prospective study of the technological branch of economics.

[17] True "capital-saving" intermediate product as discussed below.

the total. Therefore, it is, in reality, only a substitute in so far as the formula of "real costs" of the final (or other intermediate) product is concerned. But any such substitution requires indirect retaining—retaining of the intermediate product. Therefore, this indirect retention is always a deduction from the economizing of work effected by means of introducing some quantity of indirect working in place of a larger quantity of direct working; so that, in order to be justified, this economizing of total work must be great enough to exceed the added retention required. Thus, the added retention is not the effective agent in the economizing; it is rather the handicap upon the process of substitution.[18] Moreover, the added "real cost" of retaining (the quantity of retention necessary) bears no quantitative relation either to the reduction in direct work or to the increase in work in its indirect form. Finally, as we have already noted, these two kinds of effort are not inherently measured in a common unit as "real costs." In order, therefore, that one should be able algebraically to deduct the addition to the cost of retaining (the additional indirect retention) from the reduction in the total cost in work, both direct and indirect, one must find a means of relating the two units quantitatively. This means has already been outlined in previous chapters, and will be described more fully below.

The foregoing analysis of "real costs" in terms of undifferentiated effort, and the kinds of natural resistance which require this effort and determine its quantity, applies in full and without alteration to that component form of effort, work. Therefore the "real costs" of the intermediate product itself, in so far as they consist of work applied directly to the intermediate product, or indirectly via other intermediate product, are fixed by the natural resistances in the same way as has already been traced out. But that analysis did not cover the incidental component, retention. When we analyzed this latter kind of effort in

[18] One does not substitute "capital" for "labor"; one substitutes less "labor" for "more" labor, but in a way which requires more "capital" (that is, retaining).

This may be an appropriate point at which to fit this special case into our general scheme. It should be noted that, for all occasions other than the two technical options, retention is purely an added cost. This means that, in order to justify it, the product retained must have behind it a greater force either on account of the time of its use (future provisions) or its nature (durables and long processes) than has other product which is the result of the same quantity of present working. In the case of the technical options, retention is also an added cost, but not purely that; for then it is a condition for the reduction in cost of direct working. In the second technical option, but not in the first, indirect work is of the same order. The added indirect work upon the intermediate product is a condition of the reduction in direct work on the final product.

the tenth chapter we resolved the occasions which required it into several categories, the two contingencies, the three technical necessities, and the two technical options (or work economizers), large batches and intermediate product. Now it is evident that all of these except the last are occasions for direct retaining only—that is, retaining of final product. To a large extent the need for retaining in these cases is due to the action of the want system; in some cases it is in part established by natural resistances or by the facts of the environment. The seasonal element in the first technical necessity, the inherent durability of most products which are effective measures of protection in consumption, and the geographical and seasonal elements in requiring long processes place these three types in the latter category. But we have already sufficiently analyzed all these cases of direct retaining and have shown the effect on "real costs." Large batches are a special case of technique, without indirect retaining, which we shall consider under that head. At this point, therefore, we will confine our consideration to the second technical option only, intermediate product, and thus to the only occasion for indirect retaining. But we must note, at once, that it is only the fact that the retaining required becomes thereby indirect that is due to its application to intermediate product. The fact that retaining is required at all, in this case, is not due to the intermediacy of the product, but to the same reasons that make it necessary for final product. These reasons are that it may be durable, may be produced by long processes, or in large batches, and, finally, that it may be stored for future use in production on the basis of contingencies analogous to these described in connection with final product. Intermediate product may be both durable and non-durable. The former requires indirect retaining after it begins to be used in production of final product (or other intermediate); the latter does not. But both may themselves be produced by long processes or in large batches. Even non-durable intermediate product rarely constitutes a continuous stream passing instanter from production into use. Instead, it is usually produced *beforehand* and exists and moves, both during the process of production and afterwards, in large lots which are stored and from which use is gradual with periodic replenishment. Also analogies to our contingencies arise there. Furthermore, in a lesser degree the delays between the completion of production and the beginning of use may also be true of durable intermediate product.

Up to the point where it begins to be used in production, intermediate product, therefore, requires retaining, though indirect, for the same or very similar reasons for which final product requires direct retaining. In fact, this retaining is applied directly to the intermediate product, becomes part of its "real cost" and is thus only redistributed ("charged off") to the final product in connection with which it is used according to the previously described convention. It is thus treated in exactly the same way as the "real cost" of work, which has also accumulated

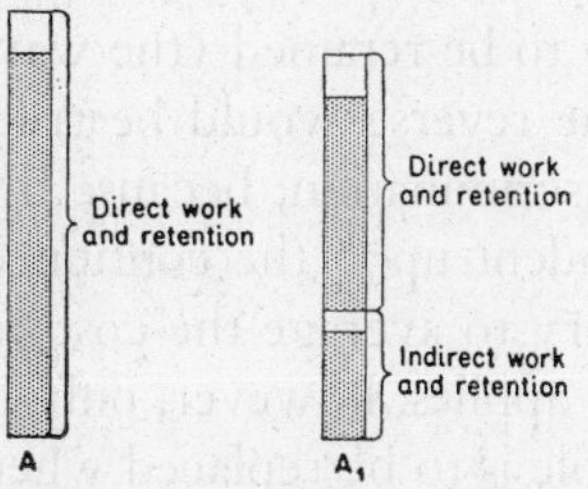

Fig. 30

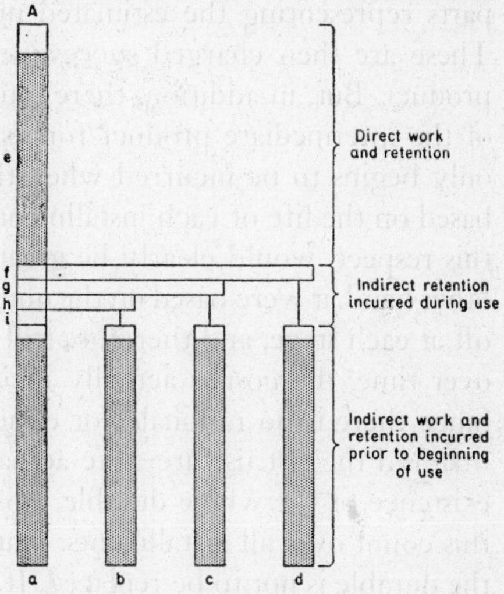

Fig. 31

during the production of the intermediate product. If this were all there was to it we could represent the connections of intermediate product in the production of final product without introducing the factor of time at all. We could show, as in Fig. 30, the "real cost" of final product A, when only direct work and retention are used (work as the black and retention as the white portion of the bar). Against that would be shown, as A_1, that of the same final product, when intermediate product was applied and effected some economizing. In the second case the "real cost" of work and the "real cost" of retention accumulated in the intermediate product, during its production and until its use, is applied *in toto* to the final product, as the cost of indirect effort. And this is all there is to it as far as non-durable (one use) intermediate product is concerned.

However, when *durable* intermediate product begins to be used in the production of final (or other intermediate) product, its accumulated "real cost" in work and retention up to that point is not all there is to it. For by the very fact of its durability it requires continued retaining throughout that use in production. This further "real cost" is usually not treated in the same way. It is not in practice accumulated as we represented it to be for final product in Fig. 30, but is charged to final product separately, directly, and as, not after,[19] it is incurred. The accumulated "real cost" of the intermediate product, in work and retention, at the beginning of use, is divided into a number of equal parts representing the estimated number of installments of its use.[20] These are then charged successively to the successive units of final product. But, in addition, there must be charged the cost of retention of the intermediate product for its whole life during use, a cost that only begins to be incurred when that use begins. If this charge were based on the life of each installment, the cost of the last installment, in this respect, would clearly be greater than that of the first. If, on the other hand, it were based on the number of installments not yet charged off at each stage, and therefore still requiring to be retained (the way, over time, the cost is actually incurred), the reverse would be true. Since there is no rationale for either such discrimination, because the first and the last use are alike actually dependent upon the continued existence of the whole durable, it is customary to average the cost on this count over all installments. This analysis applies, however, only if the durable is not to be replaced. If the durable is to be replaced when used up, the question of averaging does not arise. For then, since, in the aggregate and thus on the average, all such durables are being replaced continuously, a new installment is conceived to be added to each as fast as one is used up. In that way there comes to be no actual difference in the cost on this count per installment. Instead, because the number of extant installments of the durable which are on hand never diminishes, the "real cost" of retaining the whole durable for each year, say, is charged pro rata to each unit of final product in the production of which it is used during that year. Or, in other words, the "real cost" of retaining the whole durable during the period of time assignable to one unit of final product is charged to that unit.

We will now attempt to show, in a diagram, this combination of

[19] Or before, as would be possible.

[20] We need not confuse our presentation at this point by considering the fact that the installments are usually figured per annum, rather than per unit of final product, and that therefore the installment per unit of final product may vary widely at different times. For this purpose we are considering only installments per unit of final product and assuming them to be uniform.

charges in such a way that we can thereafter expose certain common errors. In Fig. 31, that part of the "real cost" of final product, A, which is incurred for retaining the intermediate product during use (all of which is indirect retention) is shown separately, as *f*, *g*, *h*, and *i*, from the four installments of this intermediate product, *a*, *b*, *c*, and *d*, each of which represents its share of the indirect work and retention incurred prior to beginning of use. The sum of these installments represents the "real cost" of the finished (produced) intermediate product at that time. On the assumption that each installment is replaced as fast as used, four will always be on hand. The retention involved for each during the period of time assignable to one unit of final product is thus shown here as if it were charged separately, as *i*, *h*, *g*, or *f*. But, since all four installments must always be on hand, each unit of final product A must bear the "real cost" of retaining all four during its own period of use—that is, the sum of *f*, *g*, *h*, and *i*. There is no other way of including in the cost of the final product the whole cost of retention of intermediate product during its use. Thus the whole "real cost" of a durable intermediate product, which is assignable to the final product in the production of which it is used, includes not only its own "real cost" of production in work and retention up to the time it is put to use, but also the "real cost" of retaining it during use. Therefore the latter must also be included as a deduction from the net economizing; and, in order to justify itself, the whole of bar A in Fig. 31, for instance, must be shorter than it would have been without the use of the intermediate product.

We are now in position to show the ambiguity, or even the error, in certain common interpretations of these facts. In the first place, as already noted, "capital," in the sense of intermediate product, is not actually substituted for "labor" in this process. So far as the use or effect is concerned there is no substitution at all; [21] the substitution is wholly in the make-up of "real costs." Even there most of the actual substitution (shown in Fig. 31) is that of indirect "labor" for direct "labor." Only the remainder is the cost of the kind of "capital" (retaining) which, as a function, is properly treated as the antithesis of "labor" (working). In the second place, this enables us to make clear the true distinction between "labor-saving" (work-reducing) and "capital-saving" (retention-reducing) innovations effected through intermediate product. For the sake of simplification let us ignore direct

[21] That is, working is "substituted" for working.

retention and indirect retention incurred prior to beginning of use, since these may be presumed to remain unchanged through our various permutations.

1. If the process shown in Fig. 31 was introduced in place of a wholly direct process, it is to be presumed that direct work (*e*) has been reduced, indirect work (*a*) has been increased and indirect retention (*f* to *i*) has been increased. Since, however, their sum, after the change, must needs be less than was direct work alone, before it, it is necessary that total work has been reduced by more than indirect retention has been increased. That is, the change in total work must have been negative, and negative by more than that of retention has been positive. This then was a "labor-saving" and "capital-using" innovation, in the proper sense.

2. Now let us suppose that another innovation is introduced by substituting an intermediate product which is represented by 8 bars, instead of 4, each of half the height of those in Fig. 31, but an innovation that has no other effect. Direct work (e) remains the same; indirect retention remains the same (8 bars of half the size require the same retention as did *a* to *d*); but the size of the installment, *a*, is reduced by half. Actually this is a "labor-saving" innovation because it has reduced indirect "labor" only, although it is not usually called such; and it is neither "capital-using" nor "capital-saving."

3. Next consider the introduction of an intermediate product which reduces the height of bars *a* to *d* without altering their number or affecting *e*. This is usually treated as "capital-saving" but not as "labor-saving." Actually it is both; but it is far more "labor-saving" than it is "capital-saving" because the reduction of *a* by one-half is much greater than the reduction of *f* to *i* by one-half.

4. The only exclusively "capital-saving" innovation is one which reduces the number of bars, *a* to *d*, or the period of time assignable to one unit of product, without changing their size or affecting *e*. The first alternative is due to reductions of durability. The second is due to more continuous or more intensive use.[22]

[22] An example of the second effect may be needed here. It can best be given by considering two ways of using one machine, say. Let this machine cost $1,000; suppose it will last 10 years if operated at the rate of 1,000 units of product per annum, and 5 years if at the rate of 2,000 units per annum. Depreciation, per unit of product, will be the same in both cases, for the total cost must, in either, be charged to 10,000 units. But in the second case the cost of indirect retaining per unit of product will be half what it will be in the first. Five per cent per annum, say, on $1,000, is $50. If this is divided by 1,000 units per annum, it is $.05; if by 2,000 units per annum, it is $.025. Since the machine is the same in both

4. REDUCTION OF THE TWO KINDS OF EFFORT TO A COMMON MEASURE AS "REAL COSTS"

We referred above to the fact that retention as a "real cost" must be reduced to a common measure with work as a "real cost," in order that the changes, plus or minus, produced in either by the introduction of indirect effort (intermediate product), can be algebraically added and the question whether this introduction will result in a reduction of total effort, direct and indirect, can be determined. In Chapter 10 we analyzed the two work-economizers (technical options) and saw how this common measure is established. In essence it depends on the rate of accrual of retaining as effort. If no retaining effort were involved, we might justly assume that a worker would be as willing to do an hour's working now upon a product to be enjoyed a year hence, and thus economize the hour then, as he would to wait and have the working as well as the enjoyment come then. The two hours, then and now, would be indifferent to him—in either case the enjoyment of the result would come at the same time. Since we find, however, that this is not true, we know that effort must be involved in retaining. Let us suppose that this neutral relation—indifference—is discovered to exist only when, by doing one hour's working now, the worker can economize an hour and three minutes a year from now. For any greater potential economizing then he prefers to do this working now; for any less, the reverse. This enables us to calculate that the rate of accrual of retaining as effort upon one hour's working is about 5 percent per annum—that is, the prospect of 63 minutes then = 60 minutes now. We have already analyzed the cause of this discrepancy. It is a reflection of the effort, which takes place over time, involved in retaining the product of one hour's working for one year. Assuming that the intensity of effort involved in both hours' working is the same at the respective times when they are performed, the difference between these equivalents, three minutes of working-time, is the "real cost" of the retaining. Three minutes is 1/20 of an hour. Therefore the "real cost" of retaining—the effort involved in the retention of—the product of one hour's work for one year, on this ratio, equals 1/20 of the "real

cases it cannot be more durable in one than in the other. The difference is only one between less and more continuous or intensive use. The same difference may exist between two different machines, if one be adapted to more continuous or intensive use than the other. The second costs no more; it is capable of no greater output over its life; but it is capable of steadier or faster operation.

cost" of (the effort involved in) the hour's work. If, in the formula for retaining as effort, $R_i T^{-1}$, the unit of T is taken as one year, then the unit of retention, or $R_i T^{-1} \times T = R_i$, is the amount of "real cost" of retaining involved in retaining one unit of work (W) for one year. Then R_i, as "real cost," $= \frac{W}{20}$, as "real cost," or $20\ R_i = 1\ W$. If T is taken to be 1 day, $1\ R_i = \frac{1\ W}{7{,}300}$; if both "real costs" are measured in a common denominator of time, one hour, then $1\ R_i = \frac{1W}{175{,}200}$ [23]—that is, the retention for one hour of the product of working for one hour involves, on this ratio, $\frac{1}{175{,}200}$ of the effort ("real cost") involved in that hour's working.[24] By learning, in any particular case, the neutral point between anticipation and postponement of working for future provision, where no consideration enters into the matter other than the effect of the increment of retaining upon the working itself between the two points in time, we learn, for that case, what is the ratio between the "real costs" of the two different functions, retaining and working, performed for the same length of time upon the same scale (or magnitude), so that summation of the two becomes possible. But this ratio has validity in no other respect than equivalence of effort involved. In terms of effect, even the notion of equivalence is absurd. Working, and working only, produces product; retaining and retaining only, keeps it extant.[25]

It may seem to the reader that, in developing this analysis of the very complicated way in which "real costs" in indirect effort are included among the "real costs" of the product for which they are incurred,

[23] It will be recalled that W, the unit of work, is the effect of one hour of standard working.

[24] Perhaps the most convenient concept of such a formula is that one already used which introduces a constant, K. Then $1\ R_i = 1\ WK$. But it must be noted that this constant is indeterminate until the unit of T (time) is fixed.

[25] It is important to emphasize this point. In the aspect of effect, working and retaining are disparate and incommensurable. Only in the aspect of effort are they commensurable. In that aspect, $1\ R_i$ turns out to be a minute fraction of 1 W. This must always be remembered when we compare the "producing" of 100 W with the retaining of 100 W. From the contribution angle these correspond, though they are disparate. One must have 100 R_e to retain 100 W. But, from the "real cost" angle, the 100 R_i is only equal to 5 W, say. In financial terminology, the contribution of retaining is measured in terms of "principal value," while the "real cost" of retention is measured in terms of interest on that principal per unit of time for some definite time.

we have again presented a counsel of perfection, as was suggested in the same connection in Chapter 10; that, in other words, we set up, as if it were the method in actual use in economies in general, one which imputes a greater degree of finesse and accuracy than is possible, or at least actual. Again, this point would seem to be not well taken; for the purpose of such an analysis is to present the principles upon which the practice is based and toward which it tends, rather than an inductive appraisal of the practice itself, including its errors or omissions.

A second objection may be urged even more strongly. This study is concerned exclusively with a direct economy. Yet it may seem to some that we have presented here an analysis of the system of cost accounting developed in indirect economies, operating under the exchange system and estimating and recording their costs in terms of money, and have then imputed it as a whole to a direct economy which is, by definition, without exchange or money, and whose only data, therefore, would be "real costs." The argument might continue that such a system would be impossible in terms of "real cost" (without benefit of money prices), and, moreover, that, to the extent that direct economies more nearly represent the primitive type, while indirect economies are more highly evolved, we are attributing to an earlier stage of development a system which only arose much later.[26] These possible objections are worth rebutting with some care. The countercharge must be that the supposed facts upon which these objections are based are not only untrue but are themselves impossible. Quite the contrary from these suppositions, this method must have developed first in the nearest approach to a direct economy we know of—the early isolated farm—and its operation in indirect economies must be and must always have been in terms of "real costs," of which the money

[26] Max Weber takes very dogmatically the first position and the background of his analysis includes the second (see *434*, III, 1, 46, and 53 ff., *Naturalrechnung*).

Pareto also assumes the first position in an even more positive manner. This follows automatically, for him, from his assumption that the only three ways in which economic magnitudes can be compared is in physical terms, in money terms and in terms of "ophelimity." Since, in his thinking, all economic entities, other than final product (i.e., all "land," "labor," and intermediate product) have no "ophelimity" until after they are transformed, production cannot be conceived in terms of the "sacrifice of ophelimity" (see *317*, 298–299). Thus these other (previous) entities can only be considered in physical and in money terms. As definitely limited physical quantities, constituting a stock on hand, they are "given," provided, as the data of allocation. They are not "real costs" to him; nor are they variable quantities; and his only problem is to find out how these "given" limited quantities, in view of their imputed "values" in money terms, will be allocated, in order to result in the maximum of "ophelimity." Those who deny the existence of certain real phenomena are not likely to solve the problem of their causation and way of working.

terms are a mere reflection. We know that one of the most fertile sources of the early development of intermediate product in the form of adaptation, protection, canalization (domestic animals), and tools was the isolated farm. In so far as it made its own intermediate product it was, in this regard, a direct economy. In such an economy these calculations must, therefore, have been made; and, on the other hand, they could only be made in terms of "real costs." For no other basis existed. Doubtless it is true that, in most cases, the innovations effected so great an economizing that such calculations did not need to be exact. And, doubtless, since they probably depended wholly on memory and not on records, the system could not have been applied with any high degree of precision. Nevertheless, its principles were certainly understood and developed, at this early stage; for, otherwise, no motive whatever is assignable for the evident use of intermediate product. Menger quite properly used the nearly isolated Austrian farm of his acquaintance as the basis for his analysis of this process in real terms—the first in economic literature.

As against this single and explicit relation in a direct economy, in which all working is homogeneous and the "real cost" of retaining in terms of working is established by a single influence of futurity—that of the worker-retainer—we have, in indirect economies, the diversity and confusion of as many relations as there are separate workers or retainers. Thus, here, the necessity of the system has become much less obvious to most of the participants, and its application has become much more, not less, difficult. Nevertheless, here, the effect of individual choices, made generally without benefit of perceiving their effects, is equally controlling. Those who do perceive them, and whose decisions are made in view of this insight, are nevertheless compelled to operate wholly within the framework of possibilities established by others, most of whom do not. This framework is the system of money prices fixed by the aggregate of individual choices, which is, in turn, but a reflection of the ill-informed calculations and resulting choices of these individuals. In other words, behind all money costs lies the system of preferences which establishes them. These money costs are not a reflection of given limited quantities of, nor of given "terms of trade" for, the "factors." They are entirely a reflection of the number of units of "real cost," which is determined in turn by the particular natural resistances which these must overcome. Only the "subjective value" of the unit of "real cost" is connected with and determined in the system of satisfaction of wants.

I am inclined to think that the reason economics was so slow in developing a true theory of "capital," [27] and the reason this element of "real cost"—retention—is still frequently not recognized as an actual one by those workers who do little or none of it and by those retainers who do it only for their own provision, is well demonstrated by our previous and present analysis of the way retention would usually appear in a direct economy. While work as a "real cost," in terms of its felt effort, is recognized as a separate entity and is counterposed to the product upon which it is expended, retention, as a "real cost," is not in these cases a clearly defined and separate entity; instead it takes the form merely of a dimly felt handicap on future provision as such. But, in the case of indirect retention applied to intermediate product, this is no longer possible. For, then, the intermediate product itself has no usefulness as future provision. It is purely a work-economizer. And that fact itself always compelled and still compels the recognition and calculation of retention as a "real cost."

D. "REAL COSTS" AND THE ALLOCATION OF SITES

1. ORDER OF PREFERENCE AMONG SITES FOR A SINGLE USE

We are now in position to clarify the one respect in which the environment can be treated in a quantitative way—a treatment which we have, in most unorthodox fashion, omitted hitherto. Economically speaking there are, with one exception, no units of measurement for the environment, because there are no economic aspects in which it exhibits homogeneity. The single exception is the units of measurement of space; and these have but an indirect relation with economic magnitudes, only serving as a convenient common term in which related economic magnitudes may be stated as rates and thus have their relationships reduced to quantitative terms. Otherwise, the environment is essentially diverse—a patchwork of areas of varied size and shape at each of which some one or more of the non-ubiquitous materials and powers may be available, but among which the degree of accessibility of these resources varies widely. How well this is recognized by the timber cruiser, the mining engineer, the hydroelectric engineer and even

[27] That is, the theory, the foundations of which were laid by Menger and Böhm-Bawerk.

the farmer! Why not, then, by the economist as well? "Land" is not a uniform element to be dosed out according to a chemical formula as a substitute for "labor" or "capital." Nor is the fact of the slightest importance, as we have previously noted, that the quantities of all land, and of each kind, are finite. For these potential limits do not, in any instance, constitute the effective limits. Economically speaking, land of all kinds is, at present, of unlimited extent.

The one respect in which the environment enters economic analysis in a quantitative way may be called the *density of the economic process.* This density may be conveniently conceived in terms of quantity of process per unit of space on site. But that is only proximate; for it merely relates the quantity of process to the resistances through the medium of a common measurement in terms of space. Moreover, it concerns but a limited part of the relation between the economic processes as a whole and the environment; that is, it has to do with five only of the various forms of natural resistance, the polarity between dissipation and congestion, economic depth, concentration, and economic distance. Upon a site of any size the density of process has a relation which is purely spatial. As we proceed from the pole of dissipation the resistance of economic distance or depth on the site decreases; but, after some point is reached in each process as we proceed toward the opposite pole of congestion, the resistance arising from interference among the agencies increases. At some point, or in some range, the sum of the two is least; and in either direction therefrom the sum is greater. Secondly, upon a site of any size the quantity of natural resources—materials or powers [1] —is "given" and finite. That is, there appears to enter here a relation between material (or physical) and spatial magnitudes, which also influences the density of process. But let us see. As these resources are extracted they may replace themselves continuously, or periodically, or not at all.[2] However, these finite quantities of materials and powers may exist upon each site in various concentrations and at various economic depths. To the extent that they replace themselves continuously or periodically they will still only be extracted down to such dilutions or depths as constitute the limit of "payability," to be defined later. That

[1] While powers are only canalized by intermediate product and therefore the resistance to canalization is overcome by indirect effort, we may include them with materials here, for their self-replacement and their comparative concentration and accessibility have the same effects.

[2] We say here "replace themselves" for brevity; we mean "are replaced by natural processes." Replacements by man are extant product, final or intermediate, not natural materials and powers.

means that, for any site, the output per annum will be confined to the natural replacements which come within such limit. So too, if they replace themselves partially and are partially replaced artificially (fertilizing). To the extent that they do not replace themselves at all, they will eventually be exhausted. That means that, for any site, the total output over an indefinite time will be confined to those resources which lie within the limit of payability. And this output will be spread over time according to other considerations than those mentioned here. In either case, replacement or exhaustion, the limiting point is not, then, the finite quantities of materials or powers. It is set, rather, by the purely spatial considerations of concentration and economic depth. Therefore, this constitutes no exception to the foregoing generalization. Finally, among the sites suitable for any process there is another purely spatial consideration which influences the density of process in the large. That is, the economic distance from the center to these sites, respectively, will range along a nearly continuous series or along one with wide gaps, according as the requisites for the process exist everywhere or only at certain sites. And these distances are also "given" by nature, once the consuming center is located.

On account of the first consideration, taken alone, the quantity of site chosen for any particular quantity of process will tend to be such that the density is in the optimum range. That is, dissipation will be avoided by contracting the site to the point at which the increase of congestion begins to exceed the decrease of dissipation. Thereafter, if the quantity of process is expanded, it may be expanded, within limits, against increasing resistance on account of congestion, but for other offsetting reasons. On account of the second and third considerations alone, concentration and economic depth, any particular quantity of process will tend to be applied first to the extraction of those materials and powers the sum of whose resistances on account of dilution and economic depth is least. Thereafter, if the quantity of process is expanded, it may be expanded, also within limits, against increasing resistance by reason of greater dilution or greater economic depth, but again only for other offsetting reasons. If the resource is progressively exhausted (i.e., does not replace itself), then this will occur progressively even without expansion of the process. Finally, on account of the fourth consideration alone, economic distance, any particular quantity of process will tend to be applied first to that site or those sites whose economic distance from the consuming center is least. Thereafter, if the quantity of process is expanded, it may be expanded successively to more and more economically distant sites in a continuous or discontinuous series, but again for other offsetting reasons.

It will be convenient to regard density of process in terms of superficial area only—that is, in terms of but two of the dimensions of space. Thus, for any process, other things being equal, the greater the congestion at any level and the greater the number of levels (depth, above or below the surface), the greater the density. For extractive processes the density is in part proportionate to concentration at each level and in part proportionate again to the number of levels (the range of depth) worked. Since, when not otherwise specified, we are considering economic distance only between sites, the general notion of density in this regard applies only to the degree to which all operations are, or can be, centralized around the consuming center. If the series of sites available for any purpose is discontinuous, centralization will be to that extent impossible. It may be noted, in passing, that economic distance is the only influence tending to produce centralization of economic operations around the consuming center.

However, the environmental considerations that influence density of process do not apply independently of each other. Though separately analyzable it is the sum of all these resistances which, at least in intention, determines how and where any expansion of process, or its continuation in the case of exhausting resources, will be made. If, in the case of any process, expansion to another site involves less increased resistance on account of economic distance than does expansion on the same site on account of congestion, or vice versa; if, in the case of extraction, extracting additional, or continuing to extract exhausting, materials or powers of a less degree of concentration involves a smaller increase of resistance than does extracting those at greater economic depth, or vice versa; or if, also in the case of extraction, applying the process to another site—one whose most accessible resources are sufficiently more accessible on the site—though it is at a greater economic distance, involves less increased resistance than the least that would have to be incurred at the old site, or vice versa; then expansion or continuation will tend to follow that path—in other words, the line of least resistance—or to be proportioned along all paths in such a way that the maximum total of these resistances encountered at each is the same for all sites. In respect of the first and the fourth considerations, the resistances encountered in all parts of the process will tend to be the same.

That is, the degree of congestion will tend to be uniform throughout; and the economic distance is taken as uniform for the whole site. But, in respect of the second and third considerations, which apply to extraction only, the process will not necessarily be uniform. That is, different degrees of concentration and different economic depths may apply concurrently to different parts of the process. The limit of payability, referred to above, applies only to the second and third considerations, and is fixed by the greatest resistance from dilution and depth which is worth overcoming, for any given total output, in view of the alternative of going to a further site sufficient of whose resources are more accessible on the site. From this we can deduce that, in general, those extractive processes which are applied to resources which replace themselves, continuously or periodically, are extended to sites at greater economic distance only as the quantity of process must be increased; on the other hand, those which are applied to resources which do not replace themselves and are therefore progressively exhausted, are inevitably extended to further sites in the course of time, even without any increase in the quantity of process, and perhaps even with a lessening in this quantity. Finally, we must remind ourselves that the notions of "further" and of economic distance have no meaning apart from a ground plan for a particular economy upon the consuming center of which all final product must ultimately converge.

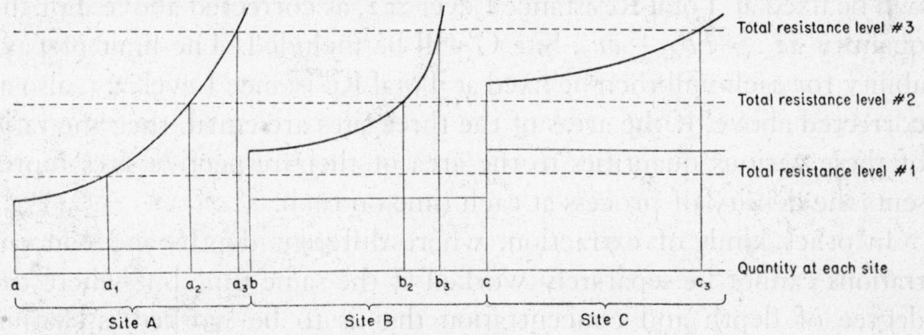

Fig. 32

While it is not possible to include therein the consideration of congestion, a diagram will help to clarify the relationship, in extraction, between the second, third and fourth considerations on sites where different depths and concentrations can be separately worked at the same time (chiefly mining). Fig. 32 shows this relation for three sites, A, B, and C; for each the resistance on account of economic distance, which is uniform throughout for each site, is shown as the solid horizontal line above the base; for each the initial (minimum) resistance on account of dilution and depth is shown as the altitude above that line of the first ordinate (on y axis); and for each the increasing resistance on account of dilution and depth is shown by the difference between the first ordinate and the ordinate to the curve at any point.[3] For the quantity aa_1 only the first site will be worked. The limit of payability will be fixed at Total Resistance Level #1—or, excluding the costs on account of economic distance, at the altitude to that level at a_1 less the section below the solid horizontal line. For the quantity $aa_2 + bb_2$, Site B will also come into operation. Then the limit of payability for each will be fixed at Total Resistance Level #2, as corrected above. For the quantity $aa_3 + bb_3 + cc_3$, Site C will be included. The limit of payability for each will then be fixed at Total Resistance Level #3, also as corrected above. If the areas of the three sites are equal, then the ratio of these various quantities to the area of their respective sites represents the density of process at each time on each.

In other kinds of extraction, where different depths and concentrations cannot be separately worked at the same time but where the degree of depth and concentration that is to be worked is, within limits, optional (chiefly agriculture), this relationship is similar. However, in this case two modifications are necessary. In the first place, we may conceive, for the sake of simplicity, that the natural resources to be extracted by biological process are evenly distributed throughout the soil (uniform concentration, in that sense) and cease at the subsoil level. Then the kind of concentration we are interested in here is the quantity of plant requirements within the reach of each plant. On this basis the greater the depth worked, down to subsoil, the greater the available plant requirements per unit of superficial area. Thus we may say, for purposes of illustration, that, down to this limit, concentration will be proportionate to depth. But, on account of the plant's minimum needs and maximum capacity, its extraction of these available requirements—and therefore the density of process—will rise, at first slowly and then sharply with increasing concentration (depth) and will finally level off gradually. Also, since the overcoming of depth must, in this case, be done at one operation each time, and not by long successive steps, the resistance per unit of depth increases as the depth increases. The combined resultant will be a curve that will show the size of the increments of plant requirements extracted per successive

[3] In many cases such curves are discontinuous (step-like) rather than as here shown.

unit of additional resistance overcome (on account of depth). This curve rises to a maximum and then declines to zero. Or, conversely, we may use a curve of resistance per unit of additional resource extracted. That curve is concave, begins to rise more and more steeply after it has passed its low point and ends with an indefinite vertical segment. In the second place, since different degrees of depth and concentration cannot be worked concurrently, but only in successive seasons or on different sites with perhaps varying "fertility," it is more difficult in this case to measure the precise additional resistance en-

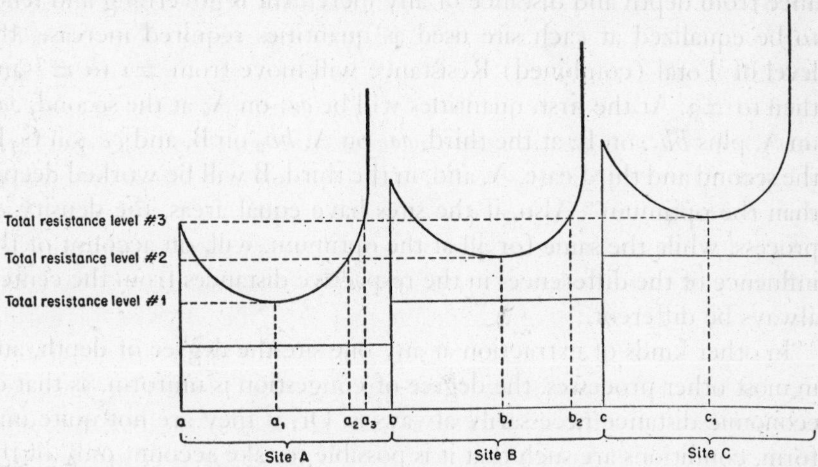

FIG. 33

countered and additional concentration achieved for each degree of increased depth. Nevertheless, even here, a rough approximation is usually made which corresponds to the limit of payability in the previous example, but which differs from it in that only one depth can be worked at a time. In Fig. 33 we show the relation between Sites A, B, and C.[4] For any site, considered alone, the tendency will be to work it to a depth at which the increment of extraction per unit of resistance is greatest—that is, to the low point of the curve.[5] If we assume that these

[4] It should be noted that these "marginal" curves, since the areas subtended represent only the successive marginal costs, may not also correctly represent the aggregate costs of each successive depth of tilling, nor, therefore, the average costs.

[5] This we may call the normal level of "extensive" agricultural operations, which, we may note, is fixed by the accessibility of resources on the site alone and is likely to be effective only at the most distant sites used. In economic analysis the range prior to this point has usually been ignored and from the range subsequent to this point, as it appears in agricultural extraction alone, has been deduced what is called the "law" of diminishing returns, as if it appeared as a common characteristic of production.

three curves are the same, but that the resistance on account of distance from the center for the three sites varies as shown by the horizontal solid lines, then Site A will be worked first for a quantity equal to aa_1, at which the incremental resistance from depth and distance combined will be the broken vertical line at a_1. If that quantity is not sufficient, a_1a_2 will be added. But from that point on, use of Site B will be preferred for the added quantity bb_1, since around the broken vertical line at b_1 incremental resistance from depth and distance is less than it is beyond a_2. And so on. Thus, because the combined resistance from depth and distance of any increment is governing and tends to be equalized at each site used as quantities required increase, the level of Total (combined) Resistance will move from #1 to #2 and then to #3. At the first, quantities will be aa_1 on A; at the second, aa_2, on A, plus bb_1, on B; at the third, aa_3 on A, bb_2 on B, and cc_1 on C. In the second and third case, A, and, in the third, B will be worked deeper than the optimum.[6] Also, if the sites have equal areas, the density of process, while the same for all at the optimum, will, on account of the influence of the differences in the respective distances from the center, always be different.[7]

In other kinds of extraction at any one site the degree of depth, and in most other processes, the degree of congestion is uniform, as that of economic distance necessarily always is. Or, if they are not quite uniform, conditions are such that it is possible to take account only of the average for the whole process on the site.[8] In some instances this is only true at a particular time, because, with exhausting resources, the degree of depth and, in other operations, even that of congestion may grow progressively greater. As to extractive operations of uniform accessi-

[6] Thus the levels reached in "intensive" agricultural operations are also dependent on the accessibility of the site and not fixed by the accessibility of the resources on the site alone.

[7] This diagram is merely illustrative and is far too simple to represent reality. As a matter of fact, the concept of overcoming depth with reference to sown crops (plowing, harrowing, etc.) is in the nature of "producing" soil; for the process changes its condition—it breaks it up and aerates it—though it does not change its composition. Also, instead of going deeper, the advantage of less distance is frequently offset by artificial fertilizing and greater cultivation (overcoming interferences and preventing spoilage). Moreover, the degree of depth to be overcome is largely regulated by the technique used in effecting it. Thus the portion of any of the broken vertical lines in the figure which lies above the distance level may represent other resistances than depth. Nevertheless, the principle upon which the quantity of such resistances overcome is determined is correctly represented here.

[8] Such kinds of extraction are quarrying, logging, etc., in so far as differences on the site are not taken account of.

bility upon the site, the relationship between different sites for any one process, with respect to depth and distance, is shown in Fig. 32 by any set of vertical lines, which, for each site, are fixed by the conditions existing there. Thus we may have, at one time, the combination of the ordinates at a_1, b_2, and c_3, showing the average (or uniform) resistance per unit at each. For then there is no reason why these Total Resistances should be the same at the different sites; nor can their differences be offset. But, in such cases, it is to be presumed that the site of least resistance is always worked to "capacity" before the next is included. Furthermore, if these are exhausting resources the shallowest of which must necessarily be worked first, each of these vertical lines may move to the right, and therefore be lengthened progressively, as time goes on. On the other hand, operations other than extraction will tend to a large extent to equalize the sum of the resistances met on account of distance and congestion by offsetting. That is, if the distances of the two sites A and C, in Fig. 32, are as shown, considerable congestion may be incurred at A to offset some part of the advantage it has on account of distance—or, in other words, to avoid adding or enlarging the operation at C.

This analysis demonstrates that we cannot utilize the magnitude "land," in economic analysis, in terms of superficial area and that we cannot by any means define *a site* in quantitative terms. A site is merely some indefinite area which is suitable or can be made suitable by reason of a certain degree of homogeneity, as the locus of a particular economic process. Within that limit the size of the process is the quantitative determinant, and that may vary indefinitely.

2. ORDER OF PREFERENCE AMONG SITES FOR ALTERNATIVE USES

Generally speaking, it is possible to use a single site, at any one time, for but a single process or the extraction of a single material or power. On the other hand, a site may be more or less suitable for many different alternative processes, and several different non-ubiquitous materials or powers may be available thereon. The scheme according to which each available site is allocated to a particular process among all alternative uses has a determining influence upon the minimum and the maximum aggregate of these resistances which will be met with for each process, and therefore upon the minimum and maximum effort per unit of product, or "real costs," which are incurred upon these counts. The resistances that enter into this further analysis are, for all processes, economic distance, congestion, suitability as site and, for extraction only, economic depth, and concentration. Let us take them up in that order.

In order to demonstrate the effect of economic distance on "real costs" it is convenient to develop a diagram (Fig. 34), highly simplified from reality. Let us at first suppose that all sites are available for all of four different uses. Also let us lay out our scheme upon the simple ground plan of a direct economy. This misrepresents the facts of an

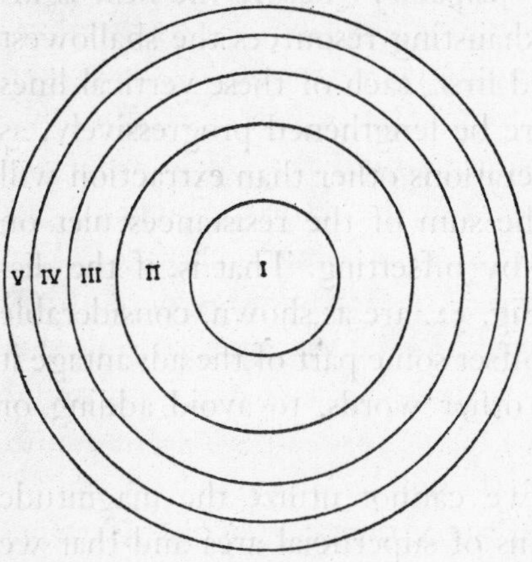

FIG. 34

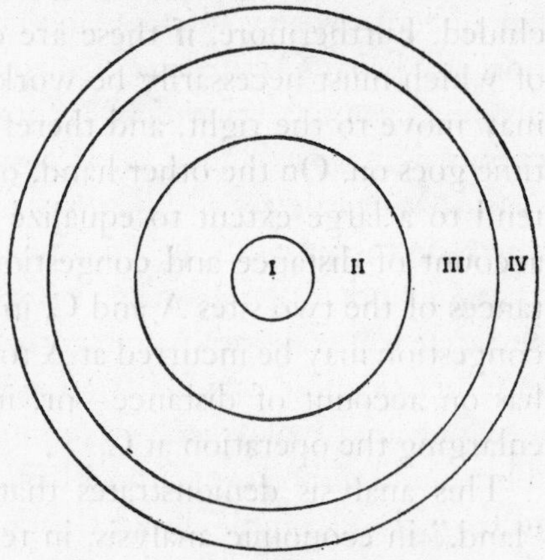

FIG. 35

indirect economy only in that the latter is a complex of these simple plans. On this plan we have a center (consuming) and increasing radial economic distances from this center as we proceed outward across a series of concentric circles. Considering only economic distance the result will be the allocation of the sites composing each of a series of concentric rings, or zones (II to V), to one of the four processes—assuming that some central circle (I) is occupied by consuming.[9] Upon what basis are these zones assigned? The factor economic distance affects each of these processes differently. Communication (going and coming) necessary per unit of product varies; the inertia of the material, if any, varies, and even its degree of concentration may be less than maximum at the earlier stages of the whole process of production.[10] These variations mean that the effort per unit of product per

[9] Each of these concentric circles is represented as of the same area as each of the others. They do not represent geographical areas but "isobars" of resistance on account of economic distance.

[10] So that much non-product (residues) must also be transported.

unit of economic distance [11] is different for the four processes, whether the product is material or not. Assuming, at first, that the density of the process (i.e., the number of units of product per square foot or per acre) is the same for all, the result will be, so far as economic distance is determining, that the innermost ring (II) will be allocated to the process whose "real cost" on account of economic distance is highest per unit of product per unit of distance; the next ring beyond (III) will be allocated to the next lower in cost; and so on to the last (V) which will go to the process with the lowest cost per unit of product per unit of distance. Under our limiting assumptions, this generalization will be true regardless of the comparative quantities of the several products wanted, regardless of their comparative "real costs" on other counts and regardless of their comparative "utilities" or usefulness.[12] And that can be readily demonstrated. Let the effort per unit of distance, on these counts, be 1 for a unit of A, and 2 for a unit of B. In Fig. 35, assume that the quantity required of A is twice that required of B, and that it can be produced in the area included in zone III plus that in either of those divided from it by broken circles—that is, II or IV —which are equal to each other in area, while B requires only one zone. The question then is whether II (and III) will be allocated to A and IV to B, or II to B and IV (and III) to A. Since the average distance from the outer ring (IV) is necessarily greater than the average distance from the inner one (II), but the difference between these average distances is the same for both of the alternative uses, it is necessarily true that the economizing of effort per unit of B, on these counts, by reason of allocating the inner ring (II) to B must be twice what it would be per unit if the inner ring (II) were allocated to A. And since, on the assumption of equal density, the number of units of A and B affected by the transposition is equal, it follows that aggregate costs on these counts for the two combined will be less if zone II is allocated to B than if it were allocated to A. Nevertheless, it also follows that the maximum, the minimum, and the average costs on this count will be higher for A and lower for B than if the arrangement were reversed. Therefore, the system of allocation determines to this extent what these costs will be.

[11] Cost per ton-mile of coal, say, compared to cost per bushel-mile of wheat, or per passenger-mile.

[12] The influence of their comparative "real costs" upon their "marginal utilities" and thus upon the quantities wanted, even where that influence exists—which we shall find reason to qualify in Part IV—will have no effect upon this order of allocation.

This first approximation requires now to be corrected for variations in density of process. If, continuing the former example, the density of process for A is more than double that for B, the situation will be reversed. For then, though the costs on these counts are, for B, double per unit those for A, the quantity of product affected per unit of area will be more than twice for A what it is for B. In other words, the total of these costs will be greater if A instead of B is produced in the outer (IV) rather than the inner zone (II); the difference in distance is the same for both; the cost per unit of product per unit of distance is half for A what it is for B; but the transposition affects more than twice the number of units of A than it does of B. Thus, economic distance only acts in conjunction with comparative density of process in its effect on zoning of sites for processes and thereby in the determination of the maxima and minima (and the averages) of "real costs" for all processes on these counts. An adequate formulation is necessarily complex. We may say that the effect of economic distance in determining to which one among the alternative uses the sites in each zone will be put, and therefore the order of the processes in succeeding zones, is to insure that the inner zone will be allocated to that process the product of which incurs the highest "real costs" on this count per unit of product per unit of distance when this is corrected by multiplying it by the number of units of product per unit of area of site (density of process).

In turn, we must recognize that density of process is not fixed for any single process. Instead, it is considerably affected, within the technical and natural limits of each process, by what we may call the optimum degree of congestion. If by increasing the density of process upon a given area of site the added resistance on account of congestion which it is necessary to overcome proves to be less than the added resistance on account of economic distance incurred by expanding to a site further from the center, increased congestion will be preferred and "real costs," though greater, will be less than they would have been had the alternative way of increasing output been chosen. For certain processes, other than extractive, it is possible, however, to increase to a considerable extent the density of process without the corresponding and usual increase in the resistances due to congestion. This is done, as has been stated, by reduplicating the superficial area in the successive stories of a building. To some extent this vertical expansion incurs its own forms of resistance on account of congestion (i.e., space for stairways, elevators, etc.) and on account of depth (transportation costs up and down). But the chief increased cost is due to the greater quantity of intermediate product required—the building. In general we have regarded the building as a means of protection for the process. But, as noted before, while added floor space requires added protection, the floor space itself is entirely designed to be a more economical means of expanding the process than the two alternatives, increased congestion on the ground area, or increased economic distance. We may say that the net added floor space (after deducting means of access) is a way of escape from (an offset to) alternative increased resistances, but that this floor space also requires protection, so that the resistances (interferences) against which protection are required are also increased by this expedient.

Given the quantity of any process, which is determined by the quantity of product wanted,[13] the area of the zone which must be allocated to that process is determined by the optimum density of the process in view of all the foregoing considerations. Since the width of each zone of equal area, as we proceed out from the center, diminishes more rapidly than the radial distance increases,[14] the economic distance to be added grows continually less to an extent proportionate to this diminution. Thus, as we proceed from one ring to another, the alternatives offering an escape from increased distance by means of increased congestion or reduplicating ground floor space become constantly less inviting. That is, the latter remain fixed, while the necessary added distance becomes continually less.

This simple ground plan in the form of zones or rings lies at the basis of all choice of alternative uses of sites and therefore of the geographical arrangement of all production processes serving a single consuming center. However, it is much confused by the entry of other factors which upset our assumption that sites are uniform in their suitability for any one process or equally suitable for all processes. It is also upset as to processes extracting or using materials and powers by the fact that non-ubiquitous materials and powers cannot, by definition, be

[13] Since "real costs" on these counts rise as quantity increases, those who hold to the usual form of demand curve will not admit that the quantity wanted is here an independent variable. We recognized this question in note 12, above, and deferred discussion of it until later. We must again defer it because it is essentially a question of the effect of different "real costs" among different part lots upon demand; and that cannot be considered apart from the want system.

[14] That is, the area of each ring is $\pi(r_1)^2 - \pi(r_2)^2$, if r_1 is the radial distance to its outer circumference and r_2 that to its inner.

available at all sites and are not in fact available with equal accessibility even where they do exist. Nevertheless, it should be realized that these other factors only distort the original plan in so far as they outweigh those which have been hitherto considered.

In so far as any site is not completely suitable to any particular process, whether dealing with materials and powers or not, consideration of it for that purpose must include the "real cost" of its adaptation to that purpose. Some installment of that "real cost," varying from the whole of it down to a small part, would then need to be considered as an addition to the "real cost" of output for some period of such a process on this site, on account of resistance to such use. But the degree of unsuitability and therefore the "real cost" of adaptation to one use has, for the most part, no bearing on the degree or cost for another use. If, now, we return to our original example and add to it the condition that this form of resistance introduces, we may find the scheme of allocation altered in whole or in part. Let us suppose that the cost of adaptation of site per unit of product, multiplied by the number of units per unit of area (density of process) is for Process A greater for some or all the sites in the outer zone (IV in Fig. 35) than for an equal number in the inner one (II), whereas that for Process B is also greater, but less so, or equal or even less. If the difference in this respect between the two alternative allocations is sufficient, in the opposite direction, to exceed the difference on the previous counts which favored the allocation of B to the inner zone (II) and of A to the outer (IV), then for the particular sites as to which this condition exists the allocation will tend to be the other way round.

Finally, when we come to consider the extraction of materials and powers and, to a certain extent, the effect of that on succeeding processes in their production, still another factor enters to alter the basic system of allocation. In the first place, these non-ubiquitous materials and powers are, by definition, not available everywhere; in the second place, upon those sites where they are available several others which cannot be extracted concurrently may also be available, so that a choice between alternative uses of these sites must be made; and, in the third place, the accessibility as resources will vary somewhat for each site as to each resource which it offers. This presents a most complex picture. Nevertheless, the principles upon which it affects the allocation of sites among alternative uses, and therefore the whole geographical scheme of allocation, follow the same lines as before.

We may start to thread our way through this complexity by considering the plan according to which the extraction of any one material or power would be organized, if alternative uses of sites upon which it was available were ignored. To all the "real costs" incurred upon the previous counts there would be added, for each possible site, the "real costs" now to be incurred by reason of the economic depth and lack of concentration of the desired resource. This would be figured per unit of product. But that figure could not be determined until the optimum density of process within the technical and natural limits—i.e., the number of units of material or power to be produced upon the area where it was available—as determined for other reasons, had been revised to include consideration of these new resistances. Presumably, the economic depth and concentration of the resource would not be uniform at all sites, and, in the cases described above, not even at a single site. If the extraction were of a material or power which replaced itself continuously or periodically, resources whose depth or dilution placed them initially beyond the limit of payability would be excluded permanently (other things remaining equal). If extraction were of an exhausting resource and the process commenced with the most accessible and concentrated materials or powers, then a future increase on these counts up to exhaustion at the limit of payability would have to be envisaged. In the former case, the quantity of initial process would be affected directly by this limit; in the latter case, it would only be affected indirectly through the consideration of optimum life of intermediate product required for adaptation and that of other immovable plant. In view of all these considerations the available sites would first be arranged in the order of increasing resistance per unit of initial (or optimum) quantity, and therefore of "real costs" on all these counts for the smallest paying operation. And, as already noted, it would be necessary in many cases also to construct a corresponding curve for each site showing the increasing resistance upon account of greater depth or less concentration. Then these sites would be applied according to their order in the first series and, where the number of deposits or the depth were optional, each would always be worked up to the point where the portion of the product with the highest cost on all counts on each site had the same cost at all sites. Such points would constitute the respective limits of payability. The greater the quantity wanted, the further along the first series would sites be applied and the higher the aggregate costs per unit which would set the limit of payability (i.e., the further also along the second series). In the case of exhaustible resources the quantity of product on the site would almost never reach the limit of payability at the start, on account of the other considerations mentioned, and this limit would only be effective in the course of time by way of stopping further use of that site for such purpose.

This analysis makes quite obvious the way the choice of alternative uses is then settled on this score. Having developed such a tentative plan for each material or power, the several plans would be found to conflict as to several or many sites. These conflicts would then be ironed out on the same principle that determined the original zoning—that is, on the principle of least aggregate costs on all counts for all products. For instance, a certain site, when used for A, could actually occasion a certain aggregate of costs on all counts for the quantity produced thereon; on the other hand, if it were not so used, the same quantity of A could be produced elsewhere by increases (along the second series) on all other sites originally included, plus the use of one or more newer sites which lay further along the first series than the last originally included (thus raising the limit of payability). The difference between the two alternatives would consist of a certain sum of "real costs." The same would be true of the alternatives presented as to B. If the difference in "real costs" from producing A on this certain site or elsewhere were greater than that between producing B here or elsewhere, the site would be allocated to A. By this method all conflicts in allocation would ultimately be resolved.

It becomes clear from all the analysis contained in this section, that the minimum, the maximum, and the average "real cost" per unit of all product, in respect of all parts of these processes of production, including extraction if any, are not fixed merely by certain absolute natural resistances to its production. Instead, many of these natural resistances vary along an extensive scale. As to all these, the optimum allocation of sites among alternative uses determines the point upon this scale which will represent the minimum resistance, and therefore minimum "real cost"; and this allocation combined with the quantity wanted will determine the maximum. Between these extremes, "real costs," on these counts, of all outputs will depend not only upon the layout according to which suitable sites and accessible resources happen to occur in the environment, but also, in each case, upon the effect of the competition for the allocation of the site to a particular use.

Thus the average "real cost" on these counts will be a weighted one and will be as much affected by allocation as is either extreme. All this is true only in so far as sites may be put to more than one use; but that applies to practically all sites.

E. "REAL COSTS" AND TECHNIQUE

So far as I know no systematic study of the economics of technology has ever been made. It is an inviting subject which should be thoroughly investigated. However, this is not the place to undertake it, and we shall have to content ourselves with a brief, and probably insufficiently penetrating, outline of the relations between technology and economics—that is, between the three elements, technique, the natural environment, in the form of resistances, and human effort, in the form of "real costs" of product. We have hitherto referred to technique as that which fixes the ratio between efforts and resistances. It is, more accurately, that analytical entity which represents each particular system of economic-physical relations, via a given sector of the resistant natural environment as medium, between the sole economic cause, effort, and the sole economic result, the satisfaction of wants. It is the way of applying the cause to achieve the result. Hence our formulation; quantity of any product varies directly with effort times technique and inversely with natural resistance.

In the first place, it should be emphasized that improved technique never reduces natural resistances. They remain what they are in any given set of conditions under which the process is conducted. What improved technique does, and all it does, is to reduce the quantity of work needed to overcome such resistances.[1] As a matter of fact such

[1] At times, in the previous pages, we have introduced the entity "effect" in connection with this ratio, work-resistance. A certain amount of confusion may have resulted from our ocasional use of the word in two different senses. In Chapter 9, when we discussed the measurement of working in terms of its effect (work), we used the term as if it meant only those effects which directly result from that particular form of human effort. In Chapter 11 (pp. 722 ff.), where we discussed the intervention of technique, we used the term as if it meant the whole effect of any production process, including that part which is the result perhaps of some form of natural "assistance." Standardization of usage is not important so long as the distinction is kept clear. The important thing is to recognize that the notion of technique has introduced a discrepancy between the total physical effects and that part of them produced by effort, and that, therefore, the measure of effect (as work) can only be used for certain kinds of comparison, while effect, in the broader sense, if it can be measured at all, is the basis of all others.

Technique also introduces the further discrepancy, already mentioned, with regard to our concept of product as a magnitude measurable only in terms of the work incorporated in it. But we must postpone this to the end of the chapter.

improvements usually, but not always, accomplish this end by adding to the total of resistances met—that is, by presenting new and otherwise unnecessary resistances which require to be overcome by effort. But they work in such a way that the effort per unit of product is nevertheless reduced, because the ratio of effort to resistances is so much smaller.[2] It would seem, then, that improved technique, if it does not reduce the natural resistances, must itself overcome them. Actually, neither is this the case. In some instances it merely increases the effectiveness of effort in overcoming the natural resistances; in most, however, it brings to bear the "assistance" of natural materials and powers in doing so.

The correctness of these generalizations can only be demonstrated by examining these relations in connection with each of the particular forms of natural resistance we have analyzed. Let us establish, first, the fact that technique never reduces natural resistances. It is not involved at all in those quantitative determinants of resistance which we have called "size" and "elaborateness." These are characteristics of the product alone. Technique cannot alter the refractoriness of materials,[3] nor their economic inertia. Concentration of materials and powers on the site is a fact which cannot be changed while these remain *in situ*. Technique does not change economic distances, nor depths, nor the facts of pre-occupation of space which present resistance to congestion of process. If it cannot alter economic distances, it cannot change the resistance to dissipation of process on the site, nor, for the worker, the distance between his locus of consumption and of working (going to and fro). Ephemeral (non-material) protection of process or product does not reduce the resistance on account of interference by natural material and powers; rather it overcomes it. Nor does it affect the result of failure of this last—that is, the resistance through spoilage to the extent that protection has not been provided or has not been successful. But protection may add to the resistances which are unavoidable some which are avoidable, and thus increase

[2] As we have noted heretofore, while such improvements decrease total effort, they usually increase the component retention, but by a less amount in terms of equivalence as "real costs" than the reduction in work.

[3] At first sight it might seem that the use of a technique which applied natural power (heat) to a material (metal) reduces the resistance of the latter. But, more precisely, the heat overcomes the resistance; for when the heat is removed the metal resumes its previous refractoriness. If the process reduces the refractoriness permanently we have a new (synthetic) material with different physical characteristics (i.e., no longer objectively indifferent).

the total quantity. Adaptation of site consists in part of overcoming certain resistances in advance. In that sense it reduces those remaining to be overcome by the subsequent production process itself. But all such a statement really means is that such resistances can be overcome more or less permanently, not that they are made actually less. On the other hand, much of adaptation meets additional resistances which, without a particular technique, would not be faced at all. Obviously, those techniques involving permanent or external protections of process and product do not reduce the influences making for interference. They merely resist (or overcome) them. It is the very battering of such continuous interfering powers against the protection that wears out the latter. And still more obviously, if the added resistance to the canalization of natural powers is incurred and overcome by reason of some technique, the diversion of such powers to productive purposes does not reduce the resistances against which they are used; it overpowers them. The same is true of tools. This somewhat detailed examination appears worth while because it leads to the following noteworthy conclusion: On the whole the natural environment is now no more hospitable to man than it was twenty thousand years ago. And there is no reason to expect that it will become more so in the future. All that has happened is that man, through intermediate product and through improvements in technique, has made himself more at home in this unchanged environment.

If technique cannot be said to reduce resistances, how does it operate? There are three general ways in which it operates; and we can best consider them separately, though the lines of demarcation are not hard and fast. In the first place, (1) improvements in technique may increase the effectiveness of effort in overcoming given resistances without bringing to bear the natural powers or utilizing materials external to the product itself—that is, without intermediate product. This may be done (1a) by planning the task. A great part of so-called scientific management is of this order. It consists in an adjustment of the expenditure of man's energy over time to fit the nature of the human organism and in the reduction of both energy and time to the minimum necessary.[4] It may deal with workers individually or col-

[4] Technique and efficiency (personal) are, in this field, of the same order—i.e., ways of reducing effort (working-time) per unit of resistance. But it is convenient to differentiate the two. For, when we come to deal with indirect economies, we will find it necessary to discriminate between the effects that are to be attributed to the worker only and those which, though they are procured through him, require another concurrent

lectively (i.e., by "division of labor"). This kind or way of technique may also be applied (1b) by arranging the work in an orderly way in space, either for individuals or groups, so that, without incurring too much resistance from dissipation, that due to congestion is also overcome (or evaded) so far as possible. An example of this is so-called straight-line production in so far as the course of the product alone is concerned. A third variety (1c) consists of ways of overcoming interferences by natural materials or powers; because of the definition of (1) this is confined to ways which are ephemeral or become part of the product (e.g., preservatives).[5] To the extent that this protection is effective it also reduces spoilage. The resistance to interference is then overcome instead of incurring that by reason of spoilage. Finally, we have that form of technical option which we have called "large-batch" production. If we separate this from (1a), then it (1d) can only be distinguished by the fact that it is a form of specialization upon each step of a process successively which requires retaining because it spreads the process over more than one working day, while the first way (1a) covers those cases which do not do so. Adaptation of site is so conglomerate an artifact that it is difficult to classify. But there are some instances of technical improvements (1e) in which effort is reduced while over-all resistances are not changed.[6] These savor of large-batch technique; for the economizing results from overcoming the same quantity of resistances but doing so in advance of operating the process. But usually even this kind of adaptation requires separate and therefore intermediate product. Therefore, it is on the border line, or should be divided, between this and the next category.

---

agency to teach, to direct, to induce or otherwise to increase the quantity or quality of his effects. Let us say, roughly, that technique is social or institutional—that is, it can be passed on from one to another person by tradition or teaching. On the other hand, efficiency is that part of the whole which is personal—that is, it is the result of personal faculties (or talents), native or acquired, which cannot be conveyed from one to another. While recognizing that the latter constitutes a reduction in the constituent effort in the person's working and probably reduces the time he requires to produce a given effect, it fits better into the framework of our analysis to treat degrees of superior efficiency as degrees of super-standard working (i.e., as the equivalent per hour of multiples of units of standard working per hour).

[5] An example of an ephemeral way is the technique of a watcher over food stores to prevent access by animals; or secondarily, the watcher over domestic animals (intermediate product) to prevent their slaughter by wild animals. This is probably a part of the function after which the *servus* (whence serve and servant) was originally named. He functioned as a "preserver" (i.e., the human equivalent of a preservative).

[6] The process of stripping surface ore beds, as an advance operation, instead of crude pit-mining, is of this general type.

The second general way of increasing the effectiveness of effort by improvements in technique (2) involves the increase of gross resistances met because it consists in the utilization of materials other than the final product itself (i.e., intermediate product) by way of "assistance" in overcoming the primary resistances. Of this, one subdivision (2a) is the tool. The tool is a material product (intermediate) through which human powers only (physical and mental) are applied to final product. In its simplest form it secures "assistance" by utilizing the greater refractoriness of one material to overcome the lesser refractoriness of some other. But that characteristic does not extend very far. It does not cover the principles of mechanics (the lever) or of hydraulics (the pump). Moreover, among tools we must include such things as technical treatises as aids to production. Thus, though this category (2a) always requires intermediate product in material form, its unifying and distinguishing feature is that it reduces effort per unit of resistance by canalizing human powers (physical and mental) so that they are more effective. Another subdivision (2b) is the utilization of materials to provide protection against interferences from other natural materials and from natural powers. Here, again, the "assistance" may be due to the characteristic refractoriness of the material so utilized. But it may also take far more subtle forms such as opacity or transparency (selective protection), impermeability, poisonous constituents, etc. Still another subdivision has been alluded to. It is (2c), the utilization of materials for the duplication of area on a site in order to overcome the primary resistance due to congestion. Also, we must include here (as 2d) all other forms of adaptation of site, since they too require, or constitute, intermediate product.

The third general way in which improvements in technique may increase the effectiveness of effort in overcoming resistances—and the one which, since the beginning of the industrial era, has probably been the most important—is (3) the utilization of natural powers so as to bring their "assistance" to bear in productive processes. It includes the utilization of such powers as are substitutes for the physical powers of man as well as of those which have no correspondent among the human faculties. This general way, like the second, increases total resistances because it must face the natural resistance to the canalization of these powers. Since the means for such canalization are themselves product, it therefore requires intermediate product. Among such powers we of course include the forms whose use is ancient, such as domestic animals, wind, gravity acting through flowing water, heat from combustion, etc., as well as those whose use is chiefly of recent date, such as the expansion of gases (explosion) or vapor (steam pressure), chemical affinities, electricity, etc.[7]

By examining in this way what technique does do, we have demonstrated that it can no more be said that it overcomes natural resistances than that it reduces them. Evidently, then, it is not itself a force or an agency in production; it is not a substitute for working; hardly is it even a *ding an sich*. Rather it is the *way of working*. Thus its application necessitates working—and usually retaining—and therefore it always requires a person, or persons, to put it into effect. This has been recognized in our formula; for we have not said that effort *plus* technique overcomes resistances, but rather that they are overcome by effort *times* technique. If the former were correct, with sufficient technique, effort might be zero. But this is not the case; if effort is zero the product is zero, regardless of the technique.[8]

Natural conditions govern the intensity of resistances and therefore the quantity to be met in producing any particular output of any particular product by any particular technique. As natural conditions vary from place to place or from time to time, some of these natural resistances will also vary in intensity, and therefore their quantity will be different for two equal outputs of the same product by the same technique. On the other hand, under any particular set of natural conditions the resistances are given in terms of intensity. Then, if the technique is varied, new and additional resistances may be encountered by reason of the use of an assistant natural process. Thus the extent of resistances encountered may be enlarged. Nevertheless, their intensity, which is given only by the natural conditions, is not changed. Thus the quantity of resistances to be met is determined by the quantity of product, its character and the technique, as to extent, and by

[7] In an article on "Economic Consequences of Technical Development" (*311*, 343), L. R. Nienstaedt calls attention to the fact that "the necessary work energy" in any process, when supplied by man or animals is "always mechanical." When it arises from other sources, however, it may be either mechanical or "nonmechanical in a physical sense." Also, "It may be nonmechanical in a chemical sense, necessary energy for the process being supplied: (1) by the reacting materials themselves with no excess or deficiency of energy; (2) by energy to be applied from without (endothermic processes); (3) by energy developing in excess (exothermic processes)."

His definition (*loc. cit.*) of technical development is approximately the same as ours; "*increasing quantity of product per productive man-hour.*"

[8] The converse is not true. Thus technique cannot be conceived as zero. Its minimum (brute force), when it has no influence at all, is unity.

natural conditions as to intensity—that is, the quantity as a whole is determined by all four factors, and the quantity per unit of product by the last three only. Thereafter, the effort required to overcome these resistances per unit of product, so fixed, is wholly determined by the technique. In so far, then, as technique can be regarded as an entity or magnitude, at all, it is a somewhat vague congeries of all the features of any "method" of applying effort which constitute the determinants of the quantity of effort required to overcome the given resistances per unit of product. In this aspect the influence of technique (A) is measured inversely as the number of units of E required per unit of N; or $A = \frac{N}{E}$.[9]

Now this construction, which seems best to enable us to deal analytically with the facts, raises two problems, both of which we must outline here, but only one of which we need to settle at this point. This formula relates two magnitudes which belong in different spheres. Natural resistances we have defined as wholly physical, though not entirely mechanical, entities. On the other hand, effort is exclusively an economic magnitude. If the formula were based on equivalence of the physical forces concerned, then most of the resistances would be said to be overcome (equalized) by the physical energy of man combined with the natural powers or even materials (the latter as static force). But then technique would not appear as a factor, and could only be deduced from the proportioning of human and natural powers. And even this would be an insufficient statement of its influence. On the other hand, if the formula were conceived wholly on the economic level, there would seem to be no way of finding a relationship between effort, not as the expenditure of physical energy but as working-time, and the resistances. In fact, the resistances cannot be conceived to exist at that level. It is the concept of technique which enables us to relate these two magnitudes each in its own sphere. Without technique—that is, at the brute-force stage—effort, consisting wholly of the expenditure of physical energy, could as well be stated in terms of ergs or foot-pounds—that is, in the same terms as the resistances to be overcome. It is the introduction of technique which makes of working something different than that, in part by substituting natural power

[9] If we conceive the unit of N to be equal to that of E at the no-technique stage, when E may be defined as the physical energy put into one hour's working, then N may be conceived to remain the same unit, while E is changing in character and quantity through the intermediation of A.

and in part by necessitating a change in the character of the working from physical to mental activities. Thus technique is the bridge which establishes a relationship between an economic entity, working-time (mental and physical activities), on the one hand, and a physical entity, the resistances, on the other; for it represents the whole transaction and all the elements through which effort overcomes resistances.

The second problem is this. Included in this intermediation is not only the introduction, usually, of a quantity of effort in the form of retaining, but also the change already noted in the character of the working. Thus technique, as the multiplier of a compound of physical and mental energy expended, which can only be measured in units of working-time and not in units of energy expended, is a multiplier of a magnitude which is itself changing in composition. As technique changes the nature of the task it comes to require more and more "skilled" work. While the technique may be generalized, its application, being wholly by way of persons, requires knowledge, expertness, and the use of a much larger component of mental activity. What we have called super-standard working consists in great part of the performance of these non-brute-force tasks introduced by improved technique. And, since that is measured as a multiple of standard working, the quantity of work performed is to that extent not reduced but merely concentrated in fewer hours. The determination of what part of the increased effectiveness per working-hour should be credited to the personal efficiency of those performing super-standard working and what part to technique is a problem with which we do not have to deal in connection with a direct economy. For, there, as we have repeatedly said, all tasks are undifferentiated and no super-standard working can be recognized. Therefore, at this stage in our analysis, we credit all reduction in working-time, incidental to a change in technique, to that technique.

As to the incidental introduction of retaining, we must remind ourselves that the greater retaining required, by reason of the usually necessary intermediate product, is in no respect the cause of the economizing of working. It is in fact only a handicap on the improvement of technique; for it causes a deduction from the economizing of work accomplished. Thus it is relegated to the function of a usually necessary adjuvant for putting into effect an improvement in technique.[10]

[10] This point is clearly made by Böhm-Bawerk (*38*, 82). He says, "The adoption of capitalist methods of production is followed by two consequences, equally character-

To technique and to technique only, must be attributed the whole of the net economizing of effort in the ways described above.

There are two inherent limitations on the economizing effect of any improvement in technique which must be mentioned here. To a certain extent in all these types of technique, but absolutely as to all those which require intermediate product, the question of scale of operations and through that the "capacity" of the intermediate product, enters. Any particular technique is usually adapted, within somewhat rigid limits, to a certain minimum scale of operations only. This is obviously true, by definition, of the first technical option—large-batch processes. With the second technical option it is true for a different reason. Each technique may require the conglomerate of intermediate product, already mentioned, to be of a fixed minimum quantity; or the economizing effect of the technique may increase, within limits, with the size of, or number of elements in, this conglomerate; or, finally, the "real cost" of the intermediate product may not increase proportionately to its increase in size. As a result of each, or a mixture, of these considerations, two different techniques for the same process and product may each be optimum at the same time for two different outputs of the product to which, for one reason or another, two different sites are limited. On the other hand, for all techniques requiring intermediate product, the "size" of the intermediate product sets also a rough limit to a maximum scale of operations. This has already been mentioned on p. 781. It is so-called "capacity."

---

istic and significant. One is an advantage [approximately equivalent to our economizing of work], the other a disadvantage. . . . The disadvantage connected with capitalist production is its sacrifice of time."

However, his definition (*ibid.*, 83) of "capitalist methods of production" ("roundabout methods") limits these to the processes in which intermediate product is used. Then they do not cover all our ways of technical improvement. For, as we have seen, there are a number of ways in which technical improvements accomplish such economizing without the use of intermediate product, or, in fact, without any retaining. Nor, on the other hand, do his "capitalist methods" include many of the other instances where there is also a "sacrifice of time." We have already noted that a great part of these do not involve intermediate product and only one of those which do not concerns technique. The "advantage" in the case of large-batch processes (one of our technical options) is also the economizing of work, but the "disadvantage" is retaining the final product. In the other occasions—the two contingencies and the three technical necessities—the retaining is also of final product only. But, there, the advantage is preferred provision for wants, not economizing of work. Therefore "capitalist" methods of production, or "roundaboutness," cannot be equivalent either to our technique or to our occasions for retaining. Obviously, they do not define the antithesis to day-to-day production. They seem to be confined to a limited number among all the instances to which his general remark (quoted above) applies, and, therefore, not to constitute a very useful analytical category.

The second limitation is partly linked to the first and partly independent. At any particular site for any process, but chiefly when that process consists of the extraction of a material or power, natural conditions may fix a maximum limit for the scale of operations and thereby compel the use of a technique which is worse than the optimum available for the largest scale. But these natural conditions may also have an influence on the selection of technique in other respects than in fixing the scale. They may also determine the kind of technique. For instance, there may exist a more economizing technique for water transportation than for any kind of land transportation. But, if there be no waterways, the optimum cannot be used. So, too, the best technique for coal mining may be the horizontal tunnel and for iron mines the stripping process. But, if the position of the coal or ore bodies and the lay of the land does not permit, these techniques cannot be used.

F. SUMMARY OF DETERMINANTS OF "REAL COSTS"

By way of recapitulation of the foregoing analysis of the causes determining the quantities of both components of "real cost" per unit of product we may append the following table, omitting therefrom some of the minor qualifications of these generalizations which were given in the text.[1]

The quantity of the two components of "real cost" per unit of product varies with, and is therefore fixed by, the following *determinants:*

Quantity of "Real Cost" in Direct Effort

- I. Demand
  - A. As to Component Work
    - 1. Characteristics of product
      - a. optional size (unit)
      - b. optional elaborateness
      - c. optional material
  - B. As to Component Retention[2]
    - 1. Optional life of product
      - a. for future provision for contingency of first type—before use
      - b. for future provision for contingency of second type—before use

[1] And also, since this is the analysis of a direct economy, assuming the uniformity of all working.

[2] It should be noted that in all cases where retaining is required there may be incurred extra "real costs" in direct work or in intermediate product by reason of the need of protection in storage and by reason of deterioration and loss.

c. for durable (partly)—elected durability within the range of choice—during use

C. As to Both Components

1. Quantity wanted, by reason of its influence on Scale of Technique
2. Quantity wanted, by reason of its influence on Maximum Resistance at Sites Used (Limit of Payability)

II. Natural Conditions

A. As to Component Work, as a result of Quantity of Resistance

1. Characteristics of product (both material and immaterial product)
   a. resistances to given size, in terms of the unit which was determined under I A 1 a, or arbitrarily
   b. resistances to given elaborateness in whatever degree was determined under I A 1 b
   c. interference (partly)
   d. spoilage (partly)
2. Characteristics of material (material product only)
   a. refractoriness
   b. economic inertia
   c. concentration (partly)
3. Channels allocated
   a. concentration (partly) (material product only)
   b. economic distance—transport of product (material product only)
   c. economic depth (material product only)
   d. dissipation *vs.* congestion (all processes)
   e. economic distance—workers going to and fro (all processes)
   f. interference (partly) (all processes)
   g. spoilage (partly) (all processes)

B. As to Component Retention

1. Necessary life
   a. imposed by conditions resulting in future provision under technical necessity of first type—before use
   b. imposed by natural features of durable product—during use
   c. imposed by necessity of long processes and incidental large-batch technique—before use
      1) intermittent working due to intervening natural processes
      2) long-time transportation

III. Technique

A. As to Component Work, Fixing Ratio of Direct Work to Resistance

1. Way of planning task
2. Way of arranging course of product

3. Way of protecting ephemerally against interferences
4. Effect of large-batch methods

B. As to Component Retention, Fixing Direct Retention
1. Necessary life
a. for large batches

Quantity of "Real Cost" in Indirect Effort

IV. Technique
A. Nature of Process: As to Both Components
1. Kind of adaptation of site required
2. Kind of permanent protection needed
3. Kind of natural power to be canalized
4. Kind (purpose) of tool

B. Characteristics of Intermediate Product Required: As to Both Components
1. Size (unit)
2. Elaborateness

C. Life of Intermediate Product (Potential Life in Use): As to Component Retention

V. Natural Conditions: As to Both Components
A. Quantity (Number of Units) of Intermediate Product Required
1. Imposed by suitability of particular sites allocated
2. Imposed by quantity of protection required on particular sites allocated
3. Imposed by quantity of resistances to canalization of natural powers on particular sites allocated

B. Production of Quantity of Natural Power Canalized to Quantity of Intermediate Product Required[3]

VI. "Real Costs" per Unit of Intermediate Product: As to Both Components.
Same determinants as for "real costs" in direct effort for final product, as analyzed above.

VII. Number of Units of Final Product to Which the Aggregate of Indirect Effort, as Determined by IV, V, and VI, Is to Be Applied
A. Determining Scale of Operations and, Thus, Technique
B. Determining Proportion of This Aggregate of Indirect Effort to Be Charged to Each Unit

N.B. Real costs of final product (other than synthetic) may be fixed by factors determining direct effort alone; those of final synthetic product may only be fixed by both sets of factors combined;[4]

[3] The effect of the use of natural power in reducing direct work depends somewhat on the quantity of it canalized per unit of intermediate product, while the indirect work added depends only on the number of units of intermediate product and their characteristics.

[4] By synthetic product we mean all product which is beyond the reach of unaided (direct) effort.

real costs of intermediate product (III above) may be fixed by determinants of direct effort alone or by both (i.e. via other intermediate product used).

Now, while the comparative "real costs" per unit of different products will be determined by the effect on each product of all of this complex set of variables, the comparative "real costs" per unit of the different part lots of a single product produced concurrently will be influenced by relatively few of them. For the purposes of our analysis in the next chapter it is necessary, at this point, to segregate these particular variables and thus to show the limited possible extent and the special reasons for differences in "real cost" per unit between such part lots—that is, to elaborate our brief mention of this subject, under the discussion of different "channels" on pp. 764 ff.

If the quantity wanted of a single product cannot be produced through the single preferred channel, either because of a "bottle-neck" in this "channel" or because a part lot imposes a different "channel" (by reason of the fact that it is wanted for a different purpose or at a different place), then the natural conditions of such other channel or channels will usually offer different quantities of some of the resistances and may necessitate a technique different in scale or kind. When technique is not affected, all of the variables listed above remain constant with the following exceptions: those determining direct effort which vary with channels allocated (II A 3 and II B c 2) and those determining indirect effort which vary with natural conditions (V). Where a technique different in scale or kind is also compelled, then, from the variables remaining constant in the first case must be deducted all of those determining direct effort under technique (III) and all the rest of those determining indirect effort (IV to VII); for then these too come into play.

Considering, first, cases where technique is not affected, the costs of extraction only, and therefore of material product only, may differ for part lots in two different ways. For certain kinds of extraction, although presumably all the other resistances listed under II A 3, II B c 2, and V are uniform for each site, two of these resistances may vary upon a single site. These are concentration and depth.[5] Thus, where it is possible to determine separately the costs of extraction of different part lots upon a single site the cost may be found to differ widely. But they will only range between a minimum (the optimum conditions on

[5] This is, of course, especially true of mining.

these two counts) and what we have called the limit of payability upon all counts. For all other kinds of extraction, where the cost upon each site is uniform, all of these resistances (II A 3 as well as the one under II B and those composing V) may vary; but they will only vary among the several part lots, as a whole, produced upon each of the several sites. Nevertheless, here, as we have seen, there will be a tendency for some comparative differences to be plus and some minus—that is, for the variations partially to offset each other and thus narrow the range.[6] This last will also be true of all later processes on material product and all processes on non-material product.[7] But, with the former, economic depth will no longer come into play, and concentration will not be an influence unless the material remains to be purified after extraction; and, with the latter, neither of these nor distance in respect of the transport of product will enter.

In extraction only, when costs differ on single sites, the notion of "channel" must be subdivided. Then the minimum cost on any part lot will be on that one derived from the optimum deposit at all the sites used; the maximum cost will be the same for all sites (uniform limit of payability); and the average cost at each will be different from that at all others, and will depend on the range between its own optimum and the limit of payability. In extraction, where costs are uniform on each site, and in all other processes concerned with material and all non-material production, the maximum, minimum, and average cost at each site will be undifferentiated; one channel as a whole will represent the minimum, some other the maximum, and the average will depend on the "shape" of a discontinuous curve composed of them all and weighted by the respective outputs of each; but the range between the minimum and the maximum cost of the part lots from different channels will here again be narrowed by offsets.

When, in addition to the above considerations, it happens that technique must be different in the different channels used, owing to the fact that natural conditions compel differences in scale or kind,[8] the

[6] That is, greater distance may be partly offset by greater concentration or less depth, etc. This is especially the case with "intensive" *vs.* "extensive" cultivation of the soil. The cultivation of the nearer site will be deep to avoid greater distance, and that of the further will be shallow on account of its greater distance.

[7] For instance, less distance may lead to greater congestion or greater protection (including reduplication of area).

[8] That is, for instance, a wind mill to supplement a water wheel, a water wheel instead of gravity irrigation (Egypt), land instead of water transportation, terrace *vs.* plain agriculture.

costs of part lots will be subject to still more variables, as noted above. And these variables may affect all processes, from extraction on, and all products, material as well as non-material. The resulting differences will almost always be confined to differences between channels as a whole. And, again, the variations will not usually be all against one channel.[9] The range will be narrowed by offsets.

This analysis covers all possible differences between the costs of part lots of a single product at one time, in a direct economy, on the assumptions of perfect allocation of sites, optimum technique for each scale or other condition, and the planned use of all intermediate product ("capacity" operation). It is evident that, where quantity wanted exceeds that which can be produced through one channel, "real costs" of part lots are not likely to be uniform. That part of the costs of material product representing the raw material costs (extractive) is likely to show the greatest net differences, in some cases between the optimum and pessimism sites and in others between the optimum deposit and the limit of payability; but differences in technique on account of scale and on account of kind of natural power available are also likely to be of considerable influence; and the latter may affect any process as to any product. Other differences will usually be of lesser importance. In this way we have explicitly defined and limited our category of comparative "real costs" of part lots of a single product and, as noted before, have made it necessary to specify, where comparative "real costs" of different products are referred to, whether the "real costs" of each are uniform and, if not, whether we are comparing the minimum, the maximum, or the average "real costs" of each specific product.

G. DISCREPANCIES IN "REAL COSTS" OF A SINGLE PRODUCT

1. DISCREPANCIES BETWEEN DIFFERENT LOTS AT ONE TIME

In this chapter we have been pursuing two parallel lines of inquiry. We have, on the one hand, examined the relation between product and its "real costs" which, in one direction, consists in determining the quantity of product contributed by any particular quantity of effort (a unit, say), and which, in the reverse direction, consists in the quantity of effort to which is to be attributed, as its economic cause, any

[9] For instance, water transport may be cheaper in work, but slower—i.e., more retention required (II B 1 c 2)—and a technique which presents more resistance to direct effort will usually present less to indirect effort—i.e., IV to VII will have less effect.

particular quantity of product (a unit, say). The latter process is, in other terms, the determination of the quantity of "real costs" (effort) which is to be assigned ("charged") to each such unit of product as a record of the past. We have, on the other hand, also examined the relation between these "real costs" and the natural resistances which necessitate them and which primarily determine their quantity, as well as the variations in this relation due to technique which, secondarily, alter such needed quantities. Along the latter lines we have demonstrated in detail the proposition previously formulated. For two units of any given product, produced by the same technique but under different natural conditions, the quantity of effort ("real cost") required for each varies with the resistance offered by each set of natural conditions (channel). Conversely, for two units of any given product, produced under the same natural conditions but by different techniques, the quantity of effort ("real cost") required for each varies with the ratio of effort to resistance fixed by each technique. Our two parallel lines of inquiry may now be united across this bridge. For this proposition recognizes that the quantity of effort necessary for the production of a unit of any single product may vary for two different reasons. This introduces what may be called the secondary problem of attribution, which may be stated as follows: If, in one case, we attribute a certain objective quantity of a certain product to the measured quantity of effort which has produced it, and, in another, we attribute an equal objective quantity of the same product to a less quantity of effort, to what do we attribute the difference in "real cost" between the two? Obviously there must be a *reason*, a *cause*, for this discrepancy. Obviously this cause cannot be found in the factor effort, but is necessarily external to that. The result is, as previously stated, an economizing of total effort. Our proposition, above, gives us the two causes of these discrepancies; they are, respectively, differences in natural conditions and differences in technique.

These discrepancies, when due to either cause, may exist under two different time relationships. Since the effect is quite different under the one from that under the other it is necessary to separate them analytically. The first time relationship is found when the discrepancy exists between two units of product compared at the same point in time; the second is found when two units are compared at two different points in time. In the first case the two units, being objectively indifferent, must have the same usefulness. Thus, in the first case, the comparison is between two units identical in every respect except that of "real cost." But, in the second case, that is not true. While the two units must still be objectively indifferent, estimates of usefulness may be different at the two points of time. That introduces a degree of vagueness into the comparison which eliminates the possibility of exact measurement.

When, from either cause, discrepancies in "real cost" between units of a single product exist at a single point in time (the first case), we may call them *differentials*. One system of differentials is due to differences in natural conditions under which the process is or has been carried on. Such differences for a single product are limited, as we have noted, to those comprised in the notion of different channels of production. The use of different sites (or deposits), or a differing set of sites, for the two units makes probable a difference in the influence of the specific natural resistances we have included generally under the terms suitability of site (including its influence on protection needed), accessibility of site, and accessibility of resources on site.[1] Obviously, if we are considering a single product, there is no possibility of more than a casual or accidental difference in any other of the natural resistances. In view of these inherent but differing characteristics, to the several sites or several systems of sites (channels) must then be assigned, as cause (or, at least, as inseparable loci of such causes), the resulting differentials in "real cost" of product. Here the base, or zero point, of the differential will be the highest average "real cost," upon the net of these counts, with the result that, among the systems of sites used, that one whose aggregate of resistances on account of suitability and accessibility causes the greatest average "real cost" on these counts per unit of product will have a zero differential.[2]

[1] As noted in the preceding section, there may be included in this latter differentials among different portions of the current material extracted from a single site due to variations in concentration and depth of the deposits upon it which are currently worked. In this case the base (see below) is the portion produced at the limit of payability.

[2] The "average" because, where costs differ on a single site, this (and not the maximum, or limit of payability) is determining. Where they do not differ the average is the same as the maximum and minimum.

It will be noted that, at this point, we are speaking of the differential per unit of product only. If this were converted into the differential per site, it would have to be multiplied by the quantity of product produced on the site (density of process). That is, the differential for the site as a whole would be the aggregate economizing of "real costs" on the whole output, due to these particular advantages, as compared with the "real costs" on these counts for an equal output at the pessimum site.

It should also be noted that we are basing these differenials on a single use only. The

The other system of differentials is due to differences in the technique used in the process, or in the several steps of the whole process, of production. The ways in which these different techniques will affect "real costs" by changing the ratio "effort to resistance" have been described so recently that it is not necessary to repeat them here. Again it is necessary, upon the assumption of uniform effort within a direct economy, to attribute to each technique or system of techniques the differentials or net economizing of effort per unit of product for which it is responsible. And again this differential is based on the poorest technique used at each step—or on the poorest combination for the whole process—and the differential of that technique is zero. In cases where a worse than optimum technique is imposed by natural conditions it will usually be recognized as a part of the first system of differentials. That is, the resulting excess of "real cost" per unit over that of the optimum technique will be regarded as a deduction from any positive differential existing on account of natural conditions on the site or in the channel concerned.[3]

Several explanatory remarks need to be made about this brief résumé of the secondary problem of attribution on account of differentials. In the first place, it may be objected that it is not proper to introduce this subject into the study of a direct economy. And this for two reasons. It may be supposed that the fact of two channels or two techniques for one product will not exist in a direct economy. Nevertheless, it must be admitted that this is possible. The supply from one channel may have to be eked out by that from some other; and a technique suitable to one set of natural conditions or one scale of operations may not be suitable to another.[4] Moreover, this is the proper place to lay the

---

fact that the base site for one use has a zero differential for that use does not preclude its having a substantial differential for some other use, as will be seen from our discussion of allocation among alternative uses above. This whole subject of differentials, as they concern sites, will be analyzed in connection with indirect economies, where the phenomenon appears in its full development.

[3] Just by way of calling attention to the frequently large magnitude of these differentials it is worth while to cite some data given by E. H. Phelps Brown in the "Third Report of the Econometrica Committee on Quantitative Production Studies" (*49*, 313). Among 21 coal mines in one district of Poland, cost of extraction and cost of sorting varied from less than 10 grosze per tonne to more than 40, and cost of loading from less than 10 to more than 60. Aggregate costs for these operations varied from something over 20 to about 100. No data is given according to which the differential could be assigned to channel (site) or to technique.

[4] For instance, product may be transported by water from one source and by hauling from another. And it must be remembered that, while technique may be available to everyone to whom it is known (and therefore to all, in a direct economy), a particular

foundations for a later treatment of the subject in connection with indirect economies; for these are facts which arise from the nature of our environment and of our relations with it and which have their influence under any technological and any institutional system. The second reason for an objection is more weighty. It is that, in direct economies, these differentials may perhaps be ignored by the want system; that is, in determining the order of preference in the satisfying of wants, each portion of a product which has a different "real cost" from other portions may be dealt with independently of the rest, or, on the other hand, they may all be lumped together so that the only "real cost" considered may be the average. But these same phenomena are possible in indirect economies if they happen to be organized in certain ways. Therefore we shall bear this caution in mind when we come to consider the question of the order of preference in Part IV and will not assume that the differentials, while they are facts, are such inexorable facts as "real costs"—which cannot be disregarded.

This introduces our second remark anent the question of the nature of these differentials. They are not necessary ingredients of the picture, as are "real costs." As to many natural resistances they do not arise at all; for these resistances are the same for all portions of the output. As to the base site (or deposits) or technique they do not exist, or are nil. Nor are they like "real costs"; nor are they substitutes for them, nor are they even quasi-"real costs." The differentials themselves are merely partial absences of "real cost." But, in a sense, they occupy the place of "real costs," and their causes are causes of such absence of "real costs." In discussing the primary problem of attribution we used the term only to cover attributing product to its causes. In connection with the secondary problem we have used it to cover attributing differences of "real cost" to their causes. But this comes to much the same thing and demonstrates the true nature of the differentials. That which causes the differential (the technique or the natural conditions) is the cause of the portion of the product corresponding to the differential (i.e., without "real cost") in the sense that it is the condition precedent

site is usually only available for one operation. A direct economy will therefore require the use of (estimates of) the differential for determining the optimum allocation of sites among alternative uses. Similarly experiments with (or estimates of) the technique differential might be necessary to determine the optimum technique. Both would be applications of the principle, though the differentials would not be continuing phenomena. They would occur only during the estimate and before the decision, if only one or the other were used.

to the existence of that portion, though not the agency which produces it. Not that better technique or more favorable natural conditions can operate alone. They are merely participants. But when they do participate the result in quantity of product is the same and the cause in the form of effort is less. Thus the nature of this kind of cause, to which in a sense may be attributed an undivided part of the product, can best be stated in a formula similar to that we used in the last chapter. In this formula we introduce the dimension P solely for the purpose of indicating the comparison of objectively equal quantities of a single objectively indifferent product;[5] we also substitute E (effort) for W (work) in order to include both "real costs" in an undifferentiated quantity. For two lots under the same technique (A_1) but under different natural conditions (N_1 and N_2), the formula reads, $1E \times A_1$ *vs.* $N_1 = 1P$, but $\frac{1}{2}E \times A_1$ *vs.* $N_2 = 1P$. The differential of N_2 with respect to N_1 is then equal to $\frac{1}{2}E$ per P (in terms of EP^{-1}). For two lots under different techniques (A_1 and A_2) but under the same natural conditions (N_1), the formula reads $1E \times A_1$ *vs.* $N_1 = 1P$, but $\frac{1}{2}E \times A_2$ *vs.* $N_1 = 1P$. The differential of A_2 with respect to A_1 is then equal to $\frac{1}{2}E$ per P (in terms of EP^{-1}). But, more usually, the improved technique will meet added resistance (for assistance, etc.). Let this increment be N_3. Then $1E \times A_1$ *vs.* $N_1 = 1P$, but $\frac{3}{4}E \times A_2$ *vs.* $N_1 + N_3 = 1P$, in which case the actual differential of A_2 with respect to A_1 will be $\frac{1}{4}E$ per P. Or, though we do not usually state differentials in such terms, all these formulae can show uniform quantities of E and the differences can be shown in terms of variable quantities of P. When that is done the cause of the differential appears as an explanation of that portion of the product which cannot otherwise be explained in view of the fact that there is no change in the quantity of the cause, effort.[6] Viewed in either way these differentials represent an intrusion of the physical aspect of production into the economic aspect because nature (the environment) and technology, while not economic agents themselves, have their influence, through conditioning the physical side of the process, in altering the purely economic picture. This does not change our conclusion that, in an economic sense, working and working only causes product to be produced and

[5] We cannot use the dimension P for different kinds of product for, as already noted, their only common denominator is E.

[6] In chemistry we have somewhat analogous semi-causative (or conducive) agents (e.g., catalytic agents, heat solvents, etc.) which increase the quantity of reaction, if, in this case, they do not precisely reduce the quantity needed of a particular reagent.

retaining and retaining only causes it to remain extant. It merely recognizes the fact that these external influences determine, and can therefore alter, the ratio between effort and product.

Finally, it must be remarked that we have broken with the traditional presentation in failing to attribute any of the economizing of effort (the differentials) to intermediate product or to retaining. Our previous analysis should have made clear why we have not done so. So far as intermediate product is concerned it is, when ready for use, a compound to which both indirect work and indirect retention are essential. There would, therefore, be no more reason for attributing its effect to retaining than to working. True, after it is once in use, only indirect retaining is required. But there is no good reason for singling out that particular stage as the only one to consider. Attribution to retention alone may, therefore, be ruled out. As to the intermediate product, as a whole, it must be regarded as an addition to "real cost" of final product in the form of indirect effort. By itself it is not an economizing, but the opposite. If there is a net economizing, it is not due to the fact of intermediate product but rather to the manner in which it intervenes and the purpose for which it is contrived in connection with the whole process. But this manner and purpose are precisely what we mean by technique. Thus we view intermediate product as a mere instrument of technique. The knowledge and the idea which conceive the purpose and devise the manner must come first. They constitute the *sine qua non;* and the execution is merely a matter of redirecting effort.

2. DISCREPANCIES BETWEEN DIFFERENT LOTS AT DIFFERENT TIMES

When discrepancies in the "real costs" of different units of a single product exist for either reason (natural conditions or technique) at two different points in time, we must use a quite different method of analysis.[7] As we noted above, the existence of a differential is predi-

[7] We are chiefly considering, here, discrepancies which arise over considerable periods of time as a result of what may be regarded as *trends*. "Real costs" may also vary somewhat fortuitously over time and in particular channels only. Among these special cases two are worthy of mention.

The first case is due to variations in quantity of product upon which a fixed conglomerate of intermediate product is being used. As a result, in accordance with our analysis on pp. 780 ff., the charge for indirect effort per unit of product may vary.

The second case is due to variations from the planned quantity of product to which is allocated a certain quantity of effort in the mass. This concerns, chiefly, the results of biological processes, the exact quantity of which cannot be foreseen. As a result, the ultimate "real cost" per unit of product will vary. So far as seems to be necessary this

cated upon the necessarily complete equivalence, objectively and in respect of usefulness, of any two units of a single product at one time. That provides the kind of basis for comparison of their "real costs" that we have found requisite. In Chapter 7 it was stated that two things must be equal (or correspond) in some one dimension (or respect) in order that the ratio of their magnitudes in some other dimension (or respect) can have meaning (i.e., a ratio between two magnitudes must have a common denominator, either implicit or explicit). Such a basis cannot be provided in the case of two units of a single product existing at two different times. Objectively they may be identical; but their subjective equivalence is indeterminate. Not only may the usefulness be stated as a different fraction of the full measure of a satisfaction but, even if their stated usefulness is the same, the bases of this statement, the usual maximum intensities of the want at two widely separated moments, become practically incomparable. Therefore, these discrepancies take the form of changes over time, in one direction or the other, whose magnitudes are exactly measurable in only one of the necessary dimensions and which do not, therefore, enable us to establish ratios—or differentials—of any very precise meaning. They are, rather, indices of favorable or unfavorable tendencies only.

We may consider first such discrepancies when they arise from natural conditions. As to those natural conditions which concern extractive processes only, we have already made the distinction between materials and powers which replace themselves and those which do not. In the latter case a tendency towards exhaustion asserts itself. If we may presume that the most accessible resources are worked first, the result will be that, over time, the optimum deposits on each site, and perhaps the optimum sites as a whole, will be worked out; the limit of payability in terms of "real costs" will rise, and therefore the pessimum deposits worked will be worse; and, presumably, the weighted average of "real costs" of the whole quantity produced will thus increase. The tendency, purely on this count, is therefore always toward higher "real costs" as time goes on. Even in the case of materials and powers which replace themselves, it remains probable that they will do so at different rates during different periods.[8] Again, as

---

discrepancy was analyzed on pp. 770 ff. It is referred to below and will appear again in Chapter 14.

[8] Rainfall, average temperature, etc., vary from season to season and, perhaps, from cycle to cycle. Winds are more or less favorable to sailing; fish and game more or less abundant; and many other fluctuations occur as between successive seasons.

to all processes, natural interferences of each variety will wax and wane.[9] Such differences for a single channel are limited, as we have noted, to those comprised in the notion of different seasons. All these influences upon the extraction of exhausting and non-exhausting materials and powers have their effect without change in the quantity of product wanted.[10] If that also increases over time, it will produce additional discrepancies in "real costs" which are to be attributed to the worse natural conditions under which the increment of production will then have to be conducted. Again, on the assumption that the most suitable and accessible sites and the most accessible resources are used first, it necessarily follows that changes in quantity will have the following effects. If the quantity is increased, then, as to all processes whatever, less accessible or suitable sites will have to be added. And these will worsen the pessimum and the average conditions of production without altering the optimum. The limit of payability will be raised (higher "real costs") at all sites. In the extraction of non-replacing natural resources the process of exhaustion will be hastened. If the quantity is decreased, the opposite effects will result. Changes of quantity may occur in both directions when these are due to changes in the nature or order of priority of wants or to changes in the terms of substitution among the available means for a single want. Then, presumably, increases in quantity wanted of one product will be accompanied by decreases in the quantity wanted of some other. On the other hand, changes of quantity wanted may also occur as a result of the *growth* of the economy. And these are likely to be all in one direction (increase) for products affected at all. Thus we see that, under any given set of natural conditions available, the optimum, the pessimum, and the average of conditions actually effective may vary widely over time. In so far as the changes in the actual conditions used arise from those of the above-mentioned causes which may work in either direction, bettering and worsening, we may regard the differences in the "real costs" over time as *fluctuations* due to natural conditions. In so far as certain of these causes produce changes only in the direction of worsening, we must regard the differences in the "real costs" over time as *deterioration* due to natural conditions.

When we come to consider those discrepancies between the "real

[9] Storms, pests, epidemics among plants and animals, etc.

[10] Nevertheless, as noted above, the result may be that the quantity produced differs from the quantity wanted by reason of the failure fully to foresee and therefore to overcome the resistances.

costs" per unit of product at two different points of time which are due to the use of different techniques it is natural to us to make the opposite assumption from that made in the foregoing. Whereas we assume, as to natural conditions, that the preference will be to use the best conditions first in point of time, we assume, on the contrary, as to technique, that the worst will be used first in point of time. The reason for these opposite assumptions is obviously the respective limitations on choice by reason of knowledge of what is available. The order of preference in both cases seems naturally to be from the best to the worst among the alternatives known to be available. So it hinges on what is known to be available. Frequently, the actual pattern of this order among natural conditions, as described above, is radically altered by the discovery of resources of greater accessibility. But, in the case of technique, we take it for granted that this process of "discovery" is all in one direction, so that the best alternative available and known is constantly improving in the course of time.[11] At least we may be sure that, with one exception, the optimum technique actually available, at any time, will, so far as it is known, always be preferred.[12] The one exception arises from the possibility that a particular technique may be available only for a certain scale of operation or under certain natural conditions. In that case, if the quantity wanted be not sufficient to justify this scale at any sites, or at supplementary sites, or if, at either, natural conditions do not permit its scale or kind,

[11] As a matter of fact, no such movement has existed during most of man's history; or, rather, it has been extremely discontinuous, with no "discoveries" whatever for long intervals. Therefore, we must be careful to treat this as an assumption only. Under "discovery" of technique we must include invention.

[12] The assumption of the equal likelihood of a preference for a regressive technique lies at the basis of one of the most unrealistic notions that has ever been conjured up by the imagination of economists whose laboratory or field work has been confined to an armchair. This is the so-called "law of the proportioning of factors" and the associated supposition as to the method of determination of the "marginal productivity of factors." In part, this arises from an erroneous analysis of "factors."

For any one technique the relative quantities of indirect and of direct effort are practically fixed, subject to one source of fluctuation, the rate of operation. The direct effort is proportionate to this rate; so is the indirect in part. But, so far as retention in use and that using up which takes place without reference to actual use are concerned, the indirect effort chargeable is not proportionate to the rate of operation. Under no circumstances, therefore, can there be an economizing by variation from the optimum rate of operation. It follows that the rate will be varied from this optimum only to conform to quantity wanted and never for the purpose of varying the proportions of direct and indirect effort chargeable, the aggregate of which can only be worsened by such procedure.

As between two different techniques no one ever reverts to the regressive technique except for the single reason mentioned in the text. And that is regressive only in an equivocal sense.

the technique will not be preferred. But, in fact, that is another way of saying that, for a single product, there may be, and usually are, different optimum techniques for different scales of operation and different natural conditions. For any given quantity, or part quantity, wanted its own optimum under available natural conditions is thus always preferred.

The general notion of the "state of the arts" comprises the entire system of optimum techniques, for various scales of production of all products and under various controlling natural conditions, which is available (discovered or invented) or known (generalized) or, perhaps, in use in any economy at some particular time. It represents in a vague way the degree to which the ratio, efforts to resistances, has been reduced at that point as compared with previous points in time; or, perhaps, as compared with a legendary maximum at the stage when no technique existed—in effect the stage of the pithecanthropus. The notion is usually confined to those methods which effect reduction of the ratio by the introduction of indirect effort (intermediate product); but it should also envisage all other methods which do so by reducing direct effort. Also, instead of limiting it to what may be called dealings with the natural environment—the "mastery" over nature—it should, in an indirect economy, be expanded to cover dealings with men so far as these constitute techniques. Thus we would include the art of organization, of "scientific management," etc. Out of the assumption, based largely on recent experience,[13] that individual optimum techniques are constantly improving in the course of time, we compound the notion that the entire system of optimum techniques, the "state of the arts" is advancing. And this improvement in the "state of arts" from period to period in the course of time is what we mean by "economic progress" in its strict sense.[14] Thus deterioration, due to natural conditions, and economic progress occupy a position with relation to discrepancies in "real costs" at different points of time similar to that occupied by the two differentials with relation to such discrepancies at the same point in time. Both are the results of the same two causes, differences in natural conditions and differences in technique. The former are apt to be generalized in any economy—that is, there is a

[13] By way of a reminder of this I have been particularly struck with Adam Smith's observation (*381*, I, 200) that, so recently as the 17th and 18th centuries, the average real wage in France was equivalent to about one fifth of a bushel of wheat. Today, only two or three centuries later, and in this country, it ranges from four to eight bushels—that is, from twenty to forty times as much.

[14] That is, in its technological, not in its institutional, sense.

general worsening of conditions or bettering of technique. The latter, by definition, cannot be generalized; for they consist in differences between the particulars of which the general is composed.

At this point, it seems well to reconcile our concepts, and the several statements already made with regard to them, as to the two magnitudes, effort, or "real cost," and product. Under our original definition of product as a magnitude that is only measurable in terms of "real cost," how is it possible that the magnitude, product, should differ from that of its "real cost"? But we have just found identical product differing in "real cost" by reason of different channels and different techniques. This is the key to the apparent contradiction, not only in our usage but in economic usage in general. A single product, of which the units are objectively and subjectively indifferent, can be measured in its own objective or subjective units. The latter may be the full measure. Terms of substitution between two products serving the same want can be established in the same dimensions. That is, a full measure of each for the same want can then be objectively determined, each in its own objective units. But that is as far as objective and subjective measurement of the magnitude product can go. The aggregate of different products is composed of incommensurables in these aspects. Therefore the magnitude of aggregate product is a concept beyond the reach of these systems of measurement.

The only common denominator of all product is its "real cost." Thus product, or production in general, must be conceived and measured in these terms, if it is to be conceived and measured at all. Nevertheless, that does not do away with the differences arising between different lots of any single product, in this aggregate, by reason of different channels and different techniques. Therefore, these differences require to be adjusted for; but the adjustment is in the magnitude of the single product in terms of its "real cost."

The way this is done when the differences exist at a single point of time, as differentials, is to select one part lot as standard and then to restate the magnitude of all other objectively equal part lots in terms, not of their own, but of this standard "real cost." The standard lot may be that one with the highest "real cost," or that one with the average, or that one with the lowest, or even some other critical level. When this restatement involves reducing the "real cost" from the actual for any lot, the reduction is "charged off" as waste; when it involves increasing it, the increase is the differential. Thus the ratio of the magnitudes of all lots of a single product, so adjusted, come to be equalized in terms of "real cost" to the ratio of their magnitudes in objective and subjective terms; but the magnitudes are then stated in terms of "real cost." In turn, this makes possible the summation of the magnitudes of the several different products—aggregate product—by reduction to commensurability.

When the differences exist at different points in time the process of restatement is more difficult. For then, as was noted above, subjective indifference is undeterminable, and therefore objective indifference is of uncertain validity. Furthermore, changes of technique resulting in economic progress over time are apt also to result in such changes in product that two lots of an article, which may continue to go by the same name, are not even objectively indifferent. The result is that comparisons of magnitude in objective or subjective terms of what may still be regarded as a single product at different points in time are difficult and sometimes impossible. In turn, that means that the basis for adjustments, such as were described above, is frequently lacking. Then the magnitude of the earlier and the later lot of each nominally uniform product must be left unadjusted and can only be stated in terms of its "real cost." Thus comparisons of aggregate product at different times come to be stated largely in terms of "production," as it is usually called, or aggregate "real cost," rather than in terms of "product" in its naïve sense. Of course, the degree to which the magnitude of any single product thus becomes assimilable only to the magnitude of its "real cost" is roughly proportionate to the interval between the two points in time. Deterioration of natural conditions and economic progress can be measured with some accuracy over short periods, but only in their effects on any single product by itself. To the extent that is or can be done, it is because the magnitude of a single product is assumed to be measurable at both times in the same objective terms and is not assimilated to its magnitude in terms of "real cost." [15]

H. THE PRINCIPLE OF MAXIMIZATION

Underlying all economic theory as to the relation of wants to efforts there has always existed the (usually) tacit assumption that human be-

[15] It should also be noted that, in the course of time, when comparisons of magnitude are not being made between current product and former product, current product tends to become assimilated to its magnitude in "real cost" even when that is less or more than it formerly was.

ings guide their economic conduct on the principle of what we have called *maximization.* This vague notion ascribes to men a motive, and maximization refers to and wholly depends on the operation of that motive. We shall, therefore, refer to it hereafter as the *motive* of *maximization.* Before we undertake to analyze and define it, it is well to note that, contrary to the tacit assumption of universal application, there may be many forms of social organization under which this motive in its fundamental and complete form cannot be observed, and is, therefore, either not present or at least not operative. The objective of this motive, which necessarily takes the form of a calculation, not an emotional urge, is sometimes stated, for example, in the form given by Courcelle-Seneuil, as follows: "à satisfaire nos besoins avec le moindre somme de travail possible." [1] But, strictly interpreted, this assumes a given and limited quantity of wants; which assumption, we have seen reason to suppose, is contrary to the facts. For this reason the objective may perhaps be better stated in the following converse form: "to satisfy as many as possible of our wants with a given quantity of efforts." [2] However, that, in turn, brings in another given limit—the quantity of effort. We recognize this at once as our notion of capacity. The notion of maximization, in any precise formulation, requires, then, the determination of capacity. In Chapter 9 the subject of this determination was considered and we established a first approximation as to the manner in which it worked. But, we saw there that, at least in the case of working, the limitation on capacity can only be determined through the relation of working, as effort, to the satisfactions to be gained by working or by not working. Thus capacity is a notion that can only be examined in connection with the intensity of wants. For that we shall have to wait until our final synthesis between the system of wants and the system of efforts, to which we proceed in Part IV. Nevertheless, since the motive of maximization may be presumed to operate all along the range of capacity, whatever its limit, the second formulation may be true, if not definitive, of any part quantity of effort as well as of the whole. That same modification could be made with reference to the first formulation by substituting "a want" for "our wants" as a whole. In this limited way, then, we

[1] Quoted by Jevons (*224*) from J. G. Courcelle-Seneuil, *Traité théorique et pratique d'economie politique*, 2nd ed. (Paris, 1867), I, 25.

[2] This, it will be recalled, harks back to Chapter 6, where we distinguished between the tendency to economize effort, in connection with future wants, as against the tendency merely to abbreviate the duration of the want, in connection with present wants.

are at liberty to consider the notion of maximization at this point.

The operation of the motive of maximization when it comes into play, as it may safely be assumed always to do in a direct economy, follows four lines of procedure. That is, the expression, motive of maximization, is only a somewhat abstract generalization of four kinds of observed behavior which we have called, respectively, the terms of substitution among means (products) for a single want, the order of preference among satisfactions (or provisions for future wants), the order of preference among the various sets of natural conditions available for the production of a single product, and the order of preference among techniques available for a single process. Since the first two depend on the want system we shall again have to wait until our final synthesis before embracing them in our scheme. The other two, however, depend wholly on comparative "real costs," assuming some given kind and quantity of product wanted. Our previous analysis has already given us the basis for stating these two lines of operation. As to the order of preference among natural conditions, the notion of maximization assumes that, in respect of natural conditions, man will always choose the line of least resistance. For each product or process he will utilize first the channel or the site upon which the sum of the natural resistances by reason of suitability and accessibility of both kinds is least.[3] Thereafter, so far as the quantity of product desired

[3] The second kind of accessibility affects the extractive processes only. Upon the extremely narrow foundation of the accessibility of resources upon the site, alone, and thus for processes of extraction only, there has been erected a so-called law of economics, the "law of diminishing returns." This was a reflection of the popularity of so-called "laws of nature" in the physical sciences, by which was understood fundamental uniformities in behavior of natural forces and entities. Unfortunately this economic "law" neither states a uniformity, nor is it for the most part the result of environmental conditioning. The first point was recognized when alternative laws were introduced—those of constant and of increasing returns—so that phenomena were conceived to have an option under which jurisdiction they should behave. As to the second point, the uniformity which is observed in this limited sector is not, with one exception, imposed by nature. We might speak of a "law of the varying accessibility of resources on site." That is almost the only natural condition bearing on the matter. The working of the most accessible resources first, the next most accessible next, and so on, is therefore, with the exception made below, entirely a matter of human preference. The corollary of that preference is that constantly less accessible resources are worked as quantities are increased or as the more accessible are exhausted. We might speak, paradoxically, of the law of human preference for diminishing returns in this particular field. But that, with the single exception, is all there is to it.

The one exception, the single ground for ascribing diminishing returns to nature, is this. The resistance which we have called economic depth necessarily increases as the depth increases. But, on account of the structure of space and the fact that we must commence operations where we are—that is, on the surface—it follows that this single form of resistance, and the effort required to overcome it, necessarily increase from first

requires him to reach, he will proceed along a series of sites or channels arranged in the order of their increasing intensity of resistance on these counts. The conflict between alternative uses will be resolved by the system of allocation described in a previous section of this chapter. As to the order of preference among techniques, the notion of maximization assumes that man will always choose, for each scale of operations or set of natural conditions, the particular technique among all those available and known to him which requires the least quantity of total effort (direct and indirect) per unit of product. Therefore, in this case, there is no arrangement of techniques in series. One and only one—the optimum—will be used; and the only effect of an increase in the quantity of product desired is to make possible, if the requisite conditions are met, the substitution of a large-scale, and therefore more economizing, technique in place of a small-scale one.

Even this limited part of the entire scope of the motive of maximization may be expanded to include two other lines of procedure that can be fruitful only adventitiously or over time. The first is the urge to discover new deposits of natural resources, hitherto unknown, the suitability and accessibility of, and on, the site of which present less combined resistances than that of the pessimum site now worked for the purpose. The second is the urge to discover, or invent or learn of, new techniques which will reduce the ratio of effort to resistances as compared with the optimum for any particular scale of operation or set of natural conditions now known or available. Thus the operation of the motive of maximization is not strictly limited to preferences. It may extend to expanding the area of choice.

One other field for the operation of this motive should be mentioned in connection with the subject of "real costs." Maximization also involves keeping waste effort at a minimum. As we have seen, waste of effort may arise from two causes. The first is objective changes in a given unit of product other than those which are the result of use (i.e., destruction, damage, spoilage, etc.); the second is subjective changes,

---

to last, or from shallowest to deepest. If the concentration is uniform from the surface down, the quantity of material extracted per unit of effort therefore necessarily represents "diminishing returns." However, this "law" may be entirely nullified by the "law" of varied concentration of resources in different bodies and at different levels. It may well happen that the returns are meager until the 5,000 ft. level is reached and then become a bonanza; and with plant "extractors" it is quite usual, as we have noted, that the returns of very superficial cultivation are small, while those deeper cultivations which make available to the plants all the resources they are capable of using constitute the optimum depth.

without objective changes, resulting in an altered estimate of usefulness. Waste only results when these changes reduce the usefulness. In the first case, in so far as the change is in the aggregate regular though in detail fortuitous, the corresponding effort may have been spread over the whole concurrent output as the "real cost" of failure to overcome the natural resistance of interferences (the cost of average spoilage). Thus the corresponding effort is not treated as waste. In the second case, in so far as this kind of obsolescence is, and can be allowed for as, a charge against prior output, the same is true. But to the extent that such effort has not been or could not be charged as a proper part of "real cost" to concurrent or prior output, which remains or remained unchanged in these respects, it is waste effort; for then, in a subjective sense, no corresponding product, or less product, remains to which to charge it. Obviously the waste of effort, and even spoilage and obsolescence, though they may not be treated as indirect waste, constitute, *pro tanto*, a reduction of the wants which can be satisfied with a given quantity of effort. To keep them at a minimum is, therefore, one of the objectives of the motive of maximization wherever that motive is operative.

without objective changes, resulting in an altered estimate of usefulness. Waste only results when these changes reduce the usefulness. In the first case, insofar as the change is in the aggregate output though in detail fortuitous, the corresponding effort may have been spread over the whole contemporary output as the "realness" of failure to overcome the natural resistance of circumstances (the "error" or "enemy spirit"). Thus the corresponding effort is not treated as waste. In the second case, in so far as this kind of obsolescence is and can be allowed for as a charge against prior output, the same is true. But to the extent that such effort has not been or could not be charged as a proper part of "real cost" to contemporary or prior output, which remains otherwise unchanged in these respects, it is waste effort; for there is, in a subjective sense, no corresponding product, or less product, to which it contributes. Obviously the waste of effort, and even spoilage and obsolescence, though they may not be treated as such as waste, constitute, *pro tanto*, a reduction of the wants which can be satisfied with a given quantity of effort. To keep them at a minimum is therefore one of the objectives of the motive of maximization wherever that motive is operative.

Part IV

SYNTHESIS

13

THE ACTUAL ORDER OF PREFERENCE—UNCHANGING "REAL COSTS"

A. INTRODUCTORY

In the three previous parts of this study we have gradually developed a scheme of economic energetics, each element of which has been drawn from an inductive examination of the data in that sector. In Part I we worked out the scheme as to the energizing of consumption as well as the most probable hypothesis with reference to the generation of the energy that is applied in production; in Part II we carried this hypothesis forward into the field of production by studying the way this energizing of production is actually applied; and in Part III we set the whole picture into its background by establishing the character of the environmental resistances which compel such application of energy and which determine the quantity required in each case. When the subject is viewed in that aspect we seem to have completed our task—to have sketched out, if only very roughly, a scheme which is self-sufficient in that it includes all the determining factors.

From another standpoint, however, we are, at the moment, very much at loose ends. At the end of Part I, in which we considered only wants and means, we had arrived at the point where we were treating pure subjective valuation as a necessarily independent process and as at least a principal factor in the making of choices. We found three conceivable types of criteria according to which such subjective valuation might be made—our three virtual orders of preference.[1] Then, in Parts II and III, we proceeded from another set of data—efforts and resistances—to construct a wholly different method of valuation—that based on comparative "real costs." And, at the end of Part III, we were

[1] More exactly we derived one criterion directly from our psycho-physiological studies and then set up two other alternative criteria which seem to include all other conceivable abstract types, when the criteria are reduced to terms of magnitudes and their dimensions.

considering the "motive of maximization" as if this second system of valuation had a great, if not predominant, bearing on the allocation of effort. But, in a direct economy, the allocation of effort is the same process, from the viewpoint of production, that the order of preference is, from the viewpoint of consumption. Thus, we appear to have imputed to our isolated economic man two independent systems of valuation of the means for the satisfaction of his wants. That makes it clear that a further task remains to us. We must discover whether the three possible systems of subjective valuation coincide with valuation in terms of comparative "real costs," or, if they do not, how their conflicts can be ironed out. In the course of doing that we shall find it possible at a rather early stage, incidentally, to settle beyond peradventure which of our three virtual orders of preference, and therefore which of the three criteria for subjective valuation, conforms to reality. For it is already evident that the influence of "real costs" is the "extraneous influence" inclusion of which we were obliged to await before we could apply this, our third, test and arrive at an analysis of the actual order of preference.

A word about this test of reality which we promised ourselves at the end of Part I. Even if the data were available—and, as yet, they certainly are not—it would be impossible, within the scope of this study, to assemble complete inductive evidence as to the various choices that are made in real life. Therefore, all that is possible is to approach the question in a more indirect fashion. The first step will be to develop what can, logically, be the interaction of this "extraneous influence" with each of our three virtual orders of preference. This will produce, for each, a combination of two interacting virtual systems of causation, one representing its hypothesis as to the influence of wants, the other representing the common hypothesis as to the influence of comparative "real costs." If these are the two preponderant influences and any of the three hypotheses is correct, one of the combinations should represent approximately the actual system of causation. We shall, in turn, compare each of these logical schemes with our general observations. If we find that man does not appear to behave as he would behave if he were impelled by one of these hypothetical systems of causation, that system must be rejected, for it cannot be used to explain behavior. If we find that, on the whole, he does behave in accord with one of them, that one becomes usable and useful. This is particularly true if it can be modified to conform to the observed facts more completely, or if the exceptions can be explained as the effects of identified and minor interfering factors. In regard to what we are calling general observations, each reader will have to depend on his own impressions and determine for himself whether to accept or reject such impressions as we cite.

In attempting this synthesis between subjective valuation and comparative "real costs," what we would like to be able to do, in terms of our previous technique, would be to establish a virtual order of preference (or of allocation of effort) based upon comparative "real costs" only. Then we could combine such a virtual order with each of our three virtual subjective orders in turn. We could see whether or not any of these respective pairs coincided in their effects so that neither member distorted the other.[2] Or we could see whether any pairing produced a combination of effects—each distorting the other—which would give us a satisfactory scheme for our actual order of preference. That would be a logical procedure. Unfortunately, for the reasons now to be described, that method is impossible, and we shall have to arrive at our goal by a much more roundabout route.

All three of our hypotheses as to subjective valuation agree in one respect—that is, all assume no other influence than the wants themselves in determining the series of choices going to make up the several virtual orders of preference. They differ only in respect of the way the want is supposed to come to bear—whether at its maximum intensity only or at discontinuous or continuous reductions in that intensity, and whether at strategic points only or *pari passu* with the process of satisfying. At the start we can ignore these differences and can treat, as the basis for all subjective valuation, the *influence of wants.* The basis for the other system of valuation is the *influence of "real costs."* Reduced to its simplest terms and treated as if it operated by itself, such an influence might be expected to result in a virtual order of preference which would follow the rising order of "real costs"—that is, an order of preference in which the least expensive means would be chosen first, the next to least next, and so on. But here arises an insuperable difficulty. What measure of each means would be used in establishing this system of comparative "real costs"? Obviously, given complete liberty in determining the quantity of each means to be used

[2] As a matter of fact we have already conceded at the end of Part I that such a result is impossible. If the two virtual orders coincided, then both would represent the actual order. But we have agreed that none of our three hypothetical virtual orders conforms to reality. Therefore none, alone, is the virtual order.

as a basis, any virtual order one chose could be demonstrated to be the order of rising "real costs." Obviously, then, the quantities of each means to be compared are of the essence of the question. Without that, the notion of an influence of "real costs" is meaningless. It is hardly necessary here to repeat our argument as to the absurdity of making such a comparison in terms of natural or arbitrary units (objective measurement) or the futility of any attempt to compare "equal" quantities of magnitudes which are incommensurable. Nevertheless, as we noted in Chapter 8, the establishment of any series of ratios of this kind requires common dimensions. Differences in one dimension are only comparable if made in terms of uniformities in some other dimension, or in terms that can be reduced to such.

We ran head on into this difficulty in Chapters 7 and 8 and in Appendix IV. Therein we found a rough basis for the subjective commensurability of different means in terms of the "satisfaction" some quantity of each would yield.[3] The basis is a rough one—comparisons of more or less or of approximate equality. But we found no basis for objective commensurability. Objective measurement only entered by way of defining the "size" of the several subjective units—different for each hypothesis—after pure subjective valuation had determined that "size." That did not permit a reversal of the process. Under two of the hypotheses one could say what objective quantities were equal subjectively. One could not say what subjective quantities were equal objectively. In the same way we developed in Parts II and III a basis for the commensurability of different means in terms of their "real costs." This basis is not a rough one. It may be quite exact. But again we found no basis for objective commensurability. Objective measurement only enters by ways of defining the "size" of some quantity of means after there has become embodied in it a certain "real cost." The certain "real cost" fixes the size. Again the process cannot be reversed. One can say what objective quantities have the same "real cost." One cannot say what quantities of "real cost" are equal objectively.

However, there the analogy between the two bases of commensurability ends. Under all three of our hypotheses as to subjective valuation it proved possible to define what we called the subjective units in such a way that there was a rational and determinate basis for making

[3] The term "satisfaction" is used here in order not to beg the question between our three possible criteria, not because we believe the judgment is made on that basis specifically.

between them a comparison of more or less, as well as of equality.[4] Thus we could derive from each a virtual order of preference that stood on its own feet and required no other comparison. But under the system of commensuration in terms of "real cost" there is no rational and determinate basis for making a comparison of more or less between quantities of different means. There is only the comparison in terms of equality.[5] But equalities do not lead to preference. Hence it follows that no virtual order of preference can be developed from the influence of "real costs" standing alone. Hence it also follows that we cannot use the technique of working out separately the virtual effects of the two influences, wants and "real costs," and then combining them into what might be an actual order of preference. The influence of "real costs" does not stand on its own feet; it is indeterminate in the sense that it cannot act in this complex as an independent criterion.

In spite of this impasse it is evident that we have now found two independent bases of commensurability for different means—one, the subjective, rough and ready, and the other, "real costs," quite exact.[6]

[4] Under the first hypothesis the subjective unit is a full measure. That is determinate. But the various full measures are not equal in terms of the criterion—normal maximum intensity. Therefore, they can be arranged in an order of preference following the order of priority. Under the second hypothesis the subjective unit is also determinate. It is the quantity of means required to change the remaining intensity of the want from one strategic level to the next. That, too, permits an order of preference, though one in which (after the first) several subjective units are equal, though preferred to all subsequent ones. Under the third hypothesis the initial subjective units are any quantities of every means that are subjectively equal. But since, thereafter, these units are fixed in objective terms, though all continue to grow smaller at various rates in subjective terms, an order of preference arises among all subsequent units.

[5] This is only the case, of course, if the "real cost" per objective unit of any one means remains constant. But that is the normal and, analytically, the basic case. The effect of differences in "real costs" of part lots of single means will be considered later. Obviously, an order of preference arising from such differences is merely the preference for the cheapest part lot first, to which we referred (p. 837), under the principle of maximization, as the third and fourth procedures. It is not an order among different means.

[6] There has been implicit in this introductory statement the assumption that we have defined a uniform unit of "real cost" for a direct economy. It is hardly necessary to review here the whole analysis in Parts II and III upon which this assumption rests. But it may be well to define our assumption more explicitly. We assume that:

1. Effort ("real cost") is the only factor of production.
2. The several expenditures of effort are, in a direct economy, reducible to, and measurable in terms of, a single homogeneous unit (e.g., atomic weight of different atoms).
3. Each of the two types of effort, working and retaining, is completely mobile and interchangeable within itself. Moreover, the second can be stated in terms of the first.
4. At this stage of the argument, working is treated as if it were a limited quantity. Later we consider changes in this limit.
5. Since we are considering here only the allocation of effort at the moment the choice is made, our analysis is realistic in a sense that Menger's (and others') is not

Thus the failure of objective measurement to serve this purpose need not stop us. For now we have the *two* necessary common dimensions which are requisite for all *systems* of ratios. Using one as the relate (inverse dimension) we can state our ratios in terms of the other as correlate (direct dimension). At least, by finding the quantity of each different means that has a certain "real cost"—the same for all—we can then compare them in terms of more or less or of equality in their subjective aspect. That much is certain. Whether the reverse is also true raises another question. For the reverse would require that we could first find the quantity of each different means that has a certain subjective value—the same for all. Our own hypothesis as to the subjective criterion does not require this capacity—in fact, is inclined to doubt its existence. But the other two hypotheses both require such a capacity—in fact, are in large part dependent upon it. Therefore, we will leave this question until we examine the three hypotheses in conjunction with the influence of "real costs."

At this point we have cleared up the possible relationship of the influence of "real costs" to the influence of wants. The only way we can take the former into account and bring it into our scheme is to determine the modifications in the several virtual orders of preference that would be produced by abandoning our previous assumption that there is no extraneous influence other than some limit on total capacity and by substituting the realistic condition that the "real cost" of the subjective unit for each want is different from that for every other. That is to say, the influence of "real costs" can only be introduced as a modifying agency—an "interfering factor"—and not as a primary determinant. We may also note that there are difficulties in the way of working in terms of ratios of which the magnitudes of both dimensions vary, as will be explained in Section C; we would prefer, therefore, to work either in terms of varying "real costs" per common unit of "satisfaction" [7] or in terms of varying "satisfactions" per unit of "real cost"; both methods might seem to be applicable to two of the hypotheses, but the first is obviously impossible for our own hypothesis, since we do not require for it a recognition of equalities, but only of

when he says "Niemand nach der Geschichte der Enstehung eines Gut fragt" (*296*, 120). That regards choices as if they were made among goods that are "given." But goods are not "given."

6. While we are considering only a direct economy and thus only acts of self, the whole analysis can be transferred to terms of acts of others, instead or as well, with rather minor modifications for interfering factors.

7 Perhaps we should say "per common unit of criterion." See note 3, above.

more or less; the most desirable and most generally applicable method would then be to set up, in each case, what would be the distortion of our virtual system, if any, if there also entered into the process a series of choices as to where each certain increment of effort (a unit of "real cost") would yield the greater "satisfaction." Thus our analytical tool, the series of choices forming an order of preference among the means for the satisfaction of all wants, would serve also for the series of choices determining the allocation of successive increments of efforts among different products.

B. WEIGHTED TERMS OF SUBSTITUTION

Before we consider the modifications which the influence of "real costs" would introduce into our three virtual orders of preference among means for different wants, which will be different for each of our three hypotheses, it is well to state its effect upon the unweighted terms of substitution among the suitable means for a single want; for this will be the same for all three hypotheses if we can assume that the unweighted terms remain the same throughout a single satisfying and that the "real costs" of all part lots are also uniform.[1] The unweighted terms of substitution consist of the ratio, in terms of objective measurement, between the subjective units of two or more means for a single want at a single stage or phase in the process of satisfying. To simplify the exposition we will use the subjective units of our own hypothesis. Thus we say that, if the several full measures of three means which are indifferent for a single want are, in terms of their respective objective measurements, as 3:2:5, that constitutes their unweighted terms of substitution.[2] It makes no difference whether or not they are objectively commensurable.[3] In the quantities given by their unweighted terms of substitution these several means are indifferent. In other words there is, in such a formula, no basis for choice. But the first task in formulating an order of preference is obviously to select the preferred means for each want. Thus we see that an essential preliminary to our virtual orders of preference is, on the basis of subjective valuation

[1] The first assumption is merely that the relation which exists between any two or more substitute means is the same for equal fractions of full measures as it is for full measures. That is, if $6a = 4a_1$, then $3a = 2a_1$, etc. The effects of abandoning the second assumption are considered in Section F, below.

[2] That is, in our formulation, $3a = 2a_1 = 5a_2$.

[3] So many cubic feet of gas, so many pounds of coal or so many kilowatt hours of electric current may serve equally well to keep you warm for a certain time. Yet they are incommensurable in objective terms.

alone, indeterminate. To select the best means for each want among indifferent substitutes under the influence of wants only is as impossible as it is to construct a virtual order of preference under the influence of "real costs" only.

The first choice, election of the optimum means for each want, becomes determinate only when the unweighted terms of substitution are weighted with the comparative "real costs." The indifferent full measures remain the basis of comparison; the differing "real costs" of these full measures become the basis of preference. That means whose full measure represents the least "real cost" is the optimum means. This is merely the second line of procedure of the motive of maximization as we gave it on p. 837. It assumes no more than was assumed there in the statement that the channel or technique involving the least effort is always chosen. The calculation is a simple one. Since the unweighted terms of substitution are stated for each means in its own objective unit, and since the "real costs" are also stated per objective unit of each, all that is necessary is to multiply the number of units of each means, under the unweighted terms, by its "real cost" per unit. Let us say that a, a_1 and a_2 are indifferent substitutes for Want A on the unweighted terms, $3a = 2a_1 = 5a_2$ (in the objective unit of each); let us say that their respective "real costs" per unit are 3, 4, and 2; then the weighted terms are $a : a_1 : a_2 = 9:8:10$. Thus a_1 is the optimum means for A. If (as is very improbable) as to any two substitutes, the weighted terms turn out to be 9:9 say, the choice is indeterminate. But where the choice is determinate it is on an *all or none* basis. That is important to bear in mind. We shall have more to say about it later.

As we have previously noted, there is, with reference particularly to a group of wants whose position is well along in the order of priority, a relation of substitutability among suitable means which cannot be reduced to terms of indifference by adjusting their respective quantities. These are the wants which are served by attributes which exist in the means in fixed quantities, not in proportion. We do not deny that such means are substitutes—we only deny that they are indifferent substitutes. Most if not all such wants are minor members of constellations, and their suitable means also serve through other attributes for the satisfying of the major members. Furthermore, the very fact that the attributes serving wants of this kind exist in fixed and different quantities in different means necessarily results in making the choice between the means involve also a choice between different degrees of satisfying the minor wants served. But that argues segmentation of the want and eliminates the possibility that any but the best of these means is a full measure for the minor wants served. All others must be regarded as part measures as far as these minor wants and these attributes are concerned. For these reasons we shall defer consideration of the terms of substitution between means with fixed attributes until we have worked out the influence of "real costs" among members of constellations, in Section D 1, and in respect of segmentation, in Section F 2.

C. THE INFLUENCE OF "REAL COSTS" ON THE THREE VIRTUAL ORDERS OF PREFERENCE

The development and exposition of a necessarily very complex scheme such as we are now attempting can best be dealt with if we first work out a basic plan under highly simplified assumptions and then, step by step, elaborate the plan by eliminating, one by one, these assumptions. By this method the abstract and, in a sense, unreal skeleton may come little by little to be clothed in flesh and blood, and thus, if the scheme is correct, ultimately approach, represent, and explain reality.[1] In this section our assumptions will be as follows:

a. Each means is suitable for a single want only.

b. The order of preference deals with current provisions only.

c. All part lots of each means required to make up a full measure have uniform "real costs."

d. The available quantity of effort—here working only, under assumption (b)—is fixed. Therefore, the effort and sacrifice per hour of working is also fixed at the level of an unchanging last hour.

It must be steadily borne in mind that our standpoint is the moment when the plan for a day's working—the allocation of a given number of hours—is being made in accordance with the actual order of preference among wants. We are assuming that this takes the form of a series of choices, an ordinal arrangement from the most to the least preferred provision. In other words, we are using as an analytical tool our notion of the limit of capacity as if it were a moving limit, including at first

[1] Or, perhaps, it is better to conceive the assumptions as limiting ones—absences of interfering factors—which, as they are successively withdrawn, permit modifications for each actual interfering factor in turn. Thus the assumptions are not untrue to reality. If they were, the analysis would be futile. They are true in the main. But they are not *quite* true. The basic plan represents the general case; but it must be modified to include the several kinds of exceptions

the first choice only, then expanding to include the second, etc., until finally it reaches the point at which the choice is for leisure.[2] Whether or not we shall thus arrive at *a* value theory for a direct economy, it is clear that this technique cannot produce a complete and sophisticated value theory for an indirect economy. Its limitations should be clearly recognized. For these are choices among non-existent provisions, still to be made and to be made by the chooser for himself.[3] In an indirect economy the allocation of resources is usually not made by consumers, and the orders of preference which are finally determining are not those of producers. Nor are the two processes then practically simultaneous—a day's working for the following night's consuming. Instead, stocks intervene which do not superficially conform to our pattern for future provisions. Nevertheless, even in an indirect economy, this process of choosing is the basic process by which valuations are made, and it will probably prove possible to allow for the distortions that arise from the separation of the two functions among persons and in time. In fact, if the basic process is kept in mind and the distortions are ascribed to these two forms of separation, the distortions themselves may much more readily be explained.

One analytical problem can be settled for all three of our hypotheses together, and therefore in advance. That is the problem of the way

[2] There are good reasons for using this analytical tool in spite of the fact that we will find it necessary to admit that observation of the facts will not enable us directly to confirm an actual order of preference. This because all we can observe is a list of wants included in, and a list of wants excluded from, the actual order. One reason for the use of the tool is that it will enable us to go over without change of structure to the actually moving limit of capacity—effect of changing "real costs"—in the next chapter. Another reason is that we will find reason to believe that the order of preference represents, in part, the order in which the several wants are considered. Still another reason is that the order of preference appears quite clearly in the matter of inclusion or exclusion of the several alternative uses of which a means may be capable. Finally, it will become clear that what we call the "base position" of any future instance, which has as much to do with its inclusion or exclusion as does the degree of futurity, is the position of the current instance in the current order of preference.

[3] At first sight it might seem that our standpoint is precisely the same as that chosen by Wicksteed (*441*, 19). He says: "We will begin with that part of our economic world which we ourselves immediately control, or which is generally accessible to observation from the inside, about which we are constantly thinking and in which we are all concerned, namely, the expenditure of our personal and domestic resources." But that, to him, is chiefly money expenditures. Ours is more nearly like Menger's in that respect. For his, which Stigler calls "an individual's budget policy for that period," is chiefly concerned with the allocation of "real" resources. Ours also resembles Pareto's in this respect. He says (*317*, 299): "Il faut au contraire considérer l'ensemble des choses qu'on a à sa disposition, et comparer les résultats que l'on obtiendra en disposant de ces choses de différentes manières, pour la production." At least, all these are nearer ours than what Stigler calls the "misleading 'dinner-table' examples . . . used by Jevons and, for that matter, most modern texts" (*386*, 240). For, then, the provisions are taken as "given."

we are going to conceive the influence of "real costs" to operate. Considered *a priori* and without reference to reality there seem to be three conceivable ways in which the influence of "real costs" might combine with that of wants. Again let us use the term "satisfaction" as the sign for an unknown criterion on the want side.

a. The influence of "real costs" may have no effect on the virtual order of preference, either because it is ignored or because "real costs" per subjective unit are all proportionate to "satisfaction." [4]

b. The influence of "real costs" may have no effect on the virtual order of preference, up to the limit of capacity, because "real costs" per subjective unit are all the same.

c. The influence of "real costs" may have the effect on the virtual orders of preference of rearranging them in a diminishing order of differences between "satisfaction" and "real cost." That is, the *surplus* of "satisfaction" over "real cost" may be governing.

d. The influence of "real costs" may have the effect on the virtual orders of preference of rearranging them in a diminishing order of "satisfaction" per quantity of "real cost." That is, the *ratio* of "satisfaction" to "real cost" may be governing.

Under (a) there is no possible limit of capacity. Therefore, we must reject this "way," out of hand. Under (b) the comparative quantities of "satisfaction," regardless of "real cost," would determine the order up to some point (the limit of capacity) at which the "real cost" equaled the "satisfaction." But the supposition of equal "real costs" per subjective unit seems to be preposterous. Therefore, we must also reject this "way." Under (c) the comparative *net* quantities of "satisfaction," after deducting the "dissatisfaction" ("real cost"), would determine the order up to the point at which this net ceased to be a positive magnitude. Under (d) the ratio of "satisfaction" to "dissatisfaction" ("real cost") would determine the order up to the point at which the value of the ratio became less than unity. On the face of the matter, (c) and (d) might seem to require a capacity on the part of the psychological apparatus concerned to subtract one psychical magnitude from another (c) or to divide one psychical magnitude by another (d). Such a capacity is manifestly impossible. Presumably, no one makes such an absurd assumption. However, we have already (end of Section A) found it possible to construe the magnitudes in such a way that they are not only not impossible but represent a process that we all recog-

[4] Or, following the same order, decline more rapidly than do the "satisfactions."

nize as the ordinary basis of choice. If we start with any certain quantity of effort ("real cost"), it seems to be possible for man to compare at least roughly the "satisfaction" to be gained from each of two, or several, alternative applications. Or—and this is only applicable on the psychological assumptions of the second and third virtual orders of preference—if it is possible to establish equal quantities among several different "satisfactions" it is certainly possible to compare their "real costs." Converted to either of these forms (c) and (d) produce the same effects on the orders of preference. That is, if we deal with surpluses or ratios of which the subtrahends or inverse dimensions are equal quantities of "real cost," then the order of surpluses and the order of ratios are the same. Or—while this method cannot be applied to the first hypothesis—if we deal with surpluses or ratios of which the minuends or direct dimensions are equal quantities of "satisfaction," the order of surpluses and the order of ratios are again the same.[5] Thus, when modified to make them psychologically possible, the two ways, (c) and (d), become one and the same.[6] That disposes of a question we raised in Chapter 10.[7] Hereafter, when we deal with the effective influence of "real cost," we shall, for convenience, refer to the basis as a ratio. But that term is used only as an analytical expression in mathematical form for the end-result of the process of choosing on this basis. All it means is that, where it is assumed that equal "satisfactions" are determinable so that the direct dimension of all ratios considered can be treated as equal, there can be a quite precise order of preference in terms of declining "real costs" per "satisfaction"; or, where it is only assumed that equal "real costs" are determinable, so that the inverse dimension of all ratios considered can be treated as equal, there can be at least a rough order of preference in terms of declining "satisfactions" per unit of "real cost."

[5] Mathematical nicety requires that the uniform dimension should be the inverse one. But we are going to ignore that in order to avoid the necessity of changing the nomenclature of the two dimensions each time we consider the two possible formulations. Our two forms are $\frac{5}{1} : \frac{4}{1} : \frac{3}{1}$. . . and $\frac{1}{0.2} : \frac{1}{0.25} : \frac{1}{0.33}$ . . . , respectively.

[6] The only basis for comparison when surpluses and ratios would not yield the same order would be one in which the units compared were neither equal subjectively or in "real cost"—say objective units of each means. While it is admitted to be possible to measure the "real cost" of an objective unit, we do not admit the possibility of measuring its subjective value under any of our three hypotheses.

[7] See p. 664, note 4.

I. THE SECOND VIRTUAL ORDER OF PREFERENCE

Since we are going to proceed by a process of elimination it will be best to deal first with the virtual order of preference which we worked out by attributing to Menger a meaning conforming to his conclusions but contrary to his statements. It will be recalled that, under that hypothesis, the order in which subjective units of different means are chosen depends upon the criterion of a static magnitude, the initial or remaining intensity of the several wants, and that the strategic points at which the remaining intensity of each want is effective are the points at which its declining intensity becomes equal to the initial intensity of some lesser want.[8] Thus the first phase of the satisfying of the prior want is completed when its remaining intensity is equal to the initial intensity of the second want in order. When we regarded subjective valuation, as the only influence, we assumed that the next choice would be for a combination of sufficient of the means for each of these two to bring them both down to the initial intensity of the third want in order. It follows that we have assumed that the "satisfaction" to be derived from these first two wants are, in that phase, equal. Thus we have here a basis for applying the influence of "real cost" by making the direct dimension of the ratio this unit "satisfaction." As soon as we do that, on the assumption that "real costs" are effective at all, we arrange these two subjectively indifferent quantities of means in an order. That one with the lower cost shows the higher value of the ratio of "satisfaction" to "real cost." Presumably it would be chosen first. The question then arises, would the other be chosen next? There is no way of settling that question by means of this form of ratio. For, as soon as we compare the more expensive of these two subjective units with the initial subjective unit of the third want in order we have lost our uniform quantity in the direct dimension. We are asking whether a lesser "satisfaction" at perhaps a lesser "real cost" is preferred to a greater "satisfaction" at a greater cost. But we have agreed above that such a calculation as that is impossible—at least in any precise terms.

Here the opposite form of ratio may come to our aid—that one in which the inverse dimension ("real cost") is the same magnitude in both alternatives. Let us say that the higher cost subjective unit was that of the second want. We wish to find a way of comparing that with

[8] See pp. 506 to 508.

the initial subjective unit of the third want, which we agree is cheaper. Now the reader must remember that this criterion is a static magnitude which cannot be related to any given quantity of means. In fact, the smaller the first quantity of means applied, the greater will be the remaining intensity of the want for the next quantity. Or, if the two quantities compared are a small first portion and the whole subjective unit, the criterion acts the same on both. Moreover, the remaining intensity of the second want is higher than that of the third want until means has been applied to reduce it to the initial intensity of the third want. If, now, we choose as our common quantity of "real cost" that of the initial subjective unit of the third want, it is obvious that we can take, as our basis of comparison, that portion of the subjective unit of the second want which has an equal "real cost." Between these two it is clear that such a portion of the subjective unit of the second want would be preferred, since the remaining intensity of that want is higher. But the same will be true of a second similar portion of the subjective unit of the second want; for, by definition, the first portion cannot have reduced the remaining intensity of the second want to the initial intensity of the third. And so on. Step by step, successive similar portions of the subjective unit of the second want are preferred until the whole unit has been preferred.

We have to conclude, I think, that the influence of "real costs" would have no effect on our second virtual order of preference, if that is strictly construed, except to the minor extent of making choices successive instead of simultaneous as between the members of each group of indifferent subjective units. However, we should probably qualify the rigor of our application of this criterion to some extent. It would seem necessary to assume that, at a sufficiently high level of "real cost" per subjective unit, some want or wants would be excluded entirely because the "satisfaction" to be procured was less than the "dissatisfaction" involved in the "real cost." It is even probable that a sufficiently wide discrepancy in "real costs" among subjective units at different stages could cause the deferment of the beginning of satisfying for a want of fairly high initial intensity even though the calculation were extremely rough. This concession to the probabilities might exclude certain wants altogether and might defer the initial satisfaction of some others until the moving limit of capacity had reached a ratio of remaining intensity to "real cost" which admitted them. If such exclusions or deferments could occur with reference to initial subjective units of certain wants, either exclusion or deferment would be even more likely to occur with later subjective units of wants with high "real costs," since, by definition, later subjective units would be wanted with less remaining intensity. And all this might extend the reach of capacity further over wants which became the beneficiaries of these exclusions or deferments. But, otherwise and in the main, it seems evident that we will have to submit this second virtual order of preference to the test of correspondence with reality—our third test—in approximately the form it took when we developed it in Part I as a purely subjective order. The influence of "real costs" makes no radical change in it.

2. THE THIRD VIRTUAL ORDER OF PREFERENCE

It will be recalled that the criterion of choice under the third hypothesis, as developed in Chapter 8, is quantities of pleasure—or what not—experienced during the consumption of quantities of means. The only basis we found for a conceivable virtual order of preference, using this criterion and depending purely on subjective valuation, is to start with a set of subjective units of the means for all wants which yield equal pleasure.[9] Having thus determined the "size" of these initial subjective units it then becomes possible to define each in terms of objective measurement. We also found it necessary to assume that it is these initially equal subjective units, thus defined in objective terms, that become the units for all subsequent choices. But thereafter they are no longer subjectively equal. In fact, on the assumption of a diminishing rate of declining intensity during the process of satisfying, each successive subjective unit yields less pleasure than its predecessor. Moreover, if wants are arranged in the order of the total pleasure which their complete satisfaction yields, from greatest to least, it is mathematically necessary that the rate of decline in pleasure per successive subjective unit becomes more rapid as we pass from the greatest toward the least want.[10] Or, in other terms, the number of such units required for a

[9] See pp. 516–518.

[10] That is—as we noted on p. 516—it is necessary if we assume a constant rate of decline for each want. To illustrate this: Let all the units of the first want add up to 10, of the second 8, of the third 6, and of the fourth 4. Let the initial subjective unit of each equal 2. Reducing this to geometrical terms we have four right-angle triangles, the altitudes of all of which are about 2 (average 2 for the first section of the base), and the areas of which are 10, 8, 6, and 4 respectively. Obviously the bases must consist of about 10, 8, 6, and 4 sections (units), respectively. Then the rate of decline for the first reduces it from 2 to 0 over 10 units, that of the second over 8 units, etc. The rate for the first must be 0.2 decline per unit, that of the second 0.25 decline per unit, etc.

complete satisfaction is proportionate to the total pleasure yielded by satiation. Thus the number of subjective units required declines along such an order of wants from first to last.

Again, as with the second hypothesis, this gives us a basis for applying the influence of "real cost" by making the direct dimension of the ratio these initial subjective units. For, by definition, all yield equal "satisfaction." We would expect to find that the "real cost" per equal "satisfaction" varies widely among them. Then they would no longer be indifferent in so far as the influence of "real cost" was concerned. Instead, there would appear an order of preference among them. The least expensive would presumably be chosen first, the next least expensive next, and so on. But would that be the order? Is it not possible that the second subjective unit of some want, if it had a low cost, would intrude before the first of another want the cost of whose unit was higher? Again, there is no way of settling this question by means of this form of ratio. For, as soon as we introduce comparisons with or among subjective units subsequent to the first, we have abandoned our common basis in equal "satisfactions." Therefore, again we must turn to the second form of ratio, which here takes the form of a comparison of more or less pleasure per quantity of different means with uniform "real cost."

With our limited objective it is not necessary to work out an elaborate representation of the order of preference that might result from this form of ratio. Nor is it possible to formulate one which we could be sure would conform to the conditions imposed on us. For different means surely vary widely in their "real cost" per subjective unit, and surely these variations have no definite relation to the "size" of the want. Therefore our best, as well as the simplest, method of demonstration, is to consider the effect of a few typical variations. For this purpose we shall arbitrarily abandon our previous assumption that the common subjective units are the least quantities which can be adjudged equal within the limits of the *minimum sensibile*. This is done only for purposes of exposition, because dividing our imaginary subjective units will be a less complex procedure than dealing in terms of multiples of them. We shall start from a basis in which the initial subjective units of all means have the same "real cost." We shall then examine in turn the effect of four exceptions to this basis—four conditions under which variation from this uniform "real cost" may occur. With these exceptions we can discover the four possible types of effect which the influence of "real cost" would produce on the virtual order of preference according to this subjective criterion.

However, before we proceed, it is necessary to make clear a by-product of our shift from a ratio based on uniform subjective units to one based on uniform "real cost" units. In Chapter 8 we used Fig. 22 to illustrate the virtual order of preference under this purely subjective criterion.[11] In that figure the several series of subjective units of each want, A to J, are overlaid on each other. The several intersections of vertical solid lines (average altitudes of sections of the base) with the curves representing the rate of decline in pleasure per successive unit, determine the order of preference. Since each section of the base represents unity—a single subjective unit—it makes no difference whether we compare the altitudes or the areas of these successive subjective units. The two ratios are the same, and that of the altitudes is more obvious in the diagram. We shall therefore continue to use the altitudes to represent quantities of pleasure, as if these were measurable. Moreover, to simplify the diagrams we shall show only the average altitude of each section of the base.

When we shift from units along the base that represent initially equal quantities of pleasure (altitudes) to units that represent equal quantities of "real cost," that may alter the initial altitudes. That is, a means which is more expensive than the average, per unit of pleasure, will have a lower initial altitude than the average; a means which is less expensive will have a higher initial altitude.[12] But that does not change the "size" of the want. Its total pleasure from a total satisfaction remains the same. Or, in terms of our diagrams, the sum of the altitudes for that want must still be what it was in Fig. 22. The result is that there are required more equal "real cost" units than subjective units, if the initial altitude is lower than that of the subjective unit, and fewer if the initial altitude is higher. In turn, that means that the rate of decline in pleasure per unit is decreased, in the first case, and increased, in the second. We show these two variations from Fig. 22 in Fig. 36. Using numbers purely for purposes of illustration, the pleasure derived from the initial subjective unit of A is 10; the total pleasure derived from all 10 units is 55. If, first, the means required for A is twice as expensive, per subjective unit, as the average, then the initial uniform "real cost" unit will

[11] See p. 517.

[12] Or, in more concrete terms, if one of these equal subjective units has a "real cost" higher than the average, it follows that its equal "real cost" unit yields less pleasure than the average.

yield half the pleasure of the subjective unit. Correspondingly, in order to derive a total pleasure of 55, 20 of these "real cost" units will be required; and the rate of decline in pleasure per "real cost" unit will be half as great. That is shown as A_1. Or, second, if the means required for A is half as expensive, then the initial uniform "real cost" unit will yield twice the pleasure of the subjective unit. The number of such units will be only half as great (5) and the rate of decline in pleasure will be twice as great. That is shown in A_2.

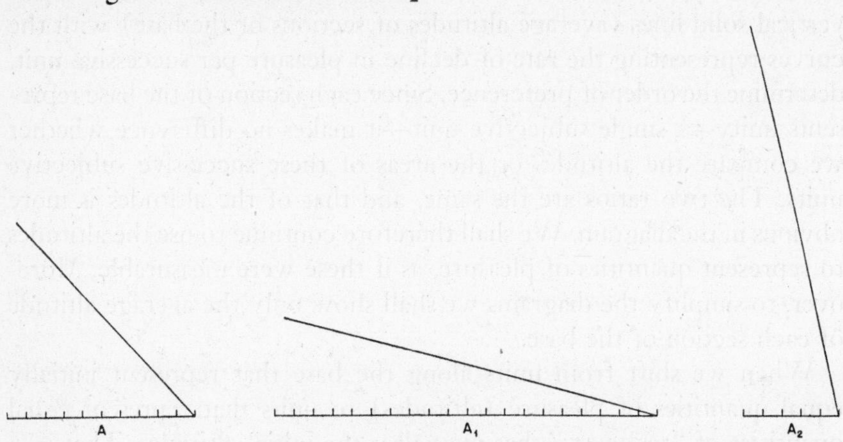

Fig. 36

Having made clear this general effect of any variation of "real cost" from the average "real cost" per subjective unit, we may now consider the particular effects of the four exceptions. In each case we set up the want whose "real cost" per subjective unit varies from the average, in contrast to the order of preference among the rest of the wants, whose "real cost" per subjective unit does not vary from the average. Since, among the latter, there are no differences in "real cost," the influence of "real cost" does not enter, and we have left simply the subjective order of preference unchanged.

1. Our first exception, or type of variation, is where the "real cost" of the subjective unit of some want is so great that "dissatisfaction" exceeds "satisfaction" even for the initial unit. We have to assume that pleasure per quantity of means can be compared with the effort and sacrifice of that part of the last hour's working required for such quantity. For that is the only possible limitation on working. The result of this effect would be altogether to exclude such a want from the order of preference within the limit of capacity so determined. This

is made clear in Fig. 37. The want shown in I has so high a cost that its initial equal "real cost" unit yields a quantity of pleasure per unit of only 2 (i.e., its cost is 5 times the average). But, in the simplified reproduction of the order of preference (taken from Fig. 22) the several wants whose "real cost" per subjective unit is average—A to E in II—consume the whole capacity when they jointly reach the level shown by the broken line. At that level, which is 2:5, pleasure per unit of "real cost" equals "dissatisfaction" per unit of "real cost" at the value of the latter which is determined by the curve of the effort and sacrifice of working. This exception, then, covers all wants whose *initial* equal "real cost" unit yields insufficient pleasure to bring it within the limit of capacity.

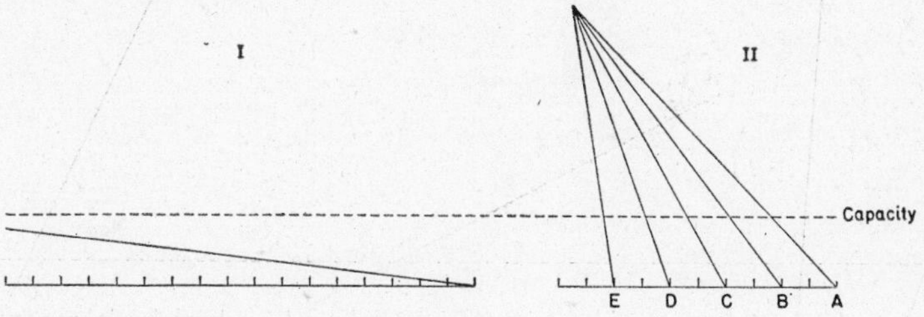

FIG. 37

2. The second exception, or type of variation, occurs where the "real cost" of the subjective unit of some want is so small that even its final subjective unit shows a ratio of "satisfaction" to "real cost" sufficiently high to include it in the order of preference within the limit of capacity. This exception is probably limited to very small wants. Very small wants, requiring, say, only two or three subjective units for their complete satisfaction, show, as we noted above, the most rapid rate of decline in pleasure per unit. Conversely, the pleasure per final unit will be further from zero than where the rate of decline is slower. In Fig. 38, I, we take a small want which, in terms of equal subjective units, requires only four units for complete satisfaction. We find that its subjective unit is only half as expensive as the average. That means that its initial equal "real cost" unit yields twice the pleasure and that, therefore, only half as many units (two only) are required. This is shown in Fig. 38 as II. While the fourth subjective unit would have been excluded by the limit of capacity shown in Fig. 37, II (yielding pleasure of only about 1) the second and final "real cost" unit will come within that limit (yielding pleasure of about 6⅔). On the other hand, we

show, in Fig. 38, III and IV, why this same effect will probably not occur with a larger want. The want—III—requires twenty subjective units. Let its subjective unit also be half the average cost. That again doubles the pleasure derived from the initial equal "real cost" unit and reduces the number required by half, as in IV. But now the final "real cost" unit will not come within the limit of capacity, as shown in Fig. 37, II (yielding pleasure of about 1 only). This exception, then, covers those small wants whose *final* equal "real cost" unit yields sufficient pleasure to bring it within the limit of capacity.

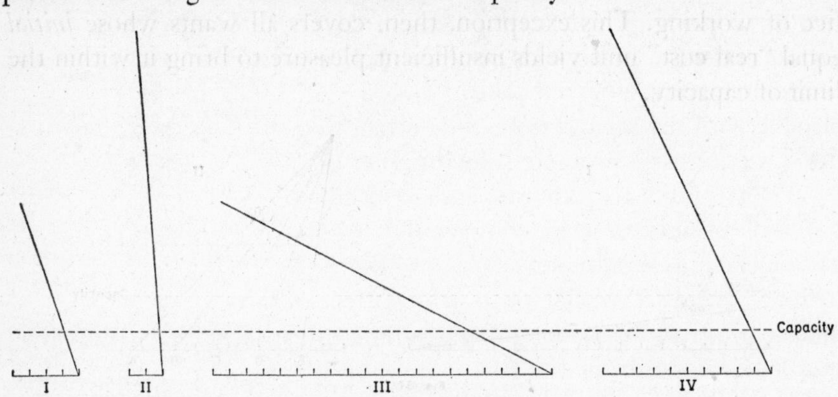

Fig. 38

3. The third exception, or type of variation, occurs where the "real cost" of the subjective unit of some want is above the average, but not sufficiently so to place the variation in the first type. The effect of this variation is to defer some number of "real cost" units to positions later in the order of preference than they would have had on the purely subjective basis. The result is that, for any given limit of capacity, a larger proportion of the total requisite means will be excluded and the want will be satisfied to a lesser extent—a lower than average percentage. To demonstrate this we may reproduce in Fig. 39 the diagram II in Fig. 37. That represents the subjective order of preference. Now suppose that Want C, as shown there, has a cost per subjective unit that is twice the rest. Whereas its subjective curve occupies the position shown by the solid line C, its "real cost" curve has a different relation to the others and becomes the broken line C_1. Whereas, under pure subjective valuation, or if its "real cost" had been the average, the limit of capacity (horizontal broken line) would have excluded only its last two subjective units, that limit will now exclude the last six "real cost"

units. The virtual (subjective) order of preference alone would have included two-thirds of the means necessary to satiate this want. Under the influence of "real costs" only one-half will be included. This exception covers all wants whose subjective units are more expensive than the average (but not of the first type), whose "real cost" units will therefore tend to be deferred in the order of preference and whose percentage of total means or total pleasure actually reached under any limit of capacity will be below the average.

4. The fourth exception is the opposite of the third. It occurs where the "real cost" of the subjective unit of some want is below the average but not sufficiently below to place it with the second type. The effect of this variation is to promote some number of "real cost" units to positions earlier in the order of preference than they would have had on the purely subjective basis and therefore to exclude a smaller proportion of the total requisite means under any given limit of capacity. Since this variation is the opposite of the last, it may be represented by the broken line A_1 in Fig. 39. Under pure subjective valuation—the solid line A—the limit of capacity would exclude the last three subjective units or three-tenths of the total means. Under this type of influence of "real cost"—A_1—the limit of capacity would exclude only the last "real cost" unit or two-tenths of the total means. This exception covers all wants whose subjective units are less expensive than the average (but not of the second type), whose "real cost" units will therefore tend to be promoted in the order of preference and whose percentage of total means or total pleasure actually reached under any limit of capacity will be above the average.

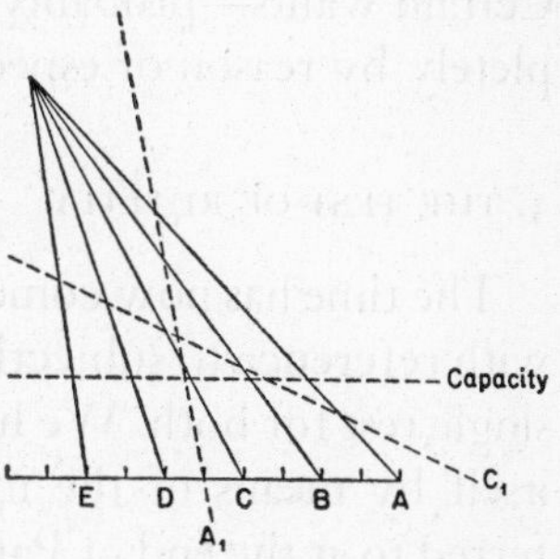

FIG. 39

To summarize, we find in the case of the third hypothesis that the influence of "real costs" is manifest without importing anything outside the criterion itself as we were obliged to do in the case of the second hypothesis. This influence consists chiefly in varying the several positions in the order of preference, and therefore the percentage of total satisfaction, of all wants the "real cost" of a subjective unit of whose means varies from the average. This variation in positions and therefore in percentage may be in either direction from the positions that would have been occupied by the several subjective units of the want and therefore from the uniform percentage of satisfaction that the subjective system alone would tend to procure. Since it can be safely assumed that all "real costs" per subjective unit will vary in one direction or the other from the average, it would follow that the influence of "real costs" would operate throughout the order of preference. The influence also includes two minor or occasional effects. Certain wants may be excluded entirely from the order of preference, by reason of especially high "real cost" per subjective unit. Certain wants—probably only very small ones—may be satisfied completely by reason of especially low "real cost" per subjective unit.[13]

3. THE TEST OF REALITY

The time has now come to eliminate our second and third hypotheses with reference to subjective valuation. That can be done by means of a single test for both. We have granted to each full opportunity to prove itself by means of the introduction of the extraneous influence—referred to at the end of Part I—which, it was thought, might so alter the virtual behavior of one of them as to make it conform to reality. It is now evident that both have failed to meet this test.

When we were considering [14] the second criterion in terms of the influence of wants only (pure subjective valuation) we found that, whatever the limit of capacity short of complete satisfaction of all wants, "there could not be any want whose satisfying had reached satiation." Similarly for the third criterion, "when the limit of capacity had been reached no wants would have been satiated." Now that we have considered the modifications produced by bringing the influence of "real costs" to bear, have we any reason to alter these virtual patterns? In Section C 1, above, we found that the influence of "real costs" should not logically produce any effect on the second virtual order of preference and that, whatever its effect might be by way of exceptions to the rule in extreme cases, there is no reason to suppose that even in these cases it would permit satiation of any want.[15] In Section C 2, above, we found a single possible exception, or type of variation, introduced into the third virtual order of preference by reason of the in-

[13] However, when we come to examine the way the limit of capacity is set, in Chapter 14, we will find that even this possibility is eliminated as soon as we eliminate the arbitrary objective unit as the minimum unit of choice. See the end of Appendix VI, Section E.

[14] See p. 527.

[15] It might permit some exclusions but no complete inclusions.

fluence of "real costs," which could produce satiation. But we saw reason to believe that this possible exception would have to be confined not only to wants with very cheap means but probably to very subordinate wants. Thus under the second hypothesis there can be no satiation, and under the third there can be none except possibly in the case of subordinate wants whose means are cheap.[16] Does this accord with reality?

If, with candor and without preconceived notions, one consults his own experience and his ordinary observation of the behavior of others, no elaborate scientific proof is necessary to settle this question. We all recognize that it is customary to satiate such subordinate wants as those which are catered to by toothbrushes and toothpaste; hairbrushes and combs; handkerchiefs; writing equipment and supplies; mousetraps, etc. If more of these means were offered free (Walras's test), no more would be taken; or, more exactly, if the extra means were accepted they would produce no greater current satisfaction but would merely be hoarded as labor-saving future provisions. Actually, this same situation rules also with reference to many prior wants. One example is sufficient. The ordinary (not rich) man, in our society, satiates his hunger three times a day. If offered another helping he declines with thanks. He has had "enough." But, upon the assumptions of these two hypothetical criteria, this would be impossible—or at least unwise. If these assumptions represented the way men *do* act, then one could never in his life have had a square meal. Or, if these assumptions represent the way men *should* act, then if one ever had had a square meal he would have proved himself an economic moron who is the creature of impulse and does not even strive toward the goal of maximization as, according to theory, he should. This is a large charge to bring against the great majority of ordinary men. In fact, it is so large a charge that it suggests a countercharge. It suggests that the assumption of declining intensity during satisfaction, which constitutes the Achilles' heel of both these hypotheses, is not in accord with the facts. If the common assumption upon which they rest is false, then, of course, both hypotheses, both possible criteria and both virtual orders of preference are equally false. They do not accord with reality.[17]

[16] See the end of Appendix VI, Section E, where we eliminate on other grounds the possibility of even this exception.

[17] In whatever form one works out the basic thesis of marginal utility theory and all its derivatives and modifications—so long as it involves *diminishing* the "whatever it is" that is derived from (and so determines choices among) successive increments of

However, it seems improper that we should dispose of the elderly and popular *idolum theatri* which lies at the base of these two hypotheses in so unceremonious a fashion. We should at least examine fully what is involved in its rejection. To that end we devote Appendix VI, Section A. The reader who is not yet convinced or the reader who finds himself with *arrières pensées* may wish to pursue the subject there.

For our own further purposes two corollaries of the elimination of these hypotheses need to be emphasized. Implicit in all "felicific calculus" and explicit in the Edgeworth-Pareto-Hicks scheme is the notion of substitutability between the "satisfactions" of different wants. Obviously, this rests on the supposition that there is a common denominator of "satisfaction"—pleasure or what not. But the fact is that, at least throughout the order of prior wants that we have studied, the satisfaction of no want is in any respect a substitute for that of another.[18] One must have air *and* warmth *and* water *and* food. A little more water is in no way a substitute for a little less food. It is true that choices may have to be made; if they can be made, there must be some basis of comparability between wants, their satisfactions, and therefore their means. But that basis is not one of substitutability; it is not a two-way or alternative relation; it is a one-way or preference relation. That one-way relation has been expressed in our order of priority. Each want in that order is greater than those which come after it; and each except the first is less than those that come before it. Moreover, if we have to give up the supposition that the intensity of the want—or other criterion—declines during the process of satisfying, it follows that each want retains its position in the order of priority until it is satiated. Or, stated in our more realistic terms, when current provision for a single order of priority is being planned, each want will be

means—the necessary result is that no important want with a means around average cost could ever be satisfied completely. For, as soon as one admits that there is some limit of capacity and therefore that the complete satisfaction of all wants is impossible, it follows that some final portion of each want must have remained unsatisfied.

[18] Different means for the same want—if the attribute is not one which exists in fixed quantity—may, on their unweighted terms of substitution, be indifferent. Satisfactions of different wants cannot be indifferent among themselves.

When the unweighted terms of substitution among different means for the same want are weighted by their respective "real costs" they are no longer indifferent. When the satisfactions of different wants are weighted by their respective "real costs" they do not become indifferent. As pointed out in Appendix IV, we cannot infer that, if bread were sufficiently expensive and wine sufficiently cheap, a normal man would choose to starve himself to death in a drunken orgy. When a man is hungry, wine at any price is no substitute for bread at any price; when he is thirsty, the reverse is true.

considered to exercise its full force until adequate provision—a full measure—is made for it.

In all fairness it should be said that our second hypothesis, derived from the construction we placed upon Menger, goes some distance toward the recognition of such an order of priority and, therefore, toward the limitation of substitutability. That is, it does so if the successive quantities of means are treated as part measures for a single satisfaction of each want. Under that hypothesis the order in which the several wants would *begin* to be satisfied is the order of priority. To that extent there would be preference rather than substitutability. However, thereafter, as second, third, etc., part measures came to be included, the order, except at the strategic want, would disappear. All forward of that position would then be on a par—indifferent—so far as subjective valuation was concerned. The effect of differences in "real cost" would not change this. It would merely introduce an order of preference among subjectively equal part measures (subjective units). But all subjectively equal parts measures would still be provided before any subjectively less part measures were considered at all. Only when the limit of capacity was reached would the order of priority appear again and substitutability disappear. Then subordinate wants whose level of initial intensity was insufficient would be excluded.

Even that little concession cannot be made with regard to the third hypothesis. There, though it is to be supposed that wants could still be arranged in an order of priority based on the total pleasure to be derived from a complete satisfaction of each, nevertheless, from the beginning and throughout the order of preference such an order of priority would necessarily be ignored. That would be equally true of the virtual order under the influence of subjective valuation only and of that order when modified by the influence of "real costs." We must admit that, though it would be ignored, this order of priority might have a certain indirect influence. For, as we found on p. 527, each want would tend, after the initial choice, to gain "cumulative pluralities" in terms of subjective units, which pluralities might accord with its rank in the order of priority (total pleasure). However, as we have seen above, even this indirect influence would be completely confused by the influence of "real costs"—that is, the pluralities would tend to be increased or decreased, from those determined by the order of priority, by reason of "real costs" per subjective unit that were less or greater than the average. Thus any preference among wants would tend to disappear. Ultimately, at the final or equilibrium state for any limit of capacity, even such a remnant of preference among wants would have entirely disappeared, and the pleasure per unit of "real cost" would be equal in all uses. In that sense there would be perfect substitutability among all the final allocations of "real cost." They would be indifferent among themselves.[19]

The first corollary is this: In rejecting the assumption upon which these two hypotheses are based—that of declining intensity of a want during its satisfaction—we are at the same time rejecting the notion of substitutability among the "satisfactions" of different wants. We hold that the initial intensities of all wants differ, so that there exists an initial order of priority, and that these initial intensities remain practically unchanged up to the point of satiation, so that this order of priority remains intact until that point. Thus there can be no phase or segment of any one want which is equal to—indifferent from—any phase or segment of any other want. As we proceed and assemble further evidence in support of this thesis it will appear that we can also, or alternatively, reject the second hypothesis on the ground that its intermediate choices require the assumption of substitutability—indifference—and the third hypothesis on the ground that all its choices require that assumption. We make this clear for one purpose only. There are back doors—e.g., the notion of satisfaction as a two-dimensional magnitude—which would permit the resuscitation of these hypotheses to save "substitutability" even if the assumption of declining intensity were allowed to die.

The second corollary serves merely to clear the ground for the next section. We have found that, under the second hypothesis, the influence of "real costs" should not logically produce any effect on the virtual order of preference except for possible exclusions and deferments. In other words, the general rule would be that subjective valuation would govern throughout without interference by the "extraneous influence." The third hypothesis would lead to the opposite result. There, the influence of "real costs" would be governing throughout, in the only way we have found that it can come to bear. That is, each choice would be made in terms of "satisfaction" per unit

[19] Incidentally, in this connection, it seems worth while to emphasize that the third hypothesis, even when it is modified by the influence of "real costs," does assume, with the few exceptions noted in Section C 2, above, that all wants will begin to be satisfied together. That, most certainly, does not meet the test of reality.

of "real cost." The greater would always be preferred to the less; but the end-result would be, at any given capacity, that "satisfaction" per unit of "real cost" would be equal among the final units applied to all wants. Thus our two rejected hypotheses involve the corollary that choices are made either all on the one basis or all on the other. In the next subsection, in which we consider our own hypothesis—the first—we shall find much evidence to indicate that neither of these extreme and contradictory positions conforms to the facts. Instead, we shall find that these two bases compete on an either-or footing; that they are in irreconcilable conflict; that one may overrule the other as to any particular choice; and that the result is something in the nature of a compromise, one basis governing some choices and the other others.

4. THE FIRST VIRTUAL ORDER OF PREFERENCE

Having excluded the possibility that either the second or the third hypothesis as to subjective valuation, when these are combined with the influence of "real cost," conforms to and thereby explains reality, we may now proceed to consider the first hypothesis based on our own analysis of wants derived from psycho-physiological data. In order to fit this in with the previous analysis we shall start with one further assumption. That is, we shall deal here in terms of full measures only and in terms of a single full measure for each want only—i.e., the single order of preference concerned with current provision. If we find the hypothesis to be tenable under these limiting conditions, we can then expand the analysis to include more than one full measure for any want on account of true future provision (Section E) and less than one full measure for any want on account of segmentation (Section F).

In the beginning of Section C, above, we considered the three possible ways in which the influence of "real costs" might combine with that of wants, and we agreed there to use the concept of a ratio of intensity to "real cost" as a purely mathematical expression for the process of choices in terms of greater or less or equal "satisfactions" per uniform quantity, or unit, of "real cost." How can the notion of such a ratio be applied under the conditions assumed for our first hypothesis? We must admit at once that these conditions preclude the possibility of determining the order of declining "satisfactions" per unit of "real cost." Under our own hypothesis, satisfactions are indivisible except as segmentation may occur. And that we will consider later. At least, we have found it necessary to conclude that intensity remains the same throughout a satisfaction, so that no part satisfaction would differ from any other in that respect. Thus it would be impossible to differentiate "satisfactions" per unit of "real cost." The only basis of subjective comparison that we have admitted is the relative normal maximum intensity of the wants. And the only correspondence established for such a maximum intensity is the full measure of means and, through that, some quantity of "real cost." But such comparisons also deny us the necessary uniform quantity in the direct dimension of our ratios. If we have neither, how make comparisons which we agree must be limited to terms of more or less per unit? That seems to be the problem. Instead of trying immediately to solve it, let us follow the procedure of assuming it to be soluble in order to try it out on reality. Let us proceed on the assumption that, under our own hypothesis, the order of ratios consists of a descending order of *values*, in which the value of each ratio is determined by the normal maximum intensity of the want, in the direct dimension, and by the "real cost" of a full measure of the preferred means in the inverse dimension.[20]

Let us see what are the possible relationships between the results of such a criterion—the influence of "real costs" combined with the influence of wants—and the results of the criterion of the influence of wants alone. It is clear from our previous analysis that a virtual order of preference based on the influence of wants alone would follow the order of priority. That is, full measures of the several means would be successively preferred in the descending order of the normal maximum intensities of their respective wants. On the other hand, a virtual order of preference based on the influence of "real costs" combined with that of wants would follow the descending order of values of the ratios—maximum intensity to "real cost" per full measure. It is evident, a priori, that there may be three possible relationships between these two virtual orders of preference.

1. If all "real costs" per full measure are equal—as we implicitly assumed in Part I and explicitly assumed in Part II—the ratios of intensity to "real cost" are all different. But the order of decreasing values for the ratios is then the same as the order of priority.

2. If all "real costs" per full measure are proportionate to the relative

[20] That involves the use of ratios with no uniform magnitude in either dimension which, it will be recalled, in so far as it involves the division of one psychical magnitude by another, we rejected as psychologically impossible. If that is the only way to bring the influence of "real costs" into our scheme, we must face squarely the difficulties it raises.

intensities of the wants, all ratios of intensity to "real cost" are the same. Then there is no descending order of values of ratios.

3. If "real costs" are neither equal among themselves nor proportionate to relative intensities, but are instead entirely irregular, then there are two independent orders which do not coincide—the order of priority and the order of decreasing values of ratios.

In the first or second case, we could say, as we did under (a) on page 853, that the influence of "real costs" could have no effect on the virtual order of preference resulting from the order of priority. Under (1) above, that would be because the two orders coincided; under (2) above, that would be because there would be no order of decreasing values of ratios. Now we know from casual observation that the first of these possible relations does not conform to the facts. The "real costs" of all full measures are not equal. On a priori grounds it seems necessary also to reject the second possibility. The likelihood that "real costs" should fit into such a neat pattern as that, when there seems to be no possible causal relation that would lead to their doing so, is so small that the theoretical possibility must be regarded as practically impossible. That leaves us with the third as the only possibility. And that, in turn, leaves us on the horns of a real dilemma. For, if the two virtual orders of preference under the third possibility do not coincide, it is impossible that any actual order of preference should accord with both. Nor, offhand, does it appear that one can find a compromise or reconciliation between their divergences. Is it possible that behavior must follow one or the other because it cannot follow both?

Before facing this issue and the various questions it raises, let us represent it diagrammatically, in order to make it quite clear. In Fig. 40, the solid lines in I represent the prior wants in the order of priority, while those in II represent subordinate wants at and around the limit of capacity. Against each want—and joined to it by a solid line along the base—is opposed the "real cost" of its full measure represented by the broken lines. All "real costs" are precisely commensurable among themselves. Therefore the series of broken lines represents the ratio among all full measures in terms of "real cost." All wants are not precisely commensurable among themselves. But they are comparable in terms of more or less. Therefore we know their order, though we do not know the precise differences between each successive pair. At the margin, the "real cost" of the last full measure, in terms of the intensity of effort and sacrifice of the last hour, is equal to the intensity of the least want included. That, we have already concluded, is the only possible way to account for the voluntary termination of the working-day. What it means is that, at that point, the direct and the inverse dimensions of our ratios become comparable (equal). (The full significance of this will be developed in Chapter 14, Section A 3.) At least that gives us a rough basis for comparability between all the solid lines and the broken ones.

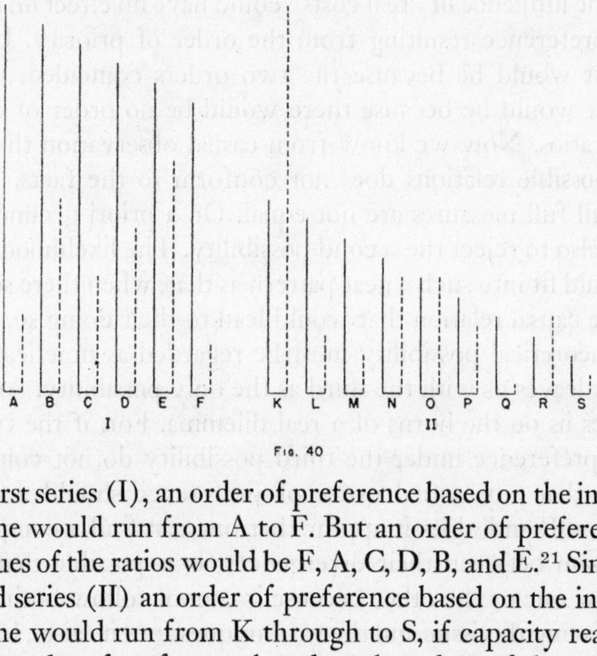

FIG. 40

In the first series (I), an order of preference based on the influence of wants alone would run from A to F. But an order of preference based on the values of the ratios would be F, A, C, D, B, and E.[21] Similarly for the second series (II) an order of preference based on the influence of wants alone would run from K through to S, if capacity reached that far. But an order of preference based on the values of the ratios would be Q, M, L, S, P, N, O. K and R would be excluded altogether, since for them the value of the ratio is less than unity—"real cost" exceeds intensity. These two virtual orders of preference do not agree. Moreover, without bringing in a limit of capacity, only the second order excludes satisfaction of any want. It would appear, then, that, without introducing the limit of capacity, the actual order of preference would, probably, not be directly observable if it followed the order of priority; and, if it followed the order of ratios, it would appear only where

[21] This diagram was originally drawn on (and has been reproduced from) cross-section paper, so that all these lines had numerical values. While we do not suppose that the relative intensities of wants can be reduced to numerical values, these numbers are useful for purposes of illustration and clarification. Therefore, in note 23, below, we give all the numerical values upon which this illustration was worked out.

some want was excluded because of high cost. The crucial nature of the actual order might then be only observable if, where, and because it sets the limit of capacity.[22]

Disregarding, for the moment, this possible connection between the order of preference and the limit of capacity, merely admitting that there must be some limit to capacity and purely for the purpose of demonstrating the effect of introducing it, let us try out two different arbitrarily chosen capacities on this series. First, we shall arbitrarily suppose that there are but 17 units of "real cost" left over to apply to the second series, II—those which represent the wants around the limit. The numerical values upon which the following conclusions are arrived at are implicit in the diagram and are given explicitly in note 23, below. On the basis of the influence of wants alone, without considering capacity, this quantity of "real cost" would have to be allotted to K only, even though, according to our numerical values, 17 units will not acquire a full measure for K. However, even on the influence of wants alone, as soon as we admit any limit to capacity, a choice is compelled between K, on one side, and L, M, N, and O on the other. On the basis of this compulsory choice we might suppose that, since the aggregate intensities of the latter are so conspicuously greater than the single intensity of the former, the 17 units would be allocated to L, M, N, and O and that K would be passed over. That would also involve the exclusion of P, Q, R, and S. On the other hand, if the actual order followed the order of ratios—combined influence—this quantity of "real cost" would be allotted to Q, M, L, S, P, and N, in order, and O would be excluded (in addition to K and R).

Now let us bring in the illustration of still another point by trying out another arbitrary capacity on the whole series. For this purpose we shall ignore the gap between F and K, since that makes no difference with regard to our point, which is to show what would be the potential effect of the ratio basis upon a prior want. If, upon the basis of the influence of wants alone, we have available for the whole series a capacity of 43 units, all of it would be used up for Wants A to F, in this order, and all the subordinate wants, K to S, would be excluded. But, upon the basis of the ratios, the virtual order of preference would be, F, A, Q, M, C, L, D, S, B, and P, in that order. Not only would K and R be excluded, as in the previous case, because the values of their ratios

[22] It is actually observable elsewhere, as described below and also in Section C, note 2, above.

are less than unity, but among the wants the values of whose ratios are here greater than unity, E, N, O, and P would be excluded because of the limit of capacity.[23] Thus, though E is one of our prior wants, it

[23] The numerical values upon which these ratios are based are as follows—direct dimension = intensity of want, inverse dimension = "real cost" (in parentheses, the values of the ratios).

The complete virtual orders of preference based on the order of priority would then be:

First series—$A = \frac{20}{4} (= 5)$; $B = \frac{19}{10} (= 1.9)$; $C = \frac{18}{6} (= 3)$; $D = \frac{17}{8.5} (= 2)$; $E = \frac{16}{12} (= 1.33)$; $F = \frac{15}{2.5} (= 6)$.

Second series—$K = \frac{10}{20} (= 0.5)$; $L = \frac{9}{3} (= 3)$; $M = \frac{8}{2} (= 4)$; $N = \frac{7}{6} (= 1.16)$; $O = \frac{6}{6} (= 1)$; $P = \frac{5}{3.66} (= 1.5)$; $Q = \frac{4}{0.8} (= 5)$; $R = \frac{3}{4} (= 0.75)$; $S = \frac{2}{1} (= 2)$.

The complete virtual orders of preference based on the values of the ratios would then be:

First series—F (6), A (5), C (3), D (2), B (1.9), E (1.33).

Second series—Q (5), M (4), L (3), S (2), P (1.5), N (1.16), O (1).

K (0.5) and R (0.75) would be excluded because the values of their ratios are less than unity.

If 17 units of capacity were applied to the second series only they would reach as below (giving effect to the exclusion of K on both bases, and of R on the second). The figures in parentheses are now the inverse dimensions of the ratios in the list above—the quantity of "real cost" per full measure.

On the basis of order of priority—L (3), M (2), N (6), O (6) = 17.

On the basis of ratios—Q (0.8), M (2), L (3), S (1), P (3.66), N (6) = 16.46.

If 43 units of capacity were applied to both series they would reach as below (the exclusion of K and R now arises only on the second basis).

On the basis of order of priority—A (4), B (10), C (6), D (8.5), E (12), F (2.5) = 43.

On the basis of ratios—F (2.5), A (4), Q (0.8), M (2), C (6), L (3), D (8.5), S (1), B (10), P (3.66) = 41.46.

On the second basis, not only will N and O be excluded, but E as well. And, be it noted, E is one of the prior wants which, as we shall judge from general observation, are never excluded.

The reader will have noted that in the foregoing examples, when the ratios are considered at all, the really critical decisions—inclusion or exclusion—have escaped the difficulty we are under by reason of lack of uniform quantities in either dimension of our ratios upon which to base comparisons. For all inclusions have had ratios with values above unity, if included, and below unity, if excluded. The capacity to determine that intensity exceeds or is less than "real cost" of a full measure is basic to our analysis and is clearly evident in real life. It is upon that comparison that the determination of the limit of capacity rests.

But the acute reader will also have noted that, in these examples, we have arbitrarily considered capacities whose limits do not, in these numerical terms, have ratios with values of unity. Whereas, in the order of ratios, when we did not consider capacity, we used the ratio with a value of unity (1:1) as the basis for inclusion or exclusion, when we introduced an arbitrary quantity of capacity we necessarily assumed a ratio with a value somewhere between N (1.16) and O (1.0)—or say 1.10—for the 17 unit limit, and one somewhere between P (1.5) and E (1.33)—or say 1.35—for the 43 unit limit. This brings in the question of the moving limit of capacity which we shall examine in Section A 3 of Chapter 14. Here it will have to suffice to say that all we mean

would seem necessary to conclude that it would be passed over under such conditions *if* the order of ratios is governing.

This demonstration makes it quite clear, I think, that the two virtual orders of preference—one based on the influence of wants alone and the other based on the order of ratios—cannot coincide and that there is no possible way of reconciling them or of finding a compromise between them. Behavior must follow one or the other. It cannot follow both at the same time. Our next task is to determine, if possible, whether behavior *always* follows one, or *always* the other, or whether it *sometimes* follows one and *sometimes* the other. As to this we seem to be able to draw several general conclusions from the abstract examples given above.

1. With regard to the first series—the prior wants—(I in Fig. 40) when considered alone, it would appear that an order of preference based on the order of ratios does not conform to the historical order in which man added provision as his capacity began to increase beyond the original point at which he was limited to the satisfying of those wants only upon which his continued animal existence depended. On the other hand, an order of preference based on the order of priority does seem to conform to that history. We do not have to accept General Walker's specific order—subsistence, clothing and shelter, wife, child.[24] But we do seem to have to accept an order of this kind, as the purely animal existence of the pithecanthropus evolved into that of early tool-using man.

2. With regard to the second series—the minor wants—(II in Fig. 40), an order of preference based on the order of priority seems to bear a considerable resemblance to the facts we observe. But, then, so does an order of preference based on the order of ratios, at least in part.

To start with, if we admit any limit of capacity at all, we recognize at once the case covered by our example of the exclusion of K. If the satisfaction of some subordinate want—even a relatively intense one—absorbs all remaining capacity, it may be passed over. Even if a man could make available $650 and therefore could buy a motor car, but, if

---

by that is that the supposition of 17 units of capacity would involve a rise of about 10% in the intensity of the last hour and that of 43 units would involve a rise of about 35% —i.e., both mean a prolongation of the working-day from its duration as assumed when the numerical values were set. Actually, we hold that the only ratio that can be recognized as the basis for the limit of capacity or for other inclusion and exclusion is that of 1:1 (or equality).

[24] Walker, *418*, 294–298. This question is considered in Appendix VI, Section G.

he did that, he would have to leave all lesser wants unsatisfied, he would usually get along without it. Here we are stating the compulsory choice in the same terms we did on p. 873. Approximately the same quantity of effort ("real cost") may serve to satisfy K only, or all of L, M, N, and O. Individually the latter are all less intense than K; but viewed in the aggregate their satisfaction might seem greater than that of K. But this compulsory choice is only set under the influence of "real costs." It consists of two alternative allocations of a single block of cost.

However, as we shall see more clearly when we come, in Chapter 14, to consider the question of the limit of the working-day, this choice may also be made in other terms, at once or eventually. For, if K is passed over, it remains unsatisfied. It has only been deferred—moved further along the order of preference. If so, the question of extending the working-day so as to include it may ultimately arise. When it does, the intensity of the want K will be contrasted with the intensity of the further effort and sacrifice (added hours) required to satisfy it. At that point the ratio must be governing. Perhaps it is so, or is sometimes so, at once. That is, it may be that K, when it is first excluded, is not excluded because it is the lesser of two alternatives of which the other alternative is the satisfaction of L, M, N, and O, but because it is the lesser of two alternatives of which the other alternative is release from the requisite hours of effort and the enjoyment of those hours of leisure —i.e., it is excluded because, at the time, its ratio has a value less than unity. Perhaps our man recognizes at once that he could earn the necessary \$650 for a motor car, if he were willing to extend his working-hours; but he is not willing. It seems likely that this type of choice is made sometimes on one of these bases and sometimes on the other—that sometimes K is squeezed out by reason of a preference for L, M, N, and O, and sometimes by reason of the fact that it seems not to be worth the effort (or money).

It will be noted that, in what we have called the "compulsory choice," we have set the alternatives as K *vs.* L, M, N, and O. That is by way of the least possible admission with regard to the interference of the order of ratios with a virtual order of preference based on the order of priority. For L, M, N, and O are only the alternatives if the tendency is to follow the order of priority. On the other hand, if such a tendency does not exist—if the order of ratios only is followed—then this question would never arise. For, in the series based on that criterion

—Q, M, L, S, P, and N—Want K does not appear at all. If the order of ratios were the order of consideration, since K only appears in that order after the limit of capacity has been reached, K would never have come up for consideration. Because this question is observed constantly to arise we must conclude that the underlying tendency is to consider wants in the order of priority, and that the influence of "real costs" (the ratios) only enters into this order of consideration as a disturbing factor.

3. In the foregoing we have suggested, as one of the two bases on which such a choice may be made, a comparison of the intensity of the want with the effort required. The critical point in this comparison only appears where the limit of capacity is being fixed, or in terms of that limit. At that point the ratio, intensity to "real cost," certainly becomes an interfering factor. But the form in which it appears there is somewhat different from the one we have presented. Prior to that point the inverse dimension of the ratio has been stated only in terms of a unit of "real cost" which is uniformly and definitely weighted in terms of a given last hour's work. But, at the point where the limit of capacity is determined, the inverse dimension of the ratio comes to be differently weighted according as the proposed last hour is at the end of a shorter, equal, or longer day, and therefore represents less, the same, or more intensity of effort and sacrifice. In view of our previous analysis of the determination of the working-day, it is clear that this means that, with the exception to be stated below, it cannot be the least want up to that point, in terms of intensity only, that is determining at the margin, but rather that it must be the want the value of whose ratio is lowest up to that point. If so, we would have to admit that, around the margin, wants are always arranged in the order of ratios, not in that of priority. And, if that is so, it seems necessary also to admit that wants lying beyond—perhaps far beyond—this general range in the order of priority might well have been brought forward, if their "real cost" were low and therefore the values of their ratios sufficiently high.

4. The question then arises whether the interfering effects of the order of ratios upon the virtual order of preference based on the order of priority is ever observed among the prior wants (I in Fig. 40), when these are considered along with the subordinate wants. In our last example (above) of a fixed capacity covering both series we found that, upon the basis of the order of ratios, Want E would be excluded

while several minor wants, Q, M, L, S, and P, would be included. This does not appear to accord with the facts. We do not observe cases where men habitually exclude such a prior want as protection, for instance, if their capacity has reached that point in the order of priority, merely because protection is as expensive as the satisfaction of many subordinate wants.[25] This suggests again (as in 1, above) that the order of ratios does not apply to the prior wants. But that raises a difficulty. If the order of ratios does not alter the order of priority through the range of prior wants, does that mean that the ratio of no prior want ever determines the limit of capacity? There we seem to have to make a qualification in the shape of a guess. It seems probable that, so long as capacity can only provide for prior wants, its limit is always set by the least intense want [26] in that range of the order of priority to which it will reach. As capacity expands along that range, the ratio of the marginal want in that order determines the fixing of the limit, or is adjusted to it. Until all prior wants are provided for, practically no subordinate wants are considered at all. And, even if, as capacity expands to cover subordinate wants as well, some of these subordinate wants prove to have a ratio with a higher value than the lowest value of any ratio among the prior wants, they will never displace any of the latter.

Let us attempt now to refine these four points into a somewhat rough generalization. If, first, we use our analytical tool of a conceptually moving limit of capacity in order to obtain a complete order of preference, we come to this conclusion: The limit of capacity must always be set in terms of the ratio of intensity to "real cost." There is no other way to account for such a limit. Thus the influence of "real costs" must always be operative, even if only at that point. This is the minimum of interference, which we have to concede for the influence of the order of ratios in the order of preference based upon the order of priority.[27] Beyond this limit all wants are excluded. That is, all wants whose ratios have a value less than unity are excluded by reason of their position in the order of ratios.

[25] In Appendix VI, Section B we consider the question whether this can be explained on the ground of relative intensity only.

[26] Not the ratio with the lowest value. This may also involve the further assumption that, at that stage in the development of technique, the marginal (least) want has allocated to it a fixed block of working equal to its intensity. On this see Appendix VI, Section H.

[27] We should also remind the reader that in Section B we have admitted that the influence of "real costs" is determining in the selection of the preferred means for each want through the process of weighting the unweighted terms of substitution.

Through the first range of the order of priority, which contains the great prior wants (necessities), the ratio has no influence except to set the limit of capacity so long as capacity is less than sufficient to provide for all prior wants.[28] As the limit of capacity is moved through this range the actual order of preference follows the order of priority—after A comes B, then C, etc.

When capacity begins to extend over subordinate wants the method of operation changes somewhat. Whenever expanding capacity reaches a want the value of whose ratio is lower than that of the ratio at the limit of capacity,[29] the order of preference passes it over and proceeds to the next, and so on. But this is the same as saying that the discard remains unsatisfied. Then, having been gauged in terms of the ratio, it must be moved forward to a range where the order of ratios obtains. For, if capacity later extends to the position in the order of ratios in which this want finds itself, the question will arise whether to expand capacity further in order to include provision for it on the basis of its ratio, intensity to "real cost," when the "real cost" is reweighted in terms of a new last hour. In other words such an excluded want may become marginal sometime.

However, now that we have introduced the moving limit of capacity, we must also recognize a possibility that did not appear before. Subordinate wants with relatively high costs, but whose ratios have nevertheless a value greater than unity, may be merely temporarily passed over and thus show a tendency, one by one, to become rearranged at some later point in the order of preference but still within the limit. Such a tendency may not work with certainty or precision. For instance, in our series above, N, the value of whose ratio is only 1.16, might be deferred to P (1.5) and Q (5), which are near it in the order of priority and whose combined "real costs" (4.44) are less than those of N (6). On the other hand, L, the value of whose ratio is 3, might be satisfied, in the course of expanding capacity, before Q, the value of whose ratio is 4, merely because, when L was reached, Q was too far along the order of priority to have been considered as yet. Thus this tendency toward deferment may be evinced only when the differences in the values of ratios are marked, and then only when

[28] We discuss possible explanations of the exemption of prior wants from this influence in Appendix VI, Section B. We also discuss the historical question of such an insufficiency of capacity in Appendix VI, Section G.

[29] That is, by definition, a value less than unity when weighted with the intensity of the last hour.

the wants are neighboring in the order of priority. But the very fact of such deferment by reason of a low value for the ratio must mean that such wants congregate among others with similar values and therefore that there is a later range in the actual order of preference which is largely determined by the values of ratios.

Let us now abandon our purely analytical tool, the conceptually moving limit of capacity, retaining it only as an historical fact, even if for one man's life. We still have left an order of preference because, for any given capacity, whether limited to or extending beyond the prior wants, the order in which the wants first come up for consideration, at least up to some range, appears to be their order of priority, not the order of their ratios. Throughout the range of prior wants, the ratios, based on minimum "real costs," have no effect. The order of preference follows the order of consideration which is the order of priority. Thereafter, among subordinate wants, whenever there appears a want with a ratio of low value—high cost—one hesitates. One compares allocation of the required quantity of "real cost" (effort) to this want alone with allocation to a group of others—probably not too much further along the order of priority—which can be satisfied with about the same quantity of "real cost." As a result this want is temporarily passed over. To this extent one makes a mass choice rather than only a series of choices. In such a choice the order of priority seems to retain some influence. But the order of ratios has interfered to defer or exclude a high cost want, though probably only in terms of rough, not precise, comparisons. Even then the deferred want may reappear further along, before the limit is reached. If it does not, that can only be because the value of its ratio is less than unity. In that event, the influence of "real costs" has been decisive. The comparison has been between this want and its own cost, not between this and other wants with about the same "real cost." This emphasis on the influence of the order of priority, as the basis of the order of consideration, should not be taken to exclude the possibility that a very subordinate want—say W—coming long after the range in the order of priority in which the limit of capacity is settled, should, given a very low cost, be made sufficiently conspicuous by the high value of its ratio to lead to its being considered, brought forward, and included in the order of preference. The final result of all these rearrangements away from the order of priority would be to group near the limit of capacity those wants the values of whose ratios were above but approaching unity, at some certain weighting. Thus, in that range, the order of ratios would have become the chief influence. Finally, we agree that the limit of capacity must always be determined by the ratio with a value of unity—i.e., solely by the order of ratios.

In fine, and to put our generalization in the most succinct form that seems possible, we hazard the hypothesis, though we cannot prove it, that man's successive consideration of his wants remains always chiefly in terms of his order of priority—crudely stated, how much he wants something. In the order of preference, the terminal point at which the limit of capacity is fixed is, in fact, that at which he wants something else (i.e., leisure) more. Therefore, that point is determined solely by the ratio. Along the course of the order of priority, and consideration, the influence of the order of ratios begins to enter, but only as an interfering factor, only when the ratio has a value less than unity or when differences in the values of the ratios are marked, and then only after what man regards as his necessities are all provided for.[30] So long as his necessities cannot be fully provided for we hold that his order of priority is subject to no interference or correction by the order of ratios in so far as current provision is concerned, except in fixing capacity.[31] Step by step along the order of priority, and of consideration, by reason of diminishing intensity of wants and therefore greater attention to their "real costs," as well as in consequence of the insertion of deferred wants, the order of ratios comes to interfere more and more effectively. Near the limit of capacity it becomes more and more governing. At the limit it governs completely, and always has. Thus, the actual order of preference emerges as the product of interferences by the influence of "real costs" in the virtual but basic order of preference resulting from the influence of wants only. This generalization, when contrasted with the one which it is intended to displace,[32] strikes one as neither neat, nor logical, nor satisfying to the susceptibilities of an intellectual aesthetic. Its only advantage seems to be that it corresponds broadly to the facts of life; whereas the other does not.

Having arrived at this tentative and rough generalization, it is now necessary to go back and remove the scaffolding by means of which

[30] As noted above, possible explanations of this last exception are considered in Appendix VI, Section B.

[31] This last phrase is intended to permit the intrusion of present wants into the planned allocation of capacity among current provisions, though only within the limits outlined in Chapter 10 (see pp. 655–656).

[32] See the first pages of Appendix VI, Section A.

it was constructed—the assumption that there can be an order of ratios with no uniform quantity in either dimension upon which to base comparisons. It is clear that our only use of the order of ratios has escaped this difficulty. We have used it to define the limit of capacity; but that is defined in terms of equality between the two dimensions of the ratio. We have used it to define the range of wants which, in the order of preference, become rearranged near the limit of capacity; but that only means that the inverse dimension is felt to be approaching close to equality with the direct dimension. We have used it to define what wants are excluded; but that only means that the inverse dimension is felt to be greater than the direct dimension. We have otherwise used it only when the alternative is offered of applying "real cost" either to one want whose satisfaction is conspicuously expensive, or to several whose positions in the order of priority are near, when the quantities of "real cost" required are approximately equal for the two alternatives—i.e., the inverse dimensions are near to equality. And, finally, we have suggested that conspicuously low costs may be recognized by bringing a subordinate want forward from its position in the order of priority to an earlier position in the order of preference; but this requires no precise estimate of the value of the ratio; it merely assumes that one knows when a little expense will produce considerably more than a little satisfaction.

D. MEANS SUITABLE FOR SEVERAL WANTS

We now proceed according to the method described at the beginning of Section C—that is, by eliminating one by one the several limiting assumptions with which we started. In this section we take the first step—the elimination of the first assumption (a) that "each means is suitable to a single want only."

1. JOINT USE FOR MEMBERS OF A CONSTELLATION

Although in Chapter 7 we outlined in some detail our analytical concept of constellations of wants, it may be well to review it briefly at this point and to elaborate it so far as that is necessary in order to examine the special ways in which the influence of "real costs" comes to bear upon the minor members of a constellation; for that is our general topic here.

So far as the usual analytical tool, complementarity, is concerned, we have found it necessary to exclude that condition from the field of finished final product. It exists, of course, in the case of intermediate product, but it is impossible to apply intermediate product to specific wants, since by definition such product does not directly serve wants. It exists, of course, as to the several materials or unfinished products that are required to composed finished final product, but only while they are not yet parts of the latter. There are only two ways of introducing complementarity into the field of final product; and neither withstands analysis. One is to define the several parts of a whole as if they were separate and complementary products. If, in order to use an automobile, gasoline is necessary, then an automobile without gasoline is not a means at all. It is, as many of us have discovered for ourselves in recent years, a white elephant. We may call it an inseparable whole when, in order to constitute a means, it must be complete. While the parts are separate they are unfinished product. The other and equally erroneous way to introduce complementarity is to ignore the fact of constellations—different wants capable of being satisfied in a joint process. If we like sugar in our tea, a spoon to stir it with and a cup and saucer to drink it out of, it is not because the tea, the sugar, the spoon, the cup and the saucer are all essential parts of a composite which satisfies a single want. For each of the wants served all but one of these means are quite dispensable. The reason we combine them is that numerous members of a constellation can then be satisfied in one process. This is an example of what we have called a conglomerate of means. But such a composite does not need to be composed of separate and independent means, as they are in this example. It may form a compound means, as we have called it, of which the several attributes serve different members of a constellation. So, in the case of the automobile we have some minimum structure which, when combined with gasoline, furnishes transportation (i.e., serves the major want). But the automobile may include attributes, or even separable parts, each of which is added to serve some minor member of this constellation. For example, we include a self-starter for convenience, tires, springs, and upholstery for comfort, and even certain attributes which are directed wholly toward the satisfaction of the want for "style" or the want for beauty. Proper analysis in terms of the want system requires that we assign each attribute of a compound means, or each separate means in a conglomerate, to the want which dictates it. On the other hand, proper analysis also requires that we assign an inseparable whole entirely to a single want, if all parts of it are indispensable for serving that want at all.

For our purposes—that is, the relation of means to wants—we may sum up these three possible types of condition as follows. Parts which constitute an inseparable whole form a single means so far as wants are concerned. When a means does not, or cannot, exist without containing more or less of several attributes which cater to different members of a constellation, it is a compound means. If the variation in quantity of any one attribute differs, beyond some minimum limit, between two or more compound means, they are different means, though substitutes for each other. When, in a single process, several separate means are used, each serving a single member, or several members, of a constellation, they do not constitute a compound means, but a conglomerate, since each can be dispensed with without affecting the others. Then each want (or group) chooses its own means independently of the others. To the extent that a composite consists of parts which are separable, each of which serves one or several members of a constellation and each of which can be dispensed with without affecting the others, the whole should be regarded as a composite of separate means (a conglomerate), similar to the previous case, not as a compound means in an analytical sense; for, again, each want (or group) may choose its own part independently of the others. What follows, therefore, does not apply to separate or composite but actually conglomerate means, which—or parts of which—can be considered separately, each for its own want or group. Such choices are affected by cost only in the way described in the previous section. This section applies only to compound means.

Let us deal first only with means whose attributes are proportionate to their quantities. This is the general case; and, so far as I can see, the only one that has been considered in the literature of subjective valuation. For this case, as we have already made clear, "substitutability," in the Pareto-Hicks phraseology, includes what are, in our version, two contradictory and mutually exclusive conditions—substitutability and preference. Strictly speaking, substitutability exists for us only when there is indifference. There is only indifference when two or more means are perfect substitutes for a single want. Even then they are indifferent only in the relative quantities which constitute their unweighted terms of substitution. There is never indifference between the satisfaction of two different wants. The satisfaction of one is never a substitute for the satisfaction of the other. The system of wants never gets on a dead center. Among the satisfactions of different wants there is always a preference; and choice is always governed by preference. True, the natural (virtual) order of preference which follows the order of priority may, in part, be overruled by considerations of relative "real costs." But that is not a substitution in any exact sense. It is also a preference, though one made in view of "real costs." So, too, is the preference which results from weighting the unweighted terms of substitution. That too does away with indifference.

That simple statement suffices for a single want and thus for the great prior wants even when each is also the major member of a constellation. But it is clear that, when the minor members of a constellation are included, the matter is greatly complicated. For, then, there is no reason to suppose that the unweighted terms of substitution for the major want among compound means will also hold good for any of the minor wants. Quantities that are indifferent for the major wants will almost certainly be subject to preferences for the minor wants—preferences which may differ for each.

We are going to confine ourselves here to the question of the influence of "real costs" on these necessarily complex choices without considering the matter of resulting segmentation, though that will be an occasional consequence where the attribute serving the minor want is proportionate to quantity, and an almost universal consequence where the attribute exists in fixed quantity. This because we are reserving the examination of the whole question of segmentation, which will be dealt with in Section F. The exposition at this point will be clarified if we consider, first and by itself, the precise nature of the conflicts in unweighted and weighted terms of substitution among the several members of a constellation, and then turn to the question of the effect of such conflicts upon the actual order of preference with due regard for the influence of "real costs."

Two compound means in which the attribute serving the minor want is proportionate to quantity may be indifferent substitutes in some quantities for both the major and the minor want; but the unweighted terms of substitution are almost certain to be different for the two wants. However, such difference does not preclude the possibility that one or the other quantity in the two ratios may be the same for both. Thus we may admit at once that, if this perhaps unusual condition subsists—if the full measure for both wants is the same for one of the means—that one will be preferred if the minor want determines. The more usual case will probably be that neither full measure will be the same for both. For example, let us suppose that, for Want A, the unweighted terms are $5af = 4a_1f_1$. That is, 5 units of *af* and 4 units of a_1f_1 constitute the full measures for A. Want F may require more or less than that quantity of either; that is, for F, full measures of *af* and a_1f_1 may be 4 and 3, or 6 and 3.5, or 4 and 5, or 6 and 5, respectively. These represent the four possible directions of variation in the two sets of terms. The last three ratios may be regarded as representing the case, for example, when, to satisfy the "sweet tooth" as well as hunger, more of either or both means (being sweet) is required.[1] If the first set of terms obtains, the two means in the quantities 5 and 4, respectively, are indifferent for both wants and either choice will be more than adequate incidentally to satiate F; if the second set of terms obtains and F determines, a_1f_1 will be elected in the quantity of 4 units and the quantity will be more than adequate to satiate F; if the third set of terms obtains and F determines, *af* will be elected in the quantity of 5 units, which is more than adequate incidentally to satiate F; but, if the fourth set of terms obtains, one more of either *af* or a_1f_1 is required for F than for A. Then, only if F is capable of inducing this additional unit of either, will it be satiated. If it is not, F will be incidentally but only partially satisfied.

Using this as a starting-point, we can now introduce the influence of "real costs" by weighting these unweighted terms. Let the "real cost" of *af* be 2 and that of a_1f_1 be 3. The weighted terms for A are now $af{:}a_1f_1 = 10{:}12$. For A, *af* will be preferred. The weighted terms for F are, for the four samples of variation, (1) 8:10.5; (2) 12:10.5; (3) 8:15; (4) 12:15. If the first ratio obtains, F is more than satiated by the choice for A, *af*, at no extra cost; the same is true if the third ratio obtains; if the second ratio obtains, F can only be satiated by substituting an excess over its own full measure of a_1f_1 at an extra cost of 0.5, or its own full measure of *af*, at an extra cost of 2; obviously a_1f_1 will be preferred by F; if the fourth ratio obtains, F can only be satiated by a larger quantity of either and therefore at an added cost of 2 or 3 respectively; obviously *af* will then be preferred by F.

[1] In the opposite direction, one can also imagine a case where the minor want's lesser requirement turns into supersatiation if one or both of the major want's full measure is chosen (e.g., it supplies too much sweetness). This negative conflict between the wants would probably not lead to a reduction in the quantity chosen, but to the election of some less sweet substitute.

We may generalize. If the preferred full measure for the major want is adequate, or more than adequate, to satiate the minor want, the minor want will not affect the choice. If it is not, but if the rejected full measure for the major want is adequate, or more than adequate, to satiate the minor want, the choice will be reversed provided the minor want affects the choice. But it will only be able to do so if it can induce the allocation of the extra "real cost" involved. If neither full measure for the major want is adequate to satiate the minor want, the choice will be made by the minor want if it affects the choice. Its choice will be made for that means which makes it chargeable with the lesser extra "real cost." But, again, it will only be able to induce this choice if it can induce the allocation of this increment of "real cost." Here we have a certain case of the entry of the influence of "real cost" so far as the minor want is concerned. Being a minor, and therefore subordinate, want the position of the want in the order of preference may be determined by the position of its ratio in the order of ratios. But the ratio itself will not be the usual one. It will, instead, be the intensity of the minor want to the *excess* cost only of its full measure of its preferred means. The effect of each minor want, in turn, will appear in the order of preference on the same basis as that described in the previous section except that the inverse dimension of its ratio will be the excess of cost of its preferred substitute only.

When we come to consider analogous choices among compound means in which the attribute serving the minor want exists in fixed quantity, we may at first ignore the quantities constituting full measures for the major want. For now, by definition, the respective quantities have no bearing on the matter so far as the minor want is concerned. Any quantities that are indifferent for the major want will nevertheless arrange themselves in an order of preference for the minor want. In a sense, the different means may still be called substitutes for the minor want; but under no conditions are they—nor can they be made—indifferent or perfect substitutes. Let us say that there are four means, af, a_1f_1, a_2f_2 and a_3f_3, which in certain quantities are indifferent for A, but which contain respectively 25 percent, 50 percent, 75 percent and 100 percent of the attribute serving F. The percentage, 100, means no more than that a_3f_3 is the most satisfying known means for F, or that it satiates F. Nor do the other percentages mean much more than an arrangement in terms of more or less. It is only for the sake of example that we state them in terms of numbers. The only case we need to consider is the one where the greater the quantity of the attribute that is contained, the more expensive is the means.[2] Therefore, let us suppose that a full measure for A of these four means costs 10, 15, 20, and 25, respectively. Obviously *af* will be preferred for A according to its weighted terms of substitution. Equally obviously, the order of preference for F, among these means will be a_3f_3, a_2f_2, a_1f_1, *af*. Since all are indifferent in the unweighted terms for A, and since *af* is preferred by A on the basis of its weighted terms, any other choice will depend on F. If F is to induce the choice of a_1f_1, at an extra cost of 5, or of a_2f_2, at an extra cost of 10, or of a_3f_3, at an extra cost of 15, it must, first, come into consideration on its own account, second, be able to induce the allocation of one of these increments of cost, and, third, be itself chargeable with whatever extra cost it is able to induce.[3] Which of the four is chosen depends, then, on whether, and how much, "real cost" is allocable by F. Hence this is again a case where the ratio is determining so far as the minor want is concerned. Hence we place wants catered to by attributes of this kind in the range of the order of preference where "real costs" are the predominating influence. However, we must recognize that these several ratios, showing different costs in the inverse dimension, no longer necessarily show the same magnitudes in the direct dimension. For, almost by definition, the different percentages of attributes seem to represent also different degrees of satisfaction. In other words, we have here a case of segmentation. Therefore, we must defer any further investigation of the factors determining the choice until we consider that subject.

Comparison of these two schemes with reality makes it clear that one further complication is necessary. In the foregoing we have treated the substitutions induced by minor wants of constellations, wherever they occur, as if they were made on an all or none basis. That is not always the case. Sometimes the effect of minor wants is to induce partial substitution—that is, an assortment of two or more substitutes in definite proportions. Since this condition can certainly arise when

[2] Obviously, when this is not so, no question of extra cost would arise, since the major want would elect the cheapest full measure.

[3] In less abstract terms, we choose according to cost among the means that cater equally to the single major want. As a result we may gain more or less incidental satisfaction of minor wants through the "overtones" of the means. But if we deliberately choose among the substitutes for the major want any means the cost of whose full measure is higher than the minimum, we do so for the sake of a greater satisfaction of the minor want. This greater satisfaction, being no longer incidental, must be at the expense of the minor want.

the attributes are proportionate to quantity, let us consider that case first. Let us suppose that, for Want A, 4 units of *af*, at a cost of 2 per unit, represent a full measure, at a total cost of 8; that for Want A, 12 units of a_1f_1, at a cost of 1 per unit, represent a full measure, at a total cost of 12; and that the corresponding full measures for Want F are 12 *af* (@ 2) = 24, or 4 a_1f_1 (@ 1) = 4. Want A, choosing first, selects *af* on the basis of its weighted terms of substitution. If F is considered, it cannot choose less than a full measure for A. To obtain a full measure for itself, therefore, its choice lies between 12 *af* and 12 a_1f_1. The first, 12 *af*, will cost 24, or 16 units of extra cost; the second 12 a_1f_1, will cost 12, or 4 units of extra cost. The first choice would show an excess of 8 units over a full measure for A; the second would be in excess, for F, by the same quantity. Now, since the unweighted terms of substitution for A can be reduced to 1 *af* = 3 a_1f_1, 3 a_1f_1 will substitute for 1 *af*. Then 3 *af* + 3 a_1f_1 will constitute a composite full measure for A. Similarly, for F, 3 *af* + 3 a_1f_1 also constitutes a composite full measure, since, for F, the unweighted terms of substitution are 3 *af* = 1 a_1f_1. But this composite full measure, 3 *af* + 3 a_1f_1, costs only 9, or 1 extra. It will therefore be preferred by F over 12 *af* or 12 a_1f_1 at extra costs of 16 or 4, respectively. It will be noted that the condition precedent to partial substitution is that the quantities required for full measures for the minor want vary in the opposite direction from those required for full measures of the major want.

It is evident that a similar situation cannot arise where the attribute serving the minor want exists in fixed but different quantities in the several substitutes. There we are not dealing with full measures for the minor want, but only with the number of natural or arbitrary units which constitute a full measure for the major want. If the terms for A are as above, let us say that the choice for F is between *af*, containing 25 percent of the special attribute, and a_2f_2, containing 75 percent. The first will yield only 25 percent satisfaction, but that will be at no extra cost. The second will yield 75 percent satisfaction at an extra cost of 10 units. The choice will then depend on whether or not F is capable of inducing this quantity of extra cost.[4] Not only may a composite of

[4] It will be well at this point to illustrate the three general conditions and their effects by examples from real life, from which the generalizations were drawn.

The pure case of extra cost for extra quantities is exemplified by housing. One room for a family and its animals does supply, and has supplied, shelter. More rooms or separate buildings are required for cleanliness, freedom from insects and noxious smells, privacy, quiet, variety, conformity, esteem, etc. Here the minor wants are served by more (and bigger) rooms. Better rooms are of the next order.

The pure case of extra cost for means with attributes in fixed quantity is exemplified

the two be impossible—e.g., half of one chair plus half of another—but, if it is possible, it might yield no satisfaction to F—e.g., half of one gown plus half of another.

In the analysis of the influence of "real costs" upon the resolution of conflicts among members of constellations as to selections among these two types of compound means, we have, already and incidentally, practically settled the question of the effect of such resolutions upon the actual order of preference—that is, the question whether the summation of the influence of the member wants of a constellation is what we have called successive or simultaneous. In the use of our analytical tool, the moving limit of capacity, we conceive that this limit moves along the order of priority so that each want is considered in turn. After the great prior wants are passed some subordinate wants may be passed over by reason of high cost. Even within the ultimate range in which the actual limit is set, some subordinate wants, still further along the order of priority but which can be satisfied at very low cost, may be included (brought forward). But, in general, the order of priority is the order of consideration. Precisely this procedure seems generally to apply to the members of a constellation. If that is the order in which the several members of a constellation which are scattered along the order of priority come up for consideration, it becomes evident that

by clothing. A single garment of a certain size and weight serves for protection. Elaborateness of various kinds is of the order of fixed attributes. These attributes serve the minor wants for comfort, beauty, conformity, esteem, etc. The demand for more (but not larger) garments is again of the order of more rooms. But the wants it serves are not only those served by better "quality"; they include adaptation to different occasions, variety, etc.

The pure case of extra cost for a composite of several means is exemplified by meals. Most economies have a basic food (such as bread, potatoes, or rice), which is usually the cheapest means to satisfy hunger. It is possible to get along on it alone. But the other specific hungers, taste, conformity, esteem, etc., as well as the want for variety, all being minor members of the constellation, may induce the partial substitution of other foods. Such substitution will reduce the quantity of the basic food used; but the reduced quantity of the basic food combined with all the substitutes must satisfy hunger whether or not they completely satisfy all the minor members of the constellation.

This may be a good point at which to define our usage of the term "want for variety." We do not know whether it is actually a separate want. It may be no more than a constantly fluctuating relationship between the intensities or the preferences of other wants. But, for analytical purposes, it is convenient to treat it as a separate want, since its effects appear as if it were. Analytically, it should be regarded as one of the causes of difference between successive orders of preference (successive days). It alters unweighted terms of substitution and even the order of priority from day to day, by throwing its weight around—perhaps by simultaneous summation—among the satisfactions of other wants. One says, "No, I had chicken for dinner last night"—and that settles it. (See Appendix VI, Section F.)

successive summation will be the usual type. Each minor want in turn will influence only the excess quantity that it requires or the change among substitutes to one that suits it better. To the extent that each in turn can be satisfied by the last choice of its predecessors, its satisfaction will be incidental, and it cannot then be said to have an influence. To the extent that it is not so satisfied and its influence leads to an excess quantity or a different substitute, it must be capable, through its own influence, of inducing the extra "real cost." True, that is summation. The total cost of the final choice is divided among the determining members of the constellation—the minimum being determined by and chargeable to the major want and each increment of "real cost" thereafter being determined by and chargeable to the minor want that has induced it. But it is successive summation, because each has exercised its influence only as it came to be considered in the order of priority. The whole force of the constellation has not combined to give its aggregate intensity a more forward position in the order of priority and thus to affect its capacity to compete with other wants or other constellations.

On the other hand, there seem to be cases where simultaneous summation occurs. This was noted in Chapter 8. There we supposed that such cases are limited to situations in which a single attribute serves—or all of several attributes serve—a number of members of a constellation. When simultaneous summation occurs, several wants are conceived to be lumped together so far as their intensity is concerned and therefore to be able to exert their influence jointly, both as to position in the order of consideration and as to the capacity to induce an allocation of "real cost." I fancy that this is confined to wants which are not clearly distinguished by the chooser and which comprise, therefore, a whole group of only the minor members of a constellation or a constellation all of whose members are minor. To the chooser it may appear that such choices are made for a number of different reasons rather than to satisfy a number of separate and distinguishable wants.[5] Actually, I suspect that each reason usually appeals to what should be defined as a separate want. If this limitation to groups of minor wants is correct, then simultaneous summation and the resulting confusion in the order of priority only influences the order of preference on special occasions and along its further reaches. But the admission

[5] This exception—simultaneous summation—is inserted chiefly to cover such choices as those among works of art, etc., in line with the discussion in Appendix VI, Section A.

that such exceptions occur seems necessary to explain the observed inclusion in the order of preference of certain somewhat expensive means which do not, apparently, serve any one want which the observer would suppose to be of considerable importance. If simultaneous summation occurs, it is not to be supposed that each of the wants is chargeable with its own excess cost. Rather the whole aggregate is chargeable with the whole undivided cost. And this, whether the chooser regards the influences as separate wants or merely as reasons for his choice.

2. ALTERNATIVE USES

The general notion of alternative uses pertains chiefly to unfinished final product and to intermediate product, rather than to finished final product. At the earlier stages of production—especially the raw material stage—unfinished product is capable of diversion to different forms of final product more often than it is not. And, if the use of an intermediate product is identified by the final product toward which it is directed, the same is true there—though perhaps to a lesser extent than formerly.[6] However, though our chief interest here is the relation of final product (means) to wants, we may, in passing, consider how choices among alternative uses are made even at earlier stages, so far as a direct economy is concerned. This will be useful also because the same principles seem to govern where final product is capable of alternative uses.

Since the number of alternative uses to be provided for is one of the chief factors determining the quantity wanted, it becomes necessary to distinguish between products which can be made in precisely the planned quantities and those which cannot. The latter are chiefly those products (including raw materials) which depend on biological processes and which therefore fluctuate in quantity from season to season, etc. Thus we treat, first, of intended quantities and, second, of unintended quantities. Moreover, since we are reserving the questions which arise when different portions of the output are produced at different "real costs," we will confine ourselves here to quantities produced at uniform "real cost."[7]

[6] That is, modern apparatus for production seems to be becoming more and more specialized. The printing plants designed for printing books no longer print newspapers, and vice versa.

[7] See Section F, below, for differential costs.

Some final products can only be made of a single material, or unfinished product, or by a single power, or by means of a single intermediate product. This is not true, however, of most cases; usually suitable materials, etc., may substitute for each other on a basis analogous to our unweighted terms of substitution, though probably they are not usually strictly indifferent even on those terms.[8] If a final product, whose quantity is intended, stands or falls according as a certain material, etc., is allotted to it or not, it is clear that the only question involved is whether that final product will be wanted at a "real cost" which includes the necessary "real cost" of its essential material, etc. If a final product does not depend on a single material, etc., the only question involved is whether it will be wanted at a "real cost" which is constituted of the aggregate attributable "real costs" of all the least cost substitutes in each set of weighted terms of substitution. This with due allowance for the difference in "quality" which the different substitutes confer. As to any particular material, etc., its uses only extend to the products in which it is the least cost substitute. In either case, a constituent material, etc., at any given "real cost," will be produced in an intended quantity sufficient to cover all its uses as thus determined.[9]

When the quantity is unintended, the process may be reversed.[10] If it is greater than would have been planned if subject to control, "real costs" may become no bar to the use of the full quantity.[11] Then, if the material, etc., is essential for some final product which was not wanted at its "real cost," that final product may nevertheless be produced if it is wanted at the "real cost" of the other constituents plus some—or even no—allowance for the "real cost" of this essential constituent. Or, if the material, etc., is one of a set of substitutes on some unweighted terms, its "real cost" may be ignored to the extent necessary to cause its substitution in sufficient cases to use up the unintended

[8] To the extent that they are not strictly indifferent they should be treated as entering into *different* final products. But we must not apply that notion too strictly. Difference and indifference are ranges along a scale, not a hard and fast dichotomy.

[9] This conclusion also applies, subject to some other extraneous influences, to "price" in an indirect economy. That is, the quantity produced will be that which, it is expected, can be disposed of at a "price" covering its "real cost."

[10] It will be reversed only in so far as the excess over the average season's production, or other fluctuating output, is not merely stored as future provision to compensate for the deficits at other times, or is not merely wasted.

[11] To the extent that "real costs" are determined by the advance allocation of effort they will, of course, be less per unit if the quantity produced is greater than the average, and more per unit if the quantity is less than the average.

quantity available. On the other hand, if the quantity is less than would have been planned if subject to control, the material, etc., may be withdrawn from a final product for which it is essential so that such product cannot be made. And, where it is one of a set of substitutes, it may be withdrawn in favor of the cheapest alternative substitute, so far as is necessary to limit its use to the quantity available.

Where the material, etc., is one of a set of substitutes in all its uses, the several weighted terms of substitution in which it appears can be arranged in a descending order of the "real costs" of the previous lowest cost substitutes, multiplied by the quantity required for each use. If the unintended quantity of the particular material, etc., is in excess of plan it will be applied as far as it reaches along that descending order. That is, this material, etc., will itself be treated as the lowest cost substitute at any arbitrary figure which will make it such, so far as the quantity reaches along this descending order—the order of successively smaller economizings. Again, all the sets of weighted terms of substitution in which this material, etc., has previously been the lowest cost substitute can be arranged in an ascending order of differences between the cost of this and the next lowest cost material, etc., again multiplied by the quantity required for each use. If the unintended quantity wanted is less than plan, it will be withdrawn along that ascending order as far as is necessary. That is, it will give place successively to the next lowest cost substitute in the order of successively greater differences.

The determination of the point, or points, in the whole order of possible additional applications or successive withdrawals of unintended quantities which will be occupied by the essential uses is more complex. For, then, the order of priority and the order of ratios enter the picture. The order of priority alone will govern the position in an order of preference which is occupied by a prior want whose only means stands or falls according to whether an essential material, etc., is assigned to it or is not. For, as we have noted, "real costs" are then ignored. But the order of ratios alone will govern the position of a subordinate want whose only reason for previous inclusion or exclusion has been that, at the previous "real cost," its ratio had a value above or below unity. The choice will be made at the point at which it is decided that using the material, etc., where it is essential, is preferable or not preferable to substituting it elsewhere, or at which it is decided that forgoing it where it is essential is preferable or not preferable, in spite of the necessary rise in "real cost" which will result if it is withdrawn from a substitution elsewhere. We will have to leave it at that.[12]

Within the limited scope in which final product is capable of alternative uses a similar analysis applies. For the most part such cases exist only where we still use, as final product, a material, etc., in approximately its natural state—though, of course, not at its extractive stage (e.g., water or milk). At given and uniform "real costs," though "real cost" per unit is the same for all uses, "real cost" per full measure will probably be different for each use. On the other hand, subjective value (usefulness) of full measures, will be different for each use, but will presumably be the same whatever substitute is used. Full measures for each of the uses will be given their respective places in the order of preference, those for prior wants in the order of priority and those for subordinate wants more and more according to their positions in the order of ratios.[13] This series of uses will include all wants for which this is the sole means and all those for which this product is preferred on the basis of its weighted terms of substitution (because it is the lowest cost among indifferent substitutes).

If the quantity produced is planned (intended), it will be so planned that it is adequate to extend along this order up to the point at which "real cost" begins to exceed subjective value—that is, where the ratio, intensity to "real cost" of a full measure, becomes less than unity. In all prior uses subjective value will exceed "real cost." We do not need to know the magnitude of this excess in any case nor the relative magnitudes in the different cases.

On the other hand, if the quantity produced is unintended—that is, if it is greater or less than what would have been planned on the basis of "real cost," as above—the matter is more complicated. For then, "real cost," being ignored more or less, it does not serve as a basis

[12] In an indirect economy, "price" will, theoretically at least, be just low enough to induce a combination of the necessary quantity of these two kinds of additional uses. To the extent that such "price" is below "real cost" the difference (loss) will be ignored. To the extent that it is above, it will produce a windfall gain. So it happens that a large crop of wheat may force the price down to a level at which it pays to use the surplus as a substitute for other stock feeds.

[13] Let us make this point clear. If the sizes of the full measures were the same for all alternative uses, the series would necessarily be arranged in the order of priority. This because the inverse dimension of all ratios would be the same—the same cost per unit of means and the same number of units per full measure. If the sizes of the full measures were different, the values of the ratios would no longer follow the order of priority. Then to the extent, but only to the extent, that the order of preference is modified away from the order of priority under the influence of the order of ratios, the series of alternative uses would also be modified from its arrangement in the order of priority.

for defining the limit of capacity. Moreover, then there may arise a question analogous to that of an essential material, etc. As remarked above, for some want in the list of alternative uses there may be no substitute final product. Taking the analysis of alternative uses of material, etc., as a basis, we seem warranted in applying it here as follows: Where alternative uses exist for a means, but for each use there is no substitute, an unintended excess quantity will probably be applied along, and in, the order of preference to wants which would have been excluded by the limit of capacity if the quantity had been as planned. To that extent "real costs" will be ignored. But this allocation will probably be affected by the different sizes of full measures if there are several such hitherto excluded wants. Thus there might be instances in which a group of the lesser among these wants, the aggregate of whose full measures is about the same as the full measure for the greatest of these wants, could divert the excess to themselves by a sort of simultaneous summation. This allocation might also be affected if the much smaller size of its full measure gave a much higher ratio to a very subordinate want. All this statement really means is that the series of alternative uses, when the means is the sole means for each, probably tends to follow the order of preference as developed in the previous section, though, if costs were entirely ignored, it would be governed wholly by the order of priority. A deficient quantity would probably be withdrawn on the same principle, subject to the same qualifications. However, unless the unintended quantity were very short of plan, it is unlikely that the withdrawals would reach back further than those wants whose position in the order of preference had been fixed by the order of ratios.

Where substitutes are available, the order in which additional uses of unintended quantities would be included, or the order in which they would be withdrawn, would be quite different and would practically ignore the order of preference. Then the whole question would depend *primarily* on the greatest saving of "real cost" of substitutes, if a means were available in excess quantity, and the least additional "real cost" to be incurred for substitutes, if it were available only in deficient quantity.[14] That would depend on the unweighted and weighted terms of substitution for each want involved, as well as on

[14] Since the question of a saving in, or an additional expenditure of, "real cost" involves also the question of the limit of capacity, which we shall discuss in Chapter 14, the term "primarily" is used here advisedly.

the relative size of full measures of each means among the different wants involved. Since substitutions of this means for others, or substitutions of others for this, would generally be made in terms of full measures,[15] correct estimates would involve some elaborate calculations. The correct basis would be application in the order of successively smaller economizings in "real cost" of substitutes, per unit of the excess means, and withdrawal in the order of successively greater additional "real cost" for substitutes, per unit of the deficient means.

In general, we may say that the order in which alternative uses for means without substitutes are excluded or included is, with due allowance for the partial ignoring of "real cost" if the quantity is unintended, the order of preference as worked out in Section C 4. The corresponding order for means with substitutes is one based chiefly on the facts which go to determine the weighted terms of substitution of the several wants involved. In neither case does any amount of inclusion or exclusion of alternative uses alter the subjective valuation of any means. For the subjective value of a means capable of alternative uses is different for each of the wants for which it is used, and the extension of its use to wants which confer less subjective value upon it does not reduce the subjective value placed upon it by those which value it more highly—nor vice versa.[16]

Since this formulation directly contradicts the customary statements which have been made on the basis of a combination of the first and second parts of the conglomerate assumption of marginal utility theory,[17] an explanation seems to be in order. It has usually been said that the allocation of a means over its alternative uses is such as to bring the final marginal increment allotted to each to a common level of subjective value.[18] If more is allotted to one than to another want, it is

[15] Except in the case of partial substitutions, as defined in Section D 1, and such other instances of segmentation as we decide to include when we come to consider that subject in Section F.

[16] In an indirect economy "price" would rise and fall as indicated in connection with raw materials, etc., above (see note 12, above). But, if the "price" rose or fell, it would no more represent subjective valuation than it does when it remains at the level of "real cost." When "price" rises or falls from the "real cost" it merely causes the exclusion or inclusion of alternative uses for wants whose subjective values come to be below the new level or were below the old level; and it merely diminishes or increases the difference between "price" and the subjective valuation conferred by those wants which remain above the new level or were above the old.

[17] See pp. 437 ff.

[18] For instance, it is stated in approximately this form by Marshall (*291*, 231). In a commonly used economic textbook (*391*, 144), the statement is similar, though applying largely to materials, etc.

assumed that this is because the first want starts at a higher level of intensity (or what not) and thus requires more to bring it down to the common level. In the first place, I think we have demonstrated that the supposition of declining intensity during a single satisfaction, upon which this construction necessarily rests, is an impossible one. In the second place, it appears that any notion is entirely unreal which assumes that the allocation of any quantity of a means which is inadequate to satiate all the wants it can serve is made in such a way that none of them is satiated.[19] Graphically speaking, we must assert that declining curves of the wants concerned are not set alongside each other and the quantity then distributed so as to reach a common level; instead, the curves are approximately rectangular, are set in series according to one or the other of the arrangements described above, and the quantity is then distributed as far along the series as it reaches—within each use, except possibly the last, on an all or none basis. No final product begins to be used for a want later in such series until sufficient of it has been used so that all wants appearing earlier have been satiated.

In conclusion we may say that, in a direct economy, the production of a means whose quantity is under control is determined, when it can serve several wants in alternative uses, in exactly the same way as if it

[19] Wicksteed's illustration of milk (*441*, 87–90) is a good example to refer to, since milk is an authentic instance of a final product capable of alternative uses—a material used as a means in approximately its natural state. I ask the reader to look at his account and to decide for himself whether any woman in her senses cuts the allowance for the baby's bottle in order to give the cat a little milk. A still better *reductio ad absurdum* might be the example of water carried on a desert journey. If there is just enough for expected needs to satisfy thirst, it is hardly probable that any would be allowed for the lesser alternative use of washing.

Most of the illustrations given in the literature deal with materials, etc., as we defined them above, not with final product. For example, Jevons (*224*, 59) refers to barley, sugar, timber, and iron, and Wicksell (*439*, I, 37) uses corn. Such illustrations only conform to the requirement that all alternative uses should be those of a single final product in the single case of grain. And, then, the different "uses" usually all apply to a single want. But we may eliminate one possible difficulty for the reader by considering the most plausible among these illustrations. Let us suppose that, in a primitive and self-dependent small economy, the crop of grain is short. Its use as seed is primary; its use as food is secondary; and its use as feed is tertiary. Nevertheless, if very short, some grain may be used as food even at the expense of seed; and, if less short, some may be used as feed even at the expense of food. But this is not a case of alternative uses for different wants. All uses concern various kinds of future provision for a single want—hunger. Any reduction of seed may mean a short crop next year; but, if the stock is not fed, it may die during the winter. Such a situation is purely an instance of what we have called a technical necessity of the first type, in which a single material is distributed over future provisions with different dates but ultimately directed to use for one and the same want.

were a different means for each want. The only novelty is that the quantities which come within the order of preference up to the limit of capacity are summated. The same is true where the quantity is uncontrolled, except that then the "real cost" of this means may be ignored so far as necessary, leaving its allocation to be determined by the most advantageous distribution of capacity within its thus expanded or contracted limits. This last construction is worked out in Chapter 14.

E. PROVISION FOR FUTURE WANTS

1. PRELIMINARY ANALYSIS

In accordance with the procedure adopted at the beginning of Section C, we now eliminate the second simplifying assumption made there—that "the order of preference deals with current provisions only." As stated there, that assumption permitted us to consider the effect of differences in "real cost" of work only, both among the substitutes for a single want and among the preferred means for different wants. For, there, we held at zero the other variable component of "real costs." Now we proceed to consider the effect of retaining as a variable—that is, the effect of differences in "real cost" of retention only. We repeat the *only*, because here we shall assume—except in connection with the technical options—that "real costs" in work are the same for a future as they are for a current provision. However, the combination of the two analyses may turn out to give us the joint effect of differences in "real costs" of both kinds or of either kind indiscriminately. That is the question. But we must wait.

In Chapter 10 we studied the effect of futurity of various degrees for wants of various rank in the order of priority. But we did it on the simplifying assumption that "real costs" in work, per day's adequate provision, were the same for the means for all wants—subject to the effect of the technical options. We have already discarded that restriction in this chapter. However, it is necessary to make clear at the start that, in doing so, we have also altered the basis of our analysis in Chapter 10 in another way. For, since the dimensions of retaining include the dimension of work, the rate at which retaining accrues per unit of time will be different according as the "real cost" in work is different.[1] Thus, in what follows, the increment of "real costs" to be

[1] It will be recalled that in Chapter 6 we found that the dimensions of interval effort, as it accrues, are a constant fraction of duration effort per unit of time. In Chapter 10 the

added on account of retention will not vary merely with the degree of futurity, as in Chapter 10, but also with the quantity of "real cost" in work.

It will be well to remind the reader briefly of the framework in which we developed our previous analysis of the influence of futurity. When we introduce future wants in addition to current wants, as potential factors in making up the current order of preference, we must, of necessity, change our conceptual diagrammatic representation from a two-dimensional to a three-dimensional one. We conceive the current order of priority, which exists in a cross-section of time, to be arranged in a vertical plane (two-dimensional) and from left to right; but, along the course of time, and therefore in the third dimension, we conceive a series of future orders of priority—each also a cross-section—receding into the distance and diagrammatically lying behind the current order of priority. Each want in the current order is repeated in each of these future orders up to some point beyond which futurity is no longer considered. According to the assumption which forms the third part of the conglomerate assumption of marginal utility theory, the present effective intensity or force of each of these more and more distant instances of any want declines regularly in proportion to its degree of futurity.[2] This would be conceived diagrammatically in the form of lines, in the third dimension, descending across the tops of the vertical lines representing the successive instances of each want from the highest (current) to the lowest (most distant). For a number of reasons we concluded in Chapter 10 that this thesis is untenable. Instead we conceive the successive instances to be of the same current force indefinitely and, therefore, that the receding lines are level. In passing, we may also say that, for our present analytical purposes, we conceive each order of priority to be a duplicate of its predecessor.

Since, for all instances of each want, the future intensity and the present force are assumed to be the same as for the current instance, and since the "real cost" in work is assumed to be the same for all instances, the general case would seem to be that provision for each fu-

dimensional formula of primary (or "simple") retaining as "real cost" was given as R_1T^{-1}; since the magnitude R_1 is equal to WK, this formula may also be stated as WKT^{-1}.

[2] This concept was referred to on p. 442. While this notion is not always stated explicitly, it seems to be always implicit. It is the theory of a "discount" on the future. Marshall states it clearly (*291*, 119–120). It is his "subjective" allowance. So, too, Pigou (*325*, 25). It is part of his "slackness of desire toward the future" (*ibid.*, 27).

ture instance can be made when and as, in the passage of time, it becomes current on exactly the same terms as those on which the current instance can be provided for now. There could be no intrinsic advantage, then, in making any provision beforehand. But, in the second place, there is an actual disadvantage—the effort involved in retaining, during the interval,what is made now for use then. This draws a veil over the future so far as the current order of preference is concerned. By itself this handicap would block all future provision. And it does so except for the occasions we have enumerated—occasions when provision either cannot be made then at all, or cannot be made then so economically. Since these exceptions constitute the only cases we have to consider, and since the three types of occasion qualify the foregoing general case and work somewhat differently among themselves, we shall have to treat them separately. Suffice it to note here that our mental diagram is altered by the fact that the only future instances considered now are those included in these occasions. We must conceive that, at most, only sections of the receding lines or, at least, only single instances appear through the apertures made by the occasions and can play parts in the present picture. For the rest it is "sufficient unto the day."

We conceive, then, that the wants clamoring for attention include the entire current order of priority plus an irregular pattern of different wants from various future orders of priority which the perception of occasions has enabled to overcome the general bar to any future provision. But the order of preference upon which this clamor is focused is a single one—the current order—and the working that is to be allocated is a single day's working. This single day's working represents capacity; and since we are reserving to Chapter 14 the question of the determination of the limit of capacity, we will here regard it as fixed. According to this conception, the order of preference under the influence of which the day's working is allocated may become a compound one, in which provisions for instances of future wants from various future orders of priority have intruded into the program for current wants based on the current order of priority. The intrusions may cause duplications of provisions that are also being made for certain wants in the current order of priority; and, as we have seen, they may include provisions which cannot be included for the current order. All instances considered of any single want that have the same present force and involve the same "real cost" in work are equal competitors so far as the allocation of working alone is concerned. And all such instances of any want compete with all instances of every other, in respect of these two elements, just as their current instances compete. But in respect of the third element—retention—each future instance of a single want is handicapped in relation to all its fellows in proportion to its degree of futurity; and instances of different wants are handicapped among themselves, if their degrees of futurity differ, in proportion to such difference.[3] But this handicap, though a "real cost," is not part of the fund which represents capacity; to permit more or less of it does not affect the quantity of working allocated; its total is not limited in a way analogous to that of capacity; and, in fact, its quantity is determined in each case independently of all others.[4] Thus the accretion of "real cost" which takes place along the third dimension (diagrammatically) is of a different order from the one represented in the two-dimensional vertical plane. The question then arises whether its effects on preference are also different and independent or whether the two summate to form a single influence. That is again the question; and, again, we must wait.

There is no need to repeat here a description of the several types of occasion. But we will have to take cognizance of the way they may qualify the foregoing scheme as well as their different effects; and we must therefore remind ourselves of the basic features of the three classes. Provision for future instances of wants as to which the first type of contingency [5] exists cannot be had at all unless they are made in advance—i.e., now. But current provision can be had, if made now. Now that we have discarded our previous assumption, the work involved in provision for each want is different from that for each other; but for a single want the work in the provision for each instance involved is always the same; then the only difference is in the retention

[3] Though the effort involved in retaining is only made during the interval, and therefore in the future so far as this current order of preference is concerned, we have agreed that it is necessary to suppose that its effect is exerted when the decision to incur it is made.

[4] This is subject to the qualification, deliberately excluded by our assumption of fixed capacity, that the greater the quantity of future as against current provision, the greater the sacrifice or extra working induced. But that is not a measure of the quantity (or limit) of retaining; for it is equal for all future provision of the same working cost, regardless of the degree of futurity.

[5] The first type of contingency exists when it is expected that, "at some date or dates within the future envisaged, all or part of the working being done to provide for current wants will have to be discontinued" (see p. 627).

involved. Future provision for contingencies of this type is handicapped by comparison with the corresponding current provision only by the "real cost" of retention required.

Where the first technical necessity exists, future provision can also not be had unless made now, though current provision can be made now.[6] But under the second contingency and the other two technical necessities no provision,[7] either current or future, can be had unless it is made in advance. When subject to this contingency or these necessities, means are either made as future provision or not at all. Moreover, since large stocks (more than one day's provision) are usually required for the seasonal material or process and in the long process, and since large units (more than one day's provision) are usually required for the durable, it is generally impossible—unlike the case of the second contingency—to deal with a single future instance of any want served by means subject to these necessities.[8] Thus, unlike both contingencies, we have practically always to deal with these cases in terms of blocks of instances and provisions. Again, the work per provision varies among different wants or remains the same for a single want, as with the two contingencies; but, since the retention involved cannot be the same for any two members of a block of provisions, we have to consider such a block in terms of its average, or of its maximum and minimum, period. Future provision for the second type of contingency or in the form of durables or long processes is not handicapped by comparison with current provision; for current provision is impossible. The "real cost" of retention only affects the length of the process before the arrival of the contingency or the beginning of uses and the number of provisions included (durability or size of lot).

[6] The first technical necessity is what we have called, generically, "seasonable materials or processes." It exists when "some natural material or power necessary for a certain product and which is available in the present will cease to be available within the future envisaged" (see p. 629).

[7] The second type of contingency exists when it is expected that "during some period within the future envisaged, an irregularly occurring want may occur without warning" (see p. 628). The second technical necessity we have called "durables" (see p. 629). The third technical necessity is generally "long-process product" (see p. 631).

[8] Of course we are not considering, in this connection, large units which are merely convenient packages covering several or many days' provision. However, it should be noted that our present admission of variations in "real cost" of work eliminates the agreement between the number of hours' working required and the number of days' provision made which resulted from our simplifying assumption in Chapter 10. Therefore the number of days on which working is applied before the beginning of use will influence the period of retaining as much as will the number of days' provision made.

All the more typical technical options include the conditions of long processes or durables.[9] They, too, must be future provision; they, too, require large stocks or large units and therefore blocks of future provision.[10] However, unlike the technical necessities, not only does the work per provision vary among different wants but also for a single want. For, the essence of the option is this: work now plus work then, per future provision, will be less than work now or work then, per current provision, if the option is not exercised. Furthermore, though the alternatives are usually either a block of future provisions or none, so that retention must be considered in terms of its average or of its maximum and minimum period, this element only goes to determine whether or not the option is worth exercising. It is not, if the retention involved exceeds or equals the work economized; only if the retention is sufficiently less is the option worth exercising. Therefore, unlike all the other cases, retention is not an added "real cost" for the technical options. It merely goes to reduce, and therefore take the place in the combined "real cost" of a part of, the work economized. Future provision in the form of the technical options is not handicapped by comparison with current provision, not only because current provision by the optional methods is almost always impossible, but because the total "real cost" must be lower than it would be if the option were not exercised. However, in spite of all these differences, the fact remains true that all the types of future provision included in our occasions require the allocation of some part of the limited fund of working available now. To that extent, whether handicapped by the retention involved or not, they involve current forgoing and, as we have seen in Chapter 10, an extra quantity of the effort and sacrifice of working.

There is one more element of the analysis in Chapter 10 that we can safely take over here, under the same limiting assumptions, and which we carry forward as a conclusion that applies throughout. Once the program for future provision for all wants is adopted, it will continue on practically the same basis if the factors which determined it remain the same. These factors are the successive future duplicates of the current order of priority, the limit of capacity, the rate of accrual of re-

[9] The first technical option is the large-batch process (see p. 634). The second technical option is intermediate product (see p. 634).

[10] In this particular connection it is, for the sake of simplicity, permissible to consider the intermediate product (indirect effort) of the second type of option as if it were future provision for the want or wants in connection with whose final product it will be used.

taining as "real cost," and now, in addition, the "real cost" in work per provision. That is, once adopted, the program for all except contingencies of the second type will probably be carried forward to each new day's working by reason of the management of replacements described in Chapter 10. As the first day's provision or installment is used up it will be replaced for the day following the last day's previous provision or installment. In the replacement process, then, retention is measured always to the maximum period of a block of provisions, not to the minimum or the average.[11]

2. THE INFLUENCE OF COMBINED "REAL COSTS" ON TERMS OF SUBSTITUTION

If both or all substitute means for a single want can be produced in the future as wanted, the relation between them will be the same then as it is now. If an occasion appears to prevent the production of all of them in the future, the current preference for the cheapest, according to the weighted terms of substitution, will merely be enhanced when all must be made now for future provision. This because any one whose "real cost" in work is higher will also have a higher rate of accrual of retaining as "real cost" than the one whose "real cost" in work is least.

Therefore, the effect of retention as "real cost" upon preferences among substitutes is limited to cases where one requires to be made in advance while the other does not, or where one requires to be made further in advance than the other. Such cases may arise under the three technical necessities. Under the first technical necessity one substitute may be available the year round while another is only available in season. Disregarding all other considerations, in spite of the fact that, in season, current provision of either can be properly weighted in terms of "real cost" of work only, future provision of the seasonable substitute for the time when it is out of season is subject to the handicap of added "real cost" of retention as compared with the all-the-year-round product. Though the seasonable means may be preferred in season, the burden of the extra cost of retention may alter the weighted terms of substitution sufficiently to reverse the preference for the period when it is out of season. For instance, let us suppose that the leader of a pas-

[11] We have seen in Chapter 10 why this should be the only period considered for replacements, though it is not the only one considered when the original block of provisions is planned.

toral tribe finds that the unweighted terms of substitution between the products of milk and the products of ripe seeds of wild grain are such that one quart of milk = one quarter pound of grain. In season the weighted terms may be such that the grain is preferred. It might be true, nevertheless, that if the leader were to direct the gathering and storing of sufficient wild grain for the winter, its "real cost" would be so enhanced by reason of the sacrifice and effort of retaining that he would prefer to fall back on a diet of milk products in the winter.[12]

In connection with long processes the same situation may arise when one substitute entails a long process and the other does not. But with long processes it may also occur that one substitute requires a longer process—period before the beginning of use—than does the other. Though the longer process product may require less work so that it is favored in terms of that "real cost" only, it is possible that the handicap of the greater retention it requires will reverse the terms, and therefore the preference, when both "real costs" are considered. The reader can work out for himself an illustration of the same situation for durables. But, in doing so, he must exclude from this particular effect differences in "real cost" of work, since these are included in the primary weighted terms, as well as differences in durability, since these involve provision for more or less instances.

Because, in the case of technical options, practically all of which require retaining, differences in the cost of retention among substitute means (methods) must always be compensated for by complementary differences in the economizing of work, the quantity of retaining required in any case can have no effect by itself on the preference among the substitutes. In fact, the effect of combining the two "real costs" may well work the other way round. Instead of being a handicap, a greater amount of retention may be a help; for, in order that its total shall show more favorable terms, the substitute involving greater retaining must involve less working; and working has to be allocated out of the limited fund of a fixed current capacity. Even with a fixed capacity, less work for future provision means less current forgoing (sacrifice).

[12] To make this illustration at all realistic we would have to assume that the food consists of milk-products, not raw milk.

3. THE INFLUENCE OF COMBINED "REAL COSTS" ON LIMITING FUTURITY OF PROVISION

Even if a certain occasion appears to warrant future provision for a want, we found, in Chapter 10, that such provision will be excluded if its combined "real costs" exceed the present force of the want. That is merely an application of a principle analogous to the one which excludes from current provision wants whose intensity does not exceed the "real cost" in work involved. But, in the first place, the principle now works differently, because we have discarded the assumption of equal work per provision; and, in the second place, this principle works on a different basis from the limit of capacity—a difference which needs to be brought out.

When all provisions were regarded as equal in the work involved, the limit of futurity was set for all wants at the point at which accruing retaining brings combined "real costs" up to the level of the force of the want. Thus the degree of futurity permitted in each case was supposed to depend only on the force of the want—the rate of accrual of retaining being the same for all. The greater the want, the greater the futurity permitted; so that the degree of futurity in each case depended on the position in the current (and each future) order of priority which it occupied. The admission of varied "real costs" in work changes this. Not only will higher or lower "real costs" in work increase or decrease that component of combined "real costs" and thus bring the limit of futurity earlier or later than otherwise; but they will also increase or decrease the rate of accrual of the other component—a rate with the formula WKT^{-1}. We have agreed that, in modern practice, the second component—retention—is usually very much smaller than the first, except for a long interval. Therefore, its differences will have less effect than those of the first. Nevertheless, to be systematic, we must take them into account. The combined effect of these two variations—$W + (WKT^{-1} \times T)$—is to make the limit of futurity different for each want. That limit for each want lies at a distance into the counterfeit future varying directly with the current intensity of the want and varying inversely with $W + WK$.

That makes it clear that the limit of futurity is not the same thing as the limit of capacity. The limit of capacity is determined in terms of W only; that of futurity in terms of $W + WK$. Both limits are also fixed in terms of the intensity or force of the wants, which is the same for both. Therefore the limit of futurity depends primarily on the difference between W and I (intensity). Moreover, secondarily, the less this difference is the more rapidly will it disappear as the degree of futurity increases, since W is also a dimension of R_1 (= WK); and the greater the difference is the less rapidly will it disappear. Converted to real terms, this analysis merely says that the greater the want and the less work involved in its provision the further into the future will a program of provision for it be entertained.

4. THE INFLUENCE OF COMBINED "REAL COSTS" ON ANY SINGLE FUTURE ORDER OF PRIORITY

The only instance we can think of where any one future order of priority is considered as a whole is when a contingency of the first type presents itself. However, an analysis of the effects of adding the "real cost" of retention in this case will help to make clear the final step we take in the next subsection. In Chapter 10, on the assumption of equal "real costs" in work and therefore of equal combined "real costs" (for a uniform degree of futurity), the potential order of preference within such a single future order of priority was conceived to follow the order of priority. In Section C 4 of this chapter, in which we dealt with the current order of priority only, and therefore with no "real cost" of retention, but where "real costs" in work were assumed to differ, the current order of preference was conceived also to follow the order of priority, but subject to interference by the order of ratios. This interference was supposed to be ineffective among the prior wants, but to become more and more effective, though in terms of rough comparisons, as one proceeds along the subordinate range of the order, until around the limit of capacity the order of ratios becomes governing. In the first analysis, the order of ratios was arbitrarily excluded because the inverse dimension of all ratios was assumed to be a uniform magnitude. In the second analysis the order of ratios was not excluded, but, at that stage of our analysis, the inverse dimension excluded the magnitude of retention. To apply the first analysis here requires, then, that the inverse dimension be changed to a set of differing magnitudes. Or, to apply the second analysis requires that retention be included in the inverse dimension. The changes produced by such inclusion have already been described in the previous subsection. Given any set of "real costs" in work, the set of combined "real costs" will diverge from each other to a greater degree, the greater the degree of futurity of the order of priority considered. This by reason of the effect of differing "real cost" in work upon the rate of accrual of retaining—WKT^{-1}. Thus any particular future order of ratios will represent lower values for each ratio than the current values; the greater the "real cost" in work the more the value of the ratio will be lowered; and the greater the degree of futurity the greater the general reduction as well as the spreading out among the values of ratios.

I am inclined to think that, when a single order of priority is, under these circumstances, considered by itself, the two influences, order of priority and corrected order of ratios (including retention), would work out very much as they seem to do in the current order (excluding retention). Of course, in such a future order, unlike the current order, some wants may come to be excluded by the limit of futurity, as above. And, as we shall see in the next subsection, it may be that the greater the degree of futurity the greater is the influence of the corrected order of ratios. Otherwise, however, in the order of preference among the wants of such a future order of priority considered as a whole, it would appear that through the range of prior wants the order of priority continues to overrule the now corrected order of ratios. Thereafter, the corrected order of ratios appears to interfere in at least rough fashion; and toward the end, where the status of the wants in terms of their ratios are critical, it may govern. Where the order of ratios does interfere or even govern the order of preference in such a future order of priority considered by itself, it seems to have an effect similar to that which it would have in the current order considered by itself. And this would seem to be a logical a priori conclusion. For, at any single degree of futurity, the relation between the various values in a future order of ratios will be the same as in the current order of ratios, in spite of the spreading out, because the increment will be the same percentage of all—that is, $KT^{-1} \times T$ is the same for all.[13]

[13] This is obviously true. If a series of ratios is $\frac{32}{8}$, $\frac{21}{7}$, $\frac{12}{6}$ and $\frac{7.5}{5}$, their values are 4, 3, 2, and 1.5. Now if $T = 100$ and $K = \frac{1}{100}$, $WKT = W$. Then $W + WKT = 2W$. The corrected ratios then become $\frac{32}{16}$, $\frac{21}{14}$, $\frac{12}{12}$ and $\frac{7.5}{10}$, which gives them the values of 2, 1.5, 1, and 0.75. The relation between these values is the same as before.

5. THE INFLUENCE OF COMBINED "REAL COSTS" ON THE CURRENT ORDER OF PREFERENCE

The most effective way to deal with this complex question is to narrow it down, step by step, and thus, in the process, to settle first the particular questions that can be answered more readily and with more certainty than can the residual question. The occasions which are included under the technical options are the simplest cases. These are chiefly alternative methods of providing for wants that are already being provided for currently. The option is not exercised unless the combined "real costs" of future provision, when the work is applied both now and then, will be less than the "real cost" in work only if made then. Since the "real cost" in the form of work only that is required for the current provision is the same as for the future provision if made then, it is clear that it is the combined "real costs" upon which hinges the position of this optional method in the current order of preference. But this position is not determined by the prospective ratio. Instead it is determined by the prospective reduction in total "real cost." And that, in turn, makes it a matter which can only be settled in terms of the change in the reach of capacity which it will produce. Those are the terms in which we analyzed the options in Chapter 10. The only change in that analysis which is necessary now is to allow for differences in "real cost" of work among the current provisions which form the bases of comparison. This being a special case involving changes in capacity, we will reserve it for Chapter 14, Section A 3. For the rest we may say that, in the options, the influence of "real cost" in retention is combined with that in work in much the same way as it is among substitute means for a single want.

That leaves us to deal only with the contingencies and the technical necessities. We may start with the conclusion that no provisions will be included whose combined "real costs" reach those at the limit of futurity, and that, since these must be greater than "real cost" in work alone, all not so excluded are within the limit of capacity.[14] Furthermore, we may here confine ourselves to a single means for each want—the preferred substitute—that selection having already been made. Of these occasions only the first contingency permits the fact of current provision. All the rest must be provided for the future or not at all.[15]

[14] If I is the same for both, then, if $I > W + WK$, it follows that $I > W$.

[15] This is true for the second contingency, because of the nature of the want (occurring sporadically), and for the technical necessities, by definition. It seems necessary to

With regard to the first contingency we may assume that the "real cost" in work of any day's future provision is the same as for the current day's provision. Our first conclusion is, then, that here a future instance of a want cannot displace in the current order of preference either its own current instance or any of its own future instances of a lesser degree of futurity. That is, its place in the current order of preference will always be subsequent to its own current or to any of its own earlier instances. In that particular regard combined "real costs" are determining. This introduces a useful diagrammatic concept. What we shall call the "base position" of each future instance of a want is the position of its current instance in the current order of preference. The degree of futurity of each future instance governs its deferment from this base position so far as its intrusion into the current order of preference is concerned. The first contingency always includes all the great prior wants. Moreover, more than one day's provision is usually considered for each want, since the contingency is viewed as likely to last at least several days. Thus the program usually envisages a block of provisions for each want provided for. Our analysis in Chapter 10 showed how the whole set of blocks is distributed over several or many days' working. It is on the principle of least sacrifice and effort. We may accept that conclusion here, treating as "given" at this point the number of orders of preference (days' working) with regard to which provisions for this contingency will be considered. There remains, then, only the question of the effect of different "real costs" in work, and so of combined "real costs," upon the determination of the particular provisions to be included in any one of the series of orders of preference (allocations of days' working) that is required.

In the previous subsection we came to the tentative conclusion, subject to the qualification below, that so far as any one of these complete future orders of priority is considered by itself, the order of corrected ratios would operate much as does the order of ratios in terms of work alone in the current order—namely, it would not interfere with the order of priority through the range of great prior wants, would come to interfere more and more in the range of subordinate wants, and would become governing around the limit of capacity. If this is true within any single future order of priority attempting to intrude as a

---

conclude that no clothing could have been worn and no produced shelter availed of by man unless it had a life of more than one day.

The question of the replacement process is dealt with below.

whole into the current order of preference, is it not likely also to be true as to the successful intrusions? Here it seems necessary to distinguish between future orders of priority of varying degrees of futurity. We may hazard the guess that great prior wants from near-by future orders will succeed in intruding without regard to the handicap of a ratio which includes retention in its inverse dimension; that in the middle range of such future orders the inclusion of retention in the inverse dimension will give the order of ratios more power to interfere than is the case in the current order of priority alone, because it reduces the value of the individual ratio; and that, toward the limit of capacity, the corrected ratio of each future want will have to compete on equal terms with the ratio of current wants which include no retention in their inverse dimensions. In competition, then, the prior future wants of near-by orders of priority may be supposed to displace subordinate current wants even if the values of the ratios of the former are lower. On the other hand, to the extent that the order of ratios does interfere, subordinate future wants of such orders probably do not displace subordinate current wants unless the values of their ratios remain higher in spite of the added component of retention in the inverse dimension. However, it would appear that, the greater the degree of futurity of the future order of priority, the greater becomes the influence of the order of corrected ratios. Thus even the prior wants of such orders come more and more to be subjected to the interference of the order of ratios, so that, at a high degree of futurity, the order of ratios governs all intrusions—prior and subordinate alike. This would seem to follow of necessity if we are to concede that the limit of futurity operates also upon prior wants—a concession enforced upon us by observation. At that limit the position of a want in the order of priority has disappeared as an independent influence and exercises its effect only as the direct dimension of the ratio.[16]

With regard to the second contingency and the technical necessities, we suppose the occasions occur with reference only to single wants—assuming minor members of constellations to have effect only by successive summation. These single wants may be prior or subordinate, and these constellations may include prior and subordinate or only subordinate wants. With all, so far as the initial provision is concerned, it is either a question of future provision or none, or—under

[16] That is, if the limit of futurity is the point at which $I = W + WK$, it is the point at which the corrected ratio has a value of unity. If so, the ratio governs there.

some technical necessities—it is a question of future provision of the preferred substitute, or acceptance of a poorer or more expensive (in work) substitute. The latter question has already been covered under the effect of retention on the weighted terms of substitution. Limiting ourselves here to the single remaining question, we may ask under what conditions the only means for a single want will intrude into the current order of preference. It might appear that the fact that a want cannot be satisfied at all except by way of future provision would tend to decrease the adverse influence of the added "real cost" of retention. The pure test case would be that of a contingency of the second type —a single provision for a single sporadically occurring want. When we consider the way future provision is made for wants whose actual occurence must be unexpected, it seems that practice generally follows the same procedure we have supposed for contingencies of the first type. If the want is a prior one—e.g., protection from wild animals— and is expected some time in the near future, combined "real costs"— corrected ratios—will have little influence. But the further in the future is the estimated probable date of occurrence, the greater becomes the influence of combined "real costs" in determining intrusion into the current order of preference even for such a prior want. On the other hand, as one proceeds along any order of priority, or as one estimates the occurrence further into the future, the influence of combined "real costs" increases, so that among wants near the limit of capacity or the limit of futurity this influence is governing. Thus it appears likely that, if the instance is of a low degree of futurity, whether the want is prior or subordinate, its intrusion is on much the same basis as the determination of the order of preference among current wants; while, if it is of a high degree of futurity, the exemption of prior wants from the influence of the order of ratios tends to disappear. If so, the fact that the want can be satisfied only by future provision seems to have no effect.

This generalization seems to be confirmed when we apply the same scheme to the three technical necessities. With them the question can frequently be resolved into the determination of how long into the future to provide a seasonable product (first type), of how durable a durable (second type) shall be when "real cost" in work is proportionate to durability, or of how long a long process (third type) shall be when its output is proportionate to its length (work remaining the same per provision). There again we seem to see a grading down of the influence of wants (priority), and a grading up of the influence of corrected ratios, both in the direction of decreasing importance of wants and in the direction of increasing length of the period provided for. A brief series of near-by instances of a prior want may be provided for pretty much regardless of the order of ratios; but the extension into the future of such a series will become increasingly subject to the place the corrected ratio of each added provision takes in the current order of ratios. And, the further along the order of priority the want lies, the more potently and the earlier will this consideration influence the decision, so that even near-by instances of subordinate wants are wholly subject to it.

Our final conclusion as to the answer to the question previously posed is this: "Real cost" in retention affects the current order of preference only as a component of combined "real costs." It never works alone or independently. The one thing it does do independently is to increase the influence of combined "real costs" as compared with the influence of "real cost" in work only, in proportion to the share of combined "real costs" which it constitutes. At first sight this conclusion seems to make necessary a somewhat radical modification of the general scheme worked out under limiting assumptions in Chapter 10. However, under ordinary conditions, it is probable that little or no change need be made in that scheme by reason of admitting variations in "real cost" in work per provision. This for two reasons. Ordinarily, the added cost on account of the retention involved in provisions for near-by instances is so small that we would not expect it to have much effect. Then our analysis in Section C 4 serves our purposes fairly well. On the other hand, our analysis in Chapter 10 may be trusted to correspond rather well to reality when the "real cost" in retention is a considerable factor, but only then. Since, for purposes of demonstration, the influence of futurity was much exaggerated there, this qualification would have been required in any case. The second reason is this: For the most part our analysis in Chapter 10 dealt with choices in terms of opposite extremes. It was therefore worked out on a basis quite different from the moving limit of capacity we have used to analyze the current order of preference when each want is compared with the next in the order of priority or in the order of ratios. In Chapter 10 the current provision which would have to be forgone to make possible a single future provision for a prior want was always that one which was last in the current order of preference within the limit of capacity, and the value of whose ratio would therefore be, by definition, just over unity. Even the proper allowance for differences in "real cost" per provision could not reverse the conditions of such a choice. Thereafter, as the current forgoing was increased to permit the intrusion of future provisions for lesser and lesser wants, the range in which the choices were made would tend necessarily to become one in which both wants were largely or wholly subject to the influence of combined "real costs" (i.e., the middle range). Thus the exemption of the prior wants from the influence of the order of ratios in inverse proportion to the degree of futurity of their instances, which we have found necessary in this chapter, would not, in fact, alter to any large extent the conclusions in Chaper 10.

It is well to serve notice here that we recognize that, in actuality, the simple choices presented above become complicated, variegated, and even altered. They are complicated when the program of provision extends, of necessity or by choice, over more than one day, so that each choice is influenced more or less by its fellows. They are variegated in that programs may be altered in process because conditions determining them have changed, so that intrusions into the current order of preference do not necessarily repeat themselves. They are altered to the extent that the program for replacements is likely to differ from the program for the initial accumulation, so that, while the component of retention may be increased, the current sacrifice and extra working are reduced. However, it does not seem necessary to pursue the subject into these details; for the principles which seem to govern choices would then remain the same; only their applications would differ.

F. SEGMENTATION AND DIFFERENTIAL COSTS

1. SEGMENTATION IN GENERAL

In Part I of this study the subject of incomplete satisfaction, and the consequent segmentation of wants and of the process of satisfying them, cropped up a number of times.[1] Each time it was considered briefly in the light of our analysis at that stage and was then referred forward to Part IV. This postponement was necessary, as we noted, because, on the hypothesis of a tendency to satiate each want in turn, there would occur no spontaneous segmentation—that is, incomplete satisfactions recognized as such and not incidental or due to inter-

[1] See particularly pp. 227 ff., pp. 402 to 404, pp. 417 ff., p. 501 and p. 529.

ference—except where complete satisfactions were impossible.[2] In such cases only the first and externally fixed segment would come into consideration at all. In order to consider the question of other occasions for segmentation, as well as of segmentation dealing with variable or multiple segments, it was necessary to wait until we could introduce the influence of "real costs," since this appears to be the only cause of what we have referred to as *deliberate* segmentation.[3]

We must admit that we are here on much less sure ground than we were in dealing with an order of preference based on the order of priority in terms of full measures and complete satisfactions. This because it is far more difficult to test our constructions as to partial satisfactions by comparison with observations of reality. Therefore, the best we can do is to do the best we can, and to hope that future investigations will serve to clarify, expand, and, so far as is necessary, correct this one. In order to make this final summary as complete as is possible for us we will commence with a brief review of our conclusions as to segmentation up to this point.

Under the influence of present wants only and excluding the influence of "real costs" we have assumed that only spontaneous segmentation would occur. The occasions for failure to satiate present wants were analyzed into three types. The first two, interference by a prior want becoming prepotent and incidental failure as to a minor want of a constellation, are due entirely to the competition between wants; the third imports an imposed external condition, but one beyond the purview of choice—an absolute limit on the immediately available supply of the necessary means, object or process. So far as the intensity of the want is concerned we found it necessary to conclude that, if such intensity remains practically unchanged throughout a complete satisfaction, it must also do so throughout a first partial satisfaction.[4] In this respect there could be no difference between the two. But, then, in this dimension, there would be no change during either the partial or the complete process of satisfying and therefore no way of distinguish-

[2] Impossible because of the insufficiency of the necessary external condition—the third reason for the failure to satiate present wants.

[3] Even spontaneous segmentation of present wants when it is due to the third cause—insufficiency of an external condition—is, in an economy advanced beyond the hand-to-mouth stage, usually due to failure to provide in advance. Thus (as remarked on p. 402, Note 10) the ultimate cause is apt to be the limitation or allocation of effort. Nevertheless, even then, it may not be deliberate if the occasion was unexpected or the yield was short of plan.

[4] This conclusion was suggested on p. 418 and was discussed at some length on p. 529.

ing between the two until the process stopped. When the process does stop short of satiation it appears that different present wants behave in different ways. In fact, these different behaviors may also occur as to a particular want according as the degree of satisfaction is less or greater. The three general possibilities for the behavior of the intensity of a want when its satisfying is stopped short of satiation are: (a) that its latent intensity should remain the same and thus be prepared to resume prepotence after the interference, etc., is over; (b) that its latent intensity should fall to a lower level and therefore be subject to further potential interference by more subordinate wants; and (c) that its intensity should disappear for the time being—becoming less than sufficient to overcome inertia—only to recur at a prepotent level sooner than usual. In view of these various possibilities it becomes difficult to conceive of any segment of the want after the first—any segment which supposedly remains unsatisfied—as if it were part of the same instance. Almost we have to think of such a subsequent segment as a new instance. Almost we have to say to ourselves that, on the one hand, if the satisfying is on an all or none basis (quasi-external wants) or is so slight that the latent intensity continues unchanged after a little of the process (storage wants), that instance of the want is not partially satisfied; practically, it is not satisfied at all.[5] If the satisfying is not on an all or none basis, partial satisfaction will delay the recurrence of the want at a prepotent level. Then, when the want again becomes prepotent it is a new instance. If it recurs quickly, it may recur at the same or at a somewhat reduced level, depending on the type. If it recurs after a considerable interval but earlier than normally, it will show at least the same intensity as did the previous instance. In fact, whenever there is a cumulative effect of deficiencies in satisfying, the new instance may even have an intensity higher than the normal maximum.

On the basis of present wants only we might conclude that what we have been calling incomplete satisfaction—satisfying a first segment only—really consists (a) in no satisfaction at all, or it consists in something which is subjectively indistinguishable from complete satisfaction but with earlier recurrence, (b) at a lower level, or (c) at the same, or (d) even at a higher level. And this in spite of recognizing that, in all the last three cases, the process of satisfying had continued for a time,

[5] Ingestion of food or drink—less than a square meal—which is nevertheless adequate, after it has been assimilated, to restore homeostasis even for a short time, will put an end to the want. But if the quantity—a *soupçon*—is too little even temporarily to raise the storage level to the normal, the want will continue unabated.

though it had stopped short of the point at which satiation and the prevention of recurrence for a normal period would result.

Now we have assumed that the dealings with the future want system, with which our order of preference is concerned, are based on experience of present wants. If so, it would seem that the tentative conclusions arrived at above would apply also to future wants. Here, however, some new factors enter. Behavior has become deliberate, not spontaneous; partly based on objective, not wholly on subjective considerations; and it deals with a program for a period of time, not merely with the impulses of the moment. In the first place, it is only as a result of these changes that the organism comes to apply what it has learned as to the objective magnitude that constitutes a full measure and thus adequate provision. But, as soon as it begins to do that, it may have an alternative dimension in which to measure a complete satisfaction and thus to discriminate that from a partial satisfaction.[6] We have already recognized that possibility. In our discussion of means in terms of quantity only, we discriminated between the static magnitude (the normal maximum intensity of the want), which is the driving force and determines the order of priority, and the dynamic magnitude (reduction of that intensity to zero), experience of which merely serves to fix the correspondence, in the process of satisfying, with a full measure of means.[7] It seems safe to assume that, wherever the subject learns what constitutes the objective magnitude of a full measure of means with proportionate attributes, he becomes capable of determining that anything less than that is a part measure and will produce less than satiation and planned recurrence, even if the behavior of the intensity of the want itself does not serve him as an accurate guide.

We must admit that the existence of at least an imaginary dimension for the process of satisfying has been implicit in every diagram or mental representation we have used; every one has included a second dimension which has been more than representational—the horizontal line denoting the unmeasured dimension of the process going on over time. This was necessary because the process itself cannot be depicted

[6] For wants which are inherently on an all or none basis—e.g., escape, being out of breath, etc.—there is no partial satisfaction. Thus we are considering here chiefly the storage wants and those that behave in a similar way.

[7] See p. 475. It was this feature that led us to say, on p. 526, that our own hypothesis occupies a middle position between the other two, since its static magnitude (like the second and unlike the third) determines the virtual order of preference, while its dynamic magnitude (unlike the second and like the third) relates it directly to the means required.

in the first dimension—the vertical dimension of the intensity of want —since intensity, under our hypothesis, remains unchanged until the end. It would be meaningless to state that the intensity of the want remained unchanged until the end of the process unless the process were conceived to have some sort of dimension of its own.[8] On the other hand, we have not pretended and do not believe that there is any subjective measure of this dimension of process short of satiation. Its only available measure is an objective one—the measure of means consumed —in terms of which part satisfactions may be imputed.

We conclude, then, that in dealing with future wants served by means with proportionate attributes man can and does use this objective measure of process as a rough way of gauging the extent of at least some first partial satisfactions which he recognizes to be less than satiation. For this purpose the objective measurement of means is the only basis which has even a pretense of quantitative accuracy. On that basis a fraction of a full measure might be supposed to yield a corresponding fraction of complete satisfaction. It is even possible that one might also infer that successive equal fractions of a full measure would yield successive equal partial satisfactions. As to that we suspend judgment for the moment. When the objective measurement of means is impossible, or too much trouble, the quantity of process may be roughly determined in terms of duration—e.g., a two weeks' vacation or an evening at the theatre.[9] But then it is recognized that time does not actually measure the process, because the rate per unit of time at which the process of satisfying actually takes place can vary so widely.[10] This exclusive dependence upon the measure of means—or, in default of that, on duration—does not deny, of course, that every process of satisfying may be, in one of its aspects, a conscious experience. Man knows when he is eating, drinking, etc. It only denies that this conscious experience can serve by itself as a measurable magnitude according to which to determine whether a satisfaction is complete or partial, and, if partial, approximately what degree of satisfaction is attained.[11]

[8] Obviously the dynamic magnitude of process cannot be measured *pari passu* in a dimension in which there is no change until the end. But it is equally obvious that the mere statement that the process takes place requires a dimension for it, even if that dimension is purely a conceptual one. In terms of our previous analogy (Chapter 8) the water moves through a siphon—there must be a measure of the flow; but that measure is not the height of the water in the siphon.

[9] Time is only an inverse dimension of any process which can actually be measured.

[10] We usually think of resting and playing in terms of elapsed time. But duration does not determine when one is "rested up" or "played out."

[11] In Chapter 4 we discussed the question of conscious "signals" such as repletion. These

Another consideration is permitted when we come to deal with future wants. We have assumed that the convenient basis for programs with regard to future wants is a day's provision. This may be more than a full measure, if the want recurs more than once a day. But this enables us to lump together the several recurrences of a day as we could not do when dealing with present wants. Therefore, even if we think of the unsatisfied portion of a present want as constituting a new instance, as was suggested above, we can agree that, for a day's program, all recurrences would be aggregated. If, therefore, a want that is only partly satisfied, recurs all the sooner, either at a level lower, the same, or higher than at its first appearance, the deficiency will become obvious as a matter of experience. Thus, in dealing with a day's program, partial satisfactions can also be judged by means of the resulting variations in the interval before, and the intensity of, recurrences.[12]

Finally, a third difference that arises in connection with future wants is that minor wants of a constellation are less apt to be confined to incidental satisfaction. For, in so far as their claims reach consciousness, they can be considered along with, not merely after, the major want.[13]

On the other hand, when we are considering a program for future wants which may involve a whole series of future orders of priority, we must bear in mind a limitation which does not arise in the case of present wants, necessarily of a single order of priority. For then, what at first sight seem to be partial satisfactions usually turn out to be adequate provision for some instances and none for others—that is, the

---

are from independent sources; they are influences which oppose the force of the want; they are brakes on the process of satisfying. But they neither measure degrees of satisfaction short of complete, nor do they diminish the force of the want. The want derives peripherally from a more recondite and unconscious source, and it only loses its force when homeostasis is restored at the strategic point.

Because of his slow process of ingestion the hunger of an infant at the breast may be satiated long before repletion. He will stop nursing. But the mother, who does not wish to adapt herself to the quick recurrence of infant hunger, urges him to go on. Then he can and will take more. If replete, he probably could not and certainly would not.

"Signals" of repletion are certainly not a sure index of restoration of homeostasis. Nor is the mere absence of repletion an index of incomplete satisfaction. It appears that, under usual conditions and after normal intervals and ordinary activity, man stops eating or drinking long before these capacity "signals" are reached.

[12] This general consideration led us to doubt (see p. 403) that over a considerable period spontaneous segmentation will produce lasting incomplete satisfaction. Interference is irregular; minor wants of a constellation may rise above their normal maxima if incidental satisfaction is continually deficient; and externally imposed shortages will tend to be overcome, if possible, because of the urging of continued prepotence or of earlier recurrence. Impossibility of overcoming shortages is probably a rare case.

[13] See p. 417.

number of instances provided for is less than the number that will actually occur over the period of the program. In such cases, satisfying is on an all or none basis as to each instance and we have no segmentation.[14]

The objective dimension in which the magnitude of a full measure of each means is stated yields us a basis for a rough measurement of the size of deliberate first segments where the means serving the want contains the required attribute in proportion to its quantity. Together with the various kinds of experience of the recurrence of the want after partial satisfaction it might serve as a way of arranging at least initial part measures of various sizes—for a single means with proportional attributes—so that the larger part measure would always be preferred over the smaller. Experience would certainly serve notice when the initial part measure was so small that it left the want completely unsatisfied—i.e., the want did not even disappear pro tem. The objective dimension might even serve, as the experiences cannot, as a rough measure of the actual differences in degree of satisfaction. But, it could not serve to compare part measures of different means or for different wants; for, as we have seen, these are objectively incommensurable.[15] Whether it also makes possible, or is used as a basis for inferring, the effects of the first half and the last half of a full measure, for instance, we shall see shortly. Theoretically, at least, it would seem that a series of segments measured off in terms of equal fractions of the full measure might be construed to be equal; in terms of differing part measures they might be construed to be proportionate.

When we come to consider attributes which exist in fixed quantity even this rough objective measure of segments fails us.[16] Nevertheless,

[14] This is what we shall call "alternation." For instance, in order to buy his child a winter coat, a man may agree with his wife to reduce his expenditures on cigarettes. He still smokes a whole cigarette at a time, and, unless he is a "chain smoker," that is all he wants at the time. However, he has agreed to budget a part of the price of the coat ahead of a package of cigarettes every other day, say. Then each package must last two days instead of one. Then he must deny himself a cigarette altogether every other time he wants one. His program for the period includes one lump of purchasing power which is assigned alternately to the two wants on successive days.

[15] Of course we have now made means for different wants commensurable in terms of their common dimension—"real cost." But that does not help us here. For no one would contend that a unit of "real cost" always produced the same quantity of the process of satisfying in every want. The very difference between the order of priority and the order of ratios denies that possibility.

[16] Neither the amount of process (wearing, looking, or thinking) nor the amount of means (dress, picture, book) necessarily varies between a means that is half-way satisfactory and one that is wholly so.

we have to admit that man does distinguish between means of more or less beauty, for instance; that he may grade them in an order of preference; and, therefore, that he must have some subjective method of gauging what may be different degrees of satisfaction attained. But, here, we must recognize at once that we are dealing with a different range of wants, chiefly minor members of constellations, and sometimes those of a constellation that is confined to subordinate wants. The physiological basis furnishes us with no more than an analogy here. However, it may still be possible to include this type of means in a little profitable speculating on the grounds of ordinary observation.

The more I explore the subject the more it appears to me that most of the instances cited of actual experience of partial satisfaction of a single instance of a single want are mythical. At least the great bulk of the examples I have examined appear not to involve segmentation at all. They seem to be cases where certain members of the constellation remain unsatisfied on each occasion, or where one or more members are satisfied on some occasions and on others not. If so, on each occasion for each individual want the satisfaction is on an all or none basis.

Take one of the most tangible constellations as an example. Shelter is a name for a joint process in which a very complex compound and durable means is aimed to serve a very large constellation of wants. To the extent that this means is successful, it prevents the wants from occuring on any occasion during its life in use—this constellation consisting chiefly of wants of prevention. But it may suffice only to prevent some—e.g., incursion by wild animals—and not others—e.g., lack of privacy. Or it may prevent a want sometimes and not at others. Ordinarily the roof may be tight; but, in a heavy downpour, it may leak. Ordinarily the chimney may draw; but, under certain atmospheric conditions, the room may fill with smoke.

Elsewhere we discuss the work of art—a durable.[17] It is suggested there that, among the innumerable members of a constellation served by such a means, satisfaction of each on each occasion may well be on an all or none basis. Having regard to the means itself, it is obvious that it is composed of a multitude of details and aspects (attributes). Some may satisfy, some annoy. Even if one is conscious only of a general impression, that impression is a very complex compound. If one is an expert, then his satisfaction is confined to the details and aspects that

[17] In Appendix VI, Section A.

he likes; those he dislikes are definite dissatisfactions. One may not distinguish these satisfactions and dissatisfactions as pertaining to different wants. They may be given the status of different "reasons" only. Nevertheless, in terms of our analysis, the response being independent for each, the wants are independent.[18] Similarly, an evening at the theater may be regarded, from the point of view of the buyer of a ticket, as a compound means serving many wants. If one analyzes the occasions which seem to him partial satisfactions, he will usually find that he must discriminate between the different attributes. Some satisfied, and some did not; the girls and their costumes may have been gorgeous; but the music may have been dull and the comedians not funny. Clearly the several wants satisfied or unsatisfied were separate wants.

Often—and particularly with the more intangible wants—what may satisfy on one occasion may not on others. On a visit home to the farm a woman's costume may satisfy her sense of beauty and conformity; at an evening in a night club the same costume may distress her. The judgment of beauty or conformity depends largely on comparisons, and the standard against which the comparison is made may be very different on different occasions.

Wherever such supposed cases of partial satisfaction have been due to faulty analysis it is only necessary to convert them into terms of compound—or even conglomerate—means serving each of the members of a constellation on an all or none basis in the way we worked out in Section D 1 of this chapter. However, we cannot deny that there may remain a residuum of cases where, for any single want, several different means each containing a different quantity of the fixed attribute may produce different degrees of partial satisfaction. Nor, if that is true, would we want to deny that man can discriminate between them and arrange them in an order of preference. Here our method of analysis leaves us *en l'air*. If he does that, we have no idea how he does it. For the subjective apparatus our physiological studies have led us to suppose does not seem capable of discriminating between different degrees of satisfaction of a single want on a single occasion by means of a single attribute. We can say that the want for beauty, for instance, like

[18] It merely happens, in such a complex case, that the individual want goes on and off with lightning rapidity as it is faced with its particular feature of the object. And this is true whether there is deliberate and discriminating examination of details or merely a cursory examination which yields a general impression composed of a jumbled myriad of impressions.

hunger, always wants more until it is satiated. But that is no more than a verbal explanation—word magic—because we do not know how such more or less can be judged.[19]

We have arrived at the tentative conclusion that there can be comparisons of the objective size of at least initial part measures of means with proportional attributes, whence can be imputed the comparative degrees of satisfaction that each will procure, and that the latter may, in some cases, be roughly confirmed by the experience of continuation or recurrence of the want. We also admit that there may be a method of judging the degree of satisfaction which will be procured by initial part measures of different means with fixed attributes. All such comparisons would be judgments of more or less, and therefore limited to the initial part measure only. Similar comparisons of a series of equal part measures may be possible. Hence might arise the imputation of equal successive segments. However, we cannot admit, for a moment, that it would be possible to set up a series of differing quantities of one means, or a set of different means, to measure the differences in the degree of satisfaction each would secure and thus to compare the sizes of a series of differing segments subsequent to the first. The capacity to subtract, from one another, existing magnitudes that cannot be measured in objective units and then to compare the non-existing remainders in quantitative terms is not one that we attribute to the human mind. Thus, in what follows, we limit ourselves to deliberate segmentation in the form of single partial satisfactions of any instance of a want, and we are only certain that our analysis applies to first segments. That, at least, enables us to consider the effect of the influence of "real costs" upon preferences among initial part measures of different size, or quantity of attribute, as well as the reasons why this influence may lead to a part measure being preferred to a full measure. Through such consideration of the operation of this influence in causing segmentation in the single want we may obtain some light on the indirect effects produced upon preferences among part satisfactions for different wants.

[19] That is, it is obvious, from our previous analysis, how man can judge quantity of means objectively so that when he says, "I want more of this," we know what is his basis for judging "more." But, when he says, "I like this better than that," we do not know what is his basis for judging "better." That is a problem for a science of aesthetics. In fact, until that problem is cleared up, the notion of satisfaction of many of our list of subordinate wants (e.g., beauty) is merely a verbal expression.

2. SEGMENTATION WITH UNIFORM COSTS

For the purpose of our analysis it is necessary to distinguish cases where segmentation may take place, although "real costs" of part measures are proportional to those of full measures (uniform costs), from cases where the same result might have to be attributed to the fact that the "real costs," per unit, of successive part lots are increasing (differential costs). Therefore, we shall deal first, in this subsection, with possible preferences for incomplete instead of complete satisfaction, on account of the greater "real cost" of the latter, and with possible preferences for a means which contains the desired fixed attributes in lesser quantities over one which contains them in greater quantities, when the latter involves a greater "real cost." It is true that this second group of preferences may involve higher costs for each successive segment added. But, in the first place, this would not be due to the existence of different costs among part lots, since, by definition, the several means are different products, not different part lots of a single product. And, in the second place, we have just stated at the end of the previous subsection, that we do not impute to man a capacity for measuring the successive increments of satisfaction gained in order to compare them with the successive increments of "real cost." Nor, as a matter of fact, would it follow of necessity that, if they were measurable and comparable, they would not all show the same relation (ratio) of part satisfaction to "real cost" per part measure.[20]

Limiting ourselves, then, to cases where various quantities of each means may be had at a uniform "real cost" per unit, let us consider first the possible influence of this "real cost" in inducing deliberate segmentation when the means concerned serves but a single want and when its attribute is proportional to quantity. This is the simplest case. It permits us to examine the question we postponed in the previous subsection. Does segmentation take place in terms of initial segments only or does it also take the form of segmentation in series? Under our hypothesis that the intensity of a want remains at approximately the same level throughout a single process of satisfying, it must also remain at that level during a partial satisfaction of any size or any succession of partial satisfactions, up to any degree less than complete.

[20] That is, they would not differ if the satisfying were always proportionate to the "real cost."

Upon this hypothesis there seem to be only two ways in which a correspondence could be established between a partial satisfaction and a part measure of means. The first way applies to segmentation in series; the second only to initial segments. According to the first, a succession of objectively determined equal fractions of a full measure of means would each be compared with this uniform intensity independently of all others; according to the second the comparison would be made in terms of successively larger fractions of a full measure. Under the first method, the first, second, and third quarters of a full measure would be judged separately; under the second a quarter, a half, and three-quarters would be judged separately. What we have been calling the *ratio* is the relation of the intensity of a want to the "real cost" of a full measure of means. Now we must introduce ratios for part measures as well. Under our hypothesis the direct dimension of all ratios for part measures, whatever their size or ordinal position, would be the same as that of a full measure. But the inverse dimension would be different from that of a full measure, and would also differ as between the two methods or bases for establishing a correspondence.

If, under the first method, the full measure were divided into quarters, the inverse dimension of each part measure ratio—the "real cost" of one-quarter—would be one-quarter that of a full measure. Then the value of the ratio of each part measure would be four times that of a full measure; but the value of all four part measure ratios would be the same. This would give no basis for segmentation. For, though the value of all part measure ratios would be proportionately higher than that of the full measure, a second, third, or fourth quarter measure would still show a higher value than any quarter measure of any want subsequent in the order of ratios. In the absence of any rationale for subdividing full measures of different wants into a different number of fractions, the influence of the order of ratios would be precisely the same as when these ratios are determined for full measures. Therefore, it seems necessary to eliminate the assumption that a series of segments does have imputed to each member a fraction of complete satisfaction on the ground that its corresponding part measure is a certain fraction of a full measure. This, not because such an inference would not be possible, but only because it would not lead to segmentation.

If, under the second method, part measures considered were one-quarter, one half, and three-quarters, the results would be quite different. The inverse dimension of the first quarter measure would be one-quarter of the "real cost" of a full measure, that of the half measure one-half, and that of the three-quarter measure three-quarters. The value of the ratio for the quarter measure would be four times that of a full measure—just as it would be by the first method. But the value of the ratio of the half measure would be only twice, and of the three-quarter measure only one and one-third times, that of the full measure. Conceivably, this would furnish a basis for segmentation. In the order of ratios the quarter measure would occupy a place far in advance of the half measure, etc. All comparisons would be made in terms of first segments only, but in terms of first segments of various sizes for each want. Conceptually, then, the order of ratios would consist, not of one ratio for each want, but of a series of such ratios, beginning with that of the smallest part measure considered and ending with that of a full measure. Actually, as stated in Section C 4, we do not believe an order of ratios is ever constructed. Instead, the ratios are considered and interfere only here and there, chiefly where particular values happen to approach unity, and around the limit of capacity, where all values are in the range just above or just below unity. Thus it would seem unlikely that the conceptually earlier position in this order occupied by a part measure would be discovered until the full measure had been considered and rejected.

Upon this basis for judging correspondences as to partial satisfactions, and assuming that the part measure would only be considered along with the full measure, the effect would be that, from the beginning of the range of wants where the order of ratios commences to have an influence and increasingly to the range where it is governing, the question might arise in many cases whether to exclude a want altogether, or to give it a deferred position because of the low value of its full measure ratio, or whether, instead, to include or prefer a part measure the value of whose ratio would be higher. In effect, the result would be the allocation of a perhaps arbitrarily determined lump sum of "real cost" on the theory that, where complete satisfaction is beyond reach, a little satisfaction, particularly of an intense want, is better than none. Such a statement seems to conform to a tendency we observe in real life. Moreover, admission of such a practice, even if it is regarded as exceptional, seems to offer a possible explanation of that residuum of instances where we find it difficult to deny that segmentation does take place. Heretofore, considering full measures only, we have concluded that the prior wants are not subject to the influence of "real costs" so long as the latter do not exceed the intensity of the wants on the basis of comparison that we have established. The supposition we now make would allow us to qualify the previous conclusion by admitting that very high "real costs" might, in this way, cause segmentation among even some prior wants. On the other hand, it is probable that experience would soon teach that plans for partial satisfactions of hunger, thirst, etc., were futile because, during the life of a day's program taken as a whole, such wants would then only recur more often and perhaps at a higher intensity. Since, in the end, they would then require about the same aggregate provision divided over frequent intervals as they would if they were satiated on each recurrence at longer and more convenient intervals, segmentation would probably be rejected as to them. However, if shelter in a certain place were only required for a short time, a provision less than adequate for complete protection might be made; or if the "real cost" of firewood were high, the want for maintenance of bodily temperature might be segmented, in the sense that it would never be quite satisfied.[21]

On its face this sounds plausible enough. However, as soon as we attempt to reduce to quantitative terms the determination of the size of the part measure which would be chosen on such a basis of segmentation we find ourselves in almost inextricable difficulties at the point beyond which our own methods of analysis can carry us no further. Since the demonstration of these difficulties requires the inclusion of factors to be examined in the next chapter and since it is itself somewhat lengthy, it has been relegated to Appendix VI, Section C. Suffice it to say here that we are unable to find any precise quantitative basis for segmentation which does not logically lead to results that are demonstrably contrary to the facts. The best we can do is to leave the matter open, to admit the possibility, and to hope that some future investigator may find an adequate rationale. But all we can honestly agree to is that in some instances a want whose intensity is high, but the "real cost" of whose full measure is higher, may have allocated to it a quantity of "real cost" based roughly on the "real cost" of full measures for other wants of similar intensity, and therefore sufficient only, in its case, for a part measure. To admit the more logical thesis that this allocation tends to bring the value of the ratio to unity, so

[21] This qualification, I think, might apply more extensively to the wants served by protection—i.e., by shelter and clothing—than to the other prior wants.

that it places the want among those marginal wants the values of whose full measure ratios are necessarily approaching unity, would bring us face to face with a complete impasse.[22]

There seems to remain one other possible basis of segmentation. In our treatment of segmentation in Part I, where we were considering the influence of wants only, we left open the possibility that successive segments of wants are each of lesser intensity.[23] Such step-like curves of intensity are all that the supposition of segmentation would require. They escape many of the difficulties attendant on the notion of continuous decline. But even the notion of continuous decline may not seem to a reader who is thoroughly inured to it to have been completely disposed of by our disproof of the two hypotheses and their virtual orders of preference which were based on it. In view of the unsatisfactory nature of our treatment of segmentation, here, the reader with such a prepossession may have thought how much simpler it would be to account for segmentation by means of the time-honored analysis, or at least by our step-like modification of it. In order to dispose of either of these alternatives we have worked out in Appendix VI, Section D the manner in which segmentation would operate if successive segments of the want were each of lesser intensity. The results hold good for continuous decline, as well, and demonstrate that both of these constructions are subject to such serious objections that they must be considered untenable.

If choices leading to segmentation could take place on the lump-sum allocation basis with regard to means whose attribute is proportional, it is obvious that, theoretically, they could occur equally readily with regard to means whose attributes are in fixed quantity. The only further difficulty this would introduce would be that of finding what is the basis according to which man arranges the various means for a single want according to the quantity of fixed attribute. That is a problem we have not tried to solve. In general, segmentation would seem to be more likely when the means have fixed attributes, due to the fact that such fixed attributes rarely exist in quantities which might be deemed sufficient to yield a complete satisfaction. On the other hand, it is hard to find an example of a single fixed attribute serving a single want, so it may well be that segmentation is unusual even here. Seemingly partial satisfactions of this kind may, in reality, always

[22] As is demonstrated in Appendix VI, Section C.
[23] See particularly Chapter 8.

involve the all or none satisfactions of individual wants of a constellation.

According to our analysis of the operation of constellations of wants, minor members come to be considered in order only after a full measure of the preferred means for the major want has been settled upon. Thereafter, each minor member in turn may either cause an increase in the quantity of the previously preferred compound means in order to make that quantity equal its own full measure, or it may cause the total or partial substitution of another means in order also to secure complete satisfaction for itself. Whether or not this can occur depends, for each minor want, on its capacity to induce the allocation of "real cost." Here again it is possible that, if any minor want lacks the capacity to procure its satiation in one of these ways, it may be deliberately assigned a definite quantity of "real cost" in order to secure a partial satisfaction rather than to exclude it altogether. Again this deliberate segmentation would seem more likely where the attribute of the means is fixed, for the simple reason that such attributes rarely exist in quantities sufficient for satiation.[24] Here, however, a further question seems to arise. If the means selected for the major want will procure a partial incidental satisfaction for the minor want, at no "real cost" chargeable to the latter, does not the choice presented to the minor want involve the psychic measurement of a second segment of satisfaction? Granted the first segment at no chargeable cost, shall a second segment be added at a given "real cost"? However, here again, when we analyze it carefully, the choice seems to resolve itself into one between first segments of different size—more or less satisfaction—and of different "real costs." The only novelty is that the smallest segment considered involves no "real cost" chargeable to the minor want. Thereafter, just as before, any larger initial segment involves an excess of "real cost" that is chargeable to the minor want, and the larger the initial segment the larger this excess of cost.[25]

[24] As we said above, this may be too broad an admission. We do not know. It may be that most means with fixed attributes which are substitutes, more or less, for the same constellation of wants, are arranged in an order of preference according to the number of these wants they satisfy *vs.* the number they do not satisfy, and, for durables, also according to the proportion of the occasions of use or consideration on which they satisfy *vs.* the occasions on which they do not. In other words, the appraisal may be on a very compound basis but, in each case, an all or none basis rather than on one of segmentation. We have suggested this and have given examples at several previous points, particularly in Appendix VI, Section A.

[25] The question may arise whether we conceive the incidental satisfaction of the minor want derived through satiating the major want to have reduced the intensity of the

The conclusion we have reached is that whenever the influence of uniform "real costs" produces deliberate segmentation, if it does, it can only be because these costs act cumulatively at each step in the increase of a small part measure up to a full measure. Thus we find that it is likely that this influence works also on consumables in much the same way as was supposed for durables in Appendix VI, Section A.[26] With durables, the successively larger provisions serve for several or many instances of the want or wants; with consumables they serve for but one. But, for both, comparisons are probably made, not in terms of measured increments of "real cost," but in terms of measured cumulative aggregates of "real cost." And the allocation of less "real cost" than is required for a full measure or complete satisfaction is probably determined by the quantity of "real cost" one is willing to assign to a want, in view of its intensity, rather than to defer its satisfaction too long or exclude it altogether. It seems to be a compromise decision reached solely on the basis of a preference for some satisfaction rather than none and a preference for more rather than less. Therefore, it can only occur in the case of those wants which will recur less often or at less intensity by reason of a partial satisfaction. In the case of wants which continue at the same intensity after the process of partial satisfying is ended, or of wants which then recur sooner or at higher intensity, it would be fruitless.

3. SEGMENTATION WITH DIFFERENTIAL COSTS

We are now prepared, during the remainder of this section, to discard that one of our initial limiting assumptions which up to this point has restricted our consideration to the influence of *uniform* "real costs" for part lots of means composing a full measure. Let us now see what changes, if any, the admission of what we have called differential "real costs" requires in our analytical scheme. It will be recalled that, at the end of Chapter 12, we defined a differential as the difference in "real cost" between simultaneous part lots of a single product (means), due either to the different aggregate of natural resistances encountered

minor want. Under our hypothesis we do not need to guess the answer to this question. Presumably the additional quantity and therefore the excess cost required to satiate it is less than would have been the case if there had been no incidental satisfaction. Then the ratio of this want is likely to be of a higher value than it would have been if the want had to start from scratch. So, too, all its ratios for part measures, yielding more than this incidental satisfaction, will have higher values than would a full measure.

[26] See under "*Rare Raw Materials*."

in the several channels required to make up the total quantity wanted, or to differences in technique used for the several part lots—chiefly differences in scale. As noted there, there are two other causes of variation in "real cost" of single products which, however, do not usually produce differences at one and the same time. These are unintended variations in output of products depending on natural processes and intended variations in output of final product which is subject to a charge for intermediate product used in so far as that "charge" is based on life rather than use. Occasionally one or the other of these might result in differences in "real cost," per unit, between part lots of simultaneously produced product. If so, they would act here in the same way as differentials. Therefore, we shall simply include them without specific mention. Here the effect of all these differential costs will be considered only when the part lots constitute parts of a full measure and may therefore lead to segmentation. In the next subsection we will take up the effect of such differences in costs among part lots each of which constitutes a full measure. Finally, there is another condition which behaves in the same way as a differential. That is the possibility that complete satisfaction of the marginal want might necessitate an extension of working-hours at a higher intensity of the sacrifice and effort of the last hour. That will prove to be a special case which we will consider below, as well as in Chapter 14 and Appendix VI, Section H.

The only means as to which segmentation could be induced by differential costs among part lots are means with proportional attributes.[27] It is conceivable that for a single instance of a single want, which is subject to the influence of the order of ratios, a first part measure might be providable at one cost, and further part measures sufficient to increase or complete the satisfaction only at different and higher costs. When and if such conditions occur, it seems safe to assume that decisions can only be made on approximately the same basis as we have supposed, in the previous subsection, for segmentation under the influence of uniform "real costs." It must be recognized that it would be even more difficult here to impute an ability to compare the values of ratios of a whole series of part measures of increasing size; for here, by definition, the "real cost" per additional objective unit changes at some point or points in the series required for a full measure.

[27] It is clear that means in which fixed attributes exist in different quantities are different means. Usually such means are inseparable wholes—i.e., a chair, a picture, a gown, etc.

On the other hand, if such a change occurs only at one point, or perhaps at two points, there would be, in this case, a more definite division in terms of which segmentation might be considered; for, here, the obvious segmentation would conform to the part lots available at different costs. Thus we incline to think that, under such a condition, the question of segmentation would resolve itself in a still more clean-cut way into a question of allocation of "real cost." Complete satisfaction would merely be under a greater handicap. The cumulative "real costs" of part measures of increasing size would, at some point or points, begin to increase at a higher rate instead of at the previous rate. That point would be quite apparent, would lead to a fresh appraisal, and therefore might, more often than in the case of uniform costs, determine the chooser to be content with less than a full measure.

However, the real question is whether differential costs ever actually occur within a single full measure of means with proportional attributes—that is, whether the question ever arises in connection with an adequate provision for a single instance of a single want.[28] One cannot state positively that it does not. But I am impressed with the fact that all the illustrations usually cited are cases of differential costs without segmentation—i.e., among full measures—with which we shall deal in the next subsection. Therefore, it may well be that our methods of analysis have so reduced the number of cases that have been put in this classification, because we have transferred them to other classifications, that the residue is negligible or even non-existent.[29]

A certain—if abstract—possibility of this kind seems to arise from our own analysis. It is conceivable, especially in a direct economy, that the rising curve of working should intersect the diagrammatic line representing the level of intensity of the marginal want at some point before the end of the period required for that want's adequate provision. Under such a condition, the full measure could only be completed at a "real cost" whose intensity exceeded that of the want. Since that, presumably, could not occur, we would necessarily have

[28] One case that can be recognized arises when some quantity is "made to last" over a period of time in such a way that one goes on short rations for the period. We shall consider that, in the next subsection, in connection with the effect of differential costs on future provision, which, in most cases, does not produce segmentation.

[29] One can imagine an example. Suppose on a camping trip you are off in your canoe at midday. You want tea with your cold lunch. But you find your tea canister almost empty. There is enough to make one cup; but to make the two or three you would like would require a trip back to camp. That extra "real cost" for complete satisfaction is too much, and you decide to get along with one cup. But how often do such quandaries arise in ordinary life?

segmentation of the marginal want. I am inclined to accept this case as an actual one under certain special circumstances. Where the completion of provision would only require a few minutes, or in the case of any provision the whole of which could be completed in a relatively short time, no such fine discriminations would be expected. But when it happens that the marginal want has a ratio whose value approaches unity and whose inverse dimension contains a considerable block of "real cost," it seems probable that a man, if he became tired long before he had finished the job, would decide to chop off work and to be content with what he had then finished even if that were recognized to yield only a partial satisfaction.[30]

4. DIFFERENTIAL COSTS WITHOUT SEGMENTATION

There seem to be three general types of condition under which the fact that part lots of a single product can only be produced at different "real costs" may have a bearing upon a program for provision without necessarily involving segmentation.

a. If such a differential exists within the full measure of the preferred means for any want, the attributes of which are proportionate, it may make the weighted terms of substitution different for the two or more part lots. Let us suppose that the unweighted terms of a and a_1 are, for Want A, $2\ a = 3\ a_1$. Let us suppose that half of a full measure of a has a cost of 2, per unit, while a second half will cost 2.5 per unit, and that both halves of a_1 cost 1.5 per unit. The weighted terms of the first halves will then be $1\ a$ @ 2 (=2) compared to $1.5\ a_1$ @ 1.5 (= 2.25). For the first half a will be preferred. But the weighted terms of the second halves are $1\ a$ @ 2.5 (= 2.5) compared to $1.5\ a_1$ @ 1.5 (= 2.25). For the second half a_1 will be preferred. Under such conditions the existence of differential costs for part lots which constitute part measures will lead to partial substitution.

b. If such a differential exists between part lots of a means—with either proportional or fixed attributes—which lots constitute full measures for each of the several wants for which the means is capable of alternative use, the lowest cost part lot will be assigned to the earliest want in the order of preference and those at successively higher costs

[30] Such instances of "high cost" means do not include durables or large batches of course, for these contain many full measures, not one, and therefore do not involve segmentation.

only to successively later wants in turn.[31] Thus, if the "real cost" of some higher-cost part lot would be greater than the intensity of the want for which it would be required, it would not be made even though, by reversing the assignment of part lots so that they ranged from highest to lowest cost, they would all be made. This statement, though in somewhat different terms, is in accord with the usual statement of marginal utility theory on this subject. It is definitely confirmed by observation. Each use of lesser importance always has to justify the increment of a means which it requires, even if that increment can be produced at uniform cost. So much the more does it need to do so if the increment must bear a higher cost.[32] In Section G, below, we suggest the probable basic explanation of this practice.

This order of assignment of part lots at differential costs is complicated, of course, by the degree to which, for each alternative use, the particular means is preferred by reason of its more favorable weighted terms of substitution. For example, when a means is useful for two wants sufficiently near to each other in the order of priority, or, later, in the order of ratios, to be considered more or less together, these terms may alter the foregoing scheme. If one part lot is available for either at a "real cost" which makes it preferred for both on the basis of their respective weighted terms, but the next part lot is too high in cost for both, the lower-cost part lot may not be assigned to the want which comes earlier in the order of preference. It may be assigned to the want whose weighted terms give it the greater advantage over the substitute for that want, provided the substitute as to which it has the lesser advantage does not have a cost so high as to exclude the want. This because such a method serves to provide for both wants at the least aggregate cost.

c. The incidence of differential costs upon future provision is of a somewhat different order, and its effects are more varied by circumstances. However, its bearing is in one respect common to all circum-

[31] It is unnecessary to consider differences in size between the several part lots and the several full measures; for it is only the "real cost" of the several full measures that would be calculated if segmentation did not take place. If segmentation did take place, the qualification would be covered under our analysis in the previous subsection.

[32] Suppose the water supply is derived from two springs, one near and one far. The nearer is adequate for drinking water; the other is needed if washing is also to be indulged in. It is quite certain that the question of going to the further spring is decided entirely on the basis of the desire for washing water, even though the "real cost" of the further spring would be justified as a means of quenching thirst and that of the nearer spring might justify washing.

stances. When, for a single want, there is contemplated a series of provisions—or, in the case of a durable, a series of installments—for a series of instances extending into the future, an expected rise in "real cost" at some point in the series will tend to reduce the number of provisions—or installments—included in the program. As the simplest example we may cite the hypothetical situation we used to illustrate a technical necessity of the first type. Let us suppose that a certain number of future provisions of ripe wild grain can be collected on a near-by prairie, but that, in order to collect more, it is necessary to go to some little distance and thus incur a higher "real cost." The question then raised is not one determined by the retention involved, as in our previous use of this example. For, here, the retention would be only slightly higher by reason of the increased "real cost"—i.e., it would be KT times the increase. Rather, the question will be settled on the basis of the increment of working necessitated, and therefore on the basis of the penalty of longer hours or more current forgoing. At the point where, or for the range after, the higher cost provisions begin, the question of further provisions will be reviewed. As a result, this series will be abbreviated to a new limit at which the reduced values of the corrected ratios somewhere in the series become too low to intrude any longer into the current order of preference.[33]

The effect is similar in the case of a durable except that, here, the actual choice is hardly ever between more or less installments (durability) in a single product, but rather between different products serving the same want whose numbers of installments differ. Previously,[34] we considered the influence of "real costs" when the cost in work per installment remains the same. That involves the assumption of a somewhat ideal situation, since it is hardly likely that two different durables for a single want whose durability is different will each involve exactly the same work per installment. If the more durable means has also a less cost per installment, it will naturally be preferred up to some point. But, here, we are supposing that the more durable means has a greater cost per installment. The question, then, is not merely that of adding a further series of installments at a higher cost for each, but of

[33] In terms of our dimensional formula, if W + WKT represents the influence of "real cost" in determining the limit of futurity for any want, the limit will obviously be nearer the higher is W per day's provision—i.e., the greater is W, the less can be T.

It is possible to conceive that the aggregate of W that is assignable to a series of provisions may remain approximately constant, so that the series is shorter the higher is W per provision. However, I doubt that the decision is made in those lump-sum terms.

[34] See p. 913, above.

adding a second series which must also bear the greater cost per installment of the first series. If a series of ten can be produced at a cost of 2 units each, but one of twenty can only be produced at a cost of 2.5 units each, the cost per installment of the added series of ten will be 3 units each. The question seems to be settled in much the same way as for the first technical necessity. It is not so much, however, that a new decision is called for under such circumstances. Rather, the initial decision will have to take account of the two alternatives. But, under these conditions, the series is likely to be shorter by reason of differential costs than it would be if costs remained uniform.

There are two possible modifications in our general analysis of future provision which this element of differential costs may introduce. When a sharp difference in "real cost" per provision or per installment puts upon a series of provisions or upon durability a limit that is notably different from what it would be at uniform "real costs," the consequent reduction in the length of the series may not always be applied at the end—that is, against the instances of the greatest degree of futurity. This because, at the limit of the reduced series—the lower cost series—the last provision or installment does not show a combined "real cost" just less than the force of the want. Instead, it may be very considerably less. As a result, in some cases, the several provisions or installments may be applied over the whole period—i.e., up to their limit of futurity—in either one of two different ways. For instance, as we have seen, it may be decided to satisfy the want completely only every other day, leaving it entirely unsatisfied on alternate days. This we call *alternation*. On the other hand, it may be decided to ration oneself by spreading the use evenly over all the days, thus satisfying a first segment only on each day.[35] This we call *spreading*. If wants actually decreased in intensity with their degree of futurity, either of these procedures would be impossible. The fact that such procedures certainly occur is one of our reasons for concluding that future instances have the same force as current ones. Such alternation or spreading involves a slightly higher cost for retaining than would the consumption of a consecutive series of full measures or uses. But, for short periods, the difference would be minutely small. And, by way of confirmation, we observe that such alternation or spreading is rarely done over long periods. When either is done over longish periods it is only done by the

[35] Strictly speaking this case belongs under our classification of segmentation with differential costs. We alluded to it in the previous subsection.

very thrifty—that is, those people whose constant, K, is particularly small.

G. SOME GENERALIZATIONS

As a result of our synthesis, in this chapter, of the influence of wants and the influence of "real costs" in determining the actual order of preference under unchanging costs, we are now prepared to combine certain conclusions which we reached in Part III with those arrived at here. We can conveniently start with an examination of the actual operation of the motive of maximization, so-called, which, it will be remembered, we dealt with tentatively in the last section of Chapter 12. In a direct economy under unchanging conditions—that is, with an unchanging set of wants of given intensity, with given "real costs" for means which can be produced in indefinitely increasing quantities at uniform "real costs," or with given "real costs" and quantities for each part lot at differential "real costs"—how does the motive of maximization work?

In the first place, under these conditions, the motive of maximization is the proximate cause which sets the limit of capacity by reason of its effect on the allocation of time. Time can be devoted to working or to leisure. As working-time increases, working becomes more effortful, its fruits less attractive, and leisure more inviting; as leisure-time passes, working appears less effortful, its fruits more attractive, and further leisure perhaps less inviting. Without repeating the details, we may say that the motive of maximization fixes the point at which the net inducements to working overbalance those of leisure so that the working-day starts; it also fixes the subsequent point at which the net inducements to working are overbalanced by those of leisure and the working-day stops. The period between these two critical points measures capacity in so far as capacity can be measured only in hours of working. However, the ultimate causes determining these critical points constitute a complex—a complex which constitutes the conditions in which the motive of maximization works. Not only does the incidence of these critical points depend on the "shape" of the curve of wants (order of priority) and on the "shapes" of the curves of working effort and of working sacrifice (leisure), as well as on the relation among them all, but it depends also on the "real costs" of a full or part measure of means for each want in turn. For the greater the "real cost" per want along the order of preference, the fewer will be the number of wants that can be provided for by any certain capacity, and vice versa. Therefore, the greater the "real cost" per want included, the greater the tendency to expand capacity, and vice versa; for the shorter the reach of any given capacity, the more intense will be the last want to which it reaches, and vice versa. The conditions under which one or the other of these opposing tendencies is effective can be more readily demonstrated in terms of changing capacity than it can in terms of different given capacities to which we are restricting ourselves here. Therefore, we reserve for the next chapter our final analysis of the determination of capacity.

In the second place, the motive of maximization is clearly the determinant of choice between substitute means for a single want which have proportionate attributes. The subjective—unweighted—terms of substitution determine the quantities of each which are indifferent. The externally given terms—weighting—determine which is the least costly. Preference for the least costly is a result of the motive of maximization. Or, from the standpoint of these particular comparisons—indifferent results for different costs—it may be said to be the result of the motive of economizing, which is the same motive viewed from the opposite standpoint.[1]

However, when it comes to the allocation of a given capacity among provisions for different wants, current or future, the motive of maximization appears not to work precisely or not to work alone. It is evident that, if this motive worked precisely and alone, the actual current order of preference would exactly follow the order of ratios. But we have seen good reason to believe that it does not do this. Instead, the order of priority appears to govern entirely in the early range, to be a chief influence in the middle range, and only to yield wholly to the order of ratios around the limit of capacity. And the order of priority most certainly does not conform to the order of ratios. Therefore, it cannot be construed to reflect the motive of maximization; it reflects, purely and simply, the intensities of the wants, perhaps combined with the concept of "necessities," for the most part without regard to costs and often without regard to consequences.[2]

Therefore, the effect of the motive of maximization upon the current order of preference seems to be limited. Its first effect is positive and

[1] The term maximization suggests preference for the greater of two satisfactions per unit of "real cost"; the term economizing suggests preference for the lesser of two "real costs" per "unit" of satisfaction.

[2] The concept of "necessities" was suggested in Appendix VI, Section B 3.

definite. It excludes any want to whose provision leisure is preferred. That is, in our technical terms, it excludes all wants the value of whose ratios is less than unity, whether these wants occupy a position in the order of priority before the general range lying around the limit of capacity, or a position in or beyond that range. And, in the current order of preference, it does frequently defer a want to a later position or bring it forward to an earlier position in so far as the order of ratios interferes.[3] That is all that we can admit for it. Since, then, we are identifying this particular effect of the motive of maximization with the influence of "real costs" and the order of ratios, it is not necessary to carry the statement further into the field of minor members of a constellation, future (beyond current) wants, or the uncertainties of segmentation. The motive of maximization works on the current order of preference only, in the form of the influence of "real costs."

There is one further effect of this motive. When differential costs exist as to part lots which constitute full measures for alternative uses, it is clearly the motive of maximization which determines that the lowest cost lot shall be assigned to the want which comes earlier in the order of preference and each successively higher cost lot only to each later want in turn. Under the influence of the order of priority alone that procedure might be reversed. Then the same series of part lots of a single means might satisfy more wants (alternative uses). It is the motive of maximization operating through an order of consideration based on the order of priority that prevents this. Or, as we stated the procedure in Chapter 12, there is an order of preference among channels and concurrently usable techniques which runs from the lowest cost to the highest.[4] Nor is this a mere matter of procedure. It is sound. The aggregate of wants satisfied is necessarily higher under this influence than it would be under the influence of wants alone.[5]

[3] It may seem, at first sight, that it is gratuitous to work out an order of preference within the limits set by exclusions. But, in our whole picture, that is not the case. See p. 852, note 2.

[4] This is the type of behavior we described on p. 837.

[5] That is, if the size of the two full measures is the same for Wants C and H and if two part lots cost 5 and 7 units respectively while the intensity of C is 8 but that of H is 6, the second part lot would be rejected for H but not for C. The first part lot would be rejected for neither. However the application of all 12 units to these two wants might preclude the application of the second 7 units to Want G with an intensity just above 7. That would yield only 14 "units" of satisfaction as against 15 +.

If the size of the two full measures is considerably different for wants whose position in the order or preference is governed by the values of their ratios—say O and R—and the full measure for R is much less than for O, the position of R in the order of preference will be considerably earlier than that of O. The calculation would then be a

Our second generalization deals with the determination of the "quantity wanted" of any means—a question which we left unsettled in Chapter 12, but which the synthesis of the influence of wants and the influence of "real costs" in this chapter has enabled us to resolve. For any means indefinite quantities of which can be produced at a uniform and given cost, the quantity wanted will depend on the following factors:

a. For what wants is it the preferred complete or partial substitute at that cost?

b. What is the sum of the full measures among such wants—including alternative uses—current provision for which will be included in the current order of preference at that cost?

c. What is the sum of the part measures among such wants that must be added because for certain wants there is partial substitution at this cost, or because only a part measure will be provided for certain wants at this cost (segmentation)?

d. What is the sum of the full and part measures that must be added by reason of the intrusion of future instances (beyond current) of any of these wants into the current order of preference at this cost?

The simplest way to conceive the quantity wanted of any means when differential costs exist is to base it on the foregoing. Applying the highest-cost part lot to the alternative want which comes last in the order of preference or to the future provision with the greatest degree of futurity—and so placing it in the ratio which will, as a result, have the lowest value—and working back, all full or part measures will be excluded or reduced the value of whose ratio is less than unity. Of course, this statement is only analytically correct. The worker-retainer does not start with a program based on uniform costs and then proceed backward, lopping off those provisions whose cost is too high. He proceeds forward, adding only those provisions whose cost is not too high. But, in either view, he is apt to add less at differential than at uniform costs. This scheme may be modified to some extent by the principle of least extra cost of substitution, as stated before.

We have not discussed in this section the effect of declining costs as quantity is increased. This because in a direct economy such a situation would never produce a differential, and therefore part lots at dif-

---

more complicated one. But it is still probable that the lower cost lot would be assigned to R, if that sufficed; for it would again be O which required the higher cost lot, or part of it, to make up its full measure.

ferent costs. Under such conditions all lots would be produced at the lower cost. Nevertheless, we should, in dealing with quantity wanted, examine briefly this effect.

Decreased costs per unit due to unplanned excess production (e.g., good crops) clearly do not concern us here. The quantity wanted was the planned or expected output. The effect of a variation from that on the allocation of the surplus means in a direct economy has been considered on pp. 893 to 894, above, and incidentally in Appendix VI, Section A.

However, in planned production, even in a direct economy, it is possible that, through some range at least, the larger the quantity the lower will be its cost per unit. This would be due either to an open alternative to use a larger scale technique or to the fact that the more continuous use of a given scale technique would involve a lower charge per unit of final product for the use of the intermediate product. Such a reduced charge applies only to that part of the cost of the intermediate product which is charged off per unit of time rather than per unit of use.[6] When such a situation exists as to any means (final product), more substitutions, more subordinate alternative uses, and more distant future provisions may be added, the lower, within these limits, will be the "real cost" per full or part measure as a result of such additions to the quantity wanted. As consideration proceeds along the order of priority, reversals in the weighted terms of substitution may result from the prospective lower costs; the greater this reduction in cost, the more delayed will be the point at which any want, served in alternative use, will be excluded by reason of a ratio with a value less than unity; and, where occasions for future provision appear, the more distant will be the limit of futurity.

It is a fine question whether, in a direct economy, it would be the marginal cost of each lower cost increment or the lower average cost produced by such increases of quantity that would be decisive in determining each of these possible inclusions. I am inclined to think that would vary according to circumstances. When the cost of the increment consisted of added direct work only—or mainly—and when the possible increase of production to cover a subordinate want presented itself for the first time, or only occasionally, it seems likely that marginal cost only would govern. That is, if it is seen that a little more

[6] Obviously the charge per unit of use remains uniform in amount. More continuous use merely charges off the whole cost of the intermediate product in a shorter period of time.

work will increase the quantity or "quality" (fixed attributes) sufficiently, the little more will act by itself. But, probably, only the first time or occasionally. After the little more work has become incorporated in a regular and repeated program, the whole cost would come to be applied to the whole output. To the extent that the marginal cost of the increment was nil, because it required merely more continuous use of intermediate product without any direct work, it seems likely that the same distinction would arise. The first time it occurred, or if it occurred only occasionally, the extra use might be conceived to have no cost. But, as soon as it became regular or frequent, the added use would be lumped in with all others. Then, when the question of replacing the intermediate product arose, the least want would probably have to bear its share of the total cost or be excluded. It will be seen that all cases come under one or the other of these headings, or under a combination of the two. No reduction in cost occurs by reason of more continuous use of intermediate product, in so far as the charge is a charge for use.[7]

In defining the quantity wanted of any means (final product) we have furnished the basis for a definite conception of the "limit of payability" which we used as an analytical tool in Section D of Chapter 12. In a direct economy, precise definition of this limit is a relatively simple matter. But, in giving it for a direct economy, we must make clear that, for an indirect economy, it is a vastly more complex matter. The "limit of payability" is defined by the highest-cost part lot that will be included in the quantity wanted.[8] We used the term "limit of payability" only in connection with our consideration of natural resistances. It applies chiefly to the extraction of natural materials and powers. Since such individual materials and powers may enter into several final products, the quantity wanted of any of them is determined by the sum of the quantity wanted of each of the final products

[7] For the substitution of a larger scale technique there would probably be some marginal cost, though, by definition, the average cost would also be reduced. For the more continuous use of the same technique and intermediate product the marginal cost, if no direct work was involved, would only be that of a use and might even be ignored. Then the average, at least, would be reduced. As an example, we may imagine our isolated farmer consenting to the use by his children of the farm horses and wagon for an occasional hay ride, because no marginal cost appears to be involved. But, if that required more horses and wagons, or their more frequent replacement, he would reject the request. And the first time they broke the wagon down, necessitating work to repair it, would be the last time.

[8] Or, as we put it on pp. 837 to 838, it is defined by the point along the order or preference for sites, and for depths and dilutions on any site, to which the quantity wanted reaches. That point is determined as described below.

in which it is one of the preferred components. For each such material or power there may be several sites in use, and more available, where accessibility varies. At each site it may be possible to work several "depths" concurrently or alternatively. Each channel of production for each final product may require a series of sites for different steps in the process. The individual sites in use, or available, for a material or power will then be related differently to these several channels of production.

For each material and power it will be possible to determine the part lot that can be produced at the lowest "real cost," including all costs for which this material or power is responsible as a component of the final product. This will represent what we called the lowest "Total Resistance Level" in Chapter 12. In judging this level, the relationship to the channel, the accessibility of and on the several sites, and the several possible depths on each site must all be taken into consideration, for the several optima may not be combined. In the same way the part lot that can be produced at the next lowest cost can be determined. And so on until one has a complete schedule.

The quantity wanted of each final product is strictly limited to the sum of the full and part measures for the wants within the limit for which it is preferred, as given on p. 941, above. Only if "real cost" of a full measure compels segmentation or results in exclusion of the want (or of alternative uses or of future provisions) does "real cost" affect the quantity wanted. For each final product the motive of maximization will select the least cost materials or powers which will produce indifferent final products. If along the schedule of part lots of any material, etc., thus preferred, the quantity of final product wanted does not require enough to reach a point where "real cost" excludes or diminishes any of its part lots, the quantity wanted will, nevertheless, have determined the maximum cost lot of material, etc. It is the highest cost lot that is required to make up that quantity. If, on the other hand, the quantity wanted does reach far enough to be limited by "real cost," it will be diminished as stated on p. 941. At that point the schedule will produce a "real cost" which causes a ratio with a value less than unity (or a smaller segment). That, too, determines the highest cost lot that is required. In both situations, all lots that can be produced at less than this highest cost are preferred by reason of the motive of maximization. The limit of payability reflects this fact. It will pay to work each site, concurrently or alternatively, down to a depth at which that resistance when added to all others (Total Resistance Level) causes a "real cost" which results in final product at this highest cost. It will not pay to work it deeper than that.[9]

[9] It will be noted that, unlike the older presentation, the limitation of quantity wanted by reason of rising "real costs" of larger quantities only occurs with us as an exception. This because, with us, the usual reason for fixing the quantity produced is that no more is wanted, not that no more can be produced at a "real cost" at which it will be wanted. This would certainly be true of a direct economy. Is it also true of an indirect economy? If, in the latter, "values" are proportionate to the highest "real cost" necessary to make up the quantity wanted of a final product in order to produce satiation of all concerned, then no one would choose deliberately to make additional quantities at still higher "real costs"; for, then, these would be higher than the "value" and still higher than the probable "price," as suggested in Section D 2, above, and in Appendix VI, Section A.

14

THE ACTUAL ORDER OF PREFERENCE—CHANGING "REAL COSTS"

In the previous chapter we have developed a scheme representing the actual order of preference as we infer it from our analysis of its apparent causes, and we have continually tested this construction as to its conformity to fact as nearly as we can determine the characteristics of the actual order by observation of reality. We have attributed to the influence of wants and to the influence of "real costs," respectively, the parts they would have to play, if they work as we think they do, in order that their combined results would conform to such an order. But, in doing so, we have treated as "given" the order of priority and the relative intensity of wants as well as the "real costs" of all full or part lots of means. That has served the purpose of a coherent, if tentative, explanation of the formation of a single day's program for the allocation of effort, or even of a series of such programs under a single set of conditions existing in the present. Now we have to take account of changes in these conditions over time, in order to bring our analysis into closer accord with a reality that never for long remains the same.

We recognize, of course, that changes take place within the want system. Even with no change in the relative intensity of wants it may be that experience gradually teaches a discrimination as to which wants to satisfy and which to leave unsatisfied for better adaptation *in toto*. Certainly the gradually acquired knowledge of particular means, which can only arise from experience of their use, leads to more successful preferences through changing their unweighted terms of substitution. Our analysis has already admitted variations in successive daily programs even with a fixed system of wants. For instance, provision for a contingency of the second type, the kind of alternation of a voluntarily limited quantity of means so that satisfactions alternate with unsatisfactions, etc., are all of this order. When it comes to changes in the want system itself, we have supposed that under unchanged circumstances of life and surroundings they are rare. Actually, however, circumstances do not remain unchanged. Relations with the environment are subject to regular and irregular fluctuations due to such factors as seasonal, cyclical, or even secular alterations in climate. Within even the minimum group (family) which we have had to recognize as the nearest approach to our direct economy, wants change with increasing age, with matrimony, with parenthood, etc. Within or between larger groups they change for frivolous reasons—fashions, fads, etc.—as well as for highly serious ones—wars, etc. However, it seems unnecessary separately to analyze the effects of such changes. Our analysis to this point has assumed no specified relations among wants or between wants and means. We have not pretended to name in their order the wants that follow the great prior wants, nor to identify the respective means and their quantities. Therefore, this analysis seems to serve quite as well for an order of priority and for estimates of usefulness that change from day to day. All that is required is to conceive a different order or different estimates and then to apply them through the scheme in the same way. There is one exception to this. Whether the want system remains the same or changes, the volume of future provision may increase or decrease due to the somewhat haphazard appearance of occasions for which future provision is required. These fluctuations have an influence which needs to be taken into account.[1] But, with that exception, we can ignore in what follows all changes in the want system and confine ourselves to the effects of changing "real costs."

A. EFFECTS OF CHANGING "REAL COSTS"

Retaining constitutes no part of the fund we have called capacity; it is subject to its own system of limitation; its quantitative effects upon the limit of capacity are therefore entirely indirect. These last will be considered as they appear.[1] Otherwise we are concerned here only

[1] Or, at least, it becomes necessary at this stage to include the account which we worked out in Chapter 10.

[1] This was made clear in Chapter 13, Section E. There is no corresponding capacity for retaining. Its quantity is decided on its own basis and separately in each instance as a matter of preference for some future as against some current provision. It is subject to the limitation of futurity only. And it is a matter of redirecting working.

In a sense the limit of working capacity is also a matter of preference. But that preference only appears critical at the limit. Thus working within that limit becomes a

with changes in "real cost" in the form of work. Moreover, we can disregard here all changes in work cost which may be called *ex post facto*—that is, all increases or decreases in work required per unit of product due to the fact that the quantity of product turns out to be less or more than was intended. This because such changes can have had no influence on the allocation of working in the plan or program. Such changes result from (a) variations in the quantity produced by a natural process below or above the amount for which the given aggregate of work was allocated; (b) variations in indirect work (intermediate product) chargeable by reason of wanting a smaller or larger quantity of final product than was expected; (c) variations in loss by spoilage, etc. That leaves us with two main types of cost change which may be taken as typical of all others. These are (a) lower costs in work by reason of improved technique; [2] and (b) higher costs in work due to the progressive exhaustion of the more accessible sites, materials, and powers, or due to the necessity of using the less accessible by reason of an increase in quantity wanted. The discovery of more accessible resources works much the same as the invention of better techniques so far as our problem here is concerned.[3] Under accessibility we may include the relative degree of all natural resistances, even congestion.

All this deals with "real cost" per unit of product measured in terms of a unit of standard work such as we developed in Chapter 9. But here we are introducing again another dimension for such "real cost." For now, having abandoned the assumption of fixed "real costs" in work we have also, of necessity, abandoned the fixed limit of capacity and therefore the fixed working-day to which we have, for the most part,

---

lump sum to be allocated, as retaining (at least in a direct economy) is not.

True, the necessity of retaining is in part imposed by the facts of the environment, as we saw in Chapter 11. But these as well as the technical options tend to merge the two "real costs" in a way that prevents our considering changes in retaining cost by itself.

[2] For the sake of logical precision we should admit here, that, in a direct economy, increases in personal skill operate in much the same way as do improvements in technique. For future use we have distinguished the two—or, at least, we have distinguished non-transmissible efficiency from transmissible efficiency. We have treated variations in personal skill as multiples or fractions of the standard unit of working—the delivery of more or less standard units of work per unit of time. But, for an individual who acquires more skill in the course of time, the number of standard units of work per unit of time will increase. The reach of his capacity is then extended without increase in the working-day. That is equivalent to a reduction in "real cost" in terms of our analysis in this chapter. Thus it should be borne in mind that the general condition, changes in technique, must, for a direct economy, be stretched to include changes in non-transmissible efficiency.

[3] That is, because greater accessibility economizes work just as the technical options do, it acts like an expansion of capacity.

confined ourselves hitherto.[4] In other words, we are now prepared to face the questions which arise when all our variables, including the intensity of the last hour's working, are allowed to vary. Since this is inherently a most complicated matter we shall approach it step by step. In subsections 1 and 2 we shall ignore the effect of changing "real costs" upon capacity and shall analyze the effects of such changes only in the revision of the preferred means for each want and in the rearrangement of the order of preference as a whole which they produce. Then, in subsection 3, we shall correct this presentation, so far as that is necessary, in the course of determining the effect of such changes of cost in altering the reach of capacity along the order of preference and in setting a new limit for the working-day.

1. EFFECTS OF CHANGING "REAL COSTS" ON PREFERENCES AMONG SUBSTITUTES

Such effects are confined to the results of the changes in weighted terms of substitution produced by changes in "real cost." The first and simplest case concerns means of proportionate attributes which are, in some set of unweighted terms, indifferent substitutes for a single want. In the example we used in Section B of Chapter 13, $3\,a = 2\,a_1 = 5\,a_2$ because these quantities are the full measures of each as means for satisfying Want A. At the several uniform "real costs" attributed there, which were 3 per a, 4 per a_1, and 2 per a_2, the weighted terms of substitution are a: a_1: a_2 = 9: 8: 10. On these terms a_1 will be the preferred means. This preference for a_1 at constant cost will remain the same so long as the "real cost" of a remains more than 2⅔ per a and the "real cost" of a_2 remains more than 1.5 per a_2. But if, for instance, the "real cost" of a declines to 2.5, the weighted terms will become a: a_1: a_2 = 7.5: 8: 10. Then a will become the preferred means. Now it should be noted that, on the original set of weighted terms, preference was on an all or none basis; a full measure of a_1 (2 units) was wanted; no a or a_2 were wanted. Correspondingly, when a becomes the preferred means, a full measure of a (3 units) is wanted; no a_1 or a_2 are wanted. That is, the effect is a shift, on the all or none basis, from a full measure of a_1 to a full measure of a. It is not necessary to repeat this analysis to illustrate the effect of a rise in the "real cost" of

[4] With the single exception of extra working induced by future provision.

a_1, for instance. If sufficient, the effect would be, of course, a shift to *a* even though the "real cost" of *a* remained unchanged. In other words, it is the relative, not the absolute, "real costs" among indifferent substitutes which are determining.

When a means with proportionate attributes is susceptible of alternative uses—that is, when it can serve more than one want, either single wants or major members of different constellations—the effect of changes in "real cost" upon each individual want served is the same as in the foregoing. Any substitution induced by such changes will be on an all or none basis—a full measure of the new, instead of a full measure of the old, preferred substitute. But here the competing substitutes, or at least the unweighted terms of substitution, will be different for each want served. Thus it will be possible that the change in relative costs will be sufficient to alter the preference, on the basis of weighted terms, for one or more wants while leaving that of others undisturbed. As a result the effect from the standpoint of the means as a whole may not be on an all or none basis. A full measure for one—or for each of more—of its uses may be added to or subtracted from the combined full measures for the others. We have heretofore concluded that the scope of alternative use for final product is a very limited one. [5] Therefore, this special case is not of major importance.

Again considering means with proportionate attributes only, and assuming that all units constituting a full measure of each are available at uniform cost, let us examine the effect of changing "real costs" where the means have attributes serving different members of a constellation. The only conditions under which this case can differ from the first one are that a minor member is not satiated by the preferred means for the major want and that it is still capable, after partial satisfaction, of inducing the allocation of sufficient extra "real cost" to insure its own satiation.[6] When these conditions are met, either the minor want can cause the substitution of a full measure for the major want of a previously rejected substitute, if that also constitutes at least a full measure for itself; or it can cause the substitution of a full measure for itself, in excess of that of the major want and among any of the indifferent substitutes for the latter; or it can cause the partial substitution of a previously rejected substitute in such a proportion that the composite of the two means will constitute a full measure both for

[5] See p. 892.

[6] Because we had not considered segmentation in Section D 1 of Chapter 13 we did not there introduce the qualification, "after partial satisfaction."

the major want and for itself. In all three situations, the actual choice will presumably be determined on the principle of least extra cost chargeable to the minor want. Now, if the "real costs" of any or several of these substitutes rise or fall, the weighted terms of substitution for the major want may be altered. A different substitute may be preferred for that want. This new preference, in turn, will change the situation presented to the minor want. If the new preference does not incidentally satiate the minor want and if that want is still capable of inducing the allocation of sufficient "real costs" to secure its satiation, the terms of choice will be reviewed and the selection made on the same principle as before—that is, least extra "real cost" chargeable to the minor want. With one minor possible exception the effect of changing "real costs," if these changes are sufficient to cause substitution of a different means, will be on an all or none basis. That is, the whole of the previously preferred substitute—or, in the case of partial substitution, all of that part—will be eliminated and such quantity of a new substitute as is equivalent to it on the basis of the unweighted terms will take its place.[7]

In the case of means with fixed attributes the case is even simpler. For then there can be no different full measures for the minor members of the constellation to which the fixed attributes appeal. Instead, there are only natural units (e.g., a tree) or artificial units (e.g., a gown). On pp. 887–888 we offered an example. Analytically, what occurs is an arrangement of full measures of all substitutes for the major want in an order of increasing content of the fixed attribute catering to the minor want. For each quantity of content only the least costly means appears in the order. Choice for the minor want depends then on how much content will be afforded for it. If the cost relations among these different means change, the order may change or it may remain the same while the difference in cost between any successive pair of means becomes larger or smaller. Either may cause a revision of the choice for the minor want; for either may enable the minor want to afford more attribute or compel it to accept less attribute. If a revision is made at all, it is always on an all or none basis. A unit of the newly preferred means takes the place of a unit of the formerly preferred means. The latter is no longer wanted at all. Since partial substitution

[7] The one exception is the case where changes of "real costs" among partial substitutes cause an alteration of the quantity of the preferred substitute for the major want. That may occur if the unweighted terms are different for two partial substitutes. Even then the effect is on an all or none basis for the partial substitute.

cannot occur as to means with fixed attributes there are, here, no exceptions to this rule.

Under all the various circumstances we have considered—with the minor exception noted—any shift from one to another substitute induced by a change in their relative "real costs" takes place at a single critical point—the point at which the weighted terms of substitution change from favoring one to favoring another substitute. There is no gradual effect; the shift does not take place by degrees. No effect at all is had until the critical point is reached; at that point the shift takes place as a whole—completely; after that point is passed there is no further effect. Furthermore, under all these circumstances, the appearance of any quantity wanted for a newly preferred substitute always has as its obverse the disappearance of all quantity wanted of the previously preferred substitute for each particular want. Only in the single case where alternative uses are included or excluded by reason of a change in relative "real cost" does the shift fail to affect the whole quantity wanted of the means. Then the appearance and disappearance may be in terms of full measures for one or more uses independently of all others. Finally, it should be emphasized that, under all these circumstances, shifts from a full measure of one to a full measure of another substitute may be induced by a change in "real cost" of either. The critical point is concerned with relative "real costs" only, not with absolute "real costs." Thus it is impossible to determine—or to show—what will happen to the quantity wanted of any one substitute by reason of changes in its own "real cost" only. If the cost of *a*, in our first example, declines from 3 to 2.5, but, at the same time that of the previously preferred substitute, a_1, declines from 4 to 3.5, there will be no shift. The quantity wanted of *a* will not increase from zero; the quantity wanted of a_1 will remain the same. That will be equally true if the "real cost" of a_1 rises from 4 to 4.75 but, at the same time, that of *a* rises from 3 to 3.2. Moreover, any changes in "real cost" insufficient to reverse a preference on the basis of the weighted terms of substitution will have no effect whatever upon that preference.

Only one modification is required in these conclusions in order to adapt them to the condition of differential costs within a full measure of means—i.e., when the two or more part measures making up a full measure are part lots at different costs. Then, as we noted in subsection F 4 of Chapter 13, partial substitution may be induced for a single want considered by itself. Since the different part lots will then have different weighted terms of substitution, a first part measure of one means may be preferred, a second part measure of another means, and so on. Changes of "real cost" may affect the weighted terms of substitution of each part lot independently of all others. While, for each, a shift, if induced, will still be on an all or none basis, it may affect the quantity wanted only in terms of part lots, not as to the means as a whole.

When these differential costs exist among full measures for alternative uses, no modification of the previous conclusions is necessary. What we said above still holds good. The weighted terms of substitution for each use, and perhaps the competing substitutes, will be different for each want capable of being served. All we need to add to that, here, is that for each want served—for each part lot—the "real cost" per unit will be different from that for each other; and, as we observed on pp. 934–935, the successively higher cost part lots will be assigned successively to wants which come later in the order of preference.

2. EFFECTS OF CHANGING "REAL COSTS" ON THE ORDER OF PREFERENCE

We shall continue, in this subsection, to examine the effects of changing "real costs" without regard to the alteration they must inevitably produce in the reach of capacity and in the duration of the working-day. If, at this point, we determine how rises and declines in cost affect the position in the order of preference of the want which is involved—how they rearrange that order—it will be much simpler, in the next subsection, to show clearly the effect they have in altering the incidence upon that order of the dividing line between inclusion and exclusion.

It is obvious that changes in "real cost" can only have effects on the order of preference in so far as "real costs" themselves have effects. Or, in our previous terms, changes in "real costs" affect primarily the order of ratios only. Only so far as the order of ratios influences the order of preference can a rearrangement of the order of ratios cause a rearrangement of the order of preference. We attempted to evaluate this influence in Chapter 13, Section C 4. It is not necessary to repeat those results. Suffice it to say now that wants whose position in the order of preference is determined solely by their position in the order of priority do not have that position altered by reason of rises or declines in their "real costs." All other wants whose position in the order of preference is subject to the interference of the influence of "real costs" may, to that extent, have their position altered by reason of such changes.

Among these latter wants let us restrict ourselves at first to cases in which choices are in terms of full measures both before and after the change in "real costs" and to choices among current provisions only. This classification covers choices determined by single wants or by members of a constellation; [8] it covers wants whose means are capable of alternative uses, provided it is borne in mind that the effect upon each want which the means serves in its alternative uses is independent of that upon all others; it even covers wants whose means show differential costs among part lots, provided the part lots each constitute a full measure for some alternative use. For all such cases the effect on an individual want will be the same. Since we are viewing the subject from the standpoint of the several wants, not that of the means, it is well to remind ourselves that a change in "real cost" which leads to a reversal of preference among substitutes will as certainly alter the ratio of the want as a change which leaves the preference undisturbed. If the ratio is changed, the position of the want in the order of preference will also be changed, in so far as the ratio is governing. Therefore, what follows applies equally to both. It is possible at least to conceive of alterations in weighted terms of substitution which will produce any of the effects we now proceed to describe.

The effect of a rise in "real cost" sufficient to reduce the value of the ratio from above to below unity will be to place that want beyond the limit of capacity—to exclude it; and the effect of a lesser rise in "real cost" will be to defer the want to a later position in the order of preference—that is, so far as the "real cost" is effective, to give it the position to which the value of its new ratio and the resulting place in the order of ratios entitles it. Conversely, the effect of a decline in "real cost" sufficient to raise the value of the ratio from below to above unity will be to bring that want from beyond to within the limit of capacity—to include it; and the effect of a decline in "real cost" for a want already within the limit of capacity will be to give the want an earlier position in the order of preference—that is, so far as the "real cost" is

[8] So far as the minor members of constellations are concerned the effect of changes of "real cost" only operates through the extra cost chargeable to the minor want. Thus, when excluded, such a want may continue to be partially satisfied and, when included, its satisfaction may only increase from a partial one to satiation.

effective, to place it in the order of preference among wants the values of whose ratios are similar and whose positions in the order of ratios are therefore neighboring.

The quantitative measure of such effects upon the quantity of means wanted will be on an all or none basis so far as the individual wants are concerned. The full measure of a want excluded will disappear from the program; that of a want included will appear *de novo*. Where the position of the want in the order of preference remains within the limit of capacity the quantitative effect will be nil. But, so far as the individual means are concerned the quantitative effects will not, in some cases, be on an all or none basis. The inclusion or the exclusion of alternative uses of any means, by reason of declines or rises of "real cost," will merely add to or subtract from the aggregate of different full measures included in the quantity wanted. Also where a minor member of a constellation would prefer its own larger full measure of the same means preferred for the major want, the quantity wanted would be increased from the smaller to the larger full measure by reason of a decline in "real cost" sufficient to reduce the chargeable extra cost to a point at which the minor want could be included; similarly, the quantity wanted would be decreased from the larger to the smaller full measure by a sufficient rise in "real cost." However, even from the standpoint of the means, such changes in quantity wanted would be discontinuous steps of considerable size.

When we introduce the subclass of future provisions into the class of choices in terms of full measures, the effects are somewhat different. It is obvious that the "real cost" in terms of work of a full measure for any want is the same whether it constitutes future or current provision.[9] Therefore, the base position (as we have called it) in the order of preference of any future provision will be the same as that of the corresponding current provision. As a result, if the position of the current provision in the order of preference is altered by a change in "real cost," the base position of all corresponding future provisions will be altered along with it.[10] However, the competitive situation of any future instance of a want—its ability to intrude in the current order of

[9] At some points we have dealt in terms of a day's future provision instead of adequate provision for a single instance of the want. Since the former is a multiple of the latter, it is easy to adjust for it.

[10] What we are calling the base position corresponds to the position in its own order of preference which a future provision would have when its instance became current. That statement relates this notion to the mental diagram we constructed in Chapter 13, Section E.

preference—is determined not only by its base position but also by its degree of futurity. In Appendix V,[11] where we gave examples of the effect of a very high rate of accrual of retaining cost, we found that, at 30 days hence, future provision for Want A could not compete with current provision for Want B but took precedence of current provision for Want C, etc.; but at 90 days hence Future Want A lost to current D and only competed on a par with current E. Thus the position in the current order of preference of any future instance of a want is deferred from that of its current instance—its base position—in proportion to its degree of futurity. In terms of our dimensional formula, this deferment, for any certain degree of futurity, is measured by $WKT^{-1} \times T$, or WK. Therefore, any change in "real cost" in work, W, will produce for each degree of futurity a change in position equal to the change in the base position plus or minus the change in the effect of futurity; and the latter will be equal to K times the change in W. Since K is normally very small the change in the deferment from the base position is correspondingly small except for high degrees of futurity.

Inserting this modification by reason of changes in "real cost" into the framework of our previous analysis of future provision, we come to the following conclusions: When no occasion exists for future provision for a want there can obviously be no effect on the quantity wanted for future provision by reason of the effect of a change in "real cost." When an occasion exists, but only for a single provision or a brief series not reaching to a high degree of futurity the effect of a rise in "real cost" is not likely to involve any alteration in the quantity wanted unless the base position is thereby brought almost to the point of incidence of the limit of capacity upon the order of preference. If brought very near that point, it is possible that the mere deferment of all future provision, as against corresponding current provision, will be sufficient to exclude the single provision or the later members of a series. When an occasion exists for a long series of provisions reaching to a high degree of futurity the effect of a rise in "real cost" is always likely to involve a change in the quantity wanted. The movement of the base position will be the chief factor, but the alteration of the degree of deferment of provisions with a high degree of futurity will come to play a part. Correspondingly, if a decline in "real cost" makes a hitherto extramarginal want sufficiently intramarginal and it happens

[11] See Section C 1.

that an occasion exists for one or a series of future provisions, these may be included as well. All alterations in quantity wanted thus induced will be in terms of full measures (adequate provisions). But, in the case of a series, the number of full measures in the whole program will be altered. Since the program which includes a considerable series is likely to extend over a considerable number of days, the effect on any single order of preference is likely to be on an all or none basis. However, when the practice of replacement is to replace each day the current day's use, a rise in cost is likely to reduce the series and thus cause postponement of the beginning of replacement; and vice versa. Once this adjustment is made the effect of the change in "real cost" will be nil.

We have admitted certain cases where the quantity wanted is less than a full measure. The effect of changes in "real cost" will, in such cases, be in terms of part measures. Under the perhaps exceptional condition of partial substitution a full measure of the preferred substitute for the major want of a constellation is replaced in part by a part measure of the preferred substitute for a minor want, and in such proportions that both wants are satiated. We have already dealt with the effects of changes in "real cost" in so far as they merely alter the preferences among partial substitutes for either of the wants concerned. The only other effect is that of causing the inclusion or exclusion of the minor want which will, in turn, cause the partial substitution, or the elimination of the partial substitution, of the preferred means for such minor want. So far as this means is concerned the effect is on an all or none basis, though the quantity wanted or not wanted is a part, not a full, measure. But the effect on the preferred means for the major want is not on an all or none basis. Partial substitution causes a reduction in the quantity wanted from a full to a part measure; and the elimination of such partial substitution causes an increase from a part to a full measure. The effect is, however, in terms of a considerable discontinuous step.

Another possible case of effects in terms of part measures would arise under our very questionable interpretation of segmentation which, if it occurs at all, seems to be confined to minor members of constellations. If we conceive that segmentation is the result of the allocation of a block of "real cost" insufficient for a full measure, by reason of a preference for partial satisfaction rather than none, it would seem to follow that a change in "real cost" of the means preferred, which nevertheless left it preferred, would merely increase or decrease the quantity which that block would provide. Since the ratio would then remain the same, we would have to assume that the position of the want in the order of ratios—and, to the extent that was determining, in the order of preference—would also remain the same. The effect would not be on an all or none basis; it would, however, consist of a discontinuous step, though perhaps a small one, from a part measure of one size to one of another size.[12]

If a whole series of daily programs and orders of preference are envisaged, one other exception should be noted. We have already mentioned the two phenomena which we called alternation and spreading out of an externally or deliberately restricted supply. When the first occurs it takes the form of satiating the want on some of its instances—full measures—and leaving it completely unsatisfied on others. In other words, successive orders of preference become different. It is possible that sometimes this process takes the second form which results in partial satisfaction of all instances—part measures. Changes in "real cost" may induce or do away with these phenomena. A rise may lead from regular satiation to either basis; a decline may lead to the opposite movement. A decline may lead from regular exclusion to either basis; a rise may lead to the opposite movement. Viewed over the whole period, the transfer of a want to or from such a basis from or to either regular satiation or regular exclusion involves a change in quantity wanted of the means concerned, though the true effect, in full measures, is a change in frequency. But, for the period as a whole, only the transfer to or from regular exclusion is on an all or none basis; that to or from regular satiation involves merely an increase or decrease in quantity wanted over the whole period.

In all but one of the instances cited, whether on an all or none basis in terms of full or part measures or on the basis of discontinuous steps in terms of number or size of full measures or shifts between full and part measures, all effects of changes in "real cost" upon quantity wanted are confined to a single critical point only.[13] That is the point at which the change of "real cost" suffices to exclude or include the particular want or future instance. Up to that point a change has no effect on quantity wanted. In this respect the effects of changes of "real cost" upon the order of preference are the same as they are on

[12] The effect of this assumption is discussed further in Appendix VI, Section H.

[13] The one exception is the doubtful case of segmentation where any change of cost may produce an effect.

preference among substitutes. But, in another respect, the two differ. When a change in cost relation reverses the preference between substitute means on the basis of their newly weighted terms of substitution, the appearance of any quantity wanted of the newly preferred substitute has as its obverse the disappearance of any quantity wanted of the previously preferred substitute for any particular want. However, in connection with the order of preference there are no such direct obverse effects. The rise in cost to a critical point which causes disappearance or discontinuous diminution in the quantity wanted of any means does not directly cause appearance or increase in the quantity wanted of any other; and vice versa. Finally, the *general* rule seems to be that the effects of changes in "real costs," both on preference among substitutes and on the order of preference, take place on an all or none basis as to each individual means. There are exceptions, as noted. But, in the course of our whole analysis in this as well as in the previous chapter, we have found reason to believe that all the exceptions are exceptional.

3. EFFECTS OF CHANGING "REAL COSTS" ON THE LIMIT OF CAPACITY

Hitherto, both in the preceding chapter and in this one, we have confined the scope of our analysis by reason of the limiting assumption of a fixed quantity of available working effort and, therefore, of a fixed limit of capacity, an unchanging duration of the working-day and an unchanging intensity of the last hour's working.[14] Now we are prepared to do away with that limiting assumption and to examine the causes which lead to changes in these magnitudes, as well as the quantitative relations which determine their size and thus limit the size of their changes. True, in order to establish an order of preference, we have used as an analytical tool, a conceptually moving limit of capacity. But, for that purpose, the moving limit was merely taken as a datum. It was not explained. We now need to discover why, how, and how far the limit actually does move. In Part II, the analysis which produced our first approximation as to the limit of capacity was predicated on the assumption of equal "real cost" in work of provisions for all wants. In Chapter 13 we constructed the actual order of preference on the assumption of haphazard but constant differences in "real cost" in work

[14] See assumption (d), p. 853.

between provisions for different wants. Then, in the last preceding subsection, we examined the effect on the order of preference of changes in such "real cost." Since changes must produce differences, what we proceed to do here will correct the analysis in Part II in both respects, and, combined with that, should give us a final and realistic picture. That is, a history of the effects of changes in "real cost" as they occur provides also a picture of the effects of differences after the changes have occurred.

So far as capacity is concerned we have seen that it consists of effort in the form of working only. Therefore, in this subsection, when we consider the effects of changing "real costs" we are usually limiting ourselves to changes in the "real cost" of working only. When retaining influences capacity we shall treat it separately. As a result, our ratios here will not be "corrected ratios," as we called them in Chapter 13, Section E. Or, more precisely, changes in the inverse dimension of our ratios are here assumed to be produced by changes in work only. In order to simplify the exposition we shall omit any special treatment of alternative uses, whether at uniform or differential costs. Thus we are dealing with the subject in terms of the preferred means for each want treated separately. If it is desired to translate this into terms of means capable of alternative uses, that can readily be done merely by adding together, or by discriminating among, the several uses. For the same reason we shall ordinarily assume that all wants are either satiated or left completely unsatisfied. The reader can allow for the doubtful matter of segmentation as far as he chooses. We shall merely point out that segmentation, if it occurs, seems to provide the one exception to the rule we shall establish.

Wherever a want is going to be satiated, so that no less and no more than a full measure is wanted at all, the effect of all changes in "real cost" in work is either to release working to elsewhere or to absorb working from elsewhere. Thus, in addition to the *direct* effect analyzed in the previous subsections, every such change has an indirect effect. Not only does it produce an effect in connection with the want as to whose preferred means the change takes place but it must also produce a *compensatory* effect elsewhere. This is necessarily true whether the direct effect is to cause a change in the preferred substitute which leads to a new position in the order of preference but not to exclusion; or whether, with the same preferred substitute, it causes transposition of the want to an earlier or later position in the order of preference, both to and from positions within the limit of capacity; or whether it causes exclusion of a hitherto included want or inclusion of a hitherto excluded want.[15] However, the quantitative relations of the compensatory effects are different in these three cases. If the direct effect is a reversal of preference among substitutes, the compensatory effect is not equal to the change of cost; it is equal to the difference between the old cost of the previously preferred substitute and the new cost of the now preferred substitute.[16] If the direct effect is only a change in position of the want in the order of preference, but within the margin, the compensatory effect is equal to the change in cost. If the direct effect is exclusion of a hitherto included want, the compensatory effect is equal to the whole previous cost. And, if the direct effect is inclusion of a previously excluded want, the compensatory effect is equal to the whole new cost.

Two modifications of these broad generalizations are required to cover two special cases. The first concerns future provision. In Chapter 10 we have already sufficiently covered the changes in the allocation and in the quantity of working as well as the increases or decreases of current forgoing which result from the appearance of occasions for future provision and the completion of such provisions. These are not consequences of changes in "real cost." Therefore, the reader should bear in mind that these effects, analogous to those we are now calling compensatory, can occur for such other reasons as well. Fluctuations in future provision, as well as changes in "real cost," may absorb working from, or release working to, elsewhere.[17] But when, to the limited degree we have admitted, fluctuations in the quantity of future provision are themselves the direct effects of changes in "real cost," we shall include the indirect effects among the compensatory ones. These

[15] We must give notice as to our terminology. Our *direct* effects of changes of "real cost" are the effects on the preference among substitutes and the position of the want in the order of preference. They should include the change in the work required where they take place. Our *compensatory* effects are the effects of the resulting release of work to, or absorption from, elsewhere. Later we shall introduce the terms primary and secondary effects—terms chosen merely to distinguish them from these. Primary effects are the effect on the quantity wanted of the means whose absolute or relative "real cost" is changed. Secondary effects are those upon quantity wanted of means at the points at which compensatory effects impinge.

[16] This is perhaps too brief a statement. The old and the new cost of either substitute may be the same. If so the change of cost is in the other substitute.

[17] The effect of increasing future provision on the reach of capacity is to retract a given capacity from the previous margin and redispose it sidewise, so to speak. The effect, via this retraction, on the extent of capacity is to increase it by inducing a longer working-day. Both tendencies are limited by the added "real cost" incurred for retaining.

statements apply equally well to future provision induced by the technical options, so far as the period before the beginning of use is concerned. But, thereafter, there is necessarily always a release of working to elsewhere, and this release is equal to the gross economizing of working, not to the net inducement—the economizing of working less the "real cost" of retaining. However, this brings us back around the circle of our analysis to its starting point. For this is the chief reason for the declines in "real cost," the effects of which we are now considering. Previously we were thinking of the train of causation which leads up to the economizing; now we are thinking of the train of causation which follows from it.

The second modification is required in order to meet the issues raised by segmentation, if that occurs. Upon our own questionable interpretation of this phenomenon we have supposed that a change in "real cost" would not affect the position of the want in the order of ratios, nor, therefore, in the order of preference. Neither would it alter allocation. It would merely result in an allocation of the same quantity of "real cost" in order to produce a larger or smaller degree of satisfaction. If so, a change in cost in such cases would neither release "real cost" to elsewhere nor absorb it from elsewhere. There would be no compensatory effects.[18]

At this point we shall make certain categorical statements which are axiomatic. There are two alternative possible regions of incidence of compensatory effect. These are, respectively, the range of the order of preference around the point to which the limit of capacity reaches and the duration of the working-day. Compensatory effects which result from releases of "real cost" to elsewhere must either take the form of extensions of the reach of capacity along the order of preference so as to include wants hitherto excluded; or they must take the form of reductions in the length of the working-day; or the effects may be a mixture of these two. Correspondingly, compensatory effects which result from absorptions of "real cost" from elsewhere must either take the form of retractions of the reach of capacity along the order of preference so as to exclude wants hitherto included; or they must take the form of increases in the length of the working-day; or, again, the effects may be a mixture of these two. The notion of expansions and contractions of capacity is, therefore, an equivocal one. The length of the working-day may be increased, but at the same time the reach of

[18] This case is considered, in its theoretical aspects, in Appendix VI, Section H.

capacity may be retracted, and vice versa. Therefore, capacity must be conceived either in terms of hours of working or in terms of the reach of capacity along the order of preference up to its limit; one conception cannot cover both. On the other hand, neither can be determined without reference to the other. They are interdependent. Recognition of this interdependence will give us our final definition of capacity (in subsection 4 below) which we left indeterminate in Chapter 12.

The essence of the question to which this leads us is the quantitative determination of the proportions of each constituent in the mixture of compensatory effects—i.e., the effects elsewhere of releases from, or absorptions to, the point at which the direct effects take place. As we found in Part II, the conclusion is inevitable that this determination rests—under the conditions we are studying—upon the variable intensity of different last hours of working and the relation of this variable to the constant intensity of the several wants around the margin. Therefore, what we need to do here is to incorporate that analysis into the framework of the analysis we are now building, which deals with changing and thus different "real costs."

The incidence of all compensatory effects upon the order of preference is at or around the margin. The margin, in our scheme, is the point to which the limit of capacity reaches along the order of preference. Within this limit, wants are included; beyond it, wants are excluded. Since this is our definition of the margin, there must always be at the margin one want the value of whose ratio is unity. And, since we have found it necessary to conclude that, around the margin, the order of ratios governs the order of preference, it follows that, within the margin, there must be a series of wants the values of whose ratios rise gradually above unity and, beyond it, a series of wants the values of whose ratios decline gradually below unity. The incidence of all compensatory effects upon the duration of the working-day is at or around the last hour's working. For each shorter working-day the intensity of the last hour is assumed to be less; for each longer day it is assumed to be more. Therefore, on this scale, intensity is held to rise gradually beyond what corresponds to the margin and to decline gradually within it.

It seems to have been generally agreed in economic literature that it is the point of coincidence of these two oppositely moving intensities which determines the number of wants satisfied and the amount of working done—at least on a voluntary basis. But the concept has been established only in the most general terms—a balance of "satisfaction" with "dissatisfaction." What is required is a precise—even if purely abstract—statement of the nature of the magnitudes compared, their dimensions and their quantitative relations.[19] We, too, have elided that question hitherto; we could do that because our analysis in Part II was based on the wholly unreal assumption that provision for all wants required equal numbers of units of work.

Our purely abstract and analytical formulation of the influence of "real costs" upon the order of preference has been in terms of the ratio of the intensity of the want to the quantity of "real cost." The basis of this non-mathematical equality or correspondence is the full measure of means. The usefulness of the full measure is equal to the normal maximum intensity of the want. That constitutes the direct dimension of the ratio. Correspondingly, the inverse dimension of the ratio is the quantity of "real cost" required for a full measure. In this connection —i.e., the uncorrected ratio—this "real cost" consists of work only. Its measure is a certain number of units of standard working-time. But, in the phrase "intensity of the last hour's work," we have recognized that, in respect of its comparability with the intensity of wants, any given quantity of work varies with the duration of the working-day. As the working-day is prolonged, the intensity of the working effort involved increases, as does the intensity of the sacrifice of leisure—the competition of an alternative use of time. Moreover, it is reasonable to

[19] As an example of the best formulation, J. B. Clark (*80*, 383) laid down the rule, precisely as we have done, though he did not define the magnitudes. He says: "In any case, it is the least of his gains for which he works last [ordinally] and hardest. Left to himself and nature, he must work during a part of the day to sustain life and he must refrain from working during a part of it for the same reason. Between the point of no-work, at which he would starve, and that of nothing-but-work, at which he would die from exhaustion, there is the point of balanced gain and loss. If he stops just there, the net gain from labor is at its greatest."

As an example of a much cruder formulation we may cite von Wieser (*442*, 197–198): "First, before undertaking any labour a man has to consider whether the utility outweighs the effort. . . . Second, when labour is once decided on, its performance must always be ordered in such a way that the toil and danger are made as light as possible. . . . Third, the fact that labour is felt to be a burden has the effect of curtailing somewhat the supply of labour as a whole."

Finally, as an example of a wholly inadequate formulation we have Wicksteed's discussion of "Diminishing Psychic Returns" (*441*, i, ii). No one sentence is quite pat for our purpose. But the defect is suggested by this statement: "Our preferences and selections as between two or more alternatives are regulated in every case by the terms on which the alternatives are offered and the supply of the desired things or experiences which we command" (*441*, 80)—in which class he includes time. The amount of working-time available is not an independent variable. It depends on the alternatives themselves.

suppose that, for any given working-day, it is this "intensity of the last hour's work" which is compared with the wants provided for by any of the hours included in it.[20] We have expressed this comparability by stating that, for any given capacity, the limit of capacity—the point at which the working-day is terminated—is defined by that ratio whose value is unity—that is, the limit is the point at which the effort and sacrifice are equal to the intensity of the want provided for. Thus, around the margin, we might conceive a series of wants whose ratios are as follows:

J	K	L	M	N	O	P	Q
$\frac{2.4}{2}$	$\frac{3.45}{3}$	$\frac{1.65}{1.5}$	$\frac{4.20}{4}$	$\frac{0.5}{0.5}$	$\frac{1.90}{2}$	$\frac{0.90}{1}$	$\frac{1.7}{2}$

The values of these ratios would then be as follows: [21]

J	K	L	M	N	O	P	Q
$\frac{1.2}{1}$	$\frac{1.15}{1}$	$\frac{1.10}{1}$	$\frac{1.05}{1}$	$\frac{1}{1}$	$\frac{0.95}{1}$	$\frac{0.90}{1}$	$\frac{0.85}{1}$

The marginal want would then be the fifth in order, or N. But, as soon as we conceive of changes in capacity—the working-day—even though we arbitrarily assume that the quantity of working-time required for each want—its "real cost"—remains the same, the "intensity of the last hour" can no longer remain the same. Thus, to allow for the effect of this variable we require a "weight" for the unit of "real cost." For purposes of demonstration the most convenient way in which to introduce such weighting is in the form of a *factor*, to be shown in parentheses and to be applied to the inverse dimension of the ratio. Unity for this factor may be conceived to be the intensity of any certain last hour. Let us then take the last hour of the fixed working-day that we have

[20] We do not need to complicate this presentation in the text by introducing the variation in intensity of effort in different tasks. That was allowed for in Chapter 9. Presumably, even in a direct economy, some working may be harder or more disagreeable than other working. Such working will not be done unless the particular want justifies it. But, otherwise, it does not affect the length of the working-day (capacity) except as it may contribute to the earlier exhaustion of the worker. In an indirect economy a whole day may be put in on such arduous working. If so, it will certainly shorten the working-day, if that is determined voluntarily. It is probably safe to assume that the critical task, so far as the determination of the working-day is concerned, is always one of average or normal arduousness. Tasks above that level are marginal as to the individual want only—exclusion or inclusion—and therefore require a want the value of whose ratio is as much above unity as the arduousness is above normal.

[21] Heretofore, the values of our ratios contain the numerators only of the following series. We are now placing in all of them the denominator 1, signifying a unit of "real cost." This is done for a reason which will appear shortly.

previously assumed. For a shorter working-day the factor will have a value less than unity, and, for a longer one, a value greater than unity, conforming to the quantitative relations among different points on our curve of working.[22] If the day is shortened to the point at which the intensity of the last hour is only 90 percent of what it was, the value of the factor will be (0.9). Then all ratios in the series above will have new values as follows:

$$\begin{array}{cccccccc} J & K & L & M & N & O & P & Q \\ \dfrac{1.2}{1(0.9)} & \dfrac{1.15}{1(0.9)} & \dfrac{1.10}{1(0.9)} & \dfrac{1.05}{1(0.9)} & \dfrac{1}{1(0.9)} & \dfrac{0.95}{1(0.9)} & \dfrac{0.90}{1(0.9)} & \dfrac{0.85}{1(0.9)} \end{array}$$

With such a factor the marginal want becomes the seventh, P, instead of the fifth in order, N. On the other hand, if the value of the factor rises to (1.1), on account of a prolongation of the working-day, the values of the ratios in this series become:

$$\begin{array}{cccccccc} J & K & L & M & N & O & P & Q \\ \dfrac{1.2}{1(1.1)} & \dfrac{1.15}{1(1.1)} & \dfrac{1.10}{1(1.1)} & \dfrac{1.05}{1(1.1)} & \dfrac{1}{1(1.1)} & \dfrac{0.95}{1(1.1)} & \dfrac{0.90}{1(1.1)} & \dfrac{0.85}{1(1.1)} \end{array}$$

Then the third want in order, L, becomes marginal.

This purely abstract formulation raises two important questions. First, does it meet the requirements of definable dimensions which we set up, in Chapter 8, as the *sine qua non* in dealing with magnitudes? Second, does it represent reality? As to the first question, it is clear that the inverse dimension of our ratios has now become one or the other of two things. It is either a fundamental magnitude with two direct dimensions—duration and intensity of working—or it is a fundamental magnitude with a single dimension. We have already had occasion a number of times to reject altogether the notion of magnitudes of the first type. And, in any case, we would be unwilling to admit a capacity upon the part of man to multiply in terms of two dimensions only one of which is measurable in units. That reduces us to the necessity of restating our formula in terms of a single fundamental magnitude which necessarily has but one dimension. Let us tentatively adopt for this

[22] See Chapter 9. It is probably necessary to remark that we cannot conceive this curve of working to remain as a fixed scale through time. Doubtless it changes from day to day according as the worker feels energetic or lazy, well or ill. Doubtless changes in technology may make working less effortful; for some this may result from decreasing the physical and increasing the mental component. Doubtless the attraction of leisure changes as improved technique makes possible more and better provision for play in place of provision for rest only.

dimension the sign X. To resolve our formula into terms of this single dimension, the type of formulation we require is that of a derived magnitude, or rate, multiplied by its own inverse dimension—e.g., $LT^{-1} \times T = L$. Along these lines, our factor—the intensity of the last hour—would be converted into a rate XT^{-1}; and the unit of "real cost" would be converted into a quantity of duration, or T. Then the inverse dimension of our ratios would become $T\,(XT^{-1}) = X$. If now we can demonstrate that this unknown dimension, X, is of the same order as, or identical with, the dimension I, in which we measure (or conceive) the intensity of wants, then our ratios can be reduced to a set of correspondences of the simplest possible type—correspondences in which the relate and the correlate have a single common fundamental dimension. Then, so long as I direct remained greater than, or equal to, I inverse, the want would be provided for; as soon as it became less—the value of the weighted ratio became less than unity—no provision would be made.

There is no difficulty in identifying the dimension of the sacrifice involved in working with the dimension of the intensity of wants; for this sacrifice consists in forgoing the satisfaction of certain present wants which, obviously, can only be measured in the same dimension. The quantity of the correlate in the correspondence—the direct dimension of our ratios—is the intensity of some future want, reinforced by volition; the non-mathematical equality which fixes the quantity of the corresponding relate—inverse dimension—is the time required to provide for that future want; in that time a certain number of present wants might be satisfied; the sum of the intensities of these present wants constitutes another correlate; that, therefore, can be substituted as one component of the inverse dimension of our ratios; it is measured in the same dimension as is the direct dimension. The longer the time required for the future want and the more intense the present wants forgone, the greater the quantity of I represented by this component of the inverse dimension. Its dimensional formula is clearly I.[23] Can we say the same of the effort involved in working? How can that question be answered, since we know nothing of the nature of effort? However, it does appear that the quantity of effort varies both with intensity and duration. That suggests that its intensity is a rate. To that extent it seems to fit our formula for the magnitude X. We can go no further than to say

[23] Be it noted that the dimension T does not enter this formula only because the quantity I is the sum of the present wants which could be satisfied in the corresponding time.

that, if man is actually capable of comparing the magnitude we have denoted by X with the magnitude we have denoted by I, it is highly probable that they are either fundamentally one and the same or have the same dimension. This for the quite convincing reason that we can find no instance of man's capacity to compare two magnitudes with different dimensions.[24] If so, the other component of our inverse dimension has also the formula $T\ (IT^{-1}) = I$.[25]

That brings us to—and resolves itself into—the question whether this abstract formulation represents reality. As to the comparability of the magnitude, sacrifice, there can hardly be any question. It consists of present wants forgone. All of our scheme would fall to the ground if such comparability does not exist. For the rest, this formulation assumes that working effort is a process that can occur at variable rates per unit of time, so that its quantity can vary not only according to its duration but also according to its rate of delivery. It assumes that this component of what we have been calling the "intensity of the last hour," the "intensity of effort," is, in reality, a rate. It assumes that what is actually compared with the intensity of a current or future want, aside from the sacrifice, is not this rate but is a quantity of effort, and that this quantity may vary both because of differences in duration and because of differences in rate. Thus this component of "real cost" becomes a rate (the factor) multiplied by a quantity of time (the hours of working). The ineluctable logic of the facts seems to prove that this is the correct abstract formulation. To suppose otherwise would require that one also suppose that man ignores either the duration of the working required to provide for a want or the duration of the working-day. On the one hand, that would mean that he requires as much of an inducement to allocate five minutes' working as he does to allocate one hour's; on the other hand, it would mean that he requires no more of an inducement, per hour, to induce him to work a twelve-hour day, than he does to induce him to work a six-hour day. The most casual

[24] I will ask the reader to tell me which is the greater magnitude, ten minutes or one mile, ten pounds or one foot.

[25] This does not mean that we are supposing that effort and intensity of want are one and the same entity. It only means that they seem to have the same dimension in the sense that they are comparable—as if intensity of want were a force and effort a resistance, or opposing force. In Chapter 8 we attempted to sketch an outline of our concept of intensity of want as a magnitude. It appeared, then, that it may be either degree of excitation or quantity of excitation, or, since these two magnitudes seem always to vary proportionately, that it may be both. The notion of quantity of excitation seems to furnish a more logical basis for comparability with quantity of effort. That is as far as we can go.

observation proves that both these suppositions are contrary to the facts.[26]

We suppose—and we observe—that man always measures the duration of his effort, at least roughly. But we do not suppose for a moment that he measures the rate at which he delivers it. Nevertheless, at the critical point where the determination of the voluntary termination of the working-day is in question it is a necessary conclusion that he has some intuitive gauge of changes in this rate. Before that point comparisons can be rough and easy. The inducement is merely felt to be excessive—the task is certainly worth while. At that point, however, comparisons may have to be made by somewhat careful balancings. Whether consciously or unconsciously, this balancing is done and the scale tips one way or the other. We know that the decision is made; we can surely impute the decision to the overbalancing of one influence by the other; we do not really need to know more than that.

Having defined the magnitudes concerned in this balancing process we are now prepared to see how the proportions of each constituent in the mixture of compensatory effects is determined—how far either the release or absorption of working as a result of changes of "real cost" at one point leads to reduction or increase of the working-day and how far either leads to extension or retraction of the limit of capacity along the order of preference. The customary, and the elegant, method of representing such a balancing process is by means of a pair of continuous curves, one of which is positively and the other negatively inclined and which therefore intersect. By moving the negatively inclined curve to the right or left to indicate a larger (absorption) or smaller (release) aggregate requirement of "real cost," or work, the point of intersection is changed on both curves. The reader is of course at liberty to conceive the matter in that neat and simple fashion. We do not choose to do so. In the first place, according to our hypotheses, both curves are discontinuous, and that makes quite a difference. In the second place, that method does not permit us to show what actually happens in the way of a rearrangement of the order of preference.[27] For these reasons we present in Appendix VI, Section E a series of diagrams which illustrate the several varieties of direct effects and the several ways the resulting compensatory effects work out. This is necessarily complex; but

[26] The first supposition hardly requires rebuttal. As to the second one does not need to revert to primitive economies for an example. It is sufficiently disproved by the necessity for "overtime" pay.

[27] The negatively inclined curve cannot move without changing its shape as well.

it seems to represent the actual facts better than does the pair of continuous curves. At this point we shall merely state our results in abstract form with numerical illustrations. It is possible that, for some, this may make the nub of the matter clearer than will the graphs in Appendix VI.

Compensatory effects resulting from releases of "real cost," if such extra available "real cost" could be wholly reapplied to other wants, should make possible the inclusion of some of the hitherto extramarginal wants next in order. For instance, for our series above, the release of 5 units of working would then permit the inclusion of Wants O, P, and Q. But, if the working-day remained the same, the factor would remain at unity—our starting-point. The values of these three ratios would then remain below unity—$\frac{0.95}{1(1)}$, $\frac{0.90}{1(1)}$, and $\frac{0.85}{1(1)}$—so that all wants would still be excluded. On the other hand, if these 5 units were applied to a reduction of the working-day, that might reduce the factor to (0.85), say. Such a factor would change the values of these ratios to $\frac{0.95}{1(0.85)}$, $\frac{0.90}{1(0.85)}$ and $\frac{0.85}{1(0.85)}$. All would be at or above unity; but only on the supposition that the working-time was not available—was all taken off. Clearly, then, it would not all be taken off. Instead, a balance would be struck at the point at which, along the order of declining values of ratios and the rising values of the factor, a weighted ratio with the value of unity was produced. This would be at some point in the declining values of ratios, at the old weighting, between $\frac{1}{1(1)}$ and $\frac{0.85}{1(1)}$, and in the rising values of the factor between (0.85) and (1). Let us say that, in the above series, that point is reached when the value of Want P, with an old ratio of $\frac{0.90}{1(1)}$ is weighted by a factor (0.9), so that its weighted ratio becomes $\frac{0.90}{1(0.9)}$. The result would be that, out of the five units of "real cost" (work) released, two would be applied to shortening the working-day and three to provision for the hitherto excluded wants O and P.

Correspondingly, compensatory effects resulting from absorptions of "real cost," if such a deficit had to be wholly made good at the expense of other wants, would necessitate the exclusion of some of the hitherto immediately intramarginal wants. In our series, above, the absorption of, say, 6 units of working would require the exclusion of Wants L, M, and N. But, for the same working-day, the factor would again remain above or at unity. The values of these three ratios would then remain above unity—$\frac{1.10}{1(1)}$, $\frac{1.05}{1(1)}$, and $\frac{1}{1(1)}$—so that all should still be included. However, that would be impossible if the working they required had been absorbed elsewhere. On the other hand, if this deficit of 6 units of working were made good by prolonging the working-day, that might increase the factor to (1.15), say. Such a factor would change the values of the ratios of L, M, and N to $\frac{1.10}{1(1.15)}$, $\frac{1.05}{1(1.15)}$, and $\frac{1.00}{1(1.15)}$, respectively. The values of all would be below unity and therefore excluded; but only on the contradictory supposition that the extra units of working were actually made available to provide for them. Obviously all of this extra time would not be added. Instead, as before, a balance would be struck. At some point in the series of values of ratios, at the old weighting, declining from $\frac{1.10}{1(1)}$ to $\frac{1}{1(1)}$, and the series of factors rising from (1) to (1.15), there would be a weighted ratio with the value of unity. Let us say that, in the above series that point is reached when the ratio of Want L, with the old value of $\frac{1.10}{1(1)}$ is weighted by a factor (1.10), so that it becomes $\frac{1.10}{1(1.10)}$. The result would be that the deficit in working would be made good by adding 1.5 units to the working-day and by withdrawing 4.5 units from Wants M and N, hitherto included, by excluding them.[28]

[28] It is perhaps well to remind the reader, at this point, of our conclusions in Chapter 13, Section C 4. We do not believe there is a hard and fast line at which the influence of "real costs" (order of ratios) supersedes the influence of wants (order of priority) in determining the order of preference. Perhaps the former never becomes completely dominant except immediately around the margin. Here we are only describing what the influence of "real costs" would be. We are not claiming that the calculations offered as illustrations in the text are made precisely. We admit that movements in or into the order of preference within the limit may be no more than rough placings. As between two wants of similar intensity the cheaper will probably have preference; as between two of similar cost the more intense will probably have preference; as between one

These two statements suffice to cover the simplest cases. That is, they serve to describe how a balance is struck between the two ways in which the compensatory effects are taken up, so long as the direct effects do not move the want whose "real cost" changes—the source of compensatory effects—to or from a position in the order of ratios which lies in the range around the margin where these effects themselves impinge. When that occurs—when any of the types of direct effect described on pp. 960 to 961, takes place among the wants in the range around the margin or leads to the insertion of a want from elsewhere into that range—the matter is complicated. Then extension or retraction of the reach of capacity does not take place along an unmodified series of ratios of declining values. Instead, the order itself within this critical range is altered. If the direct effect is to remove a want from this range, the rest may be deemed merely to close ranks. One step down in the order of ratios will merely be more discontinuous than it was. On the other hand, if the direct effect is to insert a want in this range, the rest must open ranks and, at that point, reduce discontinuity. Movement of a want from one point to another in this range will have both effects.

It is clear that a release of "real cost" to elsewhere can only occur as a result of a change in cost for a hitherto intramarginal want. On the other hand, absorption of "real cost" from elsewhere can arise as a result of a change in cost for either a hitherto intramarginal or a hitherto extramarginal want. But the only time it can arise, as to the latter, is when the value of the weighted ratio of the extramarginal want rises from a level which has excluded it to a level which permits its inclusion. Then, having required no allocation, it comes to require a certain allocation. And the "real cost" so allocated must come from somewhere. This special case being recognized, we are prepared to make five broad generalizations.

a. Declines in "real cost" among intramarginal wants cause a release of working to elsewhere and lead to a balance between the compensatory effects which includes some shortening of the working-day and some extension of the reach of capacity over immediately extramarginal wants.

b. Rises in "real cost" among intramarginal wants, if sufficient to in-

prior want and several subordinate wants that can be satisfied with about the same quantity of cost, the latter may often have preference, though their intensities cannot be summated. All this is equally true when it comes to moving a want in the order of ratios as a result of a change in its "real cost."

volve their exclusion, also cause a release of working to elsewhere, leading to the same balancing between compensatory effects. This includes some shortening of the working-day. While it also results in the inclusion of some immediately extramarginal wants, it is questionable whether it should be described as an extension of the reach of capacity. For the included wants are substituted for the excluded one, and, by reason of the shortening of the working-day, necessarily cannot require as much working.

c. Rises in "real cost" among intramarginal wants, if insufficient to involve their exclusion, cause an absorption of working from elsewhere. The resulting balancing between compensatory effects includes some lengthening of the working-day and some retraction of the reach of capacity over immediately intramarginal wants.

d. Rises in "real cost" among extramarginal wants can have no effect whatever.

e. Declines in "real cost" among extramarginal wants, if sufficient to involve their inclusion, cause an absorption of working from elsewhere, as under (c). The resulting balancing between the compensatory effects includes some lengthening of the working-day. It also involves the exclusion of some immediately intramarginal wants. But, since the newly included want requires more working than did the excluded wants, it seems proper to describe this as an extension of the reach of capacity.

Applying these generalizations to the more typical and major causes of changes in "real cost," we would expect certain observable results. Technical improvements, specific discoveries of more accessible resources, and, in a direct economy, marked increases in skill, all of which make possible reductions in "real cost," are more or less fortuitous, occur discontinuously even if they are generally progressive, and are, for the most part, specific as to a single means. If they occur with regard to means for wants which have previously been satiated, we would expect some definite and one-time shortening of the working-day and some immediate increase in the number of wants satisfied. When improvements bring the "real cost" of means for wants previously unsatisfied down to a point where they can be satiated, we would expect some definite and one-time lengthening of the working-day and some immediate forgoing as to minor wants previously satisfied. The expectation of these two opposite effects, depending on where the technical improvement, etc., arises, seems to me worthy of emphasis. Both generalizations appear to be justified by observation of reality. And the second one is a somewhat novel feature of the results of our analysis which may serve to explain certain behavior that needed explaining.[29]

Increase of natural resistances—both by reason of gradual exhaustion of the more accessible with a consequent gradually greater recourse to the less accessible resources, and, by reason of the latter alone, on account of greater quantity wanted—which occasion increases in "real cost" are also specific as to single means. But they are retrogressive, certain, and more nearly continuous. As they steadily worsen conditions for a want, we would expect that, up to the point of exclusion, they would result in a gradual lengthening of the working-day and, little by little, a reduction in the number of wants satisfied. At the point of exclusion a reversal of these effects might take place. But, if the worsening of natural conditions is widespread in its effect on means, this reversal would be likely to be only temporary, since a rise in "real cost" elsewhere would soon initiate the original process again.

Occasionally, as a result of catastrophes, natural or social, such worsenings of natural conditions also rise in sudden and severe form. More frequently they arise in milder form as a result of unfavorable seasons. Both these are temporary conditions, however, entirely discontinuous even in direction, and quite uncertain. We would expect them to lead for the time being, to the same responses as we have found likely for other increases of natural resistances. In fact, the sudden and severe worsenings might well exaggerate the responses. But, when passed, the old working-day and standard of living might be resumed. Seasonal worsenings, if mild, might be tided over without adaptation; but, if serious, they too would be expected to lead to temporary adaptation and then resumption. The question whether or not these expectations of ours as to the effects of worsenings of the environment are confirmed by observation of reality we will leave to the reader to decide for himself.

[29] We observed in the 1920s that, when the price of automobiles was being reduced to a level which brought them within the reach of the "common man," not only were all sorts of incentive wage systems, offering an opportunity to earn more money, particularly effective, but the market for men's shoes and "Sunday suits" went into the doldrums. Even the home was skimped on to scrape together the price of a car.

4. SUMMARY AND INTERPRETATION

For the purposes of the following section it seems desirable at this point to summarize briefly the conclusions of this section. With certain minor exceptions, noted below, we have found reason to conclude that the *primary* effect of a change in "real cost" of any means, or of a change in the relation of their "real costs" between any substitutes, is on an all or none basis.[30] That is, the quantity wanted of that means for a single order of preference either remains the same—a full measure—or it becomes nil, or, if none was previously wanted, it may become a full measure. It remains the same if the rise in cost does not reach the critical point, or if the change in relative costs among substitutes does not do so. It becomes nil if either absolute or relative cost reaches the critical point. Correspondingly, the quantity wanted remains nil until the decline in cost reaches the critical point or the change in relative costs among substitutes does so. At such points the quantity wanted becomes a full measure. If we assume that, for successive days, the intensities of wants as well as the "curve of working" remain the same, the primary effect, once accomplished, remains the same for subsequent days' programs.

The exceptions to this general all or none rule are, we are inclined to think, rare occurrences. Where, for the members of a constellation, partial substitution of means with proportionate attributes has taken place or is induced, the change in "real cost," if it reaches the critical point, affects a part measure only of either or of both means. Where a minor member of a constellation prefers the same means as the major member, but its full measure is larger, changes in "real cost" reaching the critical point substitute the larger for the smaller full measure, or vice versa. Where a means (final product) is capable of alternative uses, changes in "real cost," if they reach the critical points for any use, add to, or subtract from, the quantity wanted in varying amounts consisting of the several full measures making up the aggregate. Where a number of instances are included in future provision, the number of

[30] See note 15, above. What we have called the "direct effects" deal with substitutions or changes in position of a want in the order of preference. With the single exception of segmentation, under our suggested hypothesis, all changes in "real cost" have direct effects. But, under the all or none principle, they may have no effect on the quantity wanted of the preferred means, if they do not lead to substitution or exclusion. Therefore, we have to distinguish what we call "primary effects" on quantity of a particular means wanted from "direct effects" on the wants and its preferences.

full measures may be increased or decreased by reason of changes in "real cost" even if these are insufficient to reach the critical points for current provision. But, for provisions continuously replaced, there is no change in the quantity wanted, once the adjustment of the number of provisions in stock is made. Where alternation or spreading out of future provision occurs or where the want for variety induces alternation,[31] reduction or increase of frequency may take place due to changes in "real cost" reaching special critical points and thus, to the extent they are reflected in the present program, may reduce or increase the number of full measures provided. Where differential costs among part lots of a means exist, a change in "real cost" of one part lot may affect the quantity wanted in terms of that single part lot without affecting the others. The single complete exception to the rule appears to be the doubtful case of segmentation where, according to our interpretation, any change of "real cost" would induce a reciprocal change in quantity wanted.

The conclusion for the general case that for each day the quantity wanted is either a full measure, no more and no less, or it is none, is so contrary to the prevalent theory of demand that it is necessary to analyze certain commonly observed cases which seem, at first sight, to contradict it. For this we refer the reader to Appendix VI, Section F.

The compensatory [32] effects of *any* change in "real cost" produce a combination of changes in the length of the working-day and changes in the reach of capacity along the order of preference. If the intensities of wants and the "curve of working" remain the same, only one other influence also produces such changes. That influence is the increase or decrease in the diversion of current working to future provision by reason of changes in the program as described in Chapter 10. All lengthening of the working-day involves exclusion of some immediately intramarginal wants, and all shortening of the working-day involves inclusion of some immediately extramarginal wants. Whether this exclusion or inclusion is properly to be described as retraction or extension, respectively, of the reach of capacity depends on whether

[31] A little analysis of the effect of the want for variety is contained in Appendix VI, Section F.

[32] It will be seen that compensatory effects always have some secondary effects. In fact, to the extent they are not taken out in a change of the working-day, they take themselves out in secondary effects. The compensatory effects are measured in quantity of work; the secondary effects in quantity of means.

the primary effect was to include or exclude wants requiring more working or less working than is required for these secondary exclusions or inclusions. It appears that the secondary components of these compensatory effects operate, in general, on individual means in the same all or none fashion as do the primary effects, but subject to the same exceptions.

This conclusion that what we are calling the compensatory effects of changes in "real cost" are operative only around the margin, in changing the working-day or the reach of capacity along the order of preference, is also contrary to the prevalent theory of demand. It implies that, in a direct economy, progress in the state of the arts would lead man to satisfy more wants because those within the previous margin had, all along, been satiated,[33] and that progressive worsening of natural conditions would lead him to satisfy fewer wants because he prefers to continue to satiate those remaining within the new margin. It is impossible to prove that this implication is correct. Nevertheless, there is some suggestive support for it which we relegate to Appendix VI, Section G.

At the end of Chapter 12 we left for future clarification two of the cardinal concepts with which we have been dealing—capacity and the motive of maximization. They have now been implicitly defined and related and we are ready to make them explicit. Capacity is a magnitude which is determined by five variables: (1) the intensities of wants; (2) the intensities of different last hour's working (curve of working); (3) technique; (4) natural resistances; and (5) the length of the working-day. Four of these are independent variables; but the last is itself a dependable variable determined by these four. What capacity can provide—its reach along the order of preference, its scope among means, its content, so to speak—is then defined by the relation between the last variable, so determined, and the other four.

Inherent in this analysis of capacity is the fact that its limit is a matter of choice. The only actual and effective limit upon the satisfaction of man's wants is imposed by his own system of preferences. This limit is set far short of the possibilities. It is not due to imposed scarcities in any

[33] Or, conversely, the allocation of effort to the satisfying of subordinate wants occurs only as the effort required to *satiate* prior wants declines. This follows from the fact that, in our scheme, the only point at which effort allocated equals the intensity of the want is at the limit of capacity. Within that limit the intensity of every want exceeds the effort required for it. This is the opposite of the notion of equilibrium in "pleasure per dollar" for all wants.

sense. It is due entirely to the fact that, at some point, he prefers leisure. Therefore, when natural resistances are reduced by the discovery of more accessible resources, or the effort required to overcome resistances is progressively economized by better tchniques, he may prefer more leisure, or he may prefer the increase of capacity thus made possible, or he may prefer a little of both.

The motive of maximization, operating in this milieu, prefers the least costly among substitute means for each want. For such means it prefers the least costly channel in the natural environment, and the most economizing technique for any scale. These are but ways of making any specific quantity of effort go as far as possible. However, the motive of maximization appears to be qualified when it comes to the order of preference among wants. If it were not, our order of ratios would govern throughout. It is quite clear that this is not the case. On the other hand, when it comes to determining the length of the working-day and thus the incidence of the limit of capacity upon the order of preference, the motive of maximization operates precisely, so far as it is permitted to do so. For, then, whenever the next "hour" will yield greater "satisfaction" if devoted to leisure than it would if devoted to provision of produced means for some future want, preference is for the greater not the less. Thus, in the last analysis, it is the motive of maximization that creates the condition which has been called "scarcity" in economic literature. So far as it is imposed at all, such scarcity consists in the impossibility of doing two different things at the same time. That is not a condition of the external environment, like the impossibility of being in two places at the same time which we cited in Chapter 11. It is a condition of the physical organization of man himself. It is that which forces man to choose. When he chooses he should not hold his environment responsible for the fact that he cannot also have the rejected alternative.

B. ON THE "THEORY OF DEMAND"

Having concluded our analysis of the actual order of preference, it seems well, in closing, to explore briefly its relationship to two systems of economic generalizations called respectively the "theory of demand" and the "theory of value." In this section we shall deal with the first. For a direct economy the order of preference and its constituents constitute the organization and the data for a theory of demand. Of chief interest in this connection are two marked differences between our construction and those familiar in economic literature.

I. THE CONCEPT OF CONTINUITY

The concept of continuity, the view of processes in terms of continuously varying magnitudes, seems to have exercised a peculiar fascination for the human mind, so much so that it has become a prepossession of scientific thinking, at least since Newton and Leibnitz. Yet, like all our notions that are derived from other than emotional sources (present wants), it was doubtless originally drawn from experience and observation of the environment. Therefore, it had, and has, no more general validity than was conferred upon it by the degree of universality which that experience and observation reached. Apparently it was derived primarily from the observation of motion, but only of motion produced by natural forces in their natural state—chiefly the force of gravity but also, perhaps, wind and the flow of water. For the self-impelled motion of man and animals is jerky and discontinuous, because the force causing it is applied discontinuously. So, too, is practically all motion caused by man's artificial use of natural forces. The stroke of the steam piston, the explosion in the internal combustion cylinder, etc., is each a separate unit. The series can be "smoothed." As compared with the "one-lung" motor the twelve-cylinder motor approximates continuity. Nevertheless, the effects of all such applied forces are essentially discontinuous, not continuous.[1] The movement of the hands of a clock is more typical of such motion than is the movement of the sun from daybreak to nightfall.

From motion this prepossession seems to have invaded the fields of all other processes capable of being viewed in that manner. It has pervaded physics—until very recently—and thence, because physics has become a model for other sciences, it has become a prejudice in many of these others.[2] In the large, statistically, or as to the macrocosm, continuity appears to be a practicable concept for dealing with many processes. In the large, the "curve" of changing magnitudes may be so smooth that its waves or breaks are imperceptible. But the deeper the study of the microcosm is carried, the more apt the data are to reveal

[1] Perhaps exceptions should be made for the turbine and for rocket propulsion.
[2] Less so, if at all, in chemistry; for the data of chemistry are most obdurate in this respect.

discontinuity. We have recently been forcibly reminded of this by several revolutionary discoveries, one or two of which may be cited as examples. It seems that these reminders may go far to upset the prejudice.

Eddington, writing of the laws of quantum theory and its new concept of steps *vs.* continuous change, says: [3] "We must not try to build up from classical conceptions, because the classical laws only become true and the conceptions concerned in them only become defined in the limiting case when the quantum numbers of the system are very large. We must start from new conceptions appropriate to low as well as to high numbered states; out of these the classical conceptions should emerge, first indistinctly, then definitely, as the number of states increases, and the classical laws become more and more nearly true." As a result of the study of the microcosm, we are forced back "to the more fundamental conceptions out of which the classical conception (sufficient for the other types of phenomena) ought to emerge as one extreme limit."

Our phrase, the all or none principle, is borrowed from an analogous discovery in physiology. "A skeletal muscle fibre contracts to its utmost, if it contracts at all." [4] "The nerve fibre . . . fires maximally or not at all." [5] In a cross-section of time the only way variations of intensity in stimulus affect either nerve or muscle is in the number of fibers involved. As these changes in number of fibers involved take place, over time, the changes in aggregate effect are essentially step-like.

It appears that our proof of the impossibility of continuous decline of intensity of a want during a process of satisfying is adequate ground upon which to establish another incursion into the private preserve of the principle of continuity. Just as when physical systems with very low quantum numbers or individual nerve and muscle fibers came to be studied, so the study of an individual instance of a single want of a single individual leads to a new concept—that of the all or none principle—the step-like discontinuous process.

2. DISCONTINUITY

According to our hypothesis, the "shape" of the typical curve representing the process of satisfying of a want is that shown in I, Fig. 41.

[3] Eddington, *132*, 197, 198. [4] Fulton, *158*, 51. [5] Fulton, *160*, 14.

The horizontal line represents the level of the intensity (I) of the want during the process; the vertical line to the right represents the decline of that intensity to zero at the point of satiation and therefore the measure of that intensity; and the base (F.M.) represents a full measure of the means. Using this as our basis let us attempt to represent the quantity wanted at various "real costs" (the demand curve) of the one means available for a single instance of a single want.[6] Several qualifications are required. In the first place, there is only one possible case where changes in the demand for one means for one want are independent of changes elsewhere. That is, there is only one case where there are no compensatory effects. This is the somewhat imaginary case, examined in Appendix VI, Section H, where the allocation of working remains the same regardless of the change in "real cost" per unit of means. All other cases involve compensatory effects. Nevertheless, the direct effects may be said to be autonomous, in so far as the compensatory effects are permitted and are merely by-products. Therefore, we shall consider them here with reservations to be discussed in the next subsection. In the second place, we shall confine ourselves here to operations on the all or none principle which we have found reason to believe is the general rule. The reader may make for himself the adjustments necessary for the exceptions we have found to this rule—changes effective in terms of part measures or number of full measures.[7]

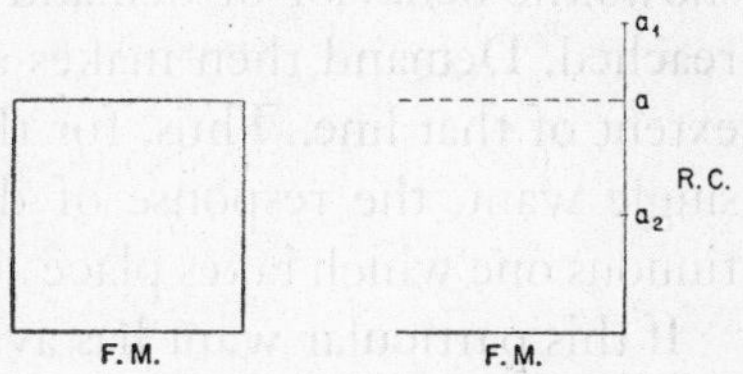

I II

FIG. 41

The only demand curve which can be fitted to this want curve is the vertical line shown in II, Fig. 41. The base (F.M.) represents a full measure, because no more and no less is wanted. The vertical line to the right represents the varying "real costs" (R.C.) of that full measure. At its full height, *a*, where it is shown as equal to the I of the want, it represents a "real cost" for the full measure which, in terms of the given factor (last hour) yields a value of unity for the ratio. At any lower "real cost," say a_2, the quantity wanted will remain exactly the same—a full measure; but the ratio will then have a value greater than unity. At any higher "real cost," says a_1, the quantity wanted will be-

[6] It is evident that this is the only case where the general curve of a want and the specific demand curve of a means are identical.

[7] The basis for doing so will appear when we consider multiple demanders below.

come nil because the value of the ratio will be less than unity.[8] If the "real cost" is conceived to decline from a_1 to a, the quantity wanted, from having been nil, will come to be a full measure. Or, if it rises from a to a_1, having been a full measure, it will become nil. But no change of "real cost" from a to a_2, or vice versa, will affect the quantity wanted. Thus the broken line shows the behavior of demand when the critical point in declining cost is reached. Demand makes a single move to the right along the full extent of that line. Correspondingly, the same line shows the behavior of demand when the critical point in rising cost is reached. Demand then makes a single move to the left along the full extent of that line. Thus, for the only means for a single instance of a single want, the response of demand to changes of cost is a discontinuous one which takes place at a single critical point.

If this particular want has available an indifferent substitute on some terms of substitution, the all or none principle obtains in the same way. But then the critical point on the demand curve will be a different one. However, that could only be shown in this diagram if the "real cost" of the substitute were assumed to remain the same. For the critical point among substitutes depends on their relative, not their absolute, costs. Since there is no reason for this *ceteris paribus* assumption, the demand curve for a means with available substitutes cannot be shown in this graphic form.[9]

In both these cases, when there is any change in quantity wanted by reason of changes in "real cost"—exclusion or inclusion of the want, or substitution of one means for another—that change necessarily involves compensatory effects—release of working to elsewhere or the absorption of it from elsewhere. But that may be equally true in reverse. Direct effects elsewhere may have compensatory effects here. This matter will be considered in the next subsection. But, here, it must be noted that, to the extent that the compensatory effects from here or from elsewhere take themselves out in a shortening or lengthening of the working-day the value of the factor in the ratio will change.

[8] To be thoroughly realistic it is necessary to note that when the means for a want becomes very cheap, some of it is apt to be wasted. Actually, no more is used or wanted; but the quantity provided may be somewhat more than the quantity used. So we may buy bread by the loaf and throw away the part that becomes stale. The thrifty never used to do this and probably do not even now.

[9] Even if the two demand curves were shown, the corresponding critical points on each would be theoretically infinite. In effect, this works out that each pair of corresponding critical points is a "line of indifference." Hence the relation could be shown by means of the graphic form used for that purpose. Hicks's form will serve.

Then our vertical line signifying "real cost," in II, Fig. 41, will change correspondingly. If the "real cost" is already close to the critical point *a*, such a change in the factor might bring it above *a*. Thus this attempt to represent by a single curve the demand for a single means is subject to this disability as well. Within limits such a curve means something; but it does not stand on its own feet very firmly.[10]

The concept of elasticity of demand has developed from the use of curves to represent "price"-demand relations and therefore only indirectly from the observations of collective demand whence these relations arise. Marshall defines the elasticity of demand as the "responsiveness" of quantity wanted to changes in "price." [11] Application of the concept of elasticity to demand curves is said to be geometrical; for "the elasticity of a curve is a geometrical conception." [12] At once this introduces the question of continuity *vs.* discontinuity, which is well exemplified in Marshall's treatment in his "Mathematical Appendix." [13] He first defines the elasticity at a point on the curve, P, as being the distance along the tangent from that point to the x axis, divided by the distance to the y axis. But, obviously, there can be no elasticity, according to his definition, when there is no movement (i.e., there can be none at *a* point). If there is a movement, it is from one point on the curve to another. If so, the movement cannot be defined in terms of the tangent, either at the initial or at the end point, unless the curve is a straight line. Any certain movement must be along an arc of the curve, or, as a whole, along the chord of that arc. For a straight line curve the chord and the arc are one and the same. There is one possible true curve, movement along any arc of which represents a constant elasticity under Marshall's definition—an elasticity of unity. That curve is a rectangular hyperbola—which Marshall uses to indicate "constant outlay demand." [14] I have seen it assumed that there are other true curves, movement along any arc of which represents a con-

[10] Provided the normal intensities and therefore the order of priority are assumed to remain the same, this general discussion applies to demand over any period chosen. Obviously, the period must be long enough to permit changes in "real cost." Also it must be long enough to include wants that only recur occasionally. Given any base period, the change in quantity wanted is for a like period.

[11] Marshall, *291*, 102. Cassel's concept, for instance, is approximately the same (*74*, 78).

[12] Robinson, *349*, 18.

[13] Marshall, *291*, 839, note III.

[14] A "rectangular hyperbola" is defined, in economic usage, as a curve which always "subtends" the same area—that is, where the product of the ordinate into the abscissa is equal at all points. Neither of these terms seems to be familiar to my expert mathematical friends though, of course, the concepts are.

stant elasticity other than that of unity. But that, I think, depends on using Marshall's definition of elasticity, which denies the fact of movement. There are only two straight-line curves, movement along the arc and chord of which represents constant elasticity. They are the straight-line curves parallel to one or the other of the axes. A vertical straight-line curve represents a constant elasticity of zero; a horizontal straight-line curve represents constant infinite elasticity. Movement along any other than these curves represents continuously changing elasticity. Then how can the elasticity represented by any particular movement along a curve be defined unequivocally?

This difficulty can be got round by adopting a different approach.[15] One solution is this. "When the changes are small," says Mrs. Robinson, elasticity is measured by "the proportional change of the abscissa divided by the proportional change of the ordinate." [16] For negative elasticity this introduces an error which, if the changes are considerable, requires correction. The simple solution for negative elasticity, as usually defined, is this: In terms of fractions, elasticity is the fraction, increment of demand over old demand, divided by the fraction, decrement of price over new price.[17] And that holds good down to the smallest change.[18] But, if we adopt this formula for elasticity we necessarily abandon all notions of continuity. We do not claim or need to know how demand might have changed in the course; we only compare the two end-points and note the effect. The correct representation is no longer a continuous curve. It is merely the two end-points. A series of such changes becomes a series of points. Moreover, we must signify which is the initial and which the final point in each movement. We might draw an arrow between them. But it must be an arrow, not a line. For a line might suggest movement in either direction, and the elasticities in the two directions are different. The more elegant solution derives what is called "arc elasticity," namely the average elas-

[15] The easiest way of maintaining the simple geometrical approach would be to adopt Marshall's representation of a series of rectangular hyperbolas (*291*, 840). If one such curve were drawn for each added unit of outlay, elasticity could be derived from (or shown by) the direction and extent of movement across these curves.

[16] Robinson, *349*, 18. We overlook the fact that this is stated to be "at any point in the curve." Of course, *at* any point in the curve there could be no changes. And, as we show below, the statement is only true of movements *from* any point on the curve if the curve represents constant elasticity.

[17] For "positive" elasticity the divisor ratio may be increment of price over old price.

[18] No formulae of this kind demonstrate neatly the concepts of "infinite" and of "zero" elasticity. Infinite elasticity is simply the case where a change occurs in the dividend ratio with no change in the divisor ratio; and zero elasticity is the case where a change in the divisor ratio involves no change in the dividend ratio.

ticity of all points on the arc, determined for each according to Marshall's formula. This gives at least the appearance of continuity and does not eliminate the need of a curve. On the face of it, it would also seem not to deny that the movement in either direction would show the same elasticity.

According to either of these formulae, except on curves showing constant elasticity, movement from any one point on the curve shows a different elasticity for each point to which the movement is made. Therefore, on any such demand curve, the elasticity of demand is different for each "price" change than for each other. It would appear, then, that elasticity can, at best, only be derived from such a curve with reference to a particular move from one definite point to another definite point. That is, we are compelled to depart from "instantaneous rates" and deal only in terms of discontinuous movements.[19]

If this discontinuity is true of the concept of elasticity of demand, is it not also true of the concept of a demand curve itself? If observation leads us to the conclusion that changes in "price" produce changes in the quantity wanted, it is only because we note that definite changes have definite results. It may quite well be that the "very small changes," in terms of which elasticity is usually defined, have no results. Then the representation of our actual observations would be confined to a series of points—the beginnings and ends of movements of demand with relation to movements of prices—fixed in relation to the two axes. It would not follow that these movements are reversible. Nor would it follow that we could fit a mathematical curve to these points. That, in the first place, would assume continuity rather than discontinuity, and would insert an interpolation for which there is no evidence. That, in the second place, would assume that some certain function or system of functions governed such a curve. But such an assumption implies that these points are determined by a relatively simple and regular conjunction of forces. Is either the interpolation, to give the appearance of continuity, or the assignment of a definite function, to give the appearance of understood (or at least measured) causation, legitimate? Does not observation, instead, give the impression of discontinuous movements with highly erratic magnitudes?

So far as our construction of individual demand in a direct economy operating on the all or none principle is concerned, the concept of

[19] True, there will be some "instantaneous rate" which represents the actual rate of the discontinuous movement. But, since it can only be discovered by first determining the actual rate, it does not seem to add any useful information.

elasticity does not seem to be a useful one. To say that, below some maximum "real cost," elasticity of demand for a means is infinite up to a full measure is hardly meaningful if the full measure is the unit of demand. To say that, below this maximum, the elasticity of demand is zero at the edge of a full measure would require so many qualifications (as we undertake to show in the next subsection) that there would not be much left of it.[20] Neither does it appear that the demand "curve" is applicable here. A single step, forward or backward, does not require such portrayal. In dealing with the microcosm, frank recognition of a complex of discontinuous change seems to be better procedure.

While we are limiting ourselves in this study to the behavior of an individual demander it is well, in passing, to make clear that, so far as discontinuity alone is concerned, we would have to admit that both these conceptions, elasticity and demand curves, like those to which Eddington refers (as quoted above), might begin to become appropriate as the number of individual demanders becomes very large. It is true that what is discontinuous in the individual case remains discontinuous in the aggregate. Nevertheless, even in our simplest general case it is possible that the critical points of different demanders are different. If so, the all or none effects for each might be arranged in so close-ordered a series and the effect in each case might be so small a proportion of the whole effect through any "price" range that, in the aggregate, the direct effects would iron themselves out into the appearance of continuity.[21] Though we count in multiples of the unit one, counting to a million may fairly be conceived and represented as a straight line. Statistically speaking, discontinuities may merge into continuities when the numbers become sufficiently large. However, we shall see in the next subsection that, unlike discontinuity, interdependence remains, in the large, as serious a bar to the application

[20] Moreover, it does not appeal to me to use a concept whose only application is to define a condition which is absent.

[21] Actually, however, all moves along a continuous curve would be the statistical average of a combination of discontinuous vertical and horizontal individual moves—i.e., a combination of a vertical move for those whose demand had an elasticity of zero for that price change with a horizontal move for those whose demand had an infinite elasticity (i.e., responded), through some range, for that price change. With the possible exception of an elasticity of unity (see Appendix VI, Section H), all elasticities will be the statistical average of various mixtures of elasticity of zero and of infinity.

Thus, while we agree with Hicks (*195*, 34) that "the change in the demand of a group is the sum of changes in individual demands," we hold that the tendency toward continuity can only appear if the critical points are different and the number of individuals becomes large.

of the concepts of elasticity and of definite demand curves as it is in the small.

Subject to that qualification, it would seem possible to make a beginning in the direction of continuity in the cases of our exceptions to the general rule of all or none change in terms of one full measure and no more. If the change affects part measures only, the discontinuities are at least smaller. If the change affects several full measures of the same or of different sizes, the discontinuities vary in size; but then we have a series of steps at a series of critical points, instead of one only. And this, in a small way, begin to suggest a demand curve. But it must be remembered that in such an adumbration of a curve, based on our findings, each tread and each riser may be different from every other. That does not lend itself to nice geometrical treatment in terms of mathematical functions. Nor does the elasticity even then resemble that of a rubber band. Rather it resembles the elasticity of a telescoping spyglass which extends one slide at a time. The one of our exceptions in which both concepts may be useful is discussed in Appendix VI, Section H.

3. INTERDEPENDENCE

General equilibrium theory has recognized that the quantity wanted of any means cannot be determined in isolation.[22] In our terms, that would mean that a change in "real cost" of any one means might affect the quantity wanted of every other means. To the extent that is true, it would obviously be impossible to draw a demand curve or determine the elasticities of demand for a single means by merely representing the reaction to its own changes of cost—our primary effects. To the extent that is true, the concept of general equilibrium precludes the concept of partial equilibrium. However, this recognition of interdependence is the result of abstract—and largely mathematical—reasoning. It is permissive rather than definite. No effort appears to have been made to determine inductively the particular conditions under which interdependence exists, nor what limitations, if any, there are upon it. While our analysis, at this stage, can no longer lay claim

[22] As Cassel states it (*74*, 77), "The individual demand of a good is generally dependent upon the prices of all goods." Or as Hicks puts it (*196*, 63), "Strictly speaking, the individual's demand for any commodity depends, not only on the price of that commodity, but also on the prices of all other commodities purchased, *and on his income*."

to being strictly inductive, it does provide us with two specific causes (and types) of interdependence, and does indicate that, for our abstraction, a direct economy, only these two causes are operative.

For any two or more means which, according to some unweighted terms of substitution, constitute indifferent substitutes for a single want, interdependence exists. As a result, it is impossible to establish a demand curve for any one without reference to the others. At any "real cost" for the now preferred substitute there will be a critical point in the relative cost of each of the other substitutes. Without change in "real cost" for the now preferred substitute a decline below the critical point in the relative cost of any of the other substitutes will reverse the preference in terms of the weighted terms of substitution. The effect will be on an all or none basis. Quantity wanted of the now preferred substitute will become nil; that of the newly preferred substitute will become a full measure. This potentiality also precludes the concept of elasticity. If at every level of "real cost" below the point of exclusion, elasticity may be zero or infinite, depending on what happens to other "real costs," elasticity is indeterminate.

While this type of interdependence exists more especially among means with proportionate attributes, it may also be conceived to exist with reference to means with fixed attributes. True, the latter are never indifferent substitutes. But it is apt to be true among them, as well, that there are critical relative costs which are based on the comparative quantity of the attribute in an otherwise fixed full measure of each. If both these classes of substitutes are to be included in establishing this type of interdependence it would seem to hold good rather generally.

The other type of interdependence is far more restricted in its scope.[23] With the single exception of possible cases where demand has an elasticity of unity (discussed in Appendix VI, Section H) every change in "real cost" of any means now used, or which causes its use,

[23] That is, it is under our construction. But it should be noted that the very idea of elasticities other than unity is inconsistent with the formation of definitive demand curves for single means. That is, movement along every arc that has an elasticity less than unity involves absorption of income from elsewhere on the rise and release to elsewhere on the decline. Conversely, with every arc that has an elasticity greater than unity. Without change in income, such absorption or release must move some or all other curves to the left or to the right, respectively. In a system of interdependent and moving curves is the concept of elasticity a definitive one? This objection does not hold good of indifference curve systems which are complete (surfaces). They evade these difficulties. They introduce "cross elasticity." But, if they do so on the false premise of general substitutability, they have saved elasticity at the cost of being unrealistic.

must have compensatory effects. This is equally true whether the direct effect includes no primary effect (is nil, so far as the means is concerned), whether it causes a substitution, or whether it leads to exclusion or inclusion of the want. However, our analysis has led us to the conclusion that the incidence of these compensatory effects is always in one range—around the margin. If so, it is limited. Moreover, it is, strictly speaking, dependence rather than interdependence, because it operates only in one direction. Changes in "real cost" within this range have no compensatory effects upon wants prior to this range. They, too, take themselves out within the range itself. It is true that the compensatory effects divide themselves, in a direct economy, between a change in the length of the working-day and a change in the reach of capacity. Nevertheless, it is not to be supposed that the change in the length of the working-day will ever produce a sufficient change in the factor (intensity of the last hour's working) to affect any wants except those in the range around the margin.[24] In fact, our very concept of this range should be defined to include all wants which can be so affected.

Recognizing this second type of interdependence we perceive that no demand curve even for the preferred means serving any of the wants in this range can be constructed without reference to all other wants. With no change in its own "real cost" the quantity wanted of the preferred means for any of these wants may become nil (exclusion) or change from nil to a full measure (inclusion), merely by reason of a change in "real cost" of some means used elsewhere. Obviously, the concept of elasticity is equally inapplicable here.

In a direct economy there seems to be no other cause of interdependence. If so, we can say that, for any want prior to the marginal range which has only one available means, it is possible to draw a demand curve of the kind shown in II, Fig. 41, on p. 981. This curve (a vertical line) represents an elasticity of zero up to a maximum—the critical point for exclusion of the want. At that point the elasticity becomes infinite for an instant while demand is disappearing. Above that point demand is nil.

Having completed our analytical scheme of the influence of changing "real costs" upon the order of preference it seems desirable to relate it to one which it resembles only superficially—that of Hicks—and to one which it resembles only fundamentally—that of Roy. Since this

[24] The possibility, suggested on p. 983, is this case.

requires a somewhat more extended treatment than is permissible in a footnote, it will be found in Appendix VI, Section I.

C. ON THE "THEORY OF VALUE"

The field which we have been exploring in this study has, in the past, been the primary concern of those who have undertaken to develop for economics a "theory of value." Yet we conclude our study without having arrived at any "theory of value." [1] Even if all qualitative connotations are removed from the term, so that "value" becomes merely an abstract system of ratios between full measures or objective units of all means,[2] we still would have no unique system of valuation ratios. For what we have uncovered is two systems of valuation ratios, each equally valid. The first is the result of subjective valuation, as we have construed it; the second is the result of comparative "real costs." The first cannot be stated in numbers; for it is based on magnitudes which cannot be measured. It is only an arrangement in terms of more or less or equality. It is constituted of full measures of all the means for each want arranged in the order of priority of these wants. Its only form of mathematical statement (in units of means) is $3a = 2a_1 = 4a_2 > 5b = 3b_1 > 2c = 4c_1 \ldots$ [3] The second system of ratios can be stated in numbers; for its magnitudes can be very accurately measured.[4] The objective unit of each means can be related to that of each other in terms of the number of units of "real cost"—their common dimension—required for each.[5] Its mathematical statement can take either of two forms. The first form is $1a\colon 1b\colon 1c = 3\colon 2\colon 4 \ldots$; the second form is $\frac{1}{3}a\colon \frac{1}{2}b\colon \frac{1}{4}c = 1\colon 1\colon 1$. Even standing by itself, either form is a perfectly valid system of valuation ratios,

[1] In the sense of the older usage, in which "value" is practically synonymous with "value in exchange," we could not develop a "value theory" for a direct economy, since by definition a direct economy excludes exchange. Or, if one conceives the sole worker-retainer to exchange his effort for product, then the only possible value system would be comparative "real costs."

The nearest thing to a "theory of value" that our study has produced is developed in Appendix VI, Section A, where we contrast our results to those of marginal utility theory.

[2] Either form can be used; $1x\colon 1y \ldots = 4\colon 2 \ldots$ or $1x = 2y \ldots$

[3] Ignoring substitutes, its realistic form of statement would be 1 day's supply of bread > 1 day's use of a house > 1 day's use of a suit of clothes, etc.

[4] That is, they can be in a direct economy where working is uniform and retaining has a fixed relation, as cost, to working.

[5] We do not need to complicate the point made here by considering differential "real costs." With them, of course, the units of each part lot take a different position in the system of ratios.

if comparative "values" are determined by "real costs." True, as we noted in Chapter 13, Section A, this yields, when standing by itself, no possible order of preference. The objective units in which it is stated are entirely arbitrary, whether natural or artificial, and are among themselves incommensurable. If the first form of statement seems to yield an order of preference—*b, a, c*—from the cheapest to the most expensive, nevertheless the second form shows that it does not. For, if I choose to conceive $\frac{1}{3}a$, $\frac{1}{2}b$ and $\frac{1}{4}c$ as being of the same "size," the "real costs" of equal quantities of all means turn out to be equal. However, this disability does not exist in connection with our present purpose. It is entirely possible to establish the natural or arbitrary unit of every means, to determine the "real costs" of such units, and then to arrange them in the order of rising or declining "real cost" per unit. If "value" depends wholly on "real cost," that would be the system of valuation ratios.

The first and least satisfactory way to relate these two systems of valuation ratios would be to find a common correspondence in terms of a defined quantity of each means which would serve to establish a non-mathematical equality between the subjective and the "real cost" value. The second and more satisfactory way would be to find a common dimension in terms of which the magnitude, subjective value, and the magnitude "real cost" could be made commensurable. The first of these steps was taken in Section C 4 of Chapter 13, where we converted the system of valuation ratios of comparative "real costs" into terms of full measures of each means. When we do this, the "real cost" of each full measure becomes the inverse dimension of our "order of ratios." Since the normal maximum intensities of the wants *correspond* to a full measure of means in the first valuation system, we can then make these magnitudes the direct dimension of our ratios. But these latter magnitudes are immeasurable. We therefore give them, to start with, a set of purely imaginary numerical values whose only significance is that they become smaller as one proceeds along the order of priority. These numbers serve only to rank the wants. However, it developed later, and particularly in Section A 3 of this chapter, that, at the limit of capacity, the two magnitudes—the direct and the inverse dimensions of our ratios—become comparable because they become equal in terms of a common dimension, I. Thus the arbitrary numbers in the direct dimension come to have another significance. While among themselves they represent only immeasurable differences

—more or less—around the margin they approach identity with the measured quantities in the inverse dimension.

By these means we found it possible to relate these two systems of valuation ratios, subjective valuation and comparative "real costs." In our order of ratios the former is the direct dimension and the latter the inverse dimension. The pivotal point which makes the two commensurable is the limit of capacity. But they are also approximately commensurable, in that range, in the actual order of preference, which contains the preferred means for those wants which are near the margin—lying within but near the limit of capacity, and probably also just beyond that limit. In that range, it would be possible to give rough extrinsic numbers to the subjective values; for the reason the want is in that range is that its intensity is approximately equal to the "real cost" of its preferred means. However, this would give us an odd assortment of numbers, because the "real costs" of these full measures may vary widely, and therefore come from widely different places in the system of valuation ratios which follows the rising order of "real costs" per unit. Moreover, such extrinsic numbers would tell us almost nothing as to the positions of these wants in the order of priority for the simple reason that the corresponding extrinsic numbers of these wants, in whose neighborhood they would presumably lie, would not serve to identify their intrinsic numbers and thus their places in the order.

Nowhere else in the actual order of preference do the two systems of valuation ratios agree—or, more precisely, do the two systems of valuation, in these senses, coincide.[6] All we know of the extent of their disagreement is this: From the beginning of the actual order of preference up to this range, relative value in subjective terms is higher than it is in terms of "real cost"—using the pivotal point as basis for both. Beyond the limit of capacity, relative value in subjective terms is

[6] Senior says (*370*, *97*): ". . . where the only natural agents employed are those which are universally accessible [our general case], and therefore are practically unlimited in supply . . . the utility of the produce, or, in other words, its power directly or indirectly, of providing gratification, or preventing pain, must be in proportion to the sacrifices [our efforts] made to produce it, unless the producer has misapplied his exertions; since no man would willingly employ a given amount of labour or abstinence in producing one commodity, if he could obtain more gratification by devoting them to the production of another."

On its face, this identification of the two systems of valuation sounds so utterly reasonable that it is hard to dispute. Nevertheless, his proof, in the last clause, proves our order of ratios equally well, and, we think, wholly fails to account for that part of the actual order of preference which is determined solely by the order of priority.

lower than it is in terms of "real cost." The very essence of our actual order of preference is this disagreement. Thus the actual order of preference is a compound of two almost wholly different and quite independent systems of valuation. It is constructed partly in terms of one only, and partly in terms of the relation between the two in each specific case. To be more precise, we have concluded that, in its earlier range—the great prior wants—the order of preference follows the order of priority (subjective valuation), and only in its later ranges is it influenced somewhat roughly by the relation between the two systems of valuation. Thus, the actual order of preference itself does not constitute a third system of valuation. It merely records the response to subjective value or to the relation of subjective value to "real cost." It is the result of a compromise between two kinds of motivation, the intensities of certain wants, which enforce their demands without reference to costs, and, with respect to all other wants, what we have called the motive of maximization which seeks to obtain the greatest possible satisfaction per unit of effort until the effort comes to exceed the satisfaction.

In striving for a unified "theory of value" one might try to conceive of the several subjective values as constituting "ceilings" and the several "real costs" as constituting "floors," so that *actual* values, if not precisely defined, would still need to be somewhere between the "ceiling" and the "floor" in each case.[7] But this gives only a delusive sense of unification. All we really know is that, in a direct economy, no means will be produced whose "floor" is higher than its "ceiling." When the "ceiling" is higher than the "floor" no unified system of values can coincide with both. If so, the determinant of actual value, between the two, would have to be some other factor or factors that we have not yet discovered. Therefore, at best, so far as a direct economy is concerned, we are obliged to content ourselves with a dual system of valuation ratios. Whether or not that can properly be called a "theory of value" we leave to the reader.

However, the qualitative connotations of the term "value" may still have so strong a hold on the minds of some that they will contend that we have proffered *a* "theory of value," because only the scheme of subjective valuation—the first system of valuation ratios—is entitled to the use of the term. We cannot argue the question, for it is not

[7] Something of this kind seems to have been in the minds of early classic economists when they used the terms "value in use" and "value in exchange."

susceptible of proof. We can only suggest that, in a direct economy, it seems probable that a qualitative connotation would attach to product in some degree by reason of its "real cost" as well as because it was wanted. Thus "value," in a sense, might be attached to a product in which effort had been invested even though, when made, it was found unsuitable to the want for which it was designed. The product might be preserved only for that reason.[8] Certainly, it is difficult to believe that product with a high "real cost" is not valued, in this sense, more highly than that with a low "real cost," even if the intensity of the wants which the two products serve are nearly equal. Observation shows that care and avoidance of waste are much greater for high cost than for low cost product. Finally, there is no value, in this sense, for means readily available for direct consumption which therefore require no effort—do not need to be produced. Yet many of these serve the most intense wants and should, therefore, have high subjective values.[9] It seems necessary to concede that there are two bases of valuation in a direct economy—one which registers how much the means is wanted and another which corresponds to the effort that has been made in order to produce it. Upon this interpretation changes in "real cost" have no direct effect on subjective valuation. They register only in the other form of valuation.

These considerations introduce some qualifications of our first general statement of the two systems of valuation ratios. It should be understood that we regard it as unnecessary to repeat here our list of exceptions to the all or none principle. We are dealing here with the general rule only. Nevertheless, it is necessary to point out that the simple statement, above, of the system of dual valuation ratios only

[8] Thus a statement like that of Wicksteed (*441*, 93) that "efforts are regulated by anticipated values, but values are not controlled by antecedent efforts" may only be true of the values subjectively conferred. It really begs the question.

[9] We have excluded the means that can be acquired at no "real cost" from our order of preference, because the latter is concerned only with the allocation of effort. That does not mean, however, that they have no subjective value.

This duality in the valuation system goes far deeper than a verbal dilemma. Take, for instance, Jevons's effort (*224*, 79) to fit Adam Smith's (*381*, I, 30) distinction between "value in use" and "value in exchange" with the categories, total and marginal utility, respectively. Smith recognized two systems of valuation; Jevons (and almost everyone since) tries to combine them in one. Of course "value in exchange" is not precisely our "real cost." But it is a distinct system of valuation.

Menger (*296*, 120) points out that "value" frequently does not coincide with "real cost" and that therefore the latter cannot be the quantitatively determining element. If by "value" he meant "exchange value" we quite agree. Where we do not agree is in identifying "exchange value" with subjective value. We can point out a great many more cases where these two do not agree.

applies, as stated, to the valuation of the quantity wanted to make up a full measure of each means. In a direct economy we may assume that there can be no more than two exceptions to the rule that the quantity made is always the quantity wanted. The first exception would cover the output of biological processes which may vary from the planned quantity in either direction.[10] If the output exceeds the planned quantity, its "real cost" per unit is less than that expected; if it falls short, its "real cost" is greater. In either case, the position of the product in the system of valuation ratios based on comparative "real costs" changes. Does its subjective valuation also change? In our scheme, for a direct economy only, it hardly ever does so. The subjective value of full measures assigned to future provision, whether longer or shorter, all have the same subjective value. Only when the shortage is so great as to require what we have called spreading does the subjective value change. And then only because a part measure comes to have the same subjective value as a full measure would normally have. Variations in output by reason of biological processes may also determine the range along a series of alternative uses to which the output will be applied. But, in our scheme and again for a direct economy only, the least important of alternative uses does not determine subjective values for all such uses. Instead, each stands on its own feet. The only effect of an excess or deficit with respect to the planned quantity is to include or exclude full measures for wants of given intensity, so that the least important full measure will have a smaller subjective value the greater the excess, and a greater subjective value the greater the deficit.

Another exception may appear necessary to cover all other deficits in quantity made as compared to quantity wanted which are due to reasons other than unwillingness to allocate the requisite effort to their production—in other words to "scarcity," so-called. In Chapter 11 we have cast doubt on the applicability of the notion of scarcity to natural resources. The other class, means that are non-reproducible because of special personal skills, cannot, of course, appear in a direct economy. If these two possibilities are eliminated here, nothing seems to remain. Moreover, the exceptional cases which might be regarded as belonging in this category have perhaps been dealt with adequately in Appendix VI, Section A. It seems unnecessary to add a further qualification to our generalization above by reason of possible exceptions of this kind.

[10] To be logically complete we may include in this all quantities that are different from what turns out to be wanted.

CONCLUSION

A study of this kind does not lend itself to any succinct summary. The conclusions reached are all tentative and they strew themselves along the whole process of examining the evidence. Nevertheless, it seems worth while, at the close, to attempt to recapitulate those particular conclusions and classifications which seem to be most positively indicated and therefore least open to question—conclusions which I am sure the progress of knowledge will modify and improve, but which I do not believe will be done away with in that process.[1] First, let us emphasize the three major theses which the study presents, and upon which, in turn, it rests.

1. Organisms, including man, are not reaction-mechanisms for response to environmental stimuli. They are, on the contrary, more or less elaborate complexes of processes, in any one of which variations from homeostasis set up corrective (balancing) responses. It is these variations which are the ultimate primary energizers of behavior. They originate in the periphery—that is, outside the brain. When their effects reach the brain, they become the excitors of integrated behavior. The effects of environmental stimuli, past as well as present, are almost wholly confined to guiding the orientation of this behavior—using the term orientation in our limited sense. However, the internal milieu is not sharply outlined against the external. It is not independent. The two milieux merge. Therefore, there is a more or less continuous exchange between them, so that the environment has other and more vital relations with the organism in addition to the limited function of affording external sensory stimuli.

2. Some organisms—chiefly man—also evince integrated behavior when these ultimate primary energizers of behavior are inoperative and when no external stimulus is apparent as cause. It seems necessary

[1] I must, for my own protection, warn the reader that this attempt at recapitulation necessarily omits all the complexities, qualifications, and exceptions presented in this study. Therefore, the nearest thing to a definitive statement which I can make is contained in the study itself. This recapitulation does not pretend to be definitive.

to infer that such behavior is energized from a secondary source in the brain itself. And, in the brain, this source appears to be related to memory and to that uncertain entity called volition, with its attendant sense of effort. To justify the supposition of a relationship between this behavior and the mnemonic-volitional system and to identify what we mean by the latter we attempted to achieve a compound, or a partial reconciliation, of views as to the characteristics of its components from several different sources—psychological, biological, and physiological—all of which are based on evidence of a very different character from that available for our first thesis. But our analysis does not depend on these identifications. Our chief reliance is placed on pure inference. Taking as our starting-point the characteristics of the behavior which appears to be energized by this secondary source, we infer what would need to be the characteristics of the wholly imputed source. Thus we arrive at a series of really unknown entities, to which we only give names because entities which they resemble have always had those names. So physics continues to use the term "gravity" for an unknown force which has characteristics quite different from those which gave it its name.[2]

[2] We could have followed Pareto's proposal and named these three necessarily to be inferred entities x, y and z. Let x stand for future wants. These, to be sure, are almost certainly to be identified as memories. Since they are assumed to be weak and, though continuing, are inoperative much of the time, there must be a reinforcing agency when and while they do become operative. Let y stand for this agency, which we have called secondary neural energy of response. This agency is instigated by x, apparently at whatever rate is required up to some limit proportional to each individual x. Such secondary energy appears to be required to overcome inertia, fatigue, and the competition of opposed primary energy, and to energize the behavior. Even then, behavior frequently fails to occur, and it always stops, temporarily or permanently. What prevents or stops it? We have elaborated the reasons for imputing a third entity, a kind of resistance. Let z stand for this resistance. It appears that z is proportionate to y. Apparently it results from y. But, as a resistance, it does not oppose y. It opposes x. That is perfectly clear. Moreover, though it opposes x chiefly in proportion to the duration (and intensity or rate) of the corresponding y during activity, it also does so, though in minute proportion, according to the futurity of the particular x (after the activity). From which we would infer that a small increment of y is required in proportion to the futurity of the particular x.

It is evident that the formula for the operation of these underlying entities is of the order of $(x - z)\ y$, where the potential maximum rate of y is a function of x and where z is a function of the actual quantity of y (rate multiplied by duration). Moreover, z varies with the quantity of y under two different sets of conditions. The quantity of y is produced at a fairly high rate during the activity itself and at a low rate during the interval between the end of the activity and the arrival of the instance. Therefore, the quantity of z accrues at a fairly high rate under the first condition and at a low rate under the second, and it is this accrued quantity of z that presents the resistance to x in each case. Such an energetic formula may be inferred from the facts of behavior even if the entities involved remain wholly unknown.

3. The fundamental economic fact of man's relation to his environment appears to be that nature imposes resistances of various kinds and degrees to man's activities in pursuit of the satisfaction of his wants. This thesis presents a view of the relation which is different from, and I think more useful than, the prevailing economic view. It makes possible a treatment of the relation in quantitative and energetic terms, and it makes clear what are the actual determinants of "real costs" in each case. This seems preferable to treatment in terms only of quantity of superficial area or other resource, with its unjustifiable corollary of "scarcity." It is not argued that one view is right and the other wrong, but merely that the view presented here is more useful in relating all our economic categories to each other in quantitative terms.

In all three theses the terms "energizer" and "energetics" must be construed in a non-physical sense. The physical energy of behavior is contributed by the muscles. Nevertheless, it is the primary and the secondary sources of the energizing of behavior which are responsible for initiating and maintaining such behavior. And such behavior includes or involves many kinds of activity which are not muscular. Neither are the natural resistances to this behavior reducible to terms of physical force. Distance, for instance, is not a force. A better term than energy might be found; I have not been able to find one that does not suffer from greater objections.

The first thesis is, of course, in no respect original with me. It seems to have become the general view of modern biologists. It seems to be replacing the external stimulus-response view in physiology and psychology. Nevertheless, in the latter fields, the older view appears still to be held in certain influential quarters. The new evidence bearing on this question should, I think, establish the first thesis on an incontrovertible basis. Partly, therefore, for the sake of rebuttal, in so far as that is still necessary, but chiefly for the more constructive purpose of building a scheme of fundamental economic motivation on this firm foundation, I have thought it worth while to digest and present this new evidence—a task, I am told, that has not yet been undertaken by anyone else.

The second thesis is not original in matter—only in manner. The study of animal behavior as a source of the objective understanding of human behavior has, I believe, led to a habit of overlooking one vast difference. In order to sharpen the point and because the difference is due to a practically unknown factor, I have chosen to state it in the form of a contrast between existent and non-existent wants—present and future. Most organisms respond only to existent wants; man, a few rodents and perhaps some birds and insects, respond also to non-existent wants. Of course, there must be a present cause for the behavior in both cases. The point is that the two systems of causation—or energizing—are evidently quite different. The dichotomy I have chosen evades all questions of intellect, morals, etc.; it is based on the simplest and most basic distinction. That, I believe, is a useful approach for the study of the organism man. It begs no questions.

The third thesis is, so far as I know, my own. It is the result of several decades of struggle with what I have found to be an entirely unmanageable concept—the factor land, as it has stood in classical economic theory—and what I have concluded is a wholly untrue concept—the notion of "scarcity" as the reason for value and price. The presentation of my different view in Chapter 11 and its illustration and conversion to quantitative terms in Chapter 12 will have to stand on their own feet. As yet I cannot cite others in support. Nevertheless, I hope that the change in the way of looking at the matter, which is all this thesis amounts to, will not prove too difficult or objectionable to prevent its becoming as useful to others as it has to me.

The chief consequences for economic analysis which arise from the examination of the data in the light of these theses may be summarized. We will confine ourselves here to those conclusions that seem to be rather definitely proven and to those analytical clarifications which seem to be nearly inescapable once they are perceived.

1. Present wants have among them an order of priority according to their normal maximum intensity and, therefore, to their power to become prepotent. Only one present want can be prepotent at a time. The prepotent want always evinces a tendency to achieve satiation, subject to certain special causes of failure to satiate.[3] Most present wants are grouped in constellations, the members of which can be satisfied in a joint process. Only the major want of the constellation, at any one time, becomes prepotent, and the satisfaction of the minor wants is incidental. Future wants duplicate present wants, but at a much lower level of intensity. They, too, have an order of priority and a system of dominance, and they, too, are grouped in constellations. But it is possible, with them, for many minor members of the constella-

[3] Of these, three were given in Chapter 4 and the fourth only appeared in Chapter 7, where we began to analyze means, because the fourth is due to a characteristic of the means rather than of the want.

tion to influence the joint process so that their ultimate satisfaction may not be incidental. The essential distinction between present and future wants is that the behavior caused by the former leads to immediate consummatory reactions (satisfying), if that is possible, while the behavior caused by the latter always stops short of immediate consummatory reactions.

2. A single means may contain one or it may contain many attributes (be compound) and, therefore, may serve one or many wants. Preparatory or consummatory reactions with regard to compound means may then constitute joint processes of members of a constellation. Certain attributes exist in means in proportion to the quantity of means; others exist in fixed quantity regardless of the quantity of means. If, regardless of the quantity of means, the fixed attribute exists in quantity too small to satiate a want, consumption of that means cannot result in satiation. Means are subject to three forms of measurement by man and, to a considerable extent, by other organisms. The first is called "subjective valuation." It is the recognition of a quantitative relation to a want, and therefore depends on some criterion by which the want itself is judged or felt. The second form of measurement is objective. Its measures are natural or artificial separate units, or they are as-if-separated units in a continuum. Man, at least, having recognized the quantity of a means necessary to satisfy a want, can thereafter reduce it to terms of objective measurement. The third form of measurement will be covered in paragraph 4 below.

3. Applying the fundamental axioms of the physicists' theory of dimensions to the magnitudes involved in paragraph 2, it becomes evident that it would be impossible meaningfully to compare quantities of different means for different wants without some method of comparing the magnitudes of the wants. We have sifted out only three possible types of energetic magnitude which might serve as criteria by which the want itself is judged or felt—i.e., ways in which the want might act. On our own (physiological) assumption of a tendency to satiation, the want acts practically undiminished throughout the process of satisfying. The first type of magnitude, then, is static, representing the intensity of the want, and declines only at satiation. On the assumption underlying all forms of marginal utility theory—even indifference systems—the want declines during the process of satisfying. This permits us to suppose either of two types of magnitude. The first is a static one which is determining (judged or felt) at several strategic

stages, but which declines from stage to stage in the process of satisfying. The second is a dynamic one which is determining (judged or felt) during the several strategic phases, but which declines from phase to phase in the process of satisfying. Therefore, if the second is also produced by the very process of reduction of intensity in the want, or by any phenomenon connected with or resembling that, it must be that the rate of decline diminishes during the satisfying.

4. In the light of our theses it seems quite clear that what we call consumption, in economics, consists of responses to present wants, while what we call production (if voluntary) consists of responses to future wants. Consumption is effortless and production is effortful, in the sense of the term "effort" used above. There may be an effortless component in effortful behavior, and vice versa. The volitional effort involved during mental or physical activity we have called working; that involved after the activity and before the instance of the want arrives we have called retaining. A quantity of each accomplished we have called work and retention, respectively. The quantity of these two performed on some certain means constitutes the "real cost" of that means. In turn, the "real cost" represents the third form of measurement of means, mentioned in paragraph 2 above.

We were unable to find any criterion by which working can be classified as effortful which did not automatically define retaining as also effortful. What makes both functions effortful is that they are energized by secondary energy of response because they are directed toward provision for future, not for present, wants. In a direct economy, beyond the hand-to-mouth stage, the only way by which most wants can be satisfied at all is by providing for them while they are still future wants—that is, by working. The "occasions" for retaining are equally unavoidable in the case of the technical necessities and the technical options, if such means are to be availed of at all. In the case of the contingencies, they are unavoidable if the wants are to be satisfied at all in the event that the contingencies occur. These "occasions" represent our analysis of the reasons for the demand for "capital" in an indirect economy, but not those for its supply. Similarly, our analysis of working represents the reasons for the demand for "labor" in such an economy, but not necessarily the reasons for its supply.

Product results from working and only from working; the fact that it remains extant results from retaining and only from retaining. Therefore, *extant product* is the result of the two functions. This distinguishes sharply between man's economic functions, working and retaining, and the result of performance of these functions, product and extant product. Product may be ephemeral; extant product must be of a nature capable of enduring for more than the moment. While working is being performed, work as effect accumulates in the product; while retaining is being performed retention as effect does not accumulate in extant product—the product remains the same and merely endures. But, as "real costs" of work and retention, both working and retaining do accumulate in product. This distinguishes sharply between the effect of performance of man's economic functions and the "real cost" of these performances.

5. The thesis that the essential economic characteristic of man's relation to his natural environment is the system of resistances imposed upon his efforts to satisfy his wants results in a general scheme. These natural resistances are the causes of the necessity of effort and, subject to the factor technique, determine the "real costs" in each case, both in direct and in indirect effort (via intermediate product). They are the reasons for the differences in "real costs" between different products and between different lots of single products, again subject to the factor technique. For different lots of a single product, man arranges the opportunities in a scale of increasing total resistances, choosing the line of least resistance first. As and if he chooses to increase quantities he must usually, therefore, meet continually increasing resistances. At some point he prefers to stop. That is all there is to the so-called "relative scarcity" of natural resources, for he always stops long before all of any particular resource that exists everywhere has been exhausted. The same principle holds good in the allocation of sites for production. As a result, there arise "discrepancies" among the "real costs" of different lots of a single product produced at the same time and, in certain respects, among those produced at different times.

6. When we combine the influence of "real costs" with the three possible criteria (paragraph 3) by which the influence of wants could be judged or felt, and then compare these syntheses with reality, it becomes evident that only one of the latter can meet this test. The assumption of declining intensity of wants during satisfaction proves to be an untenable one. Therefore, both our alternative constructions and all marginal utility theory, including indifference systems, which rest

on this assumption, must be rejected. This for the simple reason that all of them clash with the ordinary everyday experience of most human beings who regularly satiate certain of their present wants or provide for satiating certain of their future wants. Satiation would be impossible under this assumption, unless all wants were to be satiated; for, short of that, each want would always have to decline in the process of satisfying to a point at which some other would supersede it before it was satiated.

We admit no substitutability except among means serving a single want. Among these, "real costs" are largely determining. For the rest there is preference, not indifference. The actual order of preference appears to follow the order of priority through the range of the great prior wants. Thereafter "real costs" begin to have an influence. As the margin is reached, around the limit of capacity, what we have called the weighted value of the ratio seems to be governing. The terms of choice seem to be satiation, on the one hand, or, on the other, no satisfaction at all, except for cases where satiation is impossible or where the means have fixed attributes. And preferences among quantities of means so determined are on an all or none basis. Our results do not adapt themselves to a simple theory of individual demand, nor to one of value. Instead, such demand appears to be chiefly on an all or none basis and to be represented by a single step (discontinuous). Moreover, all demand among substitutes and around the margin is interdependent, so that individual demand for a single means cannot be established by itself. And, instead, we seem to arrive at two conflicting systems of valuation which are not often compromised into a resultant.

It would have been far more satisfying to have been able to produce a neat, precise, and logistic pattern for our final synthesis between subjective valuation and "real costs." But that did not prove possible. The presently available facts do not seem to warrant it. And the deeper we examine into them, the more reason there appears to doubt that future explorations will change that conclusion. On the contrary, even when we confine ourselves, as we have in Part IV, to the operation of the future-want system,[4] what becomes continually more apparent is the

[4] Our exclusive concern with future provision, so far as the actual order of preference is concerned, is due, of course, to the fact that we are limiting ourselves to a direct economy. No working and no planning are involved, there, as to present wants. In an indirect economy with money, and with stocks made available by others, a great deal of impulsive buying in response to present wants may be permitted, though, of course, such buying restricts provision for future wants. Thus, when we come to consider demand in an indirect economy, we will need the analysis of present wants as a part of

necessary inconsistencies, the jumble of conflicting influences, the immeasurability and even incomparability of many of the magnitudes, and the impossibility of anyone's accurately predicting in advance, when the plan is made, what the ultimate experience will be like. The rational, coldly calculating economic man of the classical and neoclassical schools [5] was an excellent mathematician and bookkeeper and a competent appraiser of commodities and services. But, even if we accept all that, we would have to agree that the real man, when it comes to knowing himself—a knowledge upon which everything would depend in subjective valuation—seems to be only a rather wild guesser and to be guided only by a certain amount of "common sense" derived from experience, as well as by "hunches," in making even his best-laid plans. Furthermore, his choices among satisfactions seem to result from conflict or a compromise between two motives whose objectives are mutually incompatible—the one leading to an order of preference among satisfactions in the order of importance of the wants, and the other leading to a distribution of the effort he is willing to make available in such a way as to reach as far as possible in terms of aggregate satisfaction.

Is our economic man, then, a "rational" or an "irrational" being? These terms have been little used because I do not see their precise meaning in this context. Nevertheless, something needs to be said on the subject. In respect of his responses to present wants, man's drive may be wholly emotional, or impulsive; but the direction and control, if any, is cortical. To the extent that such direction and control are not due to current external stimuli, they are due to the mnemonic-volitional system. In respect of his responses to future wants, the drive itself, as well as any internally originated direction and control, is due altogether to the mnemonic-volitional system. But, in turn, the raw material, at least, of this latter system is the product of experience. Thus it derives, originally and always in part, from the emotional system. The memories of present wants are the raw material of future wants. Can we class the emotional system as irrational and the mnemonic-volitional system as rational? Certainly not. The satisfaction of his

our whole scheme of causation. The early chapters in this study should furnish the basis for this.

[5] The economic man of the "felicific calculus" was not so certainly rational. If a man enjoys getting drunk and prefers to spend all his available funds on drink instead of food, etc., he maximizes his satisfaction according to the criterion which the hedonists establish for him. Is that an example of the rational application of "scarce" resources?

hunger, however purely it may be a response to mere "animal appetite," seems to this observer, at least, to be one of the most rational acts a man can perform.[6] The purchase and storage of a coffin at the age of twenty-one would seem to be one of the most irrational. Since our analysis does not aid us in these judgments we must perhaps content ourselves with what *understanding* we have gained and leave *appraisals* to others.

Our analytical tool, a direct economy, is an abstraction which does not exist. Conclusions with regard to it would, therefore, be of no interest whatever unless they could be made applicable to, and helpful in understanding, an actual indirect economy. In so far as the analysis of a direct economy gives us the pattern of behavior of the individual, and in so far as that pattern multiplied represents the collective behavior of many individuals, what we have found should be capable of being applied to an indirect economy. While we are reserving our study of the latter to some future time, it seems safer at this point to warn the reader in a very general way how far we believe such applicability is likely to exist.

The concept of "integrative levels," taken from the natural sciences, is appropriate here. That concept is excellently stated by the biologist Novikoff, who says that the concept

> describes the progress of evolution of the inanimate, animate and social worlds. It maintains that such progress is the result of forces which differ in each level and which can properly be described only by laws which are unique for each level. Since higher level phenomena always include phenomena at lower levels, one can not fully understand the higher levels without an understanding of the lower level phenomena as well. But a knowledge of the lower levels does not enable us to predict, *a priori*, what will occur at a higher level. Although some may have validity for a higher level, laws of a lower level are inadequate to describe the higher level. The laws unique to the higher level can [only] be discovered by approaches appropriate to the particular level.[7]

Our study of the individual biological specimen, man, in relation to his natural environment, has delved to lower integrative levels, but it

[6] This rationality may be due to insight, to his recognition of necessities. "Reason" may distinguish between "those wants which *must* be satisfied and those which need not be," as we suggest at the end of Appendix VI, Section B. If so, "reason" substitutes in part for experience, which otherwise, we have held, confers on future wants whatever capacity to dominate they have.

[7] Novikoff, *312*, 214–215. I may also refer to a paper of my own in which this concept is used in a somewhat different way (see *314*).

has culminated at that particular integrative level. When we turn to the study of a society of men—an indirect economy—we should expect to find that all the generalizations with regard to man hold good as well of men. The level of men includes the level of man. But we should also expect to find that, at the higher—the social—level, new forces and new phenomena would appear which are peculiar to that level. In the first place, we would expect to find that, at the higher level, individual behavior would be modified by reason of the introduction of a third source of excitation. Whereas the solitary man can react only to his own internal excitors and to those arising from the natural environment, social man must react also to society—to other men.[8] In the second place, we would expect that collective behavior, being a composite of widely varying patterns of individual behavior, would correspond precisely to no one of them.[9] These are the relationships between levels which exist throughout the field of science. One could not *predict* all the behavior of the periodic system of elements, as it is known to chemistry, from the knowledge of their internal constitution, as it is now known to physics. But one cannot fully *understand* the periodic system without that new knowledge of the lower integrative level. Better understanding but only limited prediction are all we can or should claim for our conclusions when they come to be applied to economies as they actually exist.

[8] Many of the subordinate wants we referred to, by way of example, at the end of Chapter 4 and which we have discussed in passing, elsewhere, could not, of course, arise except in an indirect economy. They require other men as excitors. The same is true of imposed wants. But we have only listed them. We have not pretended to analyze their nature or source.

[9] In particular, this combination of different individual patterns may mean that, just as the classical conceptions of physics and their analogue in physiology gradually emerge as larger and larger numbers are involved, so too we, in economics, may find that, subject to the effects of interdependence, certain features of the classical theory of demand will be approached when we add together the demands of innumerable individuals. The thresholds of the constituent neurons of a nerve exist in series so that, as the stimulus is increased, more and more are gradually involved. The increased aggregate effect is steplike and discontinuous; but the steps may be so small and so numerous as to give the appearance of continuous change. We may find some analogy to this in collective demand. The critical points for different men may be arranged in series so that changing "real costs" may have their effect in the mass in what appears to be a continuous process, even if it is actually composed of a discontinuous series of all or none choices many of which are determined by changes of cost elsewhere.

APPENDICES

I

THE MECHANISMS FOR THE CENTRIPETAL TRANSMISSION OF CERTAIN WANTS

Appendix to Chapter 1

A. WATER NEED

"The cause of the ingestion of water . . . has never been understood" (Hare, *180*, 417). There is even a controversy among physiologists as to the nature of the sensation called thirst. Some, like Schiff, hold that it is a diffuse sensation, while Cannon describes it as a "dry" mouth and throat due to decreased salivary flow (Gregersen, *176*, 1074). Now, "no one denies that conditions which reduce the flow of saliva in a normal animal are generally associated with thirst" (Dill, *119*, 54). Thus, secretion of adrenalin [and other effects of emotional excitement or preparedness for activity], sweating, withholding water, and the process of digestion reduce saliva and cause dryness of the mouth (Dill, *ibid.*, 54). The last, the temporary dehydration due to salivation during meals, results in a decrease in salivary flow and temporary dryness of the mouth, which disappears when the water mixed with the food is reabsorbed in the gut (Gregersen, *176*, 1076). In addition, any artificial reduction of salivation usually increases drinking (Gregersen, *ibid.*, 1074).

But a dry mouth is an equivocal signal. It may be produced by atropine injection, with reduction of salivation but no sensation of thirst. And, on the other hand, the sensation called thirst may exist as a result of the injection of pilocarpine though salivation continues to be ample (Dill, *119*, 55). Both of these conditions are, of course, independent of the water level. So, too, a dry mouth as a result of mouth breathing, of long speaking or reading aloud, of smoking, and of the first heavy breathing due to exercise, in all of which secretion does not increase sufficiently to cover the increased evaporation, does not correspond to a lowering of the water level. It is claimed that these conditions are discriminated from thirst and are usually corrected merely by wetting the mouth or by increasing salivation by chewing gum, etc. Nor does continued wetting of the mouth, at least in the absence of sufficient salivation, quench thirst, if the water level is not corrected. Claude Bernard's dog and horse, with esophagal fistulas, drank incessantly. And Dill (*119*, 60) cites cases in which dogs with similar fistulas drank up to 28% of the time. If, at the same time, water loss is abnormal, drinking is even more sustained. Van Wagenen (discussion of

Gersh, *170*, 445) says, "Animals with an esophageal fistula and a suitable hypothalamic puncture (causing loss of water from the system) will stand up and drink continuously until they fall down of exhaustion. Certainly dryness of the mouth cannot be any factor in the production of thirst in that case," because the mouth is then continuously wet. Finally, dogs continue to drink when all sensory nerves from the mouth and pharynx are sectioned, which indicates that "the desire for water is not dependent on any one of the nerves cut and is not identified with any type of sensation they mediate." Hare concludes that "thirst and the volume of water intake are not appreciably affected by the dryness of the mouth" (*180*, 417).[1]

These irreconcilable facts make it necessary to look elsewhere. For that purpose it is desirable to examine more deeply into the nature of the water level, relative and absolute. Water composes 63% of the weight of the entire body and 83%, by weight, of the blood. But, since the blood constitutes only about 5% of the total weight, while the muscles and skin constitute about 60%, approximately 70% of the total water is in the skin and muscles and only about 6% in the blood (Gregersen, *176*, 1059–1060). Thought it holds only some 40% of the quantity of water that is in the muscles, nevertheless the skin (or its connective tissue) is as important a storehouse for water because it can undergo much larger changes (Gregersen, *ibid.*, 1061). Viewed in another aspect, the blood contains about 3 liters of water, the cells themselves (the intracellular phase) about 29 liters and the interstitial or connective tissues (the inter- or extra-cellular phase) about 14 liters (Gregersen, *ibid.*, 1065). Since the blood volume is "constant with great persistence" (Gregersen, *ibid.*, 1067)[2] and "the cell volume [of water] remains approximately constant . . . the tissue spaces, [the intercellular phase] form the body's principal store of water" (Barcroft, *17*, 110). Thus we conclude that the only water stock that fluctuates freely is that in the connective tissues, chiefly of the skin. The total water balance is maintained only by exchange between the blood and the external milieu (Gregersen, *176*, 1065). The intake is "mainly in the small intestine" (Gregersen, *ibid.*, 1072) and the outflow mainly through a steady "insensible loss of water through the skin" and lungs, varying only with the metabolic rate (Gregersen, *ibid.*, 1073) and a fluctuating loss through the sweat glands and kidneys. The last is the real overflow for surplus water. And the last two are the chief agencies for conserving water, when necessary. But the internal water balance is maintained by exchange

[1] For a more complete critique of Cannon's theory, see Dill, *119*, 54–72.

[2] This statement probably holds good only as to the volume in the system as a whole, not as to that in circulation. There is some evidence for a storage of blood in the liver, the spleen and the skin, though not much is known about it (Barcroft, *17*, 169). But recently Barbour (*16*, 449) has described the water shifting in mammals in response to environmental temperature changes. By concentration of solids in cold and their dilution in heat, the availability for insensible loss is reduced or increased. The water goes to the liver, presumably as an isotonic salt solution (*ibid.*, 451). The reaction, he holds, is a sympathetic response, via adrenalin (*ibid.*, 452) and is controlled in the anterior hypothalamic nuclei (*ibid.*, 482)—that is, as a part of the heat loss mechanism.

between the blood, on one side, and the intercellular and intracellular phases, on the other (Gregersen, *ibid.*, 1065).[3] It appears, then, that the two relatively constant stocks of water, of which one, the blood, is constantly losing water, must be maintained in the interval between drinking at the expense of the third stock.[4] Only when no more water is available from this third stock do the plasma and the intracellular phase begin to be dehydrated. Until then both are adequately supplied. This fact that the intracellular and plasma (blood) water content are normally maintained so constant, suggests the presence of a very precise mechanism which relegates surplus water to storage, withdraws available water from storage to make good any deficits, and excites the organism to replenish its stores when a sufficiency is no longer available.

Identifying the critical points in the process, by means of such analysis, has led to two different suppositions. One is expressed by Gregersen (*176*, 1079). To him the facts indicate "dependence of thirst upon a reduction in the fluid volume of the blood," which he supposes is "the first step in the physiological mechanism . . . which signals the need for an increase in the water intake." Presumably this reduction is slight. It might be effective either qualitatively, as dehydration (concentration of solids), or quantitatively, in terms of total volume. The other supposition is suggested by Dill (*119*, 70): "It seems probable that the water content of tissue cells including those of the salivary glands and of the nervous system [i.e., the intracellular phase], must be depleted if an instinctive general craving for liquid [thirst] is manifested."[5] As a matter of fact these two are not necessarily mutually exclusive alternatives, since an immediate effect of dehydration of the blood might be to dehydrate the nerve cells in closest contact with it. However, since neither of these depletions can occur except when water is not available from the surplus in storage, and since presumably dehydration is rarely, if ever, carried so far as to remove all that water, it becomes necessary to inquire under what conditions the water that remains in storage may not be available.

[3] Perhaps the salivary glands also constitute a minor agency for conserving water (dry mouth due to reduction of secretion). But Cannon seems to suppose (*66*, 90 and elsewhere) that the water supply to these glands is directly from the connective tissues rather than from their blood supply only. This is an unusual view. If it is not correct, then the supply of water from the blood to these glands must reduce slightly its own volume or concentration (dehydration). Then dry mouth would be one of the symptoms of dehydration of the blood (see Gregersen's view as noted in the next paragraph of the text), and the mechanism which protected the blood from further dehydration by reducing salivation would be vasoconstriction of the glands' blood supply (see Gregersen's view as noted in note 25, below). On this basis all causes of dry mouth, those due to reduced water supply as well as all others, would be explained by known mechanisms (presumably sympathetic activity).

[4] The "water content of the blood is to a large extent preserved at the expense of changes in the fluid content of the muscles and the skin," and chiefly in that of their "loose connective tissue" (Gregersen, *176*, 1062), while that of the intracellular phase tends to remain unaltered so long as osmotic equilibrium is maintained, as it usually is (Dill, *119*, *62*). See also Cannon (*66*, 90).

[5] See also Gilman, 120 *Am. J. Physiol.* (1937) 323, and 90 *J. Physiol.* (1937) 113.

Cannon (*67*) discusses water-inhabiting vertebrates and the water supply, and notes that it is only the air-inhabiting vertebrates which have developed buccal glands. These are the chief agency for moistening the "ancient water course" when it is exposed to the air. But, as Dill points out (*119*, 62) this theory implies that "our ancestors became thirsty only when they left the sea." On the contrary, marine vertebrates (bony fishes or teleosts) also suffer thirst and quench it, though, with them, water is constantly streaming through this water course (Dill, *ibid.*, 71). The more fundamental difference between water- (marine) and air-inhabiting vertebrates seems to be that the former quench thirst with sea water while the latter cannot. Presumably, when the normal salinity of the blood was determined for our aquatic ancestors in the Cambrian period, the oceans were less salt than now.[6] Since then the salt composition of the blood of land vertebrates appears to have remained the same, while that of sea vertebrates has adapted itself to the gradual change (Bayliss, *27*, 209–210). As a result of this change, while the sodium, potassium and calcium salts have apparently become more concentrated, though remaining in much the same proportion among themselves, the magnesium salts now exist in much greater proportion to the rest. And this occasions the "chief difficulty" for the land vertebrates; for, with them, the presence of magnesium salts prevents absorption through the gut—the intestinal wall being impermeable to it. On the other hand, sodium chloride in solution is absorbed quickly and even in greater concentration than that of the blood. (Gregersen, *176*, 1072). Thus the admission of water into the system as a whole seems to depend on the solutes contained—or on these in relation to those in the body fluids—as well as on the permeability of the gut to these solutes. But the same is true of the distribution of water within the system, though here the permeability to different solutes varies. That is, the water "concentration both inside and outside the cell depends upon the attraction of other materials, chiefly electrolytes, for it, and its movements depend largely upon the movements of the materials which thus bind it" (Barcroft *17*, 3).[7]

This process works positively as well as negatively, for "the total water content of the body depends upon the retention of salts" (chiefly sodium chloride). Thus salinity governs the water level as a whole. The water level is relative to the salt content—that is, the equilibrium water level, at any time, is the quantity of water that will form an isotonic solution with the salt then in the system (or parts of it). Dehydration cannot be corrected if salt is lost (Gregersen, *176*, 1082).[8] So, if we first reduce salinity by sweat-

[6] It seems to be frequently forgotten that human beings, like all Metazoa in the animal world after they have become individualized, consist, as to a large portion of their internal milieu, of an enclosed bit of the ocean which was originally the external milieu of the segregated cell (Protozoa).

[7] Though there are advocates of the storage of bound water (hydrates) analogous to glycogen, Barcroft holds water is only "bound," so to speak, by its solutes.

[8] He speaks of "the gradual loss of body fluid which occurs in individuals living on salt-free diets" (*loc. cit.*).

ing, we cannot immediately replace the lost water by drinking except as the drinking water contains salt. Or if we drink distilled water (no salts), when no surplus of salt is already present, the water is not retained (Bayliss, *27*, 165). On the other hand, as Cannon points out, taking in salt increases retention of the water drunk (*66*, 88).[9] But, if an excess of salt is absorbed, so that hypersalinity results, only a portion of this excess is excreted at once by the kidneys. Because the salinity of the blood fluctuates but slightly and because the muscles and the liver will take up salt solution that is hypotonic but not iso- or hypertonic, only the skin takes up the excess salt. The "skin can store salt, at least temporarily, with less than enough water to dilute it to isotonicity." [10] In other words "sodium chloride not only directs the water to the skin, but tends to hold it in the body" (Gregersen, *176*, 1062)—that is, "the storage of water goes hand in hand with the storage of salt; the one cannot be retained for any considerable length of time without the other," for either one alone is usually a diuretic (Gregersen, *ibid.*, 1083).[11] However, so long as such stored water remains hypertonic it must withdraw water from any part of the intracellular phase with which it is in contact, and thus reduce cell volume (Dill, *119*, 67). This necessarily follows because sodium and chloride ions are restricted to the extracellular phase (blood and interstices), the cell walls being impermeable to them (Dill, *ibid.*, 67). Thus this excess (sodium) salinity outside cannot be equalized through the cell wall, and osmotic equilibrium can only be restored by withdrawing water from the cells.

Apart from an intake of more water to reduce the stored water to isotonicity, the kidneys work ultimately to correct this state. The tubular system there is twofold. A part reabsorbs water from the urine, presumably when salinity is excessive, and another part reabsorbs salt from the urine, presumably when salinity is low. Thus by reducing the output of whichever is deficient, the tendency seems to be toward restoring standard salinity in time. But since the kidneys work only on the blood, it seems necessary that, in the meantime, the blood should also be hypersaline, at least slightly so. Otherwise how is the excess salt transported to the kidneys? Thus we may say that the blood may receive surplus salt through

[9] He quotes Adolph, *55 J. Physiol.* (1921) 114, and *65 Am. J. Physiol.* (1923) 419, and Baird and Haldane, *56 J. Physiol.* (1922) 259, to this effect.

[10] This is proved by the edema in the skin which results when water is taken after the excess salt is stored. Cannon states (*66*, 94) that one third of all the salt from a salt-rich diet may be in the subcutaneous connective tissue. After an intravenous infusion of salt from one quarter to three quarters is there. Conversely, if the salt in the body falls 10–20%, 60–90% comes out of the skin layer. Since it is in solution there, the salt goes in and out with the water dissolving it (*ibid.*, 95).

[11] Probably absorption and release of water in and out of storage in the connective tissues is not dependent on salinity alone. As Cannon points out (*66*, 88) it is also affected by slight shifts in the direction of alkalinity (absorption) and acidity (discharge). Perhaps the thyroid also plays a role. When it is diseased or missing, albuminous matter and water collect in the connective tissue. When the condition is corrected, water and salt are released.

the gut, but that it gets rid of most of it, almost immediately, by storing it in the connective tissues and gets rid of all of it, ultimately but more gradually, by bringing it back for excretion through the kidneys.[12] In the meantime, however, before the surplus salt can be excreted it may be exerting a dehydrating influence directly on the cells with which the stored water is in contact; and, since it would seem that, then, the blood, too, would be slightly hypersaline, the stored salt might also be exerting a dehydrating influence indirectly, as well, upon the cells with which the blood is in immediate contact.

There is considerable evidence that this general hypersalinity is the cause of thirst and drinking. For instance the "intravenous injection of hypertonic salt solution gives rise to thirst" (Gregersen *176*, 1080, referring to *174*, P, p. 538). If the sweat is heavy in salt, thus rendering the stored water iso- or hypotonic, there is little thirst; if the sweat is dilute, thus rendering the stored water hypertonic, there is great thirst (see Dill, *119*, 67–68). It is said somewhere (I believe in *Arabia Deserta*) that the Arabs desalt themselves by working up a violent perspiration in the morning, then drink copiously, and thus can go all day with little thirst. On the other hand, it is said that after excessive sweating which has reduced salinity, the drinking of salt solution, usually quite distasteful, is very satisfying (Gregersen, *176*, 1082). Thus hyposalinity seems related to the "salt hunger" to which we shall refer later. If, because of hyposalinity, there is no thirst and yet the "fluid matrix," at least of the connective tissue, is reduced abnormally—while that in the cells may be increased and the blood made slightly hyposaline—it is not unlikely that it is "salt hunger" which registers this absolute need for water. At any rate, as Cannon agrees (*66*, *96*), the salt and the water control are "alike, and it is probable that they usually run parallel."[13]

It does not seem probable that hypersalinity of the stored water is itself directly responsible for thirst and drinking.[14] Nor does it seem probable that any resulting cellular dehydration, at least as to the cells in general, is directly responsible (Hare, *180*, 418). The chief reason for these conclu-

[12] Dill (*119*, 67) says dogs restore the body fluids to normal within an hour after ingesting hypersaline solution. This is done both by drinking and by the work of the kidney.

[13] And he recognizes that "salt hunger may be analogous to thirst as a means of meeting the gross requirements of the organism" (*loc. cit.*), though he does not mention the possibility that it may express the absolute need of water.

If the system has a mechanism for expressing the need of maintaining an absolute water level, it seems probable that this is salt hunger; for, apparently, the absolute water level depends on the salt content of the body. Thirst would then be the corresponding mechanism for the relative water level only (i.e., the maintenance of isotonicity of the blood). But, since the system requires this fluid intermedium bathing all parts, it must have the first mechanism; and since it also requires that this fluid intermedium be not hypertonic (to prevent loss of fluid intermedium *in* the cells themselves), it must have the second mechanism as well.

[14] Injections of glucose reduce the extracellular water, and presumably increase its salinity, without causing thirst (Dill, *119*, 71). That also proves that thirst cannot be dependent on the mere volume of the extracellular water.

sions is that both thirst and drinking cease long before the water can reach the intercellular spaces and restore their isotonicity, and still longer before any but a few strategically located cells which might have been dehydrated could have been rehydrated. This fact leads Dill (*119*, 60) to go so far as to conclude that the only way to explain the ability of a dog to drink the exact amount required to restore water balance, and then to stop, is to suppose that "as water reaches the gastro-intestinal tract, there is some rapidly acting signal [possibly "contractions of smooth muscles of the esophagus" (*ibid.*, 70)] that gauges the fluid intake."[15] Doubtless there is some such signal, perhaps a feeling of distension similar to the signal of repletion as to food, which we shall discuss. But that such a signal could be timed to the precise measure of the quantity requisite to make good the water deficit seems asking too much. On the other hand, drinking is a process which, for land mammals, requires appreciable time. It is therefore not impossible that any decrease in volume of the blood, or any decrease in its hydration (increase in plasma concentration), or any increase in its salinity might cause thirst and drinking. And these, since absorption is rapid, might quite promptly cease as soon as sufficient water had been ingested. Even if the cause of thirst and drinking were cellular dehydration in some part of the central nervous system immediately in contact with the blood stream—a dehydration consequent on the state of the blood—the speed of the circulation is such that the condition could be corrected within a few seconds of the time when it changed in the blood itself at the point of water absorption. Thus, if the critical point is either a condition of the blood, or resulting dehydration of the cells in some part of the central nervous system immediately in contact with it, or both, the exactitude of the signal to cease drinking is not so inexplicable.

In spite of the fact that the "mechanism remains to be elucidated" (Dill, *119*, 72), there are now some grounds for suspecting that the control of water balance in respect of intake—drinking—may rest in the same part of the central nervous system that is certainly of major importance in controlling it in respect of outflow. This apparatus complies with the requirement that its nerve cells should be in especially close contact with the blood stream, and it is in that subcortical region of the central nervous system which, as noted in the text, is responsible for the maintenance of the homeostasis of the blood.[16] As Bard (*24*, 198) points out, the neurohormonal apparatus concerned may be governed by nervous control from elsewhere or directly by "changes in the composition of the blood." Because of the "unique vascularity" of the nervous centers there he is inclined to favor the latter view. If this view is correct, then these centers react to humoral, not to neural, excitors.[17]

[15] Gregersen (*176*, 1079) also raises the question why a dog stops drinking when he has exactly replaced the water lost.

[16] There is considerable agreement on this double function, much of which will be referred to in Appendix II. For example, Riddoch (*344*, 102) includes the "supervision of the intake of fluids" among the functions of these centers. See also Gilman, cited note 4, above.

[17] See also notes 19 and 20, below.

At any rate, it is generally agreed that this apparatus—specifically the anterior hypothalamus and pituitary—has an important function in regulating the outflow (or retention) of water and perhaps of the excretion (or retention) of salt.[18] On its executive side it apparently consists of an alteration in endocrine balance between the two lobes of the pituitary (and also the thyroid), the posterior lobe of which, at least, is under neural control in this region (supraoptic nuclei).[19] When this balance is upset—in the condition called "diabetes insipidus"—there may be excessive loss of water, as urine, associated with excessive thirst or drinking.[20] There has been a division of opinion as to which is primary—that is, whether the loss of water causes the drinking, or the drinking causes the loss of water.[21] If the excessive thirst is primary, it would seem to identify this apparatus as the chief regulator of water intake. If, on the other hand, the excessive water loss is primary, we may be no nearer a discovery of the thirst-drinking mechanism. I have been told that, recently, evidence has become "overwhelming" that the polyuria is primary. If so, this particular part of the apparatus can hardly be responsible for water intake.

Nevertheless, there remains the possibility—not inconsistent with observations nor with the general character of such controls—that there is a second part of the complex apparatus located in that region which responds to the need of water, perhaps expressed in the form of slight—or a tendency toward—hypersalinity of the blood. If so, the first and known part (supraoptic nucleus via the posterior lobe of the pituitary) acts normally to conserve water by means of a hormone which causes the tubules of the kidneys to reabsorb it, while "the chloride-absorbing part of the tubular system remains unaffected" (Beattie, *30*, 97). The second and as yet almost wholly hypothetical part may stimulate the organism to increase

[18] As to the first, a nearly all-inclusive citation is the recent book (with its references) by Fisher, Ingram, and Ranson, *Diabetes Insipidus* (1938) Ann Arbor. As to the second, among numerous articles, see H. Broers, 18 *Arch. di. sc. biol.* (1933) 83; F. H. Lewy and F. K. Gassman, *268*, 504; Davison and Selby, *111*, 590.

[19] The most explanatory conception seems to be that of Dott (*120*, 184). He supposes water metabolism, in respect of loss at least, to be fixed at a basal metabolic rate under the balanced control of local factors and of lower nervous centers. The variations from this basal rate, one way or the other, are wholly controlled in the hypothalamus—the pressor effects by the posterior hypothalamus via the thyroid and the depressor effects by the supraoptic-hypophyseal system. While the afferent or excitor factors are unknown, he thinks the composition of the blood is the probable means.

[20] That this is due to the resulting unopposed effects of the probably general secretion of the anterior lobe of the pituitary—perhaps only via its influence upon the thyroid—is indicated by Fisher, Ranson, and Ingram in the various articles cited, by Gersh (*170*) and by various experiments of Richter, Keller, and others cited by Fulton (*152*, 245). Gregersen (*176*, 1083) concludes that the internal secretions are "complexly related" with the business of water and salt balance. And Gersh (*170*, 443–4) points out that adrenalin and even the sex hormones have their effect on water balance.

[21] We may cite as proponents of the primacy of the polyuria, Ranson (*332*, 251) and Fisher *et al.* (*141*, 125); the latter cite the "French school" in support. Supporting the primacy of the polydipsia are, among others, G. M. Curtis, 34 *Arch. Int. Med.* (1924) 801; C. P. Richter, 53 *Brain* (1930) 76; and R. T. Bellows and W. P. Van Wagenen, 88 *J. Nerv. Ment. Dis.* (1938) 417.

the supply of water—that is, lead to the behavior we call drinking.[22] Hypersalinity of the blood may well be the condition that leads to the activation of both. When either is pathologically inactive or otherwise prevented from working, sole dependence would then be on the other, with a corresponding increase in its activity.[23]

If, as Lewy and Gassman's (*268*) results suggest, the salt balance is also maintained in the same region [24] and by similar methods, one would suppose the "stimulation or paralysis" of these centers, which they obtained, to act on the chloride-absorbing part of the tubular system in the same way. At any rate, the salinity of the blood was increased and that of the urine decreased. This hypersalinity in turn could be expected to activate the water-balancing mechanism above. At least so far as a decrease in water loss was concerned, their results show that it was. They do not speak of increased thirst or drinking.

While all this is largely speculation as yet, such an hypothesis seems to fit the known facts and partly to account for them. Doubtless there are other factors in the regulation of water metabolism (Fisher *et al.*, *141*).[25] At least the known facts make plausible the hypothesis that the regulation of the water and salt balance of the system, in so far as it is neural in origin (not physical or chemical) is chiefly managed in the subcortical region mentioned, and perhaps largely as a direct response of the nerve centers to the condition of the blood as it reaches them. The facts also lead us to suspect that the regulation of water intake is a function of this

[22] It is not inconsistent with the combined vegetative and somatic controls which we find in other parts of this region to suppose such a dual activity. That the intake regulating mechanism is in this region is also hinted by one of the familiar hypothalamic syndromes, bulimia (excessive hunger), which is usually associated with excessive thirst (Riddoch, *344*, 104).

[23] That this balance is not simple is indicated by the fact that "deprivation of water decreases the polyuria" in diabetes insipidus (Fisher *et al.*, *141*, 157). The posterior lobe cannot, therefore, be solely responsible for water conservation since, in this condition, it is atrophied.

[24] I take their "paroptic ganglion (Gudden)" to be the supraoptic nucleus, since it is said to degenerate when the posterior pituitary is destroyed.

[25] To be reasonably brief we have omitted consideration of calcium, potassium, and phosphate balance, which probably play a large part in the whole system. Beattie (*30*, 97) thinks one or the other of these is controlled in the same region—the tuberomamillary nuclei.

Since it seems to relate to salivation, mention should also be made of the decrease in water loss via the kidneys during exercise, emotion, and pain (Hare, *180*, 425). This is the result of reduced glomerular filtration (*ibid.*, 430). Since the reduced water loss occurs in the same way with denervated, as with innervated, kidneys, it cannot be due to direct neural control of glomerular filtration. But it may be due to vasoconstriction of the blood supply to the kidneys—a sympathetic reaction, whether neural or hormonal (adrenalin). Similarly, Gregersen (*176*, 1078–79) finds that the reduced salivary flow in dehydration is due to vasoconstriction of the blood supply to the gland, not to the direct effects of parasympathetic or sympathetic action on the glandular secretion. Since the two outlets function similarly in respect of water loss, the possibility arises that vasoconstriction of the blood supply to the kidneys may also occur in dehydration and cause a decrease of glomerular filtration, while the same phenomenon may be responsible for the decreased salivation which is observed in exercise, emotion, and pain.

same subconscious mechanism; that systemic thirst, in so far as it reaches consciousness, probably does so in a form not strictly sensory (that is, of sensation) but of a nature to be outlined in Appendix II; and that the sensation in consciousness of a dry mouth is only a reinforcement which, if it coincides with systemic thirst, merely adds to and makes more specific, but does not substitute for, the general excitor.[26]

B. THE NEED OF FOOD

As to the place of stomach contractions in the food-replenishing system it is certain that these may occur in response to local stimuli. To what extent that is due to local reflexes or how far to reflexes whose arcs include subcortical (and supraspinal) nervous centers is not certain. But the fact that these muscular contractions seem to differ in form in hunger, in digesting, and in other cases suggests that the modified patterns in response to different stimuli are laid down, not in the muscle, nor directly via the ganglia in the visceral wall, but in some higher center, or a hierarchy of the same. Thus, in a way analogous to the other visceral organs which we shall have occasion to consider, this smooth muscle seems to have imposed upon its own automatic contractility to certain local stimuli [1] a higher control, perhaps arranged in series—the control of such higher centers being exercised over the lower ones and being in part inhibitory or facilitating (tonus) but also, in part, capable of modifying the pattern of contractions and of initiating these patterns in response to other than local stimuli.

Of these subcortical centers the lowest seems to be in the nuclei from which the vagal nerve originates (medulla). Here, or in a center superimposed upon this, there is (in the dog) a direct reaction to the concentration of blood sugar in the brain. If the latter is low (hypoglycemia) hunger contractions are at least promoted.[2] That this reaction itself takes place in a higher center and is then mediated in the nuclei of the vagi is suggested both by the general conclusion that there is in the anterior and middle regions of the hypothalamus (and preoptic region) a general vegetative mechanism—chiefly of parasympathetic character—by the fact that the metabolism of several of the nutritional constituents appears to be regulated there,[3] and by the experiments of Beattie and Sheehan, who secured a rise in intragastric pressure and usually a subsequent increase in movements of the stomach by stimulating the tuber cinereum (of a cat), while section of the vagi abolished the reaction.[4] On the other hand, there is, in the posterior

[26] Or shall we say that the two are examples of what Cannon calls "compensatory arrangements"?

[1] Cannon (*67*, 163) states that certain types of stomach contractions can occur when the stomach is isolated from the brain and the cord. Templeton and Quigley, 91 *Am. J. Physiol.* (1929) 467, state that *hunger* contractions can occur after complete denervation of the stomach.

[2] See Cannon, *67*, 164, and Fulton, *159*, 176, construing Cannon.

[3] These statements will be supported in Appendix II.

[4] See Beattie (*29*) and Beattie and Sheehan (*32*). That both the pressure and the movements are primarily controlled by the nuclei of the vagi is indicated by the fact that

hypothalamus, a sympathetic center, stimulation of which results in a slight fall of intragastric pressure and "complete obliteration of all gastric motility."[5] This effect is mediated directly to the stomach via sympathetic, and not indirectly via the vagal, nerves.[6] That gastric motility is also subject to still higher control (but perhaps only inhibitory and via control over these subcortical centers) is indicated by the results of ablation of certain cortical areas.[7] It is doubtful, however, if this higher control is in any degree "voluntary," and most authorities conclude that the hyperactivity which may result from destruction of the higher centers is a "release" phenomenon. All this suggests that stomach contractions may be largely governed by stimuli (or excitors) arising from elsewhere. To the extent that this is also true of hunger contractions, it implies that these may be an effect and not a cause of the activation of the central nervous system by the need for food.

As to the specificity of the hungers (or "appetites" in physiological terminology) and the probable strategic location of the apparatus for propagating them, existing evidence provides even less definite explanation, though it seems to preclude the possibility that gastric contractions are the primary mechanism. We have noted in the text that the nutritional wants are ultimately for glucose, protein, fat, sodium chloride, calcium (and other salts). The body appears to have means of converting some of the first three interchangeably (though it cannot make protein). It certainly can convert sugar into fat (Cannon, *66*, 103). But conversion is not possible in the case of the salts. Actually, there occur specific "hungers" (cravings). Cannon recognizes the existence of "salt hunger" in herbivorous animals—the nature of which is "quite unknown" (*66*, 96). Carlson (*71*, 14) treats it as "lack of appetite (owing to the unpalatability of the food) and some vague or general bodily distress." It is noticeable among "agricultural tribes." Beebe-Center (*34*, 281–282) cites various authorities for evidence not only of "salt hunger" but of "osteophagia" (an "inordinate desire to eat bones") representing a deficiency of phosphorus, craving for chalk (by birds), for sugar (specifically), and for sour substances (probably due to alkalinity) among animals, as well as the remarkable balanced diet achieved by children left to choose for themselves, as shown in the experiments of C. M. Davis. This last point seems confirmed, not only

stimulation of the cut ends of these nerves increased both more than did stimulation in the tuberal region, and by the fact that, on cessation of the former stimulation, the intragastric pressure fell "dramatically" and the peristalsis ceased or was much reduced (Beattie and Sheehan, *32*, 225).

[5] Beattie and Sheehan (*32*, 226). See also Sheehan (*373*, 613) who suggests that the pressor reaction can be obtained not only in the tuberal region, as above, but also in the supraoptic and preoptic. See also Kabat *et. al.* (*228*), who consider the inhibitory reaction to be only a part of a general sympathetic discharge (i.e., inhibitory to the parasympathetic system in general). That the effect on the stomach of this sympathetic reaction depends upon the state of that organ (resting or active) is suggested by the results of McCrea and McSwiney. 18 *Q. J. Exper. Physiol.* (1925) 301.

[6] It is not interrupted by section of the vagi (Beattie and Sheehan, *32*, 227).

[7] For a summary, see Fulton (*160*, especially 480–481).

as to children but also as to pigs, rats and chickens, by many recent experiments cited by Richter *et al.* (*342*). Their own experiments "showed that the rat has a special appetite not only for salt and sugar, but also for protein, carbohydrate, sodium, calcium, phosphorus, potassium and the vitamins," except perhaps for vitamin D.[8] Young, also working on rats, concludes that there cannot be a "single hunger factor" (*450*, *63*). Or, rather, he distinguishes between the "demand of hunger," depending "primarily upon the contractions of an empty stomach," and the "demand of appetite," depending more on the "nutritive state" (*ibid.*, 61). Skinner (*379*, *375*) says that "stimulation from the empty stomach . . . seems to be an emergency mechanism brought into play when the normal variation of hunger has not been efficient in obtaining food." He describes the specific hungers as "subhungers" (*ibid.*, 369–371). One of Pavlov's experiments (*320*, 139) also demonstrated the specificity of two "hungers" (or "appetites") among dogs. He found that " 'natural' conditioned reflexes, one to the appearance of meat powder and the other to the appearance of granulated sugar," increased or decreased, respectively and immediately, in their responsiveness according as alterations of the diet provided a deficit or an excess of each.

Since the evidence makes it necessary that we accept the fact of specific hungers or appetites, let us consider next in what way these may ultimately express themselves qualitatively and quantitatively. Digestion in the mouth is, in most animals, merely tentative and experimental. Its chief function seems to be to reduce enough of the starches to sugars to enable the animal to detect by taste the presence of one of the food substances it needs, glucose, which in most foods does not exist in that form. This explains the differences among animals noted by Taylor (*390*, 119), "The salivary secretion of the strictly carnivorous animals is commonly stated to be devoid of ferment"; certainly this holds for the dog, who normally forms the sugar in his system from protein and perhaps from fat (*ibid.*, 238). "The salivary secretion of the frugivora and herbivora is rich in ferment, that of the ruminantia surprisingly poor [hence, perhaps, the time taken in "ruminating"]. Human saliva is rich in ferment." Nevertheless, even with man, it is "safe to say that . . . not over one-fourth [and "often as little as 5%"] of the starch of a normal ration is digested in the mouth and in the stomach," the latter before destruction of the salivary ferment by acidity (*ibid.*, 122). A secondary function seems to be that the mixing of all other food substances with saliva, even devoid of ferment, helps to prepare them as well for absorption by the organs of taste. If what is taken into the mouth tastes "good," before and during this experimental digestion, it is accepted; if not, it is rejected. That is the point at which unlearned discrimination is made—not as to the external stimulus (the sight or smell of food), which affects the process only after conditioning.[9]

[8] As to vitamin D, see P. T. Young and J. R. Whittemore, 30 *J. Comp. Psychol.* (1940) 261.

[9] It seems that the salivary glands function exquisitely for both these purposes. Barcroft says (*17*, 318), "It is of course certain from the work of Pavlov that the nature of the saliva in the dog is regulated in sympathy with the nature of the food taken." That is

What is the reason certain substances taste "good" and are accepted, while others taste "bad" and are not? The fundamental distinction is qualitative. Roughly speaking, it appears that those substances taste "good" which, in the digested or at least dissolved condition in which they reach the taste organs, are normal constituents of the blood; those which are not, are neutral or taste "bad." But, with regard to some of the constituents, at least, certain mixtures taste "bad" if there is a deficiency or excess of one of these constituents. And, there, the standard of comparison seems to be related to the concentration of that constituent in the blood. For instance, excessive salinity is "bad"; so is insipidity, which may be due to deficient salinity.[10] Pavlov concludes from one of his most elaborate experiments (*320*, 139–140) that "in the case of nutritive substances," an "increase or decrease" is "observed in the positive or negative reactions to different substances or different quantities of them." He then says, "It is thus seen that the chemical analyser of taste in its central part forms a connecting link between the internal and external media of the organism [I presume these are, respectively, the blood or even the storage organs, on the one hand, and, on the other, the contents of the mouth as absorbed by the taste buds and the olfactory organs], and by regulating their relations one to the other secures a certain constancy of the internal medium." This strikes me as by far the most plausible and suggestive approach to the problem of specific hungers and of appetite in general that I have seen.

It is evident, then, that the gustatory system is so organized that it can compare the contents of the mouth with that of the blood (or storage organs) not only qualitatively but in some respects quantitatively. Thus it serves for the relations with the environment. But, in order that these specific hungers should express themselves as has been described above, there must exist an internal analogue of this sense of taste. It would be impossible to explain the rise and fall of these specific hungers, according as the supplies of the respective constituents become deficient or are replenished, unless there were another system capable of comparing the composition of the blood (or the storage organs), both qualitatively and quantitatively, with some still more absolute standard. The mere fact that the composition of the blood is normally maintained so uniform and that its fluctuations are regulated so closely to special needs (metabolic rate) is further evidence that its composition is compared somewhere much as the composition of the contents of the mouth is compared.

Is this still more absolute standard compared with the intermediary, the blood, or with the storage organs directly? Having no outright knowledge we can only draw an inference. Cannon argues (*69*, 435) that there is no reason to expect the "signal" (his "hunger signal") to derive from the

usually explained by the fact of the three different glands. But he says there is some evidence that the secretion of each is variable. If so, it would seem that the neural control of the several salivary glands must respond to the discriminations of the gustatory system.

[10] G. H. Parker (*319*, 136) classifies insipidity as "probably a deficiency phenomenon" producible "by the absence of several classes of substances."

blood, for, "as to the blood, there are no changes in it which are associated with actual bodily need." But since the blood is a transportation medium which is constantly losing its constituents to the tissues and, between meals, as constantly replacing them from the storage organs—liver, skin, etc.—it seems possible that it does reflect, even if ever so slightly, the increasing inaccessibility of these stores as they are drawn down. In fact, in so far as withdrawal from these stores is under central nervous control—and the weight of present opinion seems to be that they are so controlled in the hypothalamus and its subject endocrine organs—the regulation can only be exercised in response to some notice of deficiency in the blood. Thus we see reason in Pavlov's expression "hungry blood" (ascribed to him by Frolov, (*157*, 87), which, he believed, excites the cells of the "food centre," or increases their excitability. Frolov, interpreting him, supposes that "the further the exhaustion of the blood proceeds, the higher becomes the 'charge' [excitability] of the food center" (*ibid.*, 95). Along the same lines Hoelzel (*203*) assumes a "hunger center" which reflects "the nutritive condition of the blood." [11]

If the cells of such a nervous center merely reflected the effect of the slightly varying composition of the blood upon their own relatively more stable composition, they would only be performing a function similar to that which we have ascribed to the taste buds. On the other hand, if the taste buds are themselves of relatively stable composition and have the capacity to taste both ways—that is, compare the blood with themselves as well as with the contents of the mouth—and report the results to the "hunger center" in specific detail, they may perform this function as well as the other. Since it appears probable, from the evidence we shall review in Appendix II, that the "hunger center" or centers are located subcortically, while certain evidence indicates that the cortex is necessary for discrimination among oral taste signals,[12] the former supposition would seem more probable.

For our purposes the question of the precise mechanism which indicates

[11] With regard to specific "salt-hunger," referred to in Appendix I A in connection with the maintenance of the water supply, it appears that the center which controls salt loss is the same, or in the same nucleus, as that which controls water loss (see Section A, note 24, above). But this center appears to act, neurally or via a pituitary hormone, upon the adrenal cortex, whose own internal secretion is responsible for stimulating the tubules of the kidneys to reabsorb salt; see Cannon, *66*, 197, citing Zwemer and Sullivan's results—18 *Endocrinol.* (1934) 97. Salt is lost when the gland is removed, and the condition is corrected by cortin. Richter (*339*) found that all his adrenalectomized rats died, if kept on a saltless diet. They showed a greatly increased salt appetite; and most of them lived if this appetite was satisfied. The same relation seems to hold between the parathyroid and calcium (Richter *et al.*, *342*, 735). Elsewhere (*340*) Richter shows that this increased salt appetite involves a lower taste threshold for salt. The conclusion is that the taste mechanism is altered. This is suggestive, though the precise nature of these connections remains obscure.

[12] This evidence is somewhat equivocal, and no cortical gustatory area has been proved. By injecting water into the mouth of a decorticate dog, Pavlov got the same results that he got only with food in a normal one (*320*, 329). On the other hand, I have seen it reported somewhere that decorticate dogs will continue to reject dogmeat.

when to stop eating is of as much interest as that (or those) which indicates food need. While the processes of digestion require time, so, among mammals, though to a far less degree, does the process of eating. If, therefore, the deficiencies which have excited the hungers are deficiencies in the blood, these might be made good rather promptly after absorption begins in the small intestine. Thereafter, the absorbed nutriment would begin to be stored and the blood composition would reflect normal content or slight excess of these constituents. But as soon as the blood deficiencies had been made good, the hungers would have been appeased and the urge to eat would have ceased, though the process of replacing the stores would continue for some time.[13] On the other hand, there is evidence that the mere distension of the stomach provides a sense of repletion when an adequate bulk has been ingested to keep the digestive apparatus engaged; and certainly "hunger pangs," if any, are converted into the normal peristaltic movements of digestion in the stomach as soon as a modicum of food is ingested. Thus it is quite possible that the appeasement of the specific hungers ("appetites"), the change in the character of gastric contractions, and gastric distension may constitute three different but supplementary indices of sufficiency. If so, we must suppose that, if the mixture ingested does not satisfy all the specific hungers and nevertheless the other two indices are given, eating stops and the unsatisfied hungers ("appetites") remain in abeyance until the digestive apparatus is no longer fully occupied.

Most of the foregoing discussion has been purely speculative. It has been aimed only to bring out the inadequacy, for our purposes, of Cannon's and Carlson's "hunger signal," [14] to suggest the probable great complexity of the actual mechanism, and to indicate how large a part in the process is probably played by subcortical and subconscious nervous centers whose admirable and automatic control over the storage and utilization of nutriment seems also to include a considerable discriminating control over the kind, and some control (perhaps too liberal) over the quantity, of nutriment ingested. That the cortical processes, including conscious sensation, play a part is obvious. That they can be dispensed with is also clear, since decorticate animals up to and including primates can be kept alive if fed—that is, they can and do eat—and decorticate dogs continue to feed themselves adequately. It appears likely that some of the sensations in consciousness constitute only a reinforcement [15] of those which operate at lower levels, while others act as a guide to overt behavior to make it more precise in kind and in duration.

[13] This delay in replenishing the stores is a reason for rejecting the storage organs as the source of the hungers or appetites. For, as in the case of thirst, the resulting excitations actually cease long before the stores can possibly be replaced.

[14] It seems almost certain that Cannon recognized this particular inadequacy.

[15] Or, again, that the two are "compensatory arrangements."

C. THE NEED OF MICTURITION AND DEFECATION

1. MICTURITION

Since it seems to be typical of the management of vegetative functions in general and, at this stage, is somewhat better understood than most of them, it is worth while to go into some detail in describing the function of micturition. At least, this will also be suggestive as to the most likely results of further analysis of other and probably analogous functions.

Speaking broadly, micturition appears to be managed at three levels. We may at least distinguish between "automatic," involuntary, and voluntary micturition. The first is managed locally or by the lower segments of the spinal cord; the second operates in part upon the first (includes it), but is managed subconsciously in the suprasegmental and subcortical parts of the central nervous system (the brain-stem); the third operates in part upon the first and second (includes them), but is managed by the cortex—or, at any rate, involves conscious sensation, voluntary constriction or relaxation of striated muscle and perhaps the imposition and withdrawal (possibly voluntary, but probably only "reciprocal" or "associated") of inhibition over the autonomic system.

The muscular apparatus concerned consists of the smooth muscle wall of the bladder (vesicle) itself and of the ring-like or perhaps tubular (Denny-Brown, *114*, 650) internal smooth-muscle sphincter. These two are, like all smooth muscle, under neural control by the autonomic system only.[1] So volition probably has no direct influence over them. But it appears that the reciprocal relation between the bladder and the internal sphincter (by which, as the former relaxes the latter contracts and, when the former begins actively to contract, the latter relaxes) is a purely local connection and that autonomic control is exercised only over the detrusor muscle (smooth) or over the process as a whole. Beyond the internal sphincter is the external, composed of striated muscle surrounding the wall of the urethra.[2] This is subject to voluntary contraction, but not to voluntary relaxation.[3] Apparently it is also subject to involuntary contraction as an "associated movement" forming part of other reflexes.

The walls of the bladder are elastic in the sense that their tonic contraction enables them "to hold the fluid contents of the viscus at approximately the same pressure whether those contents are copious or not, because of the ability of its fibers to exert the same tension whatever the form, shorter or longer, within a certain wide range, which they have assumed" (Sherrington, *376*, 224); that is, the bladder "adapts" its size to volume of contents. The "intravesical pressure" at any time is, therefore, a function both of volume and of tonic contraction—which Sherrington likens to

[1] But see Learmonth, *264*, 171.

[2] Fearnsides, *139*, 182.

[3] Denny-Brown and Robertson, *115*, 179 and 185. They say (*ibid.*, 185) that the external sphincter will not open without active vesical contraction. Langworthy (*251*, 618) regards it as "an emergency mechanism to stop micturition temporarily."

"postural contraction" (tonus) of skeletal muscle. As the bladder fills, with any given expansion of its size, pressure increases. But since the tonic reaction of the detrusor muscle (wall of the bladder), in so far as that is due to its own stretch, is only by increment, at continuous or decreasing stretch it declines (Denny-Brown *et al.*, *116*, 452)—that is, it shortly accommodates itself to the increment of volume, by expanding another step. This tonic reaction of the detrusor muscle to its own stretch is a peripheral reflex via the vesical nerve plexus alone.[4] But tonic contraction is also subject to control from the central autonomic nervous system and, from that source, it reflects the autonomic balance at the moment. Thus, at some point in the filling, either because the bladder is so stretched that the normal limit of elasticity of the detrusor muscle is being reached or because the tonic contraction is increased by nervous influences from elsewhere, intravesical pressure rises to a point at which active (phasic) contraction sets in. When that occurs, and not till then, the internal sphincter relaxes, first; after that the external sphincter, if not voluntarily closed, relaxes (Denny-Brown and Robertson, *115*, 179, 185–186).[5] Then the bladder is forcibly and completely evacuated, at high pressure, by the active contraction of the detrusor muscle. When evacuation is complete the external sphincter closes. Thereafter, the internal sphincter closes, but only as the bladder itself relaxes (Denny-Brown and Robertson *115*, 179).

"Automatic" micturition can take place in man after spinal injury which has separated the sacral segments from the rest of the nervous system or even when the bladder is entirely disconnected from the central nervous system.[6] In the former case, the arc presumably includes the preganglionic cells of the sacral division of the parasympathetic; in the latter, it includes the intramural vesical plexus (the postganglionic cells) only.[7] But "automatic" micturition begins only after varying periods after the injury. For, at first, due to "spinal shock," retention is complete. In accordance with the current interpretation of spinal shock as a removal of facilitation,[8] one infers from this delay that, in the normal man, "automatic" micturition, though doubtless the phylogenetically first form of the process, has been superseded and relegated to the position of a compensatory mechanism,

[4] Denny-Brown (*114*) studied it in a case of automatic micturition where only the arc of the vesical plexus remained intact.

[5] Denny-Brown (*114*, 648) finds that, in automatic micturition, the sphincters open only upon active contraction of the bladder and not as a response to pressure (but see Langworthy, *251*, 618) so that a wave of contraction in the bladder produces a wave of relaxation in the sphincter (internal). Nevertheless, the internal sphincter relaxes or contracts slowly (*ibid.*, 649). Either this delay or a difference in threshold, such as Head and Riddoch supposed (*184*, 203), makes it possible, in voluntary and involuntary micturition, that resistance, or the inadequacy of the contractions to open the sphincters, causes the vesical tone to yield and the bladder to take a new tonic posture. Denny-Brown and Robertson (*115*, 188) seem to agree that adaptation is usually due to the fact that the active contractions are so inhibited that they are insufficient to open the sphincters. This inhibition is, at low volumes, subconscious.

[6] Head and Riddoch, *184*, and Denny-Brown, *114*.

[7] Denny-Brown, *114*, 648.

[8] See Fulton, *160*, 142 ff

ordinarily incapable of operating by itself or of doing so adequately.[9] When the capacity is recovered, after the spinal shock, the process is purely a direct reaction to the stretching of the detrusor muscle by a certain volume of contents, through it differs in different cases.[10] Or, if the sacral circuit remains intact, it may also be part of the "mass reflex"; that is, since the reflexes of the lower spine have then "lost their local signatures," due to the cutting off of inhibition from higher centers, stimuli capable of exciting any of them excite them all. Thus deep breathing, the flexor reflex and stimulation of various areas of the skin near the genital organs are sufficient to cause micturition.[11] In the normal man none of these local or lower spinal reflexes are sufficient to start or to carry through effectively the process of involuntary micturition.

What is called involuntary micturition is probably the normal process, subject only to voluntary influences in preventing or inducing it. It is apparently this reflex which is cut out when the sacral segments of the cord are isolated. Langworthy and his associates (*254* and *255*) have found evidence for a—presumably parasympathetic—center in the midbrain which is responsible for "reflex micturition." In this area lie centers which are known to control the tone of striated musculature; it is probable that in the same area are centers controlling the tone of all smooth muscle as well. At any rate they believe there is, there, a center which controls the tone of the detrusor muscle (presumably increasing or inhibiting its local reaction to its own stretch), and that this is the only center capable of that "prolonged and forceful contraction of the musculature necessary completely to expel the urine." If it is organized like its neighboring tonic centers, its continuous but variable excitation is doubtless caused by stimuli from the bladder wall itself.[12] Probably it is also excited, at times, by a

[9] It should be said that this is contrary to Denny-Brown's view, whom we are following so closely as to the peripheral mechanisms. He attributes retention during spinal shock to the paralysis of the external sphincter (*114*, 649). Spastic paralysis, which this would presumably have to be, is due to release of lower centers from cortical (or higher) control (see Fulton, *160*, 149). It is hard to believe that such a center exists in the lumbarsacral segments of the spine, since the others we know are all suprasegmental; if it does not, it is equally hard to believe that this voluntary muscle behaves so differently from others which, caudal to the lesion, show depression of reflexes. An explanation conforming better to the general picture and at the same time arguing for the existence of a suprasegmental tonic center, is Fulton's (*160*, 132) supposition that retention in spinal shock is due to "depression of the response to stretch of the detrusor muscle," which would, in turn, by way of the vesical plexus reflex alone, produce the abnormal restriction of the sphincters which he finds.

[10] Head and Riddoch, *184*.

[11] Head and Riddoch, *184*, 188, 199, and 202.

[12] Denny-Brown (*114*, 647) agrees that such a center exists in the cat's brain, but concludes that it is absent from dog and man because, after recovery from spinal shock, "powerful reflex micturition" recurs every six or eight hours. For this reason, he believes that, in the latter, the lumbosacral segments of the spinal cord contain "all the nervous mechanism necessary for micturition" except for the voluntary part. Not only does this differ from the usual description of automatic micturition as incomplete, but Langworthy *et. al.* (*256*) think their observations on human patients with lesions confirm the existence of this tonic center. Root (*341*, 1130) accepts it, and states that the arcs of his

superior subcortical and also parasympathetic center, responsive to other influences.[13] It is normally inhibited—or its efferents are—by other higher centers, subcortical and cortical, which appear to be responsible for the "adaptation" of the bladder; that is, for restraining micturition, and thus permitting the bladder to relax until a critical pressure is reached. There is considerable evidence that this latter function is performed chiefly[14] by the sympathetic nervous system and that the subcortical center concerned is in the posterior hypothalamus—interbrain (Beattie and Kerr, *31*, 313).[15] At any rate, stimulation of the sympathetic trunks produces "a fall of vesical pressure" and stops "the rhythmical waves of [phasic] vesical contraction" (Langworthy and Hesser, *253*, 212; Learmonth, *264*, 171). Thus, "in certain mammals they [the sympathetic nerves] have developed an inhibitory control over the detrusor muscle which enables the

two chief reflexes for bladder contraction are broken by section at the midpontine region.

[13] There is considerable evidence for such a superior center. Beattie and Kerr (*31*, 313) locate it in the anterior hypothalamus, probably in the supraoptic or preoptic region, and trace its efferent tracts to the same region—inferior colliculus—in which Langworthy's midbrain center is located. Kabat *et al.* (*229*, 954) admit the possibility of this specific—though of no general—parasympathetic center in this general region (*230*, 232). But these and others agree that its action, when excited, is pressor. Kabat *et al.* conclude (*ibid.*, 236) that it "may have nothing to do with the control of bladder tonus" and that it is "probably not concerned in the reflex contraction which occurs as a result of distension" (i.e., presumably it responds to other stimuli than that and exercises its influence upon phasic not tonic contraction).

Since "every psychical act and every sensory stimulus is apt to cause a contraction or increased tone of the bladder" (Howell, *208*, 914, quoting Mosso and Pellacani), and since this center is in the general region where emotional excitement from these acts and stimuli seems to arise, it may be that it is the function of this center to bring such excitations to bear on the detrusor muscle, via the midbrain center. We think of emotional excitement as a sympathetic phenomenon. Yet this is but one of many points which prevent our accepting the universality of the notion of "opposed action" between the two divisions into which, on purely anatomical grounds, the autonomic nervous system is divided. It is assumed that it is the sacral (parasympathetic) division of the autonomic which is, as Cannon says (*63*, 423), "serviceable in emptying the bladder and rectum of loads which might interfere with extreme physical effort—an interpretation which is consistent with the well-known effects of strong emotion (e.g., fear) in voiding these viscera as a preparation for struggle."

As to another possible mechanism for this bladder response to excitement, see below, p. 1028.

[14] It is, of course, partially performed by the parasympathetic peripheral reflex arc itself, since it occurred in Denny-Brown's case when only that arc remained intact. Apparently, however, with the midbrain center in operation, section of the sympathetic nerves to the bladder causes the loss of the ability to hold varying quantities at the same pressure, and the quantity adequate for involuntary micturition declines (Langworthy *et al.*, *257*, 290). Since these are also lost to some extent by decortication (Langworthy and Hesser, *252*, 700), it is probable that cortical inhibition is also an influence.

[15] Kabat *et al.* (*230*, 234) locate it in the lateral or medial preoptic region at the level of the anterior commissure. This is difficult to reconcile with the findings of others. But one cannot be certain whether these responses are due to the stimulation of the centers themselves or of efferent tracts from higher levels. Langworthy *et al.* (*257*, 290) believe the inhibitory effect is direct on the muscle. And Beattie and Kerr (*31*, 313) agree that it is exercised both by a direct nervous path and by adrenalin.

animal to increase the interval between micturitions by enlarging the bladder volume" (Langworthy *et al.*, *257*, 289; see also Learmonth, *264*, 165). Apparently the sympathetic influence is a coordinating one—that is, it only works when something else is going on, and, when there is no excitement, it subsides (Langworthy *et al.*, *257*, 290). Thus the combination of the two (or three) autonomic centers, the former (or the first two) parasympathetic and the latter sympathetic, seems to be a typical example of "autonomic balance." The lower parasympathetic center is excited from the periphery by the need to micturate only. It may also be excited from above by the higher parasympathetic center. However, in the presence of other and more intense excitations in the sympathetic division, this parasympathetic response is inhibited. But this balance may be still more complex. The observation by Langworthy that sympathetic inhibition appears only to be exercised in excitement or when some other activity is in progress, suggests that it is connected with the phenomena mentioned above in note 13. However, there, the effect of emotion or preparation for action was pressor, not depressor. This discrepancy may be accounted for and the two opposite reactions both attributed to the sympathetic system on the basis of the observation of Langworthy *et al.* (257, 288–289) that stimulation of the sympathetic raises intravesical pressure at first by producing a contraction of the smooth-muscle fibers at the base of the bladder, after which there is a slow fall to a lower pressure due to the inhibition of the destrusor muscle, noted above. Thus the first effect of sympathetic excitation may be pressor and the second depressor. Or the two may be simultaneous; but the reduction of pressure, requiring adaptation which, in turn, requires time, may merely appear later. Thus we are left uncertain as to which division of the autonomic system is responsible for the pressor effect of emotional excitement.[16]

Finally, there is what is called voluntary micturition. But the voluntary control seems to be exercised directly only by way of prevention, and otherwise only indirectly by deliberately achieving nervous states or initiating synergies which, as a by-product, forbid or permit the involuntary process to take place (reciprocal inhibition or "associated movement"); therefore it seems nearer the truth to conceive the voluntary act to be merely a release of the involuntary act. The sensation which appears in consciousness has been called "consciousness of tension" or "fullness" or "desire to micturate." The latter was ascribed by Mosso and Pellacani to "sensory stimulation in the bladder itself caused by the pressure of the urine, when the intravesical pressure rose to 18 cm. of water." [17] But, since

[16] It is worth while to recall Gaskell's thesis (*167*, 31 ff., 47 and *62*) that the gastro-intestinal and genito-urinary tracts are, over most of their surface, surrounded by two coats of smooth muscle and that the sympathetic system retains the capacity for spastic contractions of the outer coat. Thus sympathetic influence here may not be inhibitory, but rather excitatory of an antagonistic muscular structure (i.e., Langworthy's smooth-muscle fibers at the base of the bladder). Inhibition of phasic contraction or relaxation of tonic contraction, thereafter, may be the usual adaptation.

[17] According to Howell, *208*, 914.

this is also the point at which the involuntary process is supposed to begin by converting the tonic into active contractions, it seems more probable that Denny-Brown's and Robertson's conclusion is correct (*115*, 188–189) that the sensation which leads to voluntary micturition arises from active contractions of threshold intensity (i.e., the beginning of involuntary micturition).[18] Even then the act may be prevented by voluntary contraction of the external sphincter until the active vesical contraction subsides and there is further adaptation of the bladder (Denny-Brown and Robertson, (*115*, 188). Voluntary control can probably also be exercised to some extent upon the depressor side, in such a way that the sensation, or desire, does not arise (though within narrow limits),[19] and, upon the pressor side, in such a way that micturition can be induced to begin without the previous appearance of the sensation or desire. But these seem both to be indirect—that is, they seem to be the by-products of nervous states which can be induced by appropriate voluntary behavior or of other voluntary activities themselves.

This voluntary control seems to be represented in the cortex in the region of the motor area controlling leg movements.[20] In spite of this locus,

[18] The fact that "consciousness of tension within the bladder does not of necessity influence automatic . . . micturition" (Head and Riddoch, *184*, 196), and that one of their patients knew tension but had no desire (*ibid.*, 197), suggests also that the desire is different from tension and arises from the active process itself which, if not permitted, shortly ceases unless distension is too great. There is also described a "thrill" or "shiver" which normally accompanies the beginning of the evacuation of a full bladder and which immediately precedes automatic micturition (*ibid.*, 213). This is certainly an accompaniment of the act in process (probably relaxation of sphincter).

Finally, there is some reason to believe with Fr. Goltz and others, that the actual penetration of urine into the urethra gives rise, through a "common chemical" or a pressure sense, to the sensation of need for micturition. But this, still more than the others, is a result, not a cause, of the beginnings of involuntary micturition. However, Denny-Brown and Robertson (*115*, 182) consider that there is no evidence that this plays any part.

It has been conjectured (e.g., Kempf, *233*, 25) that the desire can be produced by contracting the abdominal muscles so that they squeeze the bladder and thus raise the pressure at the then elasticity and volume and lead to voluntary micturition. Denny-Brown and Robertson conclude (*115*, 182) that this conjecture is "unnecessary." It is worth noting, however, that Holmes (*205*, 396) thinks that the connection of the mass reflex with automatic micturition, found by Head and Riddoch, is only via the contraction of abdominal muscle which is part of that reflex.

[19] Langworthy (*250*, 342) holds that "waves of bladder contraction may be . . . partially controlled by voluntary effort."

[20] Foerster (*144*, 143) finds it in the posterior part of the paracentral lobule, and says that voluntary control is lost if there is a lesion there. Langworthy and Kolb (*254*) locate an inhibitory center in the motor cortex which, they believe, exercises its effect not on the parasympathetic center, but via extrapyramidal tracts to motor cells in the spinal cord (*ibid.*, 381; see also *257*, 290). By stimulating the motor cortex, after destroying the pyramidal and hypothalamic efferent tracts, Spiegel and Hunsicker (*384*, 269) obtained both increase of intravesical pressure and of spontaneous contractions from certain points, and inhibition of these from other points (but not the former, if the pelvic nerves—parasympathetic fibers—were severed). Kabat *et al.* (*230*, 232) find some evidence of cortical inhibitory control from the frontal pole (prefrontal area) over the pressor center noted in note 13, above. Langworthy and Kolb (*255*, 46) conclude that

which is the only one from which individual muscles can be voluntarily controlled, it is obvious that voluntary micturition is not comparable to voluntary movement. In the first place, only the whole function appears to be cortically represented.[21] In the second place, contraction of the external sphincter and contraction and relaxation of the closely associated perineal muscles are the only specific activities of voluntary musculature which are certainly concerned. Moreover, while the former acts directly, the latter appears only to act indirectly in preventing or permitting active vesical contraction.[22] In that respect the contraction of the perineal muscles seems to be the voluntary member of a large group of reflexes, all of which, when sufficiently excited, may inhibit active vesical contraction[23] and, when themselves inhibited, may permit it. Some few authorities think the internal sphincter is under voluntary control;[24] but most of the evidence seems to be opposed to this. It is possible that voluntary restraint also includes inhibition of vesical contractions. But, if so, it seems to be in the nature of reciprocal inhibition induced by other actions under voluntary control, rather than directly.[25] It is even less likely that voluntary micturition includes the voluntary contraction of the detrusor muscle.[26] For all these reasons, the position which seems least likely to be upset by further investigation is that voluntary micturition consists in the "'lifting' of voluntary restraint" (Root, *355*, 1131) upon involuntary micturition, and

"in the region of the cerebral motor cortex," there is "a single coordinated cerebral mechanism [which] may act at times to decrease vesical pressure or may elevate it to a point where micturition takes place." This is apparently near the leg center. These controls may be integrated at the level of "preganglionic cells in the spinal cord," or, in part, via "a control over the midbrain mechanism."

[21] Denny-Brown and Robertson (*115*, 182) quote Genouville to this effect.

[22] See Denny-Brown and Robertson, *115*, 182. This contraction or relaxation is itself an "associated movement" (*ibid.*, 189) of involuntary micturition. But, when voluntarily accomplished, the association seems to be reversed.

[23] This seems to be true, as well, of the closely associated external sphincter; for this contracts ("associated movement") with all reflexes other than micturition and so secures coordination with other reflexes (Denny-Brown and Robertson, *116*, 453). Since this is probably not controlled by the sympathetic, it constitutes a reinforcing mechanism for producing the same effect, in that respect, as is produced by the sympathetic. Dusser de Barenne and Ward (*128*, 340) have found a relationship of reciprocal innervation between such extensor reflexes as the knee-jerk and the presumably flexor reflex induced by distension of the bladder. As the former became gradually weaker in a narcotized monkey, involuntary micturition occurred. They presume that distension of the bladder inhibited the knee-jerk. Presumably the inhibition is mediated via motor centers in the cord.

[24] Learmonth (*264*, 171 and 173) and Rehfisch, cited by Denny-Brown and Robertson (*115*, 150). The latters' own conclusion is that it is not (*115*, 189).

[25] Root (*355*, 1131) includes inhibition of vesical contractions as one of the means of voluntary restraint, but he does not explain its mechanism.

[26] Learmonth, *264*, 169. Since the influence of cortical centers, both pressor and depressor, is proven by observations such as those cited in note 19, above, but since this influence cannot be exerted specifically by volition, we would have to assume that it appears only as part of a synergy ("associated movement") or as the "reciprocal inhibition" incidental to such. This would satisfy Root's statement that "the 'lifting' of voluntary restraint can evoke powerful contractions of the bladder" (*355*, 1131).

that it can only occur when "intravesical pressure is sufficiently great" to evoke contractions of the bladder, neither of which can be induced voluntarily.[27]

2. DEFECATION

Denny-Brown and Robertson (*117*, 306) state that the functions of micturition and defecation are almost entirely comparable. In the same way as above, the "postural tone" of the rectum and of the involuntary (internal) sphincter is a reaction to passive tension on the wall of the rectum itself. Rapidly increasing tension causes tonic contraction to give way to phasic. Thereupon, the action of the internal sphincter being reciprocal just as that of the bladder is, the sphincter relaxes and expulsion takes place. There is no "potent voluntary control over the contractions of the rectum." In this respect, they think, lies the chief difference from micturition. There is, however, voluntary control over the external (striated muscle) sphincter; but in that there is no tonic contraction so, when not voluntarily contracted, it is relaxed (*ibid.*, 305–306).

Again, there is automatic defecation without spinal connections—the active contractions arising, through the intramural plexus only, from tension on the wall (*ibid.*, 305). With the sacral segments of the cord intact but isolated by spinal section, there is what they call "reflex" defecation, analogous to the similar type of automatic micturition. The contractions are then more powerful and, as with micturition, may result from other stimuli than tension on the wall itself (mass reflex; *ibid.*, 305). And, then, the act is accompanied by all the "associated" postural and active movements, including "nettoyage," which are familiar in the normal animal (Fulton, *160*, 132–133). The sympathetic system does not mediate either automatic or "reflex" defecation (Denny-Brown and Robertson, *117*, 305) "although it is probably capable of depressing them" (Fulton, *160*, 133).

As with micturition, before either of these forms of automatic defecation begins, there is a period of spinal shock. The internal sphincter is relaxed and the rectum does not react to tension. On the other hand, "there is generally great increase in peristalsis" in the intestine. And this is due to release of vagal influences from superior control, for it "does not occur when the brain stem is severed above the vagal nucleus" (Fulton, *160*, 132). Even when, after a few days, the tone of the sphincter is recovered and, after a few weeks, the rectum begins to empty itself automatically (Fulton, *ibid.*, 132), "the general force of contraction of the rectum" is far less than in the normal subject (Denny-Brown and Robertson, *117*,

[27] This is approximately Denny-Brown's and Robertson's conclusion (*115*, 189) that "normal micturition is entirely secondary to active contraction of the bladder," and that voluntary facilitation is "indirect." They think that voluntary restraint is "direct," so that there is both "voluntary and subconscious inhibition of the mechanism of spontaneous reaction to distension." One does not know, however, the mechanism for any direct voluntary inhibition of an autonomic process, other than through the use of voluntary muscles.

304). These facts again argue the presence of tonic centers in the brain-stem, probably again under indirect inhibitory control ("reciprocal inhibition") from the cortex. One appears to act on the intestine via the cranial section of the parasympathetic (vagus) and to reinforce—and perhaps normally to be responsible for—intestinal peristalsis. And it is this which expels the contents of the intestine into the rectum and causes the local reaction there. But, since the rectal response is suspended during shock and is far less than normal after recovery, it would appear that another center in the brain-stem, acting in the same way on the rectum, but via the sacral section of the parasympathetic, is responsible at least for the force of phasic contractions and perhaps also for the maintenance of tone there.

The inference is—though not proved—that involuntary defecation is the normal process and that its management by centers in the brain-stem is superimposed upon and comes largely to replace the capacity in the storage organs themselves to perform the act. Since the existence of these centers is only postulated, it is impossible to do more than guess what might be their afferent excitants. But because of their location—the same as Langworthy's tonic center for the detrusor muscle—and because of their apparent behavior, it seems possible that they respond chiefly to impulses from the smooth muscle they control. Voluntary defecation would then, again, be in the nature of permission; that would consist generally of the withdrawal of "reciprocal" inhibition upon the tonic centers and occasionally of the relaxation of the external sphincter which had been voluntarily contracted. Perhaps it would also consist in the adoption of postures which were themselves innately, or had come by conditioning to be, stimuli to the involuntary process.[28] Finally, in this case, the sensation in consciousness which may lead to voluntary permission is even more certainly the beginning of the involuntary act itself, and therefore in no respect its cause.

[28] That is, "associated movements" which, like those suggested in connection with micturition, have come to work both ways (i.e., the excitation of either one comes to excite the other); for those postures are the same, at least in the dog, as those that Fulton describes as accompaniments of automatic defecation.

II

SYNOPSIS OF EVIDENCE ON CENTRAL BEHAVIOR MECHANISMS

Appendix to Chapter 2

In the text we present, in its broad outlines, a picture of the way the behavior mechanism is coming to be conceived to function in connection with the maintenance of homeostasis—that is, as a result of present wants. While the picture is not yet clear in many respects, and is far from complete, it may be said, I think, that it is *emerging*, largely as a result of the intensive and objective study which has been concentrated on the central nervous system in general and the brain-stem in particular, during recent decades and especially in the pre-war decade. There has been a fundamental change in the view of the whole, which seems to be in process of becoming *accepted*, so that there is a large element of novelty in this picture.

For any summary of a somewhat novel thesis, supporting evidence is required. In the text that is impossible. For that reason I have assembled in this Appendix a sort of symposium of those citations which seem most appropriate, selected from the material, chiefly journal articles, from which the picture itself was formulated. This only deals with the subject in so far as it is necessary to do so in order to bring out the relationship with the matter we have under consideration—the generation of behavior. It is, of course, not an essay on the physiology of the nervous system. Nor does it undertake to furnish more than a sample of the evidence—a fair sample, I believe. On the other hand, it should be recognized that brief statements of such a complex affair must inevitably misrepresent, to some extent, the whole body of facts; for one cannot then avoid omitting many exceptions and failing to make many qualifications. Nevertheless, this is no place to attempt a statement which would be completely accurate as to details, even within the limits of present knowledge. Probably such a statement is impossible anyway, except in the form it actually takes—that is, a long series of contributions by specialists in each of the fields touched on.

I have chosen to be specific throughout. That involves mixing together hypotheses of all degrees of uncertainty, from the relatively well-established to the almost purely speculative.[1] The reason for deliberately pur-

[1] In introducing "The Millionth Map of Hispanic America" (103 *Science*, 1946, 319–322) Isaiah Bowman states that "A significant feature of the Millionth sheets of Hispanic-America is the relative reliability diagram, introduced by the American Geo-

suing this policy is that it seems to me preferable, in a first attempt at a somewhat systematic, or schematic, synthesis of the important results of so much novel experimental and observational material, to risk being anatomically or physiologically wrong as to the details—locus, functioning, etc.—than to be so cautious that the parts of the scheme do not hang together. In any synthesis of a rapidly progressing body of knowledge this choice is unavoidable. If the skeleton of the scheme as a whole stands the test of time, it matters not, for this purpose, that its details should come to be modified, that the locus or precise nature of certain of the functions or relations turn out to be somewhat different from what now seems probable. On the other hand, if caution dictates leaving great holes in the scheme, it is no scheme at all, and does not serve even the purpose of a tentative and preliminary approach.[2]

A. THE HIERARCHICAL ORGANIZATION OF THE CENTRAL NERVOUS SYSTEM

For our purposes, the essential characteristic of the organization of the central nervous system is the hierarchical design of its organization, first recognized by Hughlings Jackson, whom Foerster (*144*, 148) calls "the father of Neurology." [1] This lies so much at the basis of our interpretation of the facts that we shall follow the same plan in arranging the evidence,

graphical Society. . . . It tells how much we do not know and the degree of accuracy of that which we do know concerning the cartography of a given sheet. . . . The highest purpose of the relative reliability diagram, if I may put it paradoxically, is to lead to new surveys that will destroy the sheet upon which the diagram appears."

I should like to have inserted a "relative reliability diagram" for the hypotheses presented here. Unfortunately, that is certainly beyond my competence and, at present, perhaps beyond that of anyone else. All I have tried to do is to suggest some discrimination and to give warning of the most speculative.

[2] To quote Isaiah Bowman again (*ibid.*, 320), "A first-class project inspires others also to reach for the stars, and though we all fail to touch them, the *effort* is what produces those powerful waves that wash the farthest shores of thought and action." There can be no doubt that this is "a first-class project," whatever the reader may think of this particular "effort." May it inspire others who are better fitted for the task.

[1] Dandy (*101*, 11) calls him "the greatest neurologist of all time." In spite of the fact that so much of the detailed knowledge of the organization of the central nervous system (particularly of the subcortical regions) has been obtained since Hughlings Jackson wrote and lectured some thirty to eighty years ago, it is noteworthy that many of the views he developed as to the general principles of this organization have become constantly more generally accepted by neurologists and physiologists. This is in part due to the fact that the new details fit so well into his general pattern or scheme. They change many of his details; they fill in the pattern; they elaborate it; but they do not fundamentally alter it.

The general scheme still rests largely on hypotheses, but on hypotheses that have proved useful. And, as he said himself, "Imagining it to be possible to investigate complex subjects without the use of hypothesis" ("the provisional conclusion which is called hypothesis," *216*, II, 476) is as "incongruously diplopic as some states in dreams" (*ibid.*, II, 361).

The concept of the "neural hierarchy" was, I believe, originally proposed by Hughlings Jackson in a series of papers in the *British Medical Journal* (1884), 591, 660, 703.

examining successively each order in the hierarchy from lower to higher and the relations between each order and those below it. A brief over-all view of this functional design,[2] in the shape of broad if rather rough generalizations, will enable the reader who is not a specialist to follow more readily the connections and significance of the details as we fill them in. At least, that has been my own experience from studying Hughlings Jackson, even where he has been outmoded. These general statements will be supported and also qualified as we proceed later to deal with the details.

The units of the hierarchy are the nervous "centers"—the nuclei, or the ganglia, of nerve cells. These are connected from level to level, and also at each level, by fiber "tracts" which, when viewed in the single direction in which the nervous impulse normally travels,[3] are often called "projections." The tracts, or projections, are composed of neurons having their cell-bodies in the nucleus or ganglion (center) and their axones in contact with some other nucleus (central cell body) or some nerve root or spinal ganglion (cell of a peripheral neuron).[4] Proceeding from the termination of the spinal cord along the segmental (spinal) portion of the central nervous system, through the brain-stem (medulla, pons, isthmus, the midbrain or mesencephalon, the interbrain or diencephalon, and the basal ganglia of the endbrain) up to the cerebral cortex, the term "higher" indicates the more rostral (i.e., nearer the cortex) and "lower" indicates the more caudal center down to the beginning of the "final common path," or the peripheral neuron. This notion of "level" is applied at times even among the "areas" of the cortex itself.[5] Jackson conceived the organization of levels to be an "evolutionary hierarchy." "The higher centres are evolved out of the lower" (*216*, I, 174). Even the very highest are no more than "developments out of lower nervous centres" (*211 ibid.*, I, 43). But, there, the process of evolution continues through life; they are "the latest evolved (the continually evolving)" (*211 ibid.*, II, 76). In turn, he conceived the converse of this process, "dissolution," to take place in the opposite direction, the highest levels becoming disordered first and most.[6]

[2] What I am calling functional, as opposed to structural, does not entirely correspond to Jackson's distinction between "anatomico-physiological" and "morphological" (see *215*, 135, note 2). Actually, the functioning (physiology) is limited by the structure (anatomy), but, within those limits, need not and does not conform.

[3] In view of the evidence for "antidromic" impulses, the one-way characteristic is not now attributed to the axone itself, but to the relation between the axones and dendrites of successive neurons in a path.

[4] As Jackson puts it (*215*, 123), a level is an "anatomico-physiological community." He says (*ibid.*, 121) "the intrinsic elements, the elements of the level itself, are a series of centres with their interconnecting fibres.' 'The term "interconnecting fibres" stands for "any sort of junction, definite or indefinite, or, so to say, for any contrivance by which different nervous elements can influence one another" (*ibid.*, 122, note 1).

[5] For details of Hughlings Jackson's definitions of the several "levels," see supplementary statement on "The 'Levels' of the Nervous System," at the end of this section.

[6] In Chapter 3 we take issue with this thesis. It is undoubtedly true that the highest level is evolved out of the next highest (subcortical). Below that level, however, development of the nervous system seems to take place from the head to the tail. Nevertheless, we can agree that all the higher centers evolve more than do the lower, though they do

In general, the division of the whole nervous system into afferent and efferent fibers is customarily carried into the central system itself and applied also to what are strictly internuncial neurons there. That is, any neurons or tracts leading to higher levels (toward the cortex) are called afferent, and any leading to lower levels are called efferent. Also, to some extent, the same terms are applied, from the standpoint of any single center, to the fibers or tracts leading to that center (afferent) or away from it (efferent), even if both be parts of the afferent system as a whole, or of the efferent system as a whole. All this on the supposition, probably universally true, that nervous impulses normally travel only one way along any specific path.[7] At the lowest level on the afferent side centers become excited because of "activities of peripheral structures from which afferent nerves pass to the central nervous system" (*216*, I, 367). Thereafter, by intermediation, higher centers may become excited wherever they are connected with the lower centers by rising afferents. Or the higher centers may be directly excited by local influences, or by neighboring centers of the same level, without direct afferent impulses from below. Similarly, on the efferent side, excitation of the centers of the lowest level produces the activities of the organism by means of impulses which these centers send out—excitatory or inhibitory and motor (muscular) or secretory—to the peripheral organs—muscular, visceral, vascular, or glandular. This excitation or inhibition may be caused directly at that level by rising afferents, by local influences, or by neighboring centers of the same level. Or it may be intermediated there, having descended from higher levels.[8]

---

not evolve out of them. Hence his comparative statement seems entirely correct, if his historical one is not.

[7] See note 3, above.

[8] Jackson used the term "impression" for all incoming excitation over the afferent system, because "it implies nothing as to sensation in the sense of mental state" (it is "an active physical . . . state only," *216*, I, 238) and because he held that the latter can arise only at the highest levels, as we shall presently see. An impression is defined as "an alteration effected at the origin of an afferent nerve [at any level] producing activity in a nervous centre because the nerve fibre is connected with that centre" (*loc. cit.*). Correspondingly, he used "movement" on the efferent side. But "movement" covered all effects, even those on the arteries and the viscera (I, 46) and included inhibition ("negative movements," *ibid.*, I, 373) as well as secretion (I, 238). That is, "under the head of movements we place effects produced through motor nerves to glands, and through inhibitory nerves" (II, 78). Presumably also they might be either "phasic" or "tonic" (postural).

While on the afferent side the term refers particularly to the peripheral cause and on the efferent to the peripheral effect, each process was conceived as a unit. For, "the nervous system is a representing system" and "the only things it can represent are Impressions and Movements" (I, 238). "Motor nervous centres represent movements of muscles, not, so to put it, muscles in their individual character" (I, 372). Or, "to speak figuratively, the central nervous system knows nothing of muscles, it only knows movements" (II, 400). And, best of all, "The nervous centres represent movements, not muscles; chords, not notes" (I, 113).

Against the prevailing theories of his day, and to some extent of ours, he contended "that the cerebral hemisphere [also] is made up of nothing else than nervous arrangements for the co-ordination of impressions and movements" (*211*, I, 40; see also *ibid.*, pp. 40–43, and elsewhere).

The first characteristic of Hughlings Jackson's "hierarchical organization" of the central nervous system is what he called "integration." Both on the afferent and on the efferent side, the functional paths from and to all parts of the body are conceived to anastomose more and more at the successively higher levels. Diagrammatically, the branches of the afferent converge as they rise; the branches of the efferent diverge as they descend. Thus the degree of integration at any level is measured by the breadth of the representation of regions of the body (including the viscera, etc.) by particular centers. At the lowest level there is detailed representation by individual centers of individual regions; [9] at the top "a great part or the whole of the body" is represented by each center.[10] Since, in general, the lowest level deals directly with the periphery, while each succeeding higher level deals only indirectly with it through the intermediation of lower levels,[11] the parts of the body are separately represented at the lowest level and then successively re-represented in larger and larger groupings at the higher levels. This fact, together with the varying number of functioning intermediations between the centers of a single level, determines the degree of co-operation or its opposite, independence, among the several centers at each level. From "considerable, not complete, independence of one another," at the lowest level, ("for local affairs") co-operation increases with integration to a "more nearly necessary concert" at the highest level.[12] But integration is a characteristic, not a geometrical rule. The functional hierarchy is multiplex—a principle, not a simple fact. There is, perhaps, no single region which is the apex, and even at the top there may be a modicum of independence among the several centers. On the efferent side this increasing co-operation is not evidenced entirely by the increasing peripheral scope involved in the movement or postural change, nor does it consist wholly of the combination of elements within the independent power of subordinate centers.[13] It is true that each spinal motor root innervates the outgrowth of its own metamere (corresponding to the segment) and that, therefore, it is only at suprasegmental levels that *general* muscular activity, either phasic or tonic, can be produced. But since finely executed (co-ordinated) movements, or those involving but one digit, for instance, require a complex background of reciprocal inhibition that is only within the capacity of the higher centers, what seems to be an independent movement is often the most co-operative in its innervation. On the afferent side, at least as one nears the highest levels, increasing integration expresses itself in the fact that the higher the level the greater is the degree to which the

[9] Since there is a certain amount of interweaving of neurons in nerve trunks, the lowest level of representation is not as detailed as it might seem.

[10] Jackson said (*216*, II, 35) that he was "neither a universaliser nor a localiser"—in other words, that he neither believed that every cortical center represented the whole body, nor that each represented a single part only.

[11] Above the lowest level the pattern of intermediation is not perfect, since there is a certain amount of by-passing of levels by "through" tracts.

[12] See Jackson, *215*, 124; and *216*, I, 46, 374; II, 29–30, 40–41, and 432.

[13] See note 40, below.

neural effects of concurrent stimuli from separate peripheral sources are compounded into one complex whole. To some extent they even come to consist of compounds of data from different senses—which are hardly interconnected at all.

The second characteristic of Hughlings Jackson's hierarchical organization may be called "differentiation." Diagrammatically, this is presented in a form the opposite of integration—that is, here, the afferent side becomes more multiplex the higher the level, while the efferent becomes less so, the lower the level. But, whereas functional integration involves the compounding of the effects of stimuli from many sources into one effect, as they rise upon the afferent side, and the wider distribution of the effects of higher excitations as the impulses descend upon the efferent (i.e., each has some effect over all available paths), the result of differentiation on either side is only to present alternative paths, which are mutually exclusive. It does not result in compounding (afferent) or spreading (efferent), as integration does; it consists in the switching of the impulses into one of many somewhat parallel paths in the ascent, each constituting a different combination of a more limited variety of effects from the original stimuli, and of the excitation from above over but one of many paths, each reaching a different combination of centers or acting on them with quantitative differences, in the descent. Thus, since the two characteristics exist together, we may say that the degree of differentiation depends on the number of alternative paths between two levels, irrespective of the degree to which all the alternatives may be integrated at either level. But since these two characteristics, though independent of each other, appear to go hand in hand in development, we find that differentiation and integration both increase from lower to higher levels.[14]

It is approximately true that each minute part of the body must be represented by at least one nerve cell at the lowest level (detailed representation), whereas it would be conceivable that a single cell should represent the whole body at the highest level. Thus the characteristic of integration, alone, would tend to result in a large number of centers at the base (next to the periphery) and a small number at the apex. In contrast to that, the characteristic of differentiation results in a small number of alternative paths at the base rising to an astronomical number at the apex. Since each alternative is represented (approximately) by at least a single neuron, it is necessarily true that the number of cells and fibers, or the extent of nervous centers, at each level must increase according to the degree of differentiation there.[15] It is this characteristic, then, that appears to explain

[14] On differentiation, see Jackson, *215*, 125; and *216*, I, 46, 374; II, 432. He regarded the result of differentiation as "complexity." In terms of Jackson's simile (see note 8, above) the fact that chords may be played at all is due to integration (the ability to play several notes at once); the variety of different chords available is due entirely to differentiation.

[15] Jackson says of the efferent side, "the greater the number of different movements the centre represents, the greater the multiplication of both cells and fibres" (*216*, I, 217); for "motor centres . . . contain more cells and fibres . . . not in proportion *to the size of the muscles* they represent; but in proportion *to the number of different movements*

the vast size of the cerebral cortex in comparison with that of lower levels.[16]
In fact, in contrast to integration, which is complete at the higher subcortical levels, most of the differentiation both on the afferent and on the efferent sides only appears in the cortex.

The third characteristic of Hughlings Jackson's hierarchical organization is the control over lower levels exercised from higher levels.[17] This control of higher over lower levels operates through three different influences. There may be direct excitation from the higher center, resulting in a further outflow of impulses from the lower center; and there may be inhibition from the higher center, which makes the lower center unresponsive to impulses which might reach it from other sources.[18] In many cases this inhibition seems to be more or less constant, though varying perhaps in degree.[19] In certain other cases the inhibition may be "reciprocal"—that is, the inhibition exerted over one center may be incidental to

of muscles which they represent" (*ibid.*, II, 438). This thesis Jackson attributes to Herbert Spencer (I, 262): "Greater differentiation of function implies greater physical separation [cf. Lashley, as cited in note 49, below]. There must be separate representation however little different the movement may be from other movements and however much of it may be a reco-ordination of other movements." This "separation is not isolation," however. But, as to both sides, "the higher the centre, the greater the number of *different* movements and impressions represented in it" (for these terms see note 8, above). "This implies a greater number both of nerve fibres and cells" (*216*, I, 46).

It has sometimes been supposed that differentiation arises from differences in the pattern of impulses rather than separation of the course they take. But, I think, both must be supposed. Otherwise, there would be no possible explanation of the selection of one path among many alternatives upon the afferent side. On the efferent side it might all be explained by difference in the combination of connections; but differences in quantitative assortments seem more likely to be due to differences in the pattern of impulses set up.

16 Thus "the cerebrum differs from the rest . . . only in being the most complicated [for his definition of complexity see note 14, above] part of the nervous system" (*216*, I, 330).

17 "Controlling as well as directive action is displayed throughout the nervous system" (Jackson, *216*, II, 481). But as Taylor puts it in his introduction (*216*, I, xiii), Jackson's evolutionary view of the hierarchy "implies that the most lately developed [level] controls and inhibits the lower levels."

18 Lashley (*262*, 375) concludes "that excitation and inhibition may be originated within the same center" throughout the central nervous system. I should say that this is less and less disputed. Probably exception should be made of the autonomic system, which seems to have separate excitatory and inhibitory fibers, at least to the periphery.

19 The existence of constant inhibition from above as the chief function of control has perhaps been overemphasized. Jackson even speaks of the whole system as a "hierarchy of inhibitory centres" (*215*, 169, and similarly elsewhere). However, it does appear that inhibition from above is one of the chief results of the evolution of the higher centers. Thus Jackson quotes Fiske (*Destiny of Man*, p. 54) to the effect that, since the cerebral organization must be completed (functionally evolved) after birth, in infancy "the lowest level will be less 'controlled' or less 'kept down' than in older persons. *Pari passu* with the later development, or evolution, of the higher levels, the lowest will be more and more 'kept down'" (*216*, I, 352). And his own analysis of nervous and mental diseases (particularly epilepsy) is considerably based on this aspect of control (see, for instance, *ibid.*, I, 369).

the excitation of another center conducting an antagonistic activity.[20] The third influence is that, in certain cases, the excitation from above may be subliminal, so that it merely "facilitates" (adds itself to the intensity of) excitation from other sources, which may also be below threshold strength; but with the result that the combined excitation is above threshold. While this control is usually thought of in connection with the efferent side, it is clear that it is also exercised upon the afferent, at least near the highest level, as will be outlined hereafter (sensory attention). Two corollaries follow from this system of control. One is that the higher the center the less the control to which it is subjected from above—the more independent it is, in this sense.[21] The other is that, in so far as this control is operative in the form of constant inhibition of lower by higher levels, withdrawal of such control does not cause, but merely *permits*, activity of the lower center.[22] Such permitted activities are then known as "release phenomena."[23] Study of these release phenomena makes possible a rough generalization. It is usually to be presumed that, before inhibitory control from above is established or after it is withdrawn for any reason, there will be overactivity of the lower center as compared with the mature and normal state.[24] Obviously, this assumes some ready source for the over-excitation of the lower level, a source which must be generally operative. We shall consider that point in the next paragraph. Our concept of the exercise of control from above should not contemplate merely the alternative exercise of one or the other of these three influences. Probably differentiation itself, on the efferent side, consists in a little more permission here, a little more inhibition there, a little more or less excitation or facilitation elsewhere, and even in the use of "contemperation"[25] (antagonists) resulting in mixtures varying largely only by reason of differences in the quantitative proportions of a more limited number of elements.

What appears to be a fourth characteristic of the hierarchical organization, if we follow Hughlings Jackson himself, was what he called (rather inadequately) "organization." Actually this is only the converse of another

[20] In some cases there is conceived to be even inhibition of inhibition—the "inhibition of a centre itself inhibitory" (Jackson, *215*, 171).

[21] Jackson says (*216*, II, 477), "Besides relation [between levels] of direction and control, the higher their evolution the more independent do centres become in their activity." See also note 48, below.

[22] See Jackson (*215*, 141) for a discussion of the difference between "cause" and "permission."

[23] Something is " 'taken off' " so the center is " 'let go' " (Jackson, *215*, 171).

[24] Jackson calls it the "principle that we get over-action of lower centres by the mere removal of the influence of higher centres" (*216*, II, 6). It is a " 'permitted' over-energising of the now uncontrolled and thus over-active nervous arrangements" (*ibid.*, II, 22). "The higher nervous arrangments inhibit (or control) their lower, and thus, when the higher are suddenly rendered functionless, the lower rise in activity" (*ibid.*, II, 30).

[25] Jackson, in fact, defines co-ordination as contemperation (*216*, I, 431). The latter (*loc. cit.*, note 1) is "the act of reducing a quality by admixture of the contrary."

characteristic. But the demonstration of that assertion involves the presentation of an actual fourth characteristic which he himself did not enumerate or describe. Within the central nervous system, for each afferent path there are several or many "connections" at different levels with paths of the efferent side. That is, each center in the hierarchy usually "connects" some particular paths of both sides, at least indirectly. It is therefore possible for afferent impulses of adequate intensity to go over to the efferent at any of these levels, even the lowest. But, normally in many cases, the control of the higher centers over the lower is imposed in such a way that this access of afferent to efferent below is prevented (inhibited), and the afferent impulses must rise to the higher centers before going over.[26] In other cases this transit is normally facilitated, so that even afferent impulses which are themselves inadequate can gain access to the efferent side at the controlled center.[27] Fulton has called the transit at lower levels "short-circuiting" and the enforced rise to higher levels "long-circuiting"—a convenient analogy. Spinal reflexes in the intact animal are cases of the shortest "short-circuiting."[28] All suprasegmental reflexes or other efferent effects of peripheral stimuli are produced by "long-circuiting" of different degrees. The two processes are often combined in various proportions and among various levels. However, it may be said that the degree of short-circuiting—and, conversely, the degree of long-circuiting—depends upon the absence, the insufficiency, or the relaxation of inhibition, or upon the facilitation, exercised by higher levels over the transit at lower levels of afferent impulses from peripheral stimuli.[29] We may call this fourth characteristic the "variable reach of the arc."

By the term "organization" Hughlings Jackson seems to have intended the certainty and speed with which, at any particular level, a single afferent path will always discharge into one specific efferent path.[30] He conceived this certainty to decline from lower to higher levels—that is, that an analogue of his differentiation (number of alternatives open) upon the

[26] And it is the withdrawal of this inhibition and the resulting transition at the lower level which, at least above the spinal cord (where facilitation seems normally required), produces the overexcitation and activity referred to above under release phenomena.

[27] This statement suffices to cover the working of normal functional paths. But, as noted, there appear to exist at all levels many anatomical connections between the afferent and the efferent which are normally in disuse (constantly inhibited from above). Nevertheless, control over these connections seems to have some limit to its possibilities. Apparently it can be taken by surprise, and it can be overcome by a sufficiently intense excitation. Thus it seems usually to be exercised to a low degree and, only with warning, to be stepped up to a high degree. Even then it can be overcome, at least above the spinal level, so that there is spreading of the excitation in unwonted directions.

[28] Not considering possible intramural reflexes, which may never occur in the intact organism.

[29] Of course, if they start at higher levels, as some certainly do, they cannot go over at lower levels.

[30] "If the sensory and motor elements be well joined, so that 'currents flow' easily from the sensory into the motor elements, then that centre, although a very simple one [having say, but two elements of sensory and two of motor] is highly organised." (*216*, II, 46)

afferent and upon the efferent sides exist between the afferent and the efferent sides. Conversely, the more alternative transits are open at any level, the more "modifiable" is that level.[31] Thus the highest centers, proceeding from the most modifiable condition, "are continually organizing through life" (*216*, II, 46), while presumably, the lowest are already completely organized and therefore no longer modifiable. Modifiability may, therefore, be construed as uncertainty among alternatives and as possible consequent delay in determining the path.

This raises an important conceptual issue which is also touched upon in the text.[32] The use of the terms afferent and efferent sides (see p. 1036) suggests that each arc consists of an afferent segment and an efferent segment with a junction at some point. Thus in the afferent segment, to use physiological terms, the impulses are supposed to be sensory, while in the efferent they are supposed to be motor. But this mental diagram is most certainly not true to the anatomical arrangements. On the contrary, even if we admit the distinction between afferent and efferent in the central nervous system, all of whose neurons are, strictly speaking, internuncial, there is almost always at least one additional internuncial neuron interposed between these so-called afferent and the efferent neurons.[33] How can one define this internuncial neuron as either afferent (sensory) or efferent (motor), since it connects the two and therefore necessarily comprises both aspects or is something different from either? Jackson evidently held that it is both. For he constantly reiterates the statement that all central nervous activities are "*sensori-motor*," not *sensory* alone or *motor* alone. But, in fact, that is a matter of terminology; for, actually, they are also *central*.[34] If, now, one alters the mental diagram from I (Fig. 42) to II, one seems to have a more realistic picture of the almost universal actual scheme. The so-called afferent and efferent segments do not meet, as in I. Instead, at the successive levels 1, 2 and 3, etc., there are internuncial segments between afferent and efferent,[35] which are themselves both or neither.

If this modification of the usual conceptual model is accepted, then Jackson's differentiation and his organization are merely the two poles of a single attribute.[36] As the number of alternative paths increases (dif-

[31] See especially *216*, II, 46, and *215*, 125. "Generally the more simple (less complex), etc., a centre the more strongly is it organized and the less is it modifiable." (*215*, 125)

[32] See pp. 98 ff.

[33] I am told that, recently, by way of providing the apparently universally necessary exception to all general statements, two spinal reflex arcs have been found which contain no internuncial neuron.

[34] Thus Sherrington (*375*, 329) regards the most purely sensory afferent system—"the path from the thalamus to the post-central convolution"—the "radiations," as internuncial.

[35] One can continue to think of the central tracts which connect level with level (above the first) as afferent or efferent, if one chooses. But actually it would be impossible, in many instances, to distinguish anatomically between those that rise or descend and those that cross over from side to side, for many (perhaps most) do both.

[36] I am inclined to think that is what he thought, though what he said seems to confine

ferentiation) from level to level, the certainty that impulses will follow any one path (organization) must decrease. Except in one respect it is all the same whether one conceives these alternative paths to be rising (afferent) or crossing (internuncial). They are central. But since, if they are rising (diagrammatically), they will lead to a level at which the number of alternatives will be still greater, one simply concludes that, generally speaking, the shorter the circuit the greater will be the degree of organization and the longer the circuit the greater will be the degree of differentiation (and therefore of modifiability).

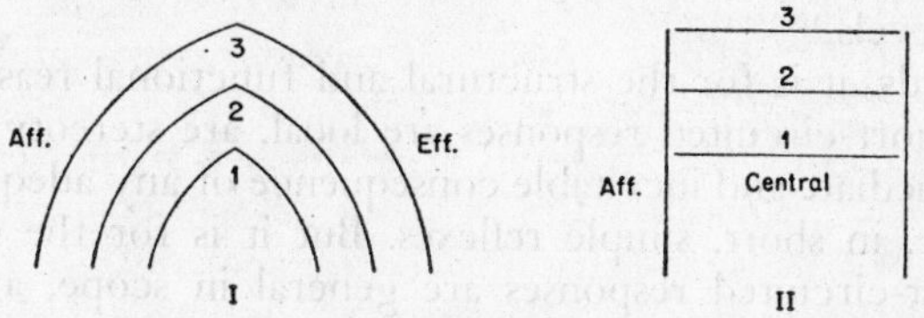

FIG. 42

If, now, we combine these several characteristics, we may deduce the nature of the hierarchical organization of the central nervous system, as conceived. As higher levels evolve more complexly than do lower levels and even, in part, evolve from lower levels, there is an increasing tendency at each higher level toward integration of the neural management of all bodily functions; but there is also an increasing tendency toward differentiation—that is, toward variability in response—and away from organization—that is, fixity of response. Since the higher levels maintain an effective, though varying control over the lower, which is perhaps primarily exercised in increasing the reach of the arc, it follows that the more control is exercised and the longer the resulting circuit, the greater will be the degree of integration evidenced in, and the greater the potential heterogeneity of, the response.[37] The fact that these deductions agree with the observed facts is confirmation of the generalizations which together form Hughlings Jackson's analytical scheme of the hierarchical organization of the central nervous system.

Since the level at which it is permitted to go over determines the extent to which these characteristics come into play with regard to any nervous activity resulting from peripheral stimuli, we expect to find and do find marked differences in such activities according to their level of transit. If relatively simple patterns of impulses from not yet differentiated or integrated paths of the afferent side pass over at spinal levels, there are available at these levels only simple patterns of movement and, normally,

"organization" to complexity of transits. But (*216*, II, 432) differentiation equals complexity, and (*ibid.*, II, 437) "the most complex . . . are the least organised; the most simple are the most organised."

[37] While we are not introducing the term here we may note, for reference in Section H 2, that Hughlings Jackson regards the polarity, voluntary *vs.* automatic, to be equivalent to the polarity, modifiable (differentiated) *vs.* organized (*216*, II, 46). Evolution is toward the voluntary; dissolution toward the automatic (*ibid.*, I, 38).

those only which deal with a single region of the body;[38] if similarly simple patterns, but from afferent paths which are now somewhat integrated, pass over at bulbar or midbrain levels, they find available a larger variety and a larger scope of patterns in the now further differentiated and integrated efferent side; if the transit takes place at interbrain levels, then, since integration on the afferent side has probably been partly completed and differentiation has been begun at this level, a considerably greater variety of afferent patterns is possible—and these, in turn, have available more efferent paths—and thus more integrated and varied responses.[39] And so on to the highest levels.[40]

In other words, it is for the structural and functional reasons we have outlined that short-circuited responses are local, are stereotyped in form, and are the immediate and inevitable consequence of any adequate stimulus—that they are, in short, simple reflexes. But it is for the same reasons that the longest-circuited responses are general in scope, are adapted,[41]

38 "In the lower centres there is a direct adjustment of few and simple movements to few and simple peripheral impressions" (Jackson, *216*, I, 60).

As to the "single region of the body" it is to be noted that the characteristic we have called integration is largely functional (paths) and only in part anatomical (fibers). That is, the canalization is largely dependent on superimposed inhibition. When this has been withdrawn *in toto* by spinal injury or transection, great numbers of connections seem to become available in the spinal cord which are normally in disuse (see note 27, above). This seems to make possible a general overflow from almost any afferent to many efferent paths at the same time. This is the "mass reflex" observed in spinal man or animals. "Sensory impulses, instead of being restricted to well defined channels as is the case when the higher centres are intact, spread diffusely throughout the spinal cord, especially along the more primitive pathways to the sympathetic and flexor centres" (Fulton, *160*, 139).

39 Of course this includes all forms of response, not merely that of skeletal muscle. Also we must remember that it may be that excitations can arise anywhere in the arc from non-neural causes, and certainly they can arise at the highest level from causes which are not current peripheral stimuli.

40 "In the very highest centres also there is a similar adjustment [to that mentioned in note 38, above]. But then it is of exceedingly special movements (representing movements of the whole organism) to the most special of impressions from the environment" (Jackson, *216*, I, 60).

It is true, of course, that "the units of the brain do represent (potentially contain) *all the lower processes* of the nervous system, as well as the higher or more special" (Jackson, *216*, I, 110). But only to the extent that such special movements are composed of lower elements in their pure form is it literally true that the "spinal cord mediates the basic reflex patterns upon which the higher centres of the nervous system operate" (Fulton, *160*, 123). If one ignores the cranial nerves and excludes the possibility of reflexes wholly within intramural plexuses, the spinal cord mediates all incoming and outgoing impulses. Therefore, it includes *all* the final common paths. Thus the details of all patterns are limited to those of which the cord is capable. But the patterns which can be constructed out of these details by the cord itself—that is, those which can be set off by a local stimulus which is short-circuited, either normally or abnormally—are of a wholly different order from those which the higher centers execute through the cord as intermediary. "It is to be remembered that the movements of which the spine [by itself] is capable are comparatively few and simple" (Horsley and Schäfer, 179 *Philosoph. Trans.*, 1888, B, as quoted by Jackson, *216*, I, 439).

41 This is what Jackson calls "speciality," "specialisation," or "definiteness"; these are better words, but he uses them in an equally purposive sense. They designate the par-

and may be long-delayed and uncertain—that they may be, as we called them in the text, "deliberate." Actually, even the latter range from the most reflex to the most deliberate because they vary widely in the extent to which they have become organized (habitual, accustomed, unconscious).[42]

To complete the description of Jackson's hierarchy, we note that "the lowest level does menial work." [43] "The very highest processes," while they "are only the most multifold and complex of all sensori-motor processes" (*216*, I, 46), "are the physical side of, or, as I prefer to say, form the anatomical substrata of, mental states (*ibid.*, I, 59)—"the anatomical basis of mind" (*ibid.*, II, 91).[44] Finally, "the highest centres are the anatomical substrata of consciousness." [45] It is through this kind of purely neurological approach, initiated by Hughlings Jackson and so generally adopted by his successors, that we arrive at the limited conclusions with reference to the locus, conditions, content and dynamic basis which underlie consciousness and the other epiphenomena we consider in Section G.[46]

This completed picture enables us to see the third characteristic of the hierarchical organization in its proper light. Control from above must not be conceived to be autonomous. It is, of course, itself a response of the higher center to some influence, continuous or temporary. This influence may itself be excitation over a long-circuited arc.[47] Or, on the other hand, it may also be entirely independent of the current excitation which is ap-

---

ticularity of ends and the appropriateness of the way these ends are served (see *215*, 127; *216*, I, 374; II, 432).

But integration, which increases along with the specialization resulting from differentiation, also serves this purpose; for the highest are also "unifying centres," "whereby the organism *as a whole* is adjusted to the environment" (*216*, II, 82).

[42] See Jackson, *216*, I, 60–61. His view of inevitability *vs.* uncertainty is outlined in *ibid.*, II, 81. The lowest centers, because they are most organized, easily transmit accustomed stimuli but resist novel stimuli, "acting in ways they have been trained to act in and resisting new ways of acting." The highest, while they "have to be forced into activity," are also, because they are least organized, "capable of being forced into new kinds of activity." At the lower levels movements are "fatally necessary"; at the higher, there is no absolute connection. At the lower levels, movements follow "with no or with little delay"; at the higher, they "will not be immediate" (I, 61).

[43] Jackson, *216*, II, 91. This includes and even emphasizes the vegetative functions.

[44] And here, as well as elsewhere, "what are physiologically reflex actions are anatomically sensori-motor arrangements" (*216*, I, 239), though, here, they are "imperfect" (I, 60).

[45] Jackson, *216*, II, 42; *215*, 127; and elsewhere. And specifically, according to his earlier definition of the highest level, the "physical basis of consciousness" is the "highest motor centres (prae-frontal lobes)" and the "highest sensory centres (occipital lobes)" (*216*, II, 79). As we shall show in Section G, while his concept still seems correct, his localization of consciousness does not seem to accord with the most recent evidence.

[46] For a comparison of Hughlings Jackson's views on "mental states" with various other theories, see supplementary statement on "The Thinking Process," at the end of this section.

[47] As Jackson puts it (*216*, II, 73), "Roughly speaking, the highest nervous states are determined from below, and not by autocratic faculties acting upon the highest parts of the highest centre."

pearing on the afferent side at some lower center and which is endeavoring to be "short-circuited" or "long-circuited." [48] Thus we qualify our picture by recurring again to the statement in Chapter 1 that all afferent impulses are projected into a complicated and variegated status of excitation and inhibition, produced by the concurrent effect of innumerable different influences, and existing throughout an interconnected (integrated) hierarchical system to which the new element adds but a single factor.[49] As Gasser puts it (*168*, 172), "Ultimately excitation in a pool of neurons is dependent upon everything which is taking place in the nervous system anywhere."

If these characteristics of the hierarchical organization of the central nervous system are recognized, it must become clear that this system is no longer susceptible of being precisely divided either along functional lines determined by peripheral sources (afferent) or peripheral effects (efferent), or along anatomical lines determined by the anatomical arrangement of peripheral nerves or even fibers. And this because the very nature of a hierarchical organization argues that these peripherally separate systems merge more and more as one proceeds to higher levels in the central nervous system, and that, after such merger, they become one or at least indistinguishable. For this reason we shall have difficulty with the customary classificatory nomenclature.

The afferent side of the nervous system as a whole has been divided by Sherrington, largely on a functional basis, into three sections according to the receptive field each serves. To follow his original classification, which is convenient, the interoceptive includes the visceral and vascular afferents; the proprioceptive includes the afferents from skeletal muscle and labyrinth, and the exteroceptive includes the afferents from cutaneous and distance receptors.[50] The distance receptors are the "projicient" senses, ocular, auditory and olfactory. Correspondingly, and also on functional

[48] To quote Jackson again (*216*, I, 375), "As evolution progresses the higher centres not only gradually develop (become increasingly complex, etc.) but also become more and more detached from, and more independent of, the lower centres out of which they have been evolved." Nevertheless, it is not true that there is "a coordinating centre" which "stands outside or above the centres which are for impressions and movements and autocratically governs them, regulates them." "The substrata of consciousness are sensorimotor arrangements re-representing all lower centres, and thus representing the whole organism. They govern it not autocratically, but *because* they represent it." "They *are* the organism in potentiality, giving out impulses to most heterogeneous movements, because they receive most heterogeneous impressions." So when this highest level loses its control, co-ordination is affected, "not from want of autocratic goverance, but from actual lack of the higher co-ordinations" (i.e., the special movements themselves) (*216*, I, 160).

[49] The "functions of every center are dependent on its anatomical relations to the rest of the intact nervous system" (Goldstein's thesis quoted by Lashley, *262*, 386). Not only this, but the functioning of each is dependent on what is going on in every other interconnected part. As Lashley suggests (*ibid.*, 386–387), this may be the basis of the physiological necessity of localization. That is, "incompatible mechanisms," which cannot function in the same nerve field without interference, must exist as separate and to a large extent disconnected centers.

[50] The sense of taste appears to be included by him in the interoceptive section. Others regard it as exteroceptive.

grounds, Cannon has divided the efferent side into the exterofective and the interofective systems. This, too, is convenient. In the former he includes all efferents to striated (skeletal) muscle, in the latter all efferents to smooth muscle and glands. The interofective system corresponds to the anatomical entity which, in its peripheral appearance, is called the "autonomic" nervous system with its two, or three, sections, thoracolumbar, or sympathetic, and craniosacral, or parasympathetic. The exterofective system corresponds to the motor portion, strictly speaking, of the anatomical division known as the sensorimotor (or cerebrospinal). If one follows a practice which is gaining favor and defines the autonomic as wholly efferent,[51] then all three of Sherrington's functional divisions of the receptive system correspond to the afferent side of the sensorimotor system. But it should be understood that, even outside the central nervous system, none of these functional divisions corresponds precisely with the actual nerves as they are observed anatomically, with the result that the functional distinctions have been imposed, in part by inference, within single structural entities. Within the central nervous system, the specific fibers mediating different functions are frequently difficult to trace, and sometimes it becomes impossible to assign known centers to any particular anatomical division of the peripheral system. Also it is beginning to appear that, even functionally, the distinctions are not as clear-cut as was at one time supposed. Even at the periphery the distinction between one of the three outflows of the autonomic (sympathetic) and the other two (parasympathetic), when applied functionally, is becoming blurred in spots.[52] And, in the central nervous system, it is becoming increasingly apparent that the interofective as a whole and the exterofective as a whole, far from being independent of each other, are intimately related at many points. We shall see some of the evidence for this when we consider the brain-stem. But even in the spinal cord Langworthy (*251*, 617) holds that the autonomic efferents are subject to afferent stimuli at any level of integration and that these "local reflexes through the spinal cord are an admixture of somatic and visceral elements"—in fact, so indistinguishable are these elements that, he says, "the designation of sensory fibers which run in autonomic nerve trunks as visceral afferents is to me unjustifiable." Finally, it is no longer possible to define the whole afferent side as functionally sensory; [53] for it is known that the impulses over many tracts cannot, and many patterns

[51] Bard, for instance, takes this position (*19*, 267, and *24*, 176). Since the visceral afferents have their cell bodies in sensory ganglia of cranial and spinal nerves (*ibid.*) and since they affect both skeletal muscle and visceral effectors (*24*), he considers that they belong in the cerebrospinal system (sensorimotor). Langworthy (*251*, 617) also holds that the autonomic is purely motor.

We have already discussed this question on pp. 60 to 61 and note 57. It seems to be entirely a matter of definition. We have therefore confined ourselves to the use of the term "visceral afferents," which does not take sides.

[52] For instance the antithesis between chemical mediation via sympathin and via acetylcholine has already run into difficulties (see Myerson, *309*). A number of other discrepancies will be mentioned as we proceed.

[53] "Sensory," with the meaning of ordinary speech—i.e., associated with sensation.

or intensities of impulses over many other tracts do not, reach the level where sensation is produced.

All this is but an exemplification of the hierarchical organization. For if, for instance, one names individually the branches of a tree with twin trunks, one will find difficulty in determining which branch shall give its name to either trunk. If one divides the Roman Catholic Church into the European and the overseas branches, to which branch shall one assign the Pope at Rome? Nevertheless, even if we do not always identify thereby a specific anatomical entity, it remains convenient to distinguish (1) between that function of the afferent system which consists in the transmission of the neural effects of movements or postures of the body itself (proprioceptive), that one which consists in the transmission of the neural effects of changes in the internal environment (interoceptive), and that one which covers the maintenance of contact with the external environment (exteroceptive); and to distinguish (2) between that function of the efferent system which results in bodily movement (exterofective) and that one which is concerned with the neural management of all other bodily functions (interofective).[54]

The "Levels" of the Nervous System. Hughlings Jackson was accustomed to speak of three levels, the lowest, the middle, and the highest; but he finally admitted (*216*, II, 425) "that the scheme of three levels is incomplete" and he actually recognized five:

1) "The periphery is the real lowest level" (*ibid.*, II, 78)—that is, there are "four levels," of which the "strictly lowest" comprises the extraspinal centers in the autonomic, the peripheral ganglia, and the ganglia of the posterior roots of the spinal cord (I, 349), and perhaps the olfactory and optic systems (II, 425).

2) He usually defines his "lowest level" (e.g., II, 80) as "any centre, bulbar or spinal, which represents a part of the body most nearly directly and in simplest ways," or (I, 372 and 413) as "all centres [i.e., in medulla and pons as well as cord] from and to which spinal and cranial nerves come and go." In effect, this includes (1) above. At first he says "I do not pretend to be able to define the upper limit of this level" (I, 413). But when, finally in his 1897 Hughlings Jackson lecture (II, 424), he defines the lowest level as extending "from the tuber cinereum to the conus medullaris," he is obliged to recognize, without treating them as a separate level, a different set of centers in the same region.

3) These are his earlier "regulating" centers, which he then thought might be "simply recombinations of elements of" simple nuclei (*216*, I, 349), but which he admitted, in 1897, to be "superior centres" representing muscles indirectly by the intermediation of those centers strictly composing his lowest level, or (2) above. These are the respiratory center and probably centers governing intestinal action, defecation, micturition, the sexual act, parturition, etc.

4) He defines his "middle level" variously as the Rolandic centers of the cortex (*215*, 120–121), the sensorimotor region of Rolando (*216*, I, 349), or

[54] Thus, for the most part, our use of these terms will be strictly in their functional sense and not as anatomical divisions.

as "Ferrier's motor region, with the ganglia of the corpus striatum, and also of his sensory region" (*216*, II, 79).

5) At first his "highest region" consists of "highest motor centres (prae-frontal lobes), and of highest sensory centres (occipital lobes)." The former is defined (*216*, II, 424) as the "region in front of the pre-central sulcus." But, as to the latter, already in 1884 he has "misgivings" (*ibid.*, II, 79); and as to this as well as the sensory parts of the middle level he has become, in 1897, uncertain (II, 424), and concludes, "of the middle and highest levels at least," their "so-called motor provinces" "are supposed to be only *chiefly motor* and their sensory provinces only *chiefly sensory*." This will be of interest to us as we proceed. At least on the motor side, the distinction between the middle and highest level was clear (I, 414). The middle level is connected with the lowest, contains most large cells and is experimentally excitable, while the prefrontal (highest) is not. Nevertheless, as we shall note, the highest level is, in Jackson's opinion, purely sensorimotor like the rest. Finally, we should note that Jackson's whole scheme is based on "degree of indirectness," not on morphological divisions (I, 349).

In the light of more recent studies but, also, on the basis of indirection, Tower (*405*, 443–444) has outlined a somewhat different scheme of four levels. These are (1) the segmental (spinal), (2) the lower brain-stem, (3) the upper brain-stem, or thalamic, and (4) the cortical. The second projects only on the first; the third projects only upon the second; but the fourth projects upon all three lower levels. In the first, presumably, she would include Jackson's (1) and the suprasegmental origins of peripheral nerves, as he does. Perhaps she would subdivide her fourth in the light of Jackson's distinction between his middle and highest, since the projections of the two parts seem to be wholly different. At any rate her second and third are important improvements.

The Thinking Process. Since Hughlings Jackson's views of the neurological basis of the thinking process, of the state of consciousness which generally attends some part of it, and of the other psychological processes whose existence we recognize from introspection, is the ground of our statements in Section G, in the text and in Chapters 5 and 6, it may be well here to enlarge on the brief statements of Jackson's which have been quoted above. As has been said he was the "father of neurology." His views, derived from direct observation of nervous and mental disease and wide-ranging studies of the work of his contemporaries, contended primarily against the current dualism. Hence his emphasis on what appears superficially to be psycho-physical parallelism. More exactly, his contention was that only the objective aspect of these processes is available to a scientific observer. Therefore, he talks in terms of this aspect only. "States of consciousness are assumed . . . to be merely concomitant with certain nervous states" (*216*, I, 367). "Consciousness has, of course, anatomical substrata, as much as speech or any other mental operation has." "These substrata are sensori-motor processes" (II, 186). So "states of consciousness attend activities of parts of this [sensori-motor] mechanism" (II, 29). Such activities are only the most special of nervous processes. Therefore, they occur in "those parts of the brain, where the most special of all nervous processes lie" (I, 186); that is in the "highest cerebral centres" (II, 400) at the "highest level" (*215*, 127). But, at any time, consciousness "arises during activity of *some*," only, of our highest nervous arrangements (*216*, I, 242). He did not suppose "one fixed seat of consciousness," nor that it is "an unvarying independent entity" (*loc. cit.*). The "nervous substrata cannot be the very same at each moment."

But even the location of consciousness within the highest level at any time is an anatomical problem (*216*, I, 241–242). Whether the active physical state produced by an impression "leads to further physical changes attended by a conscious state (that is, to a sensation) or not depends partly on the height of the centre which the current developed reaches and partly perhaps on the *amount* of disturbance it provokes there" (*216*, I, 238). In addition to height of transit and intensity, the third requirement is delay. If the connection between "impression" and "motion" is "organized," the action is a simple or compound reflex, and there is no consciousness. "If the . . . connection is not organized, then the psychical changes which come between the impressions and motions are conscious ones" (*216*, I, 111). Apparently, though, these changes that occur between are, in his view, at the same time sensory and motor. Thus, while there are, here and there, some slightly contradictory statements, I think it is correct to state that Jackson's view was that the substrata of ideation and of consciousness are combined sensorimotor action and neither sensory action nor motor action alone (see *216*, I, 171). And this in spite of the fact that he says he "adopts" Bain's "outgoing" theory. For he does that in order to include the efferent side directly in consciousness and not on the supposition that "motor sensation" has been rerouted back into consciousness through the afferent system (i.e. kinesthetic is not for him proprioceptive).

The view that the essential for thinking and consciousness is "delay" is presented in Chapter 2, Section D. It seems to me to accord also with the view of Lashley (*260*, 11), who believes that certain experiments "point to some continued neural process as the basis of thinking"—that is, "long-continued intraneural sequence of activity" (*ibid.*, 10), or "continuously maintained central processes" (*ibid.*, 12). When we develop it more fully, it will also seem to coincide to some extent with Freud's suggestion that consciousness arises in place of the memory trace (engram)—that is, that the memory trace is a lasting alteration, while consciousness only occurs where there is none as yet (*156*, 28). Bianchi (*35*, 309) makes this delay, and therefore consciousness, hinge on conflict (of ideas or impulses). Thus, since with "lower animals conduct occurs without internal conflict" it is unconscious. In men "consciousness culminates in deliberation." We shall consider this feature further in Section G.

However, the view that thinking and consciousness are always at one time sensory and motor (or neither) is not in accord with what may be called the "motor school." Thus, to Holt (*206*, 60) thought is the preceding "lambent interplay of motor attitudes, in which some *one* finally gains the ascendancy, and goes over into overt conduct." Thus "the one difference between thought and will is the difference between a motor attitude prepared and one that is touched off" (*loc. cit.*); and this difference is due to a difference in "the intensity of the nerve impulse that plays through the sensori-motor arcs" (*ibid.*, 98). As to just where or how far, on the motor side, this process reaches and how consciousness is connected with it, there are wide differences of opinion.

Kempf (*233*, 22) and others hold that "we think with our muscles" that is, with those which would be involved in the action, though usually not by overt contractions—and that the effect on consciousness is via "kinesthetic" impulses (i.e., sensory and rerouted back). So Freeman (*152*, 140) and Thorson in *J. Exper. Psychol.* (1925), 1. But is there any need for carrying the process so far toward the periphery? The motor tracts in and from the cortex are wholly central and are to be distinguished from the motor neurons (final common paths) issuing from the brain-stem or the spinal cord, which actually activate the muscles. Frolov (*157*, 7) says of Sechenov (Pavlov's predecessor and the "father of Russian physiology"), "thought, according to Sechenov's view is nothing but an 'inhibited' reflex, i.e. a reflex which had lost its last part"—that is, one which, being subliminal or for some other reason, failed to activate the final common path at all. But on this basis the relation to consciousness could not be attained by kinesthetic impulses over the only afferent system from the muscles that we know (proprioceptive), for this only responds to actual tension.

Watson's original proposal (*429*, 310–347, and elsewhere) developed the idea that thinking is "implicit language habit" (i.e., "silent talking," *ibid.*, 323) or subvocal speech. Frolov (*157*, 78 ff.) attributes to Pavlov the thesis that there are two levels of thinking and that Watson's thinking occurs in the sensorimotor areas along the central fissure, while abstract thinking occurs in the prefrontal area, where it "may bear no trace of muscular [i.e. motor] character." But there are equal objections to this view. Watson's thinking is motor, not sensorimotor; and what, pray, is abstract thinking in neurological (objective) terms?

Jackson was most explicit on this subject (*216*, II, 131–132): "Speech is a *part* of thought—a part which we may or may not exteriorise." "For its *character as speech* it matters nothing whether the proposition be said to oneself or aloud." "Verbal thinking" is merely subliminal speech; while speaking aloud reaches the articulatory and vocal muscles. But, "it is not well to say that thought is internal speech, for the man who is speechless (the man who has no internal speech) can think." True, neither can he "express himself in writing." Nevertheless, "speechlessness does not imply wordlessness"; for the speechless man can understand words of others; he "can receive propositions, but he cannot form them."

As to the nature of "silent talking," though Jackson stated earlier that "the anatomical substrata of words represent articulatory movements" (*216*, I, 51) he came to call them later (II, 139) "audito-articulatory" (that is, sensory as well as motor). But he concluded (II, 142) that "the greater part of our intellectual operations is carried on in [visual] images—in eye-derived, or, as we call them, retino-ocular processes"—thus also sensory (retino-) and motor (ocular) (see also II, 439–440). The latter is "making 'propositions of objects'" just as the whole of the former is making propositions of words (II, 140). If it is true that the greater part of our thinking is visual, it is impossible to accept the limitation of thinking to "silent talking"; and if it is true that "words" are auditory as well as articulatory and that "images" are ocular (motor) as well as retinal (sensory) then, practically, thinking is at one and the same time sensory and motor. Even among those who have adopted the recent view of thinking (and consciousness) as motor, perhaps most would agree with Tolman (*403*, 236–239) that the general view should not be "jeopardized" by assuming either motor discharges or a necessary relation to language.

In Jackson's time the general view was precisely the opposite. "Many appear to hold that the material substratum of mind is made up entirely of afferent nerves and their centres" (*216*, I, 53). Neither would he admit that ideas are purely sensory. They are always sensorimotor (I, 53–56). To define patterns of central excitation, which are, at the same time, the consequence of afferent impulses (current or prior) and the potential cause of efferent impulses, as either sensory or motor seems to me wholly illogical unless it is assumed that, at some single point, they change from sensory to motor. Since that assumption is anatomically untrue, we must fall back on defining all such patterns, while they remain in the intermediate stage, as both sensory and motor or neither. Either choice conforms in effect to Jackson's contention. Moreover, it effectively disposes of all disputes between "ingoing" and "outgoing" theories, since it makes the two of them one. The whole sensorimotor (or central) pattern of excitation in some area must *be* the sensation.

B. SUBCORTICAL MANAGEMENT OF VEGETATIVE FUNCTIONS

In line with the concept of levels within a hierarchically organized central nervous system, as propounded by Hughlings Jackson and presented in the preceding section, we shall proceed to consider some samples of the ways in which the "internal milieu" is controlled by the lowest level and, thereafter, successively, by higher levels superimposed upon that. The adoption of any particular scheme of levels is more or less arbitrary. But it will be convenient here to divide the subcortical system roughly into three levels; (1) the spinal, which must include both the nuclei giving rise to the cranial nerves, though these are actually supraspinal, and also the extraspinal ganglia of the autonomic system; (2) the lower brain-stem, including the rest of the bulb, pons, and lower midbrain; and (3) the upper brain-stem, which, as a functional division, seems to reach from some level in the midbrain through and beyond the region of the thalamus and, as to other than vegetative functions, may include the corpus striatum (the body of the endbrain).[1]

By "vegetative functions" are meant the "fundamental metabolic processes, endocrine activity, viscero-motor mechanisms, vaso-motor phenomena, etc." (Le Gros Clark, *84*, 413) as contrasted to the animal or motor functions. While, at the periphery, this conforms to the distinction between the autonomic and the motor nervous systems, we shall see that, centrally, the interofective and the exterofective functions become more and more combined or interdependent, so that motor behavior is incidental to vegetative functions, or these, in turn, accompany or result from motor behavior. Nevertheless, since even among the higher centers the distinction remains to some degree, so that all are either primarily interofective or primarily exterofective, we can more readily analyze them separately and consider the influence of each on the other (their synthesis) as incidental.

1. SPINAL

Fulton (*160*, 130) considers that "the classical account of the visceral reactions of spinal animals which has never been superseded" is that of Sherrington."[2] Those which concern micturition and defecation have

[1] All these, it will be noted, compose Hughlings Jackson's "lowest level"—that is, 2) in "The Levels of the Nervous System," above; our levels conform rather to Towers 1), 2), and 3) (see *loc. cit.*).

[2] In Schäfer's *Text-Book of Physiology* (Edinburgh, 1900), II, 849–856.

already been considered in Appendix I, Section C, and in a way which conforms on the whole to Sherrington's and to Fulton's accounts (*160*, 132–133 and 135–138). In these two cases our present knowledge indicates that the mechanism is entirely neural and consists either of intramural or of spinal reflexes in so far as it is contained within the lowest level. The short-circuited function, at least of micturition, is then performed somewhat inadequately; that is, it normally requires facilitation from above.[3] In the case of animals, the process is accompanied by its normal associated movements (posture and *nettoyage*). Therefore, the efferent path includes not only the interofective (autonomic) but also the exterofective (motor).

With regard to those reflexes which concern sexual activities the picture is not so clear. From the evidence of animal cases, after spinal transection or destruction, as reported by Sherrington and others,[4] it appears that complete coition reactions, including those of the voluntary musculature, can be induced in spinal animals, both male and female, by local manipulation—that is, spinal reflexes are apparently sufficient for coition, gestation, and parturition in the female, and for erection, ejaculation, and the copulatory posture (motor) in the male. Fulton concludes from this (*160*, 131) "that the patterns of sexual behavior are laid down in the spinal cord." But this conclusion is open to two objections. In the first place, to start the reflex by local manipulation, which was the afferent stimulus in all these cases, was beginning artificially in the middle of the normal process; for, normally, local manipulation never occurs (except in the unwilling human female) until after behavior (perhaps a prolonged sequence) has been initiated which has brought the male and female together, has produced the appropriate postures and even, usually, has already caused erection in the male. Thus these observed activities actually fall far short of effective mating behavior (Bard, *23*, 557). In the second place, spinal transection leaves the brain intact, though neurally disconnected. Therefore, the observed activities may not be entirely short-circuited spinal reflexes, but these may be reinforced or supplemented by other non-neural mechanisms. That they are not purely spinal is indicated by Bard's results; for, when all above the lower third of the midbrain is removed, "only the merest fragments of normal sexual behavior are elicitable" (*23*, 562), and some of these, in the female, are no longer certainly sexual (i.e., rather "non-specific items of response," *ibid.*, 557). Thus the effects of decerebration and of spinal transection are quite different. Doubtless among the long series of acts and activities which constitute sexual behavior (lasting in the female for months), there are many individual ones which represent short-circuiting of purely spinal—or even

[3] Langworthy and Hesser (*253*, 213) state that the isolated spinal cord causes vesical contractions too short to empty the bladder.

[4] Sherrington in Schäfer's *Text-Book of Physiology*, II, 851 ff.; for others see Fulton, *160*, 130–131. Riddoch (*343*, 264) found that his spinal man (like Goltz's dog) showed the coitus reflex, including erection and motion of the testicles and the abdominal muscles.

intramural—patterns as well as others, which are due to local vascular, not neural, transmission. On the other hand, it is equally certain that the normal initiation of the whole series lies in the supraspinal centers and presumably in those of the upper brain-stem.[5]

Among other interofective reflexes capable of being short-circuited are the pilomotor, palmar galvanic, sudorific, and vasomotor. As to the first, which, when short-circuited, is a response to cutaneous stimulation by scratching or cold, Brickner (*44*) concludes from its overaction after interruption of the spinal cord that it is a release phenomenon (i.e., normally inhibited from above). Schwartz (*365*) has obtained the palmar galvanic reflex via the stellate ganglion of the sympathetic system with no central connection (*ibid.*, 603). Since the adequate stimulus is deep pressure, the afferent segment of the arc is probably via fibers from the blood vessels or deep-lying tissues of the limb. No conclusion was reached as to whether the normal influence of the central connection is inhibiting or facilitating. On the other hand, since they disappear during spinal shock (Fulton, *160*, 133 and 139), it is apparent that general sweating and vasoconstrictor responses are normally controlled (and facilitated) from higher centers. Ultimately, after spinal transection, there is a reappearance of vasoconstrictor reflexes of which the afferent segment of the arc is an afferent nerve caudal to the lesion. And, at least as a part of the mass reflex (any local stimulus), when that occurs, paroxysmal sweating is observed below the level of the lesion.

2. LOWER BRAIN-STEM

The reader will recall that Hughlings Jackson supposed "superior and subordinate centres of the lowest level for the 'menial work'"[6] of each of the vegetative systems. The superior centers he regarded as regulative of the subordinate. Thus they constitute our second level, and we shall expect to find them dealing only indirectly with the periphery through the medium of the spinal (and cranial nerve) centers. On page 1026 we have already noted the conclusion of Langworthy and his associates that there exist, in the midbrain, centers for controlling the tone of all smooth muscle similar to those in the same region which, as we shall note later, do so for the striated musculature. It appears from their evidence that one center, around the inferior colliculi, not only controls the tonic contraction but prolongs the phasic contraction of the bladder. It is directly or indirectly under at least inhibitory control from still higher levels. This center seems to operate upon lower ones (spinal and intramural), which themselves are also eventually capable of responding to bladder stretch, but more frequently (less adaptation) and more briefly (incomplete

[5] Bard (*23*) states that "it is apparent that supraspinal levels are prepotent in the elaboration of the sexual behavior" of "male carnivores," at least (*ibid.*, 557). But his experiments show that this level is above the lower third of the midbrain. His report indicates that this is even more true of the female (cat).

[6] Jackson, *215*, 135.

emptying).[7] Thus the relation of this center to those below seems to be complex. The afferent segment of the arc which reaches it from below supposedly conducts, from the detrusor muscle itself, impulses which are normally long-circuited past the lower centers. We also suggested (p. 1032) the probability of centers in the lower brain-stem having analogous controls over intestinal and rectal contractions. Since the former (being vagal) are not depressed by spinal transection, but the latter (being spinal) are, one infers that these centers normally excite or facilitate their corresponding functions. And this seems to be confirmed, and direct inhibitory control from above established, by the results of decerebration on these activities.[8] Similarly these centers are presumably excited from below only by the stretch of smooth muscle in the intestine and rectum, which sets up afferent impulses that normally by-pass the lower centers.

From Bard's experiments (*23*, 559 and 563) one would infer the absence, at this second level, of any important centers concerned with sexual functions. As noted above, decerebration seems to depress all purely sexual reflexes and to leave other forms of usually associated behavior unrecognizable as purely sexual. Presumably this also demonstrates what is possible by way of spinal (still lower) reflexes alone.

"The most essential cardiac and vasomotor centers are situated in the bulbar and pontile portions of the brain stem" (Bazett, *28*, 471 and Fulton, *160*, 168). They are entirely adequate to keep the blood pressure and the heart rate within the normal narrow limits (Bronk *et al.*, *46*, 327). The cardiovascular reflexes are, in general, mediated here (Bard, *24*, 184) even though they may be modified by the influence of higher centers responding to other afferent excitors and exerted here. Furthermore, these centers operate upon the extraspinal ganglia of the autonomic system. But they are subject to afferent impulses from the periphery (i.e., the pressure receptors in the carotid sinus and aorta) which cannot reach these lower centers. In other words, there is evidenced here integration on the afferent side as well as long-circuiting.

As an example of a center (or a combination of centers) at this level which represents further integration on the afferent side, in that it responds to excitors which do not reach the lower centers, and which also represents differentiation, in that it has available an effector pattern which cannot be produced by lower centers, we may cite the gastric motor center. There is a center for blood sugar mobilization in the lower pontile region

[7] Root (*355*), following Barrington, seems to assume that the arcs of the reflexes whose center is in this region are independent of the spinal arcs both on the afferent and the efferent side. But, in view of automatic micturition, this can hardly be the case. Perhaps it is merely a case where the normal procedure is long-circuiting.

[8] The usual transection or ablation called decerebration, I assume from Fulton (*160*, 152–153), would leave intact the lower midbrain centers (inferior colliculi, at least) while severing the projections to them from above. Though he seems to assume a higher or lower level for such centers (interbrain or hindbrain), he infers their existence to explain the fact, as "those who have worked with decerebrate cats know," that they are likely to defecate soon after decerebration (construed as a release phenomenon); see Fulton, *159*, 177.

(Bard, *24*, 184). Presumably this operates on the liver through the adrenal medulla. Perhaps it responds to the condition of its own blood supply. Responsive to the same local (humoral) influence, and therefore perhaps in the same region, is the center, already referred to, which increases gastric activity in response to hypoglycemia, an influence which probably has no effect on (or does not reach) the extraspinal ganglia capable of producing ordinary gastric contractions. But here, or near here, there is also a gastric motor center for those peculiar gastric, esophagal, etc., movements known as vomiting. This is a reaction "foreign to the spinal animal" (Fulton, *160*, 150). It can be produced by long-circuiting afferent impulses from the stomach, which may not be, and perhaps cannot become, sensory (pain; Weiss and Davis, *436*, 532–533), by stimulation of the floor of the fourth ventricle (its location) or even manipulation of the medulla (Fulton, *160*, 167), as well as by afferent impulses from the vestibular nuclei near by (ask any poor sailor).

One of the most typical hierarchies, while unimportant in itself, will be referred to again as we proceed to consider the higher levels because it may be typical. That is the mechanism controlling the nictitating membrane in cats, which has been studied by Morison and Rioch (*307*). They find the lowest center of their "excitatory component" in the medulla near the pons. This membrane is proximately controlled by the cervical sympathetic through its extraspinal ganglia.

3. UPPER BRAIN-STEM

In respect of vegetative functions it is hardly too much to say that the level we have now reached—in what is sometimes called the "old brain"—is the *highest* level. Its chief effector portion is the hypothalamus, which is "the head ganglion of the vegetative nervous system" (Riddoch, *344*, 117). It is therefore of the first importance in our study of the want system, and we shall have to give it a more extended examination—particularly in view of the fact that its exploration is only recent.[9] We shall hereafter refer to it as the hypothalamus, as most of our authorities do, or as the hypothalamic region. But this is notice to the reader that we are including in that term whatever anatomical entities turn out to be parts of this functional whole—that is, the whole region to which will ultimately be ascribed the highest re-representation in the subcortical brain of all these functions. At present the limits of this region are not precisely defined.[10] At any

[9] "Knowledge of the functions of the hypothalamus is recent" (Fulton, *160*, 232). Chiefly, says Le Gros Clark (*84*, 407) because of the difficulty of applying experimental methods at the base of the brain. While, more than a decade ago, Harvey Cushing (*100*, 39) spoke of "the tendency to overload the third ventricle [diencephalon] with functional responsibilities," it must be conceded now that brain surgery and new experimental techniques have proved this region to be even more important than was then admitted.

[10] The functional unit probably includes other morphological entities besides the hypothalamus proper, even trespasses on other parts of the brain-stem below the interbrain, and may reach into an anomalous region rostral to the hypothalamus proper. As

rate, the region which is fundamental in discussions of the hypothalamus is a "small division of the brain" (Ranson, *332*, 241) [11] which, with the hypophysis, forms "a neuroglandular mechanism as a functional unit" (Le Gros Clark, *86*, 34) and "comprises a neural [and hormonal] apparatus through which are controlled and regulated the vegetative functions of the organism as represented by fundamental metabolic processes, endocrine activity,[12] viscero-motor mechanisms, vasomotor phenomena, etc." (Le Gros Clark, *84*, 413).[13] It "mediates the integration of visceral impulses [from the afferent side] and plays an essential part in the control of the internal milieu of the organism" (*ibid.*, 414). In other words, "the physiology of the hypothalamus is the physiology of the internal environment" (Beattie, *30*, 70).

"The hypothalamus is the chief center for the sympathetic system" (Ranson, *332*, 252).[14] Probably it occupies the same position with relation to the parasympathetic system, if this peripheral distinction can be carried so high.[15] At least, "every aspect of autonomic activity is related in

---

Le Gros Clark says (*86*, 5), "The rostral and caudal limits of the hypothalamus are ill-defined, since it passes over without any sharp demarcation into the parolfactory region in front and into the tegmental part of the mid-brain behind. Its lateral limits are similarly vague, for here it becomes directly continuous with the subthalamus." See also, for instance, Crosby and Woodburne (*97*, 81) and Riddoch (*344*, 191). It is perhaps best described, in another connection, by Bard (*23*, 566) as the "cerebral territory comprising the preoptic and septal areas, a part of the thalamus, the subthalamus, the hypothalamus and the upper portions of the midbrain." To this should be added the hypophysis.

[11] Le Gros Clark refers to "the hypothalamus, where functional mechanisms of the highest importance seem to be crowded together into an astonishingly limited space" (*86*, 1). But we would expect it to be small, for, in spite of the importance of its functions and the energy with which it can act, its reaction patterns are comparatively few (i.e., it evidences little of Hughlings Jackson's differentiation). It is also conservative. "Throughout the whole vertebrate scale there is no part of the forebrain that has maintained so constant a general arrangement" (Fulton, *160*, 234). However, Morgan finds one distinction in man, one nucleus of this region more highly developed which favors discriminating and sustained co-ordination of vegetative function (*304*, 768).

[12] The hypothalamus probably controls the hypophysis, and Cushing (*100*, 20) called the hypophysis "the 'moderator' of the endocrine series."

[13] It is worthy of note that the Scharrers (*360*, 170) suggest the possibility that, in some of these nuclei, the nerve cells themselves may have a glandular function.

[14] This conclusion is general. See also Fulton and Sherrington, *164*, 246, 259; Bard, *18*, 492; Cannon, *68*, 260.

[15] Part of the argument as to this question concerns the location of the centers which might be parasympathetic (i.e., whether these are, or are all, in the anterior hypothalamus or are, with one exception—bladder contraction—in the preoptic area). This question is not of great importance for us. See Bard (*24*, 193) for a statement in regard to it. See also Kabat *et al.* (*229*, 954 and *230*, 236) *vs.* Beattie (*30*, 100). But Riddoch (*344*, 101) cites Beattie in an earlier article (1932) in support of the assignment of the preoptic region to the parasympathetic, the posterior hypothalamus to the sympathetic and the supraoptic-infundibular group of nuclei (connected with the hypophysis) to both. Perhaps this compromise is nearest right.

The rest of the argument concerns the question whether either region belongs precisely or exclusively to either part of the autonomic system—or, as I would express it, whether the two peripheral divisions remain divided at this, their highest level. The best viewpoint seems to be that the region is not composed of discrete centers, either ana-

some way to the hypothalamus or the portion of brain immediately anterior to it" (Beattie, *30*, 69). Thus, upon the efferent side, integration of the interofective nervous system appears here to be complete. Not only that, but it appears that there is also concentrated here the highest control over the endocrine system, which is perhaps the principal effector agency through that other integrating channel, the blood. Thus, on the effector side, we have integration of the two chief integrating systems themselves. We shall examine shortly the degree to which interoceptive (neural) integration is also completed here. But at this point we should note that very exceptional vascularity, in one part, and exceptionally intimate blood supply, for the whole, argue that, on the upcoming side also, this region is the place where integration of the two integrators takes place. As a whole, this portion of the brain is "situated most advantageously with regard to its arterial blood supply," because it is surrounded by the circle of Willis (Le Gros Clark, *86*, 43). Moreover, the vascularity of one part —the supraoptic and, to a lesser extent, the paraventricular, nuclei—is greater than that of any other part of the brain.[16] These anatomical facts support the belief that, here, integration of both *internal* centripetal mechanisms as well as of the interofective outgoing mechanism is complete.

As would be expected of the highest level, even of the vegetative system alone, the peculiar characteristic of responses mediated at this level is the extent of their patterns (integration) and their increased variety (differentiation). But, in spite of this integration, it is also possible experimentally to single out centers (or tracts) which reach one region of the body only.[17] To what extent, then, the centers of this level produce ex-

tomically or physiologically, since stimulation of minute areas has widespread effects and mixed results in the two peripheral divisions of the autonomic system (Beattie, *30*, 69). This may indicate that the cell groups do not have each a single specific function (Morgan, *304*, 765, and Beattie, *30*, 100). Rather it is a "dual mechanism," one part of which can activate the parasympathetic, and the other part the sympathetic portion of the autonomic nervous system, which parts have two distinct afferent and efferent systems of paths, but which are nevertheless functionally integrated here by a reciprocal mechanism (Beattie, *30*, 69). But, better still is the way Langworthy puts it (*251*, *617*). "At the higher levels of integration there is representation of function and not of sympathetic or parasympathetic relays." On this basis we can construe the anterior region "as being chiefly concerned with growth, nutrition, and the accumulation of energy," while the posterior region "is principally concerned with the mobilization and discharge of energy" (Morgan, *304*, 766). In general, when one is activated the other is inhibited (not by peripheral antagonism but by central co-ordination,—i.e., reciprocal inhibition; see Beattie, *30*, 100). Thus they serve together a "broader co-ordinating function" (i.e., there is localized here only "reaction patterns"—Rioch, in discussion, *286*, 284) and the "specific functions are controlled by lower centers in the brain stem and spinal cord" (Morgan, *304*, 765). Moreover, "the hypophysis is part of this dual mechanism, being partially controlled by and partly controlling it" (Beattie, *30*, 100).

[16] Bard, *24*, 190; Le Gros Clark, *85*, 110; K. H. Finley, *140*, 307; and E. H. Craigie, *95*, 317. The notion that this consisted of hypophyseo-portal veins has, according to Ranson (*332*, 242), been disposed of by Wislocki and King (*445*, 452; see also Wislocki, *444*, 386).

[17] There is evidence for this—chiefly as to those centers controlling the hypophysis (see Beattie, *30*, 100). But there is also evidence against it, at least as to the neural effector

tensive patterns only through the mediation of centers, or groups of centers, at lower levels to which these are connected by descending tracts, or, on the other hand, to what extent each center at this level represents an individual region or function and the extensive patterns are due to spreading among them through their interconnections at this level, it is impossible, at present, to be certain.[18] Dott (*120*, 184) receives the impression that the hypothalamus is itself composed of higher and lower centers—"high centres for initiation of 'mass reactions' and numerous co-ordinated units below this level for the control of individual functions." These lower centers of the hypothalamus itself are "well defined functionally" and are "arranged in a very definite anatomical pattern"; for each can be singled out. But, the fact that derangement by whole groups is frequent suggests the "anatomical proximity of the neural mechanisms concerned" (i.e., in the hypothalamus itself). Thus he seems to conclude that the arrangement is a combination of the two alternatives suggested above. In addition, the extensiveness of the patterns may, of course, be greatly enhanced by the fact that, unlike other parts of the nervous system, "most—perhaps all—of its [the hypothalamus'] effects are produced through the medium of hormones broadcast through the blood circulation" (Dott, *loc. cit.*). While some of these seem to be specific and local in their effects, others are certainly quite general.

Whatever the exact anatomical organization may ultimately turn out to be, it follows from the fact that this is the chief level for the integration and differentiation of autonomic responses and for variations in the endocrine balance that, here also, such responses are co-ordinated. Physiologically, co-ordination signifies not only the combination of a number of different functions into one (extensive pattern) but also the suppression of all opposite (physiologically antagonistic) functions, while any one function is going on, and the suppression of all alternative extensive patterns involving the same agencies, when some certain extensive pattern is engaging them. That is, the very concept of extensive pattern—integration on the effector side—connotes the mutual exclusiveness of the several excitors that are capable of causing such patterns. Only one can hold the field at any one time.[19] Upon this basis we shall outline the functional capacities which are now attributed to this region. It appears probable that the rostral and the caudal portions of this region (roughly the anterior

---

apparatus. The evidence both ways will be mentioned below where the specific functions are discussed.

[18] Cushing, the great brain surgeon, seems to have supposed this latter arrangement, so that central excitation here could spread over the whole autonomic nervous system, sympathetic and parasympathetic alike (see *100*, 93).

On the other hand, it is evident that "parts of the patterns are integrated at lower levels" (Lashley, *263*, 45).

[19] But this is also proved by observation and, as we shall see in Chapter 4, by the study of the behavior of the nervous system at all levels. It is the essential characteristic of the nervous system that lies at the basis of all canalization instead of the spreading that should a priori be expected.

and the posterior hypothalamus) correspond in certain respects to the parasympathetic and the sympathetic branches of the autonomic system, respectively, or, at least, to the functional distinction they are supposed to represent.[20] It follows that, in certain respects, their control is opposed each to the other—that is, the two represent the regulation of continuous processes in opposite directions from a neutral or basic rate. In certain other respects control is vested solely in one or the other region. These represent the regulation of intermittent processes, which therefore vary from a zero rate. On the other hand, in respect of certain secretions, it seems possible that the two regions jointly control a single function, or similar functions, each through its own medium, in such a way that the function, or one of the two similar functions, may be performed by each part independently of the other. Out of these controls over individual functions there are elaborated extensive patterns in which the two regions co-operate. We shall list in order these three kinds of control, with the supporting citations, and, by way of example, shall give the details of two of the extensive patterns.

Opposite Functions

	Posterior Region	*Anterior Region*
Heart Rate and Blood Pressure	Increased	Decreased
Intragastric Pressure (Tonic) and Movement (Phasic)	Decreased	Increased
Gastric Secretion	Decreased	Increased
Intestinal Peristalsis	Decreased	Increased
Vesical Pressure (Tonic)	Decreased	Increased
Blood Sugar	Mobilized	Stored
Salt	(Uncertain)	(Uncertain)

Possibly Joint Functions

Salivation	Produced	Produced
Lacrimation	Produced	Produced (?)
Sweating, General	Produced	Produced (?)
Psychogalvanic Reflex (Palmar Sweating)	Produced	Produced (?)

Independent Functions

Piloerection	Produced	
Pupillary Dilatation	Produced	
Nictitating Membrane	Retraction	
Water Conservation		Produced
Fat Storage		Produced
Pigmentation		Produced
Sexual Functions		Produced

Heart Rate and Blood Pressure. "The most essential cardiac and vasomotor centers are situated in the bulbar and pontile portions of the brain stem" (Bazett, *28*, 471). At this level "the blood pressure is maintained

[20] For a discussion of this question see note 11, above.

within adequate limits" by a somewhat complex system of reactions to chemical environment and to afferent impulses and of efferent connections to the heart, etc. (Bronk *et al.*, *46*, 324). The hypothalamus is not an essential part of this control (*ibid.*, 327, and Bazett, *28*, 472), but instead functions only to integrate these with other organic processes, in part, if not wholly, by altering the activity of the cardiovascular centers (Bronk *et al.*, *46*, 328). As would be expected, therefore, either the two pressor effects—increase of heart rate and vasoconstriction—or the two depressor effects—the opposite—are usually combined, and these, in turn, when brought about by hypothalamic influence are usually parts of extensive patterns.[21] The combined pressor effects can be secured by stimulation of the posterior hypothalamus (Karplus and Kreidl, 1918; Ranson, *333*, 345; Kabat *et al.*, *229*, 948; Ectors, *130*, 301), and the combined depressor from the septal (Beattie, *30*, 87 and 89) or the tuberal region (Fulton, *160*, 243).[22] There is some reason to believe, however, that the vasomotor component in these opposed effects is not wholly or not only (in some patterns) mediated via the medullary centers.[23] And the possibility appears that arterial and capillary constriction may be separately reinforced by two different hormonal agencies (adrenal and pituitary respectively), which may be controlled from hypothalamic and not from lower centers (Fulton, *160*, 254). Thus

[21] Kabat *et al.* (*228*, 214) think the pressor effect can only be procured as part of an extensive pattern. If so, it is clearly the most subtle and facile part of the response, for Darrow (*102*) has used it as an index of central excitation of certain kinds, whether here or not is uncertain.

[22] Bronk *et al.* (*46*, 334) hold that both pressor and depressor effects can be produced in the latter region by varying the frequency of stimulation (electrical). Kabat *et al.* (*229*, 953) suggest that this anterior area may merely contain a descending tract inhibiting the posterior pressor mechanism.

[23] The flushing of the face and ears (cervical sympathetic inhibition) or facial pallor (cervical sympathetic excitation) may be marked and yet apparently purely local instances of vasodilatation and vasoconstriction which are undoubtedly of hypothalamic origin when they take the form of emotional expression. These are selective, not general; yet no other path for such specific action appears except that to the medulla.

Whether control of cerebral blood vessels is always exercised along with that of systemic, or whether it may be independent, and therefore to what extent its action is always a part of the same extensive patterns, remains open to question. "There is good evidence that the cerebral vessels contract on stimulation of the cervical sympathetic nerve, that they lose their tone and dilate when that nerve is cut, and that they dilate when the central end of the vagus nerve is stimulated" (Cobb, *87*, 534)—in other words, that they are controlled in the same way as elsewhere. There may also be a parasympathetic path (vasodilatation) along the facial nerve (VII) (Cobb and Finnesinger, *88*, 1256; Chorobski and Penfield, *78*, 1257) from the same or neighboring centers in the lower brain-stem. Both of these parasympathetic controls are active vasodilatators (*88*, 1253) and the latter, at least, does not appear to act merely as a consequence of the usual stimuli to the lower cardiovascular centers (*88*, 1254–1255). The pial blood vessels, at least, appear also to be controlled from the same source but not wholly (as to pressor) via the cervical sympathetic. As to them, constriction is produced, as part of an extensive pattern, by stimulation of the posterior hypothalamus and dilatation by stimulation of the ventral tuber cinereum (Stavraky, *385*, 1027 and 1028). This control of the blood supply of the brain by the hypothalamus and lower centers, and its possible independent action, is of importance for our general hypothesis.

vasodilatation in response to heat and the chronic or profuse vasodilatation observed after decortication [24] or ablation of the hypothalamus (Fulton, *160*, 248) may both be the result of higher influences which by-pass the cardiovascular centers of the medulla.

Intragastric Pressure (Tonic) and Movement (Phasic). These two pairs of opposite functions (depressor and pressor) have been observed in this region by Beattie and Sheehan (*32*, 226), by Dott (*120*, 171), by Sheehan (*373*, 613), by Kabat *et al.* (*228*, 214), and by others. Stimulation of the posterior (or lateral) region causes a slight fall in intragastric pressure and "complete obliteration of all gastric motility" (Beattie and Sheehan, *loc. cit.*). The pressor region is in the tuber nuclei. Both pressor and depressor effects are perhaps always parts of an extensive pattern.[25]

Gastric Secretion. Dott (*120*, 171) includes gastric secretion among the instances of dual control (pressor and depressor) in the hypothalamus. "There is strong support for the existence of a sympathetic [depressor] centre regulating gastro-intestinal activity" in general (Sheehan, *373*, 613). Perhaps this is in the posterior (mammillary) region. Along with the effects enumerated above, it results in "an increase in the mucous content of gastric juice and a tendency to diminish its rate of flow" (Sheehan, *loc. cit.*). On the other hand, from stimulation "more anteriorly, in the supra-optic and pre-optic areas," "greater flow and increased acidity of gastric juice" have been observed (Sheehan, *loc. cit.*).

Intestinal Peristalsis. It is evident that inhibition of intestinal peristalsis can be produced from this region (Kabat *et al.*, *228*, 225; Sheehan, *373*, 613, Ranson *et al.*, *336*, 474). It is also evident that excitation (increased peristalsis) can be produced here (Dott, *120*, 171). However, Fulton (*160*, 241) states that the latter effect has not been produced from the anterior hypothalamus proper (and see Ranson *et al.*, *loc. cit.*). Sheehan (*373*, 613) says that some have got it from the supraoptic and preoptic areas.

Vesical Pressure (Tonic). This subject has already been discussed in Appendix I, Section C, but without reference to localization in this region. While it may be true (Bard, *24*, 184) that the chief centers for this function, both pressor and depressor, are in the spinal cord and bulb, it appears that either the chief co-ordinating centers or tracts from those at still higher levels (probably the former) are in the region we are now considering. Spiegel and Hunsicker (*384*, 269) got increased vesical pressure with spontaneous contractions, as well as inhibition, from cortical stimulation when only the hypothalamic efferents were left intact. Kabat *et al.* (*229*, 954) obtained bladder contractions by stimulating the hypothalamus; and Ranson *et al.* (*336*, 474) obtained them both from the hypothalamus and from the region in front of it. Kabat *et al.* (*230*, 232–234) identify the

[24] Pinkston *et al.*, *326*, 530. But not in the monkey; see Pinkston and Rioch, *327*, 53.

[25] Kabat *et al.* (*228*, 214) conclude that, since they could never get inhibition of gastric motility from the posterior region without marked sympathetic discharge, including dilatation of pupils, inhibition of bladder, and increased blood pressure and respiration, it is "safe to assume that the single center is concerned" in all. Nevertheless, with available experimental methods, there cannot be perfect insurance against spreading.

medial preoptic region as the source (center or possibly tract) of contraction, and the lateral and medial preoptic region as the source (center or tract) of relaxation. Beattie and Kerr (*31*, 313) locate the pressor center (or possibly tract) in the anterior region, probably the supraoptic or preoptic, and trace the descending tracts to the inferior colliculi where, as already noted in Appendix I, Section C, Langworthy *et al.* have placed the tonic midbrain center. They also locate a depressor center in the posterior hypothalamus or upper midbrain, and find its effects produced both by tracts direct to the bladder and by adrenalin. The direct descending tracts conform to the findings of Langworthy *et al.* (*257*, 288–290). The effect of adrenalin is probably slight (Myerson, *309*). On the other hand, the pressor effect may also be slightly reinforced by acetylcholine (*loc. cit.*). In this case, again, it is likely that these centers are concerned in integrated patterns. Kabat *et al.* (*230*, 236) believe that the mechanism here is "probably not concerned in the reflex contraction which occurs as a result of distension" and that it "may have nothing to do with the control of bladder tonus." This indicates that its function may be wholly a co-ordinating one. Certainly that seems true of the depressor mechanism which Langworthy *et al.* (*257*, 290) believe is operative only when something else is going on. When there is no excitement (general hypothalamic excitation) this inhibition is relaxed. Nevertheless, the evidence here is somewhat contradictory, and the character of some of the integrated patterns in which these centers participate somewhat surprising. For micturition seems to be a component of an extensive pattern emanating from the posterior hypothalamus (Stravraky, *385*, 1028) or the hypothalamus in general (Kabat *et al.*, *228*, 225; citing Karplus), which also includes dilatation of the pupil, widening of the palpebral fissures, increase of blood pressure, piloerection, sweating, salivation, lacrimation, and cries. As we shall note later, these are all typical of general hypothalamic excitation. A possible reconciliation of this apparent discrepancy is along the lines of the observations of Langworthy *et al.* (*257*, 290), indicating that the first effect of sympathetic stimulation is contraction at the base of the bladder and a rise of vesical pressure, and that only later does the inhibitory effect appear. On the other hand, it may turn out that the reconciliation is that general excitation spreads throughout the hypothalamus and thence throughout the autonomic system, producing either sympathetic or parasympathetic effects according to which is locally dominant.

Blood Sugar. While the evidence on this subject is not yet adequate and seems somewhat contradictory, the best provisional thesis seems to be as follows: The mobilization of sugar from storage (liver, etc.) may be controlled in part by the sympathico-adrenalin mechanism. If so, the response can also be evoked from lower levels (Bard, *24*, 184, and *18*, 492). At this level, however, the center in control is in the tuber cinereum (ventromedial nuclei; Beattie, *30*, 98; Davis *et al.*, 108, 614); and it is this center which is largely, and perhaps wholly, responsible (Barbour, *15*, 482; Davis *et al.*, *loc. cit.*). It must be wholly responsible in so far as the effect is produced through a possible hypophyseal secretion (not adrenalin) which releases sugar from the "glycogen storehouse" (Davis *et al.*, *loc. cit.*). The shifting of blood sugar into storage (liver, etc.) appears to be caused directly by insulin (pancreatic internal secretion), which may perhaps be produced at a basic rate when induced intermittently by digestive processes. Apparently the paraventricular nuclei, in the anterior hypothalamus (Ingram and Barris, *213*, 562; Barris and Ingram, *25*, 560; Lewy and Gassman, *268*, 508), perhaps through their control over a hormone secreted by the anterior lobe of the pituitary (Ingram and Barris, *213*, 569; Beattie, *30*, 100) can regulate (increase or reduce) the secretion of insulin or its existence in the blood. These nuclei, however, seem to respond to the sugar content of the blood (Vonderahe, *415*). If so, they might be construed to stimulate or not neutralize insulin production when blood sugar is excessive and to inhibit or neutralize it when deficient. This construction fits the observation that paraventricular lesions cause a tendency to hypoglycemia—i.e., intermittent release of the insulin mechanism (Ingram and Barris, *213*, 562; Barris and Ingram, *25*, 560) whereas, when the insulin mechanism itself is in a pathological state (diabetes mellitus) these cells atrophy, as if killed by overstimulation—i.e., hyperglycemia (Vonderahe, *loc. cit.*). On the other hand, that sugar mobilization and sugar storage are opposite processes, superimposed upon a basic rate which is in balance, is indicated by the fact that destruction of the tuber nuclei (or the hypophysis) prevents hyperglycemia even if the pancreas are removed or diseased. (Davis *et al.*, *108*, 613).[26]

Salt. Little that is definite can be said on this subject. We have already referred, in Appendix I, Section A, to the probability that the mechanism of salt metabolism is associated with that of water. As noted there, Lewy and Gassman (*268*, 508) attribute it to the "paroptic ganglion" (? supraoptic nuclei). Davison and Selby (*111*, 590) also suppose a "specific nuclear control in the metabolism of mineral salts" in this region, which is involved in polyuria and polydipsia. So too Broers (1933), assigning it specifically to the supraoptico-hypophyseal system. Dott (*120*, 174) suggests that the control of gastric secretion may be part of a wide control of chloride metabolism with which is associated the hormone of the suprarenal cortex (corticin).

Salivation. We have noted already that Karplus (cited by Kabat *et al.*, *228*, 225) attributed salivation to the hypothalamus when it is part of a certain extensive pattern. Stavraky (*385*, 1028) has also observed it as part of the same pattern when produced by electrical stimulation of the posterior region. Whether it can be produced, from this region, by itself or only as part of other patterns, and whether the secretion is of the type produced by the sympathetic or that produced by the parasympathetic

[26] It should be said that Long (*272*, 497), for instance, considers that it is not proved that the hypothalamus has the predominant role in carbohydrate metabolism, and Bard (*24*, 200) only admits a possible relation. But Long assumes (*loc. cit.*) that the anterior pituitary, the adrenal cortex and the Island of Langerhans either react to their own blood supply or are controlled centrally by centers which do so.

innervation of the salivary glands, does not yet appear. It is also uncertain whether this region is concerned in the phenomenon called "psychic secretion" of the salivary glands which takes place, presumably, via the parasympathetic innervation. Nevertheless, that will be our supposition.

Lacrimation. This is also a part of the extensive pattern which includes salivation (Karplus; Stavraky). The response originates in the posterior hypothalamus. But, as in the previous case, the question whether the secretion is due to the sympathetic or to the parasympathetic innervation of the lacrimal glands remains unanswered.[27]

Sweat Secretion. This is a part of Karplus's extensive pattern but not of Stavraky's (see above). However, it is certainly a part of several others emanating from this region, which we shall discuss later. The question of the control of sweating is of especial importance for us because of the significance of palmar sweating (psychogalvanic reflex) which we mention next. But it raises difficulties, because the control is apparently anomalous. Innervation to the sweat glands seems to be wholly sympathetic; but the fibers are altogether cholinergic (characteristic of the parasympathetic system; Myerson, *309,* 101; Fulton, *160,* 216; Darrow, *104,* 654–659). In some patterns sweating is produced in association with parasympathetic effects on other structures; in others, in association with sympathetic effects elsewhere (Darrow, *104,* 658 and 662–663). Perhaps the antithesis between the two extreme outflows of the autonomic (parasympathetic) and the middle one (sympathetic) is chiefly anatomical and is functionally only a partial one. Or, perhaps, there is an as yet undemonstrated dual control of the sweat glands—that of the parasympathetic being neural or hormonal. Darrow suggests a probable center for sweat secretion in the medulla—the "region of the dorsal vagus nucleus" (*ibid.,* 662)—and admits the usual assumption of a hypothalamic center somewhere in the region from the tuber cinereum forward to the "prechiasmic" region (*ibid.,* 649). Fulton thinks the "focus" of the latter center is in the tuber nuclei (*160,* 248). Both of these locations seem more generally characteristic of parasympathetic than of sympathetic functions. Thus we can, at present, come to no clear-cut conclusion except that sweating can be produced from the hypothalamus as a part of extensive patterns.

Psychogalvanic Reflex. Whether the control of palmar sweating is independent of sweating in general (Darrow, *104,* 659) or is merely the most subtle and delicately observable part of the whole response, it is important because it appears (either sooner than, or independently of, other sweating) as part of innumerable patterns—perhaps of all extensive central activity at this level and of a large part of that at cortical levels. We have noted that Schwartz (*365,* 603) obtained palmar sweating via the extraspinal ganglion of the sympathetic with no central connection, but only in response to a local stimulus (pressure), of course. This he calls the "segmental" reflex; and he distinguishes it from the "psychogalvanic,"

[27] That both innervations exist is, I believe, generally recognized. (See Fulton, *160,* 216 and 222.) But lacrimation is usually construed as a parasympathetic reaction (*ibid.,* 482).

whose range of adequate stimuli is vastly larger and which is a long-circuited reflex (Schwartz, 367). The question whether this arc can be completed both at the hypothalamic level (decorticate animals—Darrow, *104*, 651) and at cortical, or only at the latter (Schwartz, *367*, 317–318) seems to depend on the stimulus used. That is, the degree of integration on the afferent side seems to be greater at cortical than at hypothalamic levels; but, on the efferent side, both have available an effector mechanism to produce palmar sweating, a mechanism which is of a sufficiently delicate nature to permit the use of the electrical method of detecting lowered skin resistance when general sweating does not occur or is not apparent. Whether that mechanism in the hypothalamus [28] is a specific one or consists rather of a set of centers representing different extensive patterns, all connected with some lower center, among others, which is specific for this function, is not yet known.

Piloerection. Kabat *et al.* (*228*, 225) and Stavraky (*385*, 1028) both include this in the extensive pattern producible from the hypothalamus (posterior) which has been mentioned above. While Walker (*417*, 407) is certain that there are pilomotor centers or descending paths in the midbrain, he says (*ibid.*, 414) that bilateral ablation of the hypothalamus abolishes or reduces piloerection. Fulton (*160*, 197) says that lesions of the superior colliculus (midbrain) paralyze pilomotor reflexes. But it is again uncertain whether this is due to the interruption of descending tracts from above or to the destruction of centers there. In view of Brickner's results (*44*) cited above (p. 1054) we must, I think, conclude that pilomotor reflexes to local cold and scratching are short-circuited at the spinal level and that the centers there are also directly accessible to several centers in the hypothalamus, which respond to different influences and may cause piloerection only as part of their several different extensive patterns.

Pupillary Dilatation. Active constriction of the pupil is cholinergic (Myerson, *309*, 102)—that is, parasympathetic (Fulton, *160*, 223)—and is mediated only in the pretectal region (Fulton, *160*, 200 and 202)—in the transitional area between the interbrain and the midbrain. There is no evidence connecting it with the hypothalamus. But active dilatation and passive constriction, which are the positive and negative results of sympathetic innervation (the former is adrenergic, Myerson, *loc. cit.*) are certainly chiefly controlled in the posterior hypothalamus (Fulton, *160*, 240; Spiegel and Hunsicker, *384*, 273; Stavraky, *385*, 1027; Ectors, *130*, 301). Though it may possibly be producible alone (i.e., reflex dilatation to pain), it is of interest to us chiefly as a uniform part of a set of extensive patterns which go by different names according to their different degrees and concomitants. Claude Bernard found (1851) that, among other results, stimula-

[28] Spiegel and Hunsicker (*384*, 267) found the reaction to be reduced when the hypothalamic efferents were cut, indicating that the hypothalamic mechanism always participates. Darrow (*104*, 647–649) cites indications that both hypothalamic and independent cortical tracts unite on centers in the tegmental and pontine regions. In the hypothalamus, he thinks the excitatory center is in the anterior or prechiasmic region and hence, he supposes, is parasympathetic.

tion of the cervical sympathetic trunk produces dilatation of the pupils, wide opening of the eyelids and protrusion of the eyeballs. These are the opposite of Horner's syndrome, in which the pupil is constricted, the eyelids droop, and the eyeballs are sunken into the orbit. Precisely these latter symptoms have been produced by large bilateral lesions in the posterior region of the hypothalamus (Fulton, *160*, 242). Hence one suspects this region to be responsible for the syndrome. The syndrome is evidence that the tone of all these muscles is due to these centers. When they are destroyed, the muscles relax. Conversely, the positive symptoms appear together when this area is directly stimulated, as we shall have occasion to note in Section D of this appendix. When mild, they are part of what we shall call the "alert"; when strong, of what is called "sham rage." (As to the last, see Fulton, *160*, 240 and Stavraky, *385*, 1027).

Nictitating Membrane. We have already referred to the neural control of this membrane in the cat as one of the most typical hierarchies. Morison and Rioch (*307*, 275) have found, above the excitatory (retracting) center in the pons, another excitatory component at the level of the posterior hypothalamus, presumably operating through the first. Since the innervation of the membrane itself is sympathetic (Fulton, *160*, 212) it is to be supposed that the lower of their two inhibitory centers, which is at the level of the anterior hypothalamus (Morison and Rioch, *loc. cit.*) inhibits one of these two excitatory centers rather than the muscle direct.[29] We have therefore not included this among our instances of opposition of function between the posterior and the anterior hypothalamus. But, if it turns out that such inhibition is direct, this function belongs in that classification.

Water Conservation. It is unnecessary to repeat here our discussion of this subject in Appendix I A. The hypothalamus is deemed responsible for "water balance" (Ectors *et al.*, *131*, 789; Bard, *24*, 197), or at least for the management of the outflow of water through the kidneys (Ranson, *332*, 269). Specifically, the process appears to be that, under the control of the supraoptic nuclei in the anterior hypothalamus, the posterior lobe of the pituitary secretes an antidiuretic hormone which stimulates the tubules of the kidneys to reabsorb water from the urine after this water has passed out through glomerular filtration.[30] Apparently this counteracts the diuretic action of the anterior lobe and of (or through) the thyroid (Fulton, *160*, 245; Gersh, *170*, 441). But, since that action has not been shown to be governed by any hypothalamic nuclei (at least posterior), we cannot consider it a case of opposed action between the two regions. Nor can we accept, in this respect, Dott's concept of double control (*120*, 167), in which the posterior hypothalamus acting on the thyroid is an active agent in water loss. For, according to Hare (*180*, 425), diuresis is inhibited during exercise, emotional stress, and painful stimuli, all of which, we shall see reason to believe, correspond to states of general excitation

[29] The higher of the two inhibitory centers will be dealt with in Section H I.

[30] See Fisher, Ingram and Ranson, *Diabetes Insipidus* (Ann Arbor, 1938); Beattie, *30*, 96–97; Dott, *120*, 167; Fulton, *160*, 244.

in the posterior hypothalamus. And at least pain and emotion produce this result by reducing glomerular filtration (*ibid.*, 430). Though the matter is doubtless much more complicated (Fisher *et al.*, *141*, 162), we shall confine our present thesis to a one-way control of water balance operating, when active, to conserve water and, when inactive, (passively) to permit water loss, which, in turn, is produced by other agencies that may or may not be centrally controlled at this level.[31] As to the inhibition of glomerular filtration (above) there is as yet no evidence that this is directly subject to neural control at all.

Fat Storage. While "we seem to be justified in suspecting that the hypothalamus has some relationship to the control of fat metabolism" (Bard, *24*, 199), "the part played by" it "is more obscure" than in the case of carbohydrate metabolism (Fulton, *160*, 251). Perhaps the anterior lobe of the pituitary produces a hormone storing fat in the liver, and perhaps this is under control of the tuber nuclei (Beattie, *30*, 99). But, since it is reported that "disorders in fat metabolism" have resulted from "hypothalamic lesions which spared the pituitary body," while "careful hypophysectomies which do not involve neighboring nervous tissue do not result in adiposity" (Gildea and Man, *171*, 522), it appears more likely that the effect of any such hypothalamic action is mediated through "nervous connections with the liver and possibly thyroid, adrenals and gonads." That the sexual system is concerned is evident from the fact that at least the most characteristic result of injury to the tuber cinereum is the adiposogenital syndrome ("extreme adiposity" and "atrophy of the genital glands"; Fulton, *160*, 252). Apparently tumors "involving the caudal (posterior) part of the hypothalamus may produce severe emaciation instead of obesity" (Gildea and Man, *171*, 507). But even this degree of localization may be too definite, and one may be obliged to restrict the statement to this: "Bilateral lesions involving the tuber cinereum and extending deep into the hypothalamus but without injury to the pituitary may produce either obesity or emaciation" (Gildea and Man, *171*, 521–522).

Pigmentation. Beattie (*30*, 100) includes among the hypophyseal hormones the "pigmento-effector hormone," intermedin, and attributes control over its secretion to the suprachiasmatic nucleus (in the supraoptic region).

Sexual Functions. Evidence of hypothalamic influence on sexual growth and regression seems to be limited to the adiposogenital syndrome mentioned above. But it is possible that genital dystrophy from tuberal injuries may be independent of adiposity (Fulton, *160*, 257). Certain it is that the hypophysis—the hormonal member of this neurohormonal entity we are considering—is the chief functional agency controlling sexual development.

As to the sexual functioning of the mature animal we can be even less definite. Brooks (*48*, 547) finds that the hypothalamus "mediates or in-

[31] And whose influence is probably secondary to their other and specific activities (Gersh, *170*, 436).

fluences the gonadotropic functions of the hypophysis," in some mammals and in man (*ibid.*, 546). Bard (*24*, 199) suggests that perhaps ovulation is produced by means of hypothalamic-hypophyseal action (anterior lobe). And it is evident from his experiments that overt sexual behavior (estrual) is chiefly subcortical, since it can be completed quite normally by the decorticate animal (*23*, 574–576). The region responsible appears to be the mammillary bodies (*ibid.*, 566), but the somatic part of the response "probably depends on upper mesencephalic mechanisms" (*ibid.*, 576) or is mediated there.

There are certain general characteristics of the controls over vegetative functions at this level which have appeared in numerous instances in the foregoing and which it may be well to emphasize at this point. The first is the extent to which hormonal effector mechanisms are combined with, or are the final end-product of, the neural mechanisms.[32] The second is this: While the functions or patterns which we have assigned to the posterior region seem to be largely if not wholly controlled by means of descending tracts, that appears not to be the case, at least to the same extent, with those assigned to the anterior region. From this latter region some effector mechanisms seem largely or wholly confined to paths to the pituitary body. The third characteristic is the extent to which these mechanisms operate upon lower ones which are themselves in balance, so that, at these lower levels, there is a basic rate which only varies within narrow limits as a result of such influences as reach it from short-circuiting at such levels. Imposed on these there are, at the hypothalamic level, controls which have the power of varying these basic rates through much wider ranges, and either in the pressor or depressor directions, and which themselves respond to quite different influences.[33] The fourth characteristic is the degree to which the various controls are specific as to an individual function or are evidenced only as part of an extensive pattern, two possibilities already mentioned on page 1058. And here, from the evidence cited, the two regions appear to differ. We have mentioned no cases of posterior region activity which are not parts of extensive patterns.[34] On the

[32] They may play some part in all, or nearly all, functions. But they are important enough to be mentioned above in connection with vasoconstriction, sugar mobilization and storage, salt metabolism, water conservation, fat storage, pigmentation, and sexual growth.

[33] This is Dott's interesting construction (see *120*). In many cases the details are missing or hazy. Nevertheless, there is reason to give more credence to this generalization than can as yet be demonstrated in terms of known mechanisms. Besides those we have enumerated—water metabolism, sugar metabolism, fat deposition or depletion, blood pressure, visceral motility and control, and gastric secretion—he includes three of which we have deferred consideration because they include somatic components—body temperature, respiratory rhythm and sexual activities—and one, somatic growth, as to which the evidence is as yet very slight. He assumes this last neuro-hormonal control to consist of a pressor-depressor influence of the hypothalamus upon the basic rate of the hypophysis.

[34] The mere fact that subtle changes of blood pressure and electrically detectable palmar sweating appear first or appear alone does not really show that they are separable functions here. For the very fact that they are taken as the sharpest indices of emotional

other hand, those at least which result from anterior activity but are executed largely via the pituitary appear to be capable, at that level, of specific action.[35] Since this difference between generality and specificity is held to be rather characteristic of the sympathetic and the parasympathetic divisions of the autonomic system respectively, it is an added reason for thinking of the posterior hypothalamus as having primarily sympathetic peripheral connections and of the anterior region as having primarily parasympathetic peripheral connections. But it should be noted that there is much less certainty in ascribing to the latter region the status of highest level in respect of the parasympathetic than there is in ascribing to the former that position with reference to the sympathetic division. And it should also be noted that this does not answer the question raised above (pp. 1058–1059) as to how the integration of extensive patterns is achieved even in the posterior region. Is it by spreading among adjoining but specific centers at this level, or is it by descending connections from general centers here to many specific centers at lower levels? Our hypothesis still leaves room for, or includes, both.

C. SUBCORTICAL MANAGEMENT OF MOTOR FUNCTIONS

As in the case of vegetative functions we find the control of the motor, or somatic, functions distributed along the cord and brain-stem. But since our interest in the subject is limited to the question of what somatic activities (exterofective) can be produced from the thalamic or hypothalamic levels (i.e., in the decorticate animal), we shall pass rapidly over the two lower levels—spinal and lower brain-stem—only giving attention to those cases where these are included in hypothalamic extensive patterns or consist of basic rates which can be altered from that level.

1. SPINAL

At least after recovery from spinal shock the isolated spinal cord is capable of a number of motor reflexes which are intersegmental—i.e., involve more than one segment.[1] The "flexion reflex" is usually a "reaction to a noxious stimulus" (Fulton, *160*, 102)—that is, to "impulses which would underlie pain or discomfort, if consciousness were present" (Head and Riddoch, *183*, 501)—and represents the withdrawal of an extremity from injury. The extensor stretch reflexes (postural, antigravity; Fulton,

---

or psychic states is evidence that they are parts of the extensive patterns which constitute these states, though doubtless they are the subtlest parts.

[35] See also note 17, above.

[1] Tower (*404*, 244) regards it as proved that even the "flexion reflex, the archetype of spinal reflexes, is normally under reinforcement from the cortex," via the pyramidal (direct) tracts. This facilitation—the loss of which is assumed to be the cause of spinal shock—is either continuous, or it is a long-circuited response to the same stimulus, probably the former (*ibid.*). On the other hand, the tone of the postural and the facilitation of the phasic extensor reflexes seem to be subcortical in origin, though, of course, also absent after spinal transection.

160, 109) and the extensor thrust in response to pressure or separation of the pads of the feet (*ibid.*, 116) are parts of normal posture and locomotion, respectively. Moreover, a certain degree of integration is possible at this level (Fulton, *160*, 147), such as reciprocal innervation (inhibition of antagonist muscles; *ibid.*, 121), successive induction (facilitation of subsequent excitation of antagonist muscles) making possible alternation of opposite responses,[2] and, finally, such complex and general patterns as the simultaneous but opposite reactions of the other fore- and of the ipsilateral hind-limb and vice versa (i.e., movement of progression) (Fulton, *160*, 128).

2. LOWER BRAIN-STEM

The control of respiration at this level is of chief interest to us because, though effected through striated musculature (and therefore motor), respiration is primarily a vegetative function in its nature—a part of the management of homeostasis of the blood—and because its control is more intimately allied with the interofective than with the exterofective system. The so-called respiratory center consists of cells "scattered throughout the reticular gray matter . . . of the medulla and lower pons" (Schmidt, *361*, 552). Though they react to numerous chemical and neural influences at this level, as well as to a great variety of controls from above, the fundamental reflex is the Hering-Breuer—that is, the stimulation of inflation by the collapse of the walls of the lungs and the inhibition of it by their stretch. Hughlings Jackson (*215*, 129) suggested that, on account of the numerous other purposes which it serves, this center be regarded as representing the "thoracic cage" rather than merely respiration. Certainly, there is a vast variety of modifications in the pattern. Barcroft adopts (*17*, 14) Lumsden's postulate of three evolutionary levels (three centers from lower to higher) of which the lowest—"the fundamental phenomenon"—is the gasp.[3] But above this and above the level producing normal rhythmical breathing (including expiration) it seems necessary to assume many levels (or centers) to account for such altered patterns as sneezing,[4] coughing, laughing, sighing, panting, crying, vocalizing, etc., all of which are chiefly expiratory.

In general, it may be said that the exterofective reflexes of which this level is capable by itself concern for the most part posture and position with relation to the environment, not movement.[5] Normal posture (tonic),

[2] Even such rapid rhythmic alternations as the scratch-reflex and the slower "mark-time" reflex—as reported by Sherrington (34 *J. Physiol.* 1906, and previously)—as well as the "nettoyage" following defecation, noted in Appendix I, Section C (p. 1031).

[3] Obviously this is the basic but not the rhythmic pattern (i.e., it does not include expiration). Whether this lowest level is in the "respiratory center" or not, is a question. Jackson (*loc. cit.*) presumed subordinate motor centers. But breathing ceases altogether when the connections to and from the medulla are sectioned (Schmidt, *361*, 552).

[4] The bulbo-spinal animal is capable of this one at least (Fulton, *160*, 150).

[5] What Fulton defines as "postural reflexes and the righting reactions" (*160*, 190). While many have claimed that postural contraction of skeletal muscle is produced by the sympathetic system, this is generally denied by the Sherrington school (see Forbes, *145*, 247; Fulton, *158*, 385–404 and *160*, 111 and Chapter 16).

maintained by the anti-gravity (extensor) muscles, appears to derive chiefly from the vestibular nuclei in the medulla, subject to inhibition from the red nucleus and higher levels.[6] On the other hand, the righting reflexes (phasic), due to labyrinthine as well as proprioceptive and exteroceptive impulses, are derived from the ventral midbrain (Fulton, *160*, 187) except perhaps for neck-righting (*ibid.*, 192). It is these latter which restore (phasic) or maintain (tonic) "right-side-up-ness" (*ibid.*, 192).

As a reflex to stimulation of the back of the mouth or of any branch of the taste nerve (V), swallowing, with reciprocal inhibition of respiration, has been induced in decerebrate (practically bulbo-spinal) animals (Fulton, *160*, 166–167). Doubtless other somatic movements are mediated at this level at least as parts of more extensive patterns initiated from above. But, as yet, little more that is definite can be said of the motor centers in this region.

3. UPPER BRAIN-STEM

If we exclude from consideration "the terra incognita of the striatum,"[7] the hypothalamus appears to be the highest subcortical level of the exterofective as it is of most of the interofective system. For, since the "patterned responses" obtainable from it "are made up of the integrated actions of somatic and visceral effectors, it is a mistake to regard the hypothalamus as an exclusively autonomic center."[8] These "patterned responses" are complicated performances of unmistakable significance," which require for their execution regions no more rostral than the posterior hypothalamus and perhaps the ventral thalamus and subthalamus (Tower, *405*, 433), though the primary parts of which they are composed can be got from the midbrain.[9] Thus, at some point in the midbrain we pass from fragments

[6] Thus decerebrate rigidity, which is "simply reflex standing" (Fulton, *160*, 105) or an "exaggeration of normal posture" (*ibid.*, 153) and is "quadripedal" even in human beings (*ibid.*, 154), now appears to be a release of the vestibular nuclei from the inhibition normally exerted from above by the red nucleus (midbrain) and perhaps the mammillary bodies (interbrain; *ibid.*, 153–154).

[7] Tower, *405*, 440. So far, "no definite function can be assigned the basal ganglia which is independent of cortical action" (Bard, *24*, 228). Nevertheless, they constitute an "autonomous centre" which functions independently of, and probably in a way not identical to, the cortex, and which is motor, efferent and caudal in direction (Kinnier Wilson, *443*, 477). The corpus striatum may have lost its function (*ibid.*, 489) which was, at one time, that of principal motor pathway from the forebrain (Fulton, *160*, 491; "original motor pathway," Kinnier Wilson, *443*, 478), so that it now originates nothing (Kinnier Wilson, *443*, 485) except for the prevention of action-tremor (*ibid.*, 483, and Bard, *24*, 230). On the other hand, Rioch and Brenner (*347*) have obtained a number of extensive patterns which are also obtainable elsewhere (apparently the "alert," escape, feeding and general relaxation of posture) by stimulating various regions of the striatum in a chronic decorticate preparation. Perhaps these nuclei have to do with the involuntary part of synergies ("associated movements," Fulton, *160*, 500–501). Thus they may constitute part of, or have access to, the mechanism for many extensive motor patterns.

[8] Bard, *24*, 194; Hinsey, *199*, 657; Ectors *et al.*, *131*.

[9] Since these two regions together "yield all the patterns of cortical extrapyramidal action" equally as well when the corticofugal tracts are degenerated as when intact, it is clear that the "brain-stem response depends upon intrinsic brain-stem structure" only

to such behavior as "struggling and running movements, turning of the head, spitting [cats] and other coordinated facial, vocal and respiratory movement patterns" (Hinsey, *199*, 668).

In the primates, two specific motions of which this level is capable at birth well illustrate the general system of relationships and therefore will be referred to again as we proceed. "Grasping and sucking are the first and basic functions of the hand and the mouth" (Bieber, *36*, 706). "The grasp reflex is the basic subcortical prehension pattern" (Bieber and Fulton, *37*, 450).[10] "It serves initially for support." When the use of the hand for conveying objects to the mouth (a higher motor function) begins, the grasp reflex also serves that purpose. Then, as support is relegated to the lower limbs, the first reflex (postural) becomes inhibited from above. But it returns under many conditions, as we shall note. Sucking, originally apparently a local reflex to stimulation of the mouth and surrounding areas, also disappears only to return under special conditions.

As parts of the heat-control mechanism, which we shall consider shortly, and of certain other extensive patterns, two special types of somatic reaction are either originated in the hypothalamus or are mediated for it at some lower points in the brain-stem. These are panting and shivering respectively. The heat panting of dogs (or cats) is a rapid shallow respiration which avoids absorption of oxygen and therefore heat production, but promotes heat loss through the mouth (Barcroft, *17*, 68). Apparently this type of panting (true polypneic), as a response to heat, depends on the integrity of the (caudo-dorsal) thalamus (Pinkston *et al.*, *326*, 528; Lilienthal and Otenasek, *269*, 120). But a similar motor pattern (i.e., great increase in frequency) can be procured in normal monkeys by artificial stimulation of the posterior hypothalamus. On the other hand, there is some indication that the stimulation of the anterior region produces a decrease in the rate but an increase in the amplitude of respiration (hyperpnoea) (Ectors, *130*, 301). Since the latter type of breathing is also associated with maintaining temperature against cold (Barcroft, *17*, 67), it is possible that the heat conservation mechanism uses the same effector agencies.[11] It is also

(Tower, *405*, 433). For our qualifications of this generalization as applied to primates, see Section H 2, below.

As to the inclusion of the ventral thalamus, since this is presumably an integrator of afferent patterns only, it is doubtful that it is part of the effector mechanism itself. That question will be considered later.

As to the necessary inclusion of the subthalamus, Hinsey does not agree with Tower, Ranson and Magoun (1939) and others. There may be direct descending somatic paths from the hypothalamus, so that its somatic effects, or many of them, may not be produced via the subthalamus (*199*, 668 and 683).

At any rate Ectors (*130*, 301) was able to get the struggling and running movements referred to by direct stimulation of the posterior hypothalamus in normal monkeys, so that is clearly the strategic point.

[10] Their studies indicate that it is "integrated in the brainstem somewhere between the anterior nucleus of the thalamus and the anterior border of the pons" (*ibid.*, 453).

[11] The fact that, as we shall note below (p. 1090 ff.) the heat loss mechanism is presumed to be in the anterior, and the heat conservation mechanism in the posterior, region, makes the similarity of both these patterns in the two regions, respectively, somewhat anomalous.

possible that the two similar patterns are, in both cases, independent, and that the two regions both utilize lower (midbrain) centers and to slightly different effect.[12]

Of the four causes of shivering, (1) toxic (fevers), (2) visceral (relaxation of the sphincters), (3) emotional (fright), and (4) thermal (reduction of temperature), all but the second [13] appear to be effective, chiefly if not wholly, at the hypothalamic level and presumably in the posterior region. While "an intact cerebellum appears a necessary requirement for the production of the clonic-like movements of shivering" (Uprus *et al.*, *410*, 220 and 227; and see Jung *et al.*, *227*, 31) "shivering, reflex or 'central' [also] requires . . . some central nervous mechanism anterior to the mid-brain" (Sherrington, *377*, 423). The evidence we shall adduce shows that the posterior hypothalamus has access to this mechanism, if it does not itself contain it.[14]

D. THE HYPOTHALAMUS AND EMOTIONAL STATES

While Hughlings Jackson limited his thesis almost wholly to the interofective system, and while, in his time, existing knowledge did not permit the precise localization of the "anatomical substrata of emotions," as he called them (*215*, 138), it is of interest to us, in view of our previous consideration of Jackson's generalizations, to see what he held to be the nature of the emotional system and how closely he approximated what has since been disclosed by experimentation. In general, "In emotional manifestations it is plain that the most automatic of the lower bodily processes are concerned" (*216*, II, 266). Hence he deduces that, "What on the lowest level are centres representing the circulatory, respiratory and digestive movements are evolved in the highest centres into the physical bases of the emotion" (*216*, II, 91). In more detail,

Certain parts of the body are represented directly by centres on the lowest level in simple and in general ways, in detail, and with comparatively few interconnections, as they serve in doing the menial work of digestion, circulation, respiration, etc. But all these same parts are represented indirectly, in most complex and special ways, in intricate combinations and with many interconnections in the highest centres, being represented again (re-represented) in those centres through the intermediation of the centres of the lowest level, which, as we said, represent them directly as serving in menial work. The indirect and very complex, etc., re-representation of these parts of the body by some of the nervous arrangements of the highest centres is the "emotional

[12] But panting "does not occur in the oblongata animal" (Fulton, *160*, 247).

[13] At least we noted that Head and Riddoch (*184*, 213) reported their patient experiencing a "sort of shiver" immediately preceding automatic (spinal) micturition.

[14] Fulton (*160*, 250) states that "an animal with lesions of the hypothalamus cannot shiver." On the other hand, Barbour (*16*, 483) asserts that "shivering [in response to cold] appears independent of the hypothalamus in both cats and monkeys."

Beattie (*30*, 83) finds the posterior parts of both hypothalamus and thalamus are necessary to the maintenance of temperature against cold, including shivering. Presumably this region of the thalamus, the caudal half of the medial portion (*ibid.*, 75), is only the thermo-sensitive zone, as he suggests, and not the effector mechanism.

centre."[1] The anatomical substratum of an emotion (let it not be forgotten that I am artificialising) the "emotional centre," is not the sum of those centres on the lowest level serving in menial work which I mentioned above; it is part of their evolutionary sum. The "emotional centre" so constituted has become detached from, largely independent of, the very centres of the lowest level out of which it has itself been evolved. For we can have faint emotions (without manifestations) during slight activity of the "emotional centre" whilst the lowest centres out of which that so-called centre has been evolved are at the same time steadily engaged in mere menial work. But during vivid emotions the "emotional centre" is in strong activity, and there are then manifestations. Now the centres on the lowest level are, subordinately, engaged, too; and, so far as they are engaged in this way, their service in menial work is much interfered with;[2] it is suspended when sudden fright causes fainting, and is put an end to when it kills (*216*, I, 376).

Except for its influence on the "thoracic cage" his "emotional centre" seems to be limited to the interofective system, as noted above. "Systemic sensations[3] and movements are concerned during emotional states," and these "systemic sensori-motor arrangements" "represent adjustments of parts of the organism to one another," not "betwixt the organism and its environment" (*216*, I, 241). But its influence reaches to all parts of the interofective system. "The emotional centre will then represent an exceedingly wide range of movements [in his sense]" (II, 66). The emotion itself is not identical with its "anatomical substrata," nor with its manifestations. It "arises *during* the central activities which, through the subagency of the middle and lowest centres, produce the manifestations" (II, 66).

Two of his concepts as to the energetic characteristics of these manifestations are of importance for us. In the first place, many of the manifestations are "owing to permitted activity of lower centres, consequent on removal of control" (II, 66, note 2).[4] In the second place, in this as in the general system, he evidently conceives interconnections of no utility to exist on a large scale. Therefore, what he says of the general system is also applicable to this, since "nerve fibres . . . resist as well as conduct"; "nerve cells are not only 'energy reservoirs,' but parts offering resistance" (II, 19). Because more "reservoirs" are engaged, "there is a great multiplication of energy as the [nervous] process 'goes down.'" But, because of the resistance, "currents spread in the highest centres also . . . according to the dif-

[1] The only suggestion as to localization of this 'centre' which I find in his work is the notion of two personalities of which I, or A, is *I*, or B, minus the highest layer of the highest level. This conforms, in a most remarkable way, to the scheme that is appearing out of recent investigations.

[2] For instance, the "unusual engagement [of the "thoracic cage"] during strong emotion" "is not a true respiratory service" and only interferes with its menial work (Jackson, *215*, 138).

[3] These are the "ento-peripheral" as opposed to the "epi-peripheral" sensations (*216*, I, 287).

[4] That is, "release phenomena." He conceives some to be due to the exhaustion of inhibitory fibers which, as a first effect, are suddenly and strongly active. For instance, strong sudden excitement first stops the heart and then causes palpitations; the activated sympathetic stops micturition and defecation, which then occur when it is exhausted.

ferent resistances offered." "When the lower centres are not overcome, the currents, I suppose, spread more in the highest centres." Finally, "the currents developed from a rapid discharge [5] spread in more ways [than those of a slow discharge] not only in lines of least resistance, but in lines of greater resistance" (II, 20). Extreme pathological cases are simply differences in the "degrees of discharges above the normal" (I, 355), so that, "from sudden and rapid discharges of a small part of the highest centres (in epilepsy proper) we may have from wide collateral and downward discharges universal severe convulsion" (I, 354). While these characteristics are not expressed in the terms of present-day studies of nervous impulses, they appear not to be inconsistent with present views of "release" of inhibition, of changes in excitability, or "threshold," and of "irradiation," or spreading. Moreover, they serve rather well in formulating a conceptual model of the way the subcortical nervous system, especially, behaves.

The question of localization of such an "emotional centre" in respect of its effector mechanism, appears recently to have been settled. "The hypothalamus is the center for the integration of the visceral and somatic components of emotional expression" (Ranson, *332*, 253).[6] Or, more precisely, it is "an essential element in the integration of emotional reactions and in the psychogenesis of emotional experience" (Le Gros Clark, *84*, 467), because, though essential, it is "only one of a series of areas concerned with emotional experiences and expression" (Alpers, *12*, 741). We shall consider its relation to these other areas, in this respect, as we proceed.

The terminology of this subject is confused, because there has been carried into these purely objective studies a set of terms which are largely or wholly subjective in their connotations. Therefore, we will have to be careful in reading our authorities. Three dichotomies or polarities will serve somewhat to clarify the terminology as well as to outline the relationships of this to other areas. The first is the division of emotional states into those which constitute excitement [7] and those which constitute depression. "Hyperactivity of the hypothalamus causes . . . emotional excitement. Conversely, damage to the hypothalamus produces emotional stolidity and even somnolence" (Ranson, *332*, 269–270).[8] But this seems

[5] His "discharge" is a "liberation of energy by nervous elements" (*216*, I, 412).

[6] There is wide agreement as to this. See Fulton and Sherrington, *164*, 259; Fulton and Ingraham, 162, xxvii; Cannon, *60*, 15, *62*, 877, and *64*, 259; Bard, *18*, 490; Papez, *315*, 725; Landis, *248*, 512; Monakow, *301*, 45. The various studies "leave no doubt" in Lashley's opinion (*263*, 45). Papez (*loc. cit.*) quotes M. Nathan (1931 *Presse méd.*, 857) to the effect that the idea of the region of the third ventricle as "*un cerveau affectif*" developed abroad from Haškovec (1910, 1925, 1929) to Camus (1921, 1924), Roussy and Lhermitte (1924), Rosenfeld (1925), and Küppers (1929).

[7] Excitement, in the ordinary sense, not *excitation.*

[8] It is evident from cases in which there are pathological conditions in this region that the effect may range from, or alternate between, excitement and depression. See Alpers, *12*, 740, *11*, 301; Alford, *8*, 795; Dott, *120*, 167. Sometimes, instead of excitement, there appears "elation" (Dott) or "misplaced euphoria" (Alford). Whether that is hypothalamic and, if so, of what nature, we have no present basis for even a guess.

to localize the "emotional centre" in the posterior hypothalamus only, for, while "posterior lesions are likely to be accompanied by lethargy, indifference, depression," "lesions of the anterior hypothalamus tend to produce excited states" (Fulton *160*, 255) [9]—that is, the part played by the anterior region is, in this respect, wholly inhibitory, so that its damage tends to result in release phenomena in the posterior region. Thus it appears that we have to construe the positive emotional states as various patterns, extents, and intensities of excitation (or hyperexcitation) originating chiefly in the posterior hypothalamus, and the negative emotional states as various patterns, extents, and degrees of loss of even tonic excitation in the same region. The combination of access to both interofective and exterofective mechanisms from this region, which we have already recognized, leads us to expect the second dichotomy. Emotional states, positive and negative, produce effects through the autonomic and its allied endocrine system and also through the motor (striated musculature) system. Curiously enough it is frequently the latter only which the experimentor takes as the signs of emotion.[10] Apart from these two kinds of peripheral effects (signs or manifestations) and the state itself, which is held to exist at this central level, there is the emotional experience. This is the third dichotomy. Since such experience connotes consciousness and consciousness is generally held not to be an accompaniment of neural processes at this level, but only of those at higher ones, it follows that the effects of emotional states here are supposed not only to go down (effector) but also to rise to the highest level—or cross to the other highest level—where the experience itself takes place. This hypothesis will be fully discussed as we proceed. As a result of this distinction, the term "pseudo-affective" is used with reference to emotional states and their downward effects when by reason of decortication, etc., the supposed arena of consciousness is absent or is not involved.[11]

[9] The latter statement based on Fulton and Ingraham, *162*.

[10] Thus Cannon can say (*68*, 262) that, when the sympathetic efferent trunks are completely removed, the animals "exhibit almost all the superficial signs of rage" (i.e., the somatic signs only); or (Cannon, *61*, 108) "total separation of the viscera from the central nervous system does not alter emotional behavior." Sherrington (*374*, 390) stated that cutting off the sympathetic connections left the emotional behavior apparently intact, though the hair did not rise (*ibid.*, 396). His phrase (*375*, 252), "the machinery whose concurrent action is habitually taken as outward expression of inward feeling" seems to carry the same narrow construction. Since these observations were brought forward to refute the James-Lange theory of the emotions, the limitation is perhaps natural. Nevertheless, it is well to bear it in mind since even Kabat *et al.* (*228*, 225), among others, speak of "the intense expression and violent movements typical of strong emotional reactions."

[11] The motor reaction expressive of emotion, in Sherrington's decerebrate dog, "is probably the reaction of an organic machine which can be started working though the mutilation precludes the psychosis" (i.e., affect or "feeling") (*375*, 267). See also Fulton and Bailey, *161*. Woodworth and Sherrington (*448*, 234) originally applied the term "pseud-affective" to certain reflexes short-circuited even below this level; but I think it is now generally agreed that such reflexes are only parts of patterns (*disjecta membra*) and, unless this level is involved, never combine into "a general affective state" (Bard,

With these points in mind a few illustrations will be in order. Although Bard appears to have been the first to demonstrate that the phenomenon he called "sham rage" "depends on the caudal [posterior] hypothalamus,"[12] Ranson's experiments serve our purpose better because the fact that he produced his results by direct stimulation of the hypothalamus (presumably posterior) of normal unanesthetized cats leaves out, at least for parts of the pattern, the question of what the normal stimulus is and how it is conveyed, and deals with the effector mechanism only. He says, "At the onset of stimulation the animal became alert, raising its head and opening its eyes, disclosing dilated pupils. The respiration increased in rate and depth." Examination showed "immediate cessation of gastro-intestinal peristalsis." "The animal soon began to struggle ["being restrained"], clawing, biting ["lashing its tail"] and trying to free itself." Later, "the hair on the back and tail began to bristle [and "after the stimulus had been continued for a minute or more"] sweat appeared on the pads of the feet and saliva ran from the mouth" (*332*, 254–256).[13] The whole pattern he regards as "the complete picture of ["intense"] emotional excitement" (*ibid.*, 269). But, to complete the picture, it may be necessary to add certain additional signs, noted by others, such as protrusion of claws, arching of trunk, movement of head from side to side with attempts to bite, very rapid panting with mouth open and movements of tongue to and fro,[14] snarling (Kabat *et al.*, *228*, 225), running movements (probably as an alternative to struggling), turning of the head, spitting, and "coordinated facial and vocal patterns" (Hinsey, *199*, 668)—the last probably including "occasional crying" and perhaps accompanied by tears (Kabat *et al.*, *228*, 225)—and increased blood pressure (Bard; see Fulton, *160*, 254).

At first sight this seems to be a single extensive pattern, and it has usually been so treated. But, on closer examination, it turns out to be a composite of separate patterns, which are obtainable independently of each other, and one of which did not arise, in this case, directly from the artificial stimulation. The first independent pattern is what we have called the

18, 490). Bard referred to his complex pattern, or general affective state, as "sham rage" (*ibid.*) because it was "pseudo-affective," and that term has stuck.

[12] Bard, *19*, 288. His original experiments were described in journal articles (*18*, 490, and others).

[13] In an earlier description (Ranson *et al.*, *336*, 467) the order of effects is stated somewhat differently, and some others are included which we have inserted in brackets in the text. The effects and their order appear in the earlier description as follows: Eyes open, pupillo-dilatation, increased respiration, piloerection; then the head is raised and the "animal attempts to get on its feet and, being restrained, struggles violently to free itself." In this order the somatic component of the "alert" seems not to have appeared as part of the same pattern as the autonomic. Ranson's remark that "autonomic responses appear first" (*332*, 256) which others (Hinsey, *199*, 664) have noticed as apparently inconsistent with his statement of order of events as quoted in our text, may have been based on this previous and less well known account. It suggests, however, that the two components of the "alert" may not always be parts of a single simultaneous pattern—that the autonomic part, opening of eyes, pupillo-dilatation, etc. (see above, p. 1066) is somewhat independent of the somatic part, turning the head, pricking up the ears, etc.

[14] These are among the somatic signs shown by Cannon's cats (acute cases) without special stimulus, as reported by Bard (*19*, 287).

"alert." [15] Here it appears first; evidently it can be induced without the rest by mild or brief stimulation.[16] It is composed of certain autonomic effects which we recall are usually associated with dilatation of the pupil—that is, opening of the eyelids (widening of the palpebral fissure), retraction of the nictitating membrane (cats) and, in extreme cases, protrusion of the eyeball.[17] In this case only two of these are reported. It is also composed of certain somatic effects, turning of the head, pricking up the ears, etc. Here, the only somatic sign noted was the "raising" of the head. But the whole pattern, including turning of the head and eyes and pricking up the ears, is readily induced alone by artificial stimulation anywhere along the afferent light and sound paths, in the region of the corpora quadrigemina in the dorsal midbrain,[18] and in the region of the geniculates,[19] and then it is identical to the response of the decorticate animal to actual light and sound. This leads us to conclude that there is an "alert" pattern available to the hypothalamus directly, and that it consists of two somewhat independent parts, the autonomic and the somatic motor, which, in turn, may as a whole precede or accompany more extensive patterns.[20]

It may well be that the next somatic pattern which would result from continued hypothalamic stimulation does not appear in the foregoing complex at all. Spontaneous and periodic movement, usually called "restlessness," appears in decorticate cats and dogs when left free, provided only that the posterior hypothalamus remains intact.[21] Referring to such an observation, Ranson says (*332*, 254), "Restlessness which in these unrestrained animals expended itself in walking [restlessly for a few minutes every five or ten minutes] vented itself in fits of sham rage in Bard's animals tied to a board." [22] This "restlessness" has not been demonstrated, so far as I know,

[15] Rioch calls it the "pseudo-affective . . . attention . . . reaction" (in discussion of Alpers, *12*, 748). This is a good name; but we are reserving the term attention for a cortical occurrence (in consciousness).

[16] Bard's decorticate cats turned their heads and pricked up their ears to the sound of a low whistle, scraping or clicking.

[17] See p. 1067, above.

[18] See Fulton, *160*, 194–195. Fulton interprets this as an indication that this region is "an active motor centre." But, from the evidence, it appears equally possible that the motor centers are elsewhere, and that stimulation here merely produces rising afferent impulses to such centers.

[19] See Fulton, *160*, 495–496. Again the evidence seems to indicate that, in these experiments, afferent paths were stimulated.

[20] For instance, the alert is doubtless but part of Pavlov's investigatory reflex,—"the physiological basis of attention"—for this appears to include the grasp reflex since it is "a weak form of the reflex of grasping objects" (Frolov, *157*, 65–66).

Rioch (in discussion of Alpers, *12*, 749) believes his "pseudo-affective attention reaction" is "localized well laterally in the brain stem," perhaps in subthalamic or midbrain regions. This seems more likely to be true of the motor than of the autonomic part.

[21] See Hinsey *et al.*, *200*, 3 and 22. For this item of behavior in decorticate dogs see Mettler *et al.*, *297*, 1241, and many others.

[22] Or, as Hinsey *et al.* (*200*, *26*) put it, "The somatic motor disturbances described in Bard's work were undoubtedly activities which, if the cats had been free, would have resulted in righting and walking."

as a result of artificial stimulation. But, since it depends on the hypothalamus, it must be due to some natural stimulation which reaches that region from the same or from lower levels.[23]

This observation also demonstrates that the third somatic pattern, and at least part of the autonomic, which is designated "sham rage," was not, in the above experiment, caused by the artificial stimulation, but was instead a reaction to the restraint. When there is no artificial stimulation it occurs, at least periodically, as in the case of Bard's cats (*18*) or Mettler's dogs (*297*), from restraint (prevention of movement), constraint (enforced movement) or even from touching (stroking) the animal.[24] In fact, in these decorticate animals, it is "much more easily elicited than in a normal animal" (Fulton and Ingraham, *162*, xxviii), so much so that some then call it "chronic rage." [25] On the other hand, "sham rage" does not occur if the hypothalamus is removed.[26] Though there are "certain elements of affective behavior" in the spinal cat and still more in the bulbospinal and midbrain preparations, these elements require to be "welded together to form the rage reaction" (Bard, *18*, 509).[27] When the hypothalamus is intact, they become "more expressive of an affective state" than are the pseudo-affective reflexes of the decerebrate animal; in fact, then, "sham rage" "closely resembles the behavior of the infuriated normal animal" (*ibid.*, 512).

While "a decorticate dog . . . never shows anger in response to any particular visual or auditory stimulus," it does show fear to such stimuli, though possibly only in response to loud sounds (Bard, *24*, 197). That is also true of the cat (Bard, *19*, 294). The two reactions are of course distinguishable by overt signs. The reaction called "attack" is present in rage and absent in fear, while that called "escape" is absent in rage and present in fear (Bard, *19*, 294). Other emotional responses connoting excitement have been observed in similar preparations; but these will serve our purpose as illustrations at this point.[28] The emotional states connoting depression have not, so far as I know, been reproduced artificially. Such states seem to be the converse of excitement and to have their origin in the same region. But except as to the apparent loss of peripheral tonic excitation, both

23 We shall have much to say as to these two initial motor reactions to hypothalamic excitation when we come to deal with behavior in Chapter 3, especially in Section A 2.

24 Originally Bard was not sure what started it, though he recognized that the animal was restrained—tied down to the "animal board" on its back (*18*, 509).

25 Even in human subjects with lesions in this region "easily elicited reactions of ["uncontrollable"] rage" are often reported (e.g., Alpers, *11*, 301).

26 It occurs after "ablation of hemispheres, corpora striata and the cranial half of the diencephalon" (Bard, *18*, 495) and may occur after ablation of the dorsal parts of the diencephalon (*ibid.*, 504), that is, the dorsal thalamus (*ibid.*, 512).

27 This and the others to be named are "stereotyped reaction patterns," "more complicated" but "not essentially different" from those produced by spinal reflexes (Cannon *68*, 263). Brown (*50*, 207) thinks the lashing of the tail, which is usually a sign of anger (above), can be secured by stimulating a certain spot on the neuraxis.

28 Rioch speaks of "some fifteen to twenty stereotyped behavior patterns" in the decorticate animal; but not all these are called pseudo-affective (in discussion of Alpers, *12*, 748).

sympathetic and motor, which results from them (as noted pp. 1076–1077), little can be said.

It is worth while, however, to make brief mention of some of the individual parts of emotional patterns which are supposed to emanate from this region. To consider first the somatic side, it is generally assumed that so-called emotional facial expression is controlled there,[29] and, in animals, some vocalizing such as growling and barking (Frolov, *157*, 31). We have already noted that, of the four causes of shivering, one is emotional (fright; Uprus *et al.*, *410*, 220). Laughter and weeping, as respiratory changes, are often included.[30] So is polypneic panting, which is perhaps emotional only in the intervals between—and therefore as an effect of—bursts of sham rage (Lilienthal and Otenasek, *269*, 121). Certain distinguishing characteristics of these pseudo-affective patterns are also noteworthy. For instance, in Bard's observations (*19*, 291), the response "never outlasted the stimulus; 'after-discharge' was minimal." From our evolutionary standpoint, the regressive character of the somatic patterns which strong emotion produces is typified by the frequent presence of the gasp, which Barcroft (*17*, 14) regards as the "fundamental phenomenon of respiration"; by the release of such repressed reactions as "forced grasping," which is induced, for instance, by fright (Fulton *et al.*, *163*); and by general overt characteristics such as the use of excessive force, inco-ordination, tremor and palsy, and the loss of acquired skills or language (Darrow, *102*, 573). Of this regression more later. Thus, to a degree, the somatic patterns available to emotional states are primitive ones (Bard, *19*, 285; Darrow, *102*, 573), which have been overlaid in the course of the evolution of behavior mechanisms by better adjusted reactions, but which are revived when the posterior hypothalamus has or takes control.

The same mixture of utility and inutility, of well-adapted co-ordination and of involvements which only serve to interrupt "menial" work (Hughlings Jackson), is to be observed in the effects of excited emotional states upon the interofective activities. Excitement seems to be a "shot-gun prescription." "Generalized visceral activity," via the sympathetic system, "always occurs during intense emotional excitement" (Ranson, *332*, 252).

[29] Nevertheless, Fulton (*160*, 503) states that a lesion in part of the corpus striatum (globus pallidus) causes loss of those "movements of the face appropriate to particular emotional states" which are "beyond the sphere of conscious integration." Morgan (*305*, 495) has found descending tracts thence, to motor nuclei of the pons and medulla, which are concerned with speech, mastication, swallowing, and facial expression. Though pallido-hypothalamic tracts are known, there is no evidence of any in the reverse direction. Thus any relation of the hypothalamus to facial expression must be admitted to be purely supposititious, and based on the obvious co-ordination with emotional states. But see Section H, note 50, below.

[30] Brown (*50*, 195) says that laughter "may be looked upon in great part simply as an alteration of the act of breathing." He thinks it may be related to the caudal pole of the optic thalamus (*ibid.*, 206). But Alford notes "forced laughing and weeping" from lesions there (*8*, 795). Dott (*120*, 167) considers that the hypothalamus "plays a part" in both. But, again, Alpers (*11*, 301) reports "uncontrollable laughter," among other signs, after destruction of "all the hypothalamic nuclei except the mamillo-infundibularis group."

That is, the sympathetic, which "has command over those mechanisms essential for mobilizing the resources of the body" in emergencies (Fulton, *160*, 229), is activated as a whole when this, its highest level, is in a state of intense and general excitation.[31] Each of the effects is appropriate for some kind of emergency, but none is appropriate for all kinds. Neverthless, the generality of the effect depends on the intensity of the excitement only. In great intensity the pattern seems to be indiscriminately applied to all kinds of emergencies. Not only that, but, in emotional excitement the "sacral parasympathetic appears to discharge simultaneously with the sympathetic" (Fulton, *160*, *224*).

By way of illustration we may also mention a few of the individual parts of emotional patterns which are produced by the interofective system. Among the cardio-vascular effects of excited states are the "pallor of fear and anger . . . and the palpitations of the heart" (sympathetic excitation) and the "blush of shame" (sympathetic depression) (Bard, *19*, 276). These are symptoms of the shifting of blood and of changes in blood pressure probably produced from the hypothalamic center which "discharges during strong emotion" (Kabat *et al.*, *229*, 952). In fact, changes in blood pressure, and probably from this source, may be the most delicate indicator of the degree of excitement, the slightest as well as the greatest (Darrow, *102*). Another delicate indicator of excitement, but whether always from this source is now less certain, is palmar sweating—the psychogalvanic reflex.[32] Fear and anxiety produce general "cold sweat" (sympathetic excitation). Excited emotions reduce peristalsis in the stomach and intestine (Cannon, *58*). The "depressive influence of fear and pain upon gastric secretion" has been noted (Bard, *19*, 277); and sympathetic stimulation produces the secretion of a thick viscid saliva only (Fulton, *160*, 217).[33] Yet sexual excitement has been found to increase both normal saliva and gastric juice (Bard, *19*, 277). It appears that lacrimation may occur either as part of excited or depressed states. That is difficult to construe, since lacrimation is usually regarded as a parasympathetic reaction (Fulton, *160*, 482), though the glands seem to be innervated both by that and by the sympathetic system, as noted above. Diuresis is inhibited during emotional stress (Hare, *180*, 425); there is a "rapid liberation of glucose during the emotional reactions of animals" (Beattie, *30*, 98); piloerection is a part of the expression of anger and of fear (Walker, *417*, 400); and these are signs of sympathetic activity. But "waves of bladder

[31] Beattie regards the interofective side of sham rage as "an explosive outburst of sympathico-adrenal activity" (*30*, 99).

[32] Darrow (*103*, 288) takes it as "an index of the general arousal of the organism" or as representing the relatively enduring "excitation-background" (*ibid.*, 285) for "'mobilization' or preparedness for adaptive response" (*ibid.*, 289). So far as our interpretation is concerned that is the same thing as degree of excitement, or emotional state.

[33] The general influence of the sympathetic system upon the digestive tract has not been clarified. It may be largely vasomotor, for it is to be remembered that "the blood vessels of the digestive tract between mouth and rectum and of the glands opening into that portion, receive autonomic fibers only from the sympathetic system" (Bard, *24*, 175).

contraction may be induced by emotional stimuli" (Langworthy, *250*, 342). Is this due to a sacral parasympathetic discharge?

It will be noted that all these individual elements have been reported above (p. 1060 ff.) as excitable from the general region of the hypothalamus.[34] But, as we have already acknowledged (pp. 1058 ff. and 1069), it is unknown whether each is represented there by a special center or, on the other hand, whether each individual effect has been artificially produced by itself, if it has, only by exciting a separate path descending from a center for an extensive pattern to a lower center which controls the specific function. If these hypothalamic centers are all specific, then the inclusion of more and more of them in an extending pattern, as excitation increases, must be put down to a neural phenomenon in the nature of spreading or irradiation.[35] If they are only general, then it would seem that the effect of increased excitation must be due to variations in the resistance to excitation from above on the part of the lower and specific centers.[36] In one way or the other the characteristic of emotional states is that out of specific effects, or small groups of effects, producible independently of each other at low intensities, there are integrated a considerable number of diverse extensive patterns; these, as the intensity of excitement increases to a maximum, tend toward a single pattern of intense excitement, with the result that, from this evidence alone, the source from which it developed becomes no longer determinable. For the present, Dott's hypothetical arrangement, which supposes both specific and general centers at this level, seems to be the safest; even then irradiation or spreading seems to be a necessary hypothesis to explain the near uniformity of intense excitement, whatever its particular cause.[37] The fact of such integration into diverse extensive patterns,

[34] Certain of them, it is true, are associated jointly or exclusively with the anterior region.

[35] Hilgard and Marquis (*197*, 328) criticize Pavlov on the ground that he "speaks of drainage or irradiation of 'neural energy,'" without considering the properties of nerve excitation and conduction." On this ground they should also criticize the "father of neurology," for he too conceived of a "spreading of the discharge from this focus" (Jackson, *215*, 177; and see our quotations on p. 1075). Sherrington uses the term "simultaneous combination" (*375*, *167–168*) for a similar manifestation. Because this constantly observed phenomenon cannot yet be explained in more fundamental terms is no reason for not recognizing its existence or giving it a name. As well criticize Sherrington's "c.e.s." which may turn out to be an "internuncial bombardment" (Lorente de Nó, *274*).

[36] A third possibility exists which I have not seen mentioned. We have regarded these centers as being responsive each to its own special excitor, neural or humoral. Instead, it may be that most of them respond to most of the excitors, but that their individual thresholds to particular excitors vary widely. Thus spreading would not be spreading of the excitation in one center to another, but rather the inclusion of more and more centers in the increasing influence of one common cause, as this cause increased in intensity.

[37] The phenomenon of spreading seems sometimes—though perhaps not always—to be confined within each of the chief regions, anterior and posterior, so that they maintain in some degree their generally opposed effects. For instance, Bard (*19*, *277*) noted an increase of saliva and of gastric juice in dogs under the influence of sexual excitement. That is, in the anterior region, the excitement seemed to spread to the centers for saliva-

assimilating to a single pattern in great excitement, connotes, as already stated, the mutual exclusiveness of each particular cause when it is of an intensity sufficient to produce integrated effects. But this, as we shall see from all the evidence adduced from other sources, is a general characteristic of all integration on the effector side—in fact, of all nervous activity, at least below the cortical level, and even there in a modified form.

We must conclude, from the whole body of evidence, that "the diencephalon is, without doubt, not only the head ganglion of the vegetative nervous system but is also the central nervous mechanism for emotional response" (Riddoch, *344*, 117); that such response consists of various combinations of interofective and exterofective effects; that the exterofective part consists of "stereotyped reaction patterns," "more complicated than those produced by spinal reflexes but not essentially different," especially in that "in their essential features they are not learned," but are "congenitally organized" and "natively inherent in the brain" (Cannon, *68*, 263); and that the interofective part consists of various centrally initiated combinations of alterations in rate of all the functions normally maintained in balance by the autonomic and endocrine systems. Roughly speaking, it seems to be true of the emotional states themselves that those which constitute excitement consist of various degrees of general and hypertonic hypothalamic excitation, somewhat differentiated in kind and confined chiefly to the posterior region, while those which constitute depression consist of general loss of tonic excitation in the hypothalamus, probably also confined to the posterior region and also with some differences of kind. The excited emotional states communicate themselves to and through the sympathetic system in the form of corresponding combinations of the effects of the activity of that system; conversely, the depressed emotional states result in various degrees, and combinations of various kinds, of paralysis of sympathetic functions. By way of the motor system the excited emotional states produce certain recognizable types of emotional expression (behavior); and the depressed emotional states produce loss of tone in the skeletal musculature evidenced by relaxation (postural) and inertia (phasic). It necessarily follows that the so-called "head-ganglion" of the sympathetic system is able to exert both phasic and tonic effects upon, and via, the subcortical centers of the motor system. Finally, of the total effects, interofective and exterofective, it may be said that

tion and gastric secretion. On the other hand, he also noted (*ibid.*, 292) that warm temperatures diminished, and cold temperatures increased, the "sham rage" response of his decorticate animals. As we shall note below (p. 1089 ff.), heat loss (response to warm temperatures) seems to be managed by excitation in the anterior region, and heat production (response to cold temperatures) by excitation in the posterior region. Thus we must interpret his observation to mean that the vigor of the "sham rage" reaction depends on the algebraic sum of its own excitation plus the excitation of heat production and minus that of heat loss. Then we would have spreading of excitation from the heat production to the "sham rage" mechanism (both posterior), but spreading (or continuance) of inhibition from the heat loss to the "sham rage" mechanism (anterior to posterior).

exaggerated excitement or exaggerated depression tend toward the same patterns, respectively, at their maxima, whatever the cause or name assigned to the emotion.

E. THE HYPOTHALAMUS AND PRESENT WANTS

It is quite impossible to distinguish emotional states and their manifestations from those central, integrated effects—and their manifestations—that are produced by the variations, or tendencies, away from homeostasis (wants) which we have considered in the text (Chapter 1). These wants arise from various bodily sources; so do those emotions that we can consider. All the interofective details of emotional manifestations which we have noted above are also functions for the maintenance or restoration of homeostasis; and many of the exterofective patterns are common to both. The more extensive the pattern—the greater the degree of integration—in each case, the more functions become common to the expression of these different wants and of these different emotions. The greater the degree of excitement or depression produced by either, the more nearly identical become the manifestations of both classes. We are therefore going to find it necessary to eliminate the distinction between the two classes and to consider the highest central effects of all wants—if the degree of integration reached is sufficient to produce central effects at this level—to be emotional states of various degrees of intensity, and, conversely, the causes of all emotional states, whose physiological causes can be recognized, to be wants. On this basis, we shall have to add to our list of basic wants, as presented in the text, all other causes of emotional states the physiological basis of which is at present determinable. This list appears at the end of this section.

To support the foregoing statements, let us consider first the resemblances between the effects of wants and of the emotional states we have considered. It was a part of the thesis of Cannon's book, called *Bodily Changes in Pain, Hunger, Fear and Rage*, that the interofective effects of these four conditions—and others—are too uniform in great intensity to permit their differentiation on the ground of the pattern of visceral effects (*58*, 280). Moreover, even at lower intensities, "the same visceral changes occur in very different emotional states and in non-emotional states" (Cannon, *61*, 109). These visceral changes are those produced by general sympathetic activity. They also occur on "exposure to cold, when the blood sugar is too greatly reduced, in asphyxial states and in very vigorous muscular effort" (Cannon, *68*, 262). But the same thing is true, to a considerable degree, of the exterofective effects. So both kinds of effect must be included. "One of the most peremptory causes of the discharge of energy [excited struggling] is that due to an attempt to obstruct forcibly the mouth and the nose so that asphyxia is threatened" (Crile, *96*, 23).[1] As the

[1] This may be a conditioned reflex, or it may be an example of the "freedom" reflex outlined hereafter; but it may also be a direct response to the want of air.

rectal temperature of Teague and Ranson's cats rose, they became "more and more excited," as evidenced by "frequent cries, dilated pupils, and struggling" (*392*, *565*). On exposure to cold, as Cannon notes (above), several of the interofective components of the response are the same as those of emotional states—rage, for instance. While the cold response never appears itself to reach the level of "excitement," Bard noted (*19*, 292) that cold temperatures increased sham rage (i.e., it started from a higher level of excitation in the same region), while warm temperatures diminished it (i.e., inhibited the emotional apparatus). In "insulin poisoning," which consists in a marked blood-sugar deficit, one notes sweating, dilatation of the pupils, accelerated heart beat, and even an "emotional outburst" (Cannon, *66*, 99). The need of water, food, or of getting rid of waste and refuse (micturition and defecation) is observed in animals[2] to lead to precisely the sort of restlessness (locomotion) that was presumably produced in Ranson's cats by artificial stimulation of the hypothalamus, and the restraint of which was presumably responsible for their exhibition of "sham rage." Euphoria is also manifested by restlessness, accompanied in children by at least mild excitement. Restlessness is, I think, generally taken to be an "affective reaction." Of course sexual excitement is an emotional pattern. So, too, are the responses to pain. Fulton refers to the "pain reflexes (e.g., struggling, changes in respiration, and rise in blood pressure)" (*160*, 29). Speaking of what he and Cannon call "hunger pangs," Carlson (*71*, 215) assumes that "hunger is essentially pain"; and Landis concludes that hunger in general "fits excellently in practically any usual definition of emotion" (*248*, 508). Finally, another of our basic wants, fatigue, seems to lead to various degrees of emotional depression. It is perhaps not too much to say, with Bianchi, that "hunger, thirst, the sexual need, the need of moving about, of sleeping, of avoiding high and low temperatures, are fundamental emotions" (*35*, 269) for "emotion is inherent in the modifications of the organic being" (*ibid.*, 260).[3] To this list, as causes of emotional states, we may add nearly all the other bodily wants we have enumerated.

If emotional states and the central effect of wants requiring integrated

[2] See references in the text, Chapter 3, Section A 2.

[3] In fact, to him, some of those emotions we have already considered, his "second group" such as fear, joy, anger, etc., are merely more "extra-organic." The causes of these "extra-organic" emotions are, in our terminology, the quasi-external wants. See below.

It is usual to distinguish "emotional reactions" from "instinctive impulses" (e.g., Le Gros Clark, *85*, 107). But the physiologists' difference may actually be chiefly one of degree. On the other hand, when McDougall (*284*, 48–49) said that the "peculiar and distinct" "affective quality of each instinctive process is an emotion," and that, while emotion is not prominent in the "simpler instincts," nevertheless "each of the principal instincts conditions . . . some one kind of emotional excitement whose quality is specific or peculiar to it," each being a "primary emotion," he was talking about what the physiologists call the "emotional experience"—of which more later—and not about the observable "emotional reactions," or "instinctive impulses," or automatic behavior patterns, we are now discussing. But, of course, his assumption was that "emotional" and "instinctive" (whatever that is) are adjectives that must always be used together, representing two aspects of the operations of one mechanism.

responses are one and the same thing, we naturally expect to find that the region in which those states appear is what we shall call the primary source of integrated responses to wants—of the management of maintenance of homeostasis. This is the present hypothesis of many investigators. Speaking of the hypothalamus, Harvey Cushing wrote, "Here in this well-concealed spot, almost to be covered by a thumb-nail,[4] lies the very mainspring of primitive existence—vegetative, emotional, reproductive—on which with more or less success, man has come to superimpose a cortex of inhibitions" (*100*, 56). More fully, it is "an organ of control and co-ordination of the more primitive bodily . . . functions"—the "internal environment" (Dott, *120*, 184). "Working hand in glove with the endocrine organs, especially the hypophysis . . . it supervises bodily economy—the intake of oxygen, food and fluids, their assimilation, the excretion of waste products, the regulation of body temperature and circulation, and the elimination of fatigue through sleep" (Riddoch, *344*, 102). It is concerned with the "development and maintenance of sexual functions" (Riddoch, *loc. cit.*) and with "the perpetuation of the species—sexual emotion and functional activity" (Dott, *loc. cit.*). "Consistently with its primitive place in the evolution of the brain . . . [it] contains the mechanisms of the more primitive psychic and emotional reactions. It plays a part in conditioning moods of elation and depression, and their expression in laughter or weeping" (Dott, *120*, 167). "Through it the appropriate reactions of the individual for attack and defence are evoked" (Riddoch, *loc. cit.*)—"aggression, suspicion, fear, anger" (Dott, *loc. cit.*).[5] "It ignores refinements of decency and convention, if isolated from the control of its better-educated instructor, the frontal cortex, which seems [normally] to exercise an inhibitory influence on its cruder yet vitally important functions" (Dott, *loc. cit.*).

Apparently this—the highest level of the "old brain"—is the chief locus of what Hughlings Jackson called "automatic mind—instinct" (*216*, II, 269). At any rate, it is here that there take place "the more primitive elements of mental activity, such as are represented in emotional reactions, instinctive impulses, etc." (Le Gros Clark, *85*, 107). Frolov, interpreting Pavlov (*157*, 78 ff.), describes, as the lowest of the three systems or levels that he was considering, the subcortical centers " 'most closely adjacent to the cortex.' " "This is the region of complex unconditioned reflexes or instincts, in psychological terminology the region of emotions or wishes, which is closely connected, as is recognized by endocrinologists, with the chemistry

[4] The comparatively very small size of the hypothalamus has already been commented upon (p. 1057 and note 11). But the mere fact that the gray matter in the whole brain-stem is of small extent compared with that of the cortex indicates nothing of their relative importance or influence. The areas of the brain-stem are small because they are simple, not because they are weak—that is, the number of *different* reactions possible is small. Probably the size of the cortex is due to the vast variety of its potentialities. But, there, what has been gained in variety (differentiation) may have been at the cost of power.

[5] Rioch (in discussion of Alpers *12*, 748) includes among what he calls "pseudo-affective" reactions, which have been observed in decorticate cats—rage, fear, fighting, contentment, attention (alert), seizing of prey, and female estrual behavior.

of the organism and its changes during the various cycles of life. It is these centres that give the organism a sufficiently firmly based orientation in relation to the environment and ensure equilibrium, but this orientation is strictly limited to a small number of situations (hunger, self-defence, sexual excitation) and is far from adequate for establishing higher degrees of adaptation." Specifically, he supposes that the diencephalon originates such complex movements as eating, sexual behavior, struggle, pursuit of prey and emotional facial expression (*ibid.*, 30–31).

The sufficiency of these subcortical mechanisms for the maintenance of life evidently declines according as the position of the animal is higher in the evolutionary scale and according to its degree of maturity.[6] Excepting men and monkeys, "the thalamus [decorticate] animal retains normal visceral activity, the ability to maintain normal body temperature, an apparently nearly normal control of striated muscle activity as evidenced by posture, walking, etc., and exhibits various types of pseudo-affective responses to pain, hunger, etc." (Rogers, *353*, 639). "Goltz's dog [chronic decorticate] retained . . . the entire adaptive dynamics of the body connected with the manifestation of complex *unconditioned* reflexes [including the "investigatory reflex," *157*, 63] or emotions," even including "certain elements of playfulness." In fact, it became "*predominantly* an emotional animal" (Frolov, *157*, 57). It could run, eat and drink, defecate and micturate, and mate and produce offspring (Frolov, *157*, 54). Approximately the same seems to be true of cats (Hinsey, *199*).[7] On the other hand, a decorticate mature monkey is unable to feed itself, to run or climb and, even after four months (chronic), cannot maintain a horizontal posture (Fulton, *160*, 453; Bieber and Fulton, *37*, 434).[8] But if the decortication—or at least ablation of all motor areas—is performed upon infant monkeys, they retain a motor control which "is entirely adequate to maintain the existence of the individual," in spite of a "permanent deficit." This indicates that the "relatively simple and uncoördinated movements of the animal at this age are therefore also integrated at a subcortical level" (Kennard, *235*, 145). We draw the conclusion that, among the primates, after maturation (and learning) has taken place, these subcortical regions are no longer sufficient for the exterofective performances at least. But that still lower levels are never sufficient is evidenced by the fact that all the foregoing capacities, exterofective and interofective alike, are abolished

[6] In view of the fact that precise proof of this generalization seems to have been wanting until recent years, it is of interest to note that William James said fifty years ago (*220*, I, 75), "It would seem, then, that in these higher creatures [monkeys and man] the lower centres must be less adequate [by themselves] than they are farther down in the zoological scale."

[7] Hinsey *et al.* (*200*, 1 and *21*) state that, with the cat, "for equilibration and . . . upright posture . . . the rostral portion of the tegmentum of the mesencephalon or its continuation into the hypothalamus is necessary and adequate."

Bard makes the statement (*23*, 564 and 565) that "rabbits lacking all cortex do not eat spontaneously." This may have a special (sensory) explanation.

[8] Their posture is known as "decorticate rigidity"; see Fulton, *160*, 185–187.

or altered in both birds and mammals by transection posterior to the interbrain, or in the midbrain (Rogers, *353*, 640).[9]

From these quotations it is clear that there is at present wide acceptance of the hypothesis that this, the highest level of the subcortical central nervous system, is the region of the emotional, instinctive, automatic (involuntary) life processes—in other words the primary source of integrated responses to what we have called wants. Since it is sufficient for living, however inexpertly, among lower or immature mammals, but becomes inadequate in mature primates without the cortex, we shall have to examine carefully the probable relations that arise, with evolution and maturation, between this subcortical mechanism and the cortex, as well as to try to determine whether such relations constitute a one-sided dependence of this on the "highest" level or rather an interdependence between two considerably independent and different systems. These questions will be considered in the following sections.

It is to be noted that in Riddoch's description of the supervision over the bodily economy exercised by the hypothalamus he includes practically all the, so-called, internal wants we have enumerated in the text.[10] Therefore, we should be ready to explore in some detail the relation between the use of the effector system that we have found available in this subcortical mechanism and the specific wants we are considering; in other words, to consider how far in each case the region of the hypothalamus is responsible for the behavior (and also the integrated internal activity or inactivity) which constitutes the corrective process directed toward the restoration of homeostasis in that particular respect.

Perhaps the most representative instance of the supervision exercised at this level is the regulation of body temperature. We quoted in the text (p. 49) Cannon's remark about the location of a "sensitive thermostat" in the diencephalon. The presence of this mechanism differentiates the warm-blooded from the poikilothermic animal and enables the former to maintain a normal body temperature regardless of the external temperature (within limits) and regardless of the heat it is itself generating (rate of activity). In part, the effector mechanism works to produce heat loss

[9] Lashley (*261*, 11) interprets some of the foregoing facts differently from the way they have been presented here. But he is questioning Lloyd Morgan's (*Instinct and Intelligence*, 1912) "opinion . . . that the cerebrum is not essential for the performance of any unlearned or instinctive activity" and his belief in "the reduction of automatized habits to subcortical levels" (*ibid.*, 10 and 14). As to the first point, the facts imply that "some instincts, which seem to be those requiring accurate differentiation of stimuli, are dependent upon cortical mechanisms" (*ibid.*, 11). With this we should certainly agree, though we should not go so far as to say with Frolov (*157*, 55) that the decorticate animal is "insensible to all stimuli such as light, sound, temperature, electricity, chemical substances, etc.," even if these were limited to external stimuli. As to the second point, we should say that there is no evidence supporting Morgan's "belief." The "unconscious," in the Freudian sense, may exist in or arise from these subcortical regions. Patterns of acquired motor habits which have merely become "automatic" most certainly do not.

[10] He does not mention blood neutrality or euphoria.

(cooling) or heat conservation and production (warming) by varying the rate of a single set of processes;[11] but it also utilizes, in part, different effector methods for the two opposite purposes. This latter is an a priori reason to expect dual heat regulating centers, one for heat loss and the other for heat conservation and production. The evidence seems to most of our authorities to point in that direction.[12] At any rate, all seem to be agreed that the chief temperature regulating mechanism is in the hypothalamus. And, among those who accept the theory of two centers, the more usual view locates the heat loss center in the anterior and the heat production and conservation center in the posterior region.[13] It is therefore not surprising to find that the interofective elements used in this control are among those we have already found attributable to the anterior region, as to loss, and to the posterior region, as to production (see p. 1060). Heat loss is promoted by cutaneous vasodilatation[14] and the accompanying water-shifting to the surface (increase of water available for evaporation),[15] by sweating (in primates),[16] by panting (in carnivores),[17] and is perhaps aided by the sup-

11 Thus Dott, with his pressor-depressor alterations of a basic rate (*120*, 171).

12 Among others see Bard, *24*, 195; Lilenthal and Otenasek, *269*, 116; Fulton, *160*, 248–249; Beattie, *30*, 83; Ranson, *333*, 342, *332*, 269; Ranson and Ingram, *335*, 1441; Teague and Ranson, *392*, 569; Ranson *et al.*, *334*, 465. Alpers (*10*, 30) admits the possibility. Riddoch (*344*, 111) thinks the idea "has nothing to recommend it." Morgan and Vonderahe (*306*, 91) assume "a number of cell groups rather than a single 'center,'" some of which are concerned with heat elimination and others with heat production and conservation. Balance is maintained between the two groups by mutual inhibition.

13 All of the authorities quoted in note 12, above, localize the two centers more or less precisely, the more precisely the more differently, but agree as to the two general regions concerned. Barbour agrees (*16*, 484) that the anterior hypothalamus is vital to the heat loss mechanism. But Keller and Hare (*232*, 1070), while they agree that the heat production center is in the hypothalamus, hold that heat loss is controlled below the level of the interbrain. And see their anomalous results (*ibid.*, 1067). Alpers (*10*, 30) believes the work of himself and associates indicates that the whole temperature regulating mechanism is in the infundibular region and the anterior hypothalamus. That would be in accordance with the results of Frazier *et al.* (*151*, 128)—N. hypothalamicus anterior. But, for a part of the heat loss mechanism, Fulton thinks (*160*, 248) that "the primary focus appears to be in the region of the tuber nuclei." And Davison and Selby (*111*, 589) say, "The appearance of the nuclei of the tuber and of heat regulation in mammals at about the same time suggests that the nuclei of the tuber cinereum have something to do with the regulation of body temperature."

14 Perhaps only a release phenomenon here (Fulton, *160*, 248); perhaps a reflex to cutaneous heat (Beattie, *30*, 83).

15 Barbour (*16*, 449). This results in dilution of solids (*ibid.*, 450). But sweating reconcentrates solids in spite of anti-diuresis (Beattie, *30*, 89) and shifting of water from liver (Barbour, *16*, 451). Water-shifting is controlled here (*ibid.*, 450 and 484).

16 Perhaps a different mechanism from cold (sympathetic) sweat (Beattie, *29*, 86), and produced by stimulation around the septum and anterior commissure (*ibid.*, 87) or the tuber nuclei (Fulton, *160*, 248). But Ranson (*333*, 395) considers the evidence unsatisfactory.

17 It is stated that the shallow, rapid respiration, called true polypneic panting, which serves the purpose of heat loss, while it is "an affair . . . of the hypothalamus" (Fulton, *160*, 168; Beattie, *30*, 90) is only obtainable if the caudo-dorsal thalamus is also intact (Pinkston *et al.*, *326*, 528; Lilienthal and Otenasek, *269*, 120). But see Ranson, *333*, 379. We shall have to consider what that may indicate, if it is the case.

pression of metabolism[18] and decreased heart rate.[19] Heat conservation and production is promoted by cutaneous vasoconstriction (Beattie, *30*, 84; Ranson, *333*, 395), and the accompanying water-shifting (decrease of water available for evaporation),[20] by piloerection (Ranson, *loc. cit.*; Walker, *417*, 414), by shivering,[21] and by the increase of metabolism, of the heart rate (Fulton, *160*, 248), and perhaps of the depth of respiration (Beattie, *30*, 83; Barcroft, *17*, 67). For the production of all these, except perhaps true polypneic panting and shivering, the hypothalamus seems sufficient; and for the two complete extensive patterns it is known to be essential. That is, the warm-blooded animal, when deprived of this apparatus, becomes poikilothermic.

Another but less complete and certain instance of the location in this region of the effector apparatus initiating responses to wants concerns sexual development and functioning. On page 1053 we discussed briefly the locus of the management of sexual behavior, but chiefly in a negative way in order to demonstrate that its normal course does not consist merely of spinal reflexes. We concluded there that, for "the long series of acts and activities which constitute sexual behavior (lasting in the female for months)," supraspinal levels and probably the upper brain-stem are necessary. On the basis of this evidence, sexual functions were therefore included among the vegetative functions attributed to the upper brain-stem (p. 1068)—the hypophysis as to development, and perhaps the mammillary bodies as to activities, internal and external. So far as the levels above these are concerned, "it has been demonstrated that in several species of mammals the full pattern of mating behavior can be elicited after removal of all cerebral cortex" (Bard, *23*, 575). By this process of elimination it is concluded that, while "in any mammal the presence of the cerebral cortex greatly increases the number of circumstances which are able to modify the occurrence of sexual behavior" (*loc. cit.*), the essential region for setting the whole process in motion lies below the cortex (and striatum) and above the bulb (and lower midbrain)—that is, in the interbrain and upper portions of the midbrain (*ibid.*, 566). While the connection of the hypothalamus, strictly speaking, has not been proved even for coition alone, it is obvious that sexual excitement includes many of the evidences of emotional excitement in general, as outlined above, even to so inappropriate an element as piloerection (Walker, *417*, 412). This suggests that it is a form of general hypothalamic excitation, like the rest. While the positive evidence is limited as yet, the known relation of the hypophysis to sexual development and the indications that the mammillary bodies are

[18] Fulton, *160*, 247. Beattie says (*30*, 88) that whether this occurs is unknown.

[19] At least the same region that causes vasodilatation causes slowing of the heart (Beattie, *30*, 89).

[20] Beattie, *30*, 82; Barbour (*16*, 449–450). Barbour holds (*ibid.*, 472) that this particular response to cold is from the anterior, not the posterior, hypothalamus.

[21] Though shivering appears to require an intact hypothalamus (Fulton, *160*, 250; Beattie, *30*, 83; but see Barbour, *16*, 483) it also, like panting, appears to require the thalamus—here the "caudal half of the medial portion" (Beattie, *30*, 75).

concerned in sexual functioning, as noted on p. 1070, go to support the general identification with this region.[22]

The relation of the effector system at this level to the rest of the bodily wants we have enumerated in the text has either been covered in the discussion of the vegetative and motor functions of the upper brain-stem (Sections B 3 and C 3) or can be more conveniently included as parts of the subject we now proceed to consider.[23]

I. TRANSMISSION OF INTERNAL WANTS TO THE HYPOTHALAMUS

Hitherto, we have given little or no attention to the causation of the manifold and important activities which we have found it necessary to assign to the hypothalamus. But, since it now appears that the ultimate causes are the bodily wants, we must now undertake to trace the course of these ultimate causes to this effector apparatus—that is, we must determine the way in which these wants are centripetally transmitted to this point. Because the exploration of this region of the brain has been conducted so largely by means of artificial stimulation (chiefly the Horsley-Clarke technique), there is much less detailed knowledge of the normal excitors of these extensive patterns than there is of the effects of local excitation which we have been describing. Nevertheless, there is in all cases some evidence, and in some cases rather complete evidence, as to what is the source from which, and what the mechanism of centripetal transmission by which, these excitations are normally aroused. Let us first consider the cases where the evidence shows, or suggests, that this transmission is via the vascular system of integration—the blood and lymph (and perhaps cerebrospinal fluid).

While in other cases the evidence is still incomplete, it appears almost certain that both the heat-loss and the heat-production and conservation patterns can be activated by variations away from normal of the temperature of the blood reaching the hypothalamic region itself.[24] To this extent the afferent side of the nervous system is not involved. "Among vertebrates

[22] Doubtless in the normal male there are separable constituents of the sexual act which are local reflexes; and these are accompanied by little, if any, central excitation. Thus "morning erection" (parasympathetic) or "nocturnal emission" (sympathetic). But central excitation appears to be required for normal integration of the components.

[23] In the case of all wants the relation of the effector system at this level is confined to those corrective measures which require more or less complete integration. The rest are effected at lower levels.

[24] On the basis of the experiments of Magoun *et al.* (*287*, 113), Ranson (*333*, 355 and 391) and Fulton (*160*, 249) conclude that the heat-loss mechanism (anterior nuclei) is probably responsive to the temperature of its own blood supply. For that part of the pattern which consists of water-shifting, Barbour arrives at the same conclusion (*16*, 450). Since "the respiratory centre of the medulla is not responsive to the temperature of the blood" (Fulton, *160*, 167), it is to be presumed that respiratory effects (panting, etc.) of overheated blood arise at this higher level. This is presumed by Pinkston *et al.* (*326*, 528) of their hyperpnea, but not of true polypneic panting.

On the basis of shivering only the same direct excitation by the immediate blood supply has been supposed for the heat conservation and production mechanism. Thus Sher-

nearly all specific sexual responses depend on the presence of gonadal hormones in the blood" (Bard, *23*, 552). Though "the way in which gonadal hormones activate the central [integrating] mechanisms" is still a problem (*ibid.*, 553), it is clear that "such behavior is managed by central mechanisms which are activated either directly or indirectly by gonadal hormones" (*ibid.*, 574). Conversely, at least for cats, it has been proved that "the activation of the central mechanisms responsible for the patterned sexual behavior of both sexes is not dependent on afferent impulses from the genital organs or from the erogenous zones surrounding the external genitalia"; though not necessarily "wholly independent of all afferent impulses" (*ibid.*, 553).[25] It appears to be likely, at any rate, that these central mechanisms are in the region we are considering, though not necessarily exclusively in the hypothalamus, and it is probable that their excitation, or at least facilitation, is produced directly by their own blood supply.

Instances of centripetal transmission through the integrating system of the blood of wants which exist in the blood were given in the text (pp. 47 ff). Three of these, including the regulation against excessive heat mentioned above, are of further interest to us here. Ordinarily, breathing is regulated by the respiratory center in the medulla in direct response—primarily—to the hydrogen-ion concentration in the blood. But, in the condition known as asphyxia (partial) the marked deficiency of oxygen or excess of carbon dioxide (or both) in the blood appears to produce extensive patterns which include more than respiration—patterns closely resembling those otherwise obtainable by hypothalamic excitation. "The evidence for asphyxial stimulation of the sympathico-adrenal system is overwhelming" (Cannon, *58*, 217). Probably not all of the effect is produced at this level (*loc. cit.*); but the respects in which the effects are "like pain and excitement"—the mobilization of sugar, etc.—lead Cannon to consider it among the emotional phenomena. So it appears also to Crile (see p. 1085). Whether the extensive pattern produced at this level is neurally excited by the excessive efforts of the respiratory center, or is a direct response to a marked variation in the blood, we do not know. But the latter seems more probable.

We noted above that the marked deficit in blood sugar in insulin poisoning also produces a pattern resembling that of hypothalamic (posterior) excitation, including sweating, dilatation of the pupils and accelerated heart beat, and that it may reach even to an "emotional outburst." If so, it would appear to be most likely that it is an extensive pattern spreading from the sugar-control center in the anterior region, or the sugar-

rington, *377*, 422–423; Uprus *et al.*, *410*, 230. But see Jung *et al.* (*227*, 38), who doubt that the response to blood temperature is direct.

[25] To suppose that, because among mating organisms a sex object is necessary, therefore the distance-receptors are responsible for the excitation, is superficial; first, because there is no excitation from the presence of a sex object, if the central state is not conducive; and, second, because there frequently is such excitation in the absence of a sex object.

mobilization center in the tuber cinereum, when that center is overstimulated by an excessive deficit.[26] Obviously, this reaction is direct to the condition of the blood. Finally, the same pattern was evidenced by Teague and Ranson's normal cats (p. 1086) as their blood temperature rose in spite of the activity of their heat-loss mechanism. They became "more and more excited," as indicated by "frequent cries, dilated pupils, and struggling." But these are not phenomena of the activation of the heat-loss mechanism; rather they are components of "emotional excitement"—the activation of the posterior region. In the case of blood-sugar deficit it seems possible, and in the case of heat loss it seems likely, that overexcitation of even an anterior center may spread to the posterior region.[27] Certainly the direct cause in the second case is the temperature of the blood. From these instances it would appear that specific centers in this or other regions [28] can correct minor variations from homeostasis in the blood. When, however, their efforts prove unavailing and the variations increase and become marked, these centers become so hyperexcited that something in the nature of "spreading" occurs, and the centers which express emotional excitement become engaged. It is as if the intensity of the want governed the degree of integration, not only from lower to higher levels but at this level itself.

However, there are other of the bodily wants, responses to which are certainly capable of being generated at this level, which, if intense, produce emotional behavior—restlessness—and the excitors of which may be, at least in part, the condition of the immediate blood supply. Before considering the other possible source of excitation we will give some sample facts. We have suggested in Appendices I A and I B that thirst and hunger may be fundamentally conditions of the blood—slight variations from normal salinity, hypoglycemia, etc. And, in the text (p. 56), the possibility was not excluded that a certain type of fatigue consists in the presence of an excess of the products of metabolism in the blood. Is "hungry blood" responsible for the fact that the decorticate dog becomes "restless" and walks or runs about aimlessly when hungry—that is, at feeding time? [29] Is "thirsty" blood responsible for the fact that these dogs

[26] The locus of the sugar-mobilization center would seem to make it a more likely source for such an extensive pattern.

[27] But see p. 1083, note 37. Apparently the latter supposition, here, would contradict our interpretation of Bard's observation that the activity of the heat loss (anterior) center diminishes that of the "sham rage" (posterior) center. But, in terms of the current interpretation of inhibition (see below), it would not be anomalous for inhibitory effects elsewhere, from low excitation, to change over to excitatory effects at high degrees of excitation.

[28] Possibly the respiratory center in the case of carbon dioxide (and perhaps oxygen) content of the blood, or possibly some center in the hypothalamus; probably the posterior hypothalamus itself in the case of blood sugar; and probably the anterior hypothalamus in the case of heat loss.

[29] For example, Hinsey *et al.* (*200*, 3) refer to Dresel's dog which exhibited "spontaneous" motility (involuntary) and became restless and ran about when hungry. Frolov (*157*, 57 ff.) refers to Goltz's dog which, about feeding time, began aimless movements,

drink, and drink only enough to make good their water need? [30] Is "tired" blood responsible for their maintenance of the sleep-waking rhythm? [31] At present these questions cannot be answered; but it is necessary to keep them open; for, in these cases, the means of excitation of the kind next to be considered may not be the actual or, at least, the only ones.

We come now to the cases where the centripetal transmission of wants to this region seems to be by way of the neural integrating system. While our chief concern with the thalamus will arise when we come to consider cortical functions, it appears that its phylogenetically oldest part, which Walker calls the "paleothalamus," functions only in connection with subcortical mechanisms and chiefly with the hypothalamus.[32] Thus, if we are able still to maintain the distinction between the two sides of the nervous system at so high a central level, we would regard the region we have been considering as the highest subcortical efferent, or at least internuncial, level and this "paleothalamus" as the highest subcortical afferent level at which there are direct connections from one side to the other. With two minor exceptions the hypothalamus itself appears to have no direct afferent connections from lower levels.[33] If so, all other strictly afferent (upcoming) impulses reaching it must be relayed to it from the thalamus,[34] and probably from these ancient nuclei. It is said that these and a few closely related thalamic nuclei are not connected with the cortex, and that they do not degenerate—and that they are the only ones which do not—after ablation of the cortex.[35] But, whether via the paleothalamus or direct, we are enabled to judge somewhat of the kinds of afferent paths or patterns which reach—and presumably are normally short-circuited at—these centers, and thus to distinguish the potential neural excitors of the effector region we have been examining. Though, as we shall see, they are not strictly limited to such, these afferent patterns correspond generally to Hughlings Jackson's class which produces systemic or organic sensa-

"searching" for food, which of course he could not see or smell. The fact that hunger behavior continued in Sherrington's dog after spinal transection at the cervical level leaves, as the only possible neural avenue, visceral afferents running with the vagal nerves.

[30] Since dogs continue to drink when all sensory nerves from the mouth and pharynx are sectioned (Appendix I A, p. 1010) the cause of drinking behavior must be some as yet unrecognized afferent nerves or the condition of the blood. Mettler's decorticate dog drank and "exhibited a tendency to stop drinking after a time" (*297*, 1243).

[31] Or is the latter, at least in respect of its diurnal periodicity, associated with sexual development, as we suggest in Section G 2 below.

[32] Strictly, the nuclei of the midline (Walker, *416*, 239). Their efferent tracts are mostly (five of them) to the hypothalamus (*ibid.*) and they have no cortical (only subcortical) projections (Fulton, *160*, 274).

[33] Perhaps the mammillary peduncle, if found in man, and some vago-supraoptic connections (Ingram, *212*, 239). But see note 34 below. Also there may be some tracts in the periventricular system which ascend to the hypothalamus (Le Gros Clark, *86*, 31).

[34] For a further discussion of this point, see supplementary statement on "The Paleothalamus," at the end of this subsection.

[35] On the degeneration test, see supplementary statement on "The Paleothalamus," at the end of this subsection.

tions. They yield "those vague and undefinable impressions which arise in association with all sorts of visceral activities and metabolic processes . . . by which the organism is enabled to appreciate itself as a unified being" (Le Gros Clark, *84*, 413).[36] Nevertheless, so far as this circuit itself is concerned, it is quite certain that they should be called neither sensations nor impressions (except in Jackson's sense), for "sensation . . . demands . . . consciousness" (Head, *183*, 747) and, in spite of Head, there is good reason to hold that consciousness is not a concomitant of activities in either the thalamic or the hypothalamic region. Therefore, in order that they may come to be appreciated in the field in which there is consciousness they must be mediated to that field in some other way. This point we shall have to consider in Section G. In any case, the fact that they continue to pass over to the efferent side when the cortex, the locus of consciousness, is removed[37] indicates that they also pass over—or may do so—in the normal animal, and therefore that their effects belong in the classification of automatic rather than deliberate, or volitional, behavior.[38]

On the basis of Brouwer's distinction between paleosensibility and neosensibility—the fibers for the former being carried in the anterolateral column and those for the latter in the posterior column of the cord—and the fact that the fibers of the anterolateral column which reach to this level terminate in the midline nuclei of the thalamus, Walker suggests that these ancient nuclei are concerned with paleosensibility (*416*, 262, 272). At any rate, being related chiefly to the axial portion of the body, they are concerned largely with visceral sensibility (interoceptive), which is the most primitive kind (*ibid.*, 239). But they are also "capable of a limited [?] appreciation of pain and tactile stimuli" (exteroceptive) with some (crude) localization.[39] There is reason to believe, moreover, as we shall see (p. 1102), that this exteroceptive capacity extends to all strong stimulation (light, sound, etc.) even via the distance receptors.[40]

[36] Almost the same terms are used by Papez (*315*, 729).
[37] Walker (*416*, 272) supposes that impulses "passing through the midline structures are rarely consciously appreciated." Apparently they compose the class Munk called generalized sensation, *Gemeinempfindung*, "presumably unconscious," responses to which continue to be "elicitable after complete ablation of the cortical sensory areas" (Fulton, *160*, 377).
[38] As to this dictum see Section H.
[39] Walker, *416*, 242. That is, with the cortex absent and therefore with only these nuclei remaining, an animal can appreciate (react to), with this remaining part of the thalamus, touch and pinprick (pain) on the face and heavy touch and pinprick on the body, though with bad localization (*ibid.*, 252). Head asserted that both pain and temperature sense were unimpaired, at least after ablation of the postcentral cortex (Walker, *416*, 257). See also Fulton *160*, 266.
[40] Munk's *Gemeinempfindungen* resulted from any strong stimulation. Walker (*416*, 241) says that the midline nuclei receive afferents from other thalamic nuclei. But see "The Paleothalamus," below, for Papez's suggestion of direct connection to the geniculates, which seems the more probable channel.

At any rate it appears that "strong sensory stimuli, especially if unexpected, may also sometimes release subcortical functions, apparently without the intervention of cortical activity" (Darrow, *102*, 575). And that this includes light and sound seems demonstrated

It is evident from the foregoing that we have here—and in possible but unknown direct afferent connections from below to the hypothalamic region—the other source of excitation of the subcortical effector apparatus we have been considering. That is, it is clear that when the decorticate animal shows responses appropriate to the bodily wants—so-called spontaneous behavior—the mechanism for the centripetal transmission of the variation, or tendency, away from homeostasis, is either the integrating system of the blood reaching directly to the subcortical effector mechanisms or it is this particular portion of the whole neural afferent integrating system connecting at this level with these particular effector mechanisms. And it becomes constantly more evident that this is equally true of the intact animal, so far as these functions are concerned.

The direct connection at this level between our wants and the appropriate behavior (however unskillful) is indicated by innumerable observations of decorticate animals (at least below the primates). We observed (note 29, above) that "hunger behavior" continues in dogs and cats after decortication, but only when hungry or about feeding time.[41] Thus the need of food must be productive of excitation in these subcortical effector centers either from the condition of the blood, or by means of afferent impulses,[42] or both. Distension of the bladder caused Dresel's decorticate dog to become restless and run about, exactly as hunger did.[43] In lower animals and birds, with cortex intact, the same behavior appears when the need of water[44] or the need of defecation arises. From all these instances it appears that the first effect, when the transmitted disturbance reaches, or is adequate to excite, these subcortical centers, is general and aimless

---

by Mettler's dog (*297*, 1238–1239), already referred to, as well as by others. The sense of light (brightness), with some discrimination, probably remains in subcortical visual mechanisms when the cortex is gone (Poliak, *330*, 227).

Moreover, this may include taste stimuli. Elliot Smith (*382*, 810) thinks the gustatory nerve becomes inserted into the alar lamina of the neural tube in the region which becomes the medulla. Thereafter, paths are laid down which connect it with the hypothalamus, which in turn sends a taste path to the cerebral hemispheres. If so, on its way to the sensory cortex, taste might be appreciated in the hypothalamus. But the paths are as yet almost unknown.

[41] While Mettler's decorticate dog overate when oversupplied, I am not sure that normal dogs would not do the same. At least it showed greater avidity for food when food had been withheld for several feeding periods (*297*, 1243).

[42] Carlson (*71*, 214), referring of course to "hunger pangs," holds that "the *primary hunger center* [on the "afferent pathway for the gastric hunger impulses"] is . . . the sensory nuclei of the vagi nerves in the medulla (fasciculus solitarius)"; but (*ibid.*, 215–216) the "thalamus is a very important reflex and relay station for the afferent hunger impulses." So far as it is reflex, this station must be represented by thalamic nuclei that do not degenerate after decortication.

[43] Hinsey *et al.*, *200*, 3. And they concede that "visceral stimulation may be the cause of these so-called spontaneous movements" (*ibid.*, 22). Mettler *et al.* (*297*, 1247) observed that their decorticate dog did not show incessant activity. The excitation arose only under well-defined circumstances. Spontaneous activity is not that of "a chicken with its head off."

[44] True also of decorticate dogs (see note 30, above). As noted there, this may be due to "thirsty" blood.

motion, called restlessness, and that only later does the behavior become specifically appropriate to the want which is causing it.

The best evidence that, in certain of these cases, the excitor of these subcortical mechanisms may be both neural and vascular, is furnished by the heat-regulating mechanism. In general, the autonomic components of both heat-loss and heat-production and conservation patterns seem to be producible by variations in the temperature of the local blood supply (see p. 1092). This seems also to be true of the two somatic components of such patterns, true polypneic panting for heat loss and shivering for heat production.[45] But for the former, as we noted on page 1073, the caudodorsal portion of the thalamus is held by some to be also essential: [46] and, for the latter, the same may be true of the caudal half of the medial portion of the thalamus (see Section D, note 14, above). Beattie (*30, 75*) thinks this part of the thalamus is the thermosensitive zone for the temperature gradient between the blood and the external environment.[47] His view and the general character (neural afferent) of the thalamus proper suggests that this influence on the effector mechanisms arises from skin temperature rather than from the local blood temperature. It would, therefore, be somewhat of an anomaly if these parts of the thalamus were also essential to the performance of the somatic component as a reaction to blood temperature. Moreover, it is not certain that this subcortical mechanism alone is sufficient to produce all of these reactions when external heat or cold have affected only the temperature of the skin and have not yet raised or reduced the blood temperature. And this for the reason that the evidence is somewhat equivocal as to whether the afferent nervous system reporting cutaneous heat or cold is capable of conveying these effects directly to the subcortical regions (paleothalamus) or whether it involves a mechanism included in or dependent on the cortex (thalamic relay). The question arises chiefly because of the fact that "sensory" shivering continues after decortication (Jung *et al.*, *272*, *37*), while "sensory" panting probably does not (Pinkston *et al.*, *326*, 528).[48] The difficulty could be resolved by supposing that the thalamic center concerned in sensory cold does not degenerate with decortication (i.e., is in the paleothalamus) while that one concerned in sensory heat does (i.e., is in the neothalamus).[49] This would not conform to Fulton's statement that the temperature sense (and

[45] Both occur in decorticate animals in response to changes in internal temperature. As to panting, see Pinkston *et al.*, *326*, 528. As to shivering see Sherrington, *377*, 422 and 423.

[46] Ranson (*333*, 379) definitely disputes this.

[47] As to cold, this seems to conform to Pinkston *et al.*, *326*, 529. Perhaps Beattie, also, considers it only to apply to cold.

[48] On the basis of the panting component, only, Pinkston *et al.* (*326*, 528) suggest that perhaps the sense of skin heat reaches only the cortex, while that of skin cold may go direct to the hypothalamus (*ibid.*, 529). The latter conclusion is supported by Aring (*13*, 3) and by Jung *et al.* (*227*, 37). Jung *et al.* also believe (*ibid.*, 38) that "sensory impulses are much more productive of shivering than a fall in blood temperature; and, when opposed, outweigh blood temperature."

[49] It is possible that panting is not a response to sensory (cutaneous) heat at all—only to blood heat.

pain) suffers the least impairment from cortical lesions (with, presumably, corresponding thalamic destruction). Nor would it explain the necessity of the thalamic center in the somatic response to blood temperature. We are, therefore, in somewhat of a quandary. Nevertheless, it seems evident that the effect of cutaneous cold, arriving over afferent nerves, can be short-circuited to the hypothalamic region; whether or not that is true also of cutaneous heat remains uncertain.

The Paleothalamus. In the text we followed Walker in the thesis that the part of the thalamus which he defines as the paleothalamus mediates practically all afferent impulses reaching the hypothalamus from lower levels. (See Ingram, *212*, 238). Le Gros Clark seemed at first to hold (*84*, 413) that the "hypothalamus . . . is a visceral correlation centre" which is itself the termination of ascending visceral tracts yielding impulses "on the basis of which the organism may develop an awareness of its internal organic activities" (*ibid.*, 414)—though presumably the "awareness" does not occur there. In that paper he does not consider the nuclei of the midline. But later (*86*) he assumes that the thalamus relays somatic afferent impulses to the hypothalamus via periventricular fibers; and he apparently approves Huber and Crosby (*209*) who include epithalamic centers with the hypothalamic in "the reception of visceral or interoceptive impulses and . . . their correlation and discharge to the appropriate somatic and visceral efferent centres." He also refers there to Papez (*315*, 729), who thinks the hypothalamus afferent impulses from below come partly from the "primitive sensory centers in the ventral thalamus," in which he includes the ventral parts of the lateral and medial geniculate bodies. This underlies the latter's theory of the emotional apparatus which we will discuss later. But it is of interest here, because afferents from the lateral (visual) and the medial (auditory) geniculates might explain certain responses in decorticate animals to bright light and loud noise. Mettler *et al.* (*297*, 1238) have found that a decorticate dog can learn a conditioned reflex to light and sound. Hinsey (*199*, 662) also summarizes these various views in the form of a quotation from Le Gros Clark (*86*).

As to the subthalamus, it is generally assumed to be on the somatic efferent side. Ariëns Kappers *et al.* (*231*, II, 1189) say that the "subthalamus in reality constitutes the forward continuation of the tegmentum of the midbrain" (presumably motor). Hinsey states (*199*, 663) that there is no positive evidence "that the hypothalamus deals only with visceral integrations and the subthalamus with somatic ones alone." "Such a division in terminology implies a functional separation that is not present," since stimulation of each may produce both kinds of effect. In part, these apparent differences are due to confused terminology; but in part they reflect uncertainty. Dusser de Barenne (*125*, 776) assumes that it is the "medial" thalamic nuclei acting on extrapyramidal mechanisms (not necessarily via the hypothalamus) that are responsible for the reactions (in cats) after decortication. If by "medial" is meant the nuclei of the midline, which remain after decortication, this observation may be fitted to the others (Walker, *416*, 253, so interprets him). In that case, however, his "medial" nucleus probably should not be identified with Head's "essential center," which seems to have been the dorsomedial nucleus. At any rate, it is to be doubted that these paleothalamic nuclei have direct connections to extrapyramidal mechanisms. Thus, when Dusser de Barenne notes a "high level of functional integration attained in the thalamic activity" (*125*, 770), after strychninization of the thalamus of a decorticate cat, we would assume that the activity was the result of paleothalamic excitation reaching the hypothalamus.

In Beattie's view (*30*, *69*) the posterior hypothalamus may receive most of its afferents from the thalamus, while those to the anterior hypothalamus come mostly from the prefrontal cortex via the septal nuclei. In this view the latter are part of the control system which we shall describe in Section G 4.

However, the definition of the paleothalamus on the basis of observation of degeneration after ablation of the cortex is somewhat equivocal. Ross and Woolsey (73 *J. H. Hosp. Bull.*, 1943, 65) have recently reported that the nuclei of the midline *do* degenerate, if *all* cortex is removed. And, on the other hand, others report experimental results which would indicate that the paleothalamus may also include the intralaminar nuclei, possibly some or all of the anterior group (Walker, *416*, 242–243), and possibly the centromedian nucleus of Luys (Fulton, *160*, *266*). Le Gros Clark considers the anteromedial nucleus as essentially "a part of the paleothalamus" (*84*, 438), but seems to consider the centromedian no longer a part (*ibid.*, 463).

We should note here that the fact that the neothalamus (lateral nuclear mass) and most, at least, of the dorsomedial nucleus degenerate upon decortication may mislead us into ignoring this as another possible route of afferent impulses to the hypothalamus in the normal animal. Later (Sect. G 1) we quote Walker, Fulton, and Ingram to the effect that the lateral nuclear mass is connected with the dorsomedial nucleus and that, in turn, with the hypothalamus. Thus, in the normal animal, it may be that afferent impulses to the neothalamus also reach the hypothalamus over this route. Apparently Ingram, at least, thinks that they do. On the other hand, Walker thinks (*416*, *263*) the dorsomedial nucleus synthesizes the visceral impulses from the paleothalamus and the somatic from the lateral nuclear mass and relays both to the prefrontal cortex, not to the hypothalamus. For many reasons we are, therefore, inclined to disregard this as a route for upcoming impulses to the hypothalamus. Nevertheless, it may be that it is open but usually inhibited, so that very strong stimuli, even in the channels of neosensibility, can thus reach the hypothalamus. On the other hand, it may be that paleosensibility suffices for all strong stimuli, even those from distance receptors.

2. TRANSMISSION OF QUASI-EXTERNAL WANTS TO THE HYPOTHALAMUS [50]

The question of local source of excitation (neural or humoral) also arises in connection with all the other types of emotional response that we have already noted are possible in decorticate animals and therefore must arise in these subcortical regions. Monakow concludes (*301*, 58) that a "biochemical (material) component" "is always necessary for the production of emotion arising in the immediate present." This may be true when the emotional reaction is a response to the sexual want, to asphyxia, to low blood sugar, or to overheating, for then it is doubtless solely excited by the condition (or components) of the blood. It may even be true of excessive hunger and thirst and of one type of fatigue. But these we have

[50] The explanation of our choice of the term "quasi-external wants" appears at the end of this section.

already included in our internal wants. When it comes to the other emotional reactions we have mentioned, it is difficult to believe that a humoral excitor plays any part other than that of one of the primary results and therefore only a secondary cause.[51] Then the primary centripetal transmission seems to be wholly neural and the source or cause almost wholly a somatic condition resulting from an environmental relation.

Let us consider them in the order in which they appeared in Section D. In decorticate animals, the pseudo-affective reaction which we have called the "alert" is only reported as a response to sounds, though, as we shall note, the probabilities are that it can also be elicited by the appearance of light [52] and perhaps as a result of any strong somatic stimulus. The reaction called "restlessness" has only been reported, to my knowledge, as a result of visceral causes (hunger, vesical contractions, etc.) which we have already considered. As emotional expression, therefore, it may be solely produced by internal wants. On the other hand, it may perhaps be the initial motor reaction to any low grade of excitement, whatever its cause. It seems to be generally agreed that "sham rage" is primarily a response to external restraint or constraint of bodily movement.[53] But the source and nature of the excitor is difficult to explain. It seems impossible to assign this reaction to proprioceptive impulses from the muscles; for Sherrington found proprioceptive reflexes to be the lowest in the scale so far as affective tone (emotional state produced) is concerned, whereas this produces one of the most violent states. All we can say, at present, is

[51] In other words, if we consider that the blood is the excitor in the case of most of the emotional states which have visceral causes and that neural afferents are the excitors chiefly of those which have somatic causes, we do not take issue with Cannon's statement (*61*, 108) that "total separation of the viscera from the central nervous system does not alter emotional behavior." Moreover, read in its context, Cannon's statement is only a refutation of the James-Lange theory of the emotions, and is probably not intended to mean that emotional states, as central excitation, can never have specific visceral causes with neural centripetal transmission. If that were true, visceral pain could hardly produce an emotional state.

[52] Bard's cat turned its head and pricked up its ears in response to a low whistle, scraping, or clicking (*19*, 294). Frolov reports that Goltz's dog raised its head as a response to a peculiar sound and continued in that posture as long as the sound was repeated (*157*, 57). Since this same pattern was elicited first by Ranson's direct stimulation of the posterior hypothalamus and can be obtained by excitation of the anterior (though we would expect the posterior) corpora quadrigemina (Fulton, *160*, 195) and in the region of the geniculates (*ibid.*, 495), it appears to be a subcortical response to such sound stimuli as can be completely integrated at the thalamic level, and to be procurable at any point along the afferent auditory path reaching from its source to the hypothalamus.

[53] This is suggested by Ranson's observation already quoted (p. 1079). Bard's animal was restrained (tied down on its back). But Bard was not sure what started the seemingly spontaneous reaction (*18*, 509). Any attempt to impress a movement on Mettler's dog was met by resistance (no mention of rage), but when the hand was placed on the dog's flank "the reaction began with a snarl and ended with the dog's biting viciously at the place stimulated" (*297*, 1240). It is fair to assume that this reaction is approximately equivalent to Pavlov's "freedom reflex" (*320*, 11–12, etc.) and perhaps to the defense behavior which Frolov speaks of (*157*, 57). Jennings has noted that even infusoria react to centrifugal force by swimming in the opposite direction (*223*, 150).

that it is innate (unlearned),[54] and that it occurs after "ablation of the hemispheres, the corpora striata and the cranial half of the diencephalon" (Bard, *18*, 495) and may occur after ablation of all of the dorsal thalamus (*ibid.*, 504, 512). This indicates that the reaction is not dependent on that part of the thalamus which is a relay station to the cortex, and therefore that the afferent impulses which cause it, if any, are not, strictly speaking, sensory. There remains the possibility of other afferent impulses, via the paleothalamus or direct, and the possibility of a hormonal excitor. There seems to be no basis whatever for supposing the last, since those endocrine changes we know of would appear only as effects, not as causes, of rage. So far as a physiological explanation is concerned, it must be admitted that, at present, we have none. Nevertheless, the cause of rage must be included in our list.

In respect of the effects Woodworth says that, since "the same organic state occurs in both fear and anger the difference between these two emotions must lie in the set for escape in one and for attack in the other" (*447*, 437). Bard noted that attack was present in rage and absent in fear, while escape was absent in rage and present in fear (*19*, 294). But, since he defined the two states in terms of other signs distinguishing them, the distinctions are more numerous and more subtle. Two—and perhaps a third—different causes have been suggested as innate sources of fear in human beings, causes whose afferent paths are closely allied. The first is sudden loud noise; the second is loss of equilibrium (or of support); the third is sudden bright light.[55] Obviously the origin of the first is cochlear, of the second labyrinthine, and of the third, if it can be included, retinal. That the first, as a cause of the emotional state, fear, is dependent on the integrity of the medial geniculate is suggested by the fact that, among Bard's cats, those which did not evince fear but did show rage had, unlike the others who showed both, but remnants of the medial geniculates (*22*, 202). If, then, this is the only auditory connection to the hypothalamic region, it is to be presumed that these cats had also lost the "alert" reaction to sound. As to equilibrium, or the loss of support, righting reflexes are of course obtainable in the midbrain animal at the level of the vestibular nuclei. But to produce emotional states it is likely that labyrinthine tracts direct to the hypothalamus, or paths parallel to the auditory via the medial geniculate

[54] "Hampering of . . . movements" is one of Watson's three original unconditioned stimuli which produce "emotional reactions" that belong "to the original and fundamental nature of man" (*429*, 199–201, and *430*, 121–123).

[55] See p. 1096 and note 40. The loud noise is the only cause noted by Bard for cats (*19*, 214). See also Cannon (*65*, 292). For the others we have to depend on other evidence, not appropriate perhaps to a strictly physiological enquiry. Nevertheless, it seems better to include the whole subject here. Loss of support was another of Watson's three unconditioned stimuli producing emotional reactions (see note 54), presumably of the order of fear, among newborn babes. It is mentioned by McDougall (*284*, 53) as a cause of fear equally with sudden loud noises, evidenced also in animals (and see note 56, below). The inclusion of sudden bright light is more or less of a supposition, based on observation of fear caused by it and by the fact that crude brightness discrimination is evidently adequate at subcortical levels.

(see Fulton, *160*, 366–368), must be involved.[56] Finally, since, as noted above, brightness discrimination remains in subcortical visual mechanisms in the decorticate, the effect of bright light on the hypothalamic region, if any, is presumably similarly mediated via the lateral geniculates.

Closely allied with fear is the emotional state produced by pain. As a result of the bodily want which, in the text (p. 76), we limit, so far as our consideration is concerned, to freedom from external injury, pain may be construed to be the central state produced by the centripetal transmission via afferent nerves of variations from homeostasis in this respect. The subject of pain is an important one which has received an enormous amount of attention. Nevertheless, it must be admitted that, in the aspects in which we are interested—namely, the mechanism through which the peripheral state of injury produces behavior (or internal responses)—we are, as yet, not warranted in making general statements as if they represented a consensus of opinion. The best we can do here is to outline the chief questions in dispute and, in the footnotes, give some examples of the different prevailing views with bits of confirming evidence. The chief questions are:

1. What are the natural pain stimuli? [57]

2. Are there specific receptors for pain—special end-organs or even mere fiber ("free nerve") endings, or "brushes"? Are the fibers which transmit pain impulses of a different type from others? If so, is the pain pattern their only pattern of impulses? Or is pain a special pattern for them, resulting from duration, from frequency over each fiber, or from summation (volley) over many, or from all these? If so, is pain then a pattern of some such special kind which can come over any afferent nerve? [58]

3. Is the visceral afferent system subserving pain analogous to the

[56] Rogers's (*351*, 565 and 569) results with pigeons show that, with them, lesions of the equilibratory apparatus have the same inhibitory effect on hypermotility of the crop (in hunger) that are produced by conditions causing fear or surprise, or by intrinsic painful stimuli. In this respect the results are the same in decerebrate pigeons (with thalamus intact) as they are with normal birds, so that the mechanism must be subcortical.

[57] Contrary to the assumption as to the nature of the stimulus which underlay von Frey's original specificity theory, an important body of opinion now holds that there are only, or almost only, two kinds of non-laboratory stimuli. The first is tension on, or injury to, the nerve fiber itself; the second is tension in the tissues in which its end, or end-organ, lies. See Nafe (*310*, 1037 ff. and 1063). As to visceral and vascular pain there seems to be somewhat general agreement that tension is the chief, or only, cause. See Herrick (*190*, 291), citing A. F. Hurst (*The Sensitivity of the Alimentary Canal*, London, 1911), who concludes that the "only immediate cause of true visceral pain is tension," and, in the alimentary canal, tension of the muscular coat not the lining; he also cites Livingston to the effect that a frequent cause of visceral pain is muscular spasm of the blood vessels, and F. Bremer to the effect that the same is true of cerebral blood vessels, etc.

As to both cutaneous and visceral pain, Adrian says (*3*, 101), "Most pains seem to be due to an abnormal deformation, stretching or tearing, of the tissues." But Fulton (*160*, 4) says, "the adequate stimulus for pain is any noxious agent which tends to cause tissue or cellular destruction."

[58] For a brief discussion of this question, see supplementary statement on "The Specificity of Receptors," at the end of this section.

cutaneous (or somatic)? Does it also convey unlocalized or referred pain? Or is such pain, even when from visceral causes, subserved only if the superficial (cutaneous) mechanism is brought into play? [59]

4. Where and what is the central state produced by the pain mechanism? Is it (a) a sensory modality integrated by that part of the thalamus which has direct thalamo-cortical projections and therefore represented in the cortex as such? Or is it (b) in part or *in toto* integrated in the paleothalamus, which has no cortical projections, so that it reaches the cortex, when it does at all, through a different and not strictly sensory channel?

Whereas the first three questions can remain unanswered without interfering with our present purpose, the last must be answered, at least in part. There is much evidence that the answer to (a) is negative. "The sense of pain has little if any representation in the cortex" (Penfield and Boldrey, *324*, 439).[60] If so, it would seem to follow that it has little, if any, in the part of the thalamus referred to. And, if so, it must reach the cortex in some other form and by some other channel, since it certainly can produce an effect in consciousness. These questions we will defer for consideration in Section G. The answer to (b), on the other hand, is certainly positive in part; [61] and, if the answer to (a) turns out to be entirely negative, then pain impulses must be integrated in the paleothalamus *in toto*. Thus, while we cannot as yet fully explain the source or centripetal mechanism for pain as the means of leading to behavior tending to restore homeostasis in respect of external injury, it appears that the central apparatus concerned is partly and perhaps wholly the same as it is for the other wants we have considered whose centripetal transmission is via the neural integrating system. To an equal extent it seems to be the same as for the other emotional states described. That is, pain may produce an emotional state in the subcortical regions which leads to interofective results similar to the others and to exterofective results (behavior) characteristic of excitement.[62]

Though other emotions are occasionally mentioned by our authorities, we cannot carry our list further. While Bard (*19*, 295) detected no tail-wagging or other signs of enjoyment among his decorticate preparations, he states that Bekterev did so in cases where the thalamus was intact. Frolov says (*157*, 57) that Goltz's dog showed certain elements of playfulness. Purring has been reported in decorticate cats. The decorticate dog retains Pavlov's "investigatory reflex" (Frolov, *157*, 63), which we assume is allied

59 Perhaps typical is the view of Heinbecker and Bishop (*187*, 233), who believe that the visceral is similar to the cutaneous but more specialized and sparser. But both unlocalized and referred pain, with visceral causes, raise many difficulties. As just one instance, Weiss and Davis (*436*, 532) found they could stop visceral referred pain, if localized on the skin, by applying a local skin anesthetic.

60 And many others report failure to produce it by direct stimulation anywhere in the cortex. While he made no inference from it, Cushing (*99*, 48) reports "no painful sensations."

61 See p. 1096 and note 39. Darrow (*102*, 575) concludes that, "Pain may apparently make its appeal directly to the subcortical mechanisms."

62 This is a part of the original thesis of Cannon, *58*.

with "curiosity"; and that, in turn, is generally treated as an emotion.[63] But the "investigatory reflex," though innate, is on the border line, because, in the normal animal, when the stimulus becomes familiar (on repetition), it is inhibited and disappears.[64] However, the evidence in these cases is so slight and the physiological basis at present so undeterminable that we must needs omit them from our consideration. The list that we have heretofore been able to derive from experiments in producing emotional behavior, which constitute at least gross explanations of the physiological causes of such behavior, are:

loud sounds, probably bright light, and perhaps any strong somatic stimulus, producing the "alert";

these when very strong, producing the "fear" reaction, including "escape";

loss of equilibrium or support, producing the "fear" reaction, without "escape" but probably with "forced grasping" in primates;

restraint and constraint of movement or posture, producing the "rage" reaction, including "attack";

external injury, producing the various reactions to pain.

Each of these several causes, respectively,—or the proximate condition they produce—will constitute our list of quasi-external wants. Our reasons for distinguishing these from the internal wants that we have already listed will appear more fully as we proceed to show in what respects they behave differently. Primarily, however, it is because they constitute conditions that result directly from relations with the external environment rather than from conditions of the internal environment concerned only indirectly with the external environment. On the other hand, our reason for calling them quasi-external is to distinguish them from the great mass of the external stimulus-response category. These wants consist of a very limited number of fundamental relations with the environment, as to which the organism requires homeostasis: balance and foothold, bodily freedom, freedom from injury, and freedom from excessive stimulation. The reason we call them wants is that they are innate causes of elaborate patterns of integrated, stereotyped, and automatic behavior, and that they stand on their own feet—that is, they subserve no other condition, are not dependent upon the concurrent existence of any other want, and in fact compete among themselves and with the internal wants for the opportunity of producing their especial types of "spontaneous" behavior.[65]

[63] For instance, Tower reports (*404*, 243) that the "pawing" of "curiosity," while usually diminished after section of the pyramidal tracts, becomes "indistinguishable from the normal" in excitement.

McDougall (*284*, 56–57) relates curiosity to fear, since there is fear of the "unfamiliar and strange as such." Of course the range of the unfamiliar and strange, either as cause of curiosity or of fear, is very limited in an animal which, by reason of decortication, has so largely lost contact with the external world.

[64] "The investigatory reflex . . . invariably weakens on repetition, and finally disappears altogether" (Pavlov, *320*, 255).

[65] Though the causes of all reflexes may be regarded as quasi-external wants in that they too produce innate responses to specific environmental relations, we are excluding

The Specificity of Receptors. This question is still a battle field. Nafe (*310*, 1069–1070) disagrees with Head's theory of two kinds of sensibility (protopathic and epicritic) and approaches the notion of non-specificity. Kuntz and Hamilton (*246*, 396), state that "the functional specificity of all afferent cutaneous nerve fibers . . . cannot be regarded as experimentally demonstrated." They cite the results of Nafe and of L. S. Wagoner (49 *Am. J. Physiol.*, 1937, 631, 636, and 645) as suggesting that touch, pressure, and pain may all be subserved by one set of nerves or by one morphological type, while the sense of warmth and of cold may only arise from marked or rapid local reflex vasodilatation or vasoconstriction. Waterston's results (*428*) indicate that "pressure is not a cutaneous sensation" (only from muscle or periosteum; *ibid.*, 252), and that the tactile sense must be in the epidermis (epithelium; *ibid.*, 252 and 256), while "sensibility to superficial pain . . . is subserved by the corium" only. These findings do not accord very well with the observed location of endings supposed to be specific as to these modalities. Bard (*24*, 68–73) seems to adhere to specificity, but (*ibid.*, 73) leaves the question only partly answered, and admits the possibility that the character of impulses (or patterns) may be determining (*ibid.*, 69). The older view is represented by Barcroft (*17*, 354) who believes that pain, which "has emerged from some primitive sensation of a more or less general kind," has, as its single end organ, "the simple end brush."

Recent studies of action currents have led to the differentiation of fibers according as they show rapid (A) waves (large medullated), slower (B) waves (fine medullated) or slowest (C) waves (unmyelinated). "The fastest fibers carry touch impulses but not pain, and the C fibers carry pain without touch or pressure" (Gasser, *168*, 171). There is reason to believe that localized pain is associated with the B group, while the C group carries only slightly localizable pain impulses (see Clark *et al.*, *79*, and Fulton's comments, *160*, 29). But see Hoaglund, *201*, *276*. The slightly localizable impulses are frequently associated with what has been called paleosensibility. The last two types are found with "free nerve" endings (above; see Fulton, *160*, 2).

A third distinction, which does not preclude but does not rest upon either of the foregoing, is based on the pattern of impulses. Adrian (*4*, 55) says, "poor localisation and a slow rise and decline are characteristic features of pain." All these characteristics might be explained by the assumption that the intensity of effect of impulses from any receptors, or over any fibers capable of giving rise to pain, depends upon "a summation of the changes caused by such impulse," so that pain is a function of the "amount of summation which can occur" (*loc. cit.*). Thus pain may not be distinguished by "characteristic grouping" (pattern, in the qualitative sense), or even wholly by "frequency" (Adrian, *3*, 85) but largely by the number of fibers involved (i.e., intensity and duration of stimulus). Perhaps "the summated effect of the longer discharge would allow it to break through into parts of the central nervous system which were not accessible to the brief discharge," so that felt pain would depend upon number of impulses due to all three causes—frequency, duration and number of fibers involved (*3*, 89 and 97). Nafe (*310*, 1076), going further than Adrian, concludes,

from our consideration the spinal reflexes, because they do not represent integrated behavior and therefore do not constitute our problem, and the lower brain-stem reflexes, because they have become, in the intact and normal animal, components of the behavior produced at the higher level we are considering and are rarely, if ever, produced independently of these larger patterns.

as stated above, that the same fibers which normally transmit impulses in non-painful patterns abnormally produce pain patterns. He develops (*ibid.*, 1040) the interesting hypothesis, from the observations of Adrian and others, that the result of continued intense stimulation over a considerable area is ultimately to synchronize impulses over many fibers into a succession of "volleys." Conforming to this last, but within limitations, so that it also accords with the distinction among types of fiber, is the conclusion of Heinbecker and Bishop (*187*, 226). They say "the threshold sensation induced by activation of the potential pain mechanism is not dolorous, but rather a tactile or contact sense ["a pricking touch sensation"; *ibid.*, 231], but the pathways are specific to the extent that only certain pathways and not all pathways for contact sense, are capable of conveying impulses resulting in pain" (*ibid.*, 237). These pathways are the small myelinated and the unmyelinated fibers (B and C above). "Pain ensues [as it does for Adrian] when a sufficient number of impulses resulting in a pricking touch sensation are centrally summed" (*ibid.*, 231).

These few and brief citations are not intended to answer the questions asked above. They merely suggest the compromise basis upon which they are likely to be answered.

F. CERTAIN AREAS OF THE CORTEX AND THEIR FUNCTIONS

In this vast field we shall limit ourselves to establishing a few points, some still merely the most probable hypotheses, which are required for our special purposes. These points concern, first, the specific functions of those areas of the cortex which have been most fully explored and whose relations to the regions we have just considered seem to be the most intimate; second, any differences that exist between neural events occurring at the cortical level and those which occur at lower levels; and, third, the basis for the interactions between the cortex and those highest subcortical mechanisms just considered. The first point will be dealt with in this section. The matter of the differences and interactions will be the subject of the next section. But it is well to make clear at this stage that we are assuming, in line with what has come, I believe, to be a general assumption among physiologists, that the cortex is the sole locus of the psychic epiphenomena with which, as stated in the text, we have to find some way to deal. Thus, whatever consciousness may be, it is a concomitant only of processes occurring in the cortex. Because "sensation . . . demands . . . consciousness" (Head, *183*, 747), it can only occur where consciousness occurs. Since memory, in its strict sense of recall, implies recall to consciousness, it too can occur only where consciousness occurs.[1] If, as Hughlings Jackson held (see "The Thinking Process," p. 1049), thinking (mental operations) consists chiefly of retino-ocular and considerably of

[1] In fact, Strong and Elwyn seem to be inclined to reverse the roles and to make consciousness a function of memory. They say (*Human Neuroanatomy*, Baltimore, 1943): "Those reactions usually called *conscious* are difficult to define but appear in general to represent a heightened activity of various portions of the pallial mechanism of associative memory." This comment is worth bearing in mind in connection with all our discussion of consciousness and memory in this Appendix and in Chapters 2 and 5. The essential point to note here is that both are conceded to be "pallial."

audito-articulatory sensorimotor processes in their purely central (i.e., neither peripheral afferent nor efferent) stages, and of little else, thinking too must be solely cortical, since almost the entire apparatus connecting the sensory with the motor sides of these two pairs of functions is confined to the cortex. Finally, whatever it may mean and whatever it may involve, action of any kind which is regarded as volitional, as opposed to automatic, most certainly can take its efferent origin in the cortex alone.

Certain morphological considerations are worthy of notice, not because they prove anything, but because they make us more ready to accept and understand what we find. First, in "brute bulk," the cortex "dwarfs the whole of the rest of the nervous system" (Fulton and Sherrington, *164*, 262). The neopallium alone is "a mass which makes up nearly half the total weight of the brain" (Herrick, *191*, 7). Obviously, there must be a developmental reason for this. Second, the cortex takes the form of a "mantle" (pallium), not that of a body (*corpus*) like all the large brain-stem entities (i.e., the *corpora* striata, the *corpora* geniculata, the *corpora* quadrigemina, and the thalami). The only similar structure is that of the cerebellum, which is also an outgrowth from, not in, the brain-stem. Thus the cortex seems to represent a vast increase in differentiation (Hughlings Jackson) by comparison with lower levels—that is, an immense increase in the number of slightly different but parallel alternative paths both in and out.[2] There is, however, no reason to credit it with much greater integration (Jackson) than is possible at the highest subcortical levels—integration in the sense of extent of bodily regions which can be included in a pattern—for the highest subcortical levels, the old brain, from which the cortex developed phylogenetically and still develops ontogenetically, seem already to have attained practically complete integration in this sense. Third, the rest of the bulkiness of the cortex seems to be explained by the enormous increase, as compared with lower entities, of interconnections within itself.[3] At first sight this would appear to follow from the second point. But, if differentiation means alternatives and these alternatives are of necessity mutually exclusive, one would suppose an absence of interconnections. If, however, these alternatives are not of necessity mutually exclusive but only become so by reason of the capacity of each to inhibit the others, then interconnections on a most complex scale would seem to be required.[4] Fourth, not only is all access to and from the cortex in-

[2] This is approximately Lashley's concept of "incompatible mechanisms" (see Section A, note 49, above) as a basis for spatial arrangement. Differentiation requires a great "quantity of grey matter" (Walshe, *421*, 76).

[3] Cytoarchitecture demonstrates this. But even in gross morphology, it is noteworthy that, in spite of the fact that unilateral representation exists on a large scale in the cortex, the great commissure (corpus callosum) is far greater in size than any at lower levels, where bilateral representation is the rule (e.g., commissura posterior).

[4] Obviously, differentiation also requires an enormous increase in efferent connections and perhaps also largely for the same reason (i.e., reciprocal inhibition). Thus each pyramidal tract is said to contain about 250,000 fibers (Fulton, *160*, 333).

Another reason for bulk, among higher animals and especially men, appears not to be

direct, as may also be the case neurally with the upper brain-stem, but, with one exception, there is no access to the cortex in either direction except through the subcortical and supraspinal centers of our second and third levels. The one exception is the pyramidal tract. Otherwise, as Fulton and Sherrington express it (*164*, 260), this "comparatively modern structure" "is so placed that its commerce with the body and with the external world can occur only through the medium of the archaic non-mental nervous parts."

Though in these respects different, at least in degree, the functioning (and the unit of structure) of the cortex is apparently in most respects the same as in other parts of the central nervous system.[5] As elsewhere, "the effect of impulses entering the cortex depends largely upon the impulses at that moment circulating . . . as a result of the existing cortical activity" (Fulton, *160*, 307).[6] "The cortical chains are in no way different from the chains of internuncial neurons in any part of the central nervous system" (*ibid.*, 315). In general, there are no differences of kind; so that recently Foerster (*144*, 135) was able to accept Jackson's dictum, already noted, that "there is nothing else they [the "convolutions of the brain"] can represent except movements and impressions" (i.e., sensorimotor processes).[7]

When it comes to localization of function in the cortex one must be wary. For what is a function at this level? As Poliak says (*330*, 216), "At present the difficulties in solving the problem of mental-material relations appear, on the whole, to reside less in the sphere of morphology than in the definition of the localizable elementary cortical processes." Thus, for instance, memory; "individual memories are never destroyed by small lesions" (Lashley, *262*, 373). It is doubtful that there are "separate 'intellectual' centers" (*ibid.*, 374). Perhaps such functions are "controlled by widely scattered loci contributing quite diverse elements to the whole" (*ibid.*, 373). The same difficulty may also exist, to a considerable extent, in regard to apparently definable physiological functions.[8] Nevertheless,

---

explicable either by great differentiation or great interconnection. It was Cajal's assumption "that the large number of cells with short axons was the anatomical expression of the delicacy of function of the brain of man" (at present "almost a statement of fact," Fulton, *160*, 316); for "the larger the number the higher is the brain in the series" (*ibid.*, 309). But Fulton suggests that this has to do with producing "more or less synchronous volleys of impulses" (*ibid.*, 313).

[5] Moreover, the brain, as a whole, "is like the other organs in that it is not known to deviate from physical and chemical laws in any way" (Fraenkel and Gunn, *149*, 305).

[6] This is true of the entire nervous system. See Gasser, as quoted on p. 1046 and note 49. Also see our remarks in the text, p. 45.

[7] This is approximately the same as our quotation (Section A, note 8, above) and of several other statements made by him (*216*, I, 40–43). I do not find it anywhere in precisely this form.

[8] In the discussion of Bard (*23*, 577), Lorente de Nó said: "The center of the nervous system begins to be conceded as a group of neurons connected among themselves in many different ways and it appears that center means, so to say, a junction which is a transmission of a certain set of impulses, but there is no particular function localized in

some definite localization seems to be possible, if, for the most part, in gross. We may still follow Hughlings Jackson, who said (*216*, II, 35) he was "neither a universaliser nor a localiser"—a middle-ground view which, as interpreted by Walshe (*421*, 77) "postulates no 'jig-saw' puzzle of rigidly defined, separate local elements," nor, on the other hand, an "undifferentiated cortex acting by mass." It supposes, not "differentiation without integration," nor "integration without differentiation," but "differentiation with integration." [9]

While it is no longer possible to accept Hughlings Jackson's view that "the whole anterior part of the brain [at least of the cortex] is motor, or chiefly motor" (*216*, II, 53), that appears to be true of all but the most rostral portion—the prefrontal area. However, we can accept his statement that the whole posterior part is sensory, or chiefly sensory.[10] The line of division is the central sulcus (fissure of Rolando).[11] It may be true that, in and along both margins of this fissure, motor and (somatic) sensory representations overlap—that is, that the postcentral region has some motor representation, chiefly near the fissure, and the precentral has some somatic sensory representation, also near the fissure (Penfield and Boldrey, *324*, 430). On the other hand, this is often disputed or explained away, as we shall note below.[12] As to the rest of the posterior area, the occipital and temporal lobes are, again roughly speaking, visual and auditory in function, respectively. Within these rather specific general areas, the most appealing hypothesis as to localization strikes us as being Lashley's admittedly speculative suggestion, for which we shall see further support when we consider the areas themselves. It is that strict localization within these areas exists, first, where the sensorimotor process is organized with reference to spatial relations (topognosis, stereognosis, etc.).[13] Thus "visual, tactile and motor regions have a high degree of internal specificity," because "reactions mediated by the visual and tactile areas are primarily spatial" and the motor region must conform (*262*, 377).[14] But, for instance, "olfactory experience

---

any particular center." Bard, replying said, "The function is what is represented in a center, a patterned response in this particular case. That is what is localized" (*ibid.*, 579). And there you have it.

[9] The use of these terms here does not, of course, correspond to our previous use. It signifies only localization *vs.* non-localization.

[10] Jackson, *216*, II, 80, also quoted by Fulton, *160*, 376.

[11] In Jackson's view the precentral region is preponderantly concerned with "movements" and the postcentral with "impressions" (Foerster, *144*, 146). But this preponderance is supposed to be graduated from the central sulcus, where the two are most combined, to the two poles, where they are most separate. "I suppose that in the fore part of the praefrontal lobes sensory representation is a vanishing point, and that motor representation in the occipital lobes is a vanishing point" (Jackson, *216*, I, 368).

[12] See pp. 1114–1115 and note 27.

[13] Among others, Dusser de Barenne notes this. He speaks (*125*, 773) of "loss of spatial localization and discrimination" from cortical lesions. And see Poliak, whom we quote more fully below.

[14] However, the point from which a specific response can be elicited may move in time and differs between individuals (Penfield and Boldrey, *324*, 429); also see Lashley, *259*, 585.

is lacking in spatial character," and, in turn, there is no evidence in that system of "any subordinate localization." Lashley's second suggestion is that localization is related to the "serial order of reactions." Since the "accurate timing of the separate components of an organized movement is as important as the spatial pattern" (*ibid.*, 381), its sequence may be represented in the system of localization.[15] If so, "the temporal aspects of experience [that is, memory] must therefore have a spatial basis" (*ibid.*, 382) —but not, as noted above, an individual locus (*ibid.*, 373). Finally, the fact that responses to local electrical stimulation at any one point in the motor cortex are on an all-or-none basis "suggests that mechanisms for varying intensity of reaction may have spatial and therefore local representation" (*ibid.*, 380).

1. SENSORY REPRESENTATION

We shall consider first the sensory cortex (or sensory representation in the cortex). All afferent impulses which reach the cortex, except perhaps those concerned with the sense of smell,[16] are relayed in the thalamus.[17] In fact, so far as its sensory aspect is concerned, the cortex is to be regarded, from a developmental and functional point of view, "as a dependency of the thalamus and not *vice versa*" (Le Gros Clark, *84*, 406). Therefore, the thalamus is "much more than a relay station"; it is "the anatomical equivalent of the very threshold of consciousness" (*ibid.*, 407). Nevertheless, it does serve as the "relay station through which impulses which have their origin in stimuli arising in the external environment [exteroceptive] or in such somatic structures as muscles, tendons and joints [proprioceptive] are projected on to the cerebral cortex" (Le Gros Clark,

[15] Perhaps the "production of ordered series of acts results from the subliminal excitation of many or all 'components,'" with "subsequent supraliminal excitation in predetermined order" (*262*, 382).

At any rate "some other explanation of serial acts must be sought" (*ibid.*, 382), since the "doctrine of chain reflexes is utterly without foundation" (*ibid.*, 381). That is, the notion that the sensory results of a first reflex cause the motor results of a second one, etc., is baseless.

I have never seen any discussion of Hughlings Jackson's curious suggestion with regard to this, though almost everything else he suggested has been utilized. "It is, I speculate, through the ["contraction of"] arteries that sequence of movement is developed." "When one movement follows a different movement automatically, the discharge of the nervous process for the first movement develops the second movement by fibres to the vessels supplying the nervous process for that second movement" (*216*, I, 36).

[16] Walker (*416*, 242) thinks the anterior group of thalamic nuclei may be an olfactory relay station, because of their projection to a region of the cortex which he construes as olfactory. But the function of that cortical region is very uncertain. See Le Gros Clark (*86*, 27).

[17] Bard (*19*, 305) makes almost precisely the same statement, merely qualifying the one exception. Cannon (*61*, 118) agrees, and makes no exception. Monakow states that there are no direct sensory connections with the cortex—all being mediated by the thalamic nuclei (*301*, 32). Head (*183*, 597–601) says the thalamus contains the "termination of all secondary [afferent] paths."

85, 100).[18] As stated above (p. 1095) Walker holds that the thalamus is also a relay station for interoceptive impulses, and perhaps for exteroceptive impulses conveying paleosensibility, to the hypothalamus and other subcortical regions. Therefore, it appears to play a double role which is of importance to our study.[19] So far as the sensory cortex is concerned, however, it is necessary to emphasize the fact that "the visceral, or interoceptive, senses have meager cortical representation throughout the [mammalian] series; these internal adjustments are largely taken care of by subcortical nervous apparatus." "The primary significance of the cortex, then, is to be sought in adjustments to external events as reported through the exteroceptive senses. Ancillary to these adjustments are the proprioceptive senses, which also have cortical representation" (Herrick, *191*, 9).

While the visual and auditory afferent impulses are synthesized almost independently of the rest of the thalamus, in the lateral and medial geniculates respectively, the rest—that is, the proprioceptive and the cutaneous exteroceptive (and perhaps smell and taste; [20] Walker, *416*, 242 and 265)—are integrated by reason of their locus in the thalamus itself (*ibid.*, 238) and, with the exception of taste and smell, in what we may call, for brevity, the "lateral nuclear mass." From this last, which represents, for the somatic senses, the chief cortical relay station in the thalamus proper, the proprioceptive impulses (at least the cerebellar) are then relayed direct to the motor cortex (precentral) and the exteroceptive to the postcentral convolution (*ibid.*, 246). At least as to the specific sensory modalities included in these groups, it is then true that "the thalamus and the cerebral cortex are the essential integrating sensory mechanisms" (Dusser de Barenne, *125*, 768). And, since the latter is entirely dependent on the former, complete lesions of this part of the thalamus cut off from the cortex all afferent sensory impulses—at least of these types (Harrison, *181*, 652).

Although the fact is disputed, we shall follow Walker in his statement that the whole system of thalamocortical projections is closely paralleled by corticothalamic fibers.[21] Walker thinks these latter are not merely in-

[18] This restriction (exteroceptive and proprioceptive) conforms to Walker ("stimuli from the outside world"; *416*, 277) and to Huber and Crosby (*209*, 202), "primarily, although not exclusively."

[19] On the other hand, as noted above (Section E, note 33, above), it is possible that this second role is played by the hypothalamus itself (Le Gros Clark) or by that combined with the epithalamus (Huber and Crosby, and Hinsey), or by that and the subthalamus and ventral portions of the geniculates (Papez). Which, or what combination, of these alternative theses turns out to be correct makes no difference to our construction. But, for simplicity of statement, we shall continue to use Walker's as the basis.

[20] But see Section A, note 48, above, for another view.

[21] Walker, *416*, 250. Le Gros Clark (*84*, 432) thinks there are none in primates, at least to the ventral nucleus, and therefore questions the inhibition theories based on them. Dusser de Barenne (*125*, 776) holds there are such fibers, at least to the ventrolateral nucleus; and later (*126*) he has shown, by his electrothalamograms, a "close functional interdependence of the sensori-motor cortex and the optic thalamus, for which the circuit formed by thalamo-cortical and cortico-thalamic neurones is the anatomical substratum." Fulton (*160*, 278) cites many sources to indicate that the system is fairly com-

hibitory (Head's and Holmes's theory) but serve rather as the "mechanism of sensory [cortical] attention" (*416*, 251)—that is, they modulate the sensitivity of the primary receptive centers, at any moment facilitating some and inhibiting all others. In the following section we will consider what may guide this mechanism.

The projections to the cortex from the lateral nuclear mass of the thalamus and from the geniculate bodies, which together compose the whole of the cortical relay station, take the form of "fans" (the "radiations"), with the "handle" below and the "wing" above (Poliak, *330*, 199). That one projecting the lateral nuclear mass—somatic exteroceptive and proprioceptive—spreads out to the entire precentral and postcentral agranular regions and to a considerable portion of the parietal granular region (*ibid.*, 74). But the " 'focal zone' of the entire somatic sensory region, that is, the zone receiving the greatest number of afferent fibers is . . . a narrow . . . area . . . on both sides of the central sulcus" (*ibid.*, 48), in which the fibers are densest at the floor of the sulcus, gradually decreasing up the walls "toward both lips" (*ibid.*, 75). The projection from the medial geniculate—the final auditory path—"enters the white matter of the superior temporal convolution" and reaches to its medial surface "buried in the Sylvian fossa" (*ibid.* 102). The projection from the lateral geniculate—the final visual path—terminates exclusively in the area striata of the occipital lobe (*ibid.*, 200). So Poliak finds evidence for limited "receptor fields"; and "intercalated or association areas" occupy most of the rest of the sensory cortex (*ibid.*, 212).[22]

Thus the sensory cortex is the "*immediate* projection of the external world." It is the sensory portion of Hughlings Jackson's (p. 1048) and also of Pavlov's middle or second level (Frolov, *157*, 78 ff). As suggested above (pp. 1010–1011), this projection is in part spatially organized (localized) in a way corresponding to external space. "Where the stimuli possess a 'spatial' character ["light, thermic and sound waves, gravitation, and similar forces of energy like inertia, and touch"] the receptor organs and their afferent paths when fully developed exhibit a 'spatial' arrangement of neurons. In the case of organs and paths dealing with non-localizable forms of stimuli [e.g., smell and taste] a 'spatial' arrangement of neurons is absent"

---

plete, and concludes (*ibid.*, 382) that, "All the evidence points to some type of interaction between the sensory cortical areas, including [the motor and premotor] . . . and the thalamus."

22 As to the rest of the somatic sensory area Walker says "the role of the superior and inferior parietal lobules in somatic sensibility is poorly understood" (*416*, 258). However, Poliak thinks "it must be assumed that the extensive somato-sensory region is a composite cortical organ consisting of a considerable number of suborgans, each of them with its own specific receptive [and perhaps other] function" (*330*, 77). What they are is unknown, but the difference of the parts in respect of cytoarchitecture and the independence of several projections leads to the assumption.

It is probable that the direct (?) projection of the olfactory and the possibly thalamic projection of the gustatory sense reach the allocortex (rhinencephalon). But when or how is uncertain (Fulton, *160*, 344). Probably, too, the labyrinthine sense reaches the temporal lobe (Fulton, *160*, 371).

(Poliak, *330*, 225).[23] This spatial arrangement is preserved intact through the projections to the cortex. In the somatic sensory field, at least "the tactile sensibility of each part of the body is represented in profuse topographical detail over the postcentral gyrus" (Bard, *21*, 168). And this "topical arrangement of the body segments along the postcentral convolution parallels that of the precentral convolution" (in the motor area; Walker, *416*, 257)—that is, it is arranged approximately in order from the foot (medial) to the head (lateral; Penfield and Boldrey, *324*).[24] So too, "the entire afferent visual system in primates . . . is . . . organized 'spatially,' that is, according to the 'principle of localization' " (Poliak, *330*, 205). There is a " 'mathematical projection' of the retina" upon the cortex (*ibid.*, 207). The result is that the primary visual cortex has an important non-visual function. It yields the concept of space, for it projects space also for the blind (Lashley, *262*, 385).

It is to be presumed that all modalities of exteroceptive somatic sensibility are represented in the postcentral convolution (Walker, *416*, 261). But that is difficult to prove; for when the stimulation is direct (electrical stimulation of the cortex) the sensation reported is generally tingling or numbness (Penfield and Boldrey, *324*, 433; Bard, *20*, 144).[25] So Penfield and Boldrey (*324*, 433) conclude that, while there is accurate localization of the source of the stimulus, "there is no [separate] localization of quality [modality] of sensation, either pre- or postcentral." At least, as was remarked above (p. 1104) there is considerable negative evidence to indicate that pain is not one of the sensory modalities, represented or appreciated here—which suggests that it is not ordinarily, and perhaps never, a sensory modality at all.[26] We shall consider what it probably is in the next section.

Whereas there is "complete unanimity regarding the [somatic] sensory functions of the postcentral convolution," "there is difference of opinion regarding the representation of sensation in the precentral convolutions" (Walker, *416*, 256); or, as Bard (*21*, 144) puts it, there is "some disagreement" as to whether the sensory and the motor areas overlap along the fissure of Rolando, so that there is also sensory representation in the pre-

[23] There is no reason to suppose that the olfactory or gustatory senses are so projected, since they are non-spatial (*ibid.*, 214).

[24] However, Dandy (*99*, 49) says the arrangement is only "roughly" the same as in the motor area, and "the sensory areas lack the sharp definition that is obtainable on the motor side of the paracentral region." Nor is sensation disturbed by local lesions "to the complete degree that obtains with motor function."

[25] One caution should be borne in mind in reading accounts of experimental (direct) stimulation of the nervous system and particularly of the sensory cortex. The nature of most stimuli used in laboratory work is such that they are calculated to produce much simpler or wholly different afferent patterns than those which occur in nature.

[26] Walker (*416*, 257) notes that, after ablation of the postcentral region, pain is at least the first sensation (?) to return and that Head said it remained unimpaired. He also says pain is rarely reported from stimulation in this region (*ibid.*, 256). As quoted on p. 1104 and note 60, Penfield and Boldrey (*324*, 439) say "the sense of pain has little if any representation in the cortex." Cushing (*99*, 48) reported "no painful sensations" from two stimulations of the postcentral gyri.

central and also motor representation in the postcentral area. From Bard's results (*ibid.*, 164) tactile sensibility, at least, appears to be confined to the postcentral. Thus, placing reactions to tactile stimuli seem to require the postcentral gyrus (*ibid.*, 151), but those to proprioceptive stimuli do not. This conforms to the fact that the proprioceptive projections from the thalamus appear to go only to the precentral area (motor; *ibid.*, 153; and Walker, *416*, 246), which itself suggests that sensory representation in the motor cortex is limited to the proprioceptive field.[27]

2. MOTOR REPRESENTATION

Correspondingly, then, the areas we now have to consider constitute the "chiefly motor" region of Hughlings Jackson's middle and Pavlov's second level of the central nervous system. In these areas, it will be recalled, it was Hughlings Jackson's thesis that "each movement, so far as it differs from all others, must have so far special representation in the nervous centres. Greater differentiation of function implies greater physical separation, however little different the movement may be from other movements, and however much of it may be a recoördination of other movements" (quoted by Walshe, *421*, 76). Therefore, there are no "abrupt" localizations. The "thirty muscles of the hand . . . are represented in the nervous centres in thousands of combinations—that is, as very many movements" (*ibid.*, 75). And, since there is always "co-operation of movements of different regions," even the localization of movements of the face only, for instance, is doubtful (Jackson, *216*, II, 34). While recent experimentation on the motor cortex does not controvert the first of these restrictions on localization—in fact, it makes it seem more probable—it does definitely qualify the second one; or it distinguishes in this regard between two areas of this region of the cortex, the motor area proper and the premotor area (or areas). "A mosaic of circumscribed foci can readily be demonstrated along the caudal surface of the precentral region from which . . . isolated . . . movements, sometimes of single muscles . . . can readily be obtained" (Fulton, *160*, 402). Moreover, the arrangement of this localization accords rather precisely with that of the corresponding sensory field on the postcentral side; that is, the bodily parts are represented in order from the

[27] Among others, Penfield and Boldrey (*324*, 439) find sensory effects from stimulating points in the motor area, "as if both pre- and post-central gyri are normally involved in the registering of sensation." So does Dusser de Barenne (*125*, 772). Nevertheless the latter thinks there is differentiation in function between the sensory element in the two regions; for lesions in the postcentral region always cause sensory disturbance, while those of the precentral region show no "appreciable sensory defects." "No disturbances of conscious sensibility can be attributed to lesions of area 4," at least (Fulton, *160*, 427); also "it may be inferred that the sensory function [of this region] lies in the proprioceptive sphere" (*ibid.*, 419). Le Gros Clark (*85*, 103) also believes that the motor cortex is relayed only impulses from the cerebellum and is not concerned with "sensory impulses which are brought up by the fillet system." Walker (*416*, 256) suspects that these sensory phenomena arising from the motor cortex are due to stimulation of corticothalamic neurons in the motor areas—in other words, go round his "circuit."

foot (medial) to the head (lateral). This fine localization, as compared with the synergies, which are almost the only reactions obtainable elsewhere, probably reflects the fact that the pyramidal tract, the only direct cortical projection to the spinal cord, is almost exclusively a projection of the motor area proper (area 4). Ablation of the motor area proper demonstrates that it is responsible for the "finer volitional movements" (Fulton, *160*, 425), "especially of highly organized skilled movements" (*ibid.*, 414), the most discrete, the most adapted—or, rather, that it is responsible for these qualities, since the "pattern of the movement as such is not impaired" (*ibid.*, 461). Correspondingly, section of the pyramidal tracts leaves the "basic postural mechanism intact," but "preparatory and terminal movements, movements of adjustment and correction, largely flexion, are diminished or wanting" (Tower, *404*, 241). Nevertheless, since the motor area proper also gives rise to extrapyramidal projections (Fulton, *160*, 424), the results of ablation of the motor area and of section of the pyramids cannot be and are not precisely the same.

Oriented reactions "consist of the translation of a pattern of sensory excitement into a pattern of movement with reference to bodily posture" (Lashley, *262*, 378). The skillful adaptation of a movement will therefore depend not only on discrete control of individual muscles (pyramidal tract) but also (1) on the precision of the spatial organization of those exteroceptive sensory reports, which are presumably transmitted here from the sensory cortex, as just indicated; (2) on the "graceful" adjustment of the bodily posture, by both excitation and inhibition, in order to form the best "fulcrum" for the movement; and finally (3) on the accuracy of proprioceptive reports of the movement itself while it is in process; for it is the "ring" (or circuit) formed with the proprioceptive system that "tests" the movement (Frolov, *157*, 71). It will be apparent that, in respect of (2), the motor area proper seems to have potentialities beyond the rest of the motor cortex. And, if we may judge from Tower (*404*, 252) the same may be true as to (3). Her retrograde degenerations indicate that the "pyramid, like the cortex, is a mixture of the ascending and descending systems which are the afferent and efferent pathways for the same body of reactions," so that the pyramid is "like the corresponding area in the cortex, a sensori-motor system" (*ibid.*, 254). If so, it is most probably sensory, like the motor cortex, only in respect of reports, perhaps not precisely proprioceptive, but analogous to them.

In the premotor area localization is much less precise. While, in the normal animal, it is evident that these two areas, the motor and premotor, always co-operate, nevertheless there is a radical difference between them. Practically the entire pyramidal tract—the only direct projection from the cortex to the spinal cord—originates in the motor area. On the other hand the premotor area is clearly the chief cortical representation of, and is probably evolved from, all those subcortical motor centers in the brainstem which we have discussed in Sections C, D and E. But this fact has one notable exception; there is no direct projection from the motor cortex to the hypothalamus.[28] The descending extrapyramidal tracts from the various areas of the motor cortex run to the corpora striata, the thalamus (not strictly motor), the midbrain, the nucleus ruber, the tegmentum, the substantia nigra and the pons (Fulton, *160,* 339).[29] These "extrapyramidal motor projections are primarily concerned with postural adjustments of the skeletal musculature, but they are also capable of mediating certain deep-rooted volitional synergies" (*ibid.*, 455). Generally these are "stereotyped" movements (*ibid.*, 456). But "both . . . the pyramidal area and the extrapyramidal areas co-operate when voluntary movements are performed."[30] Isolated movements can be procured by artificial excitation of the premotor area but they are mediated wholly via the motor area.[31] Thus the premotor must be able to excite (use) the motor area. On the other hand, if the premotor area is ablated, while the motor area remains, disturbances of skilled movement and posture appear. Thus the motor area must require the integrity of (use) the premotor in some way. But, if the the motor area is ablated, while the premotor area remains, "voluntary motility is by no means abolished completely." "Isolated movements" are impossible, but "distinct and typical synergies" remain.[32] For instance, monkeys, in that state, recover the ability "to carry out progression movements, to climb, and to feed themselves" (Fulton, *60,* 453). In man, purposeful movements remain possible, but they are "gross in character" (*loc. cit.*).[33]

We infer from this evidence that the premotor area has neither a larger nor a different repertory of motor patterns directly available to it than are within the scope of the several subcortical centers through which its effects are mediated.[34] On the other hand, it appears to have two advantages over these, advantages which are more important—more critical—the higher is the species in the phylogenetic series. Thus the difference between a

[28] There are several tracts from the striate bodies to various parts of the hypothalamus, which may possibly relay impulses from the cortex thus indirectly. The correctness of the statement in the text hinges, of course, on the definition of the motor cortex. If one followed Foerster, who includes parts of all three of the postcentral lobes in his extrapyramidal areas, it would be difficult to make the above assertion with any certainty.

[29] There are besides "miscellaneous motor projections from the parietal, temporal and occipital lobes" (Fulton, *160,* 339).

[30] Quoted by Fulton (*160,* 437) from Foerster. Fulton (*159,* 239) cites Jacobsen to the effect that, whereas ablation of area 4 makes execution of movements difficult, ablation of area 6 disturbs the relation of movements as patterns of response to a situation. Thus, "the premotor area plays an important role in the integration of the complex adaptive activities."

[31] If area 4 is gone or if the transcortical connections to area 4 are severed by superficial incision, they are absent.

[32] Quoted by Fulton, *160,* 437, from Foerster.

[33] While certain "specific regulatory functions" (Fulton, *160,* 455) or movements, such as rhythmic chewing and lapping, movements of the mouth and tongue (Magoun *et al.*, *288,* 295) have been assigned to other regions of the frontal lobe and elsewhere, Penfield and Boldrey "find no evidence for extending the motor cortex beyond the Rolandic areas (pre- and postcentral gyri; *324,* 436–438). This is contrary to Foerster (*144*) and others; but the issue is not germane to our particular interest.

[34] See Tower, *405,* 441.

thalamic dog and one from which only the motor area proper has been ablated is far less than it is in the case of a primate. These advantages appear to be: (1) That the premotor area has simultaneous and selective (excitatory and inhibitory) access to all these subcortical mechanisms, whereas that is far less true, and in many cases not true at all, as among the subcortical mechanisms themselves; (2) That the premotor area is intimately connected with the sensory cortex, which supplies precise and spatially organized reports of the external world, whereas the subcortical motor mechanisms are directly excited by afferent paths that carry at the best only paleosensibility, with little or no localization, in the somatic sphere, and the merest beginnings of any sensibility in the sphere of the distance receptors, with only the crudest spatial projection. Both of these advantages also exist by comparison with the hypothalamic region whose down-going somatic effects must be produced directly through, and only through, these subcortical mechanisms.

3. THE PREFRONTAL AREA

Situated rostral to the premotor area, at and around the pole of the frontal lobe, is what is usually called the prefrontal area.[35] To this region Hughlings Jackson assigned part—eventually he regarded it as the whole—of his highest level. It is also the locus which Pavlov gave to his third system or level.[36] "Despite its motor projection [all extrapyramidal] this large region of the frontal lobe is completely inexcitable [artificially] at ordinary strengths of stimulation" (Fulton, *160*, 435). That is also true of other large regions of the cortex. Furthermore, "no reflex changes in the skeletal muscles, and no obvious alterations of posture follow extirpations sharply restricted to the [pre-]frontal areas" (*ibid.*, 459–460). Judging from that, the prefrontal area is not motor in function, in our narrow sense; it is almost certainly not sensory, in our narrow sense; [37] what is its

[35] That is, areas 9, 10, 11, and 12 (Brodmann). "Prefrontal area" is used synonymously with "frontal association area" and is "sometimes inaccurately referred to as the 'frontal lobe'" (Fulton, *160*, 459).

[36] We regard these concepts of highest level and their localization as independent matters. The validity of the concept may remain, though the localization may be changed, as we think it must be, at least in large part.

[37] That is, it has apparently no exclusive motor or sensory functions. Doubtless it has transcortical effects on the motor areas. Darrow assigns to it "governing, regulating and inhibitory control over the phylogenetically older coordinating motor centers of the brain, such as the premotor center" (*104*, 661). Bianchi thinks that, at least, the connections between the prefrontal and the Rolandic area are very strong (*35*, 324). He describes the associative paths from the prefrontal to the sensory cortex (*ibid.*, 208). Walker also holds that it is probable that the prefrontal area receives transcortical effects from the sensory areas (*416*, 263). In fact, Brickner holds that the prefrontal area receives from all the rest of the cortex and makes complex associated aggregations of material (*45*, 302).

If it is not motor, in this direct way, then Hughlings Jackson's dictum that "the whole anterior part of the brain is motor, or chiefly motor" (*216*, II, 53) is subject to qualification. It does not follow from that, however, that his generalization, that the only activities of the cortex are "sensori-motor" processes, is challenged.

function? Since it cannot be experimentally excited, we are obliged to depend on inferences drawn from the effects on "behavior" of ablation or of lesions in this region.

In the first place, it is clear that there is, within this area, "no localization of function" in the ordinary sense (Brickner, *45*, 304). For this reason symptoms appear only if lesions are extensive (Goldstein, *173*, 27). Moreover, both lobes must be injured (or ablated; Brickner, *43*, 298; Fulton, *159*, 240; *160*, 468). That is, unilateral ablation has slight effect, while bilateral has a great effect (Richter and Hines, *341*, 5). While there is no difference in this respect between the right and left hemispheres in monkeys (Jacobsen, *218*, 560), Goldstein (*173*, 27) thinks that in human beings injuries on the left side have greater effect.[38] From this it is evident that, unlike the sensorimotor cortex in general, where representation is largely unilateral and rarely ipsilateral, representation in this area is almost wholly bilateral. Here, then, the "activity of the two sides is appreciated as a unitary whole," which is possible elsewhere only when one hemisphere is dominant. From these two sources, bilateral representation here and dominant unilateral representation elsewhere, probably comes "our idea of our being single individuals" (Brickner, quoting Horsley, *45*, 296).[39]

Bucy (*52*, *556*) speaks of the conviction that has grown up among neurologists "that those intellectual and social defects so common in the presence of diffuse cerebral pathologic lesions are most typically the result of damage to the prefrontal area." This may be true, in part; but we are seeking a statement in more specific terms. Brickner suggests that there may be three general types of syndromes resulting from lesions here, with some alternation among them (*45*, 28). But, when these types are analyzed, it seems possible to bring them all together under the rubric of the disturbance of a single function. The difficulty is to find the physiological key to what that function is. For that purpose we will analyze a typical group of reports on the behavioral effects of injury to the prefrontal region. It is extremely difficult to make a précis of the evidence in regard to these effects—or defects. And this because they are almost always, if not always, stated in psychological terms which prove to be extraordinarily hard to translate into anything of which the physiological basis might be identified. Nevertheless, our previous examination of the subcortical regions may make this analysis suggestive.

In his extraordinary study of a human subject, after bilateral ablation of the prefrontal areas, Brickner describes two general sets of emotional

[38] As we shall note later, the left hemisphere in right-handed human beings seems to be the exclusive seat of several of the highest functions. For instance, the motor speech center (Broca's area) is in the left hemisphere in the right-handed.

[39] If the locus of consciousness is elsewhere and is unilateral (as we shall suggest in Section G 2), but is able to appreciate both sides separately when representation is unilateral, then our ideas of ourselves as single individuals would seem necessarily to be the transcortical effects in consciousness of activities become a unitary whole in this prefrontal region, or of activities in such areas elsewhere as have complete representation unilaterally only (i.e., speech, perhaps thinking, etc.).

changes (in the behavioral sense of Section D). The first set appears to consist of release phenomena—or, as he calls it, "impairment of [emotional] restraint" (i.e., "controlling or concealing" emotional states; (*45*, 39–40). Apparently on the theory that the emotional make-up is the chief determinant of personality, he construes these phenomena as an *exaggeration* of the personality (*ibid.*, 310). In the case he observed this appeared chiefly as self-aggrandizement (*ibid.*, 40),[40] which, he suggests, may perhaps have been a form of overcompensation for an inferiority complex derived from conscious inadequacy (*ibid.*, 45). But, in general, emotional lability, irritability, rudeness, excitability, and impulsiveness are reported in other cases (*ibid.*, 28).[41] "Hatred" (Brickner, *45*, 270) and "a certain curious hostility toward family and friends" (Fulton, *160*, 466) have been observed. Restlessness is frequently noted.[42] This may be regarded as the consequence of an emotional state in the hypothalamus, due to an internal want which has not yet reached the point of directing activity to its particular behavior, as we have hitherto done. Or it may be construed as overactivity of the cortical motor regions due to release of transcortical inhibition from this area.[43] At any rate, "spontaneous" activity, whether that arises from the hypothalamus or from the motor areas of the cortex, is controlled at least in part through the prefrontal cortex (Richter and Hines, *341*, 6). Brickner's second set of emotional changes may be described as regressions in the emotional-vegetative sphere. Thus puerility,[44] incontinence,[45] and masturbation reappear as if they were ontogenetically earlier behavior patterns. As he interprets the last, the prefrontal area was concerned in the advance to an adult sex level. Thereby it became "linked with instinctual function, just as with other emotional activities." When

[40] Also Fulton, *159*, 240; *160*, 466.

[41] Great excitability and groundless excitement in some situations (Goldstein, *173*, 34).

[42] Fulton, *159*, 240; *160*, 460 and 464. Richter and Hines (*341*, 1) point out that restlessness and increased activity is observed in monkeys, but that, on the contrary, apathy and decrease in activity are commonly noted in human cases. As to a possible explanation, see below, p. 1121. Men may, and monkeys may not, be conscious of their "failure to adjust."

[43] So Darrow regards it (*104*, 661) on the ground that it is not present if both the frontal and the premotor areas are removed, though he also admits inhibitory control in this area over the hypothalamus. Bianchi (*35*, 324) supposed the connections between the prefrontal and the Rolandic area to be very strong. But Richter and Hines think much of this inhibitory effect is produced via the tip of the striatum, which was always involved in their ablations. At least the increase in activity is "much more precipitate" with striatal lesions than if only the cortex is involved (*341*, 8–9). See also Fulton, *160*, 460; tip of caudate nucleus.

[44] This is described by others as "silliness and childishness," or "childish, cheerful excitement" (Brickner, *45*, 26–27); or "levity, irresponsibility and prankishness" (Alford, *8*, 795); or euphoria (Fulton, *159*, 240); or "a rather fatuous equanimity of spirit which one encounters in a good-natured drunkard" (Fulton, *160*, 465); or the "happiness cult of the Elder Micheaux" (Jacobsen, *217*, as quoted by Fulton, *160*, 465).

[45] Vesical or rectal incontinence, or both, are generally reported (Brickner, *45*, 26–27). In his own case, however, the patient showed no incontinence except enuresis, and was then ashamed—an unusual adjunct (*ibid.*, 228).

this evolved mechanism was removed, there was an impairment of the whole instinctual function (*45*, 317).

Whether as a result of overactivity or not, Fulton reports excessive hunger and, in spite of enormous eating, a loss of weight (*159*, 240). But this is not confirmed by Richter and Hines, who observed no noticeable increase in appetite or thirst with their animals, although they always had ample food and water (*341*, 15). Neither is it mentioned by Brickner.

The next, and we think related, group of symptoms may best be approached through the external evidence of impairments in what is called the faculty of conscious attention, which recalls to us Walker's supposition as to the "mechanism of sensory attention," mentioned on p. 1113. If that faculty is impaired, the selective facilitation of some, and inhibition of all other, primary receptive centers, upon which it may depend, would be reduced or eliminated. Brickner (*45*, 41) noted a reduced capacity for the fixation of attention—that is, increased distractibility [46] or a "marked tendency to shift from one activity to another" (Fulton, *160*, 460). The ready shifting toward each new stimulus may be interpreted as an uninhibited response to external stimuli (Richter and Hines, *341*, 15). But the ready shifting away from the old stimulus to the new, and the aimlessness of the resulting activity, are due to a defect in the "reaction of fixation of attention"—that is, a "conspicuous failure to fix attention upon a stimulus before going into action" (Tower, *405*, 440). On the other hand, Goldstein (*173*, 37) reports that attention varies from distractibility to concentration according to the situation and the patient's ability to grasp its essentials. He thinks (*ibid*., 34) there is no "emotional defect," but that emotional dullness—which is probably what Brickner calls "inattentiveness," or "apathy," or "drowsiness" (*45*, 27–28)—is a consequence of failure to comprehend these essentials. All this is straight to the point of the interpretation we shall offer in the next section. As the converse of this, there appears what Brickner construes as "lack of appreciation of the gravity of the situation" (*ibid*., 315), which may be the same thing that others have called "apathy in the attitude toward oneself" (*ibid*., 26–27).[47] Thus Goldstein (*173*, 34) concludes that "the 'will,' the *Antrieb*" is not disturbed at all. It is only discouraged by the constant failure to adjust. And this may also account for any loss of motor or intellectual initiative, such as has been reported (Brickner, *45*, 26–27).

[46] Also Goldstein, *173*, 37; Fulton, *159*, 240; *160*, 460, 464, 466; Richter and Hines, *341*, 15; Tower, *405*, 440.

[47] In fact the absence of "emotional disturbance" in Jacobsen's prefrontal chimpanzee, when it made a mistake with a problem box, as compared with the "violent temper tantrum" of the normal animal when it failed, seems to be evidence of this same lack of comprehension or of interest (see *217*). Jacobsen himself noted discouragement in the normal monkey after five or six successive errors, while the bilateral prefrontal would go on indefinitely because he did not realize his failures (*218*, 564). Perseveration (inability to stop) has been reported. Richter and Hines (*341*, 15) find no evidence of other perseveration tendencies. Perhaps behavior of the order of the chimpanzee, above, has been misconstrued as perseveration.

Closely allied with this impairment of the fixation of attention and perhaps a result of it, or of the same defect, is what is usually called loss of "recent memory" (Jacobsen, *218*, 560, 564; Fulton, *160*, 462, 463, 466; Brickner, *45*, 28, 171). Since "the frontal area animal is thus unable to retain for a few seconds the memory of a recent event in the face of other oncoming sensory experience" (Fulton, *160*, 463), there is a "failure to respond in accordance with recent sensory experience" (*ibid.*, 462). Or, put in another way, "temporal patterning fails."[48] It is impossible to keep in mind several thoughts and manipulate them (Jacobsen, *218*, 565). For the same reason there is "great difficulty in executing previously acquired skilled movements requiring a series of motor acts spread out in time and occurring in definite sequence" (Fulton, *159*, 240). Memory for remote events (older than 30 minutes) remains (Brickner, *45*, 171; Goldstein, *173*, 36) or is less impaired (Fulton, *160*, 466). Fulton thinks the "difficulties lie in reproductive memory ("recall") as opposed to associative memory" (*160*, 467).[49] But what is the basis of recall except association? On the contrary, it appears that there is no lack of memory content—only what Goldstein calls a "wrong approach" (*173*, 36), a weakening of one of the major bases of association. Recognition remains; that is clear from many reports, though none speaks of it. Individual experiences are remembered (Goldstein, *173*, 27). Even the capacity to retain new impressions is still *usually* available; when the patient *cares* to use it, "he can use it well." That depends on "interest." But, if the matter is too complicated, "interest" flags and fails (Brickner, *45*, 172). Thus it seems most explanatory to assume that it is a failure of "interest" that is responsible for the defect in the "reaction of fixation of attention" (above), as well as for the weakness in associating together items of current sensory experiences which relate to the same "interest," or to file them away for future reference under that important system of classification.[50] At any rate, it is agreed—and this is important for our future reference—that, since learning is "closely identified with the function of recent retention," the result here is "little learning from experience" (Brickner, *45*, 196, 199). New acquisition is difficult (Goldstein, *173*, 36). Perhaps even the generalizations of past experience are forgotten, so that there remains little "insight" (*ibid.*, 27)—the ability to apply old generalizations to new situations.

There has been a tendency, on a priori grounds, to assign to the prefrontal area some special part in purely intellectual processes such as the

48 There is no "spatial" but some "temporal disorientation" (Brickner, *45*, 218, 312).

49 This reminds one of Bianchi's (*35*, 208) view that the "higher consciousness" in the prefrontal area can "select and recall" the images left in the sensory cortex (i.e., ransack the storehouse). We doubt that this capacity is confined to the prefrontal area.

50 Fulton refers to the fact that "with food out of sight, it is also out of mind, the animal cannot recall where it was seen" (*160*, 467), and cites Kluver's observation of a bilateral frontal monkey who, when offered grapes in rapid succession, carried each toward its mouth, but dropped that one to grasp the second when that was offered, etc., so that no grapes were eaten (*ibid.*, 460, note 2).

capacity for abstract thinking.[51] But we may remind ourselves of Poliak's caution, quoted above (p. 1109), as to the difficulty of defining what are the elementary cortical processes. Of these the psychological concept, "abstraction," is certainly not one. Or, rather, the linking together of any pair of observed phenomena by reason of similarity of any kind (recognition) constitutes an abstraction. The entire nervous system is capable of this, and certainly the rest of the cortex is capable of *conscious* recognition. It is therefore safer to confine ourselves to observed intellectual defects in actual cases. When these are carefully considered they seem to be part and parcel of the defects we have already mentioned. Fulton refers to reports of poor judgment (*159*, 24) and construes Brickner's patient as "incapable of logical thinking," going "off on tangents whenever a topic requiring sustained and simple logical analysis was brought up for consideration" (*160*, 467). But, as Brickner points out (*45*, 270 ff.), these are the same phenomena as, or are reducible to, the lack of fixation of conscious attention and of recent memory. The only strictly intellectual deficit, not already noted, appears to be what Brickner calls the "impairment of particularization"—that is, the "capacity to select and segregate units of intellectual activity" (*45*, 41). But that, too, may be connected with the cause of the defects in conscious attention and in memory. For what is the basis upon which "units of intellectual activity" are constructed?

It is evident from the foregoing that the prefrontal area is not the sole locus of consciousness; for, when it is ablated, there appears no noticeable defect in consciousness.[52] Neither does it appear likely that it is the sole locus of emotional experience—the place where the emotion, strictly speaking, is felt in consciousness; for Goldstein reports no "emotional defect" (*173*, 34). On the contrary, Brickner sums up the emotional changes he observed as a free exhibition of emotional and instinctive phenomena (*45*, 270 ff.). Nor is it the sole locus of "intellectual" operations, though these, too, seem to be affected—but, contrary to the emotional category, to be impaired rather than released. However, if we infer what the function of this region is from the defects which appear when it is removed, we may tentatively adopt Brickner's conclusions. He considers the primary

[51] Thus, as his third level or system, Pavlov supposed that there is localized here the capacity of abstraction including the abstractions of language (Frolov, *157*, 78 ff.). Darrow (*104*, 661) suggests that ideational activity is localized here in the "newest" region.

[52] As Penfield says (*323*, *66*), after citing evidence, "All of this would suggest that the frontal lobes anterior to recognized motor areas are utilized in conscious processes but that they are not indispensable to the existence of consciousness."

Of course, after the prefrontal areas have been ablated, whatever activities are normally carried on there, and which may have been available to consciousness, are no longer so, since they no longer occur. Foerster, in Bumke and Foerster, 6 *Handbuch der Neurologie* (1936), reports that artificial stimulation here may produce unconsciousness in conscious human beings. We will suggest a possible explanation of that in the next section.

symptom to be "impairment in the ability to synthesize" (*45*, 39–40)—a synthesis which relates to every process elsewhere in the cortex (*ibid.*, 291). In fact, all the other symptoms are reducible to this (*ibid.*, 270). Thus both the reduced capacity for fixation of attention and the impairment of particularization (above) are secondary to the primary "limitation of the capacity to associate or synthesize mental engrammes to a complex degree" (*ibid.*, 41).[53] Thus, too, emotional release is construed as due to defects in complex, synthetic functions dependent upon synthesis of the simple (*ibid.*, 270), for "normal restraint . . . is *composed* of the very kinds of thought processes . . . [which become] defective" (*ibid.*, 120). In other words, we may infer that the function of the prefrontal area is chiefly concerned with at least one relationship which constitutes a major basis for *association* (synthesis) "in the reception, utilization and recall of stimuli and events" (*ibid.*, 171). We shall proceed to consider, in the next section, what that one relationship may be.

G. INTERACTIONS BETWEEN THE CORTEX AND THE HYPOTHALAMUS

1. DEVELOPMENTAL CONSIDERATIONS AND THE INTERCONNECTIONS

In the development of the neural tube, "the cells of origin of the efferent nerves collect in the ventral part of the side wall"—the "basal lamina." "Most of the cells that emit afferent fibres are situated in the sensory ganglia outside the central nervous system"; "but their central processes become inserted into the dorsal part of the side wall of the tube, which is called the alar lamina." For this reason the alar lamina does not swell as much as does the basal, and this unequal swelling produces a "longitudinal groove—the sulcus limitans" (Elliot Smith, *382*, 798), which thereafter continues to mark "the line of demarcation . . . between the primary motor zone . . . and the primary sensory zone" (Kingsbury, *238*, 463).

In the region developed from the anterior brain vesicle, the hypothalamic sulcus, or sulcus of Monro, which divides the thalamus (above) from at least part of the hypothalamus (below), "was considered by His to represent" the sulcus limitans,[1] so that at least part of the hypothalamus has been held to represent the basal lamina, while the thalamus certainly repre-

[53] That is the "synthesizing of separate factors of thought into a unitary consequence or result" (*45*, 45), sometimes called "putting two and two together."

[1] Elliot Smith (*382*, 902). At least it "apparently is analogous to the sulcus limitans" (Streeter, *387*, 77), or "has been regarded as the rostral extension of the sulcus limitans" (Le Gros Clark, *86*, 3). Others are more positive. It "represents the original sulcus limitans" and continues to separate "the structures developed from the alar and basal laminae" (Whitaker, *438*, 25). "The sulcus limitans becomes the hypothalamic sulcus" (A. Kuntz, *A Text-Book of Anatomy*, 2nd ed., Philadelphia, 1936, p. 49). Lewis (in H. Gray, *The Anatomy of the Human Body*, 23rd ed., ed. W. H. Lewis, Philadelphia, 1936, p. 810) goes so far as to call it the sulcus limitans.

sents part of the alar lamina.[2] His held that the sulcus limitans terminates at the preoptic recess. So did Johnston (*225* and *226*).[3] But Kingsbury (*loc. cit.*), who cites in support Schulte and Tilney (1915), believes that it terminates at the mammillary bodies. In the former view, the whole of the hypothalamus is construed to be a development of the basal (motor) plate; in the latter view, that is held to be true only up to the anterior edge of the mammillary bodies. In either view, the basal plate is supposed to terminate with the hypothalamus and development from there forward to proceed only from the alar plate.[4] However, neither of these views seems to explain the fact that the pouch of the infundibulum, the oral pouch which joins it from below (the hypophysis), and the tuber cinereum are single structures, not paired structures such as are found in the floor of the forebrain anterior to them and perhaps also posterior to them.[5] It would be more consistent with the functional characteristics of the basal and alar plates, and with the fact that the two walls tend to produce paired structures elsewhere, to suppose that this single system of structures had intruded from below between or into the basal laminae, and that they and the paired nuclei developed from them, or from connections with them, had extruded the basal laminae, at this point, to a more lateral and dorsal position.[6]

Immediately anterior to the hypothalamus and in the ventral walls of the tube (or its "ventral surface"; Looney, *273*, 24), the paired optic evaginations form, to meet the optic nerves which insert themselves there. These two are certainly intrusions. Then "the wall adjacent to and forming the anterior border of the [optic] evagination [in each wall] forms the anlage of the corpus striatum" (Streeter, *387*, 36). Thus, the ventral walls anterior to the hypothalamus and to the optic evaginations still appear, at this stage, to represent the basal (motor) laminae. That is, they appear to do so, if the corpora striata can be construed as having chiefly motor functions and connections.[7] The development of the optic evaginations extrudes

[2] At the end of the first month, the thalamus "is continuous with and resembles the alar plate of the midbrain" (Streeter, *387*, 47). The alar plate of the interbrain, of which the thalamus represents the largest part, "is predominantly sensory" (*ibid.*, 77).

[3] So construed by Kingsbury (*loc. cit.*). Streeter (*387*, 33) says, "The region in the adult brain corresponding to the anterior end of the neural plate was placed by His at the infundibulum. Johnston (1909) from comparative embryological studies places it at the optic chiasma." That is, according to Kingsbury, they agreed on the termination of the sulcus limitans but, according to Streeter, they disagreed slightly as to the end of the neural plate, the former excluding and the latter including the optic chiasm.

[4] For a further discussion of these two views on the sulcus limitans, see supplementary statement on "The Origin of the Hypothalamus," at the end of this subsection.

[5] The mammillary bodies are paired, but they develop from a single recess.

[6] For a more detailed exposition of this hypothesis, see supplementary statement on "The Origin of the Hypothalamus," at the end of this subsection.

[7] In Fulton's view, "the paleostriatum [globus pallidus] retains its ancestral function as a motor nucleus—at one time the principal motor pathway from the forebrain" (*160*, 491). But Kinnier Wilson (*443*, 480) thinks the "original corpus striatum," the globus pallidus, represents "that part of the original cerebral hemisphere whereby impressions of smell, and no doubt other sense impressions, may bring their influences to bear on

the corpora striata to a more lateral and dorsal position. Again the basal laminae appear to be displaced. Finally, "the wall in front of the corpus striatum and adjacent to the median line (lamina terminalis) constitutes the anlage of the rhinencephalon" (*ibid.*, 40), into which the olfactory nerves will be directly inserted (Elliot Smith, *382*, 810). But, this too begins in the ventral surface of the anterior vesicle (Looney, *273*, 24).[8] It is more ventral than the corpus striatum as well as anterior to it, and is the most anterior formation in the neural tube, in fact next to the median line of the end of the tube—the suture terminalis which, when it closes, becomes the lamina terminalis (Kingsbury, *238*, 463). From this it appears that, whereas, posterior to the forebrain, sensory processes are inserted into the alar lamina (Elliot Smith, above), in this region, itself, those from two of the distance receptors seem to enter into or between the basal laminae, one immediately posterior and rostral to, and one immediately anterior and ventral to, the corpus striatum.

If these three entities, the single structures in the hypothalamus and the two paired evaginations constituting the optic vesicles and the anlage of the rhinencephalon, can be regarded as intrusions into the ventral surface of the neural tube or between the basal laminae—so as, at least, to extrude the latter to a more lateral position—rather than as developments of the basal laminae themselves, then the corpora striata would be left as the only developments from these laminae anterior to the mammillary bodies.[9] If so, the position in which we would expect to find the continuation of the sulcus limitans would be between the positions ultimately reached by the corpus striatum and the thalamus. Since the corpus striatum is anterior to, as well as ventral to, the thalamus and has been displaced laterally by the above-mentioned intrusions (particularly the rhinencephalon), this continuation of the sulcus limitans would have to take a new direction beyond the thalamus. But, instead of curving down as it is supposed to do in either of the views cited above, it would curve up. Is it possible that, at first, it follows the course along which it was originally traced—that is, to the foramen which also bears the name of Monro?[10] Is it

---

the nervous mechanisms regulating movement"—a function now gone not to return (*ibid.*, 489). But perhaps all of this region was concerned primarily with an expansion of functions as a result of the phylogenetic entry of the nerves of smell. See below. If so, the motor character of the corpus striatum would not be challenged.

[8] All parts of the rhinencephalon are formed from [or in] the basal portion of the neural tube median to (i.e., more ventral than) the corpus striatum (Streeter, *387*, 88).

[9] And even as to the latter we cannot be sure they arise from, rather than between, the basal laminae (see above, note 4).

[10] Among anatomists this has been and still is the general view. For example, see S. W. Ranson, *Anatomy of the Nervous System*, 6th ed. (Philadelphia, 1939), p. 208; J. Sobotta, *Atlas and Text-Book of Human Anatomy* (Philadelphia, 1909), III, 155; F. A. Mettler, *Neuroanatomy* (St. Louis, 1942), p. 100; A. Kuntz, *A Text-Book of Neuro-Anatomy*, 2nd ed. (Philadelphia, 1936); Elliot Smith, *382*, 902; Villiger, *414*, 19; W. H. Lewis, in H. Gray, *The Anatomy of the Human Body*, 23rd ed. (Philadelphia, 1936), p. 810.

The opportunity for a difference of opinion is obvious if one examines the data

possible that, thereafter, it is to be traced, at least in terms of a functional division, into what is construed to be a paired continuation of the lumen of the neural tube—the lateral ventricle—and is to be recognized as the deep groove (sulcus intermedius) which separates the corpus striatum from the thalamus?

There is still more to be said in regard to this hypothesis. When the optic evaginations appear, there is left, between their two dorsal borders and along the roof of the tube, the margo thalamicus which divides the anlage of the thalamus from the anlage of the pallium (Streeter, *387*, 36). At the point from which the pallium is to develop, the forebrain shows, at the end of the first month, a "prominent lateral evagination," the lumen of which is to form the lateral ventricle, connected with the neural tube by the "large foramen of Monro" and, presumably, as noted, a now paired continuation of this tube (*ibid.*, 46–47). These evaginations will form the "typical paired hemispheres opening out laterally through the foramen of Monro" (*ibid.*, 83). But "each hemisphere is formed . . . from a relatively small part of the side wall" of the forebrain (Elliot Smith, *382*, 810). The "protruding pallium [is] separated from the optic evagination by the corpus striatum and from the thalamus by the margo thalamicus" (Streeter, *387*, 40). That is, these optic evaginations and those of the rhinencephalon have extruded the corpora striata into lateral and more dorsal positions contiguous to the beginnings of the pallium. Thereafter, the corpus striatum is "closely united with the thalamus,[11] and it is through this that the connection between telencephalon and diencephalon is principally maintained" (*ibid.*, 83). The corpus striatum "shares with the thalamus in the development of the pallium," and all paths of communication to and from the cortex pass through these two (*ibid.*, 83).[12] Since the pallial walls expand laterally "from around the borders of the corpus striatum" (*ibid.*, 83), the corpora striata are withdrawn into and become essentially parts of the hemispheres.[13] Thereafter, these pallial walls expand further; they expand orally into the frontal lobe, along the extending anterior horn of the lateral ventricle; they also expand caudally, but curving down, to form the temporal lobe, along the extending inferior horn; and, lastly,

direct, for there are apparent three branchings from what is usually construed still to be the sulcus limitans anterior to the cephalic flexure. One groove descends immediately toward the mammillary bodies; the joint portion of the other two proceeds forward between the anlage of the thalamus and that of the hypothalamus; then these two divide; one branch descends between the anlage of the corpus striatum and that of the hypothalamus to the optic recess, while the other branch rises to the interventricular foramen. For a clear representation, see Mettler, *Neuroanatomy*, p. 100, Fig. 70.

[11] In fact, it is said to be "directly continuous with the thalamic plate of the diencephalon" (*387*, 85). Is it not, rather, continuous with the laterally displaced basal plate?

[12] So far as the thalamus is concerned—but apparently not so far as the corpus striatum is concerned—the phylogenetic aspect of this development is somewhat co-ordinate with that of the cortex; for "advanced development of the thalamus is characteristic of the higher vertebrates" (Streeter, *387*, 82).

[13] Literally they appear to be folded back upon the thalami as the evaginations expand caudally.

they expand again caudally, but this time dorsally, to form the occipital lobe, along the extending posterior horn. Has the fact that, of the two bodies which "share in the development of the pallium," the corpus striatum originated from a point anterior to the thalamus, and that, even when folded back, it remains largely anterior to it, anything to do with the fact that the frontal lobe is "chiefly motor," while the postcentral lobes are "chiefly sensory"?

In this connection it is interesting to note that, if on purely functional grounds (motor *vs.* sensory), we were to project into the cortex the functional division which the sulcus limitans represents in the neural tube, we would expect it to take the form of a plane intersecting the cortex approximately along the line of the Sylvian and Rolandic fissures. For the whole cortex posterior to these fissures chiefly represents functions that were dorsal in the brain tube (sensory), and the next rostral (precentral) cortex chiefly represents what was ventral there (motor).[14] On each side, the projection would have shown a change in direction of about 90°—a change from rostral to lateral and dorsal; a change from development along the axis of the neural tube to developments in a plane transverse to that axis; but the arrangement of its functional divisions would also have shown a rotation of about 90° upon these new axes.[15]

On the whole, this hypothesis seems best to accord with and therefore to explain the ultimate arrangements of the forebrain—that is, the endbrain and the interbrain—which develops from, or in, the anterior primary vesicle. It assumes that the alar plate, beyond the thalamus, has given rise only to the postcentral cortex—both being almost exclusively sensory; it assumes that the basal plate, extruded from its ventral position to a lateral

[14] To the first statement the exceptions are, as noted above, the optic evaginations and the anlage of the rhinencephalon, both of which are ventral in the neural tube.

[15] We are not suggesting, of course, that such an imaginary projection is actually an extension of the sulcus limitans. As to that, see above (pp. 1126–1127).

This change in direction is confirmed by the projections of the thalamus. Whereas projections within the central nervous system and below the diencephalon generally lie along the neural axis, here they become transverse to that axis. As Ariëns Kappers *et al.* (*231*, II, 1664) state, citing Elliot Smith (1910) and others, "the more posterior parts of the thalamus are projected on the posterior parts of the cortex, the intermediate portions of the thalamus on the intermediate cortical areas, and the anterior parts of the thalamus on the anterior part of the cortex." This is confirmed in detail, so far as the lateral nuclear mass of the thalamus is concerned, by Walker (*416*, 246–247).

The terms rostral and dorsal, as used here, may be confusing to the uninitiated. The cephalic flexure, which "persists into adult life" (Streeter, *387*, 39), and is the only flexure which does so, is "a sharp bend in the neural tube in the region of the midbrain so that the axis of the forebrain forms approximately a right angle with that of the hindbrain" (*ibid.*, 35), an angle which later increases "to an acute one" (*ibid.*, 37). Anterior to this flexure, the same terminology continues to be used as to relations with the neural axis. But, because of the flexure, in man at least, rostral as to the neural axis has become ventral as to the body axis, and dorsal has become "apical." Except in the somewhat related "cephalic indexes" of craniology, not much attention seems to have been paid to the fact that, in man, the greater flexure in the neural axis has opened roughly 270° of sagittal angle to the development of the cerebral hemispheres, whereas in quadrupeds that angle is necessarily little more than 180°, and in lower vertebrates even less.

one in the walls of the tube, has given rise to the corpus striatum and to the precentral cortex, or to those parts of the latter which are almost exclusively motor; and it assumes that the hypothalamus, or the major portion of it, is developed from neither plate and therefore takes no part in the further development, and has no direct developmental correspondent in the hemispheres. In confirmation of this it is to be noted that, whereas the motor and the sensory areas of the cortex are intimately connected, by means of elaborate and direct projections in one or both directions, with the corresponding brain-stem structures, in connection with which they developed, the hypothalamus appears to have no direct projection to the cortex and to receive but one from it (the fornix), and that from a region, not yet considered, which has generally been assigned to the olfactory cortex. Thus, both from the standpoint of further development and from that of direct interconnections the hypothalamus seems to have become almost a "dead-end."

These considerations remind us that we raised the question earlier whether it is correct to regard the new brain as, in all respects, the highest level [16] of the central nervous system or whether, on the other hand, one should admit two highest levels, the remaining highest level of the old brain and the new brain, somewhat independent of each other and with a complex system of interactions between them. In the latter view we would conceive most of the sensory portion (now concerned with neosensibility) of the old brain to have become merely a relay station for that portion of the new to which it has given rise, while we would conceive the rest (still concerned with paleosensibility) to have remained as the highest afferent level of the old brain; we would conceive the strictly motor portions (exterofective) of the old brain to have become relay stations for those among the motor portions of the new brain to which they have given rise, though continuing, in part, to be available also to the highest levels of the old brain; [17] and we would conceive the highest level of the old brain, the hypothalamus, to be the only part of it which continues to function with a considerable degree of autonomy without, or with far less, superimposition of new brain above it.

At any rate, because it has become almost a "dead-end," the hypothalamus appears to have remained almost untouched by the evolution of the rest of the forebrain. In the interbrain the hypothalamus and the epithalamus "are the most primitive in character and their fibres are the first to develop" (Streeter, *387*, 82). Moreover, the hypothalamus "retains its

[16] It should be noted that the cortex as a whole is one highest level, in our view, and that we are not separating it into two levels as Hughlings Jackson did.

[17] Since the corpora striata are "the most primitive part of the forebrain" (? endbrain) (Fulton, *160*, 489), and "at one time the principal motor pathway from the forebrain" (*ibid.*, 491) and are subcortical in spite of the fact that they lie in, and develop with, the hemispheres, they too may be regarded as having become purely relay stations, though they doubtless contribute some quality, force, steadiness, or timing, to the patterns of efferent impulse that they relay (Lashley, *262*, 380). Whether they are also relay stations for the hypothalamus in its exterofective activities is, as yet, doubtful.

primitive form and undergoes only slight change" (Elliot Smith, *382*, 893). This is true phylogenetically as well as ontogenetically. "Throughout the whole vertebrate scale there is no part of the forebrain that has maintained so constant a general arrangement" as the hypothalamus (Fulton, *160*, 234). On the other hand, the new brain, the pallium, "contrary to the rest of the nervous system, varies in its development directly according to each animal's phylogenetic position" (Streeter, *387*, 29). In the pallium, "the frontal lobe whose functional activity is the last to be required is correspondingly backward," at least ontogenetically (*ibid.*, 102). And, in the frontal lobe, it is generally conceded that, both ontogenetically and phylogenetically, the prefrontal area is the latest to develop. Thus we are presented with a marked contrast between our two highest levels. The highest level of the old brain has remained primitive; the new brain is apparently the measure of the degree of evolution; and in the new brain we find one area at least, the prefrontal, which seems to represent the latest stage in that evolution. Thus, in the forebrain, the hypothalamus and the prefrontal area appear to be at the opposite developmental poles from each other.

In spite of this contrast, there is a curious morphological analogy between these two regions which may have functional significance. We have seen that the hypothalamus ultimately occupies most of the ventral walls and floor of what remains of the anterior vesicle of the brain tube. On the other hand, the prefrontal areas of the cortex are those which surround the frontal poles of the two hemispheres—that is, the most rostral portions. If we are correct in construing the development of the hemispheres to have constituted a change in direction of 90° to each side (laterally and dorsally), then it would seem that a ventral position in the brain tube would correspond to a rostral position in the hemispheres. If morphological position has any functional meaning, the analogy in the position of these two structures may indicate some correspondence in function. At least such a correspondence is not excluded. For the most rostral cortex—the prefrontal area—is, as we noted in Section F 3, not strictly motor. Neither is the hypothalamus. Nor are either sensory (i.e., organs for integrating afferent impulses). We have already examined evidence as to the functions of the hypothalamus and have considered at least the negative evidence as to those of the prefrontal areas. The question remains whether the functions of the latter have some connection with, or correspondence to, those of the former. On this question the morphological analogy is merely suggestive.

With this consideration as to developmental relations in mind, we shall now examine those of the possible avenues of interaction between the highest levels of the old brain and the new brain which are at present known and which serve as the bases for current hypotheses. Having examined these and the hypotheses based upon them, we will take account, in Section H, of the action of the two highest levels upon lower effector levels, where, in view of the two somewhat independent systems of control, we should expect to find evidence both of co-operation and of conflicts.

The first of these avenues between the highest level of the old brain and the new brain has as its intermediary, or relay station, the dorsomedial nucleus of the thalamus, which Walker (*416*, 244) regards as the "striking development" of the primate thalamus.[18] This is what Head (*183*) called the "essential organ" of the thalamus. It is chiefly a thalamic association center, receiving "no fibres from the ascending somatic systems" (Fulton, *160*, 273). It receives from the lateral nuclear mass, which we recall is the relay station for somatic paths to the sensory cortex, and perhaps directly from the nuclei of the midline as well, which we recall is the relay station for somatic and visceral paths to the hypothalamus. It connects directly with the hypothalamus by way of the periventricular system of fibers, probably including both efferent and afferent paths. Finally, it projects to the prefrontal area of the cortex, but probably has also afferent paths therefrom.[19] Thus, in Le Gros Clark's view it is "a link between" the hypothalamus and the prefrontal areas of the cortex (*84*, 467). It is a two-way avenue.

The second of these avenues is also indirect, but consists of a somewhat miscellaneous group of paths all of which appear to be wholly afferent to the hypothalamus. Of these, the medial forebrain bundle contains the only fibers which run direct from the cortex; but these come from a region that has usually been considered olfactory.[20] The rest of this tract and some others contain afferent paths to the hypothalamus from the septum, the striatum, and the subthalamus (Ingram, *212*, 238–239). Of course all of these may, and probably do, relay impulses from the cortex. But Le Gros Clark thinks (*85*, 115) that those from the septum and the subthalamus relay

[18] Le Gros Clark (*84*, 467) says it is essentially mammalian and finds its highest development in man.

[19] Walker (*416*, 244) states that its afferent paths are from the hypothalamus and the rest of the thalamus (the adjoining lateral nuclear mass and the midline nuclei; *ibid.*, 263), while its efferent paths are to the frontal area. Fulton (*160*, 273) likewise states that it connects with the lateral nuclear mass and with the hypothalamus by way of the periventricular system (presumably afferent) and projects (efferent) to the prefrontal region (areas 9, 10 and 12). But, he holds that, in the opposite direction (*ibid.*, 238), the prefrontal, "particularly area 9," projects to the dorsomedial nucleus and thence via the periventricular system, to the posterior hypothalamic nucleus. Ingram (*212*, 238–239) also thinks the periventricular system conveys, to the hypothalamus, visceral sensory impulses from the nuclei of the midline, somatic sensory impulses from the medial (presumably dorsomedial), and, via the latter as a relay station, impulses from the neopallium (presumably prefrontal). He agrees that it also conveys impulses from the hypothalamus to the thalamus (presumably dorsomedial nucleus). Combining these elements we get Le Gros Clark's view. He holds (*86*, 36) that the connection from the hypothalamus to the prefrontal cortex via the dorsomedial nucleus is an "extremely ancient" one, and probably conducts both ways (*loc. cit.*). See also his statements in *84*, 468; *85*, 107; and *86*, 28, 31 and 32.

[20] Ingram (*212*, 238–239) derives them from the olfactory and parolfactory areas (the former presumably being a part of the orbital surface of the frontal lobe). Le Gros Clark (*86*, 31) thinks these tracts are probably olfactory; Bard (*24*, 188 and 191) doubts if they are any longer olfactory.

impulses from the frontal pole in particular; and Beattie (*30*, *69*) holds that those via the septum, coming from the frontal cortex as a whole, are the chief source of afferent impulses to the anterior region of the hypothalamus.[21] As we proceed we shall consider the various theories as to the possible and somewhat miscellaneous functions these paths underlie. But we should remember that, at present, these miscellaneous corticofugal paths are held to constitute a one-way avenue only.

The next avenue has been held to include the one direct connection—the fornix—to which we have already alluded. Papez (*315*) regards all the formations he includes in his system as constituting together a single "circuit." Actually most of his circuit takes the anatomical form of two so-called annular formations, one within the other. Both these formations are more like ram's horns than like rings, in that the base and the tip of the outer ring may not meet and those of the inner ring certainly do not meet. On the other hand, it is possible that the tips of both and the bases of both do meet. As Papez outlines his circuit, the mammillary bodies in the hypothalamus project via the bundle of Vicq d'Azyr to the anterior and anterodorsal thalamic nuclei; these in turn project to the two gyri cinguli, which are the next to innermost gyri on the dorsal portion of the medial surfaces of the cortex; these gyri look as if they were continuous (via the isthmus) with the hippocampal gyri, which are at the base of the medial hemispheric surfaces (temporal lobes). Paralleling this outer ring, the inner ring is traced in the reverse direction; the hippocampal gyri give rise to the fimbriae; these are continuous with the fornix, a paired structure, which, returning within the hemispheres and under the great commissure (corpus callosum), divides and ends, where the first projection began, in the two mammillary bodies.[22] While it is necessary to state his scheme in order to

[21] On the other hand, he holds that the posterior hypothalamus receives impulses mostly from the thalamus (*loc. cit.*).

[22] See specifically Papez's description (*315*, 725 and 743). Le Gros Clark agrees that the mammillo-thalamic tract, or bundle of Vicq d'Azyr, terminates in the anterior nucleus of the thalamus (*84*, 417–418; it is greatest in the higher mammals) and thence connects with the gyrus cinguli (*85*, 115 and *86*, 27). Also the mammillary bodies are connected via the fornix to the "hippocampal formation" (*84*, 441), or to the "whole extent of the hippocampus" (*86*, 24). Ingram (*212*, 238–239) includes the fornix in his afferent connections to the hypothalamus, connecting the hippocampus to the mammillary bodies, and, among the hypothalamico-thalamic tracts, one from these bodies to the anterior thalamic nuclei. Walker (*416*, 242) construes the entire anterior group of thalamic nuclei (anteromedial, anteroventral and anterodorsal) as olfactory, but only because they project exclusively to the anterior gyrus cinguli. Le Gros Clark (*84*, 438) excepts the anteromedial, which he thinks is a part of the paleothalamus, "differentiated from the midline nuclei" and "having no connection with the . . . cortex." The only afferent connections to these latter nuclei are from the mammillary bodies. The fornix as afferent to, and the bundle of Vicq d'Azyr as efferent from, the mammillary bodies are also agreed to by Bard (*24*, 188–191), citing Ranson and Magoun.

Fulton states (*160*, 236) that "the largest cell group [of these bodies], the medial mammillary nucleus . . . becomes highly developed in man and the higher primates." It is these which appear to be "the main terminal station of the fornix column and give rise to the mammillothalamic tract of Vicq d'Azyr . . . which links them with the anterior nucleus of the thalamus, and through this nucleus with the cingular gyri of the cerebral

borrow, as we shall do, the hypothesis he elaborates from it, we do not find it possible to regard the whole of his system as a functional unit. Instead, it seems necessary to treat his outer and his inner rings as separate units. It even appears doubtful that the morphological continuity of the gyrus cinguli and the gyrus hippocampi corresponds to a functional unity. We shall, therefore, treat the first part of the first ring up to and including the gyrus cinguli as a functional unit by itself. It is Le Gros Clark's belief that this first part also includes paths in the reverse direction (*85*, 116, and *86*, 35).[23] Thus this part alone seems to constitute a complete "circuit" in itself. We shall regard it as the third of our avenues of interaction between the hypothalamus and the cortex; and, like the first and unlike the second, we shall assume it to be a two-way avenue.

In connection with the hypotheses which will be outlined shortly it should also be noted here that the mammillary bodies, besides intimate intrahypothalamic connections, receive afferent impulses from the midbrain through the mammillary peduncle and send efferent impulses thereto via the mammillo-tegmental tract (Ingram, *212*, 238–239); thus it appears that another and descending circuit, or at least an intimate relationship, is established between these bodies and the next lower level of the brainstem.

The cortical areas included in Papez's circuit were formerly and are still frequently assigned as part of what has been variously called the rhinencephalon, the allocortex and the archipallium. These terms are intended to signify that this is the primitive, or phylogenetically first, cortex; that it is architectonically different from the isocortex or neopallium; and that its function is—or was—exclusively olfactory. Since these three terms all differentiate these regions of the cortex from those we considered in the previous section and since the developmental relation in connection with the sense of smell is of importance for our interpretations, we must proceed to review briefly the most recent theories in regard to them.

That part of the outer ring included in Papez's scheme which is formed by the gyrus cinguli and the gyrus hippocampi constituted most of Broca's limbic (circumferential) lobe.[24] Zuckerkandl assumed three concentric circles, of which the limbic lobe was the outermost, the gyrus dentatus (or more exactly, Giacomini's band-gyrus dentatus-induseum griseum-gyrus subcallosus) was the middle, and the fimbria and fornix (Papez's inner ring) was the innermost. As already noted, the hemispheres develop as evaginations around the future foramina of Monro and from the dorsolateral walls of the anterior vesicle. These evaginations come to engage and

cortex" (*ibid.*, 238). The latter is "a large projection." "Descending fibres have also been demonstrated in the mammillothalamic tract from the anterior nucleus of the thalamus, and there is a corticothalamic projection from the gyrus cinguli to the anterior nucleus" (*loc. cit.*).

[23] As to the cingular gyrus-mammillary connection, Fulton agrees (*160*, 238).

[24] Papez does not include the lobus olfactorius anterior which was part of Broca's "grand lobe limbique."

include, as their anterior and ventral edge, the evaginations of the rhinencephalon. Since the innermost circle (the fimbria-fornix above) is within the walls of the hemispheres, it is clear that the ring—or annular lobe—represented by the gyrus dentatus, the induseum and the gyrus subcallosus, being the innermost gyrus on the medial face of the hemisphere, corresponds roughly to the original edge of the evagination most proximate to the wall of the neural tube. On the other hand, the limbic lobe is next innermost and therefore next most proximate to the original wall. If, now, later development is found to take place almost wholly on the lateral walls of the budding hemispheres, as we shall see below, it is evident that these rings, while originally constituting most of the evagination, would come eventually to constitute narrow bands surrounding the region where each hemisphere adjoins the brain-stem. At least this would be true except at the base of the hemispheres, where the structures have become greatly confused. Given these conditions of growth, the earliest formed parts of the pallium become necessarily ring-like structures on the medial surface of the hemisphere, adjoining the brain-stem.

The hemispheres develop at first pre-eminently as an olfactory field, the peripheral nerves of smell being directly inserted into them (Elliot Smith, *382*, 810). But "cortex does not appear in the pallial part of the olfactory field of any lower vertebrate unless and until several strong systems of non-olfactory projection fibres penetrate the pallium and have definite and separate localization within it" (Herrick, *191*, 11). "The supposed primordium of the neopallium" (isocortex), in reptiles, "is reached by thalamic projection fibres, and these so far as is now known belong to the somesthetic system."[25] These reach into the anterior end of the dorsal area of the pallium and are inserted between the hippocampal and the pyriform areas (*ibid.*, 12). Thereafter, as the neopallium develops extensively while the archipallium develops little, the former expands laterally and comes to occupy all but the innermost medial and ventral surface.[26] Thus allocortex appears in the archipallium coincidentally with the appearance of the neopallium and its isocortex, and both arise, it would seem, as a result of interaction between the olfactory and other senses. That is, cortex seems to develop originally as the result, or means, of integration of the olfactory with other sensory modalities. What, then, is the peculiar contribution of the olfactory sense?

Summarizing Herrick's hypothesis (*loc. cit.*), we may say that the ol-

[25] It is in this way that "the cerebral hemisphere, from being essentially a receptive organ for smell impressions, ultimately becomes the terminus of all the sensory paths and the structure that is concerned with the consciousness of all kinds of sensations" (Elliot Smith, *382*, 810).

[26] See Herrick's diagrams (*191*, 8). Still later the archipallium, or part of it, is still further displaced. As Ariëns Kappers *et al.* (*231*, II, 1476) put it: "In lower mammals the archicortex occupies its primitive position in the midline, but in higher mammals, with the progressive development of the neocortex, the archicortex [at least the hippocampal area] is rolled backward, lateralward and ventralward into the temporal pole region, and only traces of it are to be found in the midline region."

factory sense is "intimately bound up with all of the nervous apparatus of feeding, nutrition and reproduction." Because of its importance for "feeding, mating and avoiding" and because "odors may be discriminated in terms of quality and intensity, but they cannot be localized in space," the olfactory sense does not give rise to its own "simple elementary reflexes," but becomes an activator of "complex sensorimotor systems whose pattern of performance is determined primarily by other senses with sharper localization." Its contribution is the determination of the reaction—whether it shall be one of seeking or avoiding—and also the degree of its intensity. Originally, then, the subcortical central connections (fornix) from the olfactory region converged on the mammillary bodies whose "main motor outflow" is "into the apparatus of mass movement"; and there its effect was "a differential inhibition or reinforcement of subcortical adjustments already in process." When the cortex develops, even in the lowest mammals, there is clear localization there of somesthetic, optic, and auditory senses, each with its own thalamic projection. The neopallium is already an analyzer in simple situations; but "here, as in the subcortical field, olfactory impulses serve as activators of complex sensorimotor systems whose pattern of performance is largely determined by the non-olfactory members of the complex"; and, at the highest, that remains the chief function of the elaborate olfactory apparatus. Thereafter the function comes to be pervasive, for "the whole cortex seems to act as a differential activator or inhibitor"; and, thereafter, the function becomes no longer dependent on the olfactory sense, for "the 'olfactory' cortex may exert a profound influence upon all neopallial activity even in an animal which is normally totally anosmic" (e.g., the dolphin). That is, "in addition to participation in its own specific way in cortical associations," the olfactory cortex serves as a "non-specific activator for all cortical activities"; and, though the latter is "one of the major functions of the olfactory cortex," "all parts of the neopallium also exhibit it to some degree." But the olfactory cortex "may act in two ways: first upon the exteroceptive systems whose localized mechanisms are adapted to execute adjustments when external orientation is demanded, and, second, upon the internal apparatus of general bodily attitude, disposition and affective tone, the " 'intimate senses' of Starbuck."

This hypothesis as to the development of a non-specific function in part, at least, in the originally olfactory cortex is of great interest to us, first, because it may dispose of the question of the specific olfactory character of some of those regions of the cortex we have been discussing and, second, because, unless we suppose the improbable explanation that the non-specific function is carried on by autogenous excitation or inhibition, we must assume some other source to be the initiator when the olfactory sense itself is no longer activating or suppressing activity. Without disputing that the middle concentric circle of Zuckerkandl—the gyrus dentatus, etc., mentioned above—may have remained specifically and exclusively olfactory, there seems to be good reason to believe that part or all of the outer ring in Papez's scheme has lost that function and is now, perhaps, the representative of Herrick's non-specific function.[27] At least as to that part of this ring which we have admitted to our third avenue of interaction —the gyrus cinguli—and as to the present origin of the non-specific excitation or inhibition, we shall accept Le Gros Clark's view (*86*, 27) that "there can be little doubt . . . that the gyrus cinguli is a neopallial projection area where the activities of the mammillary body (and through it, perhaps, the hypothalamus as a whole) find cortical representation."[28] This hypothesis would suggest that part of the function of our third avenue which is performed by the mammillocingular projection; it would leave unexplained the function of the returning projection; and it ignores the, at present, seemingly insoluble problem of the function of the hippocampus and its mammillary projection, the fornix. However, having modified Papez's scheme by omitting the less necessary and more contestible parts, and laying aside for the moment the question of the cingulomamillary projection, we have now prepared ourselves to consider the several hypoth-

[27] Papez (*315*, 732) admits that the general view has been that the hippocampus, and even the entire limbic lobe, is olfactory. So, too, with the gyrus cinguli (*ibid.*, 734). Le Gros Clark (*86*, *25*) refuses to guess the function of the hippocampus, except that he is sure it is "a structure of fundamental importance in cerebral activity" and (*84*, 441) has other than olfactory functions. For what he thinks of the function of the gyrus cinguli, see text below.

To determine whether or not the hippocampi are "essential efferent centers for the olfactory conditioned reflex," W. F. Allen (*9*, 657) transected both fornices. He found that made no difference either in establishing or continuing those conditioned reflexes (*ibid.*, 666). That argues that at least the fornix is no longer an olfactory path.

Nevertheless it should be said that the older view is still generally adhered to. Fulton holds that "the primary olfactory cortex ["the entorhinal region"] is in fact a subcortical centre comparable to the geniculate bodies, etc." (*160*, 319) and that, in man and monkey, the hippocampus represents this region (*ibid.*, 343). The latter identification is disputed. Some think the original pyriform or entorhinal region is represented in man by the lateral and medial gyrus olfactorius. But the hippocampus is even then regarded as olfactory. For instance, Streeter (*387*, 90) states that the fornix connects the olfactory apparatus with the hypothalamus and, as a more primitive commissure than the corpus callosum, serves as a commissure for the archipallium (i.e., the hippocampal gyri).

[28] If it is true, as Bard (*24*, 188 and 191) suggests, that there has been a phylogenetic shift in the function of the hypothalamus, as a whole, from an "olfactory correlation center" to an "integrating mechanism" for other purposes, then the shift may have involved the entire apparatus, cortical and subcortical. And see note 7, above, for Kinnier Wilson's suggestion. It is also worthy of note that Le Gros Clark regards the gyrus cinguli as neopallial (as quoted in text). This and our distinction from the gyrus dentatus is also confirmed by Ariëns Kappers *et al.* (*231*, II, 1479), who hold that "the cingulate and the retro-splenial areas, which are the portions of the cortex bordering on the archicortex, are really transitional areas between the neocortex and the archicortex, with which they are in intimate relation through association fibers."

This conforms to Herrick, as noted above. If the neopallium was originally developed in the lateral portion of the archipallium by the entry of somesthetic projections from the thalamus, and if the present innermost ring (gyrus dentatus, etc.) still represents the archipallium, then it appears reasonable to suppose that the next innermost ring (the gyrus cinguli, at least) was and still is the cortical area lying between these two systems and therefore, originally and still, the area of their interaction on each other.

eses as to the particular functions to be assigned to each of these avenues of interaction between the highest level of the old brain and the new.

The Origin of the Hypothalamus. The course and termination of the sulcus limitans is the key to the question of what portions of the forebrain develop from the alar lamina, what portions develop from the basal lamina, and what portions, if any, develop from neither. Of the two views as to termination which were cited above, the first would include the whole of the hypothalamus as a development of the basal lamina; the second would include only that portion posterior to the anterior edge of the mammillary bodies. But, as to the course, both views agree in one respect. That is, either view would assume what Ariëns Kappers *et al.* (*231,* II, 1190) speak of as "this extension of the alar plate forward and ventralward." And either view would conclude from the supposed curving down of the sulcus limitans that the alar plate "plays the predominant part in the formation of the cerebrum" (Elliot Smith, *382,* 893). However, Streeter (*387,* 82) holds that, at the "extreme oral end of the neural tube it is no longer possible to clearly recognize an alar plate or basal plate," as it is everywhere else. True, he says that it is usually held that the sulcus limitans curves down along the posterior border of the optic evagination to the median line just in front of the ridge caused by the optic chiasm—that is, the first view above—so that at least the whole of the endbrain is "an elaboration of the alar plate."

Le Gros Clark (*86,* 37) discusses these various theories and concludes that "In view of this uncertainty, it is perhaps best to avoid attempts at homology." And this particularly on the ground that "Arey (1926) and others believe that the basal lamina does not extend farther forwards than the junction of the mesencephalon and diencephalon and that the whole of the prosencephalon is an alar laminar product, while Frazer's (1931) reconstructions seem to demonstrate that the sulcus limitans does not reach even into the mid-brain." In these even more extreme views the whole of the forebrain, not merely the endbrain, would be a development of the alar lamina.

Nevertheless, one cannot evade the obvious anomaly that purely motor structures do develop in the forebrain. On this ground alone I am skeptical that the course and termination of the sulcus limitans is correctly envisaged in either of these views. Rather, it seems probable that it continues, and that both laminae continue, into the developed endbrain.

We have suggested the hypothesis that the single structures in the hypothalamus develop from neither the alar nor the basal lamina, but, rather, as an intrusion from below. If we construe the single structures not to include the mammillary bodies, this hypothesis would rationalize the older morphological distinction between the pars optica hypothalami (endbrain) and the pars mamillaris hypothalami (interbrain). See, for instance, Villiger (*414,* 7 and 19); and Whitaker (*438,* 25). On the other hand, on purely functional grounds I am skeptical that even the mammillary bodies are developed from the basal laminae. While they ultimately become a paired structure they actually form in the two walls of a single evagination—the mammillary recess (Streeter, *387,* 79). Thus they, too, may result from an intrusion. In that case the distinction between the two parts of the hypothalamus would remain largely arbitrary.

The morphological distinction is also rationalized by the second view above; but that view assumes that all structures arising in both dorsal and ventral surfaces of the tube and anterior to the mammillary bodies are developments of the alar plate. The hypothesis suggested avoids this difficulty or explains the apparent anomaly. Now it is true that, from the mammillary bodies (inclusive) forward, that portion of the forebrain corresponding topologically to the basal lamina "no longer contains the nuclei of origin of efferent [motor] nerves" (Elliot Smith, *382*, 893). This is admitted even by those who continue to construe it as basal lamina. "In the diencephalon, on the contrary, primary motor centers are lacking and the basal plate [as they regard it] has only a coördinative significance and is relatively less developed" (Ariëns Kappers *et al.*, *231*, II, 1190). And, again, the "hypothalamus or basal plate portion [of this region] lacks the motor elements which form so large a part of the basal plate of the epichordal system" (Streeter, *387*, 77). It is partly this difficulty which, in the absence of any other adequate explanation, has led to the supposition that the whole formation is from the alar plate. But, if we read on, we note that the principal function of the hypothalamus "seems to be in connection with the special structures which are developed in the floor plate, the hypophysis and mammillary bodies" (Streeter, *ibid.*, 78). In connection with the latter point, it has been frequently suggested that the hypothalamus is a neuroglandular apparatus of local origin and perhaps connected with the ancient mouth. And these considerations suggest the possibility of intrusion into the floor plate and between the basal laminae.

2. AWAKENESS AND CONSCIOUSNESS

The first hypothesis in regard to these interactions and their mechanisms with which we shall deal concerns sleep and its opposite state awakeness,[29] their nature, cause, apparatus, and concomitants. Sleep is cerebral (Bard, *24*, 241). However, it "is not a function essentially of the cortex, but is equally a function of lower centres. . . . Presumably there is a process in sleep which is resident in the cortex and lower centres above a certain level, the spinal centres not being involved in the process, but being affected only indirectly" (Gillespie, *172*, 219). That is, in the spinal (transected) animal, the oral end sleeps and the aboral does not (Bard, *24*, 241). The process is therefore wholly supraspinal but both cortical and subcortical. Nevertheless, there is a difference in the rhythm between the cortical and the subcortical process, or between the normal process and the subcortical when deprived of the influence of the cortex, for decorticate animals sleep, like puppies, several times daily, not diurnally (Bard, *24*, 244)—i.e., they revert to the immature state characteristic of the period before the ontological maturation of the cortex.

There are many theories of the nature, and therefore cause, of this process. One of these seems to be in the way of becoming the accepted theory.[30] It is my impression, however, that most of these other theories are not

29 Since we have in English no term for the state of being awake, I may be pardoned for coining this form instead of using other words which connote something else—e.g., wakefulness, watchfulness, or vigilance.

30 We shall, therefore, limit our reference to the others to the supplementary statement on "Other Theories of Sleep," at the end of this subsection.

mutually exclusive with the one we are presenting. Rather they describe some individual feature of a highly complex process and only err in making that single feature dominant, or in giving it causal priority in the long series of events.

"A large part of the available literature supports the view that decreased activity of the hypothalamus results in somnolence and that increased activity of the hypothalamus leads to increased bodily activity" (Harrison, *181*, 650). Thus "the evidence points to the basal grey matter as being a waking-centre and not a sleep-centre."[31] "The control of the vital vegetative functions, which are incessantly more or less in action—in waking more so, in sleeping less—is centred in the basal grey matter." The constant activity of these centers "implies a focus of excitation at the base of the brain, and this excitation will wax and wane" in the diurnal rhythm which occurs even without sleep (Gillespie, *172*, 247). In this view the "basal grey matter maintains its characteristics as a centre for vital activity" (*ibid.*, 248). It is "a focus of activity, upon which not only the cortex but the whole organism depends for stimulation" (*ibid.*, 249). Perhaps the "normal state of the cortex would be sleeping"; but excitation there is facilitated by the constant inflow of the afferent impulses from the sensory system (thalamus) as well as, independently, by this excitation from the hypothalamus (Harrison, *181*, 652).[32] The latter is not indispensable but has most effect (*ibid.*, 651). Deprived of these, the "intrinsic cortical activity (memory, abstract thinking) which [in turn] acts to facilitate incoming impulses" is not enough alone "to maintain waking very long."[33] Thus "decreased activation of the cortex by the hypothalamus directly," aided by reduction in exogenous and direct endogenous stimuli, produces sleep

[31] This phrase agrees with R. Dubois' "centre for waking" (Gillespie, *172*, 249) and with Harrison (*181*, 652). Harrison (*181*, 653) says that normal sleep seems to be associated with decreased activity of the hypothalamus and that hypersomnia is likely to result from depression of its function. He quotes (*ibid.*, 647) Serota (2 *J. Neurophysiol.*, 1939, 42) to the effect that there is a greater fall in the temperature of the hypothalamus than of the rest of the brain during sleep, which "indicates a specific diminution of activity of these centers." "Sleep . . . is due to a damping-down of hypothalamic activity" and "the hypothalamus is necessary for the state of wakefulness" (Beattie, *30*, 100). "Mechanical injury or anodal polarization of the walls of the third ventricle" causes sleep (Bard, *24*, 245). Ranson (*332*, 264) says, "It is certain that the hypothalamus is concerned in some special way with the regulation of the alternating sleep-waking rhythm." He reports that lesions there in monkeys caused somnolence at once and drowsiness for weeks (*ibid.*, 260). They "would fall asleep while eating and with the mouth full of food" (*ibid.*, 263). It is also to be noted that hypnotic drugs work almost not at all in the cortex (at least of animals) or in the centers below the diencephalon—that is, their effect is almost wholly on the diencephalon. Now their effect is depressant. That fact along with the effect of lesions proves that "these parts cannot be excitors of sleep" (Gillespie, *172*, 247). Thus sleep is a negative, not a positive, neural process.

[32] Diminution both of interoceptive and of exteroceptive stimuli favors and provokes the onset of sleep (Gillespie, *172*, 248).

[33] "The engrams of previous stimulations . . . permit the psychic functions to go on without a continuous introduction of new sensory stimuli" (Hess, *192*, 521), but presumably not without a certain degree of excitation from the hypothalamus.

(*ibid.*, 653).[34] Either directly or through the effect on the cortex this withdrawal of continuous excitation results also in a loss of tone in the motor centers of the midbrain (Gillespie, *172*, 219).[35]

As to the precise location of this mechanism in the hypothalamus it is impossible as yet to speak with certainty. Fulton (*160*, 242) says, "Within the last few years there has been a growing tendency to associate" the mammillary bodies "with the phenomenon of physiological sleep."[36] These may prove to be themselves the source of the tonic excitation, or they may turn out to be only the centers from which the general excitation of the posterior and infundibular regions begins to be distributed to the cortex,[37] or they may—the most probable view—function in both ways. In any case this points to the corticopetal part of the third of our avenues of interaction (above) as the "complicated cortico-subcortical interconnection" (Gillespie, *172*, 228) through which the cortex is kept awake or permitted to sleep.[38] And, in any case, the known existence of a subsidiary circuit connecting the mammillary bodies downward with the centers of the midbrain, which we have mentioned above, suggests that this too may play some special part in the process.[39]

The first concomitant with which we have to associate this process is consciousness. If the degree of excitation in the interbrain—or the hypothalamus—is the chief determinant of the degree of excitation in the endbrain—or the cortex—as well as in the midbrain, whence it may overflow

[34] This complies with Bremer's theory (*43*, 85) that sleep is a "more or less deep decline in cortical tonus, a tonus which is maintained principally by the incessant afflux of corticopetal excitation" (trans.)—that it is a "functional deafferentation." He recognizes that there is also a loss of tone in the interbrain, but does not assign that as the chief cause of the loss of tone in the cortex.

[35] This we discuss below.

[36] He cites Ingram, Barris and Ranson (35 *Arch. Neurol. Psychiat.*, 1936, 1175). Papez (*315*, 738) cites Ranson to the same effect. Le Gros Clark (*86*, 24) thinks possibly the sleep-regulating mechanism is in the mammillary bodies. Beattie (*30*, 100) identifies it with the region from the mammillary bodies down to the IIIrd. nerve nucleus, or the gray matter surrounding the opening of the Sylvian aqueduct (i.e., the efferent hypothalamic pathways downward). So, too, Ranson (*332*, 263), who finds that the location of his experimental lesions on cats warrants the assumption that the resulting somnolence was due to blocking impulses from the hypothalamus downward. But this midbrain involvement may perhaps be due to the breaking of the secondary circuit we suggest in the text. Sleep is primarily a matter of the forebrain.

[37] Fulton (*160*, 258) cites Ectors and Bailey (unpublished) on evidence implicating the infundibulum and posterior hypothalamus. This is approximately the region indicated by Burggren and Moberg (cited by Gillespie, *172*, 249). The same region, including "the gray matter surrounding the sylvian aqueduct" (rostral midbrain) is von Economo's sleep center (cited by Bard, *24*, 244). The anterior portion of the midbrain is included with the hypothalamus in this function by Riddoch (*344*, 129).

[38] That, of our three avenues of interaction between the old brain and the cortex, this is the one which carries the tonic influence that produces the state of awakeness, so far as the cortex is concerned, is indicated by the fact that tumors involving the anterior thalamic nuclei (Papez, *315*, 740) and tumors involving the gyrus cinguli (*ibid.*, 736) also result in drowsiness. As to the latter he cites Ironside and Guttmacher (52 *Brain*, 1929, 442).

[39] See p. 1133.

over efferent paths to the rest of the nervous system, we must recognize that several states for which we have different names actually constitute a single state, varying through different degrees of excitation over a wide range from a maximum to a minimum. Thus "an epileptic convulsion is the acme of the neural excitation of which waking activity is the normal expression," while narcolepsy is the opposite extreme of which "normal sleep is the usual manifestation" (Gillespie, *172*, 241). In this view, the degree of awakeness is graduated from the deepest sleep up to the most wide-awake state. In fact awakeness reaches to the maximum of excitation; for the epileptic in convulsions is awake—in fact, too extremely awake. Along a part of this range, the epiphenomenon—consciousness—accompanies awakeness. But "loss of consciousness is not an essential mark of sleep" (Gillespie, *172*, 219), though, in the cortical field, one of the marks of the process of sleep is loss of consciousness (*loc. cit.*) in various degrees. Consciousness is also lost in the excessive excitation of epilepsy; and, at the other extreme, loss of consciousness varies in "all conceivable degrees from slightest confusion of thought to deepest coma" (Jackson, *216*, I, 187). In fact, it is this confusion or disorientation, as opposed to "awareness" or "alertness to surroundings," which Alford (*8*, 790) takes as his criterion of observed loss of consciousness. These states of confusion may occur both as excitation increases beyond a certain limit of awakeness and as it decreases toward sleep, as well, perhaps, as from extrinsic causes.[40] Thus consciousness of various degrees of acuity seems normally to accompany a certain median range of cortical excitation which, in turn, is governed chiefly by the degree of continuous excitation supplied to it from hypothalamic regions.

It is now generally agreed that the "anatomical substratum" of consciousness is the cortex only.[41] That it is rather narrowly localized even in the cortex seems to be coming to be agreed.[42] It is certain that it is not de-

[40] As Hughlings Jackson expressed it (*216*, I, 221): "The physiology of loss of consciousness is clear. It is loss of *use of* the highest of all nervous processes." And (*ibid.*, 186), just as spasm of the arm muscles causes loss of their use as much as palsy does, so excessive excitation (epilepsy) causes loss of consciousness as much as does absence of excitation (sleep, etc.). Again (*ibid.*, II, 89), "Although consciousness arises during slight sequent discharges of nervous arrangements of the highest centres, it ceases during the sudden, etc., discharges thereof."

[41] Head seems to have assumed thalamic consciousness. Nevertheless, he also assumed that consciousness is a late arrival, phylogenetically. Thus, if not solely cortical, it exists elsewhere only in the dorsomedial nucleus of the thalamus—its "essential organ." In discussion of Harrison (*181*, 654) Bailey expressed the view that a decorticate animal could be both "conscious and awake." Harrison himself did not agree to this as far as consciousness is concerned. Older psychologists, who localized consciousness according to its content so that, if one is conscious of a pain in his big toe, consciousness exists in his big toe, were confusing the content and the locus.

[42] There is "reason to believe that consciousness is dependent upon the integrity of a certain fairly well-defined region of the brain" (Dandy, *101*, 57). Bianchi (*35*, 303), representing the older view, held that consciousness does not exist in any special part of the cerebral mantle, but in the whole brain. However, new evidence seems to be inconsistent with this conclusion.

Since this latter view remains the prepossession of many, it may be worth while to

pendent on any of the regions of the cortex which we discussed in the previous section; for ablation or destruction of those regions does not even impair consciousness.[43] It is Dandy's conclusion (*101*) that, in right-handed human beings at least, the region seems to be that portion of the gyrus cinguli of the left hemisphere which lies above the corpus callosum. The anterior limit seems to be above a point 25 mm. posterior to the genu of the corpus callosum and the posterior limit seems to be above the posterior surface of the splenium.[44] But the locus of the epiphenomenon itself and the locus of the process which enables it seem to be two different matters. It would appear that the locus itself lies in the isocortical sector of our third avenue, but the process embraces all of that avenue. That is, the process which enables consciousness in this portion of the left gyrus cinguli in right-handed human beings is the same process which produces awakeness. It is the more or less continuous excitation arising in the hypothalamus which spreads up over the path described and perhaps also spreads down over the subsidiary (midbrain) circuit from the mammillary bodies. It is a phenomenon of various degrees of tonic excitation emanating from this source and involving thereafter the whole of the brain above the hindbrain, and perhaps that, too, in part. As a necessary consequence, if at its proximate origin in the mammillary bodies, or at any point in the avenue concerned (including perhaps the descending circuit), the process is interrupted, consciousness will be impaired or disappear even if its own specific locus remains uninjured. This interpretation would explain the loss or impairment of consciousness due to conditions affecting the base of the brain and particularly the hypothalamus, as well as the fact that these ef-

---

give an example of the purely functional argument against it. Alford says (*8*, 798): "In the encephalitic child emotion suffers but consciousness escapes, and in the speech zone lesion, associated thought is affected while consciousness and emotion remain. In normal sleep consciousness is abolished, but—as we commonly assume, for instance in the case of the traditional problem solved overnight—thinking proceeds. When activities of the brain are separable in this fashion, we begin to think of them as unitary functions," which "may work alongside of one another and perhaps still other functions."

[43] The reports cited in the previous section demonstrate that ablation of the entire prefrontal area does not affect consciousness. "Foerster states that in conscious human subjects [artificial] stimulation of the prefrontal area may produce unconsciousness" (Fulton, *160*, 435). But the effect is probably due to transcortical transmission. The entire right hemisphere can be removed with no effect on consciousness; so can the left frontal, occipital, and temporal lobes (Dandy, *101*, 57). Alford (*8*, 790) agrees that many brain lesions, at least, do not affect consciousness. He also states that it "does not reside in the cortical speech zone and is independent of the cortical functions of consecutive thought" (*ibid.*, 793). He speaks of "having by means of the various lesions mentioned eliminated most of the cortex as the possible seat of consciousness" (*ibid.*, 793). He cites Dandy, as above, and agrees with Dandy that the left hemisphere "has more to do with" consciousness (*ibid.*, 791–792).

[44] So Papez (*315*, 736) construes Dandy. As to what Dandy himself has said, see supplementary statement on "The Loci of Consciousness and Thinking," at the end of this subsection.

fects cease when the condition exists below a certain point in the lower brain-stem.[45]

While any such precise localization as this of the epiphenomenon of consciousness is, as yet, very far from being proved, I have concluded that it is, at present, wiser to proceed on this specific hypothesis than to leave the matter entirely open. The evidence for *some* precise localization impresses me as strong; the evidence for this particular locus is merely the best presently available. Any or all of the limbic lobe—or even the gyrus dentatus, in the broad sense—may be concerned; and, until the function of the fornix is adequately determined, that remains an imposing structure of apparent importance which is unexplained. However, there are advantages in being explicit, even on such tentative grounds. For that enables one to define, so far as we can now go, the tests which any hypothesis on this subject must meet; it brings down to earth many vague ideas; it is something definite to shoot at; and it serves as a graphic formulation. Finally, I suspect that the most likely major change in the hypothesis is the substitution of a neighboring anatomical entity for this one, or the addition of another to this one.

Several inferences may be derived from observation or experiment as to the relation between the neural process which underlies consciousness and those underlying other cortical activities. In the first place, while "sensation demands consciousness" (Head, *183*, 747), so that the term " 'conscious sensation' is tautological" (Jackson, *216*, II, 28), it is probable that sensation does not occur in any of the regions of the cortex called sensory.[46] Rather, these appear to constitute the highest integrating mechanisms for the exteroceptive senses, the patterns of impulses from which become conscious only when they also involve the locus of consciousness by way of transcortical paths.[47] While this exteroceptive sensory stimulation undoubtedly contributes to the maintenance of the degree of excitation requisite for the state of consciousness in its own locus, it is not essential therefor, because the "most rigorous prevention of external stimuli does

[45] This makes possible a reconciliation with other views as to locus. See supplementary statement on "The Loci of Consciousness and Thinking," at the end of this subsection.

[46] As Penfield and Boldrey put it (*324*, 434), "When cortical stimulation produces a sensation the mechanism is not at all obvious." For where is the impulse carried? It has usually been presumed that it is carried to that point itself. Moreover, the fact that it is usually so different in mode (generally tingling or numbness, *ibid.*, 433) from the result of peripheral stimulation, though localization may be accurate, has led them to conclude that "there is no localization of quality of sensation, either pre- or postcentral." To them this raises the question whether there is not a "higher level."

[47] Only in this way can the fact be explained that "deep sensation is still retained when the entire sensory [presumably somatic] area has been destroyed or removed" (Dandy, *101*, 49). There must be some other avenue for the afferent impulses constituting "deep sensation" (presumably visceral). We shall consider below what that probably is. Furthermore, if these other afferent impulses continue to become sensation so long as the region of consciousness is intact, and do not when it is not, it is reasonable to presume that this is also the locus at which all other corticopetal afferent impulses are appreciated.

not lead to loss of consciousness such as we meet with in sleep" (Hess, *192*, 521). It follows that, if consciousness requires a minimal state of excitation in its locus, but continues to exist when the exteroceptive sensory region is in complete quiescence, the latter cannot be the locus of consciousness and, therefore, cannot be the locus of sensation. Conversely, this makes it probable that what goes on in the exteroceptive sensory regions of the cortex does not always involve the locus of consciousness, or may involve it with varying degrees of intensity (acuity).[48]

The second inference is that consciousness of motor actions does not take place in the regions of the cortex which are assigned a motor function. And this for several reasons. In the first place, many motor activities may take place in the absence of consciousness. Perhaps most of these are wholly subcortical; but not all; somnambulism, for instance, would seem impossible in a human being without activity of the motor cortex.[49] In the second place, most of the details of skilled, complex actions are unconscious even if the synergy as a whole is conscious. Thus associated movements, reciprocal inhibition, etc., are unconscious by-products of the main action. At least this is true once the synergy has been organized (learned or become habituated). Until then the details themselves may involve the locus of consciousness. In the third place, there is reason to believe that many proprioceptive impulses which reach the motor cortex do not involve the locus of consciousness.[50] In the fourth place, some of the so-called sensations which are reported by conscious human patients upon stimulation of motor points in the cortex are definitely neither sensory (afferent to the cortex) nor do they consist of the "sense of movement" (kinesthetic). Thus "desire-to-move . . . has been a definitely reported sensation," and was definitely contrasted to the "sense of movement" under way. So too there is "a feeling of inability to carry out some movement . . . as though the patient were made aware of stimulation of an inhibitory mechanism" (Penfield and Boldrey, *324*, 433). These "motor intuitions," as they have been called (Bianchi, *35*, and many others), appear to be the effects in the locus of consciousness of (subliminal) excitations in the motor cortex which have involved the former over transcortical paths. On these grounds we conclude that what goes on in the motor areas may or may not involve the locus of consciousness and that, even in the cortical field, "all gradations exist between wholly unconscious nervous actions and wholly conscious ones" (Jackson, *216*, I, 187, quoting Herbert Spencer).

Our third inference is that consciousness is "independent of the cortical

[48] On the other hand we have noted Walker's supposition as to cortical control of the thalamic mechanism for sensory attention. On that basis, it may be that the selectivity is exercised at this subcortical level and that what reaches the sensory cortex at all also always reaches the locus of consciousness.

[49] As we have noted above, decorticate primates cannot walk. This and the following points will be discussed further in Section H.

[50] Since the proprioceptive impulses arising from movement necessarily reach the cortex only when movement is going on, they would also necessarily pass out in large part in the same instant in which they came in.

function of consecutive thought" (Alford, *8*, 793). Laying aside for the moment the question of what "consecutive thought" may be, we may consider Dandy's conclusion as to its localization. He says (*101*) that the left parietal lobe outside the sensory areas of the paracentral region "is by far the most important part of the brain" (for the right-handed). It contains "all of the centers for sensory speech" (*ibid.*, 50), the disturbances of which constitute auditory aphasia and anomia (*ibid.*, 54). "From this [his] experiment it is obvious that the center for purposeful movements (this disturbance being apraxia) is located in the postrolandic area of the parietal lobe" (*ibid.*, 56–57) and also in the left hemisphere for the right-handed. Finally, "most, perhaps all, of the mental functions are located in the left cerebral hemisphere," for the right-handed (*ibid.*, 48), and in this same general region. Although "this statement is contrary to the teachings of physiologists and neurologists who have long taught that the left frontal lobe is the center of intellectual functions" (*ibid.*, 48), his observations exclude this latter as well as other regions.[51] But he says, "It is my impression from a series of brain tumors that the region just peripheral to the corpus striatum [in the "depths of the parietal lobe" (*ibid.*, 55) and the left one for the right-handed] and posterior to the mesial half of the rolandic area is more concerned with the mind than any other part of the brain" (*ibid.*, 55–56). "This appears to be the only part of the brain where mental changes [from damage] are the rule rather than the exception" (*ibid.*, 55). Therefore "it seems quite probable that mental functions are in large part referred to this region" (*ibid.*, 50).[52] If so, we may infer, as in the other cases, that what goes on in this region may or may not involve the locus of consciousness.

These results permit us an hypothesis of limited scope and of rather vague content as to the nature of mental functions, or "consecutive thought"—an hypothesis which has been outlined in the text and has been discussed in Section A, note 46 of this appendix. In the first place, we may adopt Lashley's conclusion that certain experiments "point to some continued intraneural process as the basis of thinking" (*260*, 11)—that is, "long-continued intraneural sequences of activity" (*ibid.*, 10). From this we would infer that all "patterns" of impulses reaching the cortex from

[51] The ablation of all the left frontal lobe except the prerolandic and Broca's speech areas (i.e., approximately ablation of the left prefrontal area) is "without any after-effect" (*101*, 48). This conforms to our previously cited reports of absence of effect from unilateral ablation of the prefrontal area. He says, "There is also reason to believe (from a single patient in whom both frontal lobes have been completely removed excepting the prerolandic and Broca's area) that no appreciable mental effects follow the extirpation of both frontal lobes" (*ibid.*, 48). This does not conform to Brickner's case; but, after all, the defects there were very subtle and certainly did not constitute the loss of all intellectual functions. Finally, "Because of negative mental results from many excisions of the right temporal lobe, both frontal and both occipital lobes, the evidence denies that any of these regions play an important part in the working of the mind" (*ibid.*, 56).

[52] For a further discussion, see supplementary statement on "The Loci of Consciousness and Thinking," at the end of this subsection.

elsewhere which immediately pass out over motor outlets do not constitute thinking and therefore do not reach, or no longer reach, the "intellectual" region. And, for the same reason, we may infer that they do not reach consciousness. In terms of our knowledge of the rest of the nervous system it would be in order to assume that incoming impulses which do not pass out at once do not do so for one of two, or possibly three, reasons: either (1) because they are of insufficient intensity, that is, subthreshold, on the motor side; [53] or (2) because they lead to an unresolved conflict of a character analogous to that between antagonistic reflexes but, resulting in mutual, rather than in one-sided, reciprocal inhibition of the motor outlets; [54] or (3) because the incoming excitation arrives at an intensity too high to be completely and immediately drawn off.[55] If prevented from outlet for the first reason, it is to be presumed that the excitation might be so slight as to remain local in other regions of the cortex—the sensorimotor or even the thinking regions—and not to invade consciousness, or, if it did, that it would be "faint" there. The second reason probably argues that, until one of the antagonistic forms of excitation overcame the other, it would be long-circuited to include the "thinking" region and also that both would then have sufficient intensity to reach consciousness. Perhaps, while in the balance, the two forms could only reach the locus of consciousness alternatively. But there is reason to believe that, at one moment, only the most intense form of excitation can involve the locus of consciousness, while, to be in prolonged conflict, both must have involved the thinking region. This picture is complicated by the conception that "the engrams of previous stimulations also permit the psychic functions to go on without a continuous introduction of new sensory stimuli" (Hess, *192*, 521). And these past patterns, when locally or generally re-excited, may also enter consciousness as "faint" (subliminal) states, or may participate in conflicts, along with the new material referred to above, and thus involve the thinking region and thence reach consciousness.[56] Thus we suppose that what is going on in the cortex, aside from instantaneous transmission in and out, includes both current and past sensory reports together with the sensorimotor integrations of various kinds which have been, or are being, made from them; that this material is long-circuited within the cortex so as to engage the

[53] And underlying this assumption would be another, that the sensory (incoming) threshold is, or can be made, lower than the motor (outgoing). As to this see note 54, below. It would also be assumed that "engrams" of previously established sensorimotor patterns, when re-excited, are, or can be, lower than the motor threshold.

[54] If we conceive inhibition to be, or to involve, the raising of the motor threshold, then these first two reasons are one and the same, except that the first is due to the "normal" threshold and the second to one that has been raised as a by-product of some special pattern of excitation.

[55] Continuing conscious pain may be of this third order. According to Hughlings Jackson's conception, excitation spreads when it cannot be immediately drawn off.

[56] In fact, in Bianchi's view (*35*, 310), it is "conflict between actual images and those furnished by the memory of past experiences," particularly, which permits consciousness.

thinking region; and that the most intense of these reports at each moment, provided its intensity exceeds some minimum, may, while it remains either subliminal or inhibited as to a motor outlet, involve the locus of consciousness. On the other hand, we suppose that those excitations which are instantaneously transmitted in and out are, so to speak, cortically "short-circuited" through regions other than the thinking region and the locus of consciousness and therefore do not involve either.[57]

We have inferred that consciousness is a concomitant of a limited range of intensity of excitation, probably in the gyrus cinguli and usually of the left hemisphere, and that, to engage consciousness, continuing forms of excitation elsewhere in the cortex must involve this region. Thus the entry into consciousness seems to necessitate transcortical transmission of these excitations in such a way as to involve the locus of consciousness. But, in discussing the phenomenon of awakeness, we concluded that awakeness involves the whole cortex, potentially at least, and that the cortical focus from which the requisite excitation is spread transcortically is this locus of consciousness itself. Thus we find ourselves to have supposed two streams of excitation flowing in opposite directions, one from the gyrus cinguli over the rest of the cortex, as the chief means of keeping it awake, and the other from the rest of the cortex to the gyrus cinguli, constituting the physiological basis of the content, or of part of the content, of consciousness. Considering the vast multiplicity and intricacy of intracortical connections, there is nothing impossible or inconsistent about the supposed dual function of this meeting point of the two streams.[58] Nevertheless, it does suggest consideration of the question whether it has some possible special significance. We shall examine that question more closely in the two following subsections.

However, before we undertake that, it will be well to explore further into the nature and ultimate source of the excitation that rises through our circuit, causes awakeness, and permits consciousness. Hitherto we have considered only one aspect of it—that of a sort of tonic excitation facilitating the activity of the cortex. In that aspect, it is of an order entirely different from the differentiated and meaningful impulses that play upon the locus of consciousness from the cortex.

Other Theories of Sleep. One group of theories has made the causation of sleep a positive neural process of some kind. It was Pavlov's conclusion "that sleep and internal inhibition are fundamentally one and the same process" (*320*, 263). "Internal inhibition during the alert state is nothing but a scattered sleep, sleep of separate groups of cellular structures; and sleep itself is nothing but internal inhibition which is widely irradiated, extending over the whole mass of the hemispheres and involving the lower centres of the brain as well" (*ibid.*, 253). Under this theory of the "irradiation of inhibition" (Gillespie,

[57] See also the supplementary statement on "The Loci of Consciousness and Thinking," at the end of this subsection.

[58] That is, it does not suppose a single neuron to be transmitting impulses in both directions at the same time.

172, 228) "sleep would simply be a special case of inhibition . . . diffusely irradiated" (*ibid.*, 242). It is conceived as "a more or less universally reduced activity," "governed by a positive brain-process," itself a "reaction to stimuli, external and internal" (*ibid.*, 229). Fatigue is construed as "one of the numerous kinds of stimuli that may set going an inhibitory process" (*ibid.*, 230). The "propagation of the inhibitory process" reaches "even to the lowest levels of the central nervous system" and includes tonelessness of muscles and inhibition of sensory nerve processes or "sensory blockade" (*ibid.*, 240). Gillespie suggests that the focus for this irradiating inhibition may be supposed to start anywhere. Since the focus is frequently held to be in the cortex, but also frequently in the subthalamic region, this theory may be in line with von Economo's thesis, according to which the latter presides over "body-sleep, while the cortex presides over brain-sleep" (*ibid.*, 228). While there can be little question that Pavlov proved the identity of sleep and what he called internal inhibition, the question remains, however, whether internal inhibition is the positive process he supposed.

Hess thought sleep was a temporary dominance of the parasympathetic system (*192*), the effect of which is a lessening of functional preparedness (*ibid.*, 315, 317, and 526), accomplished by shutting out stimuli at the point of reception (*ibid.*, 514–516), by a raising of the central threshold (*ibid.*, 526), and by inhibition over the effector system as far as the end-organs (*ibid.*, 518). But it is a positive ("neurodynamic") not a negative neural process. "In the state of sleep the cortical function is dominated by a regulative act of vegetative quality" (*ibid.*, 524). This theory was based in part on the sleep-like effects of intraventricular injections of ergotamine, which he construed as excitatory to the parasympathetic and inhibitory to the sympathetic system (*192*, 646–653 and 99, 1260–1261). While it is recognized that the parasympathetic is a system that "works while you sleep" and will therefore continue in action and become unopposed when the other systems are quiescent (see Cannon, in general, and Fulton, *160*, 225), "from pharmacological information available at present, it does not appear that the claim that sleep is due to increased parasympathetic activity is justified" (Harrison, *181*, 649).

The theory more commonly imputed to Hess, which does not seem consistent with the foregoing, resulted from his experiments in procuring sleep by electrical stimulation of an area in the diencephalon (hypothalamic region; *193*, 1260–1261). Fulton (*160*, 225) finds this indicative of "the active participation of this region in the induction of sleep." Bremer (*43*, 69) thinks the experiment "adds a notion of capital importance, if it is confirmed" (trans.). But Harrison points out (*181*, 644) that Hess is the only one who has succeeded in inducing sleep by stimulation of the hypothalamus or the brain-stem, and thinks the effect was probably due to depression, not stimulation (*ibid.*, 647). On the whole, Harrison concludes (*ibid.*, 653) that sleep does not seem to be the active inhibition of one part of the brain by another part.

Another group of theories have regarded sleep as caused by a negative neural process. When he wrote, Hess (*192*, 312) thought that the "present attitude" toward sleep was that it is "a positive adjustment" involving "the rejection of stimuli [and] the refusal to carry out sensorimotor functions" as a "protection against exhaustion." He cites E. Trömner (*Das Problem des Schlafes*, Wiesbaden, 1912) as assigning the sleep center to the thalamus and sleep as a shutting down there. Kleitman's theory (66 *Am. J. Physiol.*, 1923, 67) is based on similar grounds, a decrease of afferent impulses to higher centers raising the threshold there with the consequence that the now subthreshold impulses are not critically analyzed and no motor activity results. But, while, in sleep, there certainly is a decrease in exteroceptive impulses, and relaxation reduces proprioceptive impulses (Bard, *24*, 242), this reduction of excitation is not only in the sensory system nor wholly due to the thalamus (Hess, *192*, 518). "Lack of sensory stimulation is one of the conditions that favours sleep"—but not its cause (Gillespie, *172*, 221). "Sensory relaxation" is one of the conditions for sleep, but not the state itself (Hess, *192*, 521). Others have supposed that sleep is caused by, or is, a suspension of cortical function. But, as Hess points out (*192*, 519), decortication or "excortication" leads to enhanced reflexes, while "in sleep there is a diminution of reflex excitability" (*ibid.*, 516). Neither is the theory of cortical exhaustion tenable, because cortical activity reappears at once on sudden waking (*ibid.*, 519). It would appear, then, that if sleep is, or is due to, a negative neural process, that process does not originate in, nor is it confined to, the cortex or the thalamus.

Another group of theories have supposed sleep to be or to be caused by vascular or chemical changes. As to the first, Kleitman, following up the idea (84 *Am. J. Physiol.*, 1928, 386) "that cerebral anemia is neither the cause nor the result of sleep could be determined by direct inspection of the brain," finds no changes in the caliber of blood vessels, either of the dura or of the cortex, during sleep. But that led him back to his theory given above. Bard, too, thinks it is probably not cerebral anemia (*24*, 242), and finds no evidence to prove that it is caused by lactic acid or other fatigue substances, such as Piéron's hypnotoxin (*ibid.*, 243). Hess argues that it cannot be due to hormonal or toxic causes, because "individual functions may escape the general inhibition of sleep" (*192*, 519); and that it cannot be acidity (carbonic acid), because the waking stimulus acts quicker than the pH could change (*ibid.*, 522). On the other hand, Dott (*120*, 167), who identifies the mechanism to be the hypothalamus, in accordance with the thesis we present in the text, says, "from analogy with other hypothalamic mechanisms, it seems not unreasonable to suggest that it may receive its normal afferent stimulus from products of fatigue in the circulating blood." One such theory, allied with Demole's, fits with the one we present and may afford an underlying cause, and explanation of the proximate cause we suggest. This is outlined by Gillespie (*172*, 243–244), who suggests that the observed "fall in [ionic] calcium in the peripheral blood is compensated by its accumulation at the base of the brain." There, this "slight excess of calcium," by lessening "membrane-permeability," initiates in normal sleep an inhibited condition of the nerve-cells which "irradiates over the rest of the central nervous system"—or, we may suggest, causes a withdrawal of the normal facilitation from these centers.

The Loci of Consciousness and Thinking. We have discussed Papez's construction of Dandy's statements. Dandy himself said (*101*, 58) that there is no disturbance of consciousness from the ligation of the right anterior cerebral artery. "But if the *left anterior cerebral artery* is injured by any chance, the patient can never again regain consciousness" (*ibid.*, 57). There is no coma; the patient is awake (at least subcortically); but there is no voluntary movement and reflex movement only occurs from strong stimulation (i.e., facilitation is lost).

"The center for consciousness, therefore, must be in the left cerebral hemisphere, and in the area supplied by that part of the anterior cerebral artery that is posterior to this point of injury of the vessel [25 mm. posterior to the anterior tip of the corpus callosum], i.e., along the mesial aspect of the left hemisphere and near the corpus callosum." The left occipital and parietal lobes are not concerned. "The posterior limit of the area for consciousness therefore cannot possibly extend posterior to the splenium of the corpus callosum" (*ibid.*, 57–58). This approximately defines the left gyrus cinguli.

Though Alford, like Penfield thinks consciousness is "served by an area somewhere in the left base," he states that, "when the injury is far enough back to involve sensation, consciousness begins to be endangered." This region of the parietal lobe adjoins the locus defined above. In spite of the fact that it appears to have been Dandy who first called attention to this presently most plausible locus of consciousness, he should perhaps no longer be cited to that effect. True, his original suggestion received extensive support and is in line with indications from other sources. But he himself apparently recanted. I have examined with care his posthumously published article ("The Location of the Conscious Center in the Brain—The Corpus Striatum," 79 *J. H. Hosp. Bull.*, 35). It is evident to me that he misconstrued his new evidence. As a result, he attributed the locus to a region which seems to be quite out of the question on all other counts. Nor does this new evidence in any respect preclude the original inference. For these reasons I have decided to let the original citations stand, with this qualification.

Our hypothesis that the locus of consciousness and the source of the excitation, which chiefly maintains the state of consciousness, are separate would permit Alford's supposition that "consciouness is served by an area somewhere in the left base" (of the cerebrum) near the internal capsule (*8*, 794), provided "served" were construed to mean "energized." It would explain the observations of Ectors and Bailey and their state of "arrested consciousness" as a result of lesions in the infundibulum affecting the posterior hypothalamus, as well as Bailey's observation that "no part of the brain is so notoriously prone to cause loss of consciousness, if handled, than the posterior hypothalamus and central grey of the aqueduct of Sylvius" (both cited by Fulton, *160*, 258–259). It might even be construed to conform to Penfield's view (*323*, 68) that the "indispensable substratum of consciousness lies outside of the cerebral cortex, probably in the diencephalon," and that perhaps it "finds its topographical localization near to the representation of autonomic function in the hypothalamus and close to the third ventricle" (*ibid.*, 61). Finally, both in locus and as a circuit, it complies with Dandy's observations. "Increasing pressure on the brain stem will produce drowsiness and eventually unconsciousness" (Dandy, *101*, 58). But the effect ceases at some point in the brain just below the midbrain; for, if the lesion is at the point where the spinal cord issues from the cranial cavity, even "producing complete paralysis of the spinal cord does not produce loss of consciousness" (*loc. cit.*). "Therefore, the tracts responsible for consciousness must terminate in the region of the medulla, pons, or midbrain" (probably the second). It is "evident that nervous pathways must connect these two extremes" (the locus of consciousness and this lowest limit of contribution to its excitation), and "the interruption of these fibers at any point will be just as effective in producing loss of consciousness" as injury to the locus of consciousness itself (*loc. cit.*).

As we have previously noted, Hughlings' Jackson supposed that "the highest (chiefly) sensory centres—parts behind Ferrier's sensory region—and also the highest (chiefly) motor centres—parts in front of the so-called motor region—make up the physical basis of consciousness" (*216*, II, 54). Later (1884) he had misgivings as to whether the former included the occipital lobes (*216*, II, 79). Bianchi's "higher consciousness" was in the frontal lobes (*35*, 312).

Associated with this question of the locus of consciousness is that of the locus of the thinking process. We have cited Dandy's statements as to the probable locus of mental functions. Although Dandy does not define what he includes in mental functions, it is worth recalling here that Hughlings Jackson supposed that the main elements of that part of mind commonly distinguished as intellect from the other part called emotion or feeling are "visual and tactual ideas and words" (*216*, II, 439). The last are aural and vocal ideas (*ibid.*). "Much the greater part of mentation is carried on in visual ideas" (*loc. cit.*) which, because they are both sensory and motor, he came to call "retino-ocular" sensorimotor processes. Most of the rest of mentation, he believed, consists of words—that is, of aural and vocal ideas, or "audito-articulatory" sensorimotor processes. We would suppose that in reading and writing the two must be combined. Tactual ideas he held to constitute the smallest element.

Associated with this was "the hypothesis that large movements (those especially engaged in locomotion) are but little represented in the highest levels" (*216*, II, 441). Rather, these levels represent "very many movements of parts of the body which have small muscles" and only a few with large (*ibid.*, II, 439). Therefore his highest levels are conceived to be, "not more voluminous" but more "intricate" than his middle level (*ibid.*, II, 440). The parts of the body with small muscles are the eyes, the tongue, lips and palate, and the hands—in other words the motor executors of visual, of verbal, and of tactual ideas (*ibid.*, II, 439).

It will be recalled that he supposed the prefrontal area to be the motor part of his highest level—that is, the region of the motor element of the foregoing sensorimotor processes. Later investigation has disclosed that even these motor functions are not localized in the prefrontal area. But it is interesting to note that they are adjacent to it. Area 8, called the "frontal [motor] eye field" (Fulton, *160*, 328) and areas 44 and 45, called "Broca's area," or the "motor speech centre"—which is "no doubt an elaboration of the premotor area" (Fulton, *160*, 466)—adjoin the prefrontal area, lie between it and the premotor area, or are the most rostral parts of the premotor area, if they should be included in it. The much less important motor tactile (hand) area is elsewhere. It is the most elaborate part of the motor area proper (4b). Thus Jackson's thesis as to the nature of the motor parts of this highest level may still be valid, though its locus is evidently slightly different. Instead of the prefrontal area, it would be a number of areas between that and the premotor. The tactile (motor) area would be an exception. And the function of the prefrontal area, whatever that is, would have been left out of his accounting.

Now the location of the areas corresponding to the sensory side of these two chief processes of "mentation" are worthy of note in this connection. The first is the "primary visual cortex"—the area striata (17) which "receives the optic radiation from the external geniculate body" (Fulton, *160*, 331) and which lies at the extreme pole of the occipital lobe. Anterior to and surrounding it are two concentric areas (18 and 19) which are believed to be concerned "with visual association" (recognition). The second is the "primary acoustic cortex" (areas 41 and 42 of Brodmann) which receives the radiation from the medial geniculate and which lies in the temporal lobe along the middle part of the Sylvian fissure (Fulton, *160*, 366)—"the temporal transverse convolutions of Heschl" (*ibid.*, 330). Posterior to this in the temporal lobe (the posterior part of the gyrus temporalis superior) and in the parietal lobe (the adjoining part of the gyrus supramarginalis) is what has been called "Wernicke's centre" which is associated with "sensory aphasia" and may therefore represent auditory association (i.e., recognition). Fulton identifies the region variously as the "inferior part of the left posterior parietal lobule" or the "left angular gyrus," and includes "the base of the first and second temporal convolutions" (left lobe; *160*, 395–396). These are approximately the same areas as given in the text. Note that only the left lobes are concerned for the right-handed. That is also true of the "motor speech area."

The locus that Dandy assigns to intellectual functions, to which no function has as yet been assigned by others (to my knowledge), is situated strategically with reference to the probable lines of communication between the visual association areas and the frontal (motor) eye fields, on the one hand, and between the auditory association areas and the motor speech center, on the other. Among the so-called interlobar bundles one might guess that the fasciculus longitudinalis superior connects the second pair and perhaps also relates the two pairs (reading and writing). So far as I know, no interlobar bundle has been found which connects the first pair with each other. Nevertheless, Foerster obtained eye movements from area 19. These may have been caused by transcortical effects reaching area 8. The fact that area 19 is concerned in "visual associations involving the other sensory and motor areas of the cortex" (Fulton, *160*, 362) would suggest that. At any rate, there seems to be some basis for the suggestion that Dandy's locus is that of Hughlings Jackson's two mental types of sensorimotor process—the retino-ocular and the audito-articulatory.

Except for our different localizations and our separation of consciousness from thinking, our general hypothesis conforms approximately to that of Hughlings Jackson, as presented above and in the supplementary statement—"The Thinking Process" at the end of Section A, above. Without the specific notion of threshold, he said (*216*, II, 30), "when there is discharge of part of a higher centre giving rise to currents not strong enough to overcome the resistance of the next lower centre, the currents spread more widely in ["are boxed up in"] the higher centre." Moreover, "our highest sensory and highest motor centres [supposedly occipital and prefrontal] . . . can energise, to a large degree, independently of the lower centres" (*ibid.*, I, 375). Thus the former "can energise uninterfered with by the environment"; and the latter, "thanks to the resistance of the lower motor centres, can act without producing peripheral reactions upon the environment" (*loc. cit.*). In this way he excludes the strictly sensorimotor areas from these processes. When both afferent and efferent impulses are cut off, we have "faint states of (object) consciousness," such as dreams, reverie, reflection, etc. (*loc. cit.*). But he envisaged conflict too; for "the nervous arrangements of the highest centres, or some elements of them, are 'left to fight it out among themselves' " (*ibid.*, I, 376). To Jackson, sleep with dream is a "loss of function" of the "highest 'layer' " of the highest level, leading to "increased activities of the uncontrolled lower layers." But the fact that the dream can be remembered is due to the resistance of the middle motor level resulting in "wide irradiation of these 'boxed up' currents." If it leads to somnambulism (i.e., the motor resistance is overcome), there is no dream and therefore no remembrance (*ibid.*, II, 442).

So, too, Bianchi supposed "conflict between actual images and those furnished by the memory of past experiences" (*35*, 310). In "lower animals conduct occurs without internal conflict" and hence without consciousness (*ibid.*, 309), while, in man, "consciousness culminates in deliberation" (*loc. cit.*). Thus the content of consciousness, to him, is "arrested or inhibited motor intuitions," and the degree of consciousness corresponds to the degree of inhibition which, in turn, depends on the extent of the cortical area excited (*ibid.*, 326–327).

The term "involve," which we have used and which might be substituted by "spread to," seems to suit this thesis of Bianchi. He says (*35*, 326), "Any conscious phenomenon presupposes the propagation of an external or internal stimulus to a large number of nerve-cells in the mantle." It cannot arise if only a small number are involved (i.e., if merely local).

3. EMOTION AND DRIVES

Consideration of the nature of this stream of excitation causing awakeness and permitting consciousness brings us to the second concomitant with which we have to associate the process. This is emotion, strictly speaking—that is, the emotional experience which occurs in consciousness. With some modification of detail from its original presentation, and with some expansion by reason of more recent investigations, we are now prepared to complete the outline of Cannon's and Bard's (and also, in certain respects, Sherrington's) theory of the emotions, a part of which was developed in Sections D and E. According to this theory and upon the basis of such evidence as we summarized in Section D, the emotional state itself is held to be a condition of more or less general, and therefore less or more specific, excitation, and probably also of depression (apparently not inhibition), in the hypothalamic region (p. 1076).[59] Excitement may be construed to reflect the intensity of the excited emotional states which probably have their origin exclusively in the posterior hypothalamus (p. 1077). In low or moderate excitement (intensity) the patterns of the emotional states differ; in excessive excitement they tend to become the same, probably because all centers in the region tend to become engaged. On the other hand, depressed emotional states seem to represent depression of function (loss of excitability) also in the posterior hypothalamus, being also selective except in great depression. In what way and to what extent the anterior hypothalamus is involved in the unexcited emotional states cannot be stated. But it seems probable that the anterior region is related at least to the inactivating (unexcited) emotional states, if not to those of depression.[60]

[59] Ranson (*332*, 260) observed "emotional excitement" and "visceral and somatic activity" from the stimulation of the hypothalamus; and "emotional stolidity and even somnolence" from damage to it (*ibid.*, 270).

As originally put forward by Cannon, the central representation of emotion is "the stormy processes of the thalamus" (*68*, 265). Actually it now appears that the process occurs in the hypothalamus.

[60] Whereas Fulton (*160*, 255) concludes that "lethargy, indifference, depression" tend to accompany lesions of the posterior region, he thinks that "lesions of the anterior hypothalamus tend to produce excited states." If so, it would be natural to assume that the anterior region normally exerts an inhibitory influence on the posterior region and that the latter is "released" when the former is injured. But the anterior region includes paths from the cortex, and it may be these which normally inhibit and which are destroyed by lesions.

The individual centers in this somewhat complex subcortical system are presumed to be individually excitable by "afferent material capable of influencing the regulative functions of the hypothalamus"; and this material consists of "vague and undefined impressions from many bodily sources" (Papez, *315*, 729), rather than completely organized sensation such as that which reaches only the cortex. Evidently some of these centers are also reached by humoral excitors via the blood. It is this afferent material from both systems of integration which apparently determines the character and the intensity of the emotional state both in the direction of excitement and in that of depression. In turn, the "diencephalon discharges downward the motor influences which produce the emotional behavior" (Bard, *19*, 305). Strictly speaking, this behavior includes only the exterofective (somatic) effects. But, as Bard has repeatedly pointed out, emotional expression also includes interofective manifestations.[61] These consist of many different patterns of autonomic activity or paralysis which we find tend toward a uniform pattern of exaggeration in great excitement and to a "generalized slowing down of all body functions" in great depression.[62] Thus we find that emotional states differ in character (or pattern) and also in intensity; and the latter differences can only be conceived in terms of plus or minus variation from a normal level.

As Cannon presented his now generally accepted theory, "the neural mechanisms for the primitive emotions [the states and the manifestations] operate in a region outside the range of . . . consciousness" (*68*, 265). These "individual patterns of emotional reaction, organized in the thalamus [now believed to be organized in the hypothalamus] . . . are supposed to discharge not only to the periphery but also to the cortex and there to add 'feeling' [affective tone] to sensation" (*65*, 285).[63] "These powerful impulses originating in a region of the brain not associated with cognitive consciousness . . . explain the sense of being seized, possessed, of being controlled by an outside force and made to act without weighing of the consequences" (*61*, 123–124). Or, as Ranson puts it: "It is probable that the active hypothalamus not only discharges downward through the brain stem, spinal cord and peripheral nervous system into the body but also upward into the thalamus and cerebral cortex. This upward discharge may well be associated with emotion as a conscious experience. There are known paths between the hypothalamus and the thalamus and cerebral cortex which could account for such an interaction" (in *Ergebnisse der Physiologie*, p. 41, quoted by Harrison, *181*, 651). In this view what reaches

[61] That is, the "manifestations" of emotions are "movements" in Hughlings Jackson's inclusive sense (*216*, II, 266); they include the "bodily effects *during* emotions" (*ibid.*, II, 106)—what Cannon calls "bodily changes."

[62] This is Fulton's (*160*, 259) expression for the effect of *destruction* of the posterior nucleus.

[63] That is, for the James-Lange theory, there "is substituted the idea that they [emotional experiences] are produced by unusual [?] and powerful influences emerging from the region of the [hypo-] thalamus and affecting various systems of cortical neurones" (Cannon, *68*, 267).

the new brain over this channel is not the afferent material which has excited the afferent side of the old brain. Rather, what spreads to the new brain is only the excitation produced by that afferent material in the highest level—the effector elements—of the old brain. Thus the conscious experience is deemed to be the effect in one highest level (the cortex) of the efferent patterns independently produced in the other highest level (that of the old brain).[64] And this is the radical connotation that the recent transposition of the source of emotions from the thalamus (afferent) to the hypothalamus (efferent) has brought about. As Alpers puts it (*12*, 746), the "stimulation of the thalamus fails to produce emotional reactions" and "the thalamus is not concerned in the production of sham rage." Emotional reactions can be produced only in the hypothalamus. This reappraisal fits well into Crile's theory (*96*) that the emotional states and their results in consciousness are phenomena of "motor [effector] stimulation" rather than sensory. It also makes possible an explanation of some of the remarkable dislocations of the normal relation between stimulus and response which Pavlov produced in his conditioning experiments and which we shall consider in Chapter 3 of the text.

While consciousness and emotion are "separable to some extent" (Alford, *8*, 798), it is beginning to be believed that the cause of awakeness and the emotional state are largely one and the same thing.[65] That is, the constant inflow of excitation from the hypothalamus to the cortex, which keeps the latter awake, is construed to consist largely of these same efferent patterns which originate as emotional states in the hypothalamus. These states differ in character (pattern) as well as intensity. The degree

[64] Still speaking in terms of the original localization, now usually changed, Gardiner *et al.* (*166*, 372) say, "Emotion is awareness of the thalamic excitation."

[65] Ranson (*332*, 262) describes his monkeys with hypothalamic lesions as "somnolent." They waked easily but, if undisturbed, slept; they fell asleep while eating and with the mouth full of food; they were emotionally unreactive and showed no fear; their faces were blank and unwrinkled, with the facial muscles relaxed so that the facies "failed to register the play of emotions." "The explanation seems to lie in the loss of the emotional drive normally exerted by the hypothalamus" (*ibid.*, 264). At least, it was not due to the blocking of incoming sensory material, and it is not true of animals with thalamic lesions (Bard, *24*, 246). It appears, therefore, that "emotional drive furnished by the hypothalamus is an important factor in maintaining the waking state" (Ranson, *332*, 264). Or, as Bard puts it (*loc. cit.*), it may be that the chief function of the "central mechanism which elaborates emotional behavior of the rage type" is "to keep the animal awake and that sleep represents [its] . . . inactivity."

Both Harrison (*181*) and Papez (*315*) cite Ranson to this effect and seem to coincide with his view. The former (*loc. cit.*) also cites Serota to the effect that there is a greater rise in temperature in the hypothalamus than in the rest of the brain during excitement and a greater fall there during sleep. Thus the states of excitement and of sleep seem to be polarized.

This seems also to be Gillespie's view, since he points out that "the physical substrate of emotion is principally as far as we know" in the same region—"the basal grey matter"—as the "waking-centre" (*172*, 249).

It is also in accord with Kempf's view (*233*, 68) that "during consciousness [awakeness] an emotional or affective status continuously exists," "even during states of rest, reverie and general indifference."

of intensity, then, would determine the degree of awakeness above some minimum. But the pattern would determine the nature of the emotional experience.[66] Or, upon Sherrington's scale, the intensity would determine the degree of "affective tone" and the pattern would determine the kind. However, it is probably necessary to differentiate the emotional state in the hypothalamus, as the non-rhythmic (fortuitously variable) part of this stream of excitation, from the undercurrent of tonic excitation which is responsible for the rhythmic character of the alternations of sleep and awakeness—in spite of the fact that the proximate source of both, so far as the corticopetal tract is concerned, seems to be the mammillary bodies. In other words, it seems probable that the mammillary bodies, or some special influence operating directly on them, may be independently responsible for the rhythmic part of changes in intensity (degree), while other causes operating elsewhere in the hypothalamus, but conveyed to the mammillary bodies, determine the non-rhythmic fluctuations as well as all the specific characters (patterns). Certainly, there are differences in degree of awakeness and, within a more limited range, of its concomitant consciousness; but there are no differences in kind of awakeness. On the other hand, the emotions vary not only in degree (intensity) but also in kind. Not only that, but the depressed emotional states—at least mild ones—leave the subject awake. Thus the depressed state seems to withdraw only the non-rhythmic part of the excitation.[67] In this view, the emotional stream, at times by itself but usually only when adequately fortified in intensity (facilitated) by the rhythmic mechanism, is the cause of awakeness and a necessary condition for its concomitant, consciousness, which occurs within a limited range of awakeness. As such, it is natural to suppose that the emotional stream also constitutes a part, perhaps the larger part, of the patterns of excitation which involve the locus of consciousness, while the rhythmic component supplies, perhaps, an undifferentiated basic tone.[68]

[66] As Cannon puts it (*65*, 291), it is "quite as possible for the central integration of emotional responses, organized in the [hypo-] thalamus, to affect by its peculiar pattern the cortex in a peculiar way as for the peripheral changes [James-Lange] to do so"—or, for that matter, as for sensory patterns to do so.

[67] Possibly it even subtracts something from the rhythmic part (i.e., has a minus effect).

[68] Two entirely speculative possibilities are worth bringing out at this point. Both concern the ultimate source of the rhythmic, and tonic, excitation, the proximate source of which seems to be the mammillary bodies.

In note 22, above, we saw that it is the highly developed (in man) medial mammillary nuclei which give rise to and receive the bundle of Vicq d'Azyr. These nuclei are the efferent beginning and the afferent end of our third two-way avenue, to which we are ascribing this function, or these functions if the rhythmic and non-rhythmic excitation are actually different. But these nuclei are also "the main terminal station of the fornix column" (Fulton, *160*, 238). We have not been able to assign any specific function to the fornix and its source, the hippocampus. Is it possible that this is the ultimate source of the rhythmic factor? Probably not, for (as noted on p. 1138) this rhythm is not eliminated—it is only changed from a diurnal one to a more frequent one—in the decorticate (i.e., no hippocampus). Could this connection then be responsible for the lengthening of the rhythm which occurs with maturation? Again probably not; for, though, when lengthened, the diurnal rhythm may not produce sleep (p. 1139; i.e., there are other

It seems necessary, however, to make at this point still a third identification. The emotional state existing in the hypothalamus, whose descending efferent effects give rise to emotional manifestations, or expressions, or behavior, and whose rising or crossing efferent effects give rise to emotional experiences in the locus of consciousness, appear to many of our authorities to be one and the same thing as the various imaginary and imputed forces to which have been attributed much of behavior. Thus "drives," "urges," "instinctive impulses," "mobilization," "preparedness," and at least the directive of "orientation" seem to be identical with emotional states, their cortical effects, and their manifestations.[69] We have already reached that conclusion in Section E so far as the subcortical and peripheral elements are concerned. Now that we include the cortical elements, it begins to appear that these conditions of more or less general excitation or depression in the subcortical regions of the hypothalamus are the primary activating or inactivating forces in behavior.[70] In turn, we have also already found

---

factors) this region of the cortex and this connection are among the first to develop (before birth), and nevertheless puppies and babies continue to exhibit the short rhythm.

The second possibility seems to be more plausible. We noted on p. 1069 that "the region responsible [for overt sexual behavior] appears to be the mammillary bodies" (see Bard, *23*, *566*). Sexual excitement is certainly one of the emotional states—that is, one of the non-rhythmic factors. Has it also to do, in mild continuous form, with the rhythmic factor? If the Freudian thesis is correct, some sexual urge exists at birth. Thereafter, it develops gradually until puberty (maturation). That is also the period of the extension of the rhythmic factor to a diurnal one. It will be remembered that Freud gave the name "libido" to the force behind the sexual instinct, but he holds it also to be the force underlying "organic pleasure" or the satisfaction of wants in general—"other functions necessary for life" (see *155*, 270 ff.). Is this generalized "libido" the rhythmic factor?

That the diurnal rhythm is related to sexual development and functions is also suggested by the phenomena of "photoperiodism" and "thermoperiodism" in plant life. It is now recognized that, to induce their reproductive functions, plants require the alternation of daylight and dark and the daily rise and fall of temperature associated with daylight and dark.

Finally, we have the intimate relationship between the hypothalamus—and particularly its unpaired structures—and the hypophysis.

69 This stream is "emotional drive," to Ranson (*332*, 264). It is "powerful impulses proceeding from the region of deep-seated specific instincts" to Frolov (*157*, 140), or from the "region of complex unconditioned reflexes" (*ibid.*, 79), and these constitute the basis of orientation (*ibid.*, 78). It is the urge or impulse to activity to Bianchi (35, 283). It is identified with "instinctive impulses" by Le Gros Clark (*85*, 107). It is the source of "vital activity" to Gillespie (*172*, 248). It appears to be identical with the cause of Darrow's "'mobilization' or preparedness for adaptive response" (*103*, 289). Hess (*192*, 316) is even more explicit. He regards not only sleep, and not only "the adjustment of the degree of functional preparedness, but also its direction [i.e., kind and thereby orientation], as dependent upon vegetative influences."

Is this stream also identical—at least so far as the rhythmic factor is concerned—with Freud's "libido," as suggested above (note 68)?

70 The conspicuous feature of Ranson's somnolent monkeys was a "deficiency in motor initiative" (*332*, 262). "Lack of emotivity (apathy) produces a state of inactivity" (Gillespie, *172*, 248). On the other hand, increased hypothalamic functioning produces "excitement or increased activity" (Harrison, *181*, *653*).

it necessary (pp. 1085–1087) to regard the causes of these states as what we have, in the text, called *wants*—that is, variations or tendencies away from homeostasis.

In his original presentation (*65*, 282), Cannon showed in a diagram the general scheme of the presumed relationship between the subcortical mechanism and the cortex, on both afferent and efferent sides, that illustrated the way in which the emotional experience in the cortex was presumed to be engendered. This was reproduced and clearly explained by Bard (*19*, 305–306). In that scheme the downward (efferent) impulses from this mechanism were supposed to be also reflected upward (path 4) as "reverberations" (emotional "feelings") to the cortex, but only when the incoming afferent impulses were strong enough to reach, or were permitted to reach, the subcortical efferent outlets. That is, the "reverberations" were the result of the subcortical efferent, not of the subcortical afferent, material.[71] The actual path over which this "reverberation" was supposed to be transmitted was not then specified. Of the two known projections from the hypothalamus to the cortex, via parts of the thalamus which do not belong to the sensory relay station, the one we have described as the first avenue of interaction, which reaches only the prefrontal area, seems not to be the one involved here. Bianchi concluded that emotional reactions by-pass the prefrontal area (*35*, 269). And this seems to be clearly indicated by Brickner's case (*45*). For there, with no remaining prefrontal area, emotions seemed not to be cut off, but rather to be more influential than they are normally. Partly by default, therefore, and partly because we have already seen reason to combine the stream of excitation which causes emotional experience with that which causes awakeness and permits consciousness we are led to assign as the most probable corticopetal path in this instance the projection from the mammillary bodies via the anterior thalamus to the gyrus cinguli. As noted before, "There can be little doubt . . . that the gyrus cinguli is a neopallial projection area where the activities of the mammillary body (and through it, perhaps, the hypothalamus as a whole) find cortical representation" (Le Gros Clark, *86*, 27). If these activities of the hypothalamus are what we have concluded they are, then the gyrus cinguli is the "receptive region for the experiencing of emotion as the result of impulses coming from the hypothalamic region" (Papez, *315*, 728), as well as the cortical focus for the stream of awakeness and the locus of the concomitant of awakeness, consciousness.

In the discussion of emotional states, in Section D, we had occasion to introduce the term "pseudo-affective," which is commonly used in connection with those emotional states and manifestations which are presumed not to be accompanied by emotional experience in consciousness. At that

[71] Here we see most pointedly the fundamental difference between the Cannon and the James-Lange theory of the emotions. "Feeling" to the latter consisted of quasi-sensory reports of bodily changes from the periphery. "Feeling" to the former is a purely central "reverberation" of the centrally initiated impulses which are about to produce the bodily changes. In Cannon's theory, faint "feeling" may occur without sensible bodily changes; in the James-Lange theory it could not.

point the only reason cited for such absence was decortication—i.e., the elimination of the locus of consciousness. But, in support of the concept of a separate locus for the emotional state and the experience ("feeling"), it is worth while to indicate a few of the other conditions in which such absence of the experience may occur. "Emotional manifestations may occur without any consciousness of emotion" (Bianchi, *35*, 280).[72] Patients suffering from hemiplegia due to a lesion in a particular situation "present the outward appearance of great emotivity. They weep, laugh, and cry out on the slightest impression; yet it is evident that there is no true emotion, only the semblance of it. The weeping and laughter of such sufferers are only simulacra of the real emotions" (*ibid.*, 277–280).[73] In the chorea of Sydenham (St. Vitus's Dance) the face "assumes the strangest expressions of hatred, anger, menace, pain or joy; while the mind gives no evidence . . . of sharing in the emotion expressed by the physiognomy" (*ibid.*, 278). Masserman reports (*295*, *633*) that faradic stimulation, after intrahypothalamic injection of certain drugs, produces excitement resembling rage or fear, which he considers to be pseudo-effective partly on the ground that he could not get "emotional conditioning." In other words, he thinks that the "behavior induced" has "little or no real emotional significance to the animal." It is construed as "almost wholly automatic," on account of the apparent "absence of any affective awareness or conscious participation on the part of the animal." Such results are explicable if we assume that diseases or drugs have put some part of the rising, or crossing, pathway out of commission. On the other hand, if the pathway remains intact, "not only is the expression of emotion elicited in hypothalamic disease, but the subjective sensation commonly spoken of as affect is also involved in the experience" (Alpers, *12*, 744). Of this order appears to be encephalitis lethargica with its Parkinsonian state of "misplaced euphoria" (Alford, *8*, 795).

Conversely, it is possible for emotional states and experiences to arise without emotional manifestation. Consideration of the chief occasion for this must be deferred to the next subsection, where we consider cortical control. But it is clear from that occasion that the experience does not arise in the absence of an emotional state in the hypothalamus. It is therefore to be presumed that such a state also exists in the mild emotions which are felt but not seen. In these mild cases we suppose that the emotional state in the hypothalamus is of subliminal intensity, so far as the downward somatic paths are concerned, but of sufficient intensity to reach the locus of consciousness over the rising, or crossing, pathway.[74] That this is true is evidenced by the most subtle indicators of emotional states—blood-

[72] Or, as Bard puts it, citing Kinnier Wilson's observations, the patient's visible emotion may not correspond to his real feeling (*19*, 303).

[73] So too, "the forced laughing and weeping exhibited in lesions of the optic thalamus" (Alford, *8*, 795).

[74] As Hughlings Jackson put it, "slight anger is a faint, greater anger a vivid, element of a state of object consciousness," and the former may be too slight to produce manifestations (*216*, II, 107).

pressure and the psychogalvanic reflex, which we shall consider later—for these two autonomic (interofective) reactions are often evident in some degree even when there are no accompanying overt signs (behavior).

An even more subtle differentiation of thresholds in the various sectors of the whole emotional apparatus appears to be the explanation of dreams. Martin and Rogers (*293*, *222*) have observed hunger contractions continuing during sleep and causing restlessness. We have already construed restlessness as an affective or a pseudo-affective reaction produced by short-circuiting through the hypothalamus. The fact that it can occur in sleep indicates that the intensity of the excitation produced in the hypothalamus may be sufficient to cause a downward motor reaction and yet insufficient to awake the cortex to the degree necessary to permit consciousness.[75] It is the Freudian thesis (*155*, 107) that dreams "are called up . . . by the imperative needs of the body—hunger, thirst, sexual desire," etc., and hence are "in reaction to internal physical stimuli"—that is, they are, in our terminology, the results of emotional states produced by internal wants. Since dreams more usually produce no overt behavior, it is evident that they may also occur when the intensity of excitation produced in the hypothalamus is less than sufficient to cause a downward motor reaction. With regard to the rising, or crossing, pathway, Kempf (*233*, 68) holds that "during sleep the stream of affectivity is subliminal . . . except during dreams." That is, whatever degree of hypothalamic excitation may exist during dreamless sleep is insufficient to rise, or cross, to the cortex. But those excitations which are of sufficient strength to rise may produce dreams. Yet they are insufficient to cause awakeness and permit consciousness. Presumably the character of the emotion (stream of affectivity) which is the excitor of the dream determines what Freud calls the "latent dream thought" (*155*, 96); but what he calls the "manifest content" of the dream is clearly cortical, since it consists largely of retino-ocular and audito-articulatory material, to use Hughlings Jackson's terms, of kinds which cannot be produced subcortically.[76] Thus it appears possible that the "stream of affectivity" may be of sufficient strength to excite the cortex and yet not of sufficient strength to cause awakeness and permit consciousness. Moreover, if we follow Hughlings Jackson, the stream of affectivity may be of sufficient strength to excite the motor area of the cortex (in somnambulism) and still not be sufficient to cause awakeness or permit consciousness. Spreading is, to him, the test of whether or not there is a dream (i.e., a memory). If there is wide cortical irradiation of the

[75] Though, as we all know from experience, it may become sufficient to wake the cortex. Or it may cause an intermediate state. As Cannon puts it (*67*, *162*), hunger pangs may "interfere with sleep and thereby [sic] produce restlessness." We would say, "by producing restlessness."

[76] I take it that the hypothetical scheme we are presenting implies that Freud's "unconscious" is not subcortical nor in any certain region of the cortex. Rather it would appear to consist of emotionally endowed cortical processes either unable to reach consciousness or prevented (inhibited) from reaching it by some cortical agency such as we suppose in the next subsection.

"boxed-up" currents, the subject can remember the dream when he awakes. But if the excitation takes itself out in somnambulism (immediate motor outlet), there is no dream or remembrance (*216*, II, 442). Similarly, but on the sensory side, we have Freud's interpretation of Burdach's results. He says (*154*, 188) that he "inferred from these observations that it is not an incapability of interpreting sensory stimuli in the sleeping state which must be assumed, but a lack of interest in them." If, as we infer below, "interest" is conferred only by emotional endowment, it would not exist when the emotional stream is quiescent though, nevertheless, the sensorium might even then be sufficiently active to interpret sensation, of course without consciousness. All this differentiation of threshold seems to be evidence that the rhythmic factor in the stream of affectivity is essential to awakeness and consciousness unless the non-rhythmic factor is intense. Since the locus of consciousness is probably itself the cortical focus for the trans-cortical spreading of the stream of affectivity which is one of the factors that maintain awakeness, one would assume that the epiphenomenon, consciousness, only takes place, under the usual conditions, when the impulses passing through the locus are intensified by the rhythmic factor.

It is evident from the foregoing that the view which seems to be coming into general acceptance regards "feeling" or "affect" or "emotion" as something different from and independent of sensation.[77] Moreover, it now begins to appear that the two reach the cortex over different routes. Whereas the sensory stream, integrated in the lateral nuclear mass of the thalamus, in the geniculates and perhaps elsewhere (smell and taste), is projected direct to the sensory cortex over the radiations, where it becomes sensation when it involves the locus of consciousness, this other stream is, in effect, part of the efferent excitations of the hypothalamus. These, in turn, are partly derived from the afferent material which is integrated chiefly in the mid-line nuclei of the thalamus and partly from direct excitation by means of other (circulatory) agencies. Thence, according to Papez's localization, they are projected indirectly via the anterior nuclei of the thalamus to the gyrus cinguli. And there, or in the cortex at large, the two streams may become combined. Thus sensory excitations "receive their emotional coloring from the concurrent processes" of the affective stream, which are irradiated from the gyrus cinguli over the lateral cortex (Papez, *315*, 729).[78] Or, if the gyrus cinguli is also the locus of consciousness, the emotional

[77] In fact this is hardly its novelty. As Bard points out (*19*, 306), "Cannon's theory is in perfect accord with the view of James that emotion is a *quale* added to simple perception." And the older literature is full of similar adumbrations. As Cannon put it himself, "the peculiar quality of the emotion is added to simple sensation when the thalamic [hypothalamic] processes are roused" (*61*, 120). They "can add to sensation an aura of feeling" (*ibid.*, 121). The originality of Cannon's theory is the point that the whole emotional process originates as forebrain excitation and may be almost completely limited to that. The anatomical substrate or mechanism has been elaborated by others since he announced his theory. But nothing in that elaboration contradicts his original diagrammatic representation.

[78] That is, the irradiation from the gyrus cinguli adds "emotional coloring" to psychic processes occurring elsewhere" (*ibid.*, 728).

coloring may attach itself to sensation at this the meeting place of the two streams.[79] In Le Gros Clark's terms (*84*, 414) the sensory stream consists of "impulses on the basis of which the organism may develop an awareness of its external milieu and adapt its overt behavior accordingly," while the affective stream consists of "impulses on the basis of which the organism may develop an awareness of its internal organic activities ["appreciate itself as a unified being"; *ibid.*, 413] and through which sensory experiences are endowed with an affective tone." In similar terms it is Papez's "view that the gyrus cinguli is the seat of dynamic vigilance [awakeness] by which environmental experiences are endowed with an emotional consciousness."[80] To both these authorities, "endowment" indicates the specific combination of elements from each of the two streams. The probable basis for this "endowment," the kind of relation which seems to cause it, will be discussed in the next subsection. The evidence for this view now seems sufficiently strong to warrant its adoption as an hypothesis until a more probable one is offered. And for additional reasons, the most likely anatomical substrate of this process is the third avenue of interaction outlined above, which constitutes a part of that which Papez proposed.

As a corollary of the foregoing it should probably be assumed that, in similar fashion, emotional coloring is attached not only to sensation but also to the elements of all other cortical processes, at least those which do not pass through the cortex instanter. "Emotional manifestations . . . constantly accompany (i.e., are practically fused with) those highest manifestations which we distinguish as mental" (Jackson, *216*, II, 266). "Perhaps no thought is ever actually formed except as part of an act in which there is also an emotional component" (Brickner, *45*, 37). "Emotion or sentiment always does accompany the intellectual processes, inciting, encouraging and animating them, infusing into them the breath of interest" (Bianchi, *35*, 282). This concept of "interest" has already appeared in our discussion (p. 1122). If emotional coloring is the cortical reflection of a want, as we construe it to be, then the combining of that coloring with some elaborated sensory representation, or with some one among the several elements of a process of thinking (deliberation), is the establishment of a relation between the want and the representation of the external world or other mental process. Thus we conceive it to be the organism's interests (wants) which endow these representations or other elements with "in-

[79] In view of the fact that "stimulation of the [excitable] cortex gives rise to an emotional sensation only very rarely" (Penfield and Boldrey, *324*, 425), that only 11 times, out of 800 responses, did patients use the word pain to describe a sensation and never called it severe pain (*ibid.*, 441), and that laughing was only induced once and weeping twice (*ibid.*, 425), it becomes difficult to conceive that the "emotional coloring" exists in the pattern which is excited in the sensory cortex itself.

On the other hand, revivals of established sensorimotor patterns certainly have emotional coloring. At present we have no means of reconciling these seeming discrepancies except by supposing that the combination of emotional coloring and sensation exists in the "association areas" (including the prefrontal) or is even effected there.

[80] We have already quoted Cannon to the same effect (p. 1154).

terest." "Interest" would then be based on a synthesis (perhaps association, in the old terminology) between the cortical representation of some element of the internal environment and the cortical representation of some element of the external environment or its remaining cortical effect. But "interest" and its absence can be observed and inferred. The syntheses can be determined in detail. Then, by experiment, it may be possible to determine the apparatus that effects the synthesis. Of that more anon.

This physiological basis for the differentiation of sensation and affect requires some further examination. What are, probably, the differences characteristic of these two streams? What are we to include among affects; and what is their nature?

The first and most marked difference between the two streams seems to be in intensity. The statements and evidence we cited on p. 1139 all indicate that the stream of awakeness is, at its lowest, more intense than the sensory stream—in fact, that it is usually required to maintain awakeness. To this may be superadded, in greater or less degree, the stream of emotion. At high degrees it is, as we shall see, by far the most intense source of cortical excitation. While "sensory attention" may increase the intensity of specific sensory reports, it is probable that this occurs primarily under the influence of emotional excitement. Certainly it is reasonable to suppose, as we suggest below (p. 1173) that, in the absence of "interest," the sensory representation of the external world is the result of "a vast complex of usually mild and undifferentiated stimuli of many modalities—i.e., the scene is all background without a focus." And, in any case, any considerable degree of emotional excitement, conveyed to the cortex as affect, is certainly an excitation of far greater intensity than any sensation, strictly speaking. For our authorities have agreed that it is the chief energizer.

The second difference appears to be that the sensory stream may compound a complete representation of external reality in which the various sectors and even the various modalities are not only not mutually exclusive but are required to form the whole. True, sensory attention may not be able to concentrate on all sectors or all modalities at once. Nevertheless, they are recognized in consciousness to be there in the background. On the other hand, emotions are mutually exclusive at any one moment, though rapid shifts and even alternations are possible. Thus we must assume that, of the various emotional states, only one can exist at a time. The modes of these consist in different combinations of the parts of a single integrating system; the modalities of sensation each have their own independent integrating systems reaching through to the cortex.[81]

It would appear that we must include among affects the cortical effects of all the different modes of excitation established in the hypothalamus by the various internal and quasi-external wants we have considered in Section E. Doubtless there are many more which, because of lack of any known physiological basis, we have omitted. But this raises a question which we

[81] This point as to emotional states was made on p. 1059 and again on p. 1084. The principal evidence for it is given in Chapter 4, Section D.

have indicated above (pp. 1103–1104). Is pain an affect; or is it a sensation? Via which stream does it enter the cortex? The question cannot as yet be answered with any assurance. But present evidence indicates that it is at least chiefly, if not wholly, affect. Some of the evidence was cited in Section E. Another indication is that it appears to be one of the mutually exclusive conditions and therefore not sensory. When it is felt, it tends to engage consciousness. On the other hand, if consciousness is engaged by another strong emotion, pain is not felt.[82]

As to the nature of affects little can be said. Apparently they are generally felt as if they were part of sensation, though of a distinguishable quality. They come to be identified with, even ascribed to, concurrent sensory reports. This may be merely due to simultaneity,[83] or it may be learned through various subtle identifications leading to the attribution of

[82] Crile (*96*, 89) went so far as to construe pain—at least the conscious experience of it—to be "a phenomenon of motor stimulation." Since we consider the hypothalamus to be an effector organ that is not so far from our reading of the evidence. And the fact that an emotional state in the hypothalamus may be only a potential so far as the motor system is concerned is not an important objection to his thesis. But his and other evidence that pain comes from elsewhere in the brain and from a locus where only one emotional state can exist at one moment (mutual exclusiveness) is important for us. He cites (*ibid.*, 86) in support of his thesis the fact that pain can be suppressed by a non-painful reaction which becomes dominant (soldiers wounded in the heat of battle). We may add, perhaps, sexual masochism, ecstatic flagellation, etc., since "pain may be sought as a source of masochistic pleasure" (Lashley, *263*, 57). Crile also points out that, if two painful reflexes are absolutely antagonistic, stimulation of both appears to cause no pain (*ibid.*, 87). He says, "We believe that our experiments will prove that an equal and simultaneous stimulation of all parts of the body leaves the brain-cells in a state of equilibrium" (*ibid.*, 147), which, since "pain is an accompaniment of the release of energy in the brain cells," means that no pain would result. Confirming Crile's first point, Pavlov succeeded in conditioning to the alimentary reflex various kinds of strong nocuous stimuli which would normally produce "vigorous unconditioned defense reflexes." He was convinced that the animals then suffered no pain, for "not even the tiniest and most subtle objective phenomenon usually exhibited by animals under the influence of strong injurious stimuli can be observed in these dogs" (*320*, 29–30). In other words, the emotional state of hunger suppressed the emotional state of pain. Nafe (*310*, 395–406) concludes that, in addition to frequency (intensity) and duration of stimulation, the experience of pain requires that certain reflex activities be aroused, and perhaps only the latter (*ibid.*, 405).

Similarly fear is assumed to be the result of a motor reaction. Crile (*96*, 55) believes that "it can be shown that it is possible to elicit the emotion of fear only in those animals that utilize a motor mechanism in defense against danger or in escape from it." He finds no evidence of fear in skunks, snakes, lions, grizzly bears, elephants, turtles, or armadillos (*ibid.*, 16). M. Solomon (7 *Brit. J. Med. Psychol.*, 1927, 301) adds porcupines, and thinks fear exists only among those animals that choose between fight and flight. He includes animals who react to external stimuli by the cessation of all motion. But this, which is called "animal hypnosis" or "tonic immobility," seems to be rather due to sympathetic hyperactivity (see H. Hoagland, 1 *J. Genl. Psychol.*, 1928, 426).

These two constructions seem to belong together because we shall find, in Chapter 3, that it is probable that the want we call external injury has borrowed this inherent reaction to two or more of its fellow quasi-external wants and has made of it a learned reaction to conditioned stimuli.

[83] It will be noted in Chapter 3 that simultaneity or overlapping in point of time has much to do with conditioning—as Pavlov discovered.

the two independent streams of excitation to a common external or peripheral source which is actually localized by only one of them. It has been suggested that this is true even of the localization of pain. On the other hand, it appears that all these states can at times remain free or unassociated and therefore unlocalized—something of the order of a mood. The most common occasion for this seems to be the period when the associated sensation has ceased but the affect continues or even reappears.[84]

One more consideration arises as to these two streams. If one of them represents chiefly the external environment and the other represents almost wholly the internal environment, while the two meet in a structure which appears to be the locus of consciousness—as if the gyrus cinguli faced two ways—it is natural to suppose that their juncture there may have something to do with the psychical antithesis objective-subjective. While he did not localize this juncture where we find reason to place it and, because of that did not divide the two phases in quite the same way, Hughlings Jackson held that consciousness is dual. He said (*216*, I, 243), "Subject consciousness is first in all mentation. This half of the double substrata is made up of nervous arrangements representing the parts of the whole organism *in relation to one another*"—that is, "systemic sensori-motor arrangements," which are those "concerned during emotional states" (*ibid.*, 241). "The second half of the substrata of consciousness represents the physical side of object consciousness." So far as the external world is concerned, the first half is passive, only registering the effect of that world on the organism; but in this regard the second half is active, constituting the reaction of the organism (the "chiefly movement half"; *ibid.*, 244). He divided what he called sensation (or impressions) into the "epi-peripheral" and the "ento-peripheral"—the latter being the systemic or organic sensations (our "feelings"; *ibid.*, 287).[85]

[84] Have we not all had the experience of feeling anxiety or irritation when we can no longer immediately recall what it was that caused the affect? Perhaps this continuing emotional state occurs less, or not at all, when caused by internal wants—i.e., only when caused by quasi-external wants (the normally more intense wants).

[85] While it is impossible to identify anything in our scheme with the categories of Freud's earlier metapsychology—since the unconscious, pre-conscious, and conscious represent conditions or states through which most mental occurrences may pass, rather than functional divisions—the categories of his later metapsychology bear an interesting resemblance to those which we are outlining as a result of recent neurological work. The resemblance of the "id" to our emotional stream is obvious. What Freud called the "ego" seems allied with our sensory stream, or rather with what goes on in the whole exteroceptive-exterofective brain and its association regions. Finally, his "super-ego" bears a strong resemblance to the hypothetical function we shall attribute, in the next subsection, to the prefrontal area, and which we base on Le Gros Clark's interpretation of the physiological facts.

It should be noted that Freud's "ego" is not the subject-consciousness of Hughlings Jackson. In fact it is more closely related to the latter's object consciousness. "Ego" is an equivocal word. Poliak (*330*, 220) says the whole central nervous system "occupies the position of an 'Ego' to surrounding objects and also to the somatic part of the individual."

For an excellent analysis of the three later categories, as developed by Freud and his

It begins to appear, from recent interpretations of pathological conditions, that the cortical processes depend in some other and even more subtle way upon influences from subcortical sources, influences which may or may not be identical with the streams which produce awakeness and emotion. More and more frequently suggestions are being made such as Alford's (*8*, 798) that, perhaps, mental disorders, so-called, are primarily emotional and therefore not cortical but basal. Morgan, for instance, reports (*304*, 764–765), in cases of epilepsy, psychoses and mental deficiency, "degenerative changes" in parts of the hypothalamus.[86] Thus, while the usual view, which regards "the various manifestations of hypothalamic emotional disorders" as a release from cortical control," may be correct, it is equally possible that many of the various manifestations of mental disorders may be due to a loss or misdirection of hypothalamic influences upon the cortex. For, in these many respects, the highest level of the old brain seems to be the chief inciter and the director of the new brain. In this aspect of its relations with and interaction upon the new brain this part of the old brain cannot be considered to belong to the afferent side of the central nervous system; it must either be classed as effector (efferent) or as internuncial—and in this respect it is on a parity with most of the cortex. Evidently, as we have said before, it is itself a semi-independent highest level, vestigial in certain respects, but still the chief energizer of all the rest of the central nervous system including the cortex itself. Almost it might be said that the brain of the higher animals, at least of the primates and especially of man, has come to be organized on the two-headed principle.

If we now accept the hypothesis that the streams of emotion and awakeness, the one a non-rhythmic factor (emotional states) and the other a rhythmic factor, which arise from and represent the various degrees and kinds of excitation in the highest level of the old brain, are not only jointly responsible for consciousness and jointly constitute the "chief energizer," while the first is responsible for emotional experience and thus constitutes the "chief inciter and director" of the new brain, it becomes necessary at this point to consider whether we must amend certain of the generalizations we have used on the ground that they are no longer complete. Hitherto, having based our analysis and localization of emotional states largely upon the evidence of decorticate animals, we have repeatedly stated that the "manifestations" of these states consist of exterofective activities (behavior) and of interofective alterations in bodily processes which are short-circuited or initiated at subcortical levels—that they result, in other words, from downgoing excitation (or paralysis) from the hypothalamus to the pe-

school, which is most suggestive and striking in this connection, see Healy *et al.* (*185*, 38–57), and especially the elaborated reproduction of Freud's original diagram (*ibid.*, *56*) of their supposed topographical relationship, which conforms rather closely to our localizations.

[86] On the other hand, while Riddoch (*344*, 117) reports "placidity" as a result of damage to the hypothalamus he also notes that it is accompanied by "little intellectual impairment."

riphery. And this represents the usual view and the customary statement among our authorities. However, now that we have added to these downgoing effects a rising, or crossing, effect which produces the emotional experience in the cortex, and have recognized that this emotion constitutes one of the chief sources of excitation (energy) and one of the chief directors of the new brain, it becomes clearly necessary either to add to our other emotional manifestations those elements of behavior or bodily change which are organized in and effected by the cortex over its own channels as a result of emotion, or to find positive criteria by which to discriminate between the two classes of manifestation, or between the two components, subcortical and cortical, of jointly produced manifestations. This question of the distinction in character between the emotional manifestations, or the elements of them, which are short-circuited at the highest subcortical level, and the emotional manifestations, or elements of them, which are long-circuited over our third avenue of interaction via the cortex and its effector apparatus will be one of our chief concerns in the remainder of this appendix.

4. CORTICAL REPRESENTATION AND CONTROL OF HYPOTHALAMIC FUNCTIONS

Representation. As it has turned out, the first hypothesis as to direct interactions between the hypothalamus and the cortex has dealt exclusively with the action of the former upon the latter. On the other hand, the second hypothesis, which we will now present, is concerned for the first time also with the direct influence of the cortex upon the hypothalamus. All of the evidence we have summarized in this appendix seems to point toward this second hypothesis. Nevertheless, I have not seen it worked out precisely as it will be given here. The nearest approach and the key to it are the suggestive inferences made by Le Gros Clark. Therefore, we will commence with an outline of the scheme he has proposed.

Considering the first of the three avenues of interaction which we have outlined (see p. 1131), Le Gros Clark states that the tracts connecting the hypothalamus both ways with the prefrontal area of the cortex via the dorsomedial nucleus of the thalamus, while forming an "extremely ancient connection" (*86*, 36), are nevertheless essentially mammalian; and he finds their highest development in man (*84*, 467). Thus, in one direction, the dorsomedial nucleus forms "an intermediate station through which the whole periventricular system can be brought under the dominating influence of the frontal cortex of the cerebral hemispheres." It "provides a mechanism whereby the highest functional levels of the brain are enabled to control the more primitive elements of mental activity, such as are represented in emotional reactions, instinctive impulses, etc." (*84*, 467, and *85*, 107).[87] On the other hand, in the other direction, "it is possible also,

[87] He emphasizes this avenue, though he admits "the possibility of a cortical control of the vegetative neural apparatus in the hypothalamus" via three other avenues: (1) the

on anatomical grounds, for corticopetal impulses to reach the prefrontal areas of the cortex along the same system, so that in these areas the resultants of all the diverse activities of the cerebral cortex may be brought into close functional relation with the activities of the visceral centres of the hypothalamus." "In this way a means is provided for harnessing the impulses which are indissolubly linked up with elementary forms of emotional experience to the intentions and resolves which have their origin in ideational processes taking place at the highest intellectual levels" (*84*, 468). This interprets the prefrontal area as the place where intellectual components are equated with fundamental and primitive components (*loc. cit.*). And this interpretation of the prefrontal function and the supposition of a two-way connection with the hypothalamus seem to him to explain Fulton's and Ingraham's emotional results from a pre-chiasmal lesion (*162*). We agree, and we think that, with some modification in order to differentiate the function of this mechanism from that ascribed in our previous hypothesis to the mechanism of awakeness, emotion, and drive, it also explains all the defects of the bilateral prefrontal animals and man described in Section F 3. Thus we proceed on the assumption that the first of our avenues of interaction constitutes a two-way connection, via a relay station in the thalamus, between the hypothalamus and a specialized region of the cortex—that it is analogous to the more elaborate two-way connections between the neothalamus and the sensory cortex.

While we must admit, with Lashley (*262*, 376), that "there is no assurance that cerebral localization is anything but an accident of growth," so that the position of centers is not "a necessary consequence of their function" (*ibid.*, 375) or vice versa, nevertheless some rhyme or reason

---

reverse system of fibers of our third avenue, running from the gyrus cinguli to the anterior thalamic nuclei and thence to the mammillary bodies (p. 1133 and note 23); (2) the relay from the frontal pole (or whole frontal cortex) to the septum pellucidum and thence to the hypothalamus; and (3) the relay from the frontal pole (or whole frontal cortex) to the subthalamus and thence to the hypothalamus (*85*, 115). These are parts of our second avenue of interaction. While all these, and even the medial forebrain bundle, are possible avenues for this function, we would concur in his judgment that they seem less likely to serve the particular purpose of direct control. See our discussion on pp. 1131–1132 and notes.

The tract in the medial forebrain bundle from the olfactory (so-called) and parolfactory areas may be olfactory. Beattie thinks path (2) runs to the anterior hypothalamus only. If the subthalamus is a motor adjunct of the hypothalamus, path (3) does not seem a likely one. And path (1) seems more likely to serve a purpose quite different from this.

Moreover, the tract which descends from the dorsomedial nucleus runs chiefly to the posterior nucleus of the hypothalamus (Fulton, *160*, 238). In fact most of the periventricular fibers run to and from this nucleus (Le Gros Clark, *85*, 110). It is this system of fibers which represents the descending connection from the dorsomedial nucleus (*84*, 467). And, apparently, it is the posterior region of the hypothalamus that is chiefly related to the function we are dealing with.

While Walker (*416*, 244) mentions only the ascending part of this last tract both above and below the dorsomedial nucleus, Fulton (*160*, 238; also 278) describes the part above, at least, as "an abundant fine-fibred projection" descending from the "frontal association areas."

may be found in the accidents of growth. We have already outlined in Section G 1 the reasons why morphological analogy suggests some special relation or correspondence between the hypothalamus and the prefrontal area of the cortex. It is clear that this area is not developed from the hypothalamus in the same way that other areas of the cortex are outgrowths of their subcortical correspondents. However, there seems good reason to believe that it has come to constitute the representation in the cortex of much the same group of functions as those which pertain to the highest level of the old brain, and thus to occupy, though much less directly, the same position of re-presentation (in Hughlings Jackson's sense) with regard to the hypothalamus that the other areas occupy with regard to their subcortical correspondents. As a result of its own private path from the hypothalamaus, the prefrontal area seems to be a place, like the cingular gyrus, where the internal environment and its executory apparatus meet the external environment and its executory apparatus. But here, in contrast, they seem to meet on a parity—that is, here the special stream from the internal environment seems to be deprived of emotional force. Here, as in the case of the projections to the sensory cortex, the material seems to become organized, discriminated, differentiated, and reduced in intensity. Nevertheless, though rarefied at this level, the stream seems to be derived from the excitation of the relatively crude and potent but undeveloped level of the highest subcortical regions. If so, it could be said that the prefrontal area, more specifically, directly, and subtly than other cortical areas, represents the urges, instincts and emotions (the wants) which are the excitors of the hypothalamus. Conversely, the prefrontal area, by reason of its private path to the hypothalamus, would have a special capacity of control over its subcortical correspondent, limited in degree, not autonomous, but derived from its wider field of afferent sources and re-excitable patterns, and therefore capable of being exercised in a temporary and a graduated as well as in a constant and a uniform way. These afferent sources of the prefrontal area—the afferent aspect of this control—appear to be three-fold, yielding three types of afferent material. We would assume the prefrontal area to be excitable along with the rest of the cortex by transcortical spreading of the streams of awakeness and emotion already described, and thus to be kept awake or put to sleep by variations in the first and to be capable of becoming confused and defunctionalized by too great excitation from the second, like the rest. We would assume the excitation reaching it over its own private path, though indirectly from the same source as the emotional stream, to be, as we said above, of a more subtle and well-differentiated and therefore far less intense nature—a mere sample—corresponding rather to the character of the material which reaches the sensory cortex from the thalamus and probably subject to the same kind of "mechanism of sensory attention" which Walker (*416*, 250) ascribes to the corticothalamic projection from the sensory cortex. Thirdly, we would assume the prefrontal area to be also excitable transcortically by the sensorimotor patterns produced or re-excited elsewhere in the cortex, with their emotional endowment, if any. It would therefore be the meeting-place of three streams, not of two only, like the gyrus cinguli, nor the issue of perhaps one only like the hypothalamus. In respect of the efferent side of control we would expect, on the analogy of other re-representations, the prefrontal area to exercise a somewhat constant inhibitory effect, within limits, either upon the neural sources of afferent material coming to the hypothalamus—and at least sufficient to compel the long-circuiting of samples of that material over its own private path—or upon the hypothalamus itself, or both. Furthermore, on the analogy of the premotor cortex, we would expect the prefrontal area also to have the capacity and means of inhibiting subcortical motor centers in such a way that the excitation of its subcortical correspondent, the hypothalamus, could, within limits, be denied access downward into the exterofective (and possibly also in some degree into the interofective) system.[88] These inhibitions would presumably vary as a reflection of its own activity (reciprocal inhibition) or inactivity (general lowering of excitability)—that is, they would be a reflection of the resultant of the three streams of afferent material.

Upon the basis of these assumptions the prefrontal area would be the particular and immediate representative, in the cortex, of the internal environment. Though not developed from its subcortical correspondent, on the analogy of all other regions of the cortex, we would expect it to be a more highly evolved representative, showing a large degree of progression from the primitive character of that correspondent. Upon the afferent side, this would be chiefly due to the fact that in a way impossible to the hypothalamus it would also have available, through transcortical avenues from the sensory cortex, information about the external environment, detailed and precisely organized on spatial lines. Upon the efferent side, the prefrontal area would be capable of elaborating patterns and dealing with its material in ways that were entirely beyond the capacity of its prototype. In respect of the somatic motor apparatus, at least, it could probably influence or utilize, with little or no emotional energizing and therefore in the most precise way, the motor areas proper—thus fully realizing the potentialities of an effector mechanism capable of great differentiation and fine adjustment to the external environment. In contrast to this, the hypothalamus has directly available only the stereotyped and more or less blind synergies of the subcortical motor centers, to the extent that its excitation is short-circuited, and can only indirectly energize the cortical effector mechanism through the emotional stream, with its crude, if powerful, influences, to the extent that its excitation is long-circuited. The prefrontal area would, therefore, show marked development away from stereotyped reactions, though the original causes of the reactions might be the same. Thus we would conceive the prefrontal area

[88] We shall suggest below that these two types of inhibition—probably both originating in the prefrontal area—are not carried by the same tracts, or even by parts of the same avenues.

to be the more expert but less powerful agency for the maintenance of homeostasis, at least in respect of those features of it which require specific relations with the environment—the special cortical representative of the want system. It would be the locus of that particular type of "intellectual ascendency" which, as Barcroft points out (*17*, 88), is the means of attaining "*la vie libre*" of Bernard.[89]

Hughlings Jackson, in necessarily somewhat psychological terminology, has defined the "process of all thought" as "'stereoscopic' or 'diplopic,' being the tracing of relations of resemblance and difference" between two slightly dissimilar images (*216*, II, 359).[90] It depends mainly on memory, because "recognition (a synonym of perception) is having relations of likeness and unlikeness," and "having these relations involves revival of previously acquired states, which is memory" (*ibid.*, II, 93). Thus, even the simplest form of thought process, recognition, falls within his definition of classification (*ibid.*, II, 393). It "is the classification of things which are for the most part very different by some fundamental peculiarity each of them has." But there are other criteria besides similarity according to which the mind can classify (associate). In fact, it can do so in terms of all relations between its data which it has the capacity to detect—contemporaneity, collocation, and so on. Among these appears to be the relationship, already referred to, between some specific feature of the internal environment—an interest of the organism, a want—and some specific feature of the external environment found by experience to be related to it. The process of the establishment of this relationship between the want and the sensory presentation or representation of some specific feature of the external environment seems to be what we are calling the attachment of "interest." Externally it appears as orientation and alertness—the exteroceptive-exterofective sensorimotor process and the affective process, respectively. Internally it is probably the endowment with emotional coloring of the elaborated sensory representation—current or revived—of the particular feature of the external environment concerned. If the prefrontal area is the more special cortical representative of the want system, we would expect it to have something to do with the original establishment of this relation, with the discovery of those external details in which the organism finds reason to have an "interest." The establishment of this relationship is the fundamental element in the process called conditioning, as was demonstrated by Pavlov's experiments. When "interest" is conferred on any previously unrelated pattern of external stimuli by the demonstration to the animal that it is related to one of his wants, he reacts to that stimulus in the same way he has previously reacted to those patterns of

[89] We have already suggested (p. 1165, note 85, above) the resemblance between these functions which we are putatively assigning to the prefrontal cortex, and the functions assigned in Freud's latest metapsychology to the "Super-ego."

[90] "Mental diplopia," or "manifest diplopia," which is the existence of "two objective states for one subject," is "a caricature of the normal 'diplopia' of healthy mentation" (Jackson, *216*, II, 361, 362). This subject is discussed more fully, but from a different approach, in Chapter 5.

stimuli whose effect is innate or which he has previously learned are related, the so-called unconditioned stimuli.[91] Thus we should also expect the prefrontal area to be concerned with establishing "conditioned reflexes," or with "learning," so far as that consists of the same process.

This somewhat elaborate hypothetical statement is presented in this form only to permit us more readily to check it with the facts and determine whether it conforms sufficiently well to serve as an hypothesis. The best check we can give it is to reconsider the rather carefully examined data with reference to the defects resulting from bilateral prefrontal ablation, as presented in Section F 3—especially Brickner's acute interpretations—to see if it explains *all* the observed defects and involves *none* which were not observed. From that examination we concluded that the prefrontal area—a part of the cortex in which artificial local stimulation produces no overt effects—is neither precisely sensory nor motor, but of that order which is called internuncial (a bridge between). It is evidently not the locus of consciousness nor the cortical focus of the stream of awakeness and emotion. Neither is it the region responsible for the simplest form of thinking, recognition, nor even that for many of the more elaborate forms, which are usually called intellectual. All this because none of these functions seems to be impaired by its total removal.[92] On the other hand, it does seem to be largely responsible for the control over, and the further evolution of, the emotional-instinctive mechanisms in whatever degree such control and evolution exist. For, when removed, there become apparent certain phenomena of emotional release—"impairment of emotional restraint" [93]—and certain regressions to a more primitive stage of development in the emotional-vegetative sphere—"impairment of instinctual function." [94] In turn, this last leads directly to the relating of the external en-

[91] This statement will be explained in Chapter 3, where we distinguish between the actually innate or unconditioned stimuli and Pavlov's so-called unconditioned stimuli, many or most of which we hold have been "naturally" conditioned.

[92] The possibility that unconsciousness may be produced by artificial local stimulation here, as reported in Section F, note 52, above, might be explained, within our scheme, either as due to excessive transcortical excitation of the locus of consciousness or as due to excessive inhibition of the source of the stream of awakeness-emotion. What the true explanation is we do not know.

[93] Brickner suggests that his patient "expresses relatively freely the motivations which are ordinarily retained in the (Freudian) unconscious," so that "he actually lives out his formerly unconscious life in part, having lost some of the capacity for normal repression" (*45*, 318). And he identifies the determination of "personality" with this unconscious, since destruction of the super-psyche, imposed over and developed out of this unconscious, seemed merely to "exaggerate" the patient's personality.

[94] As Bianchi expresses it, after removal of the prefrontal areas the fundamental and intermediate emotions are preserved, though some are altered; but the higher sentiments or emotions are either absent or profoundly disturbed (*35*, 285). Both release and regression are suggested by Dott's view (*20*, 167). To him the hypothalamus "ignores refinements of decency and convention, if isolated from the control of its better-educated instructor, the frontal cortex, which seems to exercise an inhibitory influence on its cruder yet vitally important functions."

vironment to the internal.[95] If we construe "interest" as we have, then the observed "impairment of particularization" becomes an inability to select the essential feature out of a whole situation which, so far as the sensory system is concerned, consists of a vast complex of usually mild and undifferentiated stimuli of many modalities—i.e., the scene is all background without a focus.[96] This inability to select would be a by-product of the inability to confer "interest" upon some specific feature of the sensory complex by reason of discovering its relation to some internal interest. And this is described as "impairment of the faculty of conscious attention." Because no "interest" is conferred there is "inattentiveness, apathy, drowsiness," or attention is only given to each *newest* pattern of stimulation in turn (pure sensory awareness).[97] For the same reason there is inability to adjust to the environment, and hence the subject becomes discouraged by his failure in adaptation. It follows that, if "interest" is one of the chief reasons for retention of an impression, and if the connection with a particular interest is one of the chief bases for association and therefore recall, there will be a "loss of recent memory." [98] Old memories however, are re-

[95] In fact, it is part of the same process, if we construe the development of instinctual function to be learning how successfully to adapt environmental relations to the want and to adapt the want, or its behavior, to the environment—the two-way process called "adaptation," at the behavior level (i.e., not in the strictly biological sense).

[96] Though derived from a different approach, William James's interpretation exactly coincides. He says (*220*, I, 404 and 405) that the state of consciousness, without "interest" and therefore without "attention," would be "a gray chaotic indiscriminateness." The accompanying lethargy, which he describes as a "curious state of inhibition," reminding us of Pavlov's "internal inhibition," probably represents a "scattered condition of mind" which is "the usual state of brutes when not actively engaged in some pursuit"—that is, according to our interpretation, when not activated by some present want.

[97] The "faculty of conscious attention" as externally observed consists, as we said above, of orientation toward some specific feature of the scene (judged by direction of eyes, nose, ears, etc.) and of the alert. It is clear that, apart from mere strength or suddenness or other characteristic of novelty, sensory attention is not determined by the nature of the external stimuli. The selection of particular impressions from the external world to which to attend is generally determined rather by their "meaning" to the animal—that is, by the "interest" with which some one of his interests invests them. This "interest," translated into objective terms, is a relation between some particular feature of the external environment and the particular one of his interests concerned. Most of such relations are not innately organized. They are learned—the result of experience, of conditioning.

Pavlov's view, as presented by Frolov (*157*, 78 ff.) was that the subcortical centers "most closely adjacent to the cortex" "give the organism a sufficiently firmly based orientation in relation to the environment and insure equilibrium [homeostasis], but this orientation is strictly limited to a small number of situations (hunger, self-defense, sexual excitation) and is far from adequate for establishing higher degrees of adaptation." Our hypothesis is that these higher degrees of adaptation remain oriented *by* the same wants and the same subcortical centers but become oriented *toward* new and more varied external data chiefly through the instrumentality of the developed mechanism of the prefrontal areas.

[98] If one of the chief bases for making an impression revivable at all (a memory) is the amount of "interest" attached to it, if one of the chief bases for then reviving it is the fact that it is related, by reason of endowment with the same kind of "interest," to

tained. Only their revival may be defective if the connection of the current situation with them is not recognized. We would expect this nonimpairment to be true of memories laid down before the defect occurred and perhaps also of memories established by some much slower process of emotional endowment and association elsewhere in the cortex (in the awakeness-emotion mechanism). That is, we would expect this, if we assume that only the most precise part of the mechanism for originating the relationship of the internal and the external depends upon the prefrontal area.[99] Finally, if conditioning is this process of conferring "interest" *de novo* upon external facts, if learning of this kind depends on discovering the relation, and if such an investment with "interest" is one of the chief bases for retention and recall, the absence of the necessary apparatus would explain the "little learning from experience" or the difficulty in "new acquisition" that is observed. And, if only the original discovery of the relation is involved, the fact is also explained that previously conditioned responses would remain undisturbed, as they do. For we are only assuming that the prefrontal area acts as a kind of catalytic agent in establishing these relationships, and that, once established, they are relegated to other parts of the cortex as memories invested with "interest"—as more or less abstract patterns, the recognition of a new sample of which brings up corresponding memories with their emotional endowment.[100] We assume that the prefrontal area is the most precise agency for stringing the separate beads of experience upon the respective strings of the various organismic interests.

---

the current impression (association), then we should expect the data of experience to be quickly forgotten if no "interest" had been attached or, at least, not to be subject to recall if the relationship to the prevailing organic interest had not been established at the time the datum occurred.

Thus food is still recognized, but the relationship of a particular set of surroundings to a particular lot of food which has been concealed is forgotten (see Section F, note 50, above).

This suggests an explanation of Pavlov's "internal inhibition." He conceived it to be of the same nature as sleep—"essentially one and the same process" (Frolov, *157*, 107). We note that, with dogs (Pavlov's subjects), when they have no active want and are free from stimulation that arouses one (no sensory patterns to which "interest" is attached) they sleep—their stream of awakeness-emotion practically ceases. Thus absence of "interest" produces sleep. Sleep is then, perhaps, identical with internal inhibition, as Pavlov suggested, and the latter constitutes a rapid fading-away of sensory impressions which are of no "interest" and, finally, complete "adaptation" to them—the shutting of them out from sensory attention. Thus "internal inhibition" may be no more than loss of "interest," and Pavlov's dogs may have slept, not because of some mysterious effect of repetition of the single stimulus they were permitted to receive, but because they were temporarily bored to death.

99 As Brickner puts it (*45*, 303) it is evident that the prefrontal areas are "luxuries . . . from a biological standpoint," having no monopolies of any kind.

100 It will be recalled that Freud's hypothesis (*154*, 427) was that the "perception system" "is entirely lacking in memory," so that the memory system is the sole basis of association including, of course, recognition.

It will be noted that this hypothesis does not assume for the prefrontal areas any neural process foreign to other parts of the central nervous system. It merely assumes certain special connections and relations and a greater degree of refinement and development. The characteristic that this region is neither strictly sensory nor strictly motor is not new. That is true of all internuncial centers and fibers, subcortical or spinal. In fact, strictly speaking, that is the essential characteristic of the whole central nervous system and the only one which differentiates it from the peripheral system. What we call control by the prefrontal area consists in part of inhibition, and this is common to all elements of the system—a general phenomenon. Perhaps "the development of the inhibitory power in the psychic domain coincides with the appearance of the frontal lobes" (Bianchi, *35*, 318). Nevertheless, "all points of the cerebral mantle may either be inhibitory organs or may themselves be inhibited" (*ibid.*, 318); and that is true also of all the rest of the central nervous system. The only novelty at this point is expressed in the term "psychic" (i.e., restraint over the innate system exercised by the learning and learned system). Moreover "interest" is nothing novel. It exists in all lower forms of animal life, even those whose prefrontal cortex is hardly apparent. It is the explosive charge supplied, throughout the nervous system and all down the scale, from interoceptive sources, of which the great bulk of exteroceptive stimuli that are not themselves of adequate intensity to cause energetic reaction constitute merely the detonator. Here it has only moved up to the highest level and has taken advantage of other cortical developments to establish a more discriminating relationship with the external world. Here it has a new and its own special mechanism for the original integration. But the function of integrating (synthesizing) inner and outer stimuli is, as we have supposed, also general to the cortex as a whole.[101] Apparently even these special integrations, once built up by the prefrontal area, may continue to revive in other portions of the cortex. Moreover, such integration does not presume a neural process different from any other form of integration. It is of the same order as the formation of any other pattern compounded from different impulses coming over different fibers.[102]

Apparently this type of integration is intimately related to the original

[101] The capacity for conditioning is probably not even confined to the cortex, as we shall see in Chapter 3.

[102] Thus we hold that faculties which may have developed from the chief function of the prefrontal area may now serve for, or include in their scope, the whole cortex. But we also hold that these faculties are merely developments of those which have been taken over from, and previously existed in primitive form at, lower levels; so that, as Head puts it (*183*, 760), "If the functions of a lower, more primitive organization are kept under control by the activity of a higher afferent system, the removal of this dominant mechanism does not exhibit the vital processes of the phylogenetically older organs in all their primitive simplicity." For the higher, as it evolved, took along with it functions which formerly belonged in the lower organization, but which are no longer there. And this is a fact that experimenters with ablation, etc., must always keep in mind.

development of the cortex and, thereafter, to the expansion of another cortical process whose chief locus, as was suggested in the previous section, probably comes to be centered in another region. In the lower animals, already "the cortex exerts some relatively non-specific influence upon learning and remembering" (Herrick, *191*, 13). We have already suggested (p. 1135) that the non-specific influence is this endowment with emotional coloring, or "interest." Once the neopallium has become capable of "cortical representation of peripheral localization, so that the outer world is correctly and adequately mirrored in the inner (cortical) experience," "analysis of peripheral experience . . . synthetically recombined in new patterns" becomes possible (*loc. cit.*). Then the neopallium "can probably" initiate new patterns of behavior ('insight' of Kohler or 'reasoning' of Maier)" (*ibid.*, 12). Insight and reasoning are kinds of deliberation. In fact Dewey's description of deliberation (cited in the text, p. 102) is a precise definition of insight. He says, it is a "dramatic rehearsal (in imagination) of various competing possible lines of action. . . . It is an experiment in finding out what the various possible lines of action are really like. . . . Thought runs ahead and foresees outcomes, and thereby avoids having to await the instruction of actual failure and disaster." But deliberation seems usually to involve the interests. The term may be stretched to include all delayed reactions—that is, such uninhibited but subliminal continuous sequences as are represented by daydreams and such continuous excitations beyond the power of the outlets immediately to draw off as may be represented by pain. Ordinarily, however, deliberation seems to be a consequence of conflict between possible lines of action, either because one interest is contending against another, or because of uncertainty (i.e., conflict) between alternative lines of action incited by a single interest. In either process, so far as present wants are concerned, we may assume that "interest" is the inciter of the conflict, so that, if "interest" is not aroused, there is no conflict and no insight. Though he does not call the defect by that name, it is clear that all Jacobsen's bilateral prefrontal monkeys suffered a loss of the ability to apply insight to a new situation.[103] They could not initiate a successful new pattern of behavior, probably not because they had forgotten old experience, but because the details of the new situation could not be strung with the old beads. For we are not suggesting that deliberation takes place in the prefrontal areas, but only that, until "interest" has been attached by these areas, the process of deliberation elsewhere does not arise from the current external stimuli. Even this matter of deliberation does not argue a new faculty or a new neural process. Subliminal excitation is a more or less continuous state in the subcortical and spinal systems. There, it does not consist of continuous change and therefore of conflict, however mild, with the result that it does not have the concomitant of consciousness and therefore does not produce even daydreams. But even conflict is a frequent occurrence

[103] See Jacobsen, *217;* see also Jacobsen, 13 *Comp. Psychol. Monogr.*, (1936, No. 63) 3; and 82 *J. Nerv. Ment. Dis.* (1935) 1, with J. B. Wolf and T. A. Jackson.

throughout the nervous system, though elsewhere it seems to be immediately resolved or completely uninhibited, even reciprocally.[104]

Inhibitory Control. Having outlined this hypothesis as to the second and more special form of interaction between the hypothalamus and the cortex—a form which seems to be related to one cortical region only, the prefrontal areas—we are now prepared to consider the only feature of it which appears here for the first time in our analysis—that is, the reverse process which it is supposed to include—the interaction of the cortex upon the hypothalamus. As to this reverse process we cannot be so certain that the *only* cortical region involved is the prefrontal areas, though these are certainly involved. Therefore, we will begin by considering the general relation without definite cortical localization and will proceed to narrow it down to definite loci and paths as far as the evidence appears to justify that. It is generally agreed that the cortex exercises control over the hypothalamus, as it does over all subcortical mechanisms. In the case of the hypothalamus inhibitory control is at least emphasized, if it is not treated as the only form of control. But when it comes to finding any ready-made thesis which presents a picture of the specific nature of the control and the specific paths over which it is exercised, the literature does not give us full satisfaction. And yet, the outline of even a hypothetical scheme which will fit the observed facts must include such a picture. Therefore we are obliged to go into some detail as to these points.

When we examine the nature of the control exercised by higher over lower centers in the rest of the nervous system it seems to take three forms, each of which may be exerted in several different ways.

1. Inhibition. This consists in the prevention of afferent impulses from passing over to an efferent path at some level below the higher (controlling) center. It may be exerted

a. at the end of the afferent path (here the thalamus);
b. within the internuncial paths (here the hypothalamus);
c. at the beginning of the motor paths (here probably the interbrain and midbrain motor centers, and possibly the corpus striatum, through which the hypothalamus seems to have its downward motor connections, or at the point where paths to them leave the hypothalamus).

2. Facilitation. This probably consists in the subliminal excitation (c.e.s.) of lower by higher centers. It may be exerted

a. within the internuncial paths (here again the hypothalamus);
b. at the beginning of the motor paths (here again as in 1 c above).

3. Excitation. This consists in the transmission of supraliminal impulses from the higher centers to the lower centers. It may be exerted only

a. within the internuncial paths (here again the hypothalamus).[105]

104 This last is Hughlings Jackson's construction. "Convulsion is nothing other than the sum of the contentions of different movements" (*216*, II, 31). It is "the 'running up' of very many movements into a fight" (*ibid.*, II, 89).

105 Obviously if threshold excitation is exerted over corticofugal paths at the beginning of downward motor paths from the hypothalamus, or at its lower motor centers, this is in no sense control over the hypothalamus.

In general, Bard concludes (*24*, 197) that "the cortex . . . probably normally exerts both inhibitory and excitory effects either directly on the hypothalamus or upon final paths which it has in common with the hypothalamus." [106] Leaving until the next subsection the question of cortical control via excitatory effects, let us consider here the nature and probable paths of the inhibitory effects. In respect of these Bard said earlier that: "Inhibitory cortical influences normally prevent the primitive activities from dominating behavior. The subcortical processes are at all times ready to seize control of the motor reactions and when the cortical check is released they do so promptly and with elemental vigor." In such cases the reaction is certainly not due to cortical discharge, and the cortical function is negative with regard to these activities (*19*, 299). That is, the activity is a "release phenomenon" (*ibid.*, 293).[107] That this inhibition is normally a continuous affair and that it is cortical in origin is demonstrated by the fact that release phenomena always appear with decortication (*ibid.*, 286).[108] They also appear when going under ether, chloroform, or nitrous oxide, after loss of consciousness, when patients "weep and groan, sing joyously, laugh uproariously, or exhibit all the aggressive signs of rage" (*ibid.*, 297). In the latter as well as the former condition, there is of course no emotional consciousness (experience)—that is, the patients going under anesthetic become "functionally decorticates" (*loc. cit.*). That the tract which maintains at least part of this inhibitory effect runs via the thalamus is indicated by the fact that lesions affecting cortico-thalamic fibers similarly cause "excessive affective responses" (*ibid.*, 304). That the specific tract involved is that from the prefrontal area to the dorsomedial nucleus is indicated by Head's observation (*183*, 608–609). When this nucleus, his "essential organ," "has been freed from control" by removing the tract, the reaction to a slow but persistent pricking, "when it occurs, tends to be explosive; it is as if a spark had fired a magazine and the consequences were not commensurate with the cause." Some part, or all, of this inhibitory effect appears therefore to be maintained over the reverse fibers of our first avenue of interaction. Since that avenue has a relay station in the

[106] This accords with Cannon's original statement (*61*, 120) that the subcortical processes are aroused both (1) because the response initiated in the cortex is in a "certain mode or figure" which stimulates them (excitatory) and (2) because their own afferent material from below excites different reaction patterns for different affective states which are merely released from above (inhibitory).

Usually only the latter is noted, e.g., Dott (*120*, 167) and others already quoted. So Riddoch says (*344*, 117) that "emotionalism" is "a manifestation of release of the diencephalon from cortical control." Davison and Kelman (*109*, 88) conclude that pathological or involuntary laughing and crying are release phenomena due to injuries which free the hypothalamus from cortical control.

[107] Bard (*19*, 292) cites Hughlings Jackson and Head in support of the inhibitory function.

[108] Referring to Goltz's, Rothman's and Dusser de Barenne's decortications, which showed the "animal excessively prone to the display of anger," from almost any handling. In Cannon's acute cases (cats; Bard, *19*, 287) the signs are stated to have appeared without special stimulation.

thalamus, the assumption is permitted that the inhibition is exerted at the end of the afferent paths, 1a, above. But since this avenue also has descending fibers from the relay station—the dorsomedial nucleus—to the hypothalamus, these observations are also compatible with inhibition of the hypothalamus itself, 1b, above. Moreover, other evidence seems to favor the second alternative. Davison and Kelman (*109*, 88) find "excessive affective responses" as a result of lesions of cortico-hypothalamic tracts (not specified). Fulton and Ingraham (*162*, xxvii) got "chronic rage" and diffuse sympathetic discharges by separating the corticohypothalamic tracts (also not specified).[109] In Alpers' case (*11*, 301), with the cortex intact and no damage to the thalamus, but all hypothalamic nuclei destroyed except the mammillo-infundibular group, there were similar phenomena—"periods of depression, alternating at times with periods of unmotivated excitement, by easily elicited reactions of rage and by loss of inhibitory reactions in general, resulting in uncontrollable laughter or anger." He believes that either irritative or certain destructive lesions of the hypothalamus cause emotional disturbance, and prefers "to assume that the cortex exerts an inhibitory influence on the hypothalamus under normal conditions, so that expressions of rage or excitement and even of other more refined reactions in man are held normally in check" (*ibid.*, 302). Since all these statements are compatible with the supposition that this cortical inhibition is exerted upon the hypothalamus itself, while only part of them appear consistent with inhibition of the afferent paths,[110] it seems advisable merely to hold the first possibility (1a) open and to rely chiefly on the second (1b).

We have said that this inhibition is normally continuous. Yet it is clear that, even in the intact and healthy individual, it is frequently withdrawn. Under what conditions does that occur? We may have recourse to Darrow's clarifying interpretation. In his view, except in emotion, the "cortex maintains a high degree of selective inhibiting control over subcortical primitive automatic mechanisms" (*102*, 573). But "active conflict in the normal

109 "Chronic rage" is a "condition in which rage is much more easily elicited than in a normal animal" (*162*, xxviii).

110 If the inhibition were only exerted at the end of the afferent paths, then injury to direct corticohypothalamic tracts, if there are any, or to the anterior hypothalamus itself, would not necessarily "release" the posterior hypothalamus, for the afferent material necessary to excite it could remain cut off at the thalamic level. On the other hand, if it is exerted on the hypothalamus itself, then when the descending tract for control is cut at any point between its origin and its destination, inhibition ceases and, at the same time, the incoming afferent material, which does not arrive via the dorsomedial nucleus, continues to give rise to the now released reactions.

It is also possible, as mentioned before, that the anterior hypothalamus has a certain inhibitory influence on the posterior hypothalamus. If so, the influence may originate there or it may be transmitted from the cortex by way of other tracts, such as that via the septum pellucidum. This appears to be Beattie's belief (*30*, 69) as noted above (p. 1132). To the extent that this is the case, the cortical inhibition of the hypothalamus itself is probably not only transmitted by the reverse fibers of our first avenue of interaction but also by this tract and perhaps others which we included in the second avenue of interaction. On this see p. 1132 and note 21; also p. 1153, note 60.

individual is frequently the essential condition for the release of the primitive automatic subcortical mechanisms of *excited* emotion" (grief, sorrow, remorse, etc., having different mechanisms; *ibid.*, 572). This is due to the fact that "intracortical conflict" lessens the control (withdraws the inhibition). So the mechanisms are "set free" and a kind of "functional excortication" results. Reactions are then non-voluntary, relatively automatic, but not necessarily unconscious. As a consequence they leave the individual like a "by-stander astonished at his own behavior" (*ibid.*, 573). It appears that the conflict Darrow refers to must be excessive (emotionally surcharged); for we have assumed that deliberation is also a condition of cortical conflict. Yet, in deliberation, the cortical inhibition, at least of behavior, may be complete and effective. Thus "intracortical conflict" of the deliberative kind appears to be the source of the inhibition of the subcortical mechanisms *up to a certain point;* beyond that point it is the conflict itself which breaks down this inhibition. That is, the activities of the cortex appear themselves to be inhibitory to the subcortical mechanisms up to a certain degree of intensity; beyond that degree they cease to produce inhibitory effects. This supposition is in entire accord with our thesis as to the median range of excitation through which consciousness is acute, and away from which, in either direction, it becomes confused. It is also in accord with the theory of inhibition to which we shall refer on p. 1185. Jacobsen's description of the behavior of his normal but emotional female chimpanzee seems to illustrate the effect of "functional excortication." [111] There, failure to solve the problem, itself an exercise in deliberation, frequently resulted in violent temper tantrums and those, when repeated, became in a short time, in effect, an experimental neurosis.[112]

However, the supposition that this corticohypothalamic inhibition establishes "a *high* degree of *selective* control" faces two difficulties. In the first place, if it were selective, the cortex could select and permit any particular emotional state to exist in the hypothalamus or, conversely, could prevent any such specific state. I think, however, that introspective examination will convince anyone that this is definitely not the case. In respect of experiencing them or not experiencing them, emotions are beyond our control. We must suppose, then, that this type of corticohypothalamic inhibition is general rather than specific or selective. In the second place, while the degree of this constant inhibition must be sufficient to account for the wide difference in intensity of hypothalamic excitation during the times when the inhibition is being normally exerted and the times when it is entirely withdrawn by pathological or surgical interruption, it is nevertheless clear that this degree is limited and that it is never complete. For, in the normal condition, it is overcome or overridden most of the time.[113]

[111] Quoted by Fulton (*160*, 464–465).

[112] Frolov (*157*, 122) accounts for experimental neuroses, or "ruptures," as the result of confusion due to inability to discriminate stimuli with different "meanings," or inability to decide correctly (i.e., unsuccessful or unresolved deliberation).

[113] Moreover, it is not only frequently overridden in the mature, but it is much more easily overridden in the infant's brain than in the adult's. "The child's cerebral cortex,

That is, "unconditioned emotional stimuli, if adequate, are capable of directly exciting diencephalic discharge in spite of cortical inhibition" (Bard, *19*, 307).

These considerations remind us that our hypothesis has supposed that emotional states in the hypothalamus give rise to two outflows, not one, and it is evident that in respect of cortical inhibition these are somewhat independent of each other. The first is the emotional stream. An emotional state arises in the hypothalamus in spite of cortical inhibition (overriding it), and this, in turn, will then give rise to an emotion in the cortical center for experiencing emotions (probably the gyrus cinguli), whence its effect is extended transcortically. At a high degree of intensity this can result in cortical confusion (excessive intracortical conflict) which in turn suspends the cortical inhibition of the hypothalamus. Thus, unconditioned emotional stimuli of sufficient intensity to override cortical inhibition of the hypothalamus are the primary sources of emotional experience. If cortical inhibition were powerful enough to prevent these states, emotional experiences would not occur. But, since emotional experiences are a practically continuous affair, it is evident that inhibition only tempers these states of excitation and does not prevent them. Moreover, it would appear that this tempering effect is variable in strength. For, not only can the inhibition be overcome by a strong stimulus capable of producing great excitation, but it can also be overcome by suddenness, by surprise. That is, an unconditioned stimulus of sufficient strength may produce an emotional experience, if it is unexpected; whereas, if it is expected, it may have little result.[114] This argues that, with warning, this cortical inhibition can be stepped up in intensity above the customary level. It may also argue for a prefrontal attention mechanism analogous to, but the converse of, the sensory attention mechanism already referred to (i.e., raising instead of reducing thresholds). We conclude, then, that any direct inhibition of the hypothalamus by the prefrontal cortex is general in nature and mild in degree, though susceptible of some temporary increase.

The other possible outflow of emotional states in the hypothalamus is the downward discharge over the exterofective and the interofective apparatus—the first of which is usually taken to be the emotional expression, though both together actually constitute that expression. Since at least the motor component of this second outflow can be prevented altogether, even when the emotional state is giving rise to an emotional stream and causing an emotional experience of a rather high level of intensity, it is evident that cortical inhibition of the motor outlets of the hypothalamus must be

---

being functionally weaker, is frequently unable to suppress the process of excitation, especially as the latter is reinforced by powerful impulses proceeding from the region of deep-seated specific instincts, the centres of which lie in the subcortical ganglia" (Frolov, *157*, 140).

[114] For instance, a sudden loud noise, if unexpected, produces an emotional state with overt effect—a "start"—and with an emotional experience—a "fright"—of sufficient intensity, in some, to produce confusion. The same noise, expected, may cause no "start" and hardly any "fright."

exercised independently of cortical inhibition of the hypothalamus itself. The observable state of self-control under excitement proves that motor expression can be suppressed altogether. However, the fact that the excitement is observable at all suggests that the interofective expression cannot be suppressed (inhibited), or that its only form of suppression is inhibition of the state of excitement in the hypothalamus itself. We conclude, therefore, that interofective emotional expression is only controlled in so far as the emotional state is controlled and that it is, for that reason, the best overt index and reflector of the degree and character of hypothalamic excitation. This observable differentiation between cortical inhibition of the hypothalamus itself, resulting in a tempering of the emotional stream crossing to the cortex and also of the outflow of excitation over the interofective (autonomic) system, and, on the other hand, cortical inhibition of the exterofective (motor) outlets of the hypothalamus, suggests that the latter probably arrives over different paths and possibly derives from a source different from the former. Since a complete system of tracts runs from the frontal cortex to every one of the subcortical motor centers, it is natural to suppose that it is these, or some of them, which are used in blocking the access of the hypothalamus to such centers. The part of this system of tracts which arises in the motor and premotor areas—excitable cortex—has motor functions which have been carefully studied; the part which arises in the prefrontal area—non-excitable cortex—has, as yet, no function assigned to it. But, since we have seen reason to conclude that the prefrontal area is not motor in function, in our narrow sense, it seems reasonable to deduce that the tracts composing the second part are not transmitters of impulses which cause motion. It is possible, however, that they perform the function we are here considering. And, as we shall suggest in Section H, it seems probable that the inhibitory effects transmitted over the part of the extrapyramidal system arising in the motor cortex function in a different manner.[115] We, therefore, incline to the supposition that cortical

[115] If we follow Fulton in this still confused and controversial field, the extrapyramidal motor system has "two primary subdivisions," the corticopontocerebellar tracts and the corticostrionigral tracts (*160*, 501). Of the first, one part—the precentropontine—which is much the largest, arises in the motor cortex; another part—Arnold's bundle, or the prefrontopontine—arises in the prefrontal areas. Of the second, the projections to the striate bodies arise in both the motor cortex and the prefrontal areas; but, of the second, direct tracts to lower levels arise either in the motor cortex or in the prefrontal areas, not in both. Those arising from areas 4 and 6 are the corticonigral, the corticotegmental, the corticorubral and the corticosubthalamic. Entirely separate from these is the corticomesencephalic which arises in the prefrontal areas (*ibid.*, 336–337 and 491).

The corticostrionigral system is responsible for "postural adjustments and the integration of *involuntary* movement patterns" (*ibid.*, 503). That part of it which originates in the motor cortex is evidently responsible for inhibition of the substantia nigra (preventing rigidity) and of the red nucleus (preventing spasticity; *ibid.*, 502). But that part originating in the prefrontal area cannot be responsible for the latter function, at least, because ablation of the prefrontal areas "has not caused a trace of spasticity" (*ibid.*, 445–446).

This and other considerations we shall bring up later suggest that the downward access of the hypothalamus to the subcortical motor centers is independent of, and

inhibition of the motor outlets of the hypothalamus is exercised by the prefrontal area over its own tracts to the subcortical motor centers, which by-pass the hypothalamus.

There is considerable reason for supposing that these two outflows of emotional states in the hypothalamus—the one causing emotion and the other causing emotional behavior—are alternatives. As Cannon says, (*61*, 122), "there are psychologists who maintain that the emotional state [our emotion, or cortical experience] lasts only so long as there is inner conflict between the impulse to act and the hesitant or prudential check on that impulse" (cortical inhibition of motor outlets).[116] He speaks of "evidence that the emotion [cortical] increases in intensity although the expression is checked" (*ibid.*, 122), and of the "poignancy of feeling in the period of paralyzed inaction" (*ibid.*, 123). But in the denouement this disappears. There is, as Cannon says (*ibid.*, 122–123), "common testimony that intense fear, for example, may be felt, with a pathetic sense of helplessness, before any overt act occurs, and that scarcely does the appropriate behavior start than the inner tumult begins to subside and the bodily forces are directed vigorously and effectively to serviceable ends." [117] In this view the dam-

somewhat different from, the access of the motor cortex to the same centers; and that inhibition of the hypothalamic access to these centers is also independent—arising in the prefrontal area—so that it can be exercised, at least to a considerable degree, without altering the inhibitory activities of the motor cortex (antirigidity and antispasticity) and can be partially overcome (leakage) without necessarily yielding complete control of these centers to the hypothalamus.

In so far as elements of our second avenue of interaction arise from the prefrontal area it is not impossible that these are included in the cortical inhibition of the motor outlets of the hypothalamus. We have noted (p. 1131) that Le Gros Clark thinks both the tract via the septum and that via the subthalamus do so. The tract via the septum is supposed by Beattie to reach to the anterior hypothalamus. If so, it cannot serve this purpose. On the other hand, that via the subthalamus might do so. However, if that were true, we would have to suppose the inhibition to occur, not at the subthalamus, but at the beginning of the tract arriving there from the hypothalamus.

Also by way of identifying the source of this type of inhibition as the prefrontal areas, we may remind ourselves of the observations of restlessness and increased spontaneous activity after bilateral prefrontal ablation, which we noted on p. 1120 and note 43. While the authorities quoted there attributed these release phenomena to removal of transcortical inhibition of the motor cortex by the prefrontal areas, it seems more consonant with the affective nature of restlessness to suppose that its release is part and parcel of the removal of both inhibitory influences on the hypothalamus—that which reaches it directly and reduces the emotional state and that which controls its downward exterofective outflow and thereby reduces the emotional expression.

116 Or, as Gardiner, Metcalfe, and Beebe-Center put it (*166*, 362) in their interpretation of J. T. MacCurdy's thesis (see *Psychology of Emotion*, New York, 1925, especially p. 87) "the less the expression the greater the affect."

117 Cannon states in one place (*61*, 122) that "so long as the check prevails . . . the organic changes supposed to be the source of the feeling [in the James-Lange theory] are suppressed." But this effort to include cortical inhibition of the interofective expression seems neither to coincide with the facts (indicia of excitement though under motor self-control) nor to agree with his statement elsewhere (*68*, 265) that the cortex can inhibit only those bodily activities which are normally under voluntary control: "It cannot check the stormy processes of the [hypo-] thalamus which cause shivering and

ming up of excitement—an emotional state—in the hypothalamus, by reason of cortical inhibition of the subcortical motor centers to which the hypothalamus has direct access, results in an increase in the intensity of the emotional stream which rises to the cortex. Conversely, release of these motor outlets also releases the suppressed excitement.

However, this does not complete the picture. We already know what character of behavior is possible by reason of the downward flow of excitation from the hypothalamus to subcortical motor mechanisms. While, in the lower animals, this behavior is adequate, if crude, in the apes and man it is not adequate. On p. 1081 we noted the "regression of somatic patterns" that is produced by strong emotions, their primitive character showing the use of excessive force, inco-ordination, tremor, palsy, and the loss of acquired skills and language. But on p. 1088 we also noted that subcortical mechanisms are not adequate in the mature decorticated monkey (or man) to enable it to feed itself, to run or climb, or even to maintain its posture. It is clear that the regression of somatic patterns under strong emotion is due to the short-circuiting of the emotional state directly to those subcortical motor mechanisms whose activities have these characteristics. But it is equally clear that, if all the emotional state were thus short-circuited, the ape or man could not even stand up, much less run. This is only rarely the case. In its tantrum, referred to above, Jacobsen's chimpanzee rolled on the floor and beat the cage. We have all seen human beings make such displays—particularly young ones. These might be conceived to be complete short-circuiting. But far more often—nay, usually—the expression of emotional states includes behavior which is not within the competence of the subcortical motor mechanisms available directly to the hypothalamus. This observation argues that either (1) the control exercised by the cortex over the subcortical motor outlets available directly to the hypothalamus is a selective control, so that the force of the emotional state can, within limits, be canalized under cortical direction into a less crude motor pattern, or (2) a considerable part of the force of the emotional state is almost always long-circuited as emotional stream and energizes the motor cortex. While both these alternative explanations may be true to some extent, it should be said that our present knowledge does not justify us in assuming that subcortical motor mechanisms are capable of anything more precise than major synergies, even under the direction of selective cortical control; and, on the other hand, it does not now appear that the pyramidal tract, which seems to be an essential intermediary for most of those milder emotional outbursts, is available to any subcortical mechanisms whatever. We are therefore led to the tentative conclusion that, except for completely uncontrolled emotional outbursts, short-circuiting takes place only to the degree that the use of excessive force, inco-ordination, tremor, palsy, the loss of acquired skills and lan-

forcible emptying of the bladder and rectum." Or, perhaps, the first statement is only true in so far as direct cortical inhibition of the hypothalamus itself, rather than of its motor outlets, is effective. Perhaps one can "keep calm" by the first means only.

guage, etc., are observed. The rest of the somatic expression of emotion we take to be a highly energized but nevertheless long-circuited discharge, beginning as emotional stream and flowing out via the motor cortex.

In this view there is still another point at which the outflowing emotional state may be dammed up (inhibited). Our first form of cortical inhibition exerted directly on the hypothalamus is continuous, but only tempers the emotional state and does not dam it up. Our second form of cortical inhibition is exerted on the subcortical motor outlets of the hypothalamus. This inhibition, except in extreme cases, is also continuous, though perhaps never complete in real excitement. It does not, however, diminish the emotional state; it only dams it up and thus, perhaps, drives it up into the cortex. On the other hand, it appears that, again without diminution of the emotional state, damming up of the emotional stream may also occur in the region of the cortex where deliberation takes place. To the extent that the cortical motor outlets are inhibited at this point conflict arises there. And again, because the emotional stream is dammed up here, rather than allowed to flow off, the intensity of the emotional experience in the locus of consciousness is increased. But, when the conflict is resolved and the motor outflow from the cortex is permitted, this emotional experience presumably declines in intensity. At that stage, only to the extent that it surpasses the capacity of the motor outlets to drain it away would it remain intense.[118] On the other hand, whether dammed up to a certain level due to inhibition or dammed up beyond that level to a point due to lack of capacity in the outflows beyond that point, whenever "emotion [the experience] exceeds certain limits, the greater intensity is at the expense and to the detriment of intellect [deliberation]" (Bianchi, *35*, 284). As William James put it (*220*, II, 466), "it is *pent-up* emotions that 'work like madness in the brain.'" That is, if, before or after the cortical motor outlets are made available, the emotional stream ever reaches a degree of intensity sufficient to cause confusion, then the whole inhibitory capacity of the cortex is put out of commission, and the whole emotional state drains away through the subcortical motor mechanisms as well, and as fast and as far as it can. In that state, it is questionable whether enough of the long-circuited emotional stream continues even to permit acute consciousness. In other words, it is perhaps true that the intensity of this stream then drops from a degree high enough to cause the confusion which arises at the upper range of consciousness to a degree low enough to cause the confusion which arises at its lower range.

While this last form of inhibition or damming up is important for our scheme, it should not be included as an instance of corticohypothalamic control or interaction, for it occurs exclusively in the cortex. Nor should the fact that we are supposing it possible for the emotion in the cortex to

[118] Both this temporary lack of capacity and inhibition of motor outlets are covered by Janet's *théorie dynamique*. (*221*, 408) which accounts for the *énergetique de l'émotion* on the ground of "l'insufficance de l'action pour réagir à la circonstance provocatrice."

This, we recall, is the third condition, described above (p. 1146) under which what we have called delay, or even deliberation, may take place.

be drawn off via cortical motor mechanisms, as well as for the emotional state to be drawn off by subcortical motor mechanisms and thus reduce or shut off the emotional stream, lead us to forget the distinction between the two types of resulting behavior. We have already mentioned this on pp. 1166–1167 and will frequently revert to it hereafter.

So much has been said here of cortical inhibition of lower centers that it seems necessary, before leaving the topic of this form of corticohypothalamic interaction, to make clear what suppositions we are using in regard to inhibition in general. "Inhibition is a term of convenience used without exact definition in connection with a group of phenomena having certain qualities in common." "It is improper, therefore, to speak in terms implying that there is a general explanation of inhibition" (Gasser, *168*, 185). However, so far as the nervous system is concerned, "Inhibition must be a central process" (Fulton, *160*, 77); that is, it is purely a phenomenon of the central nervous system. There is no "evidence for two kinds of fibers, excitatory and inhibitory, nor for two types of ending of one type of fiber" (Gasser, *168*, 186). Moreover, "At present it is generally believed . . . that specific inhibitory impulses, even if there were specific inhibitory fibers . . . do not exist. Inhibition must, therefore, be explained in terms of processes created by the same impulses that create excitation" (Lorente de Nó, *274*, 238). At this stage in the investigation of the subject the explanation proposed by Gasser (*168*), which may be called the theory of "summation of subnormality," seems to be most satisfactory in that it requires no more than the "known properties of nervous tissue"—the "silent period" of subnormal responsiveness or raised threshold.[119] On the basis of this theory Lorente de Nó (*274*, 227) has linked c.i.s. with c.e.s. in his concept of "internuncial bombardment." This bombardment is supposed to consist in the successive arrival of impulses at a synapse due to the varying lengths of the parallel internuncial paths involved. "If the number [of parallel links involved] is small, activation of the chain may result in inhibition" (*ibid.*, 241), by reason of fractioning the volley so that the successive parts arrive at intervals longer than the effective period of summation (*ibid.*, 238) or "period of latent addition" (Gasser, *168*, 180). Thus might be maintained a continuous central inhibitory state (c.i.s.)—a continuous "summation of subnormality." On the other hand, if the number of parallel links involved is large enough, the intervals would be shorter and the result would be "sustained facilitation [central excitatory state (c.e.s.)] or discharge" (*274*, 241), depending on whether summation to threshold strength was not or was achieved.[120] Much still seems to remain obscure in this theory; but it looks promising.[121]

[119] That is, "Accumulation of subnormality in nerve is attended by augmentation and prolongation of the positive after-potential" (Gasser, *168*, 187); but this "subnormality is a matter of thresholds only; if excitation is brought to the limen, a full-sized response is obtained" (*loc. cit.*). Hence our notion of overcoming or overiding inhibition is entirely consistent with this theory.

[120] In general this corresponds approximately with Gasser's illustration (*168*, 189).

[121] It should be noted, in passing, that this theory of inhibition is of the general type

Approached from another angle—the overall viewpoint—it appears that what is called reciprocal inhibition is characteristic of all active inhibition.[122] Since, in the last analysis, the whole central nervous system is interconnected, it is obvious that the development of specific out of general activation necessarily involves canalization of impulses by shutting off all but the outlets requisite for the specific activity. In the lowest organisms excitation reverberates throughout the system. In the higher organisms sufficiently intense excitation also involves all outlets, even those which are antagonistic to each other.[123] Canalization is achieved by inhibition of antagonists and ultimately by inhibition of alternatives—that is, by recipro-

---

of "interference" theories, rather than "chemical" theories, of central excitatory *vs.* inhibitory processes. See, for instance, Fulton's excellent summary up to 1926, in Chapter XIV of his *Muscular Contraction* (*158*). It does not require an "I substance." On the other hand, it is entirely compatible with the supposition that nerve impulses are more nearly analogous to a "train of powder" than to electrical phenomena, and are thus fundamentally chemical in nature.

[122] This is not unlike the thesis developed by William McDougall, though with one important difference. In his original article in *Brain* (*281*, 153) on "The Nature of the Inhibitory Processes within the Nervous System," McDougall concluded that there are, for vertebrate skeletal muscle, no special inhibitory fibers nor passage of inhibitory impulse along the motor nerves (see also *284*, 251) such as there are for invertebrates and for the vascular-visceral (autonomic) system of vertebrates. Therefore, "inhibition of skeletal muscles in vertebrates consists always in a cutting off or diminution within the nervous system of the excitatory impulses issuing to the muscles along motor nerves" (*281*, 161). Since there is no spontaneous excitation in the motor nerves, inhibition must occur in the source of their excitation—that is, in the central system, the internuncial fibers or their synapses (*ibid.*, 162). It is thus a feature of integration (*ibid.*, 162). He also concludes that all mental, and therefore all, inhibition is the "negative or complementary result of a process of increased excitation in some other part" (*ibid.*, 169)—that is, it is reciprocal. From this he derives a "drainage theory," similar to James's, which is an unnecessary addition that we do not accept. His hypothesis is "that inhibitory effects in the nervous system result from a process of competition between the inhibiting and the inhibited tract [i.e., reciprocal], the former draining to itself a part of the energy liberated in the latter" (*ibid.*, 191). He supports this theory in his review of Sherrington's *Integrative Action* (*282*, 376); and again, in *Physiological Psychology* (*283*), inhibition of any neural system is "always a correlative effect of the excitement of some other system [i.e., reciprocal], the effect of drainage of the former by the latter" (*281*, 164).

In his *Social Psychology*, his psychological thesis conforms: "We control involuntary tendencies either by innervating [exciting] antagonistic muscles, or by directing our attention elsewhere by an effort of will; that is to say, by concentrating the energy of the mind and nervous system in one direction we withdraw it from, or prevent its flowing in [reciprocal inhibition], any other direction" (*284*, 251). Nevertheless, in consciousness, the "felt impulse" "assumes the character of an explicit desire or aversion," and this, even when inhibited as to its outlet; for "the conative aspect of the psychical process always retains the unique quality of an impulse to activity, even though the instinctive activity has been modified by habitual control" (*ibid.*, 44).

His suggestion of control by excitation of antagonistic muscles is worthy of special note. We have all observed the peculiar rigidity which, in young children, accompanies the exercise of self-control. His supposition of the presence in consciousness of the inhibited impulse to action is entirely consonant with our view of deliberation (i.e., conscious inhibition).

[123] This is Hughlings Jackson's theory of convulsions, already referred to.

cal inhibition.[124] As Frolov says (*157*, 140), this means of canalization, inhibition, is a later development both phylogenetically and ontogenetically. And it remains "a more fragile process than . . . excitation." Pavlov himself called reciprocal inhibition "external inhibition." He thought his experiments indicated that excitation irradiates and then concentrates in the areas of the cortex affected. Weak or very strong stimuli spread rapidly over the area and concentrate slowly if at all, whereas average strength stimuli concentrate at once (optimal functioning; Frolov's interpretation, *157*, 134). This concentration, or the corresponding irradiation of inhibition, constituted his "internal inhibition."[125] These irradiations and concentrations, if they are facts, would be in accord with Gasser's "summation of subnormality," and particularly with the differential results of "internuncial bombardment" contemplated in the version of Lorente de Nó.

At any rate, if we interpret, as I think we must, the inhibitory influence of the cortex upon the hypothalamus and its outlets as reciprocal inhibition, we assume by that fact that it is effective in proportion to the *concentration* of activity in the cortex itself. It is a by-product of what is going on in the cortex. The cortex, then, is not conceived as an autonomous agency for control. It is rather an agency responding to an enormous complex of influences similar to, but far weaker than, the simple influences which excite the subcortical centers, as well as to the forceful but simple forms of excitation reaching it indirectly from those centers themselves; but it responds to the combination in a different and more narrowly canalized (differentiated) way. The very fact that its activities are more canalized argues that its reciprocal inhibitory effects on lower centers will be stronger and more precise than those characteristic of the lower parts of the system. And the very fact that, in man at least, something is always going on in the cortex when it is awake (and perhaps slightly when it is asleep), even when no overt motor reaction is apparent, argues, too, for continuous inhibition (c.i.s.) of the lower centers. But, in these suppositions, we are assuming nothing that is not characteristic of the central nervous system in general. We are, however, assuming something else. At this stage of our investigation these statements will have to serve; for, at this stage, we are devoting ourselves to examining and interpreting a certain limited body of evidence. When other evidence is admitted, in Chapter 6, it will appear that we have as yet no fully adequate explanation of concentration and canalization of activity in the cortex nor, without that, any explanation of its capacity to inhibit lower centers.

[124] It should be noted that Sherrington originally used the term to apply only to the inhibition of antagonists. However, it seems equally appropriate for the inhibition of alternatives. The latter, on the basis of Hughlings Jackson's concept of differentiation, would be expected chiefly in the cortex. Pavlov seems to have assumed that his "external" and "internal" inhibition take place, at least chiefly, in the cortex.

[125] As we have suggested above, his internal inhibition may be the same thing as loss of "interest." As such it may well be the same phenomenon as "external inhibition," except that it occurs at an earlier (not yet motor) stage in the central process, the stage at which the representations and re-representations of the external world are being endowed with, or not endowed with, or are losing, emotional content and are therefore gaining, or not gaining, or losing, the force necessary to produce a motor reaction.

Release or Excitation by Conditioned Stimuli. Up to this point we have considered only the negative (inhibitory) aspects of the control exercised by the cortex over the hypothalamus. As noted above, Bard supposes that the cortex can also excite the hypothalamus.[126] This is one of the ways of explaining the effect of conditioned stimuli in producing emotional states, which we shall now consider. It is therefore necessary to proceed to the examination of the second and third forms of control exercised in general by higher over lower centers—facilitation and excitation—which were included in our synopsis on p. 1177, but were passed over at that point. But before doing so, it is necessary to state the case for conditioned stimuli. Hitherto, we have supposed that emotional states, like the rest of the excitations of the hypothalamus, are produced, and are only produced, by excitors reaching these subcortical centers directly via the blood or less directly via those parts of the neural afferent system that culminate in the paleothalamus (midline nuclei, etc.), when they are transmitted to the hypothalamus by way of the periventricular system (see pp. 1095–1097). And we carefully distinguished all these strictly speaking unconditioned stimuli (even including bright light and loud sound) from those stimuli which are construed to go to the cortex and there become sensation. But experiments with conditioning have demonstrated that innumerable other stimuli which are only conveyed by the somatic sensory system or from the distance receptors are, after learning, also capable of evoking the various forms of hypothalamic activity, even including the general excitement of emotional states. The question then arises how the impulses from these stimuli reach, or are made to affect, the hypothalamus, if they do. The supposition that they do not—that emotional states can be established in the cortex without hypothalamic involvement, seems definitely to be rejected.[127] It is contrary to all the evidence as to the nature and locus of the emotional state.[128]

There seem to be three possible known ways in which the hypothalamus might be influenced by stimuli which cannot reach it directly. The first

[126] At first this was said in a less explicit way (Bard, *19*, 307): "When an originally indifferent stimulus becomes an emotional stimulus, that is to say, when it acquires the property of eliciting diencephalic discharge [conditioning], it does so by virtue of the discriminative powers of the cortex."

In Cannon's and Bard's original scheme (see for the clearest exposition Bard, *19*, 304) afferent impulses arriving from below over path 1, if they have no direct emotional appeal, are long-circuited in the thalamus over path 1^1 to the cortex. If, however, in the cortex, they arouse a conditioned response, which inactivates (releases) the cortical inhibition upon the short-circuit, exercised over path 3, they are then short-circuited as they would have been in the beginning if they had had direct emotional appeal. As a result, whether directly or by this release, they proceed downward over path 2 to the effector mechanisms available at this level. And, as they do so, they also flow upward over path 4 to the cortex as the emotional stream which is thus simultaneous and associated with the original purely sensory report over path 1^1. While this appears now to be too simple a diagram, it represents the pioneer effort and still, in certain respects, forms the basis of the present interpretation.

[127] We may cite Bard on that; see note 126, above.

[128] Even Papez's supplementary thesis as to emotions originating in the cortex, which we shall discuss below (note 134), assumes the state to be excited in the hypothalamus.

two would constitute "release phenomena"—that is, they would consist in the withdrawal of inhibition. Only the third involves excitation of the hypothalamus from the cortex.

1. Under the first possibility it would be supposed that the long-circuiting of strictly sensory stimuli to the cortex is not a matter of anatomical structure, but that it is due to cortical inhibition of the paths between the neothalamus and the hypothalamus—an inhibition which supposedly could be withdrawn. As we noted on p. 1131, the dorsomedial nucleus of the thalamus, which Le Gros Clark takes to be "a link between" the hypothalamus and the prefrontal area of the cortex, receives also from the lateral nuclear mass of the thalamus, which is the relay station for somatic paths to the sensory cortex. It is therefore conceivable that the prefrontal cortex can permit the short-circuiting to the hypothalamus of impulses normally reaching the sensory cortex only, by relaxing inhibition in this connection between the thalamic relay station and the dorsomedial nucleus.[129] This would be supposed to occur when the prefrontal cortex had related the external stimulus to an organismic interest and thus invested the pattern with "interest"—that is, when the external stimulus had become conditioned. In this way such a conditioned stimulus would come to excite the hypothalamus directly. The difficulty with this hypothesis is that established conditioned reflexes continue after bilateral ablation of the prefrontal cortex. If it is that area exclusively which controls the dorsomedial nucleus—and this appears to be the case—then this method of selective admission of conditioned stimuli does not seem probable.

2. The second possible way is by the withdrawal of cortical inhibition over the hypothalamus of the types 1a or 1b already discussed, but here conceived to occur as a cortical response to the conditioned stimulus. In this way the conditioned stimulus is not supposed itself to reach or to excite the hypothalamus. Rather, the effect is even more purely a "release" phenomenon. This has been the chief and is still a common explanation of the phenomenon. The first difficulty with this supposition is the same as with the previous one. So far as we have been able to explore the subject, it would appear that this type of inhibition over the hypothalamus is exercised by the prefrontal area. But the prefrontal area cannot be responsible for the release of reactions to *established* conditioned stimuli. In the second place, even if it were supposed that other areas of the cortex also inhibit the hypothalamus and that responses to conditioned stimuli are due to releases of this other inhibition, the explanation, while it would be adequate in some cases, would still be subject to great if not insuperable difficulties in others. For this explanation requires the assumption that all the unconditioned reaction patterns which are innate in the hypothalamus are po-

[129] This would be in addition to the control by the prefrontal area of the afferent material reaching the hypothalamus from the paleothalamus—inhibition of the type 1a—which we recognized as a possibility on p. 1180. Of course we would assume that these impulses were not yet completely organized at the thalamic level and, therefore, that the short-circuiting was not identical with the concurrent long-circuiting.

tentially in a continuous state of excitation—that is, that all are continuously receiving excitor material from below which, when cortical inhibition is selectively withdrawn from any one center or set of centers, will immediately make this center or these centers active.[130] As we shall see, such a condition seems possible in the case of internal wants. If an animal is not hungry, it is neither possible for a new conditioned reflex to food to be established nor for an old one to be reproduced. In other words, if there is, at the time, no internal excitor to be released, this putative relaxation of inhibition due to a conditioned stimulus does not result in a reaction. But it is difficult to conceive the same condition to be true in the case of the quasi-external wants. For instance, are we to suppose that the fear and the rage mechanisms are in a continual state of potential excitation? [131] It would be necessary to assume that they are; for it is possible to produce these reactions instantly and at any time by means of a conditiond stimulus which certainly cannot reach the hypothalamus directly—i.e., patterns of impulses which produce "retino-ocular" or "audito-articulatory" sensorimotor responses in the cortex and only there.[132] But, while the evidence we have assembled above indicates that the fear and the rage reactions are more readily induced when cortical inhibition is absent (in the decorticate animal), it appears that, even then, some sort of non-continuous stimulus appreciable in the hypothalamus is necessary to set them off. They do not occur immediately and continuously when the inhibition is removed. They may be called "chronic," but they are not literally chronic. It is these facts which make the "release" explanation appear incomplete, at least, as to conditioned reflexes.

3. The third possibility is that the cortex has the capacity of directly exciting—or facilitating excitation in—the hypothalamus over one or more of the three, or four, interconnections or avenues we have outlined above (pp. 1131–1133), and that it does so, presumably, when it receives a pattern of impulses from a stimulus which has been conditioned—that is, a stimulus which the organism has learned is related to one of its wants—internal or external. Let us consider the four avenues in turn.

a. There is, first, the interconnection running from the prefrontal area via the dorsomedial nucleus. For the same reasons cited under (1) above this does not seem to be a possible route.

b. There is, second, the interconnection running from the hippocampus via the fornix to the mammillary bodies. Since, as noted in note 27 above,

130 The first possible way (above) stands on its own feet. It assumes that the conditioned stimulus itself excites the hypothalamus and that the only part the cortex plays is to permit access to the hypothalamus. The second possible way does not stand on its own feet. Like the first, it assumes withdrawal of inhibition; but, unlike the first, it offers no explanation of the excitor which is released.

131 It is for this reason that we must dismiss, as I think he has done himself, Bard's earlier supposition (*19*, 307) that, when the suitable stimulus becomes conditioned, the cortex releases the diencephalic rage mechanism.

132 Unless these patterns in their incomplete form in the thalamus can be short-circuited to the hypothalamus—a supposition we have seen reason to doubt.

severance of the fornix does not alter the process of conditioned reflexes either new or old and even when olfactory, this is obviously not the route which conditioned corticofugal impulses travel to excite the hypothalamus.

c. There is, third, the miscellaneous group of paths afferent to the hypothalamus and running directly or indirectly from various regions of the cortex, and constituting our second avenue of interaction. In so far as these paths rise in olfactory regions or in the frontal cortex (prefrontal, premotor, and motor areas)—and these are the sources generally assigned (see p. 1131)—it hardly seems possible that they serve the purpose we are considering. The olfactory tracts are clearly out; the prefrontal tracts are subject to the same difficulty recited above; and it would appear more likely that any tracts from the two motor areas serve the purpose of coordinating the hypothalamus with motor patterns, preparing or already under way, as will be outlined in the next section.

d. By a process of elimination we conclude that the most probable path for the function here in question is the remaining avenue—that is, the part of our third avenue of interaction constituted by the system of fibers running in the reverse direction from the tracts to which we have assigned the stream of awakeness and emotion. These are the tracts rising in the gyrus cinguli and passing thence by way of the anterior nuclei of the thalamus to the mammillary bodies in the hypothalamus. But there is a more positive reason for this conclusion. We have assumed that the process of conditioning consists in a synthesis between some element or elements of the current or retained cortical representation of the external world and some element of the emotional stream—between the external and the internal environments; in other words, that these sensory elements are invested with "interest" when they become related to an organismic interest, a want, or emotion. We have assumed that the chief agency for establishing these syntheses is the prefrontal cortex; but we have also recognized that, once established, the prefrontal area is not essential to their maintenance; that they are then relegated to other cortical areas. If, then, this synthesis between elements of the two streams reaching the cortex, the sensory and the emotional, is wholly intracortical and remains so, does it not seem most probable that the emotional content with which a sensory presentation is invested, if it is capable of reacting upon its original source at all, does so through the same agency by way of which it arrived in the cortex in the first place—namely the gyrus cinguli? Furthermore, if such an emotionally endowed pattern of cortical excitation must be appreciated in consciousness if it is to be effective as a conditioned stimulus to subcortical mechanisms—and this seems to be the usual case—the point at which this appreciation apparently occurs—the gyrus cinguli—would also naturally be the strategic point determining whether or not counter-excitation of the original source of the emotional stream was or was not to take place.

The energetic relations of this seemingly most plausible of the possible schemes must now be considered. We may suppose that the degree of intensity of emotional content with which cortical elements of the sensorimotor system, present and retained, are endowed varies over a wide range. And this intensity may vary according to the different kinds of emotional endowment as well as within the kinds. In the first place, we might suppose that this endowment, in the case of representations invested with the "interest" of the bodily or internal wants, is always insufficient to produce, by itself, the corresponding emotional state of hunger, etc., in the hypothalamus. This is, I think, true of all the internal wants. These, then, would require, to produce their particular hypothalamic reaction, sufficient reinforcement from the normal excitors rising from bodily sources (the innate stimuli) to raise them above the threshold. That is, we may assume, on the one hand, that, of the two subliminal excitations, the normal internal one from the body may be subliminal due to its own insufficiency at the moment, or even due to the mild continuous cortical inhibition that we have supposed to be exercised by the prefrontal area upon the hypothalamus or its afferent sources and which raises the threshold. However, when the other, the conditioned stimulus, is delivered, though by itself it is merely capable of facilitation, nevertheless when the two are combined they become supraliminal, and cortical inhibition is overcome. On the other hand, if this cortical inhibition is withdrawn or is non-existent, and is not merely overcome, the threshold will be lowered and the emotional state produced will be more intense.[133] If we credit the accounts of abnormal appetites among bilateral prefrontal primates when the inhibition is non-existent, we might suppose that, in normal cases, specific withdrawal of inhibition in response to a conditioned stimulus assists the process (i.e., that it is to this extent a release phenomenon). However, I find no evidence as yet indicating that the withdrawal of inhibition by the prefrontal area occurs in this specific way. In the second place, we might suppose the emotional endowment conferred on sensorimotor elements by reason of what we have called quasi-external wants—rage, fear, etc.—to be always of sufficient intensity to create the corresponding emotional state in the hypothalamus without being supplemented from below. At any rate, it appears to be the fact that all these latter emotional states can be aroused by conditioned stimuli from the external world (distance receptors) alone, while none of the emotional states corresponding to internal wants can be aroused by such stimuli alone, if no variation from homeostasis exists at the moment in the related respect. In the case of quasi-external wants, then, we find it necessary to reject the hypothesis of specific "release." Nevertheless, we must concede that, even in these cases, when cortical inhibition is impossible (decorticate), the reaction to such external stimuli as can be short-circuited to the hypothalamus is more violent, so that it is probable that, even in the normal organism, withdrawal

[133] As Bard puts it (*19*, 307), speaking only of unconditioned emotional stimuli which, "if adequate" in intensity, "are capable of directly exciting diencephalic discharge," such discharge can occur "in spite of cortical inhibition." But they work more violently in its absence.

of such inhibition may, in extreme intensity, play a part in the process.

Summary. What we end up with, then, is the following hypothesis which, in the present state of our knowledge, can be no more than the most plausible of several possibilities. The interaction of the prefrontal areas of the cortex upon the hypothalamus appears to be of two kinds: (1) A very limited and variable but continuous inhibition (raised threshold) in the hypothalamus itself or, possibly, of the tracts in or from the paleo-thalamus whose afferent impulses constitute the neural excitors of the hypothalamus; (2) A very powerful but variable (capacity for) inhibition of the motor (somatic) outlets of the hypothalamus which can nevertheless be overcome, in part (partial short-circuiting or leakage) and, in great excitement, as a whole (complete short-circuiting), which, to the extent it is not overcome, dams up and long-circuits the excitation as emotional experience, and which is developed with maturity and practice (self-control). The interaction of the sensorimotor areas of the cortex upon the hypothalamus, perhaps directly but probably indirectly via so-called "association" areas, seems also to be of two kinds or degrees. Sensorimotor patterns, current or even revived, which have become endowed with emotional content ("interest") can excite, or participate in exciting, the corresponding emotional state in the hypothalamus. In the case of the internal wants this is limited to facilitation (i.e., is subliminal); in the case of quasi-external wants it is sufficient by itself.

Stated more fully, and tying this in with previous conclusions, we suppose that the hypothalamus—the highest level of the old brain—is normally excited from below by excitors, humoral and neural, which create in it emotional states of various patterns and intensities; that these emotional states are potential reactions to present wants—that is, to variations from homeostasis in respect of the internal or the external environment (internal and quasi-external wants); that the hypothalamus itself is normally subject to a limited degree of continuous inhibition which raises its thresholds and thus prevents or limits its excitation by these excitors; that, differentiating this inhibition from that which is a concomitant of active motor patterns in the motor and premotor areas of the cortex (see next section), this inhibition is exercised, at least chiefly, by the prefrontal area of the cortex; that, when a sensorimotor pattern, new or old, has become related—probably through the intervention of the prefrontal area—to an organismic interest (want), it is invested in some degree with the particular kind of emotional content belonging to the latter; that, thereafter, so long as it retains this endowment ("interest"), it has the capacity of exciting the hypothalamus to some extent in its particular emotional pattern; that this secondary form of excitor operates from the cortex down, probably via an avenue which parallels that followed by the rising emotional stream; that the emotional state in the hypothalamus, roused when the excitors from above, or those from below, or both, exceed the raised threshold in the hypothalamus itself (overcome direct inhibition), may still be denied outlet to the subcortical motor mechanisms available to the hypothalamus at its own level (the other kind of prefrontal inhibition) and also, by the process of deliberation (conflict), to the cortical motor mechanisms; that to this extent it is confined and is felt as emotion (conscious experience) in the cortical area of which consciousness is a concomitant (probably the gyrus cinguli); that this emotion, operating transcortically, if it is sufficiently intense, may cause the withdrawal of direct inhibition of the hypothalamus by the prefrontal areas and thus add to the effective intensity of the emotional state and of the emotional experience; that, if in these ways the emotional stream transmitted transcortically reaches a degree of intensity which causes confusion, "excortication" occurs, even the prefrontal inhibition of the subcortical motor outlets of the hypothalamus is withdrawn, and the emotional stream is drained off by short-circuiting into primitive behavior patterns—all of which may also occur, in lesser degrees and in the form of leakage, without complete "excortication"; and, finally, that, in general and at normal levels, the intensity of the emotional state which is excited by internal wants is normally less than that excited by quasi-external wants, so that the intensity of the emotional endowment in their corresponding sensorimotor patterns, new and old, is therefore also less, with the result that those patterns related to quasi-external wants are sufficient to excite their respective emotional states alone, while those related to the internal wants are only capable of doing so if they are reinforced by the internal excitor (i.e., if the present want then exists).[134]

This hypothesis, drawn from the particular body of evidence we have been considering, by no means stands alone. As we proceed, it will, in part, serve as a basis for, and in part be supplemented by, other constructions. The interpretation of the conditioning process, here outlined, will be elaborated and reconciled with experimental studies of the conditioning process itself in Chapter 3, and then will be viewed in another aspect in Chapters 5 and 6 and Appendix III Section C. The whole scheme will also be combined with its apparently necessary supplement in Chapters 5 and 6. But, there, we have to rely on a wholly different character of evidence and of inference, for which, according to our inductive method, a different approach is needed.

The Source of Emotion. Three other schemes covering this general ground should probably be mentioned before leaving this subject.

In Papez's original presentation (*315*), much of which we have used, he supposed that there were two sources of emotion, the hypothalamic and psychic. The latter emotions, he believed, are built in the hippocampus, transmitted thence by the fornix to the mammillary bodies from which they enter the projection to the gyrus cinguli already described. Since we have found it necessary to reject the fornix as the tract conveying excitatory effects of conditioned stimuli, and since we see no reason to suppose that emotional states arise from cortical sources except as a result of conditioned stimuli, we find it impossible to use this part of his suggestion. And that, in turn, means that we are left with

[134] For a brief discussion of other theories on this subject, see supplementary statement on "The Source of Emotion," below.

no known function which can as yet be assigned to the fornix, though on morphological grounds alone it is quite evident that its function must be an important one.

I find it very difficult to construe Head's original theory in terms of our present knowledge of these regions. But it appears to have been an exclusively thalamic theory. He saw (*183*, 597–601) that the thalamus "contains the termination of all secondary [afferent] paths." He states that it regroups these sensory impulses and sends them either to the sensory cortex "for its more discriminative aspects" (*ibid.*, 664–665) or to the "grey matter" of the thalamus, "which is associated mainly with the affective side of sensation" (*ibid.*, 664–665). The "grey matter" is the "essential organ," and that is now construed to have been the dorsomedial nucleus (see Le Gros Clark, *85*, 102–103). The "lateral part" (? the lateral nuclear mass) which is presumably "its [the thalamus'] receptive mechanism" (*ibid.*, 664), where integration on functional lines is completed (*ibid.*, 664–665), is also the organ for cortical control (*ibid.*, 597–601). This "essential organ of the optic thalamus" is the center for "sensations of a change in state" (*ibid.*, 664). "It responds to all stimuli capable of evoking either pleasure or discomfort, or consciousness of a change of state" other than pleasure or discomfort (*ibid.*, 601 and 598). "The feeling-tone of somatic or visceral sensation is the product of [this] thalamic activity" (*ibid.*, 601); "the greater the affective reaction to any stimulus the more certain is its thalamic appeal" (*ibid.*, 664), and, on the contrary, "the fact that a sensation is devoid of feeling-tone shows that the impulses which underlie its production make no thalamic appeal" (*ibid.*, 601). The supposition that "each of the two great receptive centres [the essential organ and the sensory cortex] became almost exclusively occupied with the underlying basis of either the qualitative or projectional aspect of sensation" (*ibid.*, 809) makes it necessary for him to suppose that "the essential organ of the optic thalamus is the centre of consciousness for certain elements of sensation" (*ibid.*, 601)—that is, for the qualitative elements possessing feeling-tone. Finally "all stimuli which appeal to the thalamic centre have a high threshold" (*ibid.*, 609), presumably because of cortical inhibition. "Visceral insensibility" is a function of this. There is no "absence of afferent impulses"; they merely do not reach consciousness (*ibid.*, 747). But, under abnormal conditions they "can break through" (*ibid.*, 744). Or the inhibition can be withdrawn: "for with the release of the essential centre of the optic thalamus from control [by the cortex], all sensory impulses capable of exciting affective reactions exercise a preponderating influence. Sensation becomes overloaded with feeling-tone and pleasure or discomfort are evoked to an abnormal degree" (*ibid.*, 805–806).

While this pioneer proposal was most suggestive, it is hardly necessary to point out the respects in which it is now inadequate or in which the evidence presently available makes modifications necessary.

It seems also to be impossible to accept Walker's scheme as proposed. He thinks that the main medial nucleus of the thalamus (presumably the dorsomedial) is the "mechanism for the integration of synthesized somatosensory and visceral impulses from the adjoining lateral nuclear mass and midline nuclei respectively, and their relay to the cortex of the prefrontal region (*416*, 263). If so, it can hardly also be possible that this integration "has an affective quality which varies depending upon the mixture of its component factors" (*loc. cit.*); for the prefrontal area cannot be the region for the appreciation of "affective quality"—on the grounds described above in connection with bilateral ablation of the prefrontal areas—though it can and probably does sample this integration or its hypothalamic effects.

He thinks that it is probably not true, as Head and Holmes supposed (34 *Brain*, 1911), that the dorsomedial nucleus is "able to appreciate those modalities of sensation having an affective quality"; but makes the equally difficult suggestion that it is an "integrating center for somatic sensory and visceral impulses" (not "auditory and visual") "not as sensory modalities but as sensory concepts" (*416*, 245).

Developing an idea of Lhermitte and Cornil, he then suggests that, perhaps, "between these two systems—that which terminates in the lateral nuclear mass and that ending in the midline structures—there is normally an intimate relationship so arranged that the impulses through the former reach consciousness, whereas those passing through the midline structures are rarely consciously appreciated. The control of this selection probably resides within the lateral nuclear mass of the thalamus" (*ibid.*, 272). When the latter is injured, the impulses passing through the midline are short-circuited and may be appreciated there, or in the hypothalamus, or even in the opposite cortex. "Such impulses have an affective tone and are readily influenced [*sic*] by emotional states" (*ibid.*, 273). Again, as in Head's theory, this seems to confine to the thalamus a complex and extensive process which more probably embraces many elements of the forebrain, cortical as well as subcortical.

H. EFFECTOR RELATIONS BETWEEN THE CORTEX AND THE HYPOTHALAMUS

1. INTEROFECTIVE

The rest of the system of interaction between cortex and hypothalamus —the indirect portion—seems to be one purely for co-ordination, strictly speaking. The evidence we have adduced above indicates that the hypothalamus as well as the cortex has access to the extrapyramidal part of the motor (somatic) system. That situation makes it necessary that, when the motor areas of the cortex are producing overt activity, the exterofective outlets of the hypothalamus should be closed, or at least selectively controlled. This form of reciprocal inhibition is different from that already assumed to be exercised by the prefrontal areas:—it is only occasional; it appears to be exercised directly by the motor and premotor areas; it is normal long-circuiting. On the other hand, recent experimental work has also demonstrated that the motor areas of the cortex are themselves capable of originating or suppressing interofective activities, that they have means of reaching the autonomic system either directly or indirectly (via the hypothalamus), and, therefore, that there must be co-ordination between the two effector sources—the two highest levels—in that system as well.[1]

Considering first these effector relations in the interofective field, we may cite the (sometimes contradictory) conclusions of investigators as

[1] As Ectors *et al.* (*131*, 798) put it, "The hypothalamus, like frontal areas 4 and 6 [motor and premotor] . . . , thus seems to be both sympathetic and motor" (quoted with approval by Hinsey, *199*, 669).

to some of the functions. Experimenting with the heat control mechanisms, Pinkston *et al.* (*326*) found that the cutaneous vasomotor reflexes are altered by decortication. The result, in dogs and cats, was chronic vasodilatation and no vasoconstriction in response to cold (*ibid.*, 530). From this they deduce that, in dogs and cats, tonic vasoconstriction of the skin and reflex vasoconstriction on exposure to cold are of cortical origin (*loc. cit.* and Pinkston and Rioch, *327*, 49). On the other hand, observation of human beings and experiments on monkeys seem to show that the case is different there. Cortical lesions with monkeys never produce cutaneous vasodilatation, but instead produce chronic cutaneous vasoconstriction, which Pinkston and Rioch (*327*, 53) construe as a release phenomenon. Their lesions involved areas 4 and 6. With complete ablation the results were the same (*ibid.*, 54). Most studies of human beings confirm (*ibid.*, 53). Kennard (*234*, 543) got the same results, but identifies the premotor area (6) more particularly as the source (*ibid.*, 544). She also got a lag in vasodilatation in response to heat, but prompt vasoconstriction in response to cold (*ibid.*, 544). Fulton (*159*, 179) confirms Kennard's results in all respects. Both Kennard (*234*, 543) and Fulton (*159*, 181) assume the resulting chronic vasoconstriction to be a release phenomenon. Thus all three of these authorities conclude that, in monkeys and men, the cortical influence on cutaneous vasoconstriction is normally inhibitory.

Other vasomotor effects resulting in increased blood pressure and associated with increased heart rate have also been reported as a result of direct stimulation of certain regions in the cortex of cats and monkeys.[2] Crouch and Thompson (*98*, 11) report these results associated with dilatation of the pupil upon stimulation of the frontal or sigmoid gyri of cats. Hoff and Green (*204*) got increased blood pressure and heart rate from stimulating certain regions in the cortex of both cats and monkeys (*ibid.*, 420), a decline of pressure from other parts and a slowing of the heart from a few (*ibid.*, 421). Their results "cannot be due to delayed effect of muscular contraction," [3] but "clearly demonstrate the existence of two distinct cortical mechanisms. The first of these exerts control over somatic movement as shown by the normal motor response to stimulation. . . . The second influences vasomotor and other visceral activities . . . [even] in the absence of any somatic activity." Probably "afferent impulses which activate the somatic efferent will also affect the visceral efferent mecha-

[2] In spite of its contradictory nature it is worthy of note that Penfield and Boldrey (*324*, 424) found "no valid evidence of a vasomotor center on the convexity of the cerebral cortex" of human patients.

[3] Their results seem to dispose of the supposition of Kabat *et al.* (*229*) when they observed the same, but somewhat erratic, phenomena (*ibid.*, 935, 939), that the rises of blood pressure "were secondary to the somatic movements that result" (*ibid.*, 950), though they thought the depressor effects were not (*ibid.*, 953). Certainly there are also such secondary pressor effects, probably short-circuited within the autonomic system. But these cortical mechanisms appear to correspond to those Kabat *et al.* find in the hypothalamus, where increases of blood pressure are "independent of movement of skeletal muscles," and either can be initiated there without the other (*ibid.*, 950). For further evidence on this point see pp. 1206–1207.

nism" (*ibid.*, 420).[4] Further experiments (Green and Hoff, *175*) show that the pressor effects are not, or not wholly, cutaneous; for, as Fulton expresses it in his comment (*160*, 473), what happens is a "direct shift of blood from the visceral to the muscular bed." Thus it is justifiable to interpret the phenomenon as Hoff and Green did (*204*, 421). "There is a mechanism by which the cortex can influence the state of the cardiovascular system, and . . . through this mechanism the cortex may bring about a finer adjustment of the activity of the heart and circulation in accordance with the exigencies of the external environment and the immediate activities of the skeletal musculature." Whether the mechanism operates directly or via the hypothalamus is as yet uncertain (*204*, 419).[5] At present the latter seems more probable.

Since the chronic cutaneous vasoconstriction noted by Pinkston *et al.*, by Kennard and by Fulton, above, was caused by lesions of areas 4 and 6, chiefly 6, which are the motor regions, and since the rise of blood pressure noted by Crouch and Thompson and by Hoff and Green may be interpreted in the light of Green and Hoff's experiment as due in larger part to visceral vasoconstriction incidental to the shift of blood to the muscular bed, it seems not improbable that all the foregoing refer to a single phenomenon. In this interpretation, one mechanism in the motor regions of the cortex would be supposed, when the other (the motor) mechanism is quiescent, to exert an inhibitory influence on the vasoconstrictor system, or those parts of it which control the blood vessels in the skin and viscera. If these cortical regions are removed, this inhibitory influence would, of course, cease. On the other hand, when the motor mechanism in the motor regions is active, or is about to become active, the corresponding inhibitory mechanism there ceases to operate and the inhibition is withdrawn. In this view, the inhibition may be imposed upon the hypothalamus or directly upon lower centers controlled jointly with the hypothalamus. Again the former seems more probable, at present, in the case of this particular function.

There is another way in which the cortex seems to play a part in influencing blood pressure. Darrow's "studies of blood pressure in combination with records of other physiological changes have shown that the continuous blood pressure record is affected by 'disturbing ideas' more definitely than any of the other easily recorded autonomic changes" (*102*, 567). "Apparently blood pressure rise is relatively specific for those disturbing conflicting excitatory perceptual influences which may be con-

[4] But the dual system explains why the "higher tension of the blood in the arteries develops before the exercise is actually going on" (Cannon, *66*, 161), so that the activating of the sympathetic system incidental to voluntary movement (*ibid.*, 159) is not precisely caused by "nerve impulses from the cerebral cortex which initiate the effort itself" (*ibid.*, 148). The same afferent impulses may initiate both, but the efferent impulses are independent of each other.

[5] Kabat *et al.* (*229*, 953) suggest that the depressor pathway, "apparently cortical in origin," runs to the rostral end of the diencephalon and perhaps operates only to inhibit the pressor mechanism of the hypothalamus.

veyed by symbols or other stimuli involving a threat to the physical or intellectual equilibrium of the individual" (*ibid.*, 571). Here "the role of the cortex appears to be that (1) of differentiating stimulus patterns and (2) of maintaining an appropriate inhibitory control" (*ibid.*, 569). But the emotional excitation "is definitely subcortical" (*ibid.*, 568) and is assumed by him to be a release phenomenon (*ibid.*, 572). In the light of the hypothesis established in the previous section, we would construe this to be one of the subtlest indications of the excitation of an emotional state in the hypothalamus as the result of a conditioned stimulus appreciable only in the cortex, but invested there with some specific emotional endowment capable of arousing (or possibly releasing) the hypothalamus over the path described. If that interpretation is correct, this is an instance of direct interaction of the type described in section G 4, and not one of co-ordination of effector relations. If so, it becomes necessary to distinguish changes in blood pressure or other vasomotor effects which are part of the adaptation to the motor activities, impending or actual, that are initiated in the cortex—whether or not these changes are effected through the hypothalamus—from similar changes which result from and indicate an emotional state in the hypothalamus—whether the stimulus causing this state comes from below (unconditioned) or from the cortex (conditioned).

While the question is still open as far as experimental proof is concerned, I am inclined to think that the same distinction must be made with regard to the psychogalvanic reflex (palmar sweating), which we have already referred to on pp. 1054 and 1065, and which must now be examined more closely. Among experimental psychologists, though not without dispute,[6] this reflex has been taken to be an index of "affective tone," which our hypothesis describes as originating in an emotional state in the hypothalamus.[7] Since their experiments have dealt with this phenomenon in human beings, in which we are most interested, it is well to consider these results first. For that purpose we will use a restudy made by Wechsler, which is thorough if not recent.[8] He concludes that this "reflex is to be

[6] E. G. Landis (37 *Psychol. Rev.*, 1930, 381), who disputes the validity of the p.g.r. as an index of affective tone, on the ground that it is also the indirect effect of other sympathetic reactions, admits that it is "associated with the secretion of sweat" and that it is "under the control of the sympathetic division of the autonomic system" (*ibid.*, 394). His conclusion that it has "only a very limited psychological meaning" (*ibid.*, 396) would seem to me to have no bearing on our point, in view of Wechsler's exclusion (see below) of these other causative sympathetic reactions, even if it were better warranted than it is.

[7] Other "internal" indices have also been correlated quantitatively with the degree of emotion, or "affective tone." The procedure of L. N. Ziegler and B. S. Levine (169 *Am. J. Med. Sci.*, 1925, 68) demonstrated a rough correspondence between the variations from basal metabolism and the "unpleasantness" of revived memories of war experiences among veterans, even if they were unaware of emotion. And it is worthy of note that W. M. Marston (35 *Am. J. Psychol.*, 1924, 469) has found a correlation between degree of emotion and systolic blood pressure, along the lines of Darrow's thesis described above.

[8] Wechsler, 435.

taken as an index of affective tone" (*435*, 145). It is produced by stimuli which provoke emotions, by strong sensations such as loud noises and those producing pain, by "affectively toned ideational processes," either conscious or unconscious, including mental effort, if so toned, and by "changes in the state of attention" (*ibid.* 112–114). All these we have included among the causes of emotional states which operate directly on the hypothalamus or as conditioned stimuli to the same, the effect of which reaches the hypothalamus via the cortex. The reflex is independent of "awareness of any affective tone," and even "of conscious perception of the stimulus evoking the affective tone" (*ibid.*, 148), because it can be elicited in sleep, while under anesthetic, and by stimuli in regions yielding no sensation (*ibid.*, 110).[9] That is, it is not the result of a cortical effect, except indirectly where "ideational processes" are concerned, but is the result of a short-circuited process or a direct interaction (conditioned stimulus) at the subcortical level.

The magnitude of this reflex is susceptible of delicate measurement. The extent of the response "is never directly dependent on the intensity of the physical stimulus alone" and only proportionate in the degree that the more intense stimulus has become "more affectively significant" (*ibid.*, 118), so that the general conclusion "is that the magnitude of the galvanic reaction varies roughly as the intensity of affective tone which accompanies it" (*ibid.*, 121). Therefore, Wechsler assumes that "the galvanic response is obtained only in so far as the stimulus is capable of eliciting a particular kind of adaptive reaction on the part of the organism, which we have referred to as affective tone." That is, the effectiveness of the stimulus is "dependent upon an intermediate secondary effect" (not afferent, but central or efferent), which in turn is the initiator of the psychogalvanic reflex (*ibid.*, 117).[10] The term "intermediate secondary effect" coincides with our definition of the emotional state in the hypothalamus; the whole study fits neatly into our scheme; and, on this basis, the psychogalvanic reflex could be regarded as an index of hypothalamic excitement, in which the cortex plays but an occasional and accessory part.

On the other hand, recent investigations—chiefly with animals—have tended to support the view that the cortex is also—or even wholly—the originator of the psychogalvanic reflex. Considering the most extreme

[9] We said above (p. 1192) that the usual case seems to be that an emotionally endowed pattern of cortical excitation must be appreciated in consciousness if it is to be effective as a conditioned stimulus to subcortical mechanisms.This seems inconsistent with Wechsler's statement. He does not define the stimuli which produced the reaction without consciousness; but I assume they were the innate or unconditioned stimuli. Of course, this response is so subtle that it may occur without consciousness of the weakest affective tone, but hardly without consciousness of the idea in which that tone has become invested.

[10] In so far as Wechsler imputes to this "intermediate secondary effect," which he calls "affective tone," a psychic counterpart, he is making an inference based upon what his subjects tell him of their "feelings." In so far as he treats the phenomena as the same, when without consciousness, it is because of the similarity of the stimuli to those which arouse such "feeling" with consciousness.

view first, Schwartz found (*366*, 42) that the reflex in the cat was abolished contralaterally when the premotor and prefrontal areas of one hemisphere were removed. Later he concluded that "in the cat the integrity of the psychogalvanic reflex depends on the presence of . . . area 6 of Brodman" (*367*, 317),—that is, that, if that area is ablated, there is no such response to "psychic stimuli" (i.e., stimuli producing an emotional reaction), though even his completely decorticate cats showed the external signs of strong emotion after such stimuli—a loud whistle or tap on the nose (*ibid.*, 318). If these results were confirmed,[11] we would have to assume that palmar sweating is not initiated by the hypothalamus in response to emotional stimuli and that it is not an index of emotional excitement. On the contrary, however, these results seem to be contradicted by the experiments of others. Darrow (*104*, 651) found that afferent stimuli do produce the reflex in decorticate animals. Moreover, his summary of presently available evidence seems to indicate that, on the one hand, certain points in the motor area (area 4) of the forelimb and nearby points in the premotor area (area 6) are connected via an extrapyramidal path (the frontopontine fasciculus) with the centers in the tegmental or pontine regions which are concerned in the phenomenon of "forced grasping" via motor cells in the cord, and which also produce palmar sweating via their connections with preganglionic sympathetic cells. On the other hand, there appears to be another independent path from the hypothalamus which unites with the first on these same brain-stem centers. So far as the cortical path is concerned, Langworthy and Richter (*258*, 178) conclude that "this cerebral control is predominantly an inhibitory one"; but the psychogalvanic reflex can be obtained by stimulating either origin or either descending path.[12]

[11] Langworthy and Richter (*258*) and Wang and Lu (*423*) both confirm this positively, that is, they got the psychogalvanic reflex by stimulating this general region of the cat's cortex.

[12] Darrow (*104*, 642) finds the origin of the first path in that part of the motor area concerned with the forelimb and, just outside this, in the premotor area; that of the second in the anterior or prechiasmic region of the hypothalamus (hence parasympathetic; *ibid.*, 649). He cites (*ibid.*, 647–649) the various indications that both paths unite on centers in the tegmental or pontine regions. Although differing with him and among themselves in some details, these results are approximately confirmed by Langworthy and Richter (*258*), by Wang and Lu (*423*) and by Spiegel and Hunsicker (*384*); see also Fulton's interpretation of their results (*160*, 476–477).

The psychogalvanic response, which consists of a change in electrical conductivity between two points on the skin (palmar), seems to be due to the activity of sweat glands; and, since he supposes these glands to be entirely controlled, neurally at least, by the sympathetic nervous system, Wechsler concludes that "the mediation of the galvanic response by the sympathetic nervous system would then seem to have been definitely established" (*435*, 20–22, 88, 104, 109). We have already run into the anomaly, noted by Darrow (above) that sweating seems functionally parasympathetic though produced by the sympathetic system. Thus he finds the origin of this particular path in the anterior hypothalamus (*104*, 649), notes that peripheral sweat mechanisms function parasympathetically, though apparently the innervation is sympathetic, and suggests that non-palmar sweating, being primarily for the control of temperature, is managed differently. Face sweat is certainly predominantly parasympathetic (*ibid.*, 654–659). He thinks "the region of the dorsal vagus nucleus anterior to the calamus scriptorius

The most intelligible construction to place upon these data is that "forced grasping," a primitive behavior pattern (monkeys and infants)[13] had associated with it an autonomic reaction, palmar sweating, which facilitates tactual acuity and grip on objects and is thus a preparation for activity.[14] The centers for this pattern lie in the tegmentum (or the pons). In the course of time these centers have become overlaid by an inhibitory mechanism located in the premotor area (apparently a general function of this area). Voluntary grasping, or preparation for it at least, withdraws this inhibition. Ablation of the premotor area restores "forced grasping" as a response to cutaneous and proprioceptive stimuli; but it also makes these centers more responsive to hypothalamic excitation transmitted over its own path; this must be so, because such "forced grasping" is increased by fright.[15] If we suppose that the threshold of these centers for palmar sweating is low, while that for grasping is high—especially in the absence of the latter's own cutaneous and proprioceptive stimuli—then it is reasonable to expect that palmar sweating may take place from either of two causes, without grasping. The first of these causes would be subtle "intentions of movement" in the motor cortex—especially forelimb movement but, in the primate, perhaps associated with all limb movement. The second would be those affective reactions (in the absence of cortex, pseudo-affective) such as the alert or "vigilance" (Head), shifts in attention involving "interest," and anxiety or other emotional states, all of which reactions appear to originate in the hypothalamus.[16] The first of these classes

is a probable medullary center of sweat secretion" (*ibid.*, 662). And he makes the interesting suggestion, for a solution of the anomaly, that the dual control of sweating is exercised in such a way that the two influences usually neutralize each other, except under moderate excitation and in respect of palmar sweating. Hence would arise the "unique significance" of this phenomenon as an index of preparatory and facilitative processes (*ibid.*, 658). In this connection it is worthy of note that Cushing (*100*, 98) cites Hasama to the effect that "there are two kinds of centrally induced sweating, one parasympathetic associated with vaso-dilatation, and the other sympathetic or 'cold' sweating." At any rate, sweating probably occurs only by reason of nervous impulses (Kuntz, *245*, 274).

[13] Cf. Fulton, *160*, 440–444. The following statements in the text as to forced grasping are based on his summary. He does not there suggest the association with palmar sweating. But he does so in certain articles by himself and associates: 109 *Am. J. Physiol.* (1934) 37; 33 *J. Mich. Med. Soc.* (1934) 175; 57 *Brain* (1934) 69.

[14] This statement is based on Darrow's suggestion (*104*, 645) that forced grasping is allied with the psychogalvanic reflex.

[15] Based on Fulton, Jacobsen, and Kennard (*163*) and confirmed by others (see Darrow *104*, 646).

[16] Darrow contrasts the psychogalvanic reflex with the blood pressure reaction described above (pp. 1199–1200). In his judgment, whereas blood pressure shows "some disturbing or disrupting influence" (*102*, 568), the psychogalvanic reflex is "increased by conditions which arouse the organism to a state of preparedness to respond" (*ibid.*, 567, note 2). That is, the galvanic skin reflex discriminates much less clearly between disturbing and indifferent ideas and is relatively more specific for sensory stimuli and the concomitant reactions of preparation by which the organism is mobilized to a state of alertness (*ibid.*, 567). Elsewhere (*103*, 288), he calls it "an index of the general arousal

of cause, being purely cortical, would not involve the hypothalamus but would release the psychogalvanic reflex in some degree; the second, being originally or ultimately hypothalamic, would excite the psychogalvanic reflex in spite of the slight cortical inhibition. In this view, the control of the autonomic function of palmar sweating, like that of vasomotor action, would be dual; it would be initiated by the cortex, when co-ordinated with actual or intentional (supraliminal or subliminal) motor patterns; it would be initiated by the hypothalamus as a result of all preparedness which has an emotional constituent—which is the same as saying all excited emotional states. This hypothesis seems to conform to all the facts cited above—and many others—except for Schwartz's result with cats. That discrepancy may be due to the different character of stimuli he used; or perhaps, since cats have no grasp reflex, their palmar sweating has arisen wholly as a function of the motor cortex (i.e., was never a part of a primitive pattern).[17]

Since it may prove to be typical of these systems for co-ordination—that is, of the dual control of many of these autonomic functions concerned with preparation for activity—it is well to bring up again at this point one system which, while itself relatively unimportant, is of special interest because it has been more than usually clarified. Morison and Rioch (*307*, 275) found the lower brain-stem center for the excitation of reflex responses of the cat's nictitating membrane to be located in the medulla in the region of the pons. Superimposed upon this center are two areas for the excitatory components and two for the inhibitory components of the system, all of which respond to other influences than those which reach the lower center directly. The hypothalamic excitatory area is in the posterior region, and the hypothalamic inhibitory area is in the anterior region, as one would expect; in the cortex the excitatory area is chiefly along both margins in the depths of the cruciate sulcus (corresponding to the motor area), and the inhibitory area is one surrounding the pre-

---

of the organism," or (*ibid.*, 285) an "excitation-background" of a relatively enduring level, or (*ibid.*, 289) a sign of "'mobilization' or preparedness for adaptive response."

But to us these reactions of preparation seem to divide themselves into two kinds, emotional and non-emotional. Thus when he relates p.g.r. to "manipulative activity, reactions of orientation and conative functions" (*104*, 641) and even to "intention of movement" (*ibid.*, 642), we can accept the palmar sweating which results as non-emotional and the result of cortical activation over the cortical path only. On the other hand, such reactions of preparation as increase in alertness or shift in attention (if with "interest") which also produce p.g.r. (*ibid.*, 642) must be ascribed to emotional states in the hypothalamic source. Certainly chronic anxiety, which produces persistent and excessive palmar sweating (*ibid.*, 642), is an emotional state, and the sweating is to be ascribed to the hypothalamic source. Finally, the fact that when there is no preparedness, as in sleep, the palms are dry, is a neutral fact, since both regions are then quiescent.

[17] The cat has, of course, placing reactions including several which are non-visual. But these are not subcortical; or, at least, they are dependent "upon the integrity of the motor areas of the frontal lobes" (Fulton, *160*, 192). If there is an analogous association in the cats between placing reactions and palmar sweating, both may be wholly functions of the motor cortex.

sylvian sulcus and extending laterally into the gyrus orbitalis (corresponding, I take it, to the frontal eye field). The paths were not elucidated. But here, again, there appear to be two complete (excitatory and inhibitory) controls above the shortest reflex circuit; one, the hypothalamic, appears to co-ordinate the state of retraction or relaxation of the membrane with the general state of the organism, ranging between preparedness (alert), at one extreme, to unpreparedness (sleep) at the other; the other, the cortical, appears to co-ordinate the state of retraction or relaxation of the membrane with specific voluntary movements, including those of the eye.

As an example of another type of dual control over autonomic function in which the cortical influence is probably wholly inhibitory, we may cite the control of micturition, the evidence in regard to which was analyzed in Appendix I, Section C. There we concluded that the higher subcortical pressor and parasympathetic center is in the anterior hypothalamus, while the higher subcortical depressor and sympathetic center is in the posterior hypothalamus. Apparently cortical control is exercised largely by way of voluntary contraction of the external sphincter (striated muscle) and otherwise only by the voluntary or involuntary imposition or "lifting" of restraint upon involuntary micturition. The latter influence is accomplished only as to the whole function, as a part of a synergy, or by achieving an appropriate nervous state. Its mechanism is thus only indirectly voluntary,[18] but nevertheless cortical. Some have found evidence that the center for this cortical influence is near the leg center (motor area); others assign it to the frontal pole (prefrontal area). The path from the former appears to be extrapyramidal and direct to the lower brainstem; the path from the latter appears to run by way of those tracts reaching from the prefrontal area to the anterior hypothalamus.[19] Conceivably, in this complex apparatus, both may exist—the first functioning in a purely inhibitory and wholly involuntary way to prevent micturition during actual movement and the second functioning by way of the acquired voluntary inhibition of maturity (prefrontal), relaxation of which is the sole pressor factor in voluntarily inducing involuntary micturition.

There is considerable evidence that the entire gastrointestinal tract is also subject to cortical inhibition. But only in the case of defecation (see Appendix I, Section C) does a voluntary element enter.[20] And it is doubtful

[18] Thus not comparable to voluntary movement.

[19] Probably via the septum (Kabat *et al.*, *230*, 232).

[20] Fulton (*160*, 479–480) notes some of the observations of vigorous and abnormal gastric movements as a result of stimulation or ablation of the frontal lobe (chiefly premotor). Nevertheless, Sheehan (*372*, 180) found that stimulation of any point on the cortex produced no changes either in pressure or peristalsis in the "resting" (unfed) stomach, but that, in the "active" (fed) stomach, stimulation of the frontal and premotor areas (though not the motor area or the post-central gyrus) produced an initial inhibition of peristalsis, though no change in pressure. On the other hand, either extirpation or stimulation of parts of the premotor area increases intestinal peristalsis (Watts, *431*, 356–357 and Fulton, *159*, 178) and may lead to acute intussusception (Watts and Fulton, *432*, i.e., is abnormal). If the control is only inhibitory, it is hard to explain the effect of stimulation. This leads Watts (*431*, 357) to assume the presence of "both excitatory and inhibitory components."

that, in any instance, cortical influence extends to excitation or that pressor effects from cortical stimulation are other than release phenomena. It is too soon to say whether or not these gastrointestinal inhibitory and release effects are mediated via the hypothalamus or are produced directly via jointly controlled lower centers.

If, as both Brickner (*44*) and Walker (*417*) suppose, the cortical representation of the pilomotor apparatus has its descending path via the hypothalamus and not direct, Brickner's observations would make it necessary to construe the central inhibition as double—that is, normal cortical inhibition exerted on the hypothalamus and normal hypothalamic inhibition exerted on the lower sympathetic centers. For, in hemiplegia, the local reflex (to scratching or local cold) is unaffected, but the central reflex (emotional and general cold) [21] is exaggerated on the injured side. On the other hand, when there is unilateral interruption of the spinal cord, so that even the descending tract from the hypothalamus is severed, the local reflex is greatly exaggerated ipsilaterally and there is no emotional reflex.[22]

From this brief discussion it is evident that generalizations as to the relation of the cortex to the autonomic system must as yet be very tentative, if they should not be avoided altogether. Whereas, in recent decades, because of the "discovery" of the region and the resulting "tendency to overload the third ventricle with functional responsibilities" (Cushing, *100*, 39), the hypothalamus "came to be regarded as the highest center of the autonomic system" so that even the cortex was sometimes conceived to be peripheral to the hypothalamus (Spiegel and Hunsicker, *384*, 252), a revulsion has now set in, so that extremists in the opposite direction can now say that the "cortex is the controller and integrator of vegetative as of all neural functions" (Riddoch, *344*, 102). Actually, the evidence seems to indicate that neither of these positions is correct—or, rather, that each of them is correct under certain different sets of conditions. In other words, what is being uncovered is a vast complexity. Which of the two highest levels is in control at any time seems to depend on conditions.

In the first place, we may agree with Bard (*24*, 186) that "it is reasonable to suppose that the autonomic representation in the cortex is concerned with the visceral concomitants of activity in skeletal muscle induced by neural discharges of cortical origin." [23] That is, it is incidental to voluntary movement (Cannon, *66*, 159); but it is of central not peripheral origin (i.e., not secondary), so that, for instance, the "higher tension of blood in the arteries develops before the exercise is actually going on" (*ibid.*,

[21] The emotional reflex is an extensive pattern in which piloerection is combined, for instance, with a snarl, protrusion of claws, dilated pupils, and increased respiration (cat's anger), or with pallor, cold clammy hands, and shallow arrested respiration (human fear). Puppies' general cold reflex combines it with shivering and huddling (see Walker, *417*, 400).

[22] Fulton (*160*, 477–478) cites other observers to similar effect.

[23] He cites (*loc. cit.*) the effects of cortical stimulation and ablation upon arterial pressure, pupillodilatation, vasomotor, pilomotor, sudomotor responses, the inhibition of gastric peristalsis, and other gastrointestinal disturbances.

161). If so, we suppose a constant cortical inhibition, which is withdrawn specifically and in such a way as delicately to co-ordinate the needful autonomic functions with motor activities when these latter are being actually initiated.

In the second place, we know that there is also complete autonomic representation in the hypothalamus; that the sympathetic effects upon stimulation of the hypothalamus originate there; and that these, no less than those of the cortex, are "not secondary to the activity in skeletal muscle, for they precede" the latter and can be produced when the muscle is curarized (Bard, *24*, 192). If so, we suppose this representation to be concerned with regulating the autonomic system in respect of the general state of the organism and particularly in response to those excitants which constitute its wants, as heretofore outlined, and which establish in the hypothalamus emotional states of various degrees and kinds.

In the third place, we know that, besides these two, there are various kinds of specific responses which are secondary to activity; that is, responses which originate in the periphery as a result of the local effects of the activity of the skeletal musculature. The circuit of these responses may be short—they may be local reflexes. On the other hand, such circuits tend to be longer the more general the effects of activity. When they are long-circuited they may engage the hypothalamus. And, when that occurs, they become indistinguishable from the autonomic responses initiated in the hypothalamus as a result of excitors which may precede activity or even preclude it.

So far as the first two of these systems of control (i.e., the two central initiators) are concerned, there is evidently some degree of conflict. Our limited knowledge leads us to set up as the most plausible assumption the supposition that the cortical system of control includes constant inhibition in a mild degree. To that extent the cortex is normally in control. It may be conceived to remain so when, as part of the co-ordination of an autonomic function with its own motor activities, it releases this inhibition. On the other hand, it is evident that the hypothalamic system of control can, at least in a state of excitement, override this inhibition. At such times the hypothalamus is in control.

In respect of the autonomic representation in the cortex (the first system of control), we would assign much of it to the motor areas because of what Spiegel and Hunsicker refer to as the oft-noted "fact that there is a close topographical relation between the cortical areas from which certain vegetative organs can be influenced, and the cortical centers of skeletal muscles located peripherally adjacent to these organs." [24] In turn, as they point out, this argues that such representation consists of special and not general autonomic effects and, therefore, that its paths run probably direct to lower centers; for the hypothalamic responses seem to be more general in character. But the rest of the cortical representation of autonomic function, and even these special elements, by way of supplementary general in-

[24] Spiegel and Hunsicker (*384*, 252), quoting Spiegel (50 *J. H. Hosp. Bull.*, 1932, 237).

fluence, probably have paths to the hypothalamus. Thus different autonomic functions vary in the extent to which cortical representation reaches directly to the lower centers and the extent, conversely, to which it is dependent on the degree of control it exercises over the hypothalamus. When Spiegel and Hunsicker severed what they took to be the hypothalamic efferent (descending) paths, they found that autonomic responses to stimulation in the motor cortex and elsewhere in the frontal lobe ranged from one extreme, the pupillo-dilatator, which suffered the greatest impairment, to the other extreme, the bladder, which suffered the least (*384*, 273). From this they deduce (*ibid.*, 262) "that the pupillo-dilatator corticofugal impulses use the hypothalamic system to a much larger extent than [they do] the corticospinal neurones," and, presumably, that the converse is true of vesicular representation. While in both the direct and indirect cortical control it is possible that the cortical influence may be excitatory as well as inhibitory, it seems more probable, at present, that it is wholly the latter. When the inhibition is withdrawn the hypothalamic or lower centers are merely released.[25] At either level this may occur experimentally through removal of the cortex (ablation) or through its stimulation. The latter fact argues that, when a certain motor pattern is excited naturally in the intact cortex, the normal inhibition of the autonomic function, which requires to be co-ordinated with this specific activity, is withdrawn. If that activity is a specific one such as grasping, the release is also specific and therefore deals directly with the lower brain-stem center for palmar sweating. If that activity is a general one, such as running, for instance, the release must be general and therefore deals indirectly through the hypothalamic sympathetic (posterior) centers which inhibit gastric motility and which shift the blood from the skin and viscera to the muscle bed.

In a sense, then, all of this cortical inhibition and release, in so far at least as it is exercised upon the hypothalamus and thus indirectly, is hardly distinguishable from the inhibition and release which we assigned, in the previous section, to the prefrontal area especially. Nevertheless, I think it is useful to separate the two, since their relation to behavior seems to be so markedly different. The prefrontal inhibition would be classed as the agency through which what we know psychologically as "self-control" is attained—the educable focus of deliberate behavior—and also the agency for establishing a new conditioned stimulus with the faculty of exciting or releasing the hypothalamic region. On the other hand, the motor cortex inhibition would be classed as the agency for refined co-ordination of general interofective activities with the actual or impending exterofective activities initiated in the motor cortex. And this, almost certainly so far as the hypothalamus is concerned, would be assumed to operate by means

[25] Spiegel's and Hunsicker's results suggest that it may be either (*384*, 252, 270). Kennard (*234*, 543) thinks vasomotor, sudomotor, and pilomotor effects may all be release phenomena. And, as Bucy notes in his comment on Kennard (*ibid.*), this fits the fact that area 6 seems to be the inhibitory area of the cerebral cortex. In general, as Fulton puts it (*159*, 181) "the hypothalamic and medullary centers concerned in regulating visceral activities are held in check by centers lying rostrally in the forebrain."

of a constant inhibitory effect merely withdrawn when activity impended (purely by way of release phenomena).

2. EXTEROFECTIVE

In Sections C and F 2 we have already indicated something of the organization of the somatic motor branch of the central nervous system—the exterofective system. At this point, in order to clarify the relations of the two highest levels—cortical and hypothalamic—in respect of this effector mechanism, it is necessary to outline it in more diagrammatic form. As already noted (Section C), Tower (*405*, 443–444) believes that the motor "mechanism upon which the cortex acts is organized in four levels":

1. The segmental mechanism (spinal) which projects to the periphery and which is both the initial and the final site for integration.

2. The lower brain-stem motor mechanism which projects to the segmental and is the site of reintegration, producing the "elements of posture and movement."

3. The thalamic (or thalamostriatal) motor mechanism, including the hypothalamus, which projects only to the lower brain-stem mechanism and is the site of further integration, including pattern formation, producing "complicated performances of unmistakable significance" that are composed of several elements the primary parts of which can be got from the midbrain, or second level (Tower, *405*, 433).

4. The cortical motor mechanism, which projects to each of the lower levels, is the highest level of integration and pattern formation and therefore produces not only what each of the lower levels can produce but other effects impossible to them.

The projection by which the highest level reaches direct to the lowest is the pyramidal or corticospinal tract.[26] The projection by which the highest reaches to the two intermediate levels is the extrapyramidal system.[27] But, since the third level relays to the second and the second relays to the first, one must regard these indirect connections as also constituting a functional part of the extrapyramidal system, which may be set in action either from the cortex or from their level of origin. In general, Tower holds that the direct pyramidal system is predominantly excitatory (*405*, 444), including facilitation (*404*, 244).[28] On the other hand, cortical in-

[26] Tower says (*404*, 238) that the Betz cells of the pyramidal tract send off collaterals "at the level of the pons and perhaps into the corpus striatum." If so, the tract is not wholly spinal.

[27] For an up-to-date summary of recent work in this field see Fulton (*160*, 335–337). He lists five projections at least, and perhaps six, originating in the motor areas.

[28] In the monkey she finds that the pyramidal tract has no independent inhibitory action (*406*, 95). Therefore, any reciprocal inhibition via the pyramidal system must be "a property of the segmental mechanism upon which the corticospinal system must act" (*405*, 420–421).

If it is true that 80 to 90 percent of all pyramidal fibers terminate upon internuncial neurons, so that the "corticospinal tracts end at a vantage point which allows them to control all incoming sensory impulses" (Fulton, *160*, 334), it would appear that they are

fluence upon the subcortical mechanisms (the intermediate levels) via the extrapyramidal system may be either excitatory or inhibitory, "fairly equally matched" (*405*, 444). Thus the motor cortex can facilitate or inhibit activity throughout the neural axis, either at the source or at the segmental level, but always by projected action. "The prime function of the cortex itself must be so to integrate activity in these many projection systems that the final product of excitation and inhibition in the lower centres results in activity and cessation of activity in the effector mechanism, appropriate to the situation to be dealt with" (*loc. cit.*)—that is, to the completely integrated and long-circuited current stimuli.

In general, Tower finds that cortical extrapyramidal action includes inhibition of tonic (postural) contraction,[29] strong inhibition effective against movement, and a "variety of motor activities" (*405*, 409).[30] All are produced by action on the relays in the brain-stem, so that apparently each cortical area is connected with many subcortical levels (*ibid.*, 437). The motor activities are "organized in stages" (*ibid.*, 421). If, in the decorticate animal, the posterior hypothalamus, the subthalamus, and most of the ventral thalamus are intact, one can still get the "complicated performances of unmistakable significance" already referred to. Even "the tegmentum of the thalamus and mid-brain together yield all [the primary constituents of] the patterns of cortical extrapyramidal action," and do so "equally well whether the descending cortical systems be intact or degenerated." Therefore, the "brain-stem response depends upon intrinsic brain-stem structure" (*ibid.*, 433). From this she infers that, if there is a separate cortical projection system for each pattern of response, there is choice of action (differentiation—Hughlings Jackson) at the cortical level. If there is only one projection system, the particular response which results depends on conditions at the lower level, and there is no choice. "In either case the pattern which dominates extrapyramidal motor activity is probably constructed, not in the cortex, but beneath, for the activities in ques-

---

inhibitory in the sense that they are largely responsible for long-circuiting—that is, inhibitory on the afferent side. However, the matter is not clear. One has supposed the corticospinal tract to be "essentially motor" (Tower, *405*, 442). Nevertheless (*404*, 252), her retrograde degenerations indicated that the "pyramid, like the cortex, is a mixture of the ascending and descending systems which are the afferent and efferent pathways for the same body of reactions"—that is (*ibid.*, 254), "like the corresponding area in the cortex, a sensori-motor system."

29 This inhibition of tonic contraction she was able to obtain only from area 4, or at least only there to separate it from a motor excitatory pattern (*405*, 437). This may be the function of the extrapyramidal projection from that area.

30 We have already quoted Fulton (*160*, 455) along the same lines. He says, "The extrapyramidal motor projections are primarily concerned with postural adjustments of the skeletal musculature, but they are also capable of mediating certain deep-rooted volitional synergies." Foerster (*144*, 152–153) describes the latter as "stereotyped synergies," which are "unmodifiable" and "inseparable." And he cites Hughlings Jackson's concept of "compensation" to illustrate the view that the inhibitory function of the extrapyramidal system is exercised by making these synergies "recede into the background," leaving the isolated movements of the pyramidal system.

tion are those which a decorticate cat executes in stereotyped fashion, so that patterns of action must be complete in the lower centres" (*ibid.*, 441). "The cortical extrapyramidal motor mechanism may therefore be conceived as facilitating activity in lower centres, even as initiating it, but as determining form only by a limited selection of one or another pattern intrinsic in lower centres" (*ibid.*, 441).[31] It is not possible to accept these conclusions, without modification, when applied to primates, including man. Nevertheless, they serve well as a starting point, and we will defer the necessary modifications for a moment.[32]

Although "all the action which the cortex yields with this [the pyramidal] system intact has been obtained at one time or another with the system cut," nevertheless, this action is confined to the "complex synergies" (involving at least a whole extremity and often the whole animal; *405*, 442) of which the extrapyramidal system is capable. But with the pyramids intact three differences are noted. First, there can be "fractionation" of motor function—that is, "almost any fraction of such a large movement . . . may be isolated" and produced by itself. Second, there can be modification—that is, the otherwise stereotyped movement may be altered. Third, segmental reflexes are facilitated. These three make possible "discreteness of action, showing either as (1) fractionation or as (2) modification of patterns, and as (3) low threshold. The result of the first two is adaptation to a situation, and, of the third, speed and strength in execution (*ibid.*, 442). All three endow a movement with "lability and skill" (*406*, 95).

It is tempting to identify the motor area (area 4) with the pyramidal system, and the premotor area (area 6 plus others) with the extrapyramidal system. In fact, it is so tempting that it is frequently done.[33] Nevertheless, as we noted in Section F 3, the identity is by no means complete. Since the question is not germane to our present purpose we may avoid that complication here. So far as we are concerned here, the motor cortex may be treated as one. But its projections cannot be so treated? It has two systems of projection. Of these, one, the extrapyramidal, with all its synergies, inhibitory and excitatory, is also available, probably in its entirety, to the hypothalamic region—the other highest level—through descending connections from that region to all subcortical and supraspinal motor centers.[34]

[31] This limitation is proved by the fact that, after the pyramids are cut, these patterns are unmodifiable from the cortex "except by the interaction of conflicting projection" (*loc. cit.*).

[32] The apparent difference between primates and all lower animals in respect of the adequacy of subcortical mechanisms when decorticate suggests that, with primates, "something has been added" even in the extrapyramidal cortex. For our reconciliation see pp. 1218–1219.

[33] E.g., Foerster's nomenclature on his map, and Fulton's caption for Chapter XXI (*160*).

[34] In the present state of our knowledge we cannot be too specific about these connections. But experiments with local stimulation have proved they exist. In part, the connections may be by way of the subthalamus. As Le Gros Clark says (*84*, 410), "the nuclei of the subthalamus ["which may be regarded broadly as the pathway of all the

In other words, the motor cortex and the hypothalamus appear to be direct rivals for the control of the extrapyramidal system. This rivalry, however, is tempered in two ways. In the first place, the motor cortex (extrapyramidal) appears to have established a constant inhibition or suppression of these underlying primitive subcortical motor patterns, an inhibition which can only be overcome by considerable hypothalamic excitation (excitement or strong emotion), so that short-circuiting results. In the second place, as suggested in Section G 4, the prefrontal area of the cortex seems also to have an inhibitory influence, either on these subcortical motor centers or on the connections of the hypothalamus with them—and that in addition to the direct inhibition of the hypothalamus itself by this latter area. We have treated the prefrontal influences as part of the system of interaction between the two highest levels. But this shows that the distinction between that and effector relations is only one of degree or level.

On the other hand, the second of the two systems of motor projection from the cortex, the pyramidal, with its fractionation, modification, and facilitation of patterns through direct intervention at the spinal level, is not available to the hypothalamic regions through any descending connections of their own. It by-passes these regions and all the supraspinal centers which they reach. From this it is evident that the only access these regions can have to the motor apparatus that is responsible for all skillful and well-adapted movement must be by way of the motor cortex itself. Based on our analysis in Section G, we would conclude that this access is confined to the avenue over which the stream of awakeness and emotion reaches the general cortex, and to that by which an attenuated or sample stream reaches the prefrontal area.

Precisely these anatomical arrangements, then, seem to lay down the system of exterofective relationships which exist betwen the cortex and the hypothalamus, the two highest levels. So long as the state of excitement in the hypothalamus is within those ranges of intensity in which its kind is sharply differentiated (see pp. 1083–1084), the somewhat specialized stream of emotion joins the sensory, or sensorimotor, stream in the cortex, attaches "interest" to sensation and thus, by means of processes of deliberation, leads to motor activity of the adapted variety (co-operation of the pyramidal and extrapyramidal mechanisms).[35] But when that state of ex-

lateral fore-brain bundle which pass from the cerebral hemispheres to lower levels and link up the cortex and basal ganglia with the brain stem and spinal cord"] form in large part a series of relay stations for fibres which descend from the striatum, and constitute essential elements in the so-called extra-pyramidal motor system. They are also intimately related to the elements of the hypothalamus medially by fibre connections." There is some dispute as to the function of this connection. See Section C, note 9, above. Ingram (*212*, 238–239) regards it as afferent to the hypothalamus. But he includes among the efferent paths, descending from the hypothalamus to lower centers, elements of the periventricular system, of the dorsal longitudinal fasciculus, and diffuse paths mostly continuations of the medial forebrain bundle. Certainly not all of these are autonomic.

[35] For, while "area 4 contributes extensively to the extrapyramidal projection" (Fulton, *160*, 338), cortical motor activities, organized in the intact cortex, appear always to use

citement arises sharply and suddenly—or even slowly, if to a high degree—either the stream of emotion becomes so generalized and so intense that it causes confusion in the cortex, deliberation is impossible and inhibition ceases ("excortication"), or, even without that, the excitation overcomes the inhibition at the motor outlets. In both cases it is short-circuited direct by way of the hypothalamic connections to the subcortical centers of the extrapyramidal system, whence result the primitive synergies characteristic of great excitement.

While, for the sake of simplifying the statement, these alternatives have been treated above as if they were mutually exclusive, I am inclined to think that observations of animals and men justify us in concluding that they are not. In the first place, there are many indications that there can be "leakage" into the short-circuit without cutting out the long-circuit, so that many degrees of mixture of the two are possible. In the second place, examination of some of the specific exterofective activities leads to the supposition that these different activities are subject to "leakage" in widely varying degree. Thus emotional behavior of the "thoracic cage" or of the facial muscles, which is presumably due to "leakage," often accompanies highly skilled behavior of the hands, for example. In the third place, so far as mature primates are concerned, we have noted (pp. 1088–1089) that, when decorticate (even when only areas 4 and 6a are ablated), the animal can no longer walk or stand.[36] From this fact it seems to follow that, in the intact animal, the motor cortex is almost never completely cut out by short-circuiting except under pathological conditions. In other words, it seems necessary to assume that, so long as the animal can stand or walk, whatever apparently short-circuited primitive motor patterns are evident are "leakage," however extensive and intense—that is, that a mixture of long-circuiting and short-circuiting is taking place. Finally, there is some reason to think that, not only can "leakage" take place as to one motor pattern (say facial expression) while another, of which it is more or less a part, is being long-circuited

---

not only both systems but both areas. Even in cases where the pattern of action is a skilled one which cannot be carried out at all after section of the pyramidal tract, the extrapyramidal system contributes to it—at least with the motor area intact and the premotor ablated there is a "permanent deficit" in the "capacity to make skilled motor adjustments" (Fulton, *160*, 440). Perhaps this is due to the loss of the inhibitory functions of the extrapyramidal projections which are "primarily concerned with postural adjustments of the skeletal musculature" (Fulton, *160*, 455). If so, it seems plausible to suggest amendments to Lashley's statement, already quoted, by saying that oriented reactions "consist of the translation of a pattern of sensory excitement [in the cortex, where it has been endowed with specific emotional "interest" by the stream of emotion from the gyrus cinguli] into a pattern of movement [elaborated in the motor area] with reference to bodily posture [adjustments in which are made co-operatively by the premotor area]" (*262*, 378).

[36] If the consequences of "excortication" (see Darrow, as quoted, p. 1180) in the intact animal under stress of great excitement were actually the same as those of decortication (or ablation of both motor areas), we would expect reduction "virtually to the thalamic reflex status" (Fulton, *160*, 453). Apparently this does not occur in the normal animal; though something like it may occur in various pathological conditions.

and executed with skill, but that "leakage" can take place in a single pattern, so that while a long-circuited movement is under way, short-circuiting to the same lower centers may exist at the same time, adding to the energy of the movement but detracting from its skill.[37]

This matter of the hierarchical organization of the motor system is so important for our purposes, not only because it demonstrates the nature of the joint control of exterofective functions from the two highest levels but also because it forms the basis for the distinction between innate and learned motor patterns, which we examine in Chapter 3, that it is advisable to examine in some detail the results of experimental evidence as to certain elements of behavior. On p. 1073 we have already alluded to grasping and sucking. The studies of Bieber and Fulton (37, 453) "suggest that the [grasping] reaction is integrated in the brain stem somewhere between the anterior nucleus of the thalamus and the anterior border of the pons." Certainly it is among the reactions which "depend on the integrity of some centers above the pons" (*ibid.*, 435). Perhaps it is "the basic subcortical prehension pattern" (*ibid.*, 450).[38] But it seems also to be associated with feeding. For (Bieber, *36*, 705) in the new-born, both sucking and grasping are most pronounced before feeding; grasping can be elicited when sucking equally well as when the arms are stretched; and grasping cannot be elicited after feeding nor when asleep. "Grasping and sucking are the first and basic functions of the hand and the mouth," in primates (*ibid.*, 706). When hand to mouth feeding is learned, grasping also serves that purpose. Then support is relegated largely or wholly to the lower limbs, and the grasp reflex, for its other function (support), becomes inhibited by the premotor area of the cortex.[39] Apparently sucking becomes inhibited, in the same way, by the development of speech in the cortex. But "forced" grasping returns upon ablation of the premotor area, and sucking occurs when the speech area is diseased (aphasia, etc.; *ibid.*, 705–706).[40]

[37] In respect of the energy, one of Tower's experiments seems to demonstrate this. She observed (*404*, 243) that, after section of one pyramid, the two emotional reactions which she describes as the "pawing of curiosity" and the "clawing of anger" were diminished contralaterally. But, in excitement, they were "indistinguishable from normal." This is, of course, not positive proof of a mixture of short- and long-circuiting, since the reaction may have been mediated altogether from the cortex over extrapyramidal paths. Nevertheless, in view of other evidence, short-circuiting seems the more probable explanation of the increased force when under excitement. Certainly the deficiency argues the use of pyramidal paths, in part, even for such emotional reactions, so long as the excitement is not great.

[38] That is, "a postural reaction peculiar to the prehensile fingered primate" (Fulton, *160*, 457).

[39] When the motor cortex is extirpated in infancy, "forced" grasping persists, even at two years of age, because this inhibition cannot be established (Kennard, *235*, 146).

[40] Fulton is even more specific (*160*, 440–444). A lesion in area 6a causes temporary forced grasping, and this is made permanent by ablation of areas 4 and 6 as a whole. Grasping recurs due to the withdrawal of the extrapyramidal inhibition upon subcortical centers, probably the tegmentum (*ibid.*, 442). "In the presence of the cortex the grasp subserves other more highly integrated functions . . . but in the absence of

After ablation of both premotor areas, frightening causes intensification, and distraction by food is likely to cause relaxation, of forced grasping (Fulton, *160*, 442). Hence we must conclude that the degree and kind of excitement in the hypothalamus (emotional state) directly facilitates or inhibits the primitive reflex over the descending paths from the hypothalamus. Finally, in the infant, whether normal or without cerebral hemispheres, Watson (*430*, 121) lists "clutching of the hands" as a part of all responses to fear stimuli, and cites clenching of the hands as one of Darwin's signs of human terror (*ibid.*, 110). But this hardly needs authority. It is a matter of common observation among human beings that the grasp reflex is an automatic accompaniment of the fear aroused by sudden loss of support, even in adults. In these cases, since the ordinary cutaneous and proprioceptive stimuli do not come into play, it is probable that the reaction is entirely produced as a part of an extensive pattern aroused in the hypothalamus and over its own descending paths.

One of the most apt instances of dual control by the two highest levels is that over the "thoracic cage," so much so that Hughlings Jackson (*216*, I, 288) regarded respiration as both "animal" and "organic"—that is, as both an exterofective and an interofective function—in spite of the fact that its various forms of behavior are produced entirely by skeletal musculature. At any rate, the respiratory center in the medulla is "subject to regulation both from the hypothalamic and cortical levels" (Fulton *160*, 167). Of course, much (perhaps all) of the musculature that is involved in respiration is also subject to a limited degree of direct voluntary control from the cortex, presumably pyramidal. However, since the influence of the hypothalamus seems not to extend to these discrete activities, but to be confined rather to certain stereotyped synergies which are evidently extrapyramidal, we shall confine ourselves to these latter. In part, at least, they are also obtainable by cortical stimulation, and all are capable of voluntary imitation of varying degrees of accuracy. Thus, in respect of these synergies, only, do we find that an effector relation exists between the two highest levels.

Most studies of respiratory control have centered around the respiratory center in the medulla, so that the information as to these higher controls is not extensive. But, as Smith says (*383*, 55), the fact of voluntary control of the rate and duration of respiration and even, within limits, its voluntary arrest, prove that the cortex exerts an influence. Moreover, he obtained acceleration of respiration by direct stimulation of area 6a, the "frontal adversive" field (probably Foerster's 6a beta), and a deceleration from 6b, the area of mastication and deglutition (*ibid.*, 67). With sufficient stimulation of the excitatory field, he got panting, and, of the inhibitory field, cessation of breathing (*ibid.*, 66). Bucy and Case (*53*) got "sudden and marked slowing of respiratory movements," increasing with the

the cortex it reverts to the primitive group of postural reactions from which it apparently took origin" (*ibid.*, 443).

strength of stimulation until respiration ceased, by stimulation of the latter area in dog (*ibid.*, 163) and in man (*ibid.*, 165–167). When prolonged, the respiratory activity "escaped" (i.e., resumed).[41] On the basis of Tower's similar results (*405*) after section of the pyramidal tracts, Smith concludes (*383*, 66) that these effects are produced by the extrapyramidal system, and, because they are bilateral, probably operate upon the respiratory center.[42] Thus the cortical effect on that center may increase the rate of discharge there, or decrease it, or stop it; it may change the amplitude; and it may produce various combinations of all these.

Though one might argue that the cortical areas from which these effects are procured indicate that the effects, there, are strictly utilitarian coordinations with other motor activities, it is clear that they are the same synergies (same patterns) which occur as a result of hypothalamic excitation, often of a less utilitarian nature. As we have several times noted,[43] increased rate of respiration (polypnea) and increased amplitude (hyperpnea) are both patterns which are available, apparently separately or jointly, to the hypothalamus under certain kinds of stimulation—that is, both kinds occur in the decorticate animal in response to changes in blood temperature (Pinkston *et al.*, *326*, 528); "sham rage" includes polypneic panting (Lilienthal and Otenasek, *269*, 121); and decorticate polypneic panting occurs merely as a release phenomenon (*ibid.*, 122–123). The patterns are the same whether they occur as responses to the causes which excite the cortex or to the probably different causes which excite the hypothalamus.

There are, however, other alterations of normal respiration which, although they can be produced voluntarily and therefore presumably by the cortex, are not then very accurate imitations of the involuntary emotional reactions produced presumably from the hypothalamus.[44] There are, for instance, that jerky inspiration which we call sobbing and that jerky expiration which we call laughing; there is also the brief holding of the breath which, when it is followed by release, is called sighing, and which is also often an accompaniment of the "alert." The ease with which we distinguish "forced" (voluntary) laughter from real (involuntary) laughter, or the sobbing of a malingerer from that of true grief, or pain or fright, is evidence that the former, in each case, lacks in subtle ways some of the characteristics of the "natural" pattern. On the other hand, involuntary holding of the breath is apparently the same pattern as that of the cortex, which is associated with chewing and swallowing, though the former is produced for different reasons. Of course, it is not yet proved that this group of extrapyramidal respiratory patterns is not wholly cortical and

41 Dusser de Barenne *et al.* (*127*, 288) refer to "those cortical areas which control respiration." Perhaps "influence" is a better term.

42 It is worth noting, however, that Foerster (*144*, 153) holds that muscles acting chiefly bilaterally, such as these, are those which have bilateral representation in the cortex to the greatest degree.

This is more true of the proximal muscles, like these, than it is of the distal.

43 See pp. 1073–1074, 1090, 1092, 1098.

44 As to this see Section C, note 30, above.

merely distinguished by the cause—voluntary or involuntary.[45] Nevertheless, the general body of evidence as to the source of emotional reactions leads us to suppose that these two, when emotional, originate in the hypothalamus and are effected over its own descending connections to the centers of the extrapyramidal system. In fact, the difference between "natural" and artificial laughing and sobbing, and especially their jerkiness, suggests that the natural forms are parts of complex primitive patterns which are not, in the same form, available to the cortex at all.[46]

A similar situation seems to exist with reference to facial expression (facies) which is also, of course, wholly a function of the exterofective apparatus. And here observation has demonstrated the existence of descending paths from the cortex—presumably both pyramidal and extrapyramidal—as well as of an independent set of paths probably connecting with the extrapyramidal system, which, because they convey emotional expression, are presumably hypothalamic in origin.[47] As Hughlings Jackson observed (*216*, II, 121), "in some cases of disease of the hemisphere . . . intellectual expression ["what we think"] is wanting, and emotional expression ["what we feel"] is well preserved"—that is, more generally, "involuntary" use of muscles may be preserved when "voluntary" use of the same muscles is lost.[48] Bard (*19*, 297–298) carries this further. He notes not only that "paralysis of willed movement [of the face, by interruption of the voluntary paths] may not be attended by any impairment of emotional expression," but that, on the other hand, there may be emotional paralysis with retention of volitional control. In line with our suggestion above as to the extent of these emotional patterns, he quotes Kinnier Wilson to the effect that "the more severe the volitional facio-respiratory paralysis the more exaggerated is the involuntary innervation of the same mechanism," and instances the unrestrained laughing and crying which occur under these conditions.[49] In other words, the cortical influence upon the

[45] Penfield and Boldrey (*324*, 425) report laughing among their responses to stimulation of the human cortex, but remark on the fact that it only occurred once.

[46] We may remind ourselves that shivering, which also has this characteristic, is also a subcortical reaction organized in or, at least, available to the hypothalamus. See pp. 1074 and 1091.

[47] Parkinsonism, which is regarded as a syndrome of the basal ganglia, involves "expressionless" or mask-like facies. The same effect is produced by ablation of the frontal eye fields (area 8; Fulton, *160*, 451). Since, in the first, and possibly in the second, case, it appears that the corticostrionigral part of the extrapyramidal system is involved, and since the subcortical centers of this part are the globus pallidus, the subthalamic body of Luys, and the substantia nigra, it would appear that, if emotional facial expression originates in the hypothalamic region, it must be effected through this system.

[48] Also (*216*, II, 123), "a patient does things involuntarily which he cannot do voluntarily." This extends even to speech. Patients suffering from aphasia may still swear. That is "obviously not voluntary" (*loc. cit.*) for "oaths are phrases which emotion has filched from the intellect to express itself in a more definite way than it could by mere loudness of tone or manner" (*loc. cit.*). What the mechanism is, when voluntary speech is lost, is not apparent.

[49] These statements are based on case reports cited from Kirilzev (1891); Fulton and Bailey (1929); and Kinnier Wilson, 49 *J. Neurol. Psychopath.* (1924) and *Modern Problems in Neurology* (1929).

subcortical centers, in respect both of facies and respiratory changes, seems to be also inhibitory, so that these pathological responses are in part release phenomena. That reminds us of Crile's explanation of normal laughter and weeping (*96*, 93, 99–100 and 102) as release phenomena—that is, as the sudden withdrawal of cortical inhibition, ending suspense and permitting pent-up emotional excitation suddenly to flow off. In general, Bard concludes (*19*, 298) that, "It is more in accord with the evidence at hand to think in terms of a subcortical organization for emotional expression located or centered in the under part of the thalamus [presumably the hypothalamus] connected by efferent paths with the primary motor nuclei of medulla and spinal cord, and normally subject to cortical restraint." [50]

In addition to all these special instances of effector relations between the two highest levels over the exterofective system, we should recall the general behavior patterns described in Sections C 3 and D. In respect of these patterns, which are available to the hypothalamus, it is apparent that the subcortical motor centers which are used are those which are also included in the extrapyramidal projections from the cortex. Among the lower animals, when decorticate, these primitive and stereotyped synergies can be produced by excitation in the hypothalamic region and are then sufficient for the maintenance of life (p. 1088). Among the primates, however, this subcortical apparatus is no longer sufficient even for the exterofective performances (*loc. cit.*). That should not, I think, lead us to conclude that the whole process of motor behavior has, at this phylogenetic stage, been transferred from subcortical to cortical mechanisms. Rather it seems to indicate that cortical mechanisms, having become increasingly involved even in the execution of these synergies, have become strategic factors that are essential to them.[51] Thus, apparently, the primitive motor responses to the bodily wants, internal and quasi-external, which are one and the same thing as the somatic element in the expression of the emotions, can be produced in the lower animals without the assistance of cortical mechanisms. In man, on the other hand, they cannot.[52] Nevertheless,

[50] As to facial expression, Cannon (*61*, 117) also identifies this as the region. There is loss of voluntary control of facial muscles with emotional expression remaining, when the motor tract is interrupted subcortically with the "optic thalamus" intact; and voluntary control is retained, though emotional expression is lost, when the motor tract is intact and the "thalamus" is injured. But see above, Section D, note 29, which suggests that the globus pallidus is responsible or involved.

[51] Or almost essential. Lashley (*262*, 383–384) interprets the possibility of motion in cerebral paralysis under intense excitement to indicate that the pattern is not destroyed, but that the excitability of the final common path is reduced (i.e., no facilitation). Thus, even when the cortical paths are interrupted, the hypothalamic suffice, if sufficiently active.

[52] Lashley (*261*, 10–11) disputes the position which he attributes to Lloyd Morgan (*Instinct and Intelligence*, 1912) that the cerebrum is not essential for the performance of any unlearned or instinctive activity. He says the facts imply that "some instincts, which seem to be those requiring accurate differentiation of stimuli, are dependent upon cortical mechanisms." Perhaps! But we are making our distinction on the basis of the capacity to execute the corresponding motor patterns. And here it seems to depend on the phylogenetic stage of the animal.

if it is true that, in man, these wants express themselves at the highest levels via an homologous apparatus, they are also at first and primarily patterns of excitation in the hypothalamic regions. From these considerations, and in view of our whole examination of the evidence, one would deduce that, in man, responses to wants are also initiated in the hypothalamus, but that, to a large extent, they are conveyed thence to the cortex as the emotional stream, where they are executed over cortical effector paths with more or less deliberation and more or less skill. It would not be necessary, however, to assume that this is their only motor outlet. On the contrary, as we have suggested on p. 1213 and previously, observation would lead us to suppose that the indirect cortical motor component and the direct subcortical motor component are mixed in various proportions in most of these responses. The degree to which the latter component enters is taken by the observer to indicate the degree of emotionalism in the response; the degree to which the former component enters is taken by us to indicate habituated expertness, if immediate, and calculation or deliberation, if delayed. But, strictly speaking, the primary source of the whole energy of the response, via both outlets, may be emotion; so far as the subject himself is concerned, even the cortical component may be felt as such. Or, on the other hand, he may be exerting what we call self-control (i.e., canalizing or even restricting the outflow of this excitation). In that case, or to that extent, it would appear that not all the energizing can result from this primary, emotional source. But we shall leave that question to be dealt with in Chapters 5 and 6.

3. VOLUNTARY *vs.* INVOLUNTARY

Before leaving this subject of exterofective relations, one further point requires to be made for purposes of future reference. In these citations,[53] and in fact in all the literature, we see objective scientists constantly using the dichotomy voluntary *vs.* involuntary, or automatic. What do they mean by it? Physiology has always classified the musculature into "voluntary" (striated) and "involuntary" (smooth). But this is not the distinction intended in the neurological literature. For, in neurology, it is recognized that much of the action of the skeletal muscles is involuntary, while it is now sometimes suggested that there must be some form of voluntary, if indirect, influence over smooth muscle (e.g., the detrusor muscle).[54]

[53] See especially those in regard to "volitional facio-respiratory paralysis" and speech, pp. 1216–1218 and notes.

[54] In his essay on *The Feeling of Effort,* William James (*219,* 19) speaks of our "capacity to indirectly excite activities usually involuntary." "We even read of persons who can contract their pupils voluntarily by imagining a brilliant light—that being the sensation to which the pupils normally respond." So, too, with weeping and sweating. And "how easily the thought of gustatory stimuli excites the activity of the salivary glands." But weeping, sweating, and salivation are glandular, and these, as well as contraction of the pupil, are controlled autonomically. Thus the autonomic excitation is not itself voluntary; rather the idea is voluntary and the autonomic effects are involuntary accompaniments, presumably because the idea is emotionally conditioned.

Another case of indirect voluntary influence seems to be voluntary relaxation of the

The distinction in neurology involves the imputation of what psychologists mean by volition. Thus, with regard to volition, we find ourselves in the same position which we are in with regard to consciousness (see the text, Chapter 2, Section D). That is, both these are categories which cannot be ignored and which involve problems that cannot be evaded. We cannot come at them and discover their essence; but, as in the case of the "force of gravity," this is no bar to making careful observations of their appearance or effects and then, from these observations, forming some inferences as to their locus and characteristics.

It is difficult, if not impossible, to attribute to neurologists a definable distinction between voluntary and involuntary movements, since this distinction is merely implicit in their use of the terms. Nevertheless, usage, while it is not wholly consistent and is certainly not definitive, would indicate that:

1. Movement is called voluntary in proportion as it is variable—and therefore adaptable precisely to the external situation—rather than stereotyped.[55]

2. Movement, whether variable or stereotyped, is called voluntary in proportion as it is not to be explained as the consequence of an observable external stimulus; it is therefore what is called "spontaneous" activity and is to be attributed presumably to an internal and unobserved stimulus (appetite, memory, etc.).[56]

3. Movement, even if stereotyped and even if a response to, or oriented to, an external stimulus, is called voluntary in proportion as it appears to be "purposeful" (spontaneous but also adapted to the external situation in its relation to the appetite) and controlled or controllable (inhibitable, not inevitable) and is therefore construed to be the result of conscious integration.[57] In all respects, the distinction between voluntary and automatic responses is evidently one of degree.

---

general postural (somatic) musculature. At certain times this is very difficult of accomplishment; at all times it seems to be accomplished by achieving the conducive nervous state, not by direct action.

[55] For instance, Foerster, using Hughlings Jackson's term "specialized"—which I take to mean variable and adapted—says (*144*, 158) that, in the various degrees of hemiplegia, "The most specialized, most voluntary and least automatic movements are the first to suffer and the last to be restored." "The greater the number of areas destroyed in addition to the precentral convolution [area 4], the more the movements which are least specialized, least voluntary and most automatic, are involved."

[56] For instance, Kennard (*235*, 145) says, of her infant monkeys, that even after extirpation of all excitable cortical tissue (areas 4 and 6), "voluntary motor control . . . is entirely adequate to maintain the existence of the individual" (i.e., responses to wants remain). In the same way Fulton (*160*, 453) identifies as the power of making "volitional movements," the "power to carry out progression movements, to climb and to feed themselves," on the part of chimpanzees recovered from the acute affects of ablation of area 4.

[57] For instance, though "of extrapyramidal origin" (i.e., synergies), movements still may be "purposeful" (Fulton, *160*, 453). But "postural adjustments" and "associated movements such as the swinging of the upper extremities with walking . . . movements of the face appropriate to particular emotional states," etc.—though they can be

These usages seem to be acceptable as the basis of a definition of what we mean by volition, and therefore they serve as the basis of some sort of hypothesis as to its characteristics and the locus of its anatomical substrate, as Hughlings Jackson would say. Volition evidently implies choice, though it does not imply a chooser. Choice implies, first, a number of possible alternative courses of action—movements, or non-movements. Therefore, the greater the differentiation, in Hughlings Jackson's sense—that is, the larger the number of available paths upon the efferent side—the greater is the scope for volition. The spinal reflex called the knee-jerk is, in that respect, involuntary because only one response to the stimulus is possible. Therefore, choice implies, second, a conflict between the tendencies toward each of these available alternatives. If one tendency is so strong as immediately to overpower all other tendencies, there is no choice. The startled gasp is not a matter of choice.[58] Therefore choice implies, third, a delayed (suspended) reaction—that is, some period during which the various tendencies toward the various alternatives are dead-locked so far as motor outlet is concerned. Therefore, choice implies, fourth, the capacity to delay (inhibit) all reactions during such a process. While such a conflict is maintained, we conceive the very delay to be volitional. When such a conflict is resolved, we say the resulting action is volitional. But, even then, only the whole action is the subject of volition. Running is an elaborate synergy to which are attached associated movements and a vast complexity of reciprocal inhibitions, the parts of which are involuntary accompaniments of the whole. On the other hand, a discrete ("fractionated") movement such as lifting the little finger is almost wholly voluntary. Nevertheless, when this becomes part of an automatized habit,[59] as it does in playing the piano, volition is almost limited to starting and stopping the whole succession of movements—the whole action.[60]

---

reproduced or somewhat imitated voluntarily, and though some of them may be regarded as "semi-voluntary" (Fulton, *ibid.*, 501)—are, as "*involuntary* movement patterns," "automatic reactions which are beyond the sphere of conscious integration"—that is, not "in the sphere of conscious volitional movement" (Fulton, *ibid.*, 503). The term "forced" grasping indicates that it is automatic or uncontrollable and hence involuntary. Athetosis and chorea are "purposeless contortions over which the subject has no control" (Fulton, *loc. cit.*). Somnambulism is involuntary because it is unconscious.

[58] The difference between surprise and preparedness seems to be that the latter enables one to resist strong and to detect weak stimuli (the "alert"). Freud, in *Beyond the Pleasure Principle* (*156*), made interesting suggestions along these lines in regard to trauma from surprise. The essence of preparedness is, of course, to make deliberation, and hence volition, possible.

[59] Lashley (*261*, 14), in addition to disputing Lloyd Morgan's position on the exclusively subcortical nature of instinctive activities (see note 52, above), also disputes his (*Instinct and Intelligence*, 1912) "belief in the reduction of automatized habits to subcortical levels." This instance alone seems enough to confirm Lashley. Motor actions which require the pyramidal tract cannot be reduced to subcortical levels, however automatized.

[60] Motor patterns vary from synergies to fractionated or precise (modified) movements; and both may be combined in long series. Each seems to contain a chief or

These elements of a definition of volition also define for us the locus of its anatomical substrate. In our initial examination of Hughlings Jackson's generalizations we noted that the characteristic of differentiation is one that increases as we pass from lower to higher levels. As a matter of fact, almost all the increase on the efferent side takes place between the highest subcortical and the cortical levels; for we have noted that the characteristic of the hypothalamic somatic responses is that the response to each kind of stimulation is pretty much limited to a stereotyped reaction which varies only with the intensity of the stimulus and, therefore, the extensiveness of the pattern. In the second place, it appears that conflict between stimuli leading to incompatible reactions is always immediately resolved at spinal, and almost immediately at subcortical, levels and always in favor of the strongest.[61] But it is equally apparent that there is something peculiar about the organization of the cortex that permits the comparatively long continuance of unresolved conflicts—a peculiarity at the base of which undoubtedly lies its capacity for inhibition, or, shall we say, its inertia. Shall we say, in turn, that this inertia is due to the fact that all but the strongest incoming stimuli may excite in the cortex a vast complex of re-

---

strategic element, plus at least reciprocal inhibitions and perhaps a complex of associated movements. While volition initiates or terminates the whole and may, in process, slightly modify certain parts, it may be said to be exercised almost wholly as to the strategic element. The very notion of integration (and co-ordination) on the motor side involves this "wholeness."

Thus involuntary movements or involuntary elements of voluntary movements include:

a. All movements produced by short-circuiting below the cortical level, with some degree of exception, perhaps, for some of those which are immediately subcortical, especially in the immature (see note 58, above).
b. All actions, or parts, or sequences of actions which have become so habitual that no deliberation is required, or which follow automatically once the sequence has been started after deliberation.
c. All "associated movements," as parts of wholes, including autonomic excitatory effects.
d. All reciprocal inhibitions.
e. All other inhibitions, including autonomic, except to the extent that they can be voluntarily relaxed.

Therefore, the voluntary elements of movements seem to be restricted largely to initiation, to some degree of direction and variation, to continuance and to cessation of complexes, the bulk of which are involuntary.

Jackson's view is worth noting here. He said (*216*, II, 68–69), "Volition arises during activity of the least automatic nervous arrangements," but is a matter of degree without abrupt transition. The "automatic" arrangements are the best "organized"—that is, those permitting easiest transit; they are the most perfectly reflex. The "nervous arrangements just begun" are the least "organized" and therefore, conversely, the most volitional. Thus, to him, volition was not only a matter of level; it was also a matter of the degree to which a particular pattern has become "organized" even at the highest level. But degree of organization also varies with levels (see above, Section A, note 42). And the antithesis of organization, which is "modifiability," also implies "differentiation" and is the direction of "evolution" (see above, Section A, note 37).

[61] This dictum results from our examination of the evidence of reflexes in Chapter 4, Section D.

lated sensorimotor patterns established by previous stimuli, which distribute and dilute the effect and which, to the extent they are incompatible on the motor side, may establish reciprocal inhibitions, the one to the other? At any rate, while the volitional character of delay, even in the cortex, seems to be a matter of degree, and while the volitional character of movement seems also to be a matter of degree and may not be wholly excluded at subcortical levels, the cortex is at least the chief locus of volition.

"If in one hemisphere as little as 15 to 20 percent of 'agranular' frontal cortex remains intact, the animal ultimately regains some degree of volitional movement" (Fulton, *160*, 453). But, when all the motor and premotor areas are removed, voluntary movement is virtually abolished (Bieber and Fulton, *37*, 434). That tells us the proximate source of practically all voluntary movement. It does not, however, necessarily tell us the ultimate source of the movement and of the previous non-movement—the locus of volition. Hughlings Jackson supposed that, in paralysis, the highest centers may act—the patient tries—but, because the muscles are cut off, no movement occurs. May that "trying" also occur when the lesion is in the motor areas themselves? As we have already noted, among the sensations reported by Penfield and Boldrey (*324*, 433), from stimulation of the excitable cortex of conscious human patients, was "desire-to-move"; and that was contrasted with "sense of movement." Also reported was "a feeling of inability to carry out some movement . . . as though the patient were made aware of stimulation of an inhibitory mechanism." The first sensation seems identical with the sense of volition; the second, however, presumes that sense to be elsewhere. In accordance with our inferences (p. 1143) that the conflicts and their resolution (delayed reactions) take place, not in the motor cortex, but in those regions where the thinking process takes place, whence both the conflict while in process and its resolution reach the arena of consciousness, we might infer that the locus of volition is also there.[62] In fact, we might identify volition with the delay (inhibition) which produces or permits the conflict and with the resolution of the conflict, as well as with deliberation, or the process of the conflict itself.[63] In this way we might gather together our unknowns, consciousness and volition, infer that they are related to a single type of process—deliberation or delayed reaction—and attribute to them a definite locus. If the process of the conflict takes place in the thinking region and is thence conveyed transcortically to the locus of consciousness, then likewise the inhibitory elements of it and its ultimate resolution would be so conveyed. In this view both delay, in general, and volitional delay, in particular, are

[62] This appears to be approximately Penfield's conclusion. He says (*323*, 68): "The localization of those neuronal circuits most intimately associated with the initiation of voluntary activity and with the sensory summation prerequisite to it" is the equivalent of the localization of the "place of understanding."

[63] Thus, in psychological terms, we might say that an action is only voluntary when the patient knows what he is going to do before he does it, by reason of some knowledge other than past experience of his own reactions.

conceived to involve and require consciousness; perhaps, in the case of volitional delay, this is because the conflict itself, of which volition constitutes the process, its maintenance and its end, is the chief occasion for consciousness.[64]

I. SUMMARY AND GENERAL INFERENCES

On the basis of the new and revolutionary results of neurophysiological investigation which we have attempted to summarize in this appendix, it becomes necessary to revise older ideas as to the organization and functioning of the central nervous system. That is particularly true with reference to the part it plays in the maintenance of homeostasis and the causation of behavior. Subject to the numerous qualifications made in preceding pages, which will not be repeated here, we may, for purposes of clarification and simplification, set up certain broad (and necessarily rough) generalizations.

1. In the hierarchical organization of the central nervous system there are two (not one) highest levels, so-called, that of the old brain and that of the new brain.[1] They are somewhat independent of each other since the afferent material from below which excites each is different from that which excites the other—perhaps completely so. Nevertheless, the two highest levels interact directly on each other and co-operate or even conflict at lower effector levels which they control jointly. The highest level of the old brain is the hypothalamic region. We cannot yet precisely circumscribe it but have called it the hypothalamus without specific anatomical connotation. It is very small because it is very slightly differentiated (that is, hardly more than a single effect is possible from a single cause); but it is very energetic (that is, it is capable of very intense and extensive outflow of excitation). On the contrary, the new brain—the cerebral cortex—is very large because it is enormously differentiated, but corre-

[64] Certainly volition, both as inhibition and resolution of the conflict, requires consciousness. However, it is usually said that there can be unconscious thinking. If so, all thinking does not require consciousness. But if, according to our hypothesis, thinking is deliberation, deliberation is conflict, and conflict is the occasion for consciousness, there could be no unconscious thinking. But this dilemma is only apparent, not real. Unconscious thinking, if any, would certainly not be regarded as volitional. It would be involuntary as well as unconscious. As our first occasion for cortical delay, we have already included excitations which do not pass out in the form of motor action at once, not because they are in conflict and mutually inhibit each other, but merely because they are subliminal as to the motor outlet (revery, etc.). If there is unconscious thinking, it might be supposed that it too, while representing conflict and therefore mutual inhibition, consisted of so low a level of excitation as to be subliminal even as to access to consciousness. All of which is consonant with our statements on p. 1146.

[1] Hess, writing in 1932 (*193*, 1201), could say "The physiology of the central nervous system has hitherto been practically governed by the notion of a hierarchy, with the cortex as the great high priest." It was then still "almost unthinkable that psychic faculties should be placed under the influence of the autonomic nervous system."

Now it appears that the real distinction is not between an autonomic and a motor brain, but between the primarily interoceptive and the primarily exteroceptive brain.

spondingly much less energetic in proportion to its size. In respect of integration the highest level of the old and the new brain are on a par, both representing the whole body.

2. The upcoming, or afferent, system to the highest level of the old brain consists of three divisions and provides two different kinds of excitor. Probably this system has no direct access to the new brain. The three divisions are:

a. Interoceptive with humoral excitors—that is, physical conditions or chemical constituents of the blood—which reach the highest level of the old brain directly via the circulation and lymph (and possibly cerebrospinal fluid).

b. Interoceptive with neural excitors—that is, impulses over afferent nerves—which reach it for the most part indirectly via the so-called paleothalamus. There may also be some direct afferents.

c. Exteroceptive with neural excitors of a crude type which appear to reach it indirectly via the paleothalamus and possibly also, as to two distance receptors, via the corpora quadrigemina, or the geniculates, or both.

Many, perhaps most, of what we have called internal present wants are propagated centripetally to the old brain by the first division (a, above). Most of these are probably also propagated, and all the rest of the internal present wants are certainly transmitted, by the second division (b, above), which probably conveys visceral paleosensibility, including visceral and vascular pain. Some of what we have distinguished as quasi-external present wants, because they correspond to the immediate effects of relations with the environment, are probably transmitted by the third division (c, above). Whence and how the others (cause of rage, etc.) are transmitted we do not know.

3. The downgoing, or efferent, or effector, system from the highest level of the old brain also consists of three divisions and uses two different kinds of effector. The three divisions are:

a. Interofective with humoral effectors. These are the hypophyseal endocrine secretions controlled in—or in co-operation with—the hypothalamus.

b. Interofective with neural effectors. This is the autonomic system with its two divisions, the sympathetic and the parasympathetic.

c. Exterofective with neural effectors. This is that part of the somatic or motor system called extrapyramidal, which includes not only the tracts but also the subcortical but supraspinal centers through which all impulses are relayed.

4. The upcoming, or afferent, system to the new brain, on the other hand, appears to consist of one division only, with one kind of excitor. This one division includes, of course, many different sense modalities; but it is all neural; it is all relayed from the neothalamus (except perhaps taste and smell); and it is all projected thence over the radiations, chiefly to the sensory cortex, somatic and other, in the several lobes. Probably this system

has no direct access to the highest level of the old brain. It conveys all somatic neosensibility, so-called, and all but the crudest reports from the distance receptors. In general, this system is exteroceptive—that is, it relates to the external environment—though it probably also contributes all precise localization to internal sensibility by means of concurrent though independent reports. It is also proprioceptive, perhaps for all muscle and certainly for striated muscle. It may be that the proprioceptive radiations from the thalamus include all radiations which reach the motor cortex directly.

5. The downgoing, or efferent, or effector, system of the new brain, however, is probably again in three divisions, though with one kind of effector only.

a. Interofective. To a different extent for different functions the new brain appears to have direct descending paths to the hypothalamus or to the lower centers of the autonomic system with its two divisions, the sympathetic and the parasympathetic. It is entirely possible that these tracts are utilized only for inhibitory effects, so that positive effects are wholly release phenomena.

b. Exterofective. Again this includes the extrapyramidal system with its several subcortical but supraspinal centers through which all impulses are relayed.

c. Exterofective. The new brain also has available the pyramidal system, reaching directly to the spinal centers (lowest level), which cannot be reached directly by the highest level of the old brain.

6. The first of the highest levels—that of the old brain—seems to be the proximate source of a number of functional categories.

a. Certain parts of the highest level of the old brain appear to be the sole locus of emotional states. The primary causes of these states are present wants, internal or quasi-external. Thus each such state, if primary, is the central representation of a present want. Emotional states, which appear or are expressed as excitement or depression of various kinds, are to be regarded as merely the exaggeration and generalization (spreading) [2] of the excitations which produce the normal specific functions of the highest level of the old brain, or as the paralysis of these functions.

These states are of limited variety (number), but each one is specific and different from the others. Their expression, when over the old brain's own effector system, consists of easily recognized stereotyped responses, both internally (bodily changes) and externally (behavior). But this specificity, so far as the expression is concerned, tends to be reduced as extreme excitement or depression is reached. Only one specific emotional state can exist, with any considerable degree of generalization, at one time.

[2] As we have noted before, spreading is the obvious and to-be-expected result of the structure of the central nervous system. It is not that which requires explanation. Rather, what requires explanation is the fact of non-spreading—that is, of canalization of nervous impulses.

Presumably the momentarily strongest excitor or depressor determines that state.[3]

b. Other parts of the highest level of the old brain appear to be the sole locus of that rhythmic generator of excitation which is basically responsible for the central (supraspinal, at least) tonic condition we have called awakeness. What is the ultimate source or cause of this excitation we do not know. The excitation is evidently non-specific and is, in mature primates, diurnal in its rhythm. It is the general fund which underlies the special activities of the whole central nervous system and the tone of muscles.

7. The second of the highest levels—the new brain—seems to be responsible for a larger number of functional categories.

a. The sensory regions of the new brain and their subcortical relay stations appear to be the only parts of the brain where representation of the external—and perhaps also of the internal—milieu is organized spatially (the somatic sensory and the sight and hearing regions). Correspondingly, the motor regions of the new brain include the only part of the brain capable of behavior (overt sensorimotor activities) which is precisely adjusted along spatial lines to the external milieu (via the pyramidal system).

b. Certain parts of the new brain appear to be the sole locus of consciousness and therefore of sensation[4] and emotion (experience).

c. Other parts of the new brain appear to be the only portion of the central nervous system where sustained conflict between antagonistic impulses can occur without immediate effect (i.e., no behavior). Elsewhere, there can be overt vacillation between alternatives, and there can be conflict, but only in the sense of innervation of both of a pair of antagonist muscles. For this reason these parts of the new brain appear to be the sole locus of deliberation and its cause and consequence, volition (i.e., the delay of reaction and its subsequent release or resolution) and to be the source whence this material reaches and helps to produce consciousness.

d. Parts of the new brain (or perhaps only the so-called association areas) seem to contain the locus, or loci, of what we call memory, in the strict sense of previously formed impressions and movements (Hughlings Jackson) capable of recall to consciousness in a subliminal condition. Here we refer only to the revival of a sensorimotor pattern which does not correspond to, and is not directly caused by, a current internal or external stimulus. Nevertheless, this category is very difficult to define or circumscribe. As we shall note in Chapter 5, it is not readily distinguishable from other phenomena of modification, restoration and repetition.

8. The direct interaction between the two highest levels—that of the

[3] We have already postulated this on p. 1059 and p. 1084; it will be supported and elaborated in Chapter 4, Section D.

[4] The fact that, as Fulton puts it (*160*, 377), Head and Holmes demonstrated that "cortical lesions produced, not anesthesia, but a selective disruption of the discriminative and integrative functions underlying perception" is not proof, of course, that true sensation (implying consciousness) does not require the integrity of the sensory cortex.

old brain and the new brain—appears to include a number of different varieties each over its own path or avenue.

Those varieties of interaction which act upon the new brain from the highest level of the old appear to be:

a. The stream of tonic excitation which maintains what we have called awakeness and which underlies the epiphenomenon, consciousness. This is rhythmic (diurnal in the mature); it appears to spread over the cortex generally from a single focus, to have no specific character—only varying in intensity—and to arise proximately in the mammillary bodies. In other words, it is the interaction of (6b) upon the cortex.[5]

b. The stream of emotion, or affect, or drive. Apparently this forms a joint stream with that which causes awakeness. Nevertheless, it seems to be the independent result of the emotional states described in (6a); it seems to rise in the hypothalamus generally rather than in the mammillary bodies only; it seems to be composed of a considerable number of different and specific kinds of excitation, reflecting the different emotional states in the highest level of the old brain; it seems to be responsible for most of the excitation of the cortex not contributed by the rhythmic factor, awakeness (8a), and to be the chief energizing factor in so far as the present want system is concerned; and it seems to endow and to some extent energize different sets of cortical patterns—current and revived—with the different and specific kinds of excitation which correspond to the various wants (emotions).

c. Some sort of sampling of the specific excitations in the hypothalamus (6a) also appears to reach, by way of an independent path, the prefrontal areas of the cortex, where it reproduces in a precise but attenuated way the subcortical effects of the present want system. Also this interaction works, in the prefrontal areas, upon a far more highly evolved apparatus. It corresponds generally, therefore, to the effects of a lower upon a higher level rather than, like (a) and (b) to interaction between two levels that are on a par.

In some way this stream seems to be responsible for the original endowment of sensorimotor patterns in the cortex, which have been derived from the exteroceptive-exterofective system, with the specific kinds of emotion represented in the emotional stream (8b). That is, the prefrontal area, or this stream (8c), acts as a sort of catalytic agent to invest these cortical patterns with an "interest" corresponding to a specific want.

Those varieties of interaction which act upon the highest level of the old brain from the new appear to be:

d. Some general, moderate, but variable, inhibition of the hypothalamus itself or of its neural afferents (paleothalamus) by the prefrontal areas. Because of the source of this and the following form of inhibition (e) the emotivity of an animal (including man) seems to bear an inverse ratio

[5] But, as we have noted, this rhythmic effect has a far wider reach than merely to the cortex. As Foster Kennedy puts it (*236*, 864), "The hypothalamus is a neuro-glandular instrument in command of vital rhythm."

to the functional development of its prefrontal areas, phylogenetically or ontogenetically. Apparently, with warning, this inhibition can be stepped up from its ordinary level—the level existing if surprised; that is, if there is no warning.

e. Some general and also variable, but stronger, inhibition upon the immediate motor outlets (exterofective) of the highest level of the old brain, also by the prefrontal areas. The lesser strength of the forms of inhibition covered in (d) as compared with that in (e) is probably largely responsible for the emotional stream. That is, the fact that an emotional state exists at all in the highest level of the old brain argues that inhibition (d) has been overcome, or that this inhibition has merely tempered it. On the other hand, if the downgoing paths were open, most of this excitation would go down as expression rather than to the cortex as emotion (experience). Therefore, it seems to be the superior degree of control exercised as inhibition (e) that drives the surplus of excitation in excess of inhibition (d) along its other outlet, as emotional stream, to the cortex.

f. A capacity upon the part of sensorimotor patterns in the cortex in general (or perhaps only in the association areas), once they have become emotionally endowed there, to become secondary causes of the corresponding specific emotional states in the hypothalamus. In the case of what we have called quasi-external wants this secondary cause seems adequate by itself to excite the corresponding emotional state there, though of lesser intensity; in the case of the internal wants it seems to be capable of so doing only when the specific pattern of the corresponding state is already being facilitated in the hypothalamus by its primary upcoming cause.

g. Reciprocal (co-ordinating) inhibition of the immediate motor outlets (exterofective) of the highest level of the old brain by the motor cortex (probably only the premotor areas), in order, within limits, to prevent interference when the latter is itself activating, or preparing to activate, the subcortical motor centers in some specific pattern.

h. Associated (co-ordinating) excitation (or release of inhibition) of some of the specific autonomic efferent elements of the hypothalamus by the motor cortex (probably only the premotor areas). The route taken by those co-ordinating impulses, which produce, via the autonomic system, bodily changes appropriate to the motor activities (behavior) going on or being prepared, seems to be direct to the hypothalamus in certain cases and may be partly direct in all. But it is entirely possible, as noted, that all their apparently excitatory effects are purely release phenomena.

We have had to leave open the question whether or how far the effects included in (g) and (h) are produced also or only by indirect interaction (i.e., by action upon lower centers themselves rather than via tracts to the hypothalamus).

9. The indirect interaction, or effector relations, between the highest level of the old brain and the new is due to the fact that they appear jointly to control all of one effector system (interofective) and a considerable part of the other (exterofective).

a. So far as the interofective (autonomic) system is concerned, it appears that the highest level of the old brain has descending paths (3b, above) to lower centers involved in all vegetative functions. To what extent these paths are indirect to supraspinal and spinal centers or direct to the extra-spinal ganglia is also not yet known. These paths are involved in the central management of the vegetative functions and in the bodily changes which take place as a result of emotional states.

In so far as the autonomic effects producible from the cortex (probably premotor areas) are not the result of direct interaction upon the hypothalamus (8h) they argue for descending paths from the cortex to the lower centers of the autonomic system (5a, above). These putative paths are then involved in the same way as (8h) in the co-ordination of bodily changes produced by the autonomic system with motor activities (behavior) going on or being prepared. Again we must note that this co-ordination may be composed wholly of release phenomena.

b. The premotor areas of the cortex act upon—and only upon—the subcortical but supraspinal motor centers (extrapyramidal system, 5b, above) to modify bodily posture and to produce synergies which may be of considerable competence and large variety.

The hypothalamus can also act upon these centers (3c, above), and they are the only access it has to the exterofective system. Nevertheless, while the highest level of the old brain appears to have a greater energizing power there than the cortex has, the postural changes and synergies it produces are, in primates and man, notably cruder and more primitive than those produced by the cortex through the same apparatus.[6]

These joint controls over the interofective and over this one of the two exterofective systems appear to permit co-operation between the two highest levels. That is, to the extent that there is excitement—an emotional state in the highest level of the old brain—there may be leakage from the hypothalamus to its own exterofective outlets which adds energy to, while detracting from the skill of, the movement coincidently produced by the cortex. To the same extent, excitement in the highest level of the old brain may increase and spread there in such a way as to include many, even inappropriate, autonomic effects. In this case, also, the result of excitement seems generally to detract (i.e., there is an overaction which does not contribute to effectiveness). On the other hand, beyond a certain degree of excitement or in a depressed emotional state, conflict seems to arise between the two partners in control, with varied but even more untoward results. In extreme excitement this may lead to almost complete short-circuiting (i.e., the highest level of the old brain secures almost complete control of the extrapyramidal system).

However, the highest level of the old brain has no access to the pyramidal portion of the exterofective system, and is therefore incapable of produc-

[6] While this contrast between the extrapyramidal effects produced by the highest level of the old and by the new brain seems to conflict with Tower's observations, as recorded on p. 1210, it seems necessary to assume that it exists, as to primates at least, in view of the facts adduced on p. 1218 and elsewhere.

ing directly the modified and fractionated activities which are solely within the power of the areas of the cortex (chiefly motor area) in which these tracts originate. The only subcortical influence on this system is via the emotional stream (8a) to the cortex, which may provide the energy and the direction (see 11) of the cortically initiated behavior.

10. Phylogenetically and ontogenetically, the new brain, as the term implies, is late. On the other hand, all of the patterns of behavior and of autonomic effects of which the highest level of the old brain is capable are innate—that is, their paths are already laid down, and they are either available at birth, or within a few days thereafter when the new environment has had time to reach them,[7] or they develop uniformly and solely as a result of the process of maturation. True, they may come later to be somewhat modified by practice; but they never become other than primitive in their character, for they are the inheritance from the primitive stage phylogenetically. While the patterns of behavior and of the nicely coordinated autonomic by-products of which only the new brain is capable are, in part, the result of the anatomical organization of that brain, the main features of which are laid down, in the germ, at birth, it is also true that in man this brain is not functioning at birth. Unlike the old brain, it is developed in the course of, and by, contact with the external environment. We may say that it is the product of experience of that environment (of reaction to it). The fact that the external environment is somewhat uniform and the fact that all human experience is somewhat similar are responsible for such of the uniformities of the new brain among different human beings as are not merely due to the characteristics laid down in the germ (inheritance). Therefore, in the developmental as well as in the anatomical sense, it is roughly true that the highest level of the old brain is the representative and product of the internal environment, which exists at birth or develops solely from maturation, while the new brain is the representative and product of the external environment, with which the organism is only in contact after birth. But, since the internal environment, after birth, must dwell within the external environment, the two must develop a meeting place somewhere in the organism. That meeting place, or system for meeting, appears to be the system of direct interaction between the highest level of the old and the new brain,[8] which develops after birth and through to death, and which we have undertaken to examine in the foregoing so far as the limits of present knowledge permit.

11. This system of interaction between the two environments and their

[7] See pp. 1081–1083 and 1088 ff.

[8] It seems to me that the last stand of the reflexologists—the school which attributes behavior to external stimulus—is being made along the fissure of Rolando. And there, well-entrenched, they will have to fight it out. For there, and in that neighborhood, is the ultimate divide which differentiates the incoming stream from the outer world and the outgoing stream to the outer world.

From our point of view, behavior is the resultant of two streams—that from the outer and that from the inner milieu—and is determined at their confluence. The locus of that confluence is not yet established; but it is certainly not along the fissure of Rolando. In fact it may not be strictly localized at all.

representatives is evidenced by what we call orientation. For orientation has two aspects—a dual function. Orientation is direction *by* one influence and *to* another. Excluding memory, the first influence always arises internally. It is what we have called a present want. The second influence only exists externally. When driven by food-hunger an animal has a tendency to be oriented *to* any food object. Thus the tendency is internally determined. But, if a particular food object is disclosed and recognized in the environment, the animal will be oriented to that particular object. Thus the spatial direction is externally determined. Conversely, if the animal is oriented *by* sex-hunger it will not be oriented *to* a food object, but, rather, *to* a sex object. Moreover, the drive cannot be diverted from its own object —the object which has been conditioned to it.[9]

The internal determinant of orientation—the drive, or kind of emotional state, or want—is also the chief energizer of behavior in response to present wants.[10] It is, in a mechanical sense, the neural motive power operating the mechanism in their behalf. All that the exteroceptive senses do is to locate the external objective, an objective which the organism has found by example or experience is of "interest" in connection with a want. Thereafter, the exterofective apparatus, the precise part of which has developed in so close a relation to the exteroceptive senses, operates with the guidance of the latter as the mechanism for the application of the motive power.

Thus the highest level of the old brain appears to be the chief energizer of behavior, at least in response to present wants. A part of this energy is the general and non-specific tonic excitation of awakeness. But most of it —that part which varies both in degree and in kind (direction)—is itself the response of the highest level of the old brain to the different present wants of the organism; it is the emotional state produced there.[11] This

[9] But, as we shall show in Chapter 3, any external stimulus, however inappropriate, which has become conditioned to a want, becomes the object of that want if the want exists, or if a replica of it can be aroused by that stimulus.

It should be noted that our use of the term "orientation" in this appendix is a much narrower one than that in use in biology. We mean here only attention to, or motion toward some particular element in the scene, not general relations to the environment, such as posture, selection of habitat or other situations.

[10] While he did not then have the physiological grounds for his dictum which are now available, McDougall seems to have expressed the conclusion which these grounds now indicate along much the same lines. However, he seems to have made his conclusion too all-embracing, as we shall see later. He said (*284*, 45), "The instinctive impulses [approximately our wants] determine the ends of all activities and supply the driving power by which all mental activities are sustained." Morton Prince (*331*, *161–169*) expresses his hypothesis almost exactly as we have done. He suggests that emotion be regarded as energy: "It provides the drive for the response of the mechanism to the stimulus"; the discharge of energy apparently runs "synchronously with the occurrence of the emotion and continues as long as the emotion persists." He also suggests that, per Cannon, the "locus of origin of the psychical energy" may be in the "thalamus" (now the hypothalamus). He does not examine the question of the excitor from which the emotional state arises.

[11] Writing in 1866, Hughlings Jackson could say (*216*, II, 122), "It would seem that the centres for the emotional and the semi-voluntary and involuntary actions are in the

energy may explode into the old brain's own outlets, exterofective and interofective. But, except in states of extreme excitement, much of it, or most of it, is drawn off over cortical paths as emotion, or drive. Once in the new brain, though it fixes the objective, it is itself directed by a combination of the current representation of the external environment and of the past experience of that environment (revivals and recognitions) into the more skillful and adapted exterofective and interofective apparatus which is only available to the new brain.

So far as present wants are concerned, the highest level of the old brain is the chief energizer. The new brain is chiefly the applier and the restrainer of this neural energy.[12] The degree in which the latter succeeds in exercising its control varies from zero to almost complete canalization of this energy. Thus the resulting forms of behavior vary from the primitive, which are only adapted to the external environment to the extent that adapted patterns have been inherited (have become innate) due to natural selection, up to the most recently learned, which are adapted to the environment as precisely as the capacity for control, for learning and for adaptation on the part of the new brain permit.

---

pons, medulla oblongata and spinal cord, but where the power is that sets them a-going is not clear." Today the source of "emotional and energic drive" appears to be the hypothalamus (Foster Kennedy, *236*, 874).

[12] In Chapters 5 and 6 we will discuss the respects in which the new brain appears also to be an energizer. That qualification is omitted here because the evidence for it is wholly non-physiological (i.e., external observation and inference only). This appendix is concerned with the neurological evidence, only, and its reconciliation with other data.

III

DATA ON FUTURE WANTS

Appendix to Chapters 5 and 6

A. "CAPITALISM" IN THE ANIMAL WORLD

MAN IS NOT the only species of animal life which evinces the type of behavior analyzed in the fifth chapter of the text—the chapter entitled "Future Wants—Their Nature." That type of behavior is distinguished by precurrent reactions evidently suitable to the satisfying of a certain want, which behavior stops short of the appropriate consummatory reactions in the series for the apparent reason that the want does not then exist. While this behavioristic phenomenon does not extend far into the animal kingdom, we find a few cases which appear to be, or might be construed to be, of this order. It is customary to study animals, and particularly those to be mentioned here, from the standpoint of the subjective or introspective view man has of himself. This leads to the tendency, when one observes behavior like that of man, to impute it to the same causes to which we impute our own (anthropomorphism). Here we shall follow the opposite approach. We are observing animal behavior of certain types first, for the sake of getting rid of prepossessions so far as possible, and then interpreting man's behavior in terms of these results of purely objective observation. Furthermore, in order to avoid starting off with a rigidly selected and limited classification, we shall include all types of behavior which might be construed to comply with the foregoing definition and shall leave it to the final analysis to determine which types conform and which do not.

At the start, it is worthy of note that any behavior that might be construed to belong in this classification is practically confined to animal life belonging in only two of the eighteen phyla, or prime groups, and, in these two phyla, in only seven of the legion of families.[1] That is, to use the current classification in zoology, we are here concerned only with three families, Formicoidae (Ants), Vespidae (Wasps) and Apidae (Bees) within the Order Hymenoptera of Phylum 11, Appendiculata; and with three families, Sciuridae (Squirrels), Castoridae (Beavers) and Muridae (Mice) within the Order Rodentia, and one family Anthropidae (Genus

[1] The last statement does not include birds, which are considered in one connection, nor apes, which are considered in one other, since both are probably to be excluded in the last analysis.

Homo, Species Homo Sapiens, or Man) within the Order Primates, both of which orders belong within Class 4, Mammalia, of Phylum 12, Vertebrata. Both phyla, 11 and 12, belong in Grade 2, Coelomocoela, of Branch b, Enterozoa, of Grade B, Metazoa. This gives some idea of the restricted scope of such behavior. It excludes almost all of the species of the animal world.

The explanation of this extremely limited scope—the fact that capitalism is the very rare exception in the animal world—is not at all clear. Climate seems to have something to do with it; but winter works in this direction only on very few of the species whose habitat shows marked variation between the seasons. Position in the phylogenetic series certainly has something to do with it, for the families named above are notable by reason of the fact that they are always named last—as the most highly evolved—in their respective lines of descent. They represent the extreme ends of two or three branches from the main trunk of the evolutionary tree. Moreover, in each order, it is the several families whose behavior shows the greatest "plasticity," as the biologist phrases it—that is, the least stereotyped systems of reaction—which also show these characteristic forms of behavior. But there is another correlation which is more notable than any other. All of these mammals—the anthropoids (apes and men) and these rodents (squirrels, beavers, rats, and mice)—have developed the capacity to sit up (or crouch), or stand up on their hind legs, thus freeing their forelegs (or arms and hands) for other than postural and locomotive purposes. This is the permissive factor in the forehanded manipulation that is characteristic of these particular families, and of no others. Something analogous is apparent with ants, at least, among these insect families. Are this faculty and this characteristic behavior directly related; does one follow from the other? Or are they merely two independent signs of a cortical development induced by some other cause?

For purposes of analysis only we shall undertake to examine for each of the aforementioned animal families—and, at the start, for birds and apes—the evidence we can adduce from trustworthy sources as to nine types of behavior which might be construed to be of the order we are considering. These nine types will be named according to their results and will be defined as follows:

1. Self-made residences—nests, burrows, hives, etc.
2. Other adaptations of the environment that appear to make conditions more favorable for residence and living.
3. Tools, found ready-made, for aiding in activities.
4. Apparatus, self-made, for accomplishing what would otherwise be impossible.
5. Domestication of other species.
6. Care and feeding of young or queen by others than mothers.
7. Storing of food supplies for self.
8. Storing of food supplies for others than self.
9. Labor-saving devices.

BEAVERS

The beaver is a rodent "rather low in the scale, and the brain is smooth, wanting in convolutions" (*426*, 24). Its food is all vegetable, in the winter consisting of the inner bark, mostly of soft-wood deciduous trees (but also of conifers) among which the aspen is preferred (*426*, 104), so that this constitutes its principal food tree (*ibid.*, 18). In the summer the diet is varied, either for variety or conservation (*ibid.*, 104) and consists as well of berries, water lilies, and the roots of water plants (*277*). Beavers "always work at night and with great expedition" (*277*). The family usually consists of a pair, the young of the year and that of the previous year, so that there are seven or eight members (*426*, 72)—or four to twelve (*354*, 367). The colony usually consists of several families living close together (*354*, 367).

1. *Self-made Residences.* Beavers make two types of residence. The first is a mere burrow in the bank.[2] This may be the only residence, or one or more burrows may be made to serve as accessory residences, or refuges, when the true residence is of the second type (*426*, 58, and *303*).[3] Of the more artificial type, the beaver lodge, there are three sub-types, the island, bank, and lake lodge. The floor of the first is the surface of an island in the stream; that of the second is in whole or in part the soft, steep bank of a stream or pond, while the rest is, so far as necessary, built up from the bed of the stream which it overhangs; that of the third, because it is built upon hard, shelving banks, always extends for half or two thirds of its area over the stream itself and is therefore again built up from the bed (*354*, 368–370, *303* and *426*, 58). "The lodge is but a burrow above ground, covered with an artificial roof" (*303*). That is, it is a pile of sticks,[4] brushwood, and mud (*354*, 369) into which the beavers burrow up from below after the lodge is built and in which, when above water level, they burrow out a chamber. Dugmore (*121*) is quoted to the effect that there are two chambers, one a few inches below the other and entered first, which permits the draining off of water adhering to the fur before entering the main chamber. In the main chamber there is bedding of grass or shredded wood (*426*, 72). One other comfort is to be noted. Occasionally there are found small piles of beaver-cuttings on the outside walls at the ends of the lodges. "These, the trappers affirm, are purposely left there by the beavers to keep the snow loose . . . during winter for the admission of air" (*354*, 370).

All authorities agree that late each "autumn the lodges are usually plastered well with fresh mud, at least in those regions where there is severe

[2] Warren believes the beaver who lives in burrows is not a different kind, but that this adaptation or atavism occurs when beavers are attracted by plentiful food supplies in the neighborhood of a stream which is too rough, or too swift, or too wide, or too deep to permit the building of a dam and therefore of a lodge.

[3] I have not been able to consult Morgan's work (*303*) and am therefore using quotations from it, without pagination, that appear in Romanes (*354*).

[4] The sticks used are those remaining after eating the bark off the trees cut and collected.

cold" (*426*, 70–71).[5] This freezes when frost sets in and thus "becomes almost as hard as stone, so that neither wolves nor wolverines can disturb their repose" (*277*). Thus, "the whole lodge progressively increases in size"; since repair work is simultaneously conducted on the interior—removing decayed sticks, etc.—the chamber also increases; and since the same lodges may be occupied for centuries they become very large, the main chamber sometimes measuring seven or eight feet across (*354*, 368–369). On the other hand, when the food trees are exhausted, beaver ponds and lodges are abandoned (*426*, 43). The so-called beaver meadow is second growth, after the forest is cleared (*354*, 384). "A pond never becomes a beaver meadow as long as the beavers continue to occupy it. Let them abandon it however, and a meadow may be formed in a surprisingly short time"—twelve to fifteen years (*426*, 51). When the new crop is grown the beavers may return (*ibid.*, 43).

The "lodges have smooth slides or trails from their tops down to the water." Since these show no footmarks, they are apparently used for sliding quickly into the water (*426*, 72). But the entrances to the chambers are long (sometimes ten-foot) tunnels that descend from the floor into the water (after the dam is built) and which open into the stream (or a trench) below the level to which the water will freeze (*426*, 61). One, the wood entrance, is straight but not steep, to permit bringing in the sticks upon the bark of which they subsist in the winter; the other, the beaver entrance, is crooked and steep (*303*).

2. *Other Adaptations of the Environment.* Chief among these is the beaver dam. "As the dam is not an absolute necessity to the beaver for the maintenance of his life—his normal habitation being rather natural ponds and rivers and the burrows in their banks[6]—it is, in itself considered, a remarkable fact that he should have voluntarily transferred himself, by means of dams and ponds of his own construction, from a natural to an artificial mode of life." The more so, for, "when they leave their normal mode of life . . . and undertake to live in dependence upon artificial ponds of their own formation, they are compelled to prevent the consequences of their acts at the peril of their lives" (*303*). Thus, in the artificial mode of life, the dam is "necessary to their existence in many cases, and absolutely essential to their welfare" in all (*426*, 28). In otherwise shallow streams it forms an artificial pond that serves the purpose of providing a sufficient depth of water in which to move about in safety and to which

[5] Lydekker (*277*) states that this repair work does not begin until the first frost sets in and that the outer coating is never finished until the cold becomes severe. On the other hand, when a new lodge is to be built, the beavers fell the wood early in the summer, though they seldom begin building till towards the end of August.

[6] In the Cascade Mountains of Oregon and California beavers still live in their natural habitat (*354*, 370). Frolov (*157*, 35 and 36) thinks beavers' dams are unconditioned reflexes ("instincts"), since they make them also in captivity when in no danger. If so, why do beavers in certain habitats show no sign of the reflex? The slow changes from the medieval castle to the medieval chateau or from Georgian colonialism to functional modernism were (or are) not the marks of unconditioned reflexes; they were the conservatism of *idées fixes*.

to retreat as a refuge from enemies. It renders easier the transportation of food supplies. It protects the entrances to the lodge and even those of the burrows in the banks. It permits access to these entrances even when the surface water is frozen and thus also provides access to the stores of food submerged around the "wood entrance" (*426*, 51). It is, in fact, the means by which these entrances are kept two or three feet under water (*354*, 373). Again there are two types of dam, the "stick dam" and the "solid-bank dam." The first, the more common, is composed of sticks [7] and poles interlaced, in the interstices of which, on the upper face, is packed an embankment of earth; the second, while the basic structure is the same, contains much more brush and earth on both surfaces. The result is that surplus water percolates through the first, while it requires to be drawn off through a spillway in the second case.[8] This spillway is "purposely widened or narrowed with reference to the amount of water in the stream at different times, so as to insure the maintenance of a constant level in the pond" (*354*, 374–376).[9]

The site selected for the dam is the outlet of a natural pond—usually in a running stream (*426*, 44). Sometimes good judgment is shown in its location; sometimes mistakes are made and it is abandoned (*ibid.*, 42–43). Occasionally it is washed out and is then rebuilt (*ibid.*, 50). But this must usually be due to floods, for, where the current is considerable, the dam is built in a curve with its convex side toward the oncoming water (*277*). The great majority of dams are under five feet high and under fifty feet long, at first (*426*, 35 and 41). But dams have been found up to 400 or 500 feet long—one even 650 feet (*6*). The water is usually raised four or five feet (*303* and *354*, 375). "Practically all dam building is done in the fall in preparation for winter" (*426*, 44). On the authority of Dugmore (*121*), Warren states that "a week of steady work on the part of a family will see a thirty or forty foot dam raised two feet or more," but he thinks that very long dams are the "work of many generations of beavers, and probably constructed intermittently" (*426*, 43 and 35). Agassiz has estimated that some beaver dams are as much as a thousand years old (*6*). From time to time the ponds are drained, partly or wholly, by opening the dams, and then allowed to refill after closing them again (*426*, 46). The only reason suggested for this is to get rid of long stagnant water. If so, it is analogous to the provision for fresh air in the lodges, referred to above.

[7] Again the sticks used—though not the poles—are usually those remaining after eating the bark.

[8] Warren (*426*, 44) disputes Morgan's two types, holding that the solid-bank type is merely older and therefore has undergone more deposit by the stream and perhaps more repair. This sounds reasonable. But Morgan's observations led him to conclude that the "stick dam" is a "cheaper" construction deliberately used for shallow, sluggish waters, while the "solid-bank dam" is necessary when the banks are high and steep and the channel broad and deep. Warren also states he has seen no spillways, though Dugmore (*121*) also testifies to their existence.

[9] Romanes (*354*, 377) wonders what is the mechanism that leads the beavers to make these alterations in the spillway "with a more or less precise *quantitative* reference to the degree of discomfort, actual or prospective [*sic*] which they experience."

Dams are also constructed, ostensibly, for other purposes; sometimes "to provide water in which food supplies may be floated to the main [residential] pool," as supplements to, or in connection with, the canals to be mentioned below; sometimes, above the main dam, to control flood waters; and sometimes, just below the main dam, to back water up against it and thus help it to resist the pressure from water and ice. Of course both the latter may also serve the purpose of transportation (*426*, 51).[10]

The so-called "beaver slide" is another form of adaptation. "On the upper Missouri, where the banks are for miles together vertical, and rising from three to eight feet above its surface, the beavers resort to the device . . . of narrow inclined planes cut into the banks at intervals, the angle of inclination being 45° to 60°, so as to form a gradual descent from a point a few feet back from the edge of the bank to the level of the river" (*354*, 371). For a similar purpose underground passages are reported which run from under water through the bank to the surface of the ground. One was found that opened twenty feet from the edge of the bank, whence a trail led to an aspen grove (*426*, 94). These and some of those mentioned under type 9 below may be construed as labor-saving devices as well as provisions for security. Apparently they serve both purposes.

3. Tools. The beaver appears to use no tools in the sense we are giving that term. In his chief occupation, wood-cutting, he uses his powerful incisor teeth, gnawing at both ends of a section from four to seven inches long and then prying out the chips (*426*, 105). To do this he stands on his hind feet with tail stretched out behind as balance and one or both fore feet resting against the trunk (*ibid.*, 171). In water transportation wood is held in the teeth and mud and stones are brought from the bottom "by carrying them held against its chin by its fore feet, which are pretty efficient hands at such work" (*ibid.*, 29 and 122). Morgan says the latter is the way wood is transported as well (*303*). In land transportation the wood is either pushed or rolled with the fore paws (or hips, *303*), or held in the teeth and dragged, or the beaver walks on his hind legs, supporting one end of the stick with his fore paws and dragging it (*426*, 122). In land transportation of rocks or mud for lodges and dams the beaver also walks on his hind legs, holding the burden against his chest with his fore paws (*354*, 374). Warren concludes (*426*, 88) that his only tool is his fore paw. This calls attention to the important and unusual factor—the beginnings of manipulation; but we do not regard a part of the body as a tool.

4. Apparatus. Nor do we find the beaver devising apparatus which, strictly speaking, permits the accomplishment of the otherwise impossible.

10 The purposefulness of these two last kinds of dam is well supported by Morgan's observations. He notes (*303*) that since the third kind only maintains about a foot of water below the main dam, as against four or five feet above the latter, the neutralization of some of the pressure upon the latter seems to be the only possible explanation. Since the second kind is built above the beaver pond and is about two feet above the level of its lake at ordinary stages of water—whereas all others hold the water near their crests—it is evidently a provision for storage of surplus water, or at least serves that purpose.

Some of the behavior of type 9—canals—might be construed as such. But the overcoming of insuperable obstacles to dragging wood to water which this process entails seems to be entirely incidental to its other functions. The same seems to be true of road-making. That is incidental to the cutting of wood progressively back from the waterways. Occasionally there is cutting to get rid of obstacles. But the beaver goes over or under logs (*426*, 88).

5 and 6. Domestication; Care and Feeding. There is no evidence of domestication of other species among the beavers, nor of symbiosis of any kind. And, since the beaver is a mammal and, after weaning, provision of food is a joint undertaking by the whole family, there is no feeding of the young by other than mothers.

7 and 8. Storing of Food. For the same reason we must treat together the matter of provision of food for self and for others, for the beaver does not distinguish within the family either in the work or in the product.

"When the ice breaks up in spring they always leave their embankments, and rove about [feeding on summer food, as above] until a little before the fall of the leaf, when they return to their old habitations, and lay in their winter stock of food" (*277*). A tree is cut by gnawing a ring around the base, deeper on the side to which it is intended to fell it (*354*, 372). Of the large trees only the branches and upper portions are used (*426*, 124). The branches from two to six inches in diameter are then cut off, cleared of twigs, and these in turn are cut into various lengths according to thickness (weight) to permit of handling by a single beaver. The cutting of the branches is done by making semi-sections on one side, then turning the branch over and finishing from the other (*354*, 372). These lengths vary from four to eight or ten feet long (*426*, 121). The speed of this work is remarkable. Warren quotes Enos A. Mills that a four-inch aspen can be felled in one hour; Dugmore (*121*) that an eight- to ten-inch tree can be felled in one night; and Vernon Bailey that a three- to four-inch aspen can be felled, cut into sections four to eight feet long, and dragged to the water in one night (*426*, 117). But usually the work is not continuous. One colony of eight beavers was observed to have 25 to 30 trees in process at one time. Usually it requires ten to fifteen nights, working intermittently on each tree; sometimes the work lasts for years, and sometimes the beavers cannot finish the job (*ibid.*, 109). Much of the smaller brush or its bark is eaten when it is cut (*ibid.*, 121); so too some of the bark on the log itself (*ibid.*, 124). The transportation of the logs is sometimes gradual, sometimes prompt, and sometimes the harvest is completed before they are transported (*ibid.*, 123). Since the felling may be done up to 400 feet from water, the first transportation is overland (*ibid.*, 131). Thereafter, the wood is floated through the canals and downstream to the residence. There it is sunk in large piles in the stream near the "wood entrance" by piling on top and thus waterlogging the bottom of the pile (*ibid.*, 121). The pile is also anchored to the bed of the stream by transfixing it with pieces of brush stuck into the mud bottom (*354*, 373). Warren quotes Enos A.

Mills to the effect that he has seen food piles three feet deep and 124 feet in circumference which included seven or eight hundred aspen saplings and several hundred willows. The provision may be excessive. If so, it is abandoned in the spring since, then, the beaver prefers fresh provender (*426*, 122). Warren also refers to the Indian tale, current for years, that lazy beavers are exiled from the colony (*ibid.*, 137).

9. Labor-saving Devices. By far the most remarkable type of behavior among beavers—almost unique in the animal world except for man—remains to be mentioned. Its chief example is the beaver canals. These are "built for the purpose of transporting logs [or willow brush (*426*, 87)] from the place they were cut to the pond," and also to serve as a waterway which is safer than land (*426*, 80). The pond dam itself suffices at first and with some lays of the land. That is, it floods the low ground along the stream and thus gives water connection with the first high ground where the trees are, if that is near (*354*, 379). Thereafter, if the high ground is sloping and fairly smooth, the beavers roll and drag their cuttings to the ponds. But, if the high ground is not near, or the trees grow on level ground, the task of land transportation is very arduous. Hence the canal for floating the logs across the intervening rough or level ground (*303*). These are laboriously excavated trenches.[11] Romanes (*354*, 380) states that they are from three to five feet wide and three feet deep; Warren (*426*, 80) gives the dimensions of one as fifteen to eighteen inches wide, with a depth of water from nine to fifteen inches, but he observed another that was three to four feet wide and twelve to eighteen inches deep, and he quotes Morgan (*303*) as saying they are from two to four feet wide and eighteen to thirty inches deep. They run from a few feet to several hundred feet in length (*426*, 80). Morgan (303) cites a single one of 450 feet in length. All roots of trees, brush, etc., are cleared from their course; they have perpendicular sides and abrupt ends (*354*, 380). Usually they run more or less transverse to the bank of the stream or pond and connect with it, sometimes by a channel a foot or more deep, dug in the bed of the stream or pond to deep water, and sometimes by a short trail (one of 25 feet) a few feet above water level (*426*, 82 and 81). All this permits the lateral clearing away from the stream or pond that Agassiz noted (*6*). The connecting canal can be supplied with water by the stream or pond. The disconnected one must be supplied by so constructing it that it receives its own water supply from springs, rivulets, or other drainage on the banks. This problem always arises when the canal reaches to higher ground. "When the rise begins a dam is made and the canal is then continued . . . at a level . . . higher than that before." This upper lock is supplied with water by extending the dam in a wide crescent on each side to collect drainage water or springs or streams or pools at higher levels (*354*, 381).[12]

[11] Warren (*426*, 83) quotes Enos A. Mills to the effect that the excavated earth is always piled on the lower bank of the canal.

[12] Warren (*426*, 83) also says that Enos A. Mills observed a canal that had been abandoned because it would not carry water at the season the beavers needed it.

Thus a series of two or more canals may be built at successively higher levels. Morgan describes a series of four (*303*). Sometimes the first, or a higher level, canal reaches to high ground. There it may bifurcate, and each branch may be carried a hundred feet or more along the edge of the rise, "thus affording them, along this extended [frontage] . . . the great advantages of water transportation for their cuttings" (*303*). The face of the dam between canals that Warren observed "had a long gradual slope which must have greatly facilitated dragging logs over it" (*426*, 80), and "the crests of these dams where they cross the canals are depressed, or worn down, in the centre, by the constant passage of beavers over them while going to and fro and dragging their cuttings" (*303*). The observer usually notes that aspens are in process of being cut at the outer or upper end of a canal or series (*426*, 80 and 81).

Canals are also built merely to ease or shorten traveling. Warren (*426*, 83) says Mills saw one that paralleled a rocky stream descending a steep slope. Occasionally canals are found that connect ponds in series, running from below each dam to the next pond and with trails or slides over each dam into the canal (*ibid.*, 87). And Morgan observed "one or two instances where the land included in a wind or loop of a river was cut through by a beaver canal across the narrowest part 'apparently to shorten the distance in going up and down by water'" (*354*, 383).

Romanes (*354*, 372–373) mentions two instances of what may be called labor-saving behavior which go to support the construction we have placed on the building of canals. "By gnawing chiefly on the side of the trunk remote from the water they make the trees fall toward the water, with the obvious purpose of saving as much as possible the labour of subsequent transport." "Lastly, as a method whereby the beavers can save themselves the trouble of cutting, transporting and anchoring all at the same time, they are prone, when circumstances permit, to fell a tree growing near enough to their pond to permit of its branches being submerged in the water. The animals then well know that the branches and young shoots will remain preserved throughout the winter without any further trouble from them. But of course the supply of trees thus growing conveniently near a beaver-pond is too limited to last long."

SQUIRRELS AND SOME OTHER RODENTS

7. *Storing of Food.* This is the only one of the several types of behavior we are dealing with that might be attributed to the squirrel. But the evidence is equivocal. By way of samples we may cite Schmidt (quoted by William James, *220*, II, 400) who says (*362*), "In the autumn, before the winter sets in, adult squirrels bury as many nuts as they can collect, separately in the ground." He observed a young tame squirrel, supplied with nuts, go through a mimicry of the same process on a blanket, after he had eaten all he wanted, and thus construes the behavior to be instinctive (i.e., congenital). Perhaps this action is instinctive; but apparently it is not of the order we are discussing. True, the squirrel makes caches of nuts in

September and October; but then it apparently forgets about them. "Too much has been made of the Squirrel's thrift." In the winter, when food is scarce, it may *search for* these caches (*393*, II, 465); or it may merely find them again *by accident* (328). At any rate, Pitt construes the action as a "collecting impulse," without remembrance, and therefore suspects that no "foresight" or "provision for the future" is involved (*328*).

On the other hand, this does not seem to be true of the closely allied prairie dog, or of that other rodent called the rat hare. Romanes reports, on good authority, that the burrows of the former "contain a 'granary' or chambers set apart for the reception of stored food" (*354*, 366), and that the latter collects grass in August, spreads it out to make hay and then heaps it in stacks up to six feet high and eight feet in diameter in the crevices of rocks in which it lives, to serve as food in winter (*354*, 365). This does not end the list of rodents that store food for winter consumption; for, as Romanes says (*354*, 352), this practice is "more prevalent" among them "than in any other order of mammals."

MICE AND RATS

2. *Other Adaptations of the Environment.* Romanes (*354*, 363–365) records three observations—and doubtless many more could be found—which fit our classification. In one, mice piled plaster rubbish against the sides of a pot of honey in order to reach the rim. In the second, mice in Iceland are reported to have conveyed their foraged berries and themselves across intervening streams by piling the berries upon pieces of dried cow-dung which they dragged to the edge of the stream and then mounted, themselves, for the ferry ride. In the third, also in Iceland, it is stated that the mice used pieces of dried mushrooms as sacks in which to convey their provisions to the river. Both the latter cases are at least allied to tool-using.

7. *Storing of Food.* In the case of the common rat and the bank vole, Pitt (*328*) concludes that such hoarding as is observed is, as with the squirrel, the result of a "collecting impulse" and is forgotten.

OTHER MAMMALS EXCEPT PRIMATES

7. *Storing of Food.* It is sometimes asserted and sometimes denied that the fox returns to unearth the unfinished remains of a buried meal. Pitt (*328*, 205–206) agrees that they do.

Most of what the wolverine—like the jackdaw—steals and hides seems to be of no possible use. This seems to be due to a spirit of mischief, not to thrift. Nevertheless, wolverines do cache surplus food and *may* eat it later, in spite of their peculiar method of preserving (?) it (*354*, 348–350, quoting J. Rae, F.R.S., and Captain Elliot Cones of the U.S. Geological Survey).

MONKEYS AND APES

3 and 4. Tools, Ready-made, and Apparatus, Self-made. The Yerkeses state (*409*, 369) that chimpanzees use "ready-to-hand objects as implements" and also (*ibid.*, 370) go in search of non-present tools or even "make" them. They conclude (*ibid.*, 577) that "instrumentation," including utilization of objects as tools, does not exist among Prosimiae, but exists in the simplest forms among monkeys and in a variety of forms among anthropoid apes. The "tendency to construct implements, or so to modify environment that objects shall acquire instrumental value, has been observed only in anthropoid apes and man"; this "places the anthropoid apes next to man in ability to achieve adaptation through modification of environment." The tendency itself they regard as evidence of "anticipatory response or foresight"—in other words, a special form of what we have been calling deliberation or insight. The generality of this statement is subject to a few exceptions. But, beyond these, it should be noted that it rests on a very narrow definition of "instrumentation"—one that practically confines it to tools. And this in turn obviously depends on the capacity for that particular type of "manipulation" which makes possible the holding and directing of an object by the hand. All the rodents mentioned above use their forelegs for holding objects, but do not do so in a way that permits them to use these objects to extend their natural powers (i.e., they are limited to built-in tools). And as to the "ability to achieve adaptation by modification of the environment," all the evidence cited in this Appendix goes to prove that that is not at all confined to the anthropoids and man.

Romanes (*354*, 480–482) cites such authorities as Darwin, Cuvier, Rengyer, and Dampier and Wafer to the effect that monkeys have been observed to "draw things toward them with a stick" and even use a "swing" to reach something, otherwise unattainable; to draw a chair over and climb on it in order to reach a door latch; to use a stick as lever to pry open the heavy lid of a chest; to use stones as hammers to smash oyster shells; and even to lay a blanket over a door to keep it from swinging shut. He also cites (*ibid.*, 485–486) his sister's diary in regard to a pet cebu with destructive tendencies who selected the post of a brass bedstead against which to break his egg-cup; broke sticks by passing them down between a heavy chest and the wall; ripped the seams of dresses by pulling out the threads; used sticks to draw nuts toward him and to beat people when angry; and used a shawl, by flinging one end of it forward over his head, to draw nuts toward him. All these are cases of finding ready-made tools. I do not find any other evidence for the *making* of tools or instruments than the statements of the Yerkeses.

BIRDS

1. Self-made Residences. Nidification among birds may be said to be the central battle ground of instinct theory—so much so that we are not going to enter the lists. But two points require to be made. In the first place, this behavior is generally conceded to be somewhat "plastic"—that is, the nests are more or less adapted in material and architecture to the various situations in which they may be placed (e.g., *354*, 299–300). In the second place, while the art of nest-building is known to incubated birds with no experience of a nest, and while nest-building only occurs in the mating period, is absent in castrated animals, and terminates with the building of the nest, the "drive" cannot be wholly associated with the process of building, but must be also associated with the result—the nest. For, if the nest is removed, the process may be repeated up to three or more times; if an artificial nest is supplied, the process is suppressed; and, if this artificial nest is not "right," it will be reconstructed until it is so, or it will be discarded (*368*, 158). We have already suggested (p. 128 and note 2) that the "drive" may be part of the heat-regulating mechanism which arises—at least in the female—from the low generation of heat during pregnancy. That would not, however, explain the existence of unconditioned and yet skillful precurrent reactions capable of producing for each species its particular type of nest. But at this point we are considering only the motivation, not the learned or unlearned behavior.

7. Storing of Food. Pitt (*328*) holds that the behavior of jackdaws and ravens in collecting everything is an even less utilitarian instance of the "collecting impulse" than that of the rodents and carnivores cited above. It seems to have no connection with provision for the future.

ANTS

According to Ray Lankester the "little brain," of which the characteristic is "instinct" and slowness to learn, has its climax in the ant; while the "big brain," poorly endowed with instincts but with great educability, has its climax actually in the horse, the dog, the elephant, and the monkey. In proportion to the size of the body, both the size and structure of the ant's brain is superior to that of any other insect; the closest competitor is the bee (*354*, 140). Wheeler suggests that the ant owes its "social and industrial superiority" to its habitat (land), to its continued contact with its own young and to the fact that it is omnivorous. To which may perhaps be added its comparatively long life.[13]

1. Self-made Residences. The anthill and other ant burrows are familiar. The tree ant of India builds globular nests in trees, made of cow-dung worked into thin scales; in New South Wales ants live in the trunk and branches by excavating the pith of the wood (*354*, 111). One species of African ant lives in little houses built of black tenacious loam on stalks of grass growing on land that is periodically under water. These houses (or refuges) are built before the seasonal inundations; but they are built above the high water mark (*ibid.*, 110). This is remarkable.

2. Other Adaptations of the Environment. Three examples, all of them in connection with behavior to which we refer later, will suffice. "Some ants which keep aphides build out of earth covered ways, or tunnels, to the tress or shrubs where the aphides live"—occasionally, these are even

[13] The life of an ant, unlike that of many other insects, is not confined to a single season. Lord Avebury kept one for six years (*276*, *66*). A queen ant may live from twelve to seventeen years (*437*, *163*).

"continued, on a larger scale, so as to enclose the stems of the plants on which the aphides live" and thus imprison or "stable" them (*354*, 61). The doors to these tunnels are too small for aphides, but large enough for ants (*loc. cit.*). Harvester ants clear all grass and weeds in a disc, fifteen to twenty feet in diameter, above their nests, and then carefully level it by filling hollows with pellets of soil brought from elsewhere (*ibid.*, 103).

3. Tools. I find no observations of precisely this process.

4. Apparatus. Two instances are reliably recorded in which ants overcome artificial barriers to the ascent of a tree—in one case a cloth soaked in tobacco-water wound around the trunk and, in the other, a rim of bird-lime—by building across the barrier a bridge (or road) of earth, small stones, etc., brought from the ground (*354*, 135). Other bridges have been recorded: one built across tar by sticking aphides in the tar (*ibid.*, 136); one built across water by means of a straw (*ibid.*, 137); and one built across an aperture, one inch and a half wide, by dropping a straw across and anchoring both ends with a cement made of earth and saliva (*ibid.*, 138). Finally, it is recorded that ants in South America ferry themselves across rivers on bits of dry wood (*ibid.*, 139). Were these instances of instinct?

5. Domestication. The line between symbiosis and parasitism is not easy to draw. Perhaps these examples range all the way between. As Linnaeus put it, aphides (plant-lice) are the "cows of ants" who "build cowsheds over them," as we have noted (*276*, 51–52). The "milk" or "honey-dew" of the aphides is a sweet secretion which is ejected from the "abdomen upon being stroked in this region by the antennae of the ants" (*354*, 60).[14] Darwin construed this as what we would now call symbiosis, since he observed that aphides are "at last compelled to eject their secretion" of their own accord. He therefore concluded that it is a convenience to them to have it removed artificially and that "they do not excrete solely for the good of the ants" (*105*, I, 323).[15] But the next step is wholly one-sided and anticipatory. "Some ants have acquired such vested interests in certain plant-lice that they actually collect their eggs in the fall [treat them "exactly as if they were their own," *276*, 53], keep them in the nests over winter and in the spring distribute the hatching young over the surface of the plants" (*437*, 178). It is there that they may be "walled in by little 'cattle-pens' of earth," as described above (*393*, II, 518). "This dairy business is, in fact, carried on in all parts of the world" (*437*, 178).[16] Lord Avebury says, "Here are aphides, not living in the ants' nests, but outside, on the leaf-stalks of plants. The eggs are laid early in October on the food-plant of the insect. They are of no direct use to the ants, yet they are not left where they are laid, where they would be exposed to the severity of the weather and to innumerable dangers, but brought into their nests by

[14] Universally accepted, I believe. See *437*, 178; *393*, II, 517; *302*, 425.

[15] Gall insects, cocci, and even caterpillars are also kept by ants in various parts of the world for the same purpose (*354*, 64). So is the Claviger beetle (*276*, 57).

[16] Or, as Morgan states it (*302*, 425), "Hatching them out in the nest, and taking them in the spring to the daisies, on which they feed, for pasture." See also *393*, II, 517–518, and *354*, 60.

the ants, and tended by them with the utmost care through the long winter months until the following March, when the young ones are brought out and again placed on the young shoots of the daisy. This seems to me a most remarkable case of prudence. Our ants may not perhaps lay up food for the winter, but they do more, for they keep during six months the eggs which will enable them to procure food during the following summer" (*276*, 53).

"Many species of ants display the curious habit of keeping in their nests sundry kinds of other insects, which, so far as observation extends, are of no benefit to the ants, and which therefore have been regarded by observers as mere domestic pets." Most are "species which occur nowhere else," and "each species of 'pet' is peculiar to certain species of ants" (*354*, 83). Presumably "they are of some use to their hosts, although we are not yet in a position to surmise what this use can be" (*ibid.*, 84).[17] If the "pet" construction is correct this is, of course, a kind of symbiosis. In Brazil, leaf-cutting ants were observed to use certain leaf-bugs as "beasts of burden" to carry home their cuttings (*354*, 68).[18]

Several species of ants make "slaves" of other ants. Two types must be described. *F. sanguinea* carries off larvae and pupae of other species (usually *F. fusca*), "selecting those which will produce workers" (*276*, 60 ff.).[19] "When the pupae hatch out in the nest of their captors, the young slaves begin their life of work, and seem to regard their master's home as their own; for they never attempt to escape, and they fight no less keenly than their masters in defense of the nest" (*354*, 65). For this reason Wheeler (*437*, 208) thinks they should properly be called "auxiliaries," not "slaves." In England, they are few and are "strictly household slaves" (*105*, I, 338); "they never either enter or leave the nest," so that all the outdoor work of foraging, etc., is performed by the masters" (*354*, 65). In Switzerland, where they are more numerous, they help outdoors to make the nest, search for, tend, and "milk" the aphides, etc., (*105*, I, 339 and 341). "When . . . a nest has to migrate, the masters carry their slaves in their jaws" (*354*, 65). On the other hand, *F. rufescens* "assigns a much larger share of labour to the slaves, which . . . are present in much larger numbers to take it. In this species the males and fertile females do no work of any kind; and the workers, or sterile females, though most energetic in capturing, do no other kind of work" (*354*, 65). Here the master class "does not build its own nest, does not determine its own migrations, [is carried by its slaves in their jaws], does not collect food for itself or its young,

[17] Morgan (*302*, 425) admits the "pet" construction.

[18] Morgan (*ibid.*) accepts this.

[19] Darwin (*105*, II, 341–342) suggested that this "instinct" may have arisen from the capture of pupae of other ants as food—a general practice of ants—which were "unintentionally reared" and then found useful. Since the capture of adults does not seem to be practiced, this seems reasonable. On the other hand, Wheeler (*437*, 209) holds that the origin of the practice is, or was, that the *F. sanguinea* queen, "unable to found its colony independently," goes to the nest of *F. fusca* to start one. The *F. rufescens* queen also invades the nest of *F. fusca*.

and cannot even feed itself" (*105*, II, 341) or its "own larvae" (*354*, *65*); for "the structure of the animal is such as to render self-feeding physically impossible." Its jaws are for fighting only and it can only take liquid food supplied by the slaves (*ibid.*, *66*). Thus *F. rufescens* "is absolutely dependent on its numerous slaves" (*105*, II, 341), and that is evidence "of how ancient an origin the instinct of slave-making must be" (*354*, *66*). Lord Avebury says, with this and one other exception, "I know of no case in nature of an animal having lost the instinct of feeding" (*276*, *63*). But the "instinct" seems to have remained; only the behavior has been altered. For, if the masters are not fed, they remind the slaves of their duty by pulling their legs (*354*, *66*). At any rate, *F. rufescens* has become a parasite on its slaves, unable to live by itself (*276*, *61*).[20]

6. Care and Feeding of Young by Others than Mothers. The workers —sterile females—nurse the eggs, larvae, and pupae until the young ant emerges. They develop the eggs by licking them, and move them around the nest to keep them in favorable conditions of temperature and moisture. When the larvae are hatched they are fed by regurgitation into the intestinal tract, and are cleaned and kept warm and sheltered. During the pupal stage, while no food is needed, the pupae are cleaned and kept warm and dry. When the pupae are ready to emerge, the workers bite through the chrysalis, pull off the inside "skin" and wash, brush, and feed the young ant (*354*, 58–59).[21]

7 and 8. Storing of Food for Self and Others. In the case of the ant these two processes appear to be indistinguishable. With most ants, it appears that, "during the winter, when but little food is required," "certain ants are told off as foragers" and "two or three such foragers are sufficient to provide it" (*354*, 127). But with certain species food is placed in storage as a provision for the future. Honey ants use the crops of certain workers or soldiers for storing honey (*437*, 179). Harvesting ants gather nutritious seeds of grasses—either fallen or cut from the stalk—during the summer and store them in granaries for winter consumption. These granaries are separate from the nurseries for the pupae. Before storage the seeds are denuded of their husks below ground and this chaff is brought to the surface. The seeds are kept dry by bringing them out and curing them in the sun. If, even then, they begin to germinate, the tips of the radicles are gnawed off and the process is arrested (*354*, 96–105).[22] Some argue that

[20] Lord Avebury's editor (*276*, 63, note 36) ascribes this to a "behavior series, which is believed to represent also an evolutionary sequence, from ordinary predatism, leading on through slave-making to temporary and finally permanent social parasitism." But the reader of Aldous Huxley's *Brave New World* recognizes it as the process through which man is proceeding with the development of his mechanical slaves. Only, then, the slaves not being alive, we do not call the process by "bad names."

[21] Wheeler (*437*, 172) regards some of this as "reciprocal feeding." He says the substances on the eggs are "eagerly sought by the adult ants." Regurgitation also occurs between adults. Hence he supposes it is beneficial both ways. And "reciprocal feeding" also occurs between ants and guests (scavengers, predators, and parasites), as well as between ants and other insects that they milk outside their nests.

[22] Wheeler (*437*, 181) agrees and adds that some species have specialized soldiers or major workers with powerful mandibles which serve as seed crushers.

the Texas harvesting ants—those who clear the disc above their nest that was referred to above—are agriculturists. At least, ant-rice is permitted to grow on these cleared discs and is harvested, while all else is weeded before and during the growth of the desired crop (*276*, 46). Lincecum was positive that the ants sowed the seeds of the rice; others assert that it sows itself.[23] When harvested and threshed the seeds are chewed, made into little biscuits, dried in the sun and then stored (*393*, II, 518). These ants also collect termites when, during and after a rain, they have been beaten down while swarming in their marriage flight. The termites are placed, alive or dead, in the granaries, doubtless also as food provision (*354*, 108–109).

If the harvesting ant is not a true agriculturist, at least it is certain that the leaf-cutting ant is a true horticulturist, for these are "mushroom growers and eaters" (*276*, 43).[24] These ants "mount a tree in multitudes," cut off sections of leaves and then either drop them to others below or carry them down. The leaf-cutting is carried by holding one edge of it in the jaws and tossing it so that it rests on the head and back, out of the way, as a sort of banneret.[25] "The leaves the ants bring in are not eaten, but are masticated to a pulp [stored away in the nests] and used as a fertilizer [or soil] on which to grow the fungus which is their only food—indoors at least" (*393*, II, 520). This "soft whitish mould" (*loc. cit.*) is a mould-like fungus (mycelium) that is treated in some way by the smallest caste of workers so as to produce swellings (bromatia) which are eaten by the ants and fed to their larvae. Bromatia are really "anomalous growths induced by the ants" (*437*, 182). They also use the excrement of other insects, especially of caterpillars, as a substratum for their gardens (*ibid.*, 187). When they migrate they carry the ant-food with them (*354*, 95).

9. Labor-saving Devices. The leaf-cutting ants construct roads by biting off the grass close to the ground for a breadth of five inches and then throwing the grass to one side (*354*, 95). This they do the more readily to carry, from the trees where they are cut, the bulky pieces of leaves they are taking to their nest, a task that would be most difficult through thick grass.

BEES

Bees are vegetarian or "flower-wasps." The nectar of the flowers is converted in the crop into honey—that is, sucrose is digested into the invert sugars, levulose and dextrose (*437*, 98–99). The other food (for larvae only) is "bee-bread" which "consists of the pollen of flowers worked into a kind of paste by the bees." The pollen is "kneaded into a little ball and

[23] That is Lord Avebury's conclusion (*276*, 46), but his editor states that it is still an unsettled question (*loc. cit.*, note 25). Wheeler thinks they neither sow nor cultivate after the original clearing, and therefore "can hardly be regarded as true agriculturalists" (*437*, 181).

[24] Conceded by Wheeler (*437*, 159 and 181) and by Lord Avebury's editor (*276*, 46, note 25).

[25] It is for the purpose of making possible the transportation of these bulky leaf-cuttings through thick grass that these ants make the roads referred to above.

carried back to the hive in the 'pollen-basket,' a little cavity in the bee's hind-leg" (*393*, II, 524). Perhaps because they are more susceptible to cold than are wasps, their working day is shorter—only about thirteen to thirteen and one-half hours. Lord Avebury has counted 116 visits to flowers in a day, carrying 64 grains of honey (*276*, 247). Bees live from year to year (*354*, 167).[26] Whereas the queen ant "is the perfect female of her species" (*437*, 162), the worker of the stingless and honey bee is the typical female and, except in the development of her ovaries, the queen exhibits a degeneration of the typical secondary characters of her sex—that is, she is "a degenerate female, a mere egg-laying machine, entirely dependent on her worker progeny" (*437*, 122, and 137). With the honey bee, "when the queen's eggs are fertilized they develop into workers or queens according to the way the larvae are fed,[27] but when unfertilized, into males or drones, as is also the case with the eggs that are sometimes laid by workers" (*ibid.*, 133). Among the bees, as among many social insects, the workers "are very fond of eating the eggs and young larvae and these same workers or the queen not infrequently at once lay eggs in the place of those devoured" (*ibid.*, 142).

1. Self-made Residences. Of course the hive is an artificial structure provided for honey bees whose wild habitat is usually hollows in the trunks of trees. Therefore, the self-made part is limited to the honeycomb with its cells. The cells are built of wax secreted by the bees after a meal of honey and collected in heaps until the work of building starts. The cells are strengthened and also attached to the hive by means of a sticky resin called propolis (mostly from coniferous trees) collected by the bees. The perfect and regular form of the cells was explained by Darwin: "The work of construction seems to be a sort of balance struck between many bees, all instinctively standing at the same relative distance from each other, all trying to sweep equal spheres, and then building up, or leaving ungnawed, the planes of intersection between these spheres" (*105*, I, 350). "Cells are used both for storing food and rearing young" (*354*, 161); and "larger or 'royal' cells" are provided for the queen and the young queens (*ibid.*, 160). Outside the brood combs, workers make pots to hold honey, pollen, and, in some cases, propolis (*437*, 127).

2. Other Adaptations of the Environment. Three instances will suffice. After *repeated* attacks by the death's-head moth, bees have been observed to bar the entrance to their hives with a barricade, built of wax and propolis, which left an opening sufficient for a bee but too small for the moth (*354*, 184). In two cases bees have been observed to erect a scaffolding of wax and propolis to enable them to repair a damaged comb and then, when

[26] Largely because of food storing (*393*, II, 522); see below. On the other hand their industry is often exhausting. "It is said that in summer-time the average life of a worker bee is only about two months. Their brains become hopelessly fatigued. In a colony of 50,000 bees it has been estimated that there are 30,000 workers, and if each makes ten trips a day 300,000 flowers would be visited. About 37,000 loads of nectar are required for the production of a pound of honey" (*393*, II, 524).

[27] What is called "alimentary castration" (*437*, 86).

the repair was completed, to remove it (*ibid.*, 185–186). They even make "hanging bridges, chains, and ladders" for the same purpose (*ibid.*, 186). In one case, when a glass globe was superimposed on the hive, the bees, before constructing comb in it, placed a great number of spots of wax at regular distances apart which were used as footholds on the slippery glass (*ibid.*, 186).

7. *Storing of Food Supplies for Self.* "To the industry and food-storing habit of the Hive Bee is probably due their complex social life; the storing has enabled the community to survive unfavourable seasons and become permanent" (*393*, II, 522). Among hive bees, the honey is stored as winter food for the workers and the queen. As the summer wanes, "one day the decree goes forth that those that do not work shall not eat, indeed shall not live; and the massacre of the males begins. Vigorously and pitilessly the long-suffering workers at last turn on the drones and slay them all. . . .[28] The bees cease their labors and prepare for the long sleep of winter, if sleep it can be called, for the life of the hive is slackened, not completely arrested. The bees gather together in a great cluster, with their queen in their midst. . . . The bees nearest the store cupboards pass the honey to their neighbours, and so food is circulated through the drowsy mass, enough to keep the fire of life glowing, ready to burst into flame again with the return of spring" (*393*, II, 527).[29] That this honey is stored only for winter food—that is, against this contingency only—is proved by a fact that seems well-confirmed. When bees from northern climates are transported to climates without winter, so that they can get food at all seasons, they cease to lay up honey, at least after the experience of two or three years and unless the honey is abstracted as it is collected (i.e., if they are permitted to find out that they do not need it) (*354*, 187–188).

While the solitary bumble bee queen is sitting on her eggs, "in order to maintain animation and heat through the night and in bad weather when food cannot be obtained, it is necessary for her to lay in a store of honey" during fair days. It is kept in a waxen pot in the entrance passage of the nest (*437*, 113–114).

8. *Storing of Food Supplies for Others than Self.* As noted above, the queen bee of the hive is fed with honey along with and by the workers and even during the winter. The drones are provided with honey as long as it appears that they may be required. But the case of the larvae is more elaborate. The stored "bee-bread" is "partly digested by the nurses with honey, so that a sort of chyle is formed" (*354*, 160). This is fed to the larvae individually by the workers (*354*, 162). The process is called by entomol-

[28] "The massacre of the drones is not performed entirely from an instinctive impulse, but in full consciousness of the object to be gained." That is, if the queen has shown herself fertile, they are killed to the last man; if not, "all or some of the drones are left alive, in the clear prevision that their services will be required later." And bees, when transported "to a more southern country, where the time of collecting lasts longer, do not kill the drones in August, as usual, but at a later period, suitable to the new conditions" (Büchner, quoted in *354*, 166–167).

[29] That is, the bee is among the poikilothermic animals mentioned in our first chapter.

ogists "individual progressive provision," to differentiate it from the types of feeding described below (*437*, 133). Since different kinds of pollen are collected and kept separate, "there are several different kinds of bee-bread, some being more stimulating or nutritious than others. The most nutritious has the effect, when given to any female larva, of developing that larva into a queen or fertile female. This fact is well known to the bees, who only feed a small number of larvae in this manner, and the larvae which they select so to feed they place in larger or 'royal' cells, with an obvious fore-knowledge of the increased dimensions to which the animal will grow under the influence of this food" (*354*, 160–161). When the young bee finally emerges, "its nurses assemble round it to wash and caress it, as well as to supply it with food. They then clean out the cell which it has left" (*354*, 162).

The stingless-bee workers also store honey and pollen in the hive. But this is mass, not progressive, provisioning, for "the adult bees do not come into contact with the young larvae." Discrimination is merely made by providing the queen-cells "with a greater amount of pollen and honey" (*437*, 125). So too with the solitary bees who die before the young emerge (*ibid.*, 106). There "the size of the packet [of bee-bread] corresponds to the size of the particular species" (*ibid.*, 108).

9. Labor-saving Devices. Again, as in the case of the beaver, it is difficult to discriminate between labor-saving and the attainment of the otherwise impossible. But, here, it is not a question of apparatus or devices, but solely of method. "Huber's observation, since amply confirmed, of bees biting holes through the base of corollas in order to get at the honey which the length of the corollas prevents them from reaching in the ordinary way, also seems to indicate a rational adjustment to unusual circumstances." Sir Francis Darwin concluded that this was also done, even when the nectar could be reached from above, "in order to save time" (*354*, 189).

WASPS

"Our species of Vesta and Polistes each year produce a swarm of females and workers but . . . the advent of cold weather destroys the less resistant workers and permits only the dispersed queens to survive and hibernate till the following season" (*437*, 88). In fact, the parent queen also dies. "None but the young royalties survive, and the males only long enough to mate with the young queens; thereafter they also die" (*393*, II, 531). This is also true of solitary wasps (*354*, 167). Wasps "commence work early in the morning, and do not leave off till dark," with no interval for rest or refreshment. Their working day is about sixteen hours (*276*, 246).

1. Self-made Residences. Since, like the bumblebee, only the queen wasp survives the winter, the building of the nest is at first her work alone. Among the social wasps, it is made of less self-engendered materials than that of the bees.[30] Wood fiber is scraped from weather-worn surfaces, and

[30] The mason wasp builds its nest of clay; and the sphex lives in a burrow in the ground.

made into a kind of paper by mixing it with saliva. If real paper is found, that is used. The cells in the nest are used only for rearing larvae, since no honey is stored (*354*, 180). As fast as the building process proceeds, egg-depositing also proceeds; thus, as "the older grubs mature . . . a staff of worker wasps is ready [the first are always workers] to take on the manual labour and allow the queen to devote herself to egg-laying. The workers add to the original comb and suspend a new storey from it by little stalks. One storey is added after another" (*393*, II, 529).

5. Tools, Found Ready-made. The sphex wasps "tamp down the filling of their burrows with a small carefully selected pebble, held in the mandibles and used as a hammer or pestle" (*437*, 54). This is the only instance I have found of tool-using among insects.

6. Care and Feeding of Young by Others than Mothers. At first the queen wasp feeds the young in addition to laying eggs and building the nest. As the young worker appears she confines her labor at first to nest-building. "But after a week or two her salivary glands are exhausted, so that she has to give up the manufacture of paper and turn to the older wasp's task of caring for the young, feeding them with the soft parts of insects and occasional sips of fruit-juice or nectar, and cleaning them with care" (*393*, II, 530). The fact that workers come first is due to "alimentary castration," the duties of the queen being too arduous to permit of her feeding them well. And, thereafter, they are kept sterile by "exhausting labor on slender rations." Only when the colony gets large and the food becomes plentiful can it afford to raise queens. So, "as summer wanes, the workers build larger cells in the lower combs. These are the royal nurseries in which a brood of perfect females, not sterile workers, and males are reared." Then, too, some of the workers "though they are never impregnated, may occasionally lay eggs, which, like the unfertilized eggs of the queen, invariably develop into males" (*393*, II, 530).

In part, the feeding of the grubs may be reciprocal feeding (*437*, 82–85). "The first thing the fully formed young wasp does . . . is to crawl about and visit the grubs, tapping them on the head until they emit a tiny drop of fluid [salivary secretion], which the young wasp licks greedily. . . . The mother wasp also visits the grubs for this delectable drop" (*393*, II, 530). Thereafter both workers and males get this benefit in return for their labors in feeding the grubs (*437*, 82–85).

7. Storing of Food Supplies for Self. Some wasps "store a considerable amount of honey in their combs, while others are known to capture, kill and store within the nest envelope, and even in the combs, quantities of male and female termites or male ants as a supply of food to be drawn on when needed." This is done while the white ants are swarming—i.e., when food is plentiful (*437*, 79). But with none is a winter food supply stored.

8. Storing of Food Supplies for Others than Self. The solitary wasps, like the solitary bees, die before their progeny emerges, so that they never see their young (*437*, 106). "Some species of Sphex [a solitary wasp] provide the egg with a single large caterpillar, others with several small caterpillars, but in all cases with just enough food to enable the larva to grow to the full stature of a normal individual of the species." This form of mass provisioning is one of the three forms of behavior among them that "can hardly be reduced to simple physiological reflexes," for it is all properly adjusted to the requirements (*437*, 55).[31] Moreover, and more remarkable, the caterpillars or other insects so deposited are, by several species, not killed, but are merely paralyzed by stinging them through the cerebral ganglion, thus leaving them unable to escape, unresisting, and sufficiently alive to *preserve* them as "fresh meat" (*393*, II, 513, 528).[32]

9. Labor-saving Devices. So far as I know, the only form of behavior among wasps that can be construed to be of this type, though it involves no construction, is the so-called "flight of orientation." When a solitary wasp leaves her burrow or is obliged to leave such parts of her prey as she cannot transport in one journey, she will "rise into the air and fly in undulating spirals," thus making a "locality study" that "enables her to fix in her sensorium the precise position . . . in relation to the surrounding objects, so that she may find the spot again" (*437*, 53).[33] Certainly this is the investment of a few moments of time now to save much more time later.

B. MNEMIC PHENOMENA

In order to get at the fundamental elements of which the characteristics of this order of phenomena are composed, we shall briefly analyze them in the order of a "house that Jack built" and thus demonstrate the strategic changes in this connection that are made by the addition of each new element successively added to the order.

a. Plasticity. This is the capacity to receive an impression from some external agency, either passively or, by way of a reaction, actively.[1] It is common to all matter, inorganic as well as organic. The value of most of the coins in your pocket is entirely due to the fact that metals have this

[31] An instance of the way purely instinctive behavior—or, at least, behavior that is a regular response to a certain pattern of external stimuli—works in the same species may well serve, by way of contrast to this feeding behavior, to illustrate the fundamental difference. A sphex always leaves its captured prey at the mouth of the burrow and goes inside to see that nothing has intruded during its absence, before carrying in the prey. While the wasp was in its burrow, Fabre removed the grasshopper some distance away. On emerging the wasp found it again, brought it back, deposited it again and went inside again. This process was repeated forty times in succession and the wasp never omitted to go through its fixed routine (*354*, 180–181).

[32] One of the solitary wasps, the so-called mason wasp, stocks its nest "with spiders and insects paralyzed by stinging. The victims, not being wholly deprived of life, keep fresh until required as food of the developing larvae" (*354*, 180).

[33] Instances are recounted more fully by Romanes (*354*, 150–151). See also Morgan (*302*, 430).

[1] The distinction between a morphological change (impression) and a chemical change (reaction) is made here only for purposes of illustration. Neither the phenomena nor the terms are, as a matter of fact, sharply distinguishable. The terms impression and reaction are used indiscriminately hereafter.

passive capacity. The silver ones also actively react to the sulphides of the air and become tarnished with silver sulphide. Rignano refers to what we are calling plasticity as "the simple tendency to establish equilibrium with changing external conditions, that is to say to become adapted to them"; "for indeed every physico-chemical system, if its dynamic equilibrium be disturbed by external forces, tends to settle down into a new condition of dynamic equilibrium—that is, to 'adapt itself' to new external circumstances."[2] Though Jelliffe uses physiological expressions, what he says of Semon's "engram" is equally true of inorganic substances: an engram is an "alteration in reaction capacity." "An experience has been 'engraved,' 'written in.' Expressed in terms of energy this means that the substance henceforth is in a different state as regards reaction than it was before the excitement passed through it."[3] That also describes what has happened to the silver on the surface of our coin which has turned into silver sulphide. So, too, it describes what has happened to the metal in relation to the die—the original influence—once the relief has been impressed on its surface. Even Semon's "engraphic susceptibility," as he defines it, is also characteristic of the inorganic world, for it is simply plasticity of a high order as found in irritable organic substances. These latter vary in such susceptibility just as they vary in irritability. Neither is a monopoly of the nervous system; but the nervous system is most susceptible as well as most irritable, and susceptibility seems to vary with irritability.[4] This sounds reasonable, if we construe irritability to be a kind, and an intense kind of reactivity; for reactivity and plasticity seem merely to be different words for the same characteristic. If, then, mnemic phenomena are confined to the world of living organisms, the decisive criterion must be something different from, or in addition to, plasticity. Let us follow through our analysis of the elements to see what is this decisive criterion.

b. Self-restoration of status quo ante. When the silver coin becomes tarnished it cannot polish itself—that is, it cannot itself restore its surface to the state of metallic silver. Its plasticity has been permanently altered. In contrast, the living cell, after changes within certain limits, can execute its own order, "as you were." That seems to be the difference between living and dead substance—i.e., life. Whereas inorganic matter remains permanently altered by any impression or reaction, living matter has the capacity of restoring itself to its original state after many reactions.[5]

[2] Rignano, *345*, 192, 135–136. Or, as William James puts it (*220*, I, 104), "If the body be plastic enough to maintain its integrity, and be not disrupted when its structure yields," "either outward forces or inward tensions can . . . turn that structure into something different from what it was."

[3] Jelliffe, *222*, 334.

[4] Semon, *368*, 25. So that the engraphic effect is "simpler and more direct" on nerve substance than it is "on non-nervously differentiated substance" (i.e., other irritable substance; *loc. cit.*).

[5] The difference is perhaps only one of degree, for I understand that chemists are now finding inorganic—or at least non-living organic—colloid solutions which return to the previous equilibrium after the cause of disturbance ceases.

However, in general, what Rignano says in a somewhat fanciful way is correct: "As

Whereas both are plastic, one might say that living matter is also elastic. This is not a "mysterious" faculty. It is no more than the familiar feature of metabolism. It occurs in the cell; but it also occurs in the cell-systems (Metazoa). We have seen rather deep within the process in the case of the maintenance of the oxygen-CO_2 balance in the blood. Rignano describes it as the solely organic "tendency to preserve or to restore, after it is disturbed, a given condition of equilibrium, attained in a definite environment which has remained unchanged for some time." [6] The alternation of periods of repose after periods of activity in nerve fiber is well recognized to be due to such a process of self-restoration, probably conducted by the nerve cell (perikaryon). Thus the phase of self-restoration in the nervous system seems to be of the same order as in all other living cells. The *status quo ante*, then, in all these living cells consists in precisely the same kind and degree of plasticity that existed prior to the impression or reaction.

c. Repetition of original reaction. The silver on the surface of our coin, after it has been converted into silver sulphide, cannot react again with the sulphides of the air. It is permanently changed; its plasticity has been permanently altered. It cannot repeat the performance, unless one gives it a bath which releases the sulphur and restores the silver to the metallic state. Then, however, it begins to repeat the performance at once. On the other hand, all living cells, provided they have restored the *status quo ante* in the meantime, may repeat identically the same reaction that first changed them. That is, again, their plasticity having been restored to the *status quo ante*, the original impression or reaction will have the same effect as before.

d. Self-restoration to a different status. After many reactions, and particularly those of sufficient intensity or duration, or after frequent repetition, the living cell does not restore, during its period of repose, precisely the *status quo ante*. The effect of the impression or reaction has been in part temporary, in so far as the status restored resembles the original one; but it has been in part permanent, in so far as the status restored differs from the

far as the faculty of adaptation is concerned, by which is meant the power of continually reaching a condition of equilibrium with external forces . . . this power . . . is a general property of energy, shared by all forms of energy. What constitutes the difference between physico-chemical systems and organisms, is the *longing for the old environment*" (*345*, 193–194).

[6] Rignano, *345*, 192. "What, above all, strikes the biologist about assimilation [anabolism] is that it is not a process of continual production, but of continual *reproduction* since it incessantly reproduces organic substance in proportion as this is consumed. 'One might say,' writes Oscar Hertwig, 'that life is only an incessant process of destruction and renewed formation of organic substance' " (*ibid.*, 103). Perhaps the fact of reproduction is due to a factor that remains unchanged. "Thus Verworn, in his hypothesis of the living molecule or 'biogen,' imagines that in catabolism the non-nitrogenous groups of atoms are alone detached, whilst the nitrogenous groups remain and constitute the central mass of the biogen. This central mass later restores its original complexity at the expense of new non-nitrogenous groups similar to those cast off, which are contained in the surrounding nutritive medium" (*ibid.*, 97).

original one. Such cases seem in some ways to be a combination of the organic (living) with the inorganic (dead) types described under (b) above. Nevertheless, they are found only among living organisms because, both in respect of the old status and its "modification," they involve self-restoration. However changed (inorganic) the status restored may be, it is not the same as it was immediately after the impression or reaction. It is a "modification" of the *status quo ante*, being left as a trace of the impression or reaction after restoration from the *status quo post.*

e. Repetition of a modified reaction. After such a modification of the *status quo ante* the characteristics of the plasticity of the living cell or organism have been altered, with the result that the original cause of impression or reaction will now produce a somewhat different effect. Again, if one ignores the intervening restoration to a modified status, this seems to savor of the inorganic. For it is also true that the silver on the surface of our coin, once changed to sulphide, will react to a number of reagents differently than it would have reacted as metallic silver. Nevertheless, since, in living matter, the intervening process has taken place, the change in reactivity is much less simple—at some considerable further remove—than that of the inorganic substance which stays put in the interim.

f. Repetition of a modified reaction due to part only of the original cause. The cumulative basic elements of mnemic phenomena, in terms of the foregoing analysis, turn out to be, first, plasticity (a); second, a modification in the status which is restored after impression or reaction (d); third, a modification in the reaction after such change of status (e); fourth, continued restoration of the modified status thereafter (b); fifth, continued repetition of the modified reaction thereafter (c). We now come to what Semon regarded as the keystone of the arch—to the one element which differentiates mnemic phenomena from all those other phenomena that may include more or less of the foregoing elements. The common quality that distinguishes them from all other kinds of repetition is that, with them, repetition can occur when the original causative conditions that induced the modification are varied to an extreme degree. In fact, an infinitesimal portion of the original condition may suffice.[7] "The essential characteristic of all mnemic processes . . . considered as reproductions of earlier phenomena [is] that they arise without the complete repetition of the conditions which had been necessary in the case of those earlier phenomena [(a), (d) and (e)] by which they were preceded."[8] That is, the cause of (b) and (c), after (a), (d), and (e) have occurred, need no longer be the whole of the cause of (a), (d) and (e). It is as if the first process of modification had intensified the plasticity in certain ways and diminished it in others—as if it had given the organic matter greater reactivity, so that but a hint of the original conditions suffice, and at the

[7] Semon, *368*, 11.

[8] Semon, *369*, 323. This is, as he points out (*368*, 10), also another point of differentiation from inorganic repetition, even when, as is necessary in the inorganic world, some external influence has restored the original status.

same time had given it less further modifiability (susceptibility) to changes in those conditions, so that identical restorations and repetitions continue indefinitely.

g. Modification of status and reaction in series. But there is one further element which seems to us to be the most distinguishing one. Haldane [9] says, "When one regards the facts of memory from the purely physiological standpoint it is evident that memory is a phenomenon of the same nature as adaptation." But this is true only of the one change represented by elements (a), (d), and (e).[10] Once the modification is effected you no longer have adaptation; thereafter you have habit—(b) and (c). In that phase, memory is a phenomenon of the same nature as habit; and habit is restoration and repetition unchanged. Moreover, habit is not merely a physiological but also a general physical phenomenon. For, as William James says, "The laws of Nature are nothing but the immutable habits which the different elementary sorts of matter follow in their actions and reactions upon each other." [11] Thus mnemic phenomena, so far, are habits resulting from adaptations. But habits do not preclude further adaptations; nor do further adaptations erase former habits. On the contrary, each habit persists through further modification as if the modification took the form of merely overlaying a new stratum upon the old. "Every state of physiological equilibrium as it gives place to a new one always leaves a trace of itself behind." [12] Thus experience, as it changes, is conceived to leave behind it a continuous and coexisting series of permanent modifications in status and reactions, each separate from each other—and perhaps physically so—each differing from each other as the corresponding experiences differed, and each separately reproducible by a portion of its original cause. Each new state of equilibrium is an adaptation; each remaining trace is a habit. The coexistence of such an overlaid series is the essential peculiarity of mnemic phenomena. The fact that all remain potential and that any of them can be reactivated is the criterion of the mnemic character of the phenomena.

The analysis which Semon makes of the common elements of mnemic phenomena is along similar lines to the foregoing, but is expressed in his own technical terms. Memory (in the strict sense), habit, heredity, etc., are not regarded by Semon as identical. They are regarded only as manifestations of a common principle, the mnemic principle. All may be traced back to the effect of stimuli applied to the irritable organic substance. But their peculiar feature is the effect that remains after the excitement produced by the stimuli is apparently over (*368*, 11). "The external energetic

[9] Haldane, *178*, 97.

[10] But, see note 5, above. It should be noted that plasticity, in our broad use of the term, is a somewhat mechanistic notion which includes adaptation in the sense of reaching an equilibrium with the environment; on the other hand, to Thomson, "adaptation . . . is a super-mechanical concept" (*394*, 320). Just what makes it super-mechanical is a little hard to see.

[11] James, *220*, I, 104–105.

[12] Rignano, *345*, 138.

condition, forever changing, never repeating itself exactly, thus acts as a transforming factor," while "the purely conserving mnemic faculty" retains the effect of each separate condition (*ibid.*, 288).

The "first principal mnemic law," the law of engraphy, is that "all simultaneous excitations within an organism form a coherent simultaneous excitation complex which act engraphically; that is, it leaves behind it a connected engram-complex, constituting a coherent unity" (*368*, 148).[13] This "original excitation" emerges, endures and subsides as a result of "an elementary-energetic condition regarded as stimulus" (*ibid.*, 149). "Every original excitation outlines . . . the stimulus which has given it birth" (*369*, 327). The "phase of the diminishing excitation (i.e., from the moment of the cessation of the stimulus and the rapid fall of the excitation until its total extinction) may be called the 'acoluthic' phase of the excitation" (*368*, 22). In a few seconds or minutes the acoluthic excitation vanishes (*ibid.*, 23). He thinks there are no cases in which the irritable substance maintains permanently the state of excitement created by the stimulus. There ensues the "secondary state of indifference," which is identical with the primary state of indifference (prior to the stimulus) in respect of immediately manifested reactions, but not in capacity for reaction (*ibid.*, 23). There has been a "change in the capacity to react between the primary and the secondary states of indifference" (*ibid.*, 31). The organism has been "permanently affected." And this is the engraphic action (*ibid.*, 24). The permanent effect is the engram (*ibid.*, 38)—"the enduring though primarily latent modification in the irritable substance produced by a stimulus" (*ibid.*, 12). Thus "the effect of the stimulus does not entirely vanish with the synchronous [during stimulation] nor yet with the acoluthic phase." Thereafter "an engram—an enduring material change of the irritable substance—remains behind, which, though latent, can be roused to manifestation at any moment in conformity with known laws" (*ibid.*, 273). This "engram of the state of excitement produced by a stimulus" "is simply the altered disposition of the irritable substance in its relation to the repetition of the state of excitement" (*ibid.*, 39). Or, better, the engram "implies an altered disposition of the irritable substance towards a recurrence of the state of excitement produced by the original stimulus" (*ibid.*, 89). It is a predisposition. The specific modification of the irritable substance which remains fixed in the engram "is most certainly a *material* change" (*ibid.*, 112). In fact, "Without doubt, excitation is at bottom a physico-chemical process and nothing else, and the engram simply a residual physico-chemical modification" (*ibid.*, 194).[14]

The reactivation of a latent engram is called ecphory. "By the ecphory of an engram we understand the passage of an engram from a latent to a manifest state, or as we might say, the raising into action of a disposition

[13] Thus he asserts "the primary coherence of all simultaneous excitations in the organism" (*368*, 273). This "simultaneous engram-complex" is fixed in its totality, for it is "the result of the juxtaposition of co-acting stimuli" (*ibid.*, 90-91).

[14] McDougall (*283*, 119) also held that mental retention is only "a new arrangement or disposition of nervous matter," not "a continuing activity."

created by the original excitation and characterized as a permanent but usually latent change in the organism" (*368*, 138). The "state of excitement arising from the ecphorizing of an engram" is "the mnemic [as contrasted with the "original"] state of excitement" (*ibid.*, 39). "The intervention of a latent phase between the synchronous [original] and the mnemic states of excitement is highly characteristic of mnemic phenomena and presents the mnemic excitation in the light of a reproduction" (*ibid.*, 37).[15] And it is this latent phase which constitutes the proof of engraphic action, so that "it is only through ecphory that we first get to know the existence of engraphy, and there can be no ecphory unless preceded by engraphy" (*369*, 325).[16] Mnemic excitation is independent of "the elementary-energetic condition regarded as stimulus" which produced the original excitation (*368*, 149). However, "the starting of a mnemic process invariably requires an ecphoric impulse" (*ibid.*, 151). That is, the engram is not ecphorized directly by the recurring stimulus, but by the corresponding original excitation generated by that stimulus.[17] Then that engram, in turn, ecphorizes all or part of the rest of an engram-complex (*ibid.*, 142). Hence the second principal mnemic law, the law of ecphory. "The partial recurrence of the energetic condition which had previously acted engraphically, acts ecphorically on a simultaneous engram-complex. Or, more precisely described: the partial recurrence of the excitation complex, which left behind it a simultaneous engram-complex, acts ecphorically on the latter, whether the recurrence be in the form of original or mnemic excitations" (*ibid.*, 148). Thus the difference between mnemic excitation and the original excitation lies chiefly in different originating conditions (*ibid.*, 138). But it is also true that ecphory usually takes place as to a part of an engram-complex only (*ibid.*, 143) and, "in most cases, . . . the mnemic reproduction renders only the strongest lights and shadows" (*ibid.*, 149). Once started, the same mnemic excitation "may manifest itself by very different reactions. Take for example protoplasmic movements, muscular contractions, metabolism, and the phenomena of growth" (*ibid.*, 161).[18]

[15] As Rignano puts it (*345*, 188 and 190), "We have in fact defined it [this mnemonic property of living matter] as the property of reproducing by the action of internal causes given physiological states for the original production of which external causes were necessary. . . . In other words memory is not 'any after-effect of external causes,' as it is defined by Loeb . . . but rather the reproduction of dynamical effects without the renewed aid of the corresponding external conditions *and after the effects due to these conditions have completely ceased to exist*. In this sense the mnemonic property belongs exclusively and peculiarly to life."

[16] "The possibility of eliciting the mnemic phenomena (their ecphory, that is) is absolutely dependent upon the previous presence of those preceding phenomena" (*369*, 323).

[17] The recurring stimulus merely produces each time "its corresponding synchronous state of excitement." Each time it is the "original stimulus." Therefore, if an engram is ecphorized, the ecphoric influence must be different from the original stimulus (*368*, 27).

[18] As Rignano says, "the sudden variations in form which constitute the movements of plants, whether they are caused by stimuli from the environment or whether they are

"The influences which awaken the mnemic trace or engram out of its latent state into one of manifested activity" (*368*, 12), the ecphoric influences, may be (a) repetition of the original stimulus producing a similar original state of excitation, (b) the ecphory of other engrams which were produced simultaneously or just before, and (c) influences which appear as definite periods of time (chronogeneous) or of development (phasogeneous; *ibid.*, 39). All this is but an application of the laws of "association" to an enlarged field.[19] As to (a), an infinitesimal portion of the original simultaneous stimulus complex suffices (*ibid.*, 11) and, after engraphy, a feebler stimulus may produce the same effect as one of the original strength (*ibid.*, 29). Or, "The partial recurrence of the energetic condition exclusive of the original excitation which generated the engram" may produce the simultaneous ecphory of a definite engram. And this is chiefly the chronogeneous and phasogeneous influences (c, above; see *ibid.*, 145).

Semon restricts the term association to one relation only. "Association is the result of an engraphy disclosed on the occasion of an ecphory" (*369*, 325). But it seems to be limited to ecphory of type (b), above. Now the succession of excitation complexes is continuous; that is, one complex merges into the next, since it exists in its acoluthic phase while the next is in its synchronous phase. There is no break even in sleep. The connection is unilinear, being non-reversible and with the next preceding and next succeeding only (*ibid.*, 94). But the individuation of the original excitations of which the excitation-complex is composed is due to breaks. Discontinuous stimulation may produce continuous excitation. Engraphic action follows if there is stimulus-summation. On the other hand, if the interval between discontinuous stimuli is long enough so that the excitation can die down (pass out of its acoluthic phase), then the engraphic action is also discontinuous and there are a series of separate memories instead of one (*ibid.*, 34). This means that "it is only the varying components of the successive complexes, those that come and go, that allow us to apply the idea of connection and association" (*ibid.*, 99). Thus restricted, association is primarily the connection "between the several components of an engram-complex" (*369*, 325).[20] But, since "the individually acquired engram-store is formed by simultaneous engram-complexes linked to one another in a

---

produced in a mnemonic way, are effected, just as in animals, by the transmission of 'excitations' . . . which pass from certain parts of the plant to other parts." To the same kinds of excitation must be attributed "also their definite variation in form or morphological modifications" (*345*, 127).

[19] Engell, *137*, 8.

[20] In fact, Jelliffe (*222*, 336) says that Semon defines association as "the belonging together of the individual components of an engram complex." Semon says the components of an engram-complex may break up and then, under certain circumstances, unite again. This union is always association (*369*, 325). On the other hand, it is a "rule without exception" that "all simultaneously produced engrams are associated even when the effective stimuli are of different kinds and have no relationship in respect of the cause of their appearance" (*368*, 36). But, there is closer association between excitations of like stimulus quality than between those of different stimulus quality (*ibid.*, 95).

continuous series" (*ibid.*, 326), because of the overlapping of the acoluthic phase of one with the synchronous phase of the next, one may distinguish, secondarily, "successive association,"[21] though this too, because of the actual "contemporaneous conjunction of their 'ascendants'" is, in reality, also from that standpoint, "simultaneous association" (*ibid.*, 327). Thus the association of engrams is established only during the synchronous and the acoluthic stages. If it is established in the first, the basis is simultaneity and each can ecphorize the other; if in the second, the basis is succession, and ecphory takes place more strongly from the earlier to the later (*368*, 102).[22] Simultaneous and successive association leading to ready ecphory rouses engrams far more frequently than repetition of original stimuli (a, above; see *ibid.*, 143).

There is another relationship which may exist between two original excitations, between two mnemic excitations or between a mnemic and a new original excitation (*368*, 154). In *Mnemic Psychology* (*369*, 326), Semon defines "resemblance" as a "partial coincidence between the components of an actual [present] group of excitations and those of any previous engram-complex" and ascribes it as the power of the former to cause ecphory of the latter. This "resemblance" is the relationship we are referring to, but it is there stated as if it applied only in the third instance (i.e., between a mnemic and a new original excitation), whereas we can also identify this type of ecphoric influence with that mentioned under (a), above. In *The Mneme* another and broader term is used which applies to this relationship in all three of the instances above. This term is "homophony." It is defined as the "state of unison in which . . . [the excitations] may find themselves" (*368*, 154).[23] It is the basis of "the reaction of recognition; and the reaction of the perception of difference" (*loc. cit.*). Thus homophony is not only the basis of identification of similar but discrete entities; it is the basis of all classification of experience.[24]

[21] Successive association is that with the engrams "generated immediately after" (*368*, 37).

[22] As noted in the text, both are casually treated by Semon as simultaneous, for, "association, Semon insists, rests fundamentally upon the simultaneousness of different engrams or engram complexes of which this successive association [due to overlapping] is only a subordinate form" (Jelliffe, *222*, 334). Therefore, "association depends on the conjunction of single engrams; it makes its appearance during their relatively isolated ecphory, and originates simply from the presence of the respective components in the same simultaneous complex. Association, therefore, is always simultaneous association" (*368*, 148).

[23] Strangely enough Jelliffe (*222*, 336) says Semon defines it as "the simultaneous independent appearance of two sensations or sensation groups in the organism." I can neither find such a definition in Semon's works nor can I reconcile it with what Semon repeatedly says.

Homophony takes the place of what was one kind of association in the older psychology—that by similarity or contrast; e.g., William James.

[24] This because it is the basis of recognition, and re-cognition (in fact all cognition) is, in fact, classification (MacBride, *279*, 2). Thus homophony is the criterion according to which engrams are indexed and filed, so to speak, and homophonous engrams are ecphorized together or by each other, as well as by homophonous ("similar") original

Two of Semon's most important and far-reaching constructions are built upon this relationship. If new and old original excitations approach homophony, still there is perception even of the slight differences, because the re-excited engram and the new excitation are contrasted (*368*, 152–153). Even if the stimulus and its resulting new original excitation are precisely the same as were the old, still we must be able to discriminate between the original and the mnemic excitations, for we have the "reaction of recognition" (*368*, 43). In both cases this proves that the original and the mnemic excitations are separate, for they can be compared (*368*, 153). Furthermore, the several homophonous mnemic excitations must also be separate. He explains the generalization of the recollection of the appearance of a familiar person as due to the simultaneous ecphorizing of innumerable varied engrams from repetitions of many slightly different original excitations. The image blurs, like "the superposition of the pictures of different heads on one and the same plate" (composite photographs).[25] But, if one can concentrate on one engram, the picture becomes sharply defined (*368*, 163). Since it is possible thus to separate homophonous components, there can be "no perfect blending of the mnemic excitations" (*368*, 164). Instead, successive homophonous original excitations must each lay down its own engram. "At the ecphory of a combination of engrams, owing its origin to frequently repeated engraphic action, what is given is not a single indissoluble blend of the mnemic excitations—'coalescence,' some physiologists call it—but a unisonant chorus in which the single components of an apparently uniform combination of engrams, distinct indeed from each other as to their time of origin, may be individually discerned." [26] This convincing analysis proves, I think, that

---

excitations. When the latter occurs, the new excitation is "recognized" and thereby indexed and filed with its fellows.

[25] Semon calls such superimposition the "abstraction of homophony." By enlarging the sphere one gets abstractions of a higher order: "I maintain that the primary formation of abstract conceptions is based on such abstract images, and that this abstraction, created in the above-mentioned way by homophony only, is the precursor of the purely logical process. It is no monopoly of the human species for we find it manifesting itself in different ways among all the higher organized animals" (*368*, 164).

This concept of abstraction is somewhat different from, and probably more justifiable than, that of Hughlings Jackson. But it may be required to be modified by Jackson's. Jackson said (*216*, II, 205) that "propositions of symbols (verbal or pantomimic) serve in mentation." This seems to be his "arbitrary image" (*ibid.*, II, 211) or "lay figure" (*ibid.*, II, 231) and conforms to Weber's concept of "ideal type." But the essence of all these is the singling out of a single representative, not the composite photograph of all. Moreover, Semon's notion of superimposition seems foreign to Jackson. As we have already noted, he held (*ibid.*, II, 359) that "the process of all thought is 'stereoscopic' or 'diplopic,' being the tracing of relations of resemblance and difference" (Semon's homophony). But, since "it is by an alternation of two sensations and two movements that we obtain an idea of the co-existence of two external objects," he supposes that we speak and think by the "same method of parallax"—by an alternation of words and perceptions (*ibid.*, II, 228).

[26] Usually the single components differ somewhat. If they differ sufficiently, they are no longer homophonous but constitute a "dichotomy." Dichotomies are "bifurcated

recall is rarely merely the revival of a single old experience. It is usually the simultaneous revival of a whole stock of separate but homophonous experiences, which are represented, perhaps, along with a current one. But an important feature of Semon's analysis is that the process is not confined to conscious memory. It pervades all mnemic phenomena. "In the life of every human organism [and perhaps of all organisms], unconscious mnemic homophony plays at least as important a part as conscious homophony" (*368*, 160).

The second of Semon's constructions follows from this. To the extent that two excitations—both original, both mnemic, or one of each—are homophonous, they are congruous. To the extent that they are not precisely homophonous but are still related, they are incongruous. To the first extent, they produce the reaction of recognition; to the second, they produce the reaction of the perception of difference.[27] If any reaction following the latter tends to remove the incongruity, it must be guided by a contrast between a mnemic excitation and an original excitation the incongruity between which is recognized, though not necessarily in consciousness (*368*, 162). Thus he construes "the phenomena of regeneration [including healing] and regulation [restoration of homeostasis] as 'reactions for the removal of the incongruity of a homophony'" (*368*, 276).[28] In this way Semon sets up a purely physiological concept, analogous to Coghill's metabolic, and to Child's physiological, gradients (see p. 116). It is as if any thoroughly well-established group of homophonous mnemic excitations, being therefore much stronger in this respect, fixed the standard of homeostasis during its period of prepotence (i.e., until a new *status quo* is established by a new and stronger group). If, during this period, a new original excitation tending toward homophony (i.e., related) nevertheless exhibits an incongruity, a physiological gradient is thereby established tending to bring it back to congruity. Perhaps if we understood all the instances in which this occurs (see below) we would find them all due to the disturbance of a very complex physicochemical equilibrium—represented by the *status quo*, old or new—which, when the occasional and disturbing cause of incongruity ceases, tends to be restored by the interaction of the remaining and steady influences.

Such a beginning of an explanation of apparent manifestations of "pur-

---

successions of engrams which can only be ecphorized alternately"—that is, one of the two branches suppresses or alternates with the other (*368*, 166). It may be this contrast with dichotomy which led Jelliffe to his definition quoted in note 23, above. "Bifurcation" resembles more closely Jackson's "diplopic" thinking, above.

27 Semon (*368*, 156) gives an apt illustration of what he means by the detection of incongruity. One throws a ball for one's dog. After many repetitions, one goes through the motions but holds the ball. That may have to occur several times before the dog separates the congruous motion from the incongruous behavior of the ball.

28 He also uses this to explain the modification of the "phasogeneously ecphorized reactions of nest building" when an artificial or old nest is furnished. Then the reaction is limited to the correction of incongruities. If the artificial nest is satisfactory, it is congruous and the reaction is suppressed (*368*, 158). See pp. 254 and 1244.

posefulness," though it does no more than to restate the characteristics of the phenomena in terms of conceivable physiological processes, is entirely satisfactory from the standpoint we adopted in the first chapter. The phenomenon "was merely a metaphysical problem so long as one had to speak of regulation as bearing on some imagined future state" (Semon, *368*, 277). This transference of causation to the reawakened past makes of it a physiological problem—or at least brings it within the range of physiology.[29] As Rignano says, these manifestations of purposefulness[30] give "to the medium, or the environmental relations, the appearance of a pull from in front (*vis a fronte*) or 'final cause' of totally different nature from the ordinary *vis a tergo*, or 'actual cause,' which alone is operative in the inorganic world." But, in fact, "the medium, or the environmental relations towards which the animal strives, operate now like a *vis a fronte* solely because they have formerly been a *vis a tergo*, and because the physiological activities which they have then aroused in the organism have left behind them a mnemonic deposit, which now acts like a veritable *vis a tergo* in moving the living being" (*345*, 171–172).

We are now prepared to recognize these mnemic characteristics in the several phenomena in which they are said to appear. Many of these phenomena have been dealt with in previous chapters without specific reference to their so-called mnemic character. What we are now engaged in doing, therefore, is to align this thing which Semon called mneme with all that has gone before and thus interpret the latter in these terms.

a. Homeostasis. It is obvious that the processes leading toward the correction of tendencies or variations away from homeostasis—the present want system—which we have studied in previous chapters, are identical with what we have called the self-restoration of the *status quo ante*. These processes, peculiar to living matter, take place within the single cell as well as within a multicellular system. The mnemic hypothesis interprets the fact that these processes lead to a precise reproduction of the original state, giving the appearance of being guided by a model or pattern as goal, and also the fact that, when the original state is restored, they cease.[31]

[29] It converts the notion of a model (homeostasis) or a series of models, to be reattained or attained *de novo*, even generation after generation, into a notion of repetition implicit in the reappearance of the complete or partial original cause. One is reminded of Troland's "hedonism of the past." That was pure speculation, but it may have been speculation in the right direction.

[30] Rignano (*345*, 135 ff.) points out that the adaptation of physicochemical systems, after disturbance, to a new dynamic equilibrium does not serve as an explanation of apparent purposefulness. "What these mechanical and physico-chemical analogies are unable to explain even in outline is the power of anticipation by which an organism prepares to accommodate itself to conditions not yet realized." "It is just this preparation for future conditions which constitutes the purposeful character of all vital phenomena and of psychic acts" (*ibid.*, 138–139).

[31] "If we contemplate living substance which is continually undergoing decomposition in the so-called processes of organic destruction which accompany functional activity, and which is reproduced during so-called periods of functional repose, of organic reconstruction and of assimilatory synthesis, which remains through all changes identical

It requires the assumption that there remains during variation from homeostasis an engram representing homeostasis which becomes activated by that variation, and that it is the contrast between the current original excitation and the mnemic excitation resulting from that engram that, according to Semon, sets up the reaction "for the removal of the incongruity of a homophony." Such an engram, at least, might be acquired by individual experience.

b. Ontogeny. "The marvellous phenomenon of the recapitulation of phylogeny by ontogeny . . . generally known as Haeckel's 'fundamental law of biogenesis,' "[32] means "that the ancestral path of development has to be trodden by each descendant in an approximately equal manner." This "(Palinogenesis) is the obvious consequence of the action of the mnemic factor in ontogenesis."[33] The "repetition of ontogenetic facts" can be explained by "the axiom that like causes produce like effects";[34] but the attribution of a succession of causes each governing the homeostasis of a stage, and each succeeded, in turn, by a new cause which governs a new homeostasis is a more complex concept of causality. It requires the assumption that there is implicit at the beginning of ontogeny a stock of engrams not acquired by individual experience but inherited, identical for a species, and each one of which, at a certain stage, becomes activated and displaces its predecessor. Again we have the appearance of a model or pattern as goal at each stage, and again cessation of effect when that goal is achieved. But again we conceive that what actually occurs is that, when, at each stage, a new engram displaces its predecessor as the standard of homeostasis, it begins to act to remove the incongruity of the current original excitations until at last it has brought about homophony.[35]

---

with itself, and is always ready, when it decomposes, to manifest again the same functional activities, must it not appear that it is the result of an activity of a mnemonic nature?" (Rignano, *345*, 35–36; see also note 6, above). In fact, in exactly the same terms in which we conducted our study of present wants, he holds "that we must attribute a similar mnemonic nature to this fundamental tendency to preserve physiological stability whence we have derived all the most fundamental 'affective tendencies' of all organisms without exception" (*345*, 152–153).

[32] Rignano, *345*, 33–34. Someone has referred to this process as a case of the organism "climbing up its own genealogical tree."

[33] Semon, *368*, 291. As MacBride puts it (*279*, 13), the phenomenon of recapitulation "is nothing but the recurrence of old racial memories at early periods of life."

[34] Semon, *368*, 173.

[35] The chromosomes are usually regarded from the standpoint of the attributes they confer rather than the succession of stages through which development takes place. MacBride (*279*, 11) holds that "the hereditary powers of an animal, instead of being composed of so-called Mendelian units, really consist of superposed layers of memories." The proof of this fact, that superseded ways are merely submerged, is the "throw-back." Nevertheless the chromosomes must contain the engram stock, for "so long as a nucleus is capable of dividing by ordinary karykinesis it shows by its definite and typical number of chromosomes that it has retained all the potencies of the original nucleus of the fertilized egg intact" (MacBride, Introduction, *345*, 12). Semon does not identify the locus of this engram stock. He merely says that it "may be encompassed by something smaller than the cell or even the nucleus of the cell." So "we called the

c. Regeneration. The phenomenon of regeneration is difficult to classify either as a pure case of restoration of homeostasis or as a pure step in the developmental process (ontogeny). And this because its only cause is the separation of a part from the whole. That is, it is the repetition of a growth process, not the original process; it is only excited or permitted when the previous normal growth is removed; it cannot be performed by all cells, but only by those which have retained the capacity. Here the appearance of model or pattern as goal is even more explicit, for the process may be repeatedly called out by a departure from the model, whereas its re-attainment each time causes the process to cease.[36] This requires the assumption that, in the series of inherited engrams representing the stages of development under ontogeny, each engram that has been displaced as representative of homeostasis remains nevertheless capable of being activated again if homeostasis in its respects is disturbed. Since, in this case, the displaced engram also corresponds to an experience of the individual we might suppose the inherited engram to have been reinforced by an individually acquired one.[37] Here, what Semon calls the reaction for the removal of the incongruity of a homophony is most explicitly evidenced;

---

most minute morphological unit encircling it a mnemic protomer, but made no attempt at any precise morphological delineation of this unit" (*368*, 206). Rignano builds an elaborate "provisional hypothesis" that rests on so slight a foundation that it is not worth while to do more than mention it here. It assumes that "plasmatic action" is due to "nuclear energy" (from the nuclei), transmitted across the protoplasmic bridges which constitute an intercellular network throughout the body, and that this is none other than "nervous energy." It assumes that there is a "central zone of development" governing ontogeny, probably located in the spinal column and made up of "the germ-plasm," which remains unspecialized after those cells lying outside it have become gradually specialized. It assumes that, "as one element after another of the central zone enters into activity, the development of the organism will traverse all its successive stages, and it will only cease when the action of these elements is completed, because the disturbing action of the central zone on the general dynamic equilibrium of the organism will then come to an end, and the definite equilibrium of the adult stage will be established" (*345*, 72). This is pure metaphysiology, and is subject to insuperable objections as to certain details. It serves only one useful purpose—to outline the functions that appear to be performed somewhere and somehow.

36 "The tendency of organisms to restore their normal form when this has been destroyed, as happens when an amputated member is regenerated, would be nothing but the tendency to do away with the divergencies between the actual abnormal morphological condition and the normal morphological condition mnemonically recalled" (Rignano, *345*, 117).

37 "Regeneration and experimental embryology show that each cell, or rather each mnemic protomer of a developing as well as of a fully developed organism, is in possession of all those engrams which the organism as a whole inherited from its ancestors" (Semon, *368*, 136). This is not confined to the germ-plasm; for the part without germ-plasm as well as the remaining whole, with it, may have this capacity. Segments of animal or plant life of sufficient size, cut almost anywhere and anyhow are capable of full development, just as are the germ-products of the respective organisms. Therefore each of such sections must "possess in its entirety the inherited engram-store of the complete individual" (*ibid.*, 114) and "engram inheritance is not localized" (*ibid.*, 115). Single germ-cells suffice; how small sections of other cells suffice is unknown. Whatever is the minimum he calls the "protomer" (*ibid.*, 115–116).

for, not only does it not occur until the obvious incongruity appears, but it ceases as soon as congruity is restored.

d. Adaptation. During the life of an individual, the *status quo ante* which represents homeostasis may not only be changed by reason of the succession of a new stage in the inherited series, but it may also change due to the experience of the individual.[38] And in this liability the life of the individual must be treated as beginning at the stage of the egg. Such modifications we call conditioning or learning; and their fixation in the repertory of the individual we regard as habit-formation. The essential feature of conditioning to an external stimulus is that, after sufficient persistence, this minute feature of the original total energetic condition that established the engram is able to reproduce the original reaction by itself through the mnemic excitation it can revive.[39] The essential feature of learning a new reaction is that an engram comes to be formed containing the final and successful reaction in a trial and error series, so that, thereafter, repetition comes more and more habitually to be the modified instead of the original reaction.[40] The first process requires only the entry of the conditioned stimulus into the engram-complex; the second requires only the substitution of a new reaction for an old in that complex (or its addition to an old). The two combined seem to embrace the whole matter of acquiring an engram-stock from individual experience; and between them they seem to account for all acquired adaptations and modifications,

[38] "In the same way, however, as the disturbing action of the central zone was continually upsetting the equilibrium which had just been established and causing the organism to pass into a later stage of development [ontogeny], when the adult stage has been finally attained, each new external stimulus, or complex of stimuli which is not transient, in a word each persisting change in the action which the environment exerts on the organism, which, of course, induces a corresponding persisting reaction on the part of the organism, will have the effect of upsetting once more the dynamic equilibrium which would otherwise have remained fixed and definite. As a result, the organism will pass into a new physiological and morphological condition which will constitute its next phylogenetic stage" (Rignano, *345*, 88).

[39] Semon's examples of "two or more stimuli, acting simultaneously on an organism and producing synchronous effects," which "influence it engraphically in juxtaposition" and therefore become components of a single engram-complex, are examples of conditioned external stimuli (*368*, 36). The conditioned stimulus becomes the ecphoric influence (*ibid.*, 26). This specific process is described elsewhere more in detail (*ibid.*, 28 and 30).

It will be recalled that, in Chapter 3, when we described Pavlov's requisites for conditioning, one was that the to-be-conditioned stimulus must precede and overlap the unconditioned stimulus. This experimental conclusion corresponds to, and proves, Semon's law of association—that is, that association is limited to simultaneous, including just preceding, excitations.

[40] "The nerve substance preserves faithfully the memory of habitual actions" (Hering, *189*, 72). See also Semon, *368*, 47. This, or a combination of conditioning and learning, is what MacBride (*279*, 6) calls "habitudinal memory." "A voluntary action, often repeated, leaves in the motor nerve-cells and in the locomotor organs some trace of itself, which makes its repetition more and more easy, so that it is called forth by only a part of the stimulus or change in the environment which originally evoked it." This "includes series or sequences of actions (compounds)." All habitual motor action seems to have this character. It is generated along once new and modified channels for nerve impulses, which gradually become well-worn.

if one includes among reactions all impressions upon the plastic material and even morphological change due to bodily processes. Adaptation appears to include the maintenance of old models or patterns in spite of new conditions as well as the substitution of new models or patterns modified from the old by new conditions.[41] For, as we noted above, once the *status quo* has been modified and the reaction changed, the first may continue to be restored and the second to be repeated. That is, adaptation cannot be thought of as the change only; it embraces also the consolidation of the change.

e. Inheritance of Acquired Characters.[42] It is sometimes claimed that

[41] In respect of actual modification, "New characters are created exclusively by the organic reaction against stimuli, which continually spring from the ever changing external world" (Semon, *368*, 290). Thereafter, "in the Mneme there is to be found a conserving principle which is indispensable for organic development, in so far as it preserves the transformations which the external world increasingly creates" (*ibid.*, 291).

These transformations are transformations of homeostasis. They are adaptations to new conditions. "The new environmental conditions, to which the animal gradually becomes accustomed, finally become for it optimum conditions. 'Individual adaptation,' writes Dallinger (as for instance, to a new condition of salinity), 'takes place according to the law that the conditions of density under which an individual is forced to live, tend to become in time the most favorable conditions for that individual.' " Thereafter, "the new physiological condition [homeostasis] which constitutes the adaptation of the organism to the new environment, once it has been established and has lasted some time, tends to restore itself. Now this tendency to its own 'reactivation' or reproduction which is thus manifested by every former physiological state is nothing else than the tendency to its own 'evocation' shown by every mnemonic accumulation, and is therefore of a purely mnemonic character" (Rignano, *345*, 151–152).

[42] This phrase alone will act upon most biologists like a red flag to a bull; for the possibility or impossibility of such inheritance has been one of the chief battlegrounds of nearly a century, and the great majority have rejected the idea. Therefore, it would be entirely unbecoming of me to have an opinion opposed to the great majority. Neither am I competent to judge how far the negative evidence cited against it really proves that it does not occur; nor to appraise the rather exceptional cases which have been cited to prove that it does occur. That must be left to biologists themselves. But, to an outsider, it seems that biologists have not frankly faced the issue involved here. Therefore, I make the following points to justify including the hypothesis.

1. Genes cannot be unalterable. They must be subject to change; otherwise we would all still be something like paramecia.

2. If genes are alterable, such alterations must be due either (a) to spontaneous changes within themselves, or (b) to influences external to themselves.

a. The supposition of spontaneous change seems to be inconsistent with the essential character of the gene—that it is the carrier of the continuity of the species—so that we still have many species of life practically unchanged since the earliest geological ages in which they first appeared.

This supposition also seems to savor of the idea of "spontaneous generation," which, I suppose, has now been relegated to the attic storeroom.

b. Newton's first law of motion seems to be a sound postulate for all scientific thinking. Things do not change except as they are subjected to new external conditions. Since germ-cells remain in the most secluded portions of the anatomy, they cannot, during their life there, be subjected to any external conditions except through the medium of their host.

Therefore, until an alternative hypothesis is offered which consists of something more than a word—"mutations"—it seems to be the part of wisdom not to exclude the

experimental evidence is beginning to make it appear that adaptations of the foregoing type can, under certain conditions, become heritable. From this it is being argued that, not accidental variants in the germ cells, but adaptations by the whole organism are primarily responsible for establishing the several phylogenetic steps recapitulated in ontogeny and, therefore, for the whole stock of unlearned activities, including behavior, demonstrated in the history of each individual.[43] This seems to be the general position of those supporting the mnemic hypotheses. Among them, the heritable effects of the experience and adaptation of prior generations are conceived to be mnemic phenomena.[44] They suppose that the self-restoration to a different status and the repetition of a modified reaction, which are "learned" by way of adaptation (learning) during the experience of an individual, do not necessarily pass away with that individual, but may be transmitted. When they are, they become part of the unlearned stock of succeeding generations.[45] So Hering regarded "instinct as the outcome of the memory or reproductive power of organized substance" (*189*, 82).[46] However, instincts, as usually defined, would, in this interpretation, become no more than one form (behavioral) of the entire stock, not to be distinguished on any fundamental basis from internal bodily activities or from morphogenetic regularities. All would be acquired and transmitted in the same way, and only their manifestations would be distinguishable.[47]

---

equally unproved but, in some ways, more generally probable hypothesis that observed alterations in inheritance—in the genes—may be due to the prolonged influence of fairly general alterations in the host.

[43] So Rignano interprets it. "We thus see that the fundamental law of biogenetics, viz., the recapitulation of phylogeny, is an immediate consequence of the process by which acquired characters are inherited" (*345*, 90). This concept has generally commended itself to psychologists. James Ward says, "What one inherits another must have acquired" (*424*, 588). But biologists have not favored it.

[44] Rignano, in his fanciful language, says of recapitulation, "In the light thrown on it by the theory of the inheritability of acquired characters, it assumed a new aspect and one of fundamental importance, that is, it was seen to be a *mnemonic phenomenon.* It was evidence that living substance *remembered* all the modes of being through which the species had passed as a result of the continual acquisition of new characters superimposed on the old" (*345*, 34).

[45] Semon cites some of the evidence to show that acquired characters can be inherited (*368*, Chapter III). That, to him, raises the question whether heredity is the equivalent of accumulated acquired characters; and he finds that "the conclusion seems fully justified that dispositions acquired during evolution have arisen engraphically" (*ibid.*, 86).

[46] To Semon, instincts would be "engrams inherited by the organism from its ancestors (*368*, 56). He says "the 'migration impulse' innate in so many species of birds, is the motor reaction of an inherited engram, a reaction produced by chronogeneous ecphory." So, too, trees which shed their leaves regardless of temperature (*368*, 72). Others are due to phasogeneous ecphory. And to MacBride (*279*, 9) all unlearned actions are probably inherited "habitudinal memories."

[47] I have always thought that the assumption of the possibility of inheritance of structural but not of functional modifications is absurd. It treats an organism as if it consisted of structure only, which is almost the opposite of the viewpoint of Jennings, quoted in Chapter 3.

Semon regards instinct as much the same as morphological and physiological char-

Since only the germ-plasm is continuous from generation to generation, this thesis requires the supposition that adaptations may affect the germ-plasm. To start with, we may say that only those characters are actually acquired which become capable of reproduction by the soma (including the nervous system) of the organism. But this is not enough. These are learned, but may not be bequeathed. In order that these adaptations should be bequeathed, it would appear that the germ-plasm must have become capable of reproducing them. However, Semon says that "engraphic effects are subject to the same laws, whether these effects are manifested in the individual which originally experienced stimulation, or in what we call the particular inherited character of that individual's offspring" (*368*, 12). In the latter case, "the engraphic influence has been transmitted to the germ-cells of the parent generation by conduction" (*368*, 131).[48] That is, "as the germ-cells are not separated from the rest of the body by any isolating contrivance, the excitations produced in the irritable substance of the body reach them also, leaving behind, especially during the period when the germ-cells are most sensitive,[49] engrams which later become manifest" (*368*, 273). Just as the original excitation radiating along definite paths from the primary area is scarcely or not at all appreciable at the most distant irritable substance (*368*, 123), so that "certainly not every cell . . . is in full possession of the entire stock of engrams acquired during the individual organic life" (*368*, 117),[50] so at best "the

acters (*368*, 61). Rignano attributes largely to Semon the scientific success of "the idea that the instincts and the other inborn tendencies of the organism, including the morphogenetic tendencies, on account of the circumstances in which they become active and of the nature of their manifestations, are very probably nothing but 'engrams' which the ancestors of the particular individual have acquired during their lives and which they have attributed to the particular individual by heredity" (*345*, 120). Here all forms of inherited predisposition are treated as belonging in one class.

48 Semon concedes that direct stimulation of the germ-cells by such influence is impossible (*368*, 131) and questions the notion of parallel induction (i.e., effect of influence on both soma and germ-cell independently; *ibid.*, 133). Nevertheless, he holds that "from the facts as we have them we may argue to the probability of a transmission of individually acquired engrams to the irritable substance of the germ-cells, although with greatly weakened effect, and through these to the progeny" (*368*, 117).

49 Perhaps there is only a "short period during which the germ-cells of many, perhaps of all, organisms are to any considerable extent sensitive to any engraphic influence" (*368*, 84). Ordinarily they are much less susceptible than are somatic cells (*ibid.*, 118).

50 That is, engrams individually acquired act on all protomers but in vastly different strengths, and the widest difference is between the protomers of the nervous system and those of the non-nervous system (Semon, *368*, 136).

On the other hand, MacBride (*279*, 24) points out that all nuclei are derived from that of the germ. The "nucleus governs the growth and nutrition of the cell," and therefore "differentiation of the protoplasm itself is the work of the nucleus" (*ibid.*, 26). In turn the "nucleus is stimulated by the kind of protoplasm in which it finds itself" (*ibid.*, 26). Therefore, "all the nuclei of the body are potentially equivalent to one another, no matter in what organ of the body they happen to be." "The action which often repeated leads to the formation of a habit is a response of the whole animal to the situation," not the "action of the environment on one organ" (*ibid.*, 24). It follows that "in all of them [the nuclei] are harbored the same memories." Which

nervous excitations reach the germ-cells by many roundabout ways, and generally very greatly enfeebled (*368*, 137). In fact, most are not continuous or potent enough to get through (*368*, 117).[51] But frequent repetition raises them above the threshold (*368*, 137).[52] By this means it becomes possible for the strongest and most persistent external influences not only to superimpose, at the end of the existing series of phylogenetic and ontogenetic stages, various new modifications, but also to alter earlier ontogenetic stages from those which existed phylogenetically. And this permits a rational explanation of the defects in recapitulation.[53]

---

memory is activated in a particular nucleus "depends entirely on the local environment of the nucleus" (*ibid.*, 21). It is this which he considers to be the "physical basis of habitudinal memory" (*ibid.*, 24).

[51] MacBride (*279*, 26) questions whether "sensorial memories can be handed on from one generation to another." He thinks they may be, but the matter has not been explored.

[52] Rignano, as noted above, has a more specific and more elaborate, but also more purely speculative, theory as to the establishment of "the instincts and the other inborn tendencies of the organism, including the morphogenetic tendencies" (*345*, 120) as results of "the process of the hereditary transmission of acquired characters" (*ibid.*, 73). It is his centro-epigenetic hypothesis (*ibid.*, Chapters II and III) which postulates a "central zone of development (*ibid.*, 69). This zone "coincides with the least differentiated part of the nervous system," and, in vertebrates, "is probably formed by the most internal layer of the spinal cord." Thus it "would be the really *effective* germinal zone," the genital organs being merely "the place for the reception, elaboration, and re-emission of the germinal substance" (*ibid.*, 77–78). And this zone would contain the real store of racial memories. In one respect, though speculative, this theory is particularly interesting. Out of this engram store come successively the purely mnemic excitations which regulate growth, but which were inherited from ancestors who acquired them from adaptations to the environment. "Thus the ontogenetic stimulus is merely a restitution or reproduction, by internal causes, of the functional stimulus or physiological reaction which is at first produced and can only be produced by the external medium. It follows also *that ontogeny is nothing but a continual adaptation of the embryo to successive modes of the activity of the central zone*, and that the fundamental law of biogenesis, viz., that ontogeny is a succinct repetition of phylogeny, appears to be the direct consequence of the mechanism of the hereditary transmission of acquired characters" (*345*, 74). But when growth is completed, in "just the same way as, till now, the disturbing action of the central zone had interrupted the just-formed dynamic equilibrium and caused the passage of the organism from one ontogenetic stage to the next, so when the adult stage has been attained, each lasting change of functional stimulus, or of functional activity which results therefrom, will again upset what would otherwise have been the final condition of dynamic equilibrium, and cause the organism to pass to a new phylogenetic stage" (*ibid.*, 73). "The only effect, therefore, of the lasting change of functional stimulus in the species will be the addition of a new potential element to the germ-plasm" (*ibid.*, 74). In this interpretation, learning that results in acquired characters which are transmissible uses the same apparatus and is but a continuation or alteration of the same process as ontogeny itself.

[53] As expressed by MacBride (*279*, 20), "The whole of development is nothing but a series of these reminiscences or habitual memories." All stages are memories of different habits assumed at a "different crisis in the history of the race." But, though "recapitulation or the successive manifestation of ancestral memories is the essential and original core of all development," it is "blurred and obscured by many secondary causes" (*ibid.*, 14). For instance, the embryonic stage has been modified from the larval (*ibid.*, 17–18),

f. Affects. While, in the first two chapters we have associated present wants, as variations or tendencies away from homeostasis, with behavior of an emotional character or with the setting up of an emotion in consciousness, and while, above, we have included among mnemic phenomena both the tendency to maintain or restore homeostasis (a) and conditioning and learning (d), we were not then prepared to bring out the suggestion that the associated affective element is itself mnemic. As Rignano says (*345*, 152–153), "we must attribute a similar mnemonic nature to this fundamental tendency to preserve physiological stability whence we have derived all the most fundamental 'affective tendencies' of all organisms without exception." In his view, affective tendencies have several properties. The first might be called generalization. While "we have every reason to believe that each sensory mnemonic accumulation has its seat in a sole point, or, at most, in a narrowly limited area of the cerebral cortex," "every physiological state affects every point in the body." The affective tendency, being associated with the physiological state, is therefore supposedly "made up of an infinite number of elementary mnemonic accumulations deposited in each point of the body" (*345*, 155). Thus affects are associated with generalized mnemic excitations only. Partly from this follows the second property of affects—the fact that they are subjective or personal. They are subjective because they are wholly of internal origin. But that property is also "due to the fact that the organism will be endowed with certain idiosyncrasies, and with certain longings (nostalgia),[54] according to the various environments or situations to which the individual or the species has been exposed in the past for a sufficient length of time, that is to say, according to *the particular history* in each case" (*345*, 155–156). The third property also derives in part from the first.[55] "Affectivities are proportionately stronger, according to the number and persistence of the relations from which they have originated" (*349*, 159). That is, affective tendencies are proportional to habituation.[56] "In this way the nos-

---

so that an "embryo is merely a modified and concealed larva" (*ibid.*, 16). This acquired character blurs recapitulation, for certain ancestral organs are functionless in the embryo whereas the larva uses them; sometimes they are not even differentiated in the embryo" (*ibid.*, 16). The special system of embryonic nourishment was acquired (*ibid.*, 18), but the old system also remains. It would therefore, in reality, be more remarkable that a human infant has not sucked before birth than that it does so afterwards. The inheritance of acquired characters alters the picture of phylogeny. Then ontogeny appears "as if each life history were an historical record which had been blurred and which had suffered later insertions and from which pages had been lost" (*ibid.*, 19).

[54] Rignano's psychological concept of longing or nostalgia as a concomitant of any tendency to restore homeostasis—his notion that it is a *vis a fronte* as discussed below—is, in our opinion, entirely gratuitous.

[55] For "the number and persistence of the relations" is presumably also a cause of generalization.

[56] This seems to be true not only of internal physiological states but also of conditioning to external stimuli. In fact, as we have seen, the process of conditioning can be measured in its progress by the degree to which it creates a replica of the want (its corresponding emotional state or affect). The more it has become habitual, the more affect,

talgia (longing) for every customary thing which happens to be wanting, is originated" (*345*, 160). That is, affective tendencies, being tendencies to restore the *status quo ante*, are aroused by any defect (incongruity) in the whole of the customary *mise en scène*.[57] The fourth is this: "There is another special property of 'affective tendencies,' which, being essentially mnemonic in character, confirms their mnemonic origin and nature; it is what Ribot terms their power of 'transference.'" "This property of 'transference' consists in the vicarious substitution of the whole by a part." "This secondary affectivity at first awakened by the presence of a part as representative of the whole, comes in course of time, through habit, to be firmly attached to this part, which thenceforward becomes desired for itself, quite apart from its nature as a representative of the situation first desired only as a whole" (*345*, 151–162).[58]

In my judgment, this so-called biological theory of memory, presented here and in the text, hardly deserves, as yet, the name "theory." On the

---

This is what William James said in, from our present point of vantage, a curiously roundabout way. "A habit once grafted on an instinctive tendency becomes fixed on the first example" (*220*, II, 395). Translated into our terminology, that would read as follows: An habitual motor response, learned as the reaction to a want (which James regarded as a tendency with regard to miscellaneous objects) becomes fixed on the first object. That is, the first object having become conditioned to the want, and the want habitually expressing itself by a certain motor response, the stimulus of the object becomes capable of arousing a replica of the want (affect) or of raising its latent to effective intensity and thus of initiating the response. The more habituated the whole process, the greater the affective tone aroused, subject to the position of the particular want in the scale of emotivity (i.e., order of priority).

57 "Every other relation even if very specialized, which becomes established with things or persons, has no sooner become a habit than it becomes, in virtue of this very fact, a 'need.' In a word, Lehman's law of 'the necessity of the habitual,' which that author enunciated for every stimulus to which we have become accustomed, and the cessation of which gives rise to a need, can be verified in the case of every relation to the environment, general or particular" (Rignano, *345*, 159).

"Thus, for instance, persistent habit suffices to explain the origin and deeply engrained character in both animals and men of many affective tendencies, analogous to family affection, such as gregariousness, sociability, friendship and so on" (*ibid.*, 161).

"If, however, we have the opportunity of watching the most various kinds of 'affectivities' originate before our eyes—so to speak—as the results of habit, we are justified in referring to mnemonic causes of the same kind, *all* the affective tendencies, without exception, for the nature of those that are inborn is exactly the same as the nature of those that are acquired" (*ibid.*, 161).

All this consists in no more than illustrations of what Semon calls the tendency to remove the incongruities of a homophony.

58 Rignano cites the fact that "the 'conquest' of the opposite sex, which is indispensable for the satisfaction of sexual hunger,' eventually becomes in certain people an end in itself; the delight in seduction for the sake of seduction, and sexual vanity of the male as well as of the female, and other similar affectivities are further derivatives of the sexual appetite" (*345*, 163).

These last illustrations constitute a statement of the case of what we have called ancillary wants, of which our example was hunting. But, of course, it offers no explanation. On the other hand, the general statement in the text sounds more like what Semon called the ecphory of an engram-complex by an infinitesimal part of the original excitation (i.e., by a conditioned stimulus).

contrary, it seems to me to be little more than a vague synthesis of phenomena, previously regarded as discrete, among which a certain set of resemblances has been found. The very characteristics in terms of which these resemblances are defined are themselves vague. Nevertheless, I am impressed with the thesis on the ground of its suggestiveness. And it seems not impossible that the mere fact that attention has been called to these resemblances will lead to explorations which will uncover their true nature.

The reason for my adoption of this scheme for presentation in this study must already be obvious to the reader. In all the various lists of so-called mnemic phenomena, alpha is homeostasis, or its equivalent, and omega is conscious memory. Through the adoption of this scheme we have allied our two bases for human wants. Our analysis of present wants rests on Cannon's concept of variations from homeostasis. That is practically identical with Semon's concept of the incongruities of a homophony. On that basis, the present-want system might be viewed as the operation of the mnemic principle at its most primitive level. Our analysis of future wants has related them to conscious memory. On that basis, the future-want system might be viewed as the operation of the mnemic principle at its most highly evolved level.

The logical consistency of this thesis does not prove anything. However, it serves two purposes for us. In the first place, it takes out of the realm of mysticism the phenomena of conscious memory; and, in the second place, it suggests and emphasizes the probable, though not proven, relation between the two fundamental energizing mechanisms of human behavior.

C. MNEMIC "LAWS" AND THE CONDITIONING PROCESS

There is one mnemic feature, that appears at least in the case of conscious memory, which we cannot derive from Semon's presentation, though we get a few hints in regard to it from Rignano's discussion of affects (see Section B, above). A thesis as to this feature was developed in Appendix II and Chapter 3; but there, because of the order of our investigation, we did not treat it as mnemic. It is now time to attempt to reconcile and combine this thesis with that of Semon—and thus at the same time to explain more fully the construction we have been placing on Pavlov's experimental results.

According to Semon the conditioning of an external stimulus only requires that the engram produced by that stimulus become part of a simultaneously formed engram-complex. Thereafter, the revival of that engram by homophony is enough to revive the whole engram-complex by association. This merely interprets in mnemic concepts Pavlov's determination that the essence of conditioning lies in the overlapping in point of time (simultaneity) of the to-be-conditioned external stimulus and what he called the unconditioned stimulus, which we have interpreted to be an internal physiological state—a present want. Semon's thesis assumes that Pavlov's unconditioned stimulus—our present want—also leaves an engram in the same engram-complex which can thereafter be revived by association whenever the engram of the conditioned stimulus is revived. Thus, for the original conditioning, both depend on simultaneity (i.e., laying down in the same engram-complex) and on recognition through homophony and, then, on "simultaneous" association for the revival of the whole complex by the repetition of the conditioned stimulus. And, for both, this chain of events suffices.

In Appendix II, without considering conditioning in its mnemic aspect, we attributed the process to what we called the endowment of a sensorimotor process, current or revived, with the specific emotional content of a want. This original endowment also requires simultaneity—that is, the simultaneous existence of the emotion in the cortex when the sensorimotor process first occurs. But it requires more. It requires "interest." It requires, first, that the particular detail of the flat background of the whole *mise en scène*—the one that is to be conditioned—should be noticed. That usually requires conscious attention—perhaps even the focusing of conscious attention upon it; and that, in turn, seems to be directed by the current interest of the organism—its then prepotent want. In this way "interest" is conferred on the particular detail.[1] But does even this suffice; or, alternatively, what focuses this "interest" and therefore conscious attention upon the specific detail? We saw that new conditioning hardly occurs if the prefrontal areas of the cortex are not functioning, and therefore suggested that they act in some way as a sort of catalytic agent to set up, for the first time at least, the relation in which conditioning consists—or, in other words, to endow with a specific emotional content ("interest") the particular sensorimotor process resulting from the stimulus which is being conditioned. We assumed that, thereafter, the memory revived by a repetition of the stimulus continued to be endowed with the original emotion and that this combination is the essence of conditioning. Whether or not this is the correct interpretation, simultaneity, even when often repeated, does not suffice by itself to cause conditioning. An affective relationship must be established.

It would be consistent with Semon's and Pavlov's interpretation, as well as with our own, to suppose that experienced emotions lay down their "own" engrams which become parts of the engram-complexes, so that the conditioned stimulus revives such engrams by simultaneous association as part of the engram-complex, when, by homophony, it revives its "own" engram. But against this are two potent considerations. In the first place, that would presume that the engrams of a single emotion would be homophonous with each other. On that basis we could recognize our emotions

[1] It is a question whether a detail does not have to arouse or have conferred on it some "interest" in order to cause sufficient stimulation to produce an engram at all. In Appendix II, Section G4 we assumed, at least, that "'interest' is one of the chief reasons for retention of an impression."

as we experienced them. Apparently we do so. On that basis, too, homophony of emotion would be an influence producing recall of previous similar emotional experiences and thus, by association, of their respective engram-complexes (*mises en scène*). This, too, appears to be the case, at least in some degree.[2] On the other hand, that would also presume that emotions often experienced, having laid down many homophonous engrams, would become composites or abstractions which could be revived apart from their respective settings (i.e., without association). This is notoriously not the case.[3] Memories of emotions do not seem to exist alone. In the second place, if emotion had laid down separate engrams, one characteristic of conditioning would be difficult if not impossible to account for. The conditioning process grows stronger the more often it is repeated. But association with each specific occasion grows weaker the more homophonous engrams are laid down in series. They become composites or abstractions and may lose even their sense of pastness. If association of Semon's type were responsible for relating engrams of the conditioned stimulus to engrams of the emotional state, the connection would grow weaker with frequent repetition.

It appears, then, that we are safer to continue with our original thesis, that individual engrams may become endowed with an emotional content, when the emotion existed during the experience. It seems as if the very excitation pattern itself of any integrated experience may be modified or enlarged to include emotion as well as sensation. If so, emotion is only revived in memory as a part of some sensorimotor engram, not as an engram by itself; if so, the revival is not due to association in Semon's sense; and if so, the effect of a conditioned stimulus does not depend on simultaneous association among the parts of an engram-complex. In this respect Semon's interpretation seems to be wrong and Pavlov's inadequate. The revival depends, rather, upon the incorporation in the individual engram of an emotional component (endowment). On the other hand, our thesis would admit the possibility that the homophony of emotional charge might work in the same way as that of sensuous impression to revive memories. Perhaps that would depend upon whether, in a particular case, the emotional homophony was so perfect or so powerful as to overrule the usually more effective sensuous homophony. Our thesis might even be stretched to permit the recognition of recurrent emotions, though not apart from the sensorimotor processes invested with them.

There is a third set of facts, moreover, that the first of these theses cannot pretend to explain, though the second might be stretched to cover

[2] When we "feel" a certain way we are often reminded of some occasion when, under totally different and therefore non-homophonous conditions, we "felt" the same way. It is possible that some fetishism and even some symbolism has its basis in this kind of homophony.

[3] As William James (*220*, II, 474) pointed out, "The revivability in memory of the emotions . . . is very small." They arise rather as a by-product of "a lively thought" (memory) of what he calls "their exciting cause" (i.e., what we should call the sensorimotor process endowed with emotion).

them. A conditioned stimulus can revive a replica of its emotional state in the hypothalamus, in the case of quasi-external wants, or it can raise the latent intensity of an internal want to effective intensity. On the other hand, revival of the memory alone, without repetition of the stimulus (i.e., by association), cannot do either. How, then, can the conditioned stimulus be dependent for its effect on the revival of such a memory? Under the first thesis the revival of the emotion in memory would depend upon association. That is, a single engram only—the one in the same engram-complex—would be recalled either by some other memory or by the occurrence of the conditioned stimulus. Under the second thesis that would also be true if the recall were due to some other memory. In all these cases the emotional charge would be limited to that of a single engram (one experience). It would therefore be insufficient to cause a reaction in the subcortical centers in all cases, if it were insufficient in any.

But, under the second thesis, if recall were due to the conditioned stimulus, many or all homophonous engrams would be revived. If we could assume that the emotional charges of all were then summated, the difference in these two effects would be accounted for. Is this possible? We remember that Semon held that the "intensity" of memories does not summate by reason of homophony, but that there is a "notable rise in vividness" by reason of "homophonous congruence." If we were to assume that "vividness" in memory is in large part, or is largely a creature of, the emotional charge, as we did that "vividness" in current sensation is due to the focusing of conscious attention and therefore is, or is due to, "interest," then it would follow that homophonous emotional charges must be summated. As a result, we would have an explanation of the fact that conditioned stimuli, arousing a whole series of homophonous engrams with their emotional charges, are adequate to cause a reaction in the subcortical apparatus, while single engrams revived by association are not. And we would also have an explanation of the fact that conditioned stimuli cause new emotional experiences, with externality, which conceal the mere emotional revivals they probably cause in memory, while engrams coming into consciousness through association revive emotion only in memory and therefore not as a new experience, without externality, and of little force. Finally, we would have to modify that assumption to meet one other fact. Since revival by homophony is also possible between memories, without concurrent repetition of stimulus, so that many recur as composites or abstractions, it would be necessary to suppose either that the series is much briefer when revived by memory than when revived by a stimulus or that, in some way, the individual engrams, so abstracted, became detached or loosened from their respective emotional charges. At any rate, revival by conditioned stimulus produces emotional results far in excess of those that can be produced through revival by another memory only.

D. FUNDAMENTAL PREPOSSESSIONS WITH REGARD TO CONCEIVED TIME

In this connection, a little examination of the psychology of language gives not only some support to our hypotheses but some explanation of the beginnings of the process of developing "conceived" time. Our language-forming ancestors—Germanic and Italic—had two fundamental analogies according to which they conceived time. According to one, the onlooker stands still while events file by in a procession, coming from the distance of the future and going into the distance of the past. According to the other, events, having occurred, grow old, just as man does. But they do so in the opposite direction—that is, there is still relative motion between them and man. For man seems to be moving into the future, or the future to be moving toward him, while the event seems to be receding into the past. It happened once; he persists. Thus events and their times grow old as they recede into the past; but man only grows old as he proceeds into the future. As he grows old it is his youth that he sees as "old times." An examination of the following terms will demonstrate the two analogies.

Latin

Order of Events
  Procession
    Ante (before) = literally, "in front" (locative).
    Post (after) = literally, "behind," "at the back or rear."
    **Prios*, and its derivatives *prior, primus, priscus, pristinus,* contain various degrees of the idea of "ahead," up to the point of "first, foremost, leading"; thus, when used of time, they come to mean "early, earlier, earliest."
    Secundus (following), sometimes used to indicate "the following or next" period of time.
  Time Rising
    Occasionally the direction of movement was altered and time rose. Thus:
    Superior (higher) = occasionally, "earlier" (of years).
The Past
  Procession
    Antiquus (antique) < *ante-quos = literally, "in the front" time.
    Priscus (ancient) = literally, "in the leading" time.
  Life-span
    Vetus (old; of former or ancient times) = literally, "beyeared" times.
The Future
  Procession
    Posterus (future) = literally, "behind."
    Posteritas (the future) = literally, "the behind."

English

- Order of Events
  - Procession
    - Germanic Source
      - *Before* = literally, "at the front"; hence *first* (< fore-est) corresponds to Latin *primus.*
      - *After* (the comparative of *off*) = literally, "more off, further" (from the front).
      - *Following* (of times or events) = literally, those events which are coming from behind.
      - *Ahead of time,* or *of the times* = literally, "at or toward the front" of time or the times. This suggests that it is conceived to be possible—though perhaps only for "shave-tails"—to step out of the file of events and get to the present before the rest of that rank in the file arrives.
      - *Late* (indicating behind time), on the other hand, = literally, "slow" (i.e., not moving fast enough). Perhaps, as opposed to the foregoing, it connotes the straggler that has fallen out of line.
      - *Behind time* seems to have the same connotation.
    - Italic Source
      - *Preceding* (of times or events) < *praecedo,* "to go before."
      - *Subsequent* (of times or events) < *subsequor,* "to follow after."
- The Past
  - Procession
    - Germanic Source
      - *The Past* = literally, "the passed by."
      - *Former times* = literally, the "more at the front" times.
      - *Times gone by* or *bygone times* = literally, those which have already passed the reviewing stand.

        Occasionally that which moved was apparently altered, so that it was the observer who paraded past events which stood still. Or, possibly, the onlooker *faced* the future (see below) so that the past was behind him. Thus:
      - *Behind* (in "times that lie behind us") = "in times that we have passed" or "that have passed us."
    - Italic Source
      - *Antiquity* < *antiquus* (above)
      - *Ancient* (of times or events) < **ante-anus* = **ante-quos* (above).
      - *Remote* (of past time or events) = literally, "moved back or away."
  - Life-span
    - Germanic Source
      - *Old* (of times) = literally, "grown or increased" times (cognate of Latin *altus*).
      - *Eld* = old.
- The Future
  - Procession
    - Germanic Source
      - *Hereafter* = literally, "the more off, or further (back) from here."
      - *Coming* (of times or events) = "approaching" (see below).

Ahead or *before* (in "times that lie ahead of us"—or "before us").

These are subject to the same interpretation we made above us to "behind," under the past. *Before* might be appropriate to either kind of motion, but *ahead* seems definitely to connote the parade of the observer rather than that of events. So, too, does the use of "going" as an auxiliary verb to denote the future tense. In that case one is moving toward—"going to"—the event, not the reverse.

Italic Source

Posterity < *posteritas* (above).

Approaching (of times or events) < *ad* + *prope* = literally, "getting nearer to here."

Time Falling

Italic Source

Impend (of times or events) < *impendo* = literally, "to hang over."

In this somewhat figurative term, we have reversed the Roman concept evidenced in *superior* (above). There the past was above; here the future.

E. THREE PSYCHOLOGICAL VIEWS OF VOLITION OR ITS EQUIVALENT

William James's examples of pure (quasi-automatic) ideomotor actions are all initiated by external stimuli (though a chain of ideas may be associated), and they are all habitual. "The determining condition of the unhesitating and resistless sequence of the act seems to be *the absence of any conflicting notion in the mind*" (*220*, II, 522–523). On the other hand, the condition of voluntary action, chiefly deliberation, is the presence of antagonistic or inhibitory ideas—"reasons" or "motives." [1] The will itself seems to be the "express fiat, or act of mental consent," which eventually neutralizes all but one of these, or forms a resultant from them (*ibid.*, II, 526). "The essential achievement of the will . . . when it is most 'voluntary,' [2] is to ATTEND to a difficult object and hold it fast before the mind. The so-doing is the fiat" (*ibid.*, II, 561). The "effort of attention is thus the essential phenomenon of will" (*ibid.*, II, 562). It is an "effort to attend to one rather than to the other idea." The one which is less, or not at all, "intrinsically exciting" (i.e., of emotional "interest") will not "keep going of its own accord," as the other may, but "needs incessant pulses of voluntary reinforcement" (*ibid.*, I, 451).[3] The "sole achievement" of the will

[1] That is, his "reflection" is equivalent to the form of our "deliberation" that we have called "conflict." "What is reflection? A conflict between many ideas of possibility" (*219*, 27).

[2] We shall have occasion to refer to this curious expression which implies that even the will itself may be more or less voluntary.

[3] James notes, in an earlier discussion of this subject (*219*, 3), that the distinction between "passive sensation" and "one in which the elements of volition and attention are found" is recorded by popular speech in the several antitheses, "see" *vs.* "look," "hear" *vs.* "listen," "smell" *vs.* "scent," "feel" *vs.* "touch."

is "consent to the idea's undivided presence." "Its only function is to get this feeling of consent into the mind." And the only way to do so is to hold the idea "steadily before the mind until it *fills* the mind; for this filling is the consent, aided perhaps by the fact that, if held, the idea calls up "its own congeners and associates" (*ibid.*, II, 562–564). Then "the willing terminates with the prevalence of the idea" in consciousness (*ibid.*, II, 560)—that is, "when intuition or consent is there"—whether or not a motor action then results (*219*, 20). If it does, the action is merely the physiological motor consequences. But even "when the tendency of a particular motor idea to take effect is arrested or delayed" (*219*, 21), the resulting "resolve" has all the elements of "fiat" except the now. It only differs because it is contingent (*220*, II, 561). "Attention, belief, affirmation and motor volition are thus four names for an identical process, incidental to the conflict of ideas alone" (*219*, 31).

Thus the problem of the will becomes the problem of the concentration of attention. Whether that is an effect or a cause of the content of consciousness is left undetermined, as a purely metaphysical problem (*220*, Chapters 11 and 26). To Freud it is a cause; or, rather, an instrument of the cause. "The system Forec. [Preconscious] not only bars access to consciousness, but also controls the entrance to voluntary motility and is capable of sending out a sum of mobile energy, a portion of which is familiar to us as attention" (*154*, 488). But the ultimate cause is, as we shall see below, what is contained in the Preconscious. Later this metapsychology was revamped and two of these functions, repression and the control of motility, were assigned to the Ego (*185*, 38). But that in turn came to be largely controlled by the Super-ego whose effects on the Ego take the form of a "categorical imperative" and assume a "compulsive character" (*ibid.*, 44). Thus, in this later formulation, ultimate volition seems to be lodged in the Super-ego. McDougall regards volition as "a concentration of nervous energy in the neural systems whose excitement underlies" the percept or idea. "The effectiveness of this voluntary reinforcement depends upon" the free energy in the brain at the moment (*283*, 165). Either the source or the concentrating agency of this energy is not the "stronger, coarser drive of our primitive animal nature" but "the idea of self," or "the self-regarding sentiment" (*284*, 254).[4] That is, "volition or voluntary control proceeds from the idea of self and from the sentiment, or organised system of emotions and impulses, centred about that idea" (*ibid.*, 179). The effect of concentration is to "control involuntary tendencies either by innervating antagonistic muscles, or by directing our attention elsewhere by an effort of will; that is to say, by concentrating the energy of the mind and nervous system in one direction we withdraw it from, or prevent its flowing in, any other direction" (*ibid.*, 251).

To James, implicitly, and to Freud, so far as his earlier formulation was concerned, explicitly, the function of volition is merely the adjustment of the internal impulse to external fact—that is, what we are calling voli-

[4] That is, "a man's self [his "empirical self" or "idea of his self"] . . . is thrown upon the side of the motive that is made to prevail" (*284*, 253).

tion would have no "wishes" of its own. James says "both instincts and emotions . . . depend on the hemispheres." Intrinsically they are "accompanied by no forethought or deliberation" and are "irresistible." However, they are "modifiable," so that instincts, at least, come to have "less of the blind impulsive character which they had at first" (*220*, I, 76). But, apparently, his view is that conflict never ceases to be due only to them. For "nature implants contrary impulses to act on many classes of things, and leaves it to slight alterations in the conditions of the individual case to decide which impulse shall carry the day." The result is "unstable equilibrium, in the higher birds and mammals as in man." "They are all impulses, congenital, blind at first, and productive of motor reactions of a rigorously determinate sort. Each one of them, then, is an instinct, as instincts are commonly defined. But they contradict each other—'experience' in each particular opportunity of application usually deciding the issue. The animal that exhibits them loses the 'instinctive' demeanor and appears to lead a life of hesitation and choice, an intellectual life; not, however, because he has no instincts—rather because he has so many that they block each other's path" (*ibid.*, II, 392–393). To Freud the work of the Preconscious is limited to leading "the excitement emanating from the craving stimulus [perhaps our present want] by a devious path over the spontaneous motility which ultimately should so change the outer world as to allow the real perception of the object of gratification to take place." "After the second system [Preconscious] has finished its tentative mental work, it removes the inhibition and congestion of the excitements and allows these excitements to flow off to the motility" (*154*, 474–475). However, the part played by the Preconscious is "once for all restricted to the indication of the most suitable paths for the wish feelings originating in the unconscious" (*ibid.*, 478).

However, McDougall makes the act of volition, concentration, proceed from the idea of self, which is contrasted to the primitive drives. And Freud, in his later formulation, imposes upon the Ego, which includes most of the Preconscious, the Super-ego, which dominates the Ego. While Freud does not treat of volition in our sense, and while he makes the Super-ego, or Ego-ideal, a development out of the Id as the representative of the relation to parents, it is clear that he assigns to it an energy or energetic condition of its own and a potential effect, in conflict, which corresponds somewhat to our hypothetical entity—volition.

F. "FREE WILL" AND DETERMINISM

I would not wish my effort to confine this study to the objective viewpoint, including permissible inferences from observed data, nor the emphasis I have placed on automatic processes, to lead the reader to conclude that I take any stock in the automaton theory. Huxley said "We are conscious automata." [1] That strikes me as arrant nonsense. I have no patience

[1] I assume, as I believe all others have assumed, that Huxley was using this term in its derived sense to mean "living beings whose actions are involuntary." In its original

with it. It is an assertion that cannot be supported. It is not true in the sense in which it has been asserted by reflexology—the external stimulus-response viewpoint—for that leaves "spontaneous" behavior out of account. Nor, quite obviously, does it become true when we add the viewpoint of "spontaneous" behavior due to internal peripheral stimuli, for that leaves volitional behavior out of account. Finally, as we shall undertake to make clear now, it becomes not so much untrue as meaningless with the inclusion of behavior arising from the memory system, volitional behavior. Moreover, the assertion is no more than a relic of the days of Calvinistic physics—gone never to return. Therefore, I should like to reduce the whole issue between automatism and "free will" to the level of the "idola theatri" among which, I believe, it belongs.

Fraenkel and Gunn (*149*, 308) say that "the question of free will is a metaphysical one, and it cannot be answered by experimental methods." "We can get on quite well without knowing whether it exists or not." That may be a wise, if evasive, policy, provided one pursues it with complete intellectual honesty. The difficulty is that one does not. Position on one side or the other of the question is almost certain to be implicit in everyone's assumptions, even those of the "purest" and most rigorous scientist. The very term "automatism" is one of those most likely to contain such an assumption—the assumption of "determinism."

Where does the principle of determinism stand today in science? As Langmuir says (*249*, 2), many "philosophers, considering many fields other than science . . . went so far as to believe that everything was absolutely fixed by the initial conditions of the universe and that free will or choice was impossible." In the theological field this was "predetermination" according to the "will of God." In physics, "Ampere, for example, stated that if he were given the positions and velocities of all the atoms in the universe it should be possible theoretically to determine the whole history of the universe" (*loc. cit.*). Then came Planck's quantum theory and, as a result, "the uncertainty principle, developed by Bohr and Heisenberg," under which "it becomes impossible to predict with certainty the movement of a single particle," so that "Ampere's estimate of the scope of science has lost its basis," and the best that can be done is to use statistical methods "considering the average motions of the single" atoms only (*ibid.*, 2–3).

In the face of these developments, the question that H. N. Russell suggests may well be asked: "Has not modern physics abandoned determinism, and committed itself to a principle of indeterminacy?" (*358*, 249). In one aspect, nomenclature, Russell himself seems to me to give the answer. "If the great physicist who discovered the 'uncertainty principle' had only called it the 'Principle of limited measurability' (as Max Born did a few years later) we might have been spared a great part of the 'awful outbreak

---

(Greek) sense of a "thing acting of itself," "automaton" would, of course, be entirely acceptable. That is all that I claim for man.

of intellectual licentiousness' which Bridgman all too truly foresaw among the half-informed" (*loc. cit.*). Thus the seeming trend toward indeterminacy in modern physics becomes no more than a piece of honest agnosticism:[2] "We cannot measure—as yet." It is very likely still that all things are determined in the restricted sense that they are wholly the resultants of the forces then at play.

As to another aspect—the determinacy of what is only statistically measurable—Langmuir has offered an important suggestion to which we have already referred in Chapter 3. "Just as there are two types of physics, classical physics and quantum physics, which have for nearly twenty-five years seemed irreconcilable, just so must we recognize two types of natural phenomena. First, those in which the behavior of the system can be determined from the average behavior of its component parts and second, those in which a single discontinuous event (which may depend upon a single quantum change) becomes magnified in its effect so that the behavior of the whole aggregate does depend upon something that started from a small beginning. The first class of phenomena I want to call *convergent phenomena,* because all the fluctuating details of the individual atoms average out giving a result that converges to a definite state. The second class we may call *divergent phenomena,* where from a small beginning increasingly large effects are produced" (*249,* 3). Let us consider the question of "free will" from this viewpoint.

Upon the basis of our analysis in the text we have arrived at the conclusion that the process of volition takes place when there is a conflict in consciousness among memories and their accompanying sensations, both of which may be endowed with emotional qualities, or between these and emotional drives from the subcortical regions. We have also concluded that it is these several classes of excitation, and these only, which can constitute the content of consciousness during volition, and that the only part of these the presence of which is required to make the result volitional is composed of memories and coincident sensations.[3] As a result we have preferred to differentiate this latter element as the strategic one in volition (the "will" proper) and to treat the emotional element (the "wish") as no part of the criterion. We have recognized that there may be some other element that makes good the apparent deficiency in strength of the "will" against the "wish," or that tips the balance as between opposing "wills." On the other hand, we have also recognized that it may be the process of concentration itself that does this. In the latter case we have called the process automatic. In either case the process can only be determined by the specific influences at work, fortified or unfortified. Therefore, in

[2] As Langmuir says (*249, 6*), "It does not seem to me that we need be discouraged if science is not capable of solving all problems even in the distant future. I see no objections to recognizing that the field of science is limited"—or, for that matter, the field of knowledge, which may well be the same thing.

[3] Furthermore we have emphasized the connection between volition and the memory-system. Chiefly the conflict is between excitations whose origin is not peripheral to the cortex and those whose origin is so peripheral, even including most sensation.

either case suffrage is limited to the potential content of consciousness, whether that enters under its own guise or in disguise.[4] Thus the actual conflict is confined to the several elements that successively enter consciousness while it endures.

Now, let someone tell me that I have "free will." Thereafter, that memory—that verbal idea—is on a par with all others and is as capable as any of the rest of entering the fray. Suppose I decide to experiment with it to see whether or not it is true. The next time I have a strong emotional impulse the memory or idea of "free will" is revived and causes conflict. It tells me I can do the opposite of what the emotion impels me to do. I try this out and find that I can. Or, on some other occasion, after mature deliberation I come to a decision as to the wisest course of action. The memory of "free will" happens then to be revived and tells me I am entirely capable of doing the opposite of my decision. I try this out also and find it equally within my powers. It seems impossible that anyone can argue that he cannot have such an idea of "free will" and that he cannot experiment with it, or let it experiment, in these ways. Once such experiments are tried, all conflicts may become conditioned to this memory, so that it is always revived. It has then become a potent factor on precisely the same basis as all other determining factors. It is a new causative agent, but one that produces *divergent phenomena.* For, in the course of time and practice, when it is revived, along with it are also revived all its accumulating associations—experiences consequent upon all its previous participations in conflict. These are antagonistic to its exercise in certain directions and are allied in support of its exercise in certain other directions. The idea of "free will" comes to be guided by experience. Not only do these accumulating associations consist of memories of the consequences (the overt results); they come also to consist of memories of the antagonists they have met in conflicts of the past (the rest of the content of consciousness). Recognition of these antagonists when they reappear—the recall of the homophonous memories—is the process by which one comes to understand oneself. Thus "know thyself" is a prescription for the exercise of "free will" of the same order as "know thy motor car" is one for the exercise of control over that complicated mechanism. The idea of "free will" comes to be guided by recognition of the factors entering conflict.[5] These two constellations of associations built up around the idea of "free will" are what we know as character. They are the de-

[4] Even if one does not accept our restriction of the agencies of volition to a part only of the content of consciousness in the case of many conflicts, this statement seems to hold good. That is, to suppose that the influence which produces volition can be something that enters neither into one's feeling nor into one's thinking—that it is an "I" which is foreign to both fields—seems to me as impossible from the dualistic as from the monistic viewpoint.

[5] Thus it may come habitually to favor the under dog when the upper dog is emotion. I take this recognition to be the "detachment" to which Hughlings Jackson refers when he says (*216*, I, 375), "By the double process of increasing complexity [cortical] and increasing detachment we gradually 'get above' our lower mere animal selves."

terminants of the ways in which the idea of "free will" shall be exercised.

The exercise of this idea of "free will" is of course limited in two ways. It cannot reach beyond the borders fixed by one's own structure nor beyond those inherent in the way the external world works. Nor can it reach beyond one's available stock of ideas. That is, the idea of "free will" must be construed as only a reinforcing agency. If certain specific ideas are not in the mind—if they have not been previously developed or are not developed in the process of conflict—one cannot act on them. Even if such an idea is part of one's stock, but is not then revived to enter the conflict, one cannot act on it. However, within these limits, the exercise of the idea of "free will" is not eliminated by assuming a mere tipping of the scales in favor of the strongest impulses or the weightiest considerations. For the notion that one has "free will" is itself a major and potent consideration. Its own constellations of experience and recognition can mobilize it to tip the balance. Pragmatically, that capacity is "free will." If the dice can be loaded, what of the laws of chance and statistical probability? When one reacts, even originally by suggestion, against the notion of automatism, a causative factor is introduced which, as it grows thereafter from a small beginning, may make the results of conflict divergent phenomena. Once one comes to be able to react in this way, as if he had "free will," what difference does it make whether his "free will" satisfies the metaphysician? What other exercise of freedom could one desire within the limits set by the constitution of oneself and the world? [6] Once a man's mind can conceive "free will," he has it potentially to all intents and purposes.[7] The idea "I can," or "I could, if," gives one the reality of "free will," for it becomes itself a cause. Theoretically, determinacy remains; but it is a rather indeterminate determinacy, for it is only measurable and predictable in a general way (character) and it may be constantly at work altering even that degree of determinacy into divergent phenomena (development of character).

This interpretation lends itself to Russell's corollary. "Among the most obvious and important properties of man is self-determination. Whether we consider the behavior of others or our own conscious experience, a great number of varied observational data may be reduced to order and empirically 'explained' on the hypothesis that the normal human individual is a conscious person, possessing (within limits) intelligence and memory, and with a very considerable degree of control over his words and actions. We all act on these postulates every day . . . and it would be practically

[6] To the charge that this is, or may be, an illusion I would reply that, if it is, that makes no difference whatever. Illusions are, of course, as potent sources of behavior as are correct appraisals of reality. The point is that "Everybody, sane or insane, 'lives in a world of his own,'" so far as his mental life is concerned (Hughlings Jackson, *216*, I, 383). If a paranoiac thinks he is Napoleon, so far as he is concerned, that is the fact. The only unreality involved is one that derives from the external world and its hard rule that there was but one Napoleon and he is dead. "Free will" cannot exceed that limit.

[7] Conversely, one may say that, in this restricted version of "free will," man could not have had the concept had he not had this experience.

impossible to live through a day of normal human relations without acting on them" (*358*, 251). These postulates consist, then, in ascribing to others the notion of "free will" which we ourselves have acquired. "It is an immediate consequence of these postulates that the normal individual may reasonably be held responsible for his voluntary actions. Without this principle, organized society could hardly exist" (*ibid.*, 252).

However, in our view, this generalization should be qualified. Those who have the notion of "free will" and who exercise it, develop it. Thus and only thus do they become responsible in fact. Even with the extended justification of the postulate among many persons, irresponsibility may continue to attach to the actions of those who do not have or do not exercise the notion of "free will"—to the actions of animals (but not all), to those of infants, to those of the "willful," of the "self-indulgent," in short to the actions of all those who have not undertaken and succeeded in the process of self-discipline. Responsibility is thus something assumed and learned, not something innate. However, we may find it convenient in society to hold our fellows responsible for their irresponsibility—that is, to demand that they assume and learn responsibility. All that is necessary to accomplish that purpose is to state positively to all and sundry that each of them has complete "free will" within the physical limitations of his structure and his environment—that is, to implant the idea. Once that is done, the person becomes completely and solely responsible for what he makes of the idea and, given a little opportunity for practice, can thereafter justly be held to account for all his actions.

G. WALLER'S THEORY OF THE SENSE OF EFFORT

In an interesting and suggestive article, published some fifty years ago, Waller proposed a neural basis for the sense of effort which has not been much explored but which has remained familiar to neurologists ever since. He does not distinguish between what we are calling volitional effort and muscular exertion. In fact, his study is concerned wholly with the latter. But it suggests a basis for construing the sense of effort in the former case.

Waller concluded that "fatigue phenomena are manifested in the entire series of organs from centre to periphery in consequence of voluntary exertion" (*419*, 246), but that "in voluntary fatigue the degree of change is in decreasing ratio from centre to periphery" because the "cell of higher function" is relatively more exhaustible (*ibid.*, 245).[1] Thus "voluntary fatigue depends more upon central than upon peripheral change" (*ibid.*, 198), and, in fact, "fatigue is usually of central origin, and protective from peripheral fatigue" (*ibid.*, 185) so that it is impossible for the higher centers to "overdrive" their subordinates (*ibid.*, 245).[2]

[1] Waller concluded, as is I believe generally conceded, that nerve fibers themselves do not suffer fatigue and that fatigue especially involves "functional organs" (synapses) and "terminal organs" (end-plates) (*419*, 245). It is worth while to note also that Sherrington (*375*, 223) says that "the final efferent-root neurone" "seems from experimental evidence to be relatively indefatigable," while the central neurons are the most so.

[2] The experiments differentiated the "lateral" (rigor) effects and the "longitudinal"

He regards effort (exertion) as related to the "nervous emission," not to the muscular contraction or force used (*ibid.*, 219). But so are the "fatigue phenomena" that he considers purely neural. He then suggests that the sense of movement (muscle sense or kinesthesis), the sense of effort, and the sense of fatigue "are degrees of the same sensory phenomenon." The sense of effort is the "sensation accompanying muscular action," while the sense of fatigue is one "consequent upon muscular action." The "changes producing the first also produce the second." It is as if one was the effect and the other the after-effect, like an image and an after-image (*ibid.*, 187–188).

If so, since fatigue—and presumably its sense—ranges from the highest centers to the periphery but in diminishing ratio, so too would the sense of effort. Thus the sense of effort is not peripheral only nor central only but central and peripheral,[3] and, along the whole range, it is proportional to the degree of fatigability. Thus the greater the degree of participation of the highest centers in any muscular action, the greater will be the sense of effort.

On this basis we might infer that the sense of volitional effort is the same thing as the sense of muscular exertion, even though it may be confined to the highest centers and produce no overt effect,[4] and that the distinction between the two is the marked difference in the degree of intensity because of the different source—the one being on the motor side of the central nervous system, the other being in the internuncial tracts prior to the beginning of the motor tracts.

(shortening) effects of fatigue, both in respect of their prolongation and their intensification. There is "a striking prolongation of the lateral effect in voluntary fatigue," "owing to a prolongation of central discharge"; but there is a slighter prolongation of longitudinal effect (*419*, 221). "The *prolonged* lateral effect is a sign of central fatigue," while "the *increased* lateral effect (relatively to a constant longitudinal effect), is a sign of peripheral fatigue" (*ibid.*, 224). In line with the theory that, even when action is voluntary, impulses come from several or many sources (partly release), it would seem from his experiments that more of the dynamic effect (longitudinal) in a muscle is caused from a source which tires soon (i.e., from a source higher in the central system) than is the case with the rigor effect (lateral).

[3] He says (*419*, 179) that the old view "that the sense of effort is a subjective concomitant of the outgoing nerve flow," which he ascribes (just as did James), to Bain, Johannes Müller, Wundt, and Hughlings Jackson, among others, is no longer in fashion. However, his own conclusion (*ibid.*, 246) that the "sense of effort" is not peripheral (Bastian) nor central (Bain) but central and peripheral (Wundt) seems to accept this old view.

[4] In fact we might infer that it is the very fact that these cortical excitations are so weak as to be subliminal which produces or enhances the sense of effort when they persist, as they must to produce conflict or action. For Sherrington found that fatigue is like a raising of the threshold, so that it occurs earlier with weak than with strong stimuli and is actually greater in proportion to weak than it is to strong "discharges" (*375*, 219-220). If so, under Waller's construction, the same would be true of the sense of effort or exertion.

IV

THE SEVERAL SCHEMES OF MARGINAL UTILITY THEORY

Appendix to Chapter 8

A. GENERAL CONSIDERATIONS

In the examination of the various forms of marginal utility theory for our single specific purpose only, to which we may now proceed, we find it convenient to divide the chief original protagonists into four groups along lines somewhat different from the usual ones. The usual divisions are the Austrian, the French or "Lausanne," and the English schools.[1] The founder of the first was Menger and his chief nineteenth century followers were Böhm-Bawerk and Wieser. This brand of the theory has been carried into the present by Mises, Schumpeter, Hayek, and others. It is largely non-mathematical in presentation. At Lausanne, Walras was succeeded by Pareto, and since then perhaps the other most influential pupils of the school have been Wicksell and Cassel. This school is, of course, one of the chief sources of modern mathematical economics.[2] The third continuous movement was originated by Jevons, whose most direct follower and elaborator was Wicksteed. It is a little difficult to place Fisher. In respect of his methods he is obviously a disciple of "Lausanne"; in respect of his concepts he is closer to the school of Jevons. Therefore, we are placing him in the latter group. The same difficulty arises with Edgeworth. But here we find it necessary to separate both Edgeworth and Pareto—who, like Fisher, used Jevons's concepts—and put them in a group by themselves on account of the special method which they developed. And this without denying that, in certain respects, Pareto carried on the work of Walras and Edgeworth that of Jevons. The reason for our division is that we cannot admit the usually attributed homogeneity of the theory in these various hands and that, in fact, we find the difficulties of each of at least three of the four brands markedly different from those of the others.[3]

In general these difficulties arise especially in the course of applying mathematical method to this subject—but also to some extent when that

[1] We are, of necessity, ignoring the early and isolated progenitors such as Gossen and even Senior.

[2] With Cournot.

[3] Wieser, as one among many examples, treated all the different terms in use as names for the same thing (see *442*, 13).

is not done—by reason of the casual way in which the nature and dimensions of the various and heterogeneous magnitudes dealt with are determined. As to the use of mathematics in this field I think that even those who dislike "her peculiar costume," as Edgeworth calls it [4] (expression in symbols), should admit that he has successfully refuted the usual criticism, which is based on the ground that measurement in arbitrary objective units—impossible here—is necessary to such treatment. The categories of greater or less, positive or negative, maximum and minimum are also mathematical categories.[5] In fact the whole subject of magnitudes is essentially mathematical. It cannot be dealt with otherwise, with any precision of thought. Our difficulty with this treatment is a quite different one. While the higher mathematics applied to marginal utility theory may be above reproach—as to that I am not competent to judge, though I assume they are, because they have passed the test of time—the lower mathematics frequently seem highly questionable. At the point at which these lofty structures of symbols rest on the ground of premises—that is, where they come in contact with reality and the symbols require to be converted into terms of definite objects or processes [6]—there seem to arise numerous difficulties, though these are apt to be different in the different treatments.

Among the commonest difficulties is one which has to do exclusively with that one of the two axes, in the older graphic representation of the mathematical school, which is undoubtedly subject to exact and objective measurement. That is the *x* axis, when it is taken to represent quantities of means. These theories are apt to play fast and loose with the units of means. The argument is apt to pass, almost unconsciously, from the comparison of quantities of one means under different conditions (in which case the size of the unit may legitimately be indefinite, provided it remains the same and it is large enough to be measurable and provided one is dealing with

[4] Edgeworth, *133*, 3.

[5] See Edgeworth, *133*, 2–6. In spite of this, a younger Cantabrigian, Mrs. Robinson, continues to regard as a "vice" the use of a "quantitative conception that there is no known way of measuring" (*348*, 11). And she has many companions in this view. It may be true, as Knight says (*240*, 71): "It is therefore not quantities, nor even intensities, of satisfaction with which we are concerned (though the limitations of language compel the use of these terms at times), or any absolute magnitude whatever, but the purely relative judgment of comparative significance of alternatives open to choice." He holds, however, that the "psychic variables" are "ordinal," if not "quantitative"; are "variable," if not "measurable"; and can be "ranked," if not "added" (*ibid.*, 69, note 2).

[6] Curiously enough, for the purpose of examination of the entities concerned and their relations, we have, in the text, found Menger's analysis to be the most suitable for our needs. And this because—in spite of the fact that he was the only one of the three founders who did not use the mathematical mode of presentation—he was *also* the only one of the three who analyzed his primary data in an exact way. The vague and nebulous entities upon which Jevons and Walras erected their structure of higher mathematics serve no better as a ground for our analysis than they did for them as proof of their conclusions. To be sure, their conclusions are implicit in their premises, but these latter cannot be so stated as to correspond to reality or so defined that they can be observed and judged as magnitudes even in terms of their effects.

what we have called the *rate* of significance) to the comparison of quantities of different means under different conditions (in which case, without definite units, there can be no rates at all, and even with definite units there is no common basis for comparison). We have discussed that point in some detail in the text (pp. 492–493). The use of the infinitesimal notation is largely responsible; and the effect of this practical elimination of the objective dimension of means, or its inadequacy, is to lead insensibly to the point where a "little" more or less of every means could be found that would be subjectively equivalent to that of every other. The elusive quantity might become whatever quantity of each is equivalent.[7] This question will be raised again in connection with the specific theories discussed below.

More especially, however, the aforementioned difficulties have to do with the other horn of our dilemma, the y axis. What is this variously named entity whose magnitude is measured—or partly measured—along this axis? Is it maximum intensity of want; or, on the usual assumption of declining intensity during satisfaction, is it the remaining intensity of the want at some stage in the process? Or, analogous to the latter, is it "desire" for the remaining means or for the feeling of pleasure, or relief of pain, or satisfaction, that consumption of the remaining means will produce? Or is it the *rate* of such desire, whatever that may be? In any case, is it the concept of a static magnitude which is not directly related to the process shown on the x axis at all? Or, again, is it the reduction of intensity of want produced by any portion of the means through the corresponding phase of the process? Or is it something analogous to the last—the corresponding quantity of feeling of pleasure, or of relief from pain, or of satisfaction, that results from the consumption of that portion of the means? Or is it the *rate* of reduction of intensity, or the *rate* of any of these experiences? What are its dimensions? What are the effects of its variations in magnitude, from which we may infer the ways in which it does so vary? As to these questions the standard answers are so different that we will need to examine each school separately.

B. MENGER'S SCHEME

The simple and delightfully naïve method of representation which Menger used—and which Böhm-Bawerk adopted from him—consists of a set of arithmetical progressions descending in two directions.[1] The Ro-

[7] Edgeworth's warning as to a "(duly cautious) employment of infinitesimal notation" (*133*, *7*) refers to the discontinuous gaps made by the *minimum sensibile* in the changing rate of satisfaction, not to the question of comparing two infinitesimal quantities of different means.

I am not criticizing the diagrammatic use of curves, if it is done on the understanding that the units of quantity are so numerous as to make the progression take, practically, the form of a curve. My point has to do with the concept and the formula, not the representation.

[1] See Menger, *296*, 92–95, and Böhm-Bawerk, *38*, 144–145. We have found Menger's analysis of the qualitative aspects of these relations in respect of single wants the most

man numerals across the top from I to X list "*die verschiedenen Bedürfnisse der Menschen.*" The series of Arabic numerals descending down each column beneath these numbered wants denotes "*eine Scala der Bedeutung der verchiedenen Bedürfnissbefriedigungen*" for each. The Arabic series for Want I begins with 10 because that is the only one here shown containing a "*Bedürfnissbefriedigung*" "upon which our life depends." The next want, II, begins with 9, and so on down the list. Thus the other descending series across the columns, formed of the highest number in each, denotes the order of importance of the wants as a whole. It will become evident, as we examine it, that Menger's formulation was, and is, merely an impressionistic sketch of a scheme in which he tried to combine, without careful analysis, two concepts which he had inferred from his observations—that of an order of priority among wants and that of a decline of intensity during the process of satisfying a want. It will also become evident that, if we accept what he says of the magnitudes he is representing, they cannot rationally be represented by his scheme or by his numerical quantities; while, if we define the magnitudes differently, we can construe his scheme and his numerical quantities into something that we shall find usable. Moreover, it is not impossible that, when we do the latter, we shall have arrived at what Menger meant, however inconsistent that is with what he said.

What Menger said was that the successive Arabic numerals in each column represent the "significance" of each part satisfaction of that want.[2]

---

satisfactory one presented in the literature. In spite of its crudities and errors we are also going to find his treatment of many wants in quantitative terms the most suggestive and, when corrected, the most usable of all.

[2] We have adopted the term "significance" out of the miscellany of terms used in marginal utility theory. But we have given it a specific meaning that is not common to all forms of this theory. Therefore, when it is necessary to distinguish the different and particular meaning given in some form of the theory we shall use the special term of that form. Since Menger and Wicksteed both use the term "significance," we shall distinguish their special meaning by putting the word in quotation marks.

In attributing to Menger the notion of gradation in the successive parts of a single satisfaction, we must be cautious. In other words we cannot be sure just what parts or how much of the conglomerate assumption underlying the notion of declining significance (see pp. 437 ff.) he was using. His actual expression is "*die Befriedigung der einzelnen concreten Bedürfnisse*" (*296*, 94). Böhm-Bawerk uses "concrete" in the same sense. There can be no question that Böhm-Bawerk, who was by that time familiar with the work of Jevons and Walras, regarded his own "concrete" wants to be "degrees" of, or part satisfactions of, integral wants (see *38*, Book III, Chap. III). I have never been sure that this is also true of Menger. Judging from Menger's analytical statements he seems to be dealing with part satisfactions; judging from his examples he seems to be dealing in large part with different uses (assumption *b*) or with future uses (assumption *c*), of a single means (i.e., his kinds of wants are classified by the means and not at all by the wants). If so, his construction may have been adopted by his followers, and it may have been only then stated to be in terms of part satisfactions, as a result of the later influence of the other co-discoverers of marginal utility theory. If that is true, we need just as much to test the validity of the construction in this form, for it is this form which has been passed down as Menger's. But we should be careful not to attribute it to Menger.

Satisfaction of a want is a process. It is therefore a dynamic not a static magnitude. A part satisfaction is a phase of this process. If so, parts of this process must also be dynamic magnitudes. If "significance" is proportionate to the satisfaction accomplished, it is then to be measured in terms of the dynamic process. Since the whole process is the sum of its parts, the "significance" of the whole must equal the sum of the "significance" of each of its parts. Construed in this way, Menger's scheme does not represent our order of priority. Instead, it represents an order among the first part satisfactions only. To erect our own order of priority out of his, it becomes necessary to derive the "significance" of a complete satisfaction for each want. That is readily done. The "significance" of the complete satisfaction of any want becomes the sum of the figures in its column. However, that produces a decline of "significance" of complete satisfactions along the order of priority which is a very steep one, ranging from fifty-five units down to one unit.[3] That also introduces another oddity. Since there are 10 figures in the first column, 9 in the second, etc., the result is that the total satisfaction of the most important want is divided into ten part satisfactions, that of the next into nine, and so on down to the last, which consists of one part. Therefore this exposition yields the following table of equivalences within the successive orders of importance of part satisfactions:

Highest—first 10th of I
Second—second 10th of I = first 9th of II
Third—third 10th of I = second 9th of II = first 8th of III
Tenth—tenth 10th of I = ninth 9th of II = eighth 8th of III . . . = whole of X

Thus the rate of decline in "significance" of part satisfactions is presented as if it grew much less steep as we proceed down the scale in the order of wants.[4] Now I do not think either of these inferences was intended by

As to his order of priority our reading must depend on the way we construe his "concrete" wants. If these are different uses for the same means, then his order is based on the most "significant" wants for which each means may be used. On the other hand, if these are part satisfactions of single wants, then his order is based on the comparative "significance" of the initial part satisfaction of each want in turn, or on the whole satisfaction of each instance of future want in turn. On p. 97 (*ibid.*) it seems to be both. If, or in so far as, the first construction is the correct one, we could accept it, since it is identical to that extent with our own. But then his order of priority really consists of his series of arithmetical progressions and should descend in one direction only. If, or in so far as, it is the second, we cannot accept it. But since, as noted above, it has been construed to be the second, we may, without necessarily attributing it to Menger, interpret it in that manner.

It is particularly interesting to note that Menger was the only one among his contemporaries to develop the idea of the order of priority of wants.

[3] Thus the total "significance" of the satisfaction of the first want is 55; of the second, 45; of the third, 36; of the fourth, 28; of the fifth, 21; of the sixth, 15; of the seventh, 10; of the eighth, 6; of the ninth, 3; and of the tenth, 1.

[4] We have in Fig. 43, transcribed his presentation, so construed, into terms of our own. The complete satisfaction of each want in the series is shown by our vertical lines. The successively declining part satisfactions are the sections cut upon them by the broken

Menger. But it is necessary to see these points clearly in order to see the real difficulties in the way of this possible construction.

The first question is this: If these part satisfactions are divisions of whole satisfactions, what is the method used for dividing them? Means are not supposed to enter directly into this representation. Menger says he is examining part satisfactions of different wants only. But his part satisfaction ("concrete" or "different") must be divided in terms of some other dimension than "significance"; for successive part satisfactions are conceived as diminishing in "significance." This only has meaning if the parts are equal in some other respect (dimension).[5] What could that other respect

---

lines which are arranged in a reduced scale sufficient to show the successive diminution.

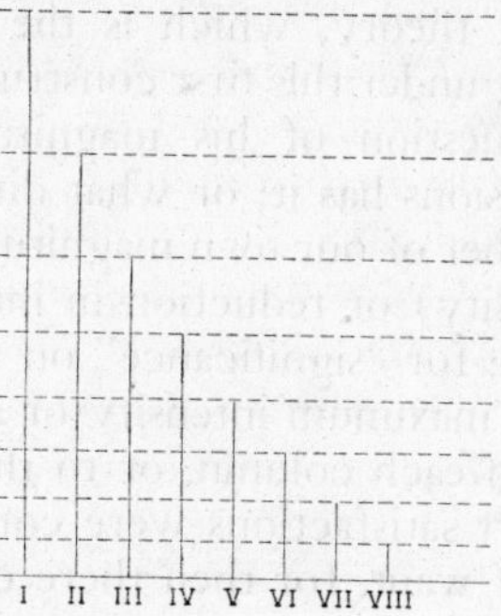

FIG. 43

If now, in Fig. 44, we divide the line of Want I into its 10 sections (on his scale) and set these sections beside each other at regular intervals (two-dimensional representation of one-dimensional magnitudes) we obtain a clearer view of the *rate* of declining "significance." But, when we also divide the sections of line of Want VI and spread

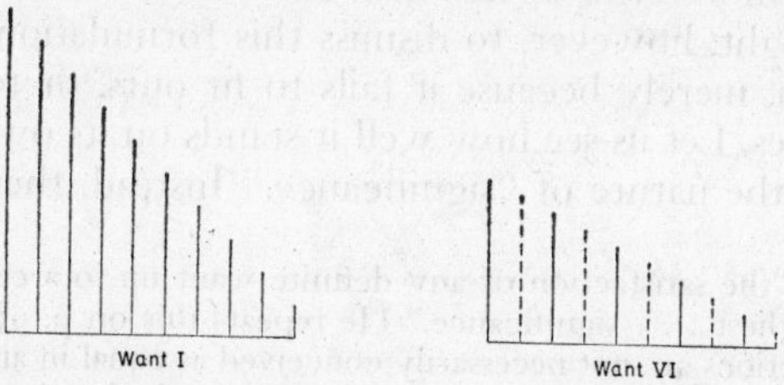

FIG. 44

them over the same, purely representational, horizontal distance we see clearly—particularly by introducing broken lines to indicate what 10 sections would look like—that the rate of declining "significance" is much less steep.

[5] We have recognized this in our illustration, in the text, of distance traversed compared with number of minutes (on pp. 469–470). In order to give meaning to the variation in distance traversed per minute it was necessary to assume that the minutes were of equal duration. Using Menger's method we could, instead of dividing a total "significance" of 10, say, into four subjectively unequal parts—4, 3, 2, and 1—divide it into four subjectively equal parts, or 2½ each, and thus prove conclusively that there is no declining "significance" as we proceed in a single satisfaction. His illustration has meaning only if he meant his parts to be equal in terms of some other dimension. But he

be? It might be time, since satisfying is a process; or it might be the dimension of means, since the quantity of means is presumably conceived to be measured in terms of uniform units; or it might be some still different dimension which will crop up later in our discussion.[6] It seems anomalous that Menger did not recognize this question, much less deal with it. Nevertheless, if he meant what he said, it is probable that he had in mind, perhaps unconsciously, the dimension of means. If so, his division into part satisfactions would correspond with the division of the full measure of means necessary for the complete satisfaction of each want into a number of equal parts or units; and it would be the "significance" of each of these successive equal parts that would be deemed to be less than that of its predecessor.

Proceeding upon that theory, which is the only one that gives the formulation any meaning under this first construction, we are immediately confronted with the question of his magnitude "significance." What measures it; what dimensions has it; or what dimension is it? First, let us attempt to relate it to either of our own magnitudes, intensity of want (including remaining intensity) or reduction in intensity of want. It cannot be the intensity of want; for "significance" on that ground would correspond, at each stage—as maximum intensity or as remaining intensity—to the sum of the figures in each column, or to the sum of these remaining after any number of part satisfactions were completed.[7] It cannot be the reduction in intensity of want, for then there could be no such order of priority among wants as he posits. In other words, as soon as part measures of means are considered, there would always be some portion of each means which would reduce intensity to the same extent as some portion of every other means, and there could be no discrimination between, or order among, them in terms of less than full measures.

We have no right, however, to dismiss this formulation, even upon the first construction, merely because it fails to fit ours, or to be convertible into our categories. Let us see how well it stands on its own feet. We have mere hints as to the nature of "significance." Instead, then, of attempting

---

says (*296*, 92) that "the satisfaction of any definite want up to a certain point has for us the relatively highest . . . significance." He repeats this on p. 93. And this suggests that the part satisfactions are not necessarily conceived as equal in any other dimension.

[6] Menger does not mention the first; and he expressly denies the second, since "significance" arises first as an attribute of part satisfactions only and is merely reflected on the means (*296*, 107, No. 1 and elsewhere). Nevertheless, that is probably what he had in mind (see *ibid.*, 107, No. 3) and may constitute the basis of his confusion of ideas.

[7] That is, it would do so as we are construing his example and provided we use remaining intensity to measure the remaining reduction of intensity, as we did in the text. Of course, if the "significance" of his first part satisfactions is taken to equal the maximum intensity of the want, and that of each succeeding part (no longer necessarily equal) to be the intensity when that segment of the want becomes prepotent, we have a rough sketch of our own later analysis. But then there is no warrant whatever for treating this as the basis of an exchange value system. This constitutes merely an order of preferences among complete satisfactions or segments of the same, without direct relation either to the process of satisfaction or the means used therein.

to understand it, we will accept it as it is presented and will confine ourselves to working out the data in the illustration. If we follow the figures in the illustration [8] and take the columns of Arabic numerals to represent the "significance" of successive equal portions of a full measure of means for each, we find that the first quarter of means for Want VII, for instance, has the same "significance" as the seventh 10th of means for Want I. Presumably, then, both these part measures will have equal positions in the order of preference among part satisfactions. If, now, we eliminate the difference in the number of parts into which each full measure of means is separated, by dividing that for Want VII also into ten parts—with the same aggregate "significance" for the full measure as before—we find that the quantities of "significance" of the first five of these parts for Want VII are $1\frac{9}{11}$, $1\frac{7}{11}$, $1\frac{5}{11}$, $1\frac{3}{11}$, and $1\frac{1}{11}$, respectively. On that basis no part satisfaction of Want VII will be preferred until after the ninth part satisfaction of Want I, and then Want VII will be half satisfied (all five tenths will be chosen) before the final tenth of Want I.[9] Thus we find that, on this basis, the order of preference depends entirely upon the number of equal parts into which each full measure of means is divided. And this makes the basis for choice perfectly arbitrary. One can get any results one chooses by this method. Nor are we saved by converting these parts into the respective objective units of each means, for we have already found that objective units are themselves also entirely arbitrary.

Now the reader inured to marginal utility analysis may regard this conclusion as due to a misinterpretation. While still adhering to our first construction, based on what Menger says he means, that "significance" is related to a part of the process of satisfying a want, he may impute to Menger a formulation in terms of "marginal significance" instead, as we have construed him, of "total significance." Menger himself did not so state his formulation. Nevertheless, we may try it out on that basis as well. If these arithmetical progressions for each want are conceived to be points on continuous curves, then the magnitude they represent is either rate of "significance" at any point—that is, the ratio between "total significance" and the corresponding quantity of means—or it is the "total significance" of a very small or infinitesimal quantity, as Jevons would say. If the magnitude is the rate of "significance," at any point, we have seen that it is immeasurable by itself—so that we are thrown back upon the "total significance" of the unit or other portion with which we have just been dealing; and if it is the "significance" of a very small or an infinitesimal quantity at that point, it would have to be very small or infinitesimal itself.

[8] Menger, *296*, 93.

[9] The reader may feel that I am practicing a little deception here and that what the chooser will do in this case is the same as before, namely that he will take the first 2½ tenths (¼) of VII, since these sum up to a significance of 4. But then why should he not elect all of VII along with the first tenth of I, since all of VII also sums up to a significance of 10?

The former we have found to be immeasurable and the latter does not fit the formulation.[10]

This analysis seems to have demonstrated that Menger's scheme cannot be construed in terms of process at all—that the concept of part satisfactions which we have imputed to him is here inapplicable—that, in fact, he was not dealing with the magnitudes of successive partial *Befriedigungen* through phases of total satisfaction, as he said he was, but with successive intensities of a *Bedürfniss* at different stages in the process of its total satisfaction. If so, he was really developing a scheme in terms of what we have called remaining intensity of want, on the basis, of course, of the assumption of declining intensity. But, if so, he was using this magnitude in its static aspect, rather than as a measure of the remaining reduction of intensity to be accomplished—its dynamic aspect. In the latter aspect, as we saw in the text (p. 478) it gives us results no different than those reached through using reduction of intensity as the criterion. But we promised ourselves (on p. 493) that we would explore another possibility with regard to it. That exploration was reserved to this point in order to give credit where credit is due. For recognition of this possibility—the use of remaining intensity as a static magnitude—was, in my case, entirely due to studying Menger.

Let us, first, construe Menger's scheme in these terms. We now find that his order of priority conforms precisely to ours. The position in this order is given by the maximum (initial) intensity of the want denoted by the first Arabic numeral in its series. But, on account of his assumption of declining intensity, we should show his order of priority in a different way from that used for our own. His order can best be represented by superimposing all wants upon each other according to the same scale. The prior want merely begins at a higher initial intensity and therefore at an earlier point on the scale. Thereafter, it continues through the several stages which represent the initial intensity of each of the other wants in turn. In fact, since we can assume continuous declines of intensity we can show the scheme as in Fig. 45. This relieves us of all the aforementioned difficulties with regard to the different number of part satisfactions—now number of stages—for the several wants, as well as of any imputed differences between the steepness of the several curves. It also relieves us of the difficulty with regard to the divisions between the several phases. The phases are now delimited by the several stages at which there comes to be equality between the remaining intensities of two or more wants. The length of this phase is fortuitous; it is not measured at all; it has, therefore, as Menger said (see note 6, above), nothing to do with quantities of means.

This gives us a consistent and self-contained order of preference among

[10] If we ignore what he says, and construe his "significance" to be the rate of "significance," we would have a formulation similar to those we discuss hereafter. We can kill two birds with one stone by postponing the more detailed analysis of that question, already raised in the text.

the several part satisfactions of the whole series of wants. Want I is dominant—has the greatest "significance"—at the start; it remains dominant through a phase of the process of satisfaction which is terminated when its remaining intensity has declined to the level of the initial intensity of Want II—here 9. At that point the two wants are of equal intensity—are of equal "significance." Since we can assume that we are dealing here with future provision—*Vorsorge*—the two wants are then jointly dominant through the next phase, which is terminated when the remaining intensity of both has declined to the level of the initial intensity of Want III—here 8. And so on, as far as capacity reaches. On this basis, we can develop a series or order of part satisfactions which only requires the ability to compare the "significance"—that is, the remaining intensity—of wants at various stages in terms of more or less or of approximate equality. The more "significant" want, at the moment, always gets the preference; equally "significant" wants, being indifferent, get joint preference, for the time being, over all wants that are then less "significant." Such preferences last through phases the limits of which are defined in terms of critical points in the "significance"—intensity—of the several wants with relation to each other only. But the scope of the phases themselves is not defined in terms of any dimension related to the process of satisfaction unless it be the reduction of intensity accomplished between two critical points. That is, we could say that the phase during which one want was more "significant" than the next was measured by that part of the process of satisfying during which the remaining intensity of the want was declining from an initial point to the level of the next. This, however, measures the phase in terms of reduction of intensity. That is one of the criteria that we have already adopted—subject to modification. Since its adoption here would necessarily involve dismissing the static magnitude as a factor—"significance" cannot be determined by both of two criteria—we must find some other way of relating remaining intensity to the process if we are to explore further the possibilities of this particular criterion. Suffice it to say, then, at this point, that this construction of Menger's scheme gives us, in itself, no basis for relating his "significance," directly and in quantitative terms, to the process of satisfaction and its dynamic magnitudes. His "significance," so construed, is therefore not our significance; it is not something conferred on means as the result of a correspondence in a joint process; it is our remaining intensity, treated as a static magnitude without relation to any other magnitude. Nevertheless, it is well worth while to carry it forward into the latter half of Chapter 8, and see what we can make of it as a criterion for the subjective valuation of means which is different from our other criteria.

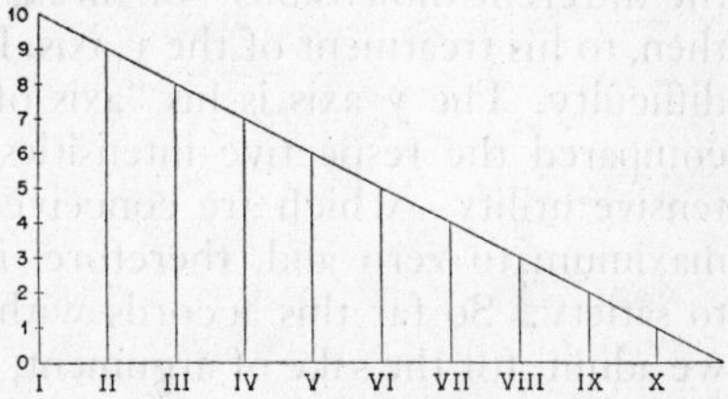

FIG. 45

C. WALRAS'S SCHEME

When we come to deal with Walras's formulation it would appear, at first sight, that his treatment of the *x* axis, in his mathematical representation, raises no difficulty for us.[1] Upon it is measured "extensive utility," which he defines as "the quantity demanded at the price of zero" (*420*, 73), and which he assumes to be a finite quantity (*ibid.*, 59). This might be taken to be the same magnitude that we have called a full measure, or, more exactly, "the number of units of a means which is required for the complete satisfaction of a want." [2] At any rate, the definition ought to justify us in assuming that this magnitude has the dimension—or at least the different dimensions—of means only. Let us pass on, for the present, then, to his treatment of the *y* axis. It is that which raises the more obvious difficulty. The *y* axis is his "axis of rarity" (*ibid.*, 76) [3] upon which are compared the respective intensities of want (*besoin*)—and thus the intensive utility—which are conceived as declining along the curve from a maximum to zero and, therefore, if this represents a single satisfaction, to satiety.[4] So far this accords with our presentation of the *y* axis, when we admit, for the sake of argument, the gradual decline of intensity during a single satisfaction. But, then, without explanation or discussion, Walras introduces the notion of "effective utility (others' "total") which is "the sum total of wants satisfied, in extension and in intensity, by a quantity of *marchandise* consumed." [5] And this proves to be represented by the area, or "surface," measured by the part quantity of means consumed multiplied by the average intensity during the consumption of that particular part quantity.

[1] Actually Walras uses the *x* axis for intensity and the *y* axis for extensity. We will ask the reader to allow us to reverse this, in dealing with his treatment, in order that our designations may conform to the general practice and continue to have the same meaning thoughout our discussion.

[2] If Walras intended by it the desired "stock," then it might include other uses and provision for future satisfactions as well. Thus, again, we cannot be sure just how much of the conglomerate assumption, described on pp. 437 ff., was in his mind. However, that makes no difference in our analysis. We have a right to transpose his limit to that of a single satisfaction for, if it did not work there, it would not work at all.

[3] Rarity was, of course, an unfortunate nickname ("pour plus de brièveté," *420*, 466) for the intensity of the last want satisfied (*ibid.*, 100). Rarity, or scarcity, being a relative matter, might have been represented as the quantity desired, at a price of zero, divided by the quantity available. His rarity is, in reality, equivalent to our remaining intensity of a want when the quantity available has been consumed. That the reduction of intensity should have stopped at that point may be the result of scarcity; but the remaining intensity is certainly not the scarcity itself. As well call unsatisfied hunger rarity.

[4] "L'intensité du dernier besoin satisfait est une fonction décroissante de la quantité de marchandise consommée"; (quoted from *420*, 466, but expressing the idea as used from *ibid.*, 73 on). As to satiety see *ibid.*, 75.

[5] Walras, *420*, 76. And this is proportionate in the same way. "The mean of the intensities of the last wants satisfied and the first wants not satisfied" is the *rareté* in the case of discontinuous curves (*ibid.*, 137). "Virtual utility" is, on the same basis, the whole content of the curve—the whole area (*ibid.*, 75).

It is evident from this that Walras did not conceive movement *along* the *x* axis (consumption of means) to be merely the representation of a correlation with a corresponding movement *down* the *y* axis (reduction of intensity), as we have represented it in the text. For, if he had so conceived it, the "effective utility" of any portion of the total means would be shown by the drop on the *y* axis (reduction of intensity) corresponding to this section of the *x* axis, and the area would have no meaning.[6] In Fig. 5 (p. 470), for example, we saw that the magnitude corresponding to the "effective utility" of unit *d* is the reduction of intensity d_1, and that of *e* is e_1. Or, upon a curve, if we estimate means according to their capacity to reduce the intensity of our wants, the degree of this capacity is represented by the "steepness" of the curve [7] between two points and not at all by the distance from the base at either point, or at any point between them. The latter shows only the remaining intensity of want at such point. According to our analysis in the text, when we treat remaining intensity as the measure of the extent of the process still to be completed, to suppose that this reflects itself on the next unit of means would be to suppose that each successive unit completely satisfies the want—that each, in turn, reduces the intensity to zero. It would be to apply to each unit the measure of effectiveness which belongs only to the whole number of units remaining necessary to accomplish satiation. It would be to use as one of the measures of satisfaction accomplished what is actually the measure of remaining dissatisfaction. And this would be absurd.

It is equally evident that Walras did not conceive the *y* axis to represent anything of the order of that which is represented in the altitude of our derived "curves of significance." These successive altitudes, it will be recalled, show the reduction of intensity of want accomplished by each unit of means in turn. Each might be supposed, then, to measure the significance of successive units of means if reduction of intensity, or anything analogous, were the criterion for significance. But, in those diagrams, the total significance of all the units of means is the aggregate of the significance of each. That is not true of Walras's scheme, since, with him, this aggregate is represented by the area, not by the sum of (with him) an infinite number of altitudes. And we have clearly demonstrated that, in our diagrams, the area can have no meaning. Finally, it is equally clear that Walras could not have intended, by his *y* axis, the magnitude we developed under our second construction of Menger's scheme. For that, as well, being a static magnitude, does not permit the imputation of meaning to the area.

On the other hand, as we have seen in the text, if the area in the diagram is given any meaning, it may be on either of two grounds. It may be because it represents a one-dimensional magnitude of the order of intensity of want. In that case the *y* axis represents, not significance, but rate of

[6] See text, pp. 467 and 470.

[7] Thus a change between successive units in this capacity per unit is shown by a change in the "steepness" (i.e., by concavity or convexity of the curve) and not at all by the respective altitudes as we move down it (or up it).

significance. Or it may be because the area represents a magnitude like a want as having two dimensions. If so, the *y* axis must represent one of these dimensions and, presumably, the *x* axis then represents the other. We would have to judge, from this, that one or both of Walras's axes did not represent what he said they did.

The most probable conclusion from this brief examination is that Walras did not clearly define to himself what his two axes and his areas represented. He called the *y* axis the "intensity of want" (*besoin*). But he also called it the "intensive utility" of the means. However, he may have thought of it as the rate of utility—that is, as a derived magnitude whose dimensions are any block of the area (representing "effective utility" or the true magnitude of the want) divided by the corresponding section of the base.[8] If so, in spite of the fact that his terminology is deceptively similar to ours, he really belongs in the group with Jevons and his successors, and we will defer consideration of that possible construction until we deal with them. If, on the other hand, he conceived the area to represent a two-dimensional magnitude "effective" and "virtual utility" whose dimensions are, on the *y* axis, "intensive utility" and, on the *x* axis, "extensive utility," we must dispute the validity of his treatment of the *x* axis; for, then, as we shall see, his characterization of that as also representing the magnitude of means, no longer remains possible. On this alternative construction we would be led to the suspicion that Walras assumed the process of satisfying wants to have two dimensions, but that, since he erroneously identified the second dimension with the entirely independent dimension of means, it did not occur to him that any further examination of this assumption was necessary. Thus he never confronted the difficulty of discovering and defining such a dimension as if it were a dimension of wants, and so failed to recognize that it probably does not exist.[9] On this

[8] His mathematics would fit that construction. In support of this view we have his slightly disingenuous introduction of a scale of measurement on the *y* axis—"a standard of measurement of the intensity of wants or of the intensive utility, common not only to similar units of the same kind of wealth but to different units of diverse kinds of wealth" (*420*, 74). This appears to be the *numéraire* (*ibid.*, 119) of which the "unit is called a standard of value." Thus he is perhaps thinking all along in terms of price on the *y* axis and quantity on the *x* axis—the old familiar viewpoint. And price, in such treatment, is a derived magnitude.

It should also be said that Walras's analysis is not as pure and subjective as his terminology would lead one to suppose. Though he distinguishes between the subjective and the objective aspects and measurements, he does not carry through the analysis of the former *by itself*. Instead, he seems to assume that the two necessarily correspond, that the former is causative and that it can be measured by its objective effects. His analysis is, therefore, not *pure*. Mixed in with the intensity of wants, he admits the influences of price as a sacrifice and of conceptually fixed limitation of quantity. These are extraneous factors which it is not proper to introduce, if value theory is to hinge on subjective valuation; for, to admit them, may be to admit that they are the determinants of value. Price is the immediate form in which cost presents itself, and limited quantities may not be data but only the secondary results of another factor. However, since we are not discussing value at this point, we will defer consideration of the effect of this impropriety.

[9] If so, he had some such vague notion as Menger's *Umfang*. Or, perhaps, he was merely

construction, as well, we can class Walras with Jevons, for Jevons was equally equivocal in this respect. His x axis is also, at times, a second dimension of wants, as we shall see.[10]

D. JEVONS'S SCHEME

1. CONSTRUED IN OUR TERMS OR IN THOSE OF HEDONISM

It is in the work of Jevons and his followers that we find most clearly exposed the underlying fallacies in the basis upon which the earlier forms of marginal utility theory have rested. Jevons starts with ostensibly different postulates from those of Menger and Walras. He deals, not with wants and their intensities, but with pleasure as an accessory of the process of satisfying wants.[1] At the beginning of his formulation[2] pleasure has two dimensions, intensity and duration.[3] If, then, time is one dimension, what is the nature of this intensity of pleasure? It is clear that it cannot be analogous in its behavior to what we have called the intensity of wants (initial or remaining). For then it would necessarily have to show a rate of decline adjusted to offset any extension beyond some minimum in the time taken in the process; otherwise, we should have the impossible result that the longer we take to satisfy a want the greater the amount of pleasure derived. In Fig. 46, we show a single want of a certain intensity represented

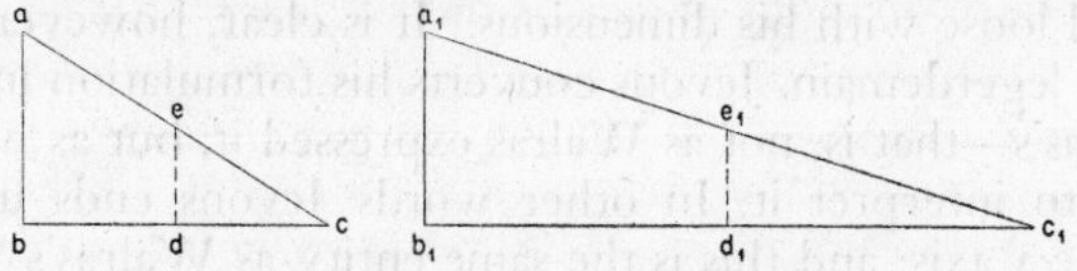

FIG. 46

in one figure as ab and, in the other, as a_1b_1. This want is satisfied over a time period bc, in the first, and over one b_1c_1, which is twice as long, in the second. If the intensity of pleasure were supposed to decline at a con-

restating the usual economic formula, as suggested in note 8, above. This formula we have attributed as the general basis for much of marginal utility theory (see pp. 437 ff.).

[10] At least we may recognize, at this point, that the fundamental trouble with Walras's analysis appears to be that each of his representational dimensions may have meant to him two or more different dimensions of different magnitudes which he assumed, without proof, to be commensurable or at least capable of being related through a correspondence.

[1] I am inclined to think that to this fact is due his limitation of his treatment to single satisfactions in a way not general among his contemporaries. Thus we seem to be able to assume that Jevons confined himself to assumption (a) (see pp. 437 ff.).

[2] We may disregard his treatment (*224*, 32–33) of pleasure and pain as positive and negative quantities (states, not changes of states). Thus he arrives at the notion that from *gross* pleasure must be deducted *gross* pain (i.e., real cost) to measure *net* pleasure. This comes perilously close to making net pleasure equal to what has come to be called the "consumer's surplus." As such it would be wholly unsuited to his purpose. Whether ingenuously or not, he drops this notion in his further analysis and treats pleasure as the *process* of having it, or that of avoiding or getting rid of pain. We discuss these hedonistic theories below.

[3] Jevons, *224*, 29.

stant rate during a satisfaction which always reached zero at the end, regardless of the duration of the process, then the amount of pleasure $b_1c_1 \times d_1e_1$ would be double that of $bc \times de$.[4] Which is absurd.[5] It is also clear that such a time dimension does not permit the supposition that Jevons's pleasure corresponds to, or results from, the reduction of intensity of want, for then its quantity would bear some fixed relation to the amount of such reduction and would again be the same regardless of the time elapsed.[6] Again, diminishing reduction of intensity would have to offset increasing duration beyond some minimum. In either case, it would have to be supposed that the intensity of pleasure varied inversely with time so that, in spite of the fact that the quantity of pleasure varied directly with time, its actual magnitude, in any instance, would depend solely on average intensity.

As a matter of fact, however, we need not trouble ourselves about the time dimension of pleasure, for it disappears at an early stage of Jevons's formulation. One might say it is conjured away by a piece of sleight of hand, and we are left with the dimension of commodity occupying its place.[7] When his notion of pleasure is applied to its source, the consumption of commodity, he relates it to the rate of supply of commodity per unit of time instead of to the quantity of commodity. Thus, having time in both elements of the ratio, he is able to cancel it out. In doing this, he plays fast and loose with his dimensions.[8] It is clear, however, that by this mathematical legerdemain, Jevons converts his formulation into a counterpart of Walras's—that is, not as Walras expressed it, but as we have found it necessary to interpret it. In other words Jevons ends up with commodity on the *x* axis; and this is the same entity as Walras's "extensity" as defined; he ends up without time as a factor; he ends up with quantity of pleasure or "total utility," corresponding to Walras's "effective utility,"

[4] The "shape" of the decline makes, of course, no real difference. Similar conclusions would hold if the curves were concave or convex.

[5] The discrimination of "brief" from "enduring" satisfaction is largely moral and ascetic. As a matter of fact the satisfactions of the most essential wants are among the briefest.

[6] In this case, moreover, while intensity of pleasure might decline—which is all he has predicated—pleasure per unit of means might remain the same throughout (as we have shown previously), if the curve of decline were a straight line; and it might increase throughout, if the curve of decline were convex. The consumption of a unit of means would merely take a longer time in one case than in another.

[7] See Jevons, *224, 65–69.*

[8] On page 65 (*224*), "intensity of feeling is only another name for degree of utility" (his U). Thus U is one of the two dimensions of pleasure, and the quantity of pleasure would be UT. Immediately above that statement U is the "instantaneous state produced by an . . . infinitesimal quantity of commodity." If the first statement is correct, the second cannot be. For the second is his way of expressing a rate. That rate, in terms of the first, would be UTC^{-1}. Again, on page 68 (*ibid.*), MU will "be greater as the time of expenditure is greater . . . because the quantity U will under those circumstances be greater." Then, here, U contains the dimension T and is equivalent to UT, or the quantity of pleasure. If, in a few pages, U means itself, UTC^{-1} and UT, it is possible to do almost anything with it.

which both represent two-dimensionally and show by area; and with intensity of pleasure or "degree of utility," corresponding to Walras's "intensive utility," which both treat in a way that permits its construction either as one of the two dimensions—commodity or "extensity" being regarded as the other—of the quantity of pleasure ("effective utility") or as the rate at which pleasure ("utility") accrues.

Since both Jevons and Walras arrived, independently of each other, at formulations that we find it necessary to reduce to the same terms, it is doubly important that we determine, if possible, what these magnitudes are, and particularly what is the magnitude or dimension measured on the *y* axis. As to this matter we find no definite clue in Walras. But we may naturally suspect that his is related to Jevons's magnitude or dimension.

In the first place, it is clear that neither the magnitude, quantity of pleasure, nor its dimension or rate, intensity of pleasure, fits, any better after removing the time factor than before, the pattern of either of our entities, intensity of want (including remaining intensity) or reduction of intensity of want.

a. Quantity of pleasure does not conform to the pattern we have found for remaining intensity of want; for, if it did, pleasure-loving people would wish it to continue as long as possible and would take pains to avoid even beginning to satisfy a want.

b. Intensity of pleasure does not conform to the pattern of remaining intensity of want, for, if it did, pleasure-loving people would choose those means which reduced intensity of want at the lowest rate (i.e., with the greatest "extensity") since in this way they could experience the greatest quantity of pleasure.

c. Quantity of pleasure might conform to the pattern of reduction in intensity of want, but only if we eliminate Jevons's second dimension, intensity of pleasure.[9]

d. Intensity of pleasure does not conform to the pattern of reduction in intensity of want, for that would leave no room for the quantity of pleasure.

Next we may consider whether this magnitude, pleasure, corresponds to that of any of the hedonistic theories which undertake to relate this conscious experience to physiological processes. If we were to follow the form of psychological hedonism mentioned in a previous chapter, we might conceive pain to be a high intensity of affective tone—or of excitation—contributed to a response by the existence of a want of high intensity, and, correspondingly, pleasure to derive from a low intensity of the same. Then the organism would be conceived to carry through the painful response "in order to" get rid of the pain, though what it actually does is to get rid of the want which is creating it. On the other hand, the organism would be conceived to enjoy pleasure—a low intensity of tone. If, therefore, it gets rid of the want which causes the pleasure, it does so,

[9] This, in a modified form, will be the basis for our third hypothesis as to the criterion for estimating means. But we cannot derive it from Jevons.

not because it wishes a discontinuance of the pleasure, but because by seeking the pleasure derived from the response, it removes, at the same time, the want which is its cause. So, in both cases, whether driven or led, it does get rid of the want. In that conception intensity of want is the determinant of pain or pleasure; arranged along the scale of intensity, pleasure is the bass and pain is the treble; and the two shade into each other as, from the least intense pleasure, increasing intensity converts the most intense pleasure into a low intensity of pain. Now, while this theory does not fit badly with our analysis, it does not conform at all to Jevons's. For Jevons construes pleasure to be the entity against which means are measured. But, in this theory, pleasure can only be conceived as incidental. If it were conceived to be the driving force that Jevons thinks it is, then, as before, that means would be selected which would prolong the pleasure to the greatest extent (i.e., reduce the intensity of the want at the lowest rate).

FIG. 47

If, on the other hand, we follow another form of hedonistic theory, we conceive pleasure to be, not a state, but the process or an accompaniment of the process of reducing, in the course of the response, the intensity of tone or of excitation (of which a high degree is pain and a low degree is merely unpleasant), then we are again, of course, brought directly back to our analysis of means in terms of their capacity to reduce intensity and thus, incidentally, yield pleasure. That, too, will not fit Jevons's formulation, for, again, there is room there for one dimension only.[10]

Finally, if we modify the foregoing by regarding pleasure as being a cumulative result of the process of reducing pain or unpleasantness, so that pleasure can be experienced even while pain or unpleasantness remains, then we might present the relations as in Fig. 47.[11] There *ac* shows the

[10] That is, that conforms to (c), above.

[11] If pleasure is cumulative, it can only be so through memory (i.e., as the recognition in consciousness of a difference between this and a previous state). Thus it would be an effect, as experienced, and then linger on as an after-effect as well. It would endure after the process is finished, so that we would be driven by an urge both to get rid of pain and by an anticipation of the pleasure to be derived from having got rid of the pain. Fig. 48 shows this diagrammatically. Here *ab* represents the magnitude of the current experience of pain while *cd* represents that of pleasure. At d_1, d_2, and d_3, as the current pain is successively diminished, current pleasure, equal to the broken lines, is felt. As this proceeds and the current pleasure, *cd*, finally eliminates the current pain, the successive areas bc_1d_1, bc_2d_2, bc_3d_3, and bcd represent the accumulated pleasure—its after-effect. But, be it noted that this assumes that pain has no after-effect (is not cumulative), or that, if it has, the after-effect of pain is only felt until pleasure begins to be currently experienced.

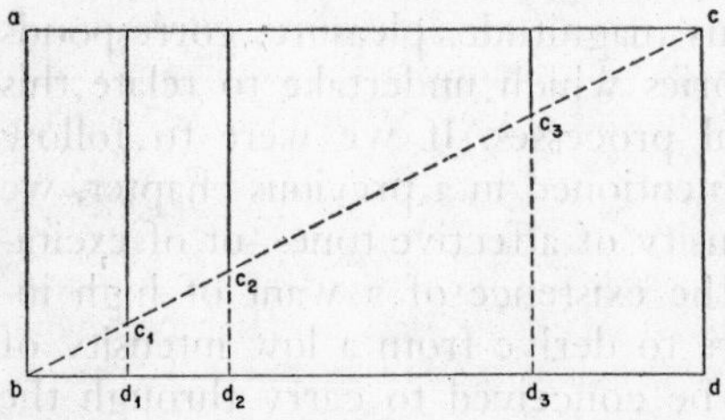

FIG. 48

Because we have treated intensity of want as the mechanism which impels the organ-

initial magnitude of pain. As this is reduced from the pole *a*, pleasure is experienced with cumulative intensity. Therefore, at *b*, *ab* = pleasure, and *bc* = remaining pain. The "net pleasure" (see Jevons) is *ab* — *bc*. But here again, the magnitude of pleasure could only be proportionate to the amount of reduction of pain (or intensity of want) which had been accomplished; and that would be true even before the appearance of "net pleasure." So even here we are forced back on the reduction of intensity of the want. Again there is room for but one dimension.

It is possible that we might be helped in getting at the nature of this entity by considering that one which has occupied the same place as Jevons's pleasure in other formulations of marginal utility analysis. Fisher and others use the term, and concept, desire. We may suspect that Walras actually had that in mind when he adopted the term "intensity of want." Now desire can be conceived in two ways. It may be (1) desire *en l'air*, an experience independent of the satisfying of a want.[12] But desire seems not to be a state one wishes to continue to enjoy, like pleasure. Instead, it seems more like one which one wishes to get rid of. In fact, this type of desire is so perilously near our concept of intensity of want that, it seems, we must identify it as the reverberation in consciousness of that entity. Therefore, it is unrelated to Jevons's concept, and must, we think, be treated as conforming to one of our two developments of the intensity of want—the dynamic one, reduction of intensity, or the static one, remaining intensity. On the other hand, desire may be conceived as (2) desire projected. If so, in so far as it is related to the process of satisfying wants, it must be conceived, in its primary projection, to be either (2a) desire for satisfaction (i.e., to get rid of the want) or (2b) desire for pleasure in the course of the process of satisfying. In either case, the desire may be thought of as projected secondarily upon the means which it is supposed will (3a) get rid of the want or (3b) yield the pleasure. Now the quantity of satisfaction is measured, as we have seen, by the reduction in the intensity of the want or some accompaniment of that process. If so, then

ism to satisfy its wants, we have found it unnecessary to confront the difficulties of treating either the "sense of satisfaction" of want or pleasure derived in the process, in their psychological aspects. Satisfaction, or amount of pleasant after-effect, would have to be described psychologically as a sense of contrast between the state at the moment and the memory of another state in the recent past (i.e., before and after using). On the other hand, satisfying, or rate of pleasure, would have to be described, not as a state, but as the process of moving from state to state—as the rate at which this change was occurring (i.e., during using). In order that these could be subjectively comparable magnitudes, it would be necessary to suppose that it is possible to remember and to anticipate, not only the difference between two states, but the difference between two rates of change of state.

[12] This seems to be the kind of desire postulated by Wundt (*Lectures on Human and Animal Psychology*, tr. J. E. Creighton and E. B. Titchener, New York, 1907, p. 229). Desire may be a "state of mind preliminary to a voluntary action" or it may be "a permanent conscious process which does not give rise to any such action." If the latter is associated with the idea that the desire cannot be realized now or later, it is what he calls a "wish."

desire (2a) for a complete satisfaction, or for any part of one, is measured by the complete, or any partial, reduction of intensity. Or, projecting this desire upon the means, as in (3a), we may say that our "curve of significance," in the text, would represent the magnitude of desire of this kind for any unit of means. Thus the ordinate on the want curve at any point would not represent the desire for the next unit of means. To suppose that it did so, as we noted in discussing Walras, would be to assign to the next unit of means the desire that is actually directed toward the whole quantity of means remaining necessary to satiety. Even a dumb animal would not so desire regardless of quantity. He would not desire the next unit with an intensity twice as great as he did the whole quantity remaining necessary for satiation.[13] Only if desire is a two-dimensional magnitude and is represented by the area, so that the *y* axis constitutes one of its dimensions, or if it is a derived magnitude, or rate, and is represented on the *y* axis, so that the area constitutes one of its dimensions, and only if, in either case, the other dimension is, or corresponds to, the quantity of means, can that difficulty be overcome. But then the entity becomes of the order of Jevons's pleasure, or Walras's effective utility, and we can best examine it with them. Finally, if desire is either of the order of (2b) or (3b), it is also measured by the pleasure upon which it is projected or that which will be derived from the means upon which it will be projected. In this view desire is only differentiated from pleasure, or for that matter from satisfaction, in that it is anticipatory and derived from past experiences rather than, as they are, the experiences themselves. We conclude that alternative concepts either become identical with our own and therefore foreign to Jevons's or that they are approximately identical with Jevons's, shed no additional light upon his and can only be included in the general examination of these to which we now proceed.

2. CONSTRUED IN JEVONS'S TERMS

Since none of our efforts to relate Jevons's concepts to entities other than those used in marginal utility theory have been successful, we can only accept his "pleasure" as an entity which stands on its own feet independent of any of the phenomena we have hitherto examined, and the knowledge of which he acquired by "direct experience," as the introspective psychologists say; and we can only agree with him that "one of the first and most difficult steps in a science is to conceive clearly the nature of the magnitudes about which we are arguing." [14] From his description of pleasure we should assume that it is something that is *derived from* the consumption of commodity.[15] Since the consumption of commodity is a process

[13] Which would be the case, for instance, as between the first unit and the average of all units if the latter were represented by the ordinate half way along a straight line curve declining to zero.

[14] Jevons, *224*, 62–63.

[15] Utility (total utility; *224*, 45) is an "addition to a person's happiness"; it is the "aggregate of the favorable balance of feeling produced—the sum of the pleasure created and the pain prevented." Total utility (MU) is (*ibid.*, 66 and 69) an amount of "abso-

and therefore a dynamic magnitude, so too the experiencing of pleasure must be a process, and therefore a dynamic magnitude. The two being related via a correspondence and the second being delimited by the first —which fixes the scope of the correspondence—the quantity of pleasure experienced, as a magnitude, can in this relation be regarded as a dependent variable, or function, of the independent variable, quantity of commodity consumed. If, then, we were to construct our own analysis of these two magnitudes, pleasure and commodity, and their relationship—independent of Jevons's—we should follow the usual method of the theory of dimensions. We would assume that the experience of pleasure, being a dynamic process, is analogous as a magnitude to motion. Therefore, let us remind ourselves of the manner in which the theory of dimensions deals with motion.

Since motion is the traversing of distance, the quantity of motion is expressed in terms of distance traversed. It is a one-dimensional magnitude whose dimension is the fundamental magnitude L (length). If now we find that the magnitude motion, or distance traversed, is a dependent variable or function of time—that is, that the distance traversed becomes greater as the time becomes greater—we must introduce another fundamental magnitude, T (time). The relation between these two is a rate, or ratio, or proportion, and is stated as so much L per T. Then we come to conceive of this relation, or rate, as if it were itself a magnitude—velocity, or rate of motion. However, this is a derived magnitude—that is, no more than a rate. As such it has two dimensions, the two dimensions—each fundamental and different from the other—of the magnitudes of which it constitutes a relation (correspondence). Now these dimensions enter into the measurement of the magnitude, velocity, in opposite ways. The larger the unit of L taken, the greater the velocity at any given numerical value; but the larger the unit of T taken, the less the velocity at any given numerical value. This is expressed by stating the dimensions of velocity to be LT^{-1}.[16]

---

lute pleasurable effect." On p. 54 (*ibid.*) commodities are held to "afford pleasure" or "enjoyment" and therefore to be "esteemed" or "desired." Intensity of feeling [i.e., of pleasure] . . . is only another name for degree of utility [U]" (*ibid.*, 65).

[16] In other mathematical terms (calculus) it is stated as $\frac{x}{y}$ when $x =$ some value of L and y some value of T. But, as we have noted in the text in connection with dimensional formulae, the fact that this ratio is stated in the same form in which an arithmetical division is stated is apt to lead to misunderstandings. As magnitudes, x and y, in this case, have numerical values in terms of different and incommensurable units of measurement. We can divide the numerical value of x by the numerical value of y, but we cannot divide the unit of x by the unit of y. If I say that there is one rider per horse, the ratio is 1:1, or $\frac{1x}{1y}$, where x and y are taken as the magnitudes of the two units. But that does not mean that I am dividing one rider by one horse; for horses do not divide riders—at least not more than half way up (though a hard trot sometimes makes one think it is going to be complete). Therefore a ratio is, in truth, not a magnitude in the usual sense at all. It is instead purely a numerical value showing a relation between the commensurable variations of each of two or more perhaps incommensurable magnitudes.

It is then well to remember our rule 11b of the theory of dimensions, as given in the

Now let us suppose this relation (velocity) between distance traversed and time to be changing. The numerical value lt^{-1} is different from that of l_1t^{-1}. That can also be expressed as a rate, a rate of change in velocity; and, in turn, can be treated as itself a magnitude (derived)—positive or negative acceleration. If we choose to measure this magnitude as a rate of change per unit of time,[17] then time enters again as a dimension, and the statement of the dimensions of acceleration becomes LT^{-2}. In Fig. 49, we show a diagram of these magnitudes and their relations. The rectangle M represents a certain quantity of motion (distance traversed). It is represented two-dimensionally, but it has only one dimension; the product of the altitude into the base equals the numerical value of its L. This two-dimensional representation is convenient for geometrical reasons; but it must be used with due caution. Having clarified this point we may now lay off on the triangle (Fig. 49) the magnitude time, with its single dimension, along the base *bc*, as if it had but this one dimension; we also lay off the magnitude velocity, with its two dimensions, along the altitude, as if it had but one dimension, *ab*. Now, since distance traversed is the product of the rate of speed (LT^{-1}) into the time (T) it is $LT^{-1} \times T$, or L. But, geometrically, it is $ab \times bc$, and therefore equals the area $abcc_1$. Analytically it is one-dimensional; diagrammatically it becomes two-dimensional—i.e., measured in terms of area, like M.[18] If now we add a change in velocity, represented by a decline in the rate from *ab* to O during the period *bc*, we conceive the rate *ab* to be represented by a continuous succession of diminishing lines parallel to *ab*, each ending at the hypotenuse, *ac*. But the rate of change of velocity, the negative acceleration, which is itself three-dimensional, is shown one-dimensionally by ab_1—the diminution of *ab* in one unit of time. Then the actual distance traversed, the quan-

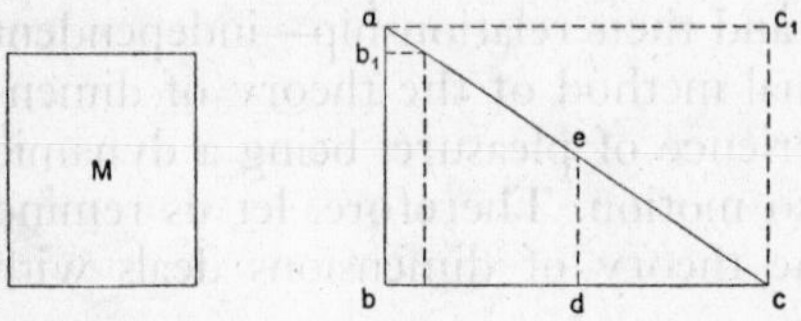

Fig. 49

text, which states that, for any values of *x* and *y*, the fraction or ratio remains the same when both are divided by the same number, up to infinity.

[17] It can also be stated as a rate of change per unit of distance just as velocity (or rate of motion) can be expressed as a rate per unit of distance.

[18] This geometrical representation makes the base seem to be a dimension of distance traversed; but it is not. We could just as well represent this relation in the forms A or B (Fig. 50) as by C. In A each separate square represents 1T and each division of the line superimposed represents 1L; in B each division along the base represents 1T and L is shown in the same way as in A; in C, T is shown in the same way as in B, but L becomes a series of squares superimposed, so that 1 square = 1L. Then, in C, the division on the base represents 1T, but, as to L, it only represents the numerical value 1, not the unit of L. And it only represents one of the two *factors* that represent the whole numerical value of L.

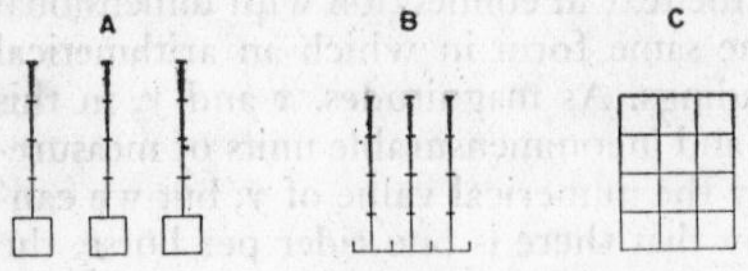

Fig. 50

tity of the one-dimensional magnitude L, is represented by the area *abc;* that is, by the product of the base, *bc*, and the average altitude *de*, or of the time elapsed multiplied by the average rate of motion (velocity). Finally, it must be noted that the two-dimensional magnitude, velocity, and the three-dimensional magnitude, acceleration, are both diagrammatically strictly one-dimensional. That is, neither is shown as a small quantity of area (distance traversed) however small (infinitesimal). Neither has any area. Both are magnitudes of wholly different order from distance traversed.

On the face of Jevons's statements as to his fundamental magnitudes we should be able to translate his system into terms of this analysis, however different that would be from his own. Let us first consider the alternative that pleasure is a fundamental (one-dimensional) magnitude. The representation of its magnitude would then correspond to distance traversed, which is the measure of motion. Pleasure is supposed to vary directly with quantity of commodity. Therefore the latter may be put in the place which time occupies in our example. The *rate* of pleasure would then be stated two-dimensionally as the rate of pleasure per unit of commodity just as the rate of motion (velocity) was stated.[19] The diminishing rate of pleasure per unit of commodity would occupy the place of negative acceleration. The dimension of pleasure being P, and that of commodity C, the dimensions of the rate of pleasure would be PC^{-1} and those of the rate of diminution of pleasure would be PC^{-2}. Interpreting this, we would conclude that the amount of pleasure varies directly with the amount of commodity in a certain proportion, or at a certain rate (let us say that this rate begins at 4 units of pleasure per unit of commodity), but that the rate diminishes through successive units (let us say that it ends at 0 units of pleasure per unit of commodity).[20]

If, then, the altitude of the triangle in Fig. 49 represents the rate at which pleasure accrues or is experienced per unit of commodity, just as it represents the rate at which distance traversed accrues per unit of time, it represents only this rate, and no more represents an amount of pleasure than it does an amount of distance. In other words, Jevons's statement that the *y* axis represents "the instantaneous state produced by an . . . infinitesimal quantity of commodity"[21] is pure mathematical nonsense—an attempt to transfer to the real world a convenient mathematical fiction. To

[19] Wicksteed (*441*, *759*) says specifically that, "'Degree of utility' stands in the same relation to 'total utility' as 'velocity' to 'space traversed.'"

[20] It may assist the reader if we apply to this translation of Jevons the same conclusions we arrived at in the case of motion.

1. Pleasure is one-dimensional, but is shown as if it had two dimensions. Then the distance along the base is not a dimension of, and its divisions do not represent units of, P. Instead, these divisions merely represent one of the two factors in its numerical value. Each represents, for it, 1, not 1P.

2. The rate of pleasure is purely a ratio; that is, it is the numerical value of a relation between two incommensurable magnitudes in terms of their respective units.

[21] Jevons, *224*, *65*. One sees here, most clearly, the confusion of the static magnitude with the dynamic.

say that velocity is an amount of distance covered in an infinitesimal period of time is no more absurd than to say that this rate at which pleasure is experienced is an amount of pleasure derived from an infinitesimal quantity of commodity. If it is true that the velocity is 1 mile per minute, and x is made to equal 1 mile, while $y = 1$ minute, then $\frac{x}{y}$ is the rate of motion. If so, then $\frac{1x}{60} \div \frac{1y}{60}$ represents the same rate of motion. This is expressed in mathematical terms by saying that $\frac{dx}{dy}$ represents the same rate as $\frac{x}{y}$. But, in the first place, it is true only if d represents the same fraction of both—here an infinitesimal fraction. And obviously the statement has no meaning whatever unless units of the original magnitudes, x and y, are defined; for, if, in terms of one set of units, $\frac{x}{y}$ had a certain numerical value, it would be absurd to suppose that the same value would hold for any other units.[22] And, in the second place, when a derived magnitude is reduced to terms of infinitesimals it becomes no longer measurable, or even appreciable, according to our dimensional rule, 9, since such measurement requires measurable quantities of the two magnitudes of which it is composed.

In spite of these divergences and the difficulties into which our interpretation has led us, it appears to me most likely that this scheme is what Jevons was driving at, and that he merely analyzed his magnitudes incorrectly and applied the theory of dimensions erroneously. If so, his M is our C, his MU is our P, and his U is our $\frac{P}{C}$, or PC^{-1}.[23] The only change we have made is to treat his U as a rate, PC^{-1}, instead of a dimension of pleasure, and therefore to convert pleasure from a two-dimensional magnitude, MU (of an unheard of type),[24] into a one-dimensional magnitude, P. Since this yields us the older generalized form of marginal utility analysis, upon which most of us were brought up, it seems worth while at this point to examine it somewhat more carefully in the light of the theory of dimensions. In spite of the fact that it has been frequently repudiated, chiefly for other reasons, we cannot yet be sure that it has been scotched for good.

22 In other words, as in our rule 11b, if all the dimensions of a rate (derived magnitude) are stated in units of half the size, the derived magnitude remains the same because it has no existence apart from its numerical value. If all the dimensions of a fundamental magnitude are stated in units of half the size, the magnitude remains the same, but its numerical value doubles or quadruples, etc.

23 Wicksteed assumes this in his two articles on "Jevons" and on "Mathematical Economics" (reprinted, *441*, 734–765). He states his reasons for using UQ^{-1} instead of Jevons's U. It is curious to me that in spite of this thorough discussion, which follows lines similar to ours, Wicksteed never stumbled upon his own underlying fallacy.

24 That is, what is the product of length and time (LT), for instance? It is a number of foot-minutes. For a further discussion of this question, see note 34, below.

In other words, let us submit it to our first test—the purely mathematical or metrical one.

In the first place, we have to decide which of the two magnitudes—that represented by the area or that represented by the altitude—determines the significance or utility of commodity. It cannot be determined by both, since they are different. In the older forms of marginal utility theory the altitude was said to show what we are calling marginal significance. But, according to the definition of marginal significance, this can also be shown as A_1, etc. (areas in Fig. 51), successively (i.e., the significance of any portion of means or commodity which happens to be marginal). According to the interpretation of marginal utility theory, if the first portion of means (B_1 in Fig. 51) and its corresponding area (A_1) are divided into halves, each half (in this particular diagram) has the same marginal significance (altitude). But it is obvious that each has only half the significance, if area shows significance. In fact, if only an infinitesimal amount of the first portion is taken, that, too, has the same marginal significance (altitude) though, clearly, it has at best only an infinitesimal amount of significance (area). If marginal significance, as defined, can behave in such an equivocal manner, it seems to be apparent that it involves a confusion between two entirely different magnitudes and an effort to treat them as one.[25] That being the case, it becomes necessary to choose between its two definitions. It cannot actually be the significance of the "edge" of a quantity of means, as it has been called. But then it cannot be the magnitude significance at all. It must be the rate of significance. It follows that commodity is "esteemed" (has significance) according to the quantity of pleasure derived from it and that this quantity of pleasure depends upon the quantity of commodity, so that only the rate of pleasure per unit of commodity can be shown on the altitude (or y axis). This conforms to the geometrical diagram (Fig. 51) where the altitude (C) represents a derived magnitude, or rate, whose dimensions are area divided by base ($\frac{A_1}{B_1}$, or

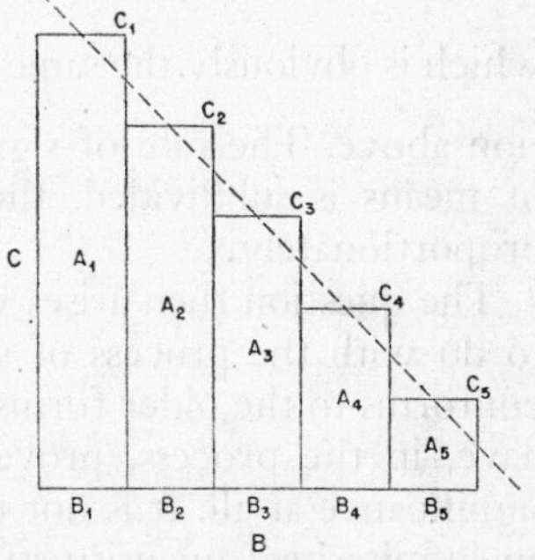

FIG. 51

[25] Elsewhere I have made this point in a slightly different way. Significance must either be represented by the area or by the altitude. It cannot be represented by both. If it is represented by area, the altitude being a geometrical line with no breadth, and therefore having no area, represents no significance. What part of a square inch is an inch? The confusion has arisen from the use of calculus; for, in that, the altitude is conceived as if it were an infinitesimal quantity of the area. That is a useful mathematical artifice. But it is not true. And it is absolutely refuted by the theory of dimensions. As soon as the line is conceived to have breadth—whether infinitesimal or "a little"—it becomes area; and, as such, it comes to represent a different magnitude—that is, here it ceases to represent the derived magnitude.

AB^{-1}).[26] That permits us to construe the successive areas A_1, etc., corresponding to successive portions of means, B_1, etc., as representing the quantity of significance of each portion of means in turn. Any altitude of any of these areas now represents its rate of significance—that is, as to the first area, A_1, any of its altitudes represents a magnitude equal to $\frac{A_1}{B_1}$. Now, if the first portion of means and its corresponding significance are divided in halves, the magnitude represented on the altitude becomes $\frac{A_1}{2} \div \frac{B_1}{2}$, which is obviously the same as $\frac{A_1}{B_1}$. Thus, we have eliminated the equivocation above. The rate of significance may remain the same, if the portion of means is subdivided, though the quantity of significance is reduced proportionately.

The question then arises what this rate of significance can actually have to do with the process of subjective valuation. While this interpretation conforms to the older forms of marginal utility theory, it is a fact that we have, in the process, proved that so-called marginal significance is not significance at all. It is not the significance of a "little more" means or of an infinitesimal quantity of means. It is, instead, a wholly different and derived magnitude—the *rate* of significance. As such it belongs to the type of magnitude that can only be measured, and derived, by measuring any corresponding pair of quantities of the two magnitudes that constitute its dimensions.

In the diagram, the successive diminutions in A_1, B_1, etc., suggest that the rate of significance may be a continuously declining one, as shown in the broken line curve drawn through the middle of the top of each area. This assumes that the rate of significance is not uniform within each portion of means, B_1, etc., but that it diminishes within them at the same rate that it diminishes between them. Nevertheless, the fact remains that we cannot know this unless we can measure the significance of each of these subdivisions of the several portions of means.

Now if we let the successive diminutions of the areas, A_1, etc. (or of any fractions of them), stand for the smallest measurable differences in such magnitudes, it is clear that the figure without the curve represents all that we could ever know by measurement of the rate of significance. The curve is then no more than a mathematical inference, the confirmation of which is impossible. It is not something which can be known by experience. It does not represent experience at all.

But, if that is true of the continuous curve, it is equally true of the successive altitudes C_1, C_2, etc., of the discontinuous steps. These, too, cannot be known as other than they are—that is, successively declining numerical expressions connoting rates of significance, or successive reductions in the

[26] The quantity of significance represented by the block of area A_1 is shown here as if it had the dimensions BC. But that is because we are using two-dimensional representation of this one-dimensional magnitude. Since A is one-dimensional, the dimensional formula is actually $C = \frac{A}{B}$.

numerical expressions connoting quantities of significance per equal portion of means. Since these rates, then, cannot be measured or apprehended directly,[27] all that is available to measurement or experience is represented by the series $\frac{A_1}{B_1}$, $\frac{A_2}{B_2}$, etc. If the magnitude represented by area could be measured in terms of objective units—as that represented by the base certainly can be—this series would be susceptible of numerical statement. If not, then all we can know is that A_2 is less than A_1, etc., or, in other words, that this series represents a diminution in the quantity of significance of each portion of means in order.

In view of this analysis it is clear that the rate of significance is a superfluous magnitude in this connection. It is not one that can have any bearing on subjective valuation. Even if it were possible to measure the magnitude represented by area in terms of objective units, so that it could be reduced to numerical statement and thus make possible a calculation, and conversion to numerical statement, of the derived magnitude, that would add nothing and alter nothing. Even then, the rate would be, in this connection, merely a convenient mathematical conception, useful in graphic representation, but not representing any part in the real process.

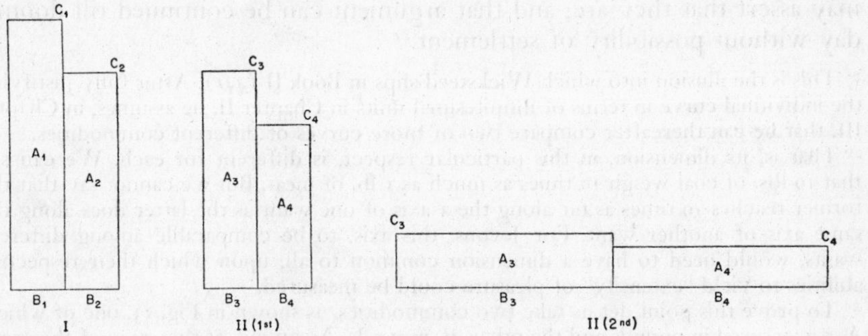

FIG. 52

This prepares us to deal with the essence of the fallacy in the older form of marginal utility representation. Fig. 51 represents only a single want and its means. We can concede, on the supposition of declining intensity of want (or desire, pleasure, satisfaction, etc.) that less significance might be reflected on successive equal portions of means for this want. We have found, however, that the altitude, having only a numerical value, cannot be used, except representationally, to signify a magnitude that is incapable of being reduced to terms of numerical value. That being the case, what basis is left for the comparison of different means for different wants? Fig. 52 represents the significance (area) of successive equal portions of two means (base) for two different wants, shown as I and II, and represents the rate of significance on the altitude. We can still assume it to be possible to compare the significance of B_1 and B_2—that is, A_1 and A_2—or that

[27] See rule 9, p. 458.

of B_3 and B_4—that is, A_3 and A_4. If so, it must also be possible to compare A_1 with A_3 or A_4. We can also assume that it is possible to measure any means (base) and to assert that B_1 and B_2 are equal, or that B_3 and B_4 are equal. It does not follow, however, that it would also be possible to determine whether B_1 and B_3 are equal.[28] For these are portions of two different commodities. We have discussed this question in the text (p. 492). All the dimensions of commodity in this respect are fundamental ones and are different for each.[29] It is as if the base of our triangle represented time in one case, mass in another, length in a third, and so on. This difficulty has been frequently noted by economists when they have attempted to conceive the real mass of wealth and to summate the incommensurables of which it is composed. The point is not merely that the two means may be measured in different physical dimensions; even if they have several physical dimensions in common, the ratios between their magnitudes in the several dimensions will be different, and it is impossible to select any one as *the* dimension for this purpose; and, finally, if they have but one common dimension, that serves only to enable us to find quantities of each that are equal in that dimension, but proves nothing as to their equality here. We may use Pareto's example. Are a kilogram of bread and a kilogram of wine of the same size in this connection? I assert that they are not; you may assert that they are; and that argument can be continued till doomsday without possibility of settlement.[30]

[28] This is the illusion into which Wicksteed slips in Book II (*441*). After fully justifying the individual curve in terms of infinitesimal units in Chapter II, he assumes, in Chapter III, that he can thereafter compare two or more curves of different commodities.

[29] That is, its dimension, in this particular respect, is different for each. We can say that 10 lbs. of coal weigh 10 times as much as 1 lb. of meat. But we cannot say that the former reaches 10 times as far along the *x* axis of one want as the latter does along the same axis of another want. For Jevons, this axis, to be comparable among different wants, would need to have a dimension common to all, upon which their respective abilities to yield "extensity" of pleasure could be measured.

[30] To prove this point, let us take two commodities, as shown in Fig. 53, one of which, A, is measured in pounds and the other, B, in yards. Assuming, at this stage of the argument, that we cannot separately measure intensity but are able to recognize the amount of pleasure engendered by a unit of each means, and that we find that, at a certain stage in the satisfaction of each want, 1 pound of A yields the same pleasure as 1 yard of B, what will enable us to determine whether, on the one hand, this is due to the fact that 1 yard of B reaches further along the base—as in unit b_1—that is, that it is actually more commodity and so yields pleasure at less intensity than A, or whether, on the other hand, equality is due to the fact that it reaches the same distance along the base and has the same intensity as A—as in unit *b*—because it is actually an equivalent quantity of commodity?

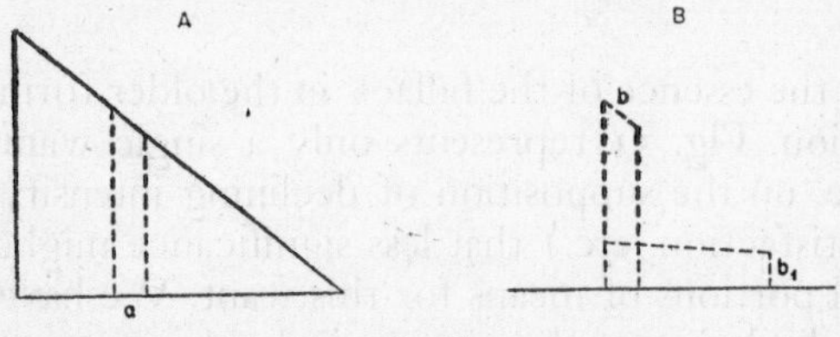

Fig. 53

In the second "posture" the base is presumed to be five times as long, and the initial altitude one-fifth as great. If you say to me that, if a yard of silk gives the same amount of pleasure as four pounds of bread, the intensity (or rate) of pleasure is, per yard of

The result is that, when we undertake to represent the magnitude of a unit of means for Want II in comparison to a unit of means for Want I, we are at liberty to use either of the two forms, II (1st) and II (2nd), shown in Fig. 52, or any other. We can show B_3 as of the same size as B_1 or we can show it as four times the size of B_1. In both figures, the significance (A_3) is the same, but in the second the rate of significance (C_3) is only one quarter that of the first.

That, being interpreted in terms of the theory of dimensions, means that before we can compare the magnitude of two rates we must reduce them to a common denominator—that is, we must find for them a common inverse dimension. But, by definition, this cannot be done in this case, for the dimension of means is here a different and fundamental dimension for each means, and different fundamental dimensions are incommensurable. It is true that, if it were possible to compare the rates of significance directly, it would also be possible to determine what were, in this respect, equal quantities of two different means. For then, if $\frac{A_2}{C_2}$ were found equal to $\frac{A_3}{C_3}$, it would needs be because $B_2 = B_3$. But, since the respective rates of significance can only be measured by measuring both of the fundamental dimensions of which they are composed, that assumption would have to be based on a novel and easy method of determining unknown quantities—one only requiring that, in order to determine them, it was necessary to know them in advance. Therefore, this argument has reduced the notion of the comparison of rate of significance as between two means for different wants, to a mathematical absurdity. It is a meaningless concept.

In the light of this analysis let us now appraise the validity of the notion of marginal significance in the usual form given it in older marginal utility theory. When it comes to the comparison of two means for different wants we find ourselves hooked on one or the other horns of a dilemma. We must be able either to compare the sizes of two infinitesimal magnitudes, or we must be able to compare the sizes of two incommensurable magnitudes. Granting the most that has been asked for marginal significance—that it represents the significance of an infinitesimal quantity of means—and is shown by altitude—the other difficulty would not bother us. For then, being able to compare the two magnitudes shown by area and then the two magnitudes shown by altitude, we could readily find equal quantities in this respect on the base, for comparison.[31] All that alternative requires is the ability to compare the significance, or any other

silk, four times that per pound of bread, I reply, "Not at all; the intensity is the same in both cases. The difference is due to the fact that a yard of silk is four times as big as a pound of bread." How can that dispute be settled? Can it be settled by seeing what happens when an infinitesimal quantity, or a "little," or even an equal fraction of both are added? What happens then is just as equivocal. In both "postures" equal additional fractions would yield the same additional amount of pleasure.

[31] That is, if the ratio between the two areas is the same as the ratio between the two altitudes the bases are necessarily equal. However, it is to be noted that, in order to determine such ratios, measurement in arbitrary units is required.

dimension, of infinitesimal quantities. On the other hand, if we could find equal quantities of two incommensurable means, this first difficulty would not bother us. For then, being able to compare the two magnitudes shown by area, we could readily compare their respective marginal significances.[32] All that alternative requires is the ability to compare, in terms of their common dimension, two magnitudes which, by definition, have no common dimension. In default of the ability to do either, the problem seems to be an insoluble one. Thus we find it necessary to reject all the schemes which take this form on the ground that they do not meet the requirements of our first, or mathematical, test.

To return to Jevons, there remains to be applied our second test, the psychological requirements implied in this version of his scheme. A word will suffice. If pleasure is a one-dimensional magnitude, then Jevons's "intensity" is no more than the rate at which pleasure is derived per unit of commodity. In order to exclude one further possibility, we must now determine whether it would be possible to escape the mathematical dilemma by assuming that it is this rate, not the quantity, of pleasure that determines significance. However, it is at once clear that even that interpretation does not obviate the psychological difficulties of his analysis. It would then be necessary to suppose that human beings could recognize the rate, apart from the quantity, of pleasure derived; for, in this interpretation of his theory, it is the rate, not the quantity of pleasure, in terms of which the marginal quantities of commodities are compared. To assume this is to assume that our feelings can do what our intelligence cannot do, namely divide one fundamental magnitude by another. Or, to make the task slightly easier, in terms of Jevons's "felicific calculus," we should have to detect not only the infinitesimal quantity of pleasure derived from an infinitesimal quantity of commodity, but also the doubly infinitesimal differences between such infinitesimal quantities of pleasure yielded by two infinitesimal quantities of commodity. Only if our psychological mensuration is equal to the task this would place upon it could we compare the "final degree of" (marginal) utility of two quantities of a single commodity, or, worse still, of two different and incommensurable commodities. If, to the reader, this seems to be a *reductio ad absurdum*, I may only add that it seems so to me as well.[33]

[32] This would not always require the same measurability required in the first case. When the conditions described on p. 456, note 4, existed, they would suffice for rough comparability.

[33] It is hardly necessary to repeat this analysis in Fisher's, Wicksteed's, or, after the foregoing, even in Walras's terms. Fisher's "desirability" is simply a forecast of the quantity of "pleasure or satisfaction to be derived" (*142*, 42–43). That is, it is either type (2b) or (3b) of desire as we analyzed the possibilities on p. 1307 ff. His "marginal desirability" is that of a unit (*ibid.*, 44 and Appendix to Chapter III). But that does not save him from comparing incommensurable units. See his "Mathematical Investigations in the Theory of Value and Prices" (9 *Trans. Conn. Acad. of Arts and Sciences* 1893). We have not disputed the presentation of a continuously declining rate, which Wicksteed is at such pains to justify (*441*, 37–94 and 439–473). Wicksteed's treatment of the margin as a "limiting rate of significance" (*ibid.*, 60 ff. and 446) is the same as our rate of pleas-

On the other hand, it is not impossible that Jevons was actually interpreting the area in his diagram as he said he was. If so, the area represents a two-dimensional magnitude of the "unheard of type" mentioned above.[34] The quantity of pleasure would then have the dimensions MU (in his notation), the "intensity" of pleasure would have the dimension U and the "extensity" of pleasure would have the dimension M. As a first step let us consider this last dimension (M). While the notion of treating the entirely extrinsic dimension of commodity as if it were a dimension of pleasure, which is involved here, might appear, at first sight, to be entirely valid so long as we are dealing with one and the same kind of unit of one and the same kind of commodity, it is immediately exploded, and, in the process, exposes the underlying fallacy of such analysis, when we come to try to measure different commodities stated in different units. For, in the first place, the identification of one of the dimensions of pleasure with the dimensions of commodity must be based on the assumption that the di-

---

ure, or what not, though he is inclined to slip in and out of the back door through which he arrived at this concept, and thus confuse the rate with the amount of "significance." We will refer the reader, for Wicksteed's practical adoption of Jevons's concepts, to pp. 415–418 (*ibid.;* though he claims, p. 435, that his analysis does not "presuppose a hedonistic theory"); and to pp. 63 ff. and p. 129, etc. (*ibid.*) for a demonstration that he assumes the relation between the "rates of significance" of two commodities to be determinable apart from any definition of the quantities to be compared, or of the relation between the size of their units, and apart from the measurability of the quantities concerned.

[34] So far as I know, no one since Jevons and Walras has assumed that the psychological entity conferring significance has itself two dimensions—"intensity" and "extensity," or what not. In the 4th edition of the *Principles* (p. 167) Marshall said, "The wants are here reckoned quantitatively, that is, with regard to their volume and intensity." The fact that this statement was deleted from the 5th and all later editions suggests that Marshall discovered the difficulties involved in defining the "volume" of a want apart from its intensity, or the "volume" as one of the two dimensions of a want.

It is worth while, however, to point out the unusual character of this supposed two-dimensional magnitude. Judging from the terms "intensity" and "extensity," it appears possible that it was conceived to be of the order of area—that is, a two-dimensional magnitude in which one dimension appears twice (like L^2). If so, that was mere illusion derived from a unique characteristic of space (or even from the form of the diagram). If, instead, it was conceived as a magnitude of which the two dimensions were different and both fundamental it would have no precedent, in dynamics at least. What is a mile-hour? As soon as one undertakes to analyze such a conceptual magnitude and to define its dimensions it becomes converted into something else which is either a rate or its underlying correspondence. What does a foot-pound, as a unit of work, turn out to be? Its dimensional formula is not ML, as would appear from its name, but ML^2T^{-2}. What does a kilowatt hour, as a unit of electrical energy (capacity for work) turn out to be? Its formula is not PT, as would appear from its name, but $ML^2T^{-3} \times T$, or also ML^2T^{-2}. Nor does either of these formulas convey the idea that ML^2 is a magnitude. Both commence with the rate, LT^{-2}, and are derived therefrom by including directly the third dimension, mass (M) and the dimension L a second time. That is, the series is built up from the formula for acceleration, LT^{-2}, by including first M, to convert it to force, and then by including L again, to convert it to energy or work. The result is unit acceleration of a unit mass over a unit distance. One cannot start with ML, for that is meaningless.

mension of commodity is the same for all commodities; whereas, as we have just shown, this dimension is different for each.

This demonstrates, I think that, if pleasure, or desire, or what not, is taken to be a two-dimensional quantity, one of which dimensions is "intensity," then, as soon as comparison of two different commodities enters, the true nature of the imputed second dimension is disclosed. It cannot be, and it never was, "commodity." [35] It must be, and it always was, some vague notion of "extensity" similar to that of Walras.

Therefore, the real difficulty is a deeper one. For, even if we admit the possibility of a magnitude with only two direct dimensions, each fundamental and different from the other, and agree to treat these two dimensions as those of the area in our diagram—the base and the altitude—we

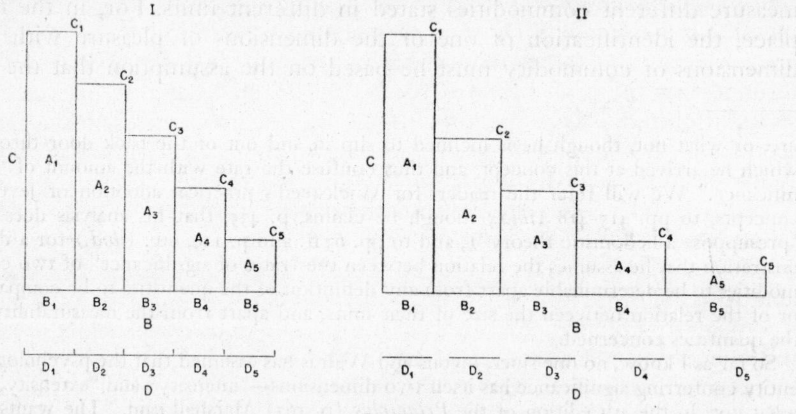

FIG. 54

still have to ask what dimension the base represents. It cannot be time (T); for, as we have already seen, that leads to results that are contrary to reality. It cannot be commodity; for, in spite of the fact that there may be a correspondence between them, as we shall see presently, correspondence does not mean—in fact denies—identity.

If it is not commodity, but there is still a second dimension in the criterion conferring significance, that necessitates a change in the meaning of that dimension in the diagrams. The base no longer represents commodity; it now represents this dimension only. Hitherto, the connection between a block of area and a section of base (A_1 and B_1 in Fig. 54, for instance) has been that of a correspondence between two incommensurable magnitudes—pleasure, or significance, and commodity—which have a relation of non-mathematical equality in a process into which they both enter. If that correspondence is still to be represented—and if it is not, the whole

[35] Theoretically it could, of course, be related to the dimension of a single commodity, if we had a right to assume that equal quantities of that commodity correspond at all times and under all conditions to equal magnitudes in this dimension. Is this a safe assumption, however, if we are also assuming that the other dimension, "intensity," has a constantly changing relation to equal quantities of that commodity?

scheme is futile—we have to bring in still a fourth magnitude to represent commodity. This is shown (in Fig. 54) as the independent line D, parallel to the base. Now the sections along D—D_1, D_2, etc.—may still show their former correspondence to the areas A_1, A_2, etc. But that does not prove that, because D_1, D_2, etc., are all of the same size, B_1, B_2, etc., are also all of the same size. That is, there is no reason to suppose that the "extensity" corresponding to each equal portion of commodity is the same as that corresponding to each other portion. The "extensity" B per unit of D might be increasing, as in the second figure (Fig. 54), though the size of the unit D remained the same throughout. On the other hand, it might be decreasing. One would not know that all of the sections of B were the same size, and thus corresponded to those on D, unless he could measure each section in the dimension represented by B independently of that in the dimension represented by D, or unless he could measure the pleasure in each area, A_1, etc., and the "intensity" in each altitude, C_1, etc., and could determine that the ratio between the series of areas and that between the series of altitudes were the same. If we do not know that the successive sections on B are equal, we have no basis in the B dimension for cutting A into sections whose comparison would have rhyme or reason.[36]

Let us see what sort of task the mathematical difficulties of such a formulation would set before our psychological apparatus in order that we might compare different quantities of different commodities. If we were able to recognize "intensity" only, we would have no means of relating it to quantity of commodity, since it is supposed to be independent of small differences in such quantity.[37] Only if the differences in these quantities were of sufficient size, so that the quantities produced notably different effects on "intensity," would we have some basis for discrimination between them. But that arrives at the scheme we developed from Menger, in terms approximately the same as the remaining intensity of wants. For, then, quantity of pleasure cannot be a factor. On the other hand, if we could recognize "extensity" only, quantities of all commodities which produced pleasure of the same "extensity" would be on a par. Again the quantity of pleasure would be undeterminable. Finally, if we were able to recognize quantity of pleasure only, there would, again, always be some certain quantity of each commodity that would give us the same quantity of pleasure as some certain quantity of every other commodity. Now all

[36] In the text we concluded that the only discontinuity in the process that we have found so far, which can be used to separate it into parts, is the consumption of successive equal portions, or units, of means.

[37] To Jevons, "the only dimension belonging properly to feeling seems to be intensity, and this intensity must be independent both of time and of the quantity of commodity enjoyed" (*224*, 65). It is only this dimension which he seems to feel sure we can measure (see top of p. 52, *ibid.*), in spite of the fact that he there confuses this single dimension with a small quantity of the area added or subtracted. As we have noted, it is pure aberration to assume, as he does (*ibid.*, 65), that "the intensity of feeling must mean, then, the instantaneous state produced by an elementary or infinitesimal quantity of commodity consumed." On that basis the length of a rectangle is the area corresponding to an infinitesimal quantity of its breadth.

these inferences may conform to the facts;[38] but, since none of these three measurements by itself does more than treat the critical magnitude as if it were actually one-dimensional, it either fails to conform to Jevons's analysis or it makes most of that analysis superfluous. Furthermore, these inferences each arrive at a different conclusion from that of Jevons.

However, all this does make it evident that, if this magnitude, pleasure, is two-dimensional, our psychological apparatus would need to be able to measure both of its dimensions, or either one of its dimensions *and* its total magnitude, in order to perform the task this analysis sets for it. If we were able subjectively to measure both the "intensity" and the "extensity" of pleasure so that we could directly compare the different "intensities" of two equal "extensities," then the area (quantity of pleasure), being the product of the two, is an unnecessary complication which we would not need to measure, and we would be able to value quantities of two different commodities, yielding the same "extensity," directly according to their yield of "intensity." If we were able subjectively to measure the dimension of "intensity" only, but also the quantity of pleasure, we would be able to value quantities of two different commodities according to the "intensity" of pleasure they yielded, provided the ratio between the quantities of pleasure they yielded was the same as that between their "intensities"; for then we could infer that their "extensities" were equal. If, finally, we could measure the dimension of "extensity" only, but also the quantity of pleasure, we could compare two quantities of commodity yielding the same "extensity" according to the quantities of pleasure which resulted. Then "intensity" would be superfluous.

These psychological requirements add a little more of the preposterous to this interpretation of Jevons's analysis, which we have already found preposterous enough. We may reasonably conclude, I think, that since there is no evidence whatever for the existence of this second dimension of pleasure, "extensity," it can be no more than a figment of the imagination conjured into existence to fill a gap in the logical processes of the analysis we have been examining.

Our conclusion is that whether area in the diagram means ultimately a one-dimensional or a two-dimensional magnitude—pleasure, or what not—what it stands for is all that we can know or need to know. Knowing that, we can find the correspondences between successive equal arbitrary units of means for a single want or of different arbitrary units of different means for different wants, on the one hand, and the quantities of pleasure, etc. derived from each. And we may assume that we can at least compare the quantities of pleasure, etc. corresponding to these several units in terms of more or less or of approximate equality. If pleasure is a one-dimensional magnitude, then the altitude is the rate of pleasure, is immeasurable by itself, and cannot by itself participate in the process. If

[38] We shall also derive an inference similar to the last from the indifference curves which we shall discuss shortly. However, this form of analysis is not that of marginal utility theory, as it used to be presented.

pleasure is a two-dimensional magnitude, neither of the two dimensions can by themselves participate in the process unless both are measurable, or unless the psychological process, knowing one, can calculate the other —dividing the area by the known dimension. These conditions appear to ask too much of the psychological apparatus.[39]

Thus, in all these different interpretations the magnitude shown on the altitude must either be construed to be a magnitude that is certainly immeasurable on mathematical grounds, or it must be construed to be a magnitude that is almost certainly immeasurable on psychological grounds. There seem to be no other alternative constructions. It appears then that all the older forms of marginal utility theory that utilize marginal significance, as defined, for their criterion of subjective valuation must be rejected on mathematical grounds. They do not pass our first test (see text, p. 452). Those older forms of the theory that assign two dimensions to the magnitude conferring significance and make of either or both of the dimensions influences on significance apart from the two-dimensional magnitude itself, must also be rejected, but this time on psychological grounds. They do not pass our second test (*loc. cit.*).

E. THE EDGEWORTH-PARETO SCHEME

Our conclusion is that, if we are to conceive significance (utility or desirability) in terms of pleasure at all, we must confine ourselves to the comparison of quantities of pleasure derived from definite objective magnitudes of various means, which quantities of pleasure are sufficiently different in size so that the difference is sensible. At the point at which we have arrived, everything depends on the respective quantities of two commodities which are being compared, since the esteem in which they will be held depends on the quantity of pleasure they will yield, not on the rate at which they yield it. It is assumed to be true that, by this means, quantities can be found of each commodity that will yield the same pleasure as some quantity of every other commodity. When these subjectively equivalent quantities are reduced to the smallest sizes which can be equated within a reasonable margin of error, they will serve as convenient subjective units—and can then be restated each in terms of its own objective unit. But, if succeeding objective units of each commodity are conceived to yield pleasure at a declining rate, then the subjectively equivalent quantities will be different according to the stage in the satisfaction of each want at which each quantity is determined. Thus we arrive at a near infinite set of objective ratios between subjective equivalents. We shall see whether there is some reasonably rational way round that difficulty. At any rate, our conclusion leads us to abandon the notion of "degree of utility," of the "marginal significance of an infinitesimal [or, vaguely, "small"] quantity," of "intensive utility," and so on, and to confine our attention to total or "effective" utility, and the significance of finite quanti-

[39] That is, they require the assumption that the hedonic apparatus is furnished with a calculating machine that can either multiply or divide.

ties.[1] And this, in turn, leads us to the method of analysis developed by Edgeworth and Pareto which, though not explicitly stated to be so, is in reality developed in these terms.

Edgeworth started with the most fantastic notions of all these protagonists with reference to the capacity of the organism to measure pleasure in units, and was the only one who believed in the possibility of relating these units as between different individuals (*133*, 8).[2] But, thereafter, following out his method of "unnumerical mathematics" (*ibid.*, 83), he proceeded to develop the least fantastic of all of these systems—one based on what he called "indifference-curves," representing various quantities of pleasure derived from combined quantities of any pair of different commodities, variations in the plus direction of either one of which pair neutralizes the variations in the minus direction of the other, so that all combinations on each curve represent equal total quantities of pleasure. Thence his "line of preference" proceeds perpendicular to the line, or curve, of indifference, and only in one direction, so that it always reaches toward preferable curves of indifference (*ibid.*, 21–22, and *134*, 457). Pareto adopted this system from Edgeworth.[3] But, instead of building it up from the notion of measurable pleasure, as Edgeworth had done, he reversed this order. Recognizing that indifference and preference were actual data of experience, fitting in with the mathematics of equality and of more or less, he used these notions as his starting point and thus avoided the difficulty of the measurement of pleasure.[4] Eventually Edgeworth rather approved Pareto's "scruples" and his procedure, indicating that he had then abandoned his own starting point.[5] We shall find it more convenient to follow Pareto's, rather than Edgeworth's somewhat different, exposition.

The essence of this method is that it deals with quantities of pleasure from compound sources in such a way that variations which are within the limits of the "*minimum sensibile*"—whatever that may actually be—

[1] We may tentatively retain the hedonism, but we must abandon the "calculus." To Jevons (*224*, 51), "degree of utility" is the "differential coefficient of total utility considered as a function of quantity"; to Fisher (*142*, 344) his equivalent is the "differential quotient"; to Walras (*420*, 76) his is a derivative of the total utility as a function of quantity consumed. All come to the same thing. All attempt to apply calculus to a field beyond its reach.

[2] His general unit of pleasure has unitary intensity for a unit of time. Pleasure is measured by the number of these units. These "*atoms of pleasure* are not easy to distinguish and discern; more continuous than sand, more discrete than liquid; as it were nuclei of the just-perceivable, embedded in circumambient semi-consciousness." This is "nice" English; but it is not so nice science.

[3] Hicks says (*196*, 52–53) that Fisher started the idea in his *Mathematical Investigations.* He also suggests (*ibid.*, 54–55) that Pareto's inconsistencies are due to the fact that his theory developed in the process of presenting it. Of how many systematic writings is that not true?

[4] Pareto, *317*, 540, note 1, and 270. He did not do so altogether. On this Hicks (*195*, 19) says, quite rightly, ". . . even after Pareto established his great proposition, he continued to use concepts derived from the earlier set of ideas."

[5] See Edgeworth, *134*, 473. On the validity of these "scruples" in particular and on the subject matter of Chapter 8 and this appendix in general, see the acute analysis by Armstrong (*14*).

are felt as no variation (equivalent combinations), and those which are beyond these limits are felt as more or less (one preferable to the other). Whatever pleasure is, this does not presume too much.[6] On this basis, Pareto constructed his well-known geographical and three-dimensional representation. His "*colline*" is a curved surface; along the various levels of this "*colline*" lie the indifference lines, corresponding to contour lines; across these contour lines lead innumerable "*sentiers*" which ascend or descend the slope of the "*colline*" in various directions, not only in one, as with Edgeworth.[7] While Pareto stated the variations in these magnitudes —or in these directions—in terms of continuous change (i.e., infinitesimals), for convenience in mathematical treatment, that is not necessary. The method deals only with the comparison of magnitudes of total significance (ophelimity). The rest is assumed to be inferred, not felt or observed.[8] Moreover, in his *examples*, he deals only with measurable quanti-

[6] In his review of Pareto's contribution to the *Encyklopädie der mathematischen Wissenschaften* (see *134*, 43), Edgeworth says: "The exercise of *choice*, the preference of the economic man for one combination of goods to another, results in a system of *indifference-curves* which are comparable with the isobars or isotherms of physical science in that each successive curve denotes a greater intensity of the attribute under consideration, but differ in that the economic, unlike the physical, curves cannot be each labelled with a number." Pareto himself does not exclude this possibility (*317*, 171); but he does not require it (*ibid.*, 661). On the other hand he does expressly exclude the "addition" of these quantities (*ibid.*, 68) or the comparison of those of different individuals (*ibid.*, 63 and 265).

[7] It should be noted at once that this diagram of quantities of pleasure does not correspond with the one we have been using. The quantity of pleasure—or index of ophelimity (total utility)—is here represented one-dimensionally by the altitude of a contour line—line of indifference—above the "*plan.*" This altitude, then, corresponds to the area in those of our diagrams in which area is given meaning. The rate of change in quantity of pleasure—his elementary ophelimity—is represented by the "*pente*" of his "*colline*"; that is, by the angle of inclination which the slope, at any point, makes with the base. This angle, at any point, corresponds to the height of the ordinate of our curve at any point. The convexity of his slope—the rate of change in this inclination (diminution of the angle)—is equivalent to the negative inclination of our curve. And the variation in the angles between each successive pair of tangents to his slope represents the "shape" of our curve; that is, its aberration from a straight line. Finally the peak of his "*colline*" represents the point where our curve intersects the x axis. (See *317*, 170–171, 264 and 283–284). On p. 268 (*ibid.*), it seems that there is no summit, but a sort of asymptote, upon which pleasure from all commodities becomes equal. (The description of passing from one level to another on p. 284 is, in the 2nd French edition, vitiated by poor proof reading.) By means of relating these correspondences it becomes possible to translate his presentation into terms of the one which we have been using for all.

"Ophelimity" is merely a different term, not a different concept. As a term, he finds it preferable to "utility," because (*316*, I, 3) he reserves the latter to cover our usefulness (a "*rapport de convenance*," *316*, I, 3), and to "desirability," because (*317*, 556, note 1) one cannot speak of the desirability of a thing already consumed. Most usually, ophelimity is to him an amount of pleasure (cf. *317*, 158, 63, etc.). But it depends on "the intensity of want (or of desire)" (*316*, I, 9 and 33). Therefore, it has nothing of the nature of a "residue," as a mere principle, an x (see his *Mind and Society*). It is identified with subjective experience, if not with objective fact.

[8] It is true that, in his earlier exposition (*316*, I, 11), he says that "men are most often conscious only of elementary ophelimity; total ophelimity remains unknown to them." But I take that to mean that they are only susceptible to differences in quantities of

ties and therefore only with ophelimity (total significance or pleasure). Let us examine his chief example of a series of indifference (*317*, 168). There, all six assortments of bread and wine are presumed to yield equal pleasure and so are indifferent among themselves.

	I	*II*	*III*	*IV*	*V*	*VI*	
Bread	1.6	1.4	1.2	1.0	0.8	0.6	kg.
Wine	0.7	0.8	0.9	1.0	1.4	1.8	kg.

It seems quite plausible to assume that these assortments are comparable and can be found to be equal, if they are so. But does it seem quite plausible that the members of this or any other series of assortments, are, as a matter of fact, indifferent among themselves? He says (*317*, 169) that the series can be prolonged indefinitely in both directions. But is that not quite absurd? Is it conceivable that man can live by wine alone; or, is it conceivable that another assortment VII, in which the only change we make from assortment VI is the addition of 0.1 kg. more of wine, would be preferred to assortment I, so that the combination of 1.9 kg. of wine with 0.6 kg. of bread is more pleasurable than any other assortment in the series? If so, the plus difference between assortments I and VII, or 1.2 kg. of wine, yields more pleasure than the minus difference, or 1 kg. of bread; and, therefore, if opportunity offered itself to one having assortment I, he would make the exchange. Something seems to be wrong with this type of analysis—or this application of it—when we attempt to fit it to reality. In this analysis every means seems to be, in some merely quantitative relation, a substitute for every other, as if the wants for food and drink were not nearly independent of one another.[9] It assumes that there would always be some quantity of bread that one would surrender—until he had no more—for a sufficient quantity of wine or of any and all other things—until satiety was reached for these other things.[10] If that were true, and sufficient quantities of these other things were available, one could be en-

pleasure (or the absence of same) and not to absolute magnitudes—whatever that may mean. Even there (*ibid.*, 21), he always compares totals, not rates. But when he defines the inverse ratio between the number of units in the respective quantities to be the elementary ophelimity of these articles, he is clearly confusing the average of the totals with the marginal, or rate of, ophelimity for the quantities. For any number of curves with differing marginal (elementary) ophelimity, can, for any definite segment, produce the same average ophelimity. If, as he says, the total ophelimity of the three units of wine were equal to that of the two units of wheat, what gain did the man procure by the exchange? On the other hand, if the elementary ophelimity of the quantities exchanged was, of wheat to wine, as three to two, why did he stop exchanging at that point? There is certainly a deeper confusion here, which I have not touched on. His elementary ophelimity is defined rather roundaboutly as a rate (see *317*, 263). But, if men are to be conscious of this, they must then be conscious of doubly infinitesimal differences between infinitesimal quantities, as above.

9 On the notion of general substitutability see below, note 25.

10 In other words, it finds sufficient to support a value theory the fact we noted above that, if pleasure is the basis, some quantity of each commodity can be found that will yield the same pleasure as some quantity of every other.

ticed gradually to pare down his supply of bread for greater pleasures elsewhere until he starved to death.

The reason this application of the notion of indifference is not so defective as it appears can only be appreciated when we discover the defect in the analysis itself. If we examine the series of assortments above, or, better, the concept of an infinite series represented by a curve (or line) of indifference, we see that at any one point on one curve there are presented an infinite number of choices as to points (assortments on another preferable curve).[11] Yet, by definition, all these choices among preferable assortments are indifferent. There is, therefore, in this analysis itself, nothing whatever which would tell us which choice would be made. When we perceive this point, it becomes clear that there has been tacitly introduced into this analysis, as an assumption, an extraneous factor, an external determinant, which at least limits if it does not fix the choice. And we can at once recognize it. It is either the "terms of trade" which are open, or it is the fact that it is assumed that only given quantities of each article are available. But, when such assumptions are admitted, we have no reason to conclude that the ultimate cause of the existing combination of available quantities or of the terms of trade offered is not the factor which determines the choice. If that were true, in turn, the dependent subjective value theory would fall to the ground; for then the cause of terms of trade or of the limitation of the respective quantities might well be the final determinant of values. The only certain influence of the line of indifference would then be that trades would never be made which merely changed assortments along that line (i.e., the indifference curve would act as the limit to quantities or values—a sort of "still pond, no more moving"). On the other hand, this discloses that the range of neutrality (indifference) is, in actual practice, very much limited by the influence of the terms of trade or the combination of quantities; and this answers our objection to Pareto's example of an indifference line. It is not so absurd to assume that the consumer might deny himself bread for other pleasures when we recognize that, as a matter of fact, a sufficiency of other pleasures may not be available to induce him to do so. It merely renders the analysis futile.

It also appears that what we have here is an analysis of trader's psychology —of that of a person who will always sell what he has if he can get enough in return for it—rather than of consumer's psychology (true subjective valuation), which, we have reason to believe, proceeds along different lines.[12] Our trader might be only too glad to exchange 1 kg. of bread for 1.2 kg. of wine, in the previous example—if he thought the latter represented greater exchange value—although our consumer might not, if he needed the bread to keep him alive. Even if we were to regard this analysis as descriptive of the combined influence of the demand and of the supply

[11] That is not true on Edgeworth's curve; his "line of preference" is single and perpendicular to the line of indifference. Also on this, see note 25, below.

[12] Cf. Aristotle's *Politics*, Chap. IX.

factors in determining values, and as explaining only the framework of potential demand values into which supply fits, we would still not be satisfied. For, if this analysis does not represent the way the final demander would behave, it does not represent the actual ultimate framework—subjective valuation—at all.

However, since this approach seems to be the most mathematically and psychologically justifiable of those we have examined, and since it constitutes the basis of the theory of subjective valuation which is probably most generally accepted today, we may proceed to consider the modifications that have been developed from it. The first and most notable is that of Hicks. Hicks ostensibly eliminates all dependence upon a scale of utility, even in terms of more or less, and relies wholly on indifference curves (equality) at successively greater distances from the origin (i.e., greater combinations of quantities) to express the absence and presence of preferences (but see note 14, below). Thus he also eliminates pleasure. In fact, he avoids all psychological entities (causation) and does not go behind the fact of choices. Substitutability remains in a slightly qualified form. It does not exist to the extent that complementarity exists; it is modified or one-directional in the case of "inferior" substitutes. But it becomes the basis for his particular contribution, the changing "marginal rate of substitution" as one moves along a single curve of indifference. This is an expression of the equivalence between the plus and minus differences in assortment among indifferent assortments.[13] In general, no limits appear to be set to substitutability, where it exists, and it seems to be assumed that it is a common relation between means for different wants as well as between substitute means for a single want.

Hicks's second innovation, or clarification, that concerns us, deals with the question of "*sentiers*" from one indifference curve to another. In his article (*196*), Hicks confirms Edgeworth and corrects Pareto as to the number of "*sentiers*" leading from one indifference line to another. There are not infinite "*sentiers*"; there is but one; and the succession of points of intersection with successive lines is the "expenditure curve" (see *196*, 61). In the book (*195*, 27–33) this becomes two "*sentiers*," one, the

[13] This concept of the marginal rate of substitution is developed somewhat differently in the earlier article (*196*) and in the later book (*195*).

In the article (*196*), Hicks's analysis is based on an antithesis between complementarity and substitutability. "Any two goods are substitutes—more or less" (*196*, 69). So "complementary" represents the polarity of less and "substitute" represents the polarity of more. The limits at each pole are as follows (*196*, 59): If two goods are perfect substitutes the rate of increase of their marginal rate of substitution is zero and their elasticity of substitution is infinite; if, on the other hand, they are so complementary that they must be used in fixed proportion, the reverse is true. In the book (*195*) this antithesis seems to have disappeared. The qualities become mutually exclusive, but are no longer opposite poles, nor necessarily relations between all goods (see *195*, 47–48). That is, "it is our definition of complementarity which draws the exact line between these two situations"—substitutability and complementarity (*195*, 46). In the article, moreover, the treatment of all means, even for different wants, as more or less competitive rests, he says (*196*, 60), on the measurability of marginal utility. In the book (*195*, 17) this is no longer necessary.

"income-consumption curve," along which one would move with any definite change in income and none in price, and a second, the "price-consumption curve," along which one would move with any definite change in price and none in income (including no "income-effect").[14] But, in the book, it is recognized more frankly (*195*, 16–17) that this determinateness is due to the market-price ratio, which is an extraneous factor, and that the indifference curves merely determine the optimum assortment at that ratio. Thus even Hicks's improved scheme cannot be made determinate when treated as a virtual pure demand system. The single optimum position on each indifference curve (*195*, 17), as well as the single intersections with other indifference curves of the income-consumption and the price-consumption curves leading from that position (*195*, 27–33) are entirely dependent upon some given "terms of trade." Therefore, this scheme cannot serve even our present purposes, much less submit itself to the kind of synthesis we will impose on our hypothesis in the final chapter.[15]

All these clarifications and modifications are improvements from our viewpoint. Nevertheless, though reduced, our fundamental objections remain. This foundation of Hicks's elaborate analytical structure, while internally logical and consistent, would rest on sand if it turns out that, to the consumer, substitutability is on an all or none basis[16] and only extends to various means that are substitutes for a single want—not to the alternative satisfactions of different wants—and if complementariness

[14] A change in price produces "income-effect" as well as "price-effect" if the elasticity of demand is other than unity.

[15] If the first hypothesis as to the order of preference in satisfying wants, which we shall establish, is found to be correct, and if it is not greatly modified when we combine it with our own analysis of the extraneous factor yet to be analyzed, it would be impossible to apply Hicks's development of the Edgeworth-Pareto scheme to consumer demand, though it might remain useful in the analysis of production—i.e., what he calls "technical complementarity and technical substitution." Even then it would be necessary to find more satisfactory definitions than those furnished either by Pareto (*317*, 268) and Edgeworth (*134*, 117), which are vitiated by the necessity of measurable marginal utility, or by Hicks (*195*, 42–44), which is vitiated by the necessity of introducing the marginal rate of substitution for money. Perhaps the proper definition is that complementarity exists between two commodities when the assortment remains unchanged regardless of changes in the price ratio, and that substitutability exists when, at either side of some certain price ratio, demand is all for one or all for the other. "Perfect" complementarity and "perfect" substitutability, both, would then eliminate indifference curves entirely, since they could only be represented by single *points*. Whether either can exist in a less than complete degree and, if so, what its definition should be remains a problem.

[16] If substitutability exists on an all or none basis it could only be represented by a pair of indifference points on the two axes. A curve joining them would not only be meaningless; it would be misrepresentation. It may be disputed that substitution, even for a single want, is on an all or none basis. But I am inclined to think alternation is due to a want for variety which, as a vacillating member of many constellations, adds complexities we shall not try to unravel.

While Hicks's modification of substitutability, including income effects and inferior goods, are in the right direction to make indifference analysis conform to the facts, the technique of that analysis still trails with it a heavy burden of inadequacy.

does not there exist for a single want, and, as between wants, is merely an optional relation within constellations of wants.[17]

Others have retained Pareto's concept of a convex surface (*colline*) representing an infinite series of indifference curves at successively higher altitudes but with diminishing increases in altitude. While this is excluded as unnecessary from Hicks's diagrams, it is really implicit in his scheme.[18] Moreover, it cannot be avoided. To accept it frankly does not require the notion of measurable pleasure, nor even the identification of the subjective criterion at all. All forms of representation seem to admit that continuous lines (curves) or surfaces are purely schematic. Actually, to be realistic, it would be necessary to convert all three dimensions into discontinuities—determinate points representing areas of indeterminateness[19] —in order to recognize the nether limits of measurability of means and of comparability (*minimum sensibile*) of utility (or what not). It has also been suggested that the limits of substitutability—equivalent to satiation —can be represented on indifference curves by making them perpendicular to one of the axes at such limits or even by reversing them (the "discommodity" of the superfluous).[20] With these minor restorations and amend-

[17] Substitutability, for Hicks, covers our terms of substitution for a single want, our successive summation (and change of means) for wants of a single constellation and our preferences among the satisfactions of independent wants. I submit that three such diverse phenomena cannot be reduced to a single proposition. The result of attempting to do so is to achieve a proposition that does not represent precisely the behavior of any of the phenomena.

We have already undertaken to show in Chapter 7 that complementarity, in Hicks's sense, does not exist. Instances cited reduce themselves either to conglomerates of means for the several members of a constellation, or to improper analysis of what constitutes a single means—i.e., treating separate but indispensable parts of a whole as if they were separate means merely because they may be replaced separately.

[18] Hicks's scheme is in terms of quantities of commodities only. Along one indifference curve it is assumed that it is necessary to add more and more of one commodity in order to induce the surrender of less and less of the other (i.e., the curves are concave in our terminology). The further from the origin lies an indifference curve the larger the combination of quantities it represents—that is, for the same quantity of one, that of the other is always larger. This suffices to represent declining marginal utility (or diminishing marginal rate of substitution) along a single indifference curve. But it merely evades the same issue as between indifference curves. That is, to show declining utility, it would be necessary to represent these curves as lying farther and farther apart in proportion to their distance from the origin, or as lying on a convex curved surface, like Pareto's *colline*. The second point seems to have been ignored by Hicks; but the underlying concept is implicit in his scheme. That is, if there is declining marginal utility as one commodity is increased while the other is decreased, there must also be declining marginal utility as one commodity is increased while the other is held constant. The declining marginal utility of one commodity is exactly neutralized by the rising marginal utility of the other, as one moves along an indifference curve. It is not neutralized as one moves to curves further from the origin. Thus our imputation is unavoidable on his premise.

[19] Or, as Edgeworth would put it, "nuclei of the just-perceivable, embedded in circumambient semi-consciousness."

[20] With that amendment (i.e., termini at the two ends of the indifference curve) we have, in fact, another possible form of representation. For then, if we invert the curve of one want on the other and ignore discontinuity, we have the pattern shown in Fig.

ments Hicks's scheme seems to be the least objectionable form to which marginal utility analysis can be reduced.[21]

By way of summary, let us now appraise this final form as a representation of subjective valuation.

a. It eliminates measurable (units of) utility or its criterion and assumes no more comparability of such magnitudes than observation warrants.

b. It does not require the determination of equal quantities of incommensurable means, for it proceeds from the basis of subjective equivalence rather than of objective equality.

c. Pareto's (and others') form returns to a one-dimensional representation of total utility or pleasure by means of the altitude of the indifference curve. Thus this magnitude is left unanalyzed as to its dimensions. At least, it does not need to be a rate. It is purely an assumption, justified by observation, and could be used to represent any basis for comparability. However, except when it is identified as pleasure, it is also unanalyzed as to its static or dynamic nature.[22]

d. The acceptance of discontinuity, difficult to represent, gets rid of the difficulty of minimum measurable or judgable magnitudes (i.e., infinitesimals or even the more modern limiting rate).[23]

---

55. All combinations of quantities have equal utility, shown along *ac*. As the quantity of A is increased along *bd* its contribution of total utility increases; as that of B is increased along *ca* its contribution of total utility increases. But, unless we know the changing rate of (marginal) utility, we cannot know how far the rate diminishes with increasing quantity and therefore whether the contribution of A reaches c_2 or c_1, for instance. Nor can we lay out on *bd* and *ca* the increments of the two means; for, in the first place, each equal section would represent a different quantity of each means; and, in the second place, that would require that we know what proportion of utility was contributed by each of the two opposite numbers of a pair of increments. Nevertheless, even with these limitations, such a figure does illustrate the concept of complementarity (in the mathematical sense) in a uniform total.

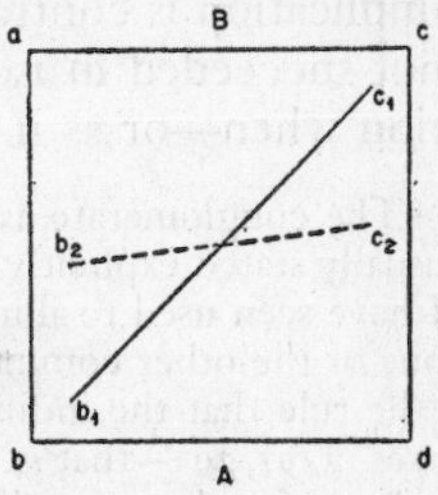

FIG. 55

[21] The most highly embroidered elaborations of Pareto's scheme use the third dimension to represent a third commodity, thus converting the indifference curve into an indifference surface, and even carry this on up to any number (*n*) of non-Euclidean dimensions among which, presumably, indifference is represented as a Riemannian manifold of n^{-1} dimensions. Since the application is the same to many as to two commodities, and since our questions concern the foundations and not the superstructures of these schemes, it is unnecessary to explore their intricacies.

[22] In general, it is for this reason that we cannot determine in any of these presentations how much to impute of the conglomerate assumption described on pp. 437 ff. Are these quantities of means within the limit of those required for single satisfactions, or do they include sufficient for alternative uses and future provision? We do not know. And, since Hicks even avoids reference to pleasure, or any other criterion for significance, we cannot, with him, even guess (see f, below).

[23] So far as metrics is concerned the conversion of infinitesimals into terms of limiting rates is pure evasion of the issue. The issue is how large the magnitude must become on its way up from zero before it will itself become actually measureable in the real world. For what we have to assume is that the subject is acting on the basis of his measurement, or at least his judgment of magnitudes.

e. The perpendicular phase or reverse in the curve corrects the most obvious error introduced by the absence of a limitation on substitutability due to satiation. It covers only such a limitation between two different wants. For substitutes for a single want, the curve would have to end at the other axis, since, then, no more of either means would be wanted. The other limit set by satiation is represented either by the summit of the curved surface or by an asymptotic finale (see p. 1325, note 7, above).

f. The scheme continues and requires the hypothesis of declining intensity during satisfaction—that is, it does so in so far as supplies are conceived to apply to a single satisfaction only. As we have noted in Chapter 7, a decline in estimation with increasing quantity must either be due to decline during one use or during successive uses (alternative uses or future wants). These other possibilities are never given as the reason for the assumption; and, in any case, it is fair to require that the scheme should be applicable to cases where they do not come into play. Therefore, it must stand or fall according as the reality of that assumption is proved or disproved.[24]

g. All forms of this scheme are indeterminate.[25] That is, at the highest indifference curve within the limit of capacity, the consumer, unless "terms of trade" are given, would be unable to make up his mind which assortment lying on that curve he would choose. It must be clear that this implication is contrary to the facts. If so, it follows that this approach has not succeeded in isolating the influence leading to pure subjective valuation when—or as if—untrammeled by interfering factors.[26]

[24] The conglomerate assumption of declining significance with increasing quantities is usually stated explicitly. But it is not analyzed into its parts. It is implicit in all examples I have seen used to illustrate the series of indifference—that is, it is necessarily true of one or the other commodity, if not of both. Hicks discusses it. In his hands it becomes "the rule that the indifference curves must be convex [concave, in our terms] to the axes" (*195*, 20)—that is, that the marginal rate of substitution is a diminishing one (*ibid.*, 20); or, for the generality of goods, that "the marginal rate of substitution must diminish for substitutes in every direction" (*ibid.*, 25). "We need the principle," for, otherwise, equilibrium will not be stable (*ibid.*, 21). But, then, he only concedes that the assumption must sometimes be true and agrees that a principle should be more than sometimes true (*ibid.*, 22). Thus, while his analysis depends on it (except, of course, for complementary goods; *ibid.*, 14) his intellectual honesty is such that he is unwilling to assume it as a proven generalization.

[25] But only Pareto admitted the fact frankly when he admitted that there were a near infinite number of "*sentiers*" leading from any point on one indifference curve to the next higher one (see p. 1325). While Edgeworth admitted only one perpendicular "*sentier*," it is clear that this was pure fallacy, since, thereafter, there would be a near infinite number of positions which could be taken on the indifference curve reached. Why not go to any of them direct?

[26] The basic, though tacit, assumption of the indifference curve technique is that consumers' preferences, standing by themselves, prescribe no definite quantities of specific means within any limit on total means—presumably less than one capable of permitting the satiation of all wants. Instead, there is a near infinite number of combinations of quantities which are indifferent (on the same curve) so that if the consumer were unconstrained except for being allowed but one choice among all and if all were available

Nevertheless, let us explore further into the possibilities of this approach, which has gone so far to correct the internal errors and external misapprehensions of earlier formulations, in order to see whether or not, by means of the technique of actually comparable quantities of pleasure, we may arrive at determinate conclusions as to what the behavior of pure, uncontaminated, and final demand would be if pleasure were the criterion of choice. For that purpose we will eliminate the admitted or tacit assumptions as to "terms of trade" or restricted quantities of particular means and, instead, will make the only assumption that we have a right to make at this stage of our analysis, namely that such quantities of every means as will yield equal pleasure are available on equal terms, and that the only limitation is on total means.[27] Implicit in Pareto's table of bread and wine, above, are the equivalences between certain increments (or decrements) of each, which can be inferred from the explicit equivalence between whole assortments.[28] If we state each increment in terms of 0.1 kg. it will be noted that the following table also represents equality in terms of equal pleasure:

---

on equal terms, his decision would have to be made by tossing a coin. Our first hypothesis identifies the means that is chosen at each stage. We claim that, on these same terms, if 1.2 kg. of bread will satiate hunger and if hunger precedes the want for wine in the order of priority, the consumer will choose the second assortment in Pareto's series (see p. 1326).

[27] We have been assuming right along that there must be some limit to the capacity to satisfy wants in general. Otherwise we would not be studying the subject.

It is worth while to point out what we are doing here. We are going back to Gossen, literally interpreted. As Jevons points out (*224*, XXXIV), Gossen assumed as a goal that the final increments of all pleasure-giving commodities should be of equal utility. Jevons does not limit himself to that (see *ibid.*, 95 ff.). Instead, he adumbrates what Schultz (*363*, 97) calls "the classic formula which states that at equilibrium the individual distributes his expenditure in such a way that a dollar's worth of any commodity yields the same utility as a dollar's worth of any other commodity." See also Fisher "Mathematical Investigations in the Theory of Value and Price" (9 *Trans. Conn. Acad. of Arts and Sciences* 1893), Wicksteed (*441*) and many others. This is implicit in Hicks's formulation and in all those based on his. Choices do not arrive at the goal of any quantity of each means which has equal marginal significance, but at that where the quantities of all means show marginal significance in the same ratio as the ratio of their costs.

This contrast discloses clearly the contrapuntal *leit-motif* that runs through most of the older marginal utility theory and of which one voice has persisted into the newest forms. It runs like this:

Given definite combinations of quantities, the relative prices of two or more means are determined by subjective valuation. The slope of the curves of utility determine the relative heights on the altitudes to which these quantities will reach.

Given definite relative prices, the combination of quantities is determined by subjective valuation. The slope of the curves of utility determine the relative distances along the bases which conform to this ratio.

If both these "givens" are excluded, the effect of the utility curves alone—or of indifference curves which imply them—becomes indeterminate. Does that represent reality?

[28] This is, in effect, stating the relation in terms of Hicks's (*196*) concept of "marginal rate of substitution."

8th increment of wine = 15th + 16th increment of bread
9th increment of wine = 13th + 14th increment of bread
10th increment of wine = 11th + 12th increment of bread
11th + 12th + 13th + 14th increment of wine
= 9th + 10th increment of bread
15th + 16th + 17th + 18th increment of wine
= 7th + 8th increment of bread

This suggests a different line of approach—one in terms of increments. If it is possible to determine various combinations of quantities of two or more means which are indifferent, it must be equally possible to determine quantities of each of two or more means which are indifferent. Let us assume that a person has at present no stock of either bread or wine, that he has completely unsatisfied wants for both, and that he has available—for the sake of the example—successive increments of his total capacity of providing means, which increments he can apply to these two wants as he chooses, without extrinsic constraint as to terms of choice. For the initial application it is obvious that there must be some small initial quantity of wine which will yield equal pleasure to some small initial quantity of bread.[29] If, now, we suppose, in accordance with the assumption of declining intensity, that the second quantities of bread and of wine, objectively equal to the first, do not yield as much pleasure as the first—that is, that the quantity of pleasure per successive objective unit of each means declines—the only competition for the first choice will be between the subjectively equal initial quantities of the two means. How, then, can the person choose between them? Since they yield equal pleasure, the natural choice would be to take out his first increment of capacity in half this quantity of each (or, for the sake of simplifying the example, his first two increments in such a quantity of each). Now let us suppose, again for the sake of simplicity, that these initial quantities which are subjectively equal, are measured objectively as 0.1 of a kilogram of bread and 0.2 of a liter of wine.[30] On two curves (Fig. 56), let the subjective unit, along the x axis of B, represent 0.1 kg. of bread and the subjectively equivalent unit (shown, of course, as of the same length on the x axis), along the x axis of W, represent 0.2 l. of wine. The corresponding amounts of pleasure,

[29] These quantities should be defined as the smallest that can be judged equal within a reasonable margin of error. They are the smallest, the subjective difference between which is less than the *minimum sensibile*, while, at the same time, the undetectable error will not constitute too large a proportion of the recognized pleasure. That is a tall order.

[30] We are changing Pareto's unit of wine in order to make our point that, here, it makes no difference whether magnitudes are objectively commensurable in one or another of their common dimensions.

The determination of these subjective units raises a difficulty. Again, at least theoretically, they must be large enough so that the margin of error in their equivalence (the *minimum sensibile*) is not great; on the other hand, they must be small enough so that the difference between their respective rates of diminution of pleasure within the units is not an important factor. So long as there is such a diminution, the person will necessarily derive more pleasure from half the quantity of each than from the whole quantity of either. But this would probably have to be inferred.

shown as the first areas on the respective curves, are then by definition, equal. Therefore, they must also have the same altitude—the bases being equal. If now the successive increments of total means may be employed to obtain one subjective unit of either of these means, the first two increments will be divided between the two wants, as above. Then, as to each, the segments marked 1–2 indicate the sum of half of each of these first two increments. But now let us suppose that, in terms of these subjective units, the rate of decline in pleasure derived is, in the case of bread, only half what it is for wine. In that event the person is faced with a choice

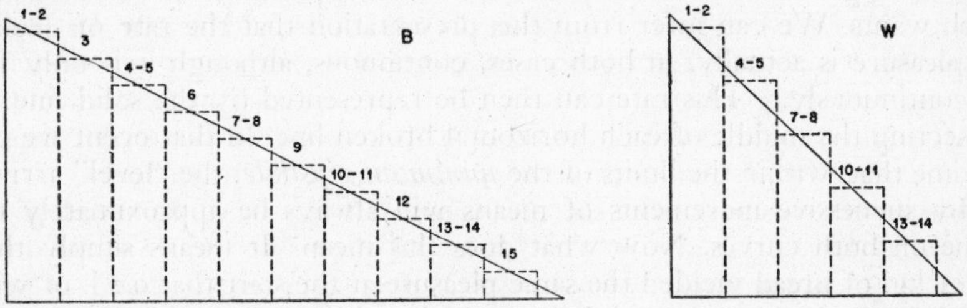

FIG. 56

as to the basis on which he is to proceed from there. He might repeat the original process and thus increase the quantity of wine in the next subjective unit in order to counterbalance its greater rate of decline in pleasure. Or he might continue to compare the two means in terms of the original subjective units. If he should adopt the first procedure it would lead him to absurd results.[31] We shall therefore assume that he will adopt

[31] There are three reasons against the first alternative, of which only the last is the *reductio ad absurdum.*

1. By choosing the first course, he would be using up total means faster than by choosing the second. If there is any reason for economizing on total means because of limitations of capacity, such a reason would be opposed to this course.

2. The first course would require a redetermination of objective quantities of the two means that were subjectively equal at each step. This would be an almost impossible complication in planning for future provision.

3. The first course would lead to the more nearly complete satisfaction of a want the more rapid the decline in the rate of pleasure; for, then, more of its means would be required to compose a subjective unit. Since, as we shall see, pleasure per original subjective unit must decline more rapidly the less pleasure is derived from the total satisfaction of a want—that is the "smaller" the want—the result would be to satisfy many "small" wants completely and leave all the "large" ones only partially satisfied.

It will be noted that Edgeworth's, Pareto's and Hicks's assumption of unlimited substitutability is an expression of the first course—i.e., the supposition that there will always be, throughout the process, some quantity of wine that will yield equal pleasure to that yielded by a quantity of bread—say the original subjective unit. They import extraneous influences to avoid the carrying of this substitutability to the above absurd conclusion. Our three reasons, above, of which only one is extraneous, are opposed to this assumption. And our own assumption that the second course will be chosen restricts the range of substitutability to certain steps in the process. This, in itself, seems to add weight to the argument for our assumption, for it seems to accord better with reality.

the second and follow it thereafter. On that basis, since, if the next increment is applied to an original subjective unit of bread, it will yield more pleasure than if applied to an original subjective unit of wine, the choice is clear-cut. The third increment will therefore go entirely for bread. On the other hand, for the fourth and fifth increments the pleasure to be derived is again equal. Therefore these two will again be divided as were the first two. And so on down.

It will be noted that, at each stage in the expansion of means, the application has been such that the amount of pleasure per subjective unit is, at the margin between the last and the next, approximately the same for both wants. We can infer from this presentation that the rate of decline of pleasure is actually, in both cases, continuous, although it is only felt discontinuously.[32] This rate can then be represented by the solid line intersecting the middle of each horizontal broken line. In that event we can assume that, within the limits of the *minimum sensibile*, the "level" arrived at by successive increments of means will always be approximately the same on both curves. Now what does this mean? It means simply that, if 0.1 kg. of bread yielded the same pleasure at the start that 0.2 l. of wine yielded—so that, in terms of their respective objective units, B:W = 2:1—total capacity would be apportioned throughout so that this ratio of equivalence would always continue approximately to hold good at the successive margins. It also means that, giving effect to the continuous curve, at every stage in the increase of total means applied, in terms of subjective units, two thirds of this total would have been applied to bread and one third to wine; and this for the simple reason that the rate of decline of pleasure per original subjective unit is, in the case of bread, only half that of wine. The demander, as he proceeds, will always tend toward choosing twice as many subjective units of bread as of wine, for any other choice would yield less pleasure; and thus he will always keep the amount of pleasure to be derived from the marginal increment of bread as nearly as possible equal to that to be derived from the marginal increment of wine. But, since, a subjective unit of wine happens to be, in this example, two tenths of an objective unit, while one of bread is one tenth of an objective unit, the total numerical value of each, in terms of its objective unit, will, in this example, always be about the same.

Thus, in the absence of any extraneous terms of choice, we conclude that the correct analysis of the influence of amount of pleasure on subjective valuation proves that objective units of every means will be valued subjectively, at the beginning of the process of satisfaction, in inverse ratio to the number required for a subjective unit which will produce an equal amount of pleasure to that produced by a corresponding subjective unit

[32] Here develops a further difficulty as to the magnitude of the subjective units. If we can only just recognize, as to each means, the difference between the amount of pleasure derived from the first subjective unit alone and the amount derived from the first and second combined, we would not be able to detect the difference, if any, between the amounts of pleasure to be derived from the two members of a pair of increments of different means. Wicksteed overlooks this (*441*, *56*).

of the chosen means for every other want; that this basic subjective unit will not be changed during satisfactions, however different may be the rate at which pleasure declines per unit for different means or wants; and that the only effect of such different rates of decline—or of any other differences between the two curves or means—will be to lead to preferences at subsequent stages of the process, tending to keep the rate of pleasure per subjective unit about equal for all and thus to take itself out in determining the ratios between the objective quantities of respective means which will have been chosen up to any point.[33]

This scheme is the result of many experiments. I have come to the conclusion that it represents the only determinate one that can be derived from the various formulations of indifference and preference that have been put forward by way of salvaging something from the older and exploded types of marginal utility theory. This scheme accepts all the assumptions, conditions, and limitations set by these various formulations except that it excludes any extraneous factor. Like those of Edgeworth and Pareto and their final development by Hicks, it does not require the measurement of pleasure, or of any other psychological entity, but only the ability to compare quantities of pleasure, or other things, in terms of more or less and of approximate equality; but, unlike them, it is determinate when isolated and it does not permit the notion of unlimited substitutability among all the means for satisfying all wants; all it permits and requires is the notion of strictly limited parity, at some times, and of sensible disparities, at others, in a series of unconstrained choices.[34]

[33] By a further inference from the foregoing we might construct a pair of curves for bread and wine in the usual form. In these we could indicate the objective units of each by abscissae which are of equal size on the two curves, as in Fig. 57. Since the satisfactions shown in Fig. 56 required 10 subjective units (0.1 kg. each) of bread and 5 subjective units (0.2 l. each) of wine, they are represented here as 10 objective units (kg. or l.) of each. It then becomes necessary to show the total pleasure per 0.1 kg. of bread as double that of 0.1 l. of wine (since subjective equivalence is $\frac{B}{W}=\frac{2}{1}$). Thus the ordinates on B are shown as if twice the altitude of those of W. But this method of representation is too apt to lead us to a further inference which would be entirely fallacious—namely, that, since all of the first five objective units of B yielded more pleasure per unit than even the first objective unit of W, therefore the demander would make his first five choices of B and only divide the sixth. And this because we have tacitly—or unconsciously—substituted objective for subjective units, as the terms of choice, without the slightest warrant for doing so. He would still, as before, make his first choice half the first unit of bread and the whole first unit of wine, which, on these terms, yield more pleasure than any others of either.

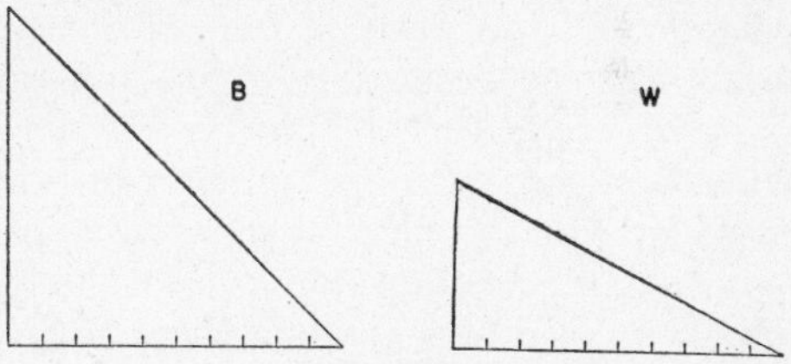

Fig. 57

[34] Parity is here distinguished from substitutability. Both are chosen when there is parity. Parity is the least that must be admitted as a condition if one introduces the assumption of declining intensity.

By means of this detailed analysis of the various original forms of marginal utility theory we have, in my judgment, arrived at two important results. We have, in the first place, demonstrated the mathematical impossibility of various of the older formulations and, in the case of Jevons (and Walras), how preposterous his psychological assumptions really were. But, in the second place, we have derived an analysis from Menger which seems to be consistent with his conclusions, if not with his presentation, and which, when some definite basis for its quantitative relationship to means is discovered, will permit us to use the static magnitude, remaining intensity, as the criterion for our second virtual order of preference in a way that supplements and complements the others. In the third place, we have also developed an analysis in terms of pleasure or desire for pleasure (or any other dynamic magnitude with the same characteristics) which is entirely consistent with the overt assumptions of the latest developments of marginal utility theory and yet arrives at results quite different from theirs. Since this method of treatment of pleasure, etc., avoids the difficulty we will find, in the text, of treating our third criterion, reduction of intensity per unit of means, as a basis, we will use it in a modification of that criterion which will serve for our third virtual order of preference.

V

WORK SHEETS ON RETAINING

Appendix to Chapter 10

A. TIME PERSPECTIVE AND DISCOUNTING THE FUTURE

During the many years in which this study has been in process my explorations have led me up a number of blind alleys. Of these perhaps none has proved so troublesome as the presupposition with which I started that the influence of futurity consists of a diminution in the present force of future wants in proportion to the futurity of their instances. Nor has the escape from any other blind alley, once I discovered that it led nowhere, turned out to be so baffling.[1] Perhaps the presupposition was, in whole or in part, one of my own construction; but I suspect that it was largely derived from the implications of economic theory—particularly the theory of interest in its more recent developments. However, it is not necessary to discover the precise source, and it is certainly not worth while to review the literature in order to determine how far my own illusion corresponded to that of others.[2] One thing only does seem to be worth while. It may save the time of other future explorers if I describe briefly what it was that I supposed—whether that was orthodox or heterodox—and then demonstrate the reasons which appear to make that supposition quite untenable.

[1] The first draft of this part of the present study was based on this presupposition and presented it as a fully developed scheme. It was not until then that I discovered its internal difficulties and its inconsistencies with the rest of the work. That necessitated a restudy of the whole subject of future wants—now presented in Chapters 5 and 6—and only that made it possible to work out, without any preconceived idea, the precise ways in which the influence of futurity must work if it is to account for the observed facts.

[2] Definite statements about the more recently current views in economics with regard to the influence of futurity are difficult if not impossible to make. This because the customary concept of a discount on "future goods" or an agio on "present goods" does not definitely ascribe this effect to any source that fits a scheme of energetics. Nevertheless, it is safe to say that those who hold that the "significance" of such goods depends on any of the criteria of marginal utility theory, as discussed in Chapter 8, imply that the particular criterion, when derived from a future want, is weaker than when derived from a present want or even than when derived from what we are calling a current want. If so, it follows that the influence of futurity is imputed to a decreasing force of the future want according to futurity and not to an increasing resistance to the present provision according to futurity.

1. THE TWO POSSIBLE PERSPECTIVES

The notion of a time perspective appears frequently in the older literature of introspective psychology. Therefore, it has probably been in the background of the thinking of many economists. It represents in visualized form the general hypothesis that future wants, as they appear or as they exert their influence in the present, do so in diminishing "size" or strength in proportion as their respective degrees of futurity increase. Since, according to all forms of subjective value theory, it is the want which gives significance to the means, it follows that the significance of each future provision, in series, for a single want is thus conceived to contract in the same proportion as the "size" or strength of the particular instance of the want contracts. Parity, or the maximum for both, is the "size" or strength of the current want and of the current provision—that is, the want or provision associated with the following consuming-day. For our purposes we may define the time element of this perspective as the rate at which the "size" diminishes as futurity increases. Thus the horizon—or the vanishing point—of the perspective is the point at which the "size" is zero. One does not see, or foresee, beyond that point.

On the analogy of visual perspective and for the sake of simplicity, let us assume that the rate of diminution is constant—a uniform quantity of shrinkage per time interval—and is therefore to be represented as a straight line. This permits two different suppositions as to the effect of perspective, if we do not follow the analogy of visual perspective too closely. If the system of time perspectives for all the different wants is conceived to be a series of parallel straight lines, then the horizon for each want would be nearer according as its current "size" is smaller. If this is correct, then the absolute quantity of shrinkage would remain exactly the same as we proceeded along the order of priority of wants. A long or short perspective, in general, would then have to be stated with reference always to the horizon of the prior want—those of the others being assumed to be dependent on or related to that. Diagrammatically, the length of perspective would be shown by the uniform obliquity of each of the lines representing the successive diminutions of "size" to zero (see Fig. 58, I).[3] On the other hand, if the system of time perspectives for all wants is conceived as a series of converging straight lines with a common horizon, the absolute quantity of shrinkage becomes less as we proceed along the order of priority of wants. It is then the percentage of decline per time interval that is the same for all. A long or short perspective would be stated with reference to the common horizon of all wants. Diagrammatically, the different obliquity of the lines representing the successive diminutions of "size" to zero would show the different effect of this horizon on the several wants

[3] The length of perspective as shown here is, of course, absurdly short, on account of the exigencies of representation in a diagram. As a matter of observation we should conclude that the length of perspective may run centuries into the future in economies which have, and expect a continuance of, social security.

(see Fig. 58, II). Under the first supposition the dimensional formula of the effect of time perspective would be IT^{-1}, while under the second it would be IKT^{-1}, where I represents the dimension, intensity of want.

The limitation of futurity is reached before the horizon is reached. It comes at the point where the future want, in the process of shrinking from its current "size," is no longer strong enough to overcome the resistance offered by working effort now to the making of such provision. The two

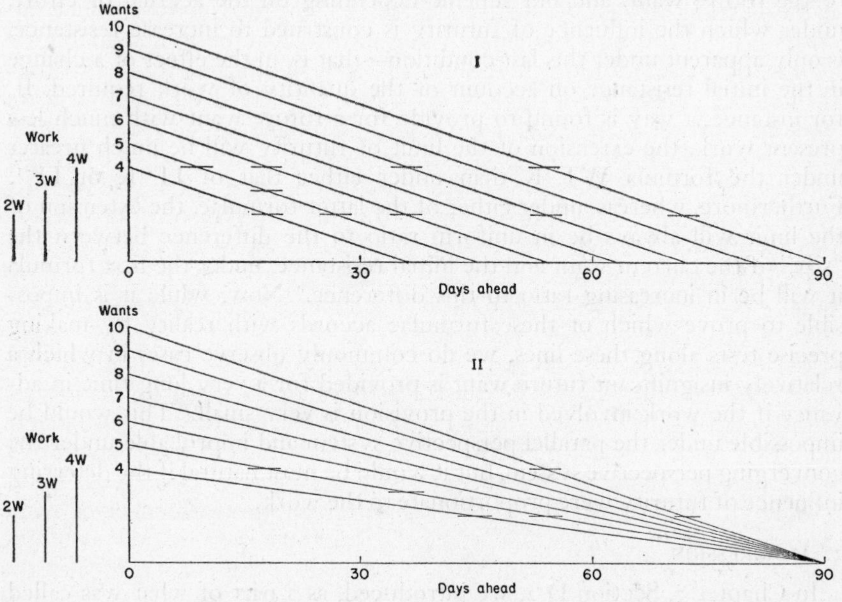

Fig. 58

forms of perspective would work differently in this respect. Giving effect only to the excess of "size" over resistance, the converging system of perspectives would tend to extend the limitation for those wants whose current "size" is small far further than the ratio of their current "size" to that of major wants would warrant. Conversely, the parallel system would evince a tendency for minor wants to drop out much earlier along the time-scale than under the converging system. In other words, the parallel system would tend to concentrate future provision on major wants to a much greater extent than would the converging system.[4]

[4] Let us, for instance and solely for the purpose of illustration, give numerical values to the quantities shown in Fig. 58. The current values of the several current wants range from 4 to 10. The resistances of the two alternative provisions are 4 and 2, respectively (4w and 2w). The time factor is shown along the base up to 90 days ahead. Under the parallel system, for resistance amounting to 2, the limit for Want 4 will run to 18 days, while that for Want 10 will run for 72 days. That is, $10 - 2 = 8$, $4 - 2 = 2$, and $8:2 = 72:18$. Limits are proportional to excess strength. Under the converging system, the limit for Want 4 will run to 45 days, while that for Want 10 will be the same as

However, the effect of diminution of resistance now—that is, an economizing in the working effort involved in the provision—would be the same under either of these systems of perspective. For instance, cutting this "real cost" in half would place the limitation further off by the same proportion for both, though not by the same amount.[5]

The critical difference between both these systems of time perspective, under which the influence of futurity is construed to diminish the force of the future want, and our scheme depending on the accrual of effort, under which the influence of futurity is construed to increase resistance, is only apparent under this last condition—that is, in the effect of a change in the initial resistance on account of the quantity of work required. If, for instance, a way is found to provide for a future want with much less present work, the extension of the limit of futurity will be much greater under the formula $WT^{-1}K$ than under either that of $IT^{-1}K$ or IT^{-1}. Furthermore, whereas, under either of the latter formulae, the extension of the limit will always be in uniform ratio to the difference between the "size" of the current want and the initial resistance, under the first formula it will be in increasing ratio to this difference.[6] Now, while it is impossible to prove which of these formulae accords with reality by making precise tests along these lines, we do commonly observe cases in which a relatively insignificant future want is provided for a very long time in advance if the work involved in the provision is very small.[7] This would be impossible under the parallel perspective system and improbable under the converging perspective system, but it would be most natural if the deterring influence of futurity were proportionate to the work.

2. A DIGRESSION

In Chapter 7, Section D 2, we introduced, as a part of what was called the "conglomerate" assumption of marginal utility theory, assumption (c)

---

before, 72 days. Then, though the excess strengths are in the same ratio, 4 to 1, the limits are in the ratio of only 1.6 to 1.

[5] That is, under the conditions recited in the previous note, a decrease of resistance from 4 to 2 would extend the limit 33⅓% for Want 10, that for Want 8 by 50% and that for Want 6 by 100%, under either system of perspectives.

[6] Using the numerical values of the previous notes, when the provision for Want 5 can be obtained for a resistance of 3 or 2 instead of 4, the limit will be extended to twice or three times what it was, under either system of time perspectives. That is, in either case, when the ratio of force over resistance is 1:2:3, the limit will be extended in the same proportion, 1:2:3 (from 30 to 60 or 90 days, and from 60 to 120 or 180 days respectively). But on the accrual of resistance basis for the influence of futurity, since the rate of accrual declines as the initial resistance declines, the extension of the limit is in increasing ratio. For Want 5 at an initial resistance of 4 the limit will be 36 days; at a resistance of 3 it will be 100 days; at one of 2 it will be 225 days. That is, the ratio of force over resistance of 1:2:3 produces extensions of the limit in the ratio of 1:3 −:6 +.

[7] Though the want served by a cudgel may now have come to be of slight importance even to an Irishman, nevertheless, because oak or blackthorn saplings are handy and the work of shaping them easy, he may still find it worth while to cut and carve a shillelagh and thus make himself a lifetime's provision for this want.

to the effect "that provisions for instances of future wants have less significance in proportion to, or as a result of, increasing degree of futurity." We now recognize that this assumption corresponds to the notion of time perspective with which we are dealing here, whether or not it includes the visual analogy. It is hardly necessary to attempt to describe the effect of applying the descending series implied in such a time perspective to either form of descending series involved in our second and third hypotheses as to the virtual order of preference. Both these are based on the supposition of declining intensity during a single satisfaction. Thus both divide a full measure or adequate provision of means into several or many parts—subjective units—each of which has less significance than the previous one. In turn, the time perspective would produce a series descending, in a third dimension, from each of these subjective units. The resulting scheme is too complex to permit of representation. Suffice it to say that the result would be, not a series of equivalent adequate provisions for different wants whose position along the time-scale was governed by the differing effect of the time perspective on the several wants, but a mass of equivalent subjective units, whose position along the time-scale was determined in the same way, but whose position in each order of preference included in the time-scale was determined in accordance with one or the other of the schemes presented at the end of Chapter 8.[8] If the complexity resulting from this compounding of the two kinds of descending series makes representation practically impossible, is it advisable to impute such a scheme as the basis of human motivation?

3. THE ANALOGY OF PERSPECTIVE

The term and concept of a time perspective may be no more than a picturesque simile adopted because there seemed to be a certain similarity between the objective datum that objects appear smaller than they are in proportion to their distance from us and the supposed conscious and subjective phenomenon that wants and efforts are less vivid or intense in proportion to their degree of futurity.[9] Nevertheless, it is useful to explore the analogy further; for an analysis of visual perspective will serve to ex-

[8] That is, diagrammatically, equivalent whole future provisions for the several wants would be shown as cut by a line parallel to the base in Fig. 58 (either I or II). But equivalent subjective units would have to be shown as cut by a plane parallel to the base in an elaboration of Fig. 58 which included a third dimension to show the declining significance of each series of subjective units making up one full measure. Even this would only be adequate representation if the two-dimensional form of representation that we used at the end of Chapter 8 is retained. There, the successive subjective units making up a full measure for each of the several wants were represented as overlapping (i.e., in a single plane). If that were converted into the more adequate form of three-dimensional representation, this would become four-dimensional.

[9] It may be related, however, to the metaphor, the "mind's eye." Those memories which are revived from the optical sensorium naturally take the form of vision. Visual memories are the most frequent; or so Hughlings Jackson supposed. Hence all memories may have been thought of in terms of their commonest manner of manifestation in consciousness.

pose the fallacy of accepting the notion of a time perspective as a factor.

As a matter of fact, we all recognize, after a certain amount of experience, that visual perspective is an optical illusion. That is, we come soon to know that objects at a distance may be, when we are there, as large as those that are now near us, here. As a result, we begin to act on that knowledge, are no longer deceived by the illusion and, in fact, come to convert it to the use of judging distance rather than size. Correspondingly, if it is true that hunger thirty days from now is presented to us with less vividness than hunger tonight, it seems impossible to suppose that we should not soon learn that, when that day arrives, the hunger will be of equal intensity. Would that not lead to our acting on the basis of the knowledge rather than the illusion? Would we not then use the time perspective merely for purposes of judging the date of the want and not its force?

Or, to approach the question in another way, let us suppose that we are moving along a single dimension in space just as we conceive ourselves to be moving along the single dimension of time.[10] As we move in space, objects at a distance grow continuously larger. Yet we are not deceived; we construe that to mean that they are becoming nearer. On the other hand, if we are to assume that we continue to act on the illusion that a future want is smaller, rather than on the knowledge that it will be equal to the current one when it itself becomes current, a strange corollary follows. Then, since the significance of any provision is supposed to be conferred upon it by the force of the want for which it is made, and since, in this case, the force of the future want would be contracted by its futurity, the significance of the provision now would be correspondingly small. But, as the date of the want approached, the want would grow in force and, as a result, the significance of the provision would increase. Thus there would occur a gradual and regular accretion in the subjective value of the provision as the time approached when it was to be used. Again it would be necessary to suppose that man is innocent of any appreciation of this process—this almost infallible form of speculation—that he does not know that his provision now will certainly be worth more to him then. For, if he did, he would discount the discount; he would act on that knowledge; the provision would have its eventual subjective value to him from the beginning.

If, obstinately, we choose to maintain our position that man is so "dumb" that he is blind to this supposed accretion of subjective value, we would have to conclude that it is a mere gratuity which is not required to overcome any resistances and is not even considered in formulating programs —that, at the end of the period of incubation, when the future has become the present and this accretion of subjective value is "realized," it constitutes a pleasant surprise due to lack of intelligence—of the order of a special compensation for one's deficiencies which is unusual in nature.

In spite of this seeming *reductio ad absurdum* it may be advisable to clinch the argument with a demonstration of the different results that would follow

[10] Perhaps the analogy would be better if we supposed the distance to be approaching us while we stood still; for that is the commonest viewpoint of the movement of time.

if the illusion, or time perspective, were the governing influence, or if the experience of accretion of subjective value determined the program; and, finally, to exhibit the quandary that would be the result of a combination of the two influences. In Fig. 59 we take our stand in the present. Using the parallel system of time perspectives for the sake of simplicity in representation,[11] we see that the instance of Want A set 90 days ahead is just sufficient to warrant the present quantity of work, W—since, at that point, it intersects the broken line projected from W—and will therefore induce provision now. On our simplified assumption that the work involved in one day's provision is the same for all wants, Want B will induce a provision for

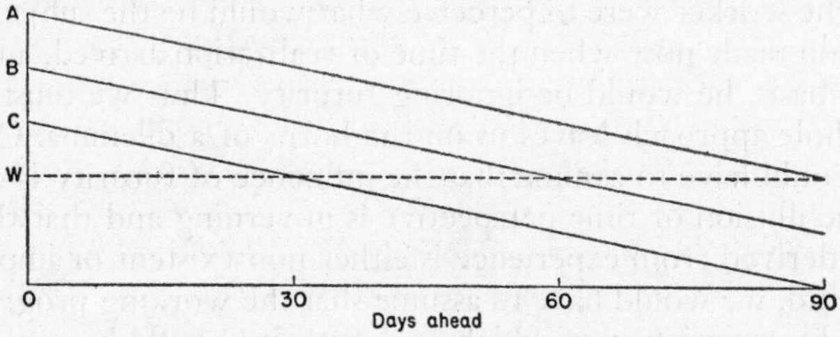

Fig. 59

60 days ahead, and Want C will induce one for 30 days ahead. The time perspective would then lead to placing the same present subjective value on all these provisions, since the discount on the future would have reduced the instance of Want A at 90 days to that of B at 60 days and that of C at 30 days, while all would just equal W now. That is, A:B:C:W = 1:1:1:1. Ignoring other factors, three hours of present work would be evenly distributed among these three provisions, for no one offers an advantage over the others. Now let time pass. At the end of 30 days the provision for Want C would have become current with a subjective value shown by the altitude to C on the scale; at the end of 60 days the provision for B would reach B on the scale; and at the end of 90 days the provision for A would reach A. Therefore, at the several times of realization, these three provisions would have attained a subjective value ratio of A:B:C:W = 5:4:3:2 (in this diagram). Imagine the worker's pleased surprise to discover his unexpected profit or, perhaps, his dismay that he had not had the sense to devote all three hours of work to provision for Want A, since that has yielded the largest profit.

Now for the quandary which would arise if both the illusion and the experience were to play their parts. A provision for C at 28 days would loom larger in the present than one for B at 60 days or one for A at 92 days. On that basis there would be no question as to choice. One hour's work would go for C. But then past experience might suggest that, in the end, the order of subjective value would be reversed, A being largest, B next, and C the smallest. How would this choice be determined? Would our worker not

[11] The results are similar, though less extreme if converging time perspectives are used.

be in the position of a thirsty wayfarer in the desert who sees the oasis and its spring in a mirage to the east, while his past experience with the landmarks and the trails tells him that it is to the west?

All this makes it seem unlikely that the illusion of perspective could ever gain the upper hand over the actual results of experience, once the latter had been acquired. However, we must recognize clearly where such a conclusion would lead us. The notion of time perspective is one way of accounting for the influence of futurity in setting a limitation on provision for future wants. That influence is one that we have inferred from observation. Something sets such a limit. But the alternative here, the actual results of experience, does not account for this influence of futurity. In fact, it eliminates it. If the worker were to perceive what would be the subjective value of a provision made now when the time of realization arrived, and were to act on that basis, he would be ignoring futurity. Thus we must conclude that this whole approach leaves us on the horns of a dilemma. On the one hand, we would have to assume that the influence of futurity is due to the fact that the illusion of time perspective is governing and that the knowledge to be derived from experience is either non-existent or impotent. On the other hand, we would have to assume that the working program would be directed by experience; in which case, futurity would have no influence whatever. The first alternative seems highly improbable in the face of the fact that the future want system is a product of experience; the second seems equally improbable since it denies the observed influence of futurity.

It was this inescapable dilemma that finally convinced me that the whole supposition of a time perspective or of an automatic time discount is untenable. That led to the exploration of the problem of conscious memory and time which is now set forth in Chapter 5, Section B 4. As the reader will recall, we found it impossible to believe that memories of the past, when projected against the flat curtain of the counterfeit future, should suffer any loss of vividness or intensity by reason merely of the futurity of the date along a purely conceptual time-scale to which they were arbitrarily assigned. Since even real pastness itself does not determine the vividness or intensity of memories, how could imaginary futurity do so? Moreover, the imaginary futurity arbitrarily assigned corresponds in no regular way to the actual pastness. These conclusions, in turn, led to a wholly different approach to the problem of assigning some cause, however inferential, to the observed influence of futurity. Out of that new approach developed the concept that retaining involves effort of a character similar to and associated with the effort involved in working; that the experience of this effort over time establishes memories; and that these memories furnish resistance, in part proportionate to time, and opposed to the force exerted by the memories of wants (future wants). In other words, it was these successive analyses that proved to me that the influence of futurity in limiting provision for future wants is through a supplement to the initial resistance and not at all through the diminution of the present force of the future wants.

B. THE "ACQUISITIVE INSTINCT"

In all the literature of the "instincts"—in itself no credit to the scientific fraternity and coming now, quite generally, to be repudiated—there is perhaps no more "awful example" than the notion of an "acquisitive instinct," so-called. It represents an aberration carried to an absurdity. We may cite two examples. In the section on "Appropriation or Acquisitiveness" in his chapter on "Instincts" (*220*, II, 422–425), William James lumps together the "proprietary instinct," or "impulse to own," with the "hoarding" or "collecting instinct." The evidence is almost wholly confined to infantile and abnormal examples. William McDougall carries this identification to an extreme. He says (*284*, 330) that "acquisitiveness . . . remains probably the most fundamental" of the complex of motives leading to the acquisition of capital. "While, in the course of satisfaction of most other desires, the point of satiety is soon reached, the demands of this one grow greater without limit, so that it knows no satiety. How few men are content with the possession of what they need for the satisfaction of all other desires than their desire for possession for its own sake." In fact, he thinks it might be maintained that economic science is concerned with the operation of this instinct rather than with enlightened self-interest.

My study of the *Institution of Property* (*313*, and see particularly Chapter VI, Section A 2) seems to me to demonstrate quite positively that the institution has developed from sources quite other than an "instinct of possession." It also shows that, in the modern world, the ultimate proprietary rights—the dominant interests in personal funds—are only to a very slight extent possessory rights of a nature which could be supposed to satisfy such an instinct. Furthermore, the analysis in Chapter 10 of this present study shows that, to the extent that property power is derived from saved income—i.e., neither from confiscation by the political powers nor from "appropriation" by individuals—and that is true originally of all "capital" other than raw land, it involves a deliberate choice. That is the antithesis of the operation of an instinct.

The three definite characteristics of an instinct are:

a. That it is found universally in a species in a single habitat.
b. That it is inborn or unlearned.
c. That it operates regardless of recognized utility.

The practice of retaining shows none of these characteristics of an instinct. It is not universal. In fact, that is one of the two chief reasons for the "inequality of wealth." It is not only not inborn, but it has been learned by the human species only at the cost of much suffering, only over aeons of time and only by a limited number. It is not only not blind, it is peculiarly discriminating. Civilized man does not "collect" what we call "extant product." In fact, one of the remarkable things about the modern economy is that he does not, because he does not need to. As to some of the basic essentials the individual can now live on an almost hand-to-mouth basis.

Hoarding among men and animals is an abnormality which we are not going to try to explain. In Appendix III, Section A, we cited a few cases of it—chiefly among wolverines, foxes, and jackdaws. The case of the squirrel is doubtful. Hoarding is a rare exception both in the animal and the human world. To ascribe collecting in the human world—ranging from boy's marble collections to men's art collections—to an undirected instinct for hoarding is too absurd to merit serious consideration. But, whatever hoarding is, we may define it here as keeping which is a satisfaction in itself while it is being done. Any "hoarding instinct" would be restricted to this very narrow sphere and would be an abnormality. It would cover the cases where objects are hoarded to an unlimited extent and without reference to future use. That differentiates it, as a rare exception, from retaining, which is limited with great precision, both in quantity and kind, by the expectation of occasions and within them, by the influence of futurity and the competition of current wants.

C. THE COMPETITION OF FUTURE WITH CURRENT WANTS

What we shall undertake here is to illustrate and graphically demonstrate the analysis upon which are based the conclusions stated in Chapter 10, Section D, as to the limitation on retaining by reason of the impingement of the several occasions for retaining, subject to the influence of futurity, upon the allocation and limitation of current working-hours. This is solely a problem in quantitative energetics. There is one homogeneous force that varies only in strength—the force of future wants. There are two forms of resistance that oppose this force. The first we have dealt with in the text. It is the present resistance offered by reason of the memory of the effort of retaining. It varies in proportion to the quantity of "real cost" retained and in proportion to the interval during which the retaining is performed. Under our simplifying assumption—one hour's work per provision—and since we are here ignoring the compounding of retaining effort, most of our examples treat retaining as varying only in the dimension of time. When, on account of labor-saving, we have to abandon our simplifying assumption, variations in the other dimension are allowed for. The second resistance turns out to be a compound one. But it can be stated in single quantitative terms. It was developed in Chapter 9, where it was found necessary to assume that some sort of balance is struck between the force of current wants—future wants with zero futurity—and the resistance of current working. The latter, in turn, is also a compound; formed of the effort of working and the sacrifice of leisure. But all of these must be comparable among themselves. We shall see, as we proceed, the several parts they play.

When we come to treat of these magnitudes we must recall that we have heretofore concluded that there is no such thing as a unit in terms of which any of them can be measured as forces or resistances—either subjectively or objectively. It follows that we cannot suppose it to be possible that our worker-retainer can calculate these forces and resistances in terms of measurement. Nevertheless, if these are forces and resistances, they must work quantitatively—their relative strengths must determine their effects. This must be true whether the subject is conscious or unconscious of the influence they have on him—whether he conceives them as comparable magnitudes or merely obeys them automatically. Therefore, it will aid us in our analysis if we attribute to these forces and resistances numerical values, however imaginary the unit, and merely for the sake of clear statement of comparisons of more or less or approximate equality. All we mean by our values is that, for instance, a force with the numerical value 4 will take precedence over one with the value 3, and will overcome a resistance of less than 4 or be restrained by one greater than 4. The generic term for these numerical values will be *weight*. Such a scale of weights is shown in Fig. 60, below.

We conceive the effort of the specific quantity of retention involved, though incurred only in the future, to offer a resistance at the time the program is made and that it is therefore summated with the resistance offered by what is to be actually incurred at the time. These two, combined, compose the resistance to future wants, or to provision for them. But, here, we are endeavoring to isolate the effects of the latter resistance only. That can be accomplished with more clarity if we treat the resistance on account of futurity as a deduction from the force of the want, leaving the resistance on account of the present factors exposed and standing alone. That is, of course, no more than to say that, if $2\,A + 2\,B = 4\,C$, then $2\,B = 4\,C - 2\,A$. Moreover, this clarifies matters for another reason. The program for future wants conflicts and competes with the program for current wants in the allocation of current working-hours. But resistance on account of retaining as effort—defined to begin the following morning—plays its part only by way of resisting the force of future wants; it has no bearing on current wants. Thus by treating such resistance as a deduction we get all the factors involving futurity on one side and contrast them sharply with the factors involving no futurity on the other.

We are considering only a direct economy which is, therefore, wholly dependent on its own efforts and in which product cannot be converted from one form to another by exchange. Also, to obtain reasonable simplicity, we must continue our limiting assumptions, which present a somewhat artificial picture, vastly oversimplified as compared with reality. We will consider only a full day's provision for each want, giving that a weight equal to the sum of its usefulness for each of the recurring maximum intensities of the want, if the want recurs more than once per day; we will treat the successive diminutions of weight of such provisions, as we proceed along the order of priority of wants, as if they were equal; and, as we have done hitherto, in order to disregard the so-called coefficients of production, we will assume, unless the exception is stated, that one hour of working is required for one day's provision for each and every want.

1. CONTINGENCIES OF THE FIRST TYPE

The necessarily complicated diagram in Fig. 60 brings into conjunction a representation of the influence of futurity upon the future-want system and a representation of the working-day highly simplified from the one we used in Chapter 9. It is important to call the reader's attention at once to the fact that, in this diagram, the influence of futurity is shown in a way which is the opposite of the way used in Figs. 25, 26, 27. The reasons for doing this were explained above. In those figures we added the accrued retention to the work as we proceeded along the time-scale, because we were aiming to show total resistance against total force at each point. As a result, the line showing the rate of accrual of retaining effort was a rising line and the differing obliquity of such lines indicated differing rates. But here, as already stated, we wish to show only the net force in the present of each of the instances of a future want; for it is only this net force that can compete with current wants which meet no resistance on account of retaining. So, here, we must deduct the accrued retention at each point in the time-scale from the force of the want at that point. To show this it is clearer to make the line representing the rate of accrual of retaining effort a declining line. Thus the several instances of Want *a*,[1] as projected into the future, show a uniform gross force equal to the altitudes up to the line marked "Obliquity Zero." But their net force in the present is shown by the altitudes only up to the line marked "Obliquity A," or, as an alternative, up to the line marked "Obliquity B." This merely reverses the previous diagrams, so that accrued retention at any point is represented by the altitudes down to Obliquity A from Obliquity Zero, for instance. While we are dealing with these diagrams we will use the term "obliquity" as an abbreviation, to signify the rate of accrual of retaining as effort; for the angle of divergence from the horizontal measures such a rate.

Let us consider, first, Future Provision A (Fig. 60). That consists of 3 days' provision for all wants included; and, since the contingency is expected to arise either at time uncertain sometime during the next 60 days or at time certain, it is dated as beginning 30 days hence. With that degree of futurity the present net weight of the future provision for *a* is less than that of the current provision for *b* but more than that for *c*, etc. The result is the following combined order of preference (future provisions in parentheses), which will govern the order in which the hours of working will be applied: *a*, *b*, (3*a*), *c*, (3*b*), *d*, (3*c*), *e*, (3*d*), *f*, (3*e*), *g*, (3*f*), *h*, (3*g*), *i* (3*h*), *j* . . . On our assumption of one hour each, the total hours required for such number of provisions is 34. Obviously this cannot be applied in one working-day. The question immediately arises, then, how many hours per day will our worker-retainer plan to apply, if he starts from scratch. That can only be determined by comparing the present weight of these current, and the net weight of these future, provisions

[1] The use of lower case letters, here, to designate wants has no significance. It is done to meet the exigencies of the diagrams.

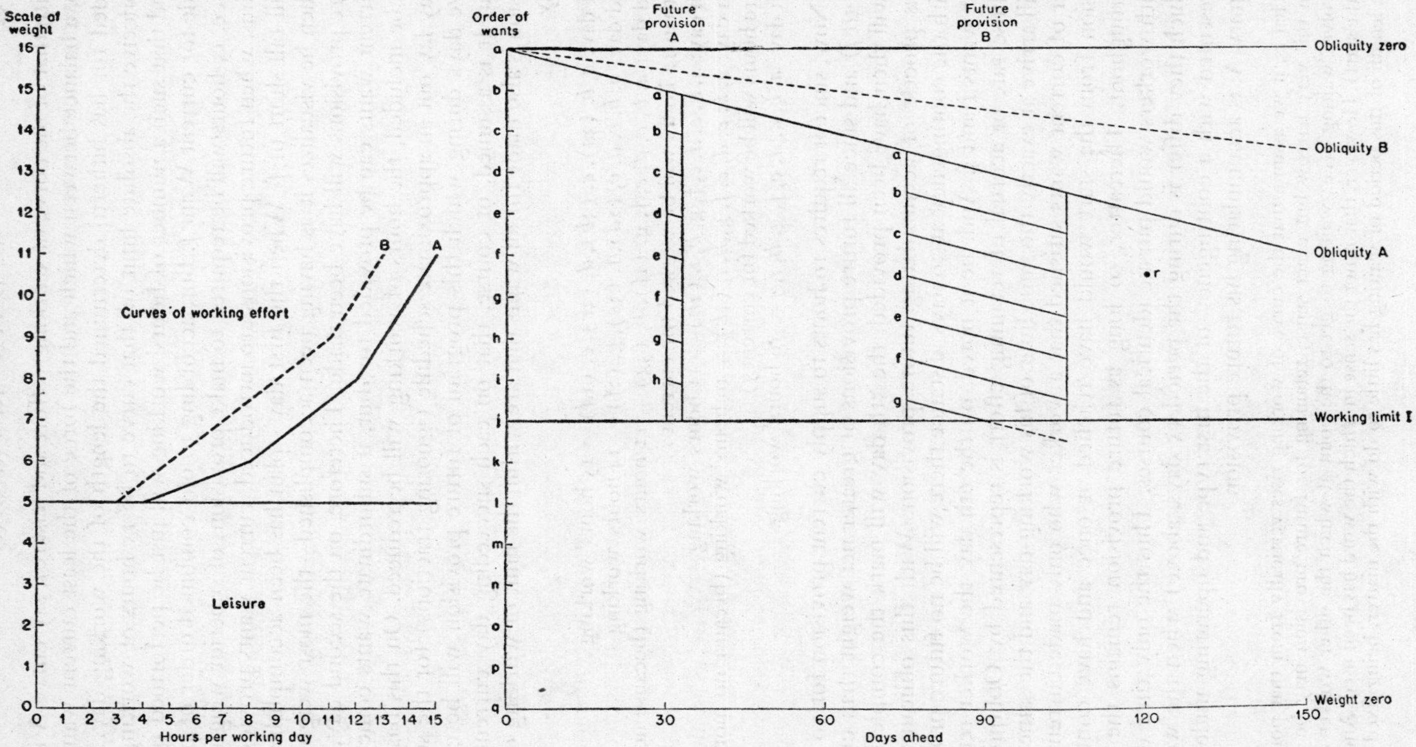
Scale of weight
Curves of working effort
Leisure
Hours per working day
Order of wants
Future provision A
Future provision B
Obliquity zero
Obliquity B
Obliquity A
Working limit I
Weight zero
Days ahead

FIG. 60

with that of the curve of working (effort and leisure), say curve A in Fig. 60, a balance between which and the force of the least current want provided for has hitherto determined the length of the working-day. If we conceive the absolute limit on that curve to be 15 hours of working,[2] we find that such a number of hours' working will just be performed to provide for current Want *f*. But, according to our combined order of preference, 15 hours will be required to make provisions of superior weight to *f*. Thus, when future provisions are introduced, current wants provided for will fall short of *f*. When the first day's plan has been accomplished—or when he visualizes it as having been accomplished—the most weighty future provisions will have been made. Therefore, on the second day, more current wants can be provided for; but, if subordinate wants come again to be included, the hours of working will be reduced. On this basis, we may lay out an approximate schedule (ignoring fractions) for the successive days during which this program of future provision will be carried out. It is assumed, of course, that on each succeeding day current provision is also made for all wants that are within the limit of working of that day.

1st day: *a*, *b*, (3*a*), *c*, (3*b*), *d*, (3*c*), *e*, (1*d*) = 15 hours' working
2nd day: *a*, *b*, *c*, *d*, *e*, (2*d*), *f*, (3*e*), *g*, (2*f*) = 14 hours' working
3rd day: *a*, *b*, *c*, *d*, *e*, *f*, *g*, (1*f*), *h*, (3*g*) = 12 hours' working (because no more than 12 hours will be worked for current *i*)
4th day: *a*, *b*, *c*, *d*, *e*, *f*, *g*, *h*, *i*, (2*h*) = 11 hours' working
5th day: *a*, *b*, *c*, *d*, *e*, *f*, *g*, *h*, *i*, (1*h*) = 10 hours' working (because no more than 10 hours will be worked for current *j*)
6th day: *a*, *b*, *c*, *d*, *e*, *f*, *g*, *h*, *i*, *j* = 10 hours' working.

Now, since it requires 10 hours to supply current provision for 10 wants (*a* to *j*) and since all future provisions of greater net weight than current *j* will then have been provided, the 5th day will mark the completion of this process of accumulating future provision. With this obliquity and with the contingency at 30 days' distance there will be no future provision for wants *i* and *j*. And, be it noted, on the 6th day the worker-retainer, whose rate of accrual of retaining effort is represented by Obliquity A, will arrive at exactly the same limit of his working-day and the same number of current wants satisfied that a worker who only made current provision from the start would have reached at once and have continued throughout. Thereafter, so long as future provision remains the same, both workers would pursue identical courses. Thus the only time during which they differ is during the period (5 days, above) when the worker, presented with a contingency of the first type and operating under Obliquity A, is accumulating his future provision.[3]

[2] That is, if we assume that the curve of working rises vertically from that point.

[3] In this very narrow but exact sense, retaining for future provision may be said to involve "waiting" (i.e., waiting to get to the point at which the other worker arrived at the start). However, that is not the sense in which the word has been used. And, since the length of this period of waiting has little to do with the matter, being fixed by the

This method of approach yields a somewhat unexpected conclusion. It is evident that the extent of future provision for this type of contingency depends as much on the limitation of the working-day as it does on the obliquity. If this worker had been governed by the same obliquity and order of wants, but by the curve of working B, where a balance is struck at 9 hours' working for 9 current provisions (*a* to *i*), his future provision for *h* would have been omitted. And, of course, the number of days required to accumulate even this lesser stock would have been lengthened. If, on the other hand, we take a more realistic example of future provision (Fig. 60, Future Provision B), where a 30 days' stock is estimated to be required at some time in every 180 days, (and therefore averages 90 days ahead), but assume the same obliquity, curve of working, and order of wants as in the first example, we find that there is no future provision for *h* and only 15 days' provision for *g*. In that case it works out that, at the end of the 28th day, the worker would still be working 12 hours daily, would have accumulated all the desired stock for wants *a* to *e* and half that for *f*. Thereafter, he would reduce his hours, fractionally, add current provisions for wants omitted, fractionally, and accumulate the 15 days' additional future provision for *f* and the 15 days' envisaged for *g*, until he ended up, with his stock complete, working 10 hours to supply 10 current wants, exactly as in the first case.

Thus it is apparent that the limitation of retaining required for this kind of future provision depends upon the interaction of the limitation of retaining as effort with the limitation of working. Or rather, the latter (limit I, for curve of working A, in Fig. 60) rules, regardless of obliquity, in one direction (downward in Fig. 60), while the limitation of retaining as effort rules in the other (to the right in Fig. 60). Given the curve of working (effort and sacrifice) and its relation with the order of priority of wants, the quantity of retaining varies with the obliquity; given the obliquity it varies with the curve of working. If we vary the obliquity—if we convert this example to the broken line, Obliquity B, which represents a lower rate of accrual of resistance on account of the effort of retaining—it is clear that more future wants will be included in the provisions—either A or B. Then, for a given curve of working, the period of accumulation will be prolonged and the reduction in working-hours to the number required for current provision alone will be slower. For the industrious (curve of working A) more retaining for this occasion will result, even with the same obliquity (A). But less obliquity (B, for instance) may balance less industriousness. It is possible that the two human tendencies go together, though I think not. Even then the reason for the expansion of such future provision in one direction would be entirely independent of the reason for its expansion in the other. Also, it must be noted that the shape of the curve of working, and the way its various levels equilibrate with those of the order of wants, entirely determine (given the co-

duration of the working required and not by the subsequent retaining required, we find it an inappropriate term for this purpose.

efficients) the period which will be required for accumulation of any given quantity of future provision (the period of 5 days in our example). The more steeply this curve rises beyond the limit available for current wants the longer will be the period of accumulation, and vice versa. Thus the willingness to work extra hours is the primary determinant of the length of this period; and the willingness to divert some of the regular hours, with its concomitant forgoing of some of the current provisions, is wholly secondary and a result of the first. Given a certain obliquity, the curve of working not only partly determines the extent of the future provision (in one direction) but it wholly determines the period which will be required to accumulate it.

This method enables us to see the only way in which the aspect of sacrifice becomes a limitation on retaining of future provision for this type of contingency. For the purpose of making this clear, let us consider the advantages and disadvantages involved in this process as they would appear in advance to our worker-retainer. The quantity of retaining as effect that is being performed at any time is an objective magnitude—just as is the quantity of working. It is measured by the quantity of product, in terms of effort, that is being retained—in this example, only the number of hours' work represented. But the magnitudes of the advantages and disadvantages involved in the process of accumulating and maintaining such future provision are—just as in the case of working only and for current provision only—entirely subjective. It is clear that the disadvantages—limited here to current working and current forgoing—will precede the advantages, just as they did in the case of working, though by a much longer time. Thus we must distinguish between all the current and future advantages and disadvantages and assume all disadvantages to occur in a less distant future than their corresponding advantages. The only way to compare the alternatives which our worker-retainer has to consider is to sum up the advantages offered and to contrast them with the disadvantages. At each stage, then, we must measure the difference between them, if any. Taking first the stage during which the stock is being accumulated, we see that, in the case of Future Provision A (Fig. 60), as compared with the alternative of satisfying 10 wants currently with 10 hours of working, extra hours' working were put in and current provisions forgone as shown in the following tabulation:

Day	*Extra Hours*	*No Current Provisions for*
1st	5	Wants *f*, *g*, *h*, *i*, *j*.
2nd	4	Wants *h*, *i*, *j*.
3rd	2	Wants *i*, *j*.
4th	1	Want *j*.
5th	0	Want *j*.
	12	12

However, since the weight of the marginal hour worked and of the marginal want forgone declined during these days, the weight of the disadvantages per day declined much more rapidly than the table shows. Following the method previously outlined, in which, for purposes of illustration, we set up an arbitrary scale of weight in terms of imaginary units, we show the current and future advantages and the current disadvantages of the two alternatives offered for each of the five days during which the process of accumulation is going on—during the time, that is, when the alternatives actually exist.

PROGRAM OF NO FUTURE PROVISION

Day	*Current Advantages (Consumption)*	*Current Disadvantages (Working)*	*Current Surplus of Advantages over Disadvantages*
1st	115	56	59
2nd	115	56	59
3rd	115	56	59
4th	115	56	59
5th	115	56	59
Total	575	280	295
6th day	115	56	59

PROGRAM OF FUTURE PROVISION A

Day	*Current Advantages (Consumption)*	*Current Disadvantages (Working)*	*Current Surplus (+) or Deficit (−)*	*Prospective Advantages*	*Less Current Deficit*	*Future Surplus*
1st	70	111.5	(−41.5)	137.37	41.50	95.87
2nd	91	90.5	+0.5	76.5		76.5
3rd	100	71.5	+28.5	39.7		39.7
4th	108	63.5	+44.5	15.9		15.9
5th	108	56	+52	7.9		7.9
Total	477	393.0	+125.5	277.37		235.87
6th day	115	56	+59	0		0

Let us first lump these advantages and disadvantages together without regard to the question whether they are assignable to the component working or to the component retaining. The net result of the choice of the second alternative, carried through for the necessary 5 days, is that the worker-retainer has secured, instead of a current surplus of 295 points, a current surplus of only 125.5 points and a future surplus (at net weights) of 235.87 points; that is, he has surrendered 169.5 points of current surplus for 235.87 points of future surplus. Or, viewed in another way, while current advantages have been reduced by 98 points, the sum of current and prospective advantages has been increased by 179.37 points at an increased cost in disadvantages of 113 for the extra working. On either basis he has made a net gain of 66.37 points. In the last analysis this represents the terms on which he has made his choice. Given the obliquity upon which our example is based there will be no question as to which alternative is chosen nor of present or ultimate gain (surplus).

As to the difference between this first pair of alternatives, these quantities seem to constitute a clear-cut gain in surplus. But when we come to assign these increased advantages, disadvantages, and surplus to working and to retaining respectively, we find ourselves in difficulties. The effect of introducing this particular contingency, subject to Obliquity A, has been to interpolate into several orders of priority of current wants a series of future wants so that, in the resulting combined orders of preference, a mass of future provisions for prior wants appears ahead of current provisions for subordinate wants. If we ignore the fact that the advantages of these future provisions are prospective only, we may apply our earlier method for determining the surplus advantages from working, and assign to working all this additional surplus. In fact, it seems that we are compelled to do so, since it requires all these extra prospective advantages to induce the extra working. Each day, during the period of accumulation, the weight of the least weighty (marginal) provision, whether future or current, is necessarily equal to (or just greater than) that of the last hour of working. Therefore, the difference between the intramarginal portions of both—the surplus—is necessarily of the same order as the surplus advantages from working in general. True, the fact that these future provisions are prospective not only differentiates this from the previous surplus from working but it involves additional effort of the kind we have called retaining. However, the effect of this additional effort has already been fully allowed for by means of Obliquity A. Of course, we have not counted as part of this increase in surplus that portion of the prospective advantages which compensate for the reduction in current advantages that arise from forgoing current satisfactions—in the above example, 98. These lost current advantages and their compensating gained prospective advantages are clearly assignable to retaining; but, since they are practically equal to each other, there is clearly no surplus involved. So far as the present is concerned, the prospective advantages preferred, with due allowance for the effort of retaining, must be as large as, or just larger than, the current ones forgone—else they would not be chosen. Moreover, we have agreed that the quantity of the current provisions forgone is purely incidental and secondary—that is, it is not determined directly, but rather by the curve of working. Thus we conclude that the entire quantity of extra advantages embodied in the second alternative as compared with the first is necessary to induce the extra working; that, by reason of the "shape" of the curve of working the choice of this alternative shows an increase of surplus from working; and that the only advantages in the second alternative which are assignable to retaining are those required to balance the loss of advantages incurred elsewhere—i.e., the advantages of current consumption forgone—which, being practically in balance, afford no surplus.

In this particular occasion for retaining another pair of alternatives also lies open from the day of completion of the process of accumulation—in fact to an increasing extent during those five days themselves. They present the choice between consuming this future provision immediately or continuing to keep it. The advantage of consuming it at once consists exclusively in being relieved for 3 days of all but 2 hours' work (that required for Wants *i* and *j*, which have no future provision) or of all but 4 hours' work, with the addition of current provision for Wants *k* and *l*. The disadvantage consists in the possibility that the contingency may occur, and that, then, the worker-retainer will go without consumption altogether (Wants *a* to *h*) for 3 days. The present weight, on each day, of the relief from 8 of the 10 hours of work for 3 days is 138; that of relief from 6 of the 10 hours of work for 3 days and enjoyment of current provision for Wants *k* and *l* for the same time is 141; the latter would be preferred. As against this the present net weight of those future 3 days without consumption is 277.37 at the start, and it keeps growing larger as the time grows nearer at which the contingency is expected actually to occur and, therefore, the deduction from the gross weight for retaining still to be performed grows less. Thus, during this second period, so long as the obliquity remains the same, there is again no doubt which alternative will be chosen, nor of present or ultimate gain. But let the present weight of this future provision fall a little more than half, due to a change in the estimate of the contingency or a change in obliquity, and the result will be a disappearance (loss) of future surplus and therefore a preference for immediate consumption. We cannot, however, regard these surplus advantages in the period during and after accumulation as a new surplus, since we have already counted them once. They merely constitute a continuing surplus. But it must be noted that, here again, the disadvantages of current working are inextricably involved in this continuance of retaining. Only the forgoing of current satisfaction of Wants *k* and *l* is, strictly speaking, the disadvantage assignable to the component retaining; for it is clear that relief from the 6 hours of working would be entirely assignable to the component working and that all of this continuing surplus is necessary as an inducement, within the margin, to procure a continuance of this working.

2. CONTINGENCIES OF THE SECOND TYPE AND TECHNICAL NECESSITIES

In considering the second type of contingency—the apprehension that an irregularly occurring want will occur without warning—we may return to Fig. 60. There we have indicated such special future provision by *r*, as if it were estimated to be a less pressing want than *b* but more pressing than *c*, and as if it were expected to recur once during the next 240 days and therefore is placed along the time-scale at a distance of 120 days. Assuming that this future provision is for one day and also involves one hour's working, it will be interpolated ahead of the current provision for Want *g* on the first day that it begins to be expected. In principle, this operates in the same way as the first type of contingency. The first difference is that it operates on a smaller scale, since it applies only to one want; the second is that this want is usually of such nature that it cannot be provided for at all when the contingency arises (i.e., it can never be satisfied with a current provision); and the third is that no sacrifice continues to be involved after the process of accumulation is once completed, since, by definition, the want does not recur until the contingency arises and the provision is therefore unusable until that time.

The effect of the first type of technical necessity—the prospect that material available now will not be available in the future—is different and more complicated. Let us suppose, as in the text, that the seed of ripe wild grain is the much preferred material with which to satisfy Want *a* (hunger), but that this seed must be picked, each season, during the 30 days after it ripens and before it falls and germinates. Provision for 360 days would then require 360 hours of working; but under the conditions of our example in Fig. 60, only provision for the next 30 days (30 hours) would, with Obliquity A, have more net weight than current provision for Want *b*. Therefore, for the first 2 days, 15 hours per day would be devoted to this work; during the two following, 1 hour per day out of 15 would go to *b* and 14 to *a*, etc. By the expiration of the 30 days available almost 270 days' future provisions would have been accumulated for Want *a*, current provision would by that time have reached to Want *i*, and working would be at the rate of 12 hours per day. Thereafter, no further provision for *a* being possible, working-hours would be reduced to 9 hours (*a* being provided for) with full current provision for *j* (since current provision for *k* does not justify 9 hours of working). It is evident, then, that the first type of technical necessity is, up to this point, the one case where the time-scale is filled in from the present as far into the future as the setting permits, up to a limit at the point where the material is expected again to be available, or at which the obliquity causes the net weight to decline below the limit of working, whichever occurs first. It is clear that this kind of future provision, like the last, does not involve continuing sacrifice after the process of accumulation is completed, for, under our premises, not more than one day's provision each day is wanted, and that one is always provided while the stock lasts. In other respects, the effects of this occasion follow much the same lines as those of the two types of contingency.

In the case of the durable, it is clear that the technical necessity for the performance of the whole block of working before the first of the resulting block of future provisions (installments) is available must distort the normal pattern of the application of working described heretofore. The first day's use of the durable would have the same weight as a current day's provision if it could be had today; but it cannot. That fact converts even the first day's use into a future provision, only available after the process of accumulation is completed. What present net weight the first day's use will have depends, then, on the number of days the process will require (on account of the shrinkage its gross weight suffers as it is put further into the future, so that longer retaining is involved); and that, in turn, depends not only on the number of hours' working the product requires, but also on the number of hours per day that it will be advantageous to devote to it. Thus we begin to see that the estimation necessary for a rational choice as to whether or not to produce a durable is a highly complex one—much more complex than our previous cases. If we assume that technical conditions fix the number of days' uses and therefore, under our simplifying assumption, the number of hours' working involved in the durable—and we must admit that such conditions always limit the range of choice—then we may establish at once two definite conclusions. The position of the future want in the order of priority will determine the maximum number of hours per day that will be available for production of the durable by way of diversion of hours from lesser wants within the limit and by way of increase in working hours. If we divide the number of hours required for the product by the number of hours per day thus available and find that, at this number of days' distance, the net weight of the first day's use of the durable remains greater than the weight of the current provision for the most intense want which will have to be displaced, we know that the maximum number of hours will be available. We may say, then, that the net weight of the first day's use of the durable, after deducting accrued retention up to the position in the future so determined, fixes the point in the current order of priority of wants at which its production will be considered at all. But, even then, the durable will only be made if the sum of the present net weight of each of its future successive uses, beginning on the day so determined, exceeds the sum of the present weight of each of the current and future extra hours or forgone satisfactions of subordinate wants entailed. Obviously, this formula works out differently the further along the order of priority of wants the durable is applicable and therefore the nearer to the limit of working at which it occurs. In order to illustrate the operation of this formula we may work out a few examples.

Reverting to Fig 60, it is clear, as to durables, say for Wants *c*, *g*, and *i*, that no one of these will be considered before current provision is made for the next subordinate want unless it can be made in less than 30 days; for a postponement of more than 30 days would subject its first use to a shrinkage greater than 1 point—that is, greater than our arbitrary difference between successive wants in the order. On the other hand, the maximum number of hours per day available to make a durable will vary greatly in these three cases. For *c* the maximum is 13 hours per day (15 hours, less 2 for current *a* and *b*); for *g* the maximum is 7 hours (13 hours less 6 for *a* to *f*); and for *i* the maximum is 2 hours, for less than 15 days' distance, and 1 hour, for 15 to 30 days (the 11th hour being eliminated at 15 days). Thus a durable for *c* would be considered before current provision for the next subordinate want if it required anything less than 390 (30 × 13) hours to make; one for *g* if it required less than 210 (30 × 7) hours; and one for *i* if it required less than 45 ($15 \times 2 + 15 \times 1$) hours. But, under the second test, a durable for *c* would be rejected if it required 390 hours to make; for the disadvantages would sum up 3,465 points, while the present weight of the advantages, less the effort of retaining which would begin, on the average, 15 days hence and extend an average of 210 ($15 + 195$) days beyond that point, would be subjected to so great a shrinkage (7 points for each) that they would sum up to 2,730 points only. So *g* too would be rejected, since the disadvantages would appear as 1,755 points and the advantages, net of retaining, only as 1,260. The same with *i*, with 375 *vs.* 303.75. In the framework which we have assumed for

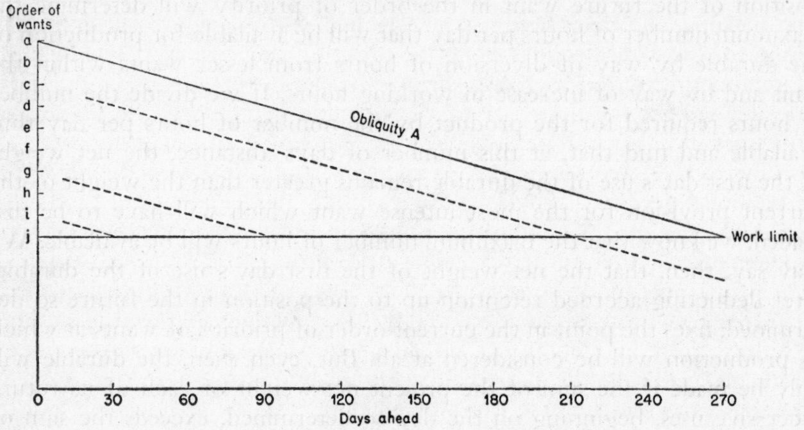

Fig. 61

this particular example no durable would be made for any want unless it passed the first test above; even if it passed this test, none would be made for *c* unless it could be made in about 250 hours and therefore had about 250 days' life under our assumption. The process of accumulation would then be condensed into about 20 days. None would be made for *g* unless it could be made in about 70 hours and therefore had about 70 days' life. The process of accumulation would then be condensed into 10 days. None would be made for *i* unless it could be made in about 20 hours and therefore had about 20 days' life. The process of accumulation would then be condensed into 10 days. These limits are represented in Fig. 61.[4]

Again, these numerical examples are not intended to represent the calculation which our worker-retainer actually makes. They are useful merely in indicating to us what are the factors at work and the result toward which that process of balancing alternatives, which we call judgment

[4] The reader should note that these limits only hold good if the necessary durability and therefore the necessary number of hours' working is treated as given, so that the question of making or not making it stands or falls as a whole. If its durability can be varied, then the installments at the end, which can be added or not, will not induce the maximum number of hours of working.

and choice, tends. It is also true, in this particular case, that this isolation of the factors for which the pure durable, per se, is accountable is more representative of the way the choice is presented in a modern and therefore indirect economy than it is of the way in which it probably appeared in a primitive economy, which was the nearest approach to our analytical entity, a direct economy. For there, probably, these issues were always mixed with the question of "labor-saving" (i.e., a change in the "coefficients of production") which we shall consider shortly. Nevertheless, the factors considered here are and have always been an essential part of the question, and they can be more clearly analyzed in isolation. So isolated, we have found that the limitation of quantity of retaining that will be done for durables is fixed by technical necessities, but only within certain maxima, and that these maxima decline as the weight of a day's provision for the want declines along the order of their priority. The quantity of retaining required increases during the period of accumulation at the rate defined by the first part of the formula, which sets the number of hours per day that will be devoted to it; thereafter, in use, it decreases according to the rate of using-up. Here again, as in the case of the first type of technical necessity above, we have a filling of the time-scale, and again it is done entirely for technical reasons. But in this case, for the first time, current provision absolutely entails future provision.[5] And even that current provision cannot be obtained until the product, with all its content of future provision, is completed. Thus the retaining involved in durables may be wholly incidental to the main purpose. Again, the sacrifice is entirely made during the period of accumulation; for, thereafter, as in all previous cases but the first, not more than one day's use is wanted and the rest are necessarily reserved once they are made. We may regard retaining as an involuntary and extra effort in this case, one which is compelled by the inherent nature of the only kinds of means which will satisfy certain wants. When man emerged from the age, or even the districts, of natural shelter he either had shelter which lasted him more than a night or he had none.

It is not necessary for us to work out a special example of long-process products. We may consider that the question of whether or not to produce them is determined by a formula of the same type as that required for the durable, except that there may be gaps in the series of working-hours on successive days which constitutes the process of accumulation of the, purely incidental, future provision. And, to that extent, the beginning of the advantages will be more deferred. The quantity of retaining is, also in this case, fixed by technical requirements; but here the length of time during which the retaining must be done is also fixed and that, perhaps, on a different basis from that which determines its quantity.[6]

[5] In the case of the second contingency the only provision is future provision.

[6] Because the period of accumulation may be extended by long gaps in the working process, while waiting for the natural process to mature.

3. TECHNICAL OPTIONS

The first of the two technical options which introduce the factor of work-economizing is the opportunity to produce in large batches. In order to analyze the effects of the exercise of such an option let us work out an example. We assume that the option becomes known after the worker-retainer has arrived at his limit of working (Fig. 60). Thereafter, it is not possible to devote any hours of working—either present or extra—to any other purpose than current provision without disturbing the balance. If any hours are diverted, the current provision to which they were applied must be given up. That will not be done unless the alternative offers greater advantages. But, if it does, not only will that current provision be given up but an increase in working-hours may be induced. How far this disturbance will go will depend on a number of factors, as we shall see. Let us assume that such a technical possibility exists with reference to Want *j*,[7] and that 15 hours' working applied by the large-batch technique will make 30 days' provision. This provision is incidentally shown by the broken line (net effort released) in Fig. 62.[8] It is clear at once that even the initial future provision of this series has not a sufficient net weight on its own account to justify it. The whole of the provision is below the present limit of working, and the first day's provision has necessarily less than the weight of current provision for *j*, the least want currently satisfied, for it is subject to obliquity, since it involves retaining. Why, then, will the process be adopted at all? The answer is that the choice offered, in this case, is not between future and current provision, nor even between future provision and none at all, as hitherto. Actually the alternatives are (1) the current satisfaction of Want *j*, as the least want satisfied with 10 hours' working, *versus* (2) the non-satisfaction of *j* for 15 days—shown by the dotted line—and thereafter the satisfaction of *j* for 30 days without working—that is, with a release from 1 hour's working each day for 30 days—shown by the broken line—(Want *k* not justifying even 9 hours' working). But this release from working is not all net gain. It involves retaining. However, the retaining is only of 15 days' work, not of 30. So the deduction is, on the average, only half what it has appeared to be in previous cases. That

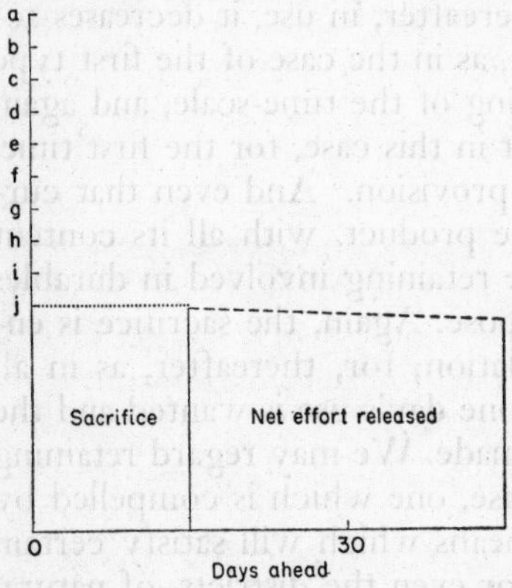

FIG. 62

[7] We are choosing, for this illustration, the least want that is being currently satisfied, in order to demonstrate, in isolation, the difference in the comparisons made in these cases from those made in the previous ones.

[8] That is, 30 days of future provision for Want *j*, beginning 15 days ahead would show the average net weight of 6⅝ points, if, as here, it only involved 15 hours' working over 15 days.

is, it becomes necessary, here, to introduce a new variable, the ratio between the hours of working and the quantity of product, a variable which has only been implicit heretofore. We have all along assumed that each hour of working produced one day's provision for any want. But now, due to introducing the factor of change in the coefficients of production, we have a series of hours which result in two days' provision each. Thus the above alternatives become:

(1) 15 days' provision for *j* with a total weight of $(7 \times 15 =)$ 105

(2) 30 days' release thereafter from the 10th hour of working with a total net weight, after deducting the effect of the retaining required (Obliquity A), of $(6\frac{5}{8} \times 30 =)$ $198\frac{3}{4}$.[9]

Obviously the game is worth the candle. We will explain in connection with the second technical option why we have regarded the forgoing of *j* for 15 days as the only sacrifice to be considered (i.e., why it is not advantageous to hasten the process by working extra hours or forgoing more than *j*). But at this point we should note several other things that this example brings out. In the first place the quantity of retaining which this example involves, at its maximum, cannot be measured in terms of 30 days' provision, but only in terms of the effect of 15 hours' working (not even 15 days' sacrifice of *j*). This confirms our decision to measure retaining as a magnitude by the quantity of work the product represents, rather than by its usefulness. Thus, the quantity of retaining involved here is only half the quantity needed for a durable involving 30 hours of working, though both consist of the same number of days' provisions. In the second place, this retaining is not done for the sake of future provision, but entirely for the sake of release from the last hour of working. The future provision, and therefore the retaining which it involves, is wholly incidental. In the third place, we have chosen, for an example, a case in which all the disadvantages consist of a sacrifice attributable to retaining—the forgoing of current satisfaction of Want *j*—and all the advantages consist of a release from working. And this because we wished to demonstrate the absence of interest in future provision as such. But we might have chosen, as an example, a process of which the disadvantages would also have included extra working; and, if the economizing of working had been sufficiently great, the advantages might well have included the future gratification of additional wants (subordinate to *j*) by diversion of future working time, as well as a release from some working then. In such an example our measurement of the advantages and disadvantages would have followed exactly the lines we used in examining future provision, with the excep-

[9] Because of the numerical values of our example the present weight of the incidental future provision for *j* and that of the hours to be saved appears to be the same. Actually, they would not often coincide. Moreover, it is clear that no part of this future provision would be wanted of and for itself. It is the economized hours that are wanted.

The deduction for the effect of the retaining required, with Obliquity A, from halfway through the period of accumulation to halfway through the period of use (the average life)—i.e., $22\frac{1}{2}$ days at the rate of 1 point per 30 days—is $\frac{3}{4}$ of a point. Applied to twice as many hours saved it becomes $\frac{3}{8}$ of a point.

tion that these advantages, though of the same weight, would have been double in number and therefore subject to only half the deduction on account of retaining (obliquity). Finally, in this case, too, the sacrifice is made altogether during the period of accumulation. Once the lot is finished, since each day is then fully provided for, there is no continuing sacrifice in not consuming the remaining provisions.

The second technical option introduces the production of intermediate product as the means of economizing working. The effects of the exercise of this type of option are along similar lines to those of the previous one, except that the working cannot all be done in advance. To work out an example, let us assume that our worker-retainer can, by putting in 60 hours working in advance, produce a machine (or tool) which will thereafter make it possible during 120 days, say, to produce daily the current provision required for two wants, that are within his present limit, in ½ hour instead of 1 hour each. Thus he is offered an option which will enable him to economize 1 hour per day. This hour, according to the curve of working in Fig. 60, he will take off, since Want *k* does not justify even 9 hours of working. But it is again not possible for him to apply this 60 hours, which has no immediate product, without working extra hours or forgoing some current provision, or both. If he concentrates these 60 hours into a few days, the benefit of the economizing will begin sooner. But since, in order to do this, he must forgo more important wants and add more effortful hours, the weight of the current disadvantages will be much higher. In Fig. 63 we illustrate the way in which this works out. We have reduced the obliquity by half, because a low rate of accrual of retaining effort is usually necessary to make this option offer any net advantage at all. Thus it corresponds with Obliquity B in Fig. 60. If our worker-retainer diverts to making the machine only the hour per day he now devotes to current provision for Want *j*—the least want currently satisfied—this forgoing will last for 60 days and the economizing of time will not begin until then. The sum of the weight of this series of disadvantages is then ($7 \times 60 =$) 420, and that of the advantages, less the effect of obliquity B is ($6\frac{1}{4} \times 120 =$) 750, affording net advantages of 330.[10] This is shown by the solid lines under the heading "advantages and disadvantages I" in Fig. 63. If he considers speeding up this process by eliminating current provision for *i*, as well, he will be forgoing *j* and *i*, with current weight of 7 and 8 respectively and will also be putting in two extra hours with current weight of 7.5 and 8, respectively. By this means he can complete the machine in 15 days, for he will work 12 hours daily, provide for 8 wants currently, and will have 4 hours a day available for this job. The sum of these disadvantages, extending over 15 days, is then 30.5 per day which,

[10] The average period of retaining begins at 30 days hence (halfway through the 60 days of accumulation) and ends at 120 days hence (halfway through the 120 days of use). It is therefore 90 days (1½ points). Applied to the hours economized (double the number retained) this means a deduction of ¾ of a point for retaining.

for 15 days, equals 457.5. This brings the beginning of the advantages closer to the present, however, and thus reduces the period of retaining and the deduction from them. That increases their net weight from 6¼ to 6⁷⁄₁₆. Multiplying the average by 120 days' life we have 772.5. But the net advantages of this quicker process are only 772.5 — 457.5 = 315. The second set of advantages could be shown in the figure, but only as an area whose altitude was slightly higher than advantages I. However, the disadvantages cannot be shown there; for they are the sum of several areas, the altitude of each of which is as great or greater than that of disadvantages I, but whose base is only one quarter as great. It is clear that the slower of these two ways of securing the machine will involve the greater net advantages. On the other hand, this does not mean that the choice will always

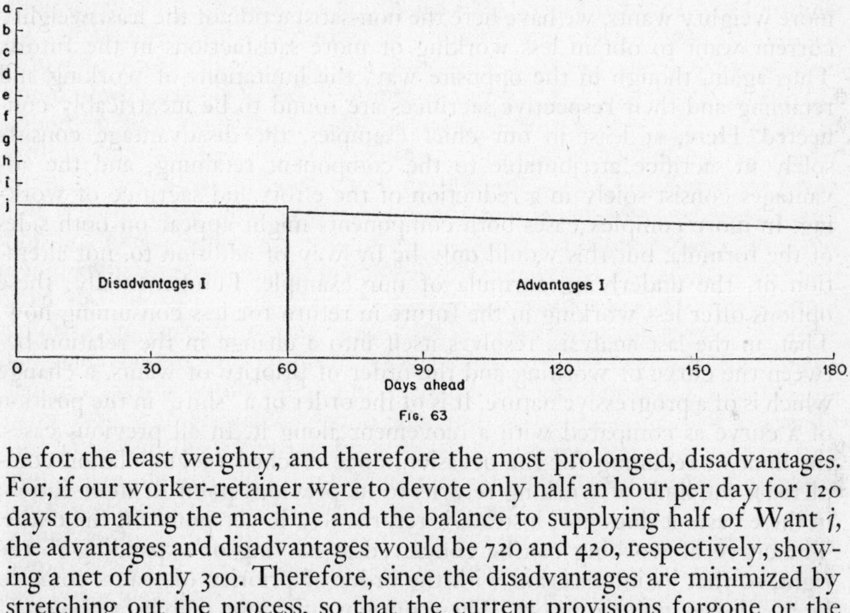

Fig. 63

be for the least weighty, and therefore the most prolonged, disadvantages. For, if our worker-retainer were to devote only half an hour per day for 120 days to making the machine and the balance to supplying half of Want *j*, the advantages and disadvantages would be 720 and 420, respectively, showing a net of only 300. Therefore, since the disadvantages are minimized by stretching out the process, so that the current provisions forgone or the extra hours worked have the least possible weight, while the advantages are maximized by shortening the process, there will be some critical point, within any given framework of weighting of wants and working and any given obliquity, at which the advantages will exceed the disadvantages by the greatest amount; and presumably this program will be chosen.

In the case of this technical option, as in most of the preceding cases, in no sense can it be said that sacrifice is involved in retaining the future uses remaining unused at any time after the process of accumulation is completed. The sacrifice is made—in fact all the current disadvantages are incurred—only while the machine is being made. In the case of both these technical options there is the same possibility of stretching out the process of accumulation until it reaches the point at which the net advantages are at a maximum and beyond which they decline.[11] Thus, in both cases, for exactly the same quantity of ultimate retaining there are various possible quantities of disadvantages. For this reason it cannot be said that the disadvantages bear any constant ratio to the quantity of retaining, even under a single set of conditions; nor even that the program calling for the least disadvantages will be chosen. Rather that one will be chosen which offers the greatest excess advantages. Thus no marginal point whatever can be defined in these terms.

These two types of technical option are obviously in a class by themselves in one respect. Hitherto, working has only appeared upon the disadvantage side of our formulae; in these cases it appears also upon the advantage side. Instead of extra working to obtain the future satisfaction of more weighty wants, we have here the non-satisfaction of the least weighty current want to obtain less working or more satisfactions in the future. Thus again, though in the opposite way, the limitations of working and retaining and their respective sacrifices are found to be inextricably connected. Here, at least in our chief examples, the disadvantage consists solely in sacrifice attributable to the component retaining; and the advantages consist solely in a reduction of the effort and sacrifice of working. In more complex cases both components might appear on both sides of the formula, but this would only be by way of addition to, not alteration of, the underlying formula of our example. Fundamentally, these options offer less working in the future in return for less consuming now. That, in the last analysis, resolves itself into a change in the relation between the curve of working and the order of priority of wants, a change which is of a progressive nature. It is of the order of a "shift" in the position of a curve as compared with a movement along it. In all previous cases, the limit of retaining for the occasion, once reached (accumulation completed), the limit of working returns to its previous point of intersection; in these cases it does not; instead, it returns to a lower point on the curve. The curve of working can be conceived as moving or expanding to the right, so that its intersection with the order of priority of wants come to be at a lower point on both. These options offer not merely a choice of the better of two alternatives; they offer also a betterment of the alternatives. They consist essentially in an enlargement of the limit of capacity to provide means.

The by-product of this difference between the technical options and other occasions for retaining is that the working-time economized by either of them must show a net advantage sufficient to make the exercising of the option worth while. In other cases the excess of advantages needs

[11] Again we find that "waiting," in the exact sense—that is, waiting for the beginning of the advantages—is increased or decreased according as the process is stretched out or concentrated. But it is apparent that this "waiting" has almost nothing to do with determining how long it will be stretched out. When retaining reaches its maximum, "waiting," in this sense, is always finished. Thus the two terms are by no means synonymous.

only to be just enough to tip the scales. In these cases, if the prospective advantages were merely just greater than the disadvantages, there would be hardly any gain in exercising the option. Therefore, in the case of both these technical options, sufficient net advantages must appear in order to induce the change of technique. It is not enough, as it was in the previous cases at the margin of choice—the least important provision in the case of future provision, and the sum of the provisions in the case of a durable—that the prospective advantages should just exceed the disadvantages. For, in the case of both these options, the choice lies, not between satisfying one want or another, which is governed by slight preferences, as it did in the previous cases, but between satisfying the same wants by two different methods, one of which is supposed to offer a release of time available for other applications, leisure or the satisfaction of a lesser want. This release of time must therefore be sufficient to be worth considering. Rejection of the chosen alternative, in all the previous cases, would have involved the possibility (in the case of future provision) or the actuality (in the case of a durable) of not satisfying, now or in the future, all the wants which were included in the limit. Such choices are, therefore, between preferred satisfactions not otherwise attainable (if the contingency occurs) and lesser satisfactions. That is not the choice these options offer. Their two alternatives are the probability of being, or that of not being, better off. The advantages they offer are, therefore, not selective within a static condition; they are advantages of "getting ahead"—a dynamic condition. They involve what we call progress. Incidentally this progress, as one after another technical opportunity is availed of, will have the effect that the weight of the prospective advantages and disadvantages of both alternatives will constantly diminish, though the quantity of total retaining required is constantly growing greater.

As we noted previously, the net advantages (or surplus) of both types of future provision for contingencies are likely to exist only intramarginally and to be assignable to working rather than to retaining; the same is true of the first technical necessity; net advantages, in the case of durables and long-process products, are likely not to exist at all—since the sum of advantages and the sum of disadvantages are likely to be practically equal; on the other hand, only those net advantages arising from the exercise of these two options exist, at least to some extent, also at the margin. And this for another reason as well. We must recognize that the quantity of retaining required by these technical opportunities is technically fixed. It is not something flexible which can be adjusted to a point where the last increment of retaining is just worth while. It is a case of all or none. And, on the other hand, these somewhat arbitrary opportunities cannot be supposed to appear in a nicely graded system, so that, up to a certain point of net advantages, all will be elected and the rest rejected. Rather, both the technical opportunities and the knowledge of them occur irregularly, almost fortuitously, and the quantity of advantages, eventually to be realized, which they offer may appear at any point along an extremely discontinuous curve. When they do appear, they are given, not variable; fixed, not adjustable. Then these advantages are subject to shrinkage by the influence of futurity and a deduction for the effort of retaining. The net advantages may be great, or they may be small. Only, to be elected at all, they must offer some considerable gain in terms of present weight.[12]

4. RETAINING FOR REPLACEMENT

In the preceding analysis of the various types of occasion for retaining we have ignored the matter of replacement.[13] Yet all these retained products will be used up more or less quickly and will therefore need to be replaced from time to time if the expectation of contingencies, the nature of seasonal changes, and such like, as well as of durables and of long processes, and the technical opportunities remain the same. However, the way this problem will then be met may be quite different from the way it was met when, in each case, it appeared as new. For, once any certain quantity of retaining has been initiated, there will, in most instances, be ways in which the replacement can be provided at a cost of less prolonged working and of less forgoing than was the case at the beginning. Thus as soon as Future Provision A for a contingency of the first type is completed on the 5th day, it will begin to appear that, when this first provision has been consumed at the end of the 33rd day, it will have to be replaced to provide against a repetition of the contingency on about the 60th day. Let us ignore, in this connection, the double deduction for retaining to which such a repetition of the contingency will be subject, at double the distance along the time-scale, and the resulting curtailment of the number of wants that would be included. A repetition of the original process—5 days of extra working and forgoing—will, in our example, have a weight of about 211 points;[14] whereas the forgoing of current provision for Want *j* and the diversion to this provision of 1 hour a day for the next 24 days will appear only as 168 points.[15] Thus it would appear that the worker-retainer will prefer to forgo Want *j* and devote that hour to a second Future Pro-

[12] This and the point discussed in the text (Chapter 10, Section G) seem to me to be the two errors in the otherwise successful Austrian capital theory. When Böhm-Bawerk says (*38*, 17–18), "We either put forth our labour just before the goal is reached or we, intentionally, take a roundabout way . . . [because] a greater result is obtained by producing goods in roundabout ways than by producing them directly," he established a wrong causal relation. The fact is that we prefer to produce directly except in those special, not general, cases, given by technical possibilities, in which we can secure, by indirection, sufficiently greater results to cover the extra "real costs" of roundaboutness and leave a considerable gain.

[13] The reader should note that our expression "continuing" future provision, etc., indicates only the not-using-up in advance of the program. In all cases but the first two this "continuing" does not involve maintenance intact during any part of the life of the provision. Even in the second case such maintenance involves no sacrifice.

[14] That is, its weight will be the sum of the differences between the two programs (p. 1355)—no future provision and Future Provision A—in respect of the lesser current advantages and the greater current disadvantages involved in the latter.

[15] It will be recalled that Future Provision A requires 3 days' provision each for 8 wants, or 24 provisions, and therefore 24 hours of working.

vision A rather than to wait and produce it again under the original conditions. Then, however, the result will be that, from its initial maximum of 24 units of retaining, the retaining involved in this future provision will rise by 1 unit per day for 24 days until it reaches 48. On the 30th, 31st, and 32nd days it will decline 8 units per day, on account of the provisions which are consumed without working. It will then stand at its initial maximum and the process will be repeated. Thus, the average of retaining performed, under this method of replacement, will be, in round figures, 36 units instead of about 24. This will add to the disadvantages of this method of replacement. But it will only add about 12 points, making the total 180, which remains less than 211. The adoption of this alternative method presupposes that the contingency is one which is expected to occur once in thirty days but not at a time certain. If it is expected to occur only at 30-day intervals, then the second, or replacing, provision, at least—and perhaps the original one as well—may be made at the rate of 1 hour per day after the first has been consumed. Then the amount of retaining required will be cut from an average of 36 to an average of 12 and the disadvantages of this method will be only 156.

With the second type of contingency such a leveling-out process may not be worth while; and with the first type of technical necessity it will be impossible. For similar technical reasons it will often be impossible as well with long processes.[16] But, in the case of the durable, the leveling can be even more perfect. For, there, as soon as the first product is finished, one day's provision will begin to be abstracted per day. By beginning at once to devote daily the hour available within the current schedule for that want—*c*, *g* or *i*—to a replacement of the durable, a new product will just be completed by the time the first one is used up.[17] Thus the necessary delay in the first use, inherent in a durable, can be rendered inoperative in the event of its continuous replacement. The disadvantages of using this hour for replacement instead of taking it off are, for our longest possible durable for Want *c*, 1,750 points, whereas the disadvantages under the original method were about 2,300. But, under this method, the average amount of retaining will be doubled as compared with a program without replacement or with one which begins replacement only when the previous durable has been used up. On the other hand, the period of waiting for the completion of accumulation will, in the latter case, be eliminated—that is, a new durable will always be ready for use as soon as the old one is used up. Against that, however, will be the fact that the average duration of retaining for each durable will be 250 days instead of 135, as in the original production.[18] The difference, being 115 days, would,

[16] Where seasonal changes are a condition of growth, or where, in a direct economy, the time of transport (being more than 1 day) or the quantity required (fermentation) precludes a continuous process, such leveling is out of the picture, and the fluctuations in quantity of retaining will always repeat the original pattern (with perhaps some overlapping).

[17] That is, it will work that way on the supposition of one hour of working to one use.

[18] The original production called for an average period of retaining of half the period

under Obliquity A, show an additional deduction for retaining of 3⅚ points per day's use, or about 958 points. This is in excess of the difference in disadvantages of the two methods—550 points. Therefore, with Obliquity A, this method of replacement would not be chosen. But, with Obliquity B (see Fig. 60), according to which the rate of accrual of interval effort is only half as great, this method of replacement would be chosen. For, then, the added retaining required would amount only to 479 points, or less than the 550 points difference.

This example makes it clear that there—and it is true in many other situations as well—lesser obliquity may lead to lesser current disadvantages, and greater obliquity may compel greater current disadvantages. But, given a degree of obliquity that permits this method of replacement of durables, this example also demonstrates that the hour that would have been devoted to current provision of the want, if it had not required a durable, can be devoted to a replacement for the durable product now being used. Each day one day's use will be subtracted from the first product; but each day one hour's working will be added to its successor. Thus, the quantity of retaining will remain unchanged, and a "perpetual succession" will be established which, while the constituent products are continually appearing and disappearing, will remain a constant aggregate. To whatever degree the technical conditions of the long process permit, the same system of determining the replacement will apply there.

In the case of the two work economizers, each, producing a saving of 1 hour a day during its life, can be replaced by devoting ½ hour a day to its replacement. This means, of course, that, if replacement is considered also, the true net of advantages turns out to be only half the quantity that appeared in the examples we worked out before taking the replacement into consideration. That deduction would have been allowed for when the original decision was made if, but only if, the rate of accrual of interval effort were sufficiently low not to nullify the time saved by the last use of the machine or the last day's provision of the large batch. Only then would the future occasion, when the same opportunity would repeat itself because the machine or large batch had been used up, appear to be one that was worth while to begin to prepare for now. If such a net advantage still appeared, then, in these cases as in the case of the durable, each day's use would be covered each day by an addition which would exactly equalize it; the quantity of retaining being done would continue at the original maximum level; and, by the time the original large batch or intermediate product was used up, a new one would be completed and ready to take its place.

---

of accumulation (20/2 = 10 days) plus half the period of use (250/2 = 125 days) or 135 days. The replacement under this method, requiring 250 days, would show (250/2 =) 125 days, plus (250/2 =) 125 days, or 250 days.

5. FORGOING AND EXTRA WORKING AS INDEPENDENT FACTORS

One point in regard to this exposition needs to be emphasized. We have been treating of the combined effect of all factors in the competition of future with current wants; we have shown their interrelations and how they modify each other's effects. But we must not leave the impression that any one of them depends on any other. Each is self-standing and self-determined. For instance, it is clear that the size of the sacrifice involved in initiating retaining for accumulation or replacement—say the forgoing of current provision for Want *j* for one day—is no greater whether it is made for one day's provision for Want *g* 30 days ahead, one day's provision for Want *d* 60 days ahead, or one day's provision for Want *a* 90 days ahead, all of which would be equal (or just preferable) alternatives if contingencies appeared to warrant them at all (Fig. 60). In other words the length of time for which the retaining is to be done has no bearing whatever on the magnitude of the sacrifice involved in the retaining. And this conforms to the fact, before noted, that the sacrifice may be—nay usually is—altogether made once for all and that at the outset (i.e., eliminating replacements, it usually does not continue during the interval at all). It is equally clear that the effort and sacrifice involved in the working necessary for a provision—here, according to our assumption, one hour for each—is no greater for any one of these three alternative provisions than it is for any other. And this regardless of whether the hour is regular or extra. In fact, the quantity of work, and therefore of working effort and sacrifice involved at the margin, is precisely the same for all three alternative provisions. Again, therefore, the degree of futurity has no relation to working in any of its aspects. There is only one entity which is proportionate to this futurity, and that is the magnitude of retention—namely, the quantity of retaining (one provision or one hour's work) per day multiplied by the time during which it is performed.

VI

NOTES ON THE ORDER OF PREFERENCE

Appendix to Chapters 13 and 14

A. IMPLICATIONS FOR THE THEORIES OF VALUE AND OF DEMAND

Since modern theories of value and of demand have been based on what we have been calling marginal utility theory, and since our analysis appears to have shown that the assumptions upon which that theory rests are untenable, it seems desirable, before leaving the subject, to consider the effect of this conclusion in its broader aspects upon the theories of value and of demand. It is particularly important and useful to show that our criticism has not been merely destructive and that we have not left large gaps in these theories merely by default. Therefore, while this section of Appendix VI was referred to first in Section C 3 of Chapter 13, in the text, we shall not confine the discussion here to matters covered up to that point, but shall, instead, include all the conclusions arrived at subsequently in Part IV which are required to make this statement complete.

The theory of value resulting from the development of marginal utility theory in general may be analyzed in the following form: Upon the side of subjective valuation it commences with what we have called the conglomerate assumption.[1] This consists of three parts: (1) Since the intensity of want—or pleasure, etc.—is assumed to decline during a single satisfaction, it follows that each successive increment of means going to make up a full measure has less significance than the previous one. (2) Since a means capable of serving several wants in alternative uses is assumed to be applied first where it has the greatest significance, and so on, it follows that successive increments applied to alternative uses will each have less significance than the previous one. (3) Since the intensity of want—or pleasure, etc.—is assumed to decline in proportion to the degree of futurity of each instance provided for, it follows that successive increments applied to more and more distant instances will each have less significance than the previous one. One or more of these three assumptions appears in each presentation of the theory, though they are often not discriminated clearly nor dealt with systematically.

Upon these assumptions, it is conceived that, as the quantity of any means increases, its marginal significance and therefore its subjective value de-

[1] See pp. 437 ff.

clines. It becomes possible, then, so to adjust the combination of quantities of all means that their relative subjective values and their relative "real costs" exactly coincide. This conjuncture may be illustrated graphically. In Fig. 64 we show the curves of relative subjective value for three means, A, B, and C. We also show the relative magnitudes of their "real costs." By applying the latter—the vertical broken lines—to the former it becomes evident that, in the quantities, *a* of A, *b* of B, and *c* of C, the ratio of subjective values will be the same as the ratio of "real costs." [2] The two systems of valuation then agree, and it is impossible to say which of the two governs. But, if the combination of quantities is not precisely *a* of A, *b* of

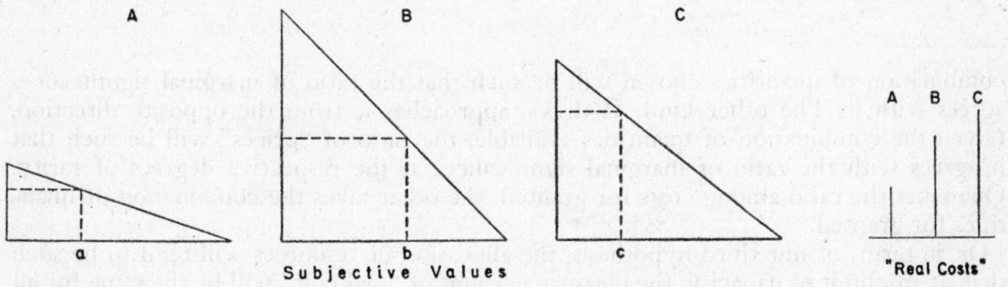

FIG. 64

B, and *c* of C, a divergence appears between the two systems of valuation. If, for instance, the quantity of A is greater than *a*, the ordinate will reach a lower point on the curve. Then subjective value will be lower than "real cost," and subjective value will govern. Or, if the quantity of A is less than *a*, the ordinate will reach a higher point on the curve. Then subjective value will be higher than "real cost," and, again, subjective value will govern. Finally, if the quantity of any means reaches to the point of incidence of the curve on the *x* axis, it will then have no subjective value regardless of whether or not it has a "real cost." This last situation has been construed to mean that the quantity is "unlimited" and, therefore, that the means must be a "free good." Since, under all these conditions, the ratio of "values" conforms to that of subjective values, whether or not the latter agrees with the ratio of "real costs," subjective value has been taken to be the criterion of value and therefore of "price."

I am under the impression that the foregoing has become an unconventional way of demonstrating the theorem.[3] It is now usually said that, at

[2] Such a representation only requires that the unit of each means represented along the *x* axis of each curve be the same unit whose "real cost" is shown by the vertical line to the right. These units need not be—in fact, cannot be—comparable as to A, B, and C. But the unit of "real cost," in terms of which the vertical lines are measured, is the same for A, B, or C. Moreover, we have to assume that the ordinates of the three curves are also commensurable.

[3] As we have before stated, subjective value theory has not been pure. There have been two kinds of impurity. One, exemplified by Wicksteed's "terms of trade" approaches the matter as we have in the first example above, now that we have introduced the influence of "real cost." On that basis, given the ratio of "real costs" (or "prices"), the

the point of equilibrium, the combination of quantities will be such that equal quantities of "real cost" in the forms A, B, and C will have equal subjective values.[4] Very well! Let us convert the representation in Fig. 64 into such terms. We do that in Fig. 65. We have chosen as our common

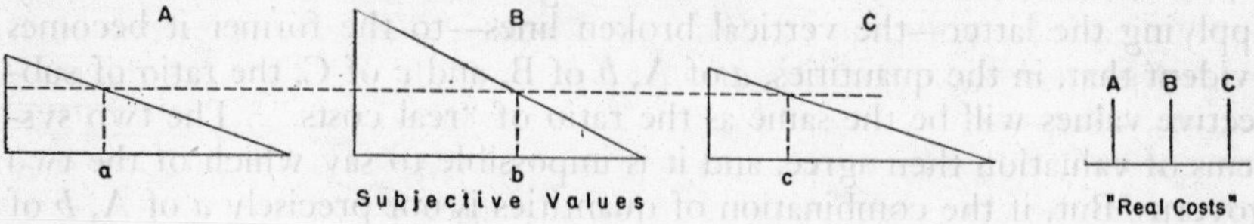

FIG. 65

combination of quantities chosen will be such that the ratio of marginal significances agrees with it. The other kind, Walras's, approaches it from the opposite direction. Given the combination of quantities available, the ratio of "prices" will be such that it agrees with the ratio of marginal significances at the respective degrees of rarity. One takes the ratio among costs for granted; the other takes the combination of quantities for granted.

[4] Or, in terms of our third hypothesis, the allocation of resources will tend to be such that, at any limit of capacity, the pleasure per unit of "real cost" will be the same for all wants. Many of the original exponents of marginal utility theory did not state it in this way, and with some the notion was not clear.

Menger is either not explicit or did not see the point. As Stigler says (*386*, 238), "This endeavor to maximize want-satisfaction by equating the 'marginal' satisfactions of all wants can take place only through the allocation of income, and indeed Menger's theory of the distribution of 'available means' seems to approach this." But (*loc. cit.*, note 17), "If the allocation of income is intended, then not marginal utilities but marginal utilities divided by prices, or in terms of units of equal value, are equated, of course. But we must not expect such refinements of statement from Menger," for he "did not see that the units of all commodities could be so defined that they have equal prices" (*ibid.*, 241, note 24). And this is "an outstanding weakness in his theory of value" (ibid., 239). The same charge holds true of Böhm-Bawerk. To him (*38*, 185) the stock of "productive instruments" will be so allocated that "wants of something like the same importance would depend on the last sample [Menger's *Teilquantität*] of the kind, and the marginal utility of every sample would therefore be approximately equal." Only, of course, if the same quantity of "productive instruments" were used for all the last "samples."

Walras uses our first form of statement. Equilibrium prices of two commodities in terms of either are equal to the ratio of their rarity (*420*, 101). And "rarity is the cause of value in exchange" (*ibid.*, 102). Jevons (*224*, 184–185) uses our second form of statement in the shape of a formula. But Wicksteed seems to think in terms of the first only (see *441*, 71, 76, 86, 373, etc.). Knight (*240*, 65) gives the second form of statement neatly: "In the utilization of limited resources in competing fields of employment, which is the form of all rational activity in conduct, we tend to apportion our resources among the alternative uses that are open in such a way that equal amounts of resource yield equivalent returns in all the fields." One notes that this statement includes, in the phrase "rational activity in conduct," the implicit assumption that underlies all these statements. As Mrs. Robinson expresses it (*348*, 10), "The fundamental assumption on which the present simple technique of analysis is based is that each individual person acts in a sensible manner from the point of view of his own economic interests." But it should be noted that this imputation is based on an a priori determination of what are "his own economic interests," not upon one which is derived from observation.

basis of "real cost" that which the unit of A represented in Fig. 64. That means that the new unit of B will be only half as large as before, and that of C will be only four tenths as large. In turn, that means that the base of B is divided into twice as many units as before, and that of C into two and a half times as many units. It also means that the ordinate (y axis) for the first unit of B is only half as high and that for C only four tenths as high. At the point where the three equal ordinates, A, B, and C, strike the three curves, the quantities *a*, *b* and *c* will have the same subjective values. But, be it noted, these quantities still represent the same proportion of their several bases—the same percentage of a full measure—that they did in Fig. 64.

Now this is a very neat and logical scheme. It complies with all the requirements of an intellectual aesthetic, and therefore meets all the needs of a science which is still at the logistic stage. The only difficulty with it is that it does not conform to the facts. So far as single satisfactions are concerned this scheme rests on the first assumption above. It requires that the intensity of want—or other criterion—should decline during the process of satisfaction in order that there may be, during the process of satisfying every want, some stage or phase at or during which the quantity of satisfaction to be derived from a dollar's worth of means is the same, and can be recognized as being the same, as that of every other. I think we have proved that the first assumption is untenable.[5]

The second part of the conglomerate assumption concerns the kind of product with which these judgments are supposed to be concerned only to a limited extent. The general concept of alternative uses applies chiefly to raw materials, to intermediate product, and to early stages of unfinished final product. The great majority of final products which are finished in our sense—ready for use, not merely ready for sale—are suitable for one want or one constellation only. When they serve several members of a constellation they do so in a single and joint process, not alternatively. In Section D 2 of Chapter 13 we discuss the question of alternative uses so far as it concerns finished final product.

The third assumption misinterprets the facts. It assigns as a diminution in the criterion for subjective valuation what, as we have shown in Chap-

[5] One can see how this whole assumption may have developed from the notion of "scarcity." But, of course, it is impossible to reconcile with the facts a scheme that depends on "scarcity." For example, Walras's extensive utility represents the quantity that would be taken at no price, so that complete satisfaction can only be had at no price ("real cost"). Thus price is either conceived as the necessary bar to complete satisfaction, or a quantity less than this is conceived as the only occasion for price. But we find men taking all they want for a complete satisfaction *at a price*, so that, at no cost, no more would be taken, unless for wastage or carelessness. Walras's limitation of quantity by reason of cost does not apply to any one want or means; it only applies to the aggregate at the point which sets the limit of capacity.

We examine the question of segmentation in Section F of Chapter 13. But even if we find it necessary to make some concession by way of admitting partial satisfactions, it does not follow that any set of segments would ever happen to be on a par with each other.

ter 10, must be regarded as—because it acts as if it were—an increment of "real cost." Thus the influence of futurity is placed by marginal utility theory upon the wrong side. Instead of its effect taking the form of a decrement of subjective value with increasing futurity, it actually takes the form of an increment of "real cost." Instead of being proportionate to the subjective criterion, it is proportionate to the "real cost" in work. Instead of acting as the influence of wants acts, it is limited to acting as the influence of "real cost" acts. Moreover, the influence of futurity is irregular in its general incidence; for it only appears at all when some one of the occasions for retaining, as we have called them, appears.

Our alternative to this theory of value, so far as a direct economy is concerned, is developed in the text at the end of Part IV. Here it will suffice to point out how it differs from—and, I think, refutes—the above-described theory in respect of the general rule, and how it explains the exceptions for the explanation of which marginal utility theory was so largely developed. According to our analysis there are two systems of valuation which hardly ever coincide. The only point at which they do approximately coincide is around the limit of capacity, where the intensities of the least wants included are construed to be about equal to their "real costs" in terms of the intensity of the last hour's working. This gives us a single range in which values under the two systems tend to become commensurable. That, in turn, enables us to say that the subjective values of all means included prior to the means for these wants are higher than their "real costs." And, in turn, that precludes the possibility that the ratio among subjective values and the ratio among "real costs" should coincide except at the marginal want.

We call that the general rule. It is the rule where the combination of quantities is precisely correct. Correctness, according to our analysis in Section C 4 of Chapter 13, and subject to the limiting assumptions there, means that full measures of each means have been provided, no more, no less. Correctness, under the other scheme, means that the quantities are so adjusted that the ratios of the two systems of valuation coincide. In a direct economy, according to our analysis, where any quantity is incorrect, that is because production has varied from plan. The effect of that is too complex and varied to describe here. The reader is referred to the several places in Chapter 13 where it is discussed. Some of these possibilities were also mentioned in Chapter 10 (pp. 659–660). But none of these possibilities affects the subjective value of that portion of the quantity that is correct for a particular use or instance. And the only effect on "real cost" is that the allocated effort is spread over more or less product than was planned.

In a direct economy "price" is inconceivable, unless one defines "price" as what is given in exchange, which would make it identical with "real cost." But, in an indirect economy, it is inherent in some form or other. And, in a single market in a free market economy, the "price" of a single indifferent means will be uniform. So far as the principles of a direct economy account for those of an indirect economy—and they do so to a considerable extent—the resulting theory of value would prescribe that the system of "prices" for a correct combination of quantities would accord with the system of "real costs" without reference to, and for the most part at a level much below, the system of subjective values. Where the quantity produced of any product was short of the quantity wanted at this "price," its "price" would rise, while its several subjective valuations would remain the same. Presumably the "price" would find its level at the bid of the marginal demander for that quantity. And, presumably, that "price" would be above the "real cost." But it would not reach the marginal demander's subjective valuation for all wants served, if there were alternative uses, nor for any one want, if there were substitutes. Similarly, when the quantity was excessive, the price of the whole quantity would fall. Presumably, it would fall to one of, or a combination of, the two following levels: (a) the level necessary to cause a reversal in the marginal demander's weighted terms of substitution with the previously preferred means, or to cause him to include a previously excluded lesser want (alternative use); (b) the level necessary to overcome the added "real cost" for retention and protection if it were held by someone for later sale to someone else for the same want (future provision). In either case, all subjective valuations by all persons would remain the same as before; "real costs"—except for the increment under (b)—would only be altered because the allocated effort would have been spread over less or more product than had been planned; but the relative "price" would be higher or lower, respectively, than the "real cost." All this follows from the general conclusion, which we present in Chapter 14, that, with the possible exception of cases of segmentation, the demand of each separate individual for each separate means (final product) for each separate instance of each separate want has either an infinite elasticity or one of zero, but never one in between these extremes.

So much for the general rule. Now let us consider the exceptions mentioned above. Like certain other features of economic theory, the marginal utility scheme seems to have been developed largely to explain the exceptions. These are, (a) the "high value" of goods when normal supplies are not available because of some kind of an emergency (e.g., war and famine); (b) the "no-value" of "free goods" (e.g., air); (c) the "high value" of non-reproducible products (e.g., art objects); (d) the "high value" of raw materials which exist in small quantities (e.g., diamonds).[6] The difficulty here is the usual one that, when one grasps for an hypothesis that explains the exceptions, he may drop the one that explains the general case. As between an hypothesis that explains the general case only, and one that explains the exceptions only, one should naturally prefer the former. True, a correct hypothesis can have no exceptions. But, in science and particularly in sciences dealing with such complicated matters as human society, where many factors enter, it is better to start with an hypothesis that works most of the time, by reason of the fact that it includes the chief and prevalent

[6] We are not defining what is meant by "value." That is the usual expression. What it means in each case will appear below.

factors, and then to proceed to hunt down the causes of the exceptions, on the theory that they are due to occasional and exceptional interfering factors.

Emergencies. The behavior of a man who is starving, when any food at all may come to have an enormously high "value" (here subjective value), proves nothing about the ordinary course of events. It is probable that the great bulk of American people have never experienced real hunger in their entire lives. The fact that the beginning of the want curve for food of a starving man is practically asymptotic to the *y* axis does not indicate that the first morsel of food in the daily dinner of a well-fed man has any such rating. The want takes a different level under abnormal conditions from what it does under normal conditions. One cannot fit a single scheme of subjective valuation to both. Nor, as we have shown in the text, can one argue, in this respect, from hunger, which is one of the great prior wants, to some subordinate want. There may be no such phenomenon as abnormal levels among the latter. We discuss this matter in more detail in Section B 1, below.

Free Goods. The reason so-called "free goods" have no "value" is not that they exist in unlimited quantities and that, therefore, the supply reaches along the *x* axis beyond the point of incidence of the want curve.[7] It is merely because, under ordinary conditions, we do not class the activity involved in making such things serve our wants as effortful activity, or working. That is, we treat them as having no "real cost." Such activities we have called "direct consumption." As a matter of fact, air—the typical "free good"—serves one of the most intense wants. But, even when one gets out of breath, so that the want rises to sufficient intensity (actual variation from homeostasis) to make one stop everything else and devote himself to breathing, the "value" of air does not rise, nor does one call the activity work. Air only becomes "valuable" when one pays an added price for one's theater ticket to cover ventilation. Then the air comes to have a cost. But, then, the want has not risen from the ordinary state of concurrent satisfaction (i.e., a mere tendency). Thus, the "value," in this sense, depends on "real cost," not on the intensity of the want. Air has no "value" when it is costless. It has "value" when it is costful. And this regardless of the intensity of the want—the subjective value—under the two conditions.

Non-reproducible Products. The "value" of non-reproducible products is, of course, not due to limited supply. There are plenty of every kind of non-reproducible products (e.g., works of art) that have little or no "value." Is it due, then, to the fact that the limited supply of some particular product happens to reach along the *x* axis of certain wants such a short distance that the ordinate reaches a very high point on the *y* axis?

Let us consider first what are the precise quantitative conditions of the supply of such products with reference to the demand curves of an individual. In the first place, there is a myriad of paintings in general. One might

[7] The distinction between limited and unlimited quantities of natural resources has already been sufficiently exploded in Chapter 11.

say that the supply is unlimited. According to that the "value" should be nil. But, you say, each picture is unique. According to that the supply is one unit in each case. One does not want half a picture or two duplicates. A single collector does not buy even two paintings of the same scene by one man (e.g., Van Gogh's two portraits of "L'Arlesienne" or his two paintings of the "Blue Room"), or two etchings from the same plate—unless he is collecting examples of the several "conditions" because of interest in their differences. If, then, the demand curve for each object of art covers but one unit along the base, it is not a descending curve. It is one of our truncated curves—that is, rectangular. One unit is wanted and no more. If so, one cannot determine the subjective valuation by finding out how far down a descending curve one unit reaches. For there is no demand for less or for more than the single unit in each case.

In that event we are dealing with what we have called a full measure or an indivisible unit. How then interpret such demand in our scheme? In the first place, the work of art is a durable. That means that it is inherently future provision. Since it is a very durable durable, the occasions on which it will satisfy or fail to satisfy the various members of the constellation to which it will cater stretch indefinitely into the future. Demand in the present must thus be based on an estimate in which all future instances are summated in some manner. This estimate is based on past experience. That teaches that, each time the work of art is viewed or thought of (each time the wants recur), some members of the vast constellation served will be satisfied and probably some will not be satisfied. Nor will the one and the other groupings necessarily be always the same on each occasion. Along these lines a rough estimate of the sum of all future satisfactions to be derived for each member want is made, and probably in this case we have simultaneous summation of the wants served (see Chapter 8).

Since durability is roughly the same for all works of art in the same category, it is probable that subjective valuation ignores this factor in appraising the several unique examples. Then, for each example, there is a different subjective valuation according to the respective number and strength of wants which will be satisfied, with possibly a deduction for wants which will be aroused and left unsatisfied (annoyance). A group of works of art in one category (i.e., comparable) will then be arranged in a series of steps representing their respective subjective valuations by an individual. Such a series represents something analogous to unweighted terms of substitution among a group of substitutes which are not indifferent because the attributes exist in fixed quantities. So far as the individual's demand for this category of works of art is concerned, this series also represents his several top bids in relative terms.[8] The top bid of no two individuals for each work of art will be precisely the same. If the artist is living and offers a work of art for sale, it will go to the bidder whose relative appraisal of the particular unique example is highest among available bidders. If the artist is dead, someone other than he must already

[8] These will also depend on the individual's capacity. See below.

possess the work of art. It will then change hands only when it ranks relatively higher along the range on someone's else scale than it does on the possessor's. In the case of non-reproducible products "value" means "price." The "price" is certainly below the subjective value of the successful bidder. Whether or not it is above or below "real cost" is a problem which will concern us when we come to examine an indirect economy.

The only direct and peculiar effect of the limitation of quantity (the fact that each example is unique) is to bring into play, in the constellation of wants served, the want for rarity *per se* (i.e., to have something no one else has). But this, without the rest of the constellation, would have no effect. For a bad and worthless picture is as unique as a good and valuable one.

Rare Raw Materials. Means made of rare raw materials (e.g., precious stones) follow somewhat the same lines. But here, of recent years, it has become impossible in most cases to class precious stones as they used to be classed. For most have become artificially reproducible out of other and not rare materials. For such artificial "precious stones," "real cost" probably sets the "value" level. However, for those that are still not artificially reproducible, and for all in former times, what has been the relation of demand to quantity?

Such gems, like works of art, are durables and they serve many wants in a constellation for an indefinite future. But, unlike works of art, each specimen—with rare exceptions—cannot be considered as unique. Nor is it true, in this case, that an individual wants only one of many duplicates. The usual way of showing this situation has been to impose on a standard declining demand curve a horizontal supply curve—assuming units of equal "real cost." Now this horizontal supply curve represents the facts in one respect. It shows that each successive diamond, for instance, costs the same as its predecessor. But, in relation to the demand curve, it is erroneous; for it treats each successive diamond as if it were applied to a single segment of the wants concerned, independently of its predecessors. Diamonds are durables. As one proceeds along these curves, preceding diamonds have not been consumed (as with food). They are still there. That is, in this case the diamonds are not arranged ordinally; they are arranged cardinally. They are cumulative.[9]

If a collector has gradually acquired ten diamonds, this constellation of wants is thereafter continuously supplied with ten diamonds at ten times the "real cost" that had been incurred when he possessed only one diamond. As the number acquired and the cumulative cost applied to this single constellation increase, there must come a time when the cumulative "real cost" exceeds what, within any given capacity, the collector is willing to assign to that constellation. If that point sets a quantitative limit to the demand of any individual, why not show the situation in the form of a horizontal demand curve (infinite elasticity) upon which is imposed

[9] In Section F of Chapter 13 we treat this as an instance of rising "real costs" of larger part measures.

a rising (cumulative) cost curve which, at some point, intersects the demand curve? [10] Why is it necessary to import the notion of a declining demand curve? One explanation is enough. It is the accumulating "real cost" to the individual (rising "real cost" of enlarging aggregate), not the declining subjective value of successive separate units, that sets the limit.

Moreover, aside from this, observation of diamond buyers disproves the declining demand curve, if we need further disproof. For example, a young man buys his fiancée a solitaire for an engagement ring. One diamond is his limit. Thereafter he makes money and wants to buy his wife a diamond bracelet or even, eventually, a diamond necklace. At that stage, one more diamond no longer interests him. He is now interested in forty or fifty more diamonds. He takes them all at one gulp. He pays the same for each (say) as for the original solitaire. But now he has reached his new limit. His new capacity [11] is forty-one or fifty-one diamonds. That quantity of "real cost" is all that he is willing to assign to this particular constellation of wants. Such a change is ordinarily shown, in terms of marginal utility theory, as a movement of his demand curve to the right. What an utterly wrong concept! The man has not changed. He is the same man with the same wants. Why assign the change to developments in his psychological make-up when it is perfectly obvious, and true by definition, that what has changed has been his capacity. His capacity having increased, he is now willing to assign to a persistently unsatiated, and perhaps in itself an almost insatiable, constellation an amount of "real cost" many times what he was willing to appropriate at first.[12]

Demand among many individuals determines the "price." If we start with completely unsatisfied demand for diamonds and with given intensity of the want and capacity for each individual, the amount each will allocate to diamonds is given. These lump-sum allocations can be arranged in descending order. If any particular quantity of diamonds is applied along this descending order, the "price" will be the top bid of the individual whose bid is necessary in order to dispose of the whole quantity.[13] If the capacity of any individual rises, his allocation may increase. The "price"

[10] In terms of our analysis of segmentation, this cumulative cost curve probably never actually intersects the curve of subjective value. Instead, it probably ends, for each capacity, at the level determined by the block of "real cost" that will be assigned to a relatively insatiable want.

[11] The use of the term capacity here should not lead the reader to suppose that we believe that individual capacity in an indirect economy is determined in the same way as in a direct economy.

[12] This process is that which we work out in Chapter 13, Section F, under segmentation—i.e., the allocation to a want of a certain quantity of "real cost" which is less than enough to satiate it.

[13] Let us say that the allocations are 1,000, 900, 800, 700, and 600. The first would cover 1 diamond @ 1,000, 2 diamonds @ 500, etc. If there are 5 diamonds, the price will be 600 because the first bidder's bid for a second diamond is only 500. On the other hand, if we add allocations of 500 and 400 and increase the number of diamonds to 7, the first bidder will bid 500 each for two and the next to last will also bid 500 for one. Those intervening will each get one at 500, and the last bidder will be excluded.

will then rise sufficiently to cause those with unchanged capacity to surrender some of their diamonds. The same scheme can be applied to a flow of new diamonds. But, there, the new demand is limited to new individuals or to increases in capacity among the old.[14]

With rare raw materials "value" means "price." "Price" will be below the subjective values of all bidders, even that of the marginal bidder. That is, it will be if we are correct in our hypothesis as to allocation to wants for which satiation is too expensive. If there are unworked deposits, it is presumably because the "real cost" of working them would be greater than "price." The "price" will be above the "real cost" of those deposits that are worked, in proportion as the general accessibility in each channel is superior to the best of the unworked channels—i.e., a series of differentials will exist.

B. THE DIFFERENCE IN THE INFLUENCE OF "REAL COSTS" ON PRIOR AND ON SUBORDINATE WANTS

We are going to consider, here, three of the possible explanations that suggest themselves for the apparent lack of influence of "real costs" in distorting the order of preference based on the order of priority so far as the great prior wants are concerned. The evidence for this lack was presented in Chapter 13, Section C 4. This procedure does not exclude other possible explanations; it merely includes all those I have been able to conceive.

1. LEVELS OF ABNORMAL MAXIMA

In our analysis of the internal present wants, both those which usually subsist as tendencies only but which may become actual variations away from homeostasis, as well as the storage wants which are always actual variations, we found that any want which is not kept satisfied (a tendency offset), or which is not satiated when it occurs or recurs, tends to rise to, or to recur at, an intensity above the level that we have called the normal maximum. Thus, the notion of normal maximum, which we have been using to define the order of priority, is only applicable to a period during which present wants can be and are kept satisfied (tendencies) or are satiated as they succeed in securing prepotence. This we have regarded as the normal process, so far as those wants are concerned whose satisfactions seem always to be preferred, within the limit of capacity, but which are otherwise not subject to the influence of "real costs." And this, we have held, governs the comparative force of these wants in relation to all others, even when they only exist as future wants—mnemonic-volitional phenomena.

We recognize, then, that the intensities of the particular wants we have chiefly studied may, under certain conditions, rise into the range of ab-

[14] All this assumes that none of the individuals concerned arrives at the point where the wants in this constellation are satiated (i.e., each one's demand retains infinite elasticity).

normal levels. In economic literature attention has often been called to the fact that hunger in a famine or in a besieged city, or thirst in the desert, will concentrate the entire attention and energy of men on that single satisfaction. "Real cost" is then no longer a consideration. There can be no question that this is the fact. In the terms of our analysis, when any such internal present want rises far beyond its normal maximum it may secure continuous prepotence over all other present wants—except for the interruptions of fear, rage, etc.—and may put an enormous force behind the drive for satisfaction. We consider such abnormal conditions from a different angle in Section F of Chapter 13, where they belong to the extent that they may be regarded as due to incomplete satisfaction (segmentation).[1]

Now our distinction between abnormal and normal levels of intensity was based entirely on the particular wants examined in our physiological study, and it is always with regard to these same wants that such conditions are cited in economic literature. It is quite possible that the same difference does not apply to subordinate wants—in other words, that wants beyond the range we have called the prior wants do not rise in intensity, or at least do so in a far less proportion, when they are not regularly satisfied. We do not know. But it is worth while to consider such a supposition, since it might serve as a basis for an explanation of the different effect of "real costs" on prior and on subordinate wants. Is it possible that the intensity of future wants, which determines their relative force in the order of preference for current provision, is not proportionate to their normal maxima but to some potential level above that up to their abnormal maxima? If so, is it also possible that there is no difference in level, or no equivalent difference, in the case of the subordinate wants?

Let us start with the first question; for, if that has to be answered in the negative, the whole supposition falls. The most important and most difficult assumption which this supposition would require is that man's actual order of preference among current provisions is not based on his experience but on hearsay or on insight. For, as a matter of fact, most modern men in civilized economies have never experienced what are described as the "tortures" of extreme hunger or thirst. If our analytical entity, a direct economy, were based on the experiences of Robinson Crusoe, we might be able to accept this assumption. But since it is not—since it is, instead, merely an abstraction from actual life around us—we are compelled to be more realistic. And realism excludes these potential abnormal intensities as actual experiences of most individuals. If, then, we would have to attribute this abnormal intensity to hearsay or insight, we

[1] We may note also that such *actual experiences* of abnormal levels cannot be used to explain the absence of influence of "real costs" upon the prior wants in the current order of preference—i.e., the allocation of the day's working. For the actual experience can only arise if there is a shortage from the planned quantity of output or where the "real cost" has become extremely high. In the latter case, the inverse dimension might have risen from normal as much as the direct dimension had; and the value of the ratio might be no higher.

face a further difficulty. It appears that, so long as he considers contingencies of our first type or technical necessities of our first type to be improbable, man does not hoard food and water. But, if his judgment seems to exclude as improbable the possibility that he will have no food or water when the time comes, why should we suppose that his judgment would permit these current wants to act on the current order of preference with the same force as they would if he had already been without food or water for some time? So much for the specific doubts that apply only to this possible explanation. For the rest it is subject to all the difficulties of the next one, to which we now turn.

2. A STEEPLY DESCENDING ORDER OF PRIORITY

Whether because the effective levels of intensity are the potential (abnormal) or the normal maxima, it would be possible to suppose that the effective levels of the prior wants are generally much higher than those of the subordinate wants. This condition could exist in either of two forms —forms which work out somewhat differently. The first form would involve the assumption that the effective levels of all prior wants are markedly higher than those of all subordinate wants—that there is a definite and wide gap in the order of priority between the least prior and the greatest subordinate want. To test that possibility let us take the series of wants included in I, Fig. 40 (p. 872), and multiply all their effective intensities by five.[2] The values of their ratios would then be changed to the following: A = 25, B = 9.5, C = 15, D = 10, E = 6.65, F = 30. Now it is clear, at once, that such a supposition would suffice to explain why all prior wants are provided for before any subordinate wants are provided for, and that it would do so on a basis that gave full effect to the order of ratios. For all these new ratios are higher than any of those in Series II, Fig. 40. But it would remain just as difficult as before to explain why the order of ratios had no effect, among these prior wants, on the successive historical orders of preference as capacity gradually expanded. For the relation among these ratios is now the same as it was before. On this new basis the order of ratios is still F, A, C, D, B, E. That certainly does not correspond to historical fact.

The same condition could exist in another form which would not only distinguish between prior and subordinate wants, but would also permit the order of ratios (the influence of "real costs") to coincide with the order of priority within the range of prior wants. This would involve the assumption that the order of priority is a very steeply descending one through the range of prior wants.[3] To test this, let us see how steeply the order would have to descend in order that, in our example I in Fig. 40,

[2] The original numerical values given this series were stated on p. 874, note 23.

[3] It appears that, if this were the situation, we could no longer assume it to be due to the fact that the effective levels among prior wants were the potential (abnormal) rather than the actual (normal) intensities. For this would require a very steep decline in the potential levels within that range, for which there appears no warrant in the facts.

the ratios of all prior wants would be higher than that of any subordinate want, but also in order to obliterate the effects of differences in "real costs" among the major wants sufficiently to make the order of ratios the same as the order of priority. If we multiply the intensities of the series A to F by a series of diminishing multipliers—A by 16, B by 15, C by 8, D by 8, E by 8 and F by 1.5—we get an order of priority (intensities) as follows: A = 320, B = 285, C = 144, D = 136, E = 128 and F = 22.5. We also get an order of ratios which arranges itself in terms of values as follows: A = 80, B = 28.5, C = 24, D = 16, E = 10⅔ and F = 9.

Evidently this assumption does the trick. But is it a reasonable or realistic one? The chief difficulty with it is one which arises from an analysis developed in Chapter 14. We have found reason to believe that the length of the working-day, if left to the choice of the worker, is fixed at the point where the effort and sacrifice involved in the last hour's working begins to exceed the intensity of the next want in the order of preference. With primitive man capacity was often limited to providing for the prior wants only. Of these, hunger, thirst, and a minimum of protection were the principal ones that required working. If we combine this with the assumption of a very steep decline in the order of priority, we find ourselves on the horns of a dilemma. Either we must assume that ratios of this order of value obtained at that period, which involves the supposition that "real costs" were then about the same as now, or we must assume that the values of the ratios in this range were then nowhere near so high, because "real costs" were then many times as great (in hours of working) as now. The first assumption runs head on into the fact that "real costs" were then many times as great as now. Even if we say that this was largely offset by the practice of allocating to each added want, at least after food and drink, only a small amount of work, and being "satisfied" with that, we are in trouble. For such an argument would assume that, nevertheless, the incentive existed for a very long working-day among primitive men which, as technique was improved, was greatly shortened. But we find evidence that the opposite was the case—and give in Chapter 14 an adequate explanation of the fact. When we face the other horn of the dilemma we see that it has the effect of eliminating, or almost eliminating the proffered explanation. For we are relying on high values of ratios to explain the matter, and this assumption reduces the values of these ratios toward, or to, their levels in the original example.

This last difficulty seems to be the real one we must face in any attempt to account for the favoritism shown the prior wants. For observation indicates that the prior wants, for food, shelter, clothing, etc., have always been and still are among the highest cost means, though not in the order named. Early men appear to have occupied practically all their available working-time in providing food, and to have afforded little or no working-time in providing shelter. Yet neither then nor now have men ignored the factor of "real costs" in considering provision for these wants. They always have chosen, and still choose, the least expensive among possible substitutes which are actually indifferent; they always have terminated, and still terminate (so far as the choice lies with them) the working-day when "real cost" exceeds the intensity of the want.

3. THE CONCEPT OF "NECESSITIES"

Man customarily distinguishes, and apparently has always distinguished, between what he regards as his "necessities" and what he regards as "comforts" and "luxuries."[4] His "necessities" cover, or have come always to include, what we are calling the prior wants. It may be that, even in the absence of personal experience, insight discloses that these wants must be satisfied in order that he may continue to live, and so differentiates them from the rest. Recognition of this differentiation would not require the concession that the effective relative level of intensity of the future wants derived from these is their potential maxima rather than their normal maxima as actually experienced. Nor would it prove that the initial range of the order of priority is much higher or much more steeply descending than the rest. Neither would it definitely exclude either of these possibilities as perhaps no more than participants in the process. It would merely introduce another factor, determining the dividing line between those wants which *must* be satisfied and those which need not be. This would be, so far as we are concerned, a purely hypothetical explanation of the apparent fact that the influence of "real costs" (the order of ratios) does not begin to conflict with the influence of wants (the order of priority) until a certain range in the order is passed. In the text we merely recognized this apparent fact without attempting any explanation. Our reason for the omission is that this hypothesis as to "necessities" does not arise from, or connect itself in any apparent way with, the system of energetics we developed inductively in Part I. If this hypothetical factor constitutes the correct explanation, it will itself have to be accounted for by other physiological or psychological studies.

The same concept could be expanded to include the observation that man's notion of "necessities" expands as his accustomed standard of living improves. It appears almost as if there were, within each standard—on almost every scale—a solid core that has become "necessities."[5] These are the *musts*. Beyond that, if the musts do not consume the whole capacity, lie the matters of choice—the means that *can* be afforded and those that cannot, and, among those which can be afforded, the ones that *will* be afforded and those that will not.[6]

[4] These general concepts will be discussed again in Section I, below.

[5] One sees this particularly among those in "reduced circumstances" who cling, often at a sacrifice that astounds the observer, to certain rather expensive provisions that must seem to them essential—their *sine qua non.*

[6] While it is not necessary to our analysis, I think it well to preserve this last distinction between wants deliberately excluded which come before the general range of incidence of the limit of capacity upon the order of priority and those that are almost automatically excluded because they lie beyond that range. Strictly speaking, both must be excluded because their ratios are too low. But there seems to be a psychological differ-

C. SEGMENTATION ON THE BASIS OF CUMULATIVE COSTS OF INCREASING PART MEASURES

In subsection F 2 of Chapter 13 we outlined as a possible basis for deliberate segmentation, the fact that successively larger part measures of a means have successively larger "real costs," while the intensity of the want is presumably the same for initial segments of all sizes. The result of distinguishing such part measures would be that, conceptually at least, we would have a more complex order of ratios and one in which part measures of each size would occupy a position in the order in advance of that of the full measure for the same want. If the ratio of the full measure were $\frac{3}{4}$, that of a quarter would be $\frac{3}{1}$, of a half $\frac{3}{2}$ and of three-quarters $\frac{3}{3}$. The quarter measure would be ranged in the order of ratios along with full measures for other wants the value of whose ratios was about 3; the half measure with those whose values were about 1.5; and the three-quarter measure with those whose values were about unity.

If we limit the application of this basis for segmentation to special cases meeting the following requirement, we run into no great difficulties. This requirement is that the want with an intensity of 3 (say) should occupy a position in the order of priority around which were arrayed wants the "real costs" of whose full measures were about 1, or even 2. When such a want came up for consideration—in the order of priority—it would be compared with neighboring wants whose intensity ranged also about 3, but the values of whose ratios were, say, 3 or even 1.5. Rather than pass over such a want it might be segmented with a quarter-measure (value of 3) or a half-measure (value of 1.5), thus putting it on a par with wants of similar intensity.

However, nothing we have developed in the course of our analysis furnishes any logical basis for limiting the effect of this principle to such cases. If it is to be so limited, that will have to be done by reason of some satisfactory explanation arrived at by others, not by us. But, if it is not so limited, it runs into insuperable difficulties. In the first place, as we pass along the order of preference we come eventually to the marginal want the value of whose full measure ratio is unity. There seems no obvious reason why this marginal want should have preference over the segmented one. To the latter there could be allocated a three-quarter measure, also with a ratio of unity. Why leave the latter one-quarter satisfied when it can be three-quarters satisfied within the limit of capacity? Once this is admitted, it becomes clear that, on the same rule, all wants whose position in the order of priority is prior to the general incidence of the limit of capacity,

---

ence between those, high in the order of priority, that remain to tease recurrently and those, lower in the order of priority, that never, or hardly ever, come up because they are always recognized to be beyond capacity.

but whose full measure ratios have a value less than unity, would be placed in the marginal range. That is, whatever segment of such wants could show a ratio of unity would be satisfied. The margin would become a wide range of partially satisfied wants whose ratios had been arbitrarily adjusted to a value of unity. And the basis of allocation would have changed to one according to which there would be allocated to each want an amount of "real cost" equal to its intensity, if less did not provide a full measure.[7]

However, in the second place, there would be no reason for stopping there. According to our thesis, the order of priority of wants extends indefinitely and far beyond the general incidence of the limit of capacity. On this principle there would be no reason for excluding such wants. So long as a want had any intensity at all it would be entitled to an allocation of "real cost" equal to that intensity. In other words, all wants would be at least partially satisfied. The order of ratios would consist of a descending order of full measure ratios up to a certain point. Thereafter, what we have called the margin, where the ratio is unity, would extend over part measures for all other wants, all of whose ratios had been brought arbitrarily to unity.

It is clear that any such extension of the principle of segmentation to its logical limit under this criterion (value of unity for the ratio) would require a vast increase of capacity. Then the effects of the mechanism for limiting capacity, which are demonstrated in Chapter 14, would have to be allowed for. Since the intensity of effort and sacrifice for the last hour's working is presumed to rise rather rapidly, the allocation of all this additional "real cost" to part measures would have rapidly reduced the values of all ratios. That is, taking the factor unity in the inverse dimension to represent the intensity of the last hour for capacity allocated to full measures only, the factor in the inverse dimension of all ratios would rise rapidly above unity.[8] Correspondingly, ratios whose values had been unity would now decline below that level. In order to adjust for this, all part measures would now need to be reduced in size to bring the value of their ratios up to unity again. But, worse than that, many full measures whose values had been insufficiently above unity would now need to be reduced to part measures.

There is no need of working out in detail the ultimate effect of such a process. The tendency would be toward—and might well reach—a situation in which all wants were partially satisfied and none were satiated. That was the rock on which were wrecked both hypotheses based on declining intensity of wants during the process of satisfying. While this

[7] An exception might be made for wants whose means are available only in what have been called "large units"—by definition indivisible. But we have already cast doubt on the existence of any want all of whose substitute means are available only in large units. In fact, upon analysis, large units usually turn out to be durables of a long life, each installment of which may be relatively small and capable of being made very small.

[8] If a unit of work at the intensity of the last hour of an eight-hour day is taken as having a factor of 1, that of a nine-hour day might be 1.25, of a ten-hour day 1.5, etc.

supposition as to segmentation denies declining intensity, nevertheless it is quite clear that, though it approaches the rock on another tack, it is equally certain to be wrecked there. Thus, as we said in the text,[9] unless someone can supply an adequate explanation why man should choose to satisfy a segment of a want—a partial satisfaction rather than none—and still stop far short of allocating to each want a quantity of "real cost" equal to its intensity, our thesis as to segmentation is in a parlous state. Apparently we cannot deny the fact of segmentation without cracking up on Scylla; apparently we cannot admit it without cracking up in Charybdis.

D. SEGMENTATION ON THE BASIS OF DECLINING INTENSITY OF WANTS

In Part I,[1] when we were dealing with the influence of wants only upon the virtual order of preference, we finally rejected the possibility, so far as our own hypothesis was concerned, that there is a continuous decline in the intensity of a want during the process of satisfying. But we left open the possibility that such intensity may decline in two or more discontinuous steps. This admission was due in part to our recognition that, in the case of some wants, intensity seems to exist or reappear at a level below the normal maximum after partial satisfaction has taken place. From these cases the inference might be drawn that the same discontinuous drop takes place at the same point in the process of complete satisfaction. Thus it is possible to conceive that, in such cases, there are two or more steps in the whole process of satisfying in which the intensity stands at successively lower levels during successive phases.[2] If so, one might suppose that deliberate segmentation takes place in terms of these phases, so that the level of intensity of each determines the drive for the satisfaction of each segment independently of each other. The admission of this possibility was also due to the fact that, as we showed there,[3] such a construction would not exclude the possibility that some wants might be satiated, while others remained partially satisfied or even excluded. In other words such an hypothesis, considering the influence of wants only, might pass that part of the test of reality.

Now, in Part IV, where we were examining the influence of "real costs" on segmentation, we disregarded this possibility in favor of the supposition that intensity continues at about the same level throughout any uninterrupted process of satisfying. It becomes necessary, therefore, to demonstrate what bearing the intrusion of the influence of "real costs" has upon this question and why that has led us to consider it not worth while to present a construction which, under the influence of wants only, we admitted might be possible.

[9] P. 928.
[1] See pp. 499–502.
[2] See Fig. 19, p. 499.
[3] See pp. 499–500 and Fig. 20.

Under the limiting conditions of Part I, while the process of satisfying each want could be objectively measured in terms of the fraction consumed of a full measure of means with proportionate attributes,[4] no comparison would be possible in that dimension as among different wants. This because different means for different wants are objectively incommensurable. But when "real costs" are introduced, all processes of satisfying become commensurable in these terms. This enables us to conceive a basis for deliberate segmentation which would depend on the supposition of step-like declines of intensity. Let us suppose that, for each want, it is possible to recognize—or, after experience, to learn—the points at which the successive drops in intensity take place during the process of satisfying. Let us suppose that, as to each want, these points could be marked off on the scale of objective units into which a full measure of such means is divided. If that could be done, the correct "real cost" could be assigned to each of the successive part measures of means which correspond to the satisfying between each pair of successive drops in intensity. The result would be that there would theoretically exist an order of ratios in which individual ratios represented the relative intensity of individual segments, so constituted, to the "real cost" of each part measure, instead of the relative maximum intensities to the "real cost" of a full measure. As before, these ratios would have neither a uniform magnitude in the direct dimension nor one in the inverse dimension. In addition, such a system of ratios would be more numerous, since for each want there would now be a ratio for each segment. However, let us pass over those difficulties at this stage and first determine how such a system would work if it were psychologically possible to compare the values of these ratios.

The first change that such a modified hypothesis would require would be in the order of priority. We might suppose that the initial segment of each want would occupy the same position that the whole want occupies in our order of priority—i.e., that given it by its normal maximum intensity. But all other segments of each want would occupy successively more subordinate positions in the order. Thus, on the supposition that the order in which wants are considered in establishing the order of preference is the order of priority, each subsequent segment of each want would only be considered when its turn came.

The second change required follows from this. Upon our tentative hypothesis in Section F 2 of Chapter 13 and in Section C of this appendix, the only question involved, if segmentation is to occur, is how large the initial segment shall be. This scheme, however, extends to all segments within capacity, and each stands on its own feet.

The third change is in the order of ratios. In order to demonstrate this

[4] It is not worth while to treat separately means with fixed attributes under these supposed conditions. For them there is no objective measure along the base—dimension of process. There is merely the measure of "real cost" of alternative means. Thus they would skip the first step in the process of measuring; but thereafter they would follow the same scheme.

clearly, let us make some simplifying and wholly artificial assumptions. Let us suppose, first, that all wants are divided into two equal segments each requiring half a full measure, and that the intensity applicable to the first part measure is the normal maximum, while that applicable to the second is half the maximum. We can then increase this subdivision to three equal part measures, the intensity corresponding to which will be the maximum, and two-thirds and one-third the maximum, respectively. We can then conceive n equal part measures for each of which the intensity is $\frac{1}{n}, \frac{2}{n}$ . . . less than the maximum, respectively. Thus we approach the continuous curve (straight line) on the criterion of remaining intensity as closely as we desire. But we cannot reach it; for a continuous curve could, by definition, have no discontinuities according to which to define successive phases in the process of satisfying.

The chief difficulty with this scheme, just as with that one analyzed in Section C of this appendix, is in the incidence of the limit of capacity. That limit is the ratio with a value of unity. The primary effect of subdivision (segmentation), no matter how great, would leave undisturbed all wants the values of whose full measure ratios are above unity. This is obvious. If that ratio is $\frac{1+}{1}$, then the ratios of two equal segments will be $\frac{1+}{0.5}$ and $\frac{0.5+}{0.5}$, respectively. This may be generalized. For any number of equal subdivisions the value of the ratio of the first part measure will be that number of times greater than the value of the ratio of the full measure, and the value of the ratio of the last part measure will be the same as that of the full measure. This is axiomatic on our simplifying assumptions.

The primary effect of such subdivision is to bring within the limit numbers of segments of wants whose full measure ratios would exclude them. Thus $\frac{1-}{1}$, if divided into two segments, gives ratios of $\frac{1-}{0.5}$ and $\frac{0.5-}{0.5}$; if divided into three segments the ratios are $\frac{1-}{0.33}, \frac{0.66-}{0.33}, \frac{0.33-}{0.33}$. Under the first, one segment (half) would come within the limit; under the second, two segments (thirds) would do so. The generalization is more complicated here. If segments are halves, half of all wants whose ratios of full measures are above $\frac{0.5}{1}$ will be included. If segments are thirds, one-third of all with full measure ratios above $\frac{0.33}{1}$ and two-thirds of all with full measure ratios above $\frac{0.66}{1}$ will be included. Obviously, the greater the subdivision the greater the reach of inclusion and the proportion of inclusion along the order of ratios of full measures.

Just as in the scheme described in Section C of this appendix, if the primary effect is to leave undisturbed all wants the values of whose full measure ratios are above unity and yet to include an indefinite number of part measures for an indefinite number of wants which, in terms of full measures only, would be excluded, it is clear that a large increase in capacity is required. This brings in, as the secondary effect, the mechanism for limiting capacity discussed in Chapter 14. Since the curve of working rises as working-hours (capacity) are extended, these ratios, requiring longer working-hours, could no longer be stated with the same factor in the inverse dimension. For the same "real cost," the magnitude in the inverse dimension would rise in proportion to the rise in the factor, and the value of the ratio would decline. Some of those wants or segments which formerly had a value of unity would no longer have it. Capacity might be expanded; but, as it expanded, it would tend to exclude more and more segments primarily included. Somewhere a new balance would be struck. But, at this point, inclusions and exclusions would be distributed somewhat differently. All inclusions of earlier segments of wants which were beyond the limit in terms of full measure ratios could now be included only at the expense of further working-hours or of the exclusion of later segments of wants within the previous limit.

Without attempting to appraise these several effects we may make a rough generalization. The greater the degree of subdivision the greater the number of wants which would be only partially satisfied—absence of satiation. This would be due to the fact that, the greater the degree of subdivision, the greater the reach of exclusion among later segments of wants whose full measures had been within the limit and, correspondingly, the greater the reach of inclusion among earlier segments of wants whose full measures had been beyond the limit. This follows from our premises. They prescribe that the larger the number of subdivisions, the larger the multiplier to be applied to the value of the full measure ratio in order to find the value of the initial part measure ratio. Thus we may say that, the greater the degree of subdivision that is supposed, the more nearly this scheme approaches the scheme based on the hypothesis of a continuous decline of intensity and, therefore, the greater the elimination of the possibility of satiation. But such an elimination is the insuperable objection to that hypothesis.

All the difficulties increase in this scheme in proportion to the degree of subdivision that is conceived to be possible. If a decline of intensity is supposed to take place about halfway through the process of satisfying, the difficulties are not great. But the more often such declines are supposed to occur the greater become our objections.

Our objections are:

1. The complication of the order of priority
2. Independent consideration of other than initial segments
3. The increased reliance on ratios with no common magnitude in either dimension

4. The questionable effect upon the limit of capacity
5. The greater extent of segmentation and, therefore, the less satiation

E. THE BALANCING PROCESS

In Chapter 14, Section A 3 [1] we stated that we would undertake to illustrate with diagrams the way the direct and compensatory effects of changes in "real cost" impinge on the reach of capacity along the order of preference and on the duration of the working-day, respectively, by striking a balance between the two. It is a question whether this complex affair can be more clearly demonstrated by the abstract statement in the text or by the graphic method. However, we shall now attempt the latter.

We shall commence with a diagram designed only to show the method of representation of each of the dimensions of each of the magnitudes concerned. In Fig. 66, the area of the five rectangles represents the in-

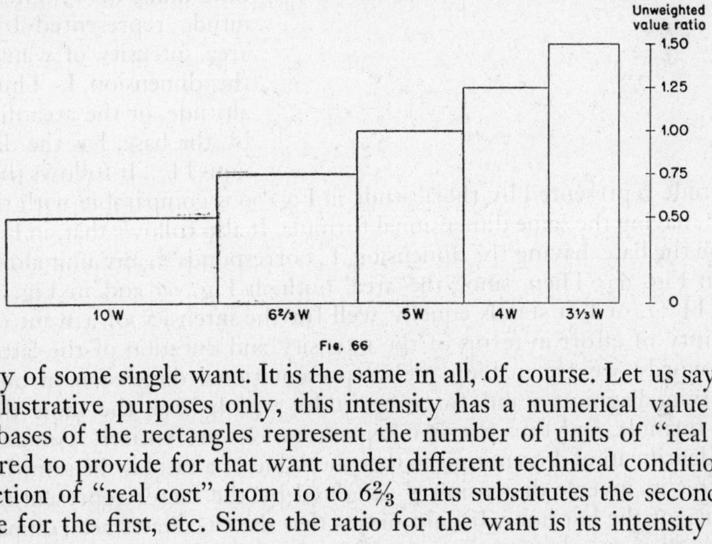

FIG. 66

tensity of some single want. It is the same in all, of course. Let us say that, for illustrative purposes only, this intensity has a numerical value of 5. The bases of the rectangles represent the number of units of "real cost" required to provide for that want under different technical conditions. A reduction of "real cost" from 10 to 6⅔ units substitutes the second rectangle for the first, etc. Since the ratio for the want is its intensity to its "real cost," the unweighted ratios of the several rectangles are $\frac{5}{10}$, $\frac{5}{6\frac{2}{3}}$, $\frac{5}{5}$, $\frac{5}{4}$, and $\frac{5}{3\frac{1}{3}}$. The values of these ratios are 0.50, 0.75, 1, 1.25, and 1.50. Since the altitude of each rectangle, geometrically speaking, is its area divided by its base, these several altitudes represent the unweighted values of the several ratios, as shown on the scale to the right.

In Fig. 67 there is shown, by the solid line, the later portion of a highly simplified curve of working. Since all hours in each day are assumed to be treated, for purposes of allocation, as if they had the same intensity as

[1] See p. 970.

the last hour, the broken lines show the intensity of all hours for each of the various working-days.[2] The relative intensity of the last hour determines the factor for weighting the inverse dimension of our ratios. Let us give the factor for an eight-hour day the value of unity—an intensity of 1. A six-hour day shows an intensity of 0.50 on the scale to the left, and so on up to the ten-hour day, which shows an intensity of 1.50. Now, in the text, we have analyzed the intensity of the last hour into a derived magnitude—the rate of delivery of effort. Its dimensions were given as XT^{-1}. But we concluded that X is identical with, or of the same dimensional order as, I. Therefore let us substitute IT^{-1}. Returning to Fig. 66, we recognize that the magnitude represented along the base, "real cost," is measured in time units, or T. The magnitude represented by the area, intensity of wants, has the dimension I. Thus the altitude, or the area divided by the base, has the dimensions IT^{-1}. It follows that the magnitude represented by the altitude in Fig. 66 is comparable with that in Fig. 67, having the same dimensional formula. It also follows that, in Fig. 66, 1 W on the base, having the dimension T, corresponds to any unit along the base in Fig. 67. Then, since the area, both in Fig. 66 and in Fig. 67, is $T \times (IT^{-1})$, or I, it stands equally well for the intensity of a want or for a quantity of effort in terms of the intensity and duration of the latter. In other words, we are making each representational dimension in both of these two diagrams stand for magnitudes which have the same dimensional formula, and thus the two representations are entirely comparable. This identification does not mean that the value of a ratio is the same before and after its inverse dimension is weighted by the factor representing the intensity of the last hour. It only means that the two states are comparable because they are changes of numerical value in the same dimension. That serves a useful purpose. It means that we can show, by compounding these diagrams, how the rising intensity of the last hour reaches a balance with the value of the ratios of wants around the margin. It means that the altitude in our diagrams can be used to show the effect of weighting, with

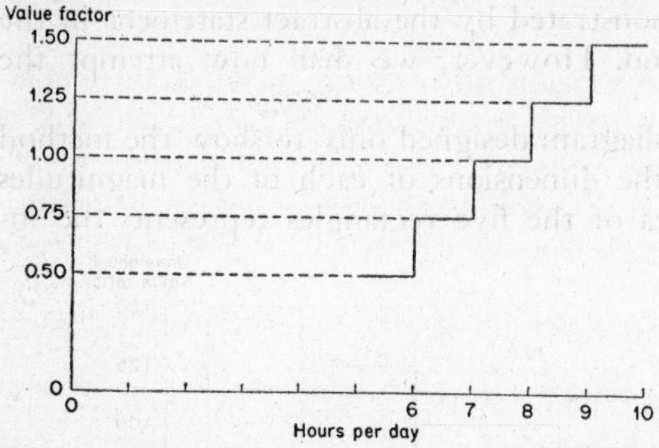

Fig. 67

[2] It should be borne in mind that each of the points on the curve of working represents the last hour of a different working-day. No two exist concurrently; and all concurrent intensities are the same (except for more or less arduous tasks). Thus, when we come to superimpose the curve of working on the order of ratios, there remains this fundamental difference in the meaning of the two. The first represents a series of mutually exclusive alternatives which cannot coexist; the second represents alternatives, in a sense, but alternatives that not only coexist but which may all be chosen.

the factor, the inverse dimension of our ratios. Hereafter, we can show on the vertical scale on one side of our diagrams the values of the unweighted ratios; and, on the scale on the other side, the values of the factor. If at any altitude the unweighted ratio and the factor coincide—that is, if the unweighted ratio and the intensity of the last hour agree—the value of the weighted ratio is unity. This because the weighted ratio is the value on the first scale divided by the value on the second. Thus an unweighted ratio of $\frac{0.50}{1}$ will not be less than unity if it can be weighted with a factor of 0.50; nor will an unweighted ratio of $\frac{1.50}{1}$ still be above unity if it has to be weighted with a factor of 1.50. In other words, if our want is marginal, at a "real cost" of 10 W (first rectangle) it will be included only in a six-hour day; at 6⅔ W (second rectangle) it will be included in a seven-hour day; or, conversely, at 3⅓ W, the unweighted value of its ratio is sufficiently high to permit it to induce a ten-hour day, if that is necessary to include it.[3]

Five different cases were recognized in Chapter 14, Section A 3. Fig. 68 illustrates case (a)—that is, the compensatory effects of a decline of "real cost" for an intramarginal want which causes a release of working to elsewhere—the sum of the compensatory effects equaling the difference in costs before and after the decline. The condition before the decline in cost is shown in I; that after the decline, in II. Since the wants here are named in the order of their positions in the order of ratios, rather than, according to our previous practice, their positions in the order of priority, we shall designate them by small, not capital, letters.[4] As such, *f* is an intramarginal want, well before the range around the margin; and *k*, *l*, *m*, *n*, *o*, and *p* are the wants in the range around the margin. In order to avoid confusing the diagram, these latter are represented by the solid horizontal lines—the tops of their respective rectangles. The name of each want is shown along the scale at the top; the length of the solid lines shows the

[3] By way of further elucidation we may say that, if the area representing intensity is greater than the area representing quantity of effort, provision will be made; if not, it will not. And this, we think, is the actual comparison in real life. But since, analytically and diagrammatically, the base of the area representing intensity and that representing quantity of effort are necessarily of the same size, since both correspond to a full measure, any differences in area must also show as differences in altitude. Thus we show that, if the altitude of the area representing intensity is greater than that of the one representing quantity of effort, the want will be included; and, if not, it will not. But that does not mean that we actually believe it possible to determine the ratio (first altitude) or the rate of delivery of effort (second altitude) and still less, then, to compare the two.

[4] Under this method of representation the order of priority would be depicted as a series of successively diminishing areas; but the order of ratios is depicted as a series of successively diminishing altitudes.

Since we are here dealing with compensatory effects and thus with wants around the margin, and since we have agreed that the order of preference around the margin follows the order of ratios, the latter is the proper basis to use.

"real cost" of each; and the distance from the base corresponds to the altitude of the rectangle. The numerical values of these altitudes are then measured on the left side of the scale under "unweighted value of ratio." Purely for convenience in demonstration, the wants around the margin are all given equal costs of 10 units each. For the same reason *f* is given a cost of 50 units. These costs are shown along the base on a scale which gives the number of units of time in the working-day. The intensities of the successive last hours are shown by the rising series of broken lines. Their relative numerical values are given on the right side of the scale under "value of factor." Before the reduction of "real cost" for *f*—shown in I—*m* is the marginal want, because its solid line, having a ratio with the unweighted value of 1.0 coincides with the broken line of the last 10 units in a 180-unit working-day with a relative intensity, and therefore a factor, of 1.0.

When a reduction of "real cost" for *f*—from 50 to 30 units, or by 20 units—takes place, 20 units are released to elsewhere. The figure for *f*, in I, represents a want of intensity 75; it has a base of 50 units and therefore an unweighted ratio of 1.5. In II, the intensity remains the same; the base has contracted to 30 units; therefore, the altitude representing the unweighted ratio has risen beyond our scale (it would be 2.5). The effect of the release of 20 units of W, shown in II, has moved the series of wants, *k* to *p*, to the left along the base scale, which, being the length of the working-day, is also the aggregate of units of cost required for the wants provided for. But of course, with relation to the base scale, the curve of working—broken lines—remains stationary. Now the solid line representing *n* coincides with the broken line representing the last 10 units of a 170-unit working-day. This coincidence means that a want the value of whose unweighted (old) ratio was 0.9 has now arrived at a weighted value of unity because the factor has also changed to 0.9.[5] The compensatory effects are divided between provision for one additional want, *n*, and a reduction of the working-day by 10 units.

The second case (b) is illustrated by Fig. 69. Here there is a rise of "real cost" for an intramarginal want sufficient to exclude it. The compensatory effects are again the result of a release of working to elsewhere, but now they are equal to the whole "real cost," before the rise of the now excluded want. Before the rise in cost (I) *f* requires 20 units of W. Since its intensity is 30, the value of its unweighted ratio is 1.5. On this basis *m* is the marginal want, with the value of an unweighted ratio of 1.0, because it coincides with the last 10 W of a working-day of 180 units, which yield a factor of 1.0. Its weighted ratio is then $\frac{10}{10(1.0)}$. The rise of cost for *f* is from 20 units to 50 units. Such a change, shown in II, reduces the value

[5] It is worth noting that this makes the value of the new weighted ratio for *f* equal to $\frac{2.5}{1(0.9)}$, or about 2.8.

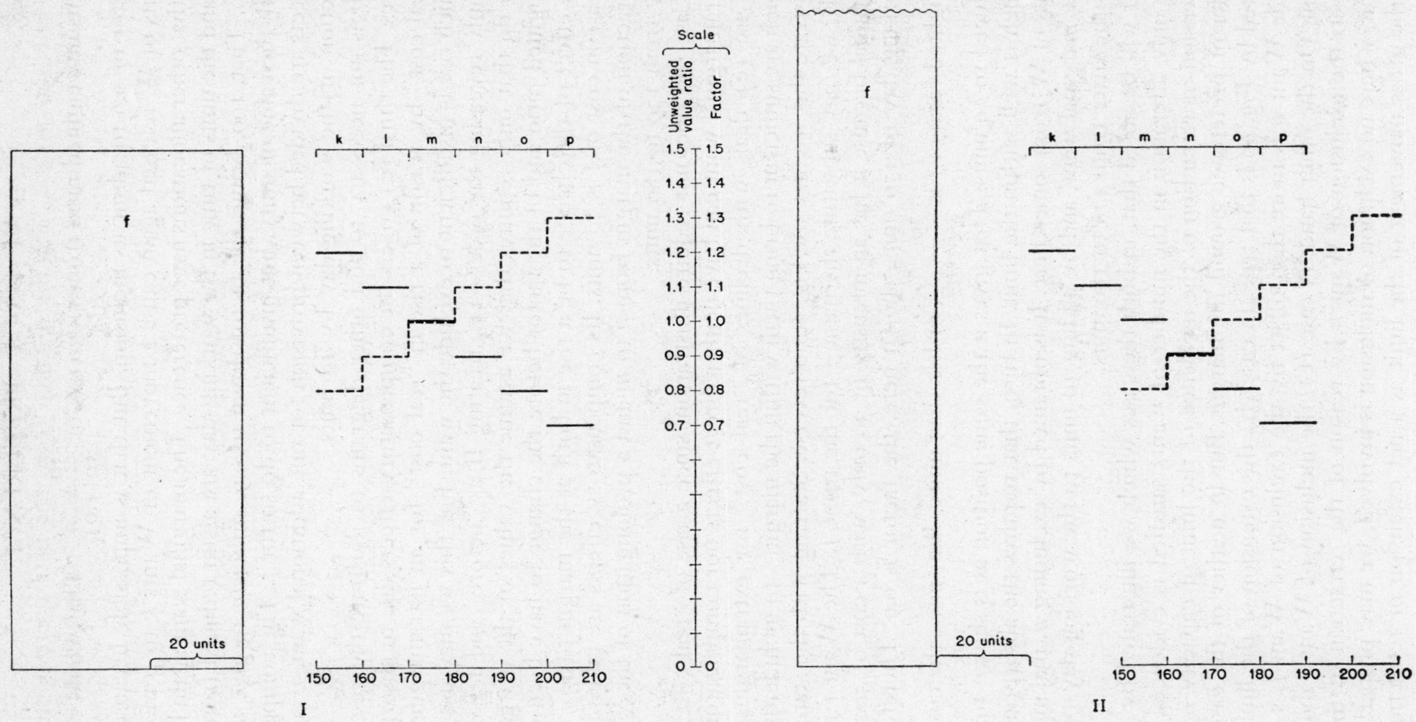

Scale
Unweighted value ratio
Factor
1.5
1.4
1.3
1.2
1.1
1.0
0.9
0.8
0.7
0
f
20 units
k
l
m
n
o
p
150
160
170
180
190
200
210
I
II

Fig. 68

of its unweighted ratio from 1.5 to 0.6, or $\frac{30}{50(1.0)}$. That would require a factor of 0.6 to admit its inclusion. But that is impossible because the 20 units of W released again cause a movement of Wants *k* to *p* to the left, so that other allocations have preference. The marginal want again becomes *n*, and the units of time in the working-day are again reduced from 180 to 170. That, too, brings the factor down to 0.9, sufficient to give *n* a ratio with the value of unity, but insufficient to do so for *f*. The compensatory effects are divided between provision for one additional want, *n*, and a reduction of the working-day by 10 units.

It is not necessary to add other diagrams to illustrate the rest of our cases. The third (c) covers the compensatory effects due to absorption of "real cost" by reason of a rise in "real cost" for an intramarginal want, which rise is insufficient to exclude the want. For this we may use Fig. 68, simply reversing the order—i.e., treating II as "before" and I as "after." To do that only requires that we assume the values of the marginal unweighted ratio and of the factor before the change to have been 0.9, and the effect of the change to be a rise in both at the margin to 1.0. The increase in cost of *f* is 20 units. Its compensatory effects are taken out in a retraction of the margin from *n* to *m* and a prolongation of the working-day from 170 to 180 units.

Case (d) does not require illustration, since a rise of "real cost" for an extramarginal want can have neither direct effects nor compensatory ones.

Case (e) deals with declines of "real cost" for extramarginal wants which are sufficient to bring them within the margin—to include them. To illustrate this we may use Fig. 69 in reverse. Starting with the state shown in II, we may substitute the name *t* for the name *f*. The Want *t* is extramarginal because it has an intensity of 30 only, with a cost of 50. With a working-day of 170 units, shown here, the factor is 0.9. Therefore, the weighted ratio of *t* is $\frac{30}{50(0.9)}$, or less than unity. But, now, the cost of *t* is reduced to 20 units. That gives it the same position as is shown for *f* in I, which is well within the limit. In turn, that requires the absorption of 20 units of W from somewhere. It is obtained by excluding *n*, making *m* the new marginal want, and by adding 10 units to the working-day—increasing the latter from 170 to 180 units.

It will be noted that, in both the cases which we illustrated by Fig. 68, the only alteration in the number of wants satisfied is evidenced by the extension or retraction of the incidence of the limit of capacity upon the order of preference around the margin. But in neither of the cases illustrated by Fig. 69 is that true. In case (b) the extension of the limit to include Want *n* is more than offset by the exclusion of Want *f*, a greater want. On the other hand, in case (e), the inclusion of Want *t* more than offsets the exclusion of Want *n* by reason of the retraction of the limit. Thus, where no exclusion or inclusion is involved, we may properly think of the gross movement of the limit as a net extension or retraction. But,

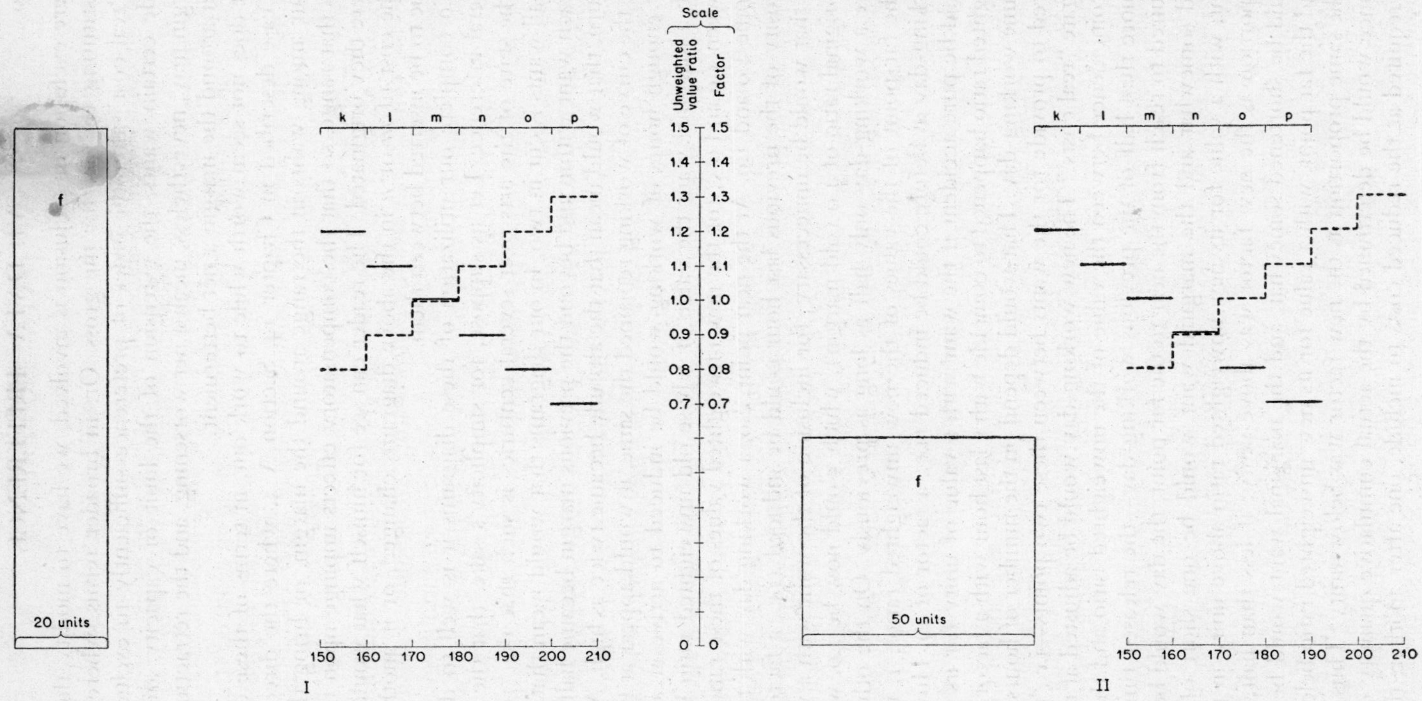
20 units
f
k l m n o p
150 160 170 180 190 200 210
I
Scale
Unweighted value ratio
Factor
1.5 1.4 1.3 1.2 1.1 1.0 0.9 0.8 0.7 0
50 units
II

Fig. 69

where exclusion or inclusion is involved, we have to modify the notion, substituting the net for the gross. Or, in broader terms, where changes in "real cost" alter the order of preference sufficiently to exclude or include certain wants, the extension of the limit of capacity around the margin may, nevertheless, mean a net worsening, and the retraction of this limit around the margin a net betterment.

It does not seem worth while to work out, in terms of these diagrams, the case described in Chapter 14, Section A 3, where the direct effects occur among wants in the range around the margin, or bring the wants into that range, so that the compensatory effects impinge upon the range where they originated. The reader can see for himself what would happen if the cost of *m* or *n* in the above diagrams changed, or if another want came to be inserted between them.

To complete our utilization of these diagrams it is well to draw one general inference. Let us suppose, for simplicity's sake, that the progress of the state of the arts over several centuries is such that the "real cost" for all wants is cut in two. In our diagrams that would mean that the base of each want within and beyond the previous margin became half as long. In turn, that would mean that the altitude became twice as high. Assuming that the curve of working remained the same, it would appear at first sight that enough hours of working would be induced to arrive at a balance with a marginal want the value of whose old unweighted ratio had been between 1.0 and 0.5; for the new unweighted values of these ratios would become 2.0 and 1.0. At the near point, 2.0, a working-day with twice the intensity of the previous last hour could be induced (i.e., a factor of 2). But that would be unnecessary; for inclusion of the want with a value for its original ratio of 1.0 (old margin), which would now be 2.0, would require a working-day only half as long as previously. On the other hand, at the far point of the values of the new unweighted ratios, 1, the same working-day as before could be induced (i.e., a factor of 1). However, it would be pure accident if the want with a value of unity for its new unweighted ratio happened to coincide with a last hour with a factor of unity —same working-day. That would depend on the number of hours now required to provide for the wants between these two points—i.e., their aggregate "real costs." The new working-day would be adjusted at the point of coincidence between the value of the unweighted ratio and the factor. If more than half of the previous working-day—the released time—were required to reach from the near to the far point, the day would be lengthened somewhat and the marginal want would be one short of the far point, with a value for its new unweighted ratio above unity in the same proportion as the new factor was above unity; if less than half, the day would be shortened somewhat, and the marginal want would be one beyond the far point, with a value for its new unweighted ratio below unity in the same proportion as the new factor was below unity. Thus the new balance would be determined by the actual cumulative quantity of working required at the reduced costs to include, one after another, the wants between the near point and the far point, or beyond. The new balance might involve a lengthening of the working-day or a shortening—either one. This constitutes a demonstration, on a more generalized basis, of the proposition we set out in Chapter 14, Section A 3, that reductions in "real cost" for intramarginal wants only tend to shorten the working-day, while those for extramarginal wants, if sufficient to include them, tend to lengthen the working-day.

We do not suppose that the curve of working does remain the same under such circumstances. For then, though the component, rate of delivery of effort, may actually decline, it is probably more than offset by a rise in the component, sacrifice. Leisure becomes more attractive than it was, at least so far as the playing, if not the resting, element is concerned.

One more point. Our demonstration of the basis on which the length of the working-day is voluntarily adjusted enables us to add one more piece of evidence that the supposition of declining intensity of wants during the process of satisfying is untenable. Since the concept of the balancing process has been generally accepted, though not in this precise form, it would appear from the following that those who have accepted it have failed to see that it is entirely incompatible with the supposition of declining intensity.

If the means necessary for a want has any "real cost" at all, then every increment has some "real cost." If the intensity of the want declines through the satisfying, there must necessarily come a point where, for the next partial satisfaction however small, the satisfaction is less than the "real cost" of the next increment. That point must come before the intensity has declined to zero, if the cost of the means is above zero. Then no want could be satiated if its means had a "real cost." Always leisure would be preferred before any want with a costful means could be satiated. The evidence for frequent and regular satiation of such wants is too strong to permit a construction that denies the possibility.

This demonstration eliminates our admission even of the exceptional possible satiations, which we conceded in Chapter 13, Sections C 2 and C 3, for the third hypothesis.

F. THE GENERALITY OF THE ALL OR NONE PRINCIPLE

In generalizing the all or none principle in connection with changes in quantity wanted of various means as a result of changes in "real cost," we found it necessary to make certain exceptions.[1] The exceptions most commonly observed seem to be due to what we have called, respectively, spreading and alternation. In spreading we have less than a full measure per instance, but part measures provided for all instances during the period; in alternation we have a full measure per instance, but no satisfaction for some of the instances during the period. Under both, changes in quantity wanted are almost always in terms of full measures or installments

[1] See Chapter 14, subsections A 3 and 4.

(durables). A rise in "real cost" may lead to increased spreading or alternation of future provision, and vice versa. In turn, that means a decrease or an increase in the number of full measures (or installments) included in the program of future provision for any certain period of time. The effect is not on an all or none basis for the period. But, for each single day's order of preference, the effect is likely to be on an all or none basis.

There are two other classes of cases where, as we noted in the text,[2] the all or none principle seems, at first sight, not to be operative. Both of these require consideration. We have limited ourselves to the examination of a direct economy—an analytical abstraction consisting of a single individual providing altogether for his own wants and for his own wants only. No such condition actually exists nor, probably, ever has. The nearest approach to it seems to be the primitive group and the isolated farmstead in which, most commonly, one elder male has been dominant. In both, provision is made for a compound, rather than a single, order of preference, which ranges from arbitrary rationing by the head to a lumping together of voluntary orders of preference independently arrived at. To the extent that the elder male dominates the joint program, it often occurs that a change of "real cost" operates to change the number of identical (or nearly identical) provisions so as to include provision for more or less of the subordinate members of the group.[3] This exception to the all or none principle is not, in reality, an exception with regard to individual demand. It is merely due to the lumping together, in actual groups of individuals, of the demands of the several individuals the effectiveness of whose demands is unequal.

The other apparent exception is the result of lack of precision in defining a single means. It occurs chiefly, perhaps only, in respect of future provision of durables, in the strict sense. As minor members of many of the constellations the means for which are durables, there are many ill-defined and, so far as we are concerned, unanalyzed wants which go by the names desire for comfort, convenience, conformity, eminence, ostentation, etc., the common denominator or characteristic of which seems to be, or to include, the want which for lack of a better term we have called the want for variety. These wants may lead to the provision of several houses, each with numerous rooms, several automobiles, many chairs, tables and beds, a plethora of ornaments and a large wardrobe. It is true, here as elsewhere, that only a single means can serve in a single

[2] P. 975.

[3] A man does not usually buy two automobiles for his own use. A lower price on automobiles may enable him to provide another for his wife or for the junior members of his family.

In the ancient Swedish farmhouses, re-erected or reproduced on Skansen, in Stockholm, there is usually one chair per house. That was for the head of the family; the rest sat on stools, benches, or the built-in beds. Today all members of a family are usually provided with chairs. But the "real cost" of these chairs is now incomparably less.

process at any one time. An individual cannot sit on more than one chair, ride in more than one automobile, or be in more than one room at a time. He does not usually wear more than one suit at a time. But these minor members of constellations may dictate that many of each of these durables be provided and in stock, to be used successively as wanted.

If the duplicates of each type of means thus collected were actually uniform (indifferent), this class of cases would fall within our exception under alternation (i.e., frequency). But they almost never are. The several houses are in different climates; the several rooms are specialized to different purposes; the furniture is a complex of disparate articles; the clothing is for different occasions and different seasons.

When the cost of any single means in this general category rises or falls, it may lead to the exclusion or inclusion of some one of the minor wants concerned or to the acceptance of a not indifferent substitute (fixed attributes). Such an effect is on an all or none basis. Almost never does a change in cost lead to the purchase of more or less of the same identical means.

The all or none direct effects lead to compensatory effects elsewhere. Sometimes these compensatory effects fall among the same constellations whence they arose. Increased cost of one means may lead to curtailing the assortment of the same type; decreased cost may lead to increasing the assortment of the same type. When the assortment is increased, it is evidence that some of the minor wants concerned have not been satisfied at all recurrences, or on all occasions of use. At such times they have been extramarginal. A woman gets tired—or is ashamed—of continually wearing the same dress; if the cost declines she may be enticed into buying another dress; but it will not be a duplicate—another of the same indifferent means. In fact, it is *only* for that reason that she increases her satisfaction by wearing one of the type one day and the other the next.

In this case, as in the one cited in the text, it is to a considerable extent true that such expansions or contractions of the stock of any one type of means, when they are once accomplished, involve no more or no less of a daily allocation of cost than was required before. The actual uses are no greater or no less; they are merely distributed over a larger or smaller number of individual means. Only in respect of the effect of Senior's "time" do these means wear out faster than at the rate of one day's use per day distributed over the whole assortment. And the decreased cost per means which induces the larger assortment may well compensate for this. To this extent, the compensatory effects go to the building-up or the thinning-down of the assortment; none are required to maintain it at the higher level, and none are permitted here once the lower level is reached. In this class of cases, then, it is true within these limits that, once the compensatory effects of changes in cost have taken place, the allocation of cost to each want concerned remains much the same as before. We may say that the very nature of the common characteristic which we have called the want for variety precludes the possibility that, for each instance of each want, the quantity wanted of one indifferent means should be on other than an all or none basis. The nature of this want requires alternation among an assortment of different means.

G. THE HISTORICAL TEST

If we have been correct in our analysis of the relation between changing "real costs" and the order of preference, as presented in Chapter 14, the same relation must have held good of the evolution of that order of preference as, from the beginning, the progress of the arts enabled man to provide for more than his "animal" wants. Let us submit it to that test.

As to one feature the historical proof is positive and self-evident. At the earliest stage, when *Homo sapiens* probably lived much as the gorilla does today, it is necessarily true that he must have satisfied the prior wants that we have listed in our physiological study. This for the very simple reason that, if he had not, his descendants would not be with us today. Or, more precisely, those who did not, died off or left no progeny. Men today must be descended from those who satisfied these wants sufficiently to survive and to continue the race. At this stage, these satisfactions were doubtless sought only under the impulsion of the present wants themselves, one of which would have been always prepotent.[1] Then, so long as it required all his time to keep alive and continuing, man certainly could not consider other and lesser wants. And, judging by his collateral relatives who remain today at that stage, he did not try to do so.[2] At that stage the range of the great prior wants in the order of priority monopolized man's attention.

At some later stage of development, and in some regions, the monopolizing of man's time for the essentials of a mere hand-to-mouth existence must have relaxed. Only then could future provision begin. Only then did man begin to "work," according to our definition, or to make others work for him. Only then did "real costs" appear. Perhaps the earliest forms of future provision were occasioned by two technical necessities—seasonal materials and durables—winter supplies of food and artificial shelter and covering.[3] Judging by the observation of present-day human beings at about that stage, working-time was entirely devoted to provision for the

[1] Or, if there were intervals when no want activated man, one would have to construe the situation as Malthus did. He says (*289*, I, 132), "A state of sloth, and not of restlessness and activity seems evidently to be the natural state of man." Observation of primates does not lead me to the same conclusion. Or, rather, I would not define their various kinds of quiescence as sloth. Neither would I define them, in Cartesian terms, as absence of external stimulus.

[2] Even up to his own time Malthus could say (*289*, I, 37) of the Andaman islanders that "their whole time is spent in search of food." A priori and from observations of animals, we must conclude that early man spent the time necessary to find enough food each day before or without doing anything else.

[3] We cannot be specific as to which came first, produced food or artificial shelter and covering. That depended partly on climate. Moreover, the use of skins—by-products of the search for food—for shelter and covering may have begun before the domestication of animals. Perhaps a minimum of shelter and covering should be regarded as a means of preserving body temperature and therefore as serving one of the great prior wants. Perhaps, before fully satisfying hunger, man wanted some shelter.

great prior wants, just as direct-consuming time had been at the previous stage. And this was done without respect to the relative "real costs" required by these and other wants.[4] Apparently the order of priority governed without interference from the influence of "real costs" except in one respect. That one respect was limitation of the working-day. Man has never worked twenty-four hours a day for any extended period.

Along with this development began, at some stage, the making of tools, a sample of our second technical option. Then "real costs" commenced to decline; working-time commenced to be released to elsewhere. That is, when man began to provide also for his subordinate wants, it was only because his technique had arrived at a point where provision for his prior wants no longer required all the time he was willing to work—at least, at some seasons.[5] Then, and only then we think, did he begin to pick and choose. Even then, the picking and choosing consisted only in giving a certain degree of weight to the relative "real costs" of satisfying the subordinate wants and was limited to this range of wants. Thereafter, as technique continued to improve, declining costs of satiating the prior wants released more and more working, a part of which might be applied to subordinate wants. In turn, the costs of satisfying subordinate wants also declined. As we said on page 973, the working-day was shortened as a result of improvements of technique in the range of prior wants; but it was maintained or even lengthened as a result of improvements in the range of subordinate wants. If that were not true, the American farmer, whose time is his own, would not be working as long hours as his ancestor did, when he can produce the same output in, say, one quarter of the time. The cost of satisfying other wants, prohibitive to his ancestor, has declined sufficiently to induce him to apply to them all the time saved.

In summary, we may say that, when the range of great prior wants required a long working-day, lesser wants were ignored. When technique reduced these requirements, time became available for subordinate wants.[6]

[4] I assume that the only causes of failure to satiate hunger, at that stage, were failure to undertake adequate future provision, crop failure and loss of stock, due to natural or human agencies.

The recency and the limited area of the release of man from the constant pressure of hunger are well brought out in E. P. Prentice's remarkable study of *Hunger and History* (New York, 1939). We are apt to forget how briefly and locally man has enjoyed "abundance."

[5] Here we may advisedly keep in our minds the example of the isolated farmstead. Elsewhere, and even there to some extent, provision for his lesser wants was exacted by one man from others. But even in that situation, it was impossible to do so unless the slaves' or servants' prior wants were provided for.

[6] In fact, as I view the matter, the *minimum* cost of satisfying the prior wants has gradually become rather low in relation to the intensities of these wants—a gradually increasing value for the ratios. This does not argue enormously high intensities for these wants—a very steeply declining order of priority. It merely assigns to their reduced costs the chief source of release of working to elsewhere. But what has enabled the enormous extension of the reach of capacity is the decline in cost of the subordinate wants. The first change enabled chiefly a shortening of the working-day; the second change offset that.

But so long as he did not get much for this work man did not work much. High costs for subordinate wants made ratios with low values, not reaching far along the curve of working. But when technical improvements became available in this range too, these costs also declined, the values of these ratios rose and they then reached further along the curve of working. Then, since he got more for his work, he worked more. Because of changes in the curve of working, the latter two stages are not clearly marked, or always successive, even in the history of independent men, if there have been such. But the two tendencies seem to underlie and, to a degree, explain certain observable phenomena.

A gradual worsening of natural conditions doubtless reverses this process. But, due to the persistence of acquired habits, it may take a long time—generations—to have its full effect. In the end, however, attention to subordinate wants will be reduced or even eliminated, and time will be exclusively devoted to the prior wants if that is necessary for their satiation. This seems to have been the course of events in regions where adverse changes of climate or exhaustion of resources have been severe.[7]

H. THE DEMAND CURVE WITH AN ELASTICITY OF UNITY

The demand curve in the form of a rectangular hyperbola, referred to on page 987, deserves some special attention from us because it is the only one that has appeared in our analysis which requires and illustrates the concept of elasticity of demand. This curve represents an elasticity of unity, or what Marshall calls "constant outlay"—in our terms, an unchanging allocation of "real cost." To us that also means that changes along such a curve would have no compensatory effects—no release of working to, or absorption of working from, elsewhere.

Theoretically, at least, there are certain situations in which individual demand might assume such a character.

a. Under our interpretation of the doubtful case in which the want is segmented we have assumed that a certain block of "real cost," insufficient to produce satiation, might be allocated to a want rather than to leave it unsatisfied. A change in "real cost" would then supposedly result in no change in the size of the block, but merely in a larger or smaller degree of satisfying to be secured by that block. If the criterion was originally the size of the block, it would remain so. For, since the want would be assumed to remain at the same intensity whatever its degree of satisfying short of satiation, there would be no incentive to increase or decrease this block.

b. The second case is the marginal want, when and if we admit that the marginal want is ever not satiated because the curve of working rises above the level of its intensity before full provision is made. That would be another case of segmentation, but this time, being marginal, the ratio would, at the point of intersection of the two curves, have a value of unity.

[7] Mesopotamia has been a favorite example.

A change in its cost, insufficient to permit satiation, would most certainly result in no change in allocation, for no change could take place without altering the value of its ratio, at the intersection, away from unity.

c. If we conceive that, at some stage in the evolution of man's order of preference, his capacity was so limited on account of poor technique that all his effort had to be applied to his single prior want—say hunger—then it might occur that this single greatest want was both segmented (a) and itself marginal (b). It is very doubtful that such was ever the case. Instead, it appears likely that the origin of working was no such clean-cut affair. Rather we must suppose that, at first, precurrent reactions to a number of prior present wants were practically merged with the initial efforts toward future provision, so that at no stage did any one want monopolize all working. However, the case is of analytical interest even if it is purely imaginary.

At first sight it seems reasonable to assign a rectangular hyperbola to represent all these instances of demand curves. Actually, however, this is the best possible basis from which to demonstrate the difficulties of assigning any definite demand curve whatever. For, as soon as compensatory effects from elsewhere are taken into consideration, the only case that permits the use of this curve is the last and least probable. In this case, no other wants being provided for, there would be no "elsewhere" from which compensatory effects could arise. In the second case, since we have concluded that the region upon which compensatory effects impinge is the range around the margin, it is necessarily true that any change in "real cost" elsewhere must alter the value of the factor here. In turn, that must alter the allocation—i.e., move the demand away from the same rectangular hyperbola. Is that not likely also to be true to a lesser extent of the first case, even if, to admit that, we would also have to admit that compensatory effects sometimes impinge on wants well within the margin if they are segmented? At least, a change in the factor, which always results from compensatory effects, would also alter the weighting of any given block of "real cost." If so, would it not lead to increasing or decreasing that block and therefore to moving demand away from the same rectangular hyperbola?

We conclude, then, that one case, the second, whose elasticity seems most likely to remain at unity, is, as a matter of fact, that one in which interdependence is at its maximum. It is, therefore, the particular case, par excellence, where no independent demand curve whatever can be drawn. We also conclude that the first case, while subject to compensatory effects to a much less degree and only indirectly, is still not likely to show an elasticity of unity or, for that matter, any definite elasticity. Only in the third case, which is perhaps entirely imaginary, could we certainly have an undisturbed elasticity of unity or any definite and independent demand curve. The application of the rectangular hyperbola serves one purpose only. It notifies us that, if there are incompletely satisfied wants within or partly within the margin, changes in the "real cost" of their own preferred means may have no compensatory effects.

From an analytical viewpoint it is also of interest to apply this same test to the equilibrium system of marginal utility theory. If "real cost" were so distributed among all wants that the *marginal* utility per unit of "real cost" were the same for all, it would necessarily follow that all wants would become to that extent marginal. If so, the compensatory effects of a change in "real cost" anywhere would affect every want. That would make it impossible to show a demand curve for any want unless all were rectangular hyperbolas—i.e., without compensatory effects. Which, being interpreted, would mean that all demand would have to have an elasticity of unity. How delightfully simple! One curve, with different scales for each, would suffice for all means. But one curve for all, or no curve for any, is the all or none principle which marginal utility theory requires. The restrictions which result from the interpretation of our own scheme, as worked out in Chapter 14, Section B 3, are not quite so severe as that.

At least, it ought to be evident that the concept of general equilibrium theory, which clearly recognizes what we are calling compensatory effects, is entirely incompatible with any notion of an independent individual demand curve unless all have elasticities of unity. Such a curve may be drawn for a single means to define the direct and primary effects of a change in cost of that means. No curve can be drawn which includes compensatory effects from elsewhere in the absence of change here. It is conceivable that it may, at times, be useful to analyze the direct or primary effects of a single change in a world of *ceteris paribus*. That uses what we have called the "virtual" method. It should be recognized, however, that it does not represent the real world.[1]

I. TWO RELATED SCHEMES

The most highly-developed form that indifference curve analysis has reached is quite definitely that of Hicks (see *195*). In certain respects his analysis seems to resemble ours. On the one hand, he uses the notion of substitutability extensively. Superficially, this resembles our analysis of substitution—at least in the use of the same term. On the other hand, he divides the effect of "price" changes into two classes, "price effects" and "income effects." This sounds like our division between direct and compensatory effects, or ours between primary and secondary effects. It is therefore worth while, in order to avoid confusion, to point out the radical differences in the two sets of ideas.

As we have already stated in Appendix IV, Section E. Hicks's concept of substitutability has a relation of polarity with his concept of complementarity.[1] To the extent that it is not impaired by the influence of the

[1] As I recollect it, Schultz recognized this and used just such a self-imposed limitation in his work on the theory of demand.

[1] Of course, the polarity, though not the names, has necessarily a mathematical validity.

opposite pole, substitutability, to him, is a relation which extends over all wants.[2] Subject to this qualification, it means that there are some terms on which partial satisfactions of each want will be preferred to partial satisfactions of each other want. On our construction, substitutability only extends, strictly speaking, to the means which are indifferent substitutes for a single want.[3] As to all others there is always preference, a preference which may only be offset by relative "real costs" to the extent that we have found it necessary to admit that the influence of "real costs" interferes with the influence of wants (order of priority).

The second difference in respect of substitutability is that Hicks conceives it in continuous terms—the marginal rate which changes continuously with the proportion each component constitutes in the assortment. Quite contrary to this, we have concluded that substitution occurs on an all or none basis and only at a single critical point in the relation between the "real costs." It is entirely discontinuous—one step.

There remains the second apparent resemblance. Hicks divides the effect of a change in "real cost" into two parts, the "price effect" and the "income effect." [4] Superficially, these seem to correspond either to our direct and compensatory effects or to our primary and secondary effects. But they do not. In the first place, the "income effect" of a single change in "real cost" is, to Hicks,[5] the movement from one indifference curve to another, while the "price effect" is the movement along the new indifference curve.[6] His "price effect" is obviously quite different from our direct or our primary effect, for it assumes general substitutability and therefore "a tendency to substitute the commodity whose price has fallen for other commodities." [7] On the contrary, we assume, as our general rule, that there will be no change in the quantity wanted of the commodity whose price has fallen and therefore no "price effect." [8] Instead, we assume that all the reduction in "real cost" will be released to produce compensatory

---

That is, any two variables, when changing, may either change in the same direction or in the opposite direction. Then, if one chooses, one can construe a less change in the same direction as an equal change minus a change in the opposite direction. However, this does not make the correlation significant nor indicate a polarity of identifiable forces.

[2] Hicks says, "Any two goods are substitutes—more or less" (*196*, 69).

[3] Thus we admit the one case which Hicks calls perfect substitutability (*195*, 49). The only difference is that we do not start with an assortment of the two means on an indifference curve. We start with the notion that, in such a case, demand was either zero for Y or for X to start with. A particular price change may reverse that situation. Otherwise there are no substitution effects.

[4] Hicks, *195*, 32.

[5] *Ibid*., 31.

[6] Hicks's case of an inferior good is the only one where the income effect is opposite to the price effect (negative; *195*, 35). That is included in our limited type of substitution where minor wants of a constellation are enabled to change the preference of the major want (see Chapter 14, Section A 1).

[7] Hicks, *195*, 32.

[8] The only "price effect" in our general case is the exclusion or inclusion of the want at the critical point in a change of "real cost."

effects elsewhere. Thus his "price effect" and our compensatory effects may often be of opposite sign. For him, a decline in price here will often absorb "purchasing power" from elsewhere; for us it will release it to elsewhere. The same differences arise if the "price" change is in the opposite direction.

Does his "income effect" have more resemblance to these compensatory effects of ours? So far as I know, Hicks was the first economist to dilate on the fact that the effects of a change in "real cost" of any single commodity actually used should include a corresponding change in "real income." Now, if the demand curve of that commodity is a rectangular hyberbola the greater or less "real income"—the "income effect"—remains absorbed in that commodity. If the curve is of any other shape, then, even for him, some part of the greater or less "real income"—"income effect"—must affect other commodities. In the first case, there is "income effect" with no compensatory effects; in the second, the "income effect" goes, at least in part, into what we call compensatory effects. This points up the first difference. "Income effect" is a category which is broader than, though of the same order as, compensatory effects. Compensatory effects are only those "income effects" which go elsewhere.

The second and chief difference is in the matter of incidence. Hicks's "income effect" is apparently divided between the commodity where the change in "real cost" takes place and all other commodities in the proportion "in which the consumer was dividing his expenditure between this commodity (X) and other goods." [9] Our compensatory effects are neither divided in that way, nor do they reach *all* other commodities. So far as they reach commodities at all, they are confined entirely to those serving the wants in the range around the margin.

Another scheme, by no means so well-known, is much more closely related to ours. Marschak says,[10] "Of all the advocates of the 'budget approach' to the study of the laws of demand, Réne Roy is the one who presented his assumptions earliest with perhaps the greatest clarity." While Roy approaches the subject from a standpoint wholly different from ours and by other methods of analysis, his "hiérarchie des besoins humains"—as presented in its recent form [11]—closely resembles our order of priority of wants. In fact, it does so to such a degree that we are tempted to cite it in support—particularly since its origin is observational rather than analytical and inferential as ours is. To him, the lower orders in the hierarchy consist of the wants whose basic means are indispensable to existence. They include our prior wants. He holds that no one proceeds to satisfy wants of a higher order—our subordinate wants—until these indispensable means have been provided. In fact, he goes so far as to say that a consumer assures himself of ability to *satiate* wants in each order before proceeding to the next. As a result, the general form which the thesis

[9] Hicks, *195*, 32.
[10] Marschak, *290*, 25.
[11] Roy, *356*.

takes is that, for various incomes—corresponding to our different capacities—the budget for essentials is not far different in amount. Increase of income—our expansion of capacity—is not applied to an increase in these essentials, and therefore the budget for them does not constitute a similar proportion of different incomes. Enlarged income is applied to extending the number of wants provided for.[12]

When price rises occur in the first group ("inferior" order), where the elasticity of demand approaches zero, the consumer is obliged to apply more of his income to this group and therefore to diminish his allocation to other groups. Conversely, when price declines occur there, income is released to more subordinate groups. On the other hand, no price changes in a "higher" group will affect demand in a "lower" one.

Finally, when we extend the use of the term to cover means with different quantities of fixed attributes which cannot be indifferent substitutes, Roy's restrictions on substitutability and the influence of changes in the relative prices of substitutes are approximately the same as ours. To him, both are confined within the single group where different articles serving the same general purpose are compared.

[12] This does not contradict what Pareto said (*317*, 274). For Roy's groups correspond to Pareto's "qualités" within the "grandes catégories de marchandises ideales"—"l'alimentation, le logement, l'habillement, les objets d'ornement, les divertissements." Roy's groups are "denrées ou services de première nécessité, produits de demi-luxe, de luxe et de grand luxe" (*356*, 21). Pareto's "qualités" and Roy's groups correspond in some degree to the several means that can be used to satisfy more or less of the members of our constellations.

LIST OF REFERENCES

LIST OF REFERENCES

Sources cited by number, in italics, are identified below

GRATEFUL ACKNOWLEDGMENT is hereby made to the publishers of journals and books listed below for their permission to make brief quotations from the authorities cited in this work.

1. Ach, N. Ueber den Willensakt und das Temperament. Leipzig, 1910.
2. Adams, Brooks. The New Empire. New York, 1902.
3. Adrian, E. D. The Basis of Sensation. New York, 1928.
4. —— The Mechanism of Nervous Action. Philadelphia, 1932.
5. Aftalion, A. "Les Trois Notions de la productivité et les revenus." 25 *Rev. d'Econ. Pol.* (1911) 145, 345.
6. Agassiz, A. "Note on Beaver Dams." *Proc. Boston Soc. Nat. Hist.* (1869) 101.
7. Åkermann, J. "Annual Survey of Economic Theory." 4 *Econometr.* (1936) 97.
8. Alford, L. B. "Localization of Consciousness and Emotion." 12 *Am. J. Psychiat.* (1933) 789.
9. Allen, W. F. "Relationship of the Conditioned Olfactory-Foreleg Response to the Motor Centers of the Brain." 121 Am. J. Physiol. (1938) 657.
10. Alpers, B. J. "Hyperthermia Due to Lesions in the Hypothalamus." 35 *Arch. Neurol. Psychiat.* (1936) 30.
11. —— "Relation of the Hypothalamus to Disorders of Personality." 38 *Arch Neurol. Psychiat.* (1937) 291.
12. —— "Personality and Emotional Disorders Associated with Hypothalamic Lesions." In *The Hypothalamus,* 20 Res. Pbl. Assn. Nerv. Ment. Dis. (Baltimore, 1940) 736.
13. Aring, C. D. "Shivering and the Cerebral Cortex." 113 *Am. J. Physiol.* (1935) 3.
14. Armstrong, W. E. "The Determinateness of the Utility Function." 49 *Econ. J.* (1939) 453.
15. Bain, J. S. "Depression Pricing and the Depreciation Function." 51 *Q. J. Econ.* (1937) 705.
16. Barbour, H. G. "Hypothalamic Control of Water Movement in Response to Environmental Temperature." In *The Hypothalamus,* 20 Res. Pbl. Assn. Nerv. Ment. Dis. (Baltimore, 1940) 449.
17. Barcroft, J. Features in the Architecture of Physiological Function. Cambridge, England, Cambridge University Press, 1934.
18. Bard, P. "A Diencephalic Mechanism for the Expression of Rage, with Special Reference to the Sympathetic Nervous System." 84 *Am. J. Physiol.* (1928) 490.
19. —— "Emotion: I. The Neuro-humoral Basis of Emotional Reactions." In Murchison, *Handbook of General Experimental Psychology* (Worcester, Mass., 1934) 264.
20. —— "Emotion: I. The Neuro-humoral Basis of Emotional Reactions." In Murchison, *Foundations of Experimental Psychology* (Worcester, Mass., 1929) 449.
21. —— "Studies on the Cortical Representation of Somatic Sensibility." 33 *The Harvey Lectures* (The Harvey Lecture Society; The Williams and Wilkins Co., Baltimore, 1938; copyright, The Science Press Printing Co., Lancaster, Pa.) 143.
22. —— "Central Nervous Mechanisms for Emotional Behavior Patterns in Animals." In *The Inter-Relationship of Mind and Body,* 19 Res. Pbl. Assn. Nerv. Ment. Dis. (Baltimore, 1939) 190.
23. —— "The Hypothalamus and Sexual Behavior." In *The Hypothalamus,* 20 Res. Pbl. Assn. Nerv. Ment. Dis. (Baltimore, 1940) 550.

24. Bard, P. "The Neuro-muscular and Central Nervous Systems." In McLeod, *Physiology in Modern Medicine* (1918; 9th ed., ed. P. Bard, St. Louis, Mo., The C. V. Mosby Co., 1941) 1.
25. Barris, R. W., and W. R. Ingram. "The Effect of Experimental Hypothalamic Lesions upon Blood Sugar." 114 *Am. J. Physiol.* (1936) 555.
26. Bastiat, F. Harmonies of Political Economy. Tr. P. J. Sterling. London, 1860.
27. Bayliss, Sir W. M. Principles of General Physiology. 1914; 4th ed., London, 1927.
28. Bazett, H. C. "The Circulation." In McLeod, *Physiology in Modern Medicine* (1918; 9th ed., ed. P. Bard, St. Louis, Mo., The C. V. Mosby Co., 1941) 295.
29. Beattie, J. "The Relation of the Tuber Cinereum to Gastric and Cardiac Functions." 26 *J. Canad. Med. Assn.* (1932) 278.
30. —— "Functional Aspects of the Hypothalamus." In *The Hypothalamus* (Edinburgh, Oliver and Boyd, Ltd., 1938) 69.
31. Beattie, J., and A. S. Kerr. "The Effects of Diencephalic Stimulation on Urinary Bladder Tonus." 59 *Brain* (1936) 302.
32. Beattie, J., and D. Sheehan. "The Effects of Hypothalamic Stimulation on Gastric Motility." 81 *J. Physiol.* (1934) 218.
33. Bechterew, V. M. Objective Psychologie. German tr. Leipzig, 1913.
34. Beebe-Center, J. G. The Psychology of Pleasantness and Unpleasantness. New York, 1932.
35. Bianchi, L. The Mechanism of the Brain. Tr. J. H. Macdonald. Edinburgh, E. and S. Livingstone, Ltd., 1922.
36. Bieber, I. "Grasping and Sucking." 37 *Arch. Neurol, Psychiat.* (1937) 704.
37. Bieber, I., and J. F. Fulton. "Relation of the Cerebral Cortex to the Grasp Reflex and to Postural and Righting Reflexes." 39 *Arch. Neurol. Psychiat.* (1938) 433.
38. Böhm-Bawerk, E. von. The Positive Theory of Capital. Tr. W. Smart. London and New York, The Macmillan Company, 1891.
39. —— "Capital and Interest Once More: Capital *vs.* Capital Goods." 21 *Q. J. Econ.* (1906) 1.
40. Boodin, J. E. "The Biological Basis of Society." 1 *J. Soc. Phil.* (1936) 301.
41. Boring, E. G. "Processes Referred to the Alimentary and Urinary Tracts." 22 *Psychol. Rev.* (1915) 306.
42. —— "The Psychological Basis of Appetite." 28 *Am. J. Psychol.* (1917) 443.
43. Bremer, M. F. "L'Activité cérébrale au cours du sommeil et de la narcose." 2 (6th ser.) *Bull. Acad. Roy. Med. Belge* (1937) 68.
44. Brickner, R. M. "Certain Characteristics of the Cortical Influence over the Sympathetic Nervous System in Man." 71 *J. Nerv. Ment. Dis.* (1930) 689.
45. ——The Intellectual Functions of the Frontal Lobes. New York, The Macmillan Company, 1936.
46. Bronk, D. W., R. F. Pitts, and M. G. Larrabee. "Role of Hypothalamus in Cardiovascular Regulation." In *The Hypothalamus,* 20 Res. Pbl. Assn. Nerv. Ment. Dis. (Baltimore, 1940) 323.
47. Bronk, D. W., and G. Stella. "Afferent Impulses in the Carotid Sinus Nerve." 1 *J. Cell. Comp. Physiol.* (1932) 113.
48. Brooks, C. McC. "Relation of the Hypothalamus to Gonado-tropic Functions of the Hypophysis." In *The Hypothalamus,* 20 Res. Pbl. Assn. Nerv. Ment. Dis. (Baltimore, 1940) 525.
49. Brown, E. H. Phelps. "Profit Experience of Producers and Their Response to Price." 4 *Econometr.* (1936) 310.
50. Brown, T. G. "Note on the Physiology of the Basal Ganglia and the Mid-Brain of the Anthropoid Ape, Especially in Reference to the Act of Laughter." 49 *J. Physiol.* (1915) 195.
51. Brun, R. "Experimentelle Beiträge zur Dynamik und Oekonomie des Triebkonflikts." 12 *Imago* (1926) 147.
52. Bucy, P. C. "Frontal Lobe of Primates." 33 *Arch. Neurol. Psychiat.* (1935) 546.

53. Bucy, P. C., and T. J. Case. "Cortical Innervation of Respiratory Movements." 84 *J. Nerv. Ment. Dis.* (1936) 156.
54. Burroughs, J. "Is Nature Beneficent?" 9 *Yale Rev.* (1920) 366.
55. Butler, Samuel. Unconscious Memory. 1880; New York, E. P. Dutton and Co., Inc., 1920.
56. Bye, R. T. "The Scope and Definition of Economics." 47 *J. Pol. Econ.* (1937) 623.
57. Canning, J. B. Economics of Accountancy. New York, 1929.
58. Cannon, W. B. Bodily Changes in Pain, Hunger, Fear and Rage. New York, 1915.
59. —— "The Physiological Basis of Thirst." 90 B *Proc. Royal Soc.* (1919) 283.
60. —— "New Evidence for Sympathetic Control of Some Internal Secretions." 2 *Am. J. Psychiat.* (1922) 15.
61. —— "The James-Lange Theory of Emotions." 39 *Am. J. Psychol.* (1927) 106.
62. —— "Mechanism of Emotional Disturbance of Bodily Functions." 198 *N.E. J. Med.* (1928) 877.
63. —— "Organization for Physiological Homeostasis." 9 *Physiol. Revs.* (1929) 399.
64. —— "The Integrative Action of the Vascular System." In Cowdry, *Human Biology and Racial Welfare.* (New York, Paul B. Hoeber, Inc., 1930) 219.
65. —— "Again the James-Lange and the Thalamic Theories of Emotion." 38 *Psychol. Rev.* (1931) 281.
66. —— The Wisdom of the Body. 1932; 2nd ed., New York, W. W. Norton and Co., Inc., 1939.
67. ——"Some Modern Extensions of Beaumont's Studies on Alexis St. Martin." 32 *J. Mich. State Med. Soc.* (1933) 155.
68. —— "Neural Organization for Emotional Expression." In *The Wittenberg Symposium* (Worcester, Mass., 1928) 257.
69. —— "Hunger and Thirst." In Murchison, *Foundations of Experimental Psychology* (Worcester, Mass., 1929) 434.
70. Carey, H. C. Principles of Political Economy. Philadelphia, 1837.
71. Carlson, A. J. The Control of Hunger in Health and Disease. Chicago, 1916.
72. Carmichael, L. "Origin and Prenatal Growth of Behavior." In Murchison, *Handbook of Child Psychology* (1931; 2nd ed., Worcester, Mass., 1933) 31.
73. Carver, T. N. Distribution of Wealth. New York, 1904.
74. Cassel, G. The Theory of Social Economy. Tr. J. W. McCabe. 1918; New York, Harcourt, Brace and Co., Inc., 1924.
75. —— On Quantitative Thinking in Economics. Oxford, England, 1935.
76. Child, C. M. Physiological Foundations of Behavior. New York, 1924.
77. —— Origin and Development of the Nervous System. Chicago, 1921.
78. Chorobski, J., and W. Penfield. "Cerebral Vasodilator Nerves and Their Pathway from the Medulla Oblongata." 28 *Arch. Neurol. Psychiat.* (1932) 1257.
79. Clark, D., J. Hughes, and H. S. Gasser. "Afferent Function in the Group of Nerve Fibers of Slowest Conduction Velocity." 114 *Am. J. Physiol.* (1935) 69.
80. Clark, J. B. The Distribution of Wealth, 1899; New York, The Macmillan Company, 1927.
81. —— "Distribution as Determined by a Law of Rent." 5 *Q. J. Econ.* (1891) 289.
82. —— "Concerning the Nature of Capital: a Reply." 21 *Q. J. Econ.* (1906) 351.
83. Clark, J. M. Economics of Overhead Costs. Chicago, 1923.
84. Clark, W. E. LeGros. "The Structure and Connections of the Thalamus." 55 *Brain* (1932) 406.
85. —— "Functional Localization in the Thalamus and Hypothalamus." 82 *J. Ment. Sci.* (1936) 99.
86. —— "Morphological Aspects of the Hypothalamus." In *The Hypothalamus* (Edinburgh, Oliver and Boyd, Ltd., 1938) 1.
87. Cobb, S. "The Cerebral Circulation." 178 (n.s.) *Am. J. Med. Sci.* (1929) 528.
88. Cobb, S., and J. E. Finesinger. "Cerebral Circulation." 28 *Arch. Neurol. Psychiat.* (1932) 1241.

89. Coghill, G. E. Anatomy and the Problem of Behavior. New York, The Macmillan Company, and Cambridge, England, Cambridge University Press, 1929.
90. —— "The Biologic Basis of Conflict in Behavior." 20 *Psychoan. Rev.* (1933) 1.
91. —— "The Structural Basis of the Integration of Behavior." 16 *Proc. Natl. Acad. Sci.* (1930) 637.
92. Commons, J. R. Legal Foundations of Capitalism. New York, 1924.
93. —— Institutional Economics. New York, 1934.
94. Craig, W. "Appetites and Aversions as Constituents of Instincts." 34 *Biol. Bull.* (1918) 91.
95. Craigie, E. H. "Measurement of Vascularity in Some Hypothalamic Nuclei of the Albino Rat." In *The Hypothalamus,* 20 Res. Pbl. Assn. Nerv. Ment. Dis. (Baltimore, 1940) 310.
96. Crile, G. W. Origin and Nature of the Emotions. Philadelphia, W. B. Saunders Co., 1915.
97. Crosby, E. D., and R. T. Woodburne. "The Comparative Anatomy of the Preoptic Area and the Hypothalamus." In *The Hypothalamus,* 20 Res. Pbl. Assn. Nerv. Ment. Dis. (Baltimore, 1940) 31.
98. Crouch, R. L., and K. Thompson. "Autonomic Responses Elicited by Stimulating the Frontal Region of the Cerebral Cortex of a Cat." 64 *Anat. Rec.* (1936 Sup.) 11.
99. Cushing, H. "A Note upon the Faradic Stimulation of the Postcentral Gyrus in Conscious Patients." 32 *Brain* (1909) 44.
100. —— Papers Relating to the Pituitary Body, Hypothalamus and Parasympathetic Nervous System. Springfield, Ill., and Baltimore, 1932.
101. Dandy, W. E. "The Brain." In 12 *Practice of Surgery,* ed. Dean Lewis (Hagerstown, Md., W. F. Prior Co., Inc., 1940) 1.
102. Darrow, C. W. "Emotion as Relative Functional Decortication." 42 *Psychol. Rev.* (1935) 566.
103. —— "The Equation of the Galvanic Skin Reflex Curve." 16 (I) *J. Genl. Psychol.* (1937) 285.
104. —— "Neural Mechanisms Controlling the Palmar Galvanic Skin Reflex and Palmar Sweating." 37 *Arch. Neurol. Psychiat.* (1937) 641.
105. Darwin, C. Origin of Species. 6th ed.; reprint, New York, 1904.
106. —— Descent of Man. 2nd ed.; reprint, New York, 1904.
107. Davenport, H. J. The Economics of Enterprise, 1913; New York, The Macmillan Company, 1936.
108. Davis, L., D. Cleveland, and W. R. Ingram. "Carbohydrate Metabolism—the Effect of Hypothalamic Lesions and Stimulation of the Autonomic Nervous System." 33 *Arch. Neurol. Psychiat.* (1935) 592.
109. Davison, C., and H. Kelman. "Pathological Laughing and Crying." *Trans. Am. Neurol. Assn.* (1938) 86.
110. Davison, C., and W. Schlick. "Spontaneous Pain and Other Subjective Sensory Disturbances." 34 *Arch. Neurol. Psychiat.* (1935) 1204.
111. Davison, C., and N. E. Selby. "Hypothermia in Cases of Hypothalamic Lesions." 33 *Arch. Neurol. Psychiat.* (1935) 570.
112. Day, C. This Simian World. New York, 1921.
113. Dean, J. "The Relation of Cost to Output in a Leather Belt Shop." *Technical Paper No. 2,* Natl. Bur. Econ. Res. New York, 1941.
114. Denny-Brown, D. "Nervous Disturbances of the Vesical Sphincter." 215 *N.E.J. Med.* (1936) 647.
115. Denny-Brown, D., and E. G. Robertson. "On the Physiology of Micturition." 56 *Brain* (1933) 149.
116. —— "The State of the Bladder and Its Sphincters in Complete Transverse Lesions of the Spinal Cord and Cauda Equina." 56 *Brain* (1933) 397.
117. —— "An Investigation of the Nervous Control of Defecation." 58 *Brain* (1935) 256.
118. Dercum, F. X. "The Thalamus in the Physiology and Pathology of the Mind." 14 *Arch. Neurol. Psychiat.* (1925) 289.

119. Dill, D. B. Life, Heat and Altitude. Cambridge, Mass., 1938.
120. Dott, M. M. "Surgical Aspects of the Hypothalamus." In *The Hypothalamus* (Edinburgh, Oliver and Boyd, Ltd., 1938) 131.
121. Dugmore, A. R. Romance of the Beaver. Philadelphia, 1914.
122. Dunbar, H. F. Emotions and Bodily Changes. 1935; 2nd ed., New York, 1938.
123. Dunlap, K. The Elements of Scientific Psychology. St. Louis, Mo., The C. V. Mosby Co., 1927.
124. —— Habits. New York, 1932.
125. Dusser de Barenne, J. G. "Central Levels of Sensory Integration." 34 *Arch. Neurol. Psychiat.* (1935) 768.
126. —— "Sensory-motor Cortex and Thalamus Opticus." 119 *Am. J. Physiol.* (1937) 265.
127. Dusser de Barenne, J. G., W. S. McCulloch, and L. F. Nims. "Functional Activity and pH of the Cerebral Cortex." 10 *J. Cell. Comp. Physiol.* (1937) 277.
128. Dusser de Barenne, J. G., and A. A. Ward, Jr. "Reflex Inhibition of the Knee-jerk from Intestinal Organs." 120 *Am. J. Physiol.* (1937) 340.
129. East, E. M. Mankind at the Crossroads. New York, 1924.
130. Ectors, L. "Stimulation of the Hypothalamus in Chronic Hemidecorticated Monkeys." 119 *Am. J. Physiol.* (1937) 301.
131. Ectors, L., N. L. Brookens, and R. W. Gerard. "Autonomic and Motor Localization in the Hypothalamus." 39 *Arch. Neurol. Psychiat.* (1938) 789.
132. Eddington, A. S. The Nature of the Physical World (Gifford Lectures). New York, The Macmillan Company, 1928.
133. Edgeworth, F. Y. Mathematical Psychics. London, 1881.
134. —— Papers Relating to Political Economy. London, 1925.
135. Ely, R. T. Outlines of Economics. 1893; 3rd ed., New York, 1918.
136. —— Property and Contract. New York, 1914.
137. Engell, B. Theories of Memory. Oxford, England, 1924.
138. Enke, S. "Space and Value." 56 *Q. J. Econ.* (1942) 627.
139. Fearnsides, E. G. "The Innervation of the Bladder and Urethra." 40 *Brain* (1917) 149.
140. Finley, K. H. "Angio-architecture of the Hypothalamus and Its Peculiarities." In *The Hypothalamus*, 20 Res. Pbl. Assn. Nerv. Ment. Dis. (Baltimore, 1940) 286.
141. Fisher, C., W. R. Ingram, and S. W. Ranson. "Relation of the Hypothalamico-Hypophyseal System to Diabetes Insipidus." 34 *Arch. Neurol. Psychiat.* (1935) 125.
142. Fisher, I. The Nature of Capital and Income. 1906; New York, 1927.
143. Flux, A. W. Economic Principles. 1903; 2nd ed., London, 1923.
144. Foerster, O. "The Motor Cortex in Man in the Light of Hughlings Jackson's Doctrines." 59 *Brain* (1936; 9th Hughlings Jackson Lecture) 135.
145. Forbes, A. "Tonus in Skeletal Muscle in Relation to Sympathetic Innervation." 22 *Arch. Neurol. Psychiat.* (1929) 247.
146. —— "The Mechanism of Reaction." In Murchison, *Foundations of Experimental Psychology* (Worcester, Mass., 1929) 128.
147. —— "The Mechanism of Reaction." In Murchison, *Handbook of General Experimental Psychology* (Worcester, Mass., 1934) 155.
148. —— "Reflex Inhibition of Skeletal Muscle." 5 *Q. J. Exper. Physiol.* (1912) 149.
149. Fraenkel, G. S., and D. L. Gunn. The Orientation of Animals. Oxford, England, The Clarendon Press, 1940.
150. Frazer, Sir J. G. The Golden Bough—the Magic Art. 1890; 3rd ed., London, 1922.
151. Frazier, C. H., B. J. Alpers, and F. H. Levy. "The Anatomical Localization of the Hypothalamic Centre for the Regulation of Temperature." 59 *Brain* (1936) 122.
152. Freeman, G. L. Introduction to Physiological Psychology. New York, The Ronald Press Co., 1934.
153. Freud, S. "A Note on the Unconscious in Psycho-Analysis." 26 *Proc. Soc. Psychic. Res.* (1912) 312.

154. —— The Interpretation of Dreams. 3rd rev. ed., tr. A. A. Brill. London, George Allen & Unwin Ltd., and New York, The Macmillan Company, 1915.
155. —— General Introduction to Psychoanalysis. Tr., New York, 1920.
156. —— Beyond the Pleasure Principle. 2nd ed., tr. C. J. M. Hubback. New York, n.d.
157. Frolov, Y. P. Pavlov and His School. London, Kegan Paul, Trench, Trubner and Co. Ltd., 1937.
158. Fulton, J. F. Muscular Contraction and the Reflex Control of Movement. Baltimore, 1926.
159. —— "Some Functions of the Cerebral Cortex." 33 *J. Mich. State Med. Soc.* (1934) 175, 235.
160. —— Physiology of the Nervous System. New York, Oxford University Press, 1938.
161. Fulton, J. F., and P. Bailey. "Tumors in the Region of the Third Ventricle." 69 *J. Nerv. Ment. Dis.* (1929) 1, 145, 261.
162. Fulton, J. F., and F. D. Ingraham. "Emotional Disturbances Following Experimental Lesions of the Base of the Brain (pre-chiasmal)." 67 *J. Physiol.* (1929) xxvii.
163. Fulton, J. F., C. F. Jacobsen, and M. A. Kennard. "A Note Concerning the Relation of the Frontal Lobes to Posture and Forced Grasping in Monkeys." 55 *Brain* (1932) 524.
164. Fulton, J. F., and Sir C. S. Sherrington. "Nervous Integrations in Man." In Cowdry, *Human Biology and Racial Welfare.* (New York, Paul B. Hoeber, Inc., 1930) 246.
165. Gantt, W. H. "Contributions to the Physiology of the Conditioned Reflex." 37 *Arch. Neurol. Psychiat.* (1937) 848.
166. Gardiner, H. N., R. C. Metcalfe, and J. G. Beebe-Center. Feeling and Emotion. New York, 1937.
167. Gaskell, W. H. The Involuntary Nervous System. London, 1916.
168. Gasser, H. S. "The Control of Excitation in the Nervous System." 32 *The Harvey Lectures* (The Harvey Lecture Society; The Williams and Wilkins Co., Baltimore, 1937; copyright, The Science Press Printing Co., Lancaster, Pa.) 169.
169. George, Henry. Progress and Poverty. 1879; 25th Anniv. ed., New York, 1916.
170. Gersh, I. "Water Metabolism: Endocrine Factors." In *The Hypothalamus,* 20 Res. Pbl. Assn. Nerv. Ment. Dis. (Baltimore, 1940) 436.
171. Gildea, E. F., and E. B. Man. "The Hypothalamus and Fat Metabolism." In *The Hypothalamus,* 20 Res. Pbl. Assn. Nerv. Ment. Dis. (Baltimore, 1940) 501.
172. Gillespie, R. D. Sleep and the Treatment of Its Disorders. London, Baillière, Tindall and Cox, 1929.
173. Goldstein, K. "The Significance of the Frontal Lobes for Mental Performances." 17 *J. Neurol. Psychopath.* (1936) 27.
174. Gonzalez, A. W. Angelo y. "The Prenatal Development of Behavior in the Albino Rat." 55 *J. Comp. Neurol.* (1932) 395.
175. Green, H. D., and E. C. Hoff. "Effects of Faradic Stimulation." 118 *Am. J. Physiol.* (1937) 641.
176. Gregersen, M. I. "The Distribution and Regulation of Water in the Body." In McLeod, *Physiology in Modern Medicine* (1918; 9th ed., ed. P. Bard, St. Louis, Mo., The C. V. Mosby Co., 1941) 1059.
177. Gregersen, M. I. (with J. H. Holmes). "A Study of the Character and the Mechanism of the Thirst Induced by the Intravenous Injection of Hypertonic Salt Solution." 126 *Am. J. Physiol.* (1939) P, 537.
178. Haldane, J. S. Organism and Environment as Illustrated by the Physiology of Breathing (Silliman Lectures). New Haven, Conn., 1917.
179. Haldane, J. S., and J. G. Priestley. Respiration. New Haven, Conn., 1935.
180. Hare, K. "Water Metabolism: Neurogenic Factors." In *The Hypothalamus,* 20 Res. Pbl. Assn. Nerv. Ment. Dis. (Baltimore, 1940) 416.
181. Harrison, F. "The Hypothalamus and Sleep." In *The Hypothalamus,* 20 Res. Publ. Assn. Nerv. Ment. Dis. (Baltimore, 1940) 635.

182. Head, Sir Henry. "Hughlings Jackson on Aphasia and Kindred Affections of Speech." 38 *Brain* (1915) 1.
183. —— Studies in Neurology. London, 1920. Vol. II.
184. Head, Sir Henry, and G. Riddoch. "The Automatic Bladder, Excessive Sweating and Some Other Reflex Conditions in Gross Injuries of the Spinal Cord." 40 *Brain* (1917) 188.
185. Healy, W., A. F. Bronner, and A. M. Bowers. Structure and Meaning of Psychoanalysis. New York, 1930.
186. Hearn, W. E. Plutology. London, 1864.
187. Heinbecker, P., and G. H. Bishop. "The Mechanism of Painful Sensations." In *Sensation: Its Mechanisms and Disturbances*, 15 Res. Pbl. Assn. Nerv. Ment. Dis. (Baltimore, 1935).
188. Henderson, W. R., and W. C. Wilson. "Intraventricular Injection of Acetylcholine and Eserine in Man." 26 *Q. J. Exper. Physiol.* (1936) 83.
189. Hering, E. "On Memory as a Universal Function of Organized Matter." In *Unconscious Memory*, tr. S. Butler (1880; New York, E. P. Dutton and Co., Inc., 1920) 63.
190. Herrick, C. J. Introduction to Neurology. 1915; 5th ed., Philadelphia, 1931.
191. —— "The Functions of the Olfactory Parts of the Cerebral Cortex." 19 *Proc. Natl. Acad. Sci.* (1933) 7.
192. Hess, W. R. "On the Interrelationships between Psychic and Vegetative Functions." 74 *J. Nerv. Ment. Dis.* (1931) 301, 511, 645, 726.
193. —— "The Autonomic Nervous System." *Lancet* (1932) II, 1199, 1259.
194. Hicks, J. R. Theory of Wages. London, 1932.
195. —— Value and Capital. Oxford, England, The Clarendon Press, 1939.
196. Hicks, J. R., and R. G. D. Allen. "A Reconsideration of the Theory of Value." 1 *Economica* (1934) 52.
197. Hilgard, E. R., and D. G. Marquis. Conditioning and Learning. New York, D. Appleton-Century Company, Inc., 1940.
198. Hinsey, J. C. "The Anatomical Relations of the Sympathetic System to Visceral Sensation." In *Sensation: Its Mechanisms and Disturbances*, 15 Res. Pbl. Assn. Nerv. Ment. Dis. (Baltimore, 1935) 105.
199. —— "The Hypothalamus and Somatic Responses." In *The Hypothalamus*, 20 Res. Pbl. Assn. Nerv. Ment. Dis. (Baltimore, 1940) 657.
200. Hinsey, J. C., S. W. Ranson, and R. F. McNattin. "The Role of the Hypothalamus and Mesencephalon in Locomotion." 23 *Arch. Neurol. Psychiat.* (1930) 1.
201. Hoaglund, H. "Specific Afferent Impulses and Cutaneous Sensibility." 6 *J. Genl. Psychol.* (1932) 276.
202. Hodge, F. A. "The Emotions in a New Role." 42 *Psychol. Rev.* (1935) 555.
203. Hoelzel, F. "Central Factors in Hunger," 82 *Am. J. Physiol.* (1927) 665.
204. Hoff, E. C., and H. D. Green. "Cardiovascular Reactions Induced by Electrical Stimulation of the Cerebral Cortex." 117 *Am. J. Physiol.* (1936) 411.
205. Holmes, G. "Observations on the Paralyzed Bladder." 56 *Brain* (1933) 383.
206. Holt, E. B. The Freudian Wish. New York, 1916.
207. —— Animal Drive and the Learning Process. New York, 1931.
208. Howell, W. H. Text-Book of Physiology. 1905; 13th ed., Philadelphia, 1936.
209. Huber, G. C., and E. C. Crosby. "Somatic and Visceral Connections of the Diencephalon." In *The Vegetative Nervous System*, 9 Res. Pbl. Assn. Nerv. Ment. Dis. (Baltimore, 1930) 199.
210. Huxley, T. H. Lessons in Elementary Physiology. 1866; ed. F. S. Lee, New York, 1902.
211. —— The Crayfish. New York, 1880.
212. Ingram, W. R. "Nuclear Organization and Chief Connections of the Primate Hypothalamus." In *The Hypothalamus*, 20 Res. Pbl. Assn. Nerv. Ment. Dis. (Baltimore, 1940) 195.

213. Ingram, W. R., and R. W. Barris. "Evidence of Altered Carbohydrate Metabolism in Cats with Hypothalamic Lesions." 114 *Am. J. Physiol.* (1936) 562.
214. Ingram, W. R., and C. Fisher. "The Relation of the Posterior Pituitary to Water Exchange in the Cat." 66 *Anat. Rec.* (1936) 271.
215. Jackson, J. Hughlings. Neurological Fragments. London, Oxford University Press, 1925.
216. —— Selected Writings of John Hughlings Jackson. Ed. J. Taylor. London, Hodder and Stoughton, Ltd., 1931–1932.
217. Jacobsen, C. F. "Influence of Motor and Premotor Area Lesions upon the Retention of Skilled Movements in Monkeys and Chimpanzees." In *Localization of Function in the Cerebral Cortex,* 13 Res. Pbl. Assn. Nerv. Ment. Dis. (Baltimore, 1934) 225.
218. —— "Functions of Frontal Association Areas in Primates." 33 *Arch. Neurol. Psychiat.* (1935) 558.
219. James, W. "The Feeling of Effort." In *Anniv. Mem. Boston Soc. Nat. Hist.* (Boston, 1880).
220. —— Principles of Psychology. 1890; New York, 1896.
221. Janet, P. "La Tension psychologique et ses oscillations." In Dumas, *Nouveau traité de psychologie,* Vol. IV, 1934.
222. Jelliffe, S. E. "The Mneme, the Engram and the Unconscious, Richard Semon: His Life and Work." 57 *J. Nerv. Ment. Dis.* No. 4 (1923) 329.
223. Jennings, H. S. Behavior of the Lower Organisms. New York, 1906.
224. Jevons, W. S. The Theory of Political Economy. 1871; 4th ed., London, 1911.
225. Johnston, J. B. "The Morphology of the Forebrain Vesicle in Vertebrates." 19 *J. Comp. Neurol.* (1909) 457.
226. —— "The Telencephalon of Selachians." 21 *J. Comp. Neurol.* (1911) 1.
227. Jung, R., J. Doupe, and E. A. Carmichael. "Shivering: a Clinical Study of the Influence of Sensation." 60 *Brain* (1937) 28.
228. Kabat, H., B. J. Anson, H. W. Magoun, and S. W. Ranson. "Stimulation of the Hypothalamus with Special Reference to Its Effect on Gastro-intestinal Motility." 112 *Am. J. Physiol.* (1935) 214.
229. Kabat, H., H. W. Magoun, and S. W. Ranson. "Electric Stimulation of Points in the Forebrain and Midbrain." 34 *Arch. Neurol. Psychiat.* (1935) 931.
230. —— "Reaction of the Bladder to Stimulation of Points in the Forebrain and Midbrain." 63 *J. Comp. Neurol.* (1936) 211.
231. Kappers, C. U. Ariëns, G. C. Huber, and E. C. Crosby. Comparative Anatomy of the Nervous System of Vertebrates, Including Man. New York, 1936.
232. Keller, A. D., and W. K. Hare. "The Hypothalamus and Heat Regulation." 29 *Proc. Soc. Exper. Biol.* (New York, 1932) 1069.
233. Kempf, E. J. Autonomic Functions and the Personality. New York, Nervous and Mental Disease Monographs, 1918.
234. Kennard, M. A. "Vasomotor Disturbances Resulting from Cortical Lesions." 33 *Arch. Neurol. Psychiat.* (1935) 537.
235. —— "Age and Other Factors in Motor Recovery from Precentral Lesions in Monkeys." 115 *Am. J. Physiol.* (1936) 138.
236. Kennedy, F. "Medical Syndromes of the Hypothalamus." In *The Hypothalamus,* 20 Res. Pbl. Assn. Nerv. Ment. Dis. (Baltimore, 1940) 864.
237. Keynes, J. M. (Lord Keynes). General Theory of Employment, Interest and Money. New York, 1936.
238. Kingsbury, B. F. "The Fundamental Plan of the Vertebrate Brain." 34 *J. Comp. Neurol.* (1922) 461.
239. Klüver, H. Behavior Mechanisms in Monkeys. Chicago, 1933.
240. Knight, F. H. Risk, Uncertainty and Profit. 1921; reprint, London School of Economics and Political Science, 1933.
241. —— "Issues in the Economics of Stationary States." 26 *Am. Econ. Rev.* (1936) 393.
242. —— "What Is Truth in Economics." 48 *J. Pol. Econ.* (1940) 1.

243. Köhler, W. Gestalt Psychology. New York, 1929.
244. Kroeber, A. L. "So-called Social Science." 1 *J. Soc. Phil.* (1936) 317.
245. Kuntz, A. The Autonomic Nervous System. 2nd ed. Philadelphia, 1934.
246. Kuntz, A. and J. W. Hamilton. "Afferent Innervation of the Skin." 71 *Anat. Rec.* (1938 Sup.) 387.
247. Kuznets, S. Commodity Flow and Capital Formation. Natl. Bur. Econ. Res., New York, 1938.
248. Landis, C. "The Expressions of Emotion." In Murchison, *Foundations of Experimental Psychology* (Worcester, Mass., 1929) 512.
249. Langmuir, I. "Address of the Retiring President of the A.A.A.S." 97 *Sci.* (1943) 1.
250. Langworthy, O. R. "A Curious Illustration of 'Mass Reflex' and Involuntary Micturition following Injury of the Spinal Cord." 60 *J. H. Hosp. Bull.* (1937) 337.
251. —— "The Influence of Suprasegmental Levels on Vesical Activity." In *The Hypothalamus,* 20 Res. Pbl. Assn. Nerv. Ment. Dis. (Baltimore, 1940) 617.
252. Langworthy, O. R., and F. H. Hesser. "An Experimental Study of Micturition Released from Cerebral Control." 115 *Am. J. Physiol.* (1936) 694.
253. —— "Reflex Vesical Contraction in the Cat after Transection of the Spinal Cord in the Lower Lumbar Region." 60 *J. H. Hosp. Bul.* (1937) 204.
254. Langworthy, O. R., and L. C. Kolb. "The Encephalic Control of Tone in the Musculature of the Urinary Bladder." 56 *Brain* (1933) 371.
255. —— "Demonstration of Encephalic Control of Micturition by Electrical Stimulation." 56 *J. H. Hosp. Bull.* (1935) 37.
256. Langworthy, O. R., L. G. Lewis, J. E. Dees, and F. H. Hesser. "A Clinical Study of the Control of the Bladder by the Central Nervous System." 58 *J. H. Hosp. Bul.* (1936) 89.
257. Langworthy, O. R., D. L. Reeves, and E. S. Tauber. "Autonomic Control of the Urinary Bladder." 57 *Brain* (1934) 266.
258. Langworthy, O. R., and C. P. Richter. "The Influence of Efferent Cerebral Pathways upon the Sympathetic Nervous System." 53 *Brain* (1930) 178.
259. Lashley, K. S. "Temporal Variation in the Formation of Gyrus Precentralis in Primates." 65 *Am. J. Physiol.* (1923) 585.
260. —— "Basal Neural Mechanisms in Behavior." 37 *Psychol. Rev.* (1930) 1.
261. —— "Integrative Functions of the Cerebral Cortex." 13 *Physiol. Revs.* (1933) 1.
262. —— "Functional Determinants of Cerebral Localization." 38 *Arch. Neurol. Psychiat.* (1937) 371.
263. —— "The Thalamus and Emotions." 45 *Psychol. Rev.* (1938) 42.
264. Learmonth, J. R. "A Contribution to the Neurophysiology of the Urinary Bladder in Man." 54 *Brain* (1931) 147.
265. Levin, P. M., and O. R. Langworthy. "Extrapyramidal Control of Micturition." 118 *Am. J. Physiol.* (1937) 483.
266. Lewin, K. "Environmental Forces in Child Behavior and Development." In Murchison, *Handbook of Child Psychology* (Worcester, Mass., 1931) 94.
267. Lewis, Sir Thomas. "The Nocifensor System of Nerves and Its Reactions." 1 *British Med. J.* (1937) 431, 491.
268. Lewy, F. H., and F. K. Gassmann. "Experiments on the Hypothalamic Nuclei in the Regulation of Chloride and Sugar Metabolism." 112 *Am. J. Physiol.* (1935) 504.
269. Lilienthal, J. L., Jr., and F. J. Otenasek. "Decorticate Polypneic Panting in the Cat." 61 *J. H. Hosp. Bull.* (1937) 101.
270. Littleton, A. C. Accounting Evolution to 1900. New York, 1933.
271. Loeb, J. Forced Movements, Tropisms and Animal Conduct. Philadelphia, 1918.
272. Long, C. N. H. "Evidence for and against Control of Carbohydrate Metabolism by the Hypothalamus." In *The Hypothalamus,* 20 Res. Pbl. Assn. Nerv. Ment. Dis. (Baltimore, 1940) 486.
273. Looney, W. W. Anatomy of the Brain and Spinal Cord. Philadelphia, 1932.

274. Lorente de Nó, R. "Analysis of the Activity of the Chains of Internuncial Neurons." 1 *J. Neurophysiol.* (1938) 227.

275. Lotka, A. J. "Some Reflections—Statistical and Other—on a Nonmaterial Universe" (Presidential Address). 38 *J. Am. Statist. Assn.* (1943) 1.

276. Lubbock, Sir J. (Lord Avebury). Ants, Bees and Wasps. Ed. J. G. Myers. London, E. P. Dutton and Co., Inc., 1929.

277. Lydekker, R. "Beavers." In *Encycl. Brit.* 11th ed., 1910–1911.

278. Macaulay, F. R. Bond Yields, Interest Rates, Stock Prices. Natl. Bur. Econ. Res., New York, 1938.

279. MacBride, E. W. The Idea of Memory in Biology (10th Earl Grey Memorial Lecture). London, Oxford University Press, and Newcastle-on-Tyne, King's College, 1928.

280. MacCurdy, J. R. Psychology of Emotion. New York, 1925.

281. McDougall, W. "The Nature of Inhibitory Processes within the Nervous System." 26 *Brain* (1903) 153.

282. —— Review of Sherrington, *Integrative Action of the Nervous System.* 30 *Brain* (1907) 376.

283. —— Physiological Psychology. London, 1905.

284. —— An Introduction to Social Psychology. 14th ed. Boston, John W. Luce and Company, 1921.

285. —— The Energies of Man. London, 1932.

286. Magoun, H. W. "Descending Connections from the Hypothalamus." In *The Hypothalamus,* 20 Res. Publ. Assn. Nerv. Ment. Dis. (Baltimore, 1940) 270.

287. Magoun, H. W., F. Harrison, J. R. Brobeck, and S. W. Ranson. "Activation of Heat Loss Mechanisms by Local Heating of the Brain." 1 *J. Neurophysiol.* (1938) 101.

288. Magoun, H. W., S. W. Ranson, and C. Fisher. "Corticofugal Pathways for Mastication, Lapping and Other Motor Functions in the Cat." 30 *Arch. Neurol. Psychiat.* (1933) 292.

289. Malthus, T. R. Principles of Population. 1798; 5th ed., London, 1817.

290. Marschak, J. "Demand Elasticities Reviewed." 11 *Econometr.* (1943) 25.

291. Marshall, A. Principles of Economics. 1890; 8th ed., London and New York, The Macmillan Company, 1920.

292. Marston, W. M. "Motor Consciousness as a Basis for Emotion." 22 *J. Abn. Soc. Psychol.* (1928) 140.

293. Martin, C. L., and F. T. Rogers. "Hunger Pain." 17 *Am. J. Roent. Rad. Therapy,* 2 (1927) 222.

294. Marx, K. Capital. 1867; tr. S. Moore and E. Arching, ed. F. Engels, London, 1887.

295. Masserman, J. H. "Effects of Analeptic Drugs on the Hypothalamus of the Cat." In *The Hypothalamus,* 20 Res. Pbl. Assn. Nerv. Ment. Dis. (Baltimore, 1940) 624.

296. Menger, C. Grundsätze der Volkswirthschaftslehre. 1871; reprint, London School of Economics and Political Science, 1934.

297. Mettler, F. A., C. C. Mettler, and E. Culler. "Effects of Total Removal of the Cerebral Cortex." 34 *Arch. Neurol. Psychiat.* (1935) 1238.

298. Mill, J. S. Principles of Political Economy. 1848; 5th ed., New York, 1909.

299. Miller, J. G. Unconsciousness. New York, John Wiley and Sons, Inc., 1942.

300. Mises, L. von. Socialism. Tr. J. Kahane. New York, n. d.

301. Monakow, C. von. The Emotions, Morality and the Brain. New York, 1925.

302. Morgan, C. L. Animal Life and Intelligence. Boston, 1891.

303. Morgan, L. H. The Beaver and His Works. Philadelphia, 1868.

304. Morgan, L. O. "Cell Changes in Hypothalamus in Major Psychoses." In *The Hypothalamus,* 20 Res. Pbl. Assn. Nerv. Ment. Dis. (Baltimore, 1940) 753.

305. —— "The Corpus Striatum." 18 *Arch. Neurol. Psychiat.* (1927) 495.

306. Morgan, L. O., and A. R. Vonderahe. "The Hypothalamic Nuclei in Heat Stroke." 42 *Arch. Neurol. Psychiat.* (1939) 83.
307. Morison, R. S., and D. McK. Rioch. "The Influence of the Forebrain on an Autonomic Reflex." 120 *Am. J. Physiol.* (1937) 257.
308. Moss, F. A. "Study of Animal Drives." 7 *J. Exper. Psychol.* (1924) 165.
309. Myerson, A. "Human Autonomic Pharmacology." 110 *J. Am. Med. Assn.* (1938) 101.
310. Nafe, J. P. "The Pressure, Pain and Temperature Senses." In Murchison, *Handbook of General Experimental Psychology* (Worcester, Mass., 1934) 1037.
311. Nienstaedt, L. R. "Economic Consequences of Technical Development." 5 *Econometr.* (1937) 342.
312. Novikoff, A. B. "The Concept of Integrative Levels and Biology." 101 *Sci.* (1945) 209.
313. Noyes, C. R. The Institution of Property. New York, 1936.
314. —— "The Law and Scientific Method." 55 *Pol. Sci. Q.* (1940) 496.
315. Papez, J. W. "A Proposed Mechanism of Emotion." 38 *Arch. Neurol. Psychiat.* (1937) 725.
316. Pareto, V. Cours d'économie politique. Lausanne, 1896–1897.
317. —— Manuel d'économie politique. French tr. A. Bonnet. Paris, Marcel Giard, 1909; 12th ed., Paris, R. Pichon and R. Durand-Auzias, 1927.
318. Parker, G. H. "The Origin and Evolution of the Nervous System." 84 *Pop. Sci. Monthly* (1914) 118.
319. —— Smell, Taste and Allied Senses in Vertebrates. Philadelphia, 1922.
320. Pavlov, I. P. Conditioned Reflexes. 1926; tr. G. V. Anrep, Oxford, England, The Clarendon Press, 1927.
321. —— Lectures on Conditioned Reflexes. Tr. W. H. Gantt. London, 1928.
322. Pearl, R. Natural History of Population. New York, 1939.
323. Penfield, W. "The Cerebral Cortex and Consciousness." 32 *The Harvey Lectures* (The Harvey Lecture Society; The Williams and Wilkins Co., Baltimore, 1937; copyright, The Science Press Printing Co., Lancaster, Pa.) 35.
324. Penfield, W., and E. Boldrey. "Somatic Motor and Sensory Representation in the Cerebral Cortex of Man as Studied by Electrical Stimulation." 60 *Brain* (1937) 389.
325. Pigou, A. C. The Economics of Welfare. 1920; 4th ed., London, 1932.
326. Pinkston, J. O., P. Bard, and D. McK. Rioch. "The Responses to Changes in Environmental Temperature after Removal of Portions of the Forebrain." 109 *Am. J. Physiol.* (1934) 515.
327. Pinkston, J. O., and D. McK. Rioch. "The Influence of the Cerebral Cortex on Peripheral Circulation." 121 *Am. J. Physiol.* (1938) 49.
328. Pitt, F. Animal Mind. London, 1927.
329. Pitts, R. F., H. W. Magoun, and S. W. Ranson. "Interrelations of the Respiratory Centers in the Cat." 126 *Am. J. Physiol.* (1939) 689.
330. Poliak, S. The Main Afferent Fiber Systems of the Cerebral Cortex in Primates. Univ. of Calif. Pubs. in Anatomy No. 2, 1932.
331. Prince, M. "Can Emotion Be Regarded as Energy?" In *The Wittenberg Symposium* (Worcester, Mass., 1928) 161.
332. Ranson, S. W. "Some Functions of the Hypothalamus" (Harvey Lecture). 13 *Bull. N.Y. Acad. Med.* (1937) 241.
333. —— "Regulation of Body Temperature." In *The Hypothalamus,* 20 Res. Pbl. Assn. Nerv. Ment. Dis. (Baltimore, 1940) 342.
334. Ranson, S. W., C. Fisher, and W. R. Ingram. "Hypothalamic Regulation of Temperature in the Monkey." 38 *Arch. Neurol. Psychiat.* (1937) 445.
335. Ranson, S. W., and W. R. Ingram. "Hypothalamus and Regulation of Body Temperature." 32 *Proc. Soc. Exper. Biol. N.Y.* (1935) 1439.
336. Ranson, S. W., H. Kabat, and H. S. Magoun. "Autonomic Responses to Electrical

Stimulation of Hypothalamus, Preoptic Region and Septum." 33 *Arch. Neurol. Psychiat.* (1935) 467.

337. Ricardo, D. Principles of Political Economy and Taxation. Everyman's ed. New York, 1917.

338. Richter, C. P. "Animal Behavior and Internal Drives." 2 *Q. Rev. Biol.* (1927) 307.

339. —— "Increased Salt Appetite in Adrenalectomized Rats." 115 *Am. J. Physiol.* (1936) 155.

340. —— "Salt Taste Thresholds of Normal and Adrenalectomized Rats." 24 *Endocrinol.* (1939) 367.

341. Richter, C. P., and M. Hines. "Increased Spontaneous Activity Produced in Monkeys by Brain Lesions." 61 *Brain* (1938) 1.

342. Richter, C. P., L. E. Holt, and N. Barelere, Jr. "Nutritional Requirements for Normal Growth and Reproduction in Rats." 122 *Am. J. Physiol.* (1938) 734.

343. Riddoch, G. "The Reflex Functions of the Completely Divided Spinal Cord in Man." 40 *Brain* (1917) 264.

344. —— "Clinical Aspects of Hypothalamic Derangement." In *The Hypothalamus* (Edinburgh, Oliver and Boyd, Ltd., 1938) 101.

345. Rignano, E. Biological Memory. Tr. E. W. MacBride. New York, Harcourt, Brace and Co., Inc., 1926.

346. Rioch, D. McK., and A. Rosenblueth. "Inhibition from the Cerebral Cortex." 113 *Am. J. Physiol.* (1935) 663.

347. Rioch, D. McK., and C. Brenner. "Experiments on the Corpus Striatum and Rhinencephalon." 68 *J. Comp. Neurol.* (1938) 491.

348. Robinson, Joan. Economics Is a Serious Subject. Cambridge, England, 1932.

349. —— Economics of Imperfect Competition. London, 1936.

350. —— "Disguised Unemployment." 46 *Econ. J.* (1936) 225.

351. Rogers, F. T. "Contribution to the Physiology of the Stomach." 41 *Am. J. Physiol.* (1916) 555.

352. ——"An Experimental Study of the Corpus Striatum of the Pigeon as Related to Various Instinctive Types of Behavior." 35 *J. Comp. Neurol.* (1922) 21.

353. —— "Studies of the Brain Stem, XI." 86 *Am. J. Physiol.* (1928) 639.

354. Romanes, G. J. Animal Intelligence. New York, 1906.

355. Root, W. S. "The Urinary Bladder." In McLeod, *Physiology in Modern Medicine* (1918; 9th ed., ed. P. Bard, St. Louis, Mo., The C. V. Mosby Co., 1941) 1127.

356. Roy R. "La Hiérarchie des besoins et la notion de groupes dans l'économie de choix." 11 *Econometr.* (1943) 13.

357. Russell, B. Analysis of Mind. New York, 1922.

358. Russell, H. N. "Determinism and Responsibility." 97 *Sci.* (1943) 249.

359. Saliers, E. A. Depreciation. New York, 1923.

360. Scharrer, E., and B. Scharrer. "Secretory Cells within the Hypothalamus." In *The Hypothalamus,* 20 Res. Pbl. Assn. Nerv. Ment. Dis. (Baltimore, 1940) 170.

361. Schmidt, C. F. "The Respiration." In McLeod, *Physiology in Modern Medicine* (1918; 9th ed., ed. P. Bard, St. Louis, Mo., The C. V. Mosby Co., 1941) 534.

362. Schmidt, H. D. "On the Structure of the Nervous Tissues and Their Mode of Action." 1 *Trans. Am. Neurol. Assn.* (1875) 71.

363. Schultz, H. "Frisch on the Measurement of Utility." 41 *J. Pol. Econ.* (1933) 95.

364. Schumpeter, J. A. The Theory of Economic Development. Cambridge, Mass., 1936.

365. Schwartz, H. G. "Reflex Activity within the Sympathetic Nervous System." 109 *Am. J. Physiol.* (1934) 593.

366. —— "The Effect of Experimental Lesions of the Cortex upon the Psychogalvanic Reflex." 64 *Anat. Rec.* (1936 Sup.) 42.

367. —— "Effect of Experimental Lesions of the Cortex on the 'Psychogalvanic Reflex' in the Cat." 38 *Arch. Neurol. Psychiat.* (1937) 308.

368. Semon, R. The Mneme. 3rd ed., tr. L. Simon. London and New York, The Macmillan Company, 1921.

369. —— Mnemic Psychology. Tr. B. Duffy. London, George Allen and Unwin, Ltd., 1923.
370. Senior, N. W. An Outline of the Science of Political Economy (from *Encycl. Metrop.* 1836). 3rd ed. London and Glasgow, 1854.
371. —— Senior's Industrial Efficiency and Social Economy. Ed. S. L. Levy. New York, 1928.
372. Sheehan, D. "The effect of Cortical Stimulation on Gastric Movements in the Monkey." 83 *J. Physiol.* (1934) 177.
373. —— "The Hypothalamus and Gastro-intestinal Regulation." In *The Hypothalamus,* 20 Res. Pbl. Assn. Nerv. Ment. Dis. (Baltimore, 1940) 589.
374. Sherrington, Sir C. S. "Experiments on the Value of Vascular and Visceral Factors for the Genesis of Emotion." 66 *Proc. Royal Soc.* (1900) 390.
375. —— Integrative Action of the Nervous System. New Haven, Conn., Yale University Press, 1906.
376. —— "Postural Activity of Muscle and Nerve." 38 *Brain* (1915) 191.
377. —— "Notes on Temperature after Spinal Transection." 58 *J. Physiol.* (1924) 405.
378. —— The Brain and Its Mechanism. Cambridge, England, 1933.
379. Skinner, B. F. The Behavior of Organisms. New York, 1938.
380. Slonaker, J. R. "The Effect of Pubescence, Oestruation and Menopause on the Voluntary Activity in the Albino Rat." 68 *Am. J. Physiol.* (1924) 294.
381. Smith, Adam. Wealth of Nations. Ed. E. Cannan. New York, 1904.
382. Smith, Sir G. Elliot. "Neurology, Central Nervous System." In Cunningham, *Textbook of Anatomy* (London, Oxford University Press, 1902; 7th ed., 1937) 791.
383. Smith, W. K. "The Representation of Respiratory Movements in the Cerebral Cortex." 1 *J. Neurophysiol.* (1938) 55.
384. Spiegel, E. A., and W. C. Hunsicker, Jr. "The Conduction of Cortical Impulses to the Autonomic System." 83 *J. Nerv. Ment. Dis.* (1936) 252.
385. Stravraky, G. W. "Response of Cerebral Blood Vessels to Electric Stimulation of the Thalamus and Hypothalamic Regions." 35 *Arch. Neurol. Psychiat.* (1936) 1002.
386. Stigler, G. J. "The Economics of Carl Menger." 45 *J. Pol. Econ.* (1937) 229.
387. Streeter, G. L. "The Development of the Nervous System." In Keibel and Mall, *Manual of Human Embryology* (Philadelphia, J. B. Lippincott Company, 1912) II, 1.
388. Sweezy, A. R. "The Interpretation of Subjective Value Theory in the Writings of the Austrian Economists." 1 *Rev. Econ. Studies* (1934) 176.
389. Swenson, E. A. "The Simple Movements of the Trunk of the Albino-rat Fetus." 38 *Anat. Rec.* (1928) 31.
390. Taylor, A. E. Digestion and Metabolism. Philadelphia, 1912.
391. Taylor, F. M. Principles of Economics. 9th ed. New York, 1925.
392. Teague, R. S., and S. W. Ransom. "The Role of the Anterior Hypothalamus in Temperature Regulation." 117 *Am. J. Physiol.* (1936) 562.
393. Thomson, Sir J. A. Outline of Science. New York, 1922.
394. —— "Is There One Science of Nature?" 10 *Hibbert J.* (1911–1912) 120, 320.
395. Thomson, Sir J. A., and Patrick Geddes. Life: Outlines of General Biology. London, 1931.
396. Thomson, M. K. The Springs of Human Action. New York, 1927.
397. Thorndike, E. L. The Psychology of Wants, Interests and Attitudes. New York, 1935.
398. —— "The Mental Life of Monkeys." *Psychol. Rev.* (Monogr. Sup.) III, No. 5, May, 1901.
399. Thünen, J. H. von. Der isolierte Staat. 1842; 3rd ed., Jena, 1930.
400. Thurstone, L. L. "The Stimulus-Response Fallacy in Psychology." 30 *Psychol. Rev.* (1923) 354.
401. —— The Nature of Intelligence. New York, Harcourt, Brace and Co., Inc., 1924.

402. Tolman, E. C. "The Nature of the Fundamental Drives." 20 *J. Abnorm. Soc. Psychol.* (1925–1926) 349.
403. —— Purposive Behavior in Animals and Men. New York, D. Appleton-Century Company, Inc., 1932.
404. Tower, S. S. "The Dissociation of Cortical Excitation from Cortical Inhibition by Pyramidal Section." 58 *Brain* (1935) 238.
405. —— "Extrapyramidal Action from the Cat's Cerebral Cortex: Motor and Inhibitory." 59 *Brain* (1936) 408.
406. —— "Pyramidal Lesion in the Monkey." *Trans. Am. Neurol. Assn.* (1938) 95.
407. Tracy, H. C. "The Development of Motility and Behavior Reactions in the Toadfish." 40 *J. Comp. Neurol.* (1926) 253.
408. Troland, L. T. The Fundamentals of Human Motivation. New York, D. Van Nostrand Company, Inc., 1928.
409. Tucker, G. The Laws of Wages, Profits and Rent. Philadelphia, 1837.
410. Uprus, V., G. B. Taylor, and E. A. Carmichael. "Shivering: a Clinical Study with Especial References to the Afferent and Efferent Pathways." 58 *Brain* (1935) 220.
411. Veblen, T. The Theory of the Leisure Class. 1899; new ed., 1918; reprint, New York, 1919.
412. —— The Theory of Business Enterprise. 1904; New York, 1936.
413. —— The Instinct of Workmanship. 1914; new ed., 1918; reprint, New York, 1922
414. Villiger, E. Brain and Spinal Cord. 3rd Am. ed., ed. W. H. F. Addison. Philadelphia, 1925.
415. Vonderahe, A. R. "Central Nervous System and Sugar Metabolism." 60 *Arch. Int. Med.* (1937) 694.
416. Walker, A. E. The Primate Thalamus. Chicago, 1938.
417. —— "The Hypothalamus and Pilomotor Regulation." In *The Hypothalamus,* 20 Res. Pbl. Assn. Nerv. Ment. Dis. (Baltimore, 1940) 400.
418. Walker, F. A. Political Economy. 1883; 3rd ed., London, 1888.
419. Waller, A. D. "The Sense of Effort: an Objective Study." 14 *Brain* (1891) 179.
420. Walras, L. Eléments d'économie politique pure. 1874; 4th (def.) ed., 1900; reprint, Paris, R. Pichon and R. Durand-Auzias, 1926.
421. Walshe, F. M. R. "On the 'Syndrome of the Premotor Cortex' (Fulton)." 58 *Brain* (1935) 49.
422. Wang, G. H. "The Relation between 'Spontaneous' Activity and Oestrous Cycle in the White Rat." *Comp. Psychol. Monogr.* (1923) Vol. II, No. 6.
423. Wang, G. H., and T. W. Lu. "Galvanic Skin Reflex Induced in the Cat by the Stimulation of the Motor Area of the Cerebral Cortex." 4 *Chin. J. Physiol.* (1930) 303.
424. Ward, J. "Psychology." In *Encycl. Brit.* 11th ed., 1910–1911.
425. Warden, C. J. Animal Motivation Studies. New York, 1931.
426. Warren, E. R. The Beaver, Its Work and Its Ways. Am. Soc. Mammalogists, Monogr. No. 2, Baltimore, The Williams and Wilkins Co., 1927.
427. Washburn, M. F. The Animal Mind. 1926; 3rd ed., New York, The Macmillan Company, 1936.
428. Waterston, D. "Observations on Sensation." 77 *J. Physiol.* (1933) 251.
429. Watson, J. B. Psychology. Philadelphia, 1919.
430. —— Behaviorism. New York, 1924.
431. Watts, J. W. "The Influence of the Cerebral Cortex on Gastro-intestinal Movements." 104 *J. Am. Med. Assn.* (1935) 355.
432. Watts, J. W., and J. F. Fulton. "Intussusception—the Relation of the Cerebral Cortex to Intestinal Motility in the Monkey." 210 *N.E. J. Med.* (1934) 883.
433. —— "The Effects of Lesions of the Hypothalamus upon the Gastro-intestinal Tract and Heart in Monkeys." 101 *Ann. Surg.* (1935) 363.
434. Weber, Max. Grundriss der Sozialökonomik. 1921; 2nd ed., Tübingen, 1925.
435. Wechsler, D. "The Measurement of Emotional Reactions." 12 *Arch. Psychol.* (1925) No. 76.

436. Weiss, S., and D. Davis. "The Significance of the Afferent Impulses from the Skin in the Mechanism of Visceral Pain." 176 *Am. J. Med. Sci.* (1928) 517.
437. Wheeler, W. M. Social Life among the Insects. New York, Harcourt, Brace and Co., Inc., 1923.
438. Whittaker, J. R. Anatomy of the Brain and Spinal Cord. 5th ed. Edinburgh, 1921.
439. Wicksell, K. Lectures on Political Economy. 1901–1906; 3rd ed., tr. E. Classen, London, 1934.
440. Wicksteed, P. H. Alphabet of Economic Science. London, 1888.
441. —— Common Sense of Political Economy. 1910; ed. L. Robbins, London, George Routledge and Sons Ltd., 1933.
442. Wieser, F. von. Natural Value. 1888; tr. C. A. Malloch, London, 1893.
443. Wilson, S. A. Kinnier. "An Experimental Research into the Anatomy and Physiology of the Corpus Striatum." 36 *Brain* (1914) 427.
444. Wislocki, G. B. "The Vascular Supply of the Hypophysis Cerebri of the Cat." 69 *Anat. Rec.* (1937) 361.
445. Wislocki, G. B., and L. S. King. "The Permeability of the Hypophysis and Hypothalamus to Vital Dyes." 58 *Am. J. Anat.* (1936) 421.
446. Woodworth, R. S. Dynamic Psychology. New York, 1919.
447. —— Psychology. 1921; rev. ed., New York, Henry Holt and Company, Inc., 1931.
448. Woodworth, R. S., and Sir C. S. Sherrington. "A Pseudaffective Reflex and Its Spinal Path." 31 *J. Physiol.* (1904) 234.
449. Yerkes, R. M., and A. W. Yerkes. The Great Apes. New Haven, Conn., 1929.
450. Young, P. T. "Reversal of Food Preferences of the White Rat through Controlled Pre-feeding." 22 *J. Genl. Psychol.* (1940) 33.

INDEX

INDEX

For the convenience of the reader, cross-references to sub-headings are capitalized when they so appear under the main heading.